LUTHER'S WORKS

American Edition

VOLUME 55

Published by Concordia Publishing House
and Fortress Press in 55 volumes.
General Editors are Jaroslav Pelikan (for vols. 1-30)
and Helmut T. Lehmann (for vols. 31-55)

LUTHER'S WORKS

VOLUME 55

Index

EDITED BY

JOEL W. LUNDEEN

FORTRESS PRESS / PHILADELPHIA

Library of Congress Cataloging-in-Publication Data
(Revised for vol. 55)

Luther, Martin, 1483–1546.
Works.

Vols. 10–16, 17–20, 24 edited by H. C. Oswald.
Vols. 31–49, 51– edited by H. J. Grimm and others. General editor: H. T. Lehmann.
Vol. 55 edited by J. W. Lundeen.
Vols. 31– have imprint: Philadelphia, Fortress Press (formerly Muhlenberg Press)
Includes bibliographical references and index (v. 55)
1. Theology—Collected works—16th century.
2. Lutheran Church—Collected works. 3. Bible—Criticism, interpretation, etc.—History—16th century.
I. Pelikan, Jaroslav, Jan., 1923– ed. II. Oswald, Hilton C., ed. III. Lehmann, Helmut T., ed.
IV. Title: Luther the expositor.
BR330.E5 1955 230′.41 55–9893
ISBN 0–570–06420–1 (v. 20)

5921D86 Printed in the United States of America 1–355

CONTENTS

Foreword vii

Names, Subjects, and Literature Index 1

Scripture Index 349

Old Testament 349

New Testament 405

Apocrypha 461

FOREWORD

To attempt a comprehensive index of the fifty-four volumes of Luther's works in English has been a formidable challenge. The task has been arduous and far more time- and energy-consuming than I had envisaged. But there is a great sense of accomplishment now that the task is completed.

This sense of satisfaction is not for myself alone, but also in feeling that I may have made a significant contribution to all those interested in Luther and Luther's theology, as well as to many others. With this index available it is hoped that the works of Luther can also be used more efficiently to help in understanding that crucial sixteenth century. His writings provide extremely useful insight into the ways of living and thinking characteristic of both upper and lower classes in that period—their daily work, their fears and hopes, their culture, their political and economic life, as well as their religious beliefs and practices. As these writings are studied, many will find, as I did, that many illusions are dispelled and prejudices moderated. One will gain, above all, a more realistic appraisal of Luther himself as both a heroic, seminal personality and a fully human person, blessed with great gifts of insight and leadership but also burdened with human failings and limited perspectives.

For myself, let me say that I can never be grateful enough for the opportunity—no, the compulsion—to read the entire fifty-four volumes before attempting the index. I am sure I join a very select company on that score. But, I am asked, do I remember all that I have read? The answer is: Not all, of course, but still a great deal. More important, I have formed some general impressions; they can be useful, I think, to pass on to the users of this volume.

My first impression is of the great variety and vitality of Luther's writings—both in style and subject matter—which is characteristic of most of them. It is plain that he often wrote in a hurry, with a strong sense of urgency and conviction, as a vitally concerned observer and participant in life around him. Seldom are either his topics or his language devoid of human interest or beyond ordinary comprehension. They reveal his full identification with the people and events of his day.

Another impression worth passing on is of the great importance of keeping in mind the chronological sequence of any one writing or statement of his. To the end of his life Luther was changing and developing in both attitudes and ideas. To take what he wrote in his earliest years as his final conclusion is therefore not safe. One has to take into account the stage in his career that a particular item represents.

A third, and related, impression is of the need always to try to keep in mind the situation, the context, or the occasion that called forth a writing or statement. Most of them were "occasional papers," addressed to a particular question or problem, frequently demanding an immediate response. He seems hardly ever to have gone back to revise anything he wrote, not even for the collection of his Latin works published in his lifetime. But there were exceptions. Chief among them, of course, was his translation of the Bible into German that he was constantly revising, working on it up to the day of his death.

There are other exceptions, too. There are a number of writings that he himself thought of as particularly definitive of his essential views; these he seems to have thought through and shaped with the greatest of care. His *Bondage of the Will* is clearly one of these. Three others, regrettably, are omitted from this American Edition of his works. These are his Small Catechism, Large Catechism, and Smalcald Articles. They are available, however, in any of the editions of the Book of Concord (the Lutheran confessional writings). Students of Luther should not fail to consult them also.

A number of comments about the index itself may be helpful to those using it.

1. The excellent, helpful, companion volume, *Introduction to the Exegetical Writings*, by Jaroslav Pelikan, was not indexed. It was thought that the comprehensive index in that volume was adequate.

2. Two indexes are to be found in this volume—the first index, note, is a *subject index,* not a word index, although such items as proper names of persons and places and many other entries could be either.

Two problems, it was felt, made the subject approach the more desirable one. First, this made it possible to bring together all entries dealing with one topic, even where Luther (or the translator) used different terminology. For instance: all references to Holy Communion, Lord's Supper, Eucharist, or Sacrament of the Altar are brought together under Lord's Supper (an arbitrary choice). The second reason, hinted at above, is that, since all these writings are in translation, the same words in original

Latin or German are frequently translated by varying, but usually synonymous, English terms; hence it was felt necessary to adopt one English word that would bring them together in the index.

3. The other index covers Scripture passages discussed or referred to. Please note that for the most part passages treated in the course of general commentaries—as of the Psalms—are not indexed; it should be obvious where such passages are discussed from the running heads at the top of each page in the commentary volumes.

4. Editors' Introductions, commentary, and notes are also indexed. It was felt that this would make it possible in many cases to move from an editor's clarifying comments to the words or ideas of Luther that called forth the comment. It also makes the often extremely valuable historical and literary commentary of the various editors available to scholars. Items indexed from Introductions to the various volumes are indicated by small Roman numeral page numbers. The "n" after a page number indicates a reference to a footnote.

But *note:* the "n" after a page number does *not* mean that a subject is mentioned *only* in the footnote; to save space it was not thought necessary to give duplicate numbers where a topic is mentioned both in the body of the page and in a footnote. Be sure to check both places!

5. Books referred to in either the body of the text, introductory comments, or footnotes are indexed usually by author, not by title. Exceptions are significant classical, patristic, or medieval writings known best by title.

6. Not all books referred to are indexed. It was not thought useful to index general reference works, such as encyclopedias, dictionaries, etc., referred to in the notes. For the most part, works of a general historical or linguistic nature, which were thought not to contribute to the essential thought of the texts, have also been omitted.

7. The extensive collections of Luther's works (Weimar Ausgabe, Wittenberg Edition, St. Louis Edition, etc.), of patristic writings (*Patrologia* both series, etc.), collections of Reformation writings (*Corpus Reformatorum*, etc.), or biographical dictionaries (*Deutsche Biographie*, etc.), and similar broad collections are *not* included in the index as such (they are, of course, indexed in each individual volume). Unless the reference is to a particular writing of Luther's in one of these collections, which is often the case, it was not thought useful to include references to them; references to other specific titles or authors are indexed, however.

8. Spellings of proper names and geographical terms vary a great deal

in the fifty-four volumes. An arbitrary choice of what seemed to be the generally accepted English form has therefore usually been made. For instance, German "Georg" is usually given as "George," "Johan" or "Johannes" as "John," etc.

9. Titles of books have been given in English where a commonly used form in English was known. Where that was not available, the German or Latin title has been used. Where several English forms of a title are in use, as with Luther's writings (*Freedom of a Christian* or *Christian Liberty*, for instance) an arbitrary choice was made.

10. The "f" after a page number usually indicates a continuation of the subject on the following page; occasionally a continuation for several pages. But the latter is usually indicated by first and last page numbers, for instance, 211–217, etc.

11. A number of entries have been broken down into subtopics—Lord's Supper, Scripture(s), God, etc. I wish this could have been done more frequently—under Faith, Grace, Word (of God), etc., for instance. But time and, to some extent, inadequate overall comprehension—a malady not unique, one hopes, to this indexer—prevented that.

12. Volume numbers are underscored for ease in locating them.

It is hoped that these comments will be found helpful. Users will need to use the index several times in order to become adept at it. They will at the same time, I am sure, find mistakes and note improvements that could be made in it. Your indexer apologizes for such things—perhaps inevitable in such a comprehensive endeavor. But be assured that I did try very hard to make the best, most useable tool for these volumes that was possible in the time allotted.

Finally some *words of appreciation*. These go first of all to my eldest son, Dr. James W. Lundeen, and his talented and patient wife, Dianne Kukkonen Lundeen: the uncounted hours, the generously contributed skills, computer time, and software, which they gave so uncomplainingly to this project, are beyond any kind of brief summary. Without them this index would still be in a larval stage.

Then thanks to the editors of Fortress Press who helped me begin and continue this project; to the libraries and library staffs of Lutheran School of Theology at Chicago; Bernadotte Library, Gustavus Adolphus College, St. Peter, Minn.; and Grand Forks Public Library, Grand Forks, N.D., all of whom have assisted in many ways.

More than to anyone else I owe thanks to my understanding and

long-suffering wife, Doris, who has endured my many months of preoccupation with this project and managed to help me see it through.

Grand Forks, North Dakota
March 1986

JOEL W. LUNDEEN

NAMES, SUBJECTS, AND LITERATURE INDEX

Aachen—22:250, 526, 31:198, 51:390, 54:240

Aachen, Council of—41:281n

Aaron—2:17, 242, 393f, 3:5, 231, 284, 300, 4:153, 275, 5:237, 6:238, 330, 7:11, 8:219, 222f, 227, 229, 9:23, 104, 108, 114, 162, 176, 11:34f, 41, 277, 313, 13:294, 305, 312, 318, 14:54f, 69, 337, 16:86, 178, 17:345, 20:205, 214, 256, 22:121, 238, 309, 23:190, 222, 24:293, 25:4, 29:22, 142, 168, 173, 199, 202, 204–206, 30:208, 307, 36:144, 187, 200, 204, 219, 222, 47:161, 222, 224, 52:31, 90, 126, 134, 150, 271

Abba—25:71, 358f

Abbesses—4:207

Abbots—3:153, 7:63, 337, 16:185, 23:134, 269, 346, 348, 24:226, 30:250, 259n, 46:5

Abbreviation—25:85

Abecedarians—4:147, 5:24, 22:125

Abel—1:80, 185, 241, 243, 245–247, 251f, 254, 257, 259, 261f, 264, 266–268, 270–274, 276, 279, 281–292, 297, 308, 312, 314, 320f, 324f, 327, 329–331, 333, 338f, 345f, 348, 2:89, 116, 140, 197, 233, 3:106, 250, 4:33, 53, 100, 344, 372f, 392, 5:74, 6:32, 119, 171, 223, 233, 296, 373f, 385, 7:86, 265, 322, 8:63, 174, 315, 11:128, 515, 13:25, 188, 412f, 417, 14:88, 197, 225, 16:207, 17:285, 401, 20:133, 212, 21:321, 22:33, 81, 427f, 430, 449f, 475, 24:202, 319, 25:3, 256, 274, 26:263–265, 271, 294, 27:146f, 211, 29:169, 229, 232–234, 30:275, 294, 33:86, 208, 34:303, 35:xi, 79, 36:51, 65f, 95n, 320, 38:290, 39:134, 40:29, 45:86, 46:233, 48:25, 51:246f, 249, 52:90, 92, 110, 123, 126, 138

Abelard, Peter—34:155n

Abiathar—27:135

Abib, Month of—9:154

Abigail—6:360

Abijah—45:207n

Abimelech, King of Gerar—2:293, 305, 3:115, 322f, 327, 330–332, 335–341, 344, 347, 349, 356–360, 4:75, 77, 81–83, 86f, 89, 91, 193f, 209, 211, 245, 5:30, 39, 51f, 55, 59, 63f, 81, 83–85, 87, 92, 6:21, 197, 227, 7:4, 114, 152, 8:133, 197, 10:158, 342, 432, 13:17, 15:153, 19:227, 45:126, 46:41

Abiram—2:58, 3:15, 17, 280, 30:324

Abishag—15:271

Abishai—13:221

Ablutions—20:143f, 27:90

Abner—5:35, 9:233, 13:154, 14:288, 25:452

Abomination—4:181, 204, 240, 283, 6:181, 239f, 9:136, 175, 190, 204, 17:54, 70, 103, 106, 145, 176f, 208, 379, 400, 411, 35:70, 198, 200f, 38:116, 118, 123, 134, 147, 150, 152, 155f, 159f, 162, 168, 174, 185–189, 191, 195f, 197f, 206f, 210, 227, 291, 303, 310, 46:177f, 184, 195, 198, 200, 243, 255f

Abortion—4:304

Abraham—1:13, 21, 89, 194, 244, 248, 256, 268f, 295, 358, 2:ixf, 12, 25, 50, 72, 83, 99, 113f, 176, 179, 197, 201, 205, 222, 230f, 234f, 238–241, 243–256, 266f, 270, 272, 275–277, 279–282, 284–287, 289–292, 295–299, 302–305, 307–309, 311f, 314, 316f, 325f, 329, 331f, 334–336, 341, 344, 349, 351–354, 357f, 360, 362f, 369, 371–375, 377, 379–382, 384f, 388–397, 399, 3:ixf, 3–7, 9–22, 24, 26, 28–36, 38, 41, 43–49, 53–55, 57–66, 71, 74–79, 81–88, 90–107, 109–116, 118–121, 123–129, 131–133, 135, 141–145, 147–150, 152–158, 161–181, 192–199, 201, 203, 205–207, 209f, 212, 216–222, 224–226, 228, 230–236, 238f, 244–248, 260f, 266f, 277, 282, 284, 294f, 302–305, 311–333, 335–341, 344–346, 348–357, 359–361, 363f, 4:ix, 3f, 9, 12–28, 30f, 33, 35–46, 48, 51, 53, 55–60, 62, 64–69, 71, 73–75, 77–81, 83–88, 90–98, 100–104, 106–115, 117–119, 121–124, 126–131, 133–135, 137–141, 149–152, 155,

157f, 160–162, 166–174, 176–185, 188–190, 192–194, 196–199, 205–212, 214–216, 218, 223, 225, 228–235, 237–242, 244–247, 249, 250n, 251–255, 258–260, 264, 266, 271, 274, 277–281, 284, 287f, 282, 294, 298, 300, 302–310, 317–321, 323–325, 327–330, 335–337, 343–345, 348–352, 359f, 362, 365, 367f, 376, 378, 380, 384, 388, 395f, 5:3, 9f, 15–23, 26–29, 51f, 55, 59, 61, 63, 72–74, 76, 78, 81, 83f, 90f, 93, 95, 105, 134, 136f, 143, 146, 149, 161, 165, 191, 197, 201f, 204, 207, 209f, 217, 224, 226, 228f, 231, 236, 242–244, 252, 262, 265, 272f, 279, 294, 325, 350, 385, 6:21, 32, 66, 71, 73, 84, 87, 89, 109, 116, 125, 132f, 146, 149, 162, 184, 223, 227, 247, 263f, 272, 280f, 283, 287f, 291, 296, 302f, 309, 315, 345, 359, 406, 7:10, 13–15, 18, 35f, 42, 56, 103, 114, 116, 133, 152, 163–166, 170, 172, 183, 186f, 199f, 225, 229, 232, 241, 263, 275, 286, 293f, 296, 303, 307, 309, 312, 327, 338, 341, 356f, 8:21, 31, 77, 80, 84, 110–112, 114, 117, 130, 132f, 135, 139f, 141, 151f, 162, 165f, 168–170, 182–184, 196f, 199, 217f, 232, 235, 242, 254, 259, 286, 303, 314–317, 9:26, 70, 103, 118, 169, 171, 241, 292, 10:76f, 146, 158, 204, 434, 447, 11:102, 542, 12:34, 273, 281, 350, 13:21, 34, 180, 299f, 308–310, 14:9, 18f, 89, 94, 152, 186, 212, 220, 270, 291, 327, 330, 332, 15:88, 93, 280, 318, 323f, 16:9f, 14, 28, 45–47, 50, 59, 64, 167, 172f, 177, 194, 250, 330, 17:28, 32–36, 40f, 76, 101, 104, 128, 137, 163f, 197, 235, 260, 263f, 272, 292, 305, 307f, 314, 345, 358–360, 381, 401, 18:95, 159, 405, 407, 19:40, 42, 50, 52, 173, 197, 20:54, 143, 208, 233, 236, 253, 21:243f, 325, 335, 346, 352–354, 22:31f, 34, 40, 42, 47, 53, 79, 92f, 96f, 99, 103, 108, 115f, 118, 120, 124, 131, 135, 195–198, 209, 231, 284, 316f, 319, 321, 354, 367, 428, 431, 449, 453, 463, 473f, 476, 523, 23:260, 266, 326, 378, 385, 395–397, 401, 403–405, 412, 414–419, 421, 24:80, 220, 302, 305, 311, 330, 25:25, 35, 37–40, 42, 80f, 95, 136, 182, 197, 199, 234, 243, 248, 255, 279–282, 384, 438, 463, 26:14, 120, 138, 226–229, 236f, 240–243, 245–247, 249, 251, 254, 257, 259–261, 264, 266, 289, 291, 293, 298f, 301–304, 328, 333, 357–360, 374, 391, 396, 399, 401, 433f, 436f, 441, 449, 454, 457, 460, 27:18, 35, 142, 222, 247, 251–255, 258, 260, 262–268, 274, 278–280, 282–284, 287, 289, 291, 310f, 322–324, 330, 334, 409, 28:49, 98, 120, 195, 271, 280, 371, 29:12, 115, 131, 141, 163, 178, 189, 190, 238f, 30:6, 21, 29, 34, 90, 94, 99, 106, 115, 210, 249, 256, 323, 31:274, 33:270f, 34:121, 223, 225, 303, 316, 321, 35:xi, 79, 83, 195, 359, 364, 373f, 396, 36:39, 43f, 48f, 65f, 321, 37:26, 65, 91, 128f, 134–136, 251, 298, 362, 38:25, 47, 80, 252, 290, 306, 40:39, 42:161, 45:23n, 48, 96, 125f, 331, 381n, 46:39, 97f, 173, 193, 233, 235, 310, 316, 47:67, 72, 77, 85, 87, 89, 92, 157n, 163, 208, 302, 48:260f, 51:29, 82, 105, 316, 338, 52:33, 52, 74, 76, 85, 126, 128, 149f, 153f, 172, 179f, 200, 266, see also **Abram**

Bosom of 4:311f, 314–316, 7:294, 296, 303 36:30, 196

Children or Seed of see **Seed, Abraham's**

His descendents see **Seed, Abraham's**

His faith 2:278, 287, 294, 306, 322, 324, 376, 3:3, 19f, 26, 28, 106, 125, 173, 177, 196, 198, 327, 335, 355, 26:121, 238f, 244, 248, 250, 252, 255

His obedience 2:268f, 3:169–171, 173, 175

His prayers 3:232, 234f, 335, 360

Promise to 47:68, 71, 74f

Sons of see **Seed, Abraham's**

Abraham, Isaac, and Jacob—47:72, 132, 201–203

Abraham's seed—see **Seed, Abraham's**

Abrahams, Israel—*Jewish Life in the Middle Ages*, New York, 1969 47:128

Abram—2:201, 228, 237f, 240, 245, 250, 277, 283, 324f, 330, 332, 335–337, 341, 345, 349, 363, 371–373, 375–378, 380, 382, 389, 392, 3:3, 10, 12, 38, 42, 45f, 61, 74, 88, 112, 4:306, 7:269, 8:84, see also **Abraham**

Absalom—1:308, 2:91, 168, 4:27, 106, 197, 5:145, 165, 206, 6:117, 176, 278, 292, 377, 7:144, 303, 8:215, 224, 238, 330, 10:86, 342, 12:242, 13:147, 154, 206, 223, 14:53, 221, 226, 270, 273, 15:25, 56, 62, 118, 143, 200, 271, 22:236, 23:301, 25:453, 456, 42:157, 45:23, 158, 46:41, 102, 193, 47:18, 52:3, 33

Absentee practice—50:116n

Absolute—10:50f, 78, 107, 160, 327

Absolution—1:11, 250, 2:46, 48, 295, 3:272, 275, 350, 4:17, 48, 67, 142,

179, 181, 202–204, 5:45f, 130, 140f, 149, 183, 197, 205, 244f, 256, 274, 355, 360, 6:128, 132, 225, 234, 300, 364, 7:155, 272, 294, 8:10, 25, 27, 33, 182, 189, 258, 267, 271, 310, 12:369, 371, 391, 13:140, 14:171, 15:233, 16:73, 17:163, 22:48, 51n, 66, 180, 202, 220, 269, 285, 301, 303, 308, 368, 420, 480, 507, 512, 515, 23:15, 206n, 319, 24:45, 179, 387, 394, 26:153f, 182, 245, 350, 27:216, 31:20f, 100, 113, 193, 322, 32:45–52, 75f, 34:347, 35:x, 6, 11f, 104, 36:8, 21f, 27, 48, 83, 88, 90, 122, 124, 172, 258, 359n, 37:368, 38:73, 87, 154, 156, 158, 177, 179, 200, 204, 41:107, 153–155, 173, 336, 42:22, 62, 110, 175n, 44:134n, 134–135, 221–229, 47:48, 48:43, 85n, 50:40, 75f, 51:53, 57, 59f, 99, 167, 299, 307, 326f, 391, 53:116–121, 54:104, 334, 394f, 463, see also **Keys, The**

Abstention—30:311f

Abstinence—2:134n, 326, 4:276, 5:3, 271, 8:172f, 15:32f, 93, 17:111, 25:112, 115, 482, 27:92, 28:313, 315, 317, 355f, 36:261f

Abstinence from meat—22:258, 441

Abstinence from sex—45:35

Abstinence from wine—46:177

Absurdities—30:290, 38:25f, 28, 57, 81, 189n, 238f

Abundance—6:5f, 174f, 10:138, 353, 16:20, 264, 28:379, 381

Abuses, Ecclesiastical—13:292, 41:222

Academic garb—34:359

Academics—33:20, 24

Accad—2:199f

Acceptance before God—18:187

Accident—18:138

Accidental blessing—5:198

Accidental mercy—see **Mercy, God's Accidental**

Accidentals—38:47f, 82, 253

Accidents vs. substance—36:29n, 31, 32n, 33–35

Accius, L.—19:126n

Accusation—28:351f, 359

Acedia—6:362, 25:456, 29:153

Achaeans (Achaians)—3:332, 25:126, 129

Achaia—see **Greece**

Achan—19:14, 62

Achatius, St.—34:24n

Achilles—2:399, 5:309, 382, 6:335, 7:164, 170, 178, 185, 13:58, 27:103, 33:145, 234, 236, 288, 47:179

Achish, King of Gath—10:158f

Achor, Valley of—17:382, 18:11

***Achtliederbuch* (Hymns)**—53:192f, 201, 217, 222, 225, 229, 232

Achzib—7:6f, 24

Acolytes—34:55, 211, 38:213f

Acquisitiveness—2:326

Acta Augustana—see **Luther, Martin, Writings of**—*Proceedings at Augsburg*

Actions—25:6, 59, 64, 82f, 104, 180–183, 190, 220, 235, 253, 263, 388f, 453, 458, 475f

Actions vs. wishes—25:64, 70, 330, 342

Actium, Gulf of—29:88n

Activity—10:249f, 254f

Acts of God—45:303

Acts of the Apostles, Book of the—2:241, 3:84, 90, 130, 359, 10:448, 14:23, 55, 333, 19:151, 24:383, 25:231, 26:69, 74f, 101, 103, 204–209, 297n, 27:143, 250, 323, 343, 35:363–365, 36:198

Ad Afros epistola synodica—2:374n

Ad generationem—1:291n

Ada—1:316–318

Adah—6:286–288, 291, 294

Adam—1:36–39, 56f, 62–72, 75–77, 80–82, 86, 88–91, 93–98, 100–103, 105–111, 115–120, 122f, 126–131, 133–142, 144–147, 151, 153f, 158f, 165–170, 172–175, 177–183, 185–187, 189–191, 193, 196f, 199, 203–211, 213–216, 218f, 221–227, 229f, 233f, 237f, 240–242, 245–247, 249f, 255, 262, 266–271, 274–276, 281–286, 290f, 293, 299f, 304, 306, 308–310, 312–314, 320f, 324, 326–328, 331, 333–335, 337–339, 341–343, 346f, 349, 351f, 2:7, 10, 28, 31, 52, 57, 71, 80, 82, 98, 114, 121n, 134, 140, 149, 209f, 219, 221–224, 233, 235, 245, 3:16f, 40, 42, 47, 56, 97, 103, 133, 138f, 141, 171, 173, 175, 179, 184, 206, 270, 272, 274, 4:61f, 97, 98n, 100–102, 144, 162f, 173, 190, 193, 236, 291f, 295, 308, 312, 318, 343, 362 369, 5:18, 24, 27, 44, 49, 74, 119, 149, 153, 163, 165, 203, 217, 222, 229, 362, 6:32, 89, 189, 223, 235, 255, 257, 281, 324, 338, 342, 7:13, 36, 181, 225, 272, 275, 276n, 277, 8:75, 95, 164, 174, 190f, 242, 254, 315–317, 326, 331, 9:51, 245, 261, 10:16, 22, 31, 224, 298, 335, 411, 434, 11:172, 182, 534, 12:110, 119, 121, 133f, 189, 243, 308f, 312, 13:34, 85, 88, 90, 97, 101, 118, 137, 236, 14:93, 169, 171f, 175, 179, 183, 300, 16:35, 165, 17:18, 36, 100, 20:211, 332, 22:30f, 33, 79, 88, 111,

116, 119, 122, 124, 131, 137, 154, 156f, 163, 168, 280, 287, 313, 340, 382, 395, 397, 420, 428, 435, 448, 450, 453, 456f, 460, 464, 469, 491, 23:8, 11, 81, 122, 166, 234, 333f, 417, 24:170, 226, 253–256, 328, 341–344, 378, 383, 25:45–47, 51, 58, 63, 273, 296–298, 304f, 308, 332, 344, 408, 513, 26:8f, 179, 240, 245, 351f, 27:181, 250, 260, 262, 288f, 368, 28:50, 97f, 176, 195f, 263, 29:129, 190, 229, 30:10, 21, 43, 109, 112, 116, 118, 189, 196, 210, 263, 272, 275, 31:89, 132, 360, 34:119, 155, 172f, 177, 185, 187, 196, 223, 303f, 316, 35:79, 83, 237, 369, 375, 36:39, 37:89, 109, 362, 366, 38:80, 86, 290, 311, 41:31, 226, 42:43, 48f, 62, 151, 45:49, 86, 88, 96, 146, 326, 46:233, 276, 47:21, 90, 145, 272, 302, 51:38f, 57, 62, 245, 316, 323, 358f, 52:27, 127f, 151, 164, 53:66, 110

Descendents of 1:312, 318, 330, 332, 336

Adam (meaning of word)—11:123

Adam and Eve—5:42, 49, 11:91, 220, 13:90, 212, 15:24, 319f, 19:77, 21:252, 25:332, 408, 27:145, 28:113–116, 118, 120, 163, 168, 192, 194–197, 204, 277–279, 291, 345, 36:345, 44:7–8, 45:202f, 207, 382, 390, 47:148

The first parents 8:11

Adam's church—1:95, 284, 321, 334f

Adam's sin—1:36, 56, 62, 140, 209, 224, 237, 15:338f

Adam, Daughters of—1:282, 312

Adam, Old—see **Old Adam**

Adam, Second—2:26, 35:375

Adders' eggs—17:297

Addis Ababa—2:195n

Additions to Esther and Daniel—35:353f

Adelmann, Bernard—39:26

Adiaphora—13:63, 26:11, 118, 27:161, 202, 34:155n, 38:313–317, 319, 41:173f

Adiaphorists—43:169f

Admah—22:423

Administration—13:151f, 197, 267, 15:7, 26f, 102, 143, 160, 242

Administrator—44:151

Admission to communion—51:137

Admonitions—14:32, 36, 228, 16:21, 94, 209, 224f, 228, 231, 17:212, 21:43 37:102, 135n, 144, 146, 368

Adolescence, adolescents—2:119, 3:279, 4:182, 334, 13:95, 16:42, 29:52, 58

Adolph, Bishop of Merseburg—31:319

Adonai—35:248

Adonijah—9:103

Adoption—8:150f, 154–157, 22:96f, 25:71, 73, 27:289, 30:255, 45:25

Adoration—3:118, 6:160f, 329, 22:64, 137, 52:198, 54:102

Adoration of the Sacrament—36:xi, 271–274, 275n, 277f, 289–293, 295, 297

Adornment—13:284, 368–370, 16:181, 20:70, 205f, 255, 28:273–275, 284f, 29:53, 219, 30:89f, 156, 296, 38:108, 114

Adrian—see also the spelling **Hadrian**

Adrian VI, Pope—34:60, 238n, 41:265n, 45:135f, 138, 46:xi, xii, 48:155n, 54:450

Adrian, Matthew—48:132, 154n, 160–162

Adrianople—50:243n

Adriatic Sea—8:274, 25:124

Adulation—13:205f

Adullam—7:5f, 24, 18:220

Adullamites—7:3f, 7, 24, 37, 47

Adulterers—2:59, 79, 122, 167, 312, 316, 3:46, 222–224, 254, 279, 324, 328, 5:29, 41, 51, 293, 302f, 341, 7:83, 85, 90, 96, 98, 233, 23:312, 314, 24:265, 279, 289, 26:70, 277, 280, 310, 423

Adulteresses—7:92–94, 202, 283, 23:312f, 317–319, 341

Adultery—1:96, 106, 138, 147, 168, 176, 238, 305, 329, 3:5, 227, 233, 254, 331, 350, 4:239, 249, 290, 304, 333, 336, 391, 5:28, 37, 39, 41, 51f, 86, 190, 193, 214, 302–304, 322, 381, 6:82, 91, 197, 300f, 377, 7:20f, 43, 84f, 88, 90, 93f, 98, 110, 115f, 175, 191f, 8:5, 18, 44, 236, 9:146, 166, 211, 219, 223–226, 14:149, 17:272f, 18:4, 23, 36, 22:96, 149f, 222, 233, 264, 274, 371f, 389, 394, 403f, 407f, 436, 439, 23:58, 63, 134, 235, 247, 270, 297, 310–312, 314, 317, 319, 399, 24:291, 339, 341, 26:36, 40f, 96, 123, 125, 139, 141, 308, 327, 340, 363f, 415, 453, 458, 27:88, 188, 219, 260, 348, 357, 368, 28:13, 34, 29:58, 84, 30:20, 26, 179, 183, 245, 250, 269, 272, 279, 288, 302, 35:366, 36:90, 100f, 104f, 165, 206f, 38:166, 191f, 202, 41:18, 113f, 124, 227, 239, 241, 246, 249, 287, 42:44, 92, 139, 45:18, 26, 30f, 32f, 115, 145, 155, 157, 46:77, 98, 262, 267, 270–272, 276, 278, 282, 294f, 297–300, 311, 313, 49:85f, 51:153–155, 191, 261, 294, 299, 374, 389, 54:24, 66, 154, 160, 218, 244, 302, 315, 335, 349, 415

Adultery, Woman caught in—23:337

Adults—3:103, 110, 112, 171, 233, 29:102, 180, 30:247
Advancing socially—21:185
Advent—16:40, 23:405n, 34:57
Advent, Second—8:15, 11:75, 16:46, 32:139f, 203, 35:299, 327, 392, 37:73n, 361
Adversaries—6:76, 147, 159, 170, 318, 397, 16:247, 29:37, 70, 35:196n, 217, 220
Adversity—9:71, 74, 92, 96, 113, 170, 11:300, 14:56f, 94, 102, 140, 144, 161, 185, 209f, 237, 305, 16:261, 288, 22:133, 252, 23:146, 179, 299, 27:68, 403, 30:9, 17f, 154, 204, 35:53, 56, 42:32, 50f, 60f, 144f, 159, see also **Trials and tribulations**
Advice—46:267, 271, 283
Advocate—27:388
Aegean Sea—50:72n
Aegidius, St.—14:45n
Aegidius of Viterbo—54:208
Aeneas—2:399, 3:359, 7:48, 203
Aeneas Sylvius—see **Pius II, Pope**
Aeneid—see **Vergil**
Aenon—22:414f, 421n, 423
Aeolians—2:191
Aepinus, John (Johannes)—7:294n, 50:30, 150n, 180
Aeschylus—37:138n
Eumenides 1:287n, 6:78n
Prometheus Bound 3:49n
Aesop—2:159f, 4:61n, 6:125, 13:200, 209, 396, 16:42n, 78n, 26:405, 34:286, 35:177, 350, 37:23n, 38:93, 40:316n, 317, 46:111n, 112n, 47:228, 49:288, 54:72, 210–213
Fables 15:61n, 96, 101, 31:xxi, 93n, 358, 36:17n, 39:104n, 163n, 213n, 41:235n
Fox and the Hedgehog 46:111n
Frogs and the Stork 46:112n
Affection—6:16f, 46, 48, 56, 82, 150, 252–256, 269, 272, 296, 312, 321, 379, 384, 386, 396, 403, 7:261, 266, 305, 315f, 340–342, 15:8, 10f, 12, 20f, 16:205, 24:102, 164, 246, 265, 29:154, 175
Affection, Natural—6:16n, 8:3, 13–16, 19–22, 50, 96ff, 328
Affinity—4:226, 306, 7:19, 84
Afflictions—2:17, 24, 50, 61f, 93, 104f, 156, 195, 204, 226, 304, 307, 310, 319f, 3:9, 18, 22, 32, 35f, 38, 63f, 68–71, 73, 101, 249, 264, 317, 320, 343–346, 4:6f, 47f, 93, 103, 131, 175, 197, 229, 249, 270, 278, 311, 314, 329f, 337f, 340, 354, 360, 5:5f, 12, 22, 57, 65, 88, 166, 171, 177, 385, 6:8–11, 38, 74, 123, 133, 310, 312, 7:61, 98, 100, 125, 133, 137, 180, 202, 208, 229, 256, 311, 327, 8:5, 13, 33, 73, 114, 121, 128, 154, 230, 236, 240, 293, 9:23, 154f, 157f, 268, 10:39, 152, 288, 320, 367, 12:404, 410, 13:113, 240, 260, 15:25, 63, 191f, 199f, 204f, 209, 235, 237, 243, 246, 16:109, 201, 208f, 213, 233, 237, 261, 343, 17:3, 49f, 104, 129, 135, 160f, 166, 194, 204, 239, 319, 332, 334, 357, 399, 20:89, 151, 156, 164, 275, 22:54, 207, 283, 302, 472, 502, 24:7, 12, 17, 145, 150, 198, 211, 242, 354f, 357, 27:12, 23f, 33, 35, 133f, 143, 231, 29:118, 128, 30:24, 40, 126, 312, see also **Trials and tribulations**
Africa—2:187, 194, 203, 364, 3:63, 10:412, 16:126, 135, 170, 183, 17:413, 25:230, 27:60, 31:281, 32:69, 34:345, 41:24, 281, 291, 334, 50:95
Africans—2:194
Africanus, Julius—54:421
Afterbirth—7:35, 8:241–243
Agag—10:16, 19:6
Agamemnon—2:399, 7:178n, 31:284n
Agape vs. eros—27:391f, see also **Love**
Agatha, St.—3:125n, 6:255, 8:255, 259, 10:251, 288, 366, 22:479, 24:118, 196, 277, 420, 28:376, 30:127, 31:199, 42:160n, 44:174n, 206, 291, 312, 52:273
Agathon—42:25n
Aged, The—see **Old people**
Agent of sin—26:147n, 155, 169, 372
Agnes, St.—3:125n, 4:396, 6:255, 7:88, 8:191, 10:252, 288, 13:333, 17:258, 20:25, 22:479, 24:118, 277, 420, 31:228, 32:258, 51:392
***Agnus Dei* (hymn)**—38:123, 41:168n, 169, 338, 53:21, 36, 57, 82, 149, 151f, 154
Agnus Dei, Luther's version of—53:151f
Agreed Statement of 1955—38:xiii
Agreements—9:144, 20:126
Agricola, Else (Elizabeth) Moshaner—48:221n
Agricola, John—1:232n, 3:243n, 6:76n, 16:210n, 34:5, 7, 37:155, 39:110, 40:266, 275n, 41:72n, 42:17n, 19n, 25n, 46:111n, 47:101–106, 108, 135f, 48:113n, 220, 236n, 49:103, 150f, 152, 180n, 182f, 212f, 285n, 291n, 299n, 330n, 338f, 347, 362, 372f, 401n, 413n, 414, 51:103, 197, 54:23, 191, 220, 233, 248, 290, 313–314, 379, 391
Agricola, Stephan—38:9f, 63, 89n, 49:238n
Agriculture—1:205, 211, 4:299, 5:267, 7:115, 16:151, 46:128, 131n, 181

Agriculture vs. commerce—44:214
Agrippa—47:243, 249f, 303
Ahab, King—2:20, 4:175, 365, 5:12, 246, 7:52, 144, 8:233, 300, 9:70, 81, 11:65, 13:59, 68, 88, 17:74, 92, 278f, 301, 18:12, 193n, 267, 19:56, 64, 25:95f, 160, 237, 422, 445, 31:316, 36:219, 222f, 46:66, 120, 131, 172, 47:276
Ahasuerus—2:264, 304, 11:265, 508, 34:130
Ahasuerus, King—35:61, 337
Ahasuerus Priscus—20:160
Ahaz, King—3:30, 216, 4:100, 102, 105, 124, 180, 7:300, 314, 341, 11:495, 16:6, 11, 14, 54, 78f, 80f, 83f, 111, 142f, 336, 18:38, 20:163, 36:44, 65, 154n, 174, 47:194f, 199, 53:21
Ahaziah, King—47:199, 208, 222f
Ahitophel—5:145, 8:330, 13:170, 172, 179f, 221, 223, 14:226, 23:301, 45:122
Ahrens, Frederick C.—indexer of Vols. 41, 45, 46
  translator of *On Marriage Matters* 46:259–319
  translator of *To the Saxon Princes* 43:251–287
Ai—1:315, 2:282, 286, 3:164, 180, 5:243, 6:223, 247, 9:258, 16:114
Air—2:94, 115, 147, 330, 388, 27:149, 284
Akeldama—11:73
Akiba, Rabbi—47:234f
Akten und Briefe zur Kirchenpolitik Herzog Georgs von Sachsen—see **Gess, Felician**
Aland, Kurt—47:10, 36n, 106, 54:xv
Aland, Kurt, ed.—*Luther Deutsch: Die Werke Martin Luther in neuer Auswahl für die Gegenwart*, Stuttgart, 1957–1969 38:94
Alaric—13:282n, 46:236n
Alb—29:22, 40:129f
Alber, Matthew—36:310, 37:xiii, 8
Albert I, Emperor and King of Austria—28:364n
Albert II, Emperor—48:189n
Albert of Brandenburg, Margrave—54:191
Albert of Mansfeld, Count—35:115, 43:49, 51, 45:80, 46:47, 247n, 48:145n, 238, 337n, 49:103n, 108f, 320n, 435n, 50:281f, 291, 295n, 302, 311f, 315, 52:3, 54:233, 272f
Albert the Great—see **Albertus Magnus**
Albertus Magnus—14:284n, 23:115n, 38:119n, 42:7n, 45:377n, 48:30n, 96n
Alberus, Erasmus—*Der Barfuser Münche Eulenspiegel und Alcoran* 17:286n
Albinus—47:250
Albrecht, Archbishop of Mainz—2:199n, 4:201, 5:365n, 6:47n, 49, 76n, 365, 371, 7:242n, 13:352n, 16:258, 22:188, 253n, 408, 465, 23:201n, 378n, 25:476, 498, 29:18n, 31:xv, 21f, 183f, 34:20n, 48n, 97, 252n, 329, 330n, 336n, 36:133n, 205, 38:141, 39:xxiii–xxv, 60n, 241–245, 269n, 41:15n, 222n, 229n, 230n, 231n, 232n, 233n, 234–239, 256n, 276, 369n, 43:101, 107n, 141, 147, 239f, 253, 260, 262, 44:147n, 151n, 245n, 45:134n, 288n, 46:90n, 227n, 47:20n, 255, 48:44f, 56n, 70, 109n, 143n, 150, 152n, 154n, 161n, 163n, 205n, 213, 214n, 234, 305n, 316, 320, 326, 339, 344f, 349, 350f, 353f, 365, 373f, 377, 381, 49:60n, 119, 181n, 182n, 189n, 198n, 350n, 354n, 389n, 416, 50:22, 41n, 44, 54n, 56, 87n, 95n, 111, 115n, 147n, 160n, 161, 224, 237n, 256f, 269, 272, 51:197, 383, 53:324, 54:60, 86, 144, 171, 230, 256, 265, 310, 357, 370, 380, 387, 405, 441, 472
  Summary Instructions 31:183–185, 236n
Albrecht, Duke of Mecklenburg—50:147
Albrecht, Duke of Prussia—9:5, 17:188n, 22:408n, 495n, 38:281, 39:xv, 49:23n, 24n, 59f, 60, 121, 122n, 152n, 312n, 321n, 50:190n, 222n, 252f
Albrecht, Grand Master of Teutonic Knights—see **Albrecht, Duke of Prussia**
Albrecht, John—50:285n, 296
Albrecht, Otto—*Die evangelische Gemeinde Miltenberg und ihr erster Prediger*, Halle, 1896 35:222n, 43:99n, 100n, 104n
  "Studien zu Luthers 'Sendschreiben an die Christen zu Riga und in Liefland vom Jahre 1524' " (in *Zeitschrift für Kirchengeschichte*, Vol. XVII, 1897), Gotha 45:316n, 324n, 335n, 348n, 354n, 356n, 360n, 362n, 365n, 366n, 369n, 371n, 376n, 377n
Albrecht of Brandenburg—see **Albrecht, Archbishop of Mainz**
Albs—13:296, 15:149, 34:55
Alcala—University of 50:27n
Alcibiades—15:105n
Alcoran—5:79, 221, 347, 13:271, see also ***Koran***
Aldhelm—*Tractatus de laudibus virginitatis* 5:304n
Aleander, Jerome—31:381, 394, 32:5, 103, 123n, 123–130, 276n, 34:80n, 233,

267, 332n, 36:8, 43:74, 44:xvii, 48:176, 216n, 220n, 223n, 255n, 272n, 49:285n
Aleppo, Battle of—46:202n
Alesius, Alexander—50:150n, 180n, 197n
Alexander I, Pope—29:17n
Alexander III, Pope—43:237n
Alexander V, Pope—54:81
Alexander VI, Pope—31:155, 32:88, 36:63n, 44:156n, 167n, 54:23
Alexander, Bishop of Alexandria—11:225n, 38:203, 41:55n, 56
Alexander de Villa-Dei—45:370n
Alexander of Hales—31:222, 32:258, 34:154n, 35:64n, 36:63n
Alexander the Great—2:191, 285, 343, 346, 351, 368, 374, 4:35, 129, 186, 5:239, 253f, 270, 6:335, 362, 7:67, 142f, 170, 178, 185, 362, 8:48, 211, 237, 274, 288, 320, 13:155, 199f, 202, 395, 14:118, 250, 15:19f, 43, 86, 101, 16:182, 184, 19:187, 217, 20:90f, 171, 284f, 22:43, 79, 25:172, 35:295, 299, 300n, 306f, 331, 47:207, 221, 223, 249, 50:156n, 54:64
Alexandria—3:217, 4:56, 5:96, 16:127, 158, 165, 18:309, 35:348, 38:308n, 47:236
Alexandria, Bishop of—41:41f, 91, 95, 290, 46:179n
Alexandria, Church of—41:41, 55f, 84, 87, 133f, 210n, 325, 348
Alexandria, Destruction of—41:42n
Alexandria, School of—13:33
Alexandria, Theology of—32:128n
Alexandrian school—9:25
Alexios III, Eastern Emperor—41:305n
Alfred IX, King of Leon—46:266n
Algeria—50:95n, 224n
Alien loveliness—12:278f
Alien purity—12:367
Alien righteousness—12:367, 16:120, 28:362
Alien work of God—2:134, 4:131, 8:5n, 13:79, 135f, 14:191, 335, 16:233f, 17:4, 50, 353, 21:341, 26:38n, 29:135f, 36:56, 44:77, 51:19–21
Alien work of the Gospel—51:20
Alien work, Christ's—51:62f
Aliens—16:194
All Saints' Day—23:x
Allah—46:183f
Allegory—1:5, 19, 87n, 90, 93, 97, 99, 121f, 132, 184f, 187–189, 201–204, 237, 2:x, 68, 108f, 144, 150–158, 160–162, 164, 386, 3:28, 32, 55, 72, 141, 192, 194, 237n, 293, 4:101, 137, 5:88, 216, 224, 253, 279, 294n, 345–348, 6:125, 146, 153–155, 322, 7:7, 49, 224, 8:146, 269, 283, 9:7f, 24, 26f, 97, 113, 126, 134, 149–151, 156, 198, 213–215, 226, 250, 12:204, 225, 248, 254f, 257f, 290f, 408, 13:26, 14:36, 297, 299, 318f, 335, 338, 15:17, 114, 179f, 196, 200, 209, 235, 252, 16:xi, 7, 12f, 22, 61, 76, 122, 125–127, 136f, 161, 173, 211, 222, 291, 296f, 322, 325n, 326–328, 17:7, 23n, 47f, 75, 125, 136, 149, 213, 235, 335, 349, 18:8, 14, 18, 20, 23, 26, 34, 36, 42, 44, 52, 66f, 70, 75, 82f, 86, 90, 114, 117f, 120, 122, 130, 132, 136, 150, 156, 160, 172, 179f, 185, 194, 214, 221, 243, 257, 268, 299, 301, 308, 313, 325, 330f, 353, 19:31, 74, 97f, 102, 210, 20:24f, 51, 62, 65, 102, 105, 143, 155–157, 181, 346, 22:114n, 414, 23:105n, 169n, 24:366, 25:xi, 141, 144, 332, 398, 26:298, 304, 347, 430, 432–436, 438, 439n, 440–442, 444, 450, 460, 27:37, 127, 226, 310–312, 315–317, 322, 324, 340, 345f, 400, 407, 28:175f, 348, 29:80, 86, 153f, 213, 222, 30:20f, 48f, 54, 115, 187, 35:66, 235n, 247, 36:30, 92, 95, 110, 219–229, 37:261, 38:24, 40, 56, 39:180, 40:188–190, 48:54, 51:23f, 35f, 253, 54:46–47, 406
Alleluia—53:21, 24, 30
Allen, N.H.—53:xviii
Allen, Percy S., ed.—*Opus Epistolarum Desiderii Erasmi Roterodami*, New York, 1906–1958 33:ix, 6n, 13n, 48:xiii
Allgau—37:244
Alliances—16:89, 91, 106f, 111, 252, 285, 349, 46:90n, 113n, 50:46
Alliances of Imperial Estates—49:xvin, 88n, 190f, 223f, 227n, 228f, 236n, 243, 244n, 246, 251, 256, 264, 266f, 272, 281n, 424, 429f, 435n
Alliteration—9:163
Alloeosis—23:101n, 28:265f, 37:xviii, 153, 156, 206n, 207–214, 218, 230–236, 247, 275, 280, 331
Allstedt—35:169n, 40:47f, 50, 105, 48:188, 49:82n, 98, 53:54
Almah (Hebrew word for virgin or maiden)—10:91, 16:84, 17:236, 45:207–210
Almonds—7:322f
Alms—2:263, 349, 3:168, 215, 4:90, 7:338, 9:138, 147n, 13:53f, 397, 14:50, 21:130f, 134–136, 162, 183, 22:81, 133, 335, 349, 521f, 23:16, 18f, 23, 49,

85f, 110f, 238, 247, 327, 401, 24:228, 26:25, 124, 204, 208–210, 286, 294, 312, 27:350, 30:230, 31:86, 34:248, 315, 35:93f, 38:173, 45:181f, 185, 259, 284, 287n
Almsgiving—41:52
Aloetus, Peter—37:42n
Alphabet—4:362
Alps—2:108, 23:168
Alsace—49:118
Altar paintings—13:434
Altar screen—42:119, 123
Altars—1:95, 284, 337, 2:112–114, 138, 192, 277, 284, 286, 332f, 363, 3:32, 143, 280f, 4:89, 112, 138, 179, 201, 231, 237, 5:78, 80f, 83, 251f, 265, 304, 6:184–186, 223–226, 233, 241, 247, 249f, 8:75f, 125, 135, 11:140–144, 150, 13:375, 16:59, 165f, 215, 18:211, 213, 23:80, 121, 138, 213, 366, 408, 24:91, 370, 26:135, 155, 27:126, 286, 352, 364, 385, 29:7, 204–206, 30:15, 185, 188, 34:55, 36:116, 172, 184, 198, 227, 233, 263, 321, 37:65n, 70, 72, 84, 123, 355f, 38:120f, 158, 160, 170, 205, 208, 316, 53:33, 69, 74, 80
Altars, Endowed—45:161, 180n, 284, 286, 304, 306
Altdorff, Herman von—33:10n
Altenburg—45:13n, 162, 288n, 48:8, 96, 100, 103n, 104n, 108, 109n, 127f, 129n, 161n, 170, 222, 264n, 49:15n, 58n, 143, 190n, 194, 212n, 334, 50:97n, 142, 154, 156n, 169n, 170n
Altenburg manuscript—18:ix–xii, 77, 387, 19:ix, 148n, 20:ix, 3n, 4n, 76n, 152n
Altenstaig, John—54:8
Altenstein Castle—48:227
Althaus, Paul—39:xvn, xviiin, 47:160n, 52:xn
"Luther auf der Kanzel," 1921 51:xin
Altmühl River—49:313n
Alveld, Augustine—27:280n, 39:xxiii, 49–104, 44:117–120, 48:164n, 183n, 194
Alveld, Augustine, Works of—*A Very Fruitful and Useful Booklet about the Apostolic See and about St. Peter* 39:xxiiif, lif, 44:117f
Concerning the Apostolic See 39:51
Treatise concerning Communion in Both Kinds 36:6f, 12n, 13n, 15–17, 23n, 24n, 25, 26n, 27n
Amalek—11:109, 121f, 125f, 26:55
Amalekites—2:78f, 355, 367f, 3:172, 293, 4:44, 5:152, 268, 6:211, 291, 295, 297, 389, 8:306, 9:37, 249, 251, 19:233, 22:397, 51:159n
Amana, Mt.—10:196, 203f, 27:315
Amaziah, King—6:265, 46:120
Amaziah, Priest of Bethel—18:176f, 19:157
Amazons—3:189n, 15:130f
Ambassador of Jesus Christ—26:16
Ambassadors—6:118f, 122
Amber—7:323
Ambiguities—6:53, 136, 181, 7:157, 168, 252, 8:141f, 195–197, 199, 209
Ambition—2:119, 125, 127, 171, 214, 338, 348, 395, 397, 3:5f, 13, 15, 65, 7:66, 185, 190, 194, 196, 236, 263, 15:69f, 96, 16:346, 27:80, 132
Ambracia in Illyricum—29:88
Ambrose, St.—1:28, 2:55, 3:165, 194, 298, 329, 4:253, 377f, 399, 7:252, 10:43, 446, 15:274n, 17:6, 101, 253, 20:184, 22:254, 256, 258–260, 263f, 267, 271, 484, 514, 23:72, 74, 25:xi, 118, 268, 327, 343, 447, 26:66, 76, 458, 27:83, 179, 214, 218, 245, 271, 368f, 373, 376, 28:317, 29:125n, 131, 31:119, 126, 208, 214, 32:9, 194, 221, 34:95, 35:197, 372, 36:15n, 37:329, 38:69, 239, 39:280n, 41:19, 52n, 80, 94n, 98, 308, 44:128, 211, 45:233n, 289n, 290n, 46:269, 48:24, 54, 51:153n, 363, 53:171, 235, 260, 286, 308, 54:8, 26, 34, 259, 335, 353, 460
Ambrose, St., Works of—*Commentaria in XII epistolas beati Pauli* 27:179n, 214n, 245n, 368n, 376n
Commentaria in epistolam ad Romanos 6:307n
De excessu fratris Satyri 5:220n
De officiis 4:399n, 16:18n, 31:208n
De paradiso 25:168, 328
De poenitentia 25:314
De sacramentis 25:261, 53:27n
De sacramento regenerationis 25:63, 327
Exhortatio virginitatis 5:323n
Hexaemeron 15:352n
Hymnus ad Completorium 8:210n
On Faith 38:239n
Vita gloriosa Agnetis 44:174n
Ambrosian Rite—38:318n
Ambrosiaster—28:14n
Commentary on the Epistle to the Romans 25:304
Ambrosius Catharinus Politus—*Apologia pro veritate catholicae et apostolicae fidei ac doctrinae adversus impia ac valde pestifera Martini Lutheri dogmata*, 1520 16:341n, 26:57n, 30:123n
Ameln, Conrad—53:xx, 58, 151, 154, 177, 181, 185f, 225, 296

Amen—11:486, 16:320, 42:76n, 77, 113

Amerbach, John—48:24n

Amerbach, Veit—38:265, 273n, 54:474

America, 20th century—26:404n

Americas, Discovery of the—1:207n, 45:234

Amittai—19:3, 28

Ammianus Marcellinus—*Res gestae* 5:191n

Ammon—6:387, 7:303, 8:238, 289, 11:121f, 125, 128, 12:258, 265, 19:235, 47:154

Ammonites—1:292, 302, 2:189, 367, 3:228, 314, 4:175, 5:171, 268, 6:283, 8:199, 237f, 285, 289, 304, 9:32–34, 83, 169, 230f, 235, 10:413, 12:306, 15:139, 16:126f, 17:72, 87, 18:9, 116, 136f, 323, 342, 27:321, 47:182

Amnon—6:267, 323, 9:224, 13:223

Amorites—1:206, 2:204, 362f, 372, 3:40, 4:246, 5:91, 6:202, 206, 214, 388, 390, 392, 7:4, 18, 35, 8:197f, 9:16, 20, 21, 24, 27, 32, 35–37, 83, 145, 204–206, 272, 16:154, 17:358, 18:89, 142f, 26:436, 27:315, 42:39, 44:274n, 46:120, 190

Amos, Prophet—2:190, 3:10, 274, 7:349, 8:301, 9:3, 125, 14:311, 18:x, 127–130, 207, 230, 19:3, 38, 157

  Commentary on his book 18:xf, 127–190 (text)

Amphibia—1:51

Amphictyones—2:202

Amplification—30:221

Amputation—46:96f

Amraphel—2:364

Amsdorf, Nicholas von—13:ix, 22:418n, 26:36n, 28:3, 32:103, 119f, 259, 34:108, 37:147n, 155, 38:94, 39:227, 42:17n, 43:116, 44:xi, 119, 45:54, 378n, 46:184n, 48:113n, 202, 213, 218, 232, 234f, 257, 262, 264, 267n, 269, 310, 352, 360, 382, 49:13, 111n, 112f, 115n, 116f, 172n, 173n, 186n, 187f, 213f, 218f, 239f, 284n, 377, 50:29n, 30, 38n, 46n, 53f, 72f, 173n, 216, 218, 220, 224n, 226n, 260, 262f, 264f, 269n, 270f, 273, 275n, 51:69, 77, 53:43, 54:xxiii, 150, 214, 219, 226, 264, 321, 391

Amulets—46:135n

Amusements—45:120n, 121, 249, 368–370

Anabaptists—1:145f, 149, 156, 160, 2:18, 43, 83, 87, 150, 162, 243, 325f, 3:5, 13, 15, 103, 191, 301, 4:71, 78, 81, 88, 392, 5:239, 249, 7:131, 152n, 200, 8:133, 12:23, 65, 74, 116, 166–168, 223, 253, 274, 278, 280, 288, 13:61, 263, 279, 14:24n, 84n, 16:188n, 17:39f, 50, 53, 74, 92, 100, 113, 173, 221, 256, 327, 391, 21:5, 254f, 257, 22:22, 173, 180, 190n, 225, 239, 383, 23:66, 71, 79, 85, 99, 157, 187, 194, 201f, 205, 257, 275, 285, 354, 358, 368, 24:13n, 69, 92, 176, 215, 229, 235, 404, 26:28n, 52, 130, 143f, 176, 192, 194, 221. 242n, 312, 395, 397, 413, 454f, 27:34, 53, 60, 62, 88, 147–149, 28:199, 233, 361–364, 367, 29:8f, 81n, 30:315n, 34:346, 354, 35:26, 37:xiii, xv, xvii, 360, 366f, 38:6, 27, 88, 97, 293, 40:227, 229f, 232f, 234, 239–241, 246, 248f, 258, 260–262, 381, 383n, 384, 386, 390, 392f, 41:xii, 45n, 46n, 66n, 126n, 191n, 241, 242n, 43:49n, 54, 116, 45:91n, 46:5n, 90n, 47:59, 110n, 116, 119, 50:16, 113n, 198n, 286, 51:187, 224, 226, 299, 325, 337, 377, 384, 53:xv, 212, 237, 292, 54:48, 113, 140, 152, 163, 174, 318, 376, see also **Antisacramentarians**; **Enthusiasts**; **Fanatics**; **Sectarians**

Anacletus II, Pope—27:218n

Anacoluthon—27:316, 318

Anagoge—1:87n, 27:312

Anagogical sense—25:xi, 26:440

Anah—6:291–293, 297, 301

Anakim—2:36, 4:193, 9:34, 86

Analogies—4:5, 313, 7:217, 8:252f, 316, 16:262, 310, 339, 26:296f, 304, 345, 350, 436, 27:23, 263–265, 283, 30:115, 37:109n, 109f, 112, 163f, 175, 227, 253–270, 343, 345f, 51:7, 10–12

Analogy of faith—2:16, 151f, 164, 3:168, 4:126, 129f, 6:131, 331, 7:173, 16:146, 248, 20:147, 25:106, 445, 25:446, 28:320, 37:262, 38:59

Ananias—4:72, 24:358, 26:62f, 74, 39:269, 41:324

Anarchy—3:130, 9:183n, 13:190f, 14:4n, 46:xii

Anarchy the ideal—45:89, 101

Anastasia, St.—6:255, 8:250, 10:366, 12:258, 22:479, 24:277, 25:462, 32:258

Anastasius, Pope—44:359n

Anastasius of Constantinople—41:05n

Anathema—15:79, 18:419, 25:380f, 26:56, 27:177–179, 183, 345, 41:226, 46:147n, 49:152

Anatomy, Knowledge of—1:125, 129

Anaxagoras—31:313, 33:166, 36:16n

Ancestors, Imitating—15:17, 21, 42, 206

Ancient of Days—7:118

Anderson, John—53:xviii, 199

Andrae, Johannes—31:149n

Andreas Bodenstein von Karlstadt—see **Barge, Hermann**
Andreas, Willy—*Deutschland vor der Reformation*, Stuttgart, 1948 34:24n
Andrew, St., Apostle—10:288, 13:28, 22:182, 184–187, 189, 192, 229, 41:162, 319
Andrew's, St., Day—23:396n
Aner—2:372, 398, 5:52, 6:227, 345
Anfechtungen—1:287n, 7:276n, 12:189n, 14:49n, 84n, 19:179f, 22:142n, 23:73n, 268n, 26:63n, 34:287n, 35:54f, 12, 15, 19, 43, 53–55, 105, 110, 260, 265, 322, 41:xii, xvi, 48n, 110n, 261, 42:71n, 181, 43:116, 44:63n, 46:149, 48:28n, 143, 147, 174, 215, 232, 257, 263, 303n, 307f, 319, 328, 366, 49:249, 50:101n, 51:179, 237n, 54:37, 50, 74
Angel—43:128f
Angelic Hymn—see ***Gloria in Excelsis***
Angelic life—1:46, 65, 111, 236, 347, 349
Angelo Carletti di Chivasso—*Summa de casibus conscientiae (Summa Angelica)* 2:314n, 17:250n, 26:406n, 31:146, 150, 36:96n, 45:22n, 252n, 46:320n, 48:187n
Angels—1:4, 12, 19, 22f, 28, 30f, 57f, 74, 86, 88, 90, 98, 106–108, 111f, 113n, 145, 173, 193f, 223f, 230–232, 235f, 244–246, 286, 296, 301, 324, 339, 341, 345f, 348, 356, 2:3, 38, 46, 82, 130, 145, 151, 169, 202, 211–213, 227, 240, 261, 284, 288, 312, 355f, 376, 378, 388, 390f, 3:5, 18, 29, 58, 60–62, 64, 66, 69, 71, 74f, 80, 99, 108, 164f, 167, 178, 181, 187f, 194, 199f, 207f, 212, 215, 218–220, 228, 232, 243f, 246–249, 252, 258, 263f, 266–275, 277, 280, 284–286, 295f, 298, 300, 305, 320, 322f, 340f, 360, 4:8, 37, 51, 56–58, 61, 63, 65, 67, 71f, 83, 106f, 120–130, 136f, 139, 155, 160f, 170, 178, 180–183, 191, 212, 221, 251–258, 260, 264–266, 272, 279–281, 285, 287, 294, 304f, 313, 315f, 319f, 322, 327, 332f, 340, 352, 372, 389, 5:20f, 23, 34, 50, 61–63, 70f, 125, 160f, 196, 215–224, 229f, 234, 236, 243f, 247–252, 260, 267, 272, 276, 283, 317, 329, 346, 353, 355, 361, 363, 385f, 6:41f, 58, 87–95, 125–127, 129, 191, 226, 329f, 350, 7:13, 55, 71, 97–99, 111, 119f, 195, 225, 279, 287, 309, 367, 375, 8:26. 30, 43, 46, 56, 60, 114, 139, 151, 162–168, 188f, 242, 254, 256, 270, 315–317, 9:57, 123, 129, 171, 188, 10:111, 120, 153, 325, 338, 345, 11:176n, 209, 226, 321–323, 13:34, 235, 241, 14:32, 82, 89, 101, 103, 120, 210, 218, 261, 288, 330, 15:81, 212, 308, 310, 313, 318, 326, 337, 16:20, 27, 58, 70, 76, 158, 212, 266f, 272, 283f, 317, 17:357, 18:377, 20:15–17, 26, 42f, 64, 74, 93, 138, 142, 167–173, 180f, 215, 248f, 327, 21:36, 242, 351, 22:10, 14, 20, 22, 27, 51, 61, 75, 88, 102–104, 109, 113, 118f, 130f, 134, 173, 179, 201–204, 206, 208–211, 246, 253, 256, 263, 266, 306, 338, 346, 359, 363, 374, 380, 392, 412, 466, 491, 503f, 506, 508, 520, 526f, 23:77, 90, 98f, 122f, 139, 191f, 238, 302, 323, 329, 348, 350, 366, 376, 390, 411, 24:21, 49, 57, 65, 68f, 90, 92, 95, 105, 108, 113, 118f, 123, 128, 141, 157f, 165f, 180, 182, 184, 198, 232, 294, 312–314, 321, 369, 373, 414, 416, 25:78, 106, 131, 143, 175, 463, 26:16, 22, 31, 33, 38, 41, 49, 55–58, 65–67, 82, 93, 98f, 106f, 136, 175, 178, 182, 210, 220, 265, 292, 294, 300, 318f, 323, 352, 362n, 372f, 382, 417–422, 458f, 27: 35, 38, 40, 45, 102, 108, 129, 143, 146, 171, 178, 180, 226f, 271f, 239, 297, 300–303, 310f, 314, 376, 391f, 28:113, 172, 178f, 187, 196, 306, 29:63, 71f, 109f, 115–117, 121f, 126f, 129, 134, 146, 167, 202, 30:24f, 90. 98, 121, 175, 177, 181, 185, 187, 195, 206f, 228, 241f, 266, 296, 312, 34:185, 225, 35:31, 144, 163, 182, 190f, 198n, 199, 266, 305, 364, 384, 401f, 407, 410, 36:82n, 109, 37:58, 70, 82, 89f, 98, 133, 202, 208, 215, 222–224, 232f, 294, 38:34, 99f, 113, 119, 161, 163, 180, 192, 197f, 200f, 232, 41:15, 17, 81, 85, 105, 116, 122, 149, 171, 178, 190, 206, 219f, 223, 226, 231, 249, 261, 267, 289, 318, 349, 359, 361, 42:104, 110, 112, 113n, 116, 141, 45:121f, 145f, 372, 46:176, 221n, 223, 225, 229, 240, 47:35, 47, 49, 51f, 89, 147, 168, 174, 176, 198, 200, 215, 240, 242, 246f, 258, 261, 273, 284, 295, 303, 48:58, 207, 49:359, 50:70f, 302, 54:172
Angels, Evil—1:22f, 112f, 150, 2:4, 105, 120, 125, 129, 256, 314, 320, 388, 24:112, 164, 168, 352
Angelus de Clavassio—see **Angelo Carletti di Chivasso**
Anger—1:163, 190, 199, 229, 261, 267, 2:13, 19, 44, 119, 141, 215, 301, 307, 321f, 355, 3:58f, 239, 309, 320, 331, 337, 354, 4:22, 24, 67, 94, 255, 5:12,

76, 82, 152, 169, 172–174, 221, 255, 300, 7:95f, 185, 254, 262, 363, 8:11, 28, 40, 179, 223, 226, 230, 232, 269, 298, 307, 330, 11:259, 294, 303, 14:27, 47, 60, 63, 71f, 106, 125, 134, 140f, 150, 156, 159, 211, 214f, 225, 293, 295, 317, 322, 323, 349, 15:28, 110, 117, 178, 20:19f, 175, 21:74–80, 83, 22:10f, 18, 95, 232–234, 270, 286, 370, 393, 398, 507, 23:59, 64, 86, 196, 251, 293, 301, 421, 24:61, 64, 70, 108, 111f, 114, 134, 157, 159, 184f, 197, 244, 248, 267, 270, 277, 320, 338, 379, 389, 420, 26:187, 317, 350, 413, 417, 27:368f, 371, 377, 410, 28:32f, 38, 272f, 374, 29:77, 139, 147, 30:31, 10f, 104, 123, 142, 186, 191, 229, 248n, 31:306, 35:53, 200, 378, 36:203, 207, 210, 227

Anger with self—10:31, 33, 64f, 67, 75

Angst—13:7n, 14:37n

Anguish—11:507f, 24:7, 58, 149, 382

Anhalt—see **Wolfgang, Prince of Anhalt**

Anhalt, Princely family and court of—48:400, 50:79, 149n, 151, 175, 288, 309

Anhalt, Principality of—50:123n

Anima—28:189

Animal life—1:56f, 65, 86f, 117

Animals—1:8, 52, 55, 63, 66–71, 73, 77, 81, 84–86, 91, 98, 102, 116f, 119–122, 125, 136, 140f, 144f, 150–153, 183, 185f, 188f, 205, 216f, 219, 221, 230, 247, 255, 319, 2:52, 58f, 66, 69f, 74–77, 88, 90, 93, 96f, 104, 106, 109, 115f, 132–139, 141–144, 324, 355, 2:58, 70, 74f, 116, 132f, 136, 139, 199, 297, 329, 347, 3:32, 66, 250, 293, 347, 6:17, 91, 119, 189, 9:134f, 137f, 306, 10:89, 11:329, 13:112, 15:125, 16:297, 21:320, 22:30, 28:193, 186, 191, 313, 325f, 348, 30:181, 45:326, 353, 46:211, 217f, 237f, 242, 252, 51:10, 249, 275, 323, 375

- Carnivorous 2:74
- Clean and unclean 2:67f, 89, 112, 114, 134f, 160, 3:250
- Kindness towards 9:220
- Land 1:5, 54f
- Strangled 41:28f, 68, 72–74, 76–77

Anna—11:474, 22:76, 347, 28:306, 338, 35:345n, 41:286

Anna, Countess of Mansfeld—50:312

Annaberg—17:235, 23:137

Annas—6:378, 380, 388f, 393, 7:89, 8:217, 233, 256, 13:339, 21:112, 302, 314, 22:128, 194, 196, 238f, 276f, 306, 356, 483, 23:210–213, 218, 223, 254, 268, 272, 24:155, 310, 40:54, 41:197, 45:274n, 275

Annas and Caiaphas—19:203

Annas, Servants of—46:102

Annates—14:333, 27:237, 385, 39:60n, 95, 41:15, 283, 294, 337, 368, 44:143f, 144n, 46:164n

Anne, St.—6:238, 13:326, 20:267, 23:137n, 24:22, 75, 34:24, 28, 35:68, 43:11n, 154n

Anne of Cleves—50:136, 192, 194

Anne of Hesse—48:272n

Anne of Hungary—48:217n

Annihilationism—13:263

Annius of Viterbo, John—27:267n, 45:224n

Anniversaries—2:161, 4:203, 27:352, 36:36n, 47, 49, 198

Annunciation—29:171, 41:64n

Anointed ones—17:122, 19:144

Anointing—5:253, 6:266, 8:320, 10:218, 21:156, 30:254–257, 261, 266, 306, 36:108, 112, 115, 122f, 150f, 197, 201f, 41:149, 152, 375n, 376, 53:100, 102, 106

Anomia—2:383

Anonymous reports of Marburg Colloquy—38:11f, 22n, 29n, 30n, 36

Ansbach—*Evangelische Ratschlag* of 1524 49:127f

Anselm, St.—2:270, 11:294, 13:90, 15:176n, 27:172n, 30:107n, 54:84

- *Cur Deus homo* 27:288n, 30:107n
- *De conceptu virginali et originali peccato* 34:154n, 155n, 185

Anselm of Laon—see ***Glossa interlinearis* of Anselm of Laon**

Ansgar, St.—32:263, 273

Anshelm, T.—48:57n, 123n, 155

Antaeus—25:300

Anthony, St.—2:355, 3:131, 196, 216f, 275n, 328f, 355, 4:56f, 109, 5:3f, 13, 7:307, 312, 9:55, 11:21, 13:33, 17:65n, 18:202, 19:207n, 22:267, 446, 23:350, 24:65, 25:353, 28:292, 322, 34:261, 36:186n, 221, 39:45n, 40:279n, 41:38n, 39–41, 125n, 126, 289n, 44:253n, 316n, 382, 46:117n, 51:217, 52:38, 137

Anthony of England—see **Barnes, Robert**

Anthropomorphisms—1:14n, 15, 2:45, 223, 3:230, 4:62, 133, 37:231n

Anthropomorphites—2:45

Anti-Semitism—47:x, 123, 131, 135

Anti-Trinitarianism—24:91n, 47:116n, 126

Antichrist—1:301, 2:34, 38, 61, 101, 181, 213, 229, 316, 3:121–123, 221, 349,

4:31, 141, 240, 363, 6:63, 404, 7:200, 8:185, 282f, 9:67, 10:114, 244, 246, 279, 282, 353, 360, 449, 11:100, 235, 476, 551, 12:115, 13:178, 188, 190, 258, 282, 330, 417, 14:11f, 17:19, 118, 222, 18:120, 270, 20:123, 127, 130, 192, 207, 264, 320, 337, 21:3, 63, 271f, 22:61, 67, 82, 84f, 102, 163, 470, 23:26, 212, 24:16, 75, 285, 308, 355, 366–369, 371, 26:24f, 86, 180, 223f, 257–259, 383, 385, 391, 408, 27:89, 110, 129, 342, 28:237, 339, 373, 29:33, 42, 30:99, 107, 138, 192, 193n, 251–254, 259, 284, 287–289, 314, 31:336, 342, 375, 391–393, 32:63, 71, 77, 79, 92, 139, 141, 147, 34:xv, 40, 79, 237, 240, 285, 35:107, 201, 306, 313, 351f, 387, 393, 407, 36:72, 83, 98, 102, 134, 158, 219, 288, 37:367, 38:173–176, 180, 183, 190f, 195, 206, 211, 232, 310, 39:60, 84, 102, 134, 161, 173, 193–5, 203, 210, 212, 279f, 307, 40:49, 58, 107, 131, 231–233, 262, 330, 349, 41:xv, 12, 205, 209–212, 274, 339, 357, 363f, 370f, 42:73n, 75, 43:68f, 44:133n, 138, 149, 169, 227, 45:60n, 61, 144n, 289n, 359, 46:8f, 180n, 181, 196, 47:40f, 53, 48:104n, 114, 137, 215, 230n, 261, 317, 319, 321, 49:13, 345, 347, 50:243, 287n, 51:80, 329, 374, 52:6, 21, 81, 83, 114, 137, 248, 256, 259, 54:101, 346f

Antichrists—36:171, 211, 251, 263

Anticipation—5:337, 341, 357f, 6:43, 282, 343, 7:268f, 16:150

Anticyra—33:21

Antidote to sin—28:204–206

Antinomian controversy—12:ix, 25:54, 33:9f, 34:xiv, 47:ix, 101–119, 48:220, 49:180n, 182f, 212f, 291n, 50:183, 309f, 54:233, 248, 289f, 308f, 313f, 391

Antinomian disputations—47:103–105

Antinomians—2:18, 3:223, 237, 239f, 243, 269, 281, 314, 336, 4:48–51, 63, 240f, 276, 405, 9:180n, 22:139, 146n, 390n, 41:72n, 113n, 114, 143, 147, 150, 153

Antioch—2:204, 317, 8:273, 9:168, 10:412, 12:295, 18:169, 20:91, 250, 282, 284, 23:306, 26:15, 79, 85, 106, 30:235, 38:307n, 47:233, 52:175

Antioch, Bishops of—41:42, 88, 91, 95

Antioch, Church in—41:88f, 92, 98, 321f, 324f, 348f

Antioch, Theology of—32:128n

Antioch of Syria—16:126

Antiochus III—13:155n, 197n

Antiochus IV Epiphanes—2:359, 3:121, 11:98, 100, 13:197n, 15:115n, 25:24, 271, 32:96, 35:350, 47:17n, 207, 221–223, 227, 229, 249

Antipater—5:160f

Antiperistasis—25:377

Antiphons—43:231, 53:12, 14, 38, 69, 195, 208, 265, 286, 321, 331, 337

Antiphrasis—4:11, 5:35f, 6:229, 7:40, 285, 8:66, 16:13, 150n, 175

Antiquitates Rerum Humanorum et Divinarum—see **Varro, Marcus Terentius**

Antiquity, Classical—9:6n

Antisacramentarians—51:213, 224, 226, 377, 379, 384, 386f

Antithesis—12:213, 346, 352, 368, 372, 378, 16:70, 100, 223, 17:54, 85, 106, 132, 145, 164, 172, 264, 312, 367, 380, 26:248, 27:20, 28:192

Antonians (Hospital brothers of St. Anthony)—48:180, 327n

Antoninus, Abbot of Buch (near Leisnig)—39:303, 45:163, 164n, 179

Antoninus, Archbishop of Florence—*Summary of Moral Theology* 20:160n, 170n, 187n, 31:146, 222

Antonomasia—11:113, 178, 12:82

Antony, Mark—15:41n, 103n, 104, 105n, 29:88n

Antwerp—16:323, 32:263f, 265n, 272, 41:340, 48:233n, 236n, 49:12, 21, 50:29, 31

Anubis—1:249

Anvils—4:43

Anxiety—3:42, 234, 237, 282, 286, 6:102f, 126f, 131, 134, 142, 226, 15:7, 10f, 24, 28, 46f, 70, 93, 150, 20:176, 316, 21:196–198, 203f, 207f, 24:7, 10–12, 15, 17, 40, 58, 97f, 110, 114, 145, 148, 211, 382f, 399f, 414f, 418–421, 25:18, 268, 390, 460, 45:325f

Apathy—7:261, 315, 342, 354, 356

Ape, God's—6:331

Ape, Satan as God's—7:121

Apel, John—49:115n, 310n

Apelles—2:150, 5:373

Apes—4:236, 328, 5:309, 7:121, 8:133

Aphaca—2:18n

Aphrodite—3:201n

Apion—35:341

Apis—2:18, 7:347, 351

Apocalypse—2:274, 22:429, 27:227, 370

Apocope—27:263n

Apocrypha—28:74, 35:337n, 338–354, 47:208n, 222n

Revised Standard Version, New York, 1957 35:349n

Apodoses—28:315n

Apollinarianism—24:91n

Apollinaris—22:110n, 37:362, 52:81

Apollo—1:249, 19:195, 25:17

Apollo, Priesthood of—36:199

Apollos—7:337, 8:178, 20:109, 309, 25:149, 496, 26:66, 29:88, 30:ix, 22, 298, 35:381, 40:37f

Apology of the Augsburg Confession—see **Melanchthon, Philip, Writings of**

Apophasis—33:100

Apoplexy—1:207, 305

Aposiopesis—1:303, 27:346

Apostasy—2:199, 212, 214, 9:27, 13:287, 23:158, 160, 162, 187–191, 24:118, 26:44–94, 197, 407, 28:308f, 314f, 29:105, 38:143, 46:180n

Apostates—2:198, 213, 234, 3:275, 4:209, 16:242, 24:216, 312, 26:19, 99, 135, 38:103, 41:33, 80, 188f, 192, 200, 212, 219, 224, 341, 49:99

Apostles—1:121, 146, 194, 221, 230, 234f, 254, 272, 295, 299, 355, 2:17, 40, 57, 76, 85f, 88, 101, 151, 192, 274, 289, 320f, 330, 354, 365, 378, 385, 398f, 3:5f, 16, 56, 63, 77, 84, 114, 125, 147, 152, 164, 185, 203, 258, 355, 4:33, 70, 96, 103, 125f, 131, 140, 159, 199, 206, 241, 316, 348, 373, 406, 5:11, 14, 19, 25, 43f, 52, 90, 131, 138, 204, 216, 227, 286, 348, 7:11, 38, 116, 135, 149, 212, 279, 304, 312, 344, 364, 8:10f, 43, 46, 75, 94, 132, 183f, 217, 222, 227, 248–250, 252, 254, 262, 265, 270, 306, 316, 9:168, 176, 179, 189, 214, 225, 299, 10:88f, 133, 136, 234, 310, 11:97, 176n, 12:5, 64, 112f, 173, 177, 179, 252, 265, 267, 295, 325, 331, 335, 350, 386, 13:5, 26, 28, 14:9, 14, 16, 23, 91, 95, 148, 154, 162, 166, 168, 180, 186f, 200, 202, 264f, 285f, 290, 303f, 307, 314n, 325, 329, 333f, 338–340, 344, 347, 349, 15:262f, 276, 287, 299, 344, 16:31, 45, 60, 94, 97, 112, 178, 186, 188–190, 193, 211, 214, 225, 281, 17:3, 15, 41, 45, 68, 84f, 92, 185, 197, 201, 320, 404f, 19:45, 20:13, 53, 100, 102f, 108, 110, 113, 126, 130, 149, 171, 184, 230, 233, 248, 251f, 287, 293f, 297, 302, 323f, 335, 21:61–63, 69, 22:7, 42, 46f, 53, 55–58, 67, 69f, 80, 84, 98, 107–109, 113, 190, 192, 199, 221, 225, 227f, 322, 332, 351, 385, 392, 401, 413, 467, 472, 478, 482, 487, 489, 510, 513, 23:8, 155, 185–187, 189–193, 218, 261, 264, 266, 280, 282, 290, 292, 297, 323, 343, 349, 365f, 369, 376–378, 380, 387, 408, 24:9, 11, 56f, 60, 64, 66f, 70f, 77f, 84, 86, 90, 122, 125f, 145, 147, 149, 155, 171, 174, 178–180, 183, 193, 196, 202–204, 206f, 211, 225, 243, 246, 256, 265, 270, 280, 283, 304f, 308, 310f, 313f, 319, 322, 324, 336f, 339, 350, 356–359, 366–369, 376–380, 383, 403f, 413f, 422, 25:3–6, 43, 50, 61, 79, 104f, 113, 123–125, 138–144, 327–335, 338, 379f, 426f, 445f, 485, 487, 498, 520–524, 26:15f, 18, 31, 44, 56, 59, 66f, 69, 71f, 74f, 78, 80f, 83, 93, 96, 98, 100f, 104, 106, 109, 114, 121, 135, 140, 148, 168–170, 187, 204f, 207, 210, 218, 220, 224, 230, 241, 256, 287, 290f, 295, 298, 305f, 330, 334, 365f, 371, 373f, 387, 419–421, 427, 429, 448, 451, 27:163, 165, 28:22–25, 60, 75f, 90f, 102, 152f, 298, 29:4–8, 13, 15–17, 29, 35–37, 67f, 70, 78, 95, 98f, 124, 134, 145, 214, 226, 229, 30:3, 5, 8, 10, 12, 16, 18f, 21, 24, 26, 29, 32, 34f, 38, 40, 42–44, 47f, 50f, 56, 58–60, 62, 65–67, 72, 79–81, 84, 87, 89, 91, 94f, 98–100, 104f, 109f, 112–117, 121–130, 132–140, 143, 149, 153, 157f, 161–163, 167, 175, 177, 179, 184, 191, 196, 198f, 203, 206, 213, 215, 219, 224, 228f, 233–235, 241–243, 251, 258, 272, 277, 279, 288, 290, 294, 297, 302, 304, 306f, 312, 317f, 320, 324, 32:74, 34:113, 35:120, 144, 152, 161, 169, 214, 246, 358, 382f, 36:13, 53, 63, 71, 91, 95, 111, 121, 137, 142, 148, 157, 163–165, 184, 198, 205, 263, 38:51n, 100, 161, 178, 186, 188, 192, 198, 207, 210n, 232, 239, 290, 41:xv, 7, 26f, 29–31, 45–47, 51, 58f, 61, 70f, 75, 78, 88f, 113, 120, 122, 125, 130, 132, 144, 154–156, 176, 190, 194–198, 200, 204f, 213, 217f, 223, 246f, 290, 302, 306, 311–316, 318–326, 345, 347–349, 351f, 354f, 359, 365, 368, 45:100f, 145, 169, 200, 359–361, 46:51, 95, 149, 151, 163, 177, 196n, 255, 265, 47:110, 112, 114, 147, 171, 175, 209, 284, 291, 295, 297f, 52:21, 38, 40f, 45, 90, 107, 133f, 166f, 175, 205f, 209, 212f, 215, 267, 276, 53:12, 20, 68, see also **Disciples**

Apostles as princes—13:27f

Apostleship—see **Apostolic office**

Apostolate—see **Apostolic office**

Apostolic blessing—25:131

Apostolic Constitution—41:45n

Apostolic Council—26:207, 28:309, 29:37,

40, 41:5, 27n, 28–33, 36, 68–75, 79, 123, 44:136, 49:90
Apostolic office—23:192, 24:209, 304, 25:123, 141–144, 26:19, 61, 69, 94, 96, 98, 107, 121, 27:163–165, 168, 180, 192, 205, 209, 38:28, 201, 41:38, 123
Apostolic poverty—46:5
Apostolic preaching—35:396
Apostolic succession—2:102, 4:28, 30, 33, 24:66
Apostolici Regiminis—47:38n
Apostolicity—35:394n, 396, 398
Apostrophe—7:113n, 17:146, 154
Apothecary—23:94
Apparitions—3:10, 166, 168, 4:125, 127, 130, 5:382, 18:108, 24:71n, 369
Appearance—10:155, 181, 303, 452, 17:27–29, 44, 54, 56, 77, 96, 119, 132, 137, 144, 167, 176, 186, 216f, 238f, 244, 311, 318, 20:56f, 150, 228, 234, 241, 334
Appearing of our Lord—29:65–67
Appellative—7:6f
Appion—14:281
Apples—2:136n, 269, 350, 3:149, 7:68, 76, 96, 138, 196, 4:115f, 131f, 21:267, 23:114, 189, 254, 257, 305, 385, 398, 24:224, 262, 275f, 343, 26:255, 417
Appolonia—2:205
April—2:92, 3:123, 9:154
Aprons—7:32, 26:103
Apuleius—*Metamorphoses* 1:268n
Apulia—4:127, 49:185
Aquila—7:7, 15:267, 16:38n, 25:129, 41:324, 347
Aquila, Caspar—49:291n
Aquileia—28:150
Aquinas, St. Thomas—see **Thomas Aquinas, St.**
Ar—16:146
Arabia—1:101n, 2:195, 283, 3:162, 4:328, 331, 5:55, 6:179, 307f, 7:323, 346, 8:109, 156, 9:35, 299, 10:412f, 16:147, 173, 18:116, 195, 202, 20:114, 251, 25:8, 26:69, 74, 77f, 27:193, 314–317, 382, 43:109, 46:202, 52:160f, 170, 198
Arabia Felix—2:195, 4:307f, 16:126, 27:317
Arabia Petraea—2:189, 367, 4:307f, 331, 7:208, 9:32, 34, 16:126, 17:352, 18:116, 195, 202, 26:438, 27: 314, 317
Arabian Gulf—1:99
Arabians—6:105n, 179, 304, 308
Arabic—26:436, 27:315, 46:183n, 232n
Arabs—2:217, 3:66, 4:71, 328, 5:155, 159, 279, 7:118, 171, 13:99, 15:201, 16:33, 126, 135, 159, 172, 174, 339, 17:72, 314f, 352, 18:116, 341, 26:436, 438, 27:315
Aragon—34:345, 48:155n
Aram—2:206, 279, 4:186
Aramaic—1:87, 235, 16:165n, 311, 20:245n, 22:182, 47:180n
Arannah—5:251
Ararat, Mt.—2:107f, 117, 207
Arba—4:193
Arbaces—2:206
Arbea—4:192
Arbitration—9:162, 46:42, 75n
Arbitrium—33:xi–xii
Arborvitae—1:95
Arcadia—50:212n
Arcadius, Emperor—41:373n
Archangels—1:235
Archbishop, Evangelical—50:97n, 170
Archbishops—27:385n, 36:110, 38:179, 197
Archbishops of Mainz, Trier, and Cologne—22:188
Archdeacons—27:153
Archers—4:80
Archippus—29:95, 105
Architects—26:257
Archiv fr Reformationsgeschichte—42:97n, 45:54n, 55n, 56n
Archpapist—38:227
Arena—24:196
Argonauts—5:312
Argos—31:237n
Arguments—28:94–96, 260f, 288, 368, 29:229, 239
Argus—25:174
Arian controversy—20:149
Arianism—3:301n, 11:225n, 13:62, 234f, 24:91n, 37:120, 361
Arians—1:10, 59, 156, 4:392, 11:87, 220n, 224, 226, 244, 526, 15:163, 268, 17:74, 187, 247, 254, 20:164, 240, 303, 22:19, 22, 75, 23:147, 150, 184n, 186n, 24:93, 96, 140, 215, 26:30f, 28:229, 303, 30:289, 308f, 316, 319f, 327, 32:73, 119, 128, 243f, 33:28, 86, 163, 173, 34:201, 203, 208n, 210, 38:255, 261, 310, 40:80n, 197n, 273n, 41:43n, 56n, 57, 60, 68, 79n, 81n, 82, 83n, 84f, 86n, 104, 117, 141, 210f, 46:179n, 54:41
Ariel—16:238f, 241
Arioch—2:365
Aristarchus—29:105
Aristarchus of Samothrace—28:294f
Aristides—26:123
Aristocrats—3:253, 16:294, 23:220

Aristophanes—*The Clouds* 41:208n
Wasps 2:161n, 25:105
Aristotelians—38:75
Aristotle—1:3, 5f, 24, 26, 27n, 29, 45, 48, 52, 58, 60, 70, 84, 122–125, 127, 131, 143, 2:121, 124, 126, 146f, 159f, 199, 207f, 297, 303, 329, 340, 4:145, 217, 227n, 5:112n, 8:14, 174, 269, 10:49n, 322, 359, 462, 11:11n, 39, 75, 174, 337, 12:207, 400, 13:54, 81, 93n, 161, 199, 14:89n, 118, 295, 15:103, 16:297, 17:70, 152, 22:91n, 293, 302, 23:115n, 24:205, 266, 25:ix, 4, 103, 235, 338m 340, 343, 434, 26:138n, 141n, 234, 248n, 256, 259n, 262n, 271n, m294, 316n, 362n, 404n, 27:181n, 219, 225, 328, 28:261, 367, 29:40, 30:105, 107, 221n, 226 264n, 31:6, 12n, 41f, 57, 70, 222, 227, 317, 32:xviii, 78, 185–187, 191, 104, 205, 209, 217, 258, 33:107n, 171, 240, 291, 34:138n, 139, 142f, 165, 186, 188, 191, 35:186, 36:16n, 29n, 33n, 62n, 153, 182, 336n, 37:30, 31n, 206n, 38:189, 240n, 245, 39:xvi, 130, 134, 144, 146, 162, 168, 197, 208f, 44:200f, 300, 45:233n, 299n, 322n, 374n, 377n, 46:111n, 253, 48:25, 37f, 42n, 58n, 59n, 95, 51:22, 64f, 54:61, 184, 243, 307, 423, 475
Aristotle, Works of—*Athenian Republic* 50:228n
Categories 1:218n, 21:125n, 25:257, 274, 299, 26:316n, 48:37n, 57n
De anima 15:59n, 179, 25:204, 364, 27:367n, 44:200, 201n, 202, 48:112
De caelo 1:24n, 26n, 30n, 44n, 2:93n
De generation et corruptione 8:211n
De generatione animalium 1:70n
Ethics 2:340, 8:171, 11:174n, 31:12
Historia animalium 1:52n, 2:162n, 4:188n, 25:230, 48:166n
Libri meteororum 30:226n
Logic 44:200–202, 201n
Metaphysics 1:61n, 124n, 2:208n, 3:50n, 122n, 4:164n, 5:294n, 11:486, 13:77, 15:183n, 21:279n, 26:271n, 27:364n, 33:171n, 36:33n, 44:200–202, 201n, 48:112
Meteorologica 2:146, 147n, 30:266n
Nicomachean Ethics 1:45n, 48n, 122n, 131n, 143n, 2:297n, 303n, 340n, 3:85n, 4:145n, 7:191n, 8:171n, 10:74n, 99n, 102n, 13:54n, 15:183n, 25:3, 152, 172, 179, 344, 385, 410f, 26:234n, 294n, 404n, 27:23n, 29n, 29:33n, 75n, 30:226n, 32:209n, 33:29n, 206, 34:130n, 165n, 186n, 36:211n, 44:200–202, 201n, 48:25, 82, 51:6n, 64n, 385
On Memory and Recollection 11:11n
On Sense and the Sensible 20:66n
On the Soul 48:112
Organon 4:259n, 29:155n, 36:33n
Peri hermeneias 48:95
Physics 1:4n, 30n, 3:226n, 4:158n, 7:205n, 8:11n, 10:186n, 25:204, 377, 31:6, 44:200–202, 201n, 48:38, 95, 107, 112
Poetics 3:303n, 44:200–202, 201n
Politics 2:126n, 199n, 329n, 4:85n, 7:16n, 13:217n, 14:118n, 19:208, 26:256n, 34:244
Posterior Analytics 30:264n, 48:95
Prior Analytics 4:102n, 7:291n, 28:261, 32:215n
Problemata 1:119n
Rhetoric 1:177n, 263n, 27:24n, 30:221n, 44:200–202, 201n
Rhetorica ad Alexandrum 14:89n, 26:362n
Sophistici elenchi 1:108n, 25:200
Topics 1:3n, 2:271n, 4:34n, 83n, 32:215n
Aristotle's God—33:171, 291
Arithmetic—3:130, 26:300, 46:215, 251, 252n
Arius—1:13f, 152, 157, 160, 164, 2:374, 3:301, 5:96, 9:164, 11:225n, 497, 12:46f, 54f, 85, 222f, 282f, 287f, 13:63, 15:187n, 303, 17:125, 327, 22:18, 20, 25, 67, 75, 110, 314, 391, 395, 493, 23:79, 85, 231, 24:131, 176, 204, 296, 26:282, 27:62, 28:253, 29:14, 35, 30:257, 33:86n, 34:201n, 228, 35:404n, 38:36, 308n, 309n, 41:43n, 55n, 56, 57n, 58–60, 79n, 80n, 82–84, 86f, 95f, 98, 120f, 123, 133f, 138, 189, 44:284n, 48:105, 178n, 51:64n, 54:314, 36, 60, 259, 333
Ark of the Covenant—6:50, 127f, 9:108, 123, 258, 297, 11:87, 96, 128, 16:109, 20:246, 347, 22:367, 24:24, 160, 29:179, 201f, 205f, 236f, 47:186, 223f
Ark, Noah's—2:28, 46, 58, 66f, 69f, 72f, 75–77, 81, 85, 89–91, 96–98, 103–105, 107–112, 114–116, 120, 152f, 155f, 158–160, 162f, 174, 182, 192, 3:19, 30:113, 115, 176, 193f
Arm (Body)—20:128f
Armaments—45:331, 350, 356
Armonia—2:107f, 189, 20, 18:151
Armenia, Greater—2:189
Armics—16:89n, 94, 167f, 191
Arminius—13:59

Armistice between evangelicals and papists—49:404n, 423, 429
Armor—9:203, 23:254, 263, 389, 25:112, 45:328, 331, 336, 46:245, 249f
Arms—see **Weapons**
Arms, Bearing—32:89
Arms, Laying down—41:274, 275n
Army, Imperial—46:120n
Arnobius—*Against the Pagans* 27:43n
Arnold—*De villa Dei* 6:331
Arnoldi, Bartholomew—48:30n, 37n, 38, 62, 139, 151, 54:127
Arnoldshain Theses of 1955—38:xiv, xviiif
Arnon—16:149
Arnon, Mt.—9:35f
Arnstadt—50:209
Aroer—9:36, 16:154
Arphaxad—1:357, 2:197, 205f, 232, 3:233, 4:3, 14:114n
Arphaxad, King—19:207f
Arras, Balthasar von—45:194
Arrogance—2:119, 225f, 371, 3:5, 14, 131, 4:209, 255f, 381, 391, 5:92f, 121f, 124, 180, 182, 336, 6:56, 328, 7:165, 167, 179, 182, 184f, 187, 345, 9:185, 14:325f, 16:183, 185, 347f, 21:216f, 308–310, 328, 333, 22:232, 23:180, 253, 328f, 350, 418, 25:10, 21, 91, 136, 141, 217f, 222, 242, 26:74, 119, 27:97, 31:48, 50, 42:26, 30–33, 35, 36f, 45:327–333
Arrows—4:71, 387, 11:199f, 216–220, 222–226, 289, 446, 538
Ars moriendi—16:337
Arsenius, papal legate—28:364
Arsenius, St.—11:69n, 25:478, 26:149n, 27:14
Arson—4:x, 281n, 41:31, 138, 182, 212n, 220f, 239, 242f, 245f, 248, 250–254, 256, 46:8, 70, 50:215, 222
Art—14:7, 46, 23:144n, 350, 42:101n
Art, Medieval—4:110n
Art, Religious—36:230, 40:99f
Artaxerxes I—20:160n, 35:303n, 304
Artaxerxes—see **Cambyses II**
Artemus—29:88
Artesian well—5:64n
Articles of Faith—28:59f, 62f, 69f, 75, 80, 82, 94, 96f, 100, 150f, 169, 201, 32:76–79, 83, 149, 154, 33:95, 173, 34:354, 356, 36:28, 30, 35, 96, 111, 167, 186, 190, 211, 276, 38:12, 25, 51, 61, 67, 70–72, 75, 79, 85–88, 141, 143, 147, 167, 173f, 176–178, 182n, 191, 224, 232, 239, 241–243, 246, 248f, 259, 277, 288f, 291, 298, 301, 306–312, 40:19, 24, 333, 351, 363, 41:5, 48, 52, 57–61, 67f, 71f, 74f, 77, 86, 92f, 96, 105, 118, 121, 123, 134, 136–138, 142, 148, 161, 174, 211, 219, 222, 224, 271, 285, 300, 310, 313, 320, 342, see also **Creeds**
Articles of Visitation—see **Melanchthon, Philip, Writings of**
Articles, Six—see ***Six Articles***
Artifices—24:369
Artisans—1:317, 26:46
Artois—34:345, 353
Arts—1:318, 11:441, 15:9, 152, 165, 183, 201f, 45:351, 358, 368f, 373f, 376f
"As much as one is able"—25:181, 186, 218, 496
Asa, King—46:173
Asaph—10:434, 441, 447, 452, 463, 11:29, 110, 152, 12:169, 31:226, 53:221
Asceticism—12:353, 13:368, 14:262, 15:4, 23:72, 349, 24:35n, 228, 232, 281, 307, 25:254, 27:10, 88, 41:126n
Asenath—7:52, 200f, 207
Ashdod—2:191, 16:168, 18:147, 340, 20:92, 285
Asher—5:339f, 351, 6:279, 319, 321, 366, 378, 7:6
Ashes—2:136, 269, 343, 11:310f
Ashkelon—18:216, 340, 342
Ashkenaz—2:109, 193
Ashor—9:307
Ashtaroth (Ashteroth)—6:230, 9:34, 41:207n
Ashteroth (place)—2:367, 9:54
Ashurbanipal—40:19n
Asia—2:108, 175, 185, 187, 193, 205, 9:34, 10:412, 20:294, 26:32, 411, 426, 27:117, 28:90, 381, 30:5f, 34:345, 36:238, 41:24, 106, 334, 46:202
Asia, Bishops of—41:24, 61, 291
Asia, Churches of—41:321, 347, 351, 358
Asia Minor—2:108, 189, 13:343, 22:137n, 38:317n
Asmodeus—3:58, 35:346
Asmus of Haubitz—40:272n
Aspergillum—51:326, 333
Asphalt—2:269, 3:222
Asps—9:297, 11:215, 25:29, 230
Assa von Kram—13:191
Assassins—41:243, 249f, 255
Assault—9:167
Assedoth—9:40, 60
Assembly of the Lord—9:229–231
Assembly, Annual community (Leisnig)—45:182, 193n
Assertions—33:19–21
Asses—3:66, 86, 149, 312, 337, 4:107f,

111, 118, 122, 128, 181, 183, 202, 246, 5:73, 76, 322, 6:51, 54, 176, 208, 293, 301, 7:10, 69, 165, 264, 268, 270, 292, 338, 9:219, 221, 224f, 233, 23:85, 97, 236, 241, 252, 24:207, 332, 351, 26:7, 116f, 261, 391

Asses, Wild—3:66, 11:329f, 337f, 18:45, 146

Asshur—2:200–202, 205f, 214, 232, 247, 16:81

Associate editors—see **Hansen, Walter A.**

Assumption of the Virgin Mary—2:21n, 16:327n, 38:173n

Assurance—4:144f, 157f, 258, 267, 356, 366, 5:43, 6:9f, 7:154f, 8:210, 9:86, 123, 12:371, 376, 380, 383, 13:136f, 139f, 322, 13:139f, 15:272f, 15:3f, 144f, 148, 227, 243, 17:61, 92f, 143, 164, 172, 245, 253, 289, 300, 340f, 388, 21:38f, 24:45, 217f, 220–222, 230f, 258, 293, 25:78, 116, 498, 26:212, 295, 377f, 335, 388, 27:26, 173, 358, 405, 28:72f, 238–240, 246, 269f, 324f, 374f, 29:15, 217, 30:159, 161, 224, 262, 279, 283, 321, 33:287f, 289, 37:30, 68, 70, 77f, 96, 103, 107, 123, 126, 303–306, 329, 366, 51:122, 54:18, 57, 182, 455

Assyria—2:202, 232, 365, 6:389, 13:270, 14:114, 273, 322, 16:82, 89f, 108, 114f, 142, 144f, 156, 159f, 162, 168, 176, 184, 218, 254, 261, 265–267, 284, 290, 309, 312, 315, 319, 324f, 328f, 336, 346, 17:3, 56, 208, 264, 301, 305, 20:114f, 179, 189, 250f, 253, 264n, 307f, 21:344, 24:366, 34:49n, 35:276, 295, 326, 45:329, 46:41, 47:173

Assyrian captivity—see **Captivity**—Assyrian

Assyrians—2:98, 200, 206, 365, 3:270, 4:356, 372f, 6:88, 157, 162, 7:15, 70, 153, 301, 11:122, 128, 191, 12:30, 265, 14:66, 16:28, 85f, 108, 113–115, 125f, 148, 150, 152, 155–158, 160, 164, 184, 220f, 252, 254, 259, 267, 269–273, 282–285, 287f, 291, 317, 325, 320f, 348, 18:9, 47, 52, 89, 103, 131–134, 148–151, 158, 172–174, 211, 245, 281–287, 291–294, 298–302, 305–308, 311, 315, 346, 392, 19:4, 26, 39f, 42, 145, 20:68, 169, 193, 23:387, 397, 27:164, 330, 29:140, 46:107n, 110

Astarte—30:219

Astral influences—13:122

Astrologers—7:110, 120, 346, 16:326n, 336, 27:295

Astrology—1:44f, 13:22n, 17:153, 25:145, 26:410n, 43:17, 54:33, 172–173, 219–220, 416–417, 449, 458

Astronomers—3:289, 4:87, 9:109n, 17:26n, 22:59n

Astronomy—1:40f, 44, 47f, 66, 2:305, 3:358, 15:9, 41:61, 62n, 65f, 348, 46:252n

Ataxia—2:30n

Athaliah, Queen—47:208, 52:3

Athanasian Creed—see **Creeds**—Athanasian

Athanasius, St.—12:49, 223, 13:63, 14:285, 310, 20:184, 27:333, 30:277, 31:105, 35:402n, 38:203, 40:273n, 41:59n, 81n, 82n, 84, 325, 43:121, 48:105, 178, 53:20, 54:314

Apology for His Flight 30:277n

Discourses against the Arians 8:164n

Epistle 15:187n

Life of St. Anthony 4:7n

Vita Antonii 15:274n

Atheists—4:391, 50:243

Athenians—25:11, 34:277n

Athens—1:88, 125, 255, 3:51n, 13:343, 24:267

Atkinson, James—47:127n

author of introduction to Vol. 44

editor of Vol. 44

presumed author of introductions to all items included in Vol. 44

translator of *Instruction to Penitents concerning the Forbidden Books of Dr. Martin Luther* 44:220–232

translator of *Judgment of Martin Luther on Monastic Vows* 44:243–399

translator of *Sermon on the Estate of Marriage* 44:3–14

translator of *Sermon on the Three Kinds of Good Life for the Instruction of Consciences* 44:232–242

Atlas—2:378, 15:143n

Atlases—3:305

Atonement—13:319, 22:132, 165, 23:58, 195, 24:98, 25:45, 284, 348, 26:29, 41:111f, 336, 342, 43:27, 44:38, 47:303f

Atonement, Feast of—1:312, 9:154, 11:101, 20:260, 21:156, 29:204f

Atreus, King—37:138

Attalus—27:280

Attentiveness—25:459f

Attic law—50:228

Attic Nights—see **Aulus Gellius**

Attila—20:187, 51:64n

Attribution—32:201, 208

Attrition—31:21, 32:41, 34:172, 306, 36:84n
Audacity—18:212
Audians—1:14n
Auerbach, Henry Stromer von—31:323, 39:242
Augsburg—12:220, 22:412, 23:217n, 255, 262n, 27:154, 157, 34:7, 35:177n, 38:9, 63, 93, 147, 297n, 39:26, 56n, 134, 211, 248n, 304, 45:135n, 162, 234, 242, 46:213n, 47:130, 48:36n, 39n, 83n, 87, 88n, 90n, 92, 94n, 99n, 105n, 124, 140, 142n, 170, 191, 205n, 230n, 249, 363n, 49:30n, 96n, 146n, 160n, 238, 282, 283n, 284n, 287, 317, 318n, 326, 339n, 373, 376n, 394n, 50:173, 264, 51:xiii, 236–238, 291, 53:193, 240, 337, 54:39, 182, 231, 285, 331, 375, 381, 417
Augsburg, Bishop of—32:116, 33:13n
Augsburg, Diet of, 1500—44:214n
Augsburg, Diet of, 1518—27:297n, 31:255–257, 34:330, 43:268n, 48:70n, 72f, 75n, 77n, 82n, 84n, 91n, 92n, 93n, 131n, 246n, 249, 49:107
Augsburg, Diet of, 1530—3:340f, 5:115n, 6:40, 13:352, 14:x, 21:19, 71, 22:408n, 412n, 23:ix, 173, 217, 219, 255f, 293, 400, 34:xii, 5, 11n, 29, 65–104, 35:177, 41:xiin, 190n, 222n, 235, 236n, 362, 375n, 38:93, 141f, 147, 40:xiv, 53, 43:169–170, 181f, 185, 265, 266n, 273n, 45:135n, 46:211, 213n, 227n, 47:5, 11f, 14–16, 20–28, 30–33, 35, 46, 108, 48:77n, 80n, 99n, 247n, 275n, 49:xviii, 51, 273, 284n, 293f, 315, 327, 332n, 334n, 340, 355n, 356, 363, 367f, 373f, 397, 414n, 419n, 420n, 422n, 424f, 429, 433, 50:3, 9, 22, 41n, 55n, 81, 82n, 140, 142n, 219n, 51:197, 217
  Business conducted 49:52, 328n, 339n, 348f, 350n, 353f, 359f, 367f, 368n, 374n, 376, 377n, 378n, 391f, 397n, 401n, 403f, 413f, 414n, 416f, 420f, 435n, 436
  Evangelicals at 49:341f, 349n, 368n, 374n, 378n, 394n, 395, 397n, 401n, 406n, 407n, 413, 416n, 420n, 423f, 425, 429f, 435n
  Mail service at 49:299n, 310n, 315n, 316f, 320, 322n, 326f, 330, 332, 334f, 339, 348, 367, 373f, 373n, 382, 399, 401n, 402, 405n, 415f, 422, 425
  Papists at 49:126n, 299n, 306f, 309, 315, 318, 332n, 340f, 349n, 350, 354, 359f, 363, 367, 369, 374n, 375, 378n, 401n, 404n, 407n, 414n, 416, 420n, 424f, 435n, 437
  Plans for 49:251n, 255n, 265n, 280f, 285n, 294n, 296n, 315n, 328n, 333 344n, 345n, 350n, 352n, 362n, 363f, 367, 377n, 403f, 413, 416
  Preaching during 49:296n, 298f, 306n, 339f, 352n, 362, 375
  Resolution of 49:423f, 429, 432n, 435
Augsburg, Imperial Edict of, 1531—see **Imperial Edict, 1531**
Augsburg, Peace of, 1555—41:xiin
Augsburg, Recess of Diet of, 1530—47:5, 24n
Augsburg, Reformation in—46:39n
Augsburg Confession—see **Melanchthon, Philip, Writings of**
Augsburg Confession, Apology of the—see **Melanchthon, Philip, Writings of**
Augsburg Interim of 1548—49:291n, 325
Augsburg Recess, 1530—34:65–67, 68n, 69–104
Auguries—5:366–368, 7:121, 9:175
August, Duke of Saxony—50:280n
Augustine of Ancona—31:146, 222
Augustine, St.—1:xi, 4, 8–10, 18, 22, 31, 41, 44, 49, 60, 93, 97, 121, 126, 184f, 188, 213, 232, 234, 252, 263, 296, 305, 2:11, 14, 39, 45, 55, 68, 76, 86, 121, 125, 148, 150–152, 164, 238, 249, 251, 253, 291, 298, 301, 317, 321, 340, 350, 371, 3:10f, 107, 130, 159f, 165, 187, 192, 194, 199, 257f, 260, 288, 298, 325f, 348, 4:4, 9, 13f, 19, 67, 68n, 126, 133, 212f, 253, 306, 311, 314, 332, 377f, 6:117, 146, 153f, 218n, 307, 343, 407, 7:70f, 76, 81, 86, 115, 119, 135, 181, 198, 233, 243, 248, 252, 254f, 268, 281, 292, 296, 329, 9:86n, 117n, 130, 164, 222, 260, 261n, 10:27, 30n, 40n, 93, 97, 99, 104, 108, 111, 116f, 122, 128, 150, 153, 166–168, 171, 175, 184, 191, 194, 201, 207, 210, 213, 219f, 222, 232, 234, 248, 255, 257, 265, 268, 270, 289f, 302f, 307, 314n, 315, 318, 324, 326, 331–333, 338, 353, 358, 361, 386n, 389n, 399n, 410, 416, 422f, 431, 439, 441, 446, 458, 11:5, 17, 19, 30, 37, 62n, 65n, 69, 75–77, 95n, 96n, 99n, 103n, 122n, 123n, 124, 126n, 130n, 139n, 178n, 180, 182, 189, 195, 196n, 204, 213, 222, 270, 273n, 274, 287, 323, 336f, 350, 366, 372, 399, 401, 425, 460, 489n, 528, 552, 12:19, 52, 223, 298, 327, 13:25, 89n, 96, 105, 163, 14:38, 51n, 149n, 285, 296, 310f, 15:63f, 268, 310, 16:9, 178,

347, 17:7, 54, 66, 70, 101, 107n, 242, 259, 318, 328, 337, 364, 18:262, 19:5, 172, 20:136, 141, 184, 21:265, 22:254, 256, 259f, 263, 270, 327n, 368f, 450, 453, 461, 512–514, 516, 23:25, 34, 38, 72, 76, 94, 203, 343, 361, 387, 24:25, 26n, 94n, 188n, 208n, 374n, 398, 402n, 25:xi, 70, 227, 263, 300, 343, 350, 366, 447, 26:58, 66f, 76, 84, 85n, 92, 107, 108n, 154, 214n, 313, 377, 389n, 410, 412, 458f, 27:x, 83, 112, 156, 173, 211n, 212, 245, 248, 271, 319, 321, 390, 406, 28:235, 261, 285, 309, 317, 323, 341, 343–345, 356, 367, 29:5, 18, 26, 31f, 104, 112, 123, 161, 181, 216n, 30:10, 69, 88, 109, 166, 227f, 232n, 239, 275, 287n, 290n, 294, 298n, 299f, 313, 322, 31:9f, 39, 44, 56, 66, 75, 89, 125, 134, 139f, 184, 193, 213f, 269, 281, 285, 322, 32:xvii, 9, 27f, 34, 41, 44, 51, 72, 74, 85f, 92, 118, 154, 156f, 167, 189, 194, 204f, 209, 216f, 221, 231, 238, 255, 33:58, 61, 72, 77, 78n, 95, 103, 108, 116, 286, 34:95, 126, 143, 155n, 164f, 169f, 180, 185, 187, 190, 194, 195n, 200, 202, 275n, 285, 334, 337, 355, 35:50n, 56n, 128n, 151, 184n, 197, 318n, 353, 363, 372, 36:19n, 100, 136, 158, 188, 221, 289, 37:55–57, 63, 72, 104–107, 123f, 172, 271, 272n, 288n, 302, 315, 363n, 38:18, 20f, 23n, 28, 31, 33–36, 50n, 51n, 52, 58f, 61f, 68f, 76, 81, 98, 163, 196–198, 240, 251n, 253, 276, 290, 303n, 39:32, 35, 55n, 78, 166, 178f, 189, 198, 268, 280, 40:80n, 245, 250n, 41:xin, 19, 21n, 22n, 23n, 24f, 43n, 44, 45n, 46f, 49n, 50n, 51n, 79n, 83n, 85n, 86, 94n, 98, 105, 117n, 125n, 130n, 132, 138n, 139n, 146n, 151n, 160n, 161, 175, 178, 194n, 281, 290, 308f, 312n, 325f, 43:21, 248f, 44:30, 104, 128, 283n, 292n, 306n, 45:25n, 81n, 82, 97n, 108, 110n, 129n, 211n, 233n, 259n, 276n, 290n, 361, 362n, 48:5, 6n, 24f, 28n, 40, 42, 52f, 54, 59n, 79n, 266, 362n, 49:7, 88n, 89n, 200, 51:xviii, 9, 16, 24, 78, 295f, 362f, 52:51, 173, 181, 53:20, 171, 318, 54:10, 18, 26, 34, 49f, 61, 111, 177, 242, 259–260, 270, 309, 315, 329, 337, 340, 344, 352, 377, 401, 454

Augustine, St., Works of—*Ad catechumenos sermo alius* 6:401n

Against Felix 39:170

Against Julian 27:361, 362n, 31:45, 49, 214, 32:27n, 92, 253n, 254n, 33:108n, 142n, 34:155n, 164n, 180n, 186n

Against Two Letters of the Pelagians 7:81n, 25:327, 27:256n, 32:194n

Against the Academics 4:206n, 30:275n

Against the Donatist Petilian 23:203n, 39:196

Against the Epistle of Parmenian 38:28n, 39:196n

Annotations in Job 31 27:175n

Anti-Pelagian Writings 48:24, 54

Christian Doctrine 2:164n, 298n, 347n, 3:192n, 5:88n, 6:24n, 146n, 7:268, 269n, 15:308n, 24:398n, 25:295, 375, 512, 26:92n, 27:236n, 312, 29:5n, 40n, 104n, 36:304n, 37:104n, 38:18n, 35n

City of God 1:252n, 263n, 302n, 305n, 2:11n, 125n, 319n, 3:81n, 4:185n, 213n, 304n, 5:11n, 12n, 30n, 338, 7:181n, 8:284n, 316n, 328n, 14:10n, 19n, 19:172n, 22:33n, 267n, 23:387n, 25:21, 60, 172, 178, 27:101n, 172n, 219, 227n, 406, 407n, 29:49n, 30:290n, 31:167n, 32:238n, 33:95n, 34:169n, 275n, 277n, 37:104n, 173n, 38:34n, 290n, 39:261, 48:207n, 49:410

Commentary on Psalm 39 (40) 42:153n

Concerning Martyrdom 31:215

Concerning Reprimand and Grace 31:50

Concerning the Origin of Man's Soul 34:186n

Confessions 1:8, 9n, 10n, 31n, 44n, 2:14n, 3:160n, 4:259n, 306n, 333n, 5:103n, 180n, 323n, 344n, 359n, 7:119n, 135n, 254n, 329, 8:318n, 10:27, 43n, 57n, 64n, 86n, 142, 394, 11:20f, 37, 13:96n, 101, 14:141n, 196n, 330n, 15:11n, 30n, 259n, 17:187n, 21:41n, 321n, 22:113n, 267n, 25:112, 374, 425, 27:101n, 337n, 29:163n, 30:88n, 298n, 31:126, 214, 266, 32:44, 85, 34:334n, 36:188n, 38:98n, 276n, 39:33n, 55n, 42:131n, 147n, 150n, 154n, 44:292n, 48:331n

Contra Epistolam Manichaei 35:150, 151n, 36:107n

Contra Faustum Manichaeum 21:66n, 35:150n

Contra Julianum 25:63–65, 268, 297, 304f, 328, 330, 337, 340–343, 375, 506, 36:20n

Contra Julianum haeresis Pelagianae defensorum 27:316n, 361n, 362n

Contra literas Petiliani 23:203n

Correction of the Donatists 30:109n, 239n

De beata vita 25:169, 402
De bono viduitatis 44:396n
De catechizandis rudibus 2:45n, 3:107n
De civitate Dei—see **Augustine, St., Works of**—*City of God*
De consensu evangelistarum 20:125n, 129
De continentia 5:37n
De correctione Donatistarum 27:169
De correptione et gratia 3:348n, 9:261n, 26:214n
De cura pro mortuis 4:311n
De dono perseverentiae 11:468n
De fide et symbolo 16:82n
De Genesi ad litteram 1:4n, 6n, 9n, 18n, 19n, 50n, 93n, 103n, 2:86n, 148n, 15:20n, 263n, 29:161n, 190n
De Genesi contra Manichaeos libri duo 1:185n
De gratia et libero arbitrio 25:348
De haeresibus 7:86n, 25:496, 44:306n
De libero arbitrio 13:108f
De mortalitate 25:65
De Natura et Gratia 34:155n
De nuptiis et concupiscentia 25:101, 261, 319, 342, 35:34, 35n
De opere monachorum 25:332
De ordine 10:335, 25:169
De peccatorum meritis et remissione 25:47f, 70, 297, 299, 302, 304, 34:155n
De Spiritu et littera 25:22, 24, 30, 32, 49f, 62, 135, 151–153, 174, 184–186, 243f, 279, 325f
De Trinitate 1:50n, 60, 2:76n, 3:191n, 193n, 298n, 4:126n, 195n, 8:165n, 10:50n, 354, 416, 11:460n, 13:105, 15:300n, 302n, 21:190n, 22:16n, 18n, 19n, 24:94n, 188n, 25:227, 310, 420, 432, 26:377n, 27:238, 288, 290n, 29:123n, 162n, 166n, 199n, 225n, 38:253n
De utilitate credendi 1:126f, 126n
De vera religione 4:126n
De vita eremitica 44:104n
Enarratio in psalmum 2 14:334n, 338n, 343n
Enarratio in Psalmum 10 1:41n
Enarratio in Psalmos 21 51:94n
Enarratio in Psalmum 89 13:95
Enarratio in Psalmum 103 6:376n
Enarrationes in Psalmos 8:121n, 11:5n, 48n, 50n, 65n, 16:103n, 25:511, 27:312n, 319n, 332n, 29:113n, 125n, 183n
Enchiridion ad Laurentium 4:314, 7:292, 8:37n, 20:170n, 25:284, 394f, 30:299n, 31:177n, 32:98n, 42:70n, 44:30n, 48:207
Epistle 130 21:143n
Epistle 147 51:130
Epistolae 34:285n, 48:370n, see also **Augustine, St., Works of**—*Letters*
Epistolae ad Bonifacium 29:163n
Epistolae ad Galatas expositio 26:108n, 389n, 410n, 27:174n, 176n, 179n, 205n, 226n, 228n, 234n, 261n, 277n, 281n, 285n, 294n, 295n, 299n, 334n, 368n, 372n, 373n, 378n, 381n, 388n
Expositio quarundam propositionum ex epistola ad Romanos 25:50, 58, 61f, 88, 99, 303, 307–309, 324, 329, 347f, 353f, 357
Exposition of Psalm 34 38:303n
Exposition of Psalm 68 38:303n
Exposition of Psalms 7:292n, 37:106, 124, 39:189n, 48:370n
Exposition of John 37:56n, 123n
Faith and the Creed 37:72n
Faith, Hope, and Charity 27:22n
First Catechetical Instruction 37:104n
Harmony of the Gospels 37:315, 42:160n
In epistolam Joannis ad Parthos 30:232n
Lectures or Tractates on the Gospel according to St. John 5:217n, 8:258n, 22:325n, 487n, 515n, 23:94n, 345n, 361n, 24:26n, 208n, 374n, 402n, 25:178, 29:172n, 210n, 31:274, 32:17n, 72n, 33:286n, 35:11n, 38:21n, 23n, 51n, 198n, 39:78n, 51:36–38, 42, 44, 45n, 187n, 189, 52:52, 57, 63, 71n
Letter 29 25:276
Letter 127 25:267
Letter to Jerome 39:166n
Letters 28, 40, 71, 82 25:489
Letters 27:310n, 32:11, 118n, 167n, 204n, 216n, 37:104n, 105, 144n, 38:33n, 52n, 303n
Nature and Grace 7:281n, 9:86n, 27:228, 379, 31:214n, 215, 34:155n
Of Holy Virginity 2:341n, 4:233n, 44:306n
On Baptism, Against the Donatists 27:84n, 38:28n
On Genesis 48:370
On Man's Perfection in Righteousness 30:228n
On Marriage and Concupiscence 7:76n, 14:299n, 27:188, 32:27n, 28n, 34:164n, 195n
On the Good of Marriage 2:301n, 44:306n
On the Good of Widowhood 7:115n

On the Grace of Christ and Original Sin 27:275n
On the Presence of God 38:31, 50
On the Spirit and the Letter 21:xii, 27:188, 219n, 274n, 314n, 30:322n, 32:92, 33:108n, 116, 39:180, 48:25n, 54, 150n
On the Unity of the Church 39:79n, 177n
Our Lord's Sermon on the Mount 39:270n
Preaching on Psalm 21 42:171n
Predestination of the Saints 31:138
Questions on the Heptateuch 4:13n, 19n, 5:292n, 6:117, 118n, 125n, 172n, 314n, 342n, 387n, 7:198n, 248n, 8:85n, 88n, 142n, 146n, 9:222n, 37:104n, 38:35n
Regula ad servos Dei 3:130n, 5:308n, 8:173n
Regula beati Augustini 10:222n, 25:112, 463
Regula tertia 11:528n
Reply to Faustus the Manichaean 2:68n, 291n, 4:14n, 21:66n, 27:97n, 30:187n, 35:150n, 39:210n
Retractions 14:140n, 25:327, 31:62f, 214, 216, 266, 32:156, 189n, 209, 34:180n
Sermo 54 25:514
Sermo 112 36:19n
Sermo 170 25:225
Sermo 355 25:465
Sermons 3:288n, 32:34n, 38:50, 52n
The Lord's Sermon on the Mount 2:318n, 8:329n, 21:3n, 69n, 99n, 29:26n
The Spirit and the Letter 31:xxi, 42f, 49, 34:337n
The Trinity 36:107n, 37:271n, 299n
Augustinian Breviary—25:356
Augustinian Canons—48:160n
Augustinian Eremites—see **Augustinians**
Augustinian Rule—18:55n, 41:129n, 130, 48:20n, 22, 39, 61n, 227n
Augustinians—5:333n, 7:192n, 10:ix, 8, 72, 222n, 14:67n, 16:317, 17:70, 90, 18:55, 323n, 22:ix, 60, 270, 330, 424, 23:274n, 27:153, 281, 30:73n, 95, 31:ix, xvi, 37, 255, 316n, 32:263, 34:272, 36:130, 133, 38:xviii, 41:127n, 42:97n, 44:172, 190, 48:3, 5, 6n, 7, 11, 14–16, 20f, 27f, 28n, 29n, 30f, 31n, 33f, 36, 39n, 41, 53, 60f, 64n, 108, 124, 125n, 135, 149, 164n, 169f, 171n, 233n, 236n, 272, 324, 356n, 357f, 358n, 364n, 40:10, 11n, 12f, 21f, 24, 48n, 93n, 140, 238n, 51:xi, 5, 61, 69, 80n, 113, 53:211, 54:18, 30, 44
Augustus Caesar—1:317, 4:193, 4:350, 6:335, 362, 7:144, 195, 9:203n, 13:155, 158, 161, 165, 199, 200, 14:280, 15:39, 42, 45, 116n, 17:184, 270, 313, 322n, 345, 18:239, 29:88n, 41:78n, 356n 373, 44:94n, 48:203
Aulus Gellius—*Attic Nights* 3:213, 214n, 4:292n, 5:182n, 10:49n, 15:296n, 31:222, 45:36n, 272n
Aulus Persius Flaccus—*Satires* 27:326n
Aunts—23:208
Aurelian, Emperor—29:73
Aurelius Prudentius—53:331
Aurelius Victor—*De viris illustribus* 17:51n
Aurifaber—see **Dring, Christian**
Aurifaber, Andrew—54:269, 324
Aurifaber, Christian—13:ix
Aurifaber, John—12:ixf, 22:xi, 23:ixf, 25:xii, 37:360n, 49:59n, 81n, 93n, 416n, 50:226n, 227n, 244n, 246n, 285n, 317f, 51:xvi, 70, 291, 54:xi–xix, xxiii, xxiv, xxv, 8, 20–22, 30, 61, 84, 88, 133, 135, 143n, 389, 397
Aurogallus—see **Goldhahn, Matthew (Aurogallus)**
Austria—1:254, 3:77, 7:152, 22:82, 28:131, 34:345, 49:156, 210n, 284n, 296, 50:101, 105n, 108, 112n, 120, 211n, 253n, 273n
Authorities—42:85, 91, 45:17, 46, 77, 107f, 249f, 258, 281f, 287, 341–343, 354f, 357, 46:xii, 21n, 25, 27, 32, 50f, 61, 99, 101, 127, 134, 209f, 227n, 272, 280–282, 285, 292–297, 306f, 309, 311f, 315
Authorities, Religious—23:212n, 36:x, 41:xi, 5–7, 86, 259, 300f
Authorities, Secular—13:44f, 146, 197, 210, 340, 370, 36:238, 244, 311, 327f, 40:89, 41:xiii, xv, 197, 269, 298, 300f, 303, 44:91f, 126f, 130–133
Authority—3:13, 69, 81, 93, 118, 213, 240, 255, 257, 259, 279, 298, 322, 326, 329, 350, 362, 4:19, 30, 78f, 106, 173, 219, 223f, 226, 233, 246f, 344, 387, 402f, 407, 7:17, 27, 29, 35, 37, 39, 44, 53, 64, 74, 77, 92n, 102n, 109, 132, 136, 143–145, 164, 166, 168, 187, 189, 192, 195, 197, 204f, 207, 240, 255, 261, 310, 351, 16:43, 180, 20:146f, 171, 242, 244, 333, 25:5, 138f, 469–472, 26:12–16, 46, 52, 57, 63, 65f, 76, 89, 83f, 96–100, 102, 104, 107, 208, 222–224, 228, 240, 267, 340, 354, 366, 370, 378, 422, 429, 439, 457, 27:4, 9, 15, 46, 61, 64, 99–101, 129, 141, 156f, 164, 166, 168, 171, 178, 191f, 196f,

207, 212, 261, 272, 283f, 297, 304, 324, 327, 337, 342, 369, 397, 29:99, 115, 131, 185, 35:7, 13, 21, 136, 148, 150–152, 215, 298, 45:xiii, 17, 61–63, 66, 77–129, 171f, 265, 278, 281f, 368, 386, 46:13, 25f, 31, 52, 74, 100, 126f, 190, 209, 226, 227n, 231, 237f, 242, 248, 256, 265f, 267f, 279, 281, 284, 314, 51:7, 109
Divine 4:8, 72, 101, 164, 179, 206, 392, 405
Authority, Abuse of—8:100
Authority, Civil—see **Government**
Authority, Ecclesiastical—38:147, 149, 171f, 174, 197, 44:80–89, 159
Authority, Resistance to—25:415, 47:ix, 6–9, 13–20, 34–55
Authority, Spiritual—44:52, 159–164
Authors of introductions and introductory comments—see **Atkinson, James; Bergendoff, Conrad J.; Caemmerer, Richard R.; Dietrich, Martin O.; Doberstein, John W.; Fischer, Robert Harley; Forell, George W.; Grimm, Harold J.; Gritsch, Eric W.; Hillerbrand, Hans J.; Krodel, Gottfried G.; Lazareth, William H.; Oswald, Hilton C.; Rupp, E. Gordon; Sherman, Franklin; Spitz, Lewis W.; Watson, Philip S.; Wiencke, Gustav K.**
Autodidacts—27:20n
Auxentius, Bishop of Milan—41:80n
Avarice—2:119, 3:233, 9:148, 196, 14:111, 23:8, 31:176, 41:18, 44:147–156, 45:239, 245–250, 261f, 270–273, 292, see also **Greed**
Ave Maria—34:25n, 37:260, 43:7–9, 39–41
***Ave praeclara maris stella* (Sequence)**—10:410n
Aven (Hebrew word)—see **Awen (Hebrew word)**
Avenger—9:195, 197, 204, 242
Averroes—1:29f, 3:306, 23:99, 115, 168, 36:336n
Averroists—34:211n
Avignon—49:17n, 50:55n
Awen (Hebrew word)—18:133, 19:140, 159, 27:350
Awl—9:149, 151
Axes—7:133, 342
Axhead—9:193
Axioms—3:213f, 16:270
Azal—20:339
Azariah, King—25:441, 46:120
Azariah, Prayer of—35:353f
Azarias—35:346f
Azekah—19:234
Azotus—2:205, 40:38
Azov, Sea of—2:188n

Baal—3:144, 320, 330, 4:123f, 128, 135, 5:12, 246, 6:230, 372, 7:155, 343f, 9:54f, 131, 10:353f, 11:372, 524, 14:348, 16:8, 51, 112, 17:236, 346, 18:10–12, 69, 193n, 321, 19:56, 24:24, 25:4, 95f, 158, 218, 422, 27:154, 176, 29:51, 30:186, 35:272, 36:133, 141, 146, 153, 219f, 222f, 226, 41:207n, 210, 214, 220, 47:165, 286, 53:21, 32
Baal, Priests of—13:59
Baal-peor—4:238, 9:52, 54f, 131n, 308, 13:185, 18:137, 39:262–265, 271, 40:16
Baalhannan—6:309
Baalites—7:344, 350, 355–358, 361, 9:130, 307, 21:5
Babbler—15:62, 162f
Babblers—16:275
Babel—3:170, 230, 13:148, 150, 17:305, 20:59, 246, 30:144
Babel, Tower of—2:ix, 180, 205, 210, 216, 382, 20:59, 27:242, 45:328
Babies—see **Infants**
Babst, Valentin—53:173, 176, 185, 194, 293, 302, 305, 308f, 332f
Babylon—1:99, 112, 310, 328, 2:17, 62, 175, 180, 199–204, 213, 216f, 225, 232, 240, 247, 250f, 274, 279, 360, 364f, 368, 2:200, 202, 232, 255, 259, 3:10, 60, 274, 280, 285, 4:188, 250, 258, 348, 5:160, 6:9, 52, 227, 353, 7:52, 137, 202, 241, 9:295, 11:83, 177f, 185, 366, 542, 12:30, 13:270, 325, 14:112, 114, 118, 129, 339, 15:227, 339, 16:35, 60, 85f, 126, 132n, 133, 135, 137–140, 142, 170–172, 175–177, 184, 279, 324, 346, 348, 17:33f, 56, 95, 123, 126–130, 133, 142, 146, 148, 151–154, 164–167, 355, 365, 372, 395, 18:91, 179, 208, 241, 246, 272f, 327, 330, 346, 19:208f, 215, 235, 20:28, 61, 68, 84, 89, 160f, 179, 183, 189–191, 245, 251, 260f, 343, 21:344, 348, 22:42, 89, 92, 246, 23:387, 389, 24:302, 366, 25:110, 26:201, 211, 249, 27:169, 281, 28:191, 30:80, 144, 31:285, 336f, 34:169f, 212, 35:226, 282, 294, 407, 36:12, 72, 77, 80, 83, 88f, 158, 200, 264f, 305, 327, 38:207, 41:xv, 42:161, 45:329, 46:194, 47:85–87, 158, 195, 48:109, 50:289f
Babylon, King(s) of—2:62, 257, 259, 276, 363, 19:185f, 188, 199–205, 210, 235,

20:75, 90, 134, 192, 250, 253, 264, 47:173, 188, 246, 258
Babylonia—2:279, 5:352, 7:140, 26:441
Babylonian Captivity—see **Captivity—Babylonian**
Babylonian Captivity of the Church—see **Luther, Martin, Writings of**
Babylonian religion—17:34, 134, 137, 145
Babylonians—1:23, 323, 2:98f, 157, 200, 371, 388, 3:278, 4:185, 350, 356, 372f, 5:208, 6:88, 206, 284, 383, 7:152f, 199, 11:546, 16:132–135, 138, 170f, 347, 349, 17:4, 33f, 95, 119, 128, 133–135, 137, 145–148, 153, 361, 18:79, 89, 92, 101, 211, 321, 344, 353, 392, 20:62, 75f, 159, 169, 193, 206, 226, 259, 341, 23:397, 47:265, 271
Babylonians and Chaldeans—19:107n, 111, 113, 116, 124, 127, 145, 153, 155, 167–173, 176, 178, 182–186, 206, 208, 235, 19:125
Bacchus—6:238, 27:371
Bacchus, Priesthood of—36:199
Bach, Johann Sebastian—53:226, 321
Bachelor in Biblical Studies—see **Cursor Bibliae**
Bachmann, E. Theodore—author of General Introduction to *Word and Sacrament*, Vols. 35–38 35:xi–xxi
author of Introduction and presumed author of introductory comments preceding each writing included in Vol. 35
editor of Vol. 35
translator of *Brief Instruction on What to Look for and Expect in the Gospels* 35:115–129
translator of *Defense of the Translation of the Psalms* 35:204–224
translator of *How Christians Should Regard Moses* 35:156–174
translator of *Prefaces to the Apocrypha* 35:336–354
translator of *The Sacrament of Penance* 35:4–22
Bachscheisse, Lecks—50:279
Backbiters—42:67–60, 73
Backs—10:331f
Backsliders—22:49
Bacon, Leonard W.—53:xviii
Baden Debate—37:8, 81, 97
Baden-Baden—49:50n
Bader, Paul—49:290n, 315n, 402n
Badia, Thomas—34:233, 267
Bag of worms—see **Worms, Bag of**
Baggage—6:22f, 59, 65, 176, 280
Bailiff—49:290n, 313n, 50:24n, 168, 295n
Bainton, Roland H.—47:x, 116n, 48:xviin, 54:43
Erasmus of Christendom, New York, 1909 33:5n
Here I Stand, New York, 1950 32:115n, 35:xiv, 37:371n, 42:181n, 45:59n
Bakers—3:197, 7:53f, 114, 161, 186, 18:35f, 23:11, 14, 39f, 94, 129, 132
Bakers, Chief—7:99, 107f, 118, 152, 157
Balaam—3:280, 4:185f, 5:207, 209, 6:34, 308, 7:348, 9:125, 230, 235f, 297, 13:146, 16:241, 21:276f, 22:187, 23:97, 25:445, 30:185–188, 208, 34:316, 36:130, 37:28, 41:120, 191, 360, 47:235
Balaam's ass—36:182
Balak—30:185
Baldness—10:194, 341, 18:182, 220
Balkans—49:240n, 50:190n
Ballad—53:196, 212, 217
Balsam—1:250, 2:344, 6:382f, 7:323, 326, 15:107n, 208f, 18:166, 258f, 322, 24:359
Bamberg—46:72n, 49:81n, 119
Bamberg, Bishop of—49:119n, 189n, 198
Bamberg Agenda—53:96
Bamberger Halsgerichtsordnung—49:18n
Ban—23:341, 24:266, 306, 311, 26:97n, 34:32–34, 37, 54, 35:51, 382n, 36:212, 219, 38:93, 191, 317, 39:xiii, xxii, 5–22, 40:311, 340, 371, 41:153, 251, 266, 278, 287, 320, 332n, 375, 44:223–229, 45:61n, 69, 84n, 172, 176n, 197, 285n, 314, 347, 46:162, 197n, 271, 273, see also **Excommunication**
Ban, Imperial—49:193, 258
Banishment—46:313, 314n
Banking in Luther's day—22:471
Bankruptcy—45:267, 268n
Banners—15:214f, 20:103, 297, 46:168f, 185, 189f, 196
Banns, Marriage—46:290n, 293, 53:111, 113
Banquets—3:195, 197f, 251, 253, 4:183, 251, 276, 295, 25:481
Bapst Hymnal—see **Wittenberg Hymnal (Bapst)**
Baptism—1:11, 94, 157, 161, 196, 223, 227f, 247, 249f, 304, 309, 2:44, 46–48, 68, 151, 153, 155, 269f, 295, 353, 3:29, 37, 82, 90, 92, 95, 101, 103–111, 124, 146f, 155, 165, 167f, 220, 272–275, 288, 4:16f, 93–96, 126f, 142, 179, 181f, 198, 201, 240, 242, 315, 323, 348f, 373, 405, 5:21f, 43, 131, 141, 145, 149, 183, 196, 205, 244–248, 250, 274, 277, 280n, 6:10, 128f, 141, 149, 234, 237,

257f, 286, 308, 330, 364, 7:64, 132, 135, 155, 234, 278, 344, 346, 349, 10:151, 342, 441, 11:53, 86, 12:39, 59, 105f, 136, 236, 250f, 255–257, 259f, 262, 264, 266, 269, 277f, 283, 297f, 327, 329, 351, 366f, 369–371, 400, 13:192, 244, 282, 303, 324, 329, 331–334, 381, 384, 14:13, 21, 31f, 35, 39, 55f, 16:73, 109, 227, 297, 17:53, 113, 163, 192, 341, 389, 18:258, 19:121, 167, 193, 20:68, 253, 331, 21:150–152, 276, 278, 285f, 22:44–46, 66, 77n, 102, 117, 119, 139, 172–175, 177, 179–181, 196f, 201, 214, 220, 240, 268, 270, 283f, 285–287, 290f, 294f, 303f, 308, 314, 318, 333, 349, 357, 381, 386, 408n, 414, 419f, 424–427, 429, 431, 433, 435, 439, 443, 447–449, 454, 464, 467, 479–481, 486, 490, 498, 505–507, 510, 512, 515f, 523, 529, 23:15, 56, 62, 79, 85, 92, 99, 123, 142, 164, 173, 206n, 224, 226, 229, 235, 257, 275, 280, 285–288, 321, 330f, 333–335, 345, 349, 355, 378, 386, 392, 405, 416, 418f, 24:12, 14, 42, 45, 51, 66, 69f, 72, 79, 84f, 99, 109, 127f, 130f, 145, 149, 151, 155, 169–171, 173–175, 179f, 182f, 185, 202, 215, 220–222, 230, 233, 236, 239, 252, 257, 268, 274, 280, 294, 296, 304, 307, 309f, 312, 320f, 326–328, 359, 368, 394, 25:6, 50–52, 57, 61, 63f, 155f, 261, 272, 276, 286, 304f, 312f, 315, 338, 340, 26:24f, 74, 104, 109, 140, 143, 199, 228, 241f, 352–356, 27:85, 93, 148, 193, 362, 401, 28:59f, 62, 66, 68, 70, 78, 84, 101, 114, 132f, 147, 149–151, 193, 267–269, 29:17, 48, 81n, 81–85, 180f, 195, 219, 227, 30:3, 40, 42, 71, 82, 96, 115, 170f, 189f, 245, 249, 286, 314–316, 32:14, 16, 18–31, 41, 51f, 60f, 157–159, 191n, 194, 203, 206–209, 220–222, 236, 251, 34:53, 125, 163, 180, 190, 193, 306, 314, 347, 354, 35:xi, xiii, 13, 25–43, 50, 55, 66f, 81, 93, 199, 201, 375, 36:7, 18, 21, 27, 48, 56–82, 86, 93, 95n, 102, 108n, 111, 118, 124, 172, 201, 215, 279, 283, 300, 345, 347, 353, 37:11, 16n, 155, 183, 188, 192f, 226, 252, 274, 286, 292, 329, 366–368, 370, 38:x, xvi, 18f, 24, 27f, 29, 36, 41, 56, 58, 65, 70, 73, 79, 81, 87f, 95, 97–101, 120f, 132, 153f, 158f, 160, 171, 177f, 183, 185–189, 193–196, 198f, 201–203, 207f, 233, 290, 309n, 313, 39:xxii, xxv, 43, 75, 171, 268, 304, 40:23, 214, 239f, 245f, 247, 249, 250, 252f, 260, 288, 41:xivf, 22, 38, 40, 44–47, 73, 93, 107, 113, 149, 151f, 154f, 160, 167f, 170–173, 175, 194f, 199f, 207–211, 218, 223, 315f, 329, 336, 342, 348, 352, 358–361, 42:11, 28, 100n, 142n, 43:37, 44:314f, 356, 384, 385, 45:8n, 24, 106, 46:51, 137, 177, 220, 227, 231, 254, 262, 294, 47:35, 52–53, 161f, 297, 48:280, 367f, 369n, 371f, 49: 98n, 219, 50:13f, 21, 74, 51:11, 22, 99, 113f, 116, 172, 182–188, 242, 247f, 294, 296, 299, 307f, 315–329, 343, 373f, 376, 379, 385, 391, 53:32, 64, 68, 93, 95–103, 106–109, 111, 117, 122, 124, 171, 200, 54:20, 287, 358, 425, 460f, see also **Christ**—His baptism; **Baptism, Infant**

Conditional 50:13f

Modes of 53:100n

Prenatal 54:61

Baptism, Infant—16:297, 25:304f, 29:8n, 172, 36:57f, 68, 73f, 301, 40:236f, 254–258, 54:55–57, 98, 113, 242

Baptism, Order of—see **Luther, Martin, Writings of**

Baptism of John—36:86

Baptism of the Spirit—42:142n

Baptista Mantuanus—*De patientia* 25:290

Baptized persons—36:99f, 46:224

Baptizing—22:38f, 45–47, 62, 65, 71, 77, 86, 120, 127, 130, 159f, 173, 175f, 180, 197, 202, 209, 218, 239, 269, 283, 286, 291, 295, 300f, 308, 312, 318, 320, 357, 381, 386, 413, 415, 419–425, 430, 433, 441, 447–449, 453, 464, 479f, 493, 22:503, 505, 509, 512–516, 523, 527

Barabbas—14:314f, 20:123, 28:130, 36:204, 207, 42:51

Barak—6:275, 9:307, 19:134, 22:274, 36:152

Barbara, St.—6:238, 13:326, 17:140n, 20:267, 22:118, 137, 142, 164f, 385, 388, 490, 23:121, 28:247, 34:24, 29n, 44:68, 74, 183

Barbarians—1:255f, 7:75, 99, 18:187, 22:85, 25:8, 38:250

Barbarism blamed on Reformation—49:11, 34, 72

Barbarossa—see **Frederick I, Emperor**

Barcelona—49:222, 245n, 281n, 286n

Barcelona, Treaty of—47:24n

Barefoot orders—23:274n

Barge, Hermann—*Andreas Bodenstein von Karlstadt,* Leipzig, 1905 45:53n, 162n, 54:107

Jakob Strauss: ein Kämpfer für das Evangelium in Tirol, Thüringen und Süddeutschland 45:240n, 241n
Luther und der Frühkapitalismus 45:238n, 239n
Barley—1:37, 210, 2:157, 161, 23:9, 40, 116, 132, 140, 24:323n
Barnabas, St., Apostle—3:320, 355, 14:23, 346, 19:27, 20:297, 21:319, 24:245, 26:75f, 79, 81f, 100, 107f, 112–115, 118f, 204f, 27:165, 190, 195, 200, 202, 208, 213f, 28:90, 29:36, 30:229, 36:149, 38:186, 41:68, 162, 325
Barnes, Robert—1:288n, 34:108, 50:27f, 28f, 30, 31n, 101n, 102n, 142n, 150n, 202n, 206, 54:384
and Henry VIII's divorce 50:28f, 28n, 98n, 106n, 137n
first mission to Saxony 50:98n, 101n
Lives of the Popes, Wittenberg, 1536 41:xiiin
second mission to Saxony 50:98n, 100f, 103f, 104n, 106n, 111, 113n, 114f, 114n, 120, 137f
Barnim XI, Duke of Pomerania—31:324, 51:53
Barns—7:159, 171, 204–206, 213, 215, 223
Baron, Salo W.—47:128n, 190n
Barrenness—16:50, 18:51
Barth, Hans—49:152n
Bartholomew, St., Apostle—22:229, 41:319, 48:17, 51:217
Bartholomew of Pisa—*De conformitate vitae beati Francisci ad vitan Dominin Jesu* 17:286n
Bartholomew's, St., Day—23:289n
Bartolus de Saxoferrato—2:313n, 54:361n
Baruch, Book of—35:349f
Basel—32:106, 37:xiv, 138, 150, 203, 271n, 38:6, 8, 15, 77, 157n, 40:75f, 41:8, 42:5, 17, 48:18n, 24n, 110, 115n, 230n, 305n, 318, 49:42, 43n, 50n, 77n, 96n, 188n, 215n, 216, 303n, 427, 50:3, 28, 145n, 191n, 227n, 228
Council of 41:266n, 294n, 48:186n
University of 31:257, 263, 47:261n, 48:79n, 132n, 194n, 219n, 305n, 49:88n
Basemath—5:93, 6:287f, 290
Bashan—3:197, 9:27, 34, 40, 293, 307, 10:198–200, 203, 338f, 16:37, 286, 18:275, 287, 20:117, 311
Basil of Caesarea, St.—41:79n
Basil the Great, St.—12:76, 23:123n, 25:268, 53:21, 54:34, 353
De Spiritu Sancto 1:146n
The Orthodox Faith 23:123n
Basilisks—11:215, 218, 16:148, 17:54, 297, 47:172, 216
Basilius—2:39
Baskets—7:72, 118
Bastards—9:230f, 235, 291
Bathsheba—3:45, 7:14, 35, 321, 13:205, 14:173, 15:296, 22:264, 29:115, 36:100, 47:197
Battering-rams—3:9, 213, 341, 7:55, 75, 77, 183, 313
Battles—9:203, 236f, 20:8, 44, 108–110, 130, 134, 302, 338f, 25:53, 63f, 112, 127, 46:133, 135
Bauer, Clemens—"Conrad Peutingers Gutachten zuri Monopolfrage: Eine Untersuchung zure Wandlung der Wirtschaftsanschauungen im Zeitalter der Reformation" (in *Archive für Reformationsgeschichte*, XLV, 1954) 45:241n, 262n
Bauer, Karl—*Luthers Anruf an den Adel, die Kirche zu Reformierten* 44:119n, 120n, 121n
Baumbach, Louis von—50:193, 200n
Baumgärtner, Jerome—49:105n, 50:263
Bäumker, Wilhelm—53:37n
Baur, Frederick—43:74
Bautzen—2:202n
Bavaria—1:254, 288, 34:98, 45:27, 77n, 112n, 49:187n, 313n, 383n, 427, 54:336, 392
Bavarian War—6:334
Bavarians—6:183, 17:188, 54:310, 387, 472
Bayezid, Sultan—4:29n
Bdellium—1:97, 101
Beads—42:23, 72
Beams and pillars—19:213, 214
Bears—1:55, 62, 103, 119, 132, 331, 2:66, 69, 74, 116, 135f, 274, 4:37, 106, 382, 390, 5:254, 327
Beast—15:3, 57f, 61
Beast, Scarlet—37:138n
Beast and riders—33:65f, 237
Beastliness—3:256
Beasts—1:54–57, 64, 66, 75, 77f, 81, 85, 91, 94, 99, 101, 125, 132f, 151, 153, 182, 185, 187, 192, 208, 210f, 255, 266f, 286f, 292, 303, 306, 309, 333, 336, 6:17f, 68, 9:248, 295, 10:89f, 171f, 430, 449, 24:82, 196, 228, 25:139, 160, see also **Animals**
Beasts of burden—2:279, 395
Beauty—10:133, 215–217, 230f, 239, 329f, 11:207, 260–266, 376f, 387, 12:280f
Becoming—25:104.
Bedbugs—1:208

Bedchambers—7:51f, 93, 303
Bede, The Venerable—32:183n, 39:211
Bedrooms—4:280, 313
Beds—10:66f, 80, 191, 305
Beelzebub (Beelzebul)—1:113, 11:112, 14:96, 18:308, 22:433, 23:158, 241, 25:422, 34:359, 37:169, 38:305, 47:232
Beer—1:210, 2:350, 7:199, 351, 23:9, 40, 128f, 137, 262f, 267, 372, 51:77, 180, 296, 323, 54:132, 172, 178
Beer, Rastrum—39:76n, 98, 211
Beern, Hans—49:417n
Beersheba—2:281, 3:180, 4:46f, 71, 77, 88, 98, 179, 183, 324, 326, 5:61, 69, 73, 209, 7:153, 18:159f, 36:87, 38:150
Bees—3:183, 7:68f, 9:293, 11:203n, 412f, 24:205
Beetle's hole—33:45, 47
Beetles—1:52
Beggar girl (parable)—11:280f
Beggars—2:175, 326, 329, 394, 3:183, 188, 209, 315, 361, 4:7, 77, 7:66, 142, 171, 338, 24:35, 84, 154f, 251, 336–338, 26:403f, 409, 37:141, 42:136n, 46:250f, see also **Mendicant orders**
Begging—7:337f, 32:98f, 44:189f, 45:xii, 161, 176n, 189n, 281f, 285–287, 54:20, see also **Stationaries (Mendicant Monks)**
Beghards—25:487, 28:338, 32:129
Beginners—25:8, 152, 245
Beginning—25:59
Behavior—29:52f, 118
Bėhavior, Christian—21:235–237
Beheim, Sebald—49:96n, 330n
Behemoth—7:371, 13:31, 14:289, 24:417, 25:472, 26:97, 428, 452, 40:42
Beier, Leonhard (Leonard)—31:37–39, 45:8n, 48:39n, 60, 90n, 54:194, 334
***Bekenntnisschriften der evangelisch-lutherischen Kirche*, Göttingen, 1952**—32:153n
Bel—17:133, 137
Bel and Nebo—19:186, 217, 224
Bel and the Dragon—19:107n, 35:327n, 353n, 354
Belgians—2:188
Belgium—1:254, 5:283, 6:x, 244, 32:135
Belgrade—16:254, 46:157, 49:240n
Belgum, Gerhard, ed.—*Luther Today*, Decorah, 1957 54:406n
The Mature Luther, Decorah, 1959 54:xxii, 54, 362, 406
Belial—5:246, 279, 9:148, 15:351, 16:262, 18:40, 292, 297, 22:377, 407, 37:27, 176, 212, 263, 49:367. 413
Belial, Children of—13:177f
Belief—30:34f, 57, 152, 282, 42:81, 110
Beliefs—23:233, 282, 288, 290, 297f, 344, 351, 408, 24:19, 181, 205, 309, 314, 317, 328, 331, 405, 408, 38:5, 12, 27f, 103f, 119, 150, 164n, 210, 262, 269, 308
Believers—2:12, 76, 153, 157, 358, 386, 3:29, 52, 87, 90, 131, 152f, 185, 188, 198, 269, 294, 321, 328, 335, 346f, 361, 4:25, 71, 103, 169, 202, 259, 313, 341, 408, 5:17, 214, 223n, 234, 271, 275–277, 7:177, 203, 220, 234, 296, 319, 370, 9:94, 97, 179, 183, 187, 225, 244, 291, 13:6, 9f, 13, 26, 14:20, 46, 51, 70, 80, 82, 92, 100, 102, 187, 219, 222, 299, 307f, 326, 331, 344, 18:12, 15, 21:247, 22:24, 275, 285, 311, 339, 344, 346, 352, 378, 23:31, 48, 70, 96, 130, 149n, 150, 233, 275, 277f, 299, 302, 306, 358, 24:57, 92, 112, 134, 169, 209, 211, 250, 264, 321, 330, 349, 385, 26:75, 81, 84, 112, 116, 151, 155, 172, 162f, 165f, 204, 212, 240, 242–244, 260, 271, 274, 282, 285, 302, 331, 334, 343, 356, 361, 371, 374–376, 378, 431, 439, 447, 449, 27:8f, 23, 30, 32, 47, 76, 83, 89, 96, 117–121, 124, 129, 136, 142, 148, 162, 167, 184, 202, 241, 245, 254, 255, 280, 290, 310, 398, 29:21, 104, 216, 226, 229, 237, 30:9, 15, 23, 35, 63, 70, 74, 76, 107, 127, 133, 149, 152, 238, 255, 311, 36:93, 316, 337, 38:x, xvf, 7, 39f, 43, 56, 71, 94n, 95, 111f, 256, 308, 41:167, 42:119, 142, 150, 46:xiv, 122, 135, 219, 224f, 236, 261, 265
Believing—23:46
Belisarius—15:115n
Bell, Henry—54:xv
Bellies, Care for—45:142, 171, 348f, 355, 371
Bells—7:300, 34:54, 56, 40:311f, 41:169, 292, 46:175n, 53:62, 260
Belly—1:353, 3:14, 149, 197, 200, 4:392, 401, 403, 405, 408f, 5:6, 14, 36, 208, 353, 372, 7:316, 9:54, 92, 94f, 118, 123, 140, 157, 174, 236, 10:142f, 207, 291, 23:5f, 8, 10, 32, 39, 43, 48, 75, 116, 132, 153, 259, 362, 403, 26:95, 458, 27:69, 131f, 296, 369, 371, 29:37–39, 210
Belly servers—15:67, 166, 18:9, 22f, 40, 57, 391, 394, 400, 20:55f, 110, 237, 276, 312, 344
Belly teachers—16:239
Belshazzar—2:17, 391, 7:141, 16:141, 22:92, 35:298

Bembo, Cardinal Pietro—54:208
Ben-ammi—3:314
Benaiah—1:299, 9:163
Benedicamus—53:30, 68f
***Benedicite omni opera* (canticle)**—35:353n
Benedict XIII, Pope—41:265n, 267n
Benedict, St.—2:113, 270, 3:165, 200n, 9:54, 17:101, 20:330, 22:163f, 254, 259, 261, 23:25, 34, 38, 273, 27:83f, 30:294, 322, 36:221n, 39:192, 211n
Rule 3:200n, 11:422n, 525n, 35:134n, 135n
Benedict of Nursia, St.—44:380n, 54:270
Benedictines—20:330, 26:33n, 27:281, 30:259n, 48:64n, 163n, 225n, 49:10, 11n, 48f, 115n, 164n
Benediction—53:30, 84, 99, 100, 109, 126
***Benedictus* (Canticle)**—22:38, 40:307, 53:28, 68
Benefactors—21:132f
Benefices—4:200f, 396f, 9:168, 27:385n, 30:212, 34:36n, 37, 92, 98, 247f, 250–253, 41:15n, 259, 270, 272, 45:174n, 180
Benefices, Incompatible—36:114n
Benefit—35:93, 120
Benefit of clergy—29:71n, 30:290f
Benevolence—9:219, 27:376
Benhadad, King of Syria—29:170, 30:289, 31:316
Benjamin—2:257, 4:55, 5:ix, 339f, 6:178, 187, 223, 270, 273, 278f, 321f, 340, 380, 7:5, 8, 211, 218, 220–222, 230, 233, 237, 241f, 244, 246f, 249, 257, 263f, 282f, 285–291, 301, 306, 310, 313, 317f, 322–331, 339–341, 352, 358f, 361–363, 366–368, 371, 376f, 9:35, 258, 306, 11:96f, 16:114f, 18:28, 203, 340, 20:342, 28:323, 45:254
Benjamin, Tribe of—13:27f, 27:155, 187, 47:187, 203
Benjaminites—3:279, 6:279, 13:151, 18:57, 46:191
Benno of Meissen, St.—4:130n, 39:107, 53:265n
Benoni—7:6
Benrath, Karl, ed.—*An den christlichen Adel deutscher Nation, von D. Martin Luther*, Halle, 1884 35:68n
Berbig—21:xvii
Berengar of Tours—37:300f
Bergendoff, Conrad J.—author of Introduction to Vol. 40 and presumed author of introductions to all writings in Vol. 40
co-translator of *The Keys* 40:321–378
editor of Vol. 40
translator of *Against the Heavenly Prophets in the Matter of Graven Images and Sacraments, Part II* 40:144–244
translator of *Concerning Rebaptism* 40:225–262
translator of *Concerning the Ministry* 40:3–44
translator of *Infiltrating and Clandestine Preachers* 40:379–393
translator of *Instructions for Visitors of Parish Pastors in Electoral Saxony* 40:263–320
translator of *Letter to the Christians at Strassburg in Opposition to the Fanatic Spirit* 40:61–72
translator of *Letter to the Princes of Saxony concerning the Rebellious Spirit* 40:45–60
Berger, Arnold E., ed.—*Die Sturmtruppen der Reformation*, Leipzig, 1931 45:58n, 125n
Luthers Werke, Leipzig, nd. 35:345n
Berlepsch, Hans von—35:127, 36:235, 48:214n, 227n, 255, 269, 276, 290n, 294, 307n, 313n, 40:13n
Berlin—40:52, 47:106, 264n, 48:160, 49:176, 50:128n
Bern—14:76, 38:7, 49:88n
Bern Disputation—37:41n
Bernard of Clairvaux, St.—2:55, 164, 268f, 321, 3:165, 225, 291, 4:82, 256, 267, 273, 305, 342, 7:83–85, 124, 307, 10:35, 123, 147, 195, 356, 421n, 11:223, 285, 451, 496, 14:38, 311, 347, 15:335, 17:298, 392n, 393, 20:142, 21:283, 23:38, 57, 24:386, 395, 25:xi, 434, 26:52n, 459f, 28:210, 323, 356, 30:27, 40, 42, 230, 232, 296, 323, 31:89, 204, 273, 337, 32:221, 34:155n, 215, 35:134n, 217n, 36:135–137, 186–190, 289, 37:172, 38:159, 178, 39:268n, 41:20n, 26f, 125n, 126n, 127n, 42:9n, 10n, 44:58n, 266n, 288–293, 309, 316, 325, 334f, 354, 288–293, 363, 45:363n, 47:110, 48:298, 49:24n, 51:186, 54:84, 105, 353, 407
Bernard of Clairvaux, St., Works of—9:130, 164, 22:52, 58, 103–105, 254f, 259, 264, 268f, 273, 335f, 360, 377, 387f, 458, 27:43, 83–85, 89
Concerning Commandment and Dispensation 25:364, 44:343
De consideratione 3:225n, 25:17, 120, 176, 270, 472, 29:165n, 202n, 31:205, 337n, 342
Epistula XCI 25:225

Epistula XCIII 10:53
Exordium magnum Cisterciense 36:189n
Homilia II super Missa est 51:375
In nativitate Dominini sermo 5:234n
In virginis nativitatem sermo 2 10:106n
Liber de praecepto et dispensatione 29:216n
Opera omnia 34:215n
Oratio devota ad Dominum Jesum et B. Mariam matrem eius 13:326
Sermo II in vigilia nativitatis Domini 25:478
Sermo 20 in Canticles 33:77n
Sermo in festo Annunciationis Beatae Mariae Virginis 29:171n
Sermones de diversis 3:291n, 4:267n, 7:83n, 27:300n
Sermones de tempore 1:23n, 4:342n, 5:220n
Sermones in Quadragesima 29:218n
Sermons on the Canticles 4:256n, 7:84n, 10:88n, 352, 11:223n, 285n, 13:245n, 14:347n, 26:5n, 370n, 27:387n, 30:296n, 34:215n
Vita prima, S. Bernardi vita et res gestae 4:273n, 5:133n, 30:27n
Vitis mystica 4:305n
Bernard (a converted Jew)—45:198, 200n
Bernard of Cluny, St.—*De contemptu mundi* 15:4n
Bernardines—22:270
Berndt, Ambrose—50:209, 209n, 212, 54:419
Bernhard, Prince of Anhalt—51:315
Bernhardi, Bartholomew—44:245, 48:94n, 95n, 115n, 142n, 148, 231, 235, 278, 291n, 342n, 378
Bernhardi, John—39:53f, 101n, 48:164n
Confutation of the Inept and Impious Booklet of Friar Augustine Alveld 39:53
Berosus—2:32
Berthold of Henneberg, Archbishop of Mainz—16:258n
Berthold of Regensburg, St.—37:370n, 53:263
Bertram, Martin H.—translator of *Christian Letter of Consolation to the People of Miltenberg* 43:97–112
translator of *Commentary on I Corinthians 15* 28:59–213
translator of *How God Rescued an Honorable Nun* 43:81–96
translator of *Letter of Consolation to all who Suffer Persecution* 43:57–70
translator of *Letter to Hans von Rechenberg* 43:47–56
translator of *Personal Prayer Book* 43:3–46
translator of *Sermons on the Gospel of St. John, Chapters 1–4* 22:5–529
translator of *Sermons on the Gospel of St. John, Chapters 6–8* 23:5–421
translator of *Sermons on the Gospel of St. John, Chapters 14–16* 24:5–421
translator of *To all Christians in Worms* 43:71–80
translator of *Treatise on the Last Words of David* 15:265–351
translator of German text of *Lectures on Habakkuk* 19:151–237
translator of German text of *Lectures on Jonah* 19:35–106
translator of all writings included in Vols. 30, 42, and 47
translator of commentary on Psalm 68 13:1–38
Beskendorf, Peter—43:189–217, 50:123, 176
Besold, Jerome—5:ix, 54:xii, 368, 467
recorder of Luther's table conversation, 1544 54:465–476
Beth-horon—47:236
Bethabara—22:415, 422f
Bethany—24:333, 42:8
Bethaven—5:242, 10:86, 11:40, 547, 18:24, 28, 34n, 43, 54, 159, 27:155, 187, 36:88n, 113, 219f, 227
Bethel—2:244, 282, 286, 332, 3:164, 180, 316, 4:178, 5:241–244, 251f, 6:39, 125–127, 183, 223f, 226f, 238, 241, 247–249, 264–268, 340, 9:188, 13:270, 14:258, 16:155, 18:24, 34n, 65f, 142, 149, 151, 154, 158–160, 20:77, 262, 264, 27:262, 344, 36:221f, 226
Bethel, John, of Spangenberg—48:29, 31n, 49:24n
Bethel, Priests of—41:220
Bethlehem—1:310, 3:216n, 4:181, 5:220, 6:267, 273f, 295, 7:214, 335, 22:109, 195, 203, 485, 511, 23:105, 243f, 279, 283–285, 287, 289, 306, 29:174, 35:360, 47:231
Bethlehem-Ephrathah—18:247f
Bethsaida—22:184, 186, 193, 390, 42:134, 45:148
Bethuel—4:184, 280, 294, 5:280, 6:307, 7:13, 199
Bethulia—35:339, 42:90
Beto, George—translator of commentary on Psalm 118 14:41–106
Betrayal—14:149
Betrothal, Parental consent for—44:392
Betrothals—1:134, 4:184, 218, 224, 251,

293, 5:193, 301, 7:27, 36:100f, 213, 44:11n, 12, 53:111, 46:262, 267–310, 297n, 320, see also **Engagements**
Betrothals, Secret—4:220, 226f, 288f, 6:299, 369, 7:5n, 36:213, 45:29, 46:220, 262, 267–288, 289n, 290f, 297, 300, 306, 308, 320
Betrothed persons—9:162, 46:262, 270f, 281, 284, 287, 289f, 292, 295f, 296–298, 306
Beulah—17:346f
Bewitchment—26:190, 192–194, 195–200, 210, 254
Beyer, Christian—45:55n, 49:274n, 349, 353f, 377n, 413n, 50:22n, 80n, 107, 112n
Beyer, Earl—co-translator of *The Keys* 40:321–378
Beyer, H.W.—13:160n
Beyschlag—21:xii
Bias of Priene—2:297f, 7:101, 9:17, 230, 13:211, 21:298
Bibbiena, Cardinal Antonio—46:188n
Bible—see **Scripture(s)**
Chaldean see **Scripture(s), Old Testament**—Aramaic version
Biblia cum glossa ordinaria—see ***Glossa ordinaria***
***Biblia iam pridem renouate pars prima*, Basel, 1502**—6:xi
Bibliander, Theodore, ed.—German edition of the *Koran*, 1543 5:79n
Bibliographical notes—48:xvii–xx, 49:xv–xix, 50:xvii–xx
Biel, Gabriel—4:220n, 10:30n, 85n, 12:342n, 25:xi, 7, 163, 372, 458, 497, 31:6, 9n, 13, 32:153n, 34:155n, 35:64, 368, 38:263n, 272, 44:275n, 45:252n, 263n 283n, 291n, 48:6n, 59n, 65n, 156n, 313n, 51:9n
Canon of the Mass 31:9n
Collectorium in quattuor libros sententiarum 10:49n, 85n, 100
Commentary on the Sentences 32:153n
Expositio canonis missae, Tübingen, 1499 54:264
Sermones de festivitatibus Christi 11:396n
Bigamists—28:23f
Bigamy—36:105n, 114, 41:156n, 157–161, 163, 183n, 241, 50:33n, 54:243, 379, 382, 387, 390
Bigwigs—7:330, 21:133, 168, 172, 184, 202, 224f, 227, 23:201, 203, 218, 240, 284, 294, 302, 417
Bildad—6:307
Bildenhauer, Claus—34:295n
Bileam—2:191
Bilhah—5:337, 340, 6:270, 275–278, 362, 393, 7:8, 218, 221, 256, 9:258
Billerbeck, Paul—see **Strack, Herman L., and Paul Billerbeck, eds.**
Billican, Theobald—31:37, 37:5, 8f
Binding and loosing—41:53f, 153, 191, 195, 293, 316–320, 329–343, 345, 357, 364, see also **Keys, The**
Bindseil, Heinrich Ernst—54:xiii
Bird traps—50:302
Birds—1:5, 29f, 39, 48f, 51–55, 66f, 74f, 77, 85, 99, 120, 132f, 139, 217, 300, 340, 2:58, 67, 69, 74, 92, 96, 109, 115n, 133f, 160, 162, 214, 236, 330, 342, 3:32–34, 179, 347, 4:71, 6:17f, 90, 133, 7:29, 118, 158, 9:95, 137, 163, 175, 225, 10:89f, 100, 11:138–142, 308, 331, 336, 337n, 342, 437n, 21:196–198, 320, 24:46, 82, 228, 28:183, 290, 46:13, 39, 238, 54:192
Birnbaum—34:25
Birth—1:46, 71, 104f, 126, 128, 186, 189, 192–194, 196, 198, 199–200, 202, 216f, 220, 243, 255, 257f, 274, 312, 314, 327, 352f, 7:6–8, 13, 35, 46–49, 51, 71, 164f, 179, 182, 261, 296, 325, 352, 360, 372, 13:302f, 15:50f, 108, 22:93f, 96, 130, 133, 281, 288, 290f, 303, 306, 310–312, 316, 319f, 254, 457, 26:351, 355, 367, 385, 392, 435, 450, 458, 42:99, 100n, 52:152f
A miracle 4:4f, 8, 355, 7:46
Birthrights—4:383, 391, 394f, 401f, 404–409, 5:113, 148, 151–155, 157, 167, 7:201, 236, 260, 9:211, 214
Births, Multiple—1:217
Bishop's cloak—34:100
Bishoprics—4:380, 396, 5:192, 7:157, 194, 9:49, 140, 11:291, 14:262f, 17:323, 23:6, 211f, 338, 24:274, 360, 27:166, 385
Bishoprics, Apostolic—16:236
Bishops—1:184, 235, 249, 261, 271f, 276, 280, 289, 2:5, 7, 12, 21, 38, 84, 88, 102, 152, 165, 181, 202, 226n, 256, 272, 284, 286f, 292, 310, 315, 334, 374, 3:5, 98, 153, 179, 222, 240, 242, 245, 280, 314, 326, 328, 338, 340, 344, 346, 4:32, 76f, 89, 105, 121f, 125, 211, 250, 282, 351, 384, 392, 396, 407f, 5:90, 122f, 155, 192, 199, 238, 272, 274, 331, 6:48, 114, 239, 347, 375, 407, 7:63, 68, 115, 147, 152, 157, 168, 194, 199f, 205, 233, 337, 9:3f, 6, 8, 171, 235, 10:222f, 330, 359, 11:3, 143f, 291, 544, 546, 13:16, 30f, 260, 296,

14:23, 57, 64, 67f, 74, 76, 91–93, 97, 103, 209, 215, 217, 225, 241, 243, 247, 260, 262f, 266, 292, 325f, 331, 333f, 337, 340, 16:22, 40, 44f, 137, 185, 193, 222–224, 232, 243f, 249, 278, 303, 333, 17:12, 14, 23, 40, 56, 78, 91, 94, 101, 105, 188f, 211, 266, 269, 323, 20:119, 129, 141, 267, 321, 324, 21:220, 22:227, 478, 23:46f, 56, 104, 150, 152, 156, 158, 191–193, 196, 201f, 212, 226, 228, 253, 255, 257f, 270, 287f, 290, 294, 296, 320, 329, 341, 363f, 369–372, 378–380, 383, 386f, 390, 394, 397, 402, 408–410, 415–418, 24:66f, 117, 122, 126, 128, 153f, 156, 172, 174f, 199, 225, 235, 246, 265f, 275, 280, 286–288, 205f, 311, 315, 318, 354f, 357, 361, 365, 370, 25:173, 441, 471f, 510, 26:14, 17, 23, 45, 52, 59f, 65, 75, 94, 97, 103, 106, 125, 140, 208, 241, 250, 308, 408f, 413, 418, 27:44, 96f, 110, 121f, 129f, 166, 208, 216, 281, 296f, 303, 346, 358, 369, 384f, 392, 398, 28:12f, 22f, 217–219, 251f, 281, 283f, 286, 288, 290, 295, 29:15–22, 24–30, 32–34, 36–39, 43, 45, 59, 95, 169, 173, 30:53, 62, 77, 86, 95, 106, 125, 132–138, 177f, 180, 183, 186, 188, 203f, 208f, 212, 237, 250, 31:360, 386, 32:52, 74, 81, 34:14, 44–47, 50f, 53, 246, 35:12f, 388f, 401, 36:42, 70, 91, 98, 101f, 105f, 108, 110, 113–116, 133–136, 144, 154–159, 164, 167f, 200, 207, 209f, 219, 222, 37:15, 364, 367, 38:99f, 114, 141, 147, 149f, 152f, 158, 161, 167, 13, 39:7f, 74, 154f, 252–259, 260–266, 269, 270–275, 277–279, 282f, 285, 289–292, 295, 299, 309, 311–313, 314n, 40:13, 35, 40f, 41:9, 12, 14, 15n, 16, 21f, 23f, 29, 32f, 36, 40–45, 55–57, 59–61, 68, 85, 87–92, 93n, 94f, 97–99, 102, 106, 115, 117, 120–122, 124f, 131–135, 138–140, 142–144, 154–164, 167, 170, 206, 211, 234–236, 251, 281, 288, 290–294, 296–300, 308, 316f, 320–322, 324–326, 328–330, 334, 337, 345, 347f, 351, 354f, 358f, 360, 363, 365–369, 376, 42:47, 55, 91, 44:88f, 128, 175, 367, 45:8, 25, 30, 105–107, 109n, 114–117, 151–153, 155, 172, 174, 200, 286, 297, 318, 356, 46:5, 19, 116, 149, 164n, 165f, 168f, 173, 179f, 186, 199, 221, 223, 236, 272f, 294, 47:15, 23f, 38–40, 48, 50, 52, 169, 175, 177, 297–299, 48:46f, 100, 218, 223n, 235, 286, 303n, 308f, 336, 341, 354f, 376, 51:73, 136f, 139f, 148, 154, 181, 184, 202, 206, 279, 295, 301, 306, 354, 363, 366, 384, 52:34, 36f, 39f, 79, 81f, 100, 112, 115, 118, 120, 145, 191, 203, 209, 216, 221, 231, 233, 249, 267f, 274f, 53:23, 25, 29f, 54:287–288, 299, 333, 380, 441, 473

Bishops, Emergency—21:280n

Bishops, Evangelical—49:135n, 138n, 159, 214, 264, 283, 334, 348, 353, 383f, 420, 50:179, 188, 218, 220, 224n, 247, 252n, 262, 265, 271, 273, 280n, 288, 309

Bishops, Play—41:142

***Bishops' Book*, England, 1537**—50:180n

Bishops' courts—44:160

Bithynia—30:5f

Bithynia, Church in—41:321, 347, 351, 358

Bitterfeld—50:41–43, 285n, 287

Bittir—47:236f

Bitumen—2:66f, 217, 344, 368, 3:243

Bizer, Ernst—*Luther und der Papst*, Munich, 1958 41:xiin

Black Death—43:115–138

Blamelessness—29:195

Blandina—36:60n

Blandishments—7:76, 78, 80, 86–88, 93

Blank, Christopher—54:214

Blankenfeld, John and Thomas—49:176n

Blasphemers—4:29, 32, 34, 24:94, 198, 312f, 323, 380, 389, 46:34, 51f, 66, 74, 162, 195, 302, 52:216, 218, 220, 254, 256, 264f

Blasphemy—1:63, 108, 114, 135, 142, 175, 177–180, 249, 260, 278, 358, 2:28, 43, 53, 60, 62, 214, 224, 262, 334, 387, 3:162, 173, 240, 278, 319, 4:31, 33, 55, 93, 144f, 158, 204, 219f, 222, 257, 352, 357, 391, 399, 5:11f, 43, 45, 206, 215, 258, 260, 6:56, 85, 132, 217, 353, 7:63, 124, 263, 327, 341, 9:5, 22, 111, 146, 198, 211, 226, 10:59–61, 13:66f, 107f, 110, 116, 187, 385, 16:x, 8, 64–66, 74, 83, 96, 308, 316, 318, 322, 324, 17:127f, 161f, 208, 297, 19:123, 177, 192, 206f, 23:238, 304, 320, 24:11, 62, 97, 222, 260, 269, 285, 303, 326, 356, 358, 394, 397, 400, 406, 25:390f, 26:35f, 40–42, 60, 69–72, 86, 125f, 135, 140, 146, 171, 176, 179, 182, 185, 224, 254, 314, 323, 326, 341, 365, 370, 377, 385, 403, 407f, 452, 458, 27:22, 69, 71, 81, 89, 102, 112, 136, 141, 158, 230, 240, 371, 28:99, 241–243, 368, 30:7, 37, 100, 128, 189,

224, 234, 266, 304, 35:69, 144, 152, 193, 281, 364, 36:6, 25, 214, 225, 311–315, 317f, 320, 324, 327f, 355, 37:67f, 72, 143, 364, 369, 371, 41:13, 57, 80, 91, 172, 198, 211, 221, 234, 236f, 239, 252, 285, 289–291, 293, 325, 327–328, 330f, 333, 338–340, 342, 344, 349, 352, 356f, 359, 361, 363, 369f, 42:26–28, 31–33, 35, 73, 78, 103, 45:38, 84, 110, 136, 145f, 148, 178, 46:19, 48, 50, 147f, 174, 178, 186, 240, 255, 49:99, 113f, 226, 232f, 263, 411, 435, 54:373

Blaurer, Ambrose—38:95

Blaurer, Thomas—21:xix

Blesilla—15:4, 31

Blessed Offspring—26:317–319, 323f, 327, 329, 334, 339, 374

Blessed ones—25:36, 256, 264f, 424

Blessedness—23:76, 106f, 339, 355, 37:24, 129, 132, 136, 190, 312f, 323

Blessing—20:276, 282, 292f, 23:14, 339, 341, 416

Blessing, Accidental—5:198

Blessings—3:9, 12–15, 25, 28, 45, 48, 54, 56f, 64f, 68, 73f, 99, 104, 107, 111, 120, 134f, 143, 145–150, 152, 154, 157f, 162f, 208, 212, 220f, 274, 313, 323, 334, 338, 342f, 4:5–8, 10f, 17, 38, 43, 45f, 52, 57, 73, 77, 88, 92, 147, 149–152, 154–167, 169f, 171–177, 202, 210f, 222, 226–229, 242, 247–250, 268, 286f, 293, 299, 303, 307, 318, 320, 323–325, 328f, 337, 344, 348, 355, 361, 365, 379, 388–392, 397, 401–405, 408f, 5:10, 18f, 21, 37, 43, 57, 59f, 64f, 76–78, 82, 84, 86f, 89, 94f, 99, 105, 108–112, 114, 116–118, 127, 129, 132–134, 136, 138–153, 155–164, 167–170, 173, 175–178, 181–184, 187, 196–206, 210, 217, 225f, 228, 230–233, 238, 240f, 272, 274, 286f, 300, 310f, 317f, 325, 328, 331f, 338, 342, 363, 366f, 369, 373f, 384, 6:12f, 18–20, 72, 165, 168, 173f, 257, 263, 7:33, 35, 38, 59, 61f, 65–68, 85, 97, 99, 112, 128, 147, 151f, 156, 161f, 175, 193, 204, 209, 211, 214, 217, 304, 325, 334, 337, 340, 347f, 361f, 10:45, 47f, 54, 85, 210, 284f, 13:398f, 15:11, 201f, 214 216, 227, 240, 17:41, 95, 103f, 187, 287f, 355f, 384f, 25:36, 107, 127, 256f, 424, 516, 29:188–190, 239, 31:189–101, 35:58, 67, 111, 38:86, 105, 137, 201, 314, 41:154, 168, 205, 42:22, 57, 70, 85f, 91, 108, 111, 120, 129, 144–165, 53:93

Blind persons—17:78f, 91, 114, 179, 265, 301, 360, 46:198, 224f, 302, 306

Blindness—3:23, 97, 102, 133, 263–266, 5:176, 6:60, 16:7, 243, 248, 25:10, 79, 97, 159, 164, 173f, 176, 30:15, 31, 36, 65, 99, 165f, 182, 186, 236, 307, 51:37–43, 104, 109

Blindness, Spiritual—15:288

Blood—9:222, 229, 231, 293, 299, 10:26, 77, 339–341, 11:73f, 82, 121n, 19:128, 205f, 214f, 20:92, 96, 133, 184, 286, 29:129, 206f, 213, 215, 232, 37:43f, 264, 42:141, 142n, 46:42, 189, 53:26f, see also **Christ, His blood**

Blood, Baptism of—2:270n

Blood, Eating—41:28f, 34, 68, 70, 72–78

Blood relationship—2:10

Bloodguiltiness—9:220, 12:390, 16:20

Bloodhounds—46:68f, 74, 180, 189, 227

Bloodshed—2:7, 60, 197, 3:13, 9:210, 32:88, 46:27, 40, 42, 49, 54, 63, 82f, 129, 157, 180, 195, 201–203, 226, 326

Blossoms—21:264f

Blum, Michael—53:141, 154, 194

Boars—1:62, 119, 132, 2:135, 197

Boas, Marcus, ed.—*Disticha Catonis*, Amsterdam, 1952 23:266n, 320n, 362n, 27:125n

Boasting—6:42, 50f, 81f, 157, 180, 262, 284, 10:9, 73, 244, 437, 16:69, 192, 239, 248, 322, 17:40, 43, 47, 62, 70, 118, 146, 156, 170, 246, 288, 339, 22:133f, 25:10, 33, 136, 138, 248, 394, 28:66, 75, 86–91, 133, 155, 217, 221f, 238f

Boasting, Christian—27:133f

Boaz—6:246, 7:200, 25:265

Boccaccio, Giovanni—54:xxii, 208

Bodily needs—28:142f, 170f

Body—4:273, 15:179f, 21:180, 230, 303f, 334f, 24:106f, 158, 180, 206, 208, 226, 232, 244, 253, 255, 268, 359, 384, 407, 419, 25:11, 51, 64f, 104–106, 112, 162, 165f, 245, 309, 313f, 317, 433, 435–437, 509, 27:69, 28:13f, 18, 20f, 46, 51, 59, 69, 100, 110–112, 123, 135, 142–144, 150f, 168, 170–173, 180f, 183–187, 189–194, 196–198, 200, 321f, 29:120, 126, 128f, 153, 164, 166, 206, 222–224, 38:45, 110, 150, 187, 192, 199, 41:130, 146, 42:92, 144, 162, 172, 44:390, 46:39, 51, 74, 96f, 108, 127, 130, 132, 146n, 150, 166, 179, 187, 224, 228, 237, 249, 266, 269, 297, 319

Body, Christian's—37:6, 71, 87, 92f, 100f, 115, 118f, 125, 132, 134f, 155

Body, Mutilation of the—21:90
Body, Resurrection of the—22:479
Body, Spiritual—30:11, 302
Body and blood of Christ—37:xii, xviii, 11, 19, 26, 28, 36–39, 43, 45, 63f, 66, 68f, 76f, 85f, 108, 111f, 117, 126f, 137, 139, 153, 164–167, 170–172, 177f, 180n, 181f, 185, 187, 197, 200, 203, 206f, 216–225, 227f, 232, 249n, 252f, 255, 258, 261f, 275f, 279f, 289n, 290n, 296, 303, 306, 309, 317, 326, 350–356, 38:xiii, xvi, 25, 27, 29, 32, 40, 44f, 53, 58, 71, 85, 95, 227, 304, 306, 316, see also **Bread and wine in the Sacrament; Breaking Bread in the Lord's Supper; Eating and drinking in the Sacrament; Flesh and blood of Christ; Lord's Supper; Sacramental elements; Words of Institution (Communion Liturgy)**
Body and soul—46:23, 25, 32, 42f, 48f, 53, 117, 136, 227, 249, 252, 254
Body and spirit, Unity of—25:340–343
Body of Christ—see **Christ, His body**
Body of Christ, The Church as—36:xi, 74, 286f
Body of sin—25:314
Boethius—48:57n, 58n
Consolations of Philosophy 2:266n
Bogler, Wilhelm—*Hartmut von Kronberg* 43:59n
Bohemia—1:254, 14:209, 309, 16:196n, 258n, 22:82, 23:379n, 25:487, 30:277n, 38:182n, 40:4f, 8, 13, 17, 38–40, 41:371, 45:173, 46:202, 203, 47:17f, 59, 266, 272, 48:137, 143, 145, 149, 153n, 189n, 272, 49:4n, 216, 320n, 50:208, 218, 228n, 51:xvn, 54:40, 367
Bohemian Brethren—17:67n, 36:xi, 20n, 23n, 24f, 27n, 167, 271–271, 275n, 276f, 298f, 39:82n, 108, 112, 173, 45:365n, 366, 49:56n, 53:63n 203, 208, 284, see also **Hussites**
Apologia 36:272, 276n, 277, 298f
Bohemian crown—2:202n
Bohemian language—37:244
Bohemians—10:242, 11:227, 14:11, 22:60n, 25:487, 27:392, 32:56, 59, 69, 44:194–200, 54:48, 220, 352, 367, 387, 394, see also **Hussites**
Böhme, F.M.—53:275n, 278n, 289n
Böhmer, Heinrich—48:xviin, 54:xxii
Luthers Romfahrt, Leipzig, 1914 39:59n
Road to Reformation, Philadelphia, 1946 31:38, 38:xviiin, 39:xxiin, xxiiin, 51:26, 35, 61
Urkunden zur Geschichte des Bauernkrieges und Wiedertäufer, Bonn, 1910 46:7n, 11n
Boils—3:270
Boineburg, George von—50:178f
Boineburg, Ludwig von—54:381
Boisset, J.—*Erasme et Luther, Libre ou Serf-arbitre?*, Paris, 1962 33:5n
Boldness—see **Courage**
Bologna—41:308n, 367n, 47:24, 49:265n, 280, 284n
University of 48:73n, 112n, 318, 49:107, 126n
Bologna, Concordat of, 1516—31:262n
Bon Christian—41:264n, 342n, 356n
Bonae literae—33:6, 15n
Bonaventura, St.—1:227, 4:117n, 297, 5:36, 323, 344, 10:414, 22:255, 333, 29:121, 31:83, 147, 172, 202, 216, 218, 222, 32:258, 35:64, 368n, 41:125n, 44:367n, 45:283n, 50:104, 51:186, 52:10n, 267, 54:112, 264
Commentaria in Ecclesiasten, Opera 15:18n, 19n
Commentaria in quattuor libros sententiarum M. Petri Lombardi 1:228n
De duodecim fructibus Spiritus 8:43n
De incarnatione verbi 5:221n
In quatuor libros Sententiarum expositio 29:121n
Meditations on the Life of Christ 52:10
Bondage—9:150f, 225, 243, 268
Bondage of sin—22:166
Bondage of the will—32:92, 33:xii, 108
Bondman—9:148
Bonds—11:300f, 319
Bones—10:142, 177, 179, 17:410f, 18:138
Bonhoeffer, Dietrich—47:x
Boniface I, Pope—31:281
Boniface II, Pope—32:152n
Boniface III, Pope—41:90n, 290n, 292, 299, 309
Boniface VIII, Pope—26:37n, 27:342, 28:364, 30:180n, 31:20, 34:236n, 35:405n, 37:14n, 39:199n, 281n, 44:171n, 202n, 48:186n, 54:239
Boniface IX, Pope—44:171n
Unam sanctam 1:233n
Boniface, Winfred, St.—10:149, 31:111, 39:281n
Bonn—53:184
Book, Flying—20:233–235
Book burning—31:381, 383–385, 32:x, 5, 47, 66, 83, 105, 137n, 150, 218, 237
Book of Common Prayer—53:xviii, 149n
Book of Concord—2:266n, 4:126n, 9:24n, 69n, 16:35n, 26:383n, 35:ixn, 26n,

37:35n, 361n, 39:xin, 45n, 42:61n, 43:181n, 45:247n, 254n, 308n, 47:5n, 116n, 51:161n

Book of Hours—43:5f

Book of life—5:45, 50, 16:51

Book of the Saints—34:24n

Books—3:37f, 69, 245, 299, 305f, 13:199, 220, 15:84f, 28:84f, 45:77n, 83, 84n, 110f, 112n, 373–377, 52:39, 206f, 54:141, 163, 213, 274, 292, 311, 326, 342, 361, 387, 440

Books, Blasphemous—44:227f

Books, Luther's—32:131

Books, Prohibited—44:223–229

Books, Publishing and reading—44:205

Books, Sacred—9:3, 6

Booths, Feast of—26:411

Bora, Florian von—50:232, 233n

Bora, Hans von—54:370

Bora, John von—50:208n, 232n

Bora, Katharine von—see **Luther, Katharine von Bora**

Bora, Magdalene von—49:271, 324, 402, 50:50, 151n, 153, 167

Bora family—50:208n

Borcherdt, H.H.—25:xiv, 47:63, 106, 136

Boredom—15:8, 10, 20, 32, 34, 155

Bornkamm, Heinrich—9:6n, 21:x, 38:178n, 47:89n, 96n, 134n, 48:xviin

Luther and the Old Testament, Philadelphia, 1969 38:178n, 39:xvn

Luther und das Alte Testament, Tübingen, 1948 35:xif, 51:xin

Luther's Doctrine of the Two Kingdoms, Philadelphia, 1966 38:233n

Luther's World of Thought, St. Louis, 1958 37:xxi, 38:x, 39:xin, xvin

Borrowing—10:175

Bosnia—50:269n

Bosom—10:445–447

Bosphorus—18:203f

Bosra—11:186

Bottles—10:155–157

Botzheim, Johann von—21:xix

Bouman, Herbert J.A.—translator of *First Lectures on the Psalms* 10:3–464, 11:3–553

translator of *Lectures on Isaiah, Chapters 1–39* 16:3–349

translator of *Lectures on Isaiah, Chapters 40–66* 17:3–416

Boundaries—9:198, 292, 10:331, 335

Bow(s)—18:40, 11:40–43, 48–50

Bowels—29:94, 98, 101, 104, 112

Bowing down—6:160f, 163

Bowling—54:320

Bows (rainbows)—see **Rainbow**

Boxwood—2:93

Boye, Nicholas—32:263, 276

Boys, Educating—45:370, 46:231, 234, 246, 257

Bozrah—16:294, 17:352f, 18:136

Bozrah (Arabia Petraea)—6:307

Brabant—34:345, 353, 41:350

Brain—17:113, 214

Branch, The—16:53, 117, see also **Zemah**

Branches—24:193–195, 198–205, 208–213, 216–227, 234–236, 239, 244, 246, 248–250, 263

Brand—20:37, 210f

Brandenburg—3:66n, 9:5, 29:170n, 41:253n, 45:112n, 138, 47:135, 48:220, 339, 49:152n, 54:407

Brandenburg, Bishop of—32:116

Brandenburg, Electoral—50:128n, 146, 214n, 254n, 280

Brandenburg-Ansbach-Kulmbach—49:xvif, 18n, 127f, 189, 190n, 209n, 246n, 50:61f, 65n

Church Ordinance of 50:13, 61f

Brandt, Karl—*Deutsche Reformation und Gegenreformation, I*, Leipzig, 1927? 34:6n

Brandt, Walther I.—author of introduction and presumed author of introductions to individual items in Vol. 45

editor of Vol. 45

translator of *Estate of Marriage* 45:11–50

translator of *Exposition of Psalm 127, for the Christians at Riga in Livonia*, 1524 45:311–338

translator of *Fraternal Agreement on the Common Chest of the Entire Assembly at Leisnig*, 1523 45:176–194

translator of *Persons Related by Consanguinity and Affinity Who are Forbidden to Marry, According to the Scriptures, Leviticus 18*, 1522 45:3–10

translator of *That Jesus Christ was born a Jew* 45:195–230

translator of *That Parents should neither Compel nor Hinder the Marriage of their Children and That Children Should not Become Engaged Without Their Parents' Consent*, 1524 45:379–394

Brant, Sebastian—*Ship of Fools* 20:238n, 37:260n, 39:167n, 41:182, 186n, 43:11

Bratwurst—50:206n

Braude, William G.—*The Midrash on the Psalms*, New Haven, 1959 35:210n, 211n, 215n, 219n

Brauer, Bruno—34:295

Braun, John—48:3
Braun, Joseph—*Die liturgische Gewandung im Occident und Orient* 13:296n
Braunschweig—21:xix, 34:107, 46:59f, 130, 210, 49:82, 160n, 50:49n, 55n
Braunschweig'sche Kirchenordnung—46:210n, 53:151
Braunschweig-Wolfenbüttel—41:181, 183, 230n, 240n
Braunsdorf, Catherine—Letter to Ursula Roth, 1539 22:417n
Brave spirit—12:388
Brazen serpent—2:113
Breachmaker—18:229
Bread—2:46, 49, 161, 243f, 270, 289, 295, 327, 331, 383–388, 3:50f, 59, 149, 159f, 181, 184–186, 190, 197f, 220, 225, 243f, 246, 250f, 267, 290, 298, 355, 4:21, 29, 36f, 39, 45, 51f, 95, 137, 227, 364, 381, 384, 396, 7:32, 63, 67–69, 104f, 108, 118, 127f, 136, 194, 213f, 216f, 219, 222f, 232, 251, 267, 285, 309, 338, 350, 367, 9:93–95, 97, 118, 140, 157f, 203, 230, 235, 272, 11:303f, 309, 334f, 23:8–11, 14, 20, 39, 32–34, 37, 44, 76, 78, 83, 110, 114, 116, 120, 123, 125, 129, 133f, 153f, 156, 164f, 256, 263, 275, 283, 356, 399, 403, 410, 24:83, 109, 266f, 354, 390–392, 399, 26:95f, 190, 315, 442, 456, 27:58, 69, 298, 340, 28:107f, 142f, 29:153f, 156, 200f, 42:53f, 56–59, 61n, 62, 79, 87f, see also **Sacramental elements**
Bread, Heavenly—23:8, 69, 83, 110, 113f, 116, 132
Bread, Holy—27:55
Bread and wine in the Sacrament—11:368f, 378, 41:168, 170f
  Luther's opponents' views 37:xiii, xviii, 11, 18, 24, 26, 40–43, 46, 52, 61n, 76f, 93n, 102f, 111–113, 126f, 131f, 142f, 146, 149f, 163f, 166, 182, 188, 202f, 261f, 294n, 295, 309, 340–345, 347, 349f, 354f, 367
  Luther's view 37:xix, 22n, 29, 33, 40–46, 61n, 64–66, 69, 72, 83, 85–88, 103–127, 129–134, 139–141, 145, 158, 189f, 216f, 227, 254, 258, 296, 299–301, 37:306, 312f, 317, 328f, 333, 343, 346, 351, 353–356, 358, 367, see also **Sacramental elements**
Bread from heaven—23:30–32, 38f, 80, 86, 118
Bread in the Sacrament—35:xin, 26n, 36:15, 20, 22, 29–35, 44, 53f, 147, 162f, 166, 168–173, 181–183, 279, 282, 285, 288, 295f, 299, 314–322, 326, 336, 341, 345f, 349, 352
Bread of life—2:386, 23:40–43, 45, 49, 51f, 54f, 77, 82, 91, 101, 109–113, 115–117, 121, 132
Bread of mourners—18:48, 336
Breaking bread in the Lord's Supper—37:43f, 130, 266, 327–329, 332f, 348–356
Breaking down—25:xi, 3, 1135f, 176, 229, 365, 392
Breasts—3:83, 30:49
Breath of God—15:301f
Breisgau—49:119
Breitenbach, George—3:66
Bremen—9:4, 30:xi, 48:233n, 236n, 49:23, 82, 50:181
Bremer, Otto—43:49n
Brenz, John—14:xi, 15:x, 3n, 31:37, 36:332, 37:xiv, 9, 24n, 360, 38:9–11, 61, 63, 71, 73, 76n, 89n, 47:46, 49:145n, 177f, 238, 332, 344n, 347, 373n, 374n, 394n, 395n, 414n, 50:63n, 65, 67n, 54:50, 311, 376, 383, 391
Brenz, John, Works of—see also ***Swabian Syngramma***
  Exposition of the Gospel of John 37:360
  The Foundation in Holy Scripture which was Treated Somewhat in the Colloquy at Marburg in Dealing with the Sacrament, 1529 38:73–74n
Breslau—48:143n, 49:216, 342, 50:301n, 53:271
Breslau, League of—28:259, 49:189f, 197f
Brethren of the Common Life—11:145n, 45:341n, 49:314n, 50:190n
Bretscher, Paul M.—translator of commentary on Psalm 90 13:73–142
Breviaries—25:495n, 44:67n, 48:28n, 51:171n
  Medieval 14:47n
Brewer—23:129
Briars—4:135–137
Bribes—9:110, 163, 170, 19:164
Bride and bridegroom—1:134, 136, 233, 355, 5:290–304, 307, 312–314, 7:27, 43, 146, 344, 9:223, 224, 241, 244, 10:11, 28, 15:193, 198, 205, 216f, 222, 227, 233, 243, 247f, 257f, 261, 17:342, 346, 406, 18:13, 83, 22:440f, 450f, 460, 27:93, 37:xii, 109, 367, 41:158–160, 163f, 205, 207f, 227, 46:181, 235, 261n, 268, 282, 289–292, 296–302, 304f, 314, see also **Betrothed persons**
Bride of God—36:223

Bridegroom and bride—see **Bride and bridegroom**
Bridegrooms—3:8, 330, 4:85, 225, 230, 248, 251, 254, 260, 297, 299
Brides—3:8, 277, 283, 330, 4:85, 225, 230, 232, 247f, 250f, 253–255, 257f, 260, 262, 270, 273, 276, 278, 288f, 295–299, 405, 23:323, 331, 24:197, 273, 308, 27:93, 184, 315, 391, 42:141
Bridesmaids—4:352
Bridget of Sweden, St.—34:25, 55, 42:21n, 22, 43:5, 11f, 271
Revelationes 5:346n, 5:346n, 348
Bridget, St., of Ireland—44:27n
Bridgettines—34:25n
Brieger, Theodor—31:80
Briessmann, John—45:137n, 138n, 318n, 49:97n, 98n, 120f, 313n
Brigands—2:36, 3:113, 150, 234
Brigitta of Sweden, St.—see **Bridget of Sweden, St.**
Brilioth, Yngve—*Eucharistic Faith and Practice*, New York, 1956 37:xxi
Brimstone—3:190, 224, 295, 307
Brisger, Eberhard—49:22n, 58n, 212n
Britain—34:247, 48:33n
Broken body, Christ's—37:xviii, 129n, 265–267, 328, 332f
Bromily, G.W., ed.—*Zwingli and Bullinger* (Library of Christian Classics), Philadelphia, 1953 38:37n, 289n
Bronze—1:317f, 20:64, 66, 128, 248
Bronze serpent—1:96, 227, 248, 9:81, 26:159, 166, 357, 30:253
Brothels—3:258f, 39:288, 290, 44:96, 214f, 49:11, 24, 72, 421
Brother, Consolation of a—13:111
Brotherhoods—14:23, 26, 23:226, 25:107, 26:222, 30:42f, 178, 279, 34:26, 54, 99, 35:47, 67f, 36:35n, 133n, 178, 41:33n, 199f, 215, 338, 42:60n, 44:192n, 45:181n, 284, 351, 48:142, see also **Sodalities**
Brothers (brethren)—21:77f, 218f, 223, 25:107, 116, 502f, 505f, 29:10, 24–26, 35, 42, 45, 66, 75, 78, 84, 88f, 93–96, 98–100, 103–105, 133, 241, 48:142
Bruchtgeld—16:45
Brück, Gregory von—35:165n, 43:257, 259n, 45:241, 47:32n, 49:50f, 51f, 247, 339n, 349n, 394f, 413n, 423, 429f, 50:22f, 41f, 42n, 43f, 48, 83, 87, 89, 90, 102f, 103n, 104n, 108n, 112, 117, 145n, 157, 190, 196n, 274n, 276, 285, 297n, 298, 54:139, 150, 228, 274, 322, 387, 391, 444
Bruges—2:137
Brunet, Gustave—54:xvn
Brunfels, Otto—48:322n
Bruno, St.—24:35n
Brunswick—see **Braunschweig**
Brussels—9:4, 32:263, 266, 34:353, 41:260, 49:12n, 50:44n, 256n, 53:211–216
Brussels, Henry and John of—9:4
Brutality—2:60
Brutus—5:236, 6:331, 13:165, 54:247
Bucer, Elizabeth—50:228n
Bucer, Martin—16:346, 31:37f, 32:103, 34:80n, 35:121n, 37:xii, xivf, 9f, 21n, 23n, 24n, 77n, 147n, 148f, 158, 38:5–8, 36n, 62, 70–72, 78, 80, 89n, 95, 281, 284, 40:63, 76, 47:123, 129, 48:247n, 275n, 305n, 49:xviiin, 88n, 124n, 199f, 226n, 238n, 303n, 50:168n, 172n, 187n, 188n, 190n, 191n, 228, 230, 254n, 54:25, 196, 205, 262, 282, 376, 379, 383, 417
And Philip of Hesse 50:xixn, 195f, 203n, 205
In Lord's Supper controversy 50:3f, 6f, 171, 171n, 173
Negotiations with English 50:28, 180n, 190, 195f, 197, 199n, 200n, 202n, 203, 205
Bucer, Martin, Works of—*Apology* 37:9, 21n, 23n, 24n, 80n, 84n, 86n, 149n
Cologne Reformation 48:248n
Compromise of the Opinions held by Martin Luther and his Opposition on Christ's Supper. A Dialog . . . 49:200f
Defense and Explanation 37:42n
Dialog 37:158, 50:4n
Fourth Volume of Luther's Postil, Translated 37:10, 148n
On the Jews 47:129
Preface 37:10, 21n, 127n, 131n, 147n, 148n
Psalter Translated (Bugenhagen's Exposition) 37:9
Translation of Luther's *Exposition of the Epistles and Gospels* 36:332
Buch, Monastery of—45:162, 164f, 179, 49:29n
Buchführer, George—32:266
Buchman—Translation of *The Koran* 43:235n
Buchwald, George—12:ixf, 16:ix, 18:x, 30:ix, x, 51:xin, xvi, 5, 136, 211, 221, 54:37n
Theologische Studien und Kritiken, Gotha, 1896 46:60n
Buchwald, George, ed.—*Luthers Werke*

für das christliche Haus, Braunschweig, 1890 36:18n, 61n, 82n, 89n, 105n, 108n, 109n, 110n, 118n, 168n, 191n, 193n, 203n, 212n 226n
Zur Wittenberger Stadt—und Universitäts-Geschichte, Leipzig, 1893 22:417n
Buchwald, Reinhard—54:xxvn
Buckler—18:25
Buda—4:28n
Budapest—49:91, 156, 240n, 50:224n, 228n, 243n
Buehner, Andrew J.—indexer of Vol. 19
Buenau, Guenther von—54:135
Bugenhagen, John—6:34, 124, 9:x, 16:ix, 17:129n, 19:95n, 21:277, 21:xix, 21:xixf, 22:ix–xi, 5, 68n, 215, 530, 23:ix–xi, 322, 422, 23:ix–xi, 322f, 422, 24:ix, 28:xi, 31:324, 34:6, 108, 148, 292, 297, 301, 315, 318, 36:9, 331, 37:xivf, 7–10, 35, 147, 155, 40:267, 41:49n, 181, 43:115f, 245, 45:313n, 343, 47:102, 48:303n, 49:xviiin, 15, 115n, 130, 151, 170, 173n, 174n, 175n, 179, 180n, 184, 186, 237, 244n, 261, 262n, 274, 315, 383, 386, 399, 401, 418f, 50:xixn, 31, 33n, 154, 159n, 216n, 250, 250n, 51:xii, xv, 121n, 357, 53:43, 151, 54:ix, xxi, 15, 23, 49, 52, 75, 89, 142, 156, 158, 180, 214–217, 231, 257, 271, 305, 316, 374, 386, 393, 416, 428, 443, 461, 470
And Wittenberg University 50:56, 63, 67, 102, 196, 204, 274, 274n, 275, 275n
Luther's friend and pastor 50:110, 156, 168n, 209, 221, 275, 281, 295, 312, 318
Builders—20:184f, 25:104
Bull Rush Sea—16:114
Bullinger, Henry—35:xii, 38:281, 284, 47:123, 50:55n, 54:89
Bulls (animals)—7:150, 3, 22, 10:320f
Bulls, Papal—1:322n, 7:162n, 14:23, 26, 225, 27:237, 34:238n, 332n, 35:217, 36:5, 8f, 75n, 77n, 125, 133, 160, 164, 166, 168, 202, 205, 212, 220, 230, 247, 38:191, 231, 39:275–278, 287, 289, 41:9, 30, 34, 42, 93, 140, 169, 272, 275, 308, 332, 342, 357, 360, 366, 368, 42:169n, 44:188f, 395, 45:54, 64n, 68n, 85n, 135n, 286f, 289, 295n, 347
Ad Dominici gregis 50:144f, 155n, 161, 163
Apostolici regiminis 27:297n
Bull of Convocation, Trent 41:263n
Clement VI's (spurious) 36:82n
Cum postquam 48:105n
De Indulgentiis contra Turcam 41:140n
Decet pontificem 31:xx, 32:xii, 276n
Decet Romanum pontificem 34:238n, 39:xxi, 40:341n, 48:179n, 192n
Execrabilis 50:219n, 267n, 289n
Exsurge, Domine 18:88n, 31:xix, 330, 381, 394, 32:ix, 5, 15n, 45, 83n, 109, 137n, 187n, 276n, 34:332n, 35:47, 407n, 36:302n, 39:113n, 123n, 247n, 248n, 41:174n, 235n, 42:xi, 169n, 43:73, 44:117n, 179n, 221, 46:162n, 213n, 48:80n, 176, 179n, 182n, 183, 185n, 186, 190n, 192f, 193n, 51:66n
Exultate Deo 44:129n
In coena domini 30:207, 31:238n, 241, 243, 36:86n, 44:162n
Laetentur coeli 4:314n
Pastor Aeternus 31:262n
Romani pontificis 31:172n
Sublimis Deus 34:238n, 50:159n, 160n, 161n
Unam sanctam 1:233n, 8:264n, 26:87n, 27:342n, 30:180n, 41:42n
Unigenitus Dei Filius 31:260–262, 264–270, 48:84n
Bundschuh—32:115n
Bunglers—15:65f, 184
Burchart, Francis—50:80n, 112n, 114n, 123f, 130f, 132, 138f
first mission to England 50:178f, 195, 198, 198n, 201, 203n
second mission to England 50:190n, 193, 193n, 200n
third mission to England 50:194f, 196, 200n
Burckhart, C.A.H.—*Geschichte der sachsischen Kirchen—und Schulvisitation*, Leipzig, 1879 46:234n
Burdens—16:132, 18:157, 283, 19:157, 20:58, 89, 91, 130–135, 200, 243, 283f, 323
Burer, Albert, Letter of—45:54n, 56
Burgensis, Paulus—see **Paul of Burgos**
Burggraf—50:237n
Burghers—2:6, 24, 3:182, 227, 249, 345, 4:74, 208, 211, 227, 276, 24:78f, 81, 83, 162, 197, 214, 265f, 288, 41:176, 228
Burgomasters—3:49, 23:98, 247, 311, 321, 323, 336, 342, 24:80f, 218, 377
Burgos, Paul of—see **Paul of Burgos**
Burgundy—34:345
Burial service—40:310
Burials—4:190, 198, 205, 217, 395, 8:157, 43:135f, 53:93, 134, 209, 222, 247, 325–331

Burning coals—25:108, 465f
Burning of books—see **Book burning**
Burnt offerings—4:92, 98, 100, 102, 108, 110–112, 114, 128, 137f, 183, 351, 9:174, 233, 258, 305, 16:15f, 29:148, 176, 204, 29:221
Buschmann, Arnolt—43:271n
Bushes—4:136, 298
Business—13:408, 20:277, 21:184, 235–237, 24:250, 45:233, 239, 240, 245, 247–295
Business practices of the 16th century—45:233–310
Businessmen—16:161, 46:244, 251f
Buszin, Walter E.—*Luther on Music*, St. Paul, 1958 53:xxn
Butcher shops—23:14, 110, 125, 163, 168
Butchers—2:133, 4:110f, 114, 7:33, 53f, 77, 186, 54:188
Butchers, Chief—7:107f, 110, 122, 157, 161, 198
Butlers—7:53f, 123f, 127, 133, 141, 165, 186, 348
Butlers, Chief—7:107f, 113f, 118, 122, 127, 157, 161
Butter—3:198, 211, 4:37, 245, 27:384
Butter letters—34:18, 54, 40:342, 345, 41:357, 44:155n
Butterflies—1:54
Buxtehude—32:275
Buying and selling—see **Trade and commerce**
Buz—4:185f
Byzantine Empire—14:333n

Cabala—10:313, 26:290, 27:221
Cabalists—6:314, 7:188, 11:459n
Caemmerer, Richard R.—co-author of Introduction to Vol. 9 9:ixf
  translator of Vol. 9, *Lectures on Deuteronomy* 9:3–311
Caesar(s)—2:365, 14:268, 16:206, 331, 24:410, 26:12, 27, 305, 452, 27:281, 385, 407
Caesar, Julius—see **Julius Caesar**
Caesar, Rendering unto—46:50f, 134, 316
Caesar Augustus—see **Augustus Caesar**
Caesarea—2:205, 16:115, 26:206, 27:197, 40:38
Caesarea Philippi—2:205
Caesarini, Cardinal Julian—44:194n, 46:167n
Cahera—see **Gallus Cahera**
Caiaphas—2:218, 221, 6:378, 380, 388f, 393f, 398, 404, 7:89, 11:113, 116, 224, 13:186, 339, 14:72, 314, 17:86, 21:276f, 302, 314, 316, 22:128f, 194, 196, 238f, 276f, 306, 356, 483, 511, 23:192, 210–213, 218f, 223, 254, 268, 272, 24:59, 155, 237, 274, 310, 412, 25:12, 28:198, 31:260, 36:138, 288, 40:66, 41:122, 197, 218, 246, 320, 51:268, 52:77, 176, 191f, 283
Cain—1:11, 78, 80, 103, 164, 185, 211, 215, 237–313, 319f, 322–327, 329, 334, 338f, 352, 354, 2:3, 6, 10, 27f, 116, 140f, 177, 180f, 185, 196f, 200, 210, 219, 221, 223, 287, 3:13, 16, 56, 96, 106, 111, 250, 272, 3:317f, 4:33, 53, 108, 327, 244, 250, 267, 372–374, 392, 402, 5:163, 177, 6:32, 119, 171, 223, 233, 269, 283, 296, 345, 358, 368, 373f, 385, 12:86, 13:186, 412, 417, 14:88, 187, 225, 270, 15:24, 319f, 16:191, 207, 17:43, 19:77, 20:212, 21:321, 22:33 81, 427, 429f, 432, 475, 24:250, 260, 319, 26:263f, 338–340, 343, 454, 27:146f, 262, 30:207, 275, 294, 33:86, 125f, 208, 34:141, 36:56, 38:157, 40:29, 41:188, 194, 314, 45:86, 46:233, 47:147, 51:246f, 52:90, 110, 127
  Descendents of 1:261, 311, 314–317, 330
Cainite church—1:320–322, 326, 344
Cainites—1:276, 309, 316, 318, 320, 322–325, 327f, 330, 334f, 342, 345, 357f, 2:10, 26f, 29f, 98, 4:44, 7:86n, 21:259
Cairo—30:144
Cajetan, Cardinal Thomas de Vio—27:154n, 156–158, 31:xvii, xix, 255, 263, 264n, 270, 275, 339, 32:ix, 34:326, 330, 331n, 36:13n, 15n, 118n, 39:56n, 134n, 248n, 40:350n, 41:xiii, 236n, 375n, 45:300n, 307n, 48:73n, 81n, 82n, 84f, 87, 90n, 91n, 92, 94n, 108n, 124, 249, 291n, 54:285, 443
Cakes—3:196–198, 7:108, 118, 216, 267
Calah—2:201f
Calais—50:194n
Calamity—16:66, 173, 175, 17:268f, 276, 278f, 292, 307, 354, 368–370
Calcutta—13:404, 45:246
Caleb—3:323, 9:20, 22, 104, 271, 11:132n, 320, 20:203, 23:113, 47:187
Calendar—41:62f, 64n, 65–67, 347, 54:307, 458
Calendar, Jewish—14:210n, 20:77
Caligula, Emperor—1:261n, 7:195, 13:210n, 19:126, 35:305, 341n, 342n, 47:181, 225, 54:278
Calixtus I, Pope—20:279n
Calixtus III, Pope—45:297n
Call—4:3n, 8, 53, 104, 132, 174, 180, 182,

342, 344, 345–351, 29:5, 13, 172, 30:158f
Call (election)—25:5f, 75, 371–374
Call of God—20:34
Call to office—13:32, 65, 80, 23:214, 226, 228, 322, 342, 344, 25:142, 447, 26:17–22, 75, 101, 260
Call to the ministry—54:80
Callings—3:30, 62n, 65, 118, 128, 130f, 142, 172, 204, 209, 267, 274, 290, 299, 301, 321f, 325, 329, 4:103–105, 142, 179, 5:36, 274, 311, 5:6, 50, 130, 238f, 245, 254, 269, 274, 280, 314, 6:10, 105, 262, 270, 325, 347f, 7:73, 154f, 221, 299, 308, 356, 367, 8:107, 109, 9:3, 84, 12:71, 73, 274, 365, 384, 407, 13:398, 14:23, 15:151, 201f, 236, 17:39, 289, 384, 18:405, 20:34, 36f, 52, 21:209, 245, 21:234, 258f, 22:286, 524, 23:323, 342n, 352, 356, 359, 24:68–70, 87, 128–130, 219–221, 240, 247, 326, 329, 377–379, 384, 394f, 25:6, 105, 446f, 26:16–21, 67, 77, 102, 117, 193, 213, 356, 379, 27:49, 61, 74, 103, 119–121, 140, 165, 167, 28:46f, 71, 337, 374, 29:62f, 30:82f, 124, 248, 269, 279, 34:103, 35:259f, 36:78, 37:365, 44:130, 269, 295, 363, 45:100, 101f, 328, 46:100, 128, 166, 236, 248 252–253, 48:395f, 52:123f, 125, 192, 230, 256f, 54:258, 281
Calliope—16:140
Calmana—1:282, 312
Calneh—2:199f, 18:169
Calvary—1:310, 4:193, 5:243, 10:194
Calves—2:214, 286, 3:196–198, 280, 4:37, 111, 114, 146, 180, 275, 5:241, 294, 7:46, 9:104, 108, 113f, 166, 10:134–137, 321, 18:43, 54f, 57, 214, 418, 23:84, 125, 146, 225, 298, 403, 29:175f
Calves, Golden—18:4, 10, 17, 34n
Calvin, John—35:318, 38:xi, 41:260n, 47:9, 50:189n, 190n, 191
Institutes 34:xvi
Calvinism—47:9, 59, 48:77n
Calvisius, Seth—53:284n
Cambrai—49:222
Cambrai, Archbishop of—see **D'Ailly, Pierre**
Cambrai, Cardinal of—see **D'Ailly, Pierre**
Cambrai, League of—3:41n, 16:349n
Cambrai, Peace of—15:39n, 50:55n
Cambridge—University of 48:247n, 50:28, 150n
Cambyses—20:6, 83, 160, 35:337n, 45:225n, 226n
Cambyses II—18:368n, 371
Camels—1:202, 2:357, 3:321, 4:259, 272f, 282, 284, 5:282f, 6:59f, 176, 280, 9:137
Camenz—2:202n
Cameracensis—see **D'Ailly, Pierre**
Camerarius, Joachim—23:xi, 46:6n, 214n, 49:77n, 81n, 401n, 50:11n, 14n, 134n, 228n, 54:319
Campano, Gianantonio—41:270n
Campanus, John—2:18, 38:298, 47:116
Campeggio, Cardinal Lorenzo—12:x, 144n, 34:8, 67, 83, 89, 40:350n, 46:xii, 188n, 47:20, 45, 49:126n, 285n, 296n, 315n, 349n, 350n, 377n, 378n, 393, 414n, 416n, 423, 54:215
Campostela, St. James of—see **James, St., Apostle**
Camps—9:232, 234, 236f, 242
Cana, Wedding at—22:110, 217, 23:114
Canaan—1:99, 243, 2:21, 174, 176, 178, 182, 194, 204, 206, 217, 237, 247, 276, 279, 281, 287–290, 292, 303, 342, 345, 358–360, 362, 374–377, 390, 396f, 3:9f, 27f, 31–34, 36, 38f, 41, 52, 66, 83, 100, 112–114, 116, 119f, 149, 151, 156, 180, 188, 190, 209, 222, 251, 317, 353, 4:38, 73f, 183, 188, 190, 195, 198, 308, 365f, 5:94, 139, 143, 198, 210, 224–226, 265, 338f, 6:145, 153, 161, 190, 288, 290, 315, 344, 353, 7:14f, 18, 171, 215, 219, 239, 244, 270, 276, 300, 306, 9:16, 32, 35, 103, 293, 299, 304, 12:268n, 16:155, 165, 184, 17:28, 252, 18:99, 203, 330, 341, 19:99, 144, 233, 20:76, 97f, 113, 117, 228, 22:31, 40, 25:39, 27:254, 314, 29:150, 36:155n, 38:113, 47:90, 94, 97, 173, 183, 185, 203, 271
Canaanite woman—4:55, 220, 6:139f, 153, 262, 7:5, 13, 17f, 22, 201, 8:85, 135, 228
Canaanites—2:9f, 176, 204, 282f, 287, 290f, 332, 336, 3:40, 4:42, 244–246, 251, 306, 379, 383, 5:10, 182, 193, 240, 6:201, 227, 243, 246, 345, 388, 392, 7:5–8, 14f, 23, 35, 37, 42, 163, 200, 218, 222f, 307, 9:34, 37, 83, 85, 89, 145, 204–206, 16:58, 155, 20:347, 25:282, 31:124, 45:331, 46:120, 125, 47:151
Candace, Queen—15:131, 20:280, 28:276
Candlemas—20:166n, 41:64n
Candles—3:273, 34:55, 58, 53:22, 25, 69, 101f, 106
Cannae—6:106
Cannibals—23:169
Cannis—16:254
Canon Law—3:121, 322, 326, 4:93, 200f,

219–223, 226–228, 289n, 396–400, 9:147n, 229n, 13:198f, 14:23, 262, 22:432f, 436f, 438, 445, 452, 464, 23:39, 27:250, 28:23f, 37, 29:18n, 54, 31:26, 32f, 83, 92f, 107–119, 152, 178f, 189, 248, 384–388, 32:67n, 83n, 34:36, 100, 35:80n, 82n, 123n, 201, 379, 36:19, 35, 71–73, 79, 136–138, 164, 199–203, 207, 212f, 217, 222, 249, 251, 253, 258, 261, 37:14n, 56n, 123n, 300, 38:99, 101f, 114f, 135, 196, 318, 39:57, 59, 61, 71, 75, 90, 100, 112, 126n, 249n, 281n, 40:354, 355n, 41:7n, 20n, 30, 33n, 34n, 36n, 42n, 47, 49, 113f, 157, 162n, 174n, 177, 200n, 267, 270, 278, 328, 337n, 338, 340, 342n, 360, 43:153–158, 44:128n, 132, 151n, 179n, 182–184, 202–204, 202n, 203n, 45:17, 22n, 54, 60, 69, 72n, 144n, 229, 238, 240, 275, 276n, 277, 297n, 305n, 381, 46:xiv, 166, 168, 226, 227n, 232n, 261, 266, 268, 272, 273n, 295, 297f, 303f, 308, 316, 319f, 47:16, 181, 48:47, 84f, 105, 114, 140n, 186n, 246n, 266n, 275f, 308n, 318, 49:29n, 62f, 85, 138n, 232, 276, 278n, 382f, 397n, 423n, 50:32n, 35n, 36n, 150, 162, 199n, 213n, 248n, 249n, 51:88n, 93n, 108, 114, 386, 52:172, 220f, 223, 232, 284f, 54:14, 144, see also ***Corpus Iuris Canonici***

Canon of the Mass—14:295, 34:83n, 35:82n, 85n, 36:37n, 41n, 51n, 52, 54n, 131, 184–186, 254, 312–328, 38:123n, 318n, 39:38f, 53:xvii, xx, 21f, 26f

***Canon of the Mass* by Gabriel Biel**—31:9n

Canones apostolorum—41:45n

Canonical Hours—3:362, 4:122, 9:55, 10:385n, 391, 11:259, 422, 455n, 525n, 12:304, 393, 14:ix, 16:331, 17:324, 21:142, 21:298, 23:25, 24:241, 325, 25:458f, 461, 25:461, 470, 493, 26:140, 305, 30:83, 322, 34:55, 100, 36:112n, 113–115, 36:193f, 39:39, 41:173, 283, 42:23n, 43:199, 44:329f, 48:28, 114n, 51:65, 107, 171, 295, 52:39, 228, 53:5, 38, see also **Breviaries**

Canonists 2:151, 4:200–202, 204f, 217f, 219f, 223f, 225, 227, 396, 400f, 7:10, 16f, 21:5, 26:20, 57, 313, 41:158, 161, 162n, 319n, 360, 45:233n, 238

Canonization—3:109, 26:423n, 32:96, 45:288n, 280

Canons—1:75n, 166, 3:197, 242, 254, 363, 5:192, 333, 7:63, 194, 27:153, 36:220, 309

Canons and Decrees of the Council of Trent—32:29n

Canons of the Holy Apostles—34:31, 41:45n

Cantate Sunday—23:185n, 197n

Canticles—19:xi, 53:176, see also names of individual Canticles

Capella, Galeatus—34:272, 275, 278

Capernaites—37:93, 99f, 124, 129, 133f, 138, 38:18, 72n, 75

Capernaum—2:315, 16:97, 22:186, 214–217, 390, 415, 23:78, 80, 104, 155f, 201, 209, 42:134, 45:148

Caphtorim—2:203

Capital—45:234

Capital letters—37:74, 144f, 162, 206f

Capital punishment—9:83, 162, 183n

Capitalism—21:184f, 22:471n, 45:xii, 233, 235, 239

Capito, Wolfgang Fabricius—3:206n, 34:80n, 281, 35:7, 37:xiv, 9, 42n, 157, 38:6, 281, 39:140, 242f, 40:76, 45:243, 48:118, 230n, 305n, 316n, 326n, 343n, 344f, 365, 372, 381, 49:303n, 50:171f, 188n, 191n, 228n

In Habacuc Prophetam enarrationes, Strasbourg, 1526 19:151n

Capitolinus, Julius—*Antoninus Pius* 33:142n

Cappadocia—30:5

Cappadocia, Church of—41:321, 347, 351, 358

Cappadocians—2:189, 9:34

Cappel, Battle of—50:46n, 55n

Capreolus, John—31:146, 321

Captatio benevolentiae (rhetoric)—3:288n

Captivities of the Church—36:7, 41, 49, 71, 78, 255

1st captivity 36:27f

2nd captivity 36:28

3rd captivity 36:35, 41

Captivity—2:26, 101, 127, 262, 264, 320, 389, 3:37, 150, 226, 11:154–156, 550–552, 16:87, 107, 137, 36:18, 73, 90, 114, 265

Assyrian 6:162, 12:119, 18:5, 17, 24, 26, 45, 48, 56f, 146, 168, 181, 183, 201n, 216n, 244, 250f, 19:116, 147, 153, 20:28

Babylonian 2:229, 360, 3:36, 6:33, 9:268, 296, 10:431, 434, 11:187n, 16:27, 60, 75, 175, 221, 255, 279, 17:3, 119, 124f, 137, 142, 165, 355, 359, 361, 368, 371, 375, 18:16, 89, 168, 193f, 199, 201, 216, 243, 320, 333f, 337, 341, 343f, 248, 252, 364, 20:3f, 10f, 18, 28, 49f, 68, 159, 189f, 213, 251, 337 25:395f, 421, 511, 28:160, 29:208, 35:276, 279f,

286, 295, 297, 321, 327f, 36:6, 17, 19, 78n, 45:214f, 220, 222, 367, 47:69, 173, 188, 194f, 201, 203–205, 209, 228, 241, 265
Egyptian 2:292, 18:275
Roman 9:296, 16:76
Captivity, Return from—18:237, 240–244, 273f, 342, 348, 364, 20:68, 97f, 161, 290f
Captivity, Spiritual—18:34
Captivity foretold—18:16, 28, 39, 44–48, 52f, 56f, 71, 88, 92, 146–148, 150f, 167–169, 171f, 175, 178–180, 182f, 219–221, 236f, 244, 250, 274, 321, 329–331, 335, 337
Capuchins—18:55n, 23:274n
Caraccioli, Marino—34:332, 326
Carafa, Cardinal John Peter—34:232, 266
Cardinal Issues—33:35, 294
Cardinals—1:213, 260, 276, 2:38, 102, 152, 202, 256, 3:153, 240, 242, 254, 268, 294, 4:32, 54, 121, 220, 396, 403, 5:35, 195, 245, 331, 333, 353, 6:40, 48, 375, 7:62f, 68, 131, 147, 233, 242, 297, 331, 21:320f, 23:192f, 288, 320, 369, 410, 418, 24:122, 126, 156, 174f, 305, 26:52, 408, 27:122, 157, 385n, 30:177, 250, 34:211, 253–255, 36:110, 113f, 158, 167, 205, 38:147, 166, 197, 230f, 41:16, 32–34, 143, 167, 191, 197, 206, 235f, 251, 254, 277–279, 282–285, 287–289, 300, 308, 322, 331–333, 336, 341f, 355–357, 360, 368, 370f, 44:141f, 46:164, 169, 47:37–40, 169, 177, 51:306, 311, 360f, 387f, 391, 52:267f
Cardinals and prelates—48:10, 83, 104
Career of the Reformer—see Vols. 31–34
Introduction 31:ix–xii
Cares—3:3, 159
Carion, John—41:23n, 106n
Chronicle 38:302n
Caritas (meaning of word)—11:447
Carletti—see **Angelo Carletti di Chivasso**
Carlstadt, Andreas—see **Karlstadt, Andreas Bodenstein von**
Carmel, Mt.—9:149, 16:247, 286, 300, 18:131, 275, 287
Carmelites—18:55n, 23:274n, 35:68n, 44:190, 48:88, 92, 49:167n
Carnal license—16:204
Carnal man—16:73, 25:327–330, 332, 334f, 25:329–333, 26:7, 30:68
Carnality—27:249, 354, 391
Carneades—54:322
Carnival mummery—23:3993
Carnival princes—13:13
Carols—53:195
Carousing—3:182, 23:5, 43, 27:91, 368, 370f
Carpenter and the ax—33:159, 176
Carpenters—13:378, 17:111f
Carrensis, Cardinal Hugo—3:26
Carrion—2:158, 160f
Carrying others in need—17:409
Cartagena, Bishops of—48:67n, 172n
Carthage—1:88, 2:194, 3:329n, 6:332, 31:245n, 36:25
Carthusians—2:338n, 339f, 3:325, 4:140, 157, 5:13, 7:134, 344, 354, 12:90, 187, 13:7, 15:32, 17:17, 23f, 27, 29, 111, 134, 140, 298, 18:183, 20:86n, 21:35, 73, 160, 22:60, 71, 87, 136, 157, 270, 278, 280, 302, 309, 369, 461, 464, 23:24, 34, 70f, 85, 117, 121, 124, 127, 129, 134, 179, 225, 263f, 288, 333, 335, 340, 346, 359, 367, 24:35, 37f, 228, 26:295, 332f, 396f, 27:88, 91, 281, 28:116, 225, 281, 356f, 29:11, 75, 30:95, 253, 255, 263, 34:214, 35:134n, 37:286n, 39:221n, 41:127n, 129n, 172, 44:99n, 46:251n, 48:322n, 51:81, 107, 109, 111, 115, 247, 52:80, 247
Cartoons in Luther's books—41:260f, 262n, 270n, 277n, 290n, 306n, 308n, 328n, 341n, 363n
Carus-Wilson, E.M.—45:266n
Carvajal, Cardinal Bernardino —48:172n
Casel, Gregory—37:xiv, 22n
Casimir, Margrave of Brandenburg-Ansbach—45:138, 46:47n, 72n, 49:xvi, 60n, 118, 127f
Casluhim—2:203
Caspians—2:189
Cassian, John—*De coenobiorum institutis* 25:482n
Cassiodorus (Pseudo-Primasius)—*In epistolam ad Titum commentaria* 29:79n
Cassiodorus, Flavius—10:94, 99, 104, 107n, 113, 116, 146, 150, 153, 167, 184, 200f, 210, 213, 246, 255, 257, 270, 307, 408, 411, 422, 431, 439, 11:17, 65, 179, 189, 306, 323, 336, 401, 40:121n, 47:117n
Expositio in Psalmos 11:65n
Historia tripartita 2:18, 272, 29:19n, 43n, 31:119, 40:121n, 41:7n, 54n, 55n, 56n, 57n, 59n, 61n, 62n, 79n, 80n, 81n, 82n, 83n, 84n, 87n, 88n, 93n, 94n, 95n, 97n, 98n, 99n, 102n, 104n, 106, 115n, 117n, 118n, 47:117n
Cassirer, Ernst—*The Renaissance Philosophy of Man* 13:77n

Cassius—5:236
Castelnuovo—50:183n, 190n
Castigations—5:13, 157
Castile—34:345, 353
Castles—24:377, 46:477, 50, 243
Castor—2:147
Castration—9:230, 46:148n, 54:177
Casuistry—39:33n, 45:22n, 234, 239
Catabaptists—16:320
Catachresis—3:192n, 6:307, 12:346, 24:26, 27:43
Catastrophe—5:113, 117, 119, 7:366, 23:12
***Catechism of Christian Doctrine: Revised Edition of the Baltimore Catechism*, 1949**—42:162n, 175n
Catechisms—7:344, 14:8, 15:247n, 304, 341, 20:156f, 22:400, 443, 481, 24:x, 26:414, 34:28, 53, 41:136, 164, 214n, 247n, 43:13, 239, 46:231f, 47:52, 109, 112, 49:214n, 233, 51:xviii, 135–193, 335, 376n, 53:64–69, 106, 110, 117, 119, 210, 271, 277, 295, 299, 54:163, 235, 258
Catechists—15:261
Catechumens—27:396, 31:211
Caterpillars—1:206, 4:89, 11:75f, 83f, 18:81, 415
Cathari—24:228, 35:403n, 37:14n
Catharinus, Ambrosius—39:167n, 48:291n
Cathedral chapters—36:178
Cathedral schools—see **Schools, Cathedral**
Cathedrals—3:245n
Catherine, St.—20:267, 22:164, 23:121, 31:219, 34:24, 26, 41:65n
Catherine of Alexandria, St.—42:119n, 54:475
Catherine of Aragon—49:223n, 265n
Catholic League—41:36n
Catholic or Christian—34:229
Catholic Union—41:181f
Catholics—1:169, 5:385, 11:209, 446, 526, 30:289, 316, 320, 34:118
Catilina—17:239n
Cato, Dionysius—54:211
Disticha moralis 2:159n, 3:11n, 4:219n, 297n, 5:237, 6:332n, 400n, 7:122n, 13:82n, 22:155n, 33:82n
Cato, Marcus—3:11, 67, 13:122, 14:118, 23:320, 362, 28:221, 31:245, 40:316n, 45:272, 47:228
De re rustica 7:67n
Disticha de moribus 2:159n, 3:11n, 4:219n, 297n, 5:237, 6:332n, 400n, 7:122n, 13:82n, 22:155n, 50:104n, 171n
Cats—2:116, 24:134, 274, 323
Cattle—1:71, 76, 79, 87f, 90, 123, 143, 243, 247, 305, 312, 2:74, 79, 88, 92, 104, 133, 135, 142, 279, 281f, 324f, 329, 336, 355, 374, 390, 396, 4:46, 74, 77, 89, 102, 122, 142, 185, 229, 245, 323, 332, 5:3f, 6–8, 13, 54f, 58–60, 132, 152, 269f, 287, 296, 324f, 337, 339, 368, 370, 376, 391, 6:6, 12–14, 19, 67f, 90, 106, 176, 280, 7:32f, 45, 82, 107, 218, 310f, 339, 347, 9:18, 43, 136, 204, 260, 11:18, 84f, 19:185, 23:222, 24:82, 27:90, 227, 245, 357, 30:84, 104
Catullus—25:481
Carmina 15:145n
Caucasus Mts.—2:108
Causes—1:124f, 127f, 131, 2:125f, 148, 5:112f, 188, 8:11, 12:350, 13:77n, 93, 49:382n, 384, 54:399f
Caves—4:216
Cecilia, St.—29:153, 44:84n, 52:273
Cedars—2:66, 93, 342, 10:134f, 11:97, 232f, 335f
Celebrations—6:35, 231, 17:367
Celestial bodies—28:184, 190, 194f, 197
Celestine I, Pope—41:94n
Celestines—26:333
Celibacy—1:118, 135, 161, 230, 238–240, 2:25, 3:44, 47, 97, 182, 202, 204, 210f, 351, 4:7, 11, 22, 303, 333, 335, 5:8, 33n, 176, 192, 292, 301, 322–324, 329f, 349, 354, 6:124, 278, 7:16, 33f, 9:74, 14:xii, 16:44, 17:11, 100, 366, 21:35, 22:434, 458, 476, 23:193, 26:141, 216, 458, 460, 27:44, 57, 67f, 82, 138, 28:ixf, 3, 9–12, 21f, 26f, 47f, 52, 231, 312, 29:10, 18f, 21, 40, 30:98, 31:389, 391, 34:40, 41n, 42–44, 48n, 92–94, 35:382, 406, 36:114, 202, 206f, 217, 37:371n, 38:88, 233, 41:156–164, 44:261–264, 45:xi, 21, 47f, 53f, 142n, 145, 153, 156, 275, 390, 46:220, 48:221n, 247n, 263n, 281n, 283f, 293f, 314n, 321f, 328, 342f, 354, 357, 363, 378, 49:11, 182n, 328n, 351, 367, 377n, 378n, 416n, 421, 425, 50:133n, 192n, 193, 198n, 199, 202, 204, 51:154, 52:273, 54:141–142, 218, 270, 335, 338, 357, 393
Celibates—1:132, 135, 3:44, 208, 4:65, 5:33, 90, 291, 323, 330, 7:344, 366
Cellarius, John—54:196, 293, 364, 405
Cellarius, Martin—40:47, 51n
Cellars—2:134, 23:14, 40f
Celsus—26:106
Cemeteries—2:340, 4:396, 24:44, 43:135–137

Cenchreae—8:305, 25:128, 26:61, 32, 156, 27:211, 343
Censorinus—3:213
Censuring—6:19, 34, 45f, 62, 211, 394
Centaurs—2:395, 6:93, 200, 8:106, 17:175, 18:315n
Centurion—26:101, 29:192, 217
Cephas—26:75, 100, 27:214, 217f, 41:314, see also **Peter, St., Apostle**
Cerberus—2:222, 4:403, 16:343, 25:300
Ceremonial—40:129f, 148
Ceremonial cleanliness—18:384f, 394n, 395
Ceremonial law—see **Law, Ceremonial**
Ceremonialists—26:10
Ceremonies—1:269, 300f, 328, 330, 2:47, 92, 159, 197, 226, 255, 257, 353, 361, 3:29, 91, 101, 144, 250, 281, 4:91, 235–237, 322f, 327, 368, 5:20, 80, 97, 109f, 125, 135f, 245, 6:231f, 247, 7:19, 152, 163, 188, 207, 337, 349, 351, 8:82, 130, 132f, 137, 146, 284, 320, 9:7, 14, 26, 48, 53, 54, 63, 79, 81, 117, 123, 134, 156, 168, 197, 210–212, 222, 254, 258, 10:75, 221, 276, 13:293, 14:14, 23, 255, 292, 301f, 341, 16:256, 299, 17:73, 98f, 284, 298, 316, 388, 20:12, 85, 102, 126, 141, 23:22, 114, 24:356, 25:337f, 25:60, 180, 489, 491, 493, 26:4, 32, 41, 87, 91f, 105, 112, 121–123, 135, 153, 180f, 222, 224, 250, 312, 330, 355, 364, 397, 429, 448, 461, 27:9, 15, 25, 31, 53–55, 59, 62, 90, 131, 138f, 161, 204, 219, 235, 276, 287, 294f, 298f, 355, 357, 383, 397, 28:150, 319, 29:7, 9, 13, 42f, 49, 191f, 217–219, 224, 30:295, 314, 31:372–376, 389, 34:54–58, 35:81f, 97f, 36:36, 66, 70, 87, 90, 92, 110f, 221, 223, 41:22, 67, 71, 75, 86, 130f, 137f, 175, 208, 211, 50:38n, 39, 63, 111, 131, 141, 201, 280n, 54:49, 68, 195, 333, 360f, 397, 436, see also **Law, Ceremonial**
Ceremonies, Ecclesiastical—38:185f, 317
Ceremonies of the Mass—36:52, 168, 239, 242f, 247, 254, 262
Ceres—6:238, 27:371
Cerinthians—30:219, 227, 251f, 284, 299, 35:393n
Cerinthus—1:146n, 17:327, 22:7, 18, 37, 57, 67, 110, 391, 30:221, 256–258, 285, 319, 44:284n, 52:53f, 61, 64, 66, 54:445
Certainty—see **Assurance**
Chaff—1:251, 2:24, 3:150, 8:63, 118, 218, 248f, 24:236, 329
Chalcedon, Council of—41:5, 8, 23n, 52, 106n, 107–119, 121, 123, 136n, 141, 280, 291n, 308, 44:137n
Chalcedonian Formula—37:213n
Chaldea—2:239, 243, 3:181, 4:198, 258, 5:279, 17:56, 92, 96, 138, 164, 167, 22:120, 30:144, 34:303
Chaldean language—7:188, 16:165
Chaldeans—2:192, 201, 242–244, 248f, 268f, 276–278, 281, 305, 349, 4:3, 185, 237, 250, 308, 348, 352, 5:10, 209f, 6:308, 7:25, 120, 140, 199, 301, 8:288, 12:34, 13:211, 14:74, 16:13, 28, 33, 85, 176, 179, 181, 184, 336, 17:134, 137, 145, 151, 153, 18:199, 209, 236, 300–305, 307, 311f, 314, 319, 325, 335, 337, 346, 20:16, 28, 68, 82, 160, 178, 193, 26:410, 27:295, 38:244, see also **Babylonians and Chaldeans**
Chalice—2:331, 338, 4:237n, 23:273, 29:7, 43, 36:26n, 116, 165f, 38:83, 114n, 119, 168, 214, 224, 54:417, see also **Cup; Sacramental elements; Wine**
Chalk—23:320n
Chamberlains—7:51–53
Chance—6:90, 93, 346, 15:132, 25:371, 387, 33:38, 171, 291
Chancel—13:365, 23:25, 53:33
Chancellor—23:392, 38:15, 63, 69
Change—13:106, 25:73, 105, 153, 217–219, 235, 246, 317, 322f
Channel—20:114, 307
Chanting—36:233, 254
Chanting of Scripture readings—18:39
Chants—2:164, 53:xvii, xixf, 13, 28, 55–60, 70–78, 82f, 147–188
Chapels—1:95, 2:332, 5:78, 252, 23:156, 413
Chapels, Devil's—see **Devil**—Builds chapel near church
Chaplains—38:166, 46:220, 234
Chaplains, Military—43:228
Character—20:22, 38
Charge—20:213f
Chariots—4:7, 9, 10:338, 342f, 18:300f, 305, 307, 20:62, 64f, 95, 247–249
Charities—49:28f, 169f, 206n
Charity—3:189, 339n, 9:241, 248, 11:18, 97, 21:130f, 172, 22:54, 23:360, 26:73, 80, 83f, 86, 91, 111, 127, 167n, 29:89, 94, 32:118, 36:104, 38:82, 45:238, 286, 355
Charlemagne, Emperor—4:193n, 10:149, 15:69n, 31:234n, 35:296n, 406n, 37:226n, 41:25n, 135n, 261, 281,

372f, 374n, 376, 44:207n, 49:348n, 53:260

Charles V, Emperor—3:340, 4:35, 371, 6:x, 244, 7:198, 349, 8:189, 12:298, 13:149n, 190n, 15:39n, 152, 16:196n, 258n, 331n, 22:83n, 409, 23:217n, 26:97n, 28:243, 31:xviii, 256, 384, 32:xiiif, 105–128, 34:xii, xvi, 5, 9, 11n, 65, 83n, 272, 332, 338, 341, 345, 360, 35:ix, 408n, 36:9, 229n, 246n, 38:93, 41:5f, 9n, 128n, 142, 181, 222, 226n, 230n, 245, 248f, 259f, 263–265, 268f, 272, 274n, 275, 276n, 277n, 280, 282, 284f, 287f, 293, 295n, 42:xi, 119, 169, 43:59, 148, 215, 253, 44:xviin, 125n, 146n, 166n, 45:xv, 134n, 242n, 271n, 272n, 347n, 46:xi, xiii, 89n, 90n, 106n, 120n, 168f, 184, 189, 198–201, 202n, 204n, 47:ix, 5f, 23f, 29–34, 222, 223n, 266, 275n, 48:97n, 99n, 129n, 140, 174n, 175f, 182, 188, 189n, 193, 195f, 198n, 200, 201f, 203, 210, 216n, 217, 220n, 226n, 234n, 255n, 270, 315, 340, 392, 395, 49:xiii, xvii, 21n, 38, 78n, 86n, 125, 144n, 155f, 161n, 185, 189, 193, 222f, 224n, 251, 252n, 254, 255n, 256f, 264, 274f, 280, 283n, 284n, 285f, 293n, 296f, 296n, 298, 315n, 317f, 327, 329n, 330, 334n, 339f, 349f, 350n, 351f, 352n, 354n, 355, 359f, 368n, 369, 374n, 375f, 376n, 377f, 397f, 397n, 401n, 403f, 406n, 416n, 420n, 422–424, 430n, 435, 50:xiii, xviii, 54n, 55n, 81f, 82n, 84, 95n, 155n, 165n, 183n, 216n, 219n, 248, 250n, 251n, 254n, 265n, 269, 272, 297, 312n, 51:150, 54:28, 143, 182, 229, 330, 336, 338, 356, 370, 417, 472

and England 50:98n, 177n, 192n

and France 50:xiii, 55n, 149n, 164n, 165n, 183n, 219n, 243n, 245n, 248n, 253n

and the Evangelicals 50:xiii, 22, 41f, 44, 54n, 56, 58n, 69n, 84, 140, 155n, 163n, 190n, 192n, 207, 216n, 219n, 221n, 245n, 248n, 250n, 251n, 254n, 256, 260, 264–267, 265n, 269n, 297, 312n, 315n

and the Turks 50:xiii, 54n, 55n, 68–70, 72n, 95n, 99, 155n, 164n, 183n, 190n, 216, 224n, 229n, 243n, 245n, 253, 267, 269f, 269n, 272, 312n

declaration vs. Luther at Worms 32:114n

Charles VI, King of France—47:265n

Charles VII, King of France—41:266n

Charles the Bold, Duke of Burgundy—45:128n, 129

Charran, Battle of—5:210, 211n

Chartres Cathedral—4:110n

Chartreuse—36:89n

Chastening—16:208, 215f, 221

Chastening, God's—14:140, 142, 156

Chastisement—3:60, 70, 6:91, 95, 150, 152, 327, 7:237, 254f, 8:9, 73, 124, 173, 11:467, 13:28, 14:142, 144f, 156, 16:25, 108, 113, 216f, 18:145, 153

Chastising the body—28:15, 17, 255, 321f, 355

Chastity—1:96, 114, 118n, 135, 339, 355–358, 2:13, 19, 165, 270n, 291, 301n, 326, 328, 3:208, 211, 216, 224, 254, 331, 358, 4:232–235, 238f, 242, 276, 307, 334–337, 378, 5:27–29, 35, 40, 54, 60, 124, 164, 195, 200, 233, 258, 263, 291f, 298f, 301, 304, 307, 323f, 330f, 341, 343, 345, 348f, 351, 356, 358, 7:16, 33, 54, 72f, 78, 80, 84, 87f, 90–92, 95f, 129, 8:18, 9:219, 222, 229, 234f, 11:306f, 369, 13:5, 17:262, 21:91, 22:232, 268, 445, 458, 464, 23:24, 134f, 182, 24:188, 227, 25:12, 55, 112, 166, 320f, 330, 482, 508, 26:70, 91, 137, 141, 171f, 175, 200, 305, 450, 27:18, 68, 84, 89, 95, 329, 346, 362, 364, 373, 378, 393, 405, 28:3, 5, 9–12, 15f, 21, 26–28, 49f, 52, 312f, 317, 328, 352, 355f, 29:46, 49, 55, 69, 30:26, 40, 61, 170, 172, 188f, 205f, 272, 35:41, 142, 382, 36:80, 96, 201, 206, 210, 224, 261, 303, 37:371, 38:176, 39:44, 148, 150, 206–214, 234, 241f, 253–268, 285, 288f, 297f, 41:43, 162, 204, 337, 44:255f, 264, 267f, 337–341, 344–346, 369f, 383, 44:8f, 103–106, 214f, 45:44, 141–150, 153, 319, 46:146f, 149, 299, 48:285, 334, 342, 51:80f, 116, 154, 171, 362, 52:12f, 58, 217, 227, 259f, 266f, 270, 272f, 284

Chastity of Clergy—41:156–164

Chasubles—4:122, 23:366, 24:361, 38:107, 119, 203, 40:129f, 148, 41:17, 147, 152, 168, 368

Cheap grace—33:268, 279

Cheating—21:235–237

Chedorlaomer—2:365

Cheerfulness—22:305

Cheering—20:47, 227

Cheese—3:211, 4:245, 7:45, 219, 8:68–70, 302, 23:225

Chemnitz, Martin—13:122n, 50:142n

Loci, I, "De peccato originis" 11:466n

Chemosh—6:230, 8:229

Cherries—23:254, 257

Cherubim—1:225, 230f, 234–236, 255,

11:95f, 277, 286, 319, 322, 13:34, 16:70, 317, 19:80, 20:59f, 233, 243f, 27:22 231

Chewing the sacramental bread—37:67, 75n, 96, 124, 130, 139n, 149n, 245, 300f, 333

Chezib—7:6

Chicks, chickens—1:102, 171, 2:116, 133, 138, 9:220, 225

Chieregati, Francesco—34:60n, 49:23n, 24n, 37n, 126n

Child communicants—see **Infant communion**

Childbirth—2:304, 311, 3:134, 136, 323, 360, 4:11, 189, 291, 363, 369f, 5:31, 289, 317, 329, 339, 7:6f, 33, 46–48, 340, 372, 8:13, 25, 56, 156, 203, 245, 303, 16:208, 18:92, 243, 249, 28:279f, 45:40, 45f

Children—1:14, 69, 82, 102, 116, 133f, 137–139, 154, 168f, 198, 200, 202, 204, 207, 210, 220, 240, 245–247, 249, 257, 273, 282f, 291, 294, 305, 311, 315, 339, 344f, 347, 355–357, 2:9, 11, 25, 27f, 37, 42, 52, 57f, 64, 66, 78f, 83, 86f, 101, 104, 111f, 115, 120f, 127, 132, 136, 140f, 145, 165, 167, 173, 179, 182, 195, 204, 220, 223, 231, 233, 243, 249, 252, 257, 268, 271f, 279, 281, 295, 301, 320, 329, 356, 373, 377, 395, 3:9, 12, 15, 19, 34, 43, 45–48, 59, 68, 93f, 96f, 100, 102, 104, 112, 122, 133f, 138, 144f, 149, 159, 162, 171, 177, 179, 181, 201, 203–205, 214, 222, 225, 231f, 238–240, 253, 257, 261, 264, 266, 269, 279, 283, 295, 302, 304, 315, 342, 360, 4:4, 11, 13, 20, 26–28, 30, 38–41, 50, 52f, 56f, 60, 68, 70, 72, 94, 97, 102f, 119, 122, 132, 182, 184, 195f, 199, 216, 218, 222–226, 228, 230, 232f, 242, 244, 248f, 251, 253f, 271f, 276, 278, 282, 285, 287, 289–292, 295, 299–302, 304–308, 323–325, 331f, 337, 342–344, 353–355, 362, 380, 384f, 5:3, 5–8, 13f, 16, 27, 29, 31, 38, 58, 66f, 71, 78, 86, 89f, 93, 99f, 102, 107f, 112, 114f, 124, 132, 138, 140, 146, 150, 160, 163–166, 168f, 174f, 185, 189f, 193f, 200, 202f, 261, 263, 267, 276, 279, 284f, 290, 304, 318f, 325, 328–330, 332, 337f, 342–344, 350, 353, 355f, 358, 371f, 6:15, 61, 94, 153, 167, 186, 198, 210f, 239, 367, 370, 7:8f, 17–19, 21–23, 33, 46, 49, 60, 83, 86, 115, 117, 124, 132, 146, 165, 179, 193, 198, 218, 226, 231f, 234, 237, 244, 249, 254f, 281, 285, 288f, 301, 304, 306f, 311, 315, 319, 326, 337, 341–343, 8:9, 20f, 32, 35f, 42, 61, 68, 72, 79, 82, 84, 95, 110, 116, 126, 147, 153, 156, 160, 163, 165, 167f, 174, 183, 192, 220, 222f, 232, 241, 244, 253, 259–262, 265, 276, 294, 309f, 322, 333, 9:18, 117, 204, 210f, 243, 250, 272, 291, 305, 11:345, 13:297, 299, 14:13, 25, 37, 51, 66, 68, 100, 114f–117, 125, 184, 187, 200, 222, 228, 249, 263–267, 299, 323, 337, 15:71, 73, 16:212, 17:15, 18:28, 70, 260, 20:271f, 306, 21:8, 22:96f, 122, 138, 236, 241, 332, 381, 418, 435, 439, 459, 468, 502, 519, 523f, 23:8, 20, 92, 100, 102, 159, 161, 166f, 204, 211, 255, 265, 275, 282, 323, 334, 339f, 378, 403f, 410–413, 418, 420, 24:64, 74, 91, 120, 136, 156, 186, 214, 220, 222, 228, 231, 238, 266f, 297, 305, 307f, 322, 329, 331, 341, 360, 392, 399, 410f, 412, 25:21, 45, 182, 488, 26:11, 44, 59, 95, 143, 188, 190, 217–219, 251, 259, 297, 352, 355, 360–362, 376, 397, 404, 417, 423, 430f, 434–436, 439–442, 444–446, 448–450, 455, 460f, 28:35, 54f, 66, 164, 279f, 286, 299, 334f, 29:21f, 54–56, 65, 68, 73, 102, 126, 131, 133, 145, 170f, 183, 30:10, 12, 20, 30, 43, 91, 94, 112, 133, 173, 187, 196, 209, 247–249, 251, 257, 276, 296, 36:80, 91, 37:55f, 141, 364, 38:160, 162, 170, 178, 180, 187, 192, 202f, 207f, 40:280f, 295, 41:154f, 161, 166, 176f, 203n, 355, 42:134f, 44:11–14, 82–88, 45:21, 29, 38, 40, 46, 48, 155, 322f, 333–336, 344, 351, 353–355, 367–370, 381, 385–392, 46:76, 97, 112, 114, 209f, 213–258, 291, 293, 295, 299, 304–309, 313f, 49:163, 203, 269, 319, 50:152f, 231f, 233f, 237f, 239f, 51:146, 151, 159, 52:217f, 219, 273, 54:157f, 163, 177, 234f, 245, 267, 296, 300, 334f, 339, 355f, 424, 429, 433

Children, Adoption as God's—25:71f

Children, Salvation of—45:349, 357

Children, Unbaptized—43:247–250

Children and faith—36:301

Children of Abraham—23:395, 403, 414–416, 419, 421

Children of Adam—23:166, 334

Children of God—1:191, 289, 310, 315, 318, 2:6, 370, 4:54, 65, 71, 91, 261, 309, 344, 348, 350, 367f, 5:199, 229, 8:9, 39, 131, 167, 185, 232, 255, 312, 14:9, 31, 55, 58, 72, 83, 106, 123, 191, 243, 246, 16:7, 9, 21:42f, 22:37, 83,

89–91, 96f, 99–102, 109, 115–118, 121, 123, 131, 134, 136, 178, 192, 203, 364, 473, 23:172, 217, 385, 415, 421, 24:87, 89, 129, 151, 157, 175, 206, 229, 272, 281, 293, 315, 322, 331, 358–360, 407, 24:87, 89, 129, 151, 175, 206, 229, 272, 281, 293, 315, 322, 331, 358f, 407, 26:81, 121, 245, 351f, 374, 458, 26:81, 121, 245, 351f, 381, 458, 29:214, 30:11, 33f, 36, 43, 45, 74, 130, 164, 178, 197, 265–268, 274, 308, 33:153, 157f, 41:82, 171, 176, 193, 42:20, 22, 28, 53f, 78, 132, 138, 162, 46:237, 248, 47:85, 95, 146, 148, 158, 162, 175, 198, 200, 288, 297

Children of Israel—2:154, 194, 277, 282, 5:139, 144, 153, 262, 385, 9:15, 35, 55, 57n, 82, 87, 114, 154, 169, 189, 230, 254, 292, 304, 23:152, 206, 24:46, 49, 51, 53, 366, 26:149, 311, 313, 321–323, 27:135, 267, 314, 407, 42:38f, 89f, 104, 159, 186, 42:38f, 89f, 104, 186

Children of this world—1:310f, 318, 322, 347, 14:66, 68

Children's Creed—see **Creeds**—Apostles'

Children's Faith (Catechism)—41:214n

Chiliasm—13:264

Chimera—42:159n

Chiron—18:315

Chislev, Month of—20:77, 259

Chittim—16:182, 184

Chivasso—see **Angelo Carletti di Chivasso**

Choice—see **Bondage of the will**

Choice, Enslaved—see **Bondage of the Will**

Choirboys—30:53n, 43:231

Choirs—24:91, 25:450, 53:xvii, 12, 28f, 74, 124, 149, 155, 172f, 185f, 193, 252, 277, 315

Chorale notation—53:xix

Chorazin—22:186, 390, 42:134

Chorus (Hebrew word)—11:187n

Chosen ones—17:103, 124

Chosen people—36:140, 143

Chremdath—see **Consolation (Chremdath) of the Gentiles**

Chrism—24:225, 38:114, 149n, 150, 152, 158, 164, 176, 185–188, 192–195, 197f, 203f, 208f, 211–214, 40:288n, 53:102

Christ—1:9, 13, 17, 22, 33, 59, 64, 68, 86, 89, 107, 111f, 128, 134f, 138f, 146, 148–150, 153, 156f, 161, 165, 170, 180, 183, 188, 190–192, 194–197, 213, 217–220, 224f, 233f, 240, 243, 246–248, 253, 255f, 259, 264f, 267, 274, 277, 280–282, 290, 292, 295, 297, 299, 303, 310, 320f, 326, 334, 336, 344, 348, 351, 354f, 2:144, 151, 163, 177, 215, 228f, 3:213f, 298, 4:25, 230, 389, 7:224, 282, 296, 335, 8:188, 250, 263, 283, 314, 9:26, 60n, 130, 134, 167, 176, 178, 186, 272, 10:38, 113, 158f, 379, 11:41, 67, 102, 118, 147n, 149, 169, 177, 179, 304, 318, 437, 477f, 534, 541, 551, 12:14, 41, 51, 73, 90, 122f, 126f, 130, 206, 208f, 211f, 213, 217, 263, 268, 363, 409, 13:4f, 6, 8, 11f, 26f, 33f, 78, 136f, 152, 228, 241, 249, 265, 284f, 320, 323, 342, 414, 14:12, 17, 21, 22–26, 31, 38, 46f, 55f, 69, 71, 86f, 89, 93, 98, 145, 151, 157, 169, 197, 324, 15:297f, 304, 313, 325f, 332f, 347f, 16:3, 29, 36, 38, 51, 53–55, 57, 73, 77, 85, 88, 104, 117, 119, 124, 166, 170, 189, 195, 200, 221, 233, 237, 241, 248, 250, 262f, 276, 279, 286, 292, 304, 17:3f, 6, 26, 46, 162, 165, 226f, 18:31, 72, 229, 248, 355, 381, 19:40f, 80, 89, 98, 102f, 111, 116n, 123, 135, 183, 189, 192, 196–198, 203, 212, 20:13, 49f, 72, 104, 112, 115, 121, 140, 195, 197, 217, 254, 295, 21:60, 66, 70, 116, 153f, 165f, 182, 219–221, 241–243, 254f, 270, 274f, 340, 350, 352–354, 22:335, 342, 355f, 23:11, 13f, 22, 28, 41, 46, 51, 55–58, 60, 71, 130, 154f, 278, 295, 311f, 336, 369, 24:8f, 24, 39, 53, 76, 78, 96, 136, 226, 237, 310, 324, 337, 344, 371, 393, 25:xi, 24, 30, 48, 68, 75, 87, 104, 112, 119f, 147, 151, 190, 208, 223, 236, 238f, 246, 267, 26:11, 24, 39, 120, 208, 273, 324, 355, 385, 27:10, 17, 43, 92, 103, 143f, 226, 396, 401, 28:34, 42, 44f, 60f, 69, 94, 108f, 111, 113–115, 121f, 128, 132, 134f, 192–194, 211, 218, 247f, 264, 333, 29:11, 15, 18, 23, 41, 49, 62, 64, 66–68, 78, 109f, 123, 131f, 135f, 142, 144, 148, 158, 168, 178, 180, 182, 189f, 193, 202f, 212, 216f, 226, 30:21, 39, 49, 51, 63, 138, 237, 300, 31:41, 84, 88, 100, 174, 189f, 192, 225, 335, 351f, 354, 366, 369, 32:17, 28f, 33, 47, 55, 62, 154, 207f, 254, 34:27, 50, 86, 112, 122, 207f, 35:84f, 119f, 173, 247, 331, 373, 391f, 396, 36:16, 48, 146, 149, 157, 167, 215–217, 219, 241, 245, 248, 294, 302, 340f, 350, 37:16, 20, 21n, 25–28, 53, 106, 124, 131, 192, 204, 209f, 231, 251, 362, 366, 369, 38:xvii, 16f, 19, 22–24, 28–30, 35, 37–39, 44, 53f, 56f, 60, 65, 81, 97, 100–103, 105, 111f, 120–126, 128,

154, 164f, 171f, 178f, 182–186, 189f, 199–202, 204, 206, 209–212, 39:12, 16, 21, 73, 76, 81–83, 96, 100, 102, 146f, 159, 169, 181, 203, 251, 40:20, 27, 36, 43, 51, 54, 57f, 70, 131–133, 207, 220, 346, 41:10–13, 16, 18f, 38–40, 44, 47f, 51, 53f, 60, 63, 65–67, 69–71, 76, 79, 87–91, 98, 110, 113–115, 119f, 122–124, 127–131, 138, 140, 143f, 146–149, 151–154, 156–158, 163–167, 169f, 172, 174, 177, 189–192, 194–198, 201–204, 209f, 212–220, 227f, 231, 245f, 256, 273, 277, 293, 295–297, 300–303, 306, 308–315, 317f, 320f, 323, 327–336, 339, 343–360, 364–367, 370, 42:5–8, 10, 12–14, 19, 23, 38, 45, 50, 57–59, 60–62, 64f, 68f, 80, 104–110, 112, 122, 129, 133, 135–137, 141–143, 149, 152, 162–166, 169, 173, 186, 44:69, 298–299, 400, 45:24, 30f, 41, 47, 59n, 60n, 65, 67–69, 71, 77, 81f, 87–93, 97f, 100–103, 105f, 11f, 114, 117f, 120, 122, 148f, 152f, 156, 164, 169, 172, 178, 201–204, 227f, 229, 234, 245, 259, 273–276, 280, 282, 289, 290, 292, 294, 297, 334, 348, 361, 372, 387, 46:9, 12, 16, 25–32, 39, 49–51, 63f, 69, 76, 81–84, 95, 97, 99, 101f, 145f, 149–151, 165f, 169, 173, 175–177, 183f, 195f, 199f, 213, 216f, 219, 220n, 224, 228, 232, 235, 242, 248, 265, 304, 47:25, 35, 40–45, 47–53, 72n, 88, 102, 104, 110–113, 116–119, 124, 134, 137, 140, 144, 175, 190–192, 216, 224, 230, 232f, 235, 238, 254–268, 273–278, 280f, 291, 292n, 299, 302, 305f, 50:19f, 53, 302, 52:3f, 7f, 10, 16f, 22–24, 27, 33f, 38f, 45f, 52f, 55f, 61, 65f, 68f, 72f, 74f, 81, 83, 88, 92f, 96, 98, 100f, 103f, 106f, 112f, 117f, 126f, 141–143, 145, 148, 152, 156, 159, 169f, 173, 175f, 187f, 191, 194, 198, 203, 205, 207, 209, 215, 237, 241, 245, 248f, 253–256, 270, 274f, 278, 280f, 283, 54:35f, 42, 45, 79, 84, 92, 111, 143, 146, 154, 371, 378f, 469–471, see also **Messiah, The; Son of God**

Abraham's child 13:20, 230f, 305
Advocate 22:75, 30:236f
Alone infallible 22:259
Alone to be trusted 32:235f, 239–241
And Aaron 39:80–83, 178
And Adam 39:64, 79
As brood hen see **Hen and chicks**
As Fish-hook 22:24
As preacher 13:270, 22:332, 23:289, 299
As the Vine 37:xii, 38, 170, 174, 252f, 262
Assumed human nature 22:37, 75, 103, 111, 113, 153, 492
At God's right hand 10:444f, 11:361, 22:416, 38:19, 43f, 66, 68, 81, 86, 163
Atonement by His blood 9:215, 11:306n, 12:360, 399, 38:100, 125, 158, 184–187, 204
Author of resurrection 7:117
Bait for Satan 5:150
Basic Christian beliefs about 8:188, 250, 263, 283, 314, 37:xvii, 49, 56, 61f, 103, 131, 137, 150, 229–231, 346
Bears our sins 32:200, 206, 42:11f, 108, 122
Bishop and pastor at Capernaum 23:104, 156
Bishop of our souls 7:99f, 8:268
Blasphemed 47:216, 268, 273f, 290
Born a Jew 45:xv, 198–213, 215–217
Breachmaker 18:229
Bridegroom 1:233
Broke down dividing wall 16:123, 230
Called a liar 35:89, 145
Called the Branch, Sprout or Bud 20:29f, 40, 215, 217, 258
Called the Stone 20:40, 50f, 150, 218
Causes offence 37:71, 202, 245, 248f, 286f
Clarifies the Law 17:81, 331
Close student of Zechariah 20:102, 150
Conquers death by dying 4:191, 13:255, 263
Content of the Gospel 25:xi, 4, 7, 131, 146, 148, 326
Cornerstone 16:100, 162, 230, 292, 21:282
Creator 14:186, 26:13, 22, 31f, 66, 107, 128, 259, 292, 297, 314, 392, 431, 41:109f, 112, 116
David's heir 13:233, 264
Defends His own 16:51, 101, 212, 234
Definition of 17:329f
Deliverer 1:68, 181, 350
Denied 35:145, 331
Desire of the nations 20:50, 71, 81
Equal to God 13:3, 6, 26, 29, 37, 234f, 22:26, 240, 23:54f, 34:222, 38:224, 253–256, 267, 275, 308n
Example and Gift 17:195
Example or model 12:76, 22:117, 27:34, 51:12, 198f
Faith in Him 39:149, 155, 41:69, 88, 310, 315, 328, 332
Faithful physician 21:231f
Firstfruits 28:100, 109–111, 122f

Foreseen in Nahum 18:295f
Forsaken by God 12:124–128, 131
Foundation 16:100, 232
Fountain of life 23:55, 278
Fulfills the Law 41:64, 66f, 114
Fulfulls promises 2:209, 219, 229, 231, 234, 236, 257, 398
Galilean 23:303–305
Glory of His tomb 25:517
God and man 3:219, 298, 12:49, 55, 84, 100, 130, 206, 231, 289, 13:20, 29, 228, 231, 234, 241, 243f, 323, 345, 16:76, 96, 17:211, 386, 18:229, 241, 248, 20:29, 195, 197, 328, 28:253f, 265f, 29:15, 66, 72, 82f, 85, 110f, 115, 133f, 136, 174, 188, 37:xv–xix, 62–64, 121, 153, 155f, 158, 166, 209–214, 218–224, 228–235, 274, 280, 292, 297–300, 316–362, 365f, 38:x, xix, 15, 29, 45–47, 50, 58, 60f, 73, 85, 103, 168, 180, 184, 198, 224, 240f, 251, 253f, 255n, 254, 256–258, 262n, 263, 266, 274f, 307n, 308n, 309n
God's annointed 13:29, 231
God's gift to us 27:34f
God's grace and mercy 14:204
God's Servant 20:40, 51, 215, 217
God's true temple 22:249
God's Word 10:228, 230, 16:31
Good Samaritan 25:260, 340, 433, 507
Great Physician 1:144, 12:76, 405, 409
Guardian of the oppressed 6:85f, 113, 126, 311
Hated by the Jews 6:326, 373
Head of His church 17:86f, 233, 29:15, 23, 117f, 136, 170, 178, 220
Heaven His home 22:321f, 324, 326f, 329, 332
His accidental function 26:373
His advent 11:75, 252, 288, 296, 396–398, 448, 456, 468, 493, 531, 551
His advent calls for faith 19:194, 208, 237
His alien work 51:62, 62f
His Ascension 10:120, 13:3f, 20, 228, 234, 320, 22:209, 318, 334, 23:162, 24:178, 13, 336, 346–348, 366, 376, 395f, 25:147, 406, 34:210, 37:xii, xix, 6, 46, 66f, 144, 155, 191, 203f, 246f, 362, 38:155, 299f
His attributes 24:105
His authority 3:114, 13:235, 239
His baptism 3:87, 193, 22:160f, 172f, 189, 201, 217–219, 41:151, 195, 199, 45:224, 226n, 51:315–319
His beauty 11:318, 387, 12:206f
His benefits 42:110f, 164f
His Betrayal 52:244
His birth and incarnation 2:261, 3:136, 5:42,78, 216f, 219–221, 223, 229, 234, 6:72f, 274, 7:x, 12f, 31, 46, 200, 296, 8:134, 9:171, 10:120, 130, 219, 297, 324, 409, 11:152, 164f, 179, 195, 206, 252, 288, 296, 314, 460, 468, 533, 548, 12:20, 37, 47, 53, 69, 84, 99, 101, 110, 123, 133, 13:132, 134, 137, 228, 234, 236f, 243, 290, 323, 16:5, 9, 38, 19:136, 21:350, 352f, 22:6, 24, 37, 73f, 103, 105f, 109–111, 113, 115f, 156, 203, 334, 352, 449, 492f, 503, 23:55, 83, 102f, 120, 148, 161f, 24:139, 25:4, 131, 146f, 26:29, 265, 269, 272, 27:268, 288, 29:5, 79, 113, 115, 190f, 195, 201, 208, 221, 30:257, 285, 294, 302, 33:47, 36:38, 219, 37:62f, 66f, 72, 76f, 85, 89, 92, 94, 98–100, 130, 172, 180, 281, 361, 38:xixf, 85, 239f, 242, 245, 254, 262–264, 266f, 270, 274f, 287n, 307, 41:15, 21, 52, 57f, 64, 68, 71, 74, 80f, 87, 95–99, 101, 104f, 100f, 117, 119, 42:21, 108, 110, 135, 45:57, 46:36, 135, 196, 199, 287, 52:8, 10–12, 18, 30f, 152, 157, 159, 163, 170, 183f, 188, 193f, 201f, 206, 208
His blood 20:96–100, 29:18, 44, 139, 169, 186, 209–211, 224, 234, 35:59, 85f, 37:43, 126, 135n, 142n, 143, 311, 315f, 319–331, 333–337, 362, 41:111, 127, 140, 204f, 209, 240, 255f, 307, 327, 332, 340, 355f, 370, 42:143, 162, 173–175, 46:12, 135, 219, 220n, 228f, 237, 256, 52:280, 282
His body 35:xiii, 51, 59, 61, 62f, 85f, 42:100, 111, 173–175, see also **Body and Blood of Christ**
His bosom 4:312–313, 316, 7:294, 296
His brothers 22:214, 23:208f, 213f, 244
His centrality 44:253f
His childhood 22:73, 46:135n, 287, 52:106, 145f
His church 2:230, 248, 256
His coming foretold 18:31f, 67, 79, 105, 116f, 121, 238, 247. 319, 409–412, 417–419
His coming reign 16:3f, 46, 280
His commands 36:14–16, 27, 169, 183, 36:87, 208f, 41:194, 196, 202, 321, 350, 366, 42:9, 41, 105, 122, 171, 45:82f, 281, 283–285, 287n, 290, 294, 305, 387, 389, 51:104–110
His cross 1:195, 260, 3:359, 4:192, 5:45, 185, 202, 220, 315, 347, 11:101f, 141f, 150, 249, 256f, 522, 13:319, 333, 344, 14:305, 309, 21:327, 25:149, 288–291, 28:230, 29:146, 31:53, 85, 90, 35:63,

230, 266, 378, 380f, 37:xviiif, 32, 35, 53, 61, 72, 83, 85, 102, 113, 123f, 129n, 131n, 136, 177, 179, 191–193, 265f, 275, 328, 330, 333, 361n, 38:xi, 19, 66, 95, 118, 187, 47:52, 112n, 48:61n, 255, 307, 387, 49:73, 249, 263, 329, 355, 51:31, 198, 208
His crucifixion 7:91, 11:102, 16:43f, 190, 337, 20:140, 328f, 23:135, 176, 206n, 254, 378, 384, 24:35, 86, 402, 26:165, 41:11f, 101f, 112–114, 116, 122, 127, 153, 232, 246, 256, 356, 42:6, 11f, 15, 65, 104–107, 108n, 109, 129, 137, 140f, 143–145, 149f, 163
His death 2:153, 215, 269, 370, 3:141, 124, 214, 9:97, 141, 197, 10:71f, 355, 364, 14:21, 321, 23:144, 161, 182, 325, 328, 330, 332, 352, 357, 360, 374f, 24:15, 34f, 40, 42, 85f, 110, 135, 140, 179, 191, 195, 211, 222, 246, 258, 260f, 271, 289, 292, 296, 309, 319, 326f, 334, 343, 348f, 375, f, 379, 381, 402, 26:140, 183–185, 224, 292, 295, 301, 303, 357, 369, 385, 398, 453, 460, 35:xi, 196f, 305, 317, 374, 52:156, 279f
His death and resurrection 25:15, 45, 50–52, 70, 89f, 146f, 284, 406, 517, 25:45, 27:10, 15, 19, 26, 49f, 76, 82f, 167f, 194, 264f, 401n, 45:217, 219, 227
His decoration 12:129
His descent into hell 2:85n, 86, 4:357, 6:379, 10:115, 363, 22:218f, 317, 325f, 328, 24:346, 25:406, 30:113n, 116, 43:27
His divine nature 4:171, 6:185, 258, 22:10f, 14, 18, 28, 37, 57, 114f, 129, 171, 185, 200, 317, 323, 325, 364, 391, 488, 493, 507, 30:221f, 223, 252, 258, 286, 319, 37:xviii–xx, 49, 61–64, 67, 85n, 120f, 129, 131, 35, 155, 209–214, 218–222, 227, 229, 238, 280f, 362, 52:41, 44, 53f, 61, 65, 69, 86f, 94, 170, 188, 278, 280
His divine-human nature 5:219, 222, 10:60f, 30:223, 36:35, 342, 41:52, 55–59, 61, 81–83, 86, 95–97, 100n, 102–112, 116–119, 121, 186, 339
His divinity hidden in humanity 10:445
His dominion 12:134
His earthly biography 22:214–217
His enemies 13:262, 284, 335, 28:128f, 131, 135–137, 46:30, 165, 176f, 180n
His exaltation 10:84, 12:129, 131
His example 35:56, 119f, 36:21, 51–52, 90, 166, 168, 171f
His face 11:295, 299
His flesh and blood 23:8, 14–19, 21, 45–47, 50, 107, 118, 120–125, 128–130, 132–138, 140–143, 147, 149, 151, 160, 163, 166, 168, 170f, 177f, 184f, 201, 234, 375, 36:275, 278, 321, 331, 336f, 38:15, 20–22, 30, 39–44, 46, 50n, 59, 72n, 76, 81, 129, 207, 277
His genealogy 1:333, 338, 5:216, 7:6, 10, 8:136, 42:14, 108–110
His gifts 36:180, 351
His glory and rule 16:37f, 24:189, 25:5, 147f, 37:22, 23n, 29, 46, 64, 70–73, 83, 131, 158, 346
His Gospel 46:30, 36, 175, 48:12, 14, 35, 62, 66, 153, 189, 286, 328, 335f, 367, 390
His grace 8:177, 37:73, 162, 363f, 371, 41:70–72, 75, 77, 113f, 123, 138f, 147, 42:40, 110, 152, 52:71, 279f
His hidden glory 25:243
His holiness 23:154
His human form 38:26, 31f, 59f, 65f
His human nature 37:xviiif, 49, 61–64, 81n, 85n, 120, 140, 158, 209–214, 229f, 280, 292, 287, 330, 362, 52:12, 55f, 61, 83, 86, 94, 147, 278, 280, 282
His humanity 23:77, 101f, 104, 124, 148f, 162, 195, 376, 26:28, 30, 39, 27:171, 289, 387, 29:82f, 111, 30:122, 210, 221, 252, 258, 30:222f, 252, 258, 34:209
His humiliation 5:219, 10:260
His humility 10:328, 12:55, 123
His image 29:138, 216
His incarnation and birth see **Christ—His birth and incarnation**
His indwelling 16:31–53, 37:120f, 132, 235
His innocence 22:139
His kingship and kingdom 27:30, 86, 94, 114, 30:3, 231, 33:287f, 36:89, 342, 42:135, 45:93, 101, 118, 206, 215–218, 221, 46:27f, 30, 39, 81, 97, 166, 175, 177, 195, 204, 219, 237, 47:53, 72n, 292
His law 25:187, 248, 511, 36:138, 199–204
His life on earth 37:61, 72, 82f, 89–91, 133, 315
His love 38:102f, 41:44, 127, 331, 351–353, 42:13, 108f, 122, 135, 143
His manger see **Manger of Christ**
His merits 30:252f, 255, 309, 322, 31:190, 212–228, 282
His ministry 22:77, 201, 218, 475
His names 6:141, 274, 11:110, 141, 149, 169f, 225, 534, 17:5, 65, 68, 90, 99, 135, 170f, 236f, 330, 36:211, 214,

37:xviif, 52, 70, 74, 88, 90f, 100, 124, 130, 139, 142, 164, 210, 274, 281, 293, 338, 359–362, 363f, 367, 370, 41:11, 73, 79, 137, 213, 277, 295, 318, 320, 330, 339, 358, 46:29, 32, 48, 165
His nature 30:221f, 275
His offices 2:388, 12:41, 63, 232, 17:63f, 170, 173, 178, 216, 331, 18:248f, 23:196, 226f, 279, 332, 335, 337–340, 343f, 368f, 375, 377, 30:76, 113, 38:117, 194, 200f, 204, 212, 214
His omnipresence 9:168, 36:16, 342f, 37:6, 56–66, 94, 155f, 207, 214, 222, 227–235, 38:45, 40:220, 54:92
His omniscience 22:185
His path or way 11:26, 28, 32–35
His patience 17:226, 232
His person 22:104, 121, 128, 247, 321, 346, 24:23, 60, 71, 98f
His power 13:233, 239, 283, 22:75, 503, 509, 38:24, 45, 86, 129, 194, 197f, 42:110n, 152, 170
His priesthood 2:381, 388, 4:151, 5:140, 142, 11:368, 13:228, 290, 304–310, 314, 319–321, 323, 328, 14:325, 20:38f, 41f, 49f, 69, 71f, 215–217, 253, 256, 26:428, 29:167f, 171, 205, 226, 31:278f, 353f, 368, 31:279f, 353–355, 388, 35:247, 395, 36:131, 137–155, 199–204, 217–221, 38:222, 224f, 231, 248, 250, 255n, 258–261, 267, 269, 273, 276f, 290, 293n, 299, 307, 308n, 312, 315f, 52:279f, 286
His priesthood prophesied 20:38f, 69, 71f, 215–217, 253, 256
His promises 37:xii, xix, 94
His redemption 37:140, 143f, 191, 194, 231, 266f, 362
His reign 16:27, 39, 101, 125, 186, 212, 222, 273, 281
His resurrection 1:110, 2:151, 3:33, 3:83, 8:54, 162, 254, 313, 316, 318, 324, 10:71, 11:4, 87, 107, 13:240, 290, 13:3, 8, 228, 236, 14:21, 83n, 96, 18:31, 355, 22:41f, 116, 118, 139, 171, 243, 321, 339, 23:162, 206n, 280, 328, 330, 384, 24:34f, 40, 85, 110, 135, 140, 142, 174, 193, 246, 296, 334, 346–348, 375f, 396, 402, 404f, 408, 25:147f, 26:21, 157, 159, 183, 185, 224, 303, 357, 369, 385, 29:47, 137, 195, 30:9f, 12, 38, 113, 34:210, 35:196f, 374, 36:68, 37:56n, 92, 144, 192, 218, 222, 283, 305, 315, 362, 38:16, 26, 29, 41, 44, 254, 41:64f, 127, 140, 241, 42:12f, 105, 143, 149, 163, 165
His righteousness 1:219, 16:29, 123, 190, 17:6, 28, 42, 48, 68, 22:59, 123, 131, 138f, 273, 25:3, 9, 30, 43, 48, 87, 137, 188, 27:51, 251, 317, 29:41f, 44, 49, 31:64, 190, 297–299
His rule 14:328, 332, 334, 340, 20:177, 323, 338, 28:60, 128f, 133
His sacrifice 2:163, 387, 37:142–144, 262, 328, 357
His sayings 46:69n, 130, 136, 145f, 153, 164, 179, 202, 222, 224, 233, 265
His scepter 13:265, 267, 277
His second Advent see **Advent, Second**
His self-sacrifice 36:147, 182, 201, 313, 321
His signs 23:10
His sinlessness 38:66, 76, 157, 225, 260
His Spirit 1:145, 338, 13:33f, 284, 35:122, 285
His subjects 13:33f, 284
His suffering and death 1:110, 179f, 248, 4:191, 200, 243, 6:103, 153, 351, 378f, 301, 8:53, 247n, 257, 11:139n, 152, 187n, 15:258, 17:194, 19:133, 135, 183, 20:41, 75, 219, 290, 22:238, 387, 23:144n, 360, 24:7, 9, 30, 34f, 40, 85, 167, 174, 183, 193, 199, 211, 222, 258, 260, 271, 282, 292, 296, 299, 326, 343, 347f, 379, 395f, 402, 412, 460, 25:382, 389f, 439, 26:62, 140, 146, 154, 270, 385, 27:82, 134, 168, 212, 238, 401n, 29:47, 66, 123, 127, 130, 165, 174, 195, 203, 210, 219f, 225, 35:60, 275, 331, 381, 391, 396, 36:38–40, 94, 124, 143, 147, 173, 178f, 183, 198, 203f, 215, 291, 320, 328, 336, 348f, 351, 37:xiii, 68n, 83–85, 92, 125f, 130, 191–194, 210, 233, 262, 266, 305, 328–331, 342, 347, 362, 366, 38:xi, 19, 23, 47, 51n, 55, 66, 86, 95, 105f, 110–112, 115–118, 121, 124–126, 128, 137, 150f, 156, 187–189, 254–274, 41:127, 347f, 358, 46:30, 134, 142, 177, 219f, 228f, 237, 255, 47:110, 112f, 230, 51:197, 234–236, 316, 52:189, 280, 282
His suffering, death, and resurrection 1:110, 17:215, 226–228, 331, 354
His sufferings 5:177, 235, 12:124f, 128, 13:345f, 375, 14:72, 80, 96, 168, 272, 320f, 329, 347, 17:100, 219–222, 231, 242, 22:139, 163, 171, 240, 253, 269, 291, 351, 360, 369, 386, 23:144, 173, 182, 30:23f, 110f, 117, 119, 127, 34:56, 85, 42:5–14, 65, 120, 141, 141, 144
His teachings 2:86, 41:40, 196, 45:71, 82n, 88, 90, 101, 256f, 259, 280–295, 46:37f, 51, 67f, 111, 114, 197

His temptations 9:250n
His titles 38:xi, 81, 86, 209, 228, 290
His twofold nature 11:180n, 376
His ubiquity see **Christ—His omnipresence**
His weakness 17:75
His will 37:69, 131f, 218, 42:45f
His wisdom 26:21, 352, 42:50f, 58f, 164
His Word 29:148, 47:53, 253f
His words 16:75, 167, 35:12f, 82, 88f, 132, 134, 146, 36:45, 57, 88, 133f, 150, 165, 168, 173, 210, 266, 38:xiii, xix, 19f, 24f, 26n, 39, 41, 44, 48f, 51, 55f, 71, 83, 86, 124f, 151, 156, 176, 180, 182f, 191, 200–202, 208, 225, 292, 305, 316, 45:88, 92, 94, 96, 101–103, 284, 286, 291, 46:9, 26, 63, 69, 164, 175, 275, 286, see also **Lord's Supper; Words of Institution**
His work 23:411, 38:117, 128–131, 158, 175, 178f, 181, 183f, 187, 189f, 199, 207, 211, 250
His works 24:75, 77, 99, 106, 115, 29:67, 93, 123, 37:26, 71, 74, 210, 213f, 45:60, 67, 69f, 54:36
History proves His victory 13:256, 342f
Identical with Jesus 19:55
Image of God 29:111f, 34:221f
In the Psalms 11:38, 187n, 189n, 400
Incarnate Son of God 25:5
Incarnate Word 37:xvi, xix, 7, 31, 62f, 133, 140, 157, 206, 361f
Intercessor 13:320
Interpreter of the Law 26:373
Jews his relatives 47:124, 305
Judge 12:156, 13:72, 326, 341f
Key to Scripture interpretation 10:xif, 3, 6f, 52
Key to the Scriptures 25:4, 15:268, 339
King and Lord 6:29, 49, 73, 101, 249, 12:35–37, 47, 58, 13:26, 228, 233, 264f, 269, 273, 365, 16:29, 102, 198, 20:3, 24, 50, 69, 71f, 82, 94–96, 150, 203, 249, 251, 253–255, 287–289, 334, 338, 340, 29:80, 118, 123, 144, 196, 203, 35:230, 287, 386, 52:187f, 210, 278, 280f, 283, 287
King of grace 27:16
King of righteousness 11:368, 393, 544
King of the ages 28:249
Lamb of God see **Lamb of God**
Light of the world 23:283, 319–321, 323–325, 327f, 330–332, 337f, 341, 353, 52:53, 61f, 80
Light to the nations 17:62f, 65, 69, 78, 175, 325
Location of his body 38:31–34, 45, 52, 59f, 66–68, 71, 76, 81f, 85
Lord of all 13:6, 13, 243
Lord of hosts 16:36f, 192
Lord of Scripture 10:xii, 3, 35:123, 287
Lord over death and grave 23:22, 130, 295, 24:138, 28:72, 74, 105, 109, 113, 204f, 211
Love for 39:97–99
Made wonderful 10:60–63, 75
Man for all seasons 14:301
Master and Teacher 23:10, 79, 36:146, 248
Mediator 1:181, 2:215, 3:26, 332, 5:21, 6:230, 7:368, 371, 8:175, 177, 268, 12:56, 67, 75, 13:320, 23:58, 60, 68, 195, 24:153, 25:43f, 25:6, 43, 45, 77, 286, 26:11, 28–30, 37–39, 131, 133, 137, 139, 141, 178, 195, 200, 232, 235f, 270, 289, 319–322, 325f, 329, 387, 27:11, 86, 268, 271f, 275, 28:263f, 266, 34:119, 35:371, 36:139, 313, 317, 320, 47:295, 51:277, 281–284
Messiah see **Messiah, The**
Minister of the circumcision 11:38, 102, 147
Noblest Jew 35:288, 296
Ordered to preach the Word 20:118, 120, 314
Our abstraction; we His concretion 11:318
Our brother 13:236, 244, 22:24, 22:24, 88, 377
Our Comforter 27:11f, 34
Our Head 14:39, 28:100, 110, 113, 120, 122f
Our leader and guide 22:305
Our Redemption 18:123
Our Righteousness 6:185, 248f, 17:6, 28, 42, 48, 68
Our Shepherd 6:9, 12:148, 152, 154–179, 212, 317, 20:122, 302, 314f, 335
Our Sun 11:101, 110, 225, 339
Papal teaching 47:48, 50, 52
Physician 23:154f
Pictures of see **Pictures of Christ**
Post-resurrection appearances 9:250n
Power hidden in weakness 17:15, 201
Prefigured 7:224
Prefigured by Joseph 6:153, 342, 379, 385–387, 392
Preserver and Protector—16:57, 122, 129
Price of His betrayal 6:391, 405
Prince of life 1:348
Promises about Him 1:78, 181, 183, 246, 325, 2:209, 219, 229, 231, 234, 236,

257, 398, 12:295, 352, 25:146, 35:22, 84, 168, 248, 254, 295, 314, 320, 327, 329
Prophet promised by Moses 9:176, 180
Prophets point to Him 19:152, 155, 189, 190, 193
Propitiator 16:231, 318, 27:11, 64, 68, 74–76, 86
Pure and holy person 7:280
Purifier 18:410f
Ransom 13:319f, 34:116
Redeemer 1:39, 166, 192, 331, 3:69, 8:10, 163, 17:5, 116f, 170, 17:5, 117, 132, 147, 166, 170, 172, 176, 240f, 306–308, 322, 21:350, 24:281, 26:37, 137, 143, 239, 288, 353, 372, 27:256, 259, 409, 34:89, 91, 35:xi, 360
Relation to the Law of Moses 21:67, 70, 72, 35:119, 123, 360
Rock 36:95, 280–282, 37:xii, 36–38, 164n, 170, 173f, 176, 253, 275, 39:78, 93, 41:12, 30, 214, 217, 309–311, 314–316, 319, 326–328, 331f, 335, 346, 352, 356f, 371
Rock of Israel 16:157, 232
Root of Jesse 25:121, 516f
Sacrifice to God 35:99, 102, 247
Salvation in Him alone 44:xii
Savior 1:229, 302, 328, 2:114, 248, 3:82, 91, 117, 122, 162, 167, 359, 4:149, 230f, 310, 312, 356, 404n, 5:17, 46, 48f, 217, 228, 248, 258, 350f, 7:12, 17, 31, 68, 298, 302, 329, 368, 8:7–10, 15, 30, 33, 60, 176, 188, 217, 253, 256, 269, 283, 294, 325, 330, 14:101, 348, 16:3, 129, 248, 17:94, 132, 134f, 170, 219, 222f, 259, 322, 340, 351, 353, 356, 397, 22:24, 24:7, 16, 25, 29, 32, 34, 42, 44, 64, 87, 91, 98, 108, 141, 143f, 147, 151, 157, 185, 215, 267, 269, 272, 274, 280f, 287, 292, 296, 310, 325, 343f, 379–381, 396, 407, 422, 26:11, 37f, 87f, 131f, 137, 141, 147, 150, 154, 173, 178, 195, 200, 247, 249, 322, 334, 347f, 355, 381, 420, 427, 453, 27:12, 27, 34f, 54, 93, 133, 142, 144, 257, 30:3, 21, 29, 39, 152, 170, 190, 237, 290f, 306, 34:164, 167, 35:59, 276, 358f, 36:216f, 38:51n, 116, 126, 128, 130, 136f, 150, 171, 178f, 287, 291, 311, 41:302, 308, 356, 41:302, 308, 358, 46:176f, 255
Seated at the Father's (God's) right hand 36:341f, 37:xviii, 11, 46–49, 55, 63–66, 69f, 73n, 77, 101f, 112, 136f, 140, 144f, 155, 178f, 198, 207, 235, 362
Servant 17:60, 93, 172, 215f, 330
Sinless 9:215n, 22:73
Sold for 30 pieces of silver 20:121, 125, 127, 318f
Son of David 25:146f
Son of God see **Son of God**
Son of Man 1:229, 336, 2:21, 84, 5:7, 217f, 228, 23:8, 11, 13–18, 40, 127, 129f, 133f, 137, 160–162, 169, 248, 374, 381, 24:93, 105f, 25:147, 26:451, 27:12, 389, 29:110, 225, 237, 30:193, 37:64, 66f, 231n, 232, 280, 41:66f, 118f, 311, 42:23, 46
Stone of stumbling 16:229f
Sun of Righteousness 14:99
Teacher 12:50, 68f
Teacher of righteousness 11:147–149
The Holy One 16:10, 322
The Image of God 34:220
The Living Stone 30:51, 53, 57, 59–63, 85, 105f, 301
The Lord 37:25, 62, 90, 98, 122f, 142, 362, 38:24, 40, 42, 115f, 125, 131f, 137, 165, 187, 198, 203, 206, 213, 221, 223f, 227f, 287, 291, 293n, 296, 303, 305, 311, 319, 41:66f, 89, 105, 119, 127, 156, 46:12, 65f, 78f, 148n, 151f, 153, 174, 191, 236, 253, 256, 258
The sole satisfaction 40:297
The Truth 11:110, 165, 170, 224
The Word 15:276, 299f, 312f, 317, 341, 37:120, 133, 206, 247
To be magnified 11:316, 326, 341
Tricked Satan 22:24, 255
True bread 42:56–59, 61
True "Miktam" 10:259, 262, 265
True God 11:107n, 119, 252n, 256, 314, 376, 415, 548, 15:287f, 299f, 312, 23:54, 77, 82f, 101f, 104f, 123, 148–150, 184, 367, 376f
True God and true man 8:140, 308, 22:25, 321, 324, 329, 362, 26:267, 272f
True man 10:11, 261, 11:6, 107, 110f, 179, 252n, 256, 277, 314, 317f, 367, 376, 412, 548, 551, 15:277, 286f, 291, 294, 305f, 330, 20:19, 26, 49, 254, 22:37, 75, 203, 111, 113, 153, 492, 23:16, 77, 38:xi, 20, 31, 38–48, 50, 59–61, 64f, 75–78, 150, 246, 254–256, 266f, 271, 274f
True pastor 22:215
True Sun 23:280, 324
Two natures 15:xii, 292f, 325, 339f, 25:147, 30:30, 57, 221f, 258, 302, 35:249, 368, 38:xii, 16, 23, 29f, 36, 46, 50n, 54, 56, 58, 73, 82, 86, 191, 247n, 254, 256, 263, 271, 274f, 287n, 307n

Unity of His person 12:131, 231
Universal Lord 12:135, 169
Victor 8:164, 12:15, 20, 127, 228, 231, 13:21, 239, 244f, 16:88, 100f, 129, 249, 305, 337, 28:202f, 210–212, 32:203, 268
Victor over sin and death 25:78, 26:22, 26f, 41, 134, 160, 224, 267, 281–283, 290, 356, 370f, 372, 27:10, 82f, 28:108f, 133f, 136f, 206f, 29:11, 123, 135, 189, 30:13, 251
Victor over sin, death, and the devil 35:358
Walks on the sea 6:151
Wrestler 6:125, 130, 138, 144, 185

Christ Child—14:114

Christ and Satan—33:282, 287–291

Christ and the church—see **Bride and bridegroom**

Christendom—13:13, 72, 241, 245f, 251, 259, 263, 266, 279, 297, 324, 340, 370, 379, 382f, 14:21, 37, 55f, 60, 64, 69f, 90, 92f, 95f, 174, 184f, 187, 202, 264, 21:57, 140, 154f, 211f, 215f, 222, 248–250, 313, 22:25f, 51, 58, 65–67, 77, 82–84, 113, 136f, 186, 204, 207, 254, 304, 360, 512f, 23:97, 107, 135, 162, 188, 192, 225, 284, 334, 418, 24:7f, 66–70, 77–79, 85, 87, 91, 101, 103, 110, 116, 118, 125, 127, 131, 134, 144, 150, 159, 161, 168, 171, 173, 176, 180, 191, 201, 204, 206–208, 210, 214–216, 221, 234–236, 244, 246, 248–250, 264, 266, 277, 283, 293f, 309, 24:313, 320, 326, 329, 339, 353, 358, 360f, 365–367, 369, 371, 383, 405, 408, 30:3, 49, 55, 126, 134, 138, 156, 158, 160, 167, 170, 182, 188–190, 209, 34:75, 79, 35:54, 71f, 128, 150f, 181, 200f, 257, 286, 289, 293, 351, 363, 388, 392, 399f, 404f, 36:208, 314f, 353, 38:ix, xvi, 27, 34, 63, 88, 119, 124, 148, 159f, 175, 187, 189, 192, 197, 310, 317n, 318, 39:55f, 57n, 58–104, 158, 171, 195, 202, 219, 252, 308, 314, 41:9f, 24f, 27f, 46, 97, 118, 138, 144f, 175, 195–197, 210, 220, 261, 266, 268, 271, 277f, 280, 285, 289–291, 300f, 303f, 306, 308f, 311, 313–315, 317, 326–328, 331f, 335, 339, 343f, 346, 352, 357f, 363–366, 42:47, 55f, 59f, 67, 79, 111, 172, 46:xiii, 158, 171, 175n, 181, 185, 187f, 192, 316f, 47:14, 39, 48, 110, 112, 128, 264, 268, 273

Christening robe(s)—41:17, 175, 211, 53:100f, 109

Christian—26:5f, 10f, 23, 26, 35, 45, 81, 97, 100, 120, 124, 130, 133f, 139, 157, 159, 163, 170–172, 178, 188, 200, 214, 217, 232f, 235, 241, 248, 256, 277, 290n, 294, 326, 334, 340–344, 356, 373, 376, 380, 391f, 394, 424, 440, 445, 447f, 451
called "Sir Christian" 46:170, 184, 192, 199

Christian II, King of Denmark—40:75, 46:106n, 107n, 113n, 115, 49:116, 143f, 157, 54:285

Christian III, King of Denmark—22:ix, 43:245, 50:147n, 250f, 54:271

Christian, Being a—51:111–117, 164f, 274

Christian Association of Peasants—see **Peasants, Christian Association of**

Christian doctrine—46:164, 170, 177

Christian duties—26:217

Christian life—4:5, 11, 22, 101, 182, 234, 277, 311, 6:147, 252, 256, 402, 9:ix, 5n, 180n, 185, 12:329, 329, 17:66, 81 224, 387f, 409, 18:354, 20:41, 47, 95, 111, 140, 278, 21:25, 34f, 37–39, 45, 67, 72, 90f, 110f, 119–121, 127f, 143–146, 149f, 153, 162–164, 173–175, 189, 193f, 196–198, 211f, 235–237, 241–243, 274, 281, 22:94, 275, 290, 302, 306, 312, 336, 23: 20, 58, 64, 68, 76, 86, 109, 134, 141, 204, 234, 262, 360, 363, 24:42, 64, 80, 167, 196, 228, 231, 234, 238, 240, 242f, 254–256, 310, 340, 361, 377, 382, 25:105, 150, 153, 262f, 268, 278, 319f, 339, 341, 383, 388, 433f, 415, 499, 28:39, 103–105, 107, 236, 294, 29:6, 57f, 61, 71, 130, 216, 224, 226, 233, 238, 29:6, 58, 71, 238, 30:17, 32, 34f, 43, 47, 71, 90, 92f, 99, 156f, 160, 165, 176, 182, 192, 197, 212, 214f, 256, 36:77, 38:44, 55, 95, 169, 173, 184, 196, 41:124–126, 238, 256, 45:35f, 68, 87, 90, 229, 46:7–10, 12f, 17, 27f, 30–33, 36–43, 52, 61, 70, 76, 78, 83, 95f, 98, 107, 122, 132f, 135, 159, 164f, 168, 170, 177, 181f, 184, 188, 192, 199, 203, 214f, 236, 257, 271, 283, 293, 50:24f, 63, 52:38, 40, 122, 242, 276, 286, see also **Process, Christian life as**

Christian name—46:28, 30–33, 36, 40–43, 130

Christian or catholic—34:229

Christian Summa—33:35f

Christianity—2:269, 8:134, 261, 9:215, 14:22, 24, 16:31, 78, 18:401, 22:81, 86, 191, 291, 23:181, 321, 412, 24:78, 131, 145, 159, 201, 227, 251, 368, 378, 26:26, 85, 91, 106, 114, 118, 126, 131,

136, 139, 189, 283, 301, 27:31, 186, 354, 29:10, 30:210, 238, 258, 269, 274, 307, 38:112, 124, 176, 183, 39:54, 69, 133, 45:98, 102, 133, 200, 239

Christianity, Description of—33:29–44

Christianity, Erasmus' description of—33:30n

Christianity, Primitive—9:6n

Christians—1:30, 166, 190, 2:60, 125, 155, 213, 263, 302, 310, 326f, 352–354, 3:38, 51, 59n, 78, 92, 110, 132f, 155, 160, 165, 168, 180, 189, 223, 240, 265, 299, 328f, 344, 364, 4:25, 28f, 41, 88, 103f, 108, 116, 118, 120, 131, 136, 165, 175, 198, 204f, 208, 242f, 266, 296, 305, 317, 356, 373, 385, 396, 403, 407, 5:18, 21f, 26, 33, 46, 48, 52, 63, 69, 71f, 77, 95, 128, 146, 185, 189f, 195, 202–204, 206, 208, 235, 240, 257, 263, 269–271, 274, 277f, 353, 359, 6:18, 142, 181, 258, 7:62, 73, 80, 88, 95, 155, 164, 175, 177, 203, 237, 255, 285, 316, 337, 344, 346, 355, 8:5, 8, 10, 21, 29, 32, 39, 50, 101, 134, 168, 182, 187, 229, 236, 251f, 262, 264f, 287, 9:6, 24, 26, 79f, 144f, 147, 167, 180n, 183, 186, 215, 225, 250, 13:20–22, 26, 36f, 112, 123, 240, 259f, 262, 275, 279f, 283, 287, 333, 403, 14:26, 59f, 71, 76, 79f, 87, 92–95, 98, 106, 111, 130, 132, 134, 141, 146, 158, 185, 202, 225, 231, 241, 243, 247f, 253, 257f, 262, 270, 274, 282, 301, 317, 321, 328, 333f, 339, 341, 16:32, 36, 52, 76, 166, 207–209, 213f, 232, 241, 343, 17:13, 43, 66f, 90, 110, 139, 115, 156, 214, 224, 239, 315, 334, 336, 345, 357f, 406, 18:118, 202, 296, 19:61f, 153, 178, 20:26, 32, 39, 96, 98, 102, 112, 115, 133, 146f, 155–157, 184, 187, 200–202, 216, 218f, 250, 270, 284, 327, 333f, 344, 346, 21:18, 21, 34f, 45f, 49f, 53f, 66, 99–101, 106–108, 110f, 115–117, 119f, 123f, 129, 136, 139f, 143f, 149f, 153, 155, 159, 170, 174, 179, 189, 195–202, 228–230, 234–237, 241–244, 247–249, 253, 267, 271, 285–287, 304, 353–355, 22:41, 60, 74f, 80–84, 86, 90, 94, 102, 106, 116, 119, 125, 137, 146, 167f, 181, 197f, 204f, 208, 210f, 230, 237, 252, 255, 257, 265, 268, 280, 286, 290f, 300, 304–306, 322, 336, 341, 344, 368, 371, 376, 386, 390, 399, 407, 411f, 442, 452, 454, 461f, 464, 472f, 479, 491, 494f, 498f, 502, 512, 517, 519f, 523, 23:6, 10, 13, 17f, 47–49, 56, 58, 60f, 65–67, 69, 75, 77f, 84f, 99f, 103, 105, 109, 111, 115, 118, 120, 124, 136, 142, 145f, 149, 158, 167f, 169–171, 176, 179–185, 189, 193, 216, 218, 221, 226, 230, 240, 242, 246f, 250f, 257–259, 262, 272, 275, 285–290, 298f, 301, 303, 327, 330–333, 364, 372, 379, 387f, 392f, 396, 398f, 400f, 408, 415, 418f, 421, 24:3, 11–13, 16–22, 24–28, 30–33, 35, 44f, 49, 51, 66, 68, 73, 77, 78–90, 98, 101, 110, 112, 114–117, 119f, 125, 127, 130–133, 135–138, 140–152f, 158–160, 162–164, 166, 168–173, 175, 176n, 183, 185, 187, 190, 192–196, 198, 202, 204, 206, 208, 210–212, 214–216, 218, 220–222, 224, 226–228, 231–234, 236, 238–241, 243, 245f, 252, 255, 257, 261–263, 267, 269–277, 282f, 287–289, 291, 293, 301–303, 309–311, 314–316, 318f, 321–323, 326f, 329f, 339, 344, 346f, 350, 352f, 357f, 360, 366, 375, 377–379, 382, 385, 389f, 394, 398–400, 406–408, 413, 415, 417–419, 421, 25:106f, 27:30–32, 35, 39, 43–45, 47, 49–52, 59, 61, 66, 68, 74, 81f, 84–86, 87, 91–93, 96, 103, 113f, 133, 136, 147, 153f, 158, 179, 182, 197, 204, 215f, 222, 225–227, 241f, 248, 250, 280f, 283, 289, 297, 308, 328, 332, 334f, 340, 357, 394, 402f, 407, 28:103–105, 114, 117f, 132f, 156, 175f, 178f, 236, 294, 29:9, 16f, 21, 25, 30, 35f, 41, 53, 55, 58, 62f, 65f 69, 71, 73–75, 87–90, 97–104, 120, 136–139, 141, 147, 150, 163, 170f, 177, 179, 192, 195, 202, 212, 216f, 224, 30:4–7, 9, 11, 13, 15–17, 23f, 32–35, 39, 42, 47–50, 52–55, 62–65, 68f, 71f, 75–84, 86f, 92f, 96–99, 101, 103f, 106, 109, 118, 128f, 131–133, 135f, 143f, 155, 167, 170f, 173, 176, 180, 183, 189, 199, 204f, 219, 224, 227, 229f, 233f, 236, 238, 240, 242f, 250, 253, 255f, 258, 261f, 265, 267–272, 278, 298f, 302–304, 306, 308, 312f, 322f, 326, 31:244, 281, 322, 354f, 358–377, 34:73, 35:57f, 197f, 288, 362f, 368, 375, 382f, 410f, 36:8, 58, 60, 71f, 76, 116, 138, 140, 142, 144, 146–154, 157, 159, 168, 179, 182f, 188, 191, 194f, 198, 201, 203, 211f, 220f, 230, 245, 254, 264f, 277, 316, 37:13f, 18, 26, 32, 42, 45, 77, 105f, 124, 131, 141–143, 147f, 162f, 166, 201, 209f, 272, 283, 359, 38:xv, 87f, 97–104, 110–114, 116, 119, 120f, 126, 131f, 136, 149, 151f, 156, 158f,

161, 164f, 169, 171f, 173–186, 186–188, 194, 198, 203, 206–208, 210, 225–227, 240, 296, 306, 310f, 39:19, 56–58, 69f, 72, 124, 127, 144, 146, 151–153, 155, 171, 208, 236, 308–310, 40:19, 31–33, 67, 69, 127, 286, 297, 356, 363, 41:xv, 10–12, 14, 16–19, 24, 28, 32f, 35–37, 41, 46f, 52, 54f, 58, 60, 63, 65, 86, 88, 93, 95, 98, 101, 103, 107, 113, 115, 118, 124–127, 130f, 135–138, 140f, 143–148, 152–155, 159, 167, 172–174, 176, 190f, 194f, 218f, 236–239, 244, 250, 263, 267, 270–274, 285, 287, 289, 293, 295f, 302, 306, 309, 314f, 318, 321, 327f, 330f, 335, 338, 341f, 351–356, 358–367, 370f, 42:xvi, 14, 28, 34, 54–56, 58, 67, 88, 103, 112, 124, 130, 147–149, 165, 45:31, 70, 77f, 83, 87–104, 106, 117f, 127, 161, 173, 177, 198f, 200, 208, 221, 229, 235, 239, 240, 257–260, 264n, 276, 278, 281–283, 286, 294, 317, 349, 362, 364, 367f, 378f, 389, 46:xiii, 12, 17, 27f, 31f, 34–37, 40, 43, 51, 54f, 70, 79, 81, 83, 89, 99, 107, 122, 145f, 150, 161, 163–166, 168–170, 173, 175f, 179f, 181f, 184, 186, 219, 224, 236, 248, 253, 255f, 265, 315, see also **Priesthood of believers**

Christians, Nominal—36:xi, 117, 202, 286, 297, 336

Christians and the state—45:xiiif, 80, 100, 126f, 291

Christians under Turkish rule—46:175n, 183n

Christocentric exegesis—25:xi

Christological heresies—34:208

Christological interpretation of Old Testament—15:xif, 267f, 343–350

Christology—38:xix, 307n

Christopher, Archbishop of Bremen—43:261n

Christopher, Duke of Brunswick—49:22n

Christopher, Duke of Württemberg—49:177, 50:83n

Christopher, St.—6:230, 238, 8:196n, 203, 13:326, 22:118, 137, 165, 347, 385, 23:121, 34:24, 37:249

Chronicles, Books of—4:101, 20:264

Chronology, biblical, according to Luther—1:319, 334n, 339n, 2:82n, 230, 239, 4:ix, 3, 184, 5:340, 6:ix, 179, 187f, 255, 282, 306, 314, 321, 340, 7:ix, 5, 8–12, 23, 269f, 8:115, 20:6n, 29n, 39:203n, 204, 41:23n, 106n, 47:78, 138n, 205n, 234n, 283f

Maccabean period 18:368

Chrosner, Alexius—39:26f

Chrysostom, John—3:298, 10:303, 21:268n, 22:484, 25:268, 297, 27:377, 28:299, 338, 355, 29:xii, 80, 136, 140, 142, 160f, 180, 184f, 214, 31:214, 37:242, 41:19, 52n, 94n, 312n, 42:60n, 43:156, 47:128, 54:33, 305

Homilae in epistolam ad Hebraeos 29:125n, 127n, 131n, 133n, 137n, 138n, 141n, 144n, 146n, 156n, 157n, 159n, 164n, 181n, 183n, 184n, 185n, 213n, 215n, 219n, 227n, 230n, 233n, 234n, 240n

Homilia X in epistulam ad Romanos 25:304f

Church, The—1:22, 41, 70, 94, 103–105, 115, 132, 135, 140, 145–148, 156, 165, 168, 179f, 183, 189, 192, 195, 200, 209, 212–214, 231–233, 235, 240f, 245, 248, 250, 252f, 255, 260, 272, 276, 284, 286, 289f, 298f, 301f, 305, 308, 312, 326–329, 2:ixf, 6, 10, 12, 15f, 20f, 23, 26–33, 35–38, 50f, 55–57, 60, 64, 68, 71, 78f, 83f, 87, 99f, 102, 109, 112f, 128, 131, 134, 152, 154, 156, 164f, 167–173, 175, 177–181, 183, 185, 192–195, 197–200, 202, 210–216, 218–230, 234–237, 243, 245, 248, 256–259, 266, 272, 274–276, 280, 283–296, 293, 297, 304, 310, 320, 325f, 332–334, 338, 353f, 356f, 359, 361, 363, 371, 378, 381–384, 386, 388–392, 395, 398, 3:3, 8, 13–17, 19f, 26f, 31, 35, 37f, 48, 50, 53–56, 58, 61, 66, 70, 72, 77, 81, 84, 98, 101, 106f, 109, 111–114, 120, 122–125, 127, 134–136, 140, 143, 145, 147, 151–153, 155, 158, 160–162, 164, 168, 170, 174, 178–182, 187–192, 196f, 202, 204, 213, 217f, 222–225, 227f, 233f, 238, 242f, 245n, 249f, 260, 263, 269, 274, 278–280, 285–287, 291, 294f, 301, 305, 314, 316, 319, 321, 324–326, 329, 335f, 338f, 341f, 344–346, 348, 356, 359–364, 4:x, 6f, 14, 17, 22–25, 31, 34, 36, 40, 42–45, 49–54, 57–60, 62, 65, 69–72, 74–77, 88–89, 98, 101, 105, 108f, 116, 118, 122, 140f, 165, 170, 179–182, 185, 193n, 199–202, 203n, 205, 209, 212, 217, 220f, 234n, 236, 237n, 239, 246f, 249f, 259, 264, 266f, 276–278, 287, 290, 292, 295, 297, 300, 306, 308, 315f, 318, 335f, 339f, 344–346, 352, 354, 359f, 362f, 365, 367, 372f, 375f, 380, 384f, 396–399, 403–405, 407–409, 5:3, 9, 15,

24f, 27f, 31, 33, 38, 41, 52f, 70, 74, 78, 80, 84, 87, 89, 92, 94, 96f, 102, 106, 109, 111–114, 115n, 116, 122f, 132, 138f, 143, 145, 147, 155f, 159, 161–163, 166, 169, 173–175, 182, 185f, 188f, 191f, 196, 200f, 204, 207–209, 214, 216, 223f, 226, 238, 240, 242, 244–251, 260f, 263–269, 271f, 274f, 284, 289f, 299, 313, 331, 333, 341–343, 345f, 348f, 352f, 355, 362, 6:20f, 23, 32, 34, 38, 52, 60, 71, 81, 90, 146f, 149, 185f, 217f, 234, 284f, 357–359, 7:10f, 28, 35, 40, 45, 62–64, 66, 68, 71, 73, 85, 89, 90f, 98, 103f, 117, 119, 124, 129, 133, 135, 138, 143, 145–147, 150, 161, 163, 167, 169, 171, 174, 176, 182, 185f, 194f, 199, 205, 214, 219, 221, 224, 227n, 248, 261, 265, 296, 301, 311f, 314, 318, 320, 332, 335, 337f, 343, 348f, 354, 364, 366, 369f, 8:26, 30, 34, 41f, 46, 54, 59–63, 65f, 69, 75f, 80–83, 90, 93–95, 101, 104, 106, 117, 130, 134–137, 140, 159, 180, 182f, 185–187, 189, 193f, 206, 212, 217–220, 223, 226, 232f, 245f, 251, 253, 255, 263–266, 268–272, 274, 277, 282–284, 289, 292, 306, 311f, 315, 9:3, 5n, 57, 135f, 150, 171, 213–215, 225f, 229, 235–237, 250f, 10:22f, 25, 30, 88f, 95, 107, 113f, 120, 125f, 156, 179, 197, 199, 203f, 225, 314, 320, 330f, 350, 389, 391, 11:3, 7, 12–14, 27, 29f, 33f, 37, 50, 67, 77, 79, 86, 92, 95–104, 106, 115, 129, 148, 159, 177f, 183n, 189, 191f, 194, 214f, 221, 226–229, 233, 246, 264–266, 289–291, 294, 309f, 314, 323, 328, 332, 336, 343, 365–370, 373f, 376, 381, 392, 427f, 437, 452–455, 457, 476f, 487, 489, 503, 509, 515–520, 535, 545, 547, 12:136, 147, 162, 173, 202, 204, 217, 234, 248, 250, 254, 257–268, 291, 295, 330, 339, 351, 363, 393, 396, 408, 13:11, 14, 20, 30, 49, 83f, 87–90, 140, 151, 241, 272f, 285f, 301, 307, 324f, 381, 383, 14:13, 21–23, 55, 87, 91–94, 96, 103, 281f, 290, 298, 301–306, 300f, 325–327, 330–333, 337, 341, 15:200f, 220f, 232, 242, 244, 260f, 282, 349f, 16:3, 22, 27–29, 32, 40, 49, 53, 76f, 123, 125, 128, 131, 198, 200, 202, 205f, 209, 212–215, 218, 222, 225, 230, 236, 246, 248f, 272n, 276, 280, 292, 295, 299f, 302f, 306, 333, 342, 17:14, 16, 18, 51, 66, 84–87, 89, 96f, 103f, 115, 157, 172, 176, 179, 181f, 186f, 189, 195, 198, 203, 209, 233–235, 237, 239, 241–243, 249, 264, 309, 317–320, 327, 338, 341, 345–347, 362, 373, 382, 390, 405, 407, 409f, 18:14f, 75, 119–121, 209, 238, 241, 243, 249, 253, 358, 409, 20:24–26, 45, 50, 66, 109, 128, 130, 133, 135, 138–141, 144, 177, 303, 327, 21:212, 248–250, 263, 312, 22:5, 55f, 59, 70, 81, 102, 144, 190, 197, 202, 208f, 220, 225, 229f, 237, 243, 254f, 258–260, 261, 265–267, 269, 274, 291, 314, 437, 440, 444, 446, 450f, 467, 470, 473, 478, 480f, 484, 490, 507, 512–514, 518, 522–524, 23:20, 27, 41f, 121, 140, 144n, 149, 151f, 156, 173, 192, 194, 213, 218, 231, 253, 284–289, 254, 258, 273n, 301, 316, 318, 322f, 327, 340f, 343, 349, 356, 376, 378–380, 384–386, 396, 415, 417–419, 421, 24:24f, 91, 121, 125–131, 144, 156f, 159f, 168, 170–174, 176n, 181, 188, 197, 202, 204f, 207, 229, 240, 242, 248, 264, 292–294, 301–313, 318, 322, 324, 327, 329–332, 350f, 356, 358, 360–362, 366f, 381, 386, 397, 405, 25:53, 104–106, 145, 263, 414, 417, 464, 469, 483, 490f, 26:10, 15, 19f, 22–26, 31, 45f, 50–53, 57f, 63, 65–69, 71, 75–79, 81, 86–89, 93, 99–101, 105f, 108f, 113, 117, 120, 125, 136, 140, 145, 152, 174, 186–188, 200, 298, 222f, 245, 257, 281, 285, 296, 302, 313, 330, 375, 377f, 402, 407, 409, 414, 418, 426, 428, 439–444, 446, 448f, 451, 457f, 461, 27:31, 36f, 42–44, 46, 53, 56, 59, 69–71, 81, 83–85, 89, 91, 97–100, 103f, 106–110, 112f, 121–124, 126–128, 133f, 139, 146, 148, 155, 156n, 159, 161, 164–166, 168f, 175, 183, 186f, 197f, 200, 206, 209f, 215f, 218f, 226f, 231, 236, 247–249, 276, 280f, 286, 287f, 304, 307, 311, 317f, 320f, 330, 338, 342, 346, 352, 354, 358, 364, 375, 382, 385, 387, 389, 392, 396–398, 401, 406, 408, 410, 28:217, 220, 281, 302f, 337, 346f, 29:8, 18, 22f, 30, 32f, 37, 56, 61, 70, 87–89, 93–96, 102, 105, 143, 151, 169, 171, 173, 179, 183f, 200, 203, 220, 226f, 229, 232, 236, 30:6, 22, 52, 58, 61, 63, 94, 98, 115f, 125, 167, 170, 178, 182–184, 188, 205f, 209, 212, 219, 256, 260, 270, 272, 284, 287f, 316, 324, 327, 31:98, 100, 117f, 175, 215f, 237, 244, 246, 33:19, 22f, 85–89, 34:39, 53, 55, 68f, 72f, 74–76, 112f, 350, 35:ixn, xiv, 50f, 143, 151f, 214f, 256f, 285, 293, 328, 405, 410, 36:8, 11,

13, 16, 18, 22f, 25f, 31, 36f, 49, 52, 56–58, 69–72, 76–78, 81f, 84, 86–88, 91, 94f, 97, 106–108, 112–116, 131, 135, 141–145, 149, 151, 155, 157, 159f, 163, 168, 178, 184, 186, 193–195, 197f, 202f, 220f, 226, 281, 283, 315, 37:xi–xiii, xvii, xx, 13, 22n, 25, 74, 105n, 107, 109, 122, 127n, 157, 275, 279, 350–355, 361, 367–369, 38:ixf, xi–xiii, xv–xvii, xxi, 15f, 30, 35f, 42, 50, 58f, 78f, 85, 95, 97, 113–115, 150–155, 161, 164f, 167, 171–182, 186f, 190, 193, 195–198, 200–204, 206–214, 228, 230f, 241, 251f, 259n, 265, 273, 293n, 295, 303f, 309n, 317n, 318, 39:xi–xvi, xviii–xxv, 10, 17, 21, 31, 34, 42, 57n, 70f, 75, 110, 139, 155, 158f, 168, 172, 180, 218, 220f, 235, 40:ixf, xiif, xv, 37f, 41, 257, 299, 349, 356, 384, 388, 391f, 41:xi, xiii, xvf, 5–7, 11–16, 18, 21, 26–28, 30–35, 40, 42f, 45–50, 52f, 55, 58–60, 63, 70–72, 89, 92, 105, 107, 117, 122, 124, 126, 131–135, 137–178, 189, 192f, 195, 198–200, 202–229, 234, 236–238, 240, 245, 251, 269f, 272f, 277f, 282, 288, 294, 298–304, 309–311, 313, 316, 323, 326, 329, 332, 335f, 339, 341, 343, 348f, 351, 358, 360, 364f, 367, 370, 42:xvi, 47, 60n, 65, 137, 160, 162f, 169, 171–173, 177, 43:28, 198, 211, 44:xiii, 87–89, 45:71, 77, 80, 106n, 108, 239, 278, 294, 304, 306, 363, 365, 46:xiv, 5, 11n, 16, 18n, 159, 163, 166, 168, 171f, 180, 185, 188, 209f, 222, 225, 256f, 261f, 268, 271, 304, 313, 47:39f, 52f, 112f, 115, 117–119, 162, 173–175, 48:69, 79f, 80n, 88f, 98, 103n, 369f, 50:7, 15, 49, 64f, 74f, 76n, 148, 170f, 188, 209, 227, 241, 247, 262, 265, 271, 286, 288, 309, 51:59, 78n, 166–168, 177, 180, 304–306, 386–388, 52:39f, 107f, 110, 112, 119, 208, 275f, 54:78f, 119, 130, 185, 195, 261f, 265, 268, 291, 299, 307, 344, 421f, 473

Abuses in 38:84n, 108, 120, 144, 159–163, 178, 206f, 50:161

Communion of saints 39:xii–xvi, xxiiif, 65, 75

In the Psalms 11:17, 37, 136, 224, 229, 288, 521

Its government and ordinances 3:53, 55, 17:86, 209, 22:93, 341, 489, 509, 34:92, 41:35, 45, 59, 135, 161f, 174f, 50:xviii, 40n, 61f, 69n, 218n

Its holiness 38:161, 175–177, 179, 185, 198, 211, 212f, 229, 301

Masks of 4:53

Must show love 3:180, 185

Pure membership impossible 8:50, 218

Reform of 46:xi, 5f, 142, 48:116, 211, 401f

Relations with the State 48:70n, 139f, 211n, 224, 309n, 399

Spiritual hospital 854

Spiritual nature 39:75, 141, 153, 218–222

True and false 1:252–254, 259f, 300, 311, 314–318, 321–325, 330, 335, 338, 342, 4:30, 32–35, 48, 64, 327, 347–351, 392, 402, 406f, 38:155f, 170–175, 197, 208f, 41:193f, 196–199, 209f, 219, 222–224, 227

Twofold 1:247

Visible and invisible 11:289, 292, 340, 373f, 41:xi, xivf

Church, The early—2:235, 270n, 14:313, 16:185, 20:31, 26:204, 374, 448, 29:43, 183, 31:211, 38:xix, 182, 41:xiv, 182, 194–205, 207f, 210f, 213, 219, 224, 347–349, 48:308, 311

Church, The old and the new—41:193, 195, 198, 200, 202, 204, 206f, 215, 222–224, 240

Church and Ministry—see Vols. 39, 40, and 41

Church and secular order—25:109

Church and state—4:76, 88, 7:145, 8:264, 13:193f, 305, 22:93, 25:469f

Church attendance—43:134

Church buildings—2:284, 13:52, 45:161, 184f, 284, 286, 288, 45:167, 184f, 284–286, 288

Church courts—46:261

Church dedications—34:54, 57, 51:333–354

Church discipline—3:281, 41:xii, 137, 152f, 176, 329

Church fathers—3:ix, 20:96f, 290, 22:256f, 264–267, 271, 273, 26:65, 68, 83, 120, 29:19f, 109, 163, 239, 31:83, 223, 32:61, 151, 189, 217, 33:57f, 82f, 228f, 33:73, 89, 34:283, 35:137, 146, 197, 341n, 347, 399, 401f, 36:25, 31, 52, 65, 110, 112, 119, 136, 163f, 168, 184–186, 190, 221, 223, 37:6f, 14f, 17, 54–57, 65, 81, 104–125, 131f, 142f, 146, 154, 206n, 211, 242, 252, 288, 294, 328–330, 371, 38:xix, 16, 20, 26, 31, 33f, 36, 41, 52, 53, 57, 62, 64, 68f, 76, 109, 122, 149, 151, 159, 161, 165, 175, 180, 186, 196, 231, 261, 276, 39:163–168, 176, 192f, 217, 222, 41:xiii, 5, 7n, 14–18, 19n, 20f, 25–29, 45–53, 55, 57f, 63–66, 68, 70, 80–82, 88–92,

94, 106f, 120, 136, 141, 143, 151, 155–157, 161f, 190, 285, 290, 309, 312, 362, 42:xiv, 44:205, 308n, 327n, 382n, 45:106, 145f, 361–364, 48:6n, 7n, 24f, 36f, 59, 94n, 105, 116, 230n, 265f, 49:68, 200, 339n, 373f, 52:176f, 200, 209, 225, 257

Church history—1:164, 12:222, 29:93, 41:xif, 7

Church members—25:150

Church militant—11:138, 259, 339, 341, 501, 538, 540, 543–545, 548

Church offices—38: 111, 123, 151, 154, 160, 176f, 179f, 187f, 192, 198–204, 214

Church Orders of Reformation Period—24:188n, 46:210n

***Church Ordinance of 1528*, Electoral Saxony**—51:136

Church polity—see **Church, The**—Its government and ordinances

***Church Postil*, Luther's**—see **Luther Martin, Writings of**

Church property—24:360, 41:xiiif, 220n, 221, 224, 227, 240, 335, 46:169

Church triumphant—11:259, 543–545

Church Year—20:74n, 25:490f, 26:106n, 27:296, 40:xiii, 53:xiv, xvi, 14, 22f, 68, 195

- Advent 53:131, 209, 235
- All Saints' Day 53:39n, 173
- Annunciation 53:14, 23
- Apostles' Days 53:23
- Ascension 53:134
- Assumption 53:14
- Candlemas 52:102, 144, 53:14, 23, 90, 210, 247
- Christmas 18:48, 362, 22:ix, 129, 362, 23:254, 26:411, 36:252n, 51:xiv, xv, 211, 53:14, 22–25, 60, 90, 129, 131, 209, 237, 240, 289, 306, 54:248f, 326f, 420
- Christmas Eve 7:176n, 34:59n
- Circumcision 53:23
- Day of St. John the Baptist 53:14
- Day of St. John, Evangelist 53:23
- Day of St. Michael and All Angels 53:90, 173, 210
- Day of St. Paul 53:1
- Day of St. Stephen 53:23
- Easter 14:333n, 51:xv, 93, 53:22, 90, 134, 255, 258
- Epiphany 53:23, 209, 242, 245, 247, 302
- Good Friday 53:24n, 90
- Holy Cross 53:23
- Holy Week 53:24, 90
- Lent 1:339, 7:x, 11:210n, 14:ix, 21:157, 22:136n, 23:125n, 24:266, 27:216, 296, 29:43f, 51:69, 87, 211, 53:24, 90, 132f, 210, 277, 321
- Martyrs' days 53:331
- Movable festivals 41:62f, 66f, 174
- Nativity see **Church Year**—Christmas
- Palm Sunday 53:90
- Pentecost 3:250, 9:144, 154–157, 254, 10:116f, 11:31, 13:20, 15:306, 310, 16:267, 280, 18:48, 107, 110, 252f, 22:86, 216, 318, 23:207, 223n, 274, 24:ix, 8, 367, 374, 26:412, 448, 27:296, 319, 30:255, 306, 35:159, 161, 319, 36:252n, 41:58, 67, 114, 144, 324, 348, 42:114, 51:296, 53:22, 72, 90, 135f, 260, 263, 265
- Pre-Lent 53:209, 229
- Presentation of Christ see **Church Year**—Candlemas
- Purification see **Church Year**—Candlemas
- Quadragesima 53:24n
- Rogate Sunday 53:136
- Saints' Days 53:xiv, 23, 38
- Thanksgiving 53:173
- Trinity 53:268
- Virgin Mary Days 53:23

Church, Marks of the—14:13, 41:xiv, 5, 148, 149n, 150–154, 156, 164–167, 170, 173, 190, 195–198, 211, 218

Church, medieval—14:ix, 47n, 45:108, 148, 150, 341f, 360

- Income and finances 45:161, 169–176, 178f, 236, 293f, 306, see also **Church buildings**

Church, Papal—see **Church, Roman**

Church, Roman—1:254, 297n, 325, 2:12, 176, 281, 314, 357, 387, 8:132, 146, 11:209, 14:282, 326, 17:18, 52, 92, 107, 115, 21:38, 158, 23:65n, 26:385, 408, 27:91, 122n, 153–159, 173, 178, 297, 389, 392, 409, 29:23, 30:300, 31:83, 152, 280, 318, 336, 338, 388, 35:xiif, 343, 379, 36:ixf, 5, 7f, 11f, 18, 22, 24f, 27, 58, 89f, 96, 108, 123, 125f, 129, 167, 202, 37:361, 38:xv, xvii, 6f, 93, 95, 120, 141f, 171, 183, 189n, 191, 210n, 293, 309n, 317n, 318n, 41:xv, 41, 89–91, 145, 148, 167, 266, 268–271, 274–279, 282, 284, 288f, 292, 293n, 294, 296–300, 311, 307, 321–326, 329–332, 334, 347–349, 351, 354, 363, 367f, 42:xi, xiii, 109n, 44:xiv, 46:xiif, 5, 164, 209f, 256, 261, 48:70n, 137, 139f, 176, 192n, 211n, 213, 224f, 233, 245f, 250, 275f, 308f, 396, 53:xv, 20, 26f, 31, 33, 62, 122

Churches—11:54, 66, 477, 36:25f, 72, 115, 41:22, 27f, 35, 81, 85, 91f, 120, 138, 160, 176, 193, 199, 202, 205, 209, 221, 238, 240, 250, 281, 291, 298–301, 307, 311f, 315f, 320f, 323–327, 329–332, 334, 338, 346–348, 354f, 363–365, 367–369, 371, 46:47, 142, 216, 256
Collegiate 48:234
Equality of 32:82
Churches, Evangelical—see **Evangelical Churches**
Churches and pastors—Condition in Luther's day 6:20f
Churches of the apostles—41:312f, 323–325
Churching of women—51:296
Chytraeus, David—13:122n
Cicero—1:45, 124, 280, 2:124, 159f, 207f, 255, 297f, 303, 308, 313f, 356, 3:67, 262n, 4:104, 202n, 216n, 5:104, 269f, 354, 7:121, 191, 281, 303, 375, 12:219, 226, 237, 309, 395, 13:98, 155, 199, 201, 14:51n, 15:5, 11, 17f, 24f, 38, 39n, 41, 104, 204, 17:239n, 19:126n, 23:51, 24:72n, 25:178, 26:44n, 123, 296, 354, 385, 403n, 424n, 28:340, 31:260, 33:87, 291, 34:130n, 143, 169f, 275n, 35:256, 38:249, 40:319n, 41:77n, 100n, 101n, 46:100n, 110n, 124n, 47:228, 51:27, 54:136, 171, 190, 223, 268, 291, 299, 307, 344, 421, 474–476
Cicero, Works of—*Actio in Verrem* 7:330n
Ad Atticum 50:230n
Consolation 7:303n
De amicitia 2:297n, 15:126n
De divinatione 1:45n, 6:90n, 7:121, 15:26n, 17:51n
De finibus 2:308, 313, 30:279n
De finitude 34:334n
De imperio Gnaei Pompei 13:224
De natura deorum 2:208n, 308, 313, 13:107n, 15:26n, 24:72n, 26:296n
De officiis 3:262n, 4:87n, 8:56n, 10:421, 13:150, 165, 15:122n, 16:118n, 25:223, 29:238n, 54:241n
De oratore 7:89n, 13:218, 25:455, 26:424n, 29:74n, 50:72n
De senectute 13:100, 122n, 16:348n, 25:19
De legibus 15:184n
Epistola ad Atticum 33:74n
Epistolae ad familiares 29:123n
First Oration against Catiline 26:44n
On Duties 2:303n, 337n
Oratio in Pisonem 16:242n
Oratio pro Flacco 29:38n
Oratio pro Milone 7:374n
Orationes Philippicae 5:66n
Orator 26:430n
Pro Milone 13:140, 19:109n, 126n, 25:182
Tusculan Disputations 7:121, 8:261n, 13:77n, 81n, 82n, 25:105, 50:116n
Verrine Orations 50:116n
Cilicia—2:191, 365, 10:412, 26:78, 27:197
Cilicia, Gulf of—2:189
Cimmerian Bosporus—2:188
Cimmerians—2:189
Cinderella—21:310, 23:146
Circle—10:335f
Circumcision—1:248, 269, 2:12, 44, 116, 146, 163, 192, 278, 361f, 3:22, 76–94, 96–99, 100, 103–106, 108–113, 115f, 120, 123–129, 131–137, 140–145, 151, 162f, 170f, 174–176, 208, 250, 338, 4:13–15, 55, 230, 237, 365, 5:20, 80, 83f, 6:10, 204f, 209f, 263, 283, 289, 307, 7:151f, 163f, 207, 346, 8:130, 133f, 137, 139, 144, 9:110f, 125, 12:268, 14:17–19, 19:41, 130, 22:40, 54, 97, 135, 182, 186, 218, 251, 284f, 330, 420, 427–429, 431f, 448, 463, 476, 523, 23:25, 237, 239f, 24:337, 25:22–25, 37, 191, 193–195, 207, 474, 488f, 26:7, 52f, 59–61, 68, 78f, 81–87, 89, 91f, 95, 101f, 104f, 111f, 120–123, 138, 145, 152, 181, 204, 206, 211, 236f, 242f, 247, 299, 330, 354, 401, 411, 433, 27:9–12, 15f, 20, 25, 30, 42, 45, 52, 59, 62, 130f, 137–139, 141, 143, 200, 203f, 209f, 251f, 256f, 280, 298, 309, 327, 329–331, 333–335, 343f, 346, 357, 402–405, 407, 28:40–42, 337, 29:6, 9, 35f, 42, 49, 60, 156, 218f, 30:233f, 34:114, 35:86, 158, 195, 374, 381, 36:44, 65f, 95n, 174, 253, 37:26, 274f, 40:139, 41:69, 71, 78, 113, 45:97n, 46:145, 47:60, 65, 81n, 83, 85–87, 133, 142, 150–152, 149–164, 166f, 254, 51:78, 87, 105f, 266, 270, 52:149f, 153f, 157f, 54:55–57
Circumlocution—16:219
Circumstances—36:61n, 88n, 89n
Cistercians—37:286n, 41:126, 127n, 49:15n, 29n, 115n
Cisterns—5:64n
Cities—1:299, 301, 305, 314f, 319, 20:186, 30:177, 45:341, 46:210, 215, 234f, 240, 243–245, 250, 257, 309, 313, 49:29f, 298
Cities, Imperial—48:70n, 49:29f, 124, 155, 189, 225, 339n
Cities of refuge—9:193–197

Citizens—1:274, 4:5, 23, 164f, 211, 216, 245, 250, 292, 333, 6:206, 209–211, 216, 7:62, 122, 159, 164, 189, 191, 199, 213, 215, 224, 338, 8:100, 102f, 115, 119–122, 124, 128, 130, 185, 197, 229f, 260, 9:145, 157, 194, 196, 221f, 242, 245, 14:57, 21:112, 256f, 24:22, 26, 123, 146, 267, 272, 277, 25:57, 46:116, 216, 294, 309
Citizens, Training of—45:344, 356f
Citizenship—3:281
Citizenship, Christian—17:271
Citizenship in heaven—22:203–206, 291
City councils—46:214, 216, 245, 294
City gates—6:209
City of Christ—35:407, 409
City of God—11:169, 19:84, 86–89
City of God—see **Augustine, St., Works of**
Civic life—27:56, 90f, 115, 219, 358, see also **Secular life**
Civil law—2:139f, 4:218f, 223f, 227f, 243f, 381
Civil order—3:230f, 8:216
To be guided by reason 3:322
Civil righteousness—13:54, 402, 34:196
Civility—6:169
Classes, Social—8:99n, 102f, 9:145, see also **Stations in society**
Classes, Upper—14:76
Classical authors, Citations from—1:xf
Classics—2:ix, 3:ix
Classics, Greek and Latin—5:x
Claudius, Emperor—2:288, 23:382n, 25:129, 27:210, 39:203f, 206, 41:324n
Claudius Claudianus—*De quarto consulati Honorii* 6:195n
De raptu Proserpinae 6:304n
Gildonic War 1:355n, 23:382n
In Rufinum 7:359n
Panegyric 3:331n
Claus Narr—13:161, 36:246n
Claws—24:382, 415, 417f
Clay—29:149
Clean things—18:384f, 395
Cleanliness, Spiritual—25:12
Cleanness, Ritual—17:213f
Cleanness of teeth—18:153
Cleansing from sin—25:322
Cleansings—12:361
Clemen, Otto—31:80, 34:13n, 45:85n, 138n, 243, 48:xiiif, 49:xv, 54:xxv
Flugschriften aus den ersten Jahren der Reformation 45:57n
Clemency—2:340, 9:138
Clement II, Pope—50:55n, 81f, 82n, 84, 127
Clement III, Pope—41:344n, 346, 349–351
Clement IV, Pope—41:277n
Clement V, Pope—35:406n, 44:166n, 207n, 349n, 48:186n, 246n
Concerning Penance and Remission 31:170, 236
Clement VI, Pope—31:260–262, 264–270, 32:75n, 36:82n, 40:342n, 44:140n, 171n, 47:51n, 48:84
Extravagante 31:260–262, 264–270, 278, 282–284
Unigenitus 31:260–262
Clement VII, Pope—1:323n, 3:144, 5:369, 8:6n, 13:149, 219, 34:5, 48n, 67, 83n, 237, 238n, 251, 41:277n, 295n, 43:265, 44:167n, 46:xiin, 169n, 199n, 47:34, 49:156, 161n, 185, 221–223, 255n, 265n, 280n, 284, 285n, 286f, 332, 350n, 374n, 54:140, 143
Clement of Alexandria—2:77, 13:33
Exhortation to the Heathen 1:4n
Clementine constitutions—14:23, 39:281n, 41:235n, 44:166n, 394n, 46:232n, 48:186, 246n
Cleopatra, Queen—4:274, 35:310n
Cleophas—27:195, 30:203
Clergy—2:152, 2:83f, 3:x, 128, 357, 4:200n, 234, 5:80, 195, 13:25, 30–32, 42, 48–50, 56, 176, 215n, 258, 329, 331f, 334, 14:4f, 557n, 64, 91, 94, 112, 116f, 326, 16:303, 18:23, 20:277, 300, 312, 344, 21:33, 63, 138, 142, 194, 226, 22:227, 23:212f, 297, 419, 24:66f, 197, 205, 233, 242, 274, 360, 25:139f, 470, 490, 26:46, 106n, 296, 458f, 27:4, 68f, 121f, 204, 215, 28:5, 313, 328, 355f, 380, 29:8, 17, 20, 28, 60, 64, 30:53, 174, 177f, 183n, 184, 186, 255, 31:370, 32:89, 34:45, 93, 214n, 35:17, 41, 201, 389f, 403, 36:8f, 16, 113, 201–206, 223, 37:90n, 364, 38:99–101, 114n, 123f, 135, 39:210, 213f, 266f, 293, 306, 309f, 312, 39:8, 14f, 18, 69, 75, 86, 218, 244, 265f, 268, 287, 41:156, 223n, 42:55, 60, 44:131f, 175–178, 366, 45:57, 58n, 60f, 62n, 64n, 67f, 71, 109, 170, 176, 256, 293f, 306, 341, 349, 46:81, 99, 112, 159, 163n, 165f, 176, 179, 181f, 186, 196, 215, 219n, 220, 222, 237, 251, 261, 315, 317, 319, 49:25f, 28, 378n, 52:34, 80, 112, 114, 117f, 120, 162, 213, 224, 227, 233f, 238f, 244, 247, 250f, 255f, 262, 265, 268, 272, 275, 282, see also **Bishops**; **Clerics**; **Ecclesiastics**; **Ministers (of the Word)**; **Pastors**; **Priests**; **Spiritual estate**
Clergy, Lower orders of—34:55n

Clergy, Marriage of—26:428, 28:22–25, 231, 312f, 339, 36:79, 114, 206, 233, 260, 303, 39:206–215, 241, 289–294, 44:175–179, 179n, 45:28, 53, 78, 136, 144n, 148, 150n, 155, 48:221, 231, 235, 342f, 344, 353n, 354, 377, 51:79–81, 88, 124, 131, 192, 361
Clergy privileges—39:249n
Clerical estate—41:223n, 301
Clericalism—44:xiiif
Clerics—8:50, 22:84, 253f, 29:60, 63, 66, 71–73, 77, 30:183, 186, 189, 203, 209, 211, see also **Clergy**
Clerics, Papal—38:114, 119, 149–152, 156, 158, 160–165, 167f, 173, 176f, 179, 181, 185–188, 190, 202, 206, 230f
Clerks—46:240f, 243f
Cleves, Duchy of—50:192, 194f
Climax—10:52
Clippers—24:194f, 198–200
Cloak and coat, Giving—45:81, 87, 96, 256, 259, 273f, 276–280, 388
Cloisters—2:339n, 3:284, 4:398, 22:51, 211, 281, 359, 368, 392, 457, 461, 486, 504, 23:6, 25–27, 34, 75, 171, 173, 182, 204f, 238, 247, 269, 335, 413, 24:62, 127, 169, 172, 181, 231, 240, 260, 268, 307, 325, 405, 30:15, 170, 174, 177f, 184, 186, 255, 30:55, 38:116–118, 121, 161, 167, 45:348f, 390, 46:109, 141, 164, see also **Convents**; **Monasteries**
Closter Neumberg—1:239
Clothing—3:50, 52, 315, 4:57, 204, 276f, 7:60, 69, 113, 124, 187, 338, 343, 8:66, 68, 94, 118, 120, 122, 133, 144, 172f, 183, 272, 283, 9:74, 94f, 111, 113, 118, 126, 149, 219, 221–226, 243, 272, 21:199f, 23:403f, 26:96, 170f, 284, 311, 352, 363, 407, 424f, 27:55, 62, 83, 122, 140, 257, 335, 383
Clothing, Origin of—1:140, 221
Clouds—2:46, 94f, 105, 129, 146f, 152, 282, 334, 3:139, 10:170f, 11:62, 322, 16:71, 195f, 30:187f, 209, 300
Clowns—1:255
Clytemnestra—31:284n
Coadjutors—44:149
Coals of fire—25:108, 465f
Coats-of-arms—19:170f
Cobblers—37:60
Coburg—14:xf, 6n, 21:xix, 19, 34:xv, xii, 5f, 35:177, 198n, 202n, 38:93f, 43:169, 181f, 46:211, 47:5, 29n, 49:282f, 284n, 287, 290n, 315n, 317n, 318n, 417n, 50:155, 51:197, 53:337, 54:11, 196
Coburg Castle—12:x, 49:xviii, 282n, 285, 287f, 306, 310n, 312f, 315n, 317n, 332n, 348, 357, 400n, 402, 410n, 420n, 422n, 426
Cochlaeus, John—3:193n, 14:76n, 17:38n, 265, 363, 23:212n, 217n, 26:238n, 32:119f, 34:70n, 95n, 314, 328n, 35:78, 38:210n, 41:150n, 189n, 190f, 43:142f, 46:60n, 47:46, 49:273, 50:185, 269n, 54:71, 94, 137, 262, 351
  Articuli CCCCC Martini Lutheri ex sermonibus eius sex & triginta, 1526 7:298n
  Confutation 34:6n, 70n, see also ***Confutation of the Augsburg Confession***
  Ein nötig und christlich bedencken auf des Luthers artickeln, die man gemeynsamen concilio fürtragen soll, 1538 30:30n
Coelius, John—54:27, 297
Coelius, Michael—50:291n, 294n, 318
Coelius Sedulius—53:237, 302
***Coelos ascendit hodie* (hymn)**—37:260n
Cognac, League of—46:204n, 49:156, 161n, 185n, 222
Cohabitation—see **Coitus**
Coitus—1:281, 2:11n, 32, 115, 3:48, 208, 261, 308, 310, 313, 4:10, 227, 232f, 247, 306, 352, 5:4, 30, 32, 37, 51, 333, 350, 7:16, 28, 31, 43, 83, 87–89, 94, 7:33, 88, 9:74, 222, 27:89, 321, 399f, 38:202, 46:261–285, 290, 293–297, 306f, 318, 320f
Coitus interruptus—7:20f
Coke, Zachary—*Logick*, 1654 4:100n
Cold—2:129, 136
Colditz—34:272, 50:111f
Cole, Henry—47:65n
  Early translator of Erasmus into English 33:xin
  Select Works of Martin Luther, London, 1824 42:120n
Collectanea rerum memorabilium—see **Solinus, Gaius Julius**
Collection for the poor—25:126
Collections—36:53
Collects—35:57, 95, 36:53f, 254, 40:121, 53:14, 21, 23, 29, 69, 72, 74, 84, 106, 127–145, 154f, 168–170
  Index of first lines of original collects 53:346f
  Index of Luther's German versions 53:346f
  Index of translations into English 53:346f
Collegiate churches—29:33
Collegium biblicum—35:206, 229, 340n
Collin, Rudolph—38:8, 11, 18n, 30n, 52, 289n
Colloquies, Religious—50:xiii

Cologne—8:264, 289, 31:381, 384, 32:264, 48:9n, 150n, 194, 262, 49:147, 50:41n, 254n, 51:xi, 54:271–272, 275
Archbishop of 41:24, 49:416
Augustinian Monastery 48:30f, 34, 236n
Diet of 44:214n
Other monasteries 48:10n, 11, 33n, 317
Theologians of 25:289, 429, 454
University of 36:14n, 204, 211n, 45:285n, 48:10n, 11, 30n, 38n, 145n, 155n, 185n, 317f, 378n, 49:148, 50:247n
Cologne Reformation—see **Bucer, Martin, Works of**
Color(s)—6:4, 12–15, 305, 323f, 20:66
Colossae, Church at—41:323
Colossians—14:39, 29:95, 105
Colossians, Epistle to the—23:28, 35:386
Colts—8:247, 262f, 266, 272, 310
Comander, John—37:158
Comedy—5:119–121, 305, 7:364, 366, 29:61
Comets—2:147
Comfort—1:190f, 214f, 220f, 233, 252, 255, 270, 281, 286–288, 327, 345–347, 349–353, 2:104, 112, 118, 131, 145f, 148, 151, 155, 157, 166f, 169f, 185, 196, 219, 221f, 225, 229, 248, 254, 273, 281, 283, 296, 306, 308, 316, 321, 325, 335, 343, 350f, 363, 375, 390, 3:3, 10, 15, 33, 38, 52, 58, 62f, 65, 73, 124, 135, 184, 241, 243, 271, 291, 305, 314, 320, 331, 337, 345–347, 355, 4:7, 16f, 51, 57, 59, 67, 69, 75, 88, 94, 96, 98, 103f, 128, 131, 138, 158, 162, 188–191, 197, 248, 257, 262, 273, 282, 292, 309–312, 315, 317, 321, 362, 366, 373f, 5:14–16, 18, 21, 23, 25–27, 31, 33f, 36f, 43, 55, 57f, 61f, 64, 69, 71, 76–78, 81, 83f, 87f, 103, 131, 136, 154, 156, 157, 172, 199, 235, 6:22, 95, 116, 7:10, 28, 48, 98, 100f, 122, 128, 176, 191, 195, 315, 331, 335, 366, 8:12, 74, 187, 9:57, 197, 221, 10:50, 11:468, 550, 14:64, 81f, 86f, 133, 142, 145, 161, 166, 170, 180, 198, 201, 204f, 209f, 213, 216, 218, 220, 233, 236, 244, 251, 253–255, 266, 323, 16:52f, 57, 77, 101, 109, 111, 113, 119, 206, 200, 214, 225f, 287, 300, 315f, 17:3, 6, 40f, 103, 130, 137f, 197, 201, 335, 18:256, 288, 300, 303, 315, 379f, 19:47, 120, 20:4, 8, 14f, 18–20, 22, 26f, 34, 36f, 42, 46, 52, 63, 65, 83, 94, 130–132, 134f, 144f, 159, 174–177, 181, 187, 323, 325, 21:290, 309, 348, 22:52, 55, 75, 105, 114f, 121, 163, 205, 209f, 484, 23:7f, 30, 44, 47, 50, 54, 67, 139, 152, 154, 157, 172, 182f, 218, 241, 256, 259, 268, 270, 274f, 278, 290, 294, 299, 301f, 316f, 336, 339f, 348, 369–371, 379, 388, 391, 396, 399, 24:7f, 10–12, 17–21, 28–30, 33f, 36, 40f, 50, 52, 57–59, 77, 98f, 101, 110f, 113–119, 126, 130, 132, 134, 137, 142, 144f, 147f, 152, 158, 161, 163–165, 167f, 171, 179, 183–187, 196, 204, 207f, 210, 218, 234, 236, 240f, 263, 275–277, 279, 285, 289f, 292, 310, 316, 318, 325, 327, 329, 332–336, 345, 347f, 353–356, 360f, 377, 379–384, 389, 399–405, 407, 411f, 414f, 417f, 420–422, 25:7, 53, 179, 368, 26:5, 7, 24, 32, 35, 42, 48, 52, 64, 108f, 113, 153, 161f, 167, 195, 276, 278–280, 283, 292, 306, 316, 329, 337, 341, 351, 372, 380f, 384, 386, 393, 440, 445, 450, 456, 461, 27:3, 19, 21f, 25–27, 32f, 71, 73–76, 78, 81, 84, 109, 111, 115, 126, 400, 30:59f, 70, 86, 103, 116, 128, 131, 140, 142, 152, 258, 280, 35:xvii, 36, 66, 97, 143, 200, 252, 207, 327f, 330, 359, 377, 383, 401, 407f, 43:103f, see also **Consolation**
Comforter, The—3:205, 24:13, 101, 103, 110–117, 127, 131, 149, 153, 167, 171f, 175, 190, 291, 297f, 334, 336, 357, 364f
Commandments—see **God, His commands**
Commandments, Conflicting—4:44
Commandments, Papal—36:202, 242, 252
Commandments of men—6:85f, 29:41–45, 36:194, 240, 37:13–17, 136, 284, 367f, 45:42, 347
Commendation—25:205–207, 44:150n
Commentaries—45:364, 376
Commentaries on the Bible—those used by Luther 25:ix
Commentariolus—29:xi
Commentators—1:3
Mistakes of 19:133
Commerce—Dangers of 8:277, see also **Trade and commerce**
Commercialism—22:220
Commodus, Emperor—15:72n
Common chest—3:178, 9:138, 254, 21:118f, 172, 22:417, 30:182, 35:57, 67, 69, 45:xii, 176–194, 49:29f, 45f, 57, 98n, 169, 50:49, see also **Treasury, Common**
Common crowd—9:233, 12:8, 188
Common fund—see **Common chest; Treasury, common**

Common man—35:90, 163, 189, 38:227, 45:57, 45:57, 62
Common people—16:66, 17:282, 289, 21:253f, 22:71, 79, 26:23, 33, 51, 84, 27:100, 29:74, 30:187, 32:145, 33:41, 48, 83, 34:363, 36:78n, 212, 253, 310f, 359, 37:xix, 5, 11, 20, 22, 24, 31, 51, 53f, 67f, 72, 74, 107, 110, 115, 138, 143, 149, 161–163, 203, 208, 230, 250, 41:137, 46:18n, 19, 21, 187, 215, 217f, 231, 251, 274, 49:46, 53f, 135, 157, 162, 209, 349, 408n
Common people, Reformers' concern for—34:363
Common prayer—16:139
Common sense—46:262, 268f, 310
Common things—25:116, 498f
Common treasury—see **Common chest**; **Treasury, common**
Common woman—46:280, 291
Commoners—2:19
Commonweal—50:180, 245, 294
Commonwealths—7:33, 67f, 151, 239, 9:233, 241–243, 248, 27:113, 409
Commotion—20:131f, 134, 324
Communes—2:199
Communicating—36:49, 54
Communicatio idiomatum—see **Communication of properties**
Communication of attributes—see **Communication of properties**
Communication of properties—5:219, 6:126, 13:236, 15:293, 22:346, 352, 361f, 491, 492n, 23:101f, 24:106, 25:147, 332, 28:265–267, 30:222, 36:35, 37:206n, 210, 212f, 38:247n, 254, 256, 263, 272, 274f, 307, 40:196f, 41:100n, 101–104, 106, 108–111, 113, 116–119, 147
Communing—25:261, 36:49, 54, 57, 123, 233, 249n, 252, 263
  Frequency of 35:58, 43:134
  Preparation for 29:172, 32:55, 35:88–109, 36:233
Communio—53:21, 29, 181–183
Communio sanctorum—24:126n
Communion—One element 16:44
Communion chant—53:181–183
Communion of properties—see **Communication of properties**
Communion of saints—11:292, 329, 541, 24:126n, 172, 41:xi, xiv, 107, 143, 199, 316, 42:xvi, 108, 111f, 135n, 138, 161f, 182
Communion with God—24:139
Communities—2:272n, 37:120, 349f, 355f, 367, 45:328, 46:9n, 10f, 13, 15, 37f, 78, 126n, 131, 215, 294, 309, 313
Community of believers—40:36, 38
Community of goods—15:68f
Community of the faithful—35:53, 58
Companus, John—34:80n
Comparisons—16:26, 233, 284, 339
Compassion—2:65, 134, 145f, 3:71, 134, 189, 240, 249, 285f, 305, 310, 331, 360, 364, 4:46, 16:218, 17:356, 18:135, 24:87, 140f, 342, 405f, 419, 25:107, 462, 29:9. 14, 140, 142, 187
Complacency—9:164, 13:113, 16:279, 24:172, 25:101, 428, 37:141
Complaints—15:211
Complenda—53:29
Compline—51:295, 53:38, see also **Canonical Hours**
Compositiones—14:280–349, 44:154n
Compostella—1:250, 3:109, 22:250, 32:41, 96, 342, 39:43n, 285n, 41:172n, 44:12n, 27, 68, 70, 86, 337–340, 50:73, see also **James of Compostella, St.**
Compostella, Santiago de—see **James of Compestella, St.**
Compulsion—29:99, 102, see also **Force**; **Tolerance**
Comus—25:481, 27:371
Conceit—1:258, 3:186, 22:96, 404, 25:464, 27:383f, 52:89
Concentration—40:117, 148
Conception—1:216f, 3:206, 4:304, 343, 351, 358, 5:380, 383, 7:33, 36, 360
Concerning the Order for Public Worship—see **Luther, Martin, Writings of**
Concerns—21:193–200
Conciliarism—48:80n, 90f, 104n, 50:82n, 254n, 267n
Concomitance—22:266n, 36:297n
Concomitance, Doctrine of—17:82n
Concord—9:221, 15:69, 228f, 233, see also **Harmony**; **Unity of Christians**
Concordance of the Discordant—13:223
***Concordia Triglotta*, St. Louis, 1921**—32:225n, 37:249n
Concubinage—49:105n, 51:357, 363f
Concubines—2:10, 305, 4:184, 301f, 306f, 5:325, 7:10, 19, 8:222, 306, 54:135, 230, 243
Concupiscence—1:114, 2:30, 4:221, 231f, 234, 238f, 241, 249, 252, 408, 5:338, 345, 380, 6:133, 7:49, 8:65, 325, 11:21, 201, 265, 301, 447, 13:81n, 95, 97, 109, 114, 24:398, 25:7, 22, 24, 49, 51, 59f, 63, 68f, 118, 220, 259, 261f,

309, 341f, 349, 381, 27:389, 31:10, 86, 136, 35:35n, 37n, 51:22, 25
Condemnation—2:16, 41, 51, 122, 5:18, 50, 52, 8:40, 331, 24:61, 121, 259, 306, 308f, 343, 345, 350–352, 379, 396, 26:58, 133, 235f, 447, 35:63, 200, 375, 377
Condign and congruent (scholastic terms)—11:396n, 424
Condignity—2:123f, 26:124–127, 131, 134f, 175f, 181, 183, 291, 293, 301, 330, 374f
Condiments—1:210
Confessing the faith—see **Witnessing**
Confessio Tetrapolitana—34:80n, 48:247n, 50:3
Confession—3:57, 118, 182f, 187, 189, 199, 241, 273, 321, 340, 5:41, 122, 146, 22:202, 395f, 401, 412, 27:13, 73, 107, 130, 146, 293, 29:45, 100, 143f, 172, 32:16, 32–36, 42–44, 54f, 159, 286, 33:48, 54, 34:19, 53, 56, 35:xvii, 6, 17f, 147, 39:xxii, 25–42, 43n, 44–47, 40:240, 296f, 323f, 339f, 52:236f, 277f, 54:394–395, 402, 404, see also **Penance**
Confession, Private—6:297, 301, 26:154, 182n, 33:48, 36:86, 358–360, 37:368, 38:87, 109, 127, 149, 177, 183, 204, 51:65, 69, 97–100, 107
Confession, Public—36:357f, 38:204
Confession, Short Order of, before the Priest for the Common Man—see **Luther, Martin, Writings of**
Confession of faith—4:33, 71, 96, 103, 166, 219, 403, 8:249, 314, 16:71, 20:152, 25:90, 411, 28:375f, 37:23, 122, 157, 163, 300f, 305f, 360, 38:xix, 5, 8, 107, 112, 117, 123, 207, 222–224, 284, 48:370
Confession of sins—1:176–178, 181, 258, 275, 1:258, 275, 2:166, 314, 3:347, 4:54, 148, 159, 5:86, 154f, 157, 6:75–77, 198f, 297f, 7:37, 47, 57f, 111, 227n, 237, 245, 257, 259f, 263, 272f, 275, 277f, 280, 287, 365, 8:52, 70, 72, 181, 189, 268, 275, 10:27, 31, 162f, 233f, 236, 238f, 317, 443, 455, 11:81, 260–266, 371f, 401, 12:339, 341, 347, 352, 357, 392, 16:341, 20:138, 25:10, 28, 62, 200f, 206, 211–216, 246f, 258, 263, 267f, 479, 25:28, 206, 214–216, 246f, 268, 339, 30:71, 190, 231n, 242, 286, 31:85, 100, 36:61, 83, 85–88, 90, 120, 123, 233, 331, 354–361, 38:19, 157f, 41:85, 336, 342, 42:62, 69, 100, 140, 43:9, 46:172, 50:75, 135, 168n, 198n, 53:34, 80, 82–93, 116–121
Confessional—27:384, 396, 44:xix, 155n, 184n, 223–225
Confessions—see **Augustine, St., Works of**
Confessors—4:41, 141, 5:156, 36:97, 46:270, 272, 286, 318, 320n
Confidence—6:62, 114f, 244f, 12:383f, 16:299, 20:44, 25:78, 116, 498, 29:172f, 177, 35:72, 89, 199, 374
Confirmation—29:180, 34:55, 87, 349, 356, 36:48, 91f, 115, 118, 45:5, 8n, 15, 24f, 53:93, 173,
Confitebor (Psalm 111)—13:363
Confitemini (Psalm 118)—3:155, 14:xi, 45, 47, 50
Conflict of faculties—1:47n
Conformity, Outward—9:164
Confraternities—see **Brotherhoods**
Confusion—8:7, 11, 34f, 47, 55, 59, 66n, 121, 160, 214, 247, 10:385–387, 390, 392, 25:401–403, 26:48, 117, 323
Confutatio Pontificia—see **Cochlaeus, John**
Confutation of the Augsburg Confession—4:166n, 16:201n, 22:447, 23:16n, 33n, 173n, 24:128n, 26:137n, 34:6n, 70n, 47:5, 14n, 21–28, 32, 49:350n, 374n, 378, 394, 400, 401n, 403f, 423f, 54:137n, 187, 355
Congregations—1:135, 4:101, 9:226, 229, 11:372–374, 13:27, 46n, 334, 357, 22:480, 482, 510, 23:156, 24:172, 235, 293, 386, 30:52, 55, 63, 132, 136, 144, 208, 257n, 35:382, 401, 39:16, 303–314, 42:xv, 60, 49:28f, 61n, 90n, 135, 159, 160n, 163n, 168n, 201n, 214, 348, 384f
Congruity—2:123, 26:124–127, 130f, 134f, 172f, 181–183, 209, 219, 230, 291, 293, 301, 330, 374f
Conjugal duty—45:20, 26, 33–35
Conquering God—6:140f, 259
Conquerors through Christ—25:78
Conrad, Duke of Massovia (Poland)—45:133
Conradi, Tilemann—32:120
Conradin of Swabia, King of Naples—41:277n, 332n
Consanguinity—7:15, 19, 84, 9:229n, 36:99, 102, 44:179n, 183f, 46:262, 310, 315f
Conscience—1:114, 159, 164, 170, 172f, 176f, 180f, 254, 274, 277, 296f, 322, 347, 2:55, 89, 115, 133, 145, 151, 158, 160f, 219–222, 248, 251, 273, 293,

295, 314, 350, 3:8n, 25, 125, 196, 214, 222–224, 326, 342, 349, 351, 4:50, 57, 93, 134f, 141, 145, 175, 192, 205, 220, 236f, 248, 279, 323, 407, 5:26, 33, 37, 47, 66, 88, 157, 254, 271, 304, 6:42, 56, 62f, 78, 84, 299, 369–371, 377, 395, 7:16, 47, 63, 65f, 74, 80, 89, 101, 103, 154, 228–230, 271, 273, 275, 290f, 312, 330f, 333, 336, 345, 8:25–27, 42, 45, 77, 80, 163, 234, 238, 251, 267, 270, 314, 324, 326f, 329, 332, 9:14, 43, 49n, 50, 57n, 58, 60, 73, 81, 83, 88f, 97, 108, 118, 123, 125f, 129f, 135–137, 151, 158, 184, 190, 197–199, 206, 213f, 232, 236–238, 244f, 267, 273, 277, 291, 298, 310, 10:21, 32, 99, 140, 191, 11:8f, 17f, 24, 107f, 114, 213f, 237, 240, 360, 389, 12:28, 44, 168, 172, 251, 270, 273f, 277, 296, 304, 310, 316, 323–325, 331f, 336, 346f, 352, 357, 362, 368, 371, 373, 375f, 390, 400, 405, 13:6f, 10, 22, 116, 137f, 150, 188, 191, 238, 242, 264, 269, 287, 353, 373f, 376, 415, 14:20, 28, 54, 60, 75, 82, 84, 91, 100f, 105, 110, 142, 148–150, 153, 156f, 159, 166, 170f, 216, 224, 262, 295, 306, 321, 15:3, 70, 80, 133, 209, 236, 273, 16:53f, 56, 72, 77, 98f, 107, 129, 137, 152, 179, 205, 223, 230, 232, 235, 246, 301, 305f, 310, 312, 321, 327, 343, 17:3–5, 42, 44f, 48, 64f, 180, 189, 207, 209, 213, 224, 237, 261, 288, 299, 323, 18:65, 95, 99, 152, 255, 277, 374, 19:60, 63, 65, 67, 69, 10, 20:3f, 8, 11f, 14, 22, 24, 35, 37f, 41, 58, 67, 85, 109, 112, 188, 205f, 211, 227, 235, 270, 272, 276, 291f, 21:35, 47, 80f, 103, 153, 236–238, 22:72, 86, 95, 150, 206, 225, 258, 369, 378, 380, 384, 401–403, 441, 456, 481, 484, 488, 525, 23:33, 44, 47f, 50, 53f, 57, 59f, 64, 66, 68, 75, 87, 122, 145, 179, 197, 201, 225, 248, 267–272, 278, 282, 295–297, 304–306, 317f, 320, 327, 336, 341, 388, 395, 399, 411, 24:7f, 11–14, 17, 50, 55, 58, 61, 74, 76, 79, 83, 98, 101, 110–112, 116, 129, 152f, 170, 181, 228f, 250, 257, 266, 271, 274, 290, 293, 295f, 298, 305, 323, 347, 349, 355, 360f, 378, 390, 399, 401, 25:6, 19f, 79, 104, 114–116, 157, 187f, 400f, 465, 499f, 502f, 506, 26:5, 8f, 10f, 20, 26–31, 33, 35–38, 44f, 51f, 54f, 60, 63, 67, 70, 72, 76, 85f, 89, 91–93, 109f, 113–118, 120, 133f, 138–140, 148–152, 158f, 161f, 164, 166, 180, 182, 195, 212, 215–218, 220f, 224f, 232, 249, 259, 286, 290, 301f, 305f, 309f, 313f, 317f, 322–324, 327, 338f, 341f, 345, 349f, 354, 356–358, 361–366, 369, 371, 375, 377, 379, 381, 386f, 389–392, 398, 403, 405f, 408–411, 414, 439f, 445, 447f, 461, 27:4f, 6f, 11–15, 21, 27, 40f, 47–49, 51, 54, 75, 87, 96, 107, 110, 115–121, 126, 130, 141, 164, 167, 169, 171, 191, 216, 220f, 237, 287, 311, 318, 321, 327–329, 334f, 340, 345, 372, 375, 381–385, 388, 392, 395, 28:11, 30, 41, 44, 69, 70f, 104, 111, 208f, 252, 310–312, 29:10, 12, 18–20, 23, 27f, 32, 34, 36, 40–43, 45–52, 58, 60, 62, 72f, 84, 95, 97, 153, 169, 172, 200, 206, 208–212, 30:8f, 50, 59, 77, 80f, 109, 116, 125, 132, 135, 152, 154, 164, 172f, 229, 232, 246f, 263, 279f, 301, 303, 308, 320, 325, 31:100, 103, 231, 32:32, 36f, 40, 55, 112f, 130, 33:48–58, 34:72, 126, 35:xvii, 6f, 14f, 36f, 90, 109f, 119, 131, 133, 136–146, 153, 193, 216, 244, 248, 278, 376f, 379, 382f, 388f, 36:xii, 5, 7, 9, 30, 57, 60f, 72, 80, 83–88, 101, 103, 133f, 142f, 165, 168, 172, 175f, 181, 184, 193–199, 203, 206, 212, 221f, 227, 230, 235, 241, 243, 247, 250, 253–256, 260–264, 290, 347, 359, 37:13, 23, 35, 77, 108, 110, 115, 118, 344, 38:8, 87, 101, 129, 157, 163, 170, 181, 183, 191, 196, 231, 295f, 299, 302, 304, 315–317, 319, 39:36f, 41:17, 25f, 29, 32, 50, 72, 77, 107, 130, 146, 153, 202, 222, 283, 307, 309, 335, 338, 340f, 357, 361, 44:223–229, 235–242, 45:xiif, 7, 17, 33, 79, 84, 296, 247–250, 260f, 392, 46:xiv, 17, 33, 39f, 42f, 52, 54, 83, 89, 93, 105, 112–115, 117, 119, 121, 129f, 134f, 159, 163f, 169, 184, 187–190, 194, 204, 226, 242, 255, 261–263, 265–267, 270–272, 275, 278f, 281–284, 286f, 289n, 299, 303, 308f, 312, 315–320, 48:205, 223, 247, 277, 279, 294, 301, 307, 310f, 337, 395f, 402, 50:8, 9, 32n, 38, 46, 77, 134, 197f, 201, 51:20, 30, 46, 59, 79, 80, 93f, 99, 129, 131, 158, 178, 273–277, 341, 52:284f, 54:25, 64, 66, 395, 442

Conscience, Evil—5:145, 190f, 194, 7:271, 274, 276f, 328f, 332, 334f, 8:25, 52, 54, 189, 191, 323, 16:30, 36:219, 313, 351, 359

Conscience, Good—3:128, 332, 4:227, 286, 5:39, 65, 191, 195, 272, 7:91, 115, 242, 304, 8:43, 268, 328, 25:522

Consciousness—9:49
Consecration—see **Sanctification**
Consecrations—5:253, 12:359, 34:55–57, 246, 53:31, 80, 54:119, 244
***Consilium de emendanda ecclesiae*, 1537**—50:159n, 176n, 191n
Consistory—34:233
Consolation—1:191, 3:54, 4:93, 106, 222, 323, 5:131, 192, 203, 205, 215, 223, 230f, 235, 247, 254f, 257, 275–277, 279, 283, 293, 313, 315–317, 320f, 353, 358, 360, 6:8–11, 23, 62, 73f, 87, 95, 99, 103, 109, 123, 149, 179f, 221, 246, 256, 260, 272, 297f, 311, 325, 353, 387, 390, 7:10–12, 15, 32, 40, 49, 64, 68, 96f, 100f, 105, 122f, 128, 133, 135, 196, 201, 226, 228, 233, 251, 304, 313, 315, 319, 8:5, 12–15, 27, 34, 37, 42f, 45f, 61, 74, 78, 80, 89, 110, 179, 185, 189, 214, 231, 234, 257f, 270, 294, 312, 324, 326, 330, 332, 9:42, 94, 112, 277, 12:12, 59, 346f, 370f, 390, 15:64, 199f, 204–207, 209f, 212, 214, 230, 233, 235, 237, 243, 246, 325, 16:6, 20, 154, 172, 209, 17:3f, 13, 15, 27, 39, 43, 49, 68, 74, 84, 88, 103, 126, 131, 133, 137, 139, 154, 176, 182f, 203f, 236f, 277, 355–357, 408, 21:206f, 292, 22:44, 61, 72, 90, 110, 114, 480, 491, 499, 23:76, 111, 117, 145, 196, 256, 259, 270, 273, 292, 299, 339, 355, 400, 24:7f, 10–12, 18, 25, 28, 31, 70, 74, 76, 83, 86, 89, 97, 109–111, 117–120, 124f, 131, 135, 140, 142, 144f, 148, 157, 161, 166, 168, 180, 183, 185, 193, 204, 249, 257, 266, 274, 278, 285, 292, 296, 322, 349f, 355, 362, 24:414, 418, 421, 26:25, 32, 37, 39, 54, 64, 77, 96, 133, 28:105, 107, 114, 118, 121, 128f, 133, 136, 146, 191, 29:12, 50, 94, 104, 129, 187, 201f, 234, 30:13, 16, 240, 275, 288, 35:297, see also **Comfort**
Consolation, Mutual—13:111
Consolation (Chemdath) of the Gentiles—47:209–229, 255, 297, 305
Conspiracy—6:388f
Constance—24:413, 34:80n, 38:95, 48:247n, 49:414n, 54:215, 263, 372, 443
Constance, Bishop of—49:41, 88n
Constance, Council of—31:321, 43:69n, 146n, 149n, 175
Constancy—7:71, 75, 80, 86, 96, 101, 12:382, 23:400
Constans I, Emperor—41:373n
Constantia—41:55, 79
Constantine I, Emperor—2:18, 3:328, 13:63, 17:322, 339, 18:203, 20:345, 27:3n, 31:228, 276n, 390n, 35:404n, 40:273n, 41:7, 22n, 23–25, 37n, 38n, 41, 54f, 56n, 57–62, 79n, 80, 82–84, 87, 88n, 134, 141, 281, 354n, 372, 373n, 48:24n, 105n, 178n
Constantine II, Emperor—41:373n
Constantinople—2:262, 380n, 7:346, 14:325, 18:197, 22:42, 23:331, 27:218, 35:300n, 37:232, 38:287n, 307n, 309n, 310, 41:371n, 372–376, 41:87, 88n, 89–90, 106f, 277, 50:95, 228n, 229n, 269n
Constantinople, Fall of—41:91n, 46:157, 200n
Constantinople, Patriarchs of—41:88–92, 93n, 94, 290, 41:92–94
Constantius I, Emperor—41:52n, 79n, 210n
Constantius II, Emperor—41:373n
Consternation—11:400–405, 408
Constitutions, Ecclesiastical—34:351
Constitutions of the Holy Apostles—41:45
Consubstantiation—37:xix, 40:196n
Consumption—23:144
Contarini, Cardinal Caspar—34:xv, 233, 266
Contemplation—3:274–277, 25:240
Contemplative life—3:275f, 5:294n, 345–349, 5:294n, 345f, 347–349, 26:287, 459
Contemporary applications—25:xi, 469–472
Contempt—4:6, 11, 18, 20, 31, 59, 61, 72, 100, 121, 141, 201, 210–213, 220, 225, 245, 319, 332, 379, 381, 406, 5:10, 14, 43, 45, 95, 107, 114, 138, 145, 148, 153, 166, 179, 200, 241f, 252, 268, 272, 286, 314–318, 321, 330, 15:4, 8f, 31, 176, 22:36, 85, 96, 23:12, 73, 238, 257n, 263, 264f, 355, 371, 390, 398, 25:500–502, 27:102f, 201, 203, 240, 360, 405
Contention—see **Dissension**; **Schisms**
Contentment—15:7, 10, 13, 21, 30, 65, 86, 101, 133, 143, 15:7, 10, 13, 65, 86, 101, 133, 143, 28:370f
Context—33:193, 205, 258
Continence—1:326, 2:165, 3:208, 210, 5:37, 291f, 323f, 330, 7:72, 77, 86, 11:307, 309, 25:166, 25:320, 30:239
Continents—2:136n
Contingency—25:373, 33:36–44
Contingency of the consequent—25:371f
Contraception—4:304f

Contracts—45:235–237, 301–308, 302n, 45:307n, see also **Zins and Zinskauf**
Contracts, Triple—45:252n, 304
Contradictions—3:119, 4:165, 26:332, see also **Scripture(s)**—Contradictory passages
Contributions—25:106, 126f, 449, 472, 494
Contrition—3:242, 4:56, 58, 7:48, 227n, 228f, 234–237, 257, 363f, 377, 8:5, 181, 189, 267f, 332, 11:8, 83, 237, 240, 249, 297, 12:370, 372, 403, 13:90, 117, 15:281, 16:59, 77, 17:277, 399, 19:87, 26:154, 182n, 27:8, 13, 222, 31:21, 99, 103, 117, 178f, 184–188, 197–199, 224, 32:32–42, 47f, 53f, 34:172–174, 193, 306, 35:6, 12, 14, 17f, 40:294–296, see also **Repentance**
Controversies, Academic—10:264
Controversies, Theological—16:262, 297n
Controversy—27:369, 375, 28:366f
Controversy with Erasmus—26:323n
Convents—3:275, 4:181, 203, 237, 14:20, 22:244, 392, 23:136, 142, 264, 408, 28:3, 10, 28, 49, 336, 39:296–299, 41:120, 294f, 46:47, 141–143, 298, 52:118, 258
Conversations—6:166f, 169
Conversion—1:17, 7:119, 135, 11:17, 37, 156–159, 162–164, 12:390, 13:8, 16:14, 17:135, 174, 306–308, 318, 336, 18:96, 100, 229, 20:9, 30, 32, 87, 100f, 280f, 22:48, 23:407, 25:253, 466, 26:75, 171, 31:96, 33:133, 35:364
Conviction, Christian—52:255f
Cooperation with God—33:155, 241–245
Copenhagen—22:x, 50:147
Copernicus, Nicholas—54:358–359
Copulation—see **Coitus**
Copyists—8:88, 198
Copyists' mistakes—7:267
Coram Deo—25:219, 33:234–241
Cordatus, Conrad—17:366n, 34:125, 147, 47:20n, 49:284n, 332n, 352, 353n, 51:xv, 54:xf, xiii, xvi, 5, 24, 121, 133, 140, 145, 169, 207, 393, 408
recorder of Luther's table conversation, 1532–1533 54:167–201
Coriander—23:31
Corinth—18:92, 22:472, 25:128, 26:23, 63, 27:123f, 29:88, 45:24
Corinth, Church in—41:323
Corinthians—3:283, 7:337, 14:127, 304, 22:344, 379, 489, 24:16, 367, 25:128f, 131, 484, 26:24, 371, 426, 27:51, 108, 122, 124, 260, 301, 406, 30:144, 37:188, 316, 342f, 347, 45:278, 46:29, 64
Corinthians, First Epistle to the—35:380–383
Corinthians, Second Epistle to the—27:299, 35:383f
Corn—1:211, 23:10f, 40
Cornelius—3:81, 355, 359, 5:27, 51, 130, 12:292, 14:23, 17:194, 26:204–207, 209–211, 239, 27:268, 30:298, 33:220, 41:40, 69, 73, 368, 45:98
Cornelius I, Pope—41:44n, 308n, 329n, 354n
Cornelius, Pope—31:281, 34:193n, 37:122
Cornerstone—20:40f, 50, 101, 108f, 150, 218–220, 30:51f, 55f, 58, 60, 301
Corollaries—29:137, 155, 192
Corpora sanctorum (Hymn)—53:331
Corporal—38:114., 214, 224
Corporate nature of life—25:499
Corposant—2:147n
Corpses—3:150, 5:381, 9:212f
Corpus Catholicorum—see index of each volume
Corpus Christi—23:82, 53:137, 252, 54:19
Corpus Iuris Canonici—4:201n, 5:154n, 188n, 13:42n, 282n, 31:xxif, 14n, 95n, 113n, 136n, 143n, 147n, 150n, 170n, 171n, 236n, 244n, 264–270, 278, 279n, 282–284, 385n, 386n, 387n, 388n, 389n, 390n, 391n, 32:81n, 88n, 110n, 34:20n, 37:14n, 300n, 40:354, 355n, 41:107n, 45:7n, 14n, 108n, 144n, 233n, 288n, 297n, 50:162n, see also **Canon law**; **Decretals, Papal**; ***Extravagantes***; **Gratian**; index of each volume
Corpus Iuris Civilis—45:262n
Corpus Reformatorum—23:xi, 101n
Correction—18:354
Corruption—4:158, 190f, 234, 244, 252, 255, 257, 5:62, 86, 130, 208, 7:36, 210f, 228, 263, 281, 294, 336, 8:16, 35, 66, 220, 240, 257, 304, 27:127, 154, 173, 276, 400
Corsica—41:41n
Cortese, Abbot Gregory—34:267
Corvinus—see **Matthias Corvinus**
Corycian cavern—33:26n, 60, 139, 188, 206
Cosmographers—7:208
Cosmography—4:5, 8:78, 96
Cosmological tables—4:87
Cosmology—1:235n
Couch—26:157f, 163
Council, German national—50:82n, 249n
Council of Regency—49:xvii, 23n, 24n, 35f, 93, 126, 191, 197n, 251n, 253n, 317n
Council proposed and indefinitely

postponed—50:82n, 83n, 84, 128n, 144, 145n, 150, 154f, 157f, 158n, 159n, 176n, 177, 184f
Councilmen—45:330, 343, 347–350, 354f, 358, 368, 46:42, 187, 218n
Councilors—24:9, 107
Councils, Decrees of—41:5, 29, 33f, 36, 43, 45f, 73, 96, 123, 290
Councils, Ecumenical—see **Councils, General Church**
Councils, General Church—2:21, 41, 3:213n, 335, 4:9, 6:x, 228, 9:168, 12:49, 14:23, 17:101, 23:27, 284, 287f, 290, 297f, 329, 378, 24:121f, 128, 351, 361, 413, 27:156, 158, 297, 29:19, 44f, 30:4, 22, 105f, 132, 167, 187, 227, 277, 31:255, 262, 284, 322, 385, 32:55, 62, 79f, 114n, 116f, 120f, 129f, 33:57, 86f, 34:125, 283, 41:xiiif, 5f, 6n, 7f, 9n, 10f, 13, 14n, 15–17, 19–23, 24n, 25–33, 35f, 41–49, 51–53, 58, 72–74, 79, 83, 87f, 91–94, 106–108, 112, 115–128, 130–143, 151, 167, 175f, 190, 223f, 236, 259, 261, 263–266, 268–276, 279–281, 284, 288–290, 293f, 296, 300, 308, 334, 341, 345, 361f, 44:xviii, 91, 121, 126, 139f, 144, 169, 45:xii, 105, 286, 314, 46:xi, 47:5, 8, , 48:90, 171, 185, 205f, 208, 49:35, 38, 64f, 68, 90, 156, 161n, 224, 257, 280n, 350n, 362n, 374n, 378n, 404n, 416n, 421, 423, 432n, 50:xiii, xv, xviii, 81f, 85n, 162f, 263, 267n, 51:82n, 93n, 53:35f, 46, 54:215f, 230f, 261–263, 273, 291, 332–333, 356f, 441
Alexandria, Council of 37:361n
Basel, Council of 31:173, 262, 32:59, 81n, 44:91n, 144n, 146n
Chalcedon, Council of 26:273n, 31:281n, 37:212n, 213n, 50:156n
Constance, Council of 8:90, 14:92, 21:320, 32:xi, 82, 83n, 87, 113, 114n, 117, 122, 129n, 33:160, 34:235, 37:173n, 38:114n, 39:127, 134, 149, 41:xiii, 7n, 120n, 121, 122n, 140n, 265n, 266n, 267, 269, 279, 308, 44:91n, 141n, 142n, 144n, 146n, 194, 47:20n, 48:147n, 153n, 189n, 249n, 50:163
Constantinople, Council of 37:372n, 41:5, 23n, 27, 52, 86–94, 96, 106n, 121, 123, 141, 280, 44:137n
Ephesus, Council of 22:323n, 32:128n, 37:212n, 363n, 40:80n, 41:5, 23n, 52, 93n, 93–105, 106n, 121, 123, 136n, 141, 308, 44:137n, 54:333
Ferrara, Council of 44:91n
Florence, Council of 35:93n, 44:129n, 48:362n
Iconium, Council of 41:44n
Jerusalem or Apostolic Council 26:207, 28:309, 29:37, 40, 35:364
Lateran Council, Fourth 38:101n, 251n, 44:179n, 227n, 51:93n
Lateran Council, Fifth 27:297n, 31:262n, 285n, 32:78n, 34:236, 38:238, 44:159n, 46:177n, 47:37f, 48:58n, 104n
Mantua, Council of 34:199, 233, 235
Milan, Council of 48:104n
Nicaea, Council of, 325 2:374, 11:225n, 13:62, 21:91n, 23:287, 29:19f, 40, 31:318, 32:128n, 243n, 33:86n, 35:402n, 37:361n, 38:85, 40:80n, 273n, 41:5, 22n, 23f, 33n, 34–40, 41n, 42–44, 45n, 46–51, 52n, 54–62, 67–68, 70–75, 79–80, 81n, 82–87, 96, 98, 106n, 120–124, 141n, 280, 281n, 299, 308, 318, 44:137n, 158f, 197, 316, 46:179n, 48:105n, 178n, 50:249, 54:333
Nicaea, Council of, 787 41:204n
Orange, Council of 33:112n, 37:363n
Orleans, Council of, Fifth 42:85
Pisa, Council of 31:155n, 285n, 44:91n, 48:104n
Poitiers, Council of 9:230n
Sardica, Council of 44:159n
Seventh Ecumenical Council 51:82n
Their authority 32:80–82, 113f, 127, 159
Toulouse, Council of 37:14n
Trent, Council of 6:x, 21:38, 22:266n, 26:377n, 27:364n, 33:112n, 34:xv, 35:37n, 36:15n, 297n, 38:318n, 41:5f, 9–11, 13, 46, 259n, 260–264, 267, 272–274, 275n, 361, 43:270n, 44:141, 185n, 45:381, 48:291n, 49:410n, 50:xiii, 82n, 249n, 250n, 251n, 254, 256n, 257n, 265n, 266, 269, 271n, 289
Vatican Council, Second 38:xvii
Vienna, Council of 46:232n
Vienne, Council of 32:129n, 48:58n, 246n
Counsel—10:11, 26, 28, 33, 11:445f, 481, 17:135, 144, 152, 164–166, 384
Counseling—17:59, 119, 135, see also **Pastoral counseling**
Counselors—3:253, 16:186, 252, 45:121–126, 46:127, 240, 243f
Counsels—15:4, 9f, 14, 24f, 34, 44, 62, 75, 16:119f, 149, 162, 176, 191, 200, 237, 265, 315f, 29:149, 164, 186, 235
Counsels, Evangelical—see **Evangelical counsels**

Counsels, Human—6:24, 74, 88, 91, 104–106, 117–119
Counsels of God—18:237
Counsels vs. commands—44:256–268, 388f, 45:82n, 83, 87f, 92, 95, 101f, 238, 256n, 275, 277, 283, 287, 291
Countenance—10:68–70, 93, 194f, 324
Counter-Reformation—41:xiv, xvi, 48:134n, 49:12f, 21f, 58f, 161, 188n, 292n, 313n, 50:253
Counterfeiting—51:124, 177
Courage—6:11, 23, 62, 103, 257, 8:13, 19, 23–25, 28, 33, 43, 52, 55, 89, 167, 191, 201, 234, 248, 252, 266, 287, 299, 9:185, 12:382f, 384, 387, 393, 395, 20:150, 24:9, 11f, 17, 20, 27f, 101, 117–120, 122, 126, 131f, 138, 142, 152, 166, 182, 184f, 276f, 290, 292, 294, 332f, 335, 357, 385, 414–416, 420, 43:287, 46:119, 167
Courland, Duchy of—45:139
Courtesy—3:186, 252, 9:204
Courtly speech—23:258n
Courts, Bishops'—44:160
Courts and courtiers—2:140, 315, 4:74f, 77, 82f, 86, 396, 8:107, 212, 13:147, 149–151, 170, 183, 201f, 204, 215, 29:199f, 204, 240, 41:xiii, 133n, 134, 239f, 249n, 253, 254n, 256, 259, 48:295, 309, 354, 383, 49:4, 69, 134, 136, 293f
Courts of law—46:81, 127, 250, 267, 301
Cousins—23:208, 258
Cousins of Christ—22:215
Covenant—3:41, 83, 85, 90–93, 99, 102, 104, 111, 115f, 123, 126–128, 138, 161, 184, 4:20f, 24, 26, 84, 86, 154, 5:264, 9:ix, 60, 63, 79, 86, 165, 182, 214, 254, 271f, 305, 11:189f, 193, 382, 13:132, 359, 361, 377, 382–384, 16:228, 329, 349, 17:69, 178, 252f, 263, 307–309, 341, 20:96f, 290, 317, 27:268, 29:169, 202, 212, 214, 35:xi, 84–87, 90f, 106, 171, 246, 280, 287f, 358, 37:275, 47:231, 251f
  Ark of the see **Ark of the Covenant**
  Baptismal 1:228
  Davidic 47:72, 192–209
  New 17:69, 308f, 25:102, 29:157, 35:xvi, 171, 287, 47:69, 87f, 143, 304
  Old 25:4, 101f, 27:314, 29:212
  With Abraham 2:283f
  With Noah 2:143f
Covetousness—2:30, 375, 4:227, 23:12, 25:63, 243, 262, 274, 299f, 26:40, 44:108, 114, 45:315–328, 336, 387
Cowardice—9:185
Cowls—2:114, 3:51, 118, 316, 322, 4:23, 41, 156, 181, 242, 253, 5:7, 260, 7:193, 323, 8:173, 186, 268, 276, 326, 14:21, 16:227, 299, 17:5, 9, 12, 17, 19, 23, 57, 59, 99, 108, 112, 137, 284, 390, 400, 23:24f, 34, 38, 68, 121, 127, 134f, 171, 179, 182, 196, 204, 261, 327, 333, 351, 409, 24:36, 38, 98, 147, 174, 225, 260, 326, 327, 356, 360f, 26:29, 85, 91f, 175, 185, 199, 238, 256, 259, 295, 29:7, 42f, 84, 30:6, 80, 96, 206, 212, 225, 227, 230f, 255, 283, 287, 38:311n, 41:125, 127f, 168f, 177, 48:12, 33, 50f, 121, 170, 332, 334f, 337
Cows—1:80f, 83, 124, 187, 346, 2:349, 3:177, 321, 347, 4:228, 5:97, 267, 269f, 7:16, 45f, 59, 66, 141, 148–150, 153, 155, 8:17, 60, 69, 224, 228, 279, 302, 318, 16:122, 147, 242, 23:84f, 92, 123, 126, 143, 164, 225, 241, 334, 403f, 24:33, 37, 55, 59, 75, 188, 194, 233, 309, 323, 26:191f, 194, 263
Cozbi—52:120f
Crabbe, Peter—41:7n, 14n, 24n, 33n, 45n, 57n, 151, 93n, 94n, 96n, 107n, 141n
Cradle—4:313
Craftsmen—15:63f, 16:161, 17:22, 37, 110f, 25:205–207, 46:131, 231, 294
Crailsham School Order—53:268
Cranach, Barbara—48:202n
Cranach, Lucas, the Elder—13:168n, 16:255n, 41:260f, 261n, 42:119n, 45:316, 345, 383, 48:200–202, 228n, 230n, 236, 309, 352n, 49:15, 72, 103n, 105n, 115n, 312n, 50:264, 271, 54:153, 217, 222, 267, 344, 435
Cranach, Lucas, the Younger—54:444
Cranach and Doering—39:303, 45:168, 198
Cranmer, Thomas, Archbishop of Canterbury—50:27, 104n, 1193n, 199, 203, 53:xix, 149
Cranz, F. Edward—54:180n
Crassus—5:210, 31:33n, 248
Cratander—48:230n
Crates—2:326, 330, 347, 15:89n
Crato—see **Mylius, Kraft**
Created things—15:4, 8, 14f, 49, 93
Creation—1:3, 12, 17–22, 26, 32, 35f, 38f, 41f, 44, 53, 66, 68, 71f, 74f, 77f, 82, 95, 99f, 104, 109, 124–126, 137, 176, 204, 209, 231f, 237–239, 337f, 354, 2:100, 117, 128, 131, 152, 348, 3:288n, 4:4, 6, 53, 137, 291, 293, 343f, 350, 355, 360, 6:242–244, 8:21, 67, 130, 9:51, 11:10, 12–17, 318, 340, 13:91f, 105f, 14:22, 126f, 344, 22:13, 26, 28n, 74,

81, 88, 91, 94, 100, 130, 149, 297, 420, 496, 25:10, 72f, 154, 360–363, 28:171f, 179–181, 183, 191, 318, 29:231, 30:38, 194, 37:xviii, 30f, 56–66, 69, 88, 119f, 133, 217–229, 236f, 292, 362, 366, 38:121, 246, 263, 268, 271, 277, 309n, 312, 41:304, 345, 43:39, 44:xi, 45:xi, 17f, 22, 25, 37, 48, 99, 46:248, 51:162–164, 358, 52:42, 47, 52, 55, 199, 54:44, 200, 245, 297, 327, 377, 400

Goodness of natural 25:362f

Subjected to vanity 25:362f

Creation, Continuous—1:77, 2:148, 21:299, 31:138

Creation, Days of—1st day 1:20, 23, 39f

2nd day 1:22f, 32f, 150

3rd day 1:33–36

4th day 1:5, 39f, 45f, 55

5th day 1:5, 39, 48, 52–54

6th day 1:5, 32, 38f, 54, 69f, 73, 81, 83, 91, 105, 120–122, 140f, 144, 173

7th day 1:70, 74, 77, 79–82

Creation, Doctrine of—3:288n

Creation, Future—25:360f

Creation, God's ordinance at—45:18–22, 41f, 45f, 150f, 155

Creation ex nihilo—1:16

Creationism—11:465, 466f, 22:327n

Creator—4:53, 60–62, 66, 119–121, 124, 136, 143, 160, 196, 228, 243, 248f, 267, 274, 328, 355, 397

Creatures—1:12f, 15, 17–19, 30, 38, 40, 42, 45–48, 50f, 53f, 56f, 63–66, 68–71, 73f, 76, 78f, 84, 86, 90f, 94–96, 100, 105, 109, 113f, 116, 122, 128, 131, 136, 142, 150–153, 160, 167, 179, 182, 212, 219f, 224, 228f, 231, 245, 287, 290, 292, 309, 327, 338, 354, 4:5, 53, 61f, 66, 68f, 90, 104, 106, 132, 142f, 145, 160, 195–197, 212, 228, 231f, 235, 249, 252, 256, 309, 6:25, 27, 30, 88, 173, 189, 349, 11:11, 15, 39, 15:8, 40, 50, 302f, 307f, 22:20–22, 28, 56, 75f, 90, 92, 95, 102, 361, 405, 496, 25:137, 183, 390, 29:154f, 161, 41:228, 318

Creatures of God—30:248

Creatures of God, Use of—16:179

Creche—16:9n

Creditors—9:243, 45:235–238, 261, 267f

Creed—1:128, 289, 2:86, 228, 333, 3:109, 333, 4:34, 5:46, 214, 6:330, 344, 7:344, 12:200, 13:296, 334, 14:8, 87, 92, 20:156f, 332, 22:75, 85, 102, 113, 249, 258, 265, 270, 316, 324, 328, 363, 366, 392, 401, 454, 459, 468, 481, 492, 499, 503, 23:17, 58, 77, 81, 101f, 163, 166, 191, 195, 284, 287, 386, 410–412, 24:91, 96, 107, 120f, 125f, 172, 222, 238, 296f, 304, 307, 309f, 325f, 365, 368, 26:31, 278, 280, 27:42, 84f, 30:118, 32:46, 78, 286, 34:74, 201, 38:165, 178, 180, 190, 40:308, 315, 318, 41:107, 137, 164, 207, 222, 42:162, 46:136, 171, 231n, 47:16, 53, 51:137, 142, 144, 162–169, 181, 188, 277, 349, 375, 53:21, 25f, 99, 109, 171, 209, 271

Apostles' 2:16n, 4:241n, 5:46n, 7:292, 11:16, 12:105, 293, 298, 13:29n, 296n, 14:307, 15:2775, 306, 309n, 342, 16:102n, 21:283, 22:24, 332, 23:77n, 284n, 26:285, 27:201n, 29:180, 34:199, 202, 35:38, 201, 410, 36:295, 37:29n, 62f, 157, 171, 178, 185f, 227, 292, 296, 38:43, 39:xii, 36n, 41:7, 106, 113n, 132n, 143f, 148, 196, 311n, 316, 362n, 43:7, 14, 25–29, 209–211, 44:23n, 54:9, 17, 333, see also **Children's Creed**

Apostles'—First article 23:77n, 37:60, 69, 361

Apostles'—Second article 5:46n, 23:77, 37:xii, xviif, 8, 29n, 55, 58, 62, 64, 67, 98, 129, 157, 361–365

Apostles'—Third article 14:87, 17:310, 318, 37:100, 115, 157, 365–372

Athanasian 15:302n, 23:284, 28:265, 32:159f, 34:199, 202, 37:212n, 213n, 40:307, 41:33n, 41:7, 33n

Children's—see **Creed**—Apostles'

Ecumenical 34:xv

Nicene 1:9n, 10:10, 13:16n, 20:80, 22:24n, 25, 103n, 105, 23:77n, 284n, 32:243n, 34:228, 38:xvi, 85, 265, 43:26n, 48:370n

Nicene – Third Article 23:77n

Creeping things—2:74

Creeping to Christ—21:72

Creighton, M.—*History of the Papacy*, Boston, 1882 32:90n

Crescent—4:274f

Crespy, Peace Treaty of—50:245n, 269n

Cretans—18:341, 26:188, 29:38–40

Crete—17:414, 20:81, 41:xi, 324

Cries—6:39f, 101, 108, 110, 135, 235

Crimes—2:127, 140, 169, 175, 343, 4:282, 351, 380, 5:11, 29, 34, 51, 110, 194, 297, 302, 382, 6:25, 35–37, 44, 94f, 207, 24:119, 250, 275, 25:272, 31:45, 120, 179

Criminals—3:113, 250, 9:212

Crisis, Prayer in time of—43:231

Crocus—16:299

Crodel, Marcus—50:152n, 230f, 231, 233f, 239f, 240n, 54:448
Cromwell, Thomas—50:29, 136f, 177n, 192n, 193n, 203
Cronberg—see **Kronberg**
Crops, Blessing of—42:86f, 91
Cross, The—30:16f, 23, 49f, 56, 84, 109, 143, 159n, 176, 179, 182, 184, 189, 212, 219, 241, 320, 31:90, 137, 226, 241, 243, 317, 355
  Meaning of 43:27, 184
  Sign of 22:256, 37:35n, 114, 38:227, 42:110, 144, 53:xix, 149, 54:462
  Theology of 25:137, 383, 31:40, 53, 55, 79, 225, 256, 38:xx, 190, 41:xi, 44:xii, 51:14, 17, 30f
Cross, Christ's—see **Christ**—His cross
Cross, Christian's—1:201, 253f, 323, 328, 345, 2:216f, 321f, 351, 369, 3:34, 65, 68, 175, 344f, 351–355, 4:6, 22, 54, 59, 101, 122, 147, 244, 248f, 255, 352, 356, 5:6, 14, 88–92, 142–146, 166, 176, 183, 186, 190, 192, 200, 215, 268, 271, 274, 298, 316, 320, 326, 347f, 353, 358, 362f, 371, 6:8, 43, 180, 192, 268, 384, 8:5, 8, 34f, 47, 61, 114, 180, 255, 294, 9:244, 267, 10:35, 110, 11:101f, 139, 141–143, 146, 150, 528, 550f, 13:263, 333, 347f, 378, 380, 14:30, 57f, 79, 96, 130, 143, 162, 179, 185f, 191, 201, 210, 305, 309, 317, 320, 339, 342, 344, 15:25, 108f, 197, 206, 235, 237f, 258f, 16:53, 119, 149, 152, 163, 166, 214–216, 225, 227, 230, 233f, 238, 263, 17:49, 67, 88, 94, 160, 166, 176, 182, 215, 233, 238f, 407, 19:177, 183, 20:30, 131f, 136, 140, 142, 150f, 155f, 304, 323, 330, 22:144, 204, 258, 312, 23:67, 24:41, 46, 55, 58, 64, 86, 107, 192, 195, 199, 210, 212, 228, 273, 280, 310, 378f, 402, 25:289f, 417, 442f, 27:25, 27, 42–45, 96f, 131, 133f, 237f, 343, 353, 391f, 29:9–11, 14, 53, 65, 83f, 115, 130, 142, 144, 147, 169, 174, 201, 227, 240, 34:121, 35:266, 299, 377f, 380f, 38:196, 40:42, 50, 41:164f, 197, 43:181–186, 46:29f, 32, 35, 220n, 255, 51:31, 40n, 41, 117, 198–208, 329, 392, 52:109, 117, 209, 233f, 246, 277, see also **Afflictions**; **Trials and tribulations**
Cross-bearers—2:37
Crosses and crucifixes—34:53, 55–57
Crossing over—29:225f, 234
Croton—2:189n
Crotus Rubeanus—27:130n, 38:143, 41:304n, 43:99, 48:93, 143n, 49:32, 54:108, 171
Crown of thorns—42:9, 13
Crown prayers—42:22n
Crowns—4:275, 5:110, 184, 206, 237, 251, 304, 353, 7:67, 182, 184, 190, 196f, 226, 9:149, 13:55, 38:107, 208
Crows and jackdaws—14:273
Crucifix—22:147, 387, 23:360, 37:273, 38:177, 40:88, 91, 96, 46:168, 51:84
Crucifixion—see **Christ**—His crucifixion
Crucifixion, Picture of the—22:170
Crucifixion, Spiritual—11:17, 102, 319
Crucifixion of the flesh—10:3, 7, 67, 105, 153, 173, 20:140, 26:165
Cruciger, Caspar—13:xi, 18:x, 24:ixf, 26:ix, 28:x, 34:108, 281f, 297, 301, 342, 35:206, 38:9, 63, 267, 284, 42:181n, 182, 49:104n, 418, 50:102, 117, 135, 173, 207, 218, 273n, 277n, 295, 312, 51:xiv–xvi, 259, 303, 333, 54:xiii, 268, 344, 360
Cruciger, Elizabeth—24:ix
Cruelty—2:70, 346, 358, 3:34, 178, 181f, 235, 252, 4:36 46, 357f, 360, 375, 6:46, 48, 56f, 62, 379, 9:233, 27:69
Crumb collector—46:250n, 251
Crusade, First—47:128
Crusades—22:51n, 31:20, 44:144n, 45:133, 234, 46:xiii, 159, 186n, 188n, 52:231
Crusades against the Turks called for—46:xiii, 157n, 162
Cruss, Johannes—32:266n
Crying to the Lord—10:60, 67
Crystal—2:69
Crystal-gazing—43:17
Cuckoo—9:135, 23:321, 37:31f, 34, 39, 56, 73, 110, 122, 235
Cud—9:136f
Cuius regio eius religio—4:403n
Culture—16:38
Cuntz Hildebrand—13:56, 52:205
Cup—7:108, 118, 237, 351–353, 360–363, 365, 367, 10:101, 106f, 109f, 458f, 16:163, 20:131f, 323f, 42:45f, 139, 183
Cup (martyrdom)—37:122
Cup, Drinking the—18:310
Cup, Sacramental—37:43, 119, 267, 310–315, 319f, 333–341, 346–349, 352f, 357, 38:114n, 132, 205, see also **Chalice**
Cup of blessing—37:248, 348, 352
Cup of salvation—11:404f
Cup of wrath—19:220, 222, 227
Cupbearer—20:90
Cupid—1:268

Curia, Roman—4:396, 8:5, 14:294, 25:472, 27:121f, 147, 157–159, 179, 375, 384–386, 392, 398–400, 31:204, 255, 276, 316, 336–338, 340, 381, 32:ix, xiii, 34:256, 35:408n, 36:18, 41:xv, 282, 287, 289, 341, 360, 362, 368, 376n, 48:10, 45, 75, 77n, 84n, 92, 96f, 105, 109n, 114, 125, 137f, 143f, 163n, 210, 272n, 50:27, 33n, 55n, 82n, 83, 158n, 159n, 176n, 190n, 251n
Curiosity—3:11, 139, 200f, 6:192, 194, 28:66f
Curriculum—45:341, 342n, 343f, 368
Currie, Margaret, trans.—*The Letters of Martin Luther*, London, 1909 35:177n, 399n, 45:318n, 344n, 48:xivn
Curses—1:78, 88–90, 97, 111, 148, 186, 188, 202, 204f, 209, 238, 290, 292f, 295, 302, 307f, 322, 325, 352–354, 2:136f, 175f, 180–183, 186, 195, 261, 265, 274, 280, 344, 389, 3:29, 99, 146, 313, 338, 6:139, 150, 201, 212f, 8:164, 206, 215, 221, 224, 227–229, 231, 233, 254f, 284, 9:83, 89, 117, 212, 215f, 258–261, 267f, 273, 290, 14:252f, 267, 290, 275f, 16:188, 20:54, 85, 209, 230, 275, 21:353, 22:230f, 23:339, 24:14, 158, 358, 25:79, 379f, 27:12, 35, 38, 46, 63, 111, 232, 256, 259–262, 275, 288, 345, 35:283, 359
Cursing—9:232, 236, 259, 267, 277, 21:101f, 25:160, 230–232 289, 359, 429, 42:26, 92, 146f, 51:142f, 155, 174
Cursor Bibliae—48:5, 135n, 173n, 233n, 236n
Curtain—29:203
Curved in on self—see **Incurvatus in se**
Cush—1:101, 2:194, 196, 364, 10:412f
Cushan—19:232
Cuspinian, John—48:199f
Custodian—26:304, 338, 345–351, 359–361, 27:16, 153, 243, 277–279, 283
Customs—9:134f, 198, 211f, 214, 220, 222f, 14:14, 16f, 20, 53, 290, 37:282f, 38:164, 177, 181, 196n, 317n, 46:132, 261f, 291f, 304
Cybele—7:52
Cyclopes—2:34, 37, 41, 138
Cynics—5:30, 7:31
Cyprian—3:191, 329, 7:80, 85, 86n, 119, 227, 9:164, 16:201, 301, 21:272, 23:74, 24:320, 25:268, 26:66, 27:84, 364n, 31:105, 112, 119, 214, 281, 35:110n, 37:54n, 72, 122f, 142, 368n, 38:69, 39:35n, 280, 41:44n, 45n, 46f, 52n, 281, 290, 308f, 312n, 43:156, 160, 44:128n, 197n, 45:41n, 48:24, 53:20, 54:357
Cyprian, Works of—*Ad Demetrianum* 17:107n
De mortalitate 29:139n
De oratione dominica 25:64f
Epistles 7:227n
On Morality 42:129, 130n
On Mortality 32:22n, 42:129, 130n
On the Lapsed 30:237, 30:237n, 35:111n
On the Lord's Prayer 42:27n, 60n
On the Vanity of Idols 17:107n
Cyprian (Pseudo)—*De duplici martyrio* 16:201n
Cyprus—19:43, 27:216
Cyrenaica—2:194
Cyrene—10:412, 16:125, 18:131, 187
Cyriacus, St.—39:215n
Cyril of Alexandria—3:194, 35:318n, 37:242, 39:232n, 41:95n, 98
Expositio sive commentarius in Joannis Evangelium 15:300n
Cyril of Jerusalem—35:399n, 41:88
Cyrus the Great—1:328, 2:100, 128, 205, 258f, 3:81, 89, 8:93, 12:34, 13:155, 16:138, 170, 172, 17:3, 52, 56, 95, 97, 117–119, 122n, 124, 131–133, 135f, 138, 143–145, 153, 156f, 159, 164, 168f, 279, 365, 18:273, 368n, 371, 392, 19:127, 218, 20:46, 83, 159–161, 22:43, 246, 35:277, 299, 329, 47:158, 203, 243, 246–249, 303

D'Ailly, Pierre—4:220n, 10:125, 25:372, 458, 31:12n
Quaestiones quarti libri sententiarum 36:28n, 29f, 31
Sententiarum 25:261
D'Etaples—see **Lefevre d'Etaples, Jacques**
***Da pacem* (hymn)**—53:286
***Da tempus acceptabile* (hymn)**—32:35n
Dabrum—8:279
Dagon—9:54, 131, 10:291, 11:87, 127, 14:66, 18:137, 328, 40:30, 53:26
Daily bread—14:121, 42:50–59, 61f, 79
Daily Office—see **Canonical Hours**
Daily prayer—see **Prayer, Daily**
Daily Services—see **Canonical Hours**
Daily worship—see **Canonical Hours**
Dalberg, John von, Bishop of Worms—5:308n, 8:173n, 41:129n
Dalman, Gustaf—22:421n
Dalmatia—25:124
Damage—9:221, 244
Damascenes—5:268
Damascus—1:89, 91, 310, 2:262, 358, 376, 381, 3:12, 16n, 181, 348, 4:55, 72,

8:291, 11:495, 13:310, 16:154, 336, 18:131–133, 148f, 20:91, 250, 282–284, 23:306, 24:276, 26:64, 74f, 77f, 125, 27:136n, 183, 190–193, 29:129, 41:324, 53:21
Damasus—see **Jerome, St., Works of**—*Letter XX*
Damasus, Pope—35:184n, 41:129n
Damiani, Peter—31:244
Damnation—1:147, 2:17, 71, 246f, 249, 275, 321, 3:70, 173, 326f, 4:60, 63, 67, 161, 316, 350, 5:45, 229, 7:36, 62, 101, 179, 181, 230, 258, 272–274, 8:6, 184, 9:199, 13:240, 261, 14:13, 84, 111, 142, 22:58, 235, 314, 324, 341f, 360, 364, 366–368, 374f, 379f, 382, 23:87, 118, 154, 167, 196f, 317, 339f, 354, 404, 24:52, 61, 141, 222, 280, 340, 342–346, 353, 361, 25:9, 79, 381f, 384, 395, 411, 443, 26:48, 94, 147, 151, 277, 310, 313f, 333, 335, 337, 347, 362f, 404, 411, 458, 27:8, 17, 19, 132, 214, 342, 29:86, 139, 30:15, 102, 175, 210, 229, 280, 35:15, 359, 37:25, 27f, 74, 88, 212, 368, 372, 41:288, 315, 369
Damned, Blessings of the—42:155, 157
Dan—2:205, 376, 4:178, 5:241, 335, 337, 340, 6:275f, 279, 319, 321, 380, 7:7, 24, 8:52, 84, 87, 102, 222, 272, 280–285, 287, 289, 292, 301, 9:307, 10:195, 13:310, 16:115, 155, 18:34n, 56, 38:150
Dan, Tribe of—22:423
Dancers, Ministers as—12:297
Dancing—4:251, 8:191, 13:26, 394, 24:21, 53, 118, 196f, 377, 420, 37:34, 57, 142, 232, 45:249, 369f, 50:279, 54:76, 207, 222
Danes—2:189
Dangers—3:3, 5f, 30f, 46, 53, 63, 76, 78, 108, 117, 120, 137f, 140, 173, 214, 256, 259–261, 264, 267, 284f, 288f, 292, 298, 302, 305–307, 320, 323, 325, 328f, 336, 355, 360f, 4:46, 58, 75, 103, 105, 107, 114, 118, 140, 143, 154, 186, 208, 214, 222, 246f, 282, 313, 319, 321–323, 359, 361, 363, 369f, 380, 390, 399, 6:22, 24, 40f, 56, 59, 78, 102, 106, 117f, 215f, 220f, 350f, 7:46–48, 56, 60, 71, 81, 87–89, 98, 101, 113f, 131, 141, 159, 169f, 177, 179, 198, 214, 220–225, 246f, 250, 256, 259, 267, 276, 282, 284, 287, 290f, 304, 306–308, 312–315, 317, 321, 324, 330f, 336, 360–363, 366f, 371, 8:17f, 31f, 36, 38, 45, 74, 76, 79, 83, 92, 94, 102, 104, 106f, 163, 167, 172, 223, 235, 282, 286f, 293, 301, 308, 310f, 317, 330, 332, 9:221, 241, 310, 15:90, 160f, 174, 211, 16:208f, 24:7, 11f, 28, 50f, 133f, 162, 215, 241, 391, 28:153–155
Daniel—2:36, 45, 58, 181, 200, 206, 229, 254, 258, 320, 359, 391f, 3:90, 121, 274, 360, 4:186, 268, 6:227, 248, 330, 333, 7:52, 56, 137, 141, 148, 187, 297, 8:11, 57, 81, 93, 208, 304, 13:34, 190, 284, 14:53f, 93, 17:124, 18:380, 19:215, 227, 21:346, 22:63, 70, 246, 347, 511, 23:17, 21, 24:80, 366, 25:52, 136, 511, 26:200, 27:167, 28:119, 131, 156, 29:13, 27, 121, 30:22, 103, 206, 35:192, 282, 294–316, 338, 350, 353f, 409, 37:298, 322, 38:161, 180, 190, 211, 232, 244, 39:281, 42:161, 45:96, 144n, 153, 220, 221n, 46:43, 224, 244, 47:85, 158, 188, 195, 204, 221, 241, 265, 281f, 298, 304f
Daniel, Book of—17:137, 140, 20:21, 62, 155f
Daniel, H.A.—*Thesaurus Hymnologicus*, 1841 32:35n, 57n
Danites—8:283f
Dante—34:xii
Danube River—46:157
Danzig—49:104
Darius, King of Persia—2:188, 258f, 3:4f, 13, 27, 30, 31n, 12:34, 35:298f, 331, 47:158, 246f, 249
Darius Hystaspis—20:160, 45:225n
Darius Longimanus—18:368, 371n, 392, 20:6, 74, 76, 160f, 45:225n
Darkness—6:123, 143, 148, 238, 268, 334f, 10:119f, 13:404, 18:80, 90, 182, 272, 290, 21:182, 26:63, 113, 136, 228, 30:165, 37:xviii, xx, 19, 37, 112–114, 168f, 259, 263, 52:68, 84
Darkness, Kingdom of—18:80
Darkness of God—29:216
Datarius—44:151n, 153, 184n
Dathan—2:58, 3:15, 17, 280, 8:222
Daughters—1:281f, 306, 316, 342, 352, 9:229f, 46:231, 269f, 277, 280–282, 285, 301f, 305–310
Daughters of the land—6:192f
Dauphin—8:178
David, House of—20:136, 138, 144, 326, 47:67, 93f, 192–209, 221–223, 261, 300f
David, King—1:132, 194, 244, 271, 298, 2:47, 59, 72, 91, 162, 168f, 224, 250, 252, 258, 264, 281, 291, 293, 306, 319, 353, 3:4f, 13f, 27, 30, 31n, 36f, 44f, 79,

117n, 141, 145, 152, 165, 235, 248, 260, 283, 290, 296, 313, 327f, 332, 339, 348, 350, 4:27, 54, 80, 103f, 106, 117, 150f, 160, 172–174, 176f, 197, 199, 206, 213, 216, 230, 233, 253, 310, 365, 381, 390f, 5:24, 40, 84, 111, 131, 144, 155, 165, 184f, 203, 206, 225, 251f, 254f, 257, 268–270, 311, 327, 355, 6:33f, 117, 162, 176, 189, 206, 223, 248, 278, 284, 292f, 303, 310, 338, 369, 377, 388f, 397, 7:11, 15, 24f, 31, 41, 65, 120, 133, 136, 145, 151, 166, 171, 181, 183, 185, 187, 195, 200, 207, 228, 232, 274f, 303, 311, 349, 360, 8:8, 10, 33f, 54, 115, 117, 129–131, 140, 143f, 146, 150, 153, 160, 203, 208, 212, 223f, 228, 234–238, 242–244, 262, 282, 285, 296, 300, 304, 332, 9:50–52, 57, 72, 87, 104f, 149, 155, 163, 169, 171, 202f, 231, 272, 10:6, 8–10, 28, 31, 42–44, 54, 147, 158f, 214, 240, 11:152n, 189, 200, 248, 544, 546–548, 12:237, 292, 305f, 310, 312, 314, 321f, 324f, 326, 329, 331–335, 338, 345, 352, 406, 13:80, 121, 147, 153–156, 161, 165–167, 172, 178, 181, 183f, 188f, 195, 197, 199f, 205f, 210, 212, 214, 216, 219, 221, 223, 228, 231f, 234f, 242f, 264, 304, 400, 14:9, 51–53, 55, 57, 61, 64, 68, 70, 75, 84, 94, 98, 105, 117, 120, 125–127, 129–133, 135, 173, 186, 221, 228f, 231–235, 238, 241, 257, 265, 273, 288, 307, 311, 313, 319f, 323f, 15:271–275, 280, 286, 294, 296f, 326, 349, 16:21, 26, 59, 62, 79–81, 83, 101, 118, 127, 143, 150, 178, 238, 329n, 332, 17:122, 173, 176, 186, 216, 252f, 278, 305, 350, 367, 370, 18:5, 17, 188f, 208, 262, 274, 325, 329, 19:85, 87, 134, 144, 234, 20:29, 136–138, 144, 192, 295, 326, 330, 21:302, 311, 313, 335, 346, 356, 22:18, 31, 65, 74, 81, 97, 99, 115f, 118, 121, 138, 188, 193, 224, 227, 236, 264, 274, 316f, 319, 346f, 354, 362, 375, 397f, 402–405, 413, 428, 449f, 453, 463, 511, 23:21, 79, 190, 243f, 249, 279, 283, 301, 346, 24:114, 116, 387, 390, 397, 418, 25:16, 61, 142, 160, 214, 255f, 263, 438, 445, 459, 516f, 26:95, 108f, 133, 260, 263, 277, 280, 293, 322, 387, 451, 27:55, 73, 77, 80f, 102, 112, 135, 165, 262, 302, 28:98, 195, 225, 240f, 272, 361, 378, 380, 29:5, 7, 27, 109, 114f, 152, 163f, 173, 176, 178, 182, 216, 227, 30:24, 32, 51, 82, 100, 210, 229–231, 244, 249, 263, 272, 280, 303, 322, 31:99, 128, 34:78, 178, 194, 285, 304, 35:83, 240, 315, 358, 374, 37:63, 172, 298, 362f, 38:50n, 130, 156, 161, 290, 41:80, 119, 122, 252, 42:46, 126, 152, 157, 161, 45:26, 44, 77, 93, 111, 122f, 159, 204, 206, 215–220, 223, 330f, 359, 373, 46:83, 97f, 102, 112, 172f, 193, 221, 285, 288f, 47:71, 78, 93f, 147, 160, 165, 182, 185, 240f, 261, 266, 301, 49:46, 74, 370–372, 51:21n, 106, 160, 275, 350, 52:3, 33, 74, 115, 126, 128f, 137, 187, 202, 271

His last words 47:192–209

David, Kingdom of—20:18, 183, 47:202, 300f

David, Promise to—47:69, 72–79, 82f, 182, 204, 222, 298, 300f

David, Rabbi—2:14

David, Seed of—25:4, 146

David, Son of—47:207f, 250, 300–303

David, Throne of—47:68, 72–79, 82f, 182, 204, 222, 298, 300f

David, Tower of—15:230

Davies, Alan T.—47:133n

Dawn—11:368, 511f

Day—11:524, 527, 18:156, 164, 25:112, 480

Day of Christ—49:13, 32, 140, 216, 289

Day of God—38:xii, 35, 70f, 78, 83, 14, 162, 302, 306

Day of Judgment—see **Judgment day**

Day of the Lord—2:84, 3:35, 18:85, 90, 94f, 110, 163f, 333f

Day of wrath—25:17, 176

Days—13:128, 26:410–412, 27:7, 52, 132, 194, 285, 295f, 331, 335, 383

Days, Observers of—9:175

Daystar—11:366, 368

De vera et falsa penitentia—39:38n

De Wette, Wilhelm M.L., ed.—*Dr. Martin Luthers Briefe*, Berlin, 1826 35:127n, 273n, 45:78n, 318n, 382n

De secretis sacerdotum—see ***On the Secrets of Priests***

Deacons—11:291, 23:196, 273n, 28:295, 297, 299, 300f, 34:53, 35:388, 38:213, 40:35, 41:124, 49:173, 183, 50:49n, 64

Dead, The—15:147f, 150f, 20:97, 290, 28:72f, 109f, 149f, 315, 38:86, 88, 134, 147, 150, 192, 46:224f, 265f, see also **Mass for the dead**

Dead, Blessings of the—42:155, 157

Dead, Commemoration of the—37:3611, 369f

Dead, Cult of the—17:360

Dead, Intercession for the—31:128, 32:97f

Dead, Preaching to the—30:121

Dead Sea—2:343f, 366, 3:298, 18:103, 20:289, 22:186, 423, 426, 35:275, 292

Deaf persons—27:248

Death—2:7, 19, 21f, 48f, 53, 77, 92f, 132, 140–143, 145, 149, 153–156, 158, 160f, 181, 196, 231, 246f, 249, 259, 261, 264, 292, 294, 311, 317, 322, 350, 375, 388, 397, 3:4, 8, 11, 28, 33, 38, 40, 62f, 79, 105, 119f, 125, 134, 136, 140, 143, 160, 173, 175, 207, 211, 215f, 223, 258, 264, 277, 305, 323, 335, 338, 340, 4:7, 16, 40f, 44, 46, 48, 51f, 55, 57f, 92, 96, 98, 103, 106, 109, 112–120, 122–124, 126, 136, 143, 146, 149f, 156, 158, 160f, 166, 173, 175–177, 181, 184, 187, 189–192, 194, 195n, 196, 198, 203n, 215, 217, 223, 226, 230, 232f, 241–243, 290–292, 299–301, 304, 307–314, 316–318, 320, 322, 329, 331, 353f, 366, 373, 376, 399, 401, 5:4f, 18f, 21–28, 39, 41, 48–50, 53, 55, 60, 63, 74–78, 100, 130–132, 143, 146, 148, 151, 154, 158, 163f, 177, 185f, 190f, 206, 219, 221, 228, 230, 233–235, 240, 273, 276, 279, 284, 315f, 328, 341, 355, 6:3f, 41, 95, 99, 236, 252, 254, 272, 384, 7:13, 24, 32, 42, 46f, 49, 62, 89f, 93, 96, 98–101, 103f, 106, 113f, 116f, 121, 124, 132, 135f, 170–172, 175–177, 179–182, 191, 194f, 212, 221f, 224–228, 231, 232, 237f, 244, 246, 249, 252, 254, 256–258, 261, 264, 269, 272–274, 281, 286f, 290f, 293, 295f, 298, 300, 302–304, 309, 313, 322, 330f, 332–334, 357, 362, 374, 8:5, 9–11, 13f, 17–19, 22, 25, 27, 31, 33, 36f, 39, 46f, 51–54, 61, 67, 80, 82f, 94, 97, 111, 113, 121, 124, 128, 138, 143, 147f, 162–166, 170, 173, 177, 182, 184, 186, 189–193, 195, 205, 210, 215, 221, 223, 244, 250–252, 255–257, 259f, 267f, 271, 281, 283, 295, 308f, 314f, 318, 323–325, 329–332, 9:5, 26, 43, 57n, 64, 95, 105, 134, 140, 147f, 163, 170f, 178, 180–182, 195f, 198f, 204, 211f, 215f, 224, 226, 233, 236, 245, 248f, 251, 259, 293, 10:115f, 197, 299, 327, 337, 363f, 371f, 11:19, 212–214, 297, 405, 449, 519f, 12:134, 174, 177f, 230f, 310f, 372, 13:21–23, 26, 76–78, 84, 94–96, 98, 102, 106f, 115f, 137, 166f, 239f, 242, 244f, 14:9, 13, 27–29, 58, 60, 66, 74, 82, 83n, 84–91, 98, 100f, 104, 120, 125f, 131, 133, 141, 143f, 169, 173, 185f, 197, 216, 234, 266f, 275, 295, 323, 329, 337, 341–343, 345, 15:44, 50f, 59, 63, 107f, 182, 258, 16:11, 28, 30f, 63, 68, 72f, 98f, 124, 129f, 152, 170, 190, 197, 207, 209, 228, 230, 305, 337f, 340, 343, 346, 18:71f, 229, 240, 364, 19:65f, 69f, 75, 79, 139, 202, 21:96, 306f, 338, 22:30, 355f, 359, 378, 382f, 385, 391f, 492, 502, 506, 23:11–14, 23, 28, 33, 41, 55, 59, 68, 71–73, 75–77, 105–110, 113, 115, 117, 122f, 127, 129–131, 134–137, 140–142, 145f, 148, 154, 170–172, 174, 176, 178f, 183, 195f, 206, 212, 236f, 243, 247, 250f, 254, 256, 262, 267, 269, 274f, 277f, 294, 310, 313, 315–319, 324, 328, 336–338, 347, 353–356, 358f, 363–366, 372, 376f, 379, 384, 399, 406f, 410–413, 416f, 419, 421, 24:7, 9, 22, 27, 36–38, 41, 44, 46, 48–52, 55, 58, 61, 71n, 73, 77, 79, 83–85, 87, 90, 102, 108f, 113, 115f, 118, 121, 123, 132, 136–146, 149–151, 153, 157f, 160, 162, 168, 175, 184–186, 189f, 192, 196–198, 200f, 212, 214f, 217f, 229, 240, 244, 246, 251, 263, 269, 279, 281f, 287, 291, 295, 315, 335, 346, 349, 359, 361, 378, 387, 395, 400f, 407, 412, 415–417, 420–422, 25:46, 51, 55, 57, 69, 245, 297f, 303f, 310f, 354–356, 26:5, 8–10, 13f, 21f, 27f, 30–32, 36–37, 39, 46, 48f, 55, 60, 64f, 72, 91f, 109, 113, 125–127, 134, 137–141, 147–151, 153, 156f, 159–168, 170, 175, 177f, 213, 224, 229, 233, 237, 246f, 251, 253, 257, 258, 262, 267, 275, 278, 280–288, 290f, 293, 295, 299, 308f, 311, 313f, 317f, 320, 324, 327, 331–333, 335, 338f, 341, 347, 350, 355–357, 361, 363, 365f, 368f, 370–373, 380–382, 384, 386, 388–393, 396f, 399, 404f, 407, 419–421, 426, 437–443, 445, 449, 456, 458, 27:4f, 7f, 14f, 21, 27, 32, 35, 44, 46, 48, 50f, 56, 65, 73n, 74, 77, 81, 83, 87, 92, 109, 117, 120, 122, 128, 134–136, 143, 145, 158, 168, 202, 212, 221, 226, 230, 232, 234f, 237, 240, 256, 268f, 273, 290, 297, 302, 313f, 320, 324, 341, 349, 356, 360, 366, 287, 408, 28:x, 69f, 71f, 80, 98, 104, 106, 108–111, 113, 115f, 118–120, 123, 126, 132f, 135f, 155, 157–159, 178f, 182, 190, 200f, 203f, 206f, 213, 29:10–12, 65, 67, 79, 81, 83, 85f, 95, 97, 130f, 134–141, 164, 170, 176, 194, 213, 215, 225, 234f, 238, 30:9, 13, 27, 29, 40, 49–52, 54, 56f, 63–65, 68, 70,

88, 106f, 110f, 113, 116, 126, 142, 152, 154f, 158f, 162, 164f, 172f, 175f, 196f, 204, 208, 219, 223–225, 230, 232, 239, 246f, 261, 263, 268, 275f, 279, 286, 298, 301–304, 308, 323, 31:69, 89, 104, 114, 116, 119–125, 131, 151, 357f, 32:24, 28, 46, 54, 34:129, 35:39f, 62, 65f, 143, 216, 242f, 252, 256, 359, 362, 401, 37:xx, 26f, 83f, 93f, 96, 100, 124, 130, 133–135, 142n, 149, 191, 238, 293, 305, 360–364, 368, 372, 38:xf, 26, 39, 63, 86, 97, 113, 118n, 125f, 128–130, 134, 157f, 175, 177, 308, 41:119, 125, 140, 146, 206, 241, 42:xv, 11, 51, 59, 61, 98n, 99, 95–115, 129f, 133, 141f, 148–151, 155, 163–165, 172, 175, 43:134f, 46:15n, 22, 39, 48–50, 52–54, 59n, 70, 77f, 81, 93, 101, 104, 133f, 194, 211, 224–226, 229, 255, 278, 297, 310, 47:51–53, 95, 214, 296f, 49:268f, 369f, 50:18f, 51f, 234n, 238, 246n, 51:41, 62, 70, 79, 93f, 112, 114f, 164f, 180, 192, 200, 233–255, 316, 319, 392, 52:55, 61f, 130, 156f, 279f, 54:33, 65, 145, 165, 190, 227, 238, 295f, 298, 312, 319, 336, 349f, 415, 429–433, 448
Like a baby's cradle 4:313
Death, Christian view of—17:269, 334, 388f
Death, Eternal—see **Eternal death**
Death, Fear of—20:98
Death of God—29:194, 41:102–105, 111, 116, 248, 253, 255
Debauchery—3:258f, 7:74, 191f, 8:248
Deborah—6:252f, 255–257, 264, 275, 279–282, 288, 312, 316, 340, 367, 380, 7:8, 125, 256, 8:13, 114, 214, 282, 285, 293, 9:307, 14:79, 283, 15:191, 19:134, 28:276, 46:193
Debt(s)—7:258f, 9:144, 150, 197, 241–245, 25:111, 49:93n
Debtors—9:148, 241f, 45:236–238, 241, 242n
Decalog—see **Ten Commandments**
Decapitation—9:211n
Decay—1:52
Deceit—4:74f, 85, 203, 283, 383, 5:113, 128, 150, 199, 300, 304f, 321, 370, 374, 385f, 25:229f, 37:18n, 27, 32, 231–233, 239, 251, 262
Decency—2:18, 32, 34, 305, 28:273f
Decently and in order—41:173
Deception—5:95, 106, 110f, 113f, 127, 129, 298, 365, 367, 10:151, 166, 181
Decet Romanum—see **Bulls, Papal**
Decision, Valley of—18:120
Decius, Emperor—3:125n, 31:199n, 34:24n
Decius, Nicholas—53:151, 184
Decomposition—28:185f
Decretals, Papal—3:155, 8:21, 181f, 185, 188, 269, 271, 283f, 14:23, 16:244, 22:185n, 27:154n, 156, 178, 218, 236, 29:7, 43, 54, 232, 31:83, 229n, 265f, 279f, 38:189n, 41:9, 30, 205n, 218n, 270n, 285f, 291, 293, 320, 342, 46:176, 197, 199, 273n, 312n, 47:181, 48:186, 51:311, 386, see also **Canon law**; ***Corpus Iuris Canonici***; **Gratian**
Cuncta per mundum 34:243n
Decretalium D. Bonifacii Papae VIII 39:12n
Decretalium D. Gregorii Papae IX 32:88n, 34:20n, 249n, 39:12n, 35n, 38n, 281n, 41:156n, 299n, 305n, 344n, 375n, 44:164n, 165n, 202n, 45:14n, 233n, 46:268n, 312n
Decreti Prima Pars 39:290n, 292n, 41:22n, 25n, 47n, 156n, 157n, 159n, 160n, 285n, 290n, 299n, 305n, 307n, 308n, 333n, 337n, 342n, 369n, 46:227n
Decreti Secunda Pars 39:210n, 249n, 41:34n, 97n, 107n
Decreti Tertia Pars 41:96n, 168n
Decretum 39:281n, 41:20n, 25f, 47, 49, 160, 45:14n, 108n, 144n, 233n, 275n, 288n, 299n
Decretum Gregorii 4:201n
Decretum of Gratian see **Gratian**
Omnes of Pope Nicholas II 41:331, 334, 345, 365
Sacrosancta 34:236n
Si Papa 50:162
Dedan—10:411, 16:173
Dedications—53:93
Deductive method—12:285
Deeds—10:26, 29, 49, 314
Deeps, The—10:155f, 171, 196, 201f, 355, 11:31, 230f, 324
Deer—1:55, 76, 188, 2:66, 74, 197, 8:248, 291
Defamation—2:171, 21:49
Defection—24:237, 249, 302, 412
Defenses—18:148, 54:279
Defiance—24:118f, 135, 137f, 159, 196, 272f, 276f, 420
Deformities, Birth—5:381
Degrees, Academic—2:220n, 5:109, 8:142f, 34:xiv, 307, 36:80, 224, 44:205, 46:209, 54:54, 320, see also **Doctor's degree**
Deifobo, Count of Anguillara—41:278n
Deities—1:42

Deity—9:54, 26:30f, 127, 227, 258, 400
Deity, Partakers of—12:281
Dejection—24:11, 114
Delilah—10:357, 15:131, 38:233
Deliverance—16:136, 336
Delphi—17:51, 35:257n
Delphic oracle—31:185
Deluge—see **Flood, The**
Demas—23:186, 29:105
Demetrius—14:14
Demon possession—24:74f
Demonology—54:279f, 298
Demons—1:61, 134f, 165, 187, 240, 249, 2:11, 119, 147, 358, 360, 4:121, 149, 266, 394, 396, 5:22, 130, 142f, 185, 218, 222, 330, 6:32f, 56, 58, 336, 395, 7:72, 115, 300, 342, 8:131, 152, 271, 316, 9:53f, 118, 294, 14:16, 16:212, 297, 21:270–272, 22:64, 23:204, 237, 24:279, 26:80, 140, 152, 174, 199, 364, 27:41, 123, 147, 149, 166, 172, 291, 311, 28:310f, 314, 373, 29:20, 170, 217, 235n, 30:106, 169, 255f, 31:238, 34:122, 38:55, 173n, 230, 307, 54:172
Demosthenes—2:255, 4:12, 104, 7:191, 194, 13:165, 199, 201, 15:5, 24, 38, 39n, 41, 84, 132, 322, 16:21n, 17:140, 26:385, 28:300, 340, 33:291, 54:223
Demuth, Nicholas—48:160n
Denck, John (Hans)—35:194n, 49:96f, 96n, 165n
Dene, Tilo—43:115
Denial—25:236, 238f
Denmark—8:321, 14:x, 22:ixf, 5n, 215, 530, 40:75, 267, 46:106n, 106–108, 113n, 114f, 202, 48:216, 236n, 303n, 50:147, 54:257, 271, 305
Denziger, Henry—*Sources of Catholic Dogma*, St. Louis, 1957 27:297n, 35:49
Denziger-Schönmetzer—*Enchiridion Symbolorum*, Barcelona, 1967 47:38n
Deo gratias—53:39
Departure—6:23, 37
Deposition—54:290, 362f
Depravity, Human—2:39, 120, 126, 299, 301, 314f, 4:5, 257, 278, 355, 371, 12:335, 337, 339, 341, 21:65, 25:245, 345f, 351
Depreciation—26:362n, 404
Depredations—2:60
Depression, Dealing with—54:16, 18, 95f, see also **Anfechtungen**
Der gantz Jüdisch glaub—see **Margaritha, Anthony**
Descent, Physical vs. spiritual—8:219, 232
Desert(s)—4:7–9, 27, 36f, 40–42, 44, 47, 49, 58, 62–64, 68, 71, 109, 111, 120, 123, 181, 10:302, 306, 457, 16:195, 254, 24:268
Desire (Karlstadt)—40:148, 179, 185
Desire, Sexual—see **Sexual desire**
Desires, Evil—46:153f
Desirous—10:100
Desolation—16:41, 86, 189
Despair—1:171, 175, 178, 191, 275, 287, 296f, 3:4, 8–10, 63, 72, 276, 294, 310, 4:48–52, 54, 57, 62f, 93f, 105, 144, 322, 353f, 360f, 378, 5:10, 13f, 43, 45, 169, 215, 254f, 320f, 327, 359f, 6:8, 39, 99, 101, 103–105, 107f, 116, 131, 151, 219, 241, 298, 404, 7:44f, 55, 94, 126–128, 132, 193, 227, 229, 257, 260, 327, 329, 363, 366–368, 8:6, 8f, 26, 46, 58, 61, 72, 80, 97, 163, 165, 167, 189f, 200, 237, 325, 329, 331f, 9:41, 59, 181f, 218, 10:140f, 12:78f, 81, 168, 193, 220f, 229, 248, 306, 311f, 316, 324f, 358, 373, 379, 402, 404f, 406f, 410, 13:110, 114, 14:254, 16:12, 54, 108, 139, 152, 156, 215, 232, 236, 314, 333, 341, 343, 17:4, 47–49, 65, 88, 129, 299, 364, 372, 388, 19:19, 25, 47, 78f, 136, 189, 199, 20:8, 49, 158, 166, 22:142, 23:12, 59, 73, 86, 221, 271, 349–351, 24:11f, 16, 44, 110, 119, 132, 148f, 166, 210, 219, 329, 361, 379, 400, 416, 25:179f, 270, 284, 290, 491, 26:5, 10f, 22, 26f, 29, 35f, 42f, 148f, 161f, 166, 195, 218, 233, 300, 310–313, 315, 318, 323, 339, 341, 345, 348, 371, 379, 381, 383f, 387, 394, 402, 405, 443, 447, 460, 27:5, 22, 26, 34, 67, 73, 78f, 81, 87, 137, 275, 361, 371, 374, 28:208f, 246, 29:184, 30:159, 173, 229f, 234–236, 280, 293, 300, 304, 312, 33:77, 190, 34:116f, 126, 35:15, 36, 53, 110, 243, 378, 39:128, 171, 186
Despair over human ability—31:51f
Despairing humility—48:54
Desperation—16:68, 26:35
Despisers—16:190f
Despotism—2:142, 219
Dessau—48:400, 50:78f, 80n, 123n, 124n, 148, 175, 235n, 51:315, 53:17n
Dessau, League of—49:82n, 119n, 123f, 126f, 144n, 154n, 155, 190n
Destruction—10:227f, 245, 272f, 431f, 441, 450f, 16:46, 107, 111, 186–188, 191, 194, 206f, 217, 222, 236, 240, 278, 288, 295f, 326, 25:232, 257, 313f, 317, 35:282, 378
Detlef, Peter—32:280
Detractors—11:354–356

Deucalion—2:131, 211, 17:198n, 33:80

Deus absconditus—see **Hidden God, The**

Deus adjutorium—10:385, 391

Deuteronomy, Book of—2:135, 3:361n, 5:200f, 8:88, 198, 307, 9:ixf, 3, 6, 7n, 14, 60, 64, 170, 259, 14:132, 15:x, 16:297, 19:26, 120, 23:121, 29:206, 50:109

Deutsche Bible—see **Luther, Martin, Writings of**—German Bible

Deutsche Messe—see **Luther, Martin, Writings of**—*German Mass and Order of Service*

Deutsche Reichstagsakten—32:104n, 113n, 114n, 45:69n, 242n, 277n

Deutsche Sprichtwörter Lexikon—see **Wander, Karl F.W., ed.**

Devastation—16:75, 176, 182, 186, 188, 190, 194, 198f, 217, 238, 264, 279, 295

Devay, Matthias Biro'—38:283

Devil—1:23, 59, 70, 74, 107, 112, 133, 140, 142f, 148f, 151, 155f, 158, 160f, 171f, 182–184, 188f, 191, 193f, 197f, 215, 218f, 222, 238f, 273, 275, 280f, 296, 301, 322, 328, 331, 355, 2:4, 11f, 19, 30, 37, 47f, 57, 99, 121, 143, 156f, 165, 197, 202, 212, 218, 261, 265, 267, 345, 348, 353, 369, 391, 3:8, 25, 49, 77, 180, 229, 252, 264f, 275, 279, 326, 344, 362, 4:7, 23, 28, 32, 72–74, 81, 93, 95, 105, 117, 120–124, 126–128, 130f, 143, 145–147, 160f, 164, 175, 179f, 182, 201, 203, 207, 210, 214, 221, 237, 248, 255–257, 263–265, 268, 277, 283, 290, 298, 305, 324, 329f, 333–338, 343f, 349f, 356, 364, 366, 372, 375f, 389, 391, 395–397, 5:5, 9–11, 16, 18, 21, 23, 26f, 32f, 34, 39f, 42f, 47f, 58, 61, 77, 111, 132, 141–143, 146, 150f, 163, 165, 168, 170, 173, 181, 185f, 191, 203–206, 208–210, 215, 219, 221f, 226–228, 230f, 233–235, 240, 248, 251f, 267, 270, 277, 279, 290, 306, 310, 313, 348, 353, 355, 382, 6:18, 31, 38, 52, 71f, 74, 88, 90, 95, 124, 132, 245, 334, 336, 380, 7:13, 16, 30, 55–58, 63, 72–77, 79–81, 85, 87–90, 93f, 96, 98f, 103f, 111, 121, 126–128, 132, 135, 161f, 165, 170, 175, 177, 179f, 182, 184f, 190–195, 200, 225f, 233, 242, 252, 255, 271f, 274, 276f, 279, 287, 290, 297, 299, 304f, 308, 311f, 326, 328f, 333, 335, 341f, 369–371, 8:30, 39, 47, 52, 56, 60, 83, 93, 114, 126, 132, 137, 152, 162–164, 166f, 177, 182–185, 187, 189, 191, 219f, 238–240, 242, 244, 250–252, 255–257, 259, 271, 274, 283, 288, 292, 294, 299, 309, 311f, 314, 316f, 324, 326, 330–332, 9:53, 55, 147f, 186, 10:29, 84, 86, 93, 114, 182, 252, 278, 347–349, 408, 11:13, 17, 185, 307, 369, 424, 435, 447, 496, 509f, 519, 530, 547, 552, 12:109, 114, 116f, 127, 134, 154, 172f, 174, 177f, 183, 212, 215, 217, 222, 228, 243, 260f, 264f, 331, 345, 347, 357, 373, 379f, 387, 394, 13:13, 21, 46, 50, 97, 111, 113f, 135, 177f, 185–187, 194, 239, 251, 262, 278, 280f, 408, 14:4, 7, 9–11, 13, 16, 24f, 27–29, 31f, 36–39, 49, 51f, 55–58, 60–62, 64, 66, 70–74, 82–84, 86f, 89, 92f, 95, 98, 100–104, 111, 116, 120–123, 127, 130, 132, 134, 140, 158, 179, 233f, 247, 251, 260f, 268, 281, 300, 304, 321, 336, 15:303f, 16:65, 123, 129, 152, 156, 177, 181, 198, 206, 211, 213, 288, 301, 308, 310, 312, 333, 17:19, 41, 361, 19:35f, 56, 139, 206, 20:x, 8, 48, 74, 93, 173, 183, 203, 205, 207, 241, 291, 314, 21:3, 5, 42, 51f, 60, 127, 133f, 138, 152f, 165, 167, 177–179, 185f, 204f, 211f, 230f, 244f, 252, 263, 271–273, 290, 22:17, 21f, 24, 41, 48f, 52, 67, 71, 74, 81, 86, 89f, 101f, 104–106, 108, 110, 114, 119, 134, 142, 152, 163, 167–169, 180, 187, 196, 201, 204f, 207, 209, 225, 227f, 231, 233, 236, 241, 245f, 247, 250, 254, 259, 262, 273, 296f, 306f, 312f, 332f, 337, 340f, 349, 354, 356–359, 361, 366, 368f, 371, 373f, 377, 379f, 384, 386, 398f, 404f, 407, 410, 416, 418, 430f, 433f, 439, 442, 445, 450–452, 458, 461, 463, 465f, 469f, 473, 475, 481, 486, 490, 497, 499–502, 507–509, 513, 525, 23:xi, 6, 11, 24, 26, 28f, 33f, 39, 44, 47, 52, 58–61, 67f, 73–75, 77–79, 81f, 87f, 93, 95, 97, 106f, 110, 115, 122, 127f, 131, 134, 136f, 139–142, 144, 146f, 157, 170f, 173–175, 179f, 183, 188, 190f, 193–197, 202, 204, 206, 213, 223, 226–228, 231, 233, 238, 240–243, 246, 249–251, 255–257, 259, 262, 264f, 274, 281f, 287, 289–294, 296, 298f, 302f, 305f, 318, 323f, 327f, 330, 336, 338–344, 346–349, 351, 353–355, 357, 359, 366–368, 371–372, 375, 377, 381, 383, 385, 389f, 395, 399, 404, 407f, 411f, 416–418, 420f, 24:7f, 11–22, 25–27, 29, 31f, 36, 39f, 43, 46, 48–50, 53, 55, 62–64, 68, 70, 72, 75–81, 82n, 83–86, 90–92, 94–96, 98, 101–103, 108–110,

121–123, 125, 128–133, 135, 137f, 140–146, 148–153, 157–164, 166, 168f, 173–175, 177–182, 184f, 189, 191f, 195f, 198–200, 204f, 209f, 213, 215–218, 222, 225, 233, 240, 244–249, 255, 258, 261, 263f, 266f, 269–274, 276f, 279–281, 284–286, 288–298, 301–303, 305, 308, 312–315, 317–323, 325, 329, 331, 343f, 346f, 350–354, 358–363, 368–371, 377–380, 382f, 385–389, 393, 399–401, 404, 411, 415–417, 419–422, 25:69, 142, 160f, 177, 254, 296f, 314, 338, 459, 26:3, 5, 10, 13, 18, 20–23, 26, 29–32, 36f, 41, 44, 46, 48–52, 54, 59f, 65, 71, 80, 87, 91, 99, 105, 114, 134, 155, 157, 160–162, 164f, 168, 174f, 178, 182, 188, 190–197, 200–202, 213, 218, 221, 224, 228, 247, 253f, 257f, 267, 273, 282, 285, 294f, 305, 307–311, 318, 332f, 341, 357, 365, 368, 371, 375, 380–382, 384, 392, 395, 397, 407f, 411, 418f, 428f, 443, 449, 455, 459, 27:4–8, 11f, 19, 21–24, 31, 33, 35, 37, 42f, 45, 47, 49, 50f, 53, 56, 58f, 70, 78, 87, 90, 92, 94, 109–111, 118, 124f, 127, 135f, 143, 145f, 170, 244f, 297, 304, 369, 384f, 387f, 28:14, 61f, 66, 70f, 74, 104, 106, 108, 111, 135, 157, 204f, 311, 29:10, 17, 20, 24f, 30, 34, 36, 41, 64, 68, 72, 89, 93, 102, 134–137, 139–141, 171, 234, 238, 30:9, 12, 29, 31, 35f, 41f, 45, 61, 67, 70–72, 83, 88, 94–96, 98, 100, 104f, 108, 114, 116, 121, 125, 135, 138, 140–143, 152, 154f, 159, 164, 173, 175, 182, 186, 188f, 191, 205–207, 209, 213, 219, 223–225, 228, 235, 240–242, 245–247, 253, 255f, 259–262, 267, 272–274, 276, 280f, 285, 287, 290, 294–297, 301, 303, 307, 309–313, 319f, 326, 31:209, 34:9, 96, 119f, 141, 366, 35:55, 60, 66, 68, 83, 90, 144, 193, 197, 200f, 214, 243, 378, 387, 391, 404n, 406, 410, 38:24, 26, 56, 77, 88, 97–99, 100f, 105, 108, 110, 112f, 119, 125–128, 130f, 137, 144, 148–158, 164, 168f, 171, 174f, 179, 181, 185, 187f, 190f, 200–202, 204, 222f, 225–228, 243, 261, 287, 292, 298, 302, 304–305, 306n, 307, 310f, 315, 39:10, 22, 34, 36, 39, 78, 93, 119, 123–125, 133, 148, 150f, 178, 195, 208–210, 247, 267, 277, 281, 284, 292–294, 296, 40:70, 80, 84, 145, 149, 197, 201, 216, 259, 261f, 271, 303, 346, 384, 393, 41:9, 11, 17, 29, 34f, 66, 71, 73, 77, 79, 81, 85–87, 91, 103, 113, 116, 119, 122, 124f, 127, 143f, 146, 150f, 155f, 161–172, 177f, 185f, 188, 190–194, 199–229, 231, 237–239, 240n, 244, 247–251, 263–265, 268, 275, 278–280, 284–286, 288, 291, 293, 295f, 298, 301–303, 306–308, 311, 318, 323, 325, 327f, 332–344, 347–351, 356n, 357–366, 369–372, 375f, 42:20, 25, 29, 31, 38–40, 46, 56, 65–67, 69, 71, 73f, 78, 101–103, 110f, 121, 135, 137, 157, 181, 184, 185n, 44:48, 54, 111, 45:xiv, 8, 21f, 26, 34, 37, 45, 64f, 68f, 106, 115f, 146, 151, 156f, 201–203, 213, 245, 279, 306, 319, 336, 342, 349–352, 358, 366f, 371, 374, 377, 385, 46:9, 18n, 21, 24, 28, 33, 41f, 49, 51–55, 63, 66–68, 70, 77, 79, 84, 117f, 121, 129, 134, 150, 162, 165, 167f, 170f, 174f, 177, 179–184, 186, 188f, 193, 195f, 200, 204, 213f, 217–219, 223–231, 240, 242, 251, 254–257, 265, 286f, 295, 301f, 305, 317, 47:13, 27f, 30, 33f, 44, 49–51, 53–55, 107, 109–111, 113–119, 137, 154, 159, 162, 190, 192, 200, 214, 217, 220f, 254, 256–258, 266, 273, 285, 290, 293f, 297–300, 303, 50:70, 96, 150, 175, 184, 215, 222, 238, 246, 296, 298, 300, 302f, 51:38, 41, 45, 48f, 62–65, 71–73, 78–80, 85f, 90, 92–94, 98, 100, 111–115, 124, 126, 128, 138f, 141, 143, 157, 165, 172, 175, 177, 180f, 184, 187, 198, 200, 203, 205–207, 212, 217, 238, 240–242, 248f, 254, 264, 286, 291f, 295, 299, 338, 360, 362, 373f, 377f, 52:57, 71, 91, 96, 98, 117f, 128, 160f, 178, 182, 184, 196, 199, 200, 216, 227, 229f, 236, 250, 255, 260, 263, 265, 270f, 273, 275, 277, 283, 53:48, 99, 101, 108, 54:16, 24, 29, 34, 51, 78, 82f, 86, 93f, 96, 105, 128f, 151, 241, 276f, 279f, 298, 313, 318, 379, 397, 453, see also **Satan**

Builds chapel near church 4:237, 5:285, 21:212, 263

Devil, Kingdom of the—26:14, 39–42, 48, 70, 152, 224, 351, 386

Devil, Works of the—7:185, 192, 195, 290

Devil's apostles—14:261

Devil's bride—12:174, 261, 24:308

Devil's children—24:322, 329, 331

Devil's icicle—7:85

Devil's martyrs—17:110, 112, 299

Devil's yeast—7:233

Devils—41:10, 12, 25, 31, 120f, 168f, 185, 189, 192, 218, 220, 224, 229, 240, 242, 244, 249, 277f, 285f, 296, 299, 301,

303, 308, 318, 328, 335, 338, 344, 351, 359, 361, 363, 370, 47:15, 29, 44, 47f, 52, 161, 163, 168–170, 172, 176, 178, 183, 230, 275, 278, 285, 297, 301, 306

Devoted things—18:269

Devotio moderna—49:24n

Devotion—10:42f, 23:7, 17, 204f, 24:260

Devotional writings by Luther—see Vols. 42 and 43

Devotions, System of—43:190f

Dew—1:83, 129, 206, 9:6, 290, 306, 308, 11:367f, 16:209

Diadem—9:149

Diakonia—25:446

Dialecticians—2:4, 126, 271, 3:101, 119, 195, 213, 308, 4:34, 100, 168, 200, 239, 5:24, 117, 148, 7:168, 310

Dialectics—1:46, 3:9, 84, 191, 194, 341, 4:239, 345, 7:90, 94, 156, 24:311, 27:23f, 30f, 32:184f, 38:239, 241, 41:118, 139, 227f, 228n, 246n, 254, 46:252n, 48:56f, 49:179, see also **Logic**

Diamonds—1:101, 24:134

Diana—6:50, 7:325, 336, 25:24

Diaspora—47:298

Dibon—16:146, 148

Dibora—1:282, 312

Dice—7:120, 338, 9:199, 24:94

Dichotomy—27:363

Dictionaries, Renaissance Latin-German—37:80

Dido—7:79, 10:159

Didymus, Gabriel—38:135n

Diehl, Karl—45:235n

Dies irae (hymn)—18:334n

Diet (food)—54:277

Diet, Imperial, 1519—42:119

Dietary rules—9:134f

Dietfurt—49:313n

Dietrich, Martin O.—author of *Introduction to the Devotional Writings* 42:ix–xi
author of Introduction to Vol. 42 42:xiii–xvi
editor of Vol. 42
presumed author of introductions to all items included in Vol. 42

Dietrich, Veit—1:ix–xii, 191n, 280n, 288n, 2:x, 3:ix, 5:ix, 7:ix, 12:viiif, 29n, 31n, 332n, 13:xi, 102, 353, 14:xi, 15:xi, 18:ix–xi, 115n, 23:xf, 26:ix, 28:21, 32:xvin, 35:206, 38:9, 12, 143, 145, 46:211, 213n, 49:282n, 283, 287, 288n, 312n, 319n, 327, 330n, 348n, 354n, 368n, 377n, 378n, 420n, 426, 50:xx, 10–12, 17n, 52, 55n, 112n, 229n, 248, 263n, 51:xivf, 197, 54:xii, xvi, xix, xxiii, 5, 23, 26, 30f, 59, 75, 79, 82, 95, 97, 102, 111, 125, 147, 156, 169, 225, 367, 383, 467
recorder of Luther's table conversation, 1531–1533 54:3–114

Dietrich of Bern—34:277, 37:340, 40:188n, 41:363n, 51:64, see also **Theodoric I, King of the Ostrogoths**

Dietrich of Bila—40:106

Diets, Imperial—6:ixf, 40, 349, 24:283, 41:9n, 134, 259, 45:310, 46:xi, 167n, 187f, 189n, 48:70n, 50:221, 263, see also cities where diets were held

Dietz, Ludwig—53:172

Difficulties—6:24, 100, 103, 109, 124, 221, 270, 312f

Digamist—22:451

Dignity—29:52, 126f, 173

Diligence—25:451, 454f

Dillenberger, John—47:209n, 54:358

Dinah—4:252, 5:90, 297, 340, 358, 6:175, 187f, 190, 192f, 215, 220f, 264, 276, 282, 305, 312, 315, 321, 340, 359, 362, 380, 7:8, 125, 310, 8:13, 56, 84–87, 92, 114, 152, 220, 30:260

Dinda, Richard J.—translator of Latin text of *Lectures on Zecchariah* 20:3–152
translator of *Lectures on I Timothy* 28:217–384
translator of *Lectures on the Minor Prophets (Hosea, Joel, Amos, Obadiah, Micah, Nahum, Zephaniah, Haggai, and Malachi)* 18:3–419

Dio Cassius—*History* 15:72n
Roman History 8:58n

Diocletian, Emperor—3:125n, 7:255f, 343, 8:105, 106n, 252, 255n, 25:462, 31:219n, 32:258n, 34:24n, 41:373n, 43:173, 45:99n

Diogenes—15:89n

Diogenes Laertes—*De vitis, dogmatibus et apophthegmatibus clarorum virorum* 15:296n
The Lives and Opinions of Eminent Philosophers 41:186n, 50:228n

Dion of Syracuse—see **Dionysius of Syracuse**

Dionysius—20:26, 64, 32:170, 259

Dionysius, Bishop of Alexandria—41:44n, 45

Dionysius, Pseudo—see **Dionysius the Areopagite**

Dionysius of Syracuse—4:202n, 205, 6:238, 15:22n, 41, 19:181, 46:110n, 50:116

Dionysius the Areopagite—1:62, 235, 237, 5:139n, 10:119, 313, 13:110, 210,

17:187n, 25:130f, 227, 287, 29:121, 39:175f, 54:112n
De divinis nominibus 3:274n, 29:132n, 217n
De mystica theologia 29:163n
Ecclesiastical Hierarchy 31:119
Epistolae 3:166n
On the Celestial Hierarchies 4:23n, 25:351, 29:121n, 179n
Dionysius the Elder—see **Dionysius of Syracuse**
Dionysius the Tyrant—see **Dionysius of Syracuse**
Dioscur, Bishop of Alexandria—41:115n
Dioscuri—2:147n
Disaster—6:187, 235, 270, 275f, 307, 351, 390, 16:23, 50, 156, 164, 177, 186, 206, 232, 279
Disbelief—24:210, 35:13, 64n
Discalced Orders—18:55
Discantus—19:148
Discerning Christ's body—37:124, 347
Discernment of spirits—16:130
Discharges, Natural—52:259f, 268, 273
Disciples—2:161, 163, 263, 327, 335, 363, 385, 3:61, 92, 104, 172, 8:26, 37, 45, 53, 146, 250, 254, 324, 14:9, 90, 274, 347, 16:92, 94, 17:173, 328, 21:73, 22:50, 52f, 55, 63, 77, 107, 161, 183, 219, 224, 228–231, 251, 350, 413, 493, 509, 512, 517, 519, 528, 23:5, 7, 10, 20, 34f, 46f, 49, 51, 76, 92, 95–97, 156, 158, 162, 188f, 28f, 214, 230, 280, 365, 392–394, 396–399, 401, 409, 24:7, 9f, 133, 16, 18, 28, 31f, 35, 40, 44, 51, 54, 56f, 71, 76f, 86f, 99, 101–103, 106, 113, 132, 135, 144f, 147f, 163, 178, 180, 183, 189, 191, 204, 206, 224, 227, 243f, 247, 249–253, 262, 265, 270, 275, 278, 288, 301, 305, 316, 331–333, 335f, 353, 355, 357, 360, 370f, 374f, 379–382, 389, 395, 399, 401f, 406–412, 414f, 419, 28:76, 29:94f, 99, 37:13f, 26, 52f, 73f, 96, 106, 180n, 248f, 262, 288, 305, 311–317, 331, 38:23, 38, 52, 56, 70, 82n, 154, 198, 205, 41:144, 311–314, 317, 319, 345, 347f, 368, 46:51, 63, 102, 52:184, see also **Apostles**
Disciples, Twelve—28:76
Disciples, Seventy-two—23:155, 157, 185–187, 190–192, 194
Discipline—2:30, 126–128, 321, 383, 3:48, 59, 98, 203, 229, 231, 245, 252–254, 256, 279, 4:5, 76, 146, 207f, 213f, 271, 281f, 331, 336, 345, 347, 5:189, 285, 287, 6:90, 130f, 150, 194, 198, 221f, 231, 239, 261, 7:16, 20, 42, 73, 152, 184, 191, 201, 226, 229, 231, 233, 237f, 254, 318, 338f, 8:9, 119, 121, 133, 161, 170f, 173, 181, 198, 251, 276, 297, 10:36, 38, 49, 289, 374, 11:459f, 14:318, 346f, 16:26, 98, 20:102, 260, 262, 278, 23:34, 24:50, 116n, 175, 176n, 228, 262, 313, 26:4, 187, 346, 350, 407, 416, 448, 459, 27:96, 278, 35:348, 42:74, 138, 46:219, 255, 309, 54:157, 235, 457
Discipline, Christian—48:13, 211n, 374f, 382f, 402
Discipline, Spiritual—44:105
Discipline of Children—7:226, 231–233, 235
Discord—4:85
Discord and dissension—27:91, 368f, 371, 375, see also **Schism(s)**
Discourses, Prophets'—20:13, 42
Discoveries—2:207n, see also **Americas, Discovery of the**
Discovery, age of—45:234, 236, 342
Diseases—1:77, 92, 110, 119, 133, 142, 160, 206, 207n, 225, 347, 3:6, 48, 65, 139, 202, 248, 271, 323, 342n, 7:76, 79, 81, 87, 130, 228, 231, 290, 295, 308, 8:54, 147, 277, 9:147, 268, 11:200, 14:259n, 38:63n, 41:75, 289n, 42:91, 130, 43:115–138, 45:44n, 46:117n, 254n, 302, 54:65, see also **Pestilence**; **Plague**; other specific diseases
Disgrace—6:43, 52, 59, 64, 180, 190f, 197, 276f, 318, 8:7, 10, 17, 24, 48, 56, 126, 218, 25:11–13, 22
Disgust—7:16
Dishonesty—4:84, 86, 229, 13:217f, 21:235–237
Dishonor—4:6, 190, 232, 234, 238
Disinterestedness—33:153
Dismas, St.—16:159n
Disobedience—1:96f, 162, 164, 166f, 171, 177, 179, 189, 210, 227, 2:12, 30, 141, 175, 273, 3:47f, 62, 135, 172, 175, 284–286, 298, 300, 305, 4:225, 286, 5:315, 6:30, 194, 367, 10:17, 28f, 189, 16:21, 22:119, 138, 174, 288, 340, 397, 399, 23:238, 24:81, 255, 260, 284, 337–339, 341, 343, 25:168, 26:20, 36, 40, 29:73, 124, 211, 30:212, 41:242, 42:38, 42–44, 66, 101f, 46:115, 269, 285, 310, 52:216, 250
Disobedience, Passive—45:xiv
Disparagement—11:353f
Dispensations—3:126, 144, 22:220, 27:215f, 226, 31:229, 36:75, 79–81, 103, 105, 217, 52:264

Dispensations, Papal—34:261, 44:154n, 155n, 184n, 46:315
Dispersion—16:284
Displeasure—2:13, 23
Disputations—28:63, 68f, 72, 31:xx, 19, 34:xiii, 38:xviiif, 6f, 150, 237f, 240, 242, 244, 269, 277n
Disputations, Academic—32:148f, 36:238n
Disputes—9:144, 25:113
Disputes, Religious—13:62f
Dissembling—15:83f, 187, 25:106, 451–454
Dissension—10:58, 25:13, 105, 117, 127, 130, 464, 476, 483, 34:212, 266, 37:13–18, 23–25, 27, 42, 167, 40:63, 66, see also **Discord and dissension; Schisms**
Dissipation—8:187
Distinction of persons—7:182, 184f, 187, 190, 201, 16:186
Distress—6:103, 136, 221, 235, 353, 14:58f, 130, 143, 16:79, 208f, 341, 18:31, 61, 21:233, 24:15, 17f, 29, 52, 82, 86, 90, 145, 149f, 183, 195, 211, 240f, 333, 391, 413, 415, 25:179f
Distributive meaning—20:47, 141, 227
Disunity—16:161
Ditmarschen—1:288, 9:5, 32:xix, 263–284
Diversity of beings—37:164, 295–303, 334f, 339
Diversity of interpretation—37:xx, 5f, 23–26, 28, 42, 154, 163–165, 167f, 236
Dives—52:172
Divination—2:271, 355, 7:110, 8:129n
Divine Majesty—see **God**—His divine majesty
Divine right—46:9n, 12n, 25
Divinity—5:42, 44, 151, 219, 221–223, 25:157f, 26:227, 229f, 233, 259, 265–267, 272f, 282, 284, 38:277, see also **God**
Divinity (divine things)—29:110f, 166, 215, 234
Divisions—see **Schisms**; **Dissension**
Divorce—3:258f, 9:210, 241, 244, 18:402, 404, 406, 21:84f, 92–94, 96–98, 28:31–34, 36f, 30:20, 34:350, 36:103f, 105n, 106, 40:98, 45:xii, 30–35, 383, 46:262, 277f, 282, 286, 296, 300, 303, 310f, 311f, 48:211n, 298, 377f, 50:31f, 51:160, 52:218, 54:349
Divorced persons—28:32f, 36f
Doberstein, John W.—54:72n
author of Introduction to Vol. 51
author of introductions and comments preceding each item in Vol. 51
editor of Vol. 51
translator of all items in Vol. 51
Doberstein, John W., comp.—*Minister's Prayer Book*, Philadelphia, 1959 43:191, 53:123n
Dobitzsch, Christopher von—50:48
Docetism—24:91n
Doctor's degree—2:220, 14:7n, 282n, 283, 26:18, 196, 440, 38:19, 48, 85, 156, 228, 262, 44:205
Doctorate, Luther's—4:220, 23:342n
Doctors (teachers)—23:102, 156f, 167, 192f, 228, 230, 264, 293, 297, 319f, 329, 411, 24:123, 156, 174, 293f
Doctors, Medical—see **Physicians**
Doctrine—1:15, 20, 59, 94, 106f, 148, 156f, 179, 214, 234, 261, 270, 272, 285, 288, 347, 351, 2:45, 55, 60, 78, 84, 123n, 151, 158, 212, 229, 243, 246, 250, 251, 253, 267, 296, 308, 315, 363, 370, 382, 398, 3:14f, 22f, 25, 77, 91, 94f, 107, 110, 124, 132f, 143, 161, 172, 183, 185f, 193, 200, 221–224, 226f, 241, 243, 252, 265, 286, 299–301, 325, 338f, 341–343, 363, 4:17, 24, 59, 70f, 89, 100, 113, 118f, 120, 127, 144, 148f, 159, 166f, 177f, 181f, 201, 205, 214, 217, 222, 220, 234, 241f, 250, 257, 266, 278, 288, 308, 317f, 321, 349, 370, 372f, 392, 404, 407, 5:11, 27, 36, 40, 71, 72, 79–81, 96, 103, 125, 158, 187f, 193, 201, 204, 206, 214, 217, 230, 232, 245, 261, 264f, 345–348, 353, 6:28, 34, 76, 105, 124, 128f, 203, 228, 230f, 253, 330, 7:38, 40, 42f, 58, 72f, 75, 80, 92, 94, 97, 106, 113, 116, 120, 125, 135, 146f, 152–155, 158, 163, 175, 182, 190, 196, 199, 205, 218, 226, 235f, 248, 250, 254, 279, 297, 299, 303, 305, 312, 333, 343, 347, 354, 357, 365, 376, 8:19, 30, 36, 39, 75, 80, 83, 90, 134f, 137, 170, 182, 185, 192, 205, 207, 212, 243, 256f, 270, 272, 275f, 299, 310, 325, 312f, 9:25, 27, 54, 89, 118f, 126, 129, 135–138, 140, 151, 157, 166f, 171, 179, 188, 197–199, 206f, 290, 297, 10:19, 11:73, 461–463, 12:352, 355, 387, 13:35, 139, 326, 336, 361, 415, 14:16, 24, 29, 36f, 64f, 70, 75, 87f, 91, 94, 102, 132, 174, 184, 200, 202, 224, 261, 288, 294, 302, 306, 310, 313, 329, 331, 338, 15:43, 116, 140, 184f, 197, 220, 230, 240, 255, 303, 16:22, 34, 72f, 94–96, 119n, 162, 166, 191, 202, 225, 246, 251, 262, 277, 346n, 17:14, 39, 47, 62, 92, 223, 350, 20:54f, 146f, 236, 297, 333, 21:211–213, 254f, 258f, 273f, 282, 353f, 22:50, 60–63, 66, 70f, 76, 80f, 85, 125, 137,

164, 206f, 235, 237, 255f, 260, 262, 284, 333, 352, 377, 380–382, 385, 389, 412, 431–433, 442, 444f, 452, 455, 458, 459n, 460f, 464, 470, 481, 489, 494, 23:17–20, 23, 27, 30, 32–36, 39, 46, 48, 56f, 62, 65f, 71, 73, 77–81, 85, 89–91, 96, 98, 100, 102f, 105, 108f, 113–115, 124f, 127, 132, 135–138, 141, 143, 152, 155, 158f, 161–163, 170f, 176, 183–189, 191–197, 204, 209, 213, 220, 223f, 226f, 229–235, 240, 247, 250, 256f, 261, 267–272, 276, 280, 284–287, 290f, 294f, 297f, 300, 305, 310f, 319–322, 324–331, 340, 344, 348f, 351f, 377, 379, 386, 388f, 392f, 396–399, 408–411, 416, 418, 420, 422, 24:7f, 21, 33, 43f, 53, 55, 62, 70, 74f, 90f, 95, 97, 107–110, 117, 119f, 122f, 126, 138, 140f, 145, 153f, 156, 166, 172, 174f, 177, 182, 202f, 209, 211–213, 215, 217, 221–224, 227f, 235f, 238, 248, 281, 285–288, 293, 295f, 301f, 308–310, 315, 317, 319–322, 326, 328f, 331, 335, 351, 356f, 360f, 368f, 384, 404f, 414, 26:3f, 7, 9f, 14–16, 20, 22f, 25, 27, 31, 39, 50, 52, 57–60, 62f, 66f, 72f, 75, 82–85, 90, 99f, 104, 106, 117f, 125, 133–135, 137–139, 146–149, 158, 169, 175f, 180, 183f, 185, 192f, 198, 200, 208, 210, 218f, 221f, 232, 250, 259, 270, 273, 280, 292, 303, 305f, 312f, 318, 368, 372, 375, 377, 379f, 386–388, 394, 397, 414f, 417, 419, 423f, 426f, 429, 443, 445f, 458, 27:3, 9f, 22, 27f, 37, 40–44, 46f, 51, 63, 71, 73–75, 81, 84f, 91, 100–109, 111f, 116, 119, 123f, 129, 135f, 145, 147f, 179f, 225, 227, 248, 281, 285f, 299, 339–341, 351, 373, 393, 396f, 400f, 408, 28:66f, 81f, 93, 96–98, 101, 107f, 175f, 217f, 221, 238f, 260, 308, 314, 320, 364, 383, 29: 3–7, 10, 12–14, 17, 31–33, 39f, 42–44, 48f, 52, 54, 57–60, 63–66, 68f, 71f, 78, 80, 83, 87, 93, 97, 118, 150, 183, 206, 30:3–5, 12, 15, 26, 36, 41, 49, 56, 65, 82, 106, 143, 149, 151, 160–165, 167, 169f, 175, 186f, 204, 207, 215, 238, 240–244, 246, 251–253, 259f, 263f, 269, 280, 282–284, 289, 291, 297, 299, 306, 310f, 318, 36:66, 70, 84, 184f, 193, 200, 222, 224, 260, 37:xvi, 21, 27, 32, 37, 42, 46, 49f, 53f, 59, 69f, 78, 117, 125, 129, 131, 137, 146, 154, 156f, 161–163, 191f, 231, 248f, 359–372, 38:xviii, 32, 36f, 70, 72, 97, 124, 156, 183n, 243, 269, 41:xiv, 5, 27, 48, 51, 111, 132, 155f, 174, 182, 190, 196, 202, 211–213, 216–219, 223–225, 229, 231, 242, 301–303, 44:52, 46:30, 164f, 177, 47:54, 111, 171, 258, 54:110, 422, 463, see also **Articles of faith**

Doctrine, Christian—35:136, 147, 153, 162, 195, 363f, 374, 380f, 384, 388f

Doctrine, Corrupt—31:383

Doctrine, Evil—29: 20, 37f, 41, 47, 50, 69, 119

Doctrine, False—see **False doctrine**

Doctrine, Human—35:131–153, 379, 386f, 406, 38:159, 164, 170, 174, 52:67, 69, 99, 172, 183, 203f, 209f, 212, 240, 258, 274f, 283

Doctrine, Lutheran—47:28, 30f, 35f, 51

Doctrine, Papal—2:218, 257, 38:88, 141, 183–185, 190, 192, 197f, 52:250

Doctrine, Pure (sound)—1:180, 232f, 235, 254, 327–329, 336, 345, 2:6, 13, 17f, 23, 33, 40, 54, 88, 172, 176, 199, 229, 234f, 240, 256, 316, 371, 388f, 3:14, 25, 57, 241, 265, 299, 338, 341, 363, 4:27, 135, 211, 236, 268, 282, 401f, 408, 5:80, 83, 97, 176, 208f, 359, 7:200, 234, 8:130, 137, 229, 301, 9:186f, 291, 12:188, 304, 407, 13:167, 185, 328, 352, 380f, 14:162, 290, 15:43, 221, 233, 16:29, 34, 18:412f, 25:485f, 26:13, 19, 201, 378, 402, 407, 27:33, 36, 44, 52, 79, 129, 133, 144, 28:62, 64, 86, 225, 43:231

Doctrines of devils—35:136f

Doctrines, Foundation—38:188, 211

Dodona—2:191

Doeg—9:163, 13:172, 183, 205, 14:232

Doelen, Bernard von—54:235

Doelsch, John—48:202n, 338n

Dog, Little black (Remorse)—6:84, 369–371

Dogma—2:218, 4:145, 166, 7:73, 337, 8:36, 14:132, 293, 26:233, 331, 427, 451, 29:7, 186

Dogmatics—44:xi

Dogs—1:63f, 81, 145, 217, 292, 2:74f, 116, 3:78, 309, 349, 4:29, 55, 348, 5:232, 364, 373, 6:18, 68, 84, 139f, 369–371, 7:14, 8:269, 292f, 9:233f, 238, 13:25, 14:247, 274, 15:61, 96, 101, 17:265f, 400, 21:223, 23:8, 55, 99, 119, 132, 168f, 238, 263, 314, 317, 403, 412, 24:71n, 109, 260, 274, 26:306, 405, 54:37, 175, 188, 421

Doing what is in oneself—6:104, 117–119, 122, 159, 32:153n, 154

Dolphins—1:51

Dolzig, Hans von—48:169n, 314n, 49:69n, 115n, 116, 132n, 134n, 135n, 295n, 296n, 299n, 431, 50:112, 194, 196, 53:221, 54:26

Dolzig, Johann—see **Dolzig, Hans von**

Dolzig, John von—see **Dolzig, Hans von**

Domel, G.—*Die Entstehung des Gebetsbuches . . . bis zum Anfang des 16. Jahrhunderts*, 1921 43:5n

Domestic matters—15:35, 37, 29: 87, 89, 93

Domestic works—6:74, 123, 347f, 364f

Domestics—5:6–8, 13f, 16, 30f, 53, 55, 57f, 138, 160, 290, 325, 342, 353, 7:66, 69, 92f, 172, 192, 218, 365, 8:16, 18, 35, 97, 126, 128, 163

Dominic, St.—2:113, 249, 251, 268f, 3:196, 8:60, 267, 9:54, 16:245, 304, 20:341, 22:50–52, 65, 70, 137, 254, 256, 267, 273, 388, 23:34, 26:459, 27:141, 36:77n, 190, 39:268n, 41:214n, 44:172n, 272n, 52:173, 249, 54:353

Dominicans—1:297n, 9:131n, 14:67n, 17:266, 22:60, 424, 30:95, 255, 275, 31:259, 289, 316n, 32:79n, 268, 278, 283, 34:28n, 335n, 41:116n, 172, 234n, 44:172n, 187n, 190, 47:46, 48:6n, 10n, 36, 70f, 109n, 247n, 291n, 54:261

Dominion—1:66f, 69, 71f, 91, 105, 133, 138f, 15:49, 277f, 291f, 345

Dominion given to mankind—1:213

Domitian, Emperor—13:68, 14:333, 17:187n

Domitius—25:455

Donation of Constantine—21:182n, 27:3n, 31:228n, 35:406n, 38:189n, 41:17n, 286n, 333n, 44:166n, 167n

Donations—23:360

Donatism—24:320n

Donatists—1:213, 5:24n, 11:220, 13:89, 23:203–205, 27:60, 30:109, 239, 31:238, 32:41, 51, 35:403n, 37:185n, 366, 38:27, 28n, 58, 39:196n, 40:250n, 41:45n, 46:179n

Donatus, Aelius—4:362, 5:24, 18:115n, 40:167n, 315n, 51:211, 235, 472
Ars minor 45:370n

Donatus, St.—36:26n

Donkeys—1:85, 128, 222, 4:98, 118, see also **Asses**

Donum superadditum—2:121n

Doomsday—24:81

Door—15:261

Doorkeeper in God's house—11:149f

Doorposts—9:149

Dorbernus, Andenus—see **Tobern, Anden**

Dordrecht—Augustinian Monastery 48:29n, 31, 236n

Doria, Andrea—50:72n

Dormice—1:51, 2:135

Dorothy of Solms, Countess of Mansfeld—50:302f, 306n

Dorothy's, St., Day—23:413n

Dorpat—53:43

Dort—32:264

Double-tongued—28:296f, 300f

Doubling—10:328f, 337, 362f, 396, 11:272, 285, 392, 20:98f, 292

Doubt—3:173, 5:327, 6:10, 101, 104, 116, 143, 12:287, 366, 368, 370, 380f, 15:3, 272, 17:92, 238, 254, 261f, 299, 19:88, 119f, 179–181, 24:129f, 218f, 222, 293f, 328f, 386, 388, 394f, 25:114, 116, 499f, 502f, 26:27, 35, 63n, 70, 212, 230, 270, 377, 379–381, 385–387, 437, 27:109, 381, 28:99, 163, 223, 240, 30:257, 31:100, 34:317f, 35:14, 61, 54:59, 61

Dough—23:94

Douglas, Winfred—53:149n, 277n

Doves—2:45f, 92, 109–111, 157, 159–163, 3:193f, 330, 8:145, 10:254f, 259f, 262, 333, 400, 11:548, 15:209, 220, 227, 241, 246, 304, 307, 17:316, 18:38, 349, 23:345, 369, 26:374, 38:31, 59

Dowries—4:225, 5:306f, 357, 6:16f, 199, 9:224, 226, 18:402f

Drach, John (Draco, Johann)—43:99–112, 45:64n, 48:223n, 49:151

Draft animals—1:353

Dragon of the Nile—16:211

Dragons—1:51, 105, 230, 2:147, 3:37, 271, 347, 11:215, 342, 16:303, 24:272, 294, 415, 418, 420, 26:453, 35:354, 369, 405

Dramatizations—24:193n

Drändorf, Johannes, von Schlieben—43:69n

Drawing near to God—18:350

Draxe, Thomas—*Bibliotheca scholastica instructissima* 26:422n

Dread, Concept of (Cf. Kierkegaard)—4:103f

Dreams—1:129, 233, 3:10–12, 18, 113, 107, 177, 275, 308, 330, 337, 340, 344, 348, 360, 4:58, 73, 126, 131, 140, 233, 5:20, 103, 122, 139, 212, 215, 217, 236n, 237–241, 244, 323, 6:14, 26, 37, 41f, 63, 89, 329, 332–336, 7:70, 102, 108, 110–112, 118–122, 127, 134–143, 147–151, 153, 155f, 189, 196, 202, 209, 224, 241, 259, 295, 319f, 323,

331, 339, 344, 357, 8:138, 221, 224, 261, 271, 316, 9:129, 131, 215, 15:77f, 81, 18:108, 23:335, 30:205f, 35:400, 54:18, 89f, see also **Visions**
Drechsel, Thomas—36:233, 51:69
Dregs—10:458, 460f, 464
Drescher, Karl—26:x
Dresden—23:201, 208, 38:157n, 40:52, 48:123n, 393n, 50:128n
Augustinian Monastery 48:23, 75n, 149
Dresden manuscript of Luther's ***First Lectures on the Psalms***—10:x, 8, 11:x
Dresden Psalter—see **Seidemann, Johann Karl**
Dress—1:222, 6:232, 261, 323f
Dress and finery—42:74
Dressel, Michael—48:20f, 31
Drewary, Benjamin—co–translator with Philip S. Watson of *Bondage of the Will*—33:xi
Drews, Paul—*Disputationen D. Martin Luthers*, Göttingen, 1895 34:135n, 38:xixn, 237n, 277n
Drink—23:9, 22, 24, 30, 40f, 43, 45, 49, 53, 119, 125, 128, 153, 158, 172, 185, 213, 267, 269–272, 277, 403f, 29: 54, 212
Drinking—13:215, 45:178, 249, 51:11, 97, 135, 157f, 291–299, 54:18, 20, 76, 205f, 210, 219
Drinking ministers—28:286, 296, 29:27
Drinking the cup—13:345f
Drones—7:68f, 338, 8:107
Droppings—24:232, 368
Dross—16:22, 24f
Drought—2:107, 136, 54:192
Drums—24:377
Drums and fifes—23:348
Drunk with the Spirit—8:249, 251, 255, 259f, 266–269
Drunkards—1:215, 8:120, 251, 260, 16:163, 191, 219, 223, 242, 19:202, 219–222, 23:402, 24:167
Drunkenness—2:166f, 169, 3:9, 233, 248, 268, 309, 8:187, 249, 251f, 259–261, 266, 270, 9:55, 11:127, 16:63, 222f, 242, 27:91, 368, 370, 384, 29: 22f, 27, 39, 30:31, 35:68, 36:209, 41:18, 237–239, 50:123n, 54:205f, 210, 278, 295, 371
Drunkenness, Blessed—12:176
Dry land—11:258f
Dryden, John—25:451n
Dualism—13:96f
Dublin, Louis I., and Alfred J. Lotka—*Length of Life* 13:122n
Ducats—50:222n, 269n
Duefel, Hans—54:341n
Dung—7:70, 142, 166, 18:336f, 27:187, 189, 219, 299
Dungerheim, Jerome (Dungersheim, Hieronymus)—37:157, 40:230n, 48:145n, 164
Duns Scotus, John—1:228, 2:124, 3:306, 4:136, 6:182, 12:345, 14:204n, 284n, 16:297, 22:255, 25:xi, 343, 372, 458, 494, 26:126, 128n, 296f, 28:223, 31:6, 9n, 146n, 321, 32:79n, 153n, 33:78n, 104, 34:27, 255n, 308, 35:64, 39:168n, 44:201n, 45:377n, 48:96n, 54:38f, 264
Duns Scotus, John, Works of—*Quaestiones in quatuor libros sententiarum* 34:308n
Sententiarum 25:260–262, 284, 325, 381
Durand, Guillaume (William)—*Rationale divinorum officiorum*, 1484 36:15n, 110n, 53:21n, 27n
Durchbrecher aller Bande, O **(hymn)**—18:229n
Dürer, Albrecht—13:168n, 16:255n, 42:101n, 43:42n, 46:247n, 49:96n, 52:160n
Düring, Christian—48:42n, 202, 230, 236, 309, 49:15, 103n, 176, 314
Düsseldorf—50:194n
Dust—10:23, 30, 207, 23:358, 369, 390, 392
Dutch—54:387
Duty—6:10, 74, 96, 105, 180, 348f, 13:174f, 21:97, 193f, 318, 329
Dying with Christ—25:312

Eagles—1:5, 62, 3:323, 9:136, 292, 18:220
Early Church—see **Church, The early**
Earring(s)—4:274f, 279, 10:189, 15:207, 18:10n, 29:154
Ears—3:136, 155, 177n, 190, 255, 294, 346, 7:29f, 103–105, 162, 164–166, 193, 211, 272, 290, 302, 10:188f, 205f, 251, 14:240, 29:221–224, 231
Ears, Piercing of—9:149, 151
Earth—1:5, 7–10, 12, 14–17, 19, 21, 23, 25f, 29f, 34–36, 38–40, 44, 46, 49, 54–58, 64–66, 68, 72–76, 78f, 82, 84f, 89, 91f, 98–100, 102, 104f, 115, 121, 125, 129, 131, 141, 144, 150f, 153, 182f, 185, 187, 189, 196, 204–208, 210, 215f, 225f, 230f, 233, 255, 284, 286f, 289–294, 303, 308–312, 314, 318, 321, 323, 334, 352f, 2:5, 32, 49, 52f, 61–66, 70, 74–76, 89, 93–98, 100–103, 106f, 109–113, 115, 117f, 129, 131, 133, 135, 142f, 145, 147f, 155, 157, 162,

177, 179, 195–197, 207f, 210f, 214, 225, 288, 330, 344, 353, 358f, 365, 378, 388, 391–393, 396–398, 3:39f, 63, 80, 89, 124, 139, 141n, 150, 168, 188, 196, 205f, 220, 229, 235, 243f, 271, 292f, 298, 307, 310, 316, 322, 338, 4:xi, 5, 47, 52f, 55, 60, 89f, 119, 121, 125, 142f, 152f, 156, 161f, 172, 175, 189f, 195, 198, 206f, 231, 234, 236, 244, 253, 267, 276, 279, 296, 310f, 314, 340, 356, 361, 364, 369, 373, 7:105, 136, 148f, 152, 162, 167, 172, 179, 182, 194, 201, 203, 205f, 210f, 216, 231, 292f, 297f, 307–309, 327, 332, 357, 370, 8:29, 32, 34, 36, 41, 60, 66–68, 79–81, 90, 95, 103, 108, 193, 217, 243, 245, 250, 253, 275, 287, 302, 304, 325, 11:267, 323n, 13:103f, 17:133, 164, 19:139, 144, 22:15, 20, 50, 75, 89, 130, 179, 203, 291, 325, 406, 455, 458, 490f, 493, 496, 501, 506, 508, 529, 23:8, 14, 25, 28, 36f, 44, 54, 71–73, 80f, 83, 95, 106, 115, 120–123, 147, 150, 154, 160–164, 167, 178f, 182, 202, 226, 228, 238, 246, 254, 282, 285, 288, 292, 312f, 327, 329f, 335f, 340, 346, 359, 361, 364, 372, 374f, 384, 387, 389, 394, 405f, 411, 421, 24:7, 10, 14, 20f, 25f, 28, 34, 36f, 41, 43, 49, 51f, 54, 62, 65, 67f, 78f, 83–85, 99, 105f, 110f, 119, 125f, 131, 133, 135, 139, 146f, 149, 157–160, 163, 166, 169–171, 175, 178, 180f, 183, 185, 187, 189f, 194, 200, 204, 214, 232, 238, 240, 242f, 251, 253, 257, 261, 266, 272, 276, 280f, 290f, 295, 304, 307, 310, 313, 315, 323–325, 328, 334, 336, 340, 346, 353, 355, 358f, 375f, 378, 380, 385, 399, 402, 408, 411, 414f, 418f, 26:6, 8, 13, 22, 27, 32, 56f, 72, 115–117, 119, 134, 151, 166, 176f, 182, 184f, 193, 211, 228, 235, 240, 243f, 247f, 265, 271, 295, 301, 303, 306, 308, 326, 329, 334, 338, 352, 362, 381–384, 399, 403, 408, 439f, 452, 27:5, 39, 41, 46, 58, 64, 83, 122, 149, 154, 161, 174, 179, 225, 253, 262, 284, 298, 319, 342, 348, 360, 376, 379, 391, 400, 405, 409, 29: 128f, 185, 30:7, 11–16, 21, 25, 30, 32, 35–37, 43, 62, 64, 67f, 98f, 102, 106, 109, 111, 114, 116, 118, 121, 128, 130, 139, 141, 153, 163, 165, 169, 178, 180f, 193–105, 197f, 208f, 213, 237, 290, 316, 37:11, 30f, 46, 49, 58f, 61f, 65f, 69, 71, 79, 88, 05, 115 117, 132f, 198–200, 232–234, 280–284, 337, 38:98, 106, 156, 158, 176, 191, 192, 202, 41:304f, 330, 42:23, 40–42, 146, 50:172n, 278n

Its four corners 20:16, 21, 24, 65, 179, 184, 191, 198, 247f, 251, 342

Earth, Age of the—1:3

Earthen vessels—29: 97

Earthquakes—1:206, 3:x, 221, 295, 18:130, 20:339

East, The—see **Orient**

East Frisia—25:440

East Prussia—45:134, 137

East wind—19:172

Easter—2:226, 5:46n, 154, 376, 7:x, 8:67, 258, 13:355, 14:100, 18:48, 24:ix, 8, 225, 374, 26:411f, 448, 35:96, 36:198, 37:144, 260n, 38:101n, 142, 177, 205, 217, 227, 317n, 41:61n, 62, 63n, 64, 65n, 66–68, 114, 54:307

Easter, Third Day of—11:80

Easter communion—36:249n, 252n, 291, 299n

Eastern Church—see **Greek Church**

Eastern Empire—41:87, 90n, 371–376

Eating and drinking—30:312

Physical 38:17f, 20f, 23, 25 27, 38–43, 46, 53–57, 65, 72, 74f, 83, 190

Spiritual 29:21, 38:16–18, 20f, 23, 25, 38–41, 46, 53–56, 75, 163, 200, 299f, 311

Eating and drinking in the Sacrament—

Both physical and spiritual 37:85f, 93, 132, 193

Physical 23:116, 123, 37:6f, 28f, 43–46, 51–52, 61n, 65n, 67–69, 72f, 79, 83–89, 92–103, 105f, 115, 118–126, 129–141, 149n, 153, 155, 188–193, 238, 245, 274, 300f, 330, 342f, 346f, 356, 358f, 367

Spiritual 23:41, 43, 46, 116, 118n, 122n, 133, 37:xiif, xvi, xx, 30, 45, 56, 83n, 84–89, 92–102, 123, 132, 136, 145, 193, 246, 248, 263, 267, 274, 322

Ebal, Mt.—2:282, 6:183, 9:117, 258f

Ebeling, Gerhard—21:xv, 47:103n

Evangelische Evangelienauslegung. Eine Untersuchung zu Luthers Hermeneutik, Munich, 1942 51:xin, xiiin, xxn

Luther: An Introduction to his Thought, London, 1970 25:4

Lutherstudien, Tübingen, 1971 10:xin, 5n

Ebeling, Harold J.—52:xn

Eben Ezra—1:270

Eber—2:205f, 209, 215, 234, 247, 371f, 388, 3:233, 4:3, 303, 343, 359, 384f,

5:20, 100f, 105, 111, 262f, 265, 272, 6:266, 288, 7:125, 8:262, 47:144
Eber, Paul—50:210n, 220n, 280n
Ebionites—22:67n, 30:251f, 257n, 284, 299, 309, 35:393n, 36:211n
Ecbatana—14:114, 19:208
Ecclesia—see **Church, The**
Ecclesiastes, Book of—1:103, 243, 7:193, 9:ix, 10:55, 29:76n, 217f, 30:248, 35:347–349
Its purpose and subject matter 15:7, 10f, 12f, 22, 46f, 92f, 144, 186, 195
Luther's *Notes* on the book 15:ixf, 4–190, 46:100n
***Ecclesiastical History*—see Eusebius of Caesarea**
***Ecclesiastical History, Eleven Books of*—** see **Rufinus**
Ecclesiastical properties, Alienation of—34:36n
Ecclesiastical revenues—1:192
Ecclesiastics—1:75n, 16:333, 31:356, 52:210, 212f, 215f, 222, 227, 235, 238, 243, 247, 253f, 256, 265f, 269, 271, see also **Clergy**
Ecclesiasticus, Book of—see **Wisdom, Book of**
Ecclesiola—2:37n
Ecclesiology, Luther's—39:xin
Eck, Johann, of Ingolstadt—see **Eck, John Maier**
Eck, Johann, secretary to the Archbishop of Trier—see **Ecken, John von der**
Eck, John Maier—6:49, 7:ix, 92n, 12:x, 144, 321n, 13:352, 23:217n, 28:242, 31:xviiif, 309–325, 338–340, 381, 32:ix, x, 5, 67n, 98f, 34:6n, 70n, 95, 310n, 326, 328, 332f, 35:178, 408n, 36:8, 14n, 37:8, 81, 97, 39:xxiii, 51, 56n, 57n, 83, 108f, 122n, 123, 145, 165, 173, 40:53n, 75, 41:8n, 54n, 150n, 183, 189, 191, 235n, 293n, 42:xi, 5, 18n, 85, 97n, 170, 44:xvii, 117n, 221, 45:64n, 71, 106n, 234, 252n, 287n, 305n, 46:5n, 47:12n, 20n, 22, 129, 48:79n, 80n, 112, 115n, 116, 134, 136, 138, 145, 149n, 152, 179n, 181, 185n, 233n, 258n , 49:7n, 71, 292n, 313n, 332n, 350, 378, 405, 408n, 410n, 50:230, 51:xivn, 53f, 55n, 212, 53:321, 54:35, 54, 137, 197, 259, 351, 415, 441, 445
Eck, John Maier, Works of—*Answer for Jerome Emser against Luther's Mad Hunt* 39:109
Attack on Luther in Behalf of Emser 48:138n
Chrysopassus 48:187
Confutation 34:6n
Defense Against Luther 48:131n
Defense Against Luther's Asterisci 48:80n
Excusatio 51:55n
Four Hundred Four Theses 34:80n
Obelisks 17:247n, 31:xvi, 309, 314, 36:12n, 48:80n
On the Primacy of Peter 39:83n
Refutation of a Jew 47:129
Theses for the Leipzig Disputation 48:107, 109f, 112
Eck, S.—45:239n
Eck of Reischach—43:266n
Ecken, John von der—32:104–124, 48:200n
Eckhart, Meister—32:95n
Eclipses—1:41–43, 2:129, 50:220n, 52:168
Eclipsis—8:214
Economics—1:94, 45:xii, 239
Ecstasy—4:48, 67
Ecumenism—38:xi, xvi
Eden—1:87–91, 97f, 101, 104, 140, 225, 229f, 307, 16:316, 22:31, 23:81, 234
Eder, Tower of—6:274, 287, 18:242
Eder Ezer—13:172
Edict of Worms—49:xiii, 24n, 35, 125f, 155f, 264n, 374n, 376
Edification—25:117, 514, 28:223f, 254, 260
Edinburgh—50:150n
Editorial manipulation—2:x
Editors—see **Atkinson, James; Bachmann, E. Theodore; Bergendoff, Conrad J.; Brandt, Walther L.; Dietrich, Martin O.; Doberstein, John W.; Fischer, Robert Harley; Forell, George W.; Grimm, Harold J.; Gritsch, Eric W.; Hansen, Walter A.; Hillerbrand, Hans J.; Krodel, Gottfried G.; Lehmann, Helmut T.; Lehmann, Martin E.; Leupold, Ulrich S.; Oswald, Hilton C.; Pelikan, Jaroslav; Poellet, Daniel E.; Schultz, Robert C.; Sherman, Franklin; Spitz, Lewis W.; Tappert, Theodore G.; Watson, Philip S.; Wiencke, Gustav K.**
Editors, general—see **Lehmann, Helmut T.; Pelikan, Jaroslav**
Edlibach, Jacob—37:8
Edom—4:365, 367f, 374, 394, 5:160, 207, 6:161f, 165, 216f, 283, 285, 290, 296, 302, 304, 307, 309f, 389, 8:11, 262, 9:32f, 304, 10:26, 284, 286, 290–292, 434, 463, 11:186, 360, 16:126, 173, 294, 17:352–354, 19:233, 235, 46:192,

47:145, 152, 154f, 264, see also **Idumea**
Edomites—2:180, 367f, 3:152, 4:331, 365, 367f, 5:155, 6:162f, 166, 283, 294, 297, 303–306, 309f, 8:228, 9:32, 34, 83, 231, 236, 10:413, 11:74, 121n, 122, 123n, 125, 17:182, 352f, 18:134f, 138, 189, 193–195, 198, 200–202, 342, 393, 20:251, 29:129, 35:321f, 47:151f, 171, 182, see also **Idumeans**
Educated persons—46:215, 244, 252
Educating boys—see **Boys, Educating**
Educating girls—See **Girls, Educating**
Education—8:42, 15:70–73, 176f, 202, 250, 37:28n, 364, 44:191n, 206f, 45:xiv, 342–344, 348–350, 356, 365n, 367f, 46:xiv, 209–211, 230, 231n, 232, 237–250, 253
Eells, Hastings—54:25
Effeminacy—3:254, 25:165f
Effort—26:26, 58, 131, 224, 369, 380, 383, 402, 449, 451
Eggs—1:53, 8:68
Egranus, John Silvius—see **Wildenauer, John Sylvius (called Egranus)**
Egypt—1:4, 89, 96, 101, 195, 209, 328, 342, 314, 2:21, 155, 194, 231, 259, 276f, 281, 288–292, 294, 299, 303, 317, 322, 324, 342, 344f, 360, 364, 367, 370, 375, 382, 3:31f, 34f, 61, 74, 81, 88, 96, 113, 154, 180f, 188, 235, 261, 318, 326, 334, 352, 4:46, 72, 186, 188, 190, 195, 198, 215, 229f, 283, 307, 322, 324, 331f, 365f, 372, 5:14f, 30, 51, 90, 131, 144, 252, 265, 276, 352, 385, 6:6, 20, 50, 101, 127, 161, 217f, 227, 268, 273, 282, 285, 308–310, 342f, 352f, 363, 367f, 378, 383, 394, 397, 401, 405f, 7:3, 5, 8f, 14, 17, 51, 53f, 64, 67, 71, 103, 105, 107, 109, 135–137, 140, 144, 148, 151–153, 156f, 159–165, 167f, 170f, 173, 176, 180f, 183, 186f, 189, 191, 197, 199f, 202, 204f, 207–209, 211–218, 220, 222–224, 236, 241, 257, 261, 268, 270, 276, 282, 284, 286, 288f, 291, 306, 309f, 313f, 318f, 321, 323, 325f, 338, 346, 348, 351, 361f, 364, 368f, 8:4, 6, 16, 17n, 18f, 21f, 29, 33, 35, 37f, 41f, 44, 46–48, 55f, 58–60, 62–64, 66, 68, 70–72, 75, 77f, 81f, 84, 87–89, 92–94, 96f, 100, 104, 108–111, 116–120, 125, 127–131, 135, 137f, 140, 150, 156, 158, 166, 188, 207, 225f, 231, 240, 242, 253, 303, 313, 320–323, 328, 333, 9:15, 23, 35, 58, 60n, 85, 117f, 141, 148, 154, 156, 169, 203, 244, 271, 310, 11:17, 511, 14:11, 19, 273, 286n, 333, 16:86, 114, 125, 127, 160–165, 167–169, 182, 218, 253–256, 259, 269, 288, 296, 308, 310, 318, 17:41, 87, 96, 128, 131, 184, 194, 200–202, 214, 258, 274, 355, 18:41, 46f, 60, 62, 64, 187, 275, 343, 353, 19:134, 138–140, 193, 231f, 20:68, 76, 90, 97, 114f, 251, 253, 260f, 280, 285, 289f, 307f, 345, 22:31, 130, 214, 309, 312, 347, 522, 23:30f, 152f, 206f, 298, 401, 403, 24:48, 80, 261, 280, 327, 330, 366, 25:156, 26:22, 149, 211, 258, 311, 320, 384, 27:226, 227n, 267f, 289, 366, 407, 28:191, 29:78, 117, 124, 144, 148, 157f, 239, 30:34, 104, 144, 185, 205, 208, 323, 34:178f, 35:165, 272, 301, 307f, 37:38, 205, 319, 333, 38:84n, 244, 41:24, 41f, 56f, 214, 251, 281, 291, 42:38, 164, 45:220, 46:120, 157, 192, 202, 248, 47:85, 231, 49:331, 50:310, 51:106, 52:144f, 155, 160, 162, 171, 238, 271
Egypt, Kings of—2:276, 296, 303, 305, 20:141
Egyptians—1:128, 187, 249, 2:18, 176, 203, 257, 296, 299, 302f, 305f, 311f, 3:32, 49, 81, 89, 259, 5:150, 159, 385, 6:19f, 24, 29, 214, 228, 304, 387, 7:15, 35, 58f, 60, 65, 68, 72, 95, 120, 136, 152, 166, 173, 187, 189, 197, 200, 207, 209, 211, 214, 249, 295, 309, 324, 334, 345–348, 350f, 8:3f, 16, 18f, 23f, 33, 36, 38, 44, 57, 61, 65n, 81, 92, 95, 98f, 102f, 105, 120, 122f, 127, 130, 132–135, 137f, 198, 250, 320f, 9:87, 134, 158, 202, 219, 231, 236, 297, 11:82, 12:265, 14:66, 338, 16:34, 85f, 88, 114, 158, 161, 163f, 166f, 211, 252, 254, 267, 269f, 17:40, 87, 96, 192, 274, 382, 22:310, 23:152, 24:323, 25:374, 26:158, 383, 384, 27:31, 126, 29:150, 240, 47:80n, 85, 151, 271
Ehses, Stephanus—*Concilii Tridentini Actorum Pars Prima*, Freiburg im Breisgau, 1904 41:259n, 263n, 269n, 282n
Eighteenth Sunday after Trinity—23:345n
Eighth Day (symbol of eternity)—3:141
Eilenburg—48:187, 380
***Ein Feste Burg* (hymn), Echoes of**—see **Luther, Martin, Biography of**
Einbeck—41:182, 242n, 253
Einhorn, Werner—48:154n, 160
Einsiedel, Haugold von—39:119, 121n
Einsiedeln—49:88n
Eisenach—5:381, 6:138, 35:158, 41:116, 45:241, 46:250n, 47:27n, 48:3f, 145,

198, 218, 223n, 226, 227n, 272, 329, 388, 49:17n, 18, 50, 118n, 50:99n, 207n, 212n, 213n, 216n, 218n, 221n
Eisleben—8:x, 23:ix, 24:75n, 31:330, 38:142, 46:47, 210, 47:101f, 107f, 48:60, 145, 171n, 220, 275n, 329, 49:59n, 103, 106, 150, 152, 212, 238n, 268n, 284n, 50:282, 283n, 285n, 286, 288n, 289n, 291n, 293, 295n, 298, 304, 307, 312n, 316–318, 51:371, 383, 54:19
Eissermann, John—see **Hess, Master John Eissermann**
Ekron—18:340, 20:93, 282n, 286
El-Bethel—6:248f
Elam—2:205, 232, 247, 365, 16:126, 171, 176
Elamites—9:34
Elbe Bridge—23:245
Elbe River—1:30, 33, 3:282, 5:256, 6:104, 309, 335, 7:266, 8:212, 279n, 15:17, 65, 17:26, 382, 23:205, 245, 274, 385, 24:267, 28:146, 316, 41:33n, 48:146n, 49:321
Elders—2:170, 173, 9:162, 168, 195, 213, 258, 272, 283, 16:41f, 46, 23:201, 24:9, 338, 403, 28:332, 347f, 350f, 29:16f, 21f, 29:16–19, 22, 30:132f, 135, 35:401, 36:118, 120f, 155, 157, 159, 41:358f, see also **Presbyters**
Eleazar the priest—9:108, 310, 29:207
Elect, The—1:301–303, 7:266, 8:37, 42, 300f, 315, 318, 13:192, 16:51, 17:40, 61, 161, 182f, 343f, 23:354, 24:215, 225, 269, 25:197, 25:73f, 78, 84, 97, 163, 197, 371f, 374, 376, 378, 423f, 26:306, 383, 27:27, 29:8f, 11, 35:31, 36:189f, 194, 227, 289, 318, 37:363, 38:159, 171, 178, 189, 207, 41:125, see also **Believers**
Election—2:72f, 3:169, 4:132, 342, 356, 9:84, 20:88, 24:263, 25:80–83, 85, 96f, 374–378, 386–389, 423f, 26:260, 30:158f, 33:11n, see also **Predestination**
Election, Imperial—48:84n, 96f, 97n, 123n, 129n, 176, 189n, 203
Electoral College—see **Electors, Imperial**
Electors, Imperial—48:49f, 70n, 129n, 244, 392, 50:41n, 254n
Electors of Saxony—3:356n, 23:226, 258, 295, 298, 35:307, 41:371, see also **Frederick the Wise, Elector of Saxony; John, Elector of Saxony; John Frederick, Elector of Saxony**
Eleemosynary activity—25:126
Elements, Four—15:15, 17, 50:278, 306
Elephants—2:135
Elert, Werner—14:334n, 47:103n, 54:358n
Morphologie des Luthertums, Munich, 1932 45:239n
Elevation of the Sacrament—35:87, 36:xi, 52f, 74, 183f, 189, 319f, 322–324, 38:166, 313n, 314–319, 40:127–130, 42:173f, 53:28, 82, 54:408, 426, 461f
Eli—9:310, 29:22
Eli and his sons—41:282, 284–288
Eliakim—16:179, 311
Elias—19:64
Eliezer—3:12, 16, 54f, 4:108, 229, 283, 306, 6:183
Eliezer, Rabbi—1:37n
Elihu—4:185, 5:207, 20:234
Elijah, Prophet—1:21, 249, 346, 358, 350f, 2:20, 76, 162, 242, 288, 3:269, 271, 320, 345, 354f, 364, 4:128, 137, 313, 370, 372, 5:10, 12, 25, 30, 6:61, 177, 7:211, 296, 349f, 8:117, 180, 290, 300, 9:93, 123, 130, 11:288, 13:88, 199, 400, 14:340, 16:64, 17:85, 158, 18:160, 193n, 419, 19:6, 14, 27, 38, 20:248, 21:346, 22:24, 99, 116, 118, 124, 131, 201, 224, 319, 340, 346f, 413, 23:369, 24:90, 25:95f, 422, 26:109, 293, 310, 425, 27:367, 388, 392, 28:122, 29:123, 234, 238, 30:162, 288, 33:85, 35:200f, 332, 36:182, 220, 37:170, 173, 253, 259, 262, 294n, 38:37, 159, 162, 178, 290, 41:139, 207n, 210, 311, 45:62, 96, 389, 46:33, 173, 235, 47:157, 51:56, 52:21, 137, 142, 248
Elim—10:344
Eliphaz—5:273, 6:288–290, 294f, 297, 307
Elisha, Prophet—1:350, 2:288, 3:89, 263, 269, 4:128, 213, 372, 5:10, 160, 6:61, 246, 7:211, 349, 370, 8:117, 288, 300, 13:79, 400, 403, 14:19, 258, 15:274, 16:130, 19:39, 64, 20:26, 188, 22:116, 210f, 224, 252, 413, 23:265, 24:90, 25:459, 26:211, 27:262, 344, 30:290, 38:290, 42:112, 163, 46:173, 192, 236
Elizabeth—11:533n, 14:101, 22:23, 38, 44, 76, 29:218, 37:260n
Elizabeth, St.—3:29, 134, 5:362f, 13:54, 17:338, 41:105
Elkosh—18:283
Ellasar—2:365
Ellipsis—5:376, 27:201, 205, 298, 300
Ellwein, Eduard—25:xiv
Elmo—see **Erasmus, St.**
Elohim—11:111
Eloquence—3:67, 154, 186, 319, 335,

7:78, 94, 9:6, 213, 26:40, 184f, 201f, 28:289f
Eloquence vs. truth—49:7
Elton, G.R.—*Reformation Europe*, Cleveland, 1964 46:59n
Elymas—45:71
Emancipation—26:359
Embalming—8:320
Ember weeks—21:159n
Embers—20:210f
Embezzlement—7:115
Embryos—3:206, 14:214
Emeralds—1:101
Emetic—7:256
Emim—2:367, 374
Emmaus—4:96, 10:162
Emmerich, John, of Goerlitz—12:203n
Emotions—10:3, 78, 80f, 92, 108, 351, 372, 16:90, 17:184, 358, 372, 411, see also **Feelings**
Emperor, Office of the—49:207f, 245, 254, 259, 274n, 275n, 276n, 430n, 432n
Emperor, Roman—13:194, 202, 23:9, 27:3
Emperor's Privy Council—48:216n
Emperors—4:24, 33, 35, 165, 275, 357, 373, 391, 403, 5:80, 94, 115, 194, 6:29f, 88, 138, 7:91, 111, 170, 188, 195, 198, 223, 369, 370n, 8:42, 47, 89, 103, 105, 205, 252, 264, 321, 12:222, 16:287, 349, 18:198, 21:80, 23:8, 13, 36, 39, 41, 44–47, 98f, 141, 147, 196, 210, 221, 226, 257f, 290, 298, 300f, 329, 331f, 371, 380, 387–389, 394f, 405–407, 417, 24:79, 80, 82f, 123, 155f, 162, 184, 198, 205, 306, 313, 315, 336, 345, 351f, 378, 413, 416–418, 30:72, 75n, 81, 181, 311, 38:110, 147, 201, 41:xii, 23–25, 35, 37, 39, 87, 93–95, 106, 134, 140f, 174, 225f, 246, 248f, 253f, 256, 259, 268, 270f, 274–276, 280–282, 284, 289f, 292f, 298, 313, 335, 344, 356, 367, 373, 45:xiii, 77, 84, 107, 268n, 272n, 277, 297, 310, 47:ix, 6–8, 30, 33f, 271, 51:78, 82, 89, 154, 160, 175, 189, 192f, 271f, 281, 307, 312, 350, 363, 374, 378, 387, 391f
Emperors, German—see **Emperors, Holy Roman**
Emperors, Holy Roman—13:342, 41:25n, 90, 246, 261n, 276f, 293f, 332, 335, 351, 356, 373–376, 48:50, 70n
titles of 34:345
Emperors and Kings—46:18n, 33, 50f, 91, 104, 105n, 114f, 125–128, 130–133, 159, 167f, 180, 184–193, 196, 200, 233, 239–243, 245, 248n, 266, 316f
Empie, Paul C., and James I. McCord, eds.—*Marburg Revisited: A Reexamination of Lutheran and Reformed Positions*, Minneapolis, 1966 38:xiin
Empie, Paul C., and Austin Murphy, eds.—*Lutherans and Catholics in Dialog, III, The Eucharist as Sacrifice*, New York, 1967 38:xvif
Empires—4:29, 36, 71, 155, 227, 291f, 350, 370, 372n, 19:172, 25:21
Empires, Four—20:62, 179
Emser, Jerome—28:244, 30:53n, 35:179, 184, 191n, 358n, 408n, 36:12n, 185n, 38:157n, 39:xxiiif, 56n, 77n, 82, 107–115, 119–135, 139, 143–146, 148, 151–153, 156, 160, 162f, 167, 171–174, 177, 179, 186, 189f, 196, 199, 202–206, 208, 211–215, 227, 230, 238, 279n, 292n, 40:22n, 155n, 41:150n, 189, 42:97n, 44:xvii, 45:64n, 71, 86n, 169n, 364n, 48:137n, 187, 192, 230, 234, 264f, 49:41, 71, 181, 183f, 53:27
Emser, Jerome, Works of—*Against Luther's "To the Nobility of the German Nation"* 48:192n
Against the Ecclesiastic, Falsely so Called, and the True Arch-heretic Martin Luther 39:244, 247n
Against the Un-Christian Book of the Augustinian Martin Luther, Addressed to the German Nobility 39:109, 121n, 127n, 132n, 135n, 139, 143n, 146n, 158n, 169n, 172n, 200n, 210n, 230n
Answer to Luther's Abominable Attack on the Sacred Secret Mass 36:310
Answer to the Raging Bull 39:197n
Assertion of the Goat against Luther's Hunt 39:109, 130
Concerning the Leipzig Debate 36:14n, 39:77n
Declaration Concerning Luther's Chasing of Goat Emser 48:137n
Formal Declaration of the Capricorn regarding the Lutheran Game 39:77n
Quadruplica against Luther's Answer to the Superchristian Book of Goat Emser 36:141n, 48:257n, 265n
Quadruplica to Luther's Recent Answer, concerning his Reformation 39:227, 230n, 231n, 232n, 233n
Reply to the Answer of the Raging Bull in Wittenberg 39:119
Reservation to Luther's First Retraction 39:228, 231n
To the Wittenberg Bull 39:110n, 119, 121, 126n, 128n, 130n, 131n, 133n, 48:192n

Emulation—25:482f
Enallage of number—8:116
***Enarratio in psalmum* 2**—see **Augustine, St., Works of**
Enchanters—7:364, 16:94
Enchiridia—see **Hymnals**
Encratites (Tatianists)—1:238n, 24:228, 27:127, 28:312, 35:138n, 402n, 39:292n, 44:283n
End of the world—10:44f, 209f, 415, 419, 433, 435, 450f, 21:184, 28:123f, 126, 129, 30:38, 122, 168, 36:225, 38:109, 199f, 46:18n, 55
Endchrist (or Endechrist)—14:11n, 22:164n, 24:367n, 30:138n
Endemann, Wilhelm—*Studien in der romanisch-kanonistischen Wirtschafts- und Rechtslehre bis gegen Ende des siebzehnten Jahrhunderts*, Berlin, 1874–1883 45:237n
Enders, Ernst Ludwig, ed.—43:249n, 47:9n, 48:xiii, 49:xv
D. Martin Luthers Briefwechsel, Frankfurt-am-Main, 1884–1932 45:56n, 74n, 79n, 166n, 198n, 240n
Luther und Emser. Ihre Streitschriften aus dem Jahre 1521, Halle, 1848 39:107n, 110n, 119n, 121n, 128n, 130n, 131n, 132n, 133n, 135n, 139n, 146., 158n, 172n, 197n, 210n, 211n, 227n, 228n, 229n
Neudrucke deutscher Litteraturwerke des 16 und 17 Jahrhunderts, Halle, 1876–1949 45:243n
Endor—11:129–132
Endowments—21:132f, 136, 182, 285, 22:518n, 23:154, 25:449f, 461, 31:247, 45:180n, 342, 351, 46:209, 234n, 254n, 49:28f, 46, 71n, 134n, 135, 169, 50:116n, 214n
Endowments, Natural—26:174f, 182
Endrisch, Nicholas—49:167n
Ends of the earth—11:258
Enduring suffering—25:178, 225, 290f, 368, 440f, 458
Enemies—10:78–80, 93, 97, 114, 11:359–362, 364–366, 480f, 17:13, 33–35, 43f, 74, 85, 87, 89, 185f, 195, 306, 321f, 325, 338, 348, 363, 393, 20:25–27, 46, 63, 65, 67, 131–133, 139, 176f, 189f, 199f, 225f, 250, 252, 295, 325, 21:118–120, 226, 248f, 25:102, 108, 289f, 431f, 466, 46:80n, 115, 123f, 132, 309
Enemies of the Gospel—25:232
Enemy, The—42:156f, 160
Engagement(s)—45:29, 381f, 387, 390f, see also **Betrothals**
Engedi—2:368
Engelhard, Andrew—48:146n
England—1:254, 288, 2:136n, 8:308n, 23:370n, 34:108, 38:63n, 41:xii, 267, 45:246, 266n, 46:202, 204n, 47:128, 272n, 49:126n, 50:27f, 104n, 127, 142, 179f, 180n, 198n, 54:332, 346, 384, 402
Papal church in 50:98n, 127, 150, 179n, 193, 195, 200n
English—54:151, 309, 317, 328
English Evangelicals—50:28n, 95n, 103f, 137f, 138n, 150f, 179f, 180n, 195, 197, 198n, 200n, 203, see also **Alesius, Alexander**; **Barnes, Robert**
English people—1:268, 51:293f
English sickness—38:63n, 49:238f, 268n
Enjoyment—25:69, 150, 295, 351f
Enlargement—10:49f, 53f, 59, 74
Enmity—1:192, 194f, 324
Ennius, Quintus—17:51n, 19:126
Annales 10:357, 18:327n, 19:109n
Enoch—1:21, 303, 310f, 314f, 324, 331–334, 342–354, 2:7, 28, 56, 180, 196, 200, 232, 3:39, 79, 4:310, 6:89, 8:315, 13:310, 26:264, 28:122, 29:234f, 238, 30:210f, 38:290, 47:148, 52:126
Enoch, City of—1:295, 310
Enos—1:326–328, 334, 343, 345, 2:28, 114
Entelechy—34:181, 195
Enthusiasts—2:162, 5:39, 16:324, 17:8, 31, 39, 60, 71, 73–75, 77, 80, 82, 87f, 115, 120, 134, 151f, 159, 163, 172, 180, 183, 185f, 194, 205, 211, 223–225, 238, 243–245, 247, 254f, 258, 326, 391, 397, 412, 415, 19:1x, 42, 20:156, 212, 223, 239, 332, 347n, 24:362, 28:79, 218, 221–223, 228, 240, 252, 281f, 285, 304f, 33:90n, 34:xivf, 13, 35:158, 164, 38:110, 217, 221–223, 41:xi, 44:xiv, 47:191, 53:17, 19, 43, 263, 316, see also **Anabaptists**; **Factious spirits**; **Fanatics**; **Radical reformers**; **Schwärmer**; **Sectarians**
Envy—1:64, 275, 334, 2:127, 143, 210, 327, 346, 4:73–75, 77, 79, 194, 5:6, 58, 68, 86, 221f, 326–328, 344, 350, 6:3–5, 7, 20–22, 7:63, 97, 136, 168, 192, 281, 8:16, 28, 38, 221, 9:185, 221, 10:86, 118, 11:259, 294, 303n, 15:63f, 98, 178, 17:12, 21:74, 80, 22:286, 24:20, 149, 161, 244, 252, 268, 272, 274, 277, 287f, 25:6, 13, 97, 231, 27:48, 66, 73, 97, 109, 141, 159, 306, 359, 367, 370f, 384, 28:300f, 367, 371,

29:24, 77f, 30:31, 48, 118f, 176, 232, 271, 273, 288, 36:207, 42:14, 151
Envy, Mr.—13:207f
Epaenetus—25:129
Epaphroditus—13:111, 26:421, 27:81, 35:385, 51:233
Epha—20:56, 59f, 122, 240f, 243–245
Ephesians—14:39, 30:168
Ephesians, Epistle to the—35:385
Ephesus—6:50, 7:325, 25:130, 36:155, 53:125
Ephod—6:33, 18:17
Ephphatha—7:277
Ephraim—5:241, 6:247, 295, 7:5, 14, 165, 200, 210, 212, 266, 8:84, 88, 107, 149f, 153–156, 158–161, 166, 168–170, 174–176, 178–180, 207, 216, 278f, 281, 293, 295f, 298, 301, 303f, 306, 326, 9:16, 258, 306, 10:281f, 284, 286, 296f, 434, 11:40f, 48f, 96f, 105, 186, 329, 16:50, 64, 81, 91, 102f, 126f, 154, 219, 220, 17:171, 18:27, 29f, 37f, 45, 47, 51f, 55–57, 63f, 69, 71, 74–76, 127, 160, 194, 203, 20:95f, 99f, 283, 288, 293, 305–307, 36:88, 40:28, 46:120, 47:203
Ephraim, Kingdom of—6:346
Ephraim, Sons of—14:344
Ephraimites—6:279, 7:165, 8:151, 285, 306, 19:233
Ephratah (or Ephrath)—6:267, 273, 8:156
Ephron—4:208, 215f
Epictetus—2:326, 330
Epicureans—1:123, 162, 348, 2:158, 346, 3:118, 242, 268, 4:5, 63, 241, 277, 317, 329, 353, 391, 404f, 5:11, 43, 45, 47, 202, 235, 327, 6:24, 89, 7:117, 336, 8:190, 13:62, 78, 81, 96, 102, 107, 112, 131, 191f, 15:3, 19:53, 22:150, 306, 30:272, 33:44, 291, 34:211, 35:267, 314, 392n, 38:167, 290f, 310, 41:211n, 221, 263, 279, 285, 287, 50:112, 243
Epicurus—1:56, 348, 3:243, 4:330, 8:189, 266, 15:88n, 33:24n, 29, 30n, 34:34n, 211n, 54:78, 475
  Fragments 15:89n
Epicycles—1:47, 9:110n
Epieikeia—29:74–77, 79
Epilepsy, epileptics—1:119, 207, 305, 7:295, 8:317, 26:403, 50:127n
Epimenides—13:199
Epiphanius—*Panarion* 1:14n
Epiphany (ies)—3:168, 4:139, 145, 8:145, 22:214, 218, 408n
Episcopacy—see **Bishops**
Episcopates—see **Bishoprics**
Epistles (liturgical)—53:xiv, 11, 13, 21, 23f, 56, 58, 68, 72–74, 78, 84–86
Epistles and Gospels (liturgical)—see **Gospels and Epistles**
Epitaph—54:227, 238
Epitasis—4:112, 5:113, 7:364, 366f, 8:4, 25:116, 27:246n
Epithalamium—28:3
Equality—9:145, 13:161, 163, 214, 32:51–53
Equality among Apostles—32:74
Equality before God—4:64f
Equality of all Christians—16:201, 18:411, 21:288f
Equality of churches—32:82
Equanimity—25:137
Equinoxes—2:92f
Equity—2:60, 9:193, 10:94f, 11:292, 382, 532f, 29:74f, 54:44, 325, 369
Equivocation—4:34, 8:146, 195f
Er—7:5f, 17–19, 21, 23, 29, 51, 8:87f
Erasmus, Desiderius—1:108, 2:44n, 125, 158, 3:67, 319n, 4:199, 5:58, 269f, 6:89, 8:61n, 9:23n, 277n, 12:225, 14:x, 16:55n, 203, 303, 332, 346, 17:4, 11, 46, 92, 150, 176, 223, 265, 331, 25:ix, xi, 81, 118f, 124f, 385, 388, 390, 392, 492, 501, 519, 523, 26:65n, 108, 150, 181, 209, 323n, 27:x, 36n, 159, 162, 175, 179, 201, 209, 212, 238, 239n, 245, 248, 307, 309, 315, 326, 336, 339, 368, 382, 387, 400, 402, 28:ix, 22, 244, 264, 285, 290, 295, 29:56n, 74n, 127, 159f, 30:248, 259, 286, 311, 316n, 31:314, 32:135, 137n, 34:80n, 163n, 164f, 260n, 35:179, 231, 264n, 394n, 399n, 36:7, 9, 118n, 229n, 37:xvi, 10, 75n, 239, 242, 260n, 327n, 331n, 363n, 370n, 39:132n, 40:272n, 317n, 42:64n, 43:99, 44:200n, 286n, 45:275n, 46:xi, 18n, 48:xiiif, xx, 23f, 40f, 52f, 77n, 98n, 99n, 114f, 116, 122f, 123n, 150, 163n, 164, 185, 191n, 205n, 230n, 247n, 275n, 282n, 305n, 306, 316n, 318, 322n, 49:xix, 6f, 42f, 76f, 88n, 89n, 90n, 140, 157n, 173, 215f, 257n, 50:xx, 136, 190n, 203n, 224n, 243n, 54:xxii, 13, 50, 68f, 71, 73, 77, 81, 84, 136, 147, 189, 245, 247, 292, 311, 401, 417
  Letters to him from Luther 33:6f, 11
  Letters to him from Melanchthon 33:10
Erasmus, Desiderius, Works of—*Adagia* 13:165, 34:121n, 130n, 36:27n, 122n, 48:26n, 62n, 63n, 72n, 258n, 318n, 351n, 354n, 383n, 49:215n, 414n,

50:94n, 156n, 202n, 228n, 230n, 237n, 249n, 293n, 296n
Against the Barbarians 33:15n
Annotationes to the Greek New Testament 25:128, 401, 406, 27:159n, 175n, 179n, 201, 209n, 212n, 309n, 326n, 29:126n, 131n, 131n, 30:259, 49:63n
Colloquies 13:107n, 34:260, 44:286n, 170n, 54:19
Complete works 7:272n, see also **Allen, P.S., ed.**
De libero arbitrio see **Erasmus, Desiderius, Works of**—*On Free Will*
Defense against Faber Stapulensis 48:55
Diatribe 1:269n, 26:209, 29:32, 33:xi, xiin, 8n, 9, 10n, 12, 100n
Enchiridion 30:259n, 33:275n, 48:118
Encomium Moriae see **Erasmus, Desiderius, Works of**—*Praise of Folly*
Greek New Testament 28:22, 33:6, 12, 36:93n, 48:23, 53n, 66n, 68n, 115n, 116, 230n, 306n, 318, 356n
Hyperaspistes 33:xi, 8n, 11n, 11f, 30n, 42n, 46n, 48n, 57n, 63n, 66n, 67n, 49:145, 153, 172
Inquisitio de Fide 49:78n, 200n
Jerome's Works, edited by Erasmus 48:18, 53n
Julius Excluded from Heaven 54:136n
Letters 33:6f, 11, 13
Novum Instrumentum see **Erasmus, Desiderius, Works of**—*Greek New Testament*
On Free Will 17:255, 20:161n, 29:32n, 33:5, 7f, 15n, 49:88, 151
Opera Omnia see **Erasmus, Desiderius, Works of**—*Complete Works*
Outline or Compendium of a True Theology 48:114, 115n
Paraphrasis 27:159n, 239n, 245n, 248n, 307n, 315n, 336n, 339n, 387n, 400n, 402n, 49:44
Periphrasis in epistolam ad Titum 29:49n
Praise of Folly 15:127n, 17:57n, 29:171n, 44:170n, 54:136n
Someone's Advice (Consilium cujusdam) 48:224
Sponge 33:7, 49:78f
The Proverb, "One must be born either a king or a fool" 36:239n
The Seraphic Funeral 44:286n

Erasmus, St.—8:203, 17:78, 22:421n, 42:119

Erasmus and Luther—Bibliography 33:5n, xin

Erech—2:199f

Eremites—6:222

Erfurt—2:339, 3:49, 50n, 5:88, 6:298, 7:69, 8:182, 12:71, 242, 16:x, 42, 159n, 196n, 22:474n, 25:ix, 476, 41:21n, 129n, 42:5, 45:xiii, 55, 62n, 64n, 46:47, 48:12n, 135n, 143n, 188n, 214, 219, 223f, 227n, 257, 262, 264, 270n, 273f, 356, 49:15n, 389, 50:99n, 167n, 194n, 51:xiif, xvn, 5, 11, 60f, 103, 53:193f, 214, 217f, 222f, 225f, 229, 235–238, 252, 255f, 260f, 271, 278, 283, 317, 54:15, 24, 29
Augustinian monastery at 42:ixn, 48:3, 5, 6n, 7, 14, 15, 27, 36, 37n, 39n, 41, 43n, 51, 60, 62, 135, 145, 149, 356
Insurrection in 16:42n
Riots in 15:159n
University of 3:50n, 6:5, 8:276n, 31:6, 41:115, 42:97n, 45:343, 46:234n, 250n, 251, 48:5, 6n, 12n, 14, 30n, 37n, 59n, 62, 115n, 136, 137n, 143n, 145, 154n, 173n, 223n, 224n, 258n, 275n, 49:15n, 32, 81n, 414n

Eric, Duke of Braunschweig-Calenberg—46:90, 49:119n

Erikson, Erik H.—54:193, 234

Eris—2:227

Erlangen edition of Luther's works—51:xiv, see also indexes in each volume

Erling, Bernhard—translator of *Against the Heavenly Prophets in the Matter of Graven Images and Sacraments, Part I* 40:73–143

Ernest II, Count of Mansfeld—50:302n

Ernest, Bishop of Saxony—21:272

Ernest, Duke of Lüneberg—13:xi, 23:219n, 49:350

Ernest, Duke of Saxony—41:222n

Ernest, Elector of Saxony—54:286

Ernst, Duke of Braunschweig-Lüneberg—46:89

Error—1:95, 121, 153, 163, 183, 219, 223, 249f, 263, 319, 336, 2:12–14, 45, 47, 54f, 60, 68, 78, 121, 125, 156, 209, 229, 239f, 242n, 244, 261f, 264, 299, 314, 328, 337, 348, 362, 3:25, 38, 97, 108, 117, 145f, 160, 168, 195, 217, 237, 240, 273, 275, 280, 295, 350, 4:14, 61, 71, 80, 83, 138, 141, 163, 179, 210, 220, 242f, 304, 5:80, 103, 106, 121, 193f, 208, 347, 356, 6:57–59, 7:x, 7n, 11, 105, 135, 154f, 207, 233, 235, 254, 269, 291, 319, 342, 349, 360, 364, 8:21f, 32, 83, 88, 118, 134, 230, 238, 330, 332, 10:13, 97, 150, 13:383, 14:7, 10, 17, 19, 25, 31, 55, 78, 82, 100, 196, 202, 204, 258f, 261, 271,

288, 341, 16:123, 191, 245, 251, 278, 17:82f, 109, 360, 20:113, 146, 243, 333, 23:83, 90, 135, 137f, 144f, 150, 154, 173, 175, 179, 223, 230, 290, 368, 384, 24:38, 43, 55, 128, 131, 144, 177, 188, 236f, 259, 271, 274, 293, 304, 309, 320–322, 353, 404, 25:9, 61, 157, 159, 164, 192, 215, 240, 291, 26:14f, 18, 30f, 41, 44, 48f, 52, 65, 67, 80, 88, 109, 111, 118, 130, 140, 174–176, 180–182, 184, 192, 197f, 233, 243, 268, 326, 356, 367f, 386, 388, 395, 413, 415, 424, 429, 448, 454, 456, 458, 27:22f, 25, 32f, 37–39, 60, 64, 76, 83f, 86, 89, 100, 104–106, 108f, 112f, 128, 135, 140, 153, 168, 213, 217, 236, 295, 303, 337, 364, 28:61–63, 67, 88, 93, 223, 255, 309f, 315, 366, 29:50, 172, 30:15, 31, 69, 105, 135, 149, 165, 168f, 173, 189, 210, 221n, 222, 228, 238f, 245, 254, 284, 292, 299, 315, 319, 325, 35:20, 65, 73, 137, 200f, 36:188–190, 192–195, 198, 335, 37:19f, 36, 39, 41f, 71, 142, 147f, 156, 162f, 167–170, 205f, 211, 220, 230, 233, 258, 260, 284, 360, 38:8, 15, 36, 39, 73, 76, 78, 87, 107, 110, 118, 129, 161, 164, 170f, 173f, 186, 224, 239, 244, 269, 294n, 301, 306f, 316, 45:27, 361, 364, 366, 388n, 46:19, 289, 303, 318, 52:248, 271, 275

Esarhaddon—2:202

Esau—1:244, 271, 297, 308, 2:230f, 3:13, 16, 56, 96, 103, 145, 148, 152, 4:24, 185, 329, 342–344, 349f, 365, 367, 369–371, 373f, 376–380, 385–393, 395, 401–409, 5:14, 70, 89–97, 99–108, 110–117, 120, 125–129, 134, 136, 143, 146–149, 151f, 154, 156f, 159–163, 165–172, 174–177, 180–182, 184, 193, 198–202, 204f, 209f, 226, 231, 269, 273, 300, 6:53, 41, 72, 96–98, 106, 115–118, 164–167, 170, 175, 224, 234, 255, 273, 281–289, 294, 308, 310, 314, 7:39, 114, 220, 8:64, 92, 114, 160, 163, 169f, 175, 178, 217, 302, 10:85, 225f, 247, 284, 290, 296, 397, 11:103, 121, 217, 517, 14:197, 17:16, 352, 18:135, 194, 198, 202, 392, 22:81, 106, 201, 208, 25:81f, 374, 386, 26:94, 237, 435, 27:267, 28:237, 30:275, 35:321, 45:392, 46:233, 47:145f, see also **Jacob**

Esauites—4:392

Esch, Johann—53:211, 217

Eschatology—48:360f, 49:359, 371f

Eschaus, Thomas—48:168, 236

Esdras, Third and Fourth—35:349, 398

Esek—5:65, 67–69

Eshcol—2:372, 398, 5:52, 6:227, 345

Esschen, John van den—13:336n, 32:263, 266, 45:347n

Essence—37:173f, 255–257

Essenes—20:54

Essential nature—37:57, 59, 61f, 120, 130, 156, 195, 230, 282, 309, 366

Esslingen—49:93, 140

Estates—see **Stations in Society**

Estergom—50:243

Esther—45:34

Esther, Queen—8:93, 143, 14:336, 21:316, 25:511, 28:274, 30:89, 33:110, 44:84, 47:157

Estonia—45:313, 317n, 53:43

Et in terra—see ***Gloria in excelsis*** **(hymn)**

Eternal death—1:96, 192, 205, 229, 340, 359, 2:71, 157, 174, 248, 280, 321, 391, 3:21, 39, 225, 342f, 357, 5:137, 229, 7:148, 228, 241, 12:372, 13:78, 137, 22:386, 391, 23:31, 39, 45, 106, 116, 194, 196, 313, 359, 24:53, 161, 319, 342, 360, 26:5, 10f, 26, 29, 36, 42, 77, 88, 92, 146, 152, 179, 218, 235f, 252, 254, 256, 292, 310, 325, 337, 347, 349, 362, 374, 381, 453, 27:18, 26, 98, 104, 124, 36:210, 38:86, 43:29, 51–55

Eternal fire—1:359, 2:24, 3:268, 4:314, 8:118, 218, 17:415f, 24:14, 85, 175, 198, 204, 222

Eternal glory—13:387

Eternal kingdom—see **Kingdom, Eternal**

Eternal life—1:46, 56, 64f, 80–82, 86, 89, 104, 110, 117, 121, 130, 161, 180, 191, 196, 198, 201, 214, 220, 226, 236, 249, 285, 330, 333, 346–348, 351f, 2:151, 153f, 160, 181, 184, 237, 256, 261, 278, 344, 390f, 397f, 3:25, 27f, 39, 41, 73, 86, 92, 99, 110f, 118, 120, 123f, 141f, 148f, 153, 155–158, 167, 214, 317, 338f, 363, 4:30, 43, 45, 52, 56f, 119, 147, 156, 164, 166, 168, 290–292, 310, 314, 316f, 329f, 345, 350, 367, 399–401, 405, 408, 5:4, 17–19, 50, 78, 89, 110, 132, 137, 140, 142, 155, 177, 183, 186f, 191f, 195, 204, 229f, 245, 247, 250, 255, 260, 286, 7:16, 64, 116f, 230, 293, 342, 8:7, 10, 12, 36, 61, 79, 140, 144, 167, 180, 183–185, 189f, 192, 195, 236, 255f, 258f, 270f, 274, 309–311, 316, 326, 12:158, 232, 251, 311, 345, 397, 402, 13:104, 124, 126f, 130f, 14:25, 55, 58, 62, 86f, 131, 181, 210, 329, 15:58, 306f, 310, 20:7, 143,

22:96, 98, 340, 345f, 349f, 353, 357, 360, 364, 367, 369f, 381, 441, 463f, 466, 471, 474, 479f, 489, 495, 499–503, 506, 513, 526, 23:5, 8–10, 12, 15, 18–20, 22, 28, 31–39, 41, 54f, 63, 71–78, 85, 87, 91, 101, 104–109, 111–119, 121, 125–144, 148, 151, 154f, 159f, 165, 169–172, 177f, 181, 193f, 197, 202, 225, 250, 277, 321, 327–331, 337, 349, 360, 364, 368, 372, 399, 24:20, 26, 34f, 37–39, 41–44, 46, 48–50, 52, 58, 60f, 77, 95, 108, 125, 135, 141, 146, 153, 159, 179, 214, 221, 228f, 238, 258, 262f, 271, 285, 296f, 307, 315, 319, 334, 346, 360f, 371f, 408, 25:45, 52, 314–316, 26:9, 11, 13f, 21, 24, 28, 31, 35, 42, 48, 77, 88, 91, 120, 124–129, 132, 135, 137–141, 144, 146f, 151, 153f, 163, 175, 177, 181, 183, 199f, 213, 218, 224f, 238, 246, 249, 251, 258, 262, 274, 303f, 331, 334f, 340f, 355f, 363, 374, 385f, 389, 392, 396, 400, 421, 431, 437, 439f, 452, 457f, 28:5, 74, 99, 101f, 120f, 126, 145f, 172f, 183–185, 191, 247, 249, 372, 374, 29:10–12, 66, 86, 98, 180, 213f, 233, 30:11, 29, 64f, 69, 107, 109, 111–113, 155f, 161, 196f, 222, 271, 319–321, 327, 32:260, 33:105f, 34:211, 35:66f, 88f, 36:45, 218f, 37:xx, 23n, 75, 87, 92–97, 100f, 115, 118f, 129–135, 140, 199f, 325, 338, 363, 366, 372, 38:38f, 43, 87, 107, 113, 165, 185, 232, 41:110, 148, 171f, 241, 301, 338, 358, 42:113, 175, 46:99, 166, 177, 181, 224, 237, 51:8, 114f, 126, 147, 166, 174, 191, 293, 52:53f, 254, 257, 272, see also **Life to come**

Eternal life, Hope of—1:80, 82, 86, 198, 201, 214, 333, 354

Eternal punishment—2:139, 196, 322

Eternal sorrow—24:17

Eternal wealth—23:13

Eternity—1:214, 3:39, 149, 4:90, 132, 137, 11:21f, 12:52f, 13:128, 17:227, 18:105, 20:11, 25:131, 47:81–84, 206f

Ethan—8:323, 10:449, 12:201

Ethics—2:303, 4:217, 25:433, 26:261, 27:225, 37:157, 364

Ethics, Contextual—25:410

Ethics, Luther's—44:xi–xvi

Ethiopia—1:101, 7:173, 10:349f, 411f, 448f, 13:33, 404, 16:126, 169, 308, 316, 18:310, 342, 344, 19:140, 232, 20:113, 126, 251

Ethiopian eunuch—16:159

Ethiopians—2:187, 194f, 259, 4:274, 5:380, 6:283, 7:171, 11:126, 185, 16:168, 333, 17:87, 131, 198, 405, 30:40

Etruscans—2:188n

Etymologies, Luther's use of—26:436n

Etymology—3:100, 4:99, 192, 306n, 6:15, 35, 141f, 145, 259, 266, 7:32n, 51, 198, 240, 250, 267f, 298, 343, 8:66f, 241

Eucharist—see **Lord's Supper**

Eucharistic controversy—see **Lord's Supper, controversy over the**

Euchit—42:24n

Euclid—15:74n

Euclio—6:5

Eugene IV, Pope—4:82, 31:205, 337, 342, 36:63n, 41:266n, 44:91n, 129n, 144n, 52:267

Eulenspiegel, Till—37:343n, 41:363n

Eunomians—12:282, 26:31

Eunuchs—3:81, 7:51–53, 110, 198, 8:192, 9:229f, 235, 17:262f, 21:6, 90–92, 23:134, 27:346, 41:42n, 43, 243n, 248, 250n, 252, 45:18–21, 27, 30, 46:149, 153

Euphrates River—1:97f, 101n, 2:234, 279, 4:186, 331, 5:210, 6:36, 84, 309, 8:38, 179, 16:86, 90, 127, 184, 218, 17:96, 19:215

Euripides—46:269n

Iphegenia in Tauris 7:329n

Europe—1:207n, 254, 288, 2:67, 185, 187, 201, 346, 7:298, 14:333, 22:82, 23:115n, 38:63n, 41:334, 46:xiii, 5, 157

Europeans—17:72, 90

Eusebius, Bishop of Nicodemia—41:81n, 84, 87

Eusebius of Caesarea—2:190, 6:260, 286, 7:343n, 27:185, 41:44n, 47:117n, 236, 298, 54:274, 305

Ecclesiastical History 9:25n, 16:127n, 251n, 20:155n, 24:196n, 26:411n, 27:195, 217, 280n, 30:144n, 198n, 31:119, 35:138n, 394n, 395n, 399n, 400, 41:7n, 44n, 54n, 56n, 94n, 106n, 47:298

Praeparatio evangelica 29:128n

Eusochium—30:40n

Eustathius, Bishop of Antioch—41:57n, 60

Eustochium, St. Julia—44:306n

Euthansia—54:397

Eutyches—15:339, 341, 342n, 38:63n, 41:107n, 108–114, 115n, 116–119, 121, 123, 126, 136, 138, 146, 163

Eutychians—32:126, 38:282, 287n, 307n

Evangelical, Meaning of—21:225f

Evangelical Churches—7:62, 46:xii, 34,

36f, 38f, 52n, 64, 90, 109, 142, 157, 252, 255, 49:xiii, xvi, 17n, 28f, 160–162, 177f, 205f, 238n, 261, 378–380, 414n
Emergence of the 49:xiii
Laws, government 49:61f, 205f, 378f
Territorial structure 46:xiii, 48:211n, 269n, 275n, 303n, 399, 49:52, 178
Theology of 49:61f, 163n, 233n, 331f, 382f
Evangelical counsels—15:64, 21:3f, 70, 74, 34:306n, 40:20n, 46:197, 49:67
Evangelical dispensations—12:320
Evangelical hermeneutics—16:xi
Evangelical way—28:15
Evangelicals—3:227, 17:74, 282, 403, 23:10f, 402, 26:221, 312, 27:48, 125, 34:65, 199, 36:x, 265n, 38:7f, 111, 141f, 183n, 217, 230, 51:202, see also **Protestants**
Evangelism—8:173, 183
Evangelists—3:205, 300, 4:126, 8:44, 240, 9:272, 11:336, 12:208, 13:12, 16:74, 97, 17:13, 58f, 330, 20:125, 127, 23:108f, 112, 156f, 184f, 189, 201, 220, 243, 259, 276, 283, 365, 372, 376, 392, 418–421, 24:7f, 32, 64, 90, 26:49, 73, 168, 30:3f, 35:357, 360, 36:31, 163, 165, 171, 37:33, 73f, 127, 289, 315, 330, 336, 38:20, 80, 41:121f, 154f, 176, 45:208, 317, 46:37, 39, 311, 52:99
Evangelists, Four—2:312, 331
Evangelus—30:204n
Eve—1:15, 37, 62–64, 66f, 69, 81f, 86, 91, 101, 103, 105, 113–115, 117f, 121, 126–128, 130f, 134–142, 144f, 147–164, 166–168, 170–173, 178–180, 182, 185f, 189–191, 193, 196f, 199f, 202f, 218–227, 233, 237f, 240–242, 245–247, 266, 271, 275, 281, 283–285, 290, 306, 308, 312, 314, 324–326, 335, 337, 339, 341f, 352–354, 2:30f, 57, 78, 80, 98, 185, 233, 3:56, 97, 133f, 139, 184, 206, 270, 282, 287, 4:162, 189, 193, 291f, 294f, 5:119, 153, 6:223, 235f, 255, 269, 324, 338, 342, 7:36, 272, 276n, 8:95, 242, 317, 326, 331, 9:21, 11:153, 13:85, 90, 16:138, 22:31, 98, 111, 124, 154, 280, 313, 340, 395, 420, 448, 453, 460, 463, 23:81, 234, 24:343, 25:332, 408, 27:260, 288f, 28:163, 194, 196, 277–279, 291, 345, 30:95, 142, 35:83, 369, 37:89, 129, 38:311, 41:314, 46:276, 47:148, 52:127f, 151, 53:110
Creation of 1:123, 128, 131
Evening—24:387
Everlasting life—see **Eternal life**; **Life to come**
Everybody, Mr.—45:63
Evil—6:59, 66, 90f, 190, 216, 235f, 271, 358, 400, 11:12f, 458, 492, 13:5, 12, 132, 135, 153, 240, 15:55, 92, 109, 117, 120, 176f, 186, 201f, 237, 19:28, 183, 25:27, 50, 65, 103, 108, 130, 160f, 201, 219–222, 244, 247, 259, 266, 371, 383f, 426, 433, 442, 453f, 464–467, 483, 488, 29:47, 79, 96, 98, 100, 140f, 155, 196, 226, 234, 237, 239, 37:81n, 133f, 238, 38:26f, 42, 85, 103, 123, 126f, 157, 167, 170, 178, 188, 193, 200, 202, 214, 231, 261n, 313, 42:11, 75f, 78, 80, 101n, 125–145, 147f, 155–157, 159, 161, 172, 45:85–88, 95f, 101, 274, 297, 387, 389, 46:24, 26, 28, 31f, 34, 41, 74, 78, 82, 95, 99f, 130f, 149, 151, 153f, 164f, 171, 204, 248, 276, 286, 300, 303, 48:375, 52:37, 58f, 226
Evil, Knowledge of—1:5, 63, 66f, 71, 73, 80f, 114, 120, 141, 143, 148, 152, 154, 298, 351
Evil, Origin of—1:144, 146
Evil, Original—7:50, 273, 278
Evil, Problem of—25:103, 160–163
Evil spirits—2:11n, 321, 14:203, 45:201f
Evil talk—28:161–165
Evil thoughts—46:130f, 149
Evildoers—2:10, 301, 369, 3:40, 235, 331, 9:144f, 166, 215, 243, 248
Evilmerodach—1:302, 2:259
Evodius—3:11n
Ex opere operato—see **Opus operatum**
Examinations—34:xiv, 66, 92
Examples—15:17f, 22, 33, 43, 49, 147, 153, 174, 186, 192, 214, 17:101, 195, 197, 272, 401, 29:54, 58, 185, 216, 220, 233, 238
Excesses—16:62, 185
Excommunication—1:284, 299, 315f, 3:57, 242, 281, 4:65, 67, 69, 71, 8:206, 246, 256, 265, 277, 9:82, 10:33f, 195, 199, 13:42, 14:55, 225, 253, 17:403, 21:124, 22:61, 84, 244, 23:50, 24:228, 304, 307, 313, 316f, 321–323, 331, 338, 25:79, 173, 379f, 414, 26:58, 87, 412, 27:110, 28:254, 286, 30:22, 80, 31:113, 229, 239f, 311, 32:ix, xiii, 5, 66f, 87n, 115, 125, 234, 276n, 34:32f, 35:47, 51, 40:341n, 371f, 41:240, 251, 278, 45:77, 116, 48:77n, 85n, 50:24, 63–65, 163, 51:42, 66, 97f, 131, 391, 54:159, 185, 346, 398, 404, 422f, see also **Ban**
Excrement—1:110, 250, 24:206–208
Excuses—10:12, 22, 26, 31

Execution—26:58
Executioners—1:109, 8:54, 99, 125, 205, 259, 9:162f, 35:258f
Executors—9:163
Exegesis, Evangelical—16:xi
Exegesis, Monastic—1:114n
Exegetes—2:ix, 13n, 150n, 164, 16:211, 25:146
Exegetes, Christian—9:308n
Exegetes, Foolish—1:191
Exegetes, Medieval—26:439n
Exegetical traditions—16:x, 69n
Jewish 3:232n
Exercise—28:321f
Exercised, To be—11:436f
Exhortation to Communicants—see **Luther, Martin, Writings of**
Exhortations—17:13, 180, 249f, 254, 349, 20:28, 231, 25:104, 105f, 111f, 119, 448, 53:78–80, 104f
Exile—7:74f, 97, 126f, 129, 196, 290, 338, 8:17f, 92, 189, 300, see also **Captivity—Babylonian**
Exiles—3:179, 182f, 20:67f, 47:66, 74–78, 96f, 137f, 188, 218, 239, 263, 269, 284, 287, 292
Exodus—1:132, 11:31, 35, 393, 16:125, 127, 17:358, 18:258, 25:72, 136, 199, 322, 36:160
Exodus from Egypt—3:35, 9:85, 271, 19:134–137, 231, 22:310, 313, 29:157f, 220, 36:160, 47:86f, 90–95, 97, 154, 158, 164, 208, 271
Exorcism—50:209f, 53:95, 97f, 106f
Exorcists—1:235, 24:264
Experience—6:10, 89, 107, 132, 361, 10:49, 303, 15:23, 28, 47, 105, 17:50, 85, 256, 277, 371, 25:105, 240, 28:71, 75–77, 80f, 97, 107, 278, 29:179, 181, 186, 33:41, 106, 225, 250, 252, 261, 265, 281, 54:7, 274, 320, 338, 371, 375
Experience, Learning from—20:12, 165f
Experience, Religious—9:93f, 12:311, 316, 319, 356, 372, 14:99, 21:307, 25:438f, 443
Experience, Subjective—48:366
Expiation—26:132, 431, 30:237, 245, 273, 295
Expositers—25:28, 52
Expostulatio—Melanchthon to Henry VIII 50:203f, 203n
Exsufflation—53:96, 106
Exsurge, Domine—see **Bulls, Papal**
External observances—44:35, 236
External things—3:272f, 275f, 17:113, 20:54, 78, 300, 37:7, 16n, 23n, 85f, 92, 99, 106, 133, 135–137, 140f, 282f, 357, 366, 41:175, 52:34f, 37, 70, 222, 259, 53:xv–xvi, 22, 90, 102
Extortion, Papal—22:220
Extravagantes—27:154, 48:84f, 186, see also ***Corpus Iuris Canonici***; **Decretals, Papal**; **Gratian**
Extreme Unction—1:229, 42:98, 100n, 108
Exultation—11:265f
Exultet (hymn)—2:154n
Eyes—3:130, 136, 150, 173, 185f, 193f, 196, 210, 215, 226, 263, 278, 294, 302–304, 341, 346, 358f, 7:29f, 49, 56, 67, 71, 78, 84, 101, 104–106, 138, 162, 164–166, 205, 211, 236, 240, 293, 340, 9:193f, 197, 199, 233, 10:99, 142f, 359f, 15:11, 19, 67, 86, 99, 100f, 133, 180, 227, 241, 244, 250, 20:30f, 51, 56f, 91, 101, 128f, 133, 194–196, 215, 219, 229, 240f, 249, 321, 21:90f, 177–180, 185f, 219f, 222, 315f, 22:436, 27:37, 39, 134, 140f, 245, 304, 338, 349, 410
Eyes, Opening of—11:426
Ezekiel, Book of—17:131
Ezekiel, Prophet—2:51, 74, 188, 191, 194, 201, 218, 3:247f, 7:25, 8:304, 19:85, 154, 22:372, 24:234, 27:111, 30:135, 177, 35:282–293, 38:40, 55f, 94, 41:208, 217n, 45:215, 272, 46:173, 47:188, 258, 265, 49:288n, 418, 52:92
Ezeongeber—9:33
Ezra—2:150, 188n, 16:221, 17:124, 126, 130, 29:208, 35:332, 337, 45:225, 47:203f
Ezra, Book of—2:188n, 20:26, 68, 274, 342, 23:21

Faber—2:385
Faber, Francis—48:230
Faber, Jacobus—see **Lefevre d'Etaples, Jacques**
Faber, John, Archbishop of Vienna—7:91n, 17:38n, 247, 23:212n, 33:84, 34:6n, 70n, 95n, 328n, 35:187, 408n, 41:150n, 190n, 191, 47:22n, 46n, 49:41n, 350, 50:186n, 219n, 54:27, 137, 351, 373, 415
Malleus in Haeresin Lutheranam 33:84n
Opus adversus nova quaedam et a christiana religione prorsus aliena dogmata Martini Lutheri, 1521 28:ix, 5f, 49:41n
Faber Stapulensis—see **Lefevre d'Etaples, Jacques**
Fabian, Pope—41:308n, 354n
Fabian, St.—3:125
Fabiola—31:119

Fabius—15:159n, 16:258

Fables—4:61n, 9:140, 198, 225, 308, 35:57, 63, 46:111n, 112n

Fabricius, Philip—12:ix, 23:x

Face of the Lord—29:165

Face(s)—10:125f, 161, 177, 195, 324, 331f, 418, 11:112f, 252, 456

Factions—3:16, 16:32, 24:31, 47, 76, 101–103, 127, 131, 133, 176, 202, 204, 207f, 215, 217, 223, 228, 251, 292, 366f, 38:228f, see also **Dissension; Schism(s)**

Factious spirits—24:95, 28:59, 61–63, 66, 72, 76f, 79–81, 93f, 100, 122, 128, 146, 148, 197, 217, 252, 326, 366, 35:137, 165f, 196, 217, 380f, 389, see also **Anabaptists; Enthusiasts; Fanatics; Radical reformers; Schwärmer**

Factotum—4:374, 392

Faintheartedness—10:100, 16:54, 30:267

Fairness—10:94f, 21:235–237

Fairness in applying law—1:27

Fairs (Yearly markets)—45:285n, 288n, 289

Fairy tales—19:68, 23:335

Faith—1:20, 39, 49f, 57, 59f, 64, 81, 87, 94, 121f, 126, 149, 152–159, 165, 168, 170f, 180f, 193f, 198, 220f, 234f, 242, 251, 257–259, 264–266, 273, 288, 318, 324f, 329f, 333, 336, 338, 344f, 347, 354, 2:27f, 30f, 38, 41, 47, 49, 52, 54–56, 59, 70f, 77, 81f, 84, 87, 90, 97–99, 101, 103–105, 107, 113f, 117f, 120, 130, 148, 152, 154, 156, 165, 175–177, 179f, 182, 192, 197, 210, 215, 221, 226, 228, 233–235, 239–244, 246, 248, 250–254, 256f, 260, 264, 267–269, 275, 280f, 283f, 286–290, 292–296, 304, 307–309, 316, 319, 321, 323, 325, 333, 335, 349f, 353, 355–357, 359, 362f, 370, 372, 374f, 377, 380, 382, 387, 389, 392, 397, 399, 3:19, 21–26, 29–31, 33, 36f, 44f, 67, 70, 72, 75, 78–80, 83, 85, 87, 89, 94–96, 102–105, 107f, 110–114, 118, 120, 124, 128, 133, 135, 137, 140–143, 146–149, 151–154, 156, 162f, 166, 168–171, 174–177, 185f, 188, 190–192, 194f, 199f, 204, 206, 208, 210, 212, 215, 218, 224, 230f, 235, 260, 264f, 270f, 289, 291, 295, 297, 300–302, 312, 315f, 318, 320–322, 325f, 328–330, 332–334, 336, 338, 344, 346, 351, 357, 362, 364, 4:6, 14, 17, 21, 24, 26–29, 32, 38f, 46, 53f, 59f, 62, 65, 68, 70–73, 78, 95–97, 101, 104–107, 112–116, 118–122, 124, 127f, 132–134, 143f, 148–150, 157, 162, 164–171, 175, 170, 182, 190–192, 205, 207, 217, 221, 234–239, 242f, 247f, 251–254, 257f, 265, 267–269, 271, 274, 277, 279, 282f, 287, 295, 302, 304, 309, 312, 314f, 317–321, 323, 325, 327–330, 336, 338f, 341, 343, 347, 349, 352, 355, 357–362, 364, 367f, 373, 377, 382, 396f, 400, 402, 404, 407f, 5:4–9, 12, 14–19, 22, 24, 26–28, 39, 41, 43f, 46, 50, 55–57, 68–70, 72, 76f, 79f, 82, 86f, 89, 116–120, 125, 127–133, 140–142, 144, 146, 158, 161, 175–177, 184, 186–188, 196f, 199–204, 205n, 207, 212, 214, 217, 220, 223f, 230, 233–236, 239, 242, 244, 247f, 255, 257, 259, 264, 266–269, 271, 274f, 277, 279, 281, 284, 292f, 310, 315, 320f, 326f, 332–335, 347f, 350, 355, 358–360, 372, 6:8, 10f, 39f, 72, 92, 102, 104, 107–109, 111, 116, 123, 135, 139, 147, 175, 218f, 241, 262f, 305, 7:10, 12, 37, 54f, 57, 61, 65, 72, 77, 89–91, 105f, 109, 111, 116–118, 123, 125, 129–139, 143, 155f, 163f, 170–178, 198f, 203, 207, 210–212, 219–222, 230, 234, 253, 257, 261, 296, 305, 307–311, 313–316, 320–327, 336, 343f, 348, 353, 356f, 360, 366, 371, 8:6–8, 12f, 15, 17–19, 26, 32–35, 37, 41f, 45, 47, 49, 53f, 58, 62, 69, 75, 80, 90, 96, 110, 114, 117, 132–134, 139, 143f, 146, 162–164, 166–168, 177–179, 181, 184–186, 188–190, 192–194, 200–204, 210, 213, 219f, 229, 235–238, 243–246, 251, 254, 256f, 261f, 268f, 274, 276f, 279, 282f, 286–288, 292, 308–316, 319f, 325f, 330, 332, 9:ix, 3f, 7f, 19–21, 24f, 33, 35, 40–42, 56f, 60n, 68–73, 75f, 84, 87–89, 93–96, 102, 104, 109, 111, 117–119, 126, 130, 134f, 137f, 140, 150, 156–158, 164–168, 170f, 175, 179f, 183–189, 197–199, 202f, 205f, 213, 219, 224–226, 232, 234–238, 241, 244f, 251, 278f, 283, 299, 305, 10:30, 69, 91, 111, 125, 140, 155, 188, 242, 273, 356, 384, 407f, 440, 452, 11:3f, 6, 8, 12–14, 18, 27–30, 35, 47f, 53, 55, 61, 95–98, 101, 103, 107, 140, 145–149, 152, 158–161, 168, 174, 177, 190, 205–210, 215f, 223, 226, 230f, 235, 245, 252, 253, 269, 291, 293, 299, 301, 318, 321, 340, 369, 401f, 406–408, 420, 438, 442, 449, 461f, 470, 477, 485, 517f, 522, 525, 529, 539, 544, 12:17f, 27, 39, 46, 104f, 108, 117f, 169f, 173, 191, 197, 203, 213, 228, 233, 247f, 250, 259,

263, 279f, 287, 289f, 293, 296, 298, 322, 324, 328f, 336, 342, 345, 353, 361f, 363–365, 367, 370, 373, 379f, 385f, 393, 401, 13:5–7, 10f, 15, 18f, 22, 26, 29, 62, 87f, 138, 177, 229, 241f, 262f, 280, 290, 377, 379f, 382, 14:9f, 12, 16f, 20, 24f, 27, 30, 36, 55, 59, 61, 65, 78, 81–84, 87f, 91, 93, 98–100, 103, 115, 119, 125, 145f, 152, 160, 168, 181, 185, 196f, 201, 203, 212f, 215, 219, 223, 227, 229, 239, 244, 245f, 258f, 276, 289–295, 297–299, 304, 306, 316f, 319, 321f, 324, 328f, 331, 334, 337, 341–343, 347, 15:208f, 218, 243, 257f, 268f, 272f, 277, 16:4, 9f, 14f, 17, 20f, 25, 29, 32, 36f, 43, 53, 59–61, 64f, 72, 75–77, 79, 82–84, 92, 100, 112f, 117, 120, 122f, 137f, 144, 152f, 157, 167–169, 171, 178, 188, 197–200, 201n, 202f, 205f, 208f, 215, 218, 223f, 227f, 230f, 233, 246, 250, 252, 262–264, 289, 302–304, 307, 309, 314, 317f, 320, 321n, 322, 325, 327–329, 331f, 347, 17:6, 27, 31, 35, 45, 50, 64f, 67, 76–78, 81, 110, 164, 168, 197, 199, 206, 213, 230, 243–245, 256, 288, 342, 345, 360, 365f, 410, 18:13f, 65–67, 96, 111f, 119, 121, 221, 240, 259, 261, 282, 284, 336, 350, 354, 363, 418, 19:5, 8, 10–13, 17, 23–25, 28, 45, 47f, 54f, 57, 65, 67, 79f, 86f, 89, 117, 119, 123f, 151, 155, 179, 180f, 196f, 225, 20:38, 44, 96, 103, 115, 137f, 147, 152, 155–157, 164, 166, 212, 223, 282, 297, 21:14–16, 29, 37, 44, 59, 62, 65–67, 141, 150, 196f, 205, 258f, 269, 285, 304–310, 338f, 341, 351, 353f, 22:8, 18, 25, 35, 48, 52, 54f, 60, 66, 70f, 74, 76f, 80, 82, 87f, 90, 100, 105, 107f, 115f, 122, 131, 140, 144f, 156, 158, 196–198, 200, 203f, 209, 211, 218, 231, 247f, 250f, 253, 264, 268, 270, 272, 274f, 285f, 298, 310, 313, 316f, 323f, 329, 331, 334f, 339, 349f, 355–358, 363f, 369, 374, 376–378, 380, 389, 392–394, 416, 418, 425, 428, 431f, 437, 439, 443, 455, 463f, 472, 474, 478, 481, 495, 498, 501–503, 507, 526, 23:12f, 19f, 22f, 25–29, 32f, 42, 44f, 47–49, 52, 54, 56, 58–60, 62f, 65–70, 72, 75f, 78–80, 84, 86f, 90, 95–97, 99, 103, 105–116, 118, 122n, 125–127f, 130f, 136f, 139, 141–144, 147, 150f, 153, 159, 161, 169–172, 177–180, 182–185, 191, 195, 207, 220, 226, 230, 234, 247, 261, 263f, 266, 275f, 282, 284, 288–290, 295–298, 303, 306, 324–326, 330f, 346, 350f, 358–360, 366, 377, 379, 381, 392f, 398, 408, 410–413, 416, 24:8, 17f, 20, 23, 33, 35–38, 40–43, 45–47, 50–55, 57, 59–61, 76f, 80, 83, 87f, 92, 96f, 113, 119, 121f, 124, 126, 129f, 135, 137, 140f, 143, 145, 147, 150, 152, 157, 168, 170–172, 196f, 202f, 205, 209–213, 217f, 220–223, 226, 230, 232, 234, 236f, 239–244, 246, 249, 252, 255, 257, 262f, 265, 273–276, 281, 287, 289, 292–294, 296f, 301, 304, 307, 309, 317–323, 325f, 329–331, 340, 342–344, 347f, 353, 358–361, 366, 374f, 378, 383, 388, 392, 394–397, 400f, 403–405, 407, 411f, 25:5–7, 26, 31–34, 39–41, 67, 71, 89, 106, 112–119, 127f, 130, 132f, 152f, 163, 204, 209, 215f, 236–239, 242f, 250f, 267, 279f, 286–289, 319f, 358f, 399, 407, 410f, 444, 446, 485, 489, 492, 498–502, 506–508, 26:3f, 10, 20, 35f, 46, 144, 146f, 167n, 172, 174, 194, 227f, 239, 252, 261, 264–266, 269, 351, 377, 459, 27:5–10, 14f, 19–32, 34, 36–42, 47f, 52–54, 56f, 61–64, 71–76, 78, 82f, 85, 88–90, 92–97, 100, 103, 107, 109, 114, 118, 120, 124, 127, 129, 132, 137, 139–141, 144–146, 153, 156, 159, 161, 168–173, 176–179, 184, 188f, 197f, 203, 210, 213–216, 218–223, 225, 227–229, 231–234, 236, 238f, 241, 246–248, 250–255, 258–260, 263, 265f, 270, 274f, 276, 278–281, 283–286, 289–291, 294, 298f, 302–304, 306, 311, 327–333, 335–338, 342f, 350, 357f, 366–268, 371, 373f, 377f, 381, 388, 391, 395f, 403f, 406, 28:20, 35, 44, 69–73, 82, 101f, 104f, 107, 124f, 126, 141, 190, 202, 206, 223–226, 236, 252–254, 296f, 304, 308, 320, 366, 372, 29:3–6, 8–14, 20f, 32, 34, 41f, 44–48, 50, 52f, 57, 62f, 68f, 71, 77, 81, 83, 85–88, 90, 93, 96–98, 100, 104, 111, 115, 117–119, 123f, 131f, 136–138, 144f, 148–152, 154–157, 160, 162, 166, 172, 178, 180, 182f, 185, 188f, 195, 202f, 207, 209–211, 217–219, 223f, 226, 228–233, 235–239, 30:3f, 6f, 10–12, 14f, 16–21, 23–35, 37, 39–43, 45–47, 50, 52, 54, 56–58, 65, 67–71, 73, 75, 77, 81f, 86, 89f, 95f, 105–109, 115–118, 120, 122–127, 130f, 141f, 148f, 151–161, 165, 167, 169–176, 179–182, 184, 186, 188–190, 192, 198f, 204, 207, 212f, 215, 224, 227–229, 232, 235, 238–240, 244f,

247, 255f, 262, 264, 267, 271, 274, 277–282, 286, 289, 296, 298, 300–307, 309, 311–313, 317f, 321–323, 326, 31:12, 55f, 131, 226, 231, 270–275, 343f, 347, 350–353, 357, 368, 32:xviif, 15, 49, 118, 130, 178, 227–233, 235f, 239–241, 33:62f, 88, 173f, 270–275, 278–288, 34:20f, 53, 91, 96, 109–114, 120f, 153, 159f, 303–321, 347f, 359, 35:xxi, 13, 17, 20–22, 25, 35f, 48f, 60f, 64n, 89, 93, 101–103, 120, 237, 240f, 358n, 359, 361f, 364, 368, 370, 374f, 384f, 36:7, 20, 27, 29, 35, 39f, 42, 44f, 47–52, 56–62, 64–67, 70–92, 94, 95n, 96f, 100, 107, 120–124, 131, 134, 143f, 162f, 164, 166, 168–171, 175–183, 187–193, 195, 198, 200f, 203–205, 208–211, 214, 221–224, 226f, 229, 241, 253, 258, 262–264, 287, 291, 293, 295–297, 300–303, 312f, 316, 324, 350, 353, 37:15, 29, 62, 76, 86n, 88–93, 102, 130–132, 134, 135n, 136f, 140, 142, 146, 153, 155, 188, 191, 194, 229, 238, 249n, 261f, 292, 296, 304–306, 308, 312, 366f, 38:xxi, 7, 15f, 17f, 21, 23, 25–27, 29f, 35f, 42, 46, 53, 56, 58f, 64, 71, 81f, 85f, 88, 95, 104, 113, 115f, 126f, 128–131, 136, 155, 163f, 167, 169–171, 173f, 181, 183n, 184n, 190, 196, 200, 203, 207–209, 211, 228, 242, 244, 257, 262, 264, 269f, 291, 295, 304f, 310, 312, 317, 40:29, 84, 90, 242f, 275f, 299, 375, 41:17, 38, 40, 47f, 50, 52, 54f, 65, 69f, 73, 77–78, 81, 85f, 89, 92f, 96, 103, 105, 110–113, 121–125, 127f, 133–137, 140, 142f, 145–147, 152, 155, 164, 167, 169, 176, 178, 185, 204, 211, 250, 261, 271, 279, 285, 287f, 296, 301f, 310, 315f, 323f, 327–329, 334, 336, 339f, 342f, 345–348, 352, 358–360, 42:xi, xv, 8n, 13, 43, 58, 62, 64, 76, 80f, 87f, 90, 93, 100f, 106f, 109–114, 127, 135, 137, 147, 150, 158, 161, 163–165, 172, 175, 185, 43:24f, 52–55, 120, 44:18, 21–114, 268–282, 275n, 285–292, 300, 348f, 398, 45:8f, 24, 39f, 72, 79, 84, 88f, 90, 97f, 105, 108, 110, 114, 116f, 126, 129, 143f, 149f, 153, 171f, 178, 199f, 203, 213, 227, 314, 317, 323, 327, 330, 332, 334, 360, 362f, 365f, 46:10, 83, 95, 135f, 150, 158n, 172, 174f, 177–179, 181, 183, 185f, 188, 195, 199, 224, 228, 306, 47:ix, 43, 48, 51–54, 85f, 101f, 110, 133, 139, 145, 150, 175, 177, 291, 48:74, 86, 90, 104, 146f, 152, 162, 183, 189, 195f, 233, 263, 267f, 391f, 49:269f, 331f, 358f, 371f, 395f, 51:59f, 66, 71, 74, 76, 89, 92f, 99, 110–116, 164, 171, 182, 187, 198, 247, 275–283, 308, 372, 52:14f, 18, 21f, 24, 28, 31f, 33f, 36f, 41, 49f, 59, 61, 67f, 72, 76, 78, 83, 88, 91, 96f, 104, 112f, 121, 127, 130f, 133f, 136, 138, 143, 146, 153–155, 157f, 163, 172f, 175, 179, 181, 192, 195f, 199f, 207f, 212, 231, 239f, 244f, 249f, 252f, 257, 276f, 282, 285f, 54:39, 74, 104, 157, 290, 453, 456, 460, see also **Articles of Faith**; **Historical faith**; **Righteousness of Faith**; **Trust**

- And the Sacrament of the Altar 36:32, 35, 38–40, 43, 46–48, 50, 53, 56, 177, 277f
- And works 25:130, 251, 44:xiii, xviii, 17–19, 23, 25f, 33, 108, 270f, 279–282, 285–287, 289, 348f
- Voluntary in nature 11:470, 28:35f, 38, 45:106–108, 114

Faith, Articles of—see **Articles of Faith**

Faith, Battle of—28:73f, 104f, 136f, 155, 157, 251, 373f

Faith, Definition of—22:369

Faith, Difficulties of—37:50, 52f, 74f, 78, 141

Faith, Doctrine of—27:19, 36, 38f, 41f, 52f, 56f, 59–61, 66, 68, 77, 99, 110, 188, 222, 311

Faith, Incarnate—26:266

Faith, Infused—26:146f, 269

Faith, Kingdom of—18:111f

Faith, Obedience of—25:5, 123f, 130f, 408

Faith, Righteousness of—see **Righteousness of Faith**

Faith, Rule of—17:114, 256

Faith, The Christian—37:xi, xx, 17, 23, 26–27, 103, 166, 229f, 360, 371, 38:xviii, 119, 168n, 169, 178, 291, 310, 41:17, 34, 38, 40, 52, 74, 107f, 111, 117, 121, 123–127, 133, 136, 140–142, 208, 241, 288, 297, 315, 325, 331, 335, 338, 346, 46:89, 95, 136, 175, 178, 188, 199, 306

Faith, Unformed—25:152

Faith alone—25:33, 44:xii, 264, 281, 284f, 287f, 292

Faith formed by love—26:88, 90, 146, 160, 168, 208, 268f, 279

Faith in Christ—42:xvf, 98, 142, 147, 149, 170, 182

Faith makes righteous—see **Justification by faith**

Faith vs. belief—25:238

Faith vs. works—25:130, 251

Faithfulness—3:4, 4:283f, 10:154f, 13:217f,

381, 16:24, 20:273, 21:269, 25:26, 139, 27:95, 119, 377, 29:60, see also **God—His faithfulness**

Falkenstein, Arnold von—49:290n, 326, 336, 360, 405

Fall, The—1:11, 62, 64, 76f, 79, 81, 95, 98, 111, 117, 128, 133, 141, 148, 150, 158, 169, 181, 196, 216, 221–224, 229–231, 255f, 2:4, 7, 65n, 74, 121, 148, 5:222, 380, 12:119, 308f, 318, 350, 13:76, 22:30, 137, 154, 340, 24:255f, 319, 29:134, 30:74n, 33:78n, 117n, 124, 174f, 272, 37:362, 366, 45:201, 203, 54:224, 426, see also **Adam**

Fault of both man and woman 2:29f

Fallacy of composition and division—4:168, 200

Fallibility of the church—22:258

False accusations—16:249

False apostles—4:131, 14:282, 24:103, 195, 330, 25:4, 113, 124, 142, 485, 487, 498, 26:14f, 19, 22–24, 42f, 45–47, 49, 51–53, 57, 60–63, 65–68, 73, 75–77, 82, 84, 86–90, 92–94, 98, 100, 103, 105, 108, 122, 142, 145, 152, 155f, 186, 194, 197f, 201, 217, 219, 221–223, 242, 253, 302–303, 351, 355, 401f, 407, 410f, 414f, 422, 424–426, 430–432, 459, 27:3, 7–9, 15, 32f, 36, 40–42, 45, 52, 99f, 108, 116, 124, 129–133, 136, 142f, 161, 165–168, 180, 183, 187, 192, 194, 196, 205, 207f, 211, 244f, 247, 280, 295, 304, 306f, 343, 402f, 29:8f, 14, 38–40, 42, 44, 47, 30:169, 284

False articles of faith—36:165, 204f, 212, 216

False bishops—24:318

False brethren—6:359, 16:205

False Christians—14:26, 37, 81, 22:362, 395, 24:76, 103, 160, 201, 203, 209, 213, 225, 230, 235f, 249–251, 264, 30:152, 264, 268, 273, 277, 303

False Christs—36:198

False churches—1:254, 261, 315f, 318, 2:10, 31, 214, 224, 231, 246, 4:30–33, 204, 347–349, 351, 408, 24:127, 280, 310

False clergy—13:25, 30f, 146, 176, 194

False disciples—23:392, 399, 401f

False doctors—23:60

False doctrine—2:59, 65, 159f, 214, 251, 334, 8:181, 251, 256, 270, 289, 9:138, 213, 10:29f, 12:166, 183, 185, 193, 216, 375, 13:177f, 186, 251, 326, 16:119n, 18:35, 37f, 57, 66, 271, 394, 398f, 412, 19:47, 20:55, 233f, 333, 22:197, 404, 406, 410f, 23:154, 180, 252, 288, 350, 24:26, 47, 129, 151, 176, 205, 216f, 219, 236, 239, 279, 293f, 313, 400, 25:29, 192, 228f, 26:18, 57, 80, 140, 152, 156, 199, 218, 285, 364, 444, 28:63f, 76, 136, 223, 30:24, 26, 135, 164, 166, 171, 199, 251, 35:138, 407, 38:178, 190, 204, 243, 40:57, 41:170, 203, 222, 288, 297, 47:41, 48, 156, 161

False gods—17:132, 134, 140, 276, 37:128n, 129, 140, 149, 359, 38:107, 112, 46:124, 135

False holiness—12:353, 13:376

False hope—24:178

False measures—18:66, 265, 328

False miracles—24:75, 181

False pastors—31:374

False piety—2:331

False preachers—23:47, 285, 30:167f

False prophets—1:106, 207, 2:161, 6:126f, 264f, 327, 7:167, 8:212, 218, 230, 276, 289, 300, 9:129, 188, 306, 14:243f, 246, 282, 290, 17:156, 209, 266, 350, 19:112, 165, 20:10f, 145–147, 164f, 233, 239, 300, 333, 21:247f, 250f, 261f, 24:302, 26:22, 425, 27:18, 166, 29:69, 71, 95, 105, 30:169, 187, 287, 35:146, 170, 246, 283, 409, 36:210, 37:20, 28, 66, 101, 113f, 132, 155, 162, 259, 361, 367f, 41:194, 303, 47:154

False religion—2:63, 13:123

False saints—12:355, 24:25, 35, 97, 203, 220, 230f, 256, 258, 370

False spirits—24:69, 362f

False spiritual government—52:204f, 214f, 222

False teachers—2:162, 243, 251, 273, 7:200, 349, 9:187, 199, 235, 15:221, 239, 260f, 16:34, 40, 249, 262, 18:8f, 35–38, 49, 254, 270f, 308, 326, 348, 20:53, 105–107, 118f, 128, 130f, 135f, 146f, 164, 173, 203, 207, 233f, 236f, 239–242, 279, 300f, 312f, 332f, 336, 21:100f, 224, 247–251, 259, 261–263, 270–272, 304f, 312, 318f, 22:52, 57, 60, 335, 346, 389, 411, 483, 491, 23:59f, 150, 189, 273, 281, 286, 363, 24:13, 144, 176, 202, 208, 224, 271, 25:425f, 26:12–14, 17f, 50, 56, 68, 94, 135, 196, 218, 258, 369, 455, 28:64, 75, 100, 220f, 227, 281, 364f, 376, 381, 383f, 29:90, 30:26, 149, 166, 168f, 174, 186, 191, 199, 204, 211, 251, 257, 319, 35:145, 201, 331, 385, 389, 391, 41:307, 349

False teachings—2:86, 15:221, 239, 25:29, 189f, 228–230
False testimony—2:9
False witnesses—36:204f
False worship—8:131, 230–232, 301, 13:127, 177, 18:4, 9f, 39, 56, 69f, 95, 142, 151, 158, 164f, 175, 184, 211, 213, 221, 337, 385, 396, 404, 24:341, 367, 25:35, 41, 158, 160, 255
False zeal—9:190, 25:404, 422f
Falsehood—see **Lies**
Fame—8:10, 17f, 20
Families—1:133, 2:28, 166, 184, 253, 260f, 264f, 270, 294, 301, 356, 381, 390f, 9:205, 241, 16:62, 23:202, 26:11, 173, 217, 236, 359n, 413, 456, 27:56, 281, 45:259, 322n, 323
Famine—1:328, 2:17, 70, 288–291, 4:137, 146, 5:9f, 12f, 16, 41, 53, 143, 170, 200, 7:70, 136, 149, 151, 153, 156, 158f, 161, 189, 206, 208, 213–217, 228, 231, 241, 250f, 253–255, 267f, 285, 306–309, 318, 8:38, 42, 45, 88, 116f, 119, 121, 123f, 126, 130, 136–138, 177, 200, 225, 256, 16:41, 23:12, 203, 406, 24:12, 14, 392, 27:123, 126, 210, 46:235f, 254, 54:344f
Famulus—48:164n, 49:158n, 402n, 50:49n, 214n
Fanatic spirit—37:xif, xx, 6, 25f, 71–73, 137–140, 150, 161–169, 222, 322
Fanatical spirits—9:80, 26:9, 14, 194, 221, 241, 343, 353, 356, 375, 378, 383, 413, 450, 454, 27:4, 8, 33, 44, 52, 72, 103f, 118f, 121
Fanaticism—13:368f, 23:272, 24:229, 47:110
Fanatics—1:21f, 107f, 145, 157, 2:12, 46n, 83, 3:110, 211, 4:103, 125, 5:34, 178, 256, 311, 6:29, 7:119f, 149, 176, 200, 261, 265, 8:133f, 251, 12:64f, 116, 189, 193, 232, 295, 393, 13:44, 51, 16:72, 188, 301, 21:224, 226, 262f, 22:49, 55, 491, 534, 23:14, 19, 46, 55f, 65f, 68, 88, 91f, 101, 119, 122, 124, 133, 147, 157f, 168, 224, 227, 230, 232, 235, 263, 323, 333, 368, 408, 24:143, 26:23, 25f, 28f, 32, 45f, 52, 56, 65, 67, 130, 143f, 150, 155f, 176f, 182, 192, 282, 288, 342, 402, 414, 418, 455f, 27:20, 38, 46, 129, 29:13, 23f, 31f, 35–37, 39, 47f, 50, 58, 89f, 97, 30:222, 227, 239, 252, 258, 261, 266, 274, 287, 289, 302, 308, 311, 313, 315, 318, 320f, 33:90, 35:380, 36:331, 337–339, 342f, 346, 37:xiif, xvi–xviii, 6, 18n, 25f, 34f, 41, 49f, 67–69, 83f, 126, 131f, 141, 153–155, 261, 326, 352, 367, 38:xx, 217, 221, 287–293, 294n, 295f, 302–307, 311–313, 316, 46:70, 179, 255, 51:xx, 158, 172f, 176, 180, 183f, 187f, 198f, 213f, 225, 227, 265, 373f, 377, see also **Anabaptists**; **Enthusiasts**; **Factious spirits**; **Radical reformers**; **Sacramentarians**; **Schism(s)**; **Schwärmer**; **Sectarians**
  Their faith 37:75, 113n, 125f, 141f, 147–149, 153, 168, 261
Farmers—2:39, 200f, 352, 4:380, 382, 5:57, 136, 7:16, 115, 193, 335, 8:38, 64, 67, 122f, 127, 302, 9:140, 167, 23:15, 222, 24:317
Farmhands—24:317
Farming—1:205, 211
Farner, Oscar—*Huldrych Zwingli*, Zurich, 1943 38:10n, 71n, 83n
Farnese, Cardinal Allesandro—46:188n, 50:265n, see also **Paul III, Pope**
Farnese, Pier Luigi—41:282n
Fast days—35:133, 137
Fasting—1:106, 2:113, 123, 134n, 161, 349, 399, 3:168, 316, 4:15, 22, 53, 57, 61, 89, 103, 141, 165, 277, 334, 336, 5:3f, 6, 13, 29, 71, 156f, 271, 6:124, 7:113, 134, 323, 354, 356, 8:69, 173, 186, 267, 326, 9:130, 197, 10:366, 11:358, 12:395, 13:7, 17:23, 27, 49f, 98, 100, 141, 158, 282, 292, 284, 18:85, 96, 100, 21:38, 81, 131, 155–161, 23:15, 23–25, 49, 58, 110f, 138, 182, 264, 287, 409, 24:24, 98, 222, 229, 240, 356, 25:482, 26:25, 29, 41, 68, 70, 72, 84, 90, 211f, 234, 283, 295, 305, 312, 27:31, 69, 84, 88, 92, 96, 138, 174, 350, 28:14f, 28, 321–323, 355, 29:7–10, 30:27f, 41, 170, 205, 232, 246, 311f, 31:86, 32:21, 34:20, 56, 35:39, 69, 133n, 134, 36:70, 76, 78, 84, 89, 202, 219, 347, 37:105, 38:105, 119, 190, 39:39f, 41:52, 124, 130, 137, 176, 198, 204, 336, 42:7, 11, 44, 74, 85, 161, 43:37, 44:74–76, 184, 45:72, 46:167, 174, 177, 189, 199, 235, 48:69n, 358, 402, 49:88n, 351, 378n, 385f, 411, 436, 50:95f, 51:62–66, 74, 86f, 105, 107, 110, 113, 116, 124, 131, 247, 270, 273, 52:138f, 205, 53:34, 54:178, 338f, 357
Fasts—20:74f, 77f, 86, 142, 259–263, 266, 276, 278f, 24:175, 228, 27:55, 68, 89, 296, 384
Fat—8:63, 10:111f, 339
Fate—7:123, 178, 308, 15:41, 55, 102, 143, 33:41, 49:410

Fate vs. promise—25:145
Fatherhood—22:91, 99
Fathers—4:3, 13–15, 17, 20, 22, 24, 26, 28, 31f, 34, 36, 40f, 44–46, 48, 50, 52, 54–57, 62, 64, 67, 71, 78, 88, 94f, 98, 100, 103, 106–117, 120f, 131–133, 137f, 143, 147–151, 156, 164f, 169, 171, 178, 181–184, 186, 189, 192f, 195–197, 218–220, 223–225, 230, 233–237, 239f, 244, 247, 251, 271, 278f, 281f, 291, 293, 302f, 305, 307–312, 317–323, 325–337, 339, 341, 344–346, 348–352, 354f, 357, 360, 364, 366–368, 376f, 379, 383f, 386f, 390f, 393, 395, 6:76f, 16:200, 215, 17:6, 41, 54, 95, 101, 125, 286, 340, 355, 360, 377, 21:8, 109, 112, 274, 312, 349, 26:11, 66f, 84, 95, 97, 108, 121, 127, 141, 152, 154, 174, 187f, 195, 197, 207, 212, 214, 228, 234–237, 239–242, 244–246, 286–288, 292, 297, 304, 307, 320, 326, 337, 346, 349, 353, 356, 358–362, 367–369, 380, 385, 389–391, 396, 398, 402, 406, 412, 415–418, 425, 430f, 434, 437, 449, 458–460, 29:14f, 66, 101, 147f, 150, 239, 36:212, 45:39–41, 173, 386f, 391–393, 46:110, 131, 151f, 222, 269, 306, 308–310, 51:137, 148f, see also **Parents**
Fathers, The—1:49f, 61, 85, 93, 109, 112, 121f, 126, 149f, 184, 232, 298, 307, 310, 312, 321, 346, 352, 357
May err 1:121
Fathers, Hebrew—20:96f
Fathers and sons—15:296
Fathers in Israel—35:199
Fathers of the Church—see **Church fathers**
Fatness—3:197
Fatness, Spiritual—11:304f
Fausel, Heinrich, ed.—54:xxvn
Faustus—2:68
Faustus, Dr. Johannes—54:241
Faustus of Mileve—39:210n
Faventinus, Didymus (Melanchthon's pseudonym)—39:110n
Favor—28:353f
Favoritism—9:211
Fear—3:7f, 10, 13f, 21, 25, 216, 242, 264, 307, 314, 320, 324, 328, 330, 336, 351f, 4:ix, 21, 40, 45, 63, 65, 79, 115f, 129, 133–135, 147, 179, 191, 242, 244, 323, 329, 341, 6:43, 55–57, 61, 70–72, 78, 83, 85f, 100, 235f, 8:9, 14, 27, 43, 46, 77f, 92, 102, 107, 119, 152, 202, 204, 230, 234, 250, 279, 282, 324, 9:58n, 73f, 84, 117, 155, 163, 213, 224, 232f, 236f, 244, 268, 271, 10:13f, 20, 38, 346, 11:69f, 99, 216–219, 221–226, 253–255, 384, 389, 444, 527f, 530, 13:78, 116, 385f, 396, 16:191, 228, 245, 17:26, 37, 41, 89, 111, 214, 240, 275f, 371, 20:34, 36, 63, 168f, 179, 24:9–11, 13f, 16, 27, 29, 42, 46, 61, 110, 112, 114, 116f, 137, 148f, 157, 166, 184f, 210, 262, 273, 285, 293, 419f, 25:357f, 382, 497, 28:104–106, 119, 311, 29:132, 141, 167, 177f, 208, 31:46f, 97, 123–130, 132, 32:31f, 44, 35:57, 217, 239, 255, 37:24, 127, 131, 54:149
Fear and love—25:140, 143
Fear and trembling—30:303
Fear of God—2:5, 11, 55, 72, 96, 148, 167, 171, 196, 210, 230, 239f, 250, 299, 322, 3:48, 128, 218, 221f, 224f, 227, 230, 233, 237, 241, 248, 252, 255, 303, 321, 327, 331, 340, 345, 4:98n, 100, 108, 130f, 226, 251, 259, 277, 279, 336, 390, 6:77, 85, 159, 7:33, 77, 79f, 88, 125, 145f, 151, 178–183, 187, 197, 241, 253, 261, 263, 357, 359f, 9:67, 76, 164, 171, 273, 12:77f, 15:55, 81f, 124, 145, 178, 186, 195, 16:56, 120, 137, 216, 18:353–354, 19:13, 44, 64, 69, 26:96, 181, 210, 321, 336, 342, 29:22, 55, 177f, 35:258, 266, 295, 345f, 36:143, 41:146f, 253, 255f, 283, 287, 44:44, 45:72, 305, 47:105, 111f, 268, 295, 51:138–141, 144, 146, 155
Fear of Isaac—see **God**—Called "Fear of Issac"
Fear of the Lord—11:9, 70, 164, 216, 442f, 446, 17:136
Fears—7:44, 47, 60, 87, 112, 141, 144, 186, 191, 204, 220–222, 244, 256, 266f, 270f, 276f, 284, 287, 290, 305, 317, 328–330, 332, 334f, 356, 359, 363, 371
Feast and fast days—25:490
Feast days—18:48, 67, 362, 41:62–64, 67, 130, 137, 174, 204
Feast of fat things—16:196
Feasting, Excesses in—25:481
Feasts—2:87, 92, 20:86, 278f, 344f, 347, 26:90, 217
Feasts, Jewish religious—9:14, 154–157
Febris—31:201
February—20:2, 166n
Feelings—6:133, 253, 271, 379, 11:512, 17:129, 183, 238f, 346, 372, 388, 28:69–72, 99, 106, 118, 177, 208–210

Feet—10:188, 276, 284, 340, 436, 11:360–362, 483, 20:110, 25:29, 231f, 417
Feilchenfeld, Ludwig—47:61n
Feilitzsch, Fabian von—13:157, 163, 46:239n, 48:98
Feilitzsch, Philip von—48:84n, 85, 88n
Feldteufel—6:296
Felix V, Pope—32:81n, 41:266n, 44:91n
Felix, St.—11:524
Felix culpa—2:154n
Fellowship—21:21, 226, 35:xvi, 50, 51f, 53f, 56f, 59–62, 65, 67, 69, 71, 36:317, 322, 37:344, 350, 356, 358f, 38:12, 78f, 109, 194, 226n, 304, 54:268, 276, 307
Fellowship, Right hand of—27:208
Fellowship with God—13:384
Felony—30:183n
Female sex—see **Women**
Females—1:69, 84, 104, 117, 123, 125–127, 136, 151, 202, 238, 255–257, 312, 338, 7:9, 9:157, 249
Fend, Melchior—54:154
Ferdinand I, Archduke of Austria, King of Bohemia, and later Emperor—4:371, 6:228, 229n, 16:196, 258n, 349n, 17:188n, 28:243, 257, 34:98, 41:274n, 43:215, 253f, 45:xv, 197, 46:203n, 47:32, 48:217, 49:71, 93, 185, 189n, 212n, 223, 240n, 242n, 248n, 251n, 265n, 332, 349n, 360n, 423, 50:41f, 45, 54n, 55n, 59, 83n, 112n, 160n, 190n, 211n, 216n, 219, 224n, 250n, 253, 267, 269n, 272, 53:304, 54:28, 46, 139, 143, 152, 159, 269, 380f, 405, 416f, 472
Ferdinand, King of Bohemia—see **Ferdinand I, Archduke of Austria, King of Bohemia, and later Emperor**
Ferdinand and Isabella, King and Queen of Aragon and Castile—47:128, 223, 268n
Ferrara—50:254
Fertility—1:53f, 133, 5:325, 6:67, 7:33, 149f, 152f, 158, 160, 202, 205f, 208, 214, 224, 251, 346, 8:38, 136, 248, 290f, 296, 302f, 11:12, 18:52
Festival of St. Peter's Throne—41:323n
Festival of Sts. Peter and Paul—41:65n, 322n
Festivals—1:48, 26:363, 411, 448, 27:296, 383, 38:214, 317n, see also **Feast days**
Festivals, Church—45:166
Festivals abolished—44:182
Festivals and seasons—see **Church Year**
Festus Porcius—27:256, 29:6
Fetuses—1:126, 200, 3:64, 205f, 360, 4:353, 361, 369, 5:75, 289, 381f, 7:14, 41, 43, 48, 325, 8:303, 316f, 17:139, see also **Embryos**
Feudal ceremonies—5:109
Feudalism—16:185n, 45:235f, 46:5, 50n, 113n, 127n, 128, 130
Fever—9:268, 295
Ficker, Johannes—25:x, xiif, 204, 29:xi
Fiction—37:72, 75–77, 82f, 88, 103–111, 117, 119, 125–132, 135f, 139f, 178–180, 189, 223, 291f, 340, 350
Fidelity—see **Faithfulness**
Fiefs—5:109, 125f, 136, 46:127f, 130
Fields—23:225, 255f, 395
Fiery furnace—4:137
Fife, Robert H.—*The Revolt of Martin Luther*, New York, 1957 31:74, 312, 37:71n, 51:5, 14, 53, 61
Fig trees—10:83, 375, 19:103, 147, 236, 21:259f, 264, 267
Fighting—2:127
Fighting wild beasts—28:156f
Figs—27:79, 373
Figurative language—12:147, 160, 224, 14:319, 16:13, 17, 43, 103, 115, 140, 295, 17:322, 335, 349, 18:136, 20:99–102, 105, 108, 116, 310, 23:116, 32:xvii, 167, 195–201
Figures (types)—4:133, 137, 176f, 230, 406, 29:112, 181, 212, 39:68n, 77n, 153n, 177, 180
Figures of speech—1:268, 2:43, 104, 156n, 396, 6:56, 182, 229, 7:7, 189, 217, 232, 268, 285f, 302, 8:116n, 196, 13:298, 15:9, 12f, 105, 107, 113, 139, 170, 193, 196, 212, 214, 249, 16:3, 12, 29, 36, 47, 57, 86, 138, 156, 207, 287, 24:234, 378, 402f, 25:116, 26:101f, 366, 27:31, 200, 229, 280, 312, 333, 336, 342, 395, 28:297, 29:35, 39, 42f, 116, 147f, 152, 155, 157, 183, 235, 255, 30:56, 114, 243f, 315, 32:xvii, 167f, 179, 195–201, 33:69, 187n, 36:65, 92, 95, 182, 279, 352f, 37:xii, 31–45, 52n, 104, 108f, 113, 141, 156, 164f, 167, 170–176, 197, 209, 231f, 234f, 252–269, 273–275, 294n, 313, 323–327, 335–337, 343, 345, 349–360, 38:16f, 22, 24, 28, 33, 37, 40, 43, 45, 80, see also **Allegory**; **Alloeosis**; **Antiphrasis**; **Antithesis**; **Hyperbole**; **Hysteron proteron**; **Irony**; **Metaphor**; **Metonymy**; **Simile**; **Synecdoche**; **Tapinosis**; **etc.**
Filth—5:6, 277, 282, 312, 329, 30:190, 268
Filthy lucre—16:278
Finances—14:305

Financial practices (Fynantze)—45:245n 267, 269

Finland, Gulf of—45:133

Fins—9:137

Fir tree—2:93, 11:337

Fire—1:8, 208, 231, 236, 252, 271, 309, 318, 351, 359, 2:46, 66, 98, 127f, 147n, 149, 192, 195, 223, 239, 242–244, 248f, 350, 358, 382, 3:190, 221–223, 225, 229, 243, 264, 270f, 273f, 278, 285, 293, 295, 300, 302, 304, 306f, 309, 315, 341, 348, 354, 4:66, 83, 102, 111f, 129, 136f, 214, 237, 313, 315, 6:64f, 7:42, 62, 79, 85, 191, 231, 237, 284, 292, 294f, 300, 333, 335, 342, 371, 8:27, 52, 90, 217, 245, 250, 255, 265f, 269, 276, 9:158, 175, 180f, 190, 194, 196, 204, 293, 295, 304, 10:102, 118, 184f, 432, 11:77f, 84, 135, 173, 413, 17:153f, 246, 411, 415f, 18:86, 91f, 133, 264f, 20:26f, 37, 76, 117, 181, 187f, 210, 259f, 311, 21:268, 23:124, 173, 253, 265, 291, 313, 315, 357, 359f, 412, 24:43, 49, 82, 109, 144, 146, 183, 197, 200–202, 213, 216, 230, 233–235, 237f, 240, 248, 266f, 271, 277, 290f, 301, 305, 361, 371, 411, 26:362, 374f, 452, 27:27, 62, 69, 276, 284, 303, 364, 388, 410, 30:17, 62, 101, 126f, 130, 153, 195, 208, 214, 46:50, 78, 182, 198

Fire, Eternal—see **Eternal fire**

Fire, Tongues of—16:168

Fire from heaven—1:249, 252, 330

Firearms—54:232, 419

Firmament—1:5, 20, 22, 25f, 29–31, 33, 42

Firs—2:66, 93

First fruits—2:22, 18:50, 84, 268, 25:73, 75, 100, 245, 341, 427, 26:196n

First fruits of the Spirit—12:33, 320, 329f, 359, 375, 382, 410, 17:388, 26:213, 230, 260, 290, 350f, 394, 461

First-born—2:3f, 190, 237–239, 276, 6:285, 312, 315, 7:4, 42, 57, 211, 220, 222, 265, 289, 294, 9:138f, 141, 150f, 158, 174, 211, 11:19, 78–80, 85

Fischer, Andreas—7:152n, 47:59

Fischer, Robert Harley—38:5n, 47:xi
- author of introduction to Vol. 37 and of introductions to each writing in that volume
- editor of Vol. 37
- translator of the writings included in Vol. 37

Fish—1:39, 48f, 51, 53–55, 66f, 71, 74–76, 85, 98f, 105, 209f, 217, 2:70, 133, 236, 330, 339, 357, 3:347, 364, 4:39, 354, 360, 5:150, 286, 7:194, 321, 8:168, 174, 225, 10:89f, 19:117, 183f, 24:46, 82, 175, 228, 26:223, 249, 308, 28:183, 384, 29:8, 45, 46:12f, 39, 204, 54:199f, 267

Fish Gate—18:329

Fish-hook, Christ as—see **Christ—as** Fish-hook

Fisher, John—17:247n, 35:128, 50:254n
- *Sacri sacerdotii contra Lutherum*, 1525 24:353n

Fishermen—5:150, 8:93, 250, 23:378, 24:337

Fists—23:382f, 386, 416, 418f

Five, Number—16:165

Flacius, Matthias—43:169, 49:325

Flagellants, flagellation—7:356, 23:347n, 51:113

Flames—2:147, 29:116f

Flanders—2:137, 34:345, 353, 41:350

Flatterer, Mr.—13:212

Flatterers—8:212, 16:347

Flattery—3:230, 7:81, 25:229–231, 26:424f, 29:94f, 98f, 104, 143, 184, 48:374f, 384

Flavian, Bishop of Antioch—41:88

Flax—3:223f

Fleas—1:77, 209, 8:172

Fleeing from God—19:45

Fleming Mts.—16:264

Flemings—54:310

Flesh—1:380, 2:23, 138, 309, 3:6, 8f, 13, 15, 19, 22, 32, 34, 40, 42, 48, 51, 63f, 77, 82, 88, 93–97, 101f, 105, 107, 112, 124, 132, 135–137, 141f, 152, 155, 158, 177f, 192, 199, 202, 205, 211, 225, 230, 252f, 261, 265, 268, 272, 276, 279, 327, 329, 332–336, 343, 355, 4:11f, 15f, 21f, 25–29, 38f, 42f, 45, 49f, 52f, 57, 59f, 62, 65f, 68, 70, 81, 93–95, 97, 102, 107, 110, 118, 123, 125, 132, 158–160, 162, 173f, 182f, 190, 205, 212, 221f, 229, 232f, 235, 239–244, 249, 252, 268f, 274, 285, 294, 299, 303, 311, 314, 317, 320f, 325–327, 332–335, 337f, 341, 343f, 346, 348–350, 358, 366–368, 370–372, 376, 379–382, 399, 408f, 5:3f, 14, 17, 21–23, 27, 33, 37, 39, 45, 47–49, 54, 59, 61–63, 71f, 93, 113, 119, 129–133, 141, 143, 145, 163f, 168, 183–189, 191f, 195, 203–205, 207f, 213, 215, 217, 220f, 223f, 227, 229f, 232–235, 247–249, 255f, 266–268, 271, 275, 284, 286, 289, 291f, 320–322, 326–328, 330f, 334f, 339, 341, 353, 360,

380, 6:8, 10, 72, 74, 100, 104, 107, 109, 116, 130, 147, 157, 172, 272, 357, 7:12–14, 16, 18, 24, 31, 36f, 57, 65, 67, 77, 80, 95, 98, 118, 126, 128f, 131, 134f, 137f, 146, 155, 177, 183, 207, 211, 221f, 229, 237, 250, 255, 264, 278, 285, 303f, 307, 312f, 316, 319, 336, 369, 376, 8:6–9, 15, 29–32, 43, 47, 50, 59, 69, 73, 75, 77, 80, 92, 139f, 145, 164, 168, 179, 184f, 202f, 215–219, 225f, 228, 232, 255, 257, 259, 266, 268, 278, 309, 314, 325, 10:32, 39, 382, 11:4, 8, 12f, 18, 83, 249, 253, 255, 260, 267, 285, 289f, 297, 301–303, 307, 318f, 324f, 359, 364, 402, 424, 435, 442f, 447, 464f, 485, 494n, 495f, 505, 510, 535, 551, 12:28, 33, 35, 65, 106, 117, 150, 188f, 207, 226, 233, 250, 267, 273f, 278, 298, 320, 327–329, 331, 337, 353, 364, 366, 375, 378, 380, 394, 410, 13:13, 115, 179, 383, 16:14, 30, 53, 57, 65, 91f, 111, 124, 130, 157, 168f, 179, 183, 189, 213, 216, 224f, 233–235, 249, 256, 258f, 270, 280, 328, 349, 17:8, 11f, 29, 38, 43, 47, 50, 66f, 70, 127, 129, 142, 160, 163f, 172, 182, 274, 287, 356, 19:28, 117, 119, 124, 20:7f, 10, 12, 101, 135, 140f, 143–145, 213, 21:230, 247, 287, 22:96f, 102f, 110f, 178, 254, 256, 259, 262f, 270–272, 274, 288, 455, 507, 522, 24:45, 55, 85, 92f, 107f, 118, 125, 129, 132f, 137, 140, 146, 152, 161–163, 168, 171, 184f, 196, 226, 232f, 244, 247, 263, 267, 269, 289, 341, 344–346, 382, 384f, 389, 396, 400, 405, 407, 415, 419, 25:3, 7, 38, 63, 68, 135f, 138, 147, 166, 245, 279, 328, 342, 348–354, 371f, 375–378, 407f, 428, 456, 484, 26:3, 9, 11, 22, 26f, 36, 42, 44, 51, 54f, 60, 64f, 74, 90, 120, 123, 125, 133, 139f, 158–160, 164f, 168, 170–172, 188–190, 193, 211, 215–219, 229–233, 236f, 243, 276, 278, 285f, 289f, 301f, 306, 308, 311, 341, 361, 366, 368–370, 372, 376, 378, 381f, 391, 393f, 397, 417–421, 429, 431, 434f, 437, 439, 449, 452–454, 456, 459, 27:3f, 7, 16, 21, 24f, 35, 48–51, 54–59, 64–71, 73–82, 84–93, 95–99, 102f, 109, 111, 113, 127, 130, 132f, 134, 137f, 140–143, 158, 170, 173f, 180, 187, 190–192, 196, 225, 227, 229, 231–239, 249f, 253, 260, 282, 288, 290, 301f, 310f, 314, 318, 320–322, 324, 328f, 331, 333f, 340f, 346–350, 360–368, 370–375, 378–380, 384, 390, 393, 399f, 402, 405f, 28:14, 26f, 135f, 183f, 192, 305f, 29:44, 54, 56, 59, 61, 65, 68, 83f, 90, 103, 114, 130, 134, 137, 154, 166, 175, 182, 193, 203, 225, 30:111, 118, 120f, 156, 160, 192, 199, 215, 267, 300f, 32:19–29, 249–256, 33:87f, 212–215, 222–228, 274f, 277, 288, 35:xi, 31, 55, 104, 236, 366, 371f, 391, 36:68, 80f, 204, 355, 37:xviif, 6f, 46, 48, 51, 55, 63, 72, 78–88, 92, 94–102, 115, 124f, 138n, 145, 200–202, 219, 233, 236f, 245–251, 282, 286–288, 355, 38:26, 35, 38, 41, 54f, 57, 59, 64f, 72n, 74–76, 107, 128f, 206–208, 241, 260, 40:203, 205, 41:312, 364, 42:14, 78, 80, 129, 147, 160, 45:202–205, 46:12, 77, 150, 153f, 178, 182, 228, 265, 305, 52:35, 54, 58, 77, 80, 194, 263, see also **Resurrection of the flesh**

Cleansed by grace 25:69

Flesh, Definition of—26:139, 216

Flesh, Desires of the—27:67, 82, 85, 87, 361

Flesh, Prudence of the—25:358

Flesh, Spiritual—37:97, 99f, 155, 245, 296n

Flesh, Wisdom of the—25:xi, 3, 9, 29, 40, 68–70, 77, 106, 135f, 211, 224, 293, 317, 345f, 348f, 351, 375, 396, 399, 407f, 428, 433, 513

Flesh and blood—11:6f, 14:89, 112, 182, 304, 327, 335, 23:8, 11, 21, 45, 399, 28:168, 189, 193f, 197f, 46:10, 41, 52, 165, 168

Flesh and blood of Christ—37:6f, 60, 65n, 68n, 75n, 70–89, 95, 97–101, 120f, 124f, 129–131, 133, 150, 155f, 236–238, 245–252, 286–288, 296n

Flesh vs. Christ's flesh—37:79–81, 95, 156, 202, 236, 249f, 288

Flesh vs. spirit—1:269f, 9:ix, 10:56, 123, 209, 296, 303, 381, 410, 425, 430, 460, 11:4, 6–8, 12, 260, 267, 285, 297f, 304f, 311, 315, 319–322, 335, 359–361, 402, 407, 443, 451, 460, 481, 495–498, 507–509, 513f, 516, 518, 520f, 523, 531, 533, 535–537, 542, 547, 550, 12:178, 235f, 343f, 357, 381, 19:28, 20:191, 21:xf, 246, 303, 25:64, 308f, 330, 332f, 339, 342, 26:217, 27:65f, 69f, 73, 75, 78f, 232, 362f, 367f, 30:232f, 272, 32:246, 250, 33:87f, 212–215, 222–227, 274f, 278, 288, 34:113, 35:366, 377, 399, 37:xvii, 7, 92, 94–99, 191, 236f, 247–251, 284, 287f, 322, 354, 38:21, 54f, 44:73f, 114, 45:153f

Fleshpots—23:30, 152

Flesner, Dorris A.—translator of *That a Christian should Bear his Cross with Patience* 43:179–186

Flies—1:52, 209, 11:18, 74f, 83

Flight—10:100, 254, 319, 25:400–403

Flippancy—3:179

Flocks—5:269f, 280–282, 284, 287, 351, 373f, 379, 384, 6:4–7, 12–14, 23, 66–68, 106, 118, 120, 175f, 289, 7:5, 7, 24, 30, 38, 66, 191, 196, 205, 20:102, 106, 118, 120, 149f, 159, 163, 296, 301f, 312

Flood, The—1:35f, 77f, 88–90, 98f, 101, 183, 194, 205–208, 231, 241, 248, 255, 291, 299, 304, 309f, 318f, 321, 323, 332–336, 341f, 354, 356–359, 2:ix, 3, 5, 10–12, 14, 23, 25, 27f, 30, 32, 36, 38–40, 43, 48, 52–55, 57f, 64–66, 70, 74–76, 81f, 86, 89, 92f, 95, 98–101, 104, 106, 110–112, 115, 119, 128f, 131n, 133, 140f, 148–151, 153–156, 162f, 165–167, 170, 175, 178, 182, 186f, 196f, 199, 204, 208, 210–213, 216f, 219, 223f, 228, 230, 232, 236, 343, 364, 368, 3:19, 140, 229, 233f, 236, 239, 241, 268, 293, 319, 4:3, 100, 193, 303, 317f, 335f, 359, 5:91, 100, 6:189, 243, 353, 7:71, 125, 8:236, 243, 11:325, 13:121f, 213, 13:97, 213, 14:126f, 17:240, 19:77, 21:282, 22:31–33, 36, 70, 23:265, 26:43, 248, 27:91, 146, 29:81n, 236f, 30:176, 183, 193, 195, 35:31f, 41:29n, 45:44, 86, 261, 46:24, 171, 47:147

Flood prayer—53:95, 97, 107, 143f

Floods—3:x, 295, 11:235

Florence—34:48n, 48:82, 49:280n, 286f, 50:82n, 54:296

Florence, Council of—45:8n, 46:262n

Florentina of Upper Weimar—43:83–96

Flour—4:404

Flowers—21:199f, 26:296, 422, 37:172, 255–258, 268

Flute—26:191

Fluttering spirits—22:330, 390, 23:326, 349, 408, 24:65, 362

Flying—10:100, 11:322

Foals—8:248f, 252f, 255, 308

Foliage—24:198f, 201

Folkemer, Carl W.—translator of *Explanations of the Ninety-five Theses* 31:77–252

Folklore—2:129n, 211n

Folksong—53:195–199, 208, 212, 218, 225, 255, 263, 275, 283, 289

Folly—6:62f, 105, 159, 196f, 206f, 209, 211, 228, 245, 275, 344, 380f, 8:9, 11, 29, 270, 294, 317, 13:60, 121, 163, 15:38f, 99, 23:144, 146, 24:57, 99, 109, 138, 280, 30:27, 187, 190, 31:54, 75, 35:259, 262, 37:18n, 72f, 81f, 103, 125, 137f, 146, 150, 263

Fomes—see **Tinder (Fomes)**

Font, Baptismal—53:100f, 108f

Food—1:210, 2:76f, 109, 132–134, 142, 231, 253, 270, 339, 350, 385, 399, 3:48, 50, 52, 146, 181, 200, 217, 222, 228, 247f, 274, 298, 316, 318, 4:14f, 36, 57, 75, 89, 98, 202, 204, 214, 242, 271, 276, 282, 323, 393, 405f, 5:7–10, 39, 54, 57, 105f, 116, 135, 138, 149n, 159, 167, 195, 219, 232, 234, 236, 249, 253f, 333, 364, 379, 386, 7:60, 66–69, 102, 113, 118, 128, 136, 158, 161, 206f, 213, 216–220, 241, 243f, 250, 267, 285, 308f, 326, 329, 338, 345, 350, 8:32, 59, 65f, 68, 94, 107, 118, 120, 122, 125, 177, 183, 200, 283f, 290, 294, 309, 13:359, 376, 16:342, 17:251f, 286, 322, 18:336, 21:196–198, 207, 349, 23:9f, 12, 14–16, 19, 22, 24, 26, 30, 32f, 36f, 40–42, 44, 51–53, 113–116, 119, 125, 128, 131–133, 135, 143f, 153, 159, 163f, 166, 170–172, 213, 403f, 410, 25:113–117, 485–487, 490, 498, 500, 502, 504, 26:90, 110–112, 117f, 128, 135, 138, 170f, 363f, 393, 411, 440, 27:15, 31, 44, 54f, 81–83, 92, 126, 138, 213, 217, 257, 275, 335, 378, 383f, 28:313, 315–317, 355f, 37:44–46, 79f, 84, 96, 98, 100, 105f, 118–121, 124, 133–135, 143, 145, 148, 150, 333, 349

Food, Everlasting—23:8f, 11–14, 17–19, 22, 27, 31, 47, 117, 132, 185, 37:71, 79, 87, 93f, 99f, 115, 132, 145

Food, Rules for use of—25:113f

Food, Spiritual—23:11, 13, 15, 19, 27, 30f, 43, 45, 47, 49, 132, 158, 170, 172, 37:40, 83n, 99–101, 114, 289, 352f

Food, Unclean—9:134

Food and drink—41:130, 137, 147, 173, 202, 338

Foods—30:28, 35, 43, 49f, 67, 80, 92, 106, 112, 155, 177, 251, 278, 302, 311, 34:66

Foods, Forbidden—35:131f, 136f, 381

Foolishness—4:14, 285, 290, 293, 314, 374, 380, 5:25, 120, 125, 127, 130, 132, 152, 208, 10:180, 325ff, 363, 16:136, 191, 228, 318, 324, 331, 25:10, 150f, 154, 214, 223, 383, 467, 29:55, 142, 144, 240

Fools—3:67, 229, 6:62f, 206, 15:38f, 65f, 75f, 78, 112, 155, 157, 159, 16:138, 232, 276, 304, 17:118f, 21:78, 29:34, 153, 237, 35:236, 259f, 271, 382, 46:65, 122n, 167, 50:163f, 311, 52:150, 197

Fools with Christ—24:99

Foot washing—3:189, 245, 7:336–338, 13:54, 28:340f, 32:158

Footstool—11:359–362, 364

Forbearance—25:32, 175, 248f

Forbidden things—25:4f, 9, 11, 18, 28, 41, 84f, 93, 98f, 121, 123, 135, 138, 143f, 155, 180–182, 185–187, 219, 419, 426f, 481, 503f, 516, see also **Foods, Forbidden**

Force—10:14f, 20, 88f, 12:216, 13:58, 21:335, 340, 45:114–118, 124f, 273, 276f, 46:7, 40, 61, 76, 103f, 305, 307, 316
- Folly of 14:75
- Ineffective 27:375
- Use of 51:76f, 81, 191
- Useless in matters of faith 44:199

Forde, Gerhard O.—*The Law-Gospel Debate*, Minneapolis, 1969 47:106n

Foreign aid—16:269f

Foreknowledge of God—see **God**

Forell, George W.—54:134n
- author of Introduction and of introductory comments on writings included in Vol. 32
- editor of Vol. 32

Foresight—46:303f

Forest fires—50:220n, 222

Forests—46:13, 39

Forever, Meaning of—18:105, 21:354f

Forgetfulness—11:13, 15, 51–53, 72, 388f, 506f, 516, 530

Forgiveness of sins—1:100, 148, 161, 177–180, 190, 221, 228f, 249, 258, 263, 265, 275, 277, 289, 297f, 331, 2:19, 41, 63, 120, 162f, 177, 184, 248f, 261, 273, 275, 320, 327, 353, 382, 387, 390f, 398, 3:7, 12, 39, 109, 118, 124, 158, 214, 222, 224, 228, 237, 265, 333, 338, 4:17, 52, 56, 82, 154, 165, 169, 202–204, 232, 241, 277, 323, 348, 397f, 405, 5:22, 141, 153, 155, 196, 213, 230, 233, 257–259, 278, 290, 6:129, 276, 298, 361, 377, 7:11, 64, 154, 227, 234, 256, 272, 278, 304, 8:10, 24, 38, 41, 43, 45f, 51, 53, 70, 136, 163, 183, 186, 194, 205, 209, 214f, 235f, 244, 252, 255, 257–259, 262, 286, 308, 310–313, 326, 330, 9:150, 198, 277, 10:145–147, 191f, 11:155f, 12:18–20, 24, 85, 89, 119, 155f, 198, 211, 241f, 261, 273f, 278, 307, 312, 322f, 324f, 327f, 331f, 334, 336, 340, 343, 345, 352, 358f, 362, 371, 376f, 379, 389, 391f, 399, 402, 13:140, 290, 383f, 407, 14:86f, 91, 99, 130, 166, 168, 191, 16:12, 20, 35, 73, 101, 129, 131, 150, 152f, 215, 226, 17:5, 7f, 27, 29, 100, 112f, 115, 163, 210f, 220f, 241, 255, 299, 308, 310, 369, 408, 19:65, 20:41, 50, 95f, 112, 137, 221, 270, 289, 332, 21:30, 46f, 75, 82, 98, 113f, 149f, 152, 155, 205, 213f, 221, 290f, 293, 22:55, 63, 65, 123, 134, 136, 139, 146, 148, 163, 169, 172, 175–179, 197, 220, 258, 261, 265, 269, 279, 287, 290, 301, 324, 368f, 383, 389, 397–399, 403f, 407, 424, 440, 458, 478, 486, 489, 501, 505, 527, 23:17, 19, 28, 48, 71f, 75, 92, 127, 136f, 147, 154f, 159, 177, 179, 202, 234f, 242, 250f, 261, 263f, 268f, 278, 310f, 317f, 325, 332, 337f, 340f, 354, 386, 24:47, 92, 95, 115, 125, 128, 147, 179, 185, 201, 210–212, 215, 217, 220, 222, 285, 287, 307, 319, 327, 330, 344, 346, 402, 25:261f, 267, 26:4, 6, 11, 26–28, 30f, 35, 42, 48, 58, 66, 82, 84, 88, 109, 116, 120, 124f, 127, 130, 132f, 135, 140f, 147f, 150–154, 159, 169, 179, 198, 200f, 209, 213f, 216, 224, 232, 234–236, 241, 260, 262, 270, 273f, 294, 304, 310, 313, 315, 317, 331f, 336, 338, 341, 347, 353, 356, 377, 392, 408, 431, 437, 439, 447f, 454, 458, 27:5f, 9f, 14, 19, 41, 61, 64, 68, 70f, 74, 76f, 79, 82, 85f, 96, 106, 109, 111f, 115, 120f, 132, 141f, 164, 184f, 222, 269, 318, 386, 28:230, 267f, 304f, 29:6, 95, 102, 123f, 168f, 175, 180, 193, 209f, 214, 220, 223, 227, 30:142, 174, 31:64, 98–107, 113, 152, 178, 191, 364, 32:27f, 44–48, 50–53, 76, 208f, 34:53, 174, 176, 306, 35:xiii, 9f, 12, 17, 19, 21f, 35, 37f, 85, 88, 109, 201, 237, 290, 36:22, 40, 43, 45, 56f, 61f, 82–85, 95n, 118, 122–124, 149, 169, 176f, 180, 183, 189f, 226, 277, 299, 320, 327, 348, 350–352, 37:44f, 85, 102, 111, 132, 135f, 153, 155, 183, 191f, 262f, 266, 292, 325–327, 335, 337f, 366, 368–370, 38:xivf, 22, 38, 46, 82, 110, 125, 129, 153, 171, 177, 183f, 194, 200, 204f, 207, 211, 229, 309, 39:28, 30, 42, 40:213–216, 274, 280, 297, 366, 41:54, 113f, 143f, 147, 153, 166, 168, 171–173, 177, 199f, 202, 209, 216, 273, 316, 310f, 338, 340,

342f, 42:63–67, 70, 74, 80, 99, 173f, 44:xiii, 45:220–223, 227, 283, 46:69, 161, 177, 312, 47:52, 241, 304, 50:59, 51:20, 22, 59, 126, 130f, 166f, 178f, 190f, 274, 277, 317f, 54:16, 34, 43, 51, 69f

Forks—24:198–200

Form—20:57, 240f, 249, 37:43, 66, 104–114, 127n, 194, 196f, 256n, 258f, 275f, 295, 298f, 333

Forming God—17:17f, 108f

Formula of Concord—1:166n, 37:158, 184n, 210n, 211n, 213n, 214n, 219n, 224n, 249n, 298n, 361n, 363n, 367n, 47:106n

  Solid Declaration 5:50n

Fornication—1:116, 118, 147f, 166, 201, 238, 2:84, 214, 3:47, 254, 259, 4:233f, 239, 244, 249, 251, 277, 304f, 333, 336, 5:34, 37, 41, 52, 86, 91, 190, 193, 343, 7:10, 30f, 40–43, 46, 76, 84, 234, 8:251, 9:223, 229, 232, 308, 21:94, 22:96, 196, 198, 371, 389, 399, 407f, 410, 23:62, 69, 171, 213, 399, 26:41, 139, 27:88, 112, 368, 384, 28:3, 5f, 9f, 12f, 24, 30:250, 272, 296, 36:206f, 224f, 227, 41:72–74, 78, 45:18f, 33, 36f, 43–45, 47, 144n, 148f, 150n, 153, 178, 320, 385, 51:154, 176, 179, 191f, 364, 374, 52:261, 273

Fornicators—27:339, 345

Förstemann, Karl Eduard, ed.—54:xiiin

  Urkundenbuch zu der Geschichte des Reichstags zu Augsburg im Jahre 1530, Halle, 1833–1835 34:8

Forstemius—see **Ziegler, Bernhard**

Forster, John—5:x, 46:142n, 50:173n, 54:xiii, 300, 304, 446

Fortifications—6:244f, 274

Fortitude—27:23–25

Fortuna—2:255n

Fortune—3:52, 226, 229, 248, 46:124f

Fortunes—21:174f, 208f

Forum of Appius and Three Taverns—26:421

Foundations—11:176, 324, 19:145, 21:282

Foundations, Religious—21:132f, 30:15, 80, 170, 174, 183, 37:363f, 371, 38:116, 118, 121, 166, 170, 181, 190, 232, 45:161, 169–175, 180, 348f, 354, 371, 373, 46:82, 220, 225f, 228, 231–235, 241, 256

Foundlings—see **Orphans**

Fountains—10:21, 344f, 11:326f, 336, 20:143f, 331

Four, Number—20:16, 21, 24, 65, 179, 247

Four Books of Sentences—see **Peter Lombard**

Fourteen Helpers in Need (saints)—34:24, 42:119n

Fourth Gospel—see **John, St., Gospel according to**

Fowler—18:146

Fox, Edward—50:104n, 114n, 115n, 117, 120, 133n, 137n, 138f, 143n, 177f, 180n, 198n

Foxes—1:77, 145, 2:74, 4:61n, 74, 15:221

Fraction in Holy Communion—40:178, 181

Fraidl, Franz Sales—47:252n

France—1:31, 254, 2:191, 3:41n, 4:371, 6:149, 7:346, 8:120, 178, 208n, 10:412, 12:16, 13:336, 14:233, 17:414, 18:203, 19:43, 22:386, 23:379n, 26:185, 28:257, 275, 30:64, 36:18, 208, 37:154, 248, 38:35, 289n, 41:xii, 127, 260, 267, 275, 294, 297, 333, 372, 374, 46:113, 130, 168, 202, 204n, 48:210, 270n, 291n, 315n, 49:17n, 125, 156, 161n, 185, 189, 221–223, 266n, 50:55, 98n, 106n, 162n, 165n, 171, 193n, 54:306, 382, 402, 421

Francis I, King of France—6:244, 13:149, 190n, 15:39n, 151, 28:257, 31:262n, 34:272, 36:229n, 38:289n, 41:6, 230n, 259f, 295n, 371n, 46:90n, 120n, 168, 199n, 48:91n, 176, 49:156, 50:183, 199, 267, 269, 272, 312, 53:304, 54:143, 299

Francis, Duke of Lüneburg—13:xi, 49:349n, 350

Francis of Assisi, St.—2:113, 249, 251, 268f, 327, 330f, 3:109, 196, 6:226, 230, 407, 8:60, 267, 9:54, 12:284, 14:99, 16:245, 304, 17:70, 101, 259, 286n, 20:330, 341, 22:50–52, 59, 65, 70, 87, 137, 163f, 254, 256, 260f, 264, 267f, 270f, 273, 320, 330, 359, 368f, 387, 446, 461, 23:25, 34, 38, 144n, 24:22, 169, 224f, 26:52n, 140, 459, 27:18, 83, 141, 28:274, 30:42, 275n, 322, 34:26, 35:135n, 36:77n, 190, 39:62, 193, 268, 41:128n, 214n, 44:172n, 255n, 256, 268, 51:217, 52:173, 192, 249, 271, 54:270

  Rule of 5:72

Franciscan crown—42:22n

Franciscans or Minorites—1:235, 239, 2:327f, 4:157, 275, 5:35, 346n, 347n, 8:230, 12:358, 389, 15:9, 16:250, 317, 17:29, 70, 90, 108, 113f, 143, 266, 18:55n, 67, 183, 323n, 22:60, 330, 424, 23:274n, 288, 27:60, 141f, 281,

28:338, 30:95, 255, 32:79n, 282n, 285, 34:214, 36:13n, 15, 16n, 78n, 89n, 223, 39:51, 53, 62n, 41:116, 128n, 172, 44:172f, 190, 329, 47:45f, 48:4n, 6n, 33n, 125n, 164n, 273n, 312f, 313n, 49:17n, 121, 169f, 54:261, 387
Francisco de Mayronis—31:146, 150
Franciscus, Petrus—39:216n
Franciscus Accursius—*Glossa Ordinaria* 8:209n, 247, 257, 282n
Franconia—2:381, 14:xi, 46:6, 19n, 47, 72n, 116, 48:124, 163n, 169n, 184, 223, 49:114, 118n, 119n, 122n, 383n, 385
Frank, Sebastian—35:205n, 46:129n
Frankenhausen—49:119n
Frankenhausen, Battle of—46:5n, 59
Frankfurt, Council of—41:281n, 332n
Frankfurt Fair—37:xv, 6, 153, 155, 45:247n
Frankfurt Truce of 1539—50:188n, 190n, 193n, 219n
Frankfurt-am-Main—3:x, 303, 8:120, 31:73, 36:229n, 47:264n, 48:123n, 129, 197, 200, 203n, 49:122n, 280, 317n, 360n, 50:111, 51:35, 54:330f
Frankfurt-an-der-Oder—48:154n, 160, 219n, 50:146
University of 49:32, 51, 121, 148, 50:150n
Frankincense—4:99, 15:231n, 234, 52:278f, 281
Franks—16:126
Franz, Adolph—*Die Messe im deutschen Mittelalter*, Freiburg–im–Breisgau, 1902 35:92n, 107n, 108n
Die kirchlichen Benediktionen im Mittelalter, Freiburg–im–Breisgau, 1902 35:96n
Franz, Günther—*Der deutsche Bauernkrieg*, Darmstadt, 1956 46:72n, 106n
Frassen, Claudius, ed.—*Scotus academicus* 4:136n
Fraternities, Religious—see **Brotherhoods**
Fratricide—5:201, 7:55, 243, 256, 264, 266, 280, 8:24, 51, 220, 224, 226, 231
Frau Hulda—37:318, 40:174n, 193f, 202, 208, 210, 215f
Fraud—5:134, 150, 305, 373, 385, 24:268, 370, 27:126, 30:77, 188
Frederick I, Emperor—41:292n, 332n, 43:237, 44:125n, 49:383n
Frederick I, King of Denmark—50:147n
Frederick II, Elector of the Palatinate—50:44, 254
Frederick II, Emperor—32:xiiin, 41:332n, 44:125n, 48:204n
Frederick III, Emperor—9:17, 13:154, 172, 15:83n, 29:75, 41:266n, 294n
Frederick, Abbot of St. Giles in Nuremberg—see **Pistorius, Frederick**
Frederick, Bishop of Magdeburg—14:67
Frederick, Margrave of Brandenburg—36:272
Frederick, Margrave of Brandenburg-Ansbach-Kulmbach—50:150
Frederick the Wise, Elector of Saxony—1:78n, 3:356n, 4:382, 7:158, 159n, 193, 10:ix, 12:ix, 13:ix, 157, 163, 213, 218, 14:65, 67, 280f, 283, 15:34n, 57n, 83n, 90n, 139n, 159, 167f, 204, 21:xviii, 29:29n, 52, 72, 31:xvi, 19, 22, 37, 255f, 261, 279, 319, 339, 32:xiii, 34:xii, 26n, 330–332, 334, 335n, 35:47, 251n, 36:130, 227n, 228f, 234, 39:22n, 25, 27n, 40:49, 41:229, 230n, 231f, 234n, 236, 245f, 250, 42:xv, 18n, 119n, 120n, 121f, 127n, 135n, 142n, 166, 43:259n, 268n, 44:245, 45:13, 54, 55n, 58n, 68n, 78, 80, 81n, 107n, 103n, 104n, 105f, 179n, 197n, 40:xii, 47, 60, 89n, 90n, 106n, 119n, 142, 163, 239n, 48:8, 28n, 33f, 49f, 56, 61, 64n, 70n, 71f, 77n, 78, 81f, 88, 90n, 91f, 94n, 96f, 101, 103, 108, 110n, 111, 115, 120, 121n, 123, 127f, 130n, 131f, 134n, 136, 138n, 142, 144n, 148, 150, 152, 154, 161, 165, 168n, 172n, 173, 174n, 176, 181f, 182n, 183, 187, 188n, 190n, 193f, 201n, 205n, 210, 227n, 263, 264n, 269n, 271f, 275n, 294f, 316n, 326, 328, 337n, 338, 344f, 352, 381, 382n, 384, 386, 388f, 393, 398n, 49:9, 14f, 18, 30n, 35f, 45f, 51, 57f, 74f, 83n, 84, 92n, 93, 107, 111n, 112n, 116n, 124, 131n, 133, 135n, 250, 273, 293n, 51:55n, 84, 231n, 53:211, 222, 54:19, 54, 164, 180, 194f, 338
Free choice—see **Free Will**
Free Will—1:61, 84f, 185, 269, 273, 2:39–42, 121f, 4:50, 405, 9:125, 164, 277n, 10:13f, 12:377, 397, 407, 14:25, 15:49, 133, 16:110, 297, 17:4f, 12, 46, 69, 96, 118, 162, 256, 293, 18:413, 19:59, 85–87, 20:9, 80, 150, 161n, 162, 22:32, 23:49, 327n, 24:226, 328, 25:375, 465f, 496, 26:26f, 41, 58, 90, 123–125, 323n, 330, 27:172, 175, 181, 220, 278, 292, 325f, 328, 338f, 364, 372, 27:364f, 29:102, 30:6, 58, 60, 293f, 299, 31:9–16, 40, 48–50, 58–70, 317, 320, 323, 32:92–94, 136, 153f, 33:68–70, 77–80,

102–117, 122, 125f, 141f, 144f, 149, 159, 234–241, 250, 280f, 288f, 34:53, 66, 87n, 88–90, 163n, 348, 357, 35:264, 368n, 36:20, 30, 215, 217, 38:116, 40:80, 301f, 42:48, 45:335, 48:117, 144, 159, 50:63n, 51:53, 56–59, 126, 128, 52:80, 88, 243, 54:260

Free woman—see **Sarah**

Freedom—9:81, 125, 136, 225, 229, 233, 10:13, 26, 325, 23:5, 397, 399, 401f, 405–407, 409, 411–414, 420f, 24:317, 25:54, 71, 73, 109, 116, 249, 363, 473–475, 487f, 493f, 500, 26:14, 48, 85, 89f, 91, 93, 156, 161–165, 177, 302, 306, 315, 340, 347, 349, 360, 389, 391, 394f, 443, 448, 461, 27:3f, 8, 17, 19, 31, 35, 48f, 51, 138, 176, 201, 203f, 213, 217, 232, 236, 248, 284, 286, 316, 324f, 329, 347–349, 383–385, 396, 33:68f, 70, 189

Freedom, Christian—2:350, 357, 4:43, 65f, 261f, 335, 8:284, 9:8f, 126, 151, 13:10, 190, 16:99, 119f, 305, 17:99, 163, 179, 207, 209, 20:292, 22:258, 452, 487f, 23:401, 403–405, 409, 414, 25:118, 26:ix, 53, 81–83, 90, 93, 110f, 116, 221, 293, 343f, 392, 411, 439, 445, 27:3, 5–7, 10f, 48, 50f, 72, 154, 198, 200, 202, 214, 248, 325f, 346, 348f, 402, 28:44–47, 52, 264, 314, 318, 29:93, 101, 30:32, 77–79, 84, 144, 173, 189, 271, 31:197, 330, 343–377, 32:223–229, 33:48–56, 34:53, 59, 358f, 35:xvii, xix, 131, 321, 376, 379, 381, 389, 397n, 36:28, 70–75, 77, 81, 89, 97–100, 102, 111, 116f, 165, 168, 241–243, 247, 254, 262, 39:183, 189f, 200–202, 40:83, 92, 127–141, 151f, 192, 286, 303f, 41:67, 131, 174, 296, 338–340, 44:xiii, 36, 184, 198, 255, 295–316, 336, 363, 376–381, 398f, 45:177, 192, 46:28, 39, 141, 175, 310, 47:53, 60, 101, 48:228, 298–300, 302, 335f, 402, 49:379, 384f, 50:63n, 51:74, 79, 80f, 86f, 90, 132, 135, 337, 339, 52:37, 258f, 270, 53:xv–xvi, 25, 30f, 47f

Freedom, Evangelical—6:240

Freedom and grace—33:9, 54f

Freemen—9:145, 149

Freewomen—9:258

Fregoso, Archbishop Frederick—34:266

Freiberg-in-Saxony—5:370, 48:399f, 49:203, 321n, 352n, 50:149n, 54:134

Freiburg-im-Breisgau—49:216n
University of 31:257, 264, 48:132n, 194n, 205n, 305n, 49:50n, 160n

Freier, Moritz—*Luthers Busspsalmen und Psalter*, Leipzig, 1918 32:268n

Freising—48:104, 109, 131n

Freitag, Albert—12:x, 54:117
Einleitung zu Luthers De servo arbitrio 33:5n

French—2:190

French Evangelicals—50:88, 190n, 191n

Frenchmen—2:214, 4:357, 5:370, 8:103, 20:269, 54:151, 306, 309, 348

Frey, Rudolph—38:8

Friars—8:173n, 22:65, 152, 154, 157, 221, 270, 309, 461, 26:35, 27:113n, 124, 32:278, 282f, 285, 36:98, 45:142, 318, 351, 375, see also **Mendicant Orders**

Friars, Barefoot—23:117, 262, 273, 333, 340, 351, 367, 24:36, 38, 170, 224

Fridays—23:409, 37:38, 45:72n

Fridericus Archbishop Solernitanus—see **Fregoso, Archbishop Frederick**

Friedberg, Aemilius Ludocius, and Emil Richter, eds.—see ***Corpus Iuris Canonici***

Friendship—14:118f, 16:22, 17:40f, 65f, 21:127f, 24:102, 118, 158, 161, 163, 178, 181, 245f, 251f, 254–258, 261, 266–268, 284, 333, 398, 420, 29:98

Friesland—49:22, 50:55

Frisia—34:345, 353

Fritzehans, John—39:54

Froben, John—48:18n, 110n, 112n, 115n, 50:145n

Froelich, Charles D.—translator of Latin text of *Lectures on Jonah* 19:3–34
translator of Latin text of *Lectures on Habakkuk* 19:109–150

Frogs—3:349, 11:18, 74f, 82f

Froschauer, Christoph—38:8

Fröschel, Sebastian—54:316

Frost—11:76f, 83, 472f, 475

Frosts—1:144, 206

Froude, J.A.—*Life and Letters of Erasmus*, London, 1900 33:5n

Frugality—8:120

Fruit—9:138, 141, 154–157, 174, 189f, 207, 221, 235, 254f, 273, 293, 297, 305f, 10:21, 23, 25, 128, 24:193–196, 200–202, 205–207, 209–214, 216–236, 239, 243f, 249f, 252, 262, 264f, 271, 324, 330f, 341, 343, 388, 397

Fruit from a tree—46:180, 199

Fruit of the vine—37:312, 314, 317, 319

Fruit trees—1:36, 38f, 91, 11:91

Fruits—21:259–261, 264–268, 285, 291

Fruits, Judging by—42:30f

Fruits of faith—4:166, 169f, 5:186f, 258f, 268f, 16:280, 18:221, 418, 19:23, 25,

86, 25:518, 26:219f, 221, 234, 35:374, 376, 40:375f
Fruits of the Gospel—9:40f, 72, 143, 179, 184f
Fruits of the Spirit—11:389, 17:258, 388, 25:68, 26:217, 220, 230, 255, 27:79, 93–96, 372–374, 379, 29:62, 135, 37:7, 24, 28, 53, 95, 137, 140n, 149, 192, 366
Fruits of the Word—6:74, 12:299, 385, 20:100, 107
Frundsberg, Caspar von—50:150n
Frundsberg, George von—12:82, 46:247n, 49:161n, 50:155n
Frying—11:301
Fuchs, Thomas—48:139
Fugger, Anton—54:28
Fugger, Jakob—45:242n
Fuggers, The—31:21, 34:329n, 41:233n, 44:155n, 213, 45:234n, 271n, 288n, 47:169, 48:45, 49:52n
Fugitives—16:191
Fuhlbohm, Margaret—53:249
Fulda—48:163n, 225n, 49:389n, 50:218
Fulfilling the law—30:39, 214
Fulfillment—21:69f, 25:64, 70, 330, 342, 29:147, 224
Fulgentius, Bishop of Numidia—38:31n, 33n, 34, 50n, 54, 59–62, 68, 83
Fragments against Fabian 38:51n
Three Books to Trasimund 38:31, 50n
Fun in marriage—5:33f, 36
Fun not forbidden—21:85
Funck, Johann—34:342
Funerals—2:160, 6:256, 273, 281, 8:82, 315, 320, 9:134, 254, 51:231
Funk, Ulrich—38:8
Fur—23:320n, 37:77, 269
Furies—7:271, 329, 331
Furnishings, Ecclesiastical—34:55
Fürstenspiegel—9:19n, 13:x
Future—29:110, 147, 151, 156
Future life—2:232, 284, 3:141, 168, 4:119, 190, 206, 309, 313, 317, 401f, 404f, 5:39, 54, 158, 245, 250, 7:16, 116f, 145, 210f, 12:105–107, 118–121

Gabalena—6:302
Gabriel, Archangel—1:109, 2:54, 3:80, 232, 4:255, 268, 6:248, 7:369, 375, 10:410, 12:111, 13:6, 150, 233, 19:193, 20:168, 170, 22:38, 88, 113, 346, 364, 529, 23:349, 369, 24:92, 27:270, 29:205, 212, 35:192, 36:341, 37:98, 260n, 262, 337, 38:226, 232, 41:105, 45:221–225, 227, 47:230, 238–241, 245f, 250f, 258, 303–305, 51:80, 376, 52:74, 103, 157
Gabriel della Volta—31:255
Gace, W.—51:121
Gad—5:339f, 349n, 350, 8:272, 289f, 292, 17:382f, 20:307
Gadarene demoniacs—37:215n
Gaiety—12:81
Gaius Caesar—see **Julius Caesar**
Galatia—26:23f, 45f, 63, 76, 186, 429, 27:97, 99, 124, 167, 177, 30:5f, 41:321, 358
Galatians—2:187, 14:91, 304, 347, 24:16, 27:ixf, 3, 7, 9, 31–33, 36, 39f, 42, 52, 54, 59, 62, 79, 99, 108, 116, 129, 131f, 144, 148, 161f, 165, 168, 174f, 177, 179, 187, 190f, 194, 196–198, 208, 217, 243–245, 249–251, 254f, 263, 292, 298, 301–308, 310, 315, 323, 331, 338f, 343f, 359, 371, 378, 403, 406, 30:261, 46:40
Galatians, Epistle to the—3:23, 35, 84, 8:165, 308, 11:121, 14:244, 294, 349, 20:212, 333, 23:28, 191, 26:264, 27:ixf, 87, 145, 29: 4, 182, 184, 193, 35:384, Note: Vols. 26 and 27 are commentaries on the Epistle
Galba, Emperor—46:105
Galileans—10:77, 11:146, 27:289, 42:133
Galilee—2:378, 8:278f, 290f, 11:494, 14:97, 16:97, 17:273, 20:118, 22:215–217, 230, 413, 415, 503, 509, 516, 23:201, 205, 208, 210, 214, 243, 245f, 278, 282–285, 289, 303, 306, 52:144
Galilee, Sea of—9:307, 22:181, 183
Gall—24:379, 401
Gall, St.—46:106, 48:75, 138, 189n, 195f, 198n, 201, 204, 207f, 208n, 210, 219n, 223, 226, 249f, 53:274
Gallows—1:351, 3:50, 123, 4:51, 8:205, 16:232, 24:399
Gallows repentance—5:152, 155, 6:43
Gallus Cahera—40:5f, 41
Gamaliel—8:241, 49:350n
Gambling—2:127, 3:182, 5:11, 54:206
Games—4:71, 7:176, 225f, 229–231, 233, 237, 243, 245, 247, 249, 253, 263, 271, 299, 317, 319, 326, 334, 352, 354f, 357f, 361f, 364–367, 8:5, 12, 16, 55, 147, 255, 259, 9:131, 54:221f
Games, God's—see **God**—Plays games with us
Ganges River—1:97–100
Gangra, Council of—41:125, 126n, 136n
Gangrene—14:259, 290, 50:48
Garb—41:124, 130, 147, 149, 174, 270, 338

Garden Brothers—16:188
Garden of Eden—see **Eden**
Gardeners—24:198
Gardens—11:23, 363, 17:290, 327, 336, 23:225, 24:333
Gardiner, Stephen—50:202n
Gargarus, Mt.—4:127
Garments—11:8f, 357, 16:48, 179, 20:37, 70, 146, 205f, 255
Garments, White—15:10, 149, 166
Gate, Narrow—21:241f, 245f
Gates—10:95f, 441–443, 11:176n, 18:161
Gates of hell—16:28f, 200
Gates of righteousness—14:91
Gath—8:151, 281, 18:216
Gauls—16:147
Gautama—18:368n
Gaza—2:205, 18:133f, 340, 20:285
Gazelle—15:217f, 222, 264
Geba—20:341
Gebal—11:121, 122n, 125
Gebhard, Count of Mansfeld—49:103n, 320n, 50:311, 51:383
Gebhardt, Friedrich—53:57n
Gebhart, Bruno—*Die gravamina der Deutschen Nation gegen den römischen Hof*, Breslau, 1895 45:277n
Gedaliah—20:76, 260
Gedud—8:288
Geese—1:67, 132, 346, 2:133
Gehenna—7:292, 298, 301–303, 11:69, 36:225n
Gelasius, Pope—43:155
Gelderland—6:x, 34:345, 353
Gellius, Aulus—see **Aulus Gellius**
Gemeinde and Gemeine—39:xiii, 57n, 205n
Gemeine—13:46n
Gems—2:195, 26:132, 134, 30:90, 98
Gemser—40:155n, 156, 165
Genealogies—1:332, 3:42, 4:3, 184, 6:179, 285, 290, 310, 314f, 7:14f, 8:18, 84–86, 89, 28:222f, 230, 270
General Church Councils—see **Councils, General Church**
Generalization—28:95
Generations, Definition of—17:36, 227, 21:324, 331
Generations, Succession of—15:15, 97
Generosity—13:418, 15:115, 171f, 28:323, 372, 380, 29:79, 88, 44:109
Genesis, Book of—1:240, 357, 2:ix, 3, 208, 374n, 3:210, 227, 4:ix, 312, 318f, 5:ixf, 99n, 101, 6:ix, 312f, 8:86, 130, 134, 243, 333, 22:8, 23:10, 339, 26:120, 238f, 263, 304, 399n, 433f
  Authorship 54:373
  Masoretic and Samaritan texts 1:270n
  Sermons on Genesis by Luther 1:345n
Genesis, Fifth book of—5:200f, see also **Deuteronomy**
Genesis, Interpreters of text of—7:6, 54, 82, 110f, 140f, 143, 149, 161, 168, 197, 205, 239, 257, 260, 301
Genesis lectures, Luther's—Chronology and authenticity 1:ixf
Geneva—47:116n, 50:191n
Genitals—9:229, 249, 251
Genitive case—26:101f
Genius—13:154f, 157f
Genoa—50:72n
Gensichen, Hans-Werner—*We Condemn*, St. Louis, 1967 39:xiiin
Gentiles—1:86, 195, 235, 291, 302, 313f, 2:91, 93, 98f, 178f, 184f, 190, 212, 227, 229, 254, 257, 274, 305, 342, 3:28, 89–99, 104–107, 110–116, 118, 121, 127–129, 131f, 142–145, 147, 151f, 162, 177, 189, 209, 261n, 319, 338f, 348, 4:9, 25, 27, 43, 55, 60, 63f, 140, 152, 155f, 160, 170, 367, 406, 5:52, 254, 259, 6:113, 212f, 228, 248, 284, 7:13–15, 18, 22, 36, 53, 108, 129, 163f, 166f, 187, 201, 207, 212, 8:14, 81, 133, 135f, 165, 168, 252, 9:21, 32–34, 42n, 79–85, 87f, 97, 102f, 105, 110, 118, 123, 145–147, 151, 155, 175, 180, 203f, 214, 225, 229f, 234, 254, 283, 292, 296, 298f, 11:44, 86, 380f, 424, 521, 542, 551, 12:268, 292f, 13:98, 285, 378, 14:96, 243, 246f, 249f, 263, 277, 301, 304, 307, 313–315, 321, 332f, 335, 342, 15:41, 212, 255, 278, 323, 338, 16:5, 26, 32, 38, 58, 64, 85, 97, 124, 154, 167, 190, 195, 225, 236, 242, 247, 278, 292f, 300, 331, 17:7, 39, 63, 69, 71, 104, 160, 169, 174f, 191, 207, 218, 246, 260, 262–264, 308, 313, 337, 376, 413f, 18:189, 202, 238, 253, 276, 359, 382, 19:40, 50f, 84, 94, 104, 20:66, 71, 87, 90, 94, 100f, 164, 170, 176, 179, 195, 197, 201, 280f, 289, 295, 343f, 21:351, 355, 22:40, 42, 53f, 97, 135, 149, 216f, 251, 344, 448, 23:201, 320, 387, 404, 406, 24:294, 340, 396, 25:39, 100, 426, 26:16, 19, 25, 29, 53, 59, 69, 73–75, 77, 79–87, 89f, 98, 101f, 104, 107–113, 117–121, 123, 204–206, 209–212, 240f, 243, 248, 275, 277, 283, 291, 305, 333f, 343, 354–357, 389, 395, 399f, 410, 418f, 423, 426f, 452, 27:42, 139, 142f, 165, 186, 194, 196f, 200, 203f, 208, 210–213, 215, 217–219, 247, 254, 260,

263–266, 281, 283, 290, 292, 295, 302, 336, 343, 357, 403, 406, 28:83, 88, 90f, 131, 270, 306, 29:6, 8, 14, 21, 36, 178, 192, 210, 212, 30:58, 66, 72, 87f, 120f, 137, 229, 270, 34:113, 35:164f, 167f, 363f, 36:187, 336, 37:71, 332, 41:51, 68f, 73, 75–78, 113, 317, 324f, 364, 42:19f, 76, 45:97, 200f, 203f, 220f, 229, 47:65–98, 111, 137–306, 49:86, 170, 386, 52:159f, 208
Gentiles, Mission to the—10:339
Gentleness—27:95, 103, 106, 111f, 298, 301, 313, 373, 377, 388, 390, 29:74–79, 182, 45:72f
Genuflection—5:264, 17:136, 18:96
Geographers—8:116, 273
Geography—2:324, 342
Geology—2:108n
Geometry—2:67
George II, Count of Mansfeld—50:311
George III, Prince of Anhalt—50:222n, 280n, 288f, 309f
George Frederick of Saxony—43:279n
George, Count of Wertheim—46:247n, 49:50n
George, Duke of Saxony—4:404, 5:x, 260, 6:34, 7:121, 13:175n, 336, 16:258n, 325, 17:34, 188n, 20:27n, 22:227n, 23:201n, 211, 370, 421, 28:6, 258, 31:310, 323, 32:116, 33:13n, 34:66, 98, 148, 333, 35:47, 179, 185n, 36:273, 38:142, 39:xxiii, 22n, 82n, 107, 119, 139, 228, 40:50, 41:150n, 181n, 182, 221n, 222, 230n, 241, 243n, 249, 253, 42:18n, 97n, 43:60, 64n, 142, 239, 44:117, 150n, 245n, 45:14n, 33n, 58n, 64n, 77n, 80, 84n, 85n, 107n, 112n, 136, 138, 152n, 199n, 46:20n, 90n, 247n, 48:xviii, 101n, 110n, 111, 123, 137n, 144n, 149, 152n, 183, 193, 201, 216f, 220, 228, 233n, 271f, 381, 388, 390f, 393, 49:xvii, 7n, 23, 71n, 119n, 120, 123, 124n, 127n, 144f, 157, 183f, 189f, 197f, 215n, 273f, 364n, 376n, 389, 50:72, 95, 128n, 134, 135n, 142n, 150, 185, 214, 51:303, 54:xvii, 38, 60, 71, 82, 86, 93f, 104, 111, 159, 181, 185, 230, 265, 273, 282, 285, 336, 349f, 352, 360, 370, 379–382, 460
George, Margrave of Brandenburg-Ansbach-Kulmbach—23:219n, 36:273, 38:142, 217, 41:141n, 43:266, 46:247n, 49:xvi, 60n, 227, 236n, 244, 246n, 251, 254, 275n, 339n, 349, 360n, 50:45n, 62, 83, 51:250, 357, 54:60
George, St.—8:203, 13:326, 22:137, 385, 390, 490, 24:90, 34:24, 40:188, 51:375f
George of Polenz, Bishop of Samland—45:152n
George the Bearded—see **George, Duke of Saxony**
Georgians—2:189
Gerar—3:303, 316, 321, 326, 330, 338, 344, 346, 352, 354, 356f, 360, 4:71, 73f, 188, 193f, 198, 215, 5:6, 58, 61f, 67, 69, 265, 7:220
Gerbel, Nicholas—37:5, 48:222, 316, 317f, 321n, 323, 328, 344, 346, 355n, 49:6n, 44n, 81f, 95n, 160n, 199f, 50:3n
His Greek New Testament 48:321n, 355n
Gerber, Rudolf—53:203n
Gereon, St.—45:99n
Gerhardt, Karl—53:185n
Gerhardt, Paul—10:397n
Gericke, Cyriacus—54:292
Gerizim, Mt.—2:282, 285, 6:183, 9:117, 259, 22:522–524, 36:220
Gerlach—see **Billican, Theobald**
German—2:395, 3:206, 248f, 4:11, 36n, 86, 87n, 101, 107n, 131n, 154, 192, 200, 216, 245n, 294, 295n, 309n, 363n, 379n, 381, 393n, 394n, 404n, 6:15, 53, 84, 119, 137, 145, 167, 195, 366, 7:6n, 20n, 40, 51, 53, 61n, 157, 161, 169, 188f, 215, 243, 252, 271, 330n, 8:3n, 143, 156, 183n, 195, 209, 216, 278, 323, 9:15, 33, 49, 56, 108n, 113, 189n, 220, 222n, 248n, 10:160, 314, 331, 16:187, 272, 276, 278n, 340n, 20:7n, 20n, 23n, 34n, 43, 44n, 52n, 60n, 64, 74n, 90f, 94, 121, 133, 163n, 167n, 174n, 183n, 211n, 212n, 213n, 215n, 227n, 238n, 247n, 304n, 330n, 22:111, 24:45, 100, 271, 349n, 399, 419, 25:69, 116, 149, 169, 208, 224, 254, 261, 369, 392, 416, 428, 436, 446, 448f, 494, 498, 510, 27:130, 244n, 341, 376, 30:5, 32, 53n, 73, 132, 135, 214, 316, 31:76, 35:xvii, 90, 189f, 194, 197, 213, 216, 250, 295f, 37:34, 38, 45n, 57n, 80n, 98n, 125n, 127n, 133n, 147n, 153, 170, 172f, 180, 239–241, 243–245, 250, 320, 327, 332f, 38:10f, 32, 48, 60, 165, 170n, 178, 185n, 207, 226, 41:269, 271, 276, 42:173, 45:189, 209f, 216, 298, 343, 353, 357, 360, 376, 46:215, 232, 251, 255, 273–275, 52:86, 185, 202, 208, 54:311, 348, 376
German Bible—see **Scripture(s)**—German translation, Luther's
German lands—22:69
German life and society—44:212–216
German Litany and Latin Litany

Corrected—see **Luther, Martin, Writings of**
German Mass and Order of Service **(Deutsche Messe)**—see **Luther, Martin, Writings of**
German nationalism—48:xx, 169n, 213, 216, 233f, 244f, 396
German Theology, A—7:133n, 31:74–76, see also **Luther, Martin, Writings of**—*German Theology*, Preface to complete edition of
Germanism—45:133
Germans—1:274, 2:94, 119, 161, 187, 189f, 214f, 226, 380, 395, 3:147, 248, 251, 283, 4:37n, 87, 98n, 153, 272, 406, 5:x, 19, 35, 66f, 88, 152, 156, 177, 211, 317, 370, 6:53, 145, 183, 201, 229, 243, 7:59, 62f, 65, 111, 145, 160, 192n, 283, 8:35, 67, 95, 103, 120, 124, 127, 137, 266, 13:203, 216, 218, 256, 14:11f, 50, 74, 238, 267, 274, 16:62, 219, 17:150, 190, 249, 18:327, 20:15, 44, 317, 22:84f, 149, 299, 338, 347, 23:21, 380, 403, 407, 25:464, 26:47, 188, 256, 27:37, 157, 28:183, 189, 191, 29:39, 31:76, 34:272, 35:295f, 406, 36:208, 275f, 40:351, 393, 41:76, 120, 139, 175, 261, 267, 270n, 283, 294, 350, 356n, 371–376, 44:139, 142–145, 164, 193, 207, 45:242f, 246f, 249, 289, 351f, 357n, 358, 360, 367, 372, 377n, 46:79, 101, 127n, 128, 129n, 136f, 161, 176, 201f, 205, 257, 262, 47:22, 29, 32, 34, 54f, 82, 140, 190, 48:86, 101, 172, 174n, 189n, 195, 197, 202, 209, 250, 267n, 270, 281, 307, 363, 396, 51:292, 296, 54:151, 262, 265, 278, 291, 309, 332, 371, 373
  Excesses in eating 25:481
Germany—1:78, 207, 288, 2:18, 20, 65, 137n, 175, 186, 193, 227, 231n, 242, 369, 3:60, 153, 249, 252, 254, 278, 319, 324, 4:214, 281, 312, 382, 6:40, 206, 243f, 383, 8:82, 109, 117–120, 125, 128, 208n, 290, 9:5, 139, 12:32, 34, 253, 13:60, 14:48n, 54, 111, 261, 267, 15:25, 444, 64, 144f, 165f, 17:55, 89, 138, 249, 297, 304f, 353, 366, 403, 18:169, 19:35, 201, 203n, 22:83, 85, 137, 207, 252, 390, 23:208, 217, 264f, 374, 380, 387, 400, 26:429, 441, 27:107, 127, 157f, 384f, 28:131, 257, 275, 34:24n, 345, 36:267, 37:xiiif, xvi, 16n, 19, 67, 109, 154, 234, 248, 39:60, 107, 296, 41:xii, 6, 142, 240, 259, 265, 267–270, 274f, 284f, 372, 374, 42:xiii, 123, 43:66, 69f, 45:xii–xiv, 58n, 84, 133, 233f, 246f, 249, 319, 347f, 352, 358, 372f, 376, 378, 46:xi, 8, 19f, 22, 40, 42, 47, 52, 78f, 116, 164, 184, 188f, 193, 198, 201f, 209, 214, 217, 234, 239, 254f, 256, 47:23f, 38, 61n, 128, 268n, 49:25, 68, 125f, 145, 165, 185, 187, 193, 220n, 265n, 368, 425, 50:54, 84n, 104n, 160, 180, 182, 192, 208, 218, 222n, 229, 254n, 296, 51:78, 223, 292, 354, 52:6, 54:229, 278, 306, 347, see also **Roman Empire, Holy**
  Roman Catholic Primate of 48:44f, 99n
  Territorial sovereigns 48:50, 70, 217n, 244, 392
Germany, South—38:9
Germany in Luther's day—Causes and effects of Reformation 3:153
  Economic and social conditions—43:220, 240, 279
  Moral degeneracy 3:227, 245, 319, 354
Gerrish, Brian A.—54:183n
  Priesthood and Ministry in the Theology of Luther 39:xviiin
  Reformers in Profile, Philadelphia, 1967 42:xiiin
Gerson, Jean—2:339n, 3:276f, 5:323, 344, 10:125, 12:270, 13:113, 27:81, 28:322, 355f, 31:108, 111, 116, 195, 262n, 32:160, 37:370n, 39:40, 44, 168, 211, 41:129n, 43:150n, 46:318, 51:48, 186, 54:42, 133, 142, 443
  De non esu carnium apud Carthusianos 17:65n
  De vita spirituali 5:323n
  Donatus moralisatus seu per allegoriam traductus 36:110n
  Mountain of Contemplation 3:276n
  Opera Omnia, Antwerp, 1706 16:311n, 32:160n
  Regulae morales 28:355
Gess, Felician—45:14n, 33n, 77n, 78n, 80n, 84n, 138n
  Akten und Briefe zur Kirchenpolitik Herzog Georgs von Sachsen, Leipzig, 1905 39:22
Gestation—1:133, 202
Gethsemane—7:302, 42:6, 14, 46
Gevatter—50:73n, 103n, 125n, 219n
Geyer, Florian—46:47n
Ghent—49:12n
Ghettoes—47:128
Ghinucci, Jerome—see **Jerome of Ascoli**
Ghosts—16:72, 24:369, 26:259, 52:178f, 54:258, see also **Poltergeists**; **Spirits**
Giants—1:299, 321, 356, 2:5, 23, 28, 32–34, 36, 38, 71, 211, 367, 4:193, 6:35,

136, 138, 9:28, 34, 40, 86f, 16:207, 209, 20:109, 112
Gibeah—16:114, 18:28, 50, 56, 45:355
Gibeon—16:234, 36:221
Gibeonites—2:177, 9:36, 79, 231, 11:359
Giberti, Cardinal John Matthew—34:233, 267
Gibon—1:97, 101
Gibraltar, Straits of—2:187
Gideon—2:258, 282, 376, 3:30, 4:104, 129, 261, 263, 6:179, 7:165, 171, 8:282, 285f, 296, 306, 9:81, 123, 10:37, 304, 11:40, 126, 129, 319, 475, 13:400, 14:114, 339, 16:98f, 102, 130, 20:190, 22:263f, 268f, 274, 316f, 319, 27:330, 364, 29:129, 35:271, 36:44, 65, 38:290, 42:106, 46:130, 192, 47:186, 52:31, 187
Gifts—6:77, 91, 96, 104, 119, 160, 169, 171, 174f, 10:9, 47, 345, 16:70f, 185, 205, 21:271, 310, 317f, 325, 25:6, 48, 106, 156, 175, 212, 296, 306, 444, 448f, 28:10–12, 16f, 26–28, 52, 137, 247, 249, 258f, 316f, 330, 45:257, 292n, 304, 322n
Gifts, Spiritual—37:21f, 50, 149
Gifts, The Wisemen's—52:278
Gifts, Variety of—20:25f, 225, 341f
Gifts of God—1:133, 245, 12:161, 166, 255, 278, 280f, 294, 397, 402, 13:165, 198, 200, 212, 214, 241, 294f, 14:117, 121, 123, 128, 133, 16:21, 25, 70, 168, 335, 20:158, 21:270, 290f, 308, 317f, 324f, 334f, 22:192, 489, 526f, 529, 26:4, 6, 29:23, 54, 67, 81, 119, 35:369, 382, 36:125, 200, 37:118, 140, 149, 366, 39:180, 42:25, 58, 88, 92, 130, 145, 148, 154, 172, 46:141, 213, 226, 237, 239, 253f
Gifts of grace—see **Grace, Gifts of**
Gifts of the Holy Spirit—see **Holy Spirit, Gifts of the**
Gilead—6:80f, 117, 8:285, 290, 296, 9:40, 10:280–282, 286, 290f, 296f, 380, 434, 18:33, 67f, 114, 132, 136, 159, 203, 259n, 275, 20:113f, 117, 306–308
Giles, St.—14:45n
Giles's, St., Day—23:299n
Gilgal—4:178, 5:241, 18:52, 67f, 151, 159f, 259, 47:187
Giliad, Mt.—6:36, 43
Gillian, St.—39:272n
Gilson, E.—*History of Christian Philosophy in the Middle Ages*, New York, 1955 38:240
Ginzberg, Louis—*Legends of the Jews*, Philadelphia, 1954 4:136n
Girdles—8:66
Girgashites—2:204
Girls—3:103, 147, 160, 183n, 257, 266, 278, 307, 310, 6:188f, 190, 193, 195, 9:162, 204, 222–224, 20:70, 104, 297f, 26:157, 163
Girls, Educating—45:188f, 344n, 370, 46:231n, 232
Girls, Schools for—44:206
Gittith—11:139n
Giuliano della Rovere—see **Julius II, Pope**
Given up by God—25:160–162, 164–168
Giving—12:291, 293, 15:115, 171f, 21:117f, 134–136, 176, 183, 25:448f, 45:280–290
Gladiators, Blind—33:104n
Glait, Oswald—47:59
Glapion, John—32:103, 36:8f
Glaser, Martin—48:124
Glass—20:66n
Glass eyes—23:241
Glatz, Caspar—49:105n, 111n
Glauchau—50:142
Glitsch, Konrad—40:113
Gloria in excelsis **(hymn)**—3:155, 7:247n, 38:290, 53:xx, 21, 23, 149, 172, 184–188, 209, 294
Gloria Patri **(hymn)**—2:365n, 53:222
Glorification—25:43, 76, 30:128
Glorification, Works of—11:10
Glorifying God—21:147f, 321, 25:283f
Glory—6:6, 49, 63, 268, 271, 311, 405, 10:84f, 133f, 346, 11:376f, 387, 433, 445, 447, 15:26, 157, 326f, 16:36, 194, 212, 17:11, 20, 29, 47, 70f, 117, 162, 172, 274, 312, 337f, 342, 408, 20:29f, 47, 70, 136, 188, 192f, 25:8, 31, 73f, 105, 153, 178f, 246, 248, 522f, 28:183–185, 201, 238, 306, 29:119, 142, 146, 165, 171, 203, 213–215, 220, 234, 33:221, 265f, 35:244f, 272, 383, 52:45, 86f
Glory, True—25:426
Glorying—25:88, 136f, 248, 251, 519f, 33:221, 226
Glorying in Christ—20:28, 25:519
Glossa interlinearis **of Anselm of Laon**—25:xi, 314, 390, 29:118n
Glossa ordinaria—5:216, 280n, 345n, 6:xi, 178n, 182n, 8:209n, 247, 257, 282n, 10:29, 37, 158, 277, 385, 439, 11:54n, 65n, 122n, 127n, 401n, 15:215n, 16:69n, 272n, 336n, 347n, 25:xi, 140, 152, 214, 390, 28:323, 29:18n, 127n, 31:142n, 51:6n, 54:14
Glosses—4:154f, 384, 397, 409, 6:170, 215, 200, 293, 10:ix–xi, 3–5, 10, 71, 84f,

102, 107, 114, 118, 135, 154, 167, 200f, 207, 227, 232, 241, 246, 248, 262, 272, 296, 300, 307, 311, 314, 328, 346, 363, 367, 397, 412, 422, 433, 449, 14:283, 338, 16:212, 311n, 23:95, 110, 118, 127, 146, 160, 168, 225, 25:ix–xi, xiiif, 1, 26:122, 136f, 181, 194f, 243, 269–271, 273, 330, 27:227, 369, 373, 397, 29:x–xii, 35:201, 366, 37:15, 120–122, 125, 146, 157, 288, 306–308, 314, 318f, 341–349, 359, 44:151n, 50:201f, 52:286

Glossolalia—see **Tongues, Speaking in**

Gluttons, gluttony—2:231, 3:248, 323f, 4:77, 276f, 314, 395n, 7:66, 74, 118, 159, 194, 214, 347, 8:106, 120, 127, 222n, 261, 10:291, 357, 417, 11:67, 127, 223, 259, 303, 310, 536, 23:5, 30, 43, 253, 25:482, 30:27, 31, 250, 36:209, 224, 41:18, 175, 42:92, 51:12, 179, 291–299, 374

Gnatho—4:375

Gnats—11:112, 203, 24:416f

Gnesio-Lutherans—50:209n, 210n, 218n

Gnosticism—44:40, 43, 388n

Gnosticism, Valentinian—23:122, 37:81, 99, 115f

Gnostics—1:238n, 22:23n, 23:186n

Goads—10:18f, 22, 43

Goats—1:255, 2:74, 88, 116, 147, 4:114, 228, 5:97, 267, 270, 284f, 310, 376f, 379, 6:13–15, 67, 119, 7:45, 66, 191, 300, 8:60, 261, 9:298

Goats' hair—11:19

Goblets—4:296

Goblins—16:297, 37:222, 224, 286, 369

God—1:13–15, 18, 33, 35, 149, 152f, 155f, 162, 173–178, 182, 187, 191, 194, 196, 201, 206f, 209, 221, 227, 230, 236–238, 243f, 246, 249, 257, 259, 266f, 270, 272, 279, 282, 285–288, 292, 296, 300, 308, 328–330, 348, 357, 359, 2:4–6, 8, 43, 45, 56, 68, 133, 141, 170, 185, 3:12, 33, 40, 103, 110, 138, 161 292, 4:57, 82, 90, 120, 132, 203, 273, 314, 5:44–46, 48, 52, 72, 6:8–10, 39, 41–43, 59f, 63, 71, 73f, 113f, 123, 128, 148, 156, 170, 180, 184f, 232, 235, 249f, 311, 343f, 347, 365, 370, 375, 7:11, 62, 83, 152, 165, 222, 231, 8:12, 30, 160, 9:41, 49, 56–58, 60n, 68, 84f, 146, 167, 10:48, 78, 118, 123, 161, 252, 258, 396, 418, 428, 449, 11:111, 159, 209f, 260, 316f, 361, 12:99, 184, 223, 281, 301, 312, 323, 344, 352, 373f, 377, 392, 403, 13:3, 7, 9, 34–37, 44f, 46, 77, 82, 85, 91, 105, 136f, 187, 161, 261, 15:40f, 54, 51, 82, 148, 193, 204, 208, 212f, 218, 240f, 263, 282, 332, 16:7, 10, 14–16, 19, 23, 35, 45f, 54, 73, 76, 81, 83f, 89, 94, 104, 106, 109f, 118, 153, 155, 161, 170, 209, 216, 236f, 241, 247, 258, 260, 262, 269–271, 279, 318f, 330, 17:29f, 58f, 81, 105, 164, 283, 308, 358, 368, 376, 394, 18:63, 160, 230, 285, 287, 306, 19:11, 28, 43, 52–55, 58, 60–62, 72–74, 84, 92, 131, 137, 139, 163, 178, 185, 225, 21:147f, 179f, 190f, 196f, 200, 261–263, 269, 298, 300f, 308–310, 317, 319, 23:6, 14f, 20, 22, 55, 63f, 100, 190, 195, 215f, 256, 301, 305, 349, 353, 408, 24:23, 381, 419, 25:12, 27, 69, 82f, 100–103, 105, 160f, 167, 175, 203, 205–207, 212, 216, 219, 238f, 374, 388f, 26:16f, 29, 60, 95, 173, 229, 311, 348, 28:45f, 53, 96–98, 117, 120, 126, 139, 160, 256, 258, 262, 379, 29:15, 23, 26, 31, 41, 57f, 65, 72f, 82, 98, 111, 120, 127, 130, 135f, 144, 146–148, 150, 153, 161, 164f, 173, 186, 189, 211, 215, 231, 235, 239, 295f, 30:6, 33, 114, 152, 229, 31:46–48, 98, 138, 233, 348–350, 33:75, 121, 145f, 176–179, 199, 208, 210, 243, 34:103, 110, 152, 154, 159, 177, 226f, 35:34f, 52, 56, 82, 104, 137, 158, 170f, 199f, 231, 248, 252, 262, 290, 358n, 371, 377, 382, 36:62, 64, 290, 313–315, 342, 37:26, 28, 53, 66, 71, 88, 124, 133, 137, 210, 38:ixf, xvif, xx, 18, 21f, 25, 27, 32, 34f, 39, 42f, 45f, 53f, 56, 60, 62, 75, 77f, 81, 83, 85–88, 95, 97–101, 104n, 105–109, 111, 113, 116, 118, 121–123, 128, 131–136, 149f, 155, 157–162, 165, 167–171, 174, 176, 180, 184f, 187f, 190f, 197, 201f, 204, 206, 208, 210, 222–233, 240, 244f, 250, 251n, 253f, 255n, 265, 289, 293n, 302f, 305–307, 309, 312f, 316, 39:xiii, xviif, 18, 20, 25, 28–30, 34, 64, 77, 83f, 86, 88, 93f, 100, 113, 125, 127f, 134, 144f, 148, 150f, 162, 176, 180, 191, 195, 231, 242, 247f, 257, 263, 268, 281, 286, 290, 41:xi–xiii, 9, 11–13, 15f, 18, 22, 28, 30f, 35, 40, 48f, 51f, 56f, 60, 69, 76–78, 81–83, 85, 87, 90n, 99–101, 103–106, 111, 310f, 313, 318, 323, 325–327, 329–332, 335, 338f, 341–344, 348f, 352–354, 356–361, 364–366, 370, 376, 42:x, 8, 11, 13, 18, 22f, 26, 28, 39, 42f, 55, 63–68, 70, 77, 88f, 101–103, 105, 109–113, 125, 129, 131, 133–136, 138, 146–148, 152–154,

156–159, 164, 175, 45:41f, 86, 126, 143, 246, 203, 253, 326, 331, 350, 359, 372–374, 386, 390f, 46:9, 12, 16, 23f, 28, 30, 32, 34, 42f, 52, 61, 75, 77, 79, 84, 91, 93, 95, 97f, 114f, 122f, 129, 133–135, 148, 152f, 167, 169–171, 174, 176, 183f, 186–189, 197f, 221, 228f, 234, 241, 246, 248, 250, 254, 256, 273, 276f, 283f, 288, 304, 309, 318, 47:6, 13, 54, 85, 112, 139, 142, 152, 162, 164f, 227–229, 251, 261, 289–291, 295, 52:7–10, 15f, 19, 27, 33f, 36, 38, 43f, 47–49, 51f, 55, 59f, 61–63, 67, 83f, 91, 104f, 128f, 149f, 155, 178f, 180f, 187, 194–196, 198–201, 209, 241f, 243, 245f, 257, 259, 266, 277, 284, 286, 54:69, 72f, 75, 78, 127f, 155, 269, 423, 429
A great cook 19:185
A Poet; we are stanzas 7:366
A witness 45:103n, 150n
Abhors presumption 4:62, 70
Active, not passive 7:104
Always comes in some "form" 16:109
Always remembers His own 2:104, 106
Always truthful 4:38, 97, 132, 47:67, 70, 72f, 78, 184, 193, 195, 200, 202, 205, 240, 249
Ancient of Days 15:291
As physician 25:202f
Author of good and evil 15:55, 120
Baked 36:336, 344
Called El 6:136, 15:288f
Called Elohim 6:54, 185, 251
Called "Fear of Isaac" 6:70–73, 10:346
Called Jehovah 6:248f, 15:290, 313, 319f, 321, 323, 328, 336
Can both speak and act 17:52, 58, 71, 94f, 105, 124, 144, 163
Carries His own 17:139, 357f
Changeableness 25:219
Chastises His own 17:319, 357, 374
Comforter in day of trouble 14:202, 252f
Commands of 41:17–19, 24, 30f, 35, 39, 61, 67, 70, 77, 111, 122, 124, 130, 139f, 145f, 171f, 195, 214, 226, 229, 247f, 287, 304f, 327, 341f, 350, see also **Ten Commandments**
Conquered by us 6:140f, 259
Conquers by the Word 25:197
Consistent in punishments 2:3
Contempt for Him 26:35f, 41, 70, 125, 230f, 309, 342, 352, 377
Creates ex nihilo 20:4f, 40, 84, 209f
Creator 1:14, 15, 17f, 37, 58, 67f, 94f, 128, 130, 142–144, 152, 171f, 175f, 179, 222, 224, 244f, 2:146, 207, 209, 227, 255, 298, 347, 5:35, 146, 184, 191f, 197, 222, 248f, 279, 314, 330, 353, 355, 363, 6:27, 30, 88, 231, 241, 243–245, 349, 7:99, 138, 152, 211, 233, 247, 298, 8:36f, 39, 80, 180, 275, 11:10, 15–17, 179, 339, 392, 465, 15:30f, 309, 17:26, 29, 50, 55, 85, 91, 93, 96, 105, 118, 18:155, 160, 186, 22:19, 21, 26f, 29, 36, 50, 74–76, 89, 104, 112, 115, 130, 153, 299, 318, 351, 359, 361, 478, 481, 23:77, 95, 117, 120f, 216, 246, 346, 367, 376, 24:25, 108, 204n, 281f, 323, 25:10, 12, 158, 27:38, 88, 297, 38:85, 245, 261, 268, 298, 309f, 312, 44:xiii, 47:90, 92, 144f, 285f, 289
Creator and Preserver 37:xviii, 30–32, 43, 49, 57–64, 69, 117, 140, 272, 361
Death of see **Death of God**
Defined 3:11f
Delays His action 11:158, 164
Depicted as female 7:325, 8:89f, see also **God**—Like a mother; **God**—Like a mother hen
Despised 46:133, 147, 185, 241, 243
Disciplines His own 8:9–11, 74, 117, 201
Divine Being 2:45
Does not sleep 3:229f
Dwells in us 13:10, 22, 20:32, 200–202, 270f
Essence of His being 15:275, 279, 301f, 305, 310f, 340, 24:100, 115, 117, 140, 290, 38:85, 252, 262, 265, 273, 307
Eternal 38:50n, 262
Fear of see **Fear of God**
Fights for us 37:21, 28, 45, 78, 143, 161f, 178
For (or with) us 18:377f
Formed by men 17:17f, 108f
Generates the Son 38:252, 257, 265, 275f
Giver of success 15:47, 73
Gives authority 46:30, 126f, 266
Gives cross to His own 2:351, 369
Giving Him thanks 38:108, 111, 123, 133, 209, 296
Glowing furnace of love 51:95
God of gods 6:184f, 249
God of Israel 16:23, 111, 250, 318
Has secret plans 6:351–354, 359f, 374, 401
He calls us 4:104, 345, 347
He repents 18:60, 97, 99, 174
Hides Himself 3:139, 4:7, 32, 36, 324, 358, 371, 5:44–46, 48, 50, 6:148, 236, 259, 354, 359, 398, 401, 7:175, 8:4, 9, 30, 9:33, 41, 10:62, 118–120, 446, 14:191, 142, 17:131f, 278f, 21:309,

23:105, 123, 139, 25:437f, 439, 28:125f, 30:267, 33:138–147, 41:171, 42:18, 44:28, 47:209, 47:209n, 49:371
Hides His face 16:93
His accidental mercy see **Mercy, God's Accidental**
His alien work see **Alien work of God**
His anger see **Wrath of God**
His arm 21:339
His arrows 19:143f, 234
His attributes 11:390f, 13:7, 34–36, 93, 99, 405
His authority 3:272f, 321, 45:99, 145–150, 156, 376, 46:26, 66, 108, 126f, 191
His benevolence 14:55, 124
His blessings 45:309, 321, 324–327, 332, 352, 46:214, 245, 305, 47:68, 78, 95, 301
His children see **Children of God**
His commandments see **God**—His commands; **God**—His ordinances; **Ten Commandments**
His commands 1:148, 150, 153–155, 161f, 202, 210, 227, 229, 276, 300f, 306, 308, 6:8, 11, 22–24, 26, 39, 96, 109f, 116, 132, 135, 162, 10:16f, 153, 171, 202, 11:452, 480, 482, 492, 498, 500, 507f, 510f, 530–533, 20:234, 236, 261–266, 276, 22:45, 82, 152f, 24:101–103, 127, 145f, 151, 156, 173, 188, 247, 249, 251–256, 259f, 264f, 296, 330, 345, 349, 354–357, 361, 389f, 25:111, 496, 28:31, 33, 47, 29:20, 41–45, 84, 102, 185f, 197, 211f, 215, 31:200, 348, 350, 353, 32:151–157, 180, 200, 210, 215, 33:9f, 128, 35:141, 145, 148f, 164f, 199f, 266f, 345, 36:78, 193f, 196f, 202–205, 221, 223, 37:26, 102n, 128, 134f, 184, 363, 38:157, 161, 163, 229, 39:39, 250, 274, 276, 278, 286, 291, 294, 41:35, 39, 111, 122, 124, 130, 171f, 195, 214, 229, 241, 272, 343, 45:31, 89, 154n, 178, 201f, 290, 293f, 304–307, 347, 353, 46:12, 26, 49, 53, 73, 76f, 98, 108, 114f, 121f, 125, 134, 186–192, 194f, 200, 276–279, 300, 305f, 312, 314, 47:12, 30, 91, 152f, 168–175, 225, 258, 48:66, 297, 302, 331f, 400n, 51:23, 187, 285f, 299, 342, 344, 52:216–220, 234, 244f, 250–252, 261, 264f, 267f
His compassion 22:133
His creation 41:81, 103, 155, 168, 192f, 197, 226, 229, 246, 304f, 359
His creatures 46:12f, 233, 238, 304
His death see **Death of God**
His decrees 46:70, 104, 110, 168
His deeds see **Works of God**
His displeasure 22:119, 123, 125, 490
His divine majesty 2:44, 47, 49, 54, 94, 247, 352, 392, 3:21, 109, 138, 148, 166, 171, 230, 270, 272, 279, 4:30, 96, 115, 118, 144, 245, 267, 285, 340, 5:132, 187, 196, 218, 6:225, 7:231, 319, 8:44, 13:35f, 91, 229, 16:55, 318, 17:17f, 20, 359, 22:6, 12, 14, 103f, 112, 308f, 314, 336, 346, 505–508, 526f, 24:67, 90, 95, 98, 100, 108, 158, 166, 290, 26:29, 31, 39, 41, 97, 119, 182, 254, 257, 33:139, 145f, 183, 47:160, 177, 295
His divine nature 3:194, 4:131, 333, 399, 22:6, 14, 74f, 118, 247, 326f, 352, 492f
His dwelling place 13:6, 36n, 83f
His enemies 1:142f, 14:218f, 41:191, 222, 243, 278, 285, 344, 357, 363, 370
His face 6:126, 130, 142, 144f, 148, 151f, 170–173, 264, 7:103, 11:99f, 252, 343, 13:3n, 195, 16:16, 17:370f, 399
His faces 1:11, 309, 3:166f
His faithfulness 6:99, 109, 112, 37:51, 139f, 143, 305
His fatherly bosom 22:148, 156, 158
His favor 14:232f
His foolishness 16:191, 228, 324, 331, 25:153f
His footprints 1:68
His foreknowledge 5:42, 44, 25:95f, 33:36–41, 42f, 184–193
His fourfold rule 20:169–171
His freedom 33:68f, 189, 37:27, 68, 94, 128f, 138, 140, 296, 306
His gifts see **Gifts of God**
His glory 9:16, 68, 73, 85, 102, 156, 234, 14:316, 331, 17:10, 71, 90f, 93, 162, 172, 217, 289, 313, 19:83, 129, 138, 166, 213, 217f, 230f, 23:7, 172, 232–234, 327, 25:27, 31, 43, 108, 248, 284, 444, 516, 26:3, 17, 20, 29, 33, 37, 58f, 61, 99, 102–104, 131, 218, 224, 227, 231, 312, 334, 355, 424, 428, 29:24, 38, 48f, 33:265, 38:63, 105–107, 109, 136, 252, 41:221, 250, 252, 255, 302, 30, 42:36, 48, 50, 79f, 113
His glory and rule 37:13, 26, 33, 40, 47, 53, 59, 61f, 70–73, 128, 133, 140, 249, 293f, 361, 365
His goodness 1:39, 41, 105, 142–144, 193, 265, 304, 3:4, 12, 103, 241, 9:5, 20f, 139, 194, 10:347, 371, 14:48–50, 53–55, 67, 122, 143, 145, 149, 168, 16:7, 83, 25:175, 42:126f, 131–133, 151f, 155f, 160, 175

His government 6:22, 59f, 92f, 105, 170, 244, 344, 361
His grace see **Grace of God**
His grief 2:49, 17:358
His hand or hands 6:13, 156, 169, 243, 245, 329, 11:533, 16:206, 17:44f, 122, 184f, 42:13, 32, 79, 130, 132, 135, 145f, 184, 46:33, 95, 112, 125, 136, 159, 179, 174, 177
His heart 22:9, 11
His help 42:ix, 11, 35, 42, 46, 49, 73, 174
His hidden judgment 43:247–250
His honor 13:385, 397, 23:5, 19, 21, 172, 219, 233, 42:21, 30–33, 35f, 48, 50, 75, 78f, 81, 88
His image 1:56f, 60–63, 65–69, 84, 86f, 90, 106, 131, 141f, 146, 150, 223f, 330, 337–339, 2:51, 141f, 227, 26:431, 34:138, 140, 177, 194
His immutability see **God—Unchangeable**
His indefinite promise 3:96
His initiative 27:294
His injustice 36:215f
His institutions 46:25, 91, 95f, 118, 243, 248, 256
His invisibility 25:9, 14, 154, 156f
His jealousy 25:483
His judgment 1:67, 76, 178, 268, 274, 297, 302, 325, 351, 2:4, 21, 100, 266, 273, 314, 373, 3:138–140, 173, 233, 236f, 241, 243, 269, 276, 299, 302, 349f, 4:57, 166, 234, 242, 371, 374, 6:55, 62, 211, 214, 7:83, 99, 146, 271, 275, 298, 349, 8:38, 43, 79, 205, 267, 9:33, 102, 140, 183, 10:206, 284, 14:28, 151, 168, 171, 190, 197, 200, 202, 205, 224, 239, 245, 252, 265, 275, 318, 16:331, 20:122, 128, 146, 243, 21:332, 25:401f, 26:6, 10, 65, 113, 120, 131, 140, 149f, 166, 179, 231, 235, 256, 287, 291, 293, 312–314, 317, 322, 324, 341, 348, 381, 387, 403, 439, 443, 445, 459f, 26:6, 10, 65, 72, 113, 120, 131, 140, 149f, 166, 179, 231, 235, 256, 287, 291, 293, 309, 312–314, 317, 324, 341, 348, 381, 387, 403, 439, 443, 445, 459f, 27:8, 15, 19, 26, 206, 217, 281, 33:206–211, 289–292, 36:166, 178, 198, 355, 39:16, 18, 33, 35, 113, 130f, 250, 42:10, 22, 30–32, 35f, 42f, 66, 80, 131, 133f, 145, 154, 156f, 158, 164, 43:247–250, 46:41, 96f, 108, 113, 131, 134, 173f, 47:47, 118, 132, 171, 177
His justice delays 19:58, 153, 178, 180, 209
His kindness 1:67, 180, 245f, 309, 8:12, 35, 53, 63, 158, 182, 234, 265, 326
His kingdom see **Kingdom of God**
His law see **Law of God**
His love 1:186, 300, 2:98, 141, 6:130, 152, 271, 9:69, 85, 12:345, 355, 373, 392, 403, 16:54, 102, 17:88f, 346, 18:33, 19:28, 21:300, 22:355f, 22:355f, 365f, 374, 376, 378f, 25:44, 29:12, 111, 134, 35:295, 42:13, 103, 184
His marvelous works 19:134f
His "masks" 4:5, 7, 61–66, 8:31, 27:43f, see also **Masks**
His mercy see **Mercy of God**
His miracles 45:21, 145, 153, 221, 349, 356
His murderers 41:104, 192, 243f
His Name 11:6, 382, 390, 501, 543f, 42:22, 26–37, 49, 75, 90, 46:24f, 33, 50, 84, 129, 136, 267, 283, 295, 301, 47:15f, 30, 39, 49, 89, 168, 226, 256, 286f, see also **Name of the Lord**
His names 3:80, 82f, 4:31, 6:54, 81, 84, 141, 248–250, 10:230, 13:16, 406, 16:14, 78, 133, 202f, 250, 259, 317, 17:52, 160, 201f, 372, 385f, 38:34, 37, 42, 78, 80, 100, 223, 225, 296, 313, 39:119, 122, 124, 128, 261f, 41:10, 298, 303
His nature and activity 3:137, 7:16, 36, 174, 210, 24:8, 65n, 91, 93, 97f, 104–106, 108, 364f, 30:30, 155, 163, 225, 50:18, 60, 152f, 175f, 184, 189, 209, 215, 225, 266
His oath 47:71, 83, 200, 205, 209, 300
His offices 46:224, 246, 248, 256f
His oracles 9:126, 215, 304f
His ordinances 38:88, 104, 111f, 124, 152, 202, 208, 210f, 225, 41:xv, 51, 151, 155, 171, 177, 197, 222, 335, 46:26, 99, 104, 108, 122, 126, 129, 132, 185f, 226, 237f, 240, 243, 248, 283, 306, 52:199
His pardon 31:48, 98–107
His patience 1:159, 289, 2:8f, 176, 285, 3:40, 156, 12:23f, 29, 25:17
His power 1:41, 49, 3:274–276, 289, 6:59f, 102f, 136, 11:13, 13:92, 266, 291, 14:52f, 82, 85, 122, 126, 209, 239, 241, 17:15, 26f, 42, 45, 87, 124f, 130, 306, 364f, 21:339f, 25:392f, 29:185, 188, 214, 38:16, 23, 32, 42, 48f, 60, 66–68, 75, 89, 104, 170, 177, 189, 262, 264, 270, 41:149, 168, 171, 212, 45:204, 207, 303

His power and presence 49:63, 101f, 114, 141, 262f, 306f
His presence 6:41, 81, 83, 99, 271, 311, 11:260, 17:42, 45, 61, 37:xix, 6, 57–64, 68, 72
His promises 2:ix, 266, 18:284, 37:68, 71, 86n, 134, 156, 323, 325, 362, 42:77, 85, 87, 89f, 109f, 174, 186, 46:33, 133, 173, 233, 47:66–82, 112, 185f, 204, 209, 231, 239–241
His promises to Abraham 17:40, 358f
His proper work 8:5n, 13:79, 16:233f, 21:341, 26:38n, 314, 44:77, 51:18f
His punishments 14:141, 157, 239, 255, 46:21, 68, 110, 116, 121, 171, 178, 198
His right hand 10:111, 420, 444f, 13:82, 15:294f, 29:120, 41:110, 119
His righteousness see **Righteousness of God**
His rod 8:73
His rule 6:22, 59f, 92f, 105, 170, 244, 344, 361
His self-revelation 37:xvii–xx, 66, 88, 135
His servants 46:52, 68, 73, 114, 221, 225, 246
His silence 3:337, 6:350f, 357, 360, 384, 386, 405, 47:75, 97, 138
His Spirit see **Holy Spirit**
His steadfast love 14:24, 28, 50f, 55, 105, 142, 146, 154, 166, 201, 203, 241, 254f, 272, 275, 320, 16:150, 169, 18:33
His strange work see **Alien work of God**
His temple 38:174, 176, 183
His truthfulness 25:26, 40f, 120f, 194–199, 201f, 205f, 208f, 213, 284, 378
His twofold will 2:44
His universal rule 20:169–173, 177, 323
His unsearchable understanding 17:19, 30
His vengeance 16:4, 12, 24, 213, 302, 323, 17:75f, 83, 147, 305, 308, 334, 353, 45:xiii, 81, 87, 46:19f, 25, 107f, 113, see also **Wrath of God**
His ways 17:256f
His will see **Will of God**
His wisdom see **Wisdom of God**
His Word see **Word (of God), The**
His words 1:21f, 47:74, 199, 246, 287
His work 51:18f
His works see **Works of God**
His wrath see **Wrath of God**
Honoring Him 9:105, 41:140, 142, 237, 287, 301
Husbandman 28:176f, 182
Ignorance of 1:114, 143, 166
In our midst 20:200–202
In the "relative sense" 3:122
Incomprehensible 38:22, 233, 306
Infinite 30:268, 38:245, 262, 306
Infinite and eternal 17:29, 36f, 163f
Invisible 38:266, 275
Judge of all 1:114, 142, 252, 274, 284, 16:46, 105, 30:85, 95, 45:107, 269f, 274, 306, 364, 46:41, 53, 74, 97, 114, 282
Judges differently from men 2:6
Justification of His acts 25:203–206
Justifier and Redeemer 12:312, 320–322, 338
Keeps bloody plans secret 6:357, 360, 384, 386, 405
Known in Christ 16:55, 318, 26:29, 30:223, 37:56, 61, 41:101–104, 106, 111
Known in His Word 12:312, 352
Let Him be God 12:187, 42:105
Liar 36:86, 355
Like a husband 17:236
Like a mother 17:16, 131, 139, 183f, 410, 24:411
Like a mother hen 52:95f
Like a potter 17:372, 25:84
Lord 6:61, 163, 169, 248, 372, 18:160, 186, 41:67, 177, 185, 187f, 286, 310, 316–319, 327, 329f, 332, 334–336, 341, 343f, 353, 355, 364, 370, 376, see also **Trinity**
Lord of body and soul 16:55, 141
Lord of hosts 20:8, 29, 134, 163, 193f, 288, 295
Loves reality and truth 14:30, 170
Loving Him 3:321, 41:17f, 146, 149, 42:78, 103, 128, 130, 175
Majesty concealed in Christ 22:504
Makes and overthrows rulers 13:67–70
May withdraw 10:40f
Meaning of being God 11:398, 403, 410f, 425
Merciful and faithful 25:194f, 201, 208f
Must die 35:84
Naked deity to be avoided 11:209f, 12:312, 16:55
Negative essence 25:383
No respecter of persons 3:64, 129, 4:33, 55, 64, 25:125, 127f, 182
Not a peddler 4:398
Nourisher and sustainer 5:197
Omnipotent 1:25, 3:137, 260, 311, 3:212, 6:102, 263, 18:155, 186, 286, 370, 19:44f, 68f, 33:175–184, 189f, 242, 37:xix, 6, 20, 47f, 52, 57–66, 69, 71, 75, 98, 132f, 139f, 144, 207–209, 217, 224–227, 277f, 362, 45:151, 213
Omnipresent 2:130, 185, 33:45f, 37:6,

57–64, 68, 71, 156, 214, 216, 220–222, 227f, 276, 54:32
One in essence 1:12, 20:341
Our Father 11:16f, 15:276f, 280, 282, 286, 293, 303–309, 311, 316, 16:105, 118, 121, 215, 248, 20:22, 32, 21:145–147, 200f, 230, 24:131, 218, 28:124f, 139–141, 29:85, 114, 133, 37:25, 55f, 61f, 64, 66, 69, 74, 142n, 143n, 222, 361, 365f, 38:29, 43f, 50n, 58, 77, 85, 184, 187, 198, 203, 224, 253f, 256–258, 262n, 267, 294n, 296, 307, 309, 319, 41:10, 13, 82, 98, 103, 106, 109, 118, 129f, 149, 172, 226, 256, 271, 302, 313, 315, 318–320, 330, 355, 42:13, 19–26, 28, 37, 51, 57, 86, 88, 113, 130, 138, 46:51, 135, 199, 235, 47:278–280, 285–287, 51:162f, 216, 52:52, 83, 87, 175
Our Guardian and Companion 20:14, 42, 131
Our Helper 11:492, 19:79, 96, 115, 136, 228, 46:34, 130, 191, 266, 47:13, 16, 74, 91, 107, 112, 244
Our Savior 7:231, 314, 348, 28:261f, 325f, 348
Our Shepherd 17:16, 181, 290
Ours through the Word and faith 13:36, 70, 191
Owner of all things 37:42, 58, 62, 65, 358
Philosophical view 4:145
Plays games with us 2:369, 4:115f, 131, 326, 5:353, 6:130f, 356, 376, 381, 7:176, 225f, 8:15
Pleasing Him 6:8–10, 73f, 110, 114, 123, 128, 148, 180, 347, 365, 370, 46:55, 84, 132, 141, 172, 241, 244, 246, 316
Plurality of Persons in Godhead 2:228, 3:276, 296f, 359, 7:109, 167, 283, 294, 8:12, 165, 168, 325, 10:60, 195, 322
Praising Him 6:86, 112, 114, 234, 237, 42:26, 36, 49, 70, 78, 105, 46:78, 148, 294, 51:142, 164, 173, 333
Prime Mover 1:42
Protector of His own 6:364, 375, 16:4, 81, 112, 252, 266, 291, 301, 316, 318, 343
Providence 2:76, 93, 8:28, 328, 9:94f, 39:17, 101, 205, 54:475
Redeemer 44:xiii
Repents 11:368
Requires silence 19:131, 225
Revealed in His Word 3:139, 7:336
Reveals Himself 5:44–46, 48, 50
Reveals self in nature 1:11
Scatters the proud 25:198, 214, 218, 404
Seems to sleep 9:59
Serving Him 12:71–73, 80f, 87, 13:72, 292f, 21:178f, 189, 269, 310, 312, 350, 23:22, 25–29, 34, 36, 25:457f, 36:214, 41:40f, 124, 157f, 160f, 165, 216, 222, 225, 250f, 327, 338f, 364, 45:144, 153f, 170, 172, 245, 306f, 349, 46:xiv, 81, 98, 129f, 133, 151, 163, 166, 178, 222, 227f, 231, 233, 236, 243f, 252f, 256, 51:246, 260–265, 327, 343, 347, 52:91f, 125, 138f, 218, 244, 246, 260, 54:84
Sets things straight 15:56f, 84f, 92, 119
Shows only His back 3:72, 4:324, 7:103, 105
Shows only His "back parts" 6:151, 185, 8:30
Sole Ruler and Judge 14:52, 65, 222, 245, 287, 328, 344
Sometimes absent 17:374
Source of good and evil 10:186, 13:35, 96, 25:160–163
Speaks 6:8, 224, 232, 257, 264
Speaks in Christ through the Word 10:285, 293f
Suffers with His own 17:358
Sun and Shield 11:150
Supreme Majesty 2:45
Sustainer, not Destroyer 3:82f
Takes care of us 6:9, 110, 123, 233, 359
Takes us in His lap 3:139
Teaches us 17:167, 243f
Tempting Him see **Tempting God**
The best marriage counselor 4:243
The crucified One 14:105
The rod of His anger 46:68, 70, 158f, 162, 170, 174, 178, 184
The uncovered God 3:276
Theological doctrines 8:59, 79, 130, 292
To be All in All 28:141–144, 146, 172
To be feared 46:21, 64, 80, 123, 125, 130, 133, 218, 303, 309
To be honored 46:132f, 148, 186, 228, 241
Triune see **Trinity, Doctrine of the**
Trusting Him 1:167, 170–172, 45:253, 260, 280f, 328–330, 51:138–141, 144–146, 156
Truth in 31:144, 350f
Two ways to know Him 4:132
Unchangeable 1:304, 17:37, 95, 106, 25:11, 41, 72, 102, 219, 432, 33:37–44, 37:62, 66, 38:253, 255f, 275
Unveiled 2:47
Wall of fire 20:26f, 181, 187f
Wants to be turned 11:40, 158, 164
Wonderful in His saints 25:246, 258, 277, 379

Works all in all 33:175f, 210
Works all things for good 25:73, 82f, 319, 360, 371, 373, 388f, 426, 468
Works inwardly 25:388f
Works of His right hand 14:88f
Works through the Word 1:11, 4:5
Worshiped by faith 16:10, 71, 109, 167, 238, 245, 317

God, His wrath—see **Wrath of God**

God, Son of—see **Son of God**

God, To have a—13:6n, 44:40

God of Abraham, Isaac, and Jacob—47:72, 86, 132

God the Father—1:9, 12, 17–19, 50, 57–60, 65, 128, 134, 144, 152, 157, 180, 189, 199, 223, 348, 351, 22:5f, 15, 27, 118

God the Son—22:15f, 26, 30, 37, 346, 352

God's Will—see **Will of God**

God's Word—see **Word (of God), The**

Goddesses—3:83

Godfathers—see **Godparents**

Godfrey of Trani—31:149

Godhead, The—37:56, 59–63, 103, 210, 212, 220f, 228–230, 233, 297f, 363, 38:xx, 84, 251n, 252, 257, 306f, 309f

Godless, The—5:7, 10–12, 74, 77, 171, 183, 236f, 239f, 272, 278, 284, 9:41, 55f, 58f, 74, 80, 84, 88, 102–104, 170, 190, 204, 268, 274, 13:179f, 220, 397, 16:22, 24, 22:86, 29:165, 171, 176, 182, 189, 35:210, 220f, 266, 268, 330, see also **Ungodly persons**

Godlessness—3:82, 5:160, 200, 367f, 370, 7:11, 121, 199, 297, 299, 348, 349, 9:22, 53, 55, 59, 75, 79, 84, 88, 102, 104, 135, 146, 149, 165, 198, 204, 206, 211f, 244f, 273, 297, 27:154, 199, 257, 260, 293, 303, 327f, 342, 358, 30:246, 248

Godliness—2:6, 12, 16, 32, 59–62, 69, 78, 170, 192f, 205, 210, 213, 251, 286, 325, 334, 349, 356, 372f, 382, 399, 3:98, 117f, 128, 170, 182, 203, 258, 261, 269, 323, 357, 4:22, 79, 88, 133, 178, 182, 213, 240, 276f, 284, 287, 295, 323, 326f, 329, 346, 382, 384, 386f, 390f, 398, 400, 404, 408, 5:6, 39, 41, 51f, 58, 80, 86, 163, 176, 178, 192, 207, 221, 233, 284f, 326, 331, 351, 358, 373, 375, 6:63, 163, 347, 7:57f, 63, 73f, 77, 88, 91f, 103, 117, 119, 167, 200, 230, 255, 318, 334, 348, 8:6, 56f, 59, 61f, 146, 180, 194, 9:3, 6, 26, 234, 273f, 294, 297, 11:444f, 13:404, 16:9, 18, 79, 119n, 120, 137, 160, 245, 247, 23:349, 376, 26:64, 91, 152, 196, 201, 443, 452f, 27:47, 53, 71, 99, 123, 372, 408, 28:321–324, 347, 364f, 369f, 372, 29:9–11, 13, 65, 214, 30:126, 153, 157, 255, 322, 324

Godly persons—2:8, 25, 27, 29–31, 33, 44, 50, 61f, 66, 82, 104, 140, 153, 154, 166, 169f, 172, 176f, 180, 192, 196–198, 204, 213, 218–223, 226, 229f, 235f, 239, 289, 296, 304, 307, 309f, 319f, 332, 347, 350f, 360, 369, 378, 380, 383, 3:8, 11, 36, 40, 63, 71, 77, 118, 129, 135, 140, 159, 179, 185, 189, 197, 221, 228–230, 236, 241, 244f, 250, 269–271, 292, 294, 307, 320, 341, 345, 347, 4:73f, 78f, 88, 101, 104, 106, 120f, 131, 142, 156, 175, 177, 184, 195f, 219, 222, 234, 259, 261–263, 267, 269, 272, 279, 310, 316, 326, 340, 342f, 355f, 363, 368, 379, 385, 407–409, 5:10, 12, 27, 47f, 56f, 62, 77, 84, 121, 138, 147, 171, 189, 200, 203, 206, 236f, 240, 265, 341, 6:74, 89, 103, 124, 217, 311, 7:11, 57, 64, 68, 73, 80, 83, 89, 103, 119, 133f, 143, 205, 226, 232, 285, 287, 292–294, 296–298, 303, 311, 316, 337f, 8:8–10, 12f, 15, 34, 46, 83, 89f, 115, 118, 135f, 177, 187, 189, 191f, 200, 202, 226, 231, 249, 252, 255, 299f, 315f, 330, 9:53, 179, 242, 268, 274, 13:179, 14:289–292, 297, 317, 16:14, 32, 57, 62, 64, 79f, 83, 91, 102, 108, 110, 120f, 129, 138, 144, 150, 152f, 162f, 173, 185, 189, 194, 197f, 202, 206–209, 213f, 216f, 223, 233–236, 241, 249f, 258, 261, 288f, 316, 17:29, 40, 74, 92, 94, 187, 242, 245, 248, 255, 287f, 300, 342, 368f, 384, 18:269, 20:134f, 146f, 333, 23:25, 31, 113, 219, 313, 24:73, 25:214, 221, 239, 246, 258f, 263, 265, 272, 275, 292, 313, 336, 26:24, 133, 181, 183, 235, 246, 450, 455, 27:40, 44, 46, 49, 51, 77, 80, 82, 99, 102, 29:11f, 233, 30:233, 244, 38:28, 42, 86, 162, 174, 202, 225

Godparents—34:54, 35:31, 45:8, 15, 21, 24, 145, 46:137, 262, 53:95–103, 108f

Gods—6:35, 49, 58, 60, 229f, 237, 11:111, 115, 13:43f, 91, 25:83, 127, 157f

Gods, Strange—41:139, 342

Gods of the pagans—34:213

Goede, Henning—3:215n, 13:158, 54:140, 246, 269

Goetz, Walter, and Paul Joachimsen, eds.—*Das Zeitalter der religiösen Umwälzung: Reformation und Gegenreformation*, Berlin, 1930 34:6n

Goetze, Alfred—36:265n
Gog—2:188, 10:411
Gog and Magog—35:177, 283, 407, 409, 46:202, 47:251, 49:217, 289n
Gogarten, Friedrich—51:xin, xix
Gold—1:97, 100, 222, 290, 2:195, 268, 279, 317, 324, 329–331, 334, 347f, 352, 395, 3:186, 190, 199, 211, 4:92, 103, 152, 201f, 211, 229, 260, 275f, 284, 287, 296, 364, 380f, 397, 6:49, 238–240, 7:40, 97, 184f, 197, 195, 231, 297, 8:123, 146, 230, 238, 245, 256, 280, 10:104, 259, 16:34, 61, 24:83f, 90, 155, 177, 359, 26:32, 95f, 177, 393, 27:51, 55, 61, 122, 171, 336, 407, 30:17, 36, 42, 90, 101, 126, 182, 186, 250, 52:278f
Gold and silver—45:234, 246n, 247, 342, see also **Metals, Precious**
Golden Bull—8:178n, 49:397n
Golden calves—5:241, 11:40f, 16:318, 23:190, 24:327, 26:258, 35:269, 272, 36:87, 219, 222, 37:22n
Golden Legend—see **Jacobus de Voragine**
Golden Meadow—1:78n, 7:299
Golden rose—31:xvii, 34:332, 334, 48:97n, 101n, 54:195
Golden Rule—21:235–237, 25:180, 183, 475, 42:68
Golden text—16:258
Golden Year—34:16, 99
Goldhahn, Matthew (Aurogallus)—35:108, 188, 206, 49:5
Goldschmidt—see **Düring, Christian**
Goldsmiths—13:401, 17:37f
Goldstein, Kilian—50:226, 54:364
Goliath—4:106, 390, 5:131, 254, 8:236, 9:202, 10:86, 11:546f, 13:156, 15:5, 20:295, 327, 26:263, 35:358, 37:63, 42:151
Gomer—2:187f
Gomorrah—1:135, 341, 2:342, 383, 388, 3:x, 131, 7:232, 9:5, 273, 297, 11:83, 16:330, 18:343, 22:36, 186, 390, 419, 423, 425, 25:86, 481, 26:24, 136, 27:48, 30:178f
Gonorrhea—2:311
Good Friday—22:49, 34:56, 42:xiv, 5, 12
Good Samaritan—25:260, 340, 433, 507, 26:260, 27:364, 30:134
Good conquers evil—25:466f, see also **Good works**
Good fortune—24:11, 80, 201, 420
Good people—11:13, 458–460, 495
Good things—11:297, 512, 515
Good works—2:119, 159, 165, 184, 268, 354, 3:24, 85f, 169, 171, 173, 185, 190, 193, 196f, 200, 203f, 217, 239, 329, 335, 347, 349, 364f, 4:74, 78, 85, 88f, 103, 105, 107, 120f, 123f, 132, 142, 149, 168f, 209, 249f, 264, 279, 284f, 336, 404, 5:70, 232, 258, 278, 6:39, 67, 7:28, 58, 89, 155, 186, 234, 286, 314, 356, 8:49, 59, 82, 167, 170, 176, 267, 9:140, 184, 237, 10:160f, 12:281, 385, 394, 409, 13:17f, 25f, 88, 183, 14:26, 28, 59, 73, 82, 85, 132, 148–150, 167, 170, 174, 191, 194, 197f, 260, 289, 292, 303, 318, 327, 15:74, 77, 107, 135, 147, 169, 172, 174, 236f, 242, 16:15, 80, 304, 319, 334, 16:54, 185, 334, 17:18, 245, 263, 271, 303, 18:221, 401, 19:23, 25, 86f, 97, 20:47, 165f, 265, 300, 321, 21:15f, 65, 136f, 261f, 291, 305, 22:51, 134, 167f, 271, 275–282, 285, 287f, 302, 320, 334f, 337, 343, 349, 352, 366–368, 370, 374, 391, 393f, 425f, 430, 451, 454, 456, 461, 487, 501, 23:15–20, 25–27, 33, 36, 57–60, 62, 65–68, 70–73, 75f, 82, 85–87, 91, 98, 105f, 108–113, 117, 126–128, 134–137, 139f, 142, 145f, 151, 154, 159, 169–173, 176f, 179, 181f, 184f, 213, 234f, 237f, 242, 246f, 251, 263, 268f, 271f, 278, 286, 324, 326, 328, 331, 335, 348, 351, 355, 360, 366, 380, 402, 413, 24:36, 42f, 52–54, 58, 64, 88, 121, 127, 167, 210, 217–219, 223f, 232, 241, 264, 291, 296, 307, 315, 321, 328–331, 340f, 344, 348, 406, 25:37, 59, 104, 108, 112, 177, 185–187, 218, 220f, 227, 235f, 244f, 246, 263, 276f, 337f, 354, 374f, 385, 407, 409, 420, 466, 488, 497, 26:7f, 11, 36, 38, 70, 84, 124–128, 130f, 133, 136f, 140, 145, 148f, 153f, 161, 169, 175, 181f, 203, 210, 214f, 220, 230f, 234, 241f, 246, 254, 260, 271, 294, 310, 328, 334f, 363, 372, 377, 404, 443, 449, 454, 27:11, 14, 17, 30, 49, 52–56, 62f, 73, 76–78, 88, 127–129, 168, 188, 221, 247f, 293, 313, 328, 347, 375, 388, 400f, 28:114, 252, 310, 380, 30:3, 14f, 32–34, 51, 61, 80, 82, 84, 93, 117f, 131, 149, 153, 155, 158, 160, 167, 174, 190, 219, 230f, 238, 240, 274, 287, 294, 313, 32:xi, 7, 36, 38, 44, 54f, 64, 76–79, 83–87, 91, 94f, 136, 154–156, 160–217, 225f, 234f, 253f, 34:21, 53, 90, 111, 348, 34:90f, 101, 161, 165, 35:12, 17, 21, 60, 67n, 79, 94, 111, 120, 346, 369, 373, 380, 385f, 392, 36:30, 35, 38f, 42, 47–57, 59, 62, 64f, 67, 73–78,

80, 83–85, 87f, 90, 94, 169f, 180f, 187, 202f, 219, 221–223, 241, 259f, 289, 313, 327, 347, 37:248f, 365, 368, 38:95, 115f, 126, 131, 156, 207, 218, 313, 39:33, 35, 185, 262, 276, 285, 287, 40:280, 287, 41:18, 71f, 85f, 92, 111–113, 121–125, 128, 139, 147, 271, 285, 296, 310, 342, 360, 41:18, 71n, 72, 85f, 92, 111–113, 121–125, 128, 136, 139, 147, 271, 285, 296, 310, 342, 360, 42:12, 30, 36, 44, 62, 72, 102, 44:21–114, 202–276, 298f, 301–303, 45:88, 98, 117, 245, 319, 46:130, 135, 178, 47:52f, 101f, 51:26, 47, 58, 60, 62–66, 105, 108, 110, 112, 115, 117, 127, 185, 191, 198f, 217, 226, 372

Follow faith 25:235

Fruit of God's grace 25:385

Rooted in grace 25:104

Good, The—25:73, 106–108, 130, 267, 319, 360, 371, 373, 426, 468, 46:66, 70, 90, 95

Goodness—11:313, 347, 410f, 458–460, 462, 513, 21:263, 310f, 25:168f, 175, 518f, 27:368, 373, 376, 395, 29:78f, 111, 134

In Christ, not self 25:267f

Goods—22:87f, 23:6, 8–10, 35, 40, 66, 145, 202, 212, 262, 277, 290, 299, 322, 330–332, 334, 344, 392, 395, 397, 400, 402f, 24:22, 24f, 29, 31, 37, 73, 79, 82–84, 112, 118f, 145f, 152, 154, 163–165, 180, 210, 215, 251, 263, 266, 271, 280, 284, 322, 389, 399, 51:6–13

Goodwill (or Good will)—2:302, 392, 395, 6:159–161, 164, 166f, 170, 174, 269, 25:88, 126

Görlitz—2:202n, 12:203

Görlitz, Martin—50:55n

Goshen—7:346, 8:48, 91, 95–97, 99, 101, 108f, 116

Goslar—49:16, 187

Gospel, The—1:12, 33, 42, 64f, 95, 111, 113, 143, 146f, 150f, 161, 170, 178, 180, 192, 207, 211, 214, 217–219, 223f, 234, 236, 262, 264, 266, 288, 323, 336, 2:24, 36, 38, 40, 48, 58, 67, 78, 84, 137, 161, 163, 177, 179, 181, 184, 185f, 190, 193, 215, 225, 250, 253, 260, 271, 275f, 285, 288, 312, 315, 327, 338, 361, 378, 398, 3:9, 66, 76f, 85, 95, 97, 121, 124f, 129, 131, 133, 167f, 189, 221, 223f, 232, 237, 263, 265, 272f, 275, 281, 290, 294, 296f, 299, 340–342, 346, 348, 363, 4:5, 30, 32, 45, 49f, 52, 54, 56, 61, 63, 77, 79, 101, 116, 121, 125, 127, 130, 159, 201f, 208, 214, 221f, 231, 240, 261, 273, 311, 348, 380, 392, 401–405, 5:10–12, 17, 35, 39, 43, 45, 47, 49, 56, 62, 74, 78, 88, 96, 115, 125, 137, 141, 156–158, 171, 186, 188, 192f, 228f, 242, 245f, 256, 261, 342, 348, 360, 6:10, 26, 40, 49, 148, 155, 158, 165, 404, 7:62–65, 68, 92, 97, 125, 134, 154, 200, 296f, 299, 303, 333, 344, 8:30, 36, 45, 62, 76, 79, 81, 125, 134, 137, 144, 146, 158, 180–182, 186–188, 202, 205, 223, 226, 229f, 235, 238, 243–246, 249, 254, 258, 263f, 271, 284, 306, 309, 312–315, 325, 9:4–6, 8, 26f, 43, 58n, 64, 94, 97, 109, 118, 130, 136f, 141, 150f, 157f, 168, 176, 178–180, 182, 187f, 194, 198, 206, 219–221, 226, 236, 242–245, 250, 278, 294, 310f, 10:30, 35–37, 70, 93, 95, 102f, 113f, 216, 401, 403, 11:4, 6, 50, 53, 60, 286–288, 291, 319f, 365, 414, 421, 441, 448, 460, 472, 498, 515, 12:6, 8, 13, 17, 19–21, 45, 60, 62f, 68, 71, 104, 106, 108f, 110, 115f, 129, 134, 136, 139f, 142f, 155f, 170, 183, 205, 217, 224f, 230, 235, 251f, 257f, 262, 266, 270, 280, 286, 292, 294f, 315, 326, 334, 340, 356, 363, 367, 384, 13:5f, 8–14, 21, 25, 35, 43, 202, 229, 249f, 266, 270, 274–276, 290f, 324f, 329, 380f, 408, 14:x, 8f, 13, 18, 20, 23f, 27, 35, 56, 80, 90, 97, 100, 111, 130–132, 140, 158, 183f, 209, 227, 236, 241, 243, 251, 258f, 263, 268, 270, 273, 329, 334n, 335–337, 339, 346, 15:65f, 74, 124, 185, 201f, 260, 262, 328, 348f, 16:27–30, 33f, 38, 60, 77, 95, 99, 106, 109, 122, 124, 126, 128–130, 137, 164, 167f, 186, 223–226, 234f, 243, 248, 250, 257, 275f, 295, 301–303, 310, 326f, 17:3f, 8f, 10–12, 15, 29, 43, 45f, 62, 72f, 80, 136, 171f, 181, 207, 210, 229, 235, 250, 292, 311, 313f, 316, 321f, 324f, 338, 18:8, 11, 16–18, 32, 61f, 74, 76, 111f, 114–119, 122f, 166, 189, 201–203, 228f, 238f, 241f, 245f, 251, 253–255, 275f, 295f, 356, 363, 382f, 408, 19:98, 132, 181, 193, 198, 203, 212, 217, 20:10, 28, 33, 51, 54, 57, 70, 93, 97f, 100, 103f, 106, 109, 119f, 122f, 126–128, 150f, 157, 182, 199, 291, 297f, 315f, 338, 21:10, 31, 51f, 70, 108, 177, 211, 225, 227, 252, 280, 338, 353f, 23:ix, 5–8, 10–12, 15, 19f, 29f, 39f, 50f, 74, 142, 151f, 157–159, 187f, 191f, 204, 206, 209, 215, 223f, 226, 232, 237f, 244, 247, 249,

257f, 261f, 269–272, 274, 277f, 280, 284–292, 296, 299, 304, 306, 310, 317, 319f, 324–327, 329f, 334–336, 341, 349, 355–357, 360, 363f, 370, 372, 374, 378–380, 386–390, 392f, 397–399, 402, 407f, 416, 418–422, 24:ix, 12, 14f, 23, 26, 30, 47, 67, 69, 79, 86, 102, 119f, 122, 127, 130, 133, 137, 140, 145, 148–151, 154–156, 169–174, 185f, 188, 197, 201, 204, 207, 209, 216, 220f, 226f, 250, 252, 263, 265f, 268, 272–275, 285, 287f, 293f, 312, 314–316, 318f, 324, 327, 329, 334, 336, 339f, 350, 352, 356–358, 268f, 383f, 389, 394–396, 400, 402f, 409, 411, 418, 25:xif, 4–9, 54, 91f, 123, 127, 131, 140, 144–146, 149f, 326f, 414, 416, 418, 521, 523, 26:13f, 66, 77, 82, 87, 102, 104, 116, 187, 208f, 313, 315, 343, 27:3, 8–10, 13, 18, 33, 35, 42–44, 47–50, 54, 62n, 82, 85, 89f, 92, 94, 99–102, 105, 107f, 116, 118f, 122–124, 126, 130, 140–142, 153, 156, 158, 162, 165, 167, 175–179, 182–184, 186–188, 190f, 193–196, 200, 204, 207–211, 214f, 217, 230, 241, 249, 263, 298f, 303, 310, 317f, 338, 340f, 344, 355, 366, 375f, 397, 28:64–67, 74f, 82, 93f, 96, 108, 129–131, 193, 206, 238, 268, 308, 29:5, 7–9, 19f, 23, 31, 36f, 39, 59, 65–67, 79, 81, 94–96, 99, 101f, 105, 109, 118f, 123f, 130, 132, 134, 142f, 145, 153, 165, 188, 192, 197, 203, 239, 30:3–5, 8, 10, 12, 17–19, 21f, 25, 28f, 31f, 38f, 41, 44–46, 48, 50, 52, 54, 61, 76, 78, 82, 87, 94, 98, 109, 114f, 117, 121, 124, 126, 130, 134f, 144, 151, 154, 158, 160, 163f, 165f, 169f, 173, 175, 179, 190f, 193, 204f, 210, 212, 221n, 229, 234, 239, 241f, 252f, 257, 259, 270, 272, 274, 280f, 283, 295, 308f, 315, 317, 321, 31:175f, 180f, 197, 210, 230, 241, 243, 391, 394, 32:136, 177, 226–229, 257f, 33:136, 34:16, 29, 53, 35:106, 115, 117f, 123, 162, 171f, 248, 331, 358n, 359–361, 379, 383, 387, 36:xii, 48, 51, 55f, 71–73, 86, 91, 100, 103, 107, 111, 115f, 118, 131, 153, 158, 171f, 177, 183, 185f, 190, 198, 201f, 204, 211, 214, 225, 229, 237, 245–256, 265, 279f, 288, 296, 298f, 303–305, 339, 347, 351, 355, 37:xif, xvif, 5, 13, 19, 26f, 32f, 126, 138n, 140, 143, 153, 163f, 255, 325, 335, 366–369, 38:ix–xi, xx, 9, 86f, 98f, 112, 120f, 124, 141, 161, 166, 177, 182, 189–192, 190, 194, 198, 200, 204, 211f, 222, 224, 230–232, 258, 261n, 264, 290, 307, 39:xvi, 75, 82, 86f, 95, 129, 133, 155, 169f, 173, 184, 194, 251, 285, 295, 298, 305, 40:42f, 41:68, 73, 76, 88f, 105, 155, 168, 170, 178, 190, 207, 248, 252, 315f, 345, 347–349, 352–354, 358, 42:xivf, 56, 64n, 79, 91, 44:111f, 256–258, 45:xiiif, 13, 21, 24, 46, 62, 67f, 70–72, 77f, 88f, 91f, 94–96, 110, 113, 136f, 142f, 147, 149, 154, 158, 169–172, 199, 204, 219, 224, 228, 239, 241, 245, 249, 258, 260, 264, 273, 276–278, 292, 307, 317, 332, 336, 348f, 351, 358–361, 365, 373, 386, 388, 393, 46:xi, xiii, 8, 9n, 10, 12, 18n, 19, 20n, 21–23, 25f, 28, 30f, 33, 35–37, 39–41, 47n, 48–52, 64, 70, 78f, 81, 82n, 104f, 115, 130, 135f, 145, 161f, 166, 169, 172, 175, 177, 180, 185, 192, 195, 197, 199, 204, 216, 222, 228f, 232f, 235f, 254f, 261, 265f, 294, 306, 308f, 315, 47.7, 11, 35, 50, 52f, 101 104, 220, 48:12, 14, 35, 62, 66, 153, 189, 286, 328, 335f, 367, 390, 50:76f, 51:18, 20, 111–115, 126, 129, 165, 175f, 198, 207, 242, 52:4f, 8f, 11, 14, 16, 18–20, 22, 24f, 39, 41, 46, 55, 65, 67–69, 73, 78, 88, 102, 119, 197, 205, 207f, 240f, 274, 54:42, 106, 111, 127, 147, 157, 275f, 344, 402, 404, 427, see also **Law and Gospel**

And Christ 52:23, 66, 98, 104

Called Light 1:223, 249, 303, 332

Definition 25:148, 153–156

God's womb 52:79

Has reached all nations 20:24, 63, 87, 89, 113, 182, 247

Its power 25:149

Its proper office 51:20

Its simplicity 52:56, 62, 66, 148

Gospel, Paul's—25:20, 125, 131, 149

Gospel in Isaiah—6:x

Gospels (liturgical)—36:51, 116, 53:xvii, 13, 21, 24f, 28, 56, 58–60, 63, 68, 74–78, 86–90, 98f, 106

Gospels, The—7:24, 216, 242, 280n, 336, 12:208, 246, 30:4, 34:66, 35:116–124, 36:24, 140

Their unity 35:357–360

Gospels, The four—46:196

Gospels, Synoptic—2:337n, 30:4

Gospels and Epistles (liturgical)—12:199f, 51:viif, xiv, 122, 221, 371n, see also **Epistles (liturgical)**; **Gospels (liturgical)**

Gossip—21:41f

Gotha—5:242, 8:ix, 38:11, 94, 46:210,

48:202n, 224, 227n, 50:166n, 168n, 169n, 170n, 178, 54:374, 383
Augustinian Monastery 48:16
Gotha-Torgau, League of—13:xi, 49:155
Goths—1:7, 2:190f, 5:11, 12:33, 13:258, 282, 14:74, 118, 18:200, 281, 23:388, 28:130, 41:356, 372, 44:208n, 46:107, 110, 236
Göttingen—50:252n
Götzel, Wolfgang—50:98
Gout—1:305
Government—1:103–105, 109, 115, 173, 212, 214, 246, 260f, 285, 294, 305f, 317, 319, 2:32, 35f, 38, 42, 79, 84, 141f, 165, 172, 175, 197, 212, 216, 219, 226f, 258, 261, 263, 272, 275, 292, 297, 301, 312, 314, 317, 319, 331, 339, 343, 353, 356, 366f, 369, 382, 3:36, 113, 122, 130f, 143, 150, 226f, 233, 255f, 259, 271, 279–281, 313, 325, 328, 4:7, 23, 35, 42, 76, 78–85, 87f, 105, 109, 164f, 179, 202, 259, 264, 278, 281f, 286, 290, 335f, 347, 354, 362, 365f, 380, 386f, 392, 5:4–6, 15, 31, 39f, 71, 80, 104, 111f, 114–116, 122–124, 139, 141, 155, 177, 183f, 201f, 204, 207, 238–240, 267, 272, 308, 326, 333, 6:9, 52, 89f, 93, 7:66, 71, 109, 144f, 158, 160, 180, 183f, 186, 188, 190–193, 195f, 201, 204–207, 227, 254f, 308, 312, 338, 349, 355, 364, 9:7, 14, 17–19, 80f, 129, 139, 144, 161, 174, 176, 182, 186, 193, 195f, 230f, 242, 12:57, 67, 74, 104, 230, 240–242, 279, 349f, 13:43–45, 51f, 72, 140, 148, 193, 195, 197–199, 201f, 204, 207, 212f, 216, 238, 250, 267f, 287, 361, 370, 14:14f, 20, 22, 24, 51–54, 56, 68f, 75f, 86, 113f, 184, 245, 262f, 276f, 15:5, 8, 24, 27, 43, 56f, 64f, 119, 123f, 130f, 136f, 143, 158f, 167–169, 196, 205, 225f, 245, 248, 16:22, 26, 43, 163, 169, 180f, 184, 186, 198, 200, 217, 219, 221, 273f, 278, 289, 17:66, 79, 143, 167, 170, 368, 19:101, 162, 20:79, 171f, 215, 265, 277, 21:25, 40–43, 76, 79f, 93f, 96, 99f, 106, 107n, 108f, 113–115, 120, 168–170, 184, 231, 254, 276f, 337, 22:96, 122, 132, 157, 168, 221f, 224f, 237, 314, 341, 372, 397, 405, 410f, 417f, 436, 446, 469, 509, 513, 524, 23:25, 57f, 62f, 65f, 134, 203, 205, 213, 220, 222, 226, 238, 247f, 310, 312f, 321f, 336, 345, 370, 385, 395, 397, 407, 412, 24:37, 70, 81, 133, 154, 180, 216, 228, 303, 308, 310f, 313, 317, 337f, 345, 351, 360, 366, 377, 25:109f, 468–471, 473, 26:48, 116n, 174, 250, 378, 427, 440, 27:91, 98, 28:78, 92, 108, 124, 126–130, 143, 256f, 29:72–74, 77, 79, 103, 132, 30:20, 73–76, 78, 80f, 86, 124, 138, 180, 183, 206, 271, 324, 31:369, 385, 34:60, 35:289, 378f, 37:xvii, 27, 67, 137, 188, 227, 283, 364f, 38:87, 105, 230, 233, 39:18, 40:xiiif, 51f, 57, 89f, 104f, 113, 265, 283, 285f, 305f, 41:39, 130, 134, 136, 154, 175n, 176f, 205, 247, 293, 44:xiiif, 91–97, 103, 131, 45:xiv, 31f, 34, 62, 80, 91–93, 235, 240, 264, 271, 273, 278–280, 289, 293, 295, 333, 46:xiii, 18, 27, 48, 65, 75, 80, 91, 95, 99, 104, 107, 112, 118, 163, 166, 178, 181–183, 195, 210, 231n, 237f, 242f, 245, 256f, 288, 317, 47:6–8, 52, 91, 96, 143, 181f, 272, 274, 288, 49:46, 53, 98n, 106f, 135f, 138, 230, 233, 254, 307f, 265, 383f, 409, 411, 50:24, 36, 40, 62n, 64f, 66, 141, 200f, 51:149, 159f, 170, 177, 181, 235, 295, 354, 385, 388f, 54:179, 199, 307, 315, 363, 395
Authority of 48:178, 211n, 258f, 392, 395
Government, Church—see **Church, The**—Its government and ordinances
Government, City—41:176f
Government, Imperial—48:70n, 77n, 83, 85n, 139, 188n, 247n, 388, 394f
Governors—23:7
Goyim—15:321, 324, 326, see also **Gentiles**
Grace, Definition of—33:136f
Grace, Effective signs of—36:66f, 119
Grace, Gifts of—27:144, 231, 238, 289, see also **Growing in grace**; **Sanctification**
Grace, Infused—24:347n, 31:99–101, 32:49
Grace, Irregular—2:119, 177–179, 4:44
Grace, Means of—see **Means of grace**
Grace, Prevenient—25:181f
Grace, Sacramental—38:xv, 105
Grace alone—25:371, 25:81, 96, 242, 44:xii
Grace and freedom—33:9, 54f
Grace of Christ—38:xx, 45, 105, 107, 109, 111, 113, 115–117, 119, 125, 132, 169, 224
Grace of God—1:69, 135, 141, 178, 180f, 189f, 213, 220, 224, 248–250, 258–260, 264, 301n, 304, 326f, 358, 2:4, 19, 39–41, 48, 53, 72f, 82, 87, 103, 105f, 111, 104, 117f, 120, 121n, 122–124, 140, 147, 155f, 162f, 169, 184, 197, 213, 223, 240, 246, 250, 314,

332f, 348, 352–354, 376, 380, 3:7f, 21f, 44, 68f, 77, 90, 95–97, 99, 102, 104, 107, 111f, 124f, 130f, 133f, 136, 142f, 146, 155f, 161, 165, 167, 169, 182, 206n, 222, 228, 237, 265, 296, 336f, 339f, 344, 363, 4:16, 42f, 49–52, 54f, 57–62, 64–70, 95, 146f, 151, 160, 168f, 174, 176, 200, 202, 214, 226, 238, 240–245, 248, 310, 368, 376, 397–400, 405, 5:31, 56, 59, 74, 77, 79, 94, 140, 154–157, 183, 196f, 199, 229f, 233, 255, 257–259, 261, 263, 278, 284, 316, 332, 337, 354, 361, 6:96f, 115, 172, 252, 370, 391, 406, 7:11, 4, 57, 101, 106, 122, 131, 142f, 145, 151, 155, 180, 196f, 226, 230, 235, 253–256, 261, 274, 301, 303, 325f, 339, 366, 371, 8:11f, 15n, 16, 24, 40, 44f, 73, 117, 161, 165, 170f, 174, 176–178, 192f, 205, 219f, 227, 229, 231–233, 254, 257, 271, 283, 312, 314, 317, 323–325, 329–331, 9:3f, 20, 24, 26, 43, 48, 53, 64, 70, 84, 97, 103–105, 108–110, 114, 118, 126, 136, 141, 150, 178, 181, 184, 190, 194, 206, 226, 244, 251, 272, 277, 296, 306, 10:34, 46f, 146, 162f, 215f, 218, 236, 258, 305, 403f, 410, 417, 11:111, 168f, 264, 312, 357, 369, 441, 445, 447f, 457, 493, 512, 12:61, 140, 155f, 160, 162, 207, 214f, 218, 230, 239, 277, 280, 303f, 306, 308, 311, 316f, 320, 323, 325–328, 331, 334, 336, 340, 345, 355, 358f, 366, 371, 374, 376f, 379f, 383f, 390, 392f, 408, 13:7, 36, 93, 130, 135, 137f, 153, 185, 251, 341, 364, 373, 376, 405f, 14:5, 24–32, 34–39, 41, 50, 55f, 58, 60, 70f, 81f, 91, 99, 101f, 104f, 111, 134, 140, 143, 148–152, 157f, 160, 163, 166–168, 170–173, 178–180, 182–186, 189–191, 194, 196, 198–205, 209, 211, 214, 222, 241, 250f, 253–255, 300, 304, 331, 335, 339, 349, 16:60, 66, 71f, 101, 121, 204, 218, 243, 281, 17:7, 71, 83, 102, 115, 157, 162f, 19:6, 27f, 30, 46–49, 51, 80, 87f, 92, 115, 134, 141, 166, 176, 277, 20:9, 24, 28, 46f, 57, 89, 123, 128, 137f, 140, 144, 227, 270f, 304, 21:38, 151f, 285, 288f, 294, 321–323, 325, 341, 351f, 22:18, 54, 63, 69, 87, 118–122, 124, 126, 131, 133, 136f, 139, 145, 150f, 156f, 169, 189–191, 220–222, 225, 288, 355, 373, 382, 410, 426, 460 463, 479, 488f, 495, 23:19, 21, 23, 26, 36, 47, 52, 58, 60, 76, 83, 98, 112, 125, 137, 166, 172, 181, 196, 233f, 250f, 262f, 265f, 268, 270f, 278, 281, 310, 316, 319, 321, 330, 339, 341, 355f, 361, 381, 409, 24:15f, 23, 50, 58, 60, 62, 64, 72f, 88f, 98, 100, 110f, 122, 129, 133, 136, 140, 141, 147, 153, 158, 164, 166, 171, 178–182, 185, 192, 194, 213n, 218–220, 223, 226, 230, 239f, 254, 257–259, 261, 263, 269–271, 282, 287, 292, 305, 308f, 319f, 328, 343, 347, 360, 368, 389, 405f, 411, 419, 422, 25:5f, 25, 36, 43, 47f, 50, 69, 80–82, 85, 96, 98, 101, 104, 106, 111f, 162, 185f, 191f, 202, 234, 241f, 261f, 266f, 284, 305f, 315f, 323, 346–348, 352, 368f, 387f, 418f, 26:4f, 7, 42, 48, 54f, 162–164, 167, 240, 315, 362, 27:3, 7, 11, 14–16, 18f, 24, 38, 42, 48, 61, 85f, 88, 90, 102, 108, 117, 120, 140–144, 146, 149, 164, 170–172, 175–177, 180, 184–189, 203, 209, 212, 219f, 223f, 226, 234f, 238, 240, 242, 246, 249, 252, 256, 260f, 264, 266, 273–277, 279, 283–285, 287, 291–294, 301, 308, 311–314, 317–322, 324, 327, 330–333, 335, 346f, 349, 353, 356, 359, 362, 364, 366f, 372, 380, 390n, 407, 28:89–91, 113, 120f, 245, 29:15, 39, 48, 50, 66, 69, 80f, 85, 95, 115, 125, 131, 142, 149, 168, 171f, 192, 197, 205, 214, 216, 219, 226, 232, 30:3f, 8, 18, 29f, 32, 36, 40, 42, 49, 58, 77, 100, 124, 143, 145, 151–154, 158, 174, 190, 198f, 204f, 208, 210f, 223, 232, 246–248, 252, 257, 263–267, 274, 280–282, 293, 295, 300, 304, 311, 313, 315, 323, 325, 31:11, 13–15, 40f, 50–52, 65, 67, 178, 183, 187, 233f, 353f, 364, 32:13, 23, 28, 38, 40, 45, 49, 86, 136, 153f, 157, 177f, 208f, 221, 225–232, 251, 254f, 257, 33:61f, 78n, 112–117, 219f, 240–244, 253f, 266n, 267f, 272, 276, 278–286, 34:53, 111, 193, 35:xiv, 11, 14f, 17, 19, 42f, 54, 64, 70, 84, 89, 101f, 109, 181, 198, 237, 244–246, 277, 364–367, 368n, 369–381, 389, 36:30, 40, 60f, 63–65, 67–69, 74f, 84n, 92, 94, 107, 149, 166, 169, 174, 176, 180, 182, 200, 204, 214, 217f, 226, 228, 327, 38:x, xv, xixf, 86, 88, 104, 106–108, 113, 115–117, 119, 128, 135–137, 157, 169, 171, 175, 184, 204, 221, 238, 272, 39:67, 126, 130, 247, 276, 41:17, 22, 49, 69–72, 75, 77f, 85, 110, 113f, 120, 123, 138f, 144, 147, 171f, 187, 199, 206, 210, 213, 232, 236f, 246, 252, 263, 280, 297, 302, 307, 316, 338, 340, 344, 351, 364,

42:ix, 11, 20, 31, 35, 40f, 49, 51, 55, 61, 70, 74, 79f, 89, 92, 103–110, 114f, 119, 130, 139, 144, 152, 174–176, 184, 186, 45:21, 57, 113, 142, 164, 177f, 182, 191, 193, 350–353, 356, 369, 373, 388, 46:10, 33, 42, 53, 69, 72, 74, 79, 83f, 94f, 102, 110, 123f, 133f, 137, 177, 190, 197, 200, 214, 235, 305, 47:ix, 12, 73, 76, 85, 102, 104f, 111, 114, 117, 132f, 145, 171, 175, 186, 209, 228, 239, 241f, 274, 302, 304f, 48:24f, 46, 48n, 144, 156f, 282, 51:29, 43, 47, 53, 56–60, 112, 114f, 122, 187, 278, 328, 52:12, 23, 55, 57, 75, 88, 133, 152, 175, 209, 239, 241f, 249, 252f, 272, 274, 280, 282

Grace vs. law—25:234

Graces—34:251

Graciousness—11:378f, 387f

Gradual—53:xvii, 21, 24, 36

Graduations, Academic—34:xiv

Graetz, Heinrich—47:129, 235n

Gräfendorf, Hans von—49:132n, 134n, 135n

Grain—1:36, 72, 251, 318, 2:24, 161f, 288, 290, 3:150, 177n, 319, 5:10, 13, 58, 138, 141, 274, 7:32, 53, 70, 148f, 153, 155, 157–159, 161, 171, 186, 201, 205f, 213–220, 223f, 236, 239, 241, 247, 260, 267f, 270, 286, 306, 309, 328, 333, 8:66, 68, 108, 112, 116, 119–122, 124f, 195, 224f, 267, 277, 290f, 302, 323, 23:6, 9–11, 14, 41, 226, 256, 286, 24:47, 196, 236, 323n, 329, 410, 27:55, 329, 36:287, 339, 352f

Grammar—1:152, 266, 2:15, 104, 139, 3:70, 72f, 87, 357f, 4:13, 99, 154, 351, 5:102, 209, 293, 312, 336, 352, 356, 6:52–54, 7:134, 147, 188, 216, 240, 251f, 267, 283, 285, 288, 323, 343, 8:143, 147, 211, 243, 246, 262, 16:3, 47, 338, 17:48, 96, 165, 228, 277, 22:299, 23:160, 24:104, 109, 26:92, 100, 139, 267f, 294, 27:202, 357, 397, 28:265, 267, 315, 31:163, 38:17n, 43, 53, 45:376n, 50:231–233

Grammarians—2:15, 104, 3:262, 4:10, 153, 192, 306, 362, 393, 6:52f, 181f, 266, 321, 340, 7:53, 79, 168, 189, 207, 215, 258, 285, 301, 8:66n, 143, 195f, 208, 215, 246, 261, 273, 278, 289, 27:28, 278, 31:47f

Gran—see **Estergom**

Granaries—2:24, 7:157–160, 213–215, 23:10f, 14f, 40f

Grandchildren—8:84, 259, 333

Grandmothers—6:255

Grapes—8:247–249, 253, 257–259, 267, 272, 9:293, 297, 16:189, 325, 18:119, 24:198, 203, 223–225, 227, 232f, 27:79, 373, 36:287, 352f

Grass—11:230, 233, 301f, 311, 313, 333, 498, 17:11, 25, 391

Grass, Hans—54:407n

Grasshoppers—2:33, 17:24, 18:79, 312–314

Gratian—43:157f, 54:26, see also **Decretals, Papal**

Decretum Magistri Gratiani 4:201n, 27:154n, 218n, 32:81n, 110n, 48:186, 266n

Discordantium canonum concordia 13:232n

Gratian, Emperor—41:23n, 24f, 38n, 86n

Gratitude—3:49, 51, 73, 157, 227, 4:215, 278f, 285, 5:331, 6:112, 114, 7:97, 322f, 8:144, 256, 23:26, 234, 25:160, 26:43, 138, 283, 376f, 27:273, 28:258

Graubünden, Switzerland—50:83n

Gravamina—27:157n, 34:14n, 33n, 39:14n, 41:265n, 44:120, 160n, 185n, 45:277n, 49:155, 350n, 374n, 414n, 50:161n, see also **Gebhart, Bruno**

Grave, The—24:51, 76, 86, 90, 132, 137, 198, 370, 402, 26:157–159, 163, 247, 384, 28:110, 119, 132f, 151, 186–188

Graves—see **Sepulchers**

Great Schism—44:167n, 173n

Great Sea—18:103

Great ones—18:281, 333

Greece—1:28n, 294, 2:108, 191, 193, 380, 3:63, 5:71, 339, 7:32, 140, 8:56, 9:55, 10:412, 13:325, 343, 14:114, 20:114, 293, 21:344, 22:246, 478, 513, 25:124, 126, 129, 27:98, 29:38, 38:324, 41:24, 281, 45:224, 329, 359, 46:200n, 202, 50:99, 172n, 52:162, 54:402, 474

Greed—1:163, 221, 336, 350, 2:17, 19, 65, 127, 246, 326, 328, 330, 348, 395, 397, 3:6, 182, 223, 231, 364, 4:145f, 182, 207, 214, 227, 5:5, 11, 268, 295, 306, 367f, 370–372, 375, 378f, 386, 6:3–7, 12, 14, 18, 22, 28, 36, 48, 50, 211, 7:66, 69, 159f, 205, 281, 8:62, 106, 109, 229, 311, 9:70, 82, 139, 163, 185, 193, 204, 221, 10:55f, 59, 355, 11:69, 99, 219, 223, 259, 303, 307, 498, 13:392f, 16:35, 61f, 182, 346, 17:266f, 278, 18:140f, 147, 150, 161, 180f, 221, 226, 233, 308, 330f, 350f, 373, 391, 393f, 396, 398–400, 19:127f, 161, 187f, 202, 207, 209, 20:55, 118f, 237, 241, 268, 312, 318, 21:16, 166–168, 172, 177–179, 182–184, 201–203, 23:11,

30, 24:14, 162–164, 26:342, 350, 352, 27:31, 48, 61, 67, 125f, 154, 257, 337, 384f, 399, 28:287f, 296, 369f, 372, 378, 30:31, 53, 137, 142, 174, 184, 187, 42:39, 73, 44:107, 45:170, 173, 233, 263, 265f, 294f, 298, 305, 307, 342, 46:130f, 132, 52:222, see also **Avarice**

Greed, Squire—13:395

Greedy Bellies—21:186, 189, 196, 201

Greedy persons—6:3–7, 28, 61f, 15:43, 87f, 92

Greek—2:15, 6:87, 137, 144, 168, 174, 282, 7:32n, 251f, 314, 8:34, 64n, 198, 209, 261, 302, 9:49, 67, 82, 113, 16:254, 276, 297, 333n, 22:298f, 421, 23:20n, 25, 196, 25:125, 481, 27:125, 163, 175, 179, 201, 212f, 246, 290f, 307, 315, 319, 326, 336, 348, 369, 376f, 380, 394, 396, 29:59, 74, 109, 111, 113, 129, 132f, 135, 146, 151f, 155, 156n, 157, 159, 165, 166, 173, 177, 179, 197, 204, 30:73, 132, 268, 37:26n, 34, 43, 75, 80, 239–241, 321, 326–329, 331–333, 38:21, 32n, 60, 72n, 226, 292n, 46:102, 232n, 52:202, 53:63, 54:310, 373, 376

Greek and Persian kingdoms—45:222, 224n, 225n

Greek Anthology—4:334n

Greek Church—1:146, 2:226, 14:326, 333n, 31:152, 228n, 322, 32:59f, 68f, 96, 36:24n, 25, 63n, 167, 39:150n, 171, 53:21, 26f

Greek drama—46:235n

Greek kingdoms—2:255, 259

Greek text of Bible—see **Scripture(s), New Testament**—Greek text

Greeks—1:4, 28n, 249, 255f, 276, 323, 2:190, 202, 206, 208, 227, 300, 305, 320, 346, 352, 3:48, 281, 324, 4:152, 237, 372, 5:24, 291n, 297, 341n, 349, 353, 6:206, 209, 211, 276, 283, 7:178, 189, 283, 325, 350, 353, 8:95, 152, 216, 237, 250, 9:15, 11:521, 13:218, 14:50, 74, 94, 301, 16:28, 66, 277, 347, 17:7, 35, 122f, 148, 151, 18:183, 281, 20:62, 114, 193, 22:50n, 97, 251, 426, 23:254, 377, 24:267, 25:8, 481, 26:29, 77, 98, 139, 228, 354, 356, 457, 27:274, 371, 28:130, 149f, 162, 183, 339, 29:21, 27, 38f, 43, 74, 30:290, 34:69, 38:317f, 45:352, 359, 367, 370, 377, 46:104, 107n, 108, 110, 123, 196, 269, see also **Achaians**

Greetings—6:98, 121, 169, 25:128–130

Greff, Jochim—*Lazarus* 53:338

Gregorian calendar—41:61n, 62n

Gregorius, Abbot—see **Cortese, Abbot Gregory**

Gregory I, Pope—1:239, 2:198n, 3:114, 168, 188n, 299, 349f, 4:9, 127, 234n, 5:216, 7:296f, 8:246, 10:123, 126, 297, 11:19, 304, 14:23, 38, 302, 348, 17:54, 21:29, 59, 22:254–256, 259, 273n, 24:370, 25:466f, 26:459f, 27:83–85, 89, 110, 388, 390, 28:309, 29:17n, 136n, 202, 31:57f, 136, 143, 152, 281, 32:xviii, 85f, 91, 95f, 158f, 221, 242, 257, 34:22, 95, 35:131n, 135n, 36:26n, 52n, 55n, 56, 135, 186, 190–193, 37:329, 38:118n, 143, 159, 178, 39:33n, 40:337, 362f, 41:90n, 291n, 292, 296n, 297, 299, 308, 326, 334, 44:148n, 51:45, 52:173, 175, 181, 183, 192, 53:21n, 260, 54:xxin, 8, 26, 85, 104, 259, 347

Gregory I, Pope, Works of—*Dialogorum libri quatuor* 3:168n, 15:58n, 32:95n, 42:155n, 156n

Epistles 32:158n

Homiliae in Evangelia 7:297n, 14:302n, 25:512

Homily on Ezekiel 25:435f, 484

In Primum Regum expoositiones 6:260n, 34:22n

Liber regulae pastoralis 3:349n, 5:216f

Luther's estimate of 30:134, 297

Moralia 1:184, 14:348n, 29:203n, 32:85n, 91, 34:22n

Moralia in Job 6:209n, 400n

Pastoral Care 4:403, 9:102, 103n, 10:391

Super Cantica Canticorum expositio 15:231n

Works 32:242n

XL homiliae in Evangelia 17:64n

Gregory II, Pope—39:281n, 51:82n

Gregory IX, Pope—22:185n, 41:20n, 116n, 44:202n

Decretalia 5:154n

Decretalium 36:79n, 137n, 138n

Gregory VII (Hildebrand), Pope—3:188n, 34:34n, 41n, 39:211n, 41:332n, 43:237n, 44:164n, 54:407

Gregory VIII, Pope—44:167n

Gregory XII, Pope—39:252n, 41:265n, 267n

Gregory XIII, Pope—41:61n, 62n, 54:307

Gregory, St.—see **Gregory I, Pope**

Gregory Nazianzen, St.—41:79n, 120, 46:221n, 54:353

Sermon against the Arians 31:222

Gregory of Nyssa, St.—26:267n, 41:79n

Fifteen Homilies on the Song of Songs 4:48n

Orationes Catecheticae 13:346n, 26:267
Gregory of Rimini—31:322
Gregory of Tours, St.—41:291n
Greifenklau, Richard von, Archbishop of Trier—48:104n, 109, 127, 128f, 138, 163n, 200n, 205n, 208n, 244, 49:59, 198n, 54:139
Greifswald—6:x
Greussen—50:209n
Grickel—see **Agricola, John**
Grickel and Jeckel—6:76
Grief—2:141, 145, 217, 225f, 304, 325, 368, 3:12, 14, 68, 134, 228, 242, 252, 302, 304, 312, 314, 329f, 346, 356, 4:4, 39–42, 45, 56, 60, 68, 98, 110, 112, 187, 194f, 197, 223, 249, 286, 299, 325, 337–339, 354, 5:90, 95, 97, 152, 154, 162–165, 175, 180, 209–212, 240f, 296, 298, 300, 314f, 358, 6:102, 190f, 196, 253, 256, 269f, 272, 275, 312f, 362, 7:5, 47, 49, 54f, 73, 99, 125, 128, 130f, 138, 165, 210f, 228, 230, 232, 236, 249f, 256, 262–264, 271, 277, 280, 288f, 291, 293, 305, 313, 315, 327, 332, 353, 363f, 368, 371, 374, 376f, 8:6f, 9, 12–14, 21, 24–27, 39, 43, 46, 52f, 55, 74, 97, 113, 219, 221, 234, 318, 20:140–142, 173, 275, 24:11f, 26, 45, 117, 133, 146, 204, 354, 358, 377, 379f, 415, 51:232–235, 249
Griffins—2:190
Grimm, Harold J.—52:xn
author of Introduction and presumed author of introductory comments to writings included in Vol. 31
author of Introduction to *Career of the Reformer* (Vols. 31–34) 31:ix–xiii
editor of Vol. 31
translator of *Disputation against Scholastic Theology* 31:3–16
translator of *Heidelberg Disputation* 31:35–70
translator of *Preface to the Complete Edition of a German Theology* 31:71–76
translator of *Proceedings at Augsburg* 31:253–293
translator of *The Leipzig Debate* 31:307–326
Grimm, Jacob and Wilhelm, eds.—
Deutches Wörterbuch, Leipzig, 1854–1954 32:38n, 35:60n, 88n, 120n, 191n, 214n, 247n, 275n, 333n, 343n, 37:127n
Grimm and Wirsung—48:230n
Grimma—31:325, 38:196, 50:154, 156n, 169n
Augustinian Monastery 48:193
Grimmenthal (Grimma Valley)—17:22n, 34:25, 28, 44:185n, 46:142n
Grisar, Hartmann—54:xxin
Luther, St. Louis, 1916 46:60n
Gritsch, Eric W.—47:14n, 235n
author of Introduction to *Church and Ministry* (Vols. 39–40) 39:xxi–xxv
author of introduction to Vol. 39
co-translator with Ruth C. Gritsch of all writings in Vol. 39
editor of Vols. 39 and 41
presumed author of introductions to individual writings in Vols. 39 and 41
Reformer without a Church: The Life and Thought of Thomas Münzer, 1488(?)–1525, Philadelphia, 1967 39:xvin
translator of *Against Hanswurst* and *Against the Roman Papacy, an Institution of the Devil* 41:179–256, 257–376
Gritsch, Ruth C.—co-translator with Eric W. Gritsch of all writings in Vol. 39
Groaning—6:107f, 110–112, 156, 158f, 180, 352f, 362, 371, 10:140, 142, 25:73f, 245, 252, 264, 277, 361, 365f
Groningen—34:345, 353
Groote, Gerard—25:300
Groping for God—37:69, 134
Grossness—9:185
Growing—20:40, 69, 72, 217, 255
Growing in faith—38:126, 128, 130, 171, 194, 209, 261
Growing in grace—12:375, 379, 381, 25:6, 43, 47f, 127, 153, 178, 232, 246, 507, 27:21, 32, 227, 289, 28:206, 224, 30:17, 27, 69f, 118, 158f, 199, 215, 230, 34:181, 35:32f, 377f, 41:166
Growing in holiness—26:350f, 360
Growing in knowledge of God—25:225
Growing in righteousness—25:137, 225
Growth, Life as—14:285
Grub, Tender—A figure of faith 8:54
Grumbach, Argula von—49:93, 313n, 317f
Grunau, Simon—45:137
Grünenberg, Johann—10:ixf, 6, 25:ix, 132, 31:22, 74, 80, 258, 382, 35:8, 25, 128, 39:6, 26, 52, 120, 141, 228, 43:7, 45:6, 15, 139, 48:19n, 40, 69n, 75n, 77n, 94n, 113n, 114n, 121n, 130n, 131n, 136n, 149n, 150n, 174n, 177, 180n, 192n, 229n, 230n, 238, 242, 246n, 252n, 258n, 288n, 292f, 296, 324, 49:4n, 52:xiii, 54:141
Gruner, Johann—39:303, 45:165, 187n
Booklet to Comfort all Poor Consciences, Wittenberg, 1524 45:163n

Grym Valley—21:272, 22:526, 23:174, 327
Grynaeus, Symon—50:28n, 228n
Gübert, Arnold—translator of *The Seven Penitential Psalms* 14:137–206
Guettel, Caspar—43:9, 47:105n, 107, 111
Guidance—9:5
Guilt—7:238, 258, 271, 8:223, 16:45f, 106, 154, 156, 177, 188, 25:46, 63f, 163, 340, 29:17f, 175, 32:27, 50–53, 34:15n, 195n, 347, 35:9f, 244, 37:16n, 26, 86, 342–345, 362
Guilt vs. weakness—25:340
Guilt-offering—5:52
Guinegate, Battle of 1513—50:135n
Gulden—40:144, 185, 46:131n, 183, 274, 48:11n, 12, 130, 160, 203n, 216, 222, 255, 49:58, 84n, 88, 158, 198n, 211, 50:49, 109, 213f, 220
Gum—6:382f
Guns—6:244f, 24:117, 417
Günterrode, Appolonia—50:135n
Gunther, Count of Schwartzburg-Sondershausen—50:209n
Günther, Francis—48:173n, 174
Günther, Franz—11:171n, 31:6
Gurk, Cardinal Raymund von—39:107
Gutknecht, Jobst—53:191, 222, 232, 265, 287
Guzzling—13:216
Gymnasia—see **Schools, Latin**
Gypsies—16:191, 37:77, 46:294, 54:234

Habakkuk, Prophet—8:72, 17:123, 19:x, 107f, 121, 124, 144, 151n, 155f, 160, 216, 20:158, 183, 283, 24:383, 25:391, 26:238, 268, 35:327f, 354
  Commentary on his book 19:107–236
  His vision 19:120f, 192–194
Habits—14:14, 16, 20
Habitus—44:26n
Hadad—6:308f
Hadadrimmon—20:141, 329
Hadar—6:308–310
Hadas, Moses—47:141n
Hades—7:293, 25:300
Hadrach—20:283
Hadrian—see also the spelling **Adrian**
Hadrian VI, Pope—4:130n, 49:23n, 24n, 35f
Hadrian, Emperor—47:234n, 237, 298f
Hagar—1:234, 3:42, 44–46, 53–65, 68–76, 99, 192, 208, 4:17–22, 36–40, 43–50, 58f, 62, 64f, 67f, 72, 109, 155, 300–302, 305, 324, 327, 335, 337, 376, 5:92, 335, 6:66, 87, 146, 387, 7:103, 200, 8:30, 9:241, 11:124, 366, 18:407, 25:80, 26:433–442, 444–446, 457–459, 461, 27:310f, 314f, 317, 322f, 29:62
Hagarenes, Hagarites—see **Hagrites**
Hagenau—16:210n, 34:345, 49:33n
Hagenau, Colloquy of, 1540—50:190n, 207n, 212n, 215f, 218f, 221
Haggai, Prophet—8:229, 16:221, 20:3, 6f, 83, 160f, 224f, 35:329f, 45:215, 228n, 46:221, 47:221, 239, 241, 281f, 298, 305
  Commentary on his book 18:ix, xi, 367–387 (text)
Hagrites—6:389, 11:121f, 124f, 18:89
Haikola, Lauri—47:106n
Hail—1:140, 11:18, 76–78, 83f, 16:234, 267, 315, 330, 24:216
Hail Mary—see **Ave Maria**
Hailperin, Herman—47:66n, 134n, 178n, 190n
Haimo of Auxerre—*Commentaria in Esaiam* 16:252n, 265n
Hainaut—34:345, 353
Hair—15:228, 241, 244f, 251
Hair shirts—23:34, 68, 124, 182, 263, 367, 409, 27:13, 84, 88
Hair styles—28:275
Halberstadt—4:192f, 41:33n, 35, 46, 240, 46:210, 48:44, 160, 377
Half-Christians—10:353
Half-mass—34:56
Half-sacrament—32:56, 58f
Halle—2:94, 95n, 23:208, 211, 26:195, 34:97, 36:205, 38:114n, 142, 167f, 217, 46:227n, 48:143n, 160, 275n, 316n, 320, 326f, 340f, 365, 372f, 49:151, 181n, 50:41n, 163n, 226n, 227, 237n, 275n, 280n, 284n, 285n, 286f, 307, 51:xvn, 84, 357, 371
  Evangelical church in 50:224n, 225f, 236f, 247, 275n, 317
  Roman Catholic Church in 50:95, 115, 147, 160, 224n, 237, 249n
Halle manuscript of Luther's lectures on Minor Prophets—18:x
Hallelujah—13:356
Halley, Edmund—13:122n
Hallische Kirchenordnungen—46:210n
Haloes (Krönlein)—28:48n, 51
Ham—1:355, 357f, 2:25, 58, 72, 120, 167–178, 180–182, 185, 194–196, 200f, 204, 210, 212, 222, 230, 364, 367, 3:56, 97, 4:3, 7:15, 18, 200, 16:125, 17:413, 52:174, 226
Ham, Descendants of—2:186, 211, 213f, 216, 219–221, 223, 228, 11:82
Haman—11:508, 47:264, 273
Hamann, Johann Georg—34:xi, 51:25n

Hamath—2:204, 16:126, 313, 18:169, 20:91, 284
Hamburg—38:63n, 49:22, 50:30, 150n, 180n, 197
Hamburg codes—53:123
Hamburger Kirchenordnungen—46:210n
Hamilton, Patrick—50:150n
Hamites—3:97
Hamor—6:193, 196f, 200, 207f, 346, 8:114, 197
Hananiah—8:300, 52:192, 270
Hananiah, Azariah, and Mishael—52:192, 270
Hand of the Lord—see **God**—His hand or hands
Handbooks—see **Hymnals (Enchiridia or handbooks)**
Handkerchiefs—26:103
Hands—10:30, 102, 111, 128, 130f, 154, 172, 420f, 444f, 11:489f, 533, 16:17f, 206
Hanes—16:254
Hangman—8:54, 99, 219, 224, 23:86, 336, 340, 412, 24:111, 399, 46:68, 303, 314n
Hanna (also called Anna)—31:273, 52:102
Hannah (mother of Samuel)—3:134, 4:339, 5:359, 6:323, 14:79, 247, 15:191, 25:377f, 26:442, 27:322, 28:335, 338, 46:148n, 153
Hannaniah, Prophet—25:445
Hannibal—2:343, 374, 5:270, 353f, 6:106, 157, 244, 309, 331f, 8:237, 10:37, 13:155f, 161, 197n, 19:115n, 20:171, 46:119n, 124
Hannover—50:181n
Hans of Jena—41:322n, 323
Hanseatic League—32:274n, 46:113n, 114f
Hansen, Paul G., et al.—*Engagement and Marriage*, St. Louis, 1959 46:261n, 262n, 270.
Hansen, Walter A.—associate editor of Vols. 4, 5, 7, 8, 26, 27, 29, and 30
death of 29:xii
indexer of Vols. 1–5, 7–9, 14, 22–24, 26, 27, and 30
translator of *Lectures on Hebrews* 29:109–241
Hanswurst—41:182, 185–187, 188n, 189, 218n, see also **Luther, Martin, Writings of**—*Against Hanswurst*
Happiness—15:30–32, 37f, 53f, 92, 111f, 114, 120, 177, 209f, 214, 240, 20:49, 112, 188, 28:11f, 28, 106, 141f, 144, 173, 185
Happy age—17:367f
Hapsburgs—46:106n, 48:175f, 199, 217n, 49:27n, 110n, 128n, 144n, 185n, 240n, 251n, 266n, 50:41n, 55n, 83, 104n, 107n, 108n, 112n, 114n, 128n
Haran—1:244, 358, 2:238f, 241f, 244, 276–278, 281f, 290, 303, 3:352, 4:184f, 188, 250, 5:209f, 269, 279f, 6:308, 7:241, 269, 8:84, 16:316, 45:23n, 46:316
Harbison, E. Harris—*Age of the Reformation*, Ithaca, N.Y., 1955 46:157n
Hardening—6:341, 395, 17:306, 360, 20:246, 268
Hardening (hardness) of heart—16:11f, 96, 103, 156, 25:17, 82f, 97, 101, 139, 163, 168, 175f, 192, 232, 374, 376, 394, 33:164–175, 178f, 181f
Hares—1:55, 2:133, 197, 4:71
Harland, J. Penrose—"Sodom and Gomorrah II. The Destruction of the Cities of the Plain" in *Biblical Archaeologist*, VI, 1943 2:136n
Harlotry—see **Prostitution**
Harlots—see **Prostitutes**
Harmon—18:151
Harmony—4:19, 210, 248, 24:102, 246, 25:64, 107, 120, 27:42, 59–61, 91, 106f
Harnack, Adolph—*History of Dogma*, Boston, 1902 35:138n
Harpies—6:21, 23, 240
Harps—1:317f, 10:152–154, 265, 11:103n, 104, 233, 272, 275, 285–288, 14:311
Harry—see **Henry, Duke of Braunschweig-Wolfenbüttel**
Hartfelder, Karl—*Melanchthoniana paedagogica* 38:264n
Philipp Melanchthon als Praeceptor Germaniae Berlin, 1889 45:343n, 345
Harvest, Prayers for—42:85
Harvests—2:129, 136, 288
Harz Mts.—46:121n
Hasdrubal—13:156
Haste—17:214
Hate, hatred—1:74, 143, 166, 171, 180, 193, 195, 275, 280, 282, 2:20, 35, 37, 43, 57, 102, 168, 171–174, 213f, 248, 286f, 302f, 334, 336, 358, 3:6, 50, 57, 115, 129, 152, 158, 179, 189, 203, 281, 309, 319, 328, 359, 4:5, 65, 74, 85, 93, 176, 188, 194, 211, 218, 220, 226, 323, 334, 344, 360, 5:5, 10, 16, 45, 58, 60, 68f, 86, 88f, 151f, 154f, 181, 222, 252, 290, 298, 317f, 326, 344, 379, 382, 6:29, 36, 172, 252, 326, 373, 8:5, 16, 18, 34, 38, 169, 185, 189, 221, 298, 325, 9:134, 163, 185, 222f, 231, 235, 10:170, 11:82, 253f, 12194, 16:245n, 20:133, 139, 175, 21:74, 77, 80, 118f,

122f, 190, 22:81, 234, 236, 286, 370, 393, 395, 398, 507, 24:20, 116, 149, 157f, 161, 181, 191, 244, 246, 248, 252, 265, 268, 270–274, 276f, 279, 286–288, 301, 315, 396, 25:51, 65, 247, 284, 309, 312, 328, 334, 380, 382, 442, 453f, 484, 512, 26:35f, 40f, 49, 58, 60, 70, 81, 125, 231, 320, 326, 352, 387–389, 407, 413f, 423, 27:31, 42f, 47, 53, 58, 66f, 69, 71, 78, 81, 102–104, 172, 179, 181, 233, 276f, 284, 301, 348, 353, 360, 369, 374f, 387, 399, 30:31, 43, 53, 118f, 122f, 159, 176, 243f, 275f, 292f, 35:53, 372f, 36:207, 227, 42:14, 44

Hätzer, Ludwig—35:194n, 49:165n, 187n

Haughtiness—2:8, 36, 248, 3:54, 56, 59, 65, 5:92, 94

Haupt, Hermann—35:190n

Hausmann, John—50:149n

Hausmann, Nicholas—20:x, 34:108, 234, 35:399n, 36:234, 37:102n, 104n, 38:142, 145, 218, 39:299n, 40:119n, 45:5, 15, 46:158n, 159, 263, 48:399–402, 49:55f, 87f, 135n, 140n, 150n, 159f, 167f, 202f, 240n, 264f, 280f, 327n, 348f, 353, 355n, 419f, 429n, 50:50, 122f, 148f, 174f, 53:17, 19, 53f, 105f, 153, 54:24, 145, 319

Hausmann, Valentin—49:352, 355n

Hausschein—see **Oecolampadius, John**

Hausteufel—3:58n

Havilah—1:97, 100f, 2:195, 4:331

Having a god—44:40

Hawks—2:138

Hay—2:74, 14:211, 214

Hazael, King—19:39

Hazazon-tamar—2:368

Hazlitt, William, translator—*Table Talk or Familiar Discourses of Martin Luther*, London, 1848 54:xv, xviii, xxn

He-goats—4:398–400, 403

Headley, John M.—47:110n, 54:407n

Heads—10:341, 11:176n, 46:249

Healing—17:331

Healing, Life a process of—25:262f

Health—2:77, 3:129, 248, 7:ix, 81, 97, 132, 180, 228, 339, 350, 15:11, 23:203, 339, 348, 24:12, 76, 178, 206, 208, 229, 370, 392, 28:356f

Hearing—10:188f, 12:368–372, 375f, 388f, 25:91f, 97, 243, 418, 420, 29:145, 148, 216, 37:29, 138n, 272

Hearing the Word—11:159–162, 20:267f, 25:92

Heart—11:15f, 50, 417–419, 442f, 12:378f, 403, 13:5, 185, 204, 264, 269, 396, 405, 416, 14:223, 18:96, 19:87, 202, 21:11, 13f, 32–35, 37, 39, 74, 80f, 91, 111–114, 123, 143–145, 172–175, 179–181, 247, 257, 308, 325, 342, 357, 22:9, 12, 83, 128, 174, 198, 235, 253, 374, 25:189f, 27:220f, 349f, 29:50, 98, 101, 139, 152–155, 160, 164, 172, 185, 189, 192, 196, 198, 208, 212, 216f, 232, 237, 35:190n, 369, 37:27–29, 47, 51f, 65, 75f, 83n, 85–94, 96, 100, 103, 127, 131, 134, 148, 161, 272, 337, 38:39, 86, 102f, 106–109, 115, 121, 125, 127, 129f, 132, 134, 137, 149f, 164f, 172, 178, 190, 198, 207, 209f, 222, 224, 227, 305, 307, 46:133, 177, 278, 52:58

Heart, Cleanness of—29:152, 193

Heart, Deep—10:307–309

Heart, Speaking the—10:73f

Hearts, curdled—11:463–465

Heat—2:129, 136

Heath, Nicholas—50:104n, 114n, 115n, 119, 120n, 133n, 137n, 138f, 142n, 179n, 193n, 198n

Heathen—1:138, 166, 197, 200f, 240, 244, 249, 256, 274, 278, 295, 323, 2:12, 17f, 42, 52, 114, 116, 125–127, 132f, 147, 152, 160, 178, 196, 242, 248, 255, 258, 260, 264f, 270, 293, 299, 305, 320, 330, 333, 335f, 342f, 351f, 363, 371, 374, 389, 397, 399, 3:32f, 35, 41, 43, 60, 64, 76, 82–85, 88f, 96, 100, 110, 113, 116f, 123, 128, 135, 145, 160, 175, 201, 203, 221, 245, 259, 283, 293, 316, 321f, 332, 344, 346, 355, 4:14, 69, 85, 107, 116, 118f, 129, 160, 165, 183, 205, 209f, 221, 223, 226, 232, 248, 250, 256, 274, 297, 305, 318f, 328, 335, 351, 370, 375, 377, 400, 5:37, 83f, 89, 119, 138, 157, 165f, 167, 176, 190, 235, 238, 252, 269–272, 298, 317, 340, 342, 353f, 363, 382, 6:3, 33, 73, 88, 170, 191, 227f, 238, 244, 332, 335, 343, 7:4, 12, 15, 27, 33, 46, 52, 72, 75, 79f, 95, 117, 135f, 171, 191, 194, 198–200, 203, 207, 218, 240, 261, 307, 309, 311, 314f, 342, 345, 359, 8:41, 129, 135f, 140, 201, 203, 220, 225, 247, 256, 277, 279, 281, 286, 304, 313, 9:137, 171, 205, 294, 14:8–10, 12f, 15–25, 29f, 33, 39, 64, 66, 69, 74f, 77, 98f, 114, 119, 132–134, 183, 185, 187, 199, 225, 313f, 316, 16:83, 263, 18:229, 275f, 21:201, 273, 22:76, 81, 119, 122, 152–154, 157, 168, 196, 306, 363, 389, 426, 432, 475, 520, 23:56, 62, 99, 120, 142, 167, 169–

171, 195, 301, 320, 341, 358, 378, 387, 421, 24:67, 71f, 97, 168, 175, 197, 205, 214, 219f, 223, 231, 233, 251, 267, 269, 286–288, 303f, 311, 323, 328, 335, 337, 339f, 345, 349, 356, 405, 408, 26:32, 80, 123, 261f, 330, 363, 376, 396, 419, 27:91, 94, 99, 124, 146f, 157, 172, 245, 293, 325, 345, 369, 382, 391, 401, 28:94f, 103f, 161, 185, 29:8, 12, 39, 45, 57f, 60, 63f, 76, 99f, 103, 210, 238, 30:6, 8, 20, 22, 34, 37, 75, 80, 92, 94, 189f, 269, 290, 33:87, 34:20, 48, 35:144, 382, 390, 410, 36:93, 148, 176, 178, 37:16n, 30, 32, 53, 72, 128, 272, 359, 38:98, 103f, 113f, 150f, 156, 183, 189, 195, 203, 290f, 306, 41:11, 46, 143, 153, 165, 167, 191, 220, 365f, 42:88, 103, 134, 45:25, 73, 100, 102, 155f, 159, 289, 353, 378, 46:27–29, 32, 34f, 41, 76, 81, 104, 106, 110, 122f, 132, 150, 154, 163, 177, 186, 226, 236n, 251, 269, 50:74, 52:57, 83

Heaton, E.W.—47:252n, 153

Heaven—2:5f, 12, 16, 40, 45, 52, 58, 61, 70, 76, 82f, 86, 88f, 93–95, 103, 106f, 127, 129, 146–148, 151, 152n, 155, 167, 211, 213, 224f, 236, 242, 256f, 269, 273f, 282, 284, 301, 334, 359, 378, 382, 392, 397f, 3:17f, 50f, 121, 138f, 143, 147, 165, 186f, 190, 193, 196, 199, 202, 217, 224, 228, 230, 239, 242f, 255, 268, 270f, 273–276, 278, 291, 293, 298, 302, 305–307, 316, 320, 322, 328, 340f, 345, 4:47, 51, 53–55, 57, 59f, 69, 107, 111, 114, 119, 121–123, 125, 127, 129f, 139, 142–144, 146f, 152f, 156, 161f, 172, 175, 179, 195, 212, 214, 222, 231f, 236, 244, 251–257, 267, 279, 282, 285, 295f, 311f, 314, 316, 324, 340, 343, 356, 358, 360f, 364, 396, 398, 404, 5:15, 45, 47–49, 74, 76, 119, 123, 138, 143, 157f, 167f, 185, 214–217, 220–225, 236, 249, 258, 264, 267, 269, 276, 309, 312, 315, 327, 348, 354f, 7:64, 68, 71, 100, 103–105, 127, 135, 138, 152, 167, 174, 179, 186, 219, 247f, 296, 298, 308f, 320, 325, 327, 332, 348, 362f, 370f, 8:12, 25, 27, 29f, 32, 34, 37f, 52, 66f, 79, 90, 103, 115, 133, 145, 152, 163f, 167, 183f, 186, 193, 217, 250, 256, 271, 275, 287, 290n, 300, 302, 312, 315, 325, 9:4, 18, 33, 51, 54, 57n, 58n, 73f, 93f, 97f, 104, 109f, 118, 129, 157f, 161, 211, 277, 279, 290, 298, 306, 308, 11:12, 284, 318, 320, 428, 13:103f, 372, 14:9, 13, 21f, 25–29, 37, 48–51, 61, 73f, 82f, 89, 95, 98, 120, 145, 149, 181, 184f, 187, 201, 210, 262, 267, 271, 287, 292, 295, 297, 313, 321f, 331, 333, 336, 340, 21:73, 153, 173, 203f, 268, 22:15, 20, 50, 52, 56, 60, 65, 67, 71f, 75, 78, 98, 103, 110, 118f, 130, 136, 156, 200–205, 208–211, 249f, 303, 305, 307, 317, 361, 404f, 455, 474, 481, 490, 493, 496, 501, 504, 506, 508f, 517, 520, 529, 23:8, 10, 16, 18, 25, 28, 31, 33–38, 42, 44, 52, 54, 58, 61f, 67f, 71, 73f, 78, 80f, 83, 85f, 89, 92f, 95, 97, 101, 103f, 106, 114, 117, 120f, 123, 129, 132, 139, 147, 150, 159, 161, 167, 175, 182, 192, 213, 226, 230, 239, 246, 263f, 266, 270, 275, 282, 294, 302f, 327–329, 333, 339f, 346, 349, 357, 359–362, 364, 366, 372, 375f, 385, 389f, 394, 401, 411f, 421, 24:13, 21, 25f, 28f, 35f, 38–40, 42–44, 46, 48, 50–53, 62f, 65, 67–71, 84f, 92, 102, 106, 108, 110, 115f, 128, 134, 136f, 139, 141, 143, 147–149, 152f, 157–160, 163–167, 169f, 178f, 183–185, 187, 190, 193, 214, 222, 228, 233f, 243, 251, 257f, 261, 266, 271, 277, 280f, 286, 291, 295, 310, 313f, 321–323, 325f, 328, 334, 336, 339f, 342–345, 359, 362, 366, 369, 371, 376, 386, 395f, 398, 408, 414–416, 419, 421, 26:8, 11, 16, 22, 27, 29f, 32, 38, 55–58, 66f, 72f, 82, 93, 98, 101, 103, 106f, 115–117, 120, 129, 134, 148f, 164, 166, 171, 176f, 182, 184f, 200, 228, 231f, 235, 247–249, 257, 265, 271, 292, 295, 297, 301, 303, 306, 312, 317, 331f, 334, 336, 338, 340f, 345, 352, 356f, 363, 381–384, 389, 391, 393, 399, 403, 408, 415, 421, 427f, 439f, 451, 453, 459f, 27:5, 18, 20, 22, 27, 33, 38–41, 44–46, 64, 83f, 86, 93, 108, 129, 225f, 292, 297f, 311, 316, 318f, 329, 337, 348, 388, 391, 408–410, 28:142–144, 171, 29:117, 145, 177, 185, 215, 217f, 30:6f, 11–15, 21, 24–26, 29–31, 38, 42, 45, 58, 67, 98, 101, 109f, 113, 115f, 118, 152f, 161, 166, 170, 172, 180–182, 184, 188, 194f, 197f, 213, 236f, 296f, 310, 316, 31:46, 51, 62, 32:20–31, 36:69, 75, 95, 175, 207, 214f, 343, 37:xviiif, 11, 46–49, 55–62, 66, 70, 73, 84, 100, 114–117, 129, 138n, 158, 195, 198, 202, 207, 213, 222, 232–234, 280–282, 294, 38:28–31, 32, 38, 43f, 47, 51, 55f, 58, 60, 75f, 81,

101, 107, 113, 115, 156f, 160f, 163–165, 171, 174f, 191f, 203, 230, 41:13, 59, 89, 112, 330, 334, 343, 348, 42:9, 22f, 41f, 66, 99, 103, 134, 147, 176, 46:36, 54, 66, 70, 81f, 83, 153, 191, 224, 254, 257, 47:49, 114, 143, 297, 50:172n, 54:416, see also **Kingdom of heaven**

Heaven, Doors of—11:62

Heaven, Host of—16:192

Heaven and earth—41:54, 109f, 116, 172, 202, 300, 304f, 314, 331, 345f, 46:230, 254, 301, 310

Heavenly Jerusalem—22:203

Heavenly prophets—9:7n

Heavenly things—29:215, 225, 231

Heavens—1:5, 7f, 10, 12, 14–17, 19–21, 23, 25f, 28, 30f, 33–36, 38–40, 43, 45f, 48f, 54, 65, 68f, 73–76, 78f, 83, 86, 90, 99f, 115, 120, 124, 149, 156, 161, 186, 188, 201, 215n, 231, 233, 235, 244, 249, 275, 286–289, 292, 294, 341, 350f, 10:88f, 118, 120, 234, 29:115, 183, 199

Hebart, S.P.—translator of Sermon for the Festival of the Epiphany 51:159–286

Hebel Vorik—47:257, 285f, 296

Hebraisms—2:312, 5:280, 305, 7:38, 252, 8:116, 295, 9:293, 10:37f, 41, 44, 65, 224, 307, 328, 15:13, 40, 53, 97, 101, 117, 120, 136, 147, 152, 164, 166, 180, 16:28, 50, 149, 175, 17:4, 7, 15, 48, 55, 117, 171, 176, 193, 208, 211, 217, 228, 236, 287, 290f, 321, 335, 340, 345, 349, 362, 364, 370f, 379f, 385, 389, 391, 399, 410, 413, 19:9, 18, 24, 20:43, 46, 52, 64, 84f, 98, 117, 121, 123, 147, 191, 227, 23:10, 21, 26:139, 293, 27:165, 208, 29:94, 98, 101, 112, 148, 30:233, 257, 33:215, 265, see also **Hebrew idiom**

Hebraists—2:14, 7:168, 258, 291, 8:141, 208, 241n, 262, 47:244

Hebrew—2:16, 22, 37, 68, 108, 117, 122, 137, 234, 311, 332, 371, 373, 387, 3:100, 164, 197, 266, 296, 330, 352, 360n, 361, 4:59, 70n, 87n, 100f, 132, 136, 138, 153f, 158, 216, 265, 275, 282, 294, 298, 306, 330, 351, 370, 383, 393, 6:42, 52–54, 63, 112, 130, 181, 209, 229f, 232, 248, 250, 266, 268, 271, 301, 308, 319, 322f, 372, 7:7, 32n, 39f, 68, 82, 87, 95, 112, 134, 148, 157, 173, 188f, 205, 207, 215f, 222, 240, 250–252, 257, 260, 267, 283, 285f, 288, 292, 301, 320, 323, 326, 339, 343, 346–348, 8:141f, 146–148, 262, 289, 8:22, 25, 28, 34, 64, 67, 71, 90, 99, 101, 104, 119, 141f, 147, 149, 158, 161, 195f, 206, 213, 216, 225, 241, 243, 260, 262, 287–290, 298f, 323, 9:18, 26, 33, 35, 40, 48–50, 71, 76n, 82, 96f, 113, 134, 156, 163, 175, 220, 272, 277, 310, 10:41, 44, 329, 12:32, 42, 185f, 198–200, 324, 346, 13:351, 368, 410, 14:252n, 253, 15:7, 105, 112f, 213, 267f, 287, 320f, 322, 16:8, 13, 22f, 25f, 37, 42, 58, 72, 84, 90, 92, 97, 100, 104, 120, 122n, 124, 126, 130, 133, 136n, 145n, 156, 158, 162, 164, 166, 171f, 185, 187, 207, 212, 214n, 219, 224, 228–230, 234, 242, 244, 246, 248f, 252, 254, 267, 272, 276f, 16:282, 289f, 292–294, 296, 301, 304, 316, 322f, 326, 337, 341, 347, 17:34, 44, 54, 80, 86, 99, 104, 109n, 122f, 304, 18:9, 13, 82f, 116, 214, 264, 298, 311, 345, 386, 19:26, 30, 94, 109–111, 130, 151, 157, 179, 195, 197f, 200, 210, 212, 216, 218f, 225, 228–230, 232, 235, 237, 20:21, 47, 49, 80, 141, 22:198, 230, 288n, 298f, 23:20f, 132, 145, 28:189, 191, 204, 29:117, 126–129, 132, 135, 145–148, 151f, 155, 174, 188, 190, 195, 201, 214, 221–223, 30:186, 233, 32:183, 196–199, 33:125f, 215f, 218, 226, 35:194f, 213, 216, 249, 36:34, 197, 223, 229, 286, 37:17n, 43, 113, 320–323, 363, 42:51, 53f, 61, 73, 76n, 45:208–210, 329n, 343, 357, 359, 376, 46:183, 232n, 47:81, 83, 191f, 248, 256f, 48:66, 123, 132, 161, 225, 255, 49:5n, 149n, 238n, 291n, 369n, 372, 52:33, 141, 157, 185, 198, 202, 53:63, 198, 54:43, 348, 375n

Hithpael voice 11:312n

Pointing 8:141f

Hebrew, Ignorance of—26:319

Hebrew alphabet—Used as headings in Psalm 119 11:414n

Used as verse heading in Psalm 111 13:363–386

Hebrew Bible text—see **Psalms—Hebrew text; Scripture(s), Old Testament—**Hebrew text; **Scripture(s), Old Testament**—Masoretic text

Hebrew commentators—29:113

Hebrew conjugations—4:153

Hebrew custom—29:174

Hebrew grammar—2:34n

Change of persons 12:42f

Hebrew idiom—20:6f, 11, 15, 20f, 47, 70n,

84, 112, 178, 29:112f, 118, 143, 145, 152

Hebrew words—17:4, 13, 15, 16n, 18f, 21f, 25, 30, 45, 49, 51n, 56, 59, 99, 107, 109n, 113, 127, 134n, 135f, 139, 144f, 147, 149, 159n, 167, 175, 180, 182f, 186, 208, 214–216, 220, 236, 245, 265f, 272–274, 303, 305, 308, 314, 321f, 329, 336, 17:338, 344–346, 350, 356, 363, 367, 371, 373, 377, 382, 398, 400f, 413f

Hebrew writers—16:331

Hebrews—1:3f, 20, 26, 51, 55, 4:11f, 99, 134, 139, 198, 320, 5:36, 67, 72, 84, 88, 211, 281, 283, 293n, 336, 356, 375, 380, 384, 6:53, 70, 160, 178, 181, 193, 214, 295, 307, 365, 7:24f, 32, 37, 49, 77, 87, 116, 134, 136, 147f, 157f, 161, 187–189, 198, 208, 217, 240, 248, 252, 260, 264, 267f, 285f, 323, 339, 348, 351, 8:16, 19, 48, 50, 56, 64, 67, 71, 98, 221, 9:14f, 27, 34, 43, 55, 109, 154, 156, 207, 308, 15:14–16, 36f, 50, 58, 81, 120, 136, 166, 272f, 276, 288f, 319–324, 329, 345, 348–352, 16:5, 8, 27, 75, 80f, 215, 19:13, 37, 64, 24:330, 26:43, 238, 27:32, 163, 178, 187, 191, 210, 345, see also **Jews**

Hebrews, Epistle to the—2:252, 383, 387, 389, 3:19, 4:145, 151, 8:111, 114, 132, 146f, 178, 236, 9:23, 27, 13:306, 16:27, 19:197, 25:xii, 4, 26:198n, 199, 264, 267, 294, 320, 27:272, 29:ix, xi, 109–241, 30:ix

Hebron—2:200, 281, 287, 362, 381, 3:180, 316, 318, 351, 4:190, 192–194, 208–210, 298, 5:6, 9, 13, 59, 61, 6:184, 204, 267f, 280, 282, 285, 315, 344–346, 358, 386, 402, 405, 7:4, 105, 178, 208, 208f, 218, 250, 270, 8:156, 323

Hebronites—4:211f, 214, 7:223

Heckel, Johannes—13:160n

Hector—5:309, 382, 6:335, 7:164, 8:134, 13:58, 16:330n, 19:200, 27:103, 39:149n, 40:199, 45:329

Hecuba—39:149

Hedge masses—36:xii

Hedgehogs—11:337f, 18:345

Hedio, Caspar—38:8, 11, 15n, 30n, 36n, 61n, 71, 89n, 49:238n

Heemantic letters—7:188

Hefele, Karl Joseph von—*Conciliengeschichte*, Freiburg, 1873–1890 20:208n, 32:59n, 152n

Heide—32:278, 280, 284

Heidelberg—8:173n, 23:x, 31:37, 48:60f

University of 43:69n, 49:100, 414n, 50:213n

Heidelberg Disputation—38:xviii, 48:39n, 60f, 247n, 49:100, 177, 371, 414n, 50:266n

Heifers—9:213, 29:207f

Heights—11:258, 390f

Heinrich of Lüneburg—34:307

Heinz, Simon—51:xii

Heirs—4:17, 19, 21, 25, 27f, 30, 33, 43–45, 50–52, 54, 117f, 124, 144, 168, 224, 226, 231, 300, 302, 306, 308, 343, 345, 349, 366f, 371, 374, 388–390, 399, 13:157, 393, 14:9, 20, 25, 187, 333, 15:45, 94f, 22:90, 97, 100f, 110, 118, 136, 203, 26:304, 346, 352, 357, 359–361, 392–393, 401, 435, 437f, 441, 444f, 449, 457f, 27:243, 264, 282f, 289, 291, 323f, 29:98, 213

Heitner, Robert R.—translator of *Commentary on the Alleged Imperial Edict* 34:63–104

translator of *Counsel of a Committee of Several Cardinals with Luther's Preface* 34:231–268

translator of *The Three Symbols or Creeds of the Christian Faith* 34:197–230

Held, Matthias—43:266n, 50:155, 163n, 164n, 189n

Heldai—20:67f, 72, 253, 256

Helding, Michael—50:272n

Helen of Troy—2:29, 6:201, 204, 207

Helena—20:345

Heling, Moritz—7:ix

Heliodorus—4:181

Heliogabalus, Emperor—15:72n

Heliopolis—7:270, 16:165

Hell—1:10, 58, 173, 176, 190, 215n, 244, 275, 318, 2:6, 48, 64, 127, 156, 196, 220, 235, 241, 260f, 273, 275, 283, 340, 344, 351, 369, 3:9, 19, 28, 40, 89, 132, 139, 143, 230, 304, 338, 4:4, 50, 54f, 103, 106, 117, 119, 146f, 149, 160, 175, 191, 201, 203, 211, 232, 242, 312–315, 357f, 400, 5:19, 21, 24–27, 32, 48, 74, 130, 132, 142f, 149, 151, 158, 168, 191, 202, 206, 219–221, 224, 231, 234f, 244, 251, 254, 295, 355, 359, 7:63, 73, 99–102, 125, 127, 129, 132, 167, 172, 177, 194, 221, 225, 228, 247, 249f, 257, 292, 294, 296–298, 301–303, 320, 333, 361f, 366f, 369, 8:5f, 8, 10, 25, 27, 29, 31, 37, 39, 43, 52, 97, 137, 162f, 166, 177, 182f, 186, 193, 217, 238, 240, 251f, 255f, 267, 277, 283, 315f, 325, 330, 332, 9:4, 24,

57n, 87, 279, 295, 11:12, 135, 175n, 177, 248, 284, 341, 519, 13:93, 107f, 123, 242, 14:31, 73, 80, 82–85, 89, 95, 125, 142–144, 149, 172, 201, 217, 253, 269, 295, 324, 329, 335, 16:152f, 228, 267, 321, 18:72, 98, 364, 371, 19:5f, 17, 20, 44, 71f, 74f, 80, 125, 154, 157, 20:96, 268, 290, 21:153, 268, 270–272, 22:49, 52, 59, 61, 86, 90, 96, 133, 186, 195, 245, 291, 311, 314, 317f, 325f, 328, 350, 359, 366, 368f, 373, 375f, 382, 384, 390, 397f, 401, 405, 425, 446, 457, 461f, 471, 486, 505f, 23:18, 26–28, 33f, 43, 52, 60f, 71, 73, 77, 86, 106f, 110, 127, 136, 139–141, 147, 183, 206, 220, 231, 238, 263, 263, 270, 313, 315, 317, 324, 327f, 332, 336, 339–341, 355, 357, 359, 363–366, 370, 372, 375f, 402, 404, 413, 419, 24:17, 20, 36f, 39, 42, 44, 50, 53, 55, 62, 64, 70, 79, 85, 100, 102, 108f, 111–115, 132, 138, 140f, 143, 146, 149, 152, 158, 160, 163, 165, 175, 179, 185f, 189, 200, 217f, 220, 222, 237, 268f, 271, 276, 280, 286, 289, 291f, 296f, 302, 307, 310, 315, 322, 328, 334, 346, 350, 352, 360f, 376, 379, 387, 399, 411, 417, 420, 422, 26:10, 20, 22, 31, 37, 60, 72, 91, 119f, 153, 155, 157, 159–162, 167, 176, 218, 224, 252, 258, 282, 292f, 327, 331, 337, 340f, 345f, 350, 363, 382, 408, 415, 439, 453, 27:4, 8f, 21, 31, 33, 46, 69, 133, 154f, 158, 167, 221, 311, 385, 408, 28:100, 102, 105, 116, 144f, 204f, 30:9, 13, 29, 45, 49, 52, 57, 63–65, 101, 104–106, 113n, 154, 166, 172, 191, 197, 243, 253, 261, 263, 281, 291, 301, 303f, 326, 31:90, 32:31, 33:47, 153, 34:174, 35:102, 256, 359f, 405, 409, 36:39, 117, 166, 175, 202f, 214, 225, 350, 352, 37:25, 28, 58, 133f, 139, 293, 38:86, 99, 113, 125, 158, 160, 191, 223, 225, 243, 41:10, 12, 119, 140, 206, 209f, 214, 220, 226, 236f, 242f, 249f, 262, 265, 268, 270, 273, 278f, 285f, 288f, 293, 301, 303, 306, 308, 313, 315, 326, 328f, 340, 352, 354, 356, 361, 366, 42:75, 101n, 102, 103, 105–111, 114f, 125, 130, 133f, 155f, 164, 172, 175, 183, 46:19, 36, 40, 51, 54f, 66, 70, 84, 132, 134, 161, 181f, 219, 223f, 228–230, 254, 257, 47:15, 42, 49, 139, 143, 214, 293, 296f, 51:62, 73, 92f, 114, 164, 200, 52:69, 121, 196, 204

Hellenists—27:197

Hellespont—20:114

Helme River—7:299n

Helmstedt—University of 50:178n

Help, Human—16:255

Helplessness—16:314n

Helt, Conrad—48:125n, 129n, 219n, 236n, 325, 337n

Helt, George—34:148

Helvidius—38:20n, 54f, 45:211n, 213

Heman—11:187, 53:221

Hemmingstedt—32:283f

Hen and chicks (figure of Christ)—1:53, 67, 132, 6:129, 10:78, 11:181, 22:257, 261, 376, 379, 490, 23:325

Henneberg—46:141n, 142n, 143

Henning, Dr.—see **Goede, Henning**

Henry I, Emperor—41:375

Henry III, Emperor—41:126n, 53:255

Henry IV, Emperor—36:212n, 41:126n, 332n, 43:237, 44:164n, 54:407

Henry V, Emperor—41:126n, 332n

Henry VI, Emperor—8:288, 45:162

Henry VI, King of Bohemia and Poland—28:364n

Henry VIII, King of England—13:190n, 17:246n, 247n, 23:370n, 28:257, 32:122n, 34:83n, 35:128, 36:9, 105n, 41:xiiin, 43:10, 48:194n, 49:71, 78n, 116, 126n, 157, 185, 223n, 265, 266n, 50:106n, 114n, 117, 136f, 142n, 150, 162n, 179, 192n, 194, 198f, 54:284f, 317, 362, 384, 387, 420

and the religious situation in England 50:101, 103f, 115, 134n, 138n, 150n, 177n, 179f, 189f, 192f, 193n, 194–196, 198f, 200n, 201–204, 205f

his divorces and remarriages 50:27f, 31f, 98n, 104f, 104n, 106n, 114n, 118f, 120n, 121, 124n, 126f, 131n, 134n, 137n, 142n, 150n, 177n, 310

Henry, Duke of Braunschweig—43:221, 239–241, 253–288

Henry, Duke of Braunschweig-Wolfenbüttel—6:76n, 41:181n, 182n, 183–193, 198, 202, 211, 212n, 213, 218f, 220n, 221, 224f, 227–229, 230n, 231, 234f, 239, 241f, 243n, 244–256, 46:90n, 47:181, 254f, 40:82n, 110n, 124n, 350, 351n, 50:222n, 224, 225n, 282n, 54:217, 279, 370, 373, 406

Rejoinder against the Elector of Saxony 41:182n, 183, 185n, 186f, 188n, 189–193, 224n, 225, 229n, 237n, 241n

Henry, Duke of Saxony—5:x, 260, 34:148, 40:267, 50:73, 185, 51:303

Henry of Segusio—31:149n, 158

Golden Summary 31:164n

Henry of Zütphen—1:288, 9:4, 32:xviii, 261–286, 43:74n, 48:31, 236n, 49:21, 53:211
Hephzibah—17:345–347
Heracles—50:156n, 295n
Heraclitus—34:xvii
Heralds—17:13f, 58
Herbipolensis, Jakob Thanner—31:23
Herborn, Nicholas—*Locorum communium adversus huius temporis haereses enchiridion* 4:125n, 134n, 5:257n, 22:451n
Herbs—1:36–38, 40, 53–55, 63, 66, 73, 75, 83, 86, 91–93, 99, 102, 183, 187, 205, 210, 225, 2:74f
Hercules—3:189, 5:309, 312, 8:134, 10:136, 13:58, 199f, 205, 210, 15:5, 143n, 20:12, 31n, 25:300, 26:309, 27:154n, 371n, 31:237n
Hercynian Alps—2:108n
Hercynian forest—2:108, 17:20, 20:116
Herdsmen—7:166, 179, 181, 8:99, 103
Heredity—8:91
Heresy—1:95, 146, 213, 238, 2:45, 84, 87, 230, 240, 327n, 354, 3:56, 97, 271, 280, 301, 5:96, 124, 359, 8:32, 101, 9:130, 206, 251, 10:114, 144, 165, 389f, 13:61f, 178, 185, 236, 380, 14:11, 15f, 24f, 31, 55, 65, 78, 98, 100, 102, 209, 258, 271, 15:80f, 120, 155, 163f, 182f, 187, 219, 221, 230, 304, 349f, 16:28, 205, 241, 256, 17:12, 49, 94, 150, 375, 20:54, 136, 147, 151, 163, 207, 333f, 21:29f, 74, 163, 248–250, 262f, 265, 274f, 288, 22:11, 17f, 20, 25, 28, 58, 61, 67, 80, 82, 84, 110, 243, 252, 271, 332, 351, 361–363, 365, 389, 393, 408, 433, 450, 469, 475, 479, 481, 510, 524f, 23:79, 101, 189, 212, 227, 233, 236, 268, 319f, 326, 347, 386, 397, 414, 24:24, 43, 105, 131, 138, 169, 176, 202, 204f, 215, 224, 228n, 279, 303, 315, 320f, 366, 25:228f, 26:26, 135, 140, 156, 228, 365, 427, 443, 454f, 27:22f, 25, 32, 67, 72, 89, 97, 109, 364, 367f, 370, 389, 392n, 29:8f, 14, 33, 96, 182, 226, 30:119, 173, 204, 213, 227, 230, 239, 252, 284, 290, 311, 31:172, 185, 245, 33:163, 35:197, 372, 36:17, 25, 135, 214, 216, 271, 295, 347, 37:13f, 19f, 27n, 77, 81, 96, 99, 108, 110, 119, 131, 157, 162f, 169, 361, 368, 38:20, 39, 74, 98, 120, 129, 182, 224, 243, 288, 293, 307, 40:xiv, 57, 230, 41:13, 58, 61, 66f, 86–88, 96, 107n, 108, 117f, 120, 138, 141, 146, 167, 234, 242, 273, 278, 294, 320, 331, 362, 45:114f, 117, 199, 46:5, 228f, 233, 294, 47:16f, 31, 107, 154, 216n, 220, 297, 49:96f, 232f, 255n, 296n, 375, 398, 416n, 52:49, 59, 88, 54:41
Heretic(s)—1:13, 148, 169, 183, 253, 2:18, 37f, 60, 88, 108, 167, 182, 213, 354, 3:8, 14, 147, 272f, 4:31, 108, 122, 125, 304, 307f, 336, 345, 379, 382, 392, 407f, 5:16, 36, 96, 345, 6:27, 32, 52, 56, 81, 147, 293, 7:73, 86, 89, 94, 131, 135, 205, 256, 265, 355, 8:32, 59, 132f, 266, 270, 311, 9:111, 137, 171, 183, 187, 235f, 250, 10:7, 18, 58, 102f, 135, 144f, 150, 172, 219, 242, 274, 276, 278f, 351f, 375, 387, 390, 425f, 441, 11:27, 46f, 49, 62, 64, 68, 74f, 77, 87, 110, 124, 136, 157, 167, 169, 197, 201, 208, 210f, 215, 220, 224, 235, 243f, 251, 279, 284, 289f, 292, 294, 308, 328n, 338f, 348, 363, 415f, 418, 424f, 428–430, 447, 461, 469–471, 476, 479, 481, 492f, 495, 498, 503, 512, 522, 526–528, 535f, 546f, 12:371, 13:44, 61f, 185, 187, 204, 414, 14:11, 16, 55f, 73, 92, 94, 102, 225, 243, 245–247, 251–253, 256, 261, 266, 271, 276, 290, 293, 305f, 309f, 327, 16:28, 35, 57, 60, 123, 202, 205, 216, 234, 249, 269, 332, 17:16, 152, 159, 185, 246f, 276, 23:77, 79, 122, 124, 126, 137, 184, 223, 225, 230–232, 235, 242, 285f, 288f, 300, 363, 397, 405, 408, 24:8, 21, 71, 91, 93, 103, 107, 168, 176, 187, 205, 207f, 216, 228, 246, 275, 281, 287, 290, 296, 303f, 312, 318, 322, 324, 331, 365, 25:16, 61, 78, 88, 91, 96, 138, 142, 167, 176, 182, 230, 235–237, 244f, 337, 398, 404, 413f, 428, 510, 26:31, 49, 52, 67, 70, 88, 99, 156, 198, 335, 365, 375, 387, 394, 418, 437, 453f, 456f, 27:19, 43, 53f, 83f, 91f, 123f, 131–136, 148, 153, 169, 178, 239, 303, 370, 382, 399f, 408, 28:69f, 193, 198, 230f, 254, 344, 365, 374, 29:4, 8, 15, 30, 33, 35, 87, 89, 97, 182, 30:19n, 51, 61, 105, 107, 219, 222, 228, 239, 241–243, 252, 254, 257, 260–262, 269, 287, 289, 292, 299, 306, 308, 310, 317, 319, 324, 32:xiiin, 87–89, 126, 35:103, 151, 197, 269, 317, 328, 390, 402, 410, 36:20, 24, 26, 28, 30, 134, 166f, 211, 222, 227, 229, 276n, 287f, 299, 304, 351, 38:20, 50, 147f, 182f, 192, 196, 223, 229f, 258f, 282, 303f, 308, 309n, 310, 312f, 39:58, 67, 73, 75f, 79, 87f, 101, 170f, 174, 181, 205, 207, 211, 234, 247, 268, 41:6, 10, 12f, 22, 31,

45–48, 50, 52, 66, 68, 70, 83f, 91, 93f, 108, 115, 117f, 120, 133, 165, 170, 188, 192–196, 198, 200, 210–212, 219, 224, 229, 301, 307, 309, 313, 320f, 331, 345, 347, 349, 361–363, 42:24, 46:90n, 225, 227, 231f, 240, 51:175, 320, 373, 52:49, 53, 81f, 115, 175f, 206

Heritage of the Reformation—see **Pauck, Wilhelm**

Herman—13:59

Hermaphrodites—41:272, 282n, 287, 289, 296f, 300, 362n

Hermelink, Heinrich—34:135n

Hermeneutics, Scholastic—10:xi

Hermes—20:60

Hermes Trismegistus—34:143

Hermit(s)—2:103, 3:66, 113, 131, 139, 202, 217, 315, 328f, 4:56, 123, 181, 5:4n, 7:326, 342, 13:56, 23:24, 139, 204, 25:419, 26:149, 332, 333n, 459f, 27:9, 68f, 75, 83, 85, 36:115, 220f, 223, 41:38n, 40, 52, 124, 125n, 42:73, 139

Hermon, Mt.—9:40, 60, 10:34, 136f, 195–199, 203, 19:223, 22:422, 25:380, 26:436, 27:177, 315

Hermonim (name for Christians)—10:195f, 198f, 204

Herod, King—1:195, 2:32, 321, 3:88, 167, 4:358, 5:160f, 6:162, 389, 401, 7:130, 195, 301, 11:31, 100n, 456, 13:184, 339, 346, 14:97, 231, 266, 313, 321, 16:45, 106, 118, 17:367, 20:192, 314, 22:49, 127, 129, 413, 415, 493, 511, 23:210, 24:21, 59, 155, 237, 274, 412, 25:271, 28:358, 29:34, 34:52, 39:18, 124, 41:122, 243, 256, 42:139f, 160, 45:112, 214, 215n, 46:51, 199f, 47:181, 183f, 192, 194–197, 200, 203–205, 221–225, 231, 250, 263, 298, 300f, 51:89, 160, 52:35, 115f, 145, 159, 163, 170f, 183f, 189f, 198, 201, 207f, 215, 218, 235, 239f, 243f, 249f, 259, 270, 273f, 283f, 286

Herodias—7:99, 19:185, 22:127, 52:90

Herodotus—2:188n, 54:155
History 3:281n 324n, 7:65n, 345n, 346n, 15:42n, 16:132n, 158n, 161n, 163n, 17:122n

Heroes—3:39, 13:58, 164f, 20:109f, 112, 302, 305

Herr Omnes—45:63n

Herring—1:51

Herrmann, Fritz—*Die Prozess gegen D. John Drach und die Unterdrücking der Evangelischen Bewegung in Miltenburg* 43:100n

Hersfeld—48:225f, 235

Herte, Adolf—54:137n

Hervais of Bourg-Dieu—*Commentaria in Esaiam* 16:100n, 25n, 265n

Herwagen, John—36:332, 37:10, 77n, 148n

Herzberg—48:28

Heschel, Abraham Joshua—47:128n

Heshbon—9:27, 16:151

Hesiod—5:291, 341n
Opera et dies 20:79n
Theogonia 29:38n
Works and Days 3:332, 5:291n, 7:162n, 15:63n

Hess, Eoban—14:xf, 33:12n, 46:214n, 49:32f, 51:61
Letter from Luther 33:12

Hess, John—36:234, 37:10, 43:116, 119–138, 48:143n, 49:122n, 175n, 196f, 216, 343, 54:470

Hess, Master John Eissermann—48:166n

Hesse—38:26, 57, 63, 74, 83, 46:59, 90, 48:225n, 247n, 49:17n, 50:00n, 178

Hessians—54:310, 331

Hewers of wood—9:193, 272

Hexapolis—2:202

Heydemreich, Caspar—54:xiii, 368, 413
recorder of Luther's table conversation, 1542–1543 54:411–464

Heymann, F.G.—47:18n

Hezekiah, King—2:258, 3:156, 270, 278, 4:261, 263, 7:52, 8:299, 304, 9:81, 11:520, 12:30, 238, 292, 13:130, 14:143, 186, 16:6, 80, 83, 85f, 90, 113, 115, 117, 142f, 150, 178, 252f, 273, 278, 280–282, 285, 307, 309f, 312, 314, 316f, 322, 332, 334, 336–338, 344, 347f, 18:63, 210, 283f, 19:154, 21:232, 22:347f, 27:43, 29:128, 164, 30:172, 38:290, 45:208n, 46:173, 47:160, 203, 51:82, 52:217, 53:90

Hiddekel—1:97, 101

Hidden God, The—3:139, 5:44–46, 48, 50, 6:148, 236, 259, 354, 359, 398, 401, 7:175, 8:4, 9, 30, 9:33, 41, 10:62, 118, 14:142, 191, 16:93, 17:131f, 278f, 21:309, 23:105, 123, 139, 25:437–439, 28:125f, 30:267, 33:62f, 136–147, 41:171, 42:18, 44:28, 47:209n, 49:371

Hiddenness—10:91, 98, 107, 112, 120, 125, 155f, 166, 445, 25:44, 105, 223, 278, 296, 356, 359f, 365f, 368, 371, 424, 437, 504f, 37:xx, 66, 92, 101, 118, 129, 178, 228, 366

Hierarchies—1:235, 13:30f, 174f, 27:398, 36:109–110

Hierarchies, Three—5:139, 15, 260

Hieroglyphics—4:87
Hieronymous, Archbishop—see **Aleander, Jerome**
High places—18:56, 211–213
High priests—5:19f, 313, 13:346, 26:178, 180, 182, 288, 381, 387, 428, 29:196
Highwaymen—45:270, 46:39, 178
Hilarion, St.—2:355, 3:329, 355, 4:109, 5:4, 13, 13:56n, 23:76, 139, 269
Hilarity—12:81
Hilary, Pope—43:156
Hilary of Arles—31:154
Hilary of Poitiers, St.—1:22, 37, 50, 69, 121, 3:191, 194, 298, 12:222, 283, 14:285, 288, 305, 17:396, 406, 18:170f, 20:184, 22:514, 23:184n, 24:187, 30:320, 31:214, 276, 32:144, 194, 244, 34:95, 35:402n, 37:54n, 59, 61n, 75, 120f, 132, 39:280n, 40:289, 41:52n, 53n, 59n, 80n, 83n, 994n, 308, 45:361n, 54:26, 34, 271
Against Constantius 32:244n
De Trinitate 3:61n, 297n, 6:380n, 10:18, 74, 144, 185, 11:422n, 15:300n, 310, 17:131n
On the Trinity 1:4n, 21n, 263n, 278n, 22:362, 23:184n, 24:187n, 30:320, 32:144n, 194n, 33:205n
Tractatus super Psalmos 14:288n, 305n
Hildebrand—see **Gregory VII, Pope**
Hildesheim—41:230n, 240n
Hilgenfeld, A.—22:67n
Hill, Charles L., translator—*Loci Communes of Philip Melanchthon*, Boston, 1944 54:260n
Hillerbrand, Hans J.—author of Introduction to Vol. 52
editor of Vol. 52
Hilten, John—41:116
Himalaya Mts.—2:108n
Himmel, Augustin—50:111n
Hind—8:291–293
Hinnom, Valley of—7:301
Hinnom and Topheth—36:224
Hinrichs, Carl—*Thomas Münzer: Politische Schriften mit Kommentar* 5:311n
Hinschius, Paul—*Das Kirchenrecht der Katholiken und Protestanten in Deutschland*, Berlin, 1888 32:87n
Hippo—22:512, 41:132, 325n, 326
Hippocrates—5:381
Hippolytus—54:306
Hiram, King of Tyre—3:112, 18:135, 47:86
Hirelings—21:319, 26:10
Hirsch, Emanuel—52:xn
Mitteilung der Luther gesellschaft 51:xin, xvn
Predigen, CL, Berlin, 1932 51:xin, xiv, 121
Hirschfeld, Bernhard von—48:33n, 50, 314n
Historia Tripartita—see **Cassiodorus**
Historians—2:94, 134, 7:3, 270, 45:370, 376
Historical approach—12:54
Historical criticism—25:129
Historical faith—5:131, 22:153n, 369, 26:168, 27:28n, 34:122
Historical perspective—35:231
Historical order—6:314f
Historical sense—6:125, 134
Histories—6:16, 206, 213, 244, 253, 297, 332, 335, 343, 16:137, 169, 41:57, 60, 79, 93, 107, 112, 120, 126f, 276f, 290, 331, 372f, 47:199, 208, 217, 224, 231, 236, 246f, 251, 288, 299
History—2:176, 188, 190, 200, 215, 234–236, 265f, 4:3, 366, 395, 7:7, 9, 15, 10:3–5, 314, 14:52, 95, 214, 265, 267, 331, 15:43, 71, 102f, 349, 16:3, 137, 173, 325, 327, 24:159, 254, 320, 27:28, 60, 97f, 268, 31:315, 395, 34:275, 277, 35:230, 258, 38:308–310, 44:95, 45:198, 224n, 228, 368f, 376n, 46:41, 124, 203, 238, 245, 54:407
History, Church—see **Church history**
History, Faith and—32:69
History in Genesis, General and special—2:ix
Hittites—2:204, 5:96f, 102, 146, 167, 6:286, 288, 290f, 294, 8:85
Hivites—8:198
Hobah—2:376
Hoboes—17:287
Hoeck, Wilhelm—22:xi
Hoelty-Nickel, Theodore—*Luther and Music*, Decorah, 1960 53:xxn
Hoelzel, Hieronymous—31:22
Hoen, Cornelius—36:279n, 40:68n
A Most Christian Letter 37:xii, xvi
Hoerschelmann, D.F.—*Andreas Kropken, der Reformator Rigas* 45:314n
Hoes—24:194f, 198–200
Hoettges, Valerie—*Typenverzeichnis der deutschen Riesen- und Riesischen Teufelssagen*, Helsinki, 1937 8:288n
Hoffmann, Melchior—53:43
Hofheim—50:51
Hofmann, Hans—54:381
Hofweise—53:196, 292
Hogs—13:366, 376
Hohenstaufens—41:277n

Hohndorf, John—54:54, 188, 281
Holewind—2:106
Holidays—24:175, 26:411f, 27:62, 296
Holiness—1:65, 135, 2:60, 63, 79, 172, 349f, 355, 4:49, 56, 123, 157f, 178, 181, 235, 238f, 242, 247, 5:4, 8, 39, 195, 214, 232, 242, 267, 275, 329, 355, 7:58, 96, 108, 230, 261f, 284, 311, 313, 341, 344, 347, 351, 362, 366, 8:56, 59, 139, 9:27f, 56, 254, 11:261, 264–266, 12:38–40, 234f, 353f, 362, 388, 14:15, 22, 24f, 29, 39, 61, 78, 85f, 93f, 97, 105, 151, 172, 196, 198, 327f, 22:55, 63, 71f, 87, 89, 107, 118, 122, 130f, 163, 166, 254, 321, 335, 361, 463, 487, 490, 523, 23:47, 53, 64f, 70, 72, 85, 120, 124, 144, 148, 179, 182, 205, 242, 267, 284, 315, 318, 329, 331, 334f, 347, 357–359, 366, 375, 377, 387, 24:58, 64, 72, 88, 109, 120, 126, 139, 154, 169f, 172, 177, 210, 221, 226f, 229, 236, 246, 260, 290, 294, 315, 322f, 25:435f, 26:25, 32, 34f, 38, 40f, 52, 70, 109, 112, 122n, 152, 182, 199f, 259–261, 288, 307, 313, 320, 331, 355, 360, 396, 428, 458, 27:14, 53, 60f, 68, 77, 82f, 85–89, 91, 115, 140f, 156, 277, 280, 302, 342, 346, 394, 405f, 28:35, 83f, 29:30, 50, 143, 152, 30:6–8, 16, 50, 60, 103, 232, 244, 255, 256, 263, 268, 270, 295, 35:144, 215, 383, 411, 37:99, 101, 107, 112, 118, 131f, 161, 163, 188, 202, 236–238, 355, 364f, 367f, 370f, 41:17, 19, 40, 128, 130, 145–148, 199, 214, 218, 272, 300, 357, 42:67, 140, 46:173, 183, see also **Saintliness**
Holiness, Excessive—11:502
Holiness, Invented—41:145, 172
Holl, Karl—21:xv, 47:9n
Cultural Significance of the Reformation, New York, 1959 45:344n
Gesammelte Aufsätze zur Kirchengeschichte, Tübingen, 1932 10:75n, 21:157n, 32:153n, 35:231n, 232n, 39:xiin, 41:xin, 45:128n, 259n, 276n, 270n, 283n, 287n
Holland—32:135, 34:345, 353, 38:xiii
Holm, John—32:282, 286
Holmio, Armas K.E.—47:124n, 51:239n
Lutheran Reformation and the Jews 47:124n
Holofernes—20:160
Holstein—3:249n, 45:308
Holy, Definition of—21:329f
Holy City—24:302
Holy Communion—see **Lord's Supper**
Holy days—38:190, 40:298, 304, 309, 376
Holy Ghost—see **Holy Spirit**
Holy Land—1:78n, 2:368, 3:74, 4:71, 331, 7:208, 8:177, 194, 247, 291, 9:32n, 14:xi, 23:378, 47:128, 48:33n, 204n, 227n, 50:73
Holy League of 1511—50:206n
Holy League of 1537—50:183n, 190n
Holy of Holies—11:96, 29:199f, 203–205
Holy One of Israel—16:10, 23, 65, 131, 155, 250, 256f, 269, 322, 17:47, 49, 86, 96, 176, 322, 19:115, 178f, 230
Holy Place—29:199f, 203f, 38:174, 176f, 179f, 182, 187, 190, 192f, 197f, 204, 208, 211
Holy Saturday—2:154n
Holy Scriptures—see **Scripture(s)**
Holy Spirit—1:5, 9, 12, 15, 17, 19, 30, 47, 50f, 57–60, 64, 66, 127, 134, 136f, 139, 146, 149, 157, 185, 194, 220, 223, 228, 238–240, 243, 247, 262, 273, 276f, 283, 286, 290f, 311, 344, 2:5, 7, 13, 17, 19f, 23, 25f, 28, 33f, 37–41, 43f, 47, 49–52, 54, 57, 59, 64, 82f, 103f, 112, 120, 124, 128, 130, 141, 153, 156, 163, 165f, 169, 174, 176f, 179, 182, 184, 186, 193, 198, 215, 219, 224f, 231, 235, 239, 241, 245, 250, 252, 254f, 261, 267, 287, 293, 295f, 300f, 305, 307f, 311, 316, 319f, 323, 325, 329, 331n, 335, 344, 349, 364, 372, 374–376, 379, 386–388, 393, 3:4, 8f, 11f, 20f, 24, 30, 35f, 38, 52f, 56, 58, 69, 97, 102, 113, 115, 124, 138, 161, 165, 167, 194f, 200, 206, 208, 211f, 217, 219, 224, 237, 241–244, 247f, 265, 275, 281, 288, 293, 296f, 312, 316, 320–323, 338, 347, 353, 355, 363f, 4:10f, 14, 19, 31f, 34, 44, 58, 60, 62, 67, 72, 78, 83f, 101, 106, 117, 119, 121, 124f, 128, 130, 141f, 151, 160–162, 168f, 173, 195n, 196, 198–203, 207–209, 217, 220, 229, 232, 238, 249, 259, 272, 274, 276, 278, 282–286, 288, 293–295, 297, 304, 310, 318, 343, 361f, 376, 380–382, 392, 397–399, 5:24, 27–30, 33, 39, 67, 72, 84, 95, 102, 104f, 111, 114, 117f, 129, 133–136, 140f, 148, 158, 168, 187, 196, 220, 223, 226f, 258, 266f, 275, 277, 281–283, 286, 288–291, 311f, 320, 327, 329–331, 333f, 352–355, 358, 372, 380, 6:58f, 74, 97, 106–108, 123, 128, 135, 159, 333–335, 7:10, 12f, 15–18, 31, 35–37, 40, 46f, 54, 56f, 71–74, 77, 81, 87, 90, 100–102, 105, 110–112, 114, 128f, 139, 142f, 148–150, 153f, 156, 158f,

163f, 170, 172, 191, 203, 205, 212, 222, 226, 235, 256, 261, 263, 273, 276, 278, 282, 304f, 310, 314, 316, 319f, 340, 343, 354, 356, 365–367, 370, 8:3, 10, 12f, 16, 19f, 22–24, 27, 29, 34, 40, 45f, 49f, 62, 68f, 75f, 87, 92, 94, 110f, 129, 139f, 144f, 149, 153, 155–158, 160, 164f, 168, 170, 179, 182, 192, 215–217, 221, 237, 244f, 247–252, 254f, 257–260, 264–272, 274f, 279, 283, 295, 308, 310, 312, 314, 9:15, 19, 52, 109n, 110n, 158, 184f, 198, 10:4, 12, 15, 50, 275, 348f, 399, 456, 11:6, 90, 367, 551, 12:10f, 18, 20, 22, 34, 37f, 43, 50, 58, 63, 65, 68f, 72, 74f, 81–83, 89, 91f, 118, 120f, 129, 134f, 157, 176f, 197f, 205, 229, 232, 246f, 252, 263, 269f, 273, 275, 277f, 281, 284, 296, 299, 303–305, 319f, 323f, 330–333, 339f, 344, 351–353, 358f, 365f, 368f, 372, 374, 377–385, 388f, 394–397, 401, 407, 13:3f, 15–17, 20, 79, 87, 111, 134, 139, 179, 188, 271, 290f, 293–295, 302, 351, 364, 370, 404, 14:8f, 12–14, 21, 25, 37, 39, 55, 59, 62, 77, 81, 87, 89, 130, 170, 172, 203f, 210, 217, 222, 265, 267, 270, 285, 313, 315, 325, 328f, 333, 15:43, 47, 185, 197, 209, 218f, 231, 233, 249, 275–277, 279, 286f, 289, 295, 297f, 303–308, 316, 16:6, 27, 34, 36, 43, 45, 51f, 54, 60, 71, 73, 97–99, 101, 106, 117–120, 122f, 130f, 135, 178, 242, 280, 299, 302f, 309, 312, 315, 319, 327, 330, 17:3f, 8, 11f, 29, 54, 62, 117, 124, 129, 171f, 192, 219, 243f, 256, 309f, 329, 356, 358, 388, 408f, 18:67, 73, 75, 89, 97, 100, 105–108, 349, 414, 19:11, 45, 54f, 72–74, 79, 87, 97, 124, 151f, 230, 20:12f, 36, 40–45, 49–51, 58, 67, 100f, 112, 137, 139, 144f, 162, 205, 212, 219, 222–224, 229, 240, 252, 294f, 312, 328, 331f, 337, 340, 21:138, 154, 249, 299f, 302, 314, 325, 353, 22:5f, 10, 13–16, 20, 23, 30, 38f, 44, 54f, 62, 65, 75f, 78, 80, 83, 88, 108, 116, 123, 127, 133, 138, 144, 146, 160, 166, 170–173, 179f, 201, 209, 223, 248, 256, 261, 263, 265, 272, 280, 284, 286, 300, 302f, 415, 427, 432, 443, 454, 462, 468, 472f, 478, 487–490, 495–498, 503, 527, 24:ix, 10, 13, 89, 92–94, 103f, 110–118, 121–131, 135, 137, 139, 142, 168–177, 179, 187, 212, 221, 226, 280, 290–292, 294–298, 304, 316, 320–322, 330, 334–340, 349–368, 371–374, 376, 382, 402, 404f, 422,
25:44, 71, 74, 122, 124, 147, 167, 294, 296, 326, 333, 356, 360, 365f, 504, 26:5, 15, 46, 73, 79, 81f, 92, 98f, 104, 109, 111, 119, 133, 135f, 139, 141, 146, 148, 154f, 169, 171f, 181, 184, 188f, 197, 203–215, 221, 226, 228, 236f, 239, 243, 255, 260, 264, 266, 269f, 274, 279, 286, 289, 301, 315, 345, 353, 362, 364, 374–379, 381, 383–385, 387, 389, 393, 401, 413f, 429f, 438–440, 446, 451, 457, 27:9, 23, 28, 32, 46, 82, 110, 121, 131, 137, 140f, 144, 165, 168, 172, 185, 221, 226, 234, 247f, 252, 261, 263, 276, 288, 290, 318f, 326, 335, 355, 362, 366f, 370, 373, 376, 387f, 390, 28:66f, 69, 87, 178f, 197, 244, 289, 292, 296f, 299, 306, 312, 314, 337, 29:10, 26, 31, 38, 42, 56, 60, 62, 81–83, 85, 98, 102, 114, 129, 135, 137, 161, 186, 197f, 214, 236, 30:22–24, 29, 38, 44, 49, 58, 112, 121, 128, 138, 164–168, 183, 194, 210, 214f, 236, 248f, 254–256, 297–299, 306f, 309, 315f, 321, 327, 31:45, 60, 90, 114, 184, 206, 269, 358, 367, 384, 32:23f, 35f, 79, 95f, 163f, 173–175, 33:6, 18, 21, 24, 28, 60f, 65, 83, 90f, 105f, 155, 158, 242f, 260, 34:53, 66, 68f, 72, 101, 168, 173, 217, 35:xiii, 83n, 110, 136f, 161, 214, 218, 221, 230, 254, 293, 319, 339, 344, 367f, 370–372, 376f, 380f, 397f, 407, 36:20, 34, 40, 74, 76f, 81, 91, 93, 107f, 112, 115, 142, 145f, 149, 151–153, 155–160, 163–165, 167, 179, 185–187, 192, 194–196, 200–203, 211, 217–223, 229, 297f, 301, 344f, 355, 37:xviii, 16n, 58, 61, 77, 89, 94f, 98f, 107, 112, 126, 130, 137, 163, 165, 169, 193, 210, 236f, 279, 289f, 292, 325, 333f, 338, 343, 352, 361f, 365f, 368, 38:xiv, 9, 18, 23, 25, 30f, 44, 46, 51n, 54f, 59, 85–89, 126, 129, 131, 137, 153, 157, 169, 178f, 185f, 188, 192f, 196, 198, 208, 224, 231, 250, 252, 262n, 295–297, 305, 308, 317, 319, 39:xiv, 67, 75, 77, 79, 83, 86, 103, 144, 155, 160f, 170, 175f, 178, 182f, 197, 199, 203, 220, 237, 268, 277f, 281, 289, 40:25, 29, 33, 52, 55–57, 82, 118, 144, 146f, 208, 41:xiv, 10, 27–31, 41, 43, 49, 51f, 58, 60, 68–70, 73f, 86n, 87, 89, 91–93, 106, 114, 120–123, 139, 143–149, 151, 153f, 156f, 164–167, 169–172, 174, 177f, 189, 202, 223, 249, 271–273, 289, 299, 301, 309, 311, 315, 319, 324, 326f, 330, 342f, 346, 355, 358, 360,

364, 370, 42:23, 25, 32, 56, 88, 114, 124, 162, 175, 186, 43:191, 198, 201f, 44:xiii, 91, 234, 241f, 269, 284, 288, 45:8, 24, 39, 41, 67, 69, 84, 89, 91–93, 97f, 100f, 103f, 122, 147, 151, 158, 204f, 208, 211, 219, 287, 321, 343, 358–362, 365f, 46:41, 102, 136, 150, 153, 161, 166, 177, 209, 220, 228f, 242, 254, 305, 47:11, 17, 19, 35, 51f, 54f, 107, 119, 183, 300, 48:53f, 303, 49:62, 79, 141, 179, 271, 51:46, 74, 81, 110–112, 128, 130, 132, 162, 165–169, 183, 186, 192, 216, 222, 224f, 227, 235, 248, 298, 304, 306, 317–324, 373f, 376, 392, 52:44f, 98, 103, 105, 131

Comes only with the Word 5:111

Comforter 23:230, 30:236

Transforms minds 25:438

Holy Spirit, Anointed by the—38:185f, 192f, 208

Holy Spirit, Baptism of the—22:82, 161, 171, 239, 283, 285, 438, 42:142n

Holy Spirit, Drunk with the—8:249, 251, 255, 259ff, 266–269

Holy Spirit, Gifts of the—4:122, 8:269f, 11:423, 12:33, 377, 381f, 386, 20:25f, 40f, 45, 50f, 157, 182, 219, 229, 249, 25:296, 26:376, 40:55f, 41:114, 326

Holy Spirit, Indwelling of the—25:68

Holy Spirit, Office of the—24:175, 295, 336, 349, 357, 362, 323, 372

Holy Spirit, Paraclete—3:69, 16:119, 17:278

Holy Spirit, Seven gifts of the—11:444

Holy Spirit, Sin against the—3:296, 8:330, 9:198, 14:76f, 272, 16:35, 18:414, 19:47–49, 20:145, 240, 312, 21:80, 28:244, 292, 312, 32:95f, 35:14f, 37:25f, 115, 147n, 47:11, 17, 51

Holy Spirit, Works of the—see **Works of the Holy Spirit**

Holy Supper—see **Lord's Supper**

Holy things—16:203

Holy water—1:229, 51:321, 326f

Holy Week—see **Passion Week**

Holy Writ—see **Scripture(s)**

Holy year—54:239f

Homburg, Synod of—49:17n

Homer—1:247, 5:353, 9:6, 13:199f, 23:51, 26:296, 406n, 49:34, 50:156

Iliad 2:192n, 227n, 4:119n, 5:382n, 13:119n, 202n, 14:280n, 15:130n, 156n, 16:330n

Iliad and *Odyssey* 33:171n, 234n, 42:159n

Odyssey 1:206n, 2:42n, 192n, 4:208n, 364n, 7:159n, 26:406n, 28:85n, 31:277n, 50:228n, 289n

Homes—2:32, 83, 140, 165, 169, 216, 228, 251–253, 267f, 270, 272, 296, 314, 319, 371, 26:48, 174, 28:128, 41:176f, 45:190n, 323f, 335, 369f

Like nests for birds 1:132f

Homicide—2:142, 4:102, 375, 9:167, 193f

Homilia in Evangelia—see **Gregory I, Pope**

Homily—40:389n, 53:38, 78

Homoousion—32:243f

Homosexuality, Homosexuals—3:251–255, 25:165f

Honesty—20:277, 21:235f, 27:95, 377, see also **Truthfulness**

Honesty, Civic—12:354, 356f

Honey—3:140, 183, 7:69, 85, 322f, 8:254, 256, 261, 9:293

Honius, Cornelius—see **Hoen, Cornelius**

Honor—21:12, 132f, 136f, 143, 183f, 322, 329f, 25:7, 107, 120f, 158f, 179, 226, 410, 448f, 455, 29:119, 173, 46:15, 77, 117, 132f, 185, 226, 237, 244, 246, 255, 309

Honor, Womanly—see **Womanly honor**

Honorius, Emperor—41:372n, 373n

Honorius, Pope—39:62n

Hoods—3:146

Hoofs—20:66, 127f

Hooker, Richard—41:xivn

Hooks—4:47, 360

Hooves—9:136f

Hope—1:57, 60, 177f, 180, 186, 191, 193, 196f, 220, 224f, 236, 242–246, 315, 328, 334, 353, 3:19, 24, 33, 37, 40, 44, 58, 63, 99, 123f, 129, 134, 149, 154, 167, 179, 208, 210–212, 237, 255, 260, 292, 300, 303f, 315, 321, 324, 329, 331, 344f, 351, 355, 357, 4:4, 21, 24, 39, 45, 54, 59, 65f, 71, 92, 94, 97, 103, 108–110, 115f, 144, 146, 190, 205, 217, 258, 262, 268, 294f, 311, 315, 318, 320, 322f, 325, 327, 329f, 336–338, 343, 352f, 355, 357, 359, 362, 373, 392, 402, 404, 5:8, 14, 27, 53, 62, 69, 77, 79f, 82, 167–169, 171, 177, 184, 186, 192, 202–204, 208, 255, 275, 282, 295–297, 315, 321, 326–328, 332, 334, 343, 345, 347, 359, 361f, 364, 386, 6:35, 37, 52, 92, 99, 116, 272, 402, 7:11f, 23, 29, 33, 44, 48f, 54f, 61, 64f, 97, 99f, 105f, 114, 116f, 122f, 125f, 130, 132, 134f, 137f, 141, 170f, 176f, 194, 202, 209f, 219, 221, 250, 253, 265, 289, 310, 315, 327, 331, 344, 351, 353, 357, 366, 368, 371, 8:6, 8, 12, 15,

18f, 32, 36, 47, 74, 82, 90, 114f, 140, 144, 157f, 162, 170, 174, 186, 190, 235f, 257, 289, 294, 304, 315, 318–320, 9:57n, 244, 277, 10:249, 260f, 283, 288, 395, 398, 11:18, 39, 97, 253, 449f, 452f, 471f, 484, 529, 12:7, 29f, 50, 85, 89, 220, 359, 404, 406, 409f, 14:320, 322, 15:146, 16:31, 137, 144, 169, 198, 200f, 209, 226, 315f, 20:98, 101, 290f, 22:84, 121, 24:11, 151f, 196f, 25:40, 44, 72, 74, 78, 88, 107, 120, 122, 127, 283, 292f, 364, 458, 515f, 518, 26:7, 62, 193, 219f, 318, 342, 353, 356, 360, 365, 434, 443, 449, 27:20–27, 46, 64, 68, 72f, 97, 100, 218, 314, 326, 328, 332f, 374, 401, 405, 28:60f, 114, 218, 242, 245f, 325, 335, 29:10–12, 66, 69, 129, 162, 181, 188, 230, 30:9, 11, 13f, 16, 28f, 39, 107, 159n, 179, 214, 224, 232, 268, 280, 283, 289, 321, 31:48, 51, 34:53, 320, 35:286, 374, 380, 385, 36:42, 37:11, 100f, 116, 118, 124, 132, 38:29, 41:146f, 165, 42:148, 161, 1172, 43:103, 52:243, see also **Eternal life, Hope of**

Hopelessness—16:285, 25:270

Hoppe, A.F.—12:viii, x, 54:xiv, xvn

Horace—3:68f, 14:280n, 32:141, 195n, 34:43n 129n, 211n, 37:172f, 176, 39:129n

Art of Poetry 3:68n, 4:188n, 192n, 5:336n, 7:72n, 13:174, 15:117n, 241n, 16:287n, 17:247n, 296n, 29:144n, 32:195n, 33:21n, 33n, 141n, 193n, 54:249

Carmina 5:16n, 66n, 6:9n, 344n, 13:92, 26:406n

Epistles 2:22n, 3:128n, 332n, 4:345n, 5:172n, 369n, 6:47n, 206n, 370n, 7:54n, 159n, 8:103n, 189n, 294n, 9:267n, 10:86, 13:120n, 14:317n, 15:133n, 20:27n, 25:105, 448, 26:106n, 158n, 27:116n, 32:141n, 33:76n, 50:230n

Epodes 18:83n

Odes 10:102, 15:87n, 157n, 240n, 19:125n, 28:292f

Satires 4:197n, 219n, 15:68n, 16:11n, 25:448, 30:250n, 33:21n, 34:283n, 332n, 40:205n, 49:34n, 341n, 50:245n

Sermones 11:280n, 15:10n, 28:293, 300, 28:300n

Horeb, Mt.—9:15–17, 180, 182, 271, 11:54, 17:252

Horites—2:367, 6:291, 294–297, 302–305

Horn (musical instrument)—11:101f, 272–275, 286–288

Horn, Johann—36:275

Hornets—9:87f

Horns—3:62, 10:113f, 11:101, 19:138, 24:377, 382, 413

Horns, Meaning of—20:21–23, 179, 185

Hornsby, Roger A.—translator of *Luther at the Diet of Worms* 32:101–132

Hornung (February)—20:166n

Hornung, Wolf—49:326n, 348, 353, 425

Horsemen—19:171

Horses—1:67, 81, 2:66, 75, 135, 147, 244, 380, 3:149, 218, 4:205, 250, 283, 317, 342, 5:121, 208, 271, 289, 370, 381, 6:15, 293, 301, 7:139, 169, 172, 193, 205f, 208, 332, 8:253, 282, 9:169f, 202, 220, 11:4, 9, 15, 13:171, 16:64, 269, 310, 18:254, 20:15f, 24, 44, 62, 64–66, 95, 108, 110, 134, 167–169, 183f, 247–250, 23:84, 241, 389, 403f, 24:37, 167, 188, 383f, 46:94, 136, 191

Horses and mules—10:148f, 190, 428

Hortulus animae—43:6, 10

Hosanna—11:271, 14:101f, 105

Hosea, Book of—5:252, 17:345, 20:151, 156

Hosea, Prophet—3:70, 330, 6:126f, 223, 264, 8:253, 282, 9:55, 11:40, 13:284, 16:5n, 88, 197, 18:x, 3f, 16f, 26, 54, 63, 69, 127f, 207, 19:3, 23, 25:84–86, 26:281, 27:385, 35:317f, 36:221–223, 41:208, 217n

Commentary on his book 18:x, 3–76 (text)

Hosea, Prophet, Luther's lectures on—Basel text 18:x, 12n, 13n, 21n, 33n, 39n, 41n, 47n, 51n

Hosius, Bishop of Cordova—41:56n

Hospitality—3:177–182, 183n, 184f, 187–189, 196–199, 244–246, 249, 258, 326, 4:269, 271f, 278, 281f, 8:60, 65, 9:229, 25:107, 462f, 25:120f, 485–487, 492, 501, 25:125, 28:285, 340, 29:94f

Hospitals—13:53f, 22:133, 166, 34:53, 43:126, 45:180n, 54:296

Host—see **Sacramental elements**

Host, Desecration of the—47:131, 264n

Hostages—7:284, 287–289

Hostiensis—see **Henry of Segusio**

Hostility—35:179, 217, 367

Hour, The—15:50, 350

Hour Services—see **Canonical Hours**

Hourglass—23:257, 259

House Postils, Luther's—51:xv

House of God—15:74, 77, 139, 281f, 284f, 338, 20:138, 177, 327

House spirits—16:297
Household gods—6:25, 58, 88, 296
Household matters—6:9, 74
Householders—13:169f, 180, 20:171, 27:113, 119
Households—2:64f, 79, 81, 83f, 137, 165, 167, 172, 215n, 227f, 242, 251, 253f, 259, 268, 275, 278, 280, 288, 297, 304, 313, 319, 330, 332, 349f, 363, 391, 398, 4:7, 15, 18f, 21–23, 29, 38, 42, 46, 61, 72, 88, 90, 109, 121, 127, 164f, 180f, 188, 194, 197, 199, 202, 217, 223, 227, 229, 246, 249, 252, 254, 259, 276, 278, 282, 284, 286–288, 297, 299, 302, 308, 335, 365, 370, 384, 392, 5:3, 5–9, 12–15, 31, 38f, 54f, 58, 60f, 69, 77–80, 82f, 85, 89f, 92f, 95, 97, 100, 108, 111, 122, 124, 138f, 141, 143f, 160f, 163, 166–168, 171, 175, 191f, 194, 200–202, 210, 245f, 250, 252, 262, 267–269, 273–275, 280, 285, 287, 313–315, 317f, 320f, 328, 330–333, 335, 341, 343, 345, 350, 363, 365f, 370–372, 376, 6:3, 8, 16, 22, 102, 116, 123f, 176, 205, 215, 221, 227f, 312, 318, 339, 358, 7:19f, 32, 34f, 37f, 42f, 45–47, 51, 55–60, 64–68, 76, 78, 80–83, 90–93, 96, 99f, 102, 107, 115, 146f, 175, 188, 190–193, 206, 218f, 221, 226, 249f, 253f, 258, 270, 280, 285, 306f, 309, 311–313, 316, 318, 338, 349f, 7:352, 366, 376f, 8:4, 37, 45, 55f, 59–62, 64, 66, 68, 72, 75–77, 82, 84, 91, 95, 98, 106, 110, 114, 116, 120, 128, 135–138, 150, 152, 159, 171f, 194, 207, 212, 221, 225, 253, 269, 280, 297, 26:11, 137, 187, 212, 355, 376, 440, 29:55–57, 61f, 71, 75, 77, 126, 30:89, 160, 208, 278, 45:233n, 322–325, 328, 336, 368, 46:102f
Houses—9:220f, 223–225, 241f, 250, 29:176f, 46:237, 254, 265, 313
Housewives—26:128, 27:61
Housing—17:291
Hoyer of Mansfield, Count—54:272
Hübmaier, Balthasar—40:227, 229n, 46:5n, 6n
Hübner, Friedrich, ed.—*Gedenkschrift für Werner Elert*, Berlin, 1955 41:xin
Hugh (or Hugo) of St. Cher, Cardinal—11:180n
Postillae in vetus et novum testamentum, Venice, 1487 3:26n
Hugh of St. Victor—25:484, 44:346n
In Ecclesiasten Homiliae 15:49n
Noah's Ark 8:14n
Hugo de Sancto Caro, Cardinal—see **Hugh (or Hugo) of St. Cher, Cardinal**
Huldah, Prophetess—18:329, 28:276, 280
Hulls—see **Shells**
Human beings—1:5, 12f, 33, 36, 39, 44, 46, 54–57, 61f, 65–67, 68n, 69f, 73, 77, 79, 82–88, 90–95, 100–104, 110–112, 115, 120–131, 133f, 136f, 138, 140–143, 147, 150–152, 154, 156, 165, 170f, 173, 175, 178, 182–187, 189f, 193f, 196, 198, 200, 202, 204–206, 215, 218f, 222, 229–231, 238, 241f, 249, 255–257, 259, 262, 267, 270, 273, 282, 286, 290, 297, 304f, 327, 330, 332, 337f, 346, 349, 352–354, 9:136, 219, 224f, 10:11, 27f, 50, 52, 87f, 224, 307f, 13:94, 98, 102–105, 115, 123, 125, 128, 155, 243, 14:192f, 196, 201, 239, 273, 289, 299f, 335, 15:175f, 319, 21:84–86, 91, 235–237, 286, 303f, 331, 333, 340f, 351–353, 22:29f, 73, 91, 102, 110, 124, 252, 291, 295, 315, 327, 336, 346, 363, 437, 491, 506–508, 23:8, 25:36, 71, 78, 82, 143, 150f, 256f, 264f, 322f, 327–330, 332, 334f, 362, 424, 26:7f, 164, 172, 186, 210, 269, 307, 354, 373, 376, 396, 450, 461, 28:25, 171–173, 194, 203, 29:162, 166, 199f, 207, 215f, 225, 233f, 238, 31:10f, 39–41, 43–46, 55, 59f, 63, 67, 69, 299–306, 344f, 359, 32:182, 33:11n, 17, 67, 118f, 130, 215–221, 222n, 223–229, 233, 275–277, 283f, 34:116, 135–144, 152, 36:49, 59, 62, 94, 96, 195, 214, 299, 303, 37:22, 25f, 32, 49, 52, 71, 81, 85n, 91, 96, 100, 101, 115, 121, 127, 148, 278, 307, 360, 362f, 38:103f, 125, 136, 157, 159, 172, 185, 223, 225, 227, 245–247, 251, 271f, 277, 41:112, 327, 42:13, 54, 72f, 148, 150, 45:89, 143–146, 153, 155f, 202f, 253, 256, 304, 390f, 46:77, 104, 130, 238, 248, see also **Will, Human**
Creation of 1:55, 57f, 69, 115
God's creation 9:51
Natural endowments 2:121
Natural powers of 12:309f, 314, 351, 359
Their inner selves 11:455, 460, 483, 485, 514, 525
Tripartite concept of 25:473, 33:275
Two kinds of 33:264, 274
Used by God 25:143
Human nature—1:114, 143, 151, 178, 189, 193, 196, 221, 228, 257, 3:276, 322, 4:7, 173, 195, 235, 238, 240, 255f, 304, 333, 5:169, 204, 208, 218–222, 229, 348, 7:13, 16, 18, 55, 235, 263, 290,

314, 355, 359, 10:185, 12:74f, 133, 309, 335, 339, 341, 345, 347, 355, 361, 377, 13:289, 18:50, 19:72–74, 80, 22:104, 247, 327, 345, 352, 493f, 24:8, 56, 74, 97, 104–106, 108, 213, 221, 227, 342f, 375, 25:10, 69, 157, 191, 245, 291f, 313, 345–347, 351f, 434, 25:185f, 465f, 25:344–346, 26:265, 326, 349, 367, 27:261f, 362f, 28:12, 29:126f, 29:142, 148, 226, 30:30, 101, 255, 31:363, 376, 35:377, 35:41, 60, 199, 243f, 375, 42:23, 45:89, 155f, 202f, 253, 256, 304, 52:58f, 60, 88, 115

Human nature, Depravity of—12:335, 337, 339, 341, 35:34, 53, 57, 192

Human opinions—36:37, 49, 55, 75, 84, 195

Human ordinances—36:58, 62, 76, 79, 101–103, 134, 142, 147, 193f, 299, 303

Human power—25:151

Human relationships—21:84–88, 98, 235–237

Human sacrifice—see **Sacrifice, Human**

Human speech—25:145

Human spirit—20:131, 145, 332f, 21:303, 305, 307, 332, 25:7, 68, 71, 97, 107, 357f, 424, 456

Humanism—26:290n, 32:135, 33:6, 25n, 34:162n, 163n, 45:341, 342n, 344, 351n, 358n, 48:3n, 23f, 53n, 66, 80n, 96n, 99n, 101, 105f, 116, 119n, 122, 143n, 150n, 163n, 165n, 222n, 230n, 305n, 314n, 49:7f, 32f, 43n, 44, 73f, 78, 81n, 88n, 148, 160n, 220n, 223, 236n, 257n, 280n, 350n, 351n, 50:28, 82n, 83n, 190n, 191n, 210n, 224n, 231, 264n

Humanists—37:xv, 363n, 370n, 38:xviii, 6, 32n, 41:xiii, 110n, 46:xi, 18n

Humanists, Italian—13:77n

Humanitarian service—13:54

Humanity—5:151, 219, 222f, 377f, 6:19, 57, 86, 189f, 254, 256, 403, 16:137, 26:265–267, 273, 284, 29:110, 126f, 188, 234, 46:42, 248

Humiliation—11:453, 515f

Humility—4:19, 21, 24, 34, 62, 121, 141, 144, 208f, 213, 217, 248, 271, 277, 282, 378, 5:79, 91, 94f, 121, 153, 192, 224, 227, 233, 270, 319–321, 6:98, 119, 121, 159, 161, 163, 166f, 169, 174f, 284f, 7:114, 144, 146f, 151, 166, 178, 181–185, 187, 191, 305, 322f, 356, 364f, 8:52, 58, 70, 105, 143, 151, 160, 328, 9:271f, 10:27, 35, 38, 41, 88f, 162, 205, 250, 393, 404, 406, 457, 11:264, 279f, 306f, 325, 367, 391f, 462, 464f, 498, 500, 526, 535f, 547f, 12:80f, 14:94f, 169, 16:169, 347, 18:261–263, 339f, 354, 20:147, 21:27f, 283, 308–310, 312–316, 321f, 329, 22:71, 87, 98, 160, 166, 277, 232f, 505, 507, 520, 23:328, 351, 25:3, 100, 108, 136f, 139–141, 182f, 191f, 204, 217, 223, 226, 232, 239, 271, 300f, 335, 353, 394, 420, 433f, 441, 463f, 477, 26:21, 34, 99, 106, 114, 140, 154, 196, 235, 329, 394, 435, 459, 27:52, 86, 99, 216, 302, 28:88, 365, 29:26, 30:82, 139, 272, 31:47, 348, 365, 33:61f, 35:142, 372, 390, 37:127, 131, 38:195, 42:70, 51:14–17, 43, 73, 130, 351f, 52:4f, 34f, 58

Humility, False—25:301

Humors—15:180n

Hungarians—14:11, 16:254, 40:306, 46:158n, 167, 202n, 54:311

Hungary—1:254, 4:28n, 8:103, 12:32, 14:x, 209, 16:196n, 22:82, 28:131, 32:260, 38:283, 41:374, 46:166, 167n, 202n, 203n, 49:37, 156, 185, 221n, 222, 241, 242n, 251n, 284n, 50:219n, 224n, 228f, 243n, 253n, 269n, 54:402

Hunger—3:179f, 184, 232, 4:20, 41, 44, 47, 49, 77, 275, 393, 408, 5:6, 9f, 13, 16, 144, 262, 264, 286, 332, 371, 386, 7:40, 62f, 69, 128, 136, 159, 215, 218, 306, 309, 8:14, 32, 39, 107, 122, 125, 184, 204, 225, 255, 328, 9:92–94, 147, 268, 295, 24:24, 400f, 26:329, 419, 450, 27:126, 143, 385, 30:50, 177

Hunger, Saturnine—3:306n

Hunger cloths—34:55

Hunger for righteousness—21:26f, 347, 349

Hungry ones—21:346, 348

Hunt, J. Eric—53:149n

Hunt, John—53:xviii

Hunters—2:197–199

Hunting—4:379–381, 382n, 383, 385, 390, 393, 5:167, 9:194n, 14:xii, 110, 274, 25:172, 50:262f, 54:279, 313

Hur—17:34, 153

Husbandmen—28:176f, 182

Husbands—1:118, 133–139, 151, 160, 163, 185, 192, 198–200, 202–205, 210f, 219, 233, 239, 270, 308, 312–314, 320, 326, 338, 344, 352, 358, 3:42, 44, 46f, 49, 53–58, 133f, 201, 203–205, 207–212, 216f, 288, 298, 300, 330, 354, 4:12, 18–20, 23f, 67, 69, 121f, 188, 194, 226, 233, 246f, 271, 278, 291, 305, 307, 326, 336–339, 351, 362, 388f, 5:3, 14, 30–32, 35–37, 39, 41,

51, 72f, 77, 94, 100–102, 104, 111–114, 134, 176, 180, 191f, 282, 284, 290f, 293, 302, 314f, 317, 320–322, 324f, 328f, 331f, 339f, 343f, 351f, 354, 356, 358f, 363, 371, 381f, 6:61, 199, 7:20, 22, 26f, 29, 40, 43, 45, 85, 90n, 95f, 146, 200, 343f, 8:85, 169, 272, 303, 9:145f, 206, 210f, 222f, 235, 241, 244, 249, 12:131, 260, 21:87, 94–97, 109, 171, 258f, 23:203–205, 224, 295, 323, 24:161, 186, 220, 231, 245, 25:57–59, 26:117, 120, 168, 305, 355, 425, 434, 442, 444f, 448, 27:61, 68, 114, 232, 281, 320f, 345f, 28:51, 128, 276–278, 284, 299, 338f, 29:10, 18–20, 54–56, 65f, 30:20, 55, 71, 86–89, 91–93, 98, 271, 35:391, 52:217

Husbands and wives—4:222, 228, 233f, 247f, 289f, 298, 304, 378, 20:82, 175, 21:87, 94f, 97–100, 36:193f, 44:98, 178f, 45:23f, 33, 38, 144, 46:141, 151f, 261, 268f, 271f, 274, 278, 283, 294–296, 298f, 306f, 311f, 314f

Hushai—2:292, 23:301, 303

Huss, John—2:21, 87, 184n, 4:396, 8:90, 226, 266, 10:125, 12:10, 13:59, 413–415, 417, 420, 14:88, 92, 224, 253, 309n, 16:210n, 256, 283, 17:36, 44, 93, 177, 234, 268f, 21:165, 23:376, 24:413, 26:70, 27:392n, 28:242f, 29:33, 80, 89n, 31:xvi, xviii, 315, 321, 32:xif, 56n, 71, 74f, 82f, 87, 117, 127, 129, 33:96, 34:104, 35:50, 36:27n, 37:173, 370n, 38:182n, 39:20n, 73n, 108, 127n, 134, 149, 172n, 173, 40:x, 4, 16n, 39, 256, 41:7n, 140n, 365n, 43:69, 146, 149n, 154, 173, 175, 44:184–196, 197n, 227, 45:173n, 47:17, 48:114n, 143, 147n, 153, 189n, 224n, 49:56n, 408n, 51:55n, 186, 52:6, 53:63n, 82, 208, 242, 249, 54:40, 81, 83, 94, 110, 220, 372

On the Church 33:96n, 48:153n, 249, 272n

Hussgen—see **Oecolampadius, John**

Hussite Wars—45:173n

Hussites—14:309n, 17:234, 27:392n, 31:265n, 314, 321, 34:50, 36:30, 39:73n, 82n, 108, 47:17f, 48:80n, 144n, 149n, 153, 189n, 249, 272n, see also **Bohemians**

Husum—50:49n

Huts—3:184, 199

Hutt, Johannes—53:237

Hutten, Ulrich von—32:xii, 35:406n, 41:183, 42:xi, 43:70, 45:58n, 270n, 285n, 288n, 46:158n, 48:xx, 150n, 163n, 169n, 193, 216n, 231, 247, 322n, 49:xixn, 78

Expostulation 33:7, 50:203n

Ulrichs von Hutten Schriften, Leipzig, 1860 44:170n

Hutzelprediger—40:199n

Hybridization—6:293, 301

Hydra—16:314n

Hyena—16:297

Hyma, Albert—34:xi

The Christian Renaissance: A History of the "Devotio Moderna," New York, 1925 45:342n

Hymen—9:222

Hymn indexes—53:206–210, 348–350, see also Table of Contents 53:viii–ix

Hymn writing rules—49:68f

Hymnal prefaces by Luther—53:313–334

Hymnals (Enchiridia or handbooks)—47:53, 53:193f, 212, 218, 222, 225, 229, 235, 237, 245, 252, 255, 258, 260f, 265f, 271, 275, 278

Hymns—12:201, 13:351, 356, 15:191f, 273f, 16:76, 203, 34:53, 56, 37:144n, 172n, 260n, 38:123, 178, 206–208, 293n, 40:300, 307, 42:114n, 137, 43:74, 231, 49:6, 53:189–341

Use in worship 3:7, 155

Hymns based on Ten Commandments, Luther's—47:109n

Hymns, Luther's—53:191–210

Bibliography of 53:xx

English versions, Bibliography of 53:xviii

Index of English translations 53:348–350

Index of first lines of German originals 53:348–350

Liturgical and topical index 53:209f

Melodies, Sources of 53:208

Metrical index 53:206f

Texts and tunes 53:211–309

Hyperbole—3:259, 4:370, 8:38, 10:92, 27:31, 304

Hyperdulia—9:71f, 17:112

Hypocrisy—1:234, 275, 278, 2:59, 172, 218, 251, 270, 274f, 299, 331, 3:189, 4:154, 209, 328, 346, 375, 409, 5:6, 9, 107f, 199, 232, 7:89, 113, 229, 244, 260, 274, 284, 337, 345, 349, 356, 369, 8:22, 9:24, 26, 63n, 165, 225, 261, 273, 294, 10:28, 55, 58, 66f, 74f, 268, 426, 14:308, 16:19, 21f, 24, 43, 82, 112, 160, 187, 204, 223, 247, 276, 18:15, 41, 95–97, 144, 147, 221, 260f, 269f, 367, 400, 408, 412f, 20:57f, 79, 86, 237, 242, 268, 271, 21:79f, 139, 156–158, 160, 183f, 187, 220, 223, 239f, 255, 342, 22:59, 121, 123, 125,

131, 141, 23:19, 67, 76, 86, 209, 213, 252, 25:264, 26:29, 65, 136, 259, 322, 335, 363, 395, 429, 443, 459, 27:31, 131, 188, 192, 204, 212–215, 217, 274, 340, 28:10, 310f, 314, 316, 30:42, 48, 53, 173, 277, 292, 298, 319, 32:34–38, 34:189, 35:137, 366, 384, 36:76f, 100, 114, 201, 210, 291, 293, 37:147, 284, 38:99, 115, 188, 51:27, 76, 112, 127, 272, 52:40, 59

Hypocrites—1:235, 271f, 275–278, 280, 335, 2:59, 160f, 168, 214, 224, 251, 3:89, 182, 203, 246, 269, 275, 4:15, 109, 159, 209, 269, 275–277, 321, 375, 379, 385, 392, 408f, 5:6f, 13, 35, 39, 107f, 147, 199, 208, 213, 232, 268, 285f, 290, 366, 370, 6:41, 43–45, 48, 51, 55, 57, 66, 69, 75–77, 79, 81f, 84f, 385, 7:89, 113, 229, 244, 260, 274, 284, 337, 345, 349, 356, 369, 8:131, 9:26, 60, 137, 141, 185, 226, 260, 272f, 305f, 11:428f, 482, 507f, 526, 542, 12:192f, 313, 327, 343f, 355, 13:186, 384, 386, 14:93, 98, 163, 170, 173, 211, 213, 215, 236, 241, 244, 262, 266, 283, 294, 322, 344, 16:12, 17, 64, 79, 83, 105, 150, 152, 155, 160, 187f, 203, 216, 222, 226, 232, 244, 263, 288, 308, 17:9, 199, 207, 269, 271, 275–277, 284f, 295–298, 390, 21:28f, 39, 105, 119f, 133f, 158f, 183f, 253f, 342, 345, 22:54, 72, 125, 132, 143, 458, 23:20, 127, 135, 211, 213, 249, 265, 400, 24:58, 88f, 129, 144, 217, 234, 25:16, 216, 256f, 269, 287, 323f, 335, 357, 26:34, 41, 60, 65, 70, 107, 125f, 148, 153, 202, 253, 256–259, 264, 266–269, 295, 307, 309, 324, 344f, 347f, 362, 376, 402f, 27:30, 54, 75, 79, 92, 96, 172, 174, 214–216, 220, 223, 258, 284, 321, 324, 334, 390, 29:119, 219, 232, 240, 30:26, 51, 231, 270, 272, 274, 299, 303, 31:345, 32:256, 35:79f, 333, 367, 372, 36:194, 221, 356, 41:333, 339, 42:20, 31, 35, 46:148, 184, 229

Hypostatic union—37:210

Hyrcanus—see **John Hyrcanus**

Hyrcanus II—52:183

Hyssop—12:366, 29:207f

Hysteron proteron—4:300, 302, 5:210, 259, 337f, 343, 358, 6:282, 343, 7:3, 51, 8:247

Iago, St.—see **James of Compostella, St.**

Ibn Rushd—see **Averroes**

Icarus—54:65

Icarus and Daedalus—37:220

Iconoclasm—35:173n, 40:xf, 56, 67, 81, 45:54

Iconoclastic controversy—41:204n, 51:82n

Iconoclasts—9:79–82, 19:42, 29:44, 37:371, 43:43, 46:183n, 48:401

Ideas—15:4f, 33, 21:36f, 178

Idleness—2:126, 9:55, 220, 15:65, 106f, 114, 123, 150, 238, 21:117f, 54:281, 295

Idleness, Dangers of—42:92

Idolaters—6:32, 61, 84, 8:95, 129, 131, 134, 180, 203, 229, 275f, 292, 300, 16:25, 81, 89, 26:53, 258, 283, 328, 395, 397–399, 423, 460, 27:51, 90, 369

Idolatry—1:146, 149, 159, 183, 192, 229, 327, 358, 2:12, 19f, 24, 28, 30, 33, 60, 63, 84, 99, 125, 137, 172, 186, 192, 201f, 205, 214f, 223, 230, 232, 240, 242–244, 246, 248–253, 275, 284–286, 355f, 371f, 382, 3:13, 60, 164, 221f, 272, 296, 320, 4:3n, 35, 88, 165, 171, 207, 210, 235, 236n, 237, 239, 243, 246, 252, 328, 381, 390, 407, 5:12, 72, 96f, 114, 170, 204, 207, 241f, 259, 268, 286, 304, 366, 6:4, 28, 32–34, 49f, 96f, 113, 127, 129, 228f, 239f, 294, 372, 7:63, 72, 75, 91, 96, 110f, 163, 199, 300, 307, 336, 341, 348f, 8:25, 93, 132, 135, 137, 179, 200, 229, 231, 250, 300f, 9:53, 68, 70–72, 75, 125, 140, 165, 273, 290, 296–298, 306f, 10:129, 12:87, 360, 378, 13:123, 169, 177, 182f, 185, 409, 14:9–11, 17, 25, 34, 39, 66f, 103, 168, 345, 15:232, 16:35, 78, 160, 185, 215f, 331, 346, 17:16f, 19, 22, 34, 39, 70, 105, 107f, 112f, 134, 140, 273, 18:4, 9f, 33, 39f, 42, 44f, 50, 54, 56, 59, 138f, 167, 184, 214, 239, 255, 321f, 394, 397, 413f, 19:11, 20, 56, 115, 131, 160, 186, 223f, 186f, 207, 20:10, 145, 301, 22:34, 51, 58, 70, 77, 130f, 196, 235, 237, 273, 275, 347, 371, 397, 405f, 431, 433, 442, 489, 502, 23:206f, 232, 374, 378, 387, 401, 24:19, 24, 62, 74, 79, 97, 151, 229, 285, 305, 309, 323, 328, 335, 369, 25:10, 86, 157–160, 164f, 192, 338, 346, 351, 26:135, 224, 254, 377, 396f, 399, 400f, 409, 427, 454, 27:31, 67, 69, 87f, 90f, 141, 148, 188, 293, 368, 369, 30:26, 119f, 186, 207, 246, 319, 327, 31:201, 32:136, 34:305, 354, 35:199, 268–270, 272f, 278, 301, 317f, 324, 343, 350f, 364, 372, 406, 36:31, 42, 88, 144, 148, 168, 176, 178, 198, 201f, 219, 263, 342, 37:xiif, 22, 27, 32, 122, 356, 370n, 38:149, 174, 186, 291,

41:10–12, 111, 124, 130, 140, 147, 201, 203f, 206, 209f, 215, 217, 221–223, 237, 271, 283, 287f, 296f, 302f, 306–308, 318, 323, 344f, 349, 357, 359f, 369f, 44:30f, 46:186, 215f, 233, 243, 47:226, 269, 283, 286, 290f, 51:17, 84f, 139, 204, 294, 327, 346, 374, 380, 52:59, 84, 91, 252
Idols—3:216, 330, 4:109, 130, 146, 159, 179, 235f, 381, 5:36, 241, 260, 304, 364, 368, 377f, 6:32–34, 58, 60, 127, 230f, 237f, 239f, 7:87f, 163, 300, 336, 343, 348f, 351, 8:25, 76, 200, 230, 245, 250, 277, 301, 9:4, 53, 58n, 71, 79, 81, 82, 84f, 130f, 167, 171, 290f, 11:398f, 12:389, 14:10, 202, 222, 348, 16:17, 25f, 35, 37f, 78, 109f, 155f, 160, 165, 215f, 245, 262f, 271, 17:38f, 50, 78, 107, 110f, 134, 137, 140, 158, 276, 382f, 401, 18:22f, 43f, 54, 57, 67–70, 76, 214, 255, 391, 413f, 20:106, 145, 170, 300, 321, 332, 21:135, 177f, 104, 216f, 312, 328f, 24:277, 25:7, 122, 139, 145, 338, 346, 350f, 500, 26:92, 98, 226f, 254, 258, 395, 397–399, 401, 454, 460, 20:40, 211, 35:168, 270f, 36:12, 76, 76, 91, 113, 146, 148f, 151f, 154–156, 158, 167, 178, 200, 219–224, 284f, 299, 38:106f, 165, 213, 226, 232, 41:122, 161f, 221f, 303, 360
Meat sacrificed to 41:28, 68, 72–78
Idumea—6:283, 291, 302f, 307f, 310, 7:239, 16:169, 173, 294, 17:352, 33:199f, see also **Edom**
Idumeans—4:331, 394, 5:160, 170, 6:309f, 7:14, 10:26, 18:113, 116, see also **Edomites**
Iekel—see **Schenk, Jacob**
Iglau—36:272
Ignatius, St.—24:196, 37:101n
Ignominy—24:314f
Ignorance—2:312–316, 326, 4:62, 81–83, 118, 5:302f, 6:57, 8:118, 170, 246, 11:303, 508, 15:80f, 16:223, 17:69, 19:133, 227, 24:33, 44, 57, 81, 233, 248, 282f, 285–287, 328, 26:35, 40f, 70, 110–112, 114, 118, 125, 175, 189, 309f, 319, 342, 352, 376, 397, 27:292f, 342, 384, 28:243f, 29:170, 206, 30:31, 239, 253, 297, 31:370, 46:78, 225
Iken, J. Friedrich—32:274n
Iliad—see **Homer**
Illegitimacy—9:230n
Illness—see **Disease**
Illuminations—4:125, 17:312f, 325f, 18:108
Illustration—16:198, 274
Illyricum—2:185, 25:124f
Image of God—see **God**—His image
Images—4:5, 35, 87, 135, 148, 6:33, 61, 230f, 237–240, 9:63f, 75f, 79–82, 84n, 88f, 164, 171, 11:268, 16:35, 215, 262n, 17:22, 70, 78, 107, 109, 141, 18:17, 54, 214, 25:11, 157–159, 26:222f, 284, 430f, 454, 29:44, 132, 179, 215f, 34:55, 351, 35:173n, 271, 398, 400, 36:233, 259f, 262, 37:161, 168, 226, 260, 371, 40:47, 52, 58, 67, 69, 81, 85–88, 96, 45:54, 289, 46:183, 48:401n, 49:129, 51:41, 69, 75, 81–85, 88, 328, see also **Statues**
Images of Christ—see **Pictures of Christ**
Imaus Mts.—2:108, 207
Imitating Christ—22:265, 30:117
Imitation of Christ—23:325n
Imitation style—18:213, 217, 299
Imitators—13:159, 162
Immaculate Conception—22:333n, 32:79f, 48:291n
Immersion—35:29f, 36:64, 68
Immolations—4:122
Immorality—8:59, 46:153f
Immorality, Pagan—45:37, 39, 44, 367
Immortality—1:44f, 80f, 84, 86, 111, 115–117, 125, 231, 330f, 333, 348, 2:130, 232, 3:11, 28, 110, 123, 149, 268, 5:xii, 73, 77f, 7:116f, 8:82, 140, 258, 315, 317, 10:337, 13:415, 15:59f, 23:45, 25:73, 27:297n, 28:203, 249, 29:135, 30:312, 32:77f, 78n, 37:99–101, 118, 124, 130, 132, 46:177n, 47:38, 54:401, 447
Immortality, Hope of—1:80f, 87, 104, 201, 229, 332
Immunities—27:3
Impanation—37:290–292
Impartiality—10:76f, 83, 94f, 404
Impatience—3:9, 25, 217, 347, 5:5, 13f, 30, 59, 163, 215, 319f, 327, 7:54, 58, 61, 74, 97, 126f, 135, 229, 262f, 320, 357, 13:117, 15:5, 106, 115f, 26:230, 340–342, 350, 27:2, 323
Impenitence—1:171, 178, 2:38f, 49, 3:230, 365, 6:195, 199f, 7:236, 282, 24:61, 318, 33:35
Impenitent persons—13:376
Imperial Edict, 1531—34:5, 11n, 65–104
Impiety—8:21, 23:260, 408
Impossibility—25:163f, 266
Imposters—7:168, 337f
Imposture—5:295f, 299, 301
Impotence, Sexual—36:102–105
Imprisonment—8:17, 55
Improperia—53:274
Impudence—7:73, 78, 84, 299

Impurity—26:141
Imputation—25:36, 56, 79, 256f, 259–261, 263, 268f, 272, 274, 26:6, 132f, 229f, 232f, 2345, 245f, 260, 274, 30:255, 34:166f, see also **Righteousness, Imputed**
In coena domini—see **Bulls, Papal**
Incarnation—see **Christ**—His birth and incarnation
Incense—1:106, 5:242, 304, 7:135, 175f, 8:200, 18:11, 397, 53:25, 260
Incest—2:9f, 3:254, 310–314, 324, 346, 5:91, 304, 6:275–277, 279, 291, 293, 299, 313, 377, 7:8–10, 12f, 20, 28, 31, 36, 43f, 48, 84, 125, 201, 260, 264, 286, 310, 318, 8:91, 204, 213, 215f, 218, 220, 222, 307, 9:229, 236, 50:32f, 37, 121
Inclinations—25:164, 168, 219, 275, 299, 348
Incompatibilia—34:252
Incomprehensibility—37:xviii, 53n, 59f, 69f, 207, 214, 220f, 223f, 228, 230, 276–278, 296
Inconstant spirits—see **Radical reformers**
Incorruptibility—25:11, 41, 72, 102, 219, 432
Incubi—2:11
Incurvatus in se—10:241, 25:245, 291f, 313, 345, 351, 513, 33:175f
Indecency—3:171; 30:68, 120
Indelible character—36:111n, 117, 160, 201, 40:x, 35, 44:129
Indemnity, Double—9:242
Index, Printer's—37:74, 183, 244
Indexers—see **Ahrens, Frederick C.; Buehner, Andrew J.; Hansen, Walter A.; John, John H.; Lueker, Erwin L.; Oswald, Hilton C.; Poellet, Luther; Reed, Elizabeth S.; Robbert, George S.; Spitz, Lewis W., Sr.**
India—1:97, 100, 2:108, 207, 19:44, 20:250, 26:441, 38:224, 41:271, 45:246, 54:474
India, South—38:xiii
Indian Gulf—2:195
Indies—34:345, 45:234
Indifference—3:23, 6:362
Indignation—6:42f, 61f
Individual differences—13:161, 163, 200
Individualism—10:135, 285, 11:294, 25:176, 271, 337, 398, 422
Indoctrination—25:450
Inductive argument—16:308
Indulgence Controversy—48:68f, 97f, 181n, 208, 211n, 339f
Indulgence preachers—48:45f, 68, 98, 101f, 339
Bibliography 31:23
Indulgences—2:275, 290, 314n, 386, 5:354, 8:230, 9:64n, 10:362, 12:371, 387, 13:325, 14:23, 67, 76, 282, 18:36, 21:68f, 79f, 204f, 22:51, 644, 220, 254, 257f, 274, 405, 23:26, 82, 127, 207, 263, 370, 409, 24:265, 268, 275, 279, 315, 325, 328, 356, 363, 25:276, 409, 26:106n, 180, 182, 221f, 28:312, 30:8, 174, 31:xv–xxi, 17–33, 73, 79f, 93, 108, 120, 131, 144, 147, 150, 153, 162, 175–177, 179–185, 188, 191–196, 199, 201, 203, 205–208, 212–228, 232–234, 237–239, 267, 291f, 322, 334–343, 32:xi, 32–34, 51n, 62–68, 88, 90, 103, 136, 257, 34:14, 15n, 16–18, 54, 99, 263, 329, 35:7f, 67, 133n, 406, 36:9, 11f, 30, 58, 89f, 133, 182, 291, 37:369, 38:103, 147–149, 164, 173, 175, 178, 183, 231, 39:25, 127, 134, 241–244, 273, 275f, 289, 40:323, 338, 345, 41:34, 115n, 120, 140, 199f, 209n, 215, 222, 232n, 233–237, 271–273, 280, 323, 338, 340, 357, 42:12, 22n, 62f, 64n, 65n, 69, 43:11, 44:171n, 179, 45:180n, 351, 46:90n, 164, 186n, 187, 201, 306, 47:39–42, 51, 50:55, 95n, 270, 272, 51:26, 31, 35, 54, 55, 77, 142, 179, 390, 52:222, 231, 54:160, 174, 264, 324, 341f
Theory and practices 48:44f, 68f, 74n, 89, 101–104, 105n, 118, 139, 316n, 320, 326n, 339f, 344f
Industry—2:5, 160, 344, 23:33
Inebriation—see **Drunkenness**
Ineffable manner—37:139n
Inequality—9:145
Infallibility—22:255, 34:113
Infancy—2:126
Infant baptism—see **Baptism, Infant**
Infant communion—35:111, 36:21, 25, 38:208, 41:152
Infantry—46:248n
Infants—1:104, 128, 202, 235, 239, 274, 332, 3:103–105, 110, 133, 137f, 140, 161, 174, 206, 274, 318, 5:75f, 100f, 173, 312, 334, 381, 7:41, 46f, 130, 295, 296n, 8:33, 112, 182, 241, 316, 18:363, 25:182, 337, 488, 36:83, 45:41
Infants, Hideous—2:11
Infants, Unbaptized—8:316, 32:54
Infirmities—10:105
Inflation—43:220–222, 240
Ingolstadt—7:92n, 40:52
Battle of 46:47n

University of 34:310n, 48:80n, 99n, 123n, 154n, 166n, 168n, 314n, 49:96n, 160n, 313n

Ingratitude—2:289, 354, 380, 3:49, 51f, 146, 196, 218, 227, 234, 288, 319, 345, 5:16, 82, 365, 6:7, 61f, 67, 236, 7:64, 80, 82f, 97f, 124, 126, 258, 8:33, 117, 133, 185, 9:294, 13:190, 364, 367, 372, 14:51, 281, 15:106, 115f, 119, 141, 145, 170, 16:7f, 83, 17:173, 358, 360, 22:36, 23:12, 38, 152, 260, 263, 265, 336, 355, 361, 398, 24:133, 247, 254, 267f, 358, 25:72, 159f, 26:35, 44, 125, 140, 247, 387f, 452, 27:154, 272, 28:62f, 131, 244, 258, 348, 36:76, 38:137, 46:171, 243, 255, 258

Inheritance—6:16f, 31f, 373, 7:42, 44, 164, 209, 211, 255f, 10:106f, 110, 333, 11:380f, 490, 26:298, 303f, 333, 346f, 359f, 364, 374, 391–395, 438, 441f, 446, 449f, 454, 457, 461

Inhospitality—3:178, 182

Iniquity—10:79, 83, 145–147, 167, 170, 177f, 192, 267f, 273f, 380f, 422f, 11:292, 294, 346, 438, 463, 469f, 485, 513f, 521f, 533, 536, 14:149–151, 157, 169, 185, 265, 334, 348, 25:168, 272, 274, 276f, 292, 313, 430, 29:176f, 183, see also **Sin**

Iniquity vs. unrighteousness—25:168

Initium theologiae Lutheri—10:ix

Injury—23:13, 149

Injustice—2:7f, 34, 142, 337, 339f, 5:65f, 182, 376, 6:55, 62, 9:19, 161, 234, 249, 12:237, 349, 16:25, 18:29, 19:161, 21:114, 25:440f, 30:75, 84f, 101, 46:7, 27f, 30f, 35, 42, 61, 100f, 106, 108, 114, 118, 270, 292

Inn—26:260

Inn River (valley)—41:231, 49:50n

Inner darkness—25:109, 168, 287

Inner man—25:68, 109, 220, 309f, 322, 331f, 334

Innkeepers—3:198, 204

Innocence—1:86, 90, 94, 98, 102f, 105, 109f, 112, 114, 117f, 130, 133f, 136, 141, 146, 166, 240, 2:74, 6:58, 62f, 8:11, 18, 16:120, 19:133f, 19:227, 24:52, 255f, 46:72, 78, 101, 180, 292f, 311f

Innocent I, Pope—31:214, 36:20n, 48:24

Innocent III, Pope—2:152n, 32:61, 41:305n, 332n, 44:132n, 144n, 45:133, 46:200n, 270n, 51:93n

Sicut universitatis Conditor 2:152n

Innocent IV, Pope—31:143

Innovations—41:204–206, 209, 227

Innsbruck—41:231, 48:217, 49:119, 295n, 296n, 299n, 315, 332n, 53:337

Inquisition—2:327n, 33:87, 47:60, 116n, 123, 128, 48:9, 10n, 11, 64n, 154n, 155n

Inquisitiveness—3:201, 282, 299

Inquisitors—30:214, 41:116n

Insanity—8:118, 223, 310

Insects—1:72, 206, 16:284

Insignificant days—20:48–50, 190, 227–229

Inspiration—4:389f, 13:81, 201

Institutes—see **Justinian, Emperor**

Institutions—14:20, 25f

Instruction—10:194, 206–209, 215, 280, 373, 452, 24:249, 306, 353, 357, 25:7, 106, 111f, 120, 123, 189, 243, 394, 29:31f, 89f, 102, 180

Instructions for the Visitors of Parish Pastors in Electoral Saxony—see **Melanchthon, Philip, Writings of**

Insurance—45:64, 252n, 307

Insurrection—16:42, 74, 89, 106, 46:xii, 8, 61, 76, 142, 47:7, 14f, 19f, 29

Insurrectionists—26:375

Intellect—2:203, 20:174f, 287

Intemperance—13:122, 216

Intention—25:24, 88, 160, 404, 440f, 459, 476, 494f

Intentions, Secret—10:98, 121

Intercession—see **Prayer, Intercessory**

Intercessors—24:24, 69, 98, 292, 307

Interchange—25:317

Intercommunion—38:xiif

Intercourse, Sexual—see **Coitus**

Interdict—22:84f, 24:266, 44:132n

Interesse—45:293f, 298n, 299f

Interest—9:145f, 150, 45:174n, 234, 236–238, 240f, 299–303, 305n, 308f, 54:316, 369, 398, see also **Usury**

Interest on money—13:191

Interest rates—35:157

***Interim* (1548)**—50:218n

Intermediary—26:319f, 322–324, 326f

Interpreters—2:13, 15, 71, 93, 137, 164, 182, 6:125, 333–335, 10:ix, 8, 18f, 235, 431, 456, 53:38

Intinction—38:114n

Intolerance—2:104

Intoning—51:190

Intoxication—see **Drunkenness**

Introits—13:ix, 355, 53:22f, 25, 55, 57f, 181, 209

Investiture—44:164n

Invisible things—6:10, 305, 29:181, 199, 216, 229, 231, 237f

Invocation—4:6

Inward manner—37:13, 16n, 99, 133, 290, 366
Inwardness—25:257
Ionia—10:412
Ionian Sea—50:72n
Ionians—2:188
Ir—2:202
Irad—1:303, 315
Irascibility—3:51
Irenaeus—14:326n, 25:268, 26:411, 30:221n, 31:214, 37:54n, 115–120, 132, 142f, 38:317n, 39:280n, 41:62n, 43:156, 48:24
Against Heresies 1:60n, 7:81n, 8:282n, 22:7n, 24:196n, 27:127n, 208n, 364n, 30:221n, 50:5
Irene, Empress—41:374n
Iron—1:317, 3:191, 4:107, 174, 343, 9:149, 307, 10:35f, 23:123–125, 380, 26:266, 426
Iron wall—37:78f, 81–84, 88, 95f, 286f
Ironsmith—17:110f
Irony—7:285, 16:149, 151, 171, 287, 315, 322, 344, 26:271f, 300f
Is, Meaning of word—38:22, 24, 40, 56
Isaac—1:295, 308, 2:25, 176, 230, 256f, 288, 294, 311, 359, 362, 380, 3:16f, 34, 63, 65, 74, 80, 92, 94–96, 112, 118, 147f, 152, 154, 156, 161–163, 176f, 192, 205f, 324, 327, 338, 4:4, 7, 10, 13f, 16f, 19–22, 24–26, 30f, 33–35, 40, 42, 45, 49, 51, 53, 65, 73, 75, 91f, 95–98, 102, 106, 108f, 110n, 111–114, 117–120, 122f, 128, 137, 180, 184, 190, 193f, 206, 216, 218, 220, 223, 225, 231f, 246, 251, 255f, 262, 265, 270, 277, 287f, 294f, 298–302, 308, 310, 319–321, 323–330, 332–345, 348–352, 359–361, 365, 367f, 376–378, 387–389, 5:ix, 3, 6–10, 12–17, 20f, 24–28, 30–32, 36, 39–42, 49, 51–65, 67–70, 73f, 77–87, 89–93, 95–108, 110f, 113f, 116, 118–120, 125–129, 133–143, 146, 148f, 155, 159, 162f, 165–167, 174–177, 179f, 182, 192–197, 199–201, 207, 209, 217, 224f, 229, 238, 241f, 252, 256, 262, 265, 272f, 283, 300, 350, 385, 6:ix, 21, 23, 32, 70–73, 109, 116, 149, 166, 170, 184, 187f, 196, 204, 223f, 255–258, 264, 268, 280, 282f, 285, 287f, 290f, 295–297, 302, 306, 309f, 314f, 325, 342, 345, 357, 367, 382, 403f, 7:3f, 10, 13, 17, 25, 42, 70, 114, 116, 125, 130, 133, 163, 186, 220, 229, 270, 307, 312, 327, 356f, 8:31, 65, 75–77, 80, 111f, 114, 117, 130, 132f, 139–141, 151, 153, 156, 160, 162, 166, 169f, 175, 182, 184, 199, 217, 232, 242, 259, 286, 302f, 314, 9:32, 169, 292, 310, 11:103, 13:180, 355, 14:197, 212, 327, 16:59, 17:77, 233, 235, 18:135, 175, 271, 19:40, 52n, 20:54, 102, 21:325, 346, 22:31, 81, 92, 116, 120, 196, 209, 284, 316, 354, 367, 463, 25:80f, 255, 374, 384–386, 438, 26:116f, 138, 236f, 304, 391, 433–436, 441, 445, 450, 454, 457, 28:280, 29:239, 278, 31:274, 34:321, 35:83, 37:91, 128, 134–136, 251, 38:290, 42:161, 45:48, 331, 381n, 390, 392, 46:233, 235, 269, 305, 310, 47:140, 146f, 151f, 208f, 264, 302, 52:33, 52, 74, 85, 126, 200, 266
Isaac, Jules—47:139n
Isaac and Ishmael—33:86
Isabella, Queen of Hungary—43:215
Isabella of Portugal, Empress—7:355n
Isaiah, Prophet—1:7, 15, 23, 85, 193f, 251, 265, 2:45, 162, 246, 3:37, 59, 69–71, 82, 107, 121, 123, 155f, 164, 169, 193, 222, 249, 255, 283, 4:6, 117, 151, 161, 233f, 316, 5:111, 7:149, 156, 176, 351, 366, 370, 8:63, 217, 224, 262, 293, 9:54, 182, 268, 13:150, 199, 284, 14:63f, 67n, 77, 88, 99, 144, 151, 180, 273, 294, 298, 302, 335, 337, 16:5n, 6, 12, 65, 71–74, 78, 80, 89, 132, 140, 162, 178, 253, 261, 282, 285–287, 320, 331, 17:3, 44, 95, 126, 137, 165f, 169, 284, 308, 18:207, 225, 236, 19:121, 154, 157, 193, 196, 208, 20:35, 67f, 73, 127, 218, 21:301, 22:18, 24, 32, 69, 79, 81, 99, 101, 111, 120, 124, 163, 195, 216, 222, 244, 247, 311, 321, 341, 346–348, 420, 450, 463, 483, 486, 494, 23:89, 97, 258, 262, 265, 369, 24:80, 259f, 340, 366, 411, 25:85f, 92, 396, 26:260, 277, 292, 442, 446, 449f, 28:158, 174, 29:109, 113f, 30:xi, 21, 51, 56, 60, 85f, 104f, 119, 35:273–278, 36:44, 53, 65, 174, 197f, 38:22, 107, 225, 290, 41:119, 229, 45:23n, 207–212, 222, 271f, 347f, 372f, 46:38, 47:93, 119, 160, 165, 173, 186, 195, 202, 218, 263, 298, 302, 52:92f, 182f, 207, 281
For commentary on his book see Vols. 16 and 17
Iscah—2:240f
Ishmael—1:295, 3:13, 56, 63–66, 69f, 75f, 78, 80, 89, 93–95, 98f, 111f, 114, 126, 145, 147, 153f, 157f, 161–163, 175, 192, 316, 4:14, 16f, 19–22, 24–26, 28, 30f, 33–39, 41–43, 46, 49–51, 53–57,

59f, 62, 64f, 68, 72, 91f, 97, 102, 108, 155, 301, 310, 320, 324–329, 331f, 343–345, 348–350, 367f, 387–390, 403, 5:36, 73, 93f, 105, 165, 199, 269, 6:32, 72, 166f, 283f, 287, 303, 382, 389, 7:42, 8:160, 169f, 217, 228, 235, 314f, 14:194, 197, 16:172f, 17:72, 182, 233, 315, 18:116, 175, 20:102, 22:81, 196, 25:80, 374, 384, 386, 26:94, 237, 304, 433–437, 441, 445f, 449–451, 454, 457, 46:233, 47:146, 150–152

Ishmael and Isaac—33:86

Ishmaelites—2:368, 3:69, 161, 163, 4:235, 237–242, 328, 367, 6:161, 303, 306, 356, 359, 374, 382, 387–391, 396, 405, 7:51, 198, 340, 10:413, 11:121–125, 16:136, 158, 17:352, 20:251, 21:259, 26:453f, 456f, 47:150–152, 293

Isidore of Seville—29:116n

Islam—see **Mohammedans**

Islands—17:72, 414

Isolani, Isidoro—*Revocatio Martini Lutheri Augustiniani ad sanctam sedem*, 1519 36:6f, 12–14, 18

Israel—1:35, 132, 244, 295, 2:ix, 20, 29, 50f, 77, 101, 110, 130, 152–154, 160, 176–178, 257, 277, 285, 359, 3:28, 32, 36, 82, 89, 133, 146, 292, 320, 332, 334, 4:70, 98, 105, 128, 173–175, 186, 206, 279, 316, 322, 356, 365, 5:12, 94, 139, 144, 153, 157, 161, 184, 209, 219, 241, 261f, 270, 385, 6:140–142, 144, 153, 162f, 247, 258–260, 263f, 277f, 280, 7:6, 14f, 20, 35, 40, 109, 121, 152, 156, 165, 170, 174, 190, 200f, 303, 349, 8:32f, 78, 84, 131–133, 142f, 146, 149, 152, 154–156, 159f, 162, 176, 179f, 185, 199f, 218, 227, 231, 236f, 242, 276, 281f, 285f, 289f, 292, 294f, 297, 304, 306, 333, 9:ix, 6, 14f, 25, 32f, 35f, 40, 48, 52, 55, 58f, 63, 67, 79, 83, 87, 97, 103, 105, 108–110, 141, 174, 181, 195f, 202f, 229–231, 233, 242, 249, 250n, 292, 296f, 299, 304–308, 11:12, 17, 121n, 123, 189n, 260, 292n, 312n, 511, 520, 542f, 13:27, 35f, 47f, 48n, 151, 14:24, 51f, 54, 69, 131f, 135, 193f, 291, 304, 313f, 324f, 332f, 341, 347, 16:10, 12, 79, 81, 83, 93, 137–139, 143, 149, 154f, 184, 214, 218f, 221, 229, 300, 307, 315, 317, 17:90, 96, 117, 120, 148, 175, 264, 306–308, 345, 352, 356, 360, 364, 371, 18:7, 16f, 55, 134f, 139f, 148f, 160, 168, 176, 178, 188, 194, 201, 203, 225, 232, 248, 20:4, 7, 10, 15f, 53, 85, 91, 95, 110f, 126, 130, 144, 275, 303, 307, 21:349–351, 24:53, 261, 309, 327, 334, 359, 26:22, 80, 150, 204, 241, 258, 263, 265, 311, 320f, 326, 383, 436, 449, 460, 27:16, 80, 111, 135, 142, 146, 187, 268, 323, 330, 344, 350, 370, 375, 392, 406, 409, 29:117, 133, 140, 149, 168–170, 178, 183, 202, 207, 30:60, 66, 186, 231, 246, 289, 34:49n, 201, 35:245f, 269f, 272, 287, 292, 382, 37:131, 355, 38:84n, 131, 178, 207, 41:51, 70, 225, 288, 318, 42:156, 45:96, 104, 125, 201, 323, 331, 359, 367, 372f, 46:9, 35, 41, 97, 104, 120, 125, 151, 171, 174, 190–192, 233, 47:85, 94, 132, 155, 157, 160, 165, 170, 185, 198, 203, 208, 218, 263, 298, 302, 49:179, 331, 52:114, 119, 134, 187f, 200, 248, 250

New name for Jacob 6:256f

Israel, Blessing of—6:98, 121, 143f, 161–163, 258, 267f, 328, 342f

Israel, Children of—1:35, 342, 6:33, 64, 101f, 127, 154, 214, 7:202, 222, 300, 348, 8:50, 117, 123, 132, 137, 184, 217, 275, 287, 301, 323, 29:142, 147, 149, 157, 168, 186, 192, 206f, 30:185f, 205, 323, 36:39, 60, 102, 115, 147, 173, 182, 195, 213, 222, 47:90, 151–153, 165, 170, 185, 208, 218, 263, 298, 302

Israel, Destruction of—18:28, 43, 79, 89, 91f, 101, 106, 188, 215f

Israel, Kingdom of—5:160, 241, 6:162, 206, 216, 218, 346, 7:211, 8:118, 130, 241, 300f, 16:5, 59, 91, 102, 108, 117, 126, 154, 156, 219, 18:3, 5, 28, 57, 89, 160, 170, 174, 200–202, 227, 291, 19:39f, 52, 199, 204, 47:194, 201, 203f

Israel, Kings of—6:162, 165, 246, 278, 41:139, 214, 318, 45:370

Israel, New—35:288, 290, 47:72n

Israel, Orders in—18:129, 320

Israel, People of—see **Israelites**

Israel, Posterity of—6:153, 263f, 267

Israel, Tribes of—11:86, 542f, 18:202

Israel, True—14:193, 24:154, 25:81

Israelites—2:152, 310, 4:356, 365, 372, 5:150, 217, 241, 6:19, 34, 50, 162, 230, 239, 259–262, 276, 279, 284f, 292, 307, 353, 366, 368, 377, 389, 7:15, 95, 8:86, 95, 134, 136, 156, 185, 217, 219, 224, 277, 286, 292, 9:35, 40, 83f, 88, 231, 259, 284, 10:434f, 16:138, 220, 17:77, 128, 273, 308, 364, 19:50, 57, 81, 83, 134, 142, 231f, 22:43, 45, 62, 67, 69, 76–78, 83, 120, 130, 189, 195, 200, 211, 223, 303, 308–310, 313,

337f, 343f, 346–348, 372, 396, 403, 447n, 448, 458, 504, 511, 522, 23:31f, 208, 222, 301, 24:305, 330, 26:14, 47:68, 93, 140, 142, 151, 161, 165f, 169n, 203f, 225, 232, 241, 271, 52:7, 19, 35, 57, 66, 73f, 80, 82f, 87, 90, 92, 95f, 99f, 105, 112, 131, 136, 142, 146f, 149f, 153, 159, 163, 168f, 189f, 202f, 207f, 228, 238, 254, 260

Israelitish victory—6:167

Issachar—5:340, 356, 6:321, 366, 378, 380, 8:51f, 70, 102, 106, 222, 278–280, 291, 9:258, 306f

Italian campaign—46:89n

Italians—2:188, 190, 215, 4:272, 6:276, 331f, 7:331, 8:95, 103, 260, 13:192, 218, 222, 14:273, 17:412, 25:464, 26:188, 34:247, 41:xvi, 240, 47:141, 275, 51:294, 297, 54:140, 151, 207, 256, 262, 266, 296, 309f

Italy—1:31, 294, 2:189, 191, 193, 346, 353, 3:63, 252, 254, 5:11, 29, 6:67, 157, 331, 8:109, 120, 10:412, 11:177, 12:16, 13:191, 17:89, 414, 22:357, 25:124, 26:441, 27:147, 28:62, 90, 30:193, 37:154, 248, 38:35, 166, 318, 40:4, 8, 41:267, 291, 350, 371f, 374f, 46:107n, 198n, 202, 47:275n, 48:143n, 230n, 49:78n, 156, 161, 185n, 198, 220n, 221n, 265n, 284n, 350n, 414, 50:183n, 191, 206n, 248, 54:229, 238, 265, 291f, 306, 402

Itch (remorse)—6:369

Itch (sexual desire)—5:323f, 7:80, 46:149

Iudocus de Langenhove—34:352

Ivory—10:218

Ivory palaces—12:255

Ivy—19:29n, 30

Iwand, Hans J.—39:xiin

Jabbok, Brook of—6:117, 122

Jabesh Gilead—3:228

Jabin—11:129–131

Jack Ketch—13:66, 203, 22:402, 411, 28:126f, 147, 51:140, 157, 294

Jackasses—23:157, 181, 26:187, 263, 350

Jackson, Doris, translation assistant—41:262

Jacob—1:132, 194, 244, 271, 295, 2:20, 176, 230f, 256f, 284–286, 288, 360, 362, 382, 3:16f, 65, 92, 103, 118, 145f, 148, 154, 235, 4:24, 69, 134, 139, 178, 184, 190, 193, 195, 216, 228, 230, 289, 306, 310, 317, 319, 322, 326, 329, 332, 342–344, 248–350, 354, 365–372, 374, 376f, 379f, 382–388, 390–395, 401–403, 405f, 409, 5:ix, 3, 10, 14, 17, 27, 61, 73, 89f, 6:ix, 3, 7, 23, 31, 37, 61f, 66f, 112, 118, 124, 136, 139–141, 161, 175, 204, 215, 221, 255, 258f, 292, 295, 310, 312f, 315, 322, 340, 342f, 346, 359, 362, 381, 403, 7:4, 7f, 11, 17, 25, 30, 39, 42, 50, 54f, 57, 61, 65f, 70, 103, 114, 125, 132f, 163, 166, 175, 186, 207, 211f, 215–222, 225, 229, 246–248, 256f, 261, 263, 267f, 270f, 275, 284, 287–291, 293, 303–307, 310, 313–315, 318–327, 330, 7:339, 341, 356f, 262, 266, 271f, 8:12f, 23, 30f, 33f, 41, 47f, 50f, 55f, 59–63, 68–70, 72–78, 80–88, 90, 92–97, 104, 107, 110–117, 130, 133f, 136–140, 142–144, 147–168, 170, 176–179, 182, 184, 188–194, 196–199, 202f, 207f, 210–223, 225–229, 231–238, 241–249, 253, 259–261, 264f, 268, 272–274, 280–282, 284–293, 295f, 298f, 301–304, 306–310, 314f, 319f, 323, 328, 9:67, 104, 113, 175, 292, 304f, 308, 310, 10:71, 120f, 153, 193, 225, 247, 284, 290, 296, 325, 373, 397, 421, 11:29f, 40, 220n, 360, 367, 517, 13:154, 298, 310, 14:24, 34, 131, 197, 212, 227, 273, 288, 336, 16:50, 118, 134, 138, 155, 214f, 250, 17:16, 40, 61, 83, 98, 102, 104f, 115, 201, 346, 18:64f, 135, 159, 213, 227–229, 329, 392, 19:40, 183, 233, 20:30, 64, 191f, 211, 21:346, 351, 22:31f, 69, 79, 81, 92, 116, 120, 195f, 208f, 367, 448, 453, 522, 528, 24:79, 25:75, 81f, 374, 386, 391, 393, 450, 26:30, 237, 357, 437, 27:267, 28:14, 74, 191, 374, 29:13, 117, 133, 178, 202, 222, 239, 30:126, 249, 275, 35:199, 36:134, 37:333, 38:290, 41:51, 42:54, 109, 161, 164, 45:27, 48, 201, 213, 215, 217f, 254, 331, 359, 381n, 388, 390, 46:233, 235, 269, 299, 47:140, 145f, 151, 165, 178–192, 196, 200, 210, 218, 239, 241, 281f, 298, 300–302, 52:33, 52, 74, 129, 131, 159f, 225, 266

Jacob, Bishop of Nisibis—41:56n, 60

Jacob, House of—16:33f, 250

Jacob and Esau—33:86, 195–202
  Typify Evangelicals vs. Rome 4:392

Jacob de Compostella—see **James of Compostella, St.**

Jacob of Voragine—see **Jacobus de Voragine**

Jacob's ladder—6:87, 89, 126, 11:321, 22:200, 207f

Jacob's sons—6:213, 215, 276, 278f, 358

Jacobins—32:278, 283

Jacobites—6:52, 263, 8:161, 220

Jacobs, Charles Michael—45:237, 47:6n
translator of *Admonition to Peace, A Reply to the Twelve Articles of the Peasants in Swabia* 46:3–44
translator of *Against the Robbing and Murdering Hordes of Peasants* 46:45–56
translator of commentary on Psalm 82 13:39–72
translator of *Defense and Explanation of All the Articles* 32:3–100
translator of *Ninety-five Theses* 31:17–34
translator of *On the Councils and the Church* 41:3–178
translator of *On Translating: An Open Letter* 35:175–202
translator of *On War against the Turk* 46:155–206
translator of *Open Letter on the Harsh Book against the Peasants* 46:57–86
translator of *Prefaces to the New Testament* 35:335–411
translator of *Prefaces to the Old Testament* 35:233–334
translator of *Sermon on Keeping Children in School* 46:207–258
translator of *The Holy and Blessed Sacrament of Baptism* 35:23–44
translator of *To the Christian Nobility of the German Nation* 44:115–219
translator of *Trade and Usury* 45:231–310
translator of *Whether Soldiers too can be Saved* 46:84–138
Jacobs, Charles Michael, and Preserved Smith, eds.—*Luther's Correspondence and Other Contemporary Letters*, Philadelphia, 1913–1918 34:6n, 43:74n, 46:18n, 20n, 51:40n, 49n, 55n
Jacobs, Henry Eyster—47:5n
The Lutheran Movement in England, Philadelphia, 1891 51:121, 161n
Jacobus de Voragine—*Golden Legend* 3:325n, 16:338n, 17:253n, 24:147n, 277n, 370n, 29:79n, 153n
30:237n, 35:253n, 36:186n, 43:12, 45:25n, 289n, 371n, 48:17, 280n
Jacopo de Vio—see **Cajetan, Cardinal Thomas de Vio**
Jaeger, John—see Crotus Rubeanus
Jael—11:129f
Jaffa—see **Joppa**
Jagow, Matthias von, Bishop of Brandenburg—50:280n, 54:219
***Jahrbuch fur Liturgik und Hymnologie*, Kassel, 1955–1965**—53:xxn, 225n, 296n
Jailers—24:11, 114, 185, 199
Jairus, Daughter of—22:46
Jakob of Hochstraaten—48:10n
James, St., Apostle—3:109, 159, 292, 348, 18:183, 23:327, 357, 25:234–236, 402, 505, 26:64, 76, 100, 102, 110, 27:167, 200, 208, 213, 388, 30:ix, 162, 249, 260, 322, 35:10n, 39:43n, 285f, 41:65n, 72–79, 162, 172n, 319, 42:40n, 46, 64n, 46:33, 173f, 47:208, see also **James of Compostella, St.**
James, St., Epistle of—2:277n, 4:92, 96, 132–134, 340, 30:12, 34:317, 36:118n, 119–122, 37:26, 52:206, 264, 54:424f
James and Jude, Epistles of—35:395–398
James of Compostella, St.—2:354, 4:130n, 179, 5:247, 6:128f, 7:299, 8:212, 18:183n, 22:51, 136, 142, 250n, 287, 365, 405, 421, 502, 504, 23:24, 43, 121, 178f, 261, 263, 268, 26:40, 27:337n, 29:63n, 31:198, 32:41, 96, 38:110n, 172, 40:157n, 51:61, 109, 179, 217, 327, 45:287n, 52:264, 54:148, 238, 247
James the Just, St.—35:397n
James the Less, St., Apostle—13:28, 20:249f, 27:195, 27:195f, 30:203, 31:265
James the Younger, St.—see **James the Less, St., Apostle**
James's, St., Day—23:266n
Janiculum—2:188
Janissaries—7:72n
Jannes and Jambres—52:212, 238f
Januarius—41:21n, 130n, 138n
Janus—2:188
Japetus—2:189
Japheth—1:355, 357f, 2:25, 58, 120, 170, 175f, 178–180, 184, 187, 189f, 192, 194f, 201, 205, 236, 3:97, 4:3, 7:15, 35, 17:413, 22:33, 36, 47:147f, 52:174
Jareb, King—18:30, 55
Jared—2:28
Javan—2:188f, 192
Jaws—9:174, 189f, 310
Jazer—16:151
Jealousy—2:119, 338, 20:19f, 82, 175, 22:232, 234f, 237, 25:93, 97, 99, 231, 426f, 483f, 27:369, 371
Jebus—4:99
Jebusites—2:204, 6:33, 223, 9:80, 10:242, 381, 17:72, 20:93, 286, 25:247, 31:124
Jechoniah, King—see **Jehoiakim, King**
Jedaiah—20:68, 72, 253f
Jedidoth (Hebrew)—10:208–210
Jedin, Hubert—*History of the Council of*

Trent, St. Louis, 1957 41:259n, 260n, 263n

Jeduthun (Hebrew Psalm title)—10:183, 185, 290, 11:21, 36, 12:201, 14:231, 53:221

Jehoiada, High Priest—1:299, 13:155, 184, 47:208, 222f, 52:93f

Jehoiakim, King—8:288, 18:208, 327, 342, 25:237, 45:214n, 47:188, 195, 49:279, 52:90, 93

Jehoram, King—13:68, 46:192

Jehoshaphat, King—6:141, 216–218, 7:183, 9:163, 237, 13:44, 45:121, 46:173, 192, 47:222f, 49:386

Jehoshaphat, Valley of—18:114, 118f

Jehosheba—47:208

Jehovah—41:xvi, 314

Jehu, King—8:290, 18:4f, 12, 19:38, 41:220, 47:194, 208

Jena—1:ix, 16:ix, 107n, 30:xi, 37:155, 41:322n, 323, 49:70, 84n, 168n, 175n, 50:38n, 85f, 87n, 88, 90f, 93n, 103n, 106n, 107n, 108n, 111n, 112n, 113n, 114n, 117n, 118n, 119, 126, 129, 51:xvn

University of 30:ix, 49:51, 140, 414n, 50:74n, 213n

Jena edition of Luther's works—23:ix

Jenny, Markus—53:296n

Jephthah—6:309, 7:165, 171, 8:150, 282, 285, 296, 11:40, 46:120

Jeremiah, Book of the prophet—3:269

Jeremiah, Prophet—1:259, 2:26, 190, 229, 3:36, 41, 70, 82, 237, 269, 348, 4:117, 156, 233, 7:103, 176, 216, 302, 8:295, 9:58n, 110, 182, 13:108, 172, 14:77, 16:12, 74, 168, 184, 255, 17:47, 127f, 149, 155, 173, 176, 289, 295, 308, 343f, 364, 368f, 383, 18:193f, 320, 19:83, 134, 154, 166, 193, 203, 207, 20:35, 63, 68, 125, 127, 141, 321f, 22:253, 375, 420, 483, 486, 23:89, 276, 291, 369, 387f, 24:301–303, 305, 366, 25:142, 144, 237f, 346, 391, 396, 445, 26:109, 310, 341, 27:166, 189, 220, 234, 262n, 29:8, 30:19f, 322, 35:279, 280n, 35:279–282, 337, 349, 37:113f, 41:119, 216, 311, 45:215, 46:43, 79, 171, 176, 236, 47:154, 160, 163, 165, 188, 202–204, 207, 258, 265, 296, 49:279, 288n, 52:90, 92, 238

Jericho—1:310, 2:282, 286, 6:183, 247, 11:523, 25:399, 26:55, 30:68

Jericho vs. Jerusalem—25:399f

Jeroboam I, King—2:286, 4:146, 5:241, 6:49, 183, 226, 264f, 346, 7:211, 8:150, 179, 229, 233, 242, 300, 306, 11:40, 13:68, 17:17, 24:327, 26:258, 27:350, 35:269, 272, 36:87, 113, 219, 222, 38:150, 40:19, 41:288

Jeroboam II, King—18:3, 5, 128, 130, 174–177, 19:3, 38f, 56, 35:272, 323

Jerome, St.—1:3, 28, 51, 91, 232, 264, 271, 296f, 302, 320, 2:13, 23, 25, 36f, 109, 151, 164, 189, 191, 253, 291, 324, 342, 355, 3:66, 199, 216, 257, 355, 358, 4:99, 101, 181, 192f, 274, 301, 303, 331, 5:40, 52, 84, 88, 111n, 162, 207, 344f, 349, 380, 6:5, 28, 119, 140, 153, 253, 267, 326, 378, 7:6f, 10, 24f, 37, 52f, 80–82, 118, 124, 161, 189, 198, 205f, 213, 235, 267, 288, 298, 302, 8:20, 50, 71, 86, 149, 211, 245, 252, 282n, 289, 307, 9:7, 15f, 34, 36, 60, 130, 164, 167, 213, 215, 308, 10:38, 65, 104, 130, 134, 146, 149, 153, 171, 194, 210, 213, 215, 217, 230f, 237, 257–259, 307f, 317, 350, 363, 413, 11:3n, 69, 95n, 123n, 126n, 127n, 128n, 129n, 130n, 152n, 187n, 204, 271, 306, 337n, 12:62, 82f, 221, 316, 325, 13:56, 79n, 108, 14:23, 36, 283, 285, 335, 15:4, 31, 79f, 107n, 108, 247, 267, 272n, 16:xi, 178, 214, 290, 327, 17:6f, 11, 52, 54, 242, 284, 286, 318, 337, 366f, 373, 18:xii, 80, 89, 145, 217, 246, 334, 341, 352n, 19:3n, 5, 22, 107, 110, 112, 114, 120, 133, 20:73, 77, 103f, 121, 131f, 142, 149, 155, 282, 22:254, 256, 260, 264, 266, 268, 271–273, 23:72–74, 76n, 24:245, 25:xi, 61, 85, 113, 276, 402, 447, 481, 483, 489, 26:85, 108, 111f, 121, 123, 180, 199, 252, 287, 313, 410n, 412, 433, 458–460, 27:x, 35, 36n, 68f, 84f, 92, 95, 101, 167, 174, 175n, 182, 207, 209, 211–213, 215, 222, 228, 250, 257, 262, 270f, 291, 296, 302f, 318, 369f, 377, 380f, 28:x, 11, 13f, 28, 49, 284, 309, 322f, 334f, 341–343, 356f, 364, 29:17, 29, 32, 80, 117f, 131, 181, 221, 30:10, 40, 69, 166, 204, 206n, 227, 245, 311–313, 31:45n, 119, 163, 184, 197, 208, 238, 283, 32:9, 21, 36, 152, 156, 161n, 188f, 192, 221, 243, 244n, 268n, 33:12, 84, 167–169, 196, 198, 212–214, 216, 219, 221, 258, 34:22, 95, 186n, 275n, 282, 285, 312, 355, 35:221, 249f, 372, 36:118n, 289, 37:75n, 38:20n, 69, 77n, 196n, 39:29n, 155, 176, 181, 203, 210, 40:80n, 187n, 190, 41:7n, 19, 25n, 26n, 51n, 52n, 79n, 82n, 94n, 120n, 125n, 160, 290n, 308, 312n, 44:81n, 84n, 281n, 282n, 306n, 307n, 346,

45:23n, 97n, 210n, 211n, 259n, 290n, 361, 362n, 370n, 48:24, 40, 52f, 306n, 51:49, 58, 78, 52:93, 155, 53:171, 318, 54:8, 33, 44, 47, 49, 72, 104, 177, 259, 270, 274, 357, 474
as Biblical scholar 35:58n, 117n, 174n, 184n, 284n, 318n, 322n, 323n, 340n, 341n, 349n, 350n, 360n, 394n, 399n
Jerome, St. Works of—*Against Helvidius* 27:196
Against Jovinian 4:304n, 11:336n, 17:262n, 27:82n, 28:11, 13f, 284, 29:17n, 21n, 39:210n, 44:306n
Against Vigilantius 38:77n
Breviarum in Psalmos 13:99n, 104, 14:342n, 346n, 29:125n
Commentaria in Abdian prophetam 18:193n
Commentaria in Biblia 10:12
Commentaria in epistola ad Philemonem 29:96n
Commentaria in Epistola S. Pauli ad Galatas 17:307n, 26:24n, 47n, 61n, 68n, 69n, 74n, 77n, 84n, 92n, 103n, 107n, 249n, 275n, 276n, 362n, 367n, 418n, 27:55n, 96n, 130n, 163n, 166n, 168n, 169n, 173n, 176n, 177n, 179n, 183n, 186n, 187n, 190n, 193, 194n, 199n, 201n, 202n, 205n, 208n, 210n, 217n, 219n, 223n, 226n, 239n, 241n, 243n, 244n, 245n, 247n, 248n, 253n, 259n, 261n, 263n, 268n, 269n, 283n, 285n, 287n, 288n, 290n, 295n, 298n, 299n, 300n, 301n, 304n, 305n, 307n, 308n, 309n, 310n, 312n, 314n, 317n, 327n, 331n, 332n, 333n, 338n, 339n, 340n, 343n, 344n, 345n, 346n, 348n, 350n, 357n, 363n, 368n, 373n, 376n, 379n, 394n, 399n, 400n, 401n, 402n, 406n, 29:131n, 156n, 166n, 231n, 33:262n
Commentaria in Evangelium S. Matthaei 7:10n, 20:125n, 29:197n, 43:193, 48:266
Commentaria in Jesaiam prophetam 16:6n, 13n, 23n, 38n, 47n, 51n, 57n, 58n, 59n, 85n, 112n, 135n, 154n, 211n, 219n, 221n, 233n, 240n, 267n, 273n, 286n, 292n, 295n, 336n, 17:7n, 11n, 12n, 34n, 25:517, 29:204n, 44:28n
Commentaria in Jonam 19:29n, 38n, 95
Commentaria in Osee prophetam 18:3n, 34n, 42n
Commentaria in Zacharium prophetam 20:26n, 38n, 75n, 87n, 89n, 90n, 92n, 96n, 114n, 231n, 280n
Commentarii in Ezechielem 13:95n
Commentariorum in Ieremiam Libri VI 7:298n, 8:142n
Commentarium in Epistolam ad Ephesios libri tres 3:83n
Commentarius in Ecclesiasten 15:4n, 15n, 63n, 147f
Commentary on the Epistle to Titus 14:141n, 196n, 330n, 29:27n, 29n, 38:196, 39:155n
Contra Rufinum 25:52
De Poenitentia 34:22n
Dialogue against Pelagius 32:152n, 188n, 189n
Editions of complete works 48:18n
Epistle 34, Ad Marcellam 10:97
Epistola 122, Ad Rusticum 14:31, 34:22n
Epistola 77, Ad Oceanum 34:22n
Epistola LXXIII 13:310
Epistola ad Paulinum 9:25n, 10:200, 15:53n, 27:194, 35:399n
Epistula ad Nepotianum 25:455
Jerome to Augustine 32:161n
Letter 48:17, 25, 54
Letter XX (to Damasus) 11:271n
Letter to Ageruchia 28:342
Letter to Algasia 25:45
Letter to Eustochium 28:28, 44:346n
Letters 6:5n, 24:128n, 245n, 25:465, 27:194n, 30:40n, 204n, 33:84n, 258n, 36:58n
Letters from St. Augustine 32:11, 118n, 204n
Liber Hebraicarum quaestionum in Genesim 1:91n, 2:13n, 23n, 119n, 187n, 190n, 4:138n, 185n, 193n, 275n, 301n, 331n, 405n, 5:374n, 381n, 6:141n, 266n, 272n, 274n, 301n, 7:7n, 25n, 26n, 189n, 198n, 8:96n, 150n, 198n, 220n, 253n, 273n, 278n, 280n, 296n, 29:144n, 173n
Lives of the Hermits 42:25n, 73n, 139n
On Hebrew Place Names 3:199n, 5:210n, 6:247n, 302n, 7:302, 9:35n, 40n, 60, 10:20, 23, 195, 412n, 27:161n, 177n, 191n, 321n
On Illustrious Men—9:25n, 27:161n, 185n, 195n, 30:206n, 35:396n, 48:17
On the Perpetual Virginity of the Blessed Mary 27:196n, 38:20n
Opera, IX, Paris, 1579 11:69n
Praefatio in libros Salomonis 29:231n
Preface to the Books of Samuel and Malachi 32:96n
Prefaces in Vulgate Bible version 35:231
Prolog 15:322

Psalterium iuxta Hebraeos 10:237, 257–259, 308, 346, 363, 388, 409, 436, 438, 448, 452, 11:5n, 11n, 75n, 77n, 83n, 99n, 107n, 139n, 144n, 162n, 178n, 191n, 196n, 197n, 198n, 201n, 204n, 205n, 208n, 212n, 217n, 219n, 261n, 265n, 273n, 290n, 299n, 312n, 314n, 315n, 317n, 332n, 335n, 337n, 357n, 366n, 376n, 400n, 413n, 419n, 435n, 437n, 439n, 443n, 453n, 456n, 460n, 462n, 463n, 464n, 479n, 483n, 491n, 494n, 506n, 508n

Regula monachorum 11:306n

Vita S. Hilarionis eremitae 3:355n, 23:76n

Vita S. Pauli primi eremitae 7:81n, 28:322

Jerome of Ascoli—31:286, 289

Jerome of Prague—2:21, 87, 8:266, 32:87, 39:134, 149, 40:16n, 41:265n, 43:69, 44:194f, 52:6, 54:372

Jerusalem—1:7, 89, 95, 195, 244, 253, 280, 310, 323, 2:50, 99f, 175, 179, 184, 225, 243f, 255, 258, 282, 342, 344, 360, 378, 381, 3:77, 84, 89, 91, 94, 164, 169, 233f, 345, 4:29, 94, 99, 101, 110, 128, 190, 193, 373, 375, 5:160f, 240–245, 250, 6:41, 80f, 183–185, 206, 223f, 226, 247, 267, 274, 307f, 353, 383, 7:24, 171, 231, 248, 298–301, 339, 375, 8:11, 60, 78, 117, 156, 183, 200, 209, 239, 241, 244f, 249, 254, 293, 296f, 301, 9:60, 73, 102, 164, 167, 213, 215, 221, 295, 308, 10:29, 77, 84, 150, 230f, 314, 367, 431, 441, 11:6f, 177f, 186, 189, 539f, 542, 13:34f, 208, 269, 271f, 339, 14:6, 9, 14, 19f, 22, 72, 97, 101, 105, 111, 112, 135, 174, 183, 185, 262–264, 325–327, 15:23, 141n, 235, 285, 352, 16:5, 13, 21f, 27, 31f, 40f, 43, 45, 51–53, 78, 80, 89–91, 111, 113–116, 126, 138, 141, 144f, 149, 153, 155, 159–161, 164, 175–177, 187, 189, 192, 194, 196, 199, 202, 216–219, 221, 238f, 247, 261, 264, 272, 281, 286, 288f, 291, 293–295, 300, 302, 316, 326f, 336, 349, 17:1, 4, 14, 58, 71f, 90, 119f, 124, 126f, 131f, 142, 147, 156f, 212, 268, 309, 311, 315, 321, 345, 364, 372f, 389, 414, 18:7, 14, 92, 112, 121, 210, 213, 218, 236, 238, 242, 329, 348f, 19:85, 89, 127, 130, 147, 154, 165, 168, 173, 190, 195, 203, 206, 20:18–21, 24, 26f, 29, 32, 61, 75f, 82–84, 93, 95, 113f, 126, 131f, 135–137, 141, 144, 175–178, 181–183, 186f, 189, 259, 271, 279, 323f, 337f, 342, 21:104, 311, 313, 22:35, 41–43, 46, 54, 73, 84, 86, 128, 189, 191f, 195, 198f, 201, 203, 208, 210, 215–219, 221, 223f, 229, 236–238, 240, 248–251, 253, 262, 280, 282, 347, 367, 384, 390, 415, 448, 465, 468, 499, 506, 522–524, 23:120f, 207–210, 214f, 217–220, 243, 254, 256f, 276, 283, 310, 352–354, 362, 366, 369f, 378, 380f, 386–388, 390f, 409, 24:9, 11, 14, 24, 156, 159, 169, 171, 237, 262, 276, 280, 301–303, 338f, 25:24, 124, 126f, 399, 429, 445, 516, 26:23, 61f, 74–77, 81–83, 86f, 101, 105f, 112f, 204, 206f, 437f, 439n, 440f, 444, 27:93, 155, 193, 196, 199f, 208n, 296, 311, 314–319, 337, 344, 382, 391, 410, 28:90, 29:36, 61, 167, 171, 173, 214, 237, 30:68, 177, 257n, 31:198, 393, 32:162f, 34:216, 35:220, 273f, 283, 289, 291, 303f, 328–331, 384, 37:284f, 38:22, 40, 110, 150, 165, 207, 40:10, 41:5, 13, 27–29, 30–34, 64, 68, 72, 74–77, 79, 113, 206, 228, 256, 321–324, 347, 42:7f, 64, 107, 112, 133, 45:214, 221, 222n, 223, 228n, 46:148, 171, 47:66, 73, 79f, 83, 86, 94, 96, 143, 145, 154, 176, 195, 203f, 212, 221, 224f, 233, 236f, 242, 249, 251, 255, 266, 271, 276, 282f, 303f, 48:109, 204, 216, 52:9, 89, 92, 134, 140, 143f, 163, 170f, 176, 183, 193f, 198, 207f, 239, 264, 53:63, 54:238

Jerusalem, Destruction of—47:75f, 84, 97, 138f, 174, 183, 190, 200, 230, 245–247, 251f, 262, 265, 267, 281

Jerusalem, Bishops of—41:42, 59, 88f, 91f

Jerusalem vs. Jericho—25:399f

Jeshurun—2:345, 9:308

Jesse—2:72, 5:255, 7:210, 15:271, 275, 16:117, 21:301f

Jesse, Root of—1:194, 16:124, 21:301f, 25:121, 516, 29:132, 178, 202

Jesters—54:194, 334

Jesting—3:283

Jesu—47:257

Jesuits—50:82n

Jesus—11:271, 288, 14:102, 105, 47:88, 134, 139, 234, 237, 256f, 262f, 267, 271, 274f, 279, 285–288, 298, 300, 303, 305, see also **Christ**

Redeemer of men 36:215f

Jesus Christ—see **Christ**

Jesus Sirach—see **Sirach**

Jethro—8:133, 136, 9:17, 21, 163, 25:181, 45:378

Jewell, John, Bishop of Salisbury—41:xivn

Jewels—3:29, 20:103, 105, 24:359
Jewels, Christians as—17:242
Jewish conversions—Historical examples 47:85, 157
Luther's expectations 47:62, 95f, 124, 137, 177, 191, 253
Jewish converts—47:130, 176n, 228, 299
Jewish doctrine—47:149, 269
Jewish fathers—20:10f, 161, 163–165, 189
Jewish kingdom—14:69
Jewish myths—29:41–44, 52
Jewish nation—9:7, 20, 108, 23:29, 148, 206, 372, 377
Jewish prayers—47:143–145, 149–151, 156, 167, 169, 228, 274, 286–288
Jewish priesthood—47:66, 73f, 79f, 83f, 97, 138, 173, 187, 198, 207, 233, 239, 272, 298
Jews—1:10, 12, 14, 16, 20, 38, 57–59, 74, 96, 138, 195, 218–220, 234, 240, 249–251, 255f, 258, 260, 264, 268, 291f, 294, 296, 302, 312f, 317, 319, 323, 326, 330f, 337–339, 350, 353, 356, 358, 2:10, 12–14, 17, 40, 42, 46, 52f, 69, 71, 77, 82, 92f, 98–101, 107, 109f, 112, 129, 137, 160, 170, 174, 178f, 182, 184f, 190, 201, 203, 205, 226–228, 237f, 240, 243f, 248, 250, 256f, 260–266, 288, 290, 292f, 304f, 311f, 326, 342f, 352, 359–361, 363f, 370, 384, 393, 396, 3:12, 21, 34, 36–38, 42, 46–48, 59, 64, 66–68, 71, 76–100, 102, 104, 106–113, 115f, 121f, 125, 129, 131, 133, 135f, 142–145, 148, 150–152, 162–164, 176f, 190–194, 197, 208, 210, 219, 232, 248, 250f, 258, 261n, 263, 274, 296–298, 304f, 308, 312f, 337, 341, 345, 348, 352f, 358, 4:9f, 13, 25–29, 31–33, 43f, 50, 52, 55, 60, 63–66, 71, 88, 97, 100, 102, 108, 114, 121, 124, 136, 145f, 149, 152, 155f, 160, 171f, 178, 182, 184, 187, 203, 221, 230, 233, 237, 241, 260, 262f, 265, 280, 295, 311, 322, 327, 341, 343, 346f, 349, 351f, 359, 366f, 372, 373, 375, 383–385, 393, 400, 406, 5:19, 30, 32, 36, 56, 71–73, 83, 101, 104, 134, 141, 149, 157, 160–162, 171, 178, 212, 259, 273, 303, 320, 336, 349, 352, 6:9f, 32, 53, 96, 113, 119, 127, 129, 136, 144f, 154f, 161, 179, 181, 197, 203, 210, 212, 228, 232, 248–250, 276, 283f, 291–293, 297, 301, 324, 326, 351, 353, 366, 373, 385, 387–389, 391, 393, 7:4, 10, 13–16, 18, 21, 30f, 50–53, 67f, 108, 112f, 115, 123, 142, 149, 152, 160, 166f, 169, 171, 173, 187, 196, 198, 200f, 207, 209, 212, 216, 231, 250, 253, 267, 283, 298f, 301, 308, 325, 330, 338, 343, 345–348, 350, 354, 8:35, 60, 65, 81, 102f, 105, 127, 129, 133f, 136, 139, 141, 144, 152, 155, 165, 167f, 176, 195, 200f, 207, 213, 216f, 225, 229, 238–241, 245f, 248, 252, 256, 261f, 280, 287f, 291f, 303f, 9:7, 21, 25, 27f, 34, 53, 58n, 59, 74, 81, 83, 84n, 102, 110, 145f, 158, 175, 180, 187, 203f, 210, 214f, 221, 225, 234f, 249, 261, 294–296, 298, 310, 10:3–5, 7, 11–13, 17, 19, 23f, 28–31, 34, 36f, 46, 54, 56, 59, 61, 67, 77, 85, 89, 92, 98, 106, 124, 149f, 245, 272, 11:8, 10, 13, 31, 35, 39–44, 48f, 51, 56f, 59, 61, 65, 67, 70, 72f, 75, 77–79, 81f, 86f, 98–100, 110, 113, 115, 121–124, 132, 134–136, 155–157, 167, 173, 189, 193f, 197, 200–202, 208, 215, 220, 224, 242, 251, 253, 255–258, 279, 284, 286, 289f, 292f, 320, 329, 348, 357, 363, 377, 381, 412, 415, 417f, 424f, 428, 430, 442, 447, 461, 471, 479, 481, 492, 494n, 495, 498, 500f, 503, 508, 512, 517, 519, 521f, 527, 535f, 542f, 551, 12:64, 70, 88, 90f, 104, 115, 124, 139, 201f, 209, 245, 253f, 265–267, 276, 283, 285, 292, 341, 343, 352, 354, 356, 363, 365, 396, 399, 403, 13:3, 19, 21, 23, 86, 169, 234, 236, 264f, 281, 283–286, 292, 301, 304, 341, 363, 398, 14:8–11, 14, 17–20, 22, 24–27, 29f, 33–35, 37f, 64, 72, 74, 89, 92, 94–96, 98f, 102–104, 118, 132, 183, 185, 187, 202, 235, 243, 247, 253, 255, 261–271, 275, 290f, 293, 301, 305f, 309, 314f, 320–323, 332f, 342, 15:44, 141, 219, 225, 254f, 263, 267f, 314f, 321, 323, 326, 334, 339f, 344, 346, 351, 16:10, 17, 14, 23, 26–29, 32–35, 38, 40, 44–46, 49, 55, 58f, 62, 64, 66–70, 73–75, 78, 84–86, 89f, 95, 97, 101, 104, 107–109, 114, 117, 125f, 132, 138f, 141–144, 146, 154, 156, 159, 162, 164–167, 170–172, 176, 190–194, 196, 198, 206f, 211, 217, 224–230, 235f, 239–243, 246, 248, 262, 272, 292–296, 300, 302, 318, 330f, 17:3, 7, 10, 39, 53, 55, 63, 69, 71, 78, 93–95, 98, 105, 120, 125, 134, 140f, 143, 156, 163, 165, 169, 174f, 190f, 197f, 216f, 220, 222, 234, 236, 241, 244, 263, 274, 306–308, 323, 346, 352n, 354, 375, 381, 385f, 404, 411, 413, 18:6, 13, 16f, 51, 56, 62, 113, 115, 138, 140, 173, 185f, 188,

194, 198, 200, 203f, 208, 236, 241, 283, 300, 332, 369, 380f, 383, 397f, 19:37, 93f, 97f, 160, 163, 171f, 193, 199, 205f, 217f, 221, 225, 20:12, 19, 22, 27, 49, 56, 58, 60f, 63, 71, 73, 75f, 78, 80f, 86f, 100, 103, 107f, 116, 121f, 126, 140, 145, 148, 159f, 163, 166, 184, 199, 214, 216, 236, 239f, 243, 245f, 258, 268, 275, 278–281, 303, 305, 337, 21:11, 17, 30, 33, 67, 81, 118f, 129f, 177f, 186f, 333, 342, 353–355, 22:7, 17, 39–45, 47, 49, 53f, 57, 68, 75, 78–81, 84, 86, 89, 91f, 97f, 107, 113, 122, 126, 135, 142, 157, 159f, 175f, 182, 187, 193, 196f, 207, 214, 217, 223, 228–231, 238f, 242–248, 251, 275f, 284, 301, 319f, 334, 338, 340, 343, 359, 366, 391–393, 405, 416, 423f, 426, 428f, 432, 448, 450, 454, 457, 462, 465, 468f, 476, 480, 485f, 494, 505, 508, 510–512, 514f, 522, 525, 23:5, 8, 12f, 25, 28f, 34, 37f, 40–43, 45, 48, 50, 52f, 56, 66, 70, 72, 78–80, 82f, 86f, 94, 99f, 103f, 108f, 112, 114–118, 120f, 124–128, 132f, 135, 139, 153, 155f, 162, 167, 169f, 181, 196, 201, 206–208, 215–219, 222–224, 228, 230, 234–236, 240–244, 246, 248, 251–256, 261, 263–265, 267, 269, 277, 283–285, 292, 304, 310, 320, 324–326, 328, 338, 343, 345–347, 352–355, 358–363, 365–369, 373–375, 378, 380f, 383–389, 391, 394–396, 399, 401, 403–409, 412–415, 418f, 421, 24:9, 11, 21f, 24, 33, 47f, 55, 71f, 74, 85f, 88, 93, 97, 103, 107f, 140, 168, 194, 227–229, 243, 256, 259, 280f, 308, 310, 323, 327, 329f, 332, 335, 337, 340f, 345, 349, 372, 396f, 405f, 414, 25:3, 9, 16, 18, 22–26, 29f, 79–103, 135f, 138, 143, 163, 182, 190, 193, 196, 207f, 219, 232, 246, 289, 324, 379–432, 26:9f, 14, 26, 28f, 53, 58f, 73, 76, 80–85, 98, 102, 104f, 107, 109–111, 114f, 117–121, 123, 125, 130, 138, 140, 147, 205–209, 211, 228, 236f, 239–241, 243f, 246–248, 251, 288f, 290n, 292f, 298f, 301, 304f, 327f, 330, 332, 345, 351, 354–357, 389, 395f, 398–400, 403, 410, 418f, 423, 425–428, 433, 435–437, 443, 452, 454, 456f, 27:9, 15f, 30, 38, 42, 55, 111, 117, 123, 130, 138f, 142f, 147, 167, 177, 180, 190, 197, 200, 203–204, 208, 210–211, 213, 215, 217f, 221, 246f, 250, 252, 265, 274, 279–281, 284f, 290, 295f, 302, 306, 309, 320, 322, 334f, 343f, 355, 357, 383, 401–403, 406, 28:9, 21f, 29, 31, 40f, 83, 109, 130, 163, 222, 271, 277, 299, 313, 29:5f, 8, 13, 21, 33–36, 40, 43, 49, 60, 123, 148, 153, 170, 174, 176, 178f, 186, 191, 203, 210, 239, 30:6–8, 12, 19f, 22, 29, 34, 58, 61f, 66, 88, 116, 152, 165, 207, 222, 229, 246, 285, 306, 308, 314, 31:187, 373, 32:170, 34:20, 110, 175, 225, 304, 35:63, 142, 164f, 194, 215, 240f, 271f, 286f, 290, 331, 348, 363f, 372f, 36:6, 9, 19, 143, 148, 176, 187, 195, 203, 279f, 288, 290, 292, 336, 37:13, 31f, 37f, 42, 53n, 71, 77, 96, 113, 128, 141, 202, 238, 272, 284, 286f, 319, 326, 337f, 359, 38:xi, 18, 23, 38f, 53, 57, 97, 100, 105, 113f, 159, 168n, 222, 287, 303, 307, 315, 39:xvii, 67, 69, 77–79, 82, 85, 123, 125, 145, 161, 180f, 185, 204, 247, 287, 290, 41:9, 11, 21f, 28, 29n, 51, 61, 63, 67, 69, 75–79, 99, 101, 104, 113, 139, 165, 177, 202, 207, 220, 229, 256, 273, 324, 348, 42:6, 7n, 9f, 51, 103, 107, 111, 134, 43:67, 103, 156, 175, 226, 262, 275, 277, 45:25, 59, 75, 98, 102, 115, 152, 155f, 198, 200f, 207–221, 229, 281, 352, 362, 46:20, 27, 64, 79, 81, 94, 97, 104, 107, 110, 130, 145f, 150, 177, 186, 195f, 199f, 236, 277, 293, 315, 47:59–98, 123–306, 49:74, 102, 170, 193, 259, 379, 50:99, 145n, 290f, 302, 317, 52:xi–xii, 114, 54:43, 208f, 238, 241, 306, 340, 348, 373, 420, 426, 434, 436f, 455, see also **Hebrews**; **Israelites**

Christian relationship to 25:102
Have lost the promise 3:113
Luther's proposals 47:124f, 135f, 268–274, 285–290, 292
No longer God's people 3:113
Reactions to the Reformation 47:60, 126
Rejection not final 25:99f
Seen as tools of the devil 47:141, 164, 174, 213f, 228, 232, 253, 277f, 282, 284, 289, 291
Should be treated kindly 21:354f
Situation in 16th century Germany 47:61n, 128, 268n
Superstitions concerning 47:131, 217, 242, 277
Their impenitence 47:139, 149, 172, 242, 298
Their lineage 47:140–149, 300–302
Their traditional stories 1:319, 326

Jews, Defense of—Agricola 47:135f
Melanchthon 47:264n

Osiander 47:129n, see also **Dorothy of Solms, Countess of Mansfeld**
Jews, Government of—47:66, 73, 79, 84, 87, 174, 178, 193, 202
Jews, Kingdom of the—16:51, 192, 47:66, 73, 78–80, 83, 97, 272
Jews and Gentiles—One fold 20:66, 71, 94, 201, 289
Jews called saints (irony)—47:172, 176, 213, 232, 239, 243, 261, 263, 265–267, 277
Jezebel, Queen—2:29, 3:320, 355, 5:25, 8:229, 273, 290n, 297, 11:112, 13:59, 183, 17:74, 18:12, 193n, 45:389
Jezreel—18:4f, 7, 14–16, 43
Joab—1:299, 308, 4:107, 5:35, 8:209, 9:163, 13:154, 221, 223, 22:236, 25:452, 42:157, 45:123
Joachim, Erich—*Die Politik des letzen Hochmeister in Preussen, Albrecht von Brandenburg*, Leipzig, 1892–1895 45:135n
Joachim, Prince of Anhalt—38:142, 217, 43:189, 50:79, 51:259, 315
Joachim, St.—22:347, 40:88
Joachim I, Elector of Brandenburg—20:27n, 32:116, 119, 34:107, 43:216n, 266n, 45:112n, 135n, 136, 138, 46:90, 47:12n, 24, 26, 33, 106, 135, 270n, 48:56, 205n, 217n, 220n, 49:60n, 119n, 123, 176, 189n, 202, 326n, 50:69n, 175n, 54:359, 475
Joachim II, Elector of Brandenburg—34:148, 50:68f, 69n, 110n, 149n, 228n, 54:62, 86, 219, 336
Joachim Frederick, Margrave of Brandenburg—25:xii
Joachim of Fiore—5:346n, 38:251n
Joachimsen, Paul, and Goetz, Walter, eds.—*Das Zeitalter der religiösen Umwälzung: Reformation und Gegenreformation, 1500–1660*, Propyläen Weltgeschichte, V, Berlin, 1930 34:6n
Joachimstal—8:x, 67, 17:235, 38:xix, 40:88
Joanna of Castile—47:223n
Joash, King—13:183, 46:173n, 47:194, 208f, 52:3, 156, 171
Job—1:144, 2:178, 259, 276, 321, 3:44, 81, 89, 106, 264, 270, 348, 5:209, 6:95, 149f, 288, 307f, 324, 7:85, 238, 8:9, 131, 133, 162, 247, 9:41n, 10:159, 162, 202, 297, 348, 368, 380f, 398, 11:242, 467, 13:101, 108, 112, 14:19, 50, 89, 180, 292, 344f, 348, 16:62, 17:47, 125, 127, 201, 303, 19:133, 219, 21:11, 313, 333, 22:375, 403, 23:77, 25:69, 181, 275, 278, 346, 376, 391, 497, 26:193, 211, 341, 27:230f, 245, 287, 335, 28:373, 30:104f, 142, 244, 303, 33:291, 38:130, 41:335, 42:32, 128, 45:280, 46:43, 78, 47:86, 113, 157, 49:74, 52:170f, 54:79
Job, Book of—4:38, 7:321, 16:96, 17:194, 35:251
Jobab—6:307
Jochebed—6:293, 8:88, 89n
Joel, Prophet—16:5n, 18:xf, 79–81, 113, 19:3, 38, 25:91, 30:22, 35:318f, 46:221
Commentary on his book 18:xf, 79–123 (text)
Joerger family—49:141n, 154, 210n
Joest, Wilfrid—47:103n
Johannan—25:387
Johannessegen (John's toast)—19:39n
Johannine Comma (I John 5:7)—30:316
Johannine writings—30:221n
John I, Emperor—41:374n
John VI, Bishop of Meissen—38:119n
John XXI, Pope—41:304n
John XXII, Pope—2:327n, 41:304n, 332n, 44:173n, 46:232n, 48:186n
John XXIII, Pope—2:327f, 4:220n, 34:236n, 41:265n, 267n, 268n, 269
John, Bishop of Antioch—41:95n
John, Elector of Saxony—3:341n, 356n, 13:x, 216n, 218, 23:ix, 152n, 219n, 321–324, 342, 27:125n, 34:6n, 66, 332, 37:155, 38:8, 93, 39:26, 43:115, 121n, 181, 45:79, 80n, 81n, 83, 104n, 127n, 240, 243, 382, 383n, 46:89n, 93n, 143, 47:6f, 23f, 27n, 48:181, 264n, 269n, 270n, 275n, 307, 313n, 314, 381n, 398n, 49:15n, 52, 83n, 84, 111n, 117, 118n, 119n, 122n, 123, 124n, 125f, 130f, 137f, 144n, 145, 154f, 159, 168n, 169f, 175n, 180n, 182, 189f, 199n, 210f, 221f, 229, 231n, 236, 240n, 243–245, 252–255, 272f, 281, 283n, 284n, 285, 295f, 303n, 305f, 315n, 317n, 326, 329n, 335f, 338n, 339f, 349n, 352, 354n, 355, 359f, 367n, 399, 403f, 413, 416n, 418n, 420n, 422n, 423f, 425n, 429n, 430, 433n, 435n, 50:3f, 22–24, 41f, 41n, 43n, 47f, 50, 56f, 160n, 278n, 51:103, 177, 197, 231f, 235–237, 239, 241, 53:222, 54:54, 180, 182, 195, 217, 228, 372
John, Epistles of—35:393–395
John, First Epistle of—23:183, 28:xi, 29:ix, 3n
John, Henry, Count of Schwarzburg—50:285n

John, John H.—Indexer of Vols. 6, 10, 20, 25, and 28
John, Margrave of Brandenburg-Küstrin-Neumark—50:149n, 54:263
John, Prince of Anhalt—38:142, 145, 217f, 45:197, 50:175, 54:279
John, St., Apostle and Evangelist—3:127, 129, 159, 297, 299, 300n, 333, 14:92, 101, 168, 194, 299n, 308, 329, 15:299f, 17:90, 22:182, 23:x, 14, 35, 38, 42, 54, 57, 61, 64, 76, 78, 108–110, 112, 117, 120, 125, 127, 132, 140, 160f, 174, 184f, 201, 218f, 243, 245, 252f, 259, 276f, 283, 343, 353, 360, 365f, 372, 376, 405, 411, 414, 422, 24:ix, 32, 64, 90, 94, 124, 161, 196, 205, 339, 375, 383, 391, 25:148, 26:31, 40, 66, 100, 102, 162, 282, 317, 27:52, 65, 136, 167, 185, 195, 200, 208, 230, 372, 388, 29:14f, 30:ix, 11, 162, 219, 221, 223, 225–227, 233, 235f, 238–241, 244, 246–248, 251–254, 256f, 259f, 263–265, 267, 272, 274f, 277–281, 284, 288f, 292–297, 299, 302–306, 308f, 311–318, 320–323, 325, 327, 37:233, 267, 38:180, 183f, 198, 258, 274, 276, 295f, 41:58, 62, 64n, 65n, 121, 157, 160, 191, 319, 42:6, 46, 46:33
John, St., Gospel according to—8:165, 21:65, 23:77, 82f, 129, 148, 24:ixf, 21, 60, 26:42, 243, 52:178
John, The name—6:309, 7:301, 50:175n
John Boaster—8:126
John Frederick the Magnanimous—see **John Frederick, Elector of Saxony**
John Frederick, Elector of Saxony—2:21n, 3:182n, 356n, 4:210f, 5:263, 6:21, 7:206n, 8:63n, 106, 178, 13:x, 171n 215n, 21:xviif, 297, 356f, 22:ixf, 205n, 418n, 512, 23:295, 27:125n, 28:x, 34:272, 292f, 296, 325, 328, 341, 35:294n, 36:234, 40:49, 103n, 107n, 115n, 265, 271n, 41:14n, 181, 182n, 185, 187f, 192, 224, 228, 231, 237–240, 242, 260, 43:215, 259–288, 44:18n, 21, 47:61, 105, 135, 255, 48:8, 181f, 218, 255n, 269n, 49:3, 15, 73, 84, 131f, 195f, 212n, 329, 349, 356f, 361n, 367n, 420, 422f, 430f, 50:42, 45n, 57, 80n, 87f, 93n, 97n, 99n, 104n, 108n, 112n, 139n, 144n, 186, 197, 205, 214n, 215, 222, 224n, 228n, 237n, 255, 271, 274n, 275n, 280n, 294n, 51:103, 231, 53:123, 54:164, 218, 226, 233, 239, 255, 257, 263, 270, 272, 283, 345, 388, 456, 472
official contacts with Luther 50:41n, 46n, 57, 81f, 89, 100f, 105, 114, 117f, 119n, 121n, 132f, 139f, 153f, 156–158, 185f, 192f, 195f, 197f, 203, 207, 224n, 255f, 258f, 278, 297n, 298, 314n, 316
personal contacts with Luther 50:94n, 95n, 122, 130n, 135, 156, 167f, 204f, 210f, 246n, 275f, 278, 318
John George, Count of Mansfeld—50:282f, 302n
John Hyrcanus—47:221
John of Damascus—23:123n, 27:131n
Barlaam and Joasaph 27:136n
De haeresibus compendium 4:70n
The Orthodox Faith 22:149n
John of Jena (name for a fool)—50:129, 219, 292
John of Salisbury—50:xv
John of Wesel—31:157, 41:115n
John of the Burned Tower—see **Torquemada, Juan de**
John the Baptist, St.—1:334, 2:357, 396, 399, 3:96, 107, 134, 150, 202, 284, 5:161, 349, 362, 6:254, 7:99, 254, 8:208, 218, 227, 9:27, 10:206, 268, 280, 401, 431, 11:112, 172, 12:254, 261, 394, 13:184, 14:273, 340, 15:27, 304, 16:79, 17:7, 141, 208, 222, 256, 262, 277, 298, 18:381, 408, 419, 19:55, 225, 20:31, 121, 146, 196, 317, 22:24, 32, 37, 39f, 44f, 47, 53f, 57, 62, 66, 71, 77f, 92f, 99, 109, 124–127, 129, 131, 134, 158, 171, 174, 181, 188, 195, 239f, 242, 260, 364, 413–415, 419, 421, 423, 429, 431f, 437, 447, 454, 459, 462, 475, 490, 22:495, 501, 509, 515, 24:40, 283, 307, 395, 25:41, 156, 282, 26:19, 57, 278, 27:35, 235, 29:194, 205, 31:96, 34:304, 35:332, 37:170, 173, 253, 262, 290, 294n, 337, 38:31, 37, 290, 39:188, 203, 41:39f, 84, 227, 311, 42:139n, 176, 45:77, 87, 98, 224, 259, 46:97f, 129, 145, 221, 289, 47:41, 141, 231f, 254, 263, 277, 48:22, 261, 321, 49:34, 52:3f, 30, 44, 46f, 51f, 56f, 60f, 63–71, 73f, 78f, 86, 89f, 105, 129, 133, 156, 206
John the Constant—see **John, Elector of Saxony**
John the Hermit, St.—41:125n
John the Steadfast (or Constant)—see **John, Elector of Saxony**
John van den Esschen—43:74
John von der Ecken—see **Ecken, John von der**
John-Baptist de Gratia-Dei—47:176n
Johnston, O.R.—co-translator with J.I.

Packer of Luther's *Bondage of the Will*, London, 1957 33:xin
Joints—6:137f, 153
Jonadab—25:250, 488, 27:229
Jonah, Book of—commentary 19:3–106 (text)
Jonah, Prophet—2:26, 77, 90, 202, 276, 3:81, 89, 232, 6:227, 8:93, 225n, 300f, 14:19, 16:74, 84, 17:76, 383, 414, 18:3, 281f, 19:x, 15, 27f, 30, 36–38, 40, 42, 44, 49f, 52, 57f, 63–66, 71–82, 92, 94, 96, 100f, 104, 22:359, 24:387, 26:109, 211f, 35:323, 46:120, 176, 47:85, 157
Jonah, Sign of—10:15, 373, 22:241–243
Jonas, Justus—9:x, 13:352n, 14:xi, 17:247n, 22:x, 23:ix, 26:195n, 28:ix, 3, 6, 31:23, 32:xvi, 103, 120, 137, 259, 33:11n, 34:5–7, 71n, 35:185n, 206, 38:6, 9, 61, 63, 79f, 89n, 141f, 145, 217f, 242f, 39:242, 40:106n, 275n, 41:8, 261, 43:191, 44:247n, 45:8n, 147n, 47:8, 16n, 20n, 29n 63, 48:262, 275n, 338n, 49:xviiin, 71n, 82n, 115n, 130, 151, 171f, 180f, 185f, 219n, 221n, 236n, 238n, 240n, 274, 282n, 283, 285n, 287, 291n, 292n, 295n, 299n, 310n, 318n, 326n, 327n, 330n, 332n, 334n, 335, 339n, 345, 347f, 349n, 350n, 351n, 352n, 353, 356, 366f, 372f, 373n, 374n, 378n, 388n, 392, 395n, 401n, 405, 431n, 50:xixn, 47n, 144n, 154n, 159n, 207n, 225f, 236f, 269n, 271n, 51:69, 80, 197, 303, 312n, 53:245, 54:ix, xiii, 49, 136, 138, 155, 184, 222, 287, 294, 319, 421, 428, 451
 and Luther 50:47, 80n, 87n, 93f, 94n, 95n, 107f, 109f, 144f, 153f, 163n, 168, 207n, 210, 225f, 236f, 237n, 246n, 247f, 268f, 275n, 280n, 285n, 289, 291n, 294n, 297, 306, 312, 317f
 and Wittenberg University 50:56, 63, 67, 93f, 102, 144n, 204, 248n
Jonas, Justus, Jr.—49:175, 324, 50:237f, 247f
Jonathan—8:285, 9:202, 17:192, 46:193
Jonathan ben Uzziel—20:245n
Joppa (Jaffa)—2:205, 8:273, 19:9, 44, 99
Joram, King—5:160, 6:162, 303, 310, 7:52, 47:194f, 208
Jordan River—1:342, 2:282, 342, 344f, 348f, 366, 4:5, 370, 6:117, 175, 179, 182, 8:73, 143, 145, 198, 279, 285, 323, 9:14, 26f, 42f, 81, 283f, 10:20, 34, 195–199, 203f, 319, 327, 342, 11:394, 14:299, 340, 16:114, 17:96, 120, 18:287, 19:223, 233, 20:117f, 289, 311, 22:38, 45f, 119, 127, 159–161, 180, 186, 201, 216, 313, 414n, 415, 419, 421–426, 512, 25:26, 137, 156, 520, 26:374, 27:177, 35:66f, 36:86, 37:83, 299, 40:87, 41:302, 42:109, 52:134
Josel of Rosheim, Rabbi—47:61f, 135
Joseph—1:196, 314, 328, 2:258, 276, 288, 324, 3:81, 88, 96, 115, 154, 177, 182, 235, 280, 334, 4:ix, 190, 195, 229, 283, 296, 5:10, 90, 286–288, 303n, 337–340, 342f, 357f, 6:ixf, 3, 118, 202, 212f, 217f, 227, 229, 247, 268, 270, 273, 277–279, 282, 292, 295, 308, 312–314, 321, 328–330, 336f, 341, 343f, 353, 358, 372f, 376, 378f, 386, 389, 7:ixf, 5f, 14, 45, 52–57, 59–62, 64f, 68–70, 72f, 76–84, 86f, 89–103, 105–117, 120, 122–135, 137, 140–147, 149f, 153, 155–161, 164–166, 168–178, 180f, 183–186, 188–192, 196–199, 201–205, 207–212, 214–216, 220, 222–225, 227, 230–233, 235–245, 247 250, 253–257, 259–261, 263–268, 270f, 278, 282–286, 288, 291, 305, 310, 313, 316f, 319, 322f, 326–331, 333, 338–341, 343, 345–348, 350–352, 354–358, 361–368, 371–374, 376f, 8:3f, 6f, 12–14, 15–31, 33–39, 41, 43–59, 61f, 64–66, 68–74, 76, 78f, 81f, 87f, 91–98, 100–105, 107f, 111f, 115f, 119–124, 127n, 128–136, 138–140, 142–144, 146, 148, 150, 153–155, 157–161, 168–170, 174, 178, 184, 188, 192, 194, 202, 204, 207f, 220–225, 227, 234, 242, 295–297, 300, 303, 305f, 314, 318, 320–324, 326f, 329, 332f, 9:258, 306, 308, 11:29f, 40, 95, 105–107, 392, 474, 12:273, 13:170, 180, 207, 14:19, 101, 227, 288, 320, 336, 15:70, 97f, 17:184, 265, 291, 18:160, 201, 19:40, 20:318, 21:171, 23:78, 80, 283, 296, 300, 366, 24:34, 80, 197, 25:75, 430, 27:155, 165, 195, 267, 29:27, 182, 36:74, 41:158, 42:164, 46:192, 235, 248, 269, 47:85, 158, 51:139, 350, 390f, 52:9f, 37, 39f, 103f, 107f, 111, 119, 126, 140f, 144, 157, 160, 171, 198, 225, 271
Joseph (Jacob's son)—45:96, 262, 263n, 264, 309
Joseph, House of—20:110f, 303–305
Joseph, St. (Mary's husband)—6:226, 21:86f, 22:24, 76, 128, 187f, 194, 214f, 239, 463, 37:76, 82, 98, 236, 45:xv, 31f, 197, 199, 211f
Joseph and Mary—46:289, 300, 311
Joseph of Arimathea—22:276, 37:20

Joseph's brothers—6:312, 318–320, 325, 338, 345, 358, 366, 371f, 374, 394f, 397, 404
Josephites—8:156, 161
Josephus, Flavius—2:32n, 108, 285, 305, 4:xi, 369, 7:302, 47:208n, 224, 233, 251
Against Apion 19:215n
Antiquities of the Jews 2:108n, 285n, 305n, 4:331n, 369n, 5:160n, 6:192n, 213n, 8:58n, 16:219n, 18:310n, 19:206n, 20:87n, 280n, 25:24, 29:129n, 30:294n, 35:342n, 45:23n
Jewish Wars 4:375n, 5:160n, 10:441, 16:35n, 187n, 238n, 293n, 20:90, 120n, 314n
Joshua—1:323, 2:34, 239f, 243, 245f, 249, 258, 282, 367, 395, 3:280, 289, 323, 4:193, 214, 5:109, 243f, 311, 325f, 6:183, 211, 247, 7:171, 211, 8:159, 175, 185, 241, 278, 297, 9:20, 22, 42f, 51, 52, 63, 82, 104f, 162, 258f, 271f, 283f, 310, 11:359, 14:101, 16:184, 17:358, 19:62, 233, 20:70n, 22:116, 523, 23:113, 26:55, 29:115, 38:290, 41:210, 45:96, 256, 373, 46:97f, 47:187, 52:156, 171
Joshua, Book of—1:315, 6:247, 16:5n, 267, 20:17
Joshua, High Priest—20:34–38, 45, 50–52, 60, 68f, 204, 207–211, 216f, 220, 230, 253f
Joshua, Rabbi—1:37n
Josiah, King—7:293, 343, 8:186n, 9:81, 203, 12:292, 16:45, 18:319, 321, 323, 328n, 19:85, 20:68, 72, 141, 253f, 256, 329, 29:206, 34:31, 36:152, 38:290, 41:220, 46:120, 173n, 47:160
Josquin de Prez—54:130
Jotham, King—16:6, 13, 78
Journeys—6:24f, 87
Jove—2:116
Jovian, Emperor—41:38n
Jovinian—39:210n, 44:306n
Joy—3:154f, 4:4f, 11, 6:87, 92, 94, 99, 103, 144f, 174, 186, 226, 8:14f, 17, 25, 31, 43, 46f, 49, 52, 71, 73, 83, 96f, 249f, 256f, 309, 10:69f, 152, 160, 208, 288, 359, 393, 11:253, 518–521, 539, 12:78–81, 164, 176, 198, 246, 264, 289, 296f, 368, 371f, 375f, 383, 392, 403, 13:5f, 14:79f, 100, 154, 170, 212, 249, 345f, 15:176f, 17:36, 47, 67, 74, 182, 201, 215, 258, 294, 335, 339, 341f, 367f, 388f, 19:147, 20:15, 24, 32, 50f, 86, 101, 112, 138, 227, 270, 305, 21:300, 302, 22:254f, 382, 25:18, 43, 44, 117, 127, 278, 379, 504f, 516, 518, 26:9, 11, 133, 214, 27:374, 30:9, 17f, 24f, 40, 50, 100, 103, 118, 127, 155, 197f, 225, 261, 280, 296, 298, 304, 35:53, 109, 212f, 255, 290, 310n, 316, 342n, 374, 44:242, 48:91, 49:359, 52:36, 147, 54:96
Jubal—1:317
Jubilate—23:165n
Jubilate Sunday—30:ix
Jubilee years—9:144, 26:411, 27:296, 40:98, 342n, 41:338, 44:170, 171n, 45:240, 310, 351n, 377, 54:239f
Jud, Leo—35:340n, 36:332, 37:10, 68n, 44:247n, 49:89n, 200n
Judah—2:175, 203, 257, 344, 367, 3:74, 145, 251, 318, 4:71, 176, 186, 332, 5:61, 91, 161, 225, 258, 337, 340, 6:175, 212, 227, 246, 273, 278, 282, 287, 292, 313–316, 321, 328, 339f, 342, 345, 366, 372, 377, 383, 385, 394, 404, 7:3–12, 14–32, 34f, 37–51, 55, 136, 187, 200f, 218, 223, 265f, 268f, 301, 310, 317–321, 362f, 367f, 370–374, 376f, 8:3f, 50n, 51f, 91, 94, 96, 104, 155, 198, 200, 216, 219, 222f, 227f, 233–235, 238, 240f, 246f, 253, 255, 263, 272, 274, 281, 285, 288f, 291–293, 295, 298, 300, 304–307, 323, 9:16, 20, 50, 60, 153, 237, 259, 298, 305f, 308, 10:23, 46, 79, 91, 108, 281f, 11:3, 6, 8, 123, 15:249, 272f, 280f, 16:5, 12, 27, 57, 81, 83, 85, 90f, 106, 112f, 118, 127, 139, 149, 164, 170, 176, 180, 219, 308, 17:133, 380, 18:5, 14, 24, 27–29, 34n, 57, 63f, 138, 148f, 176, 189, 201f, 321, 340, 19:154, 204, 206, 223, 20:20f, 29f, 32, 51, 68, 85, 93, 99f, 107, 126, 131f, 134, 144, 178, 202, 275, 293, 303, 305, 22:200, 252, 415, 448, 511, 23:222, 283, 288, 25:246, 29:117, 144n, 36:88, 143, 200, 227, 45:254, 47:154f, 160, 195f, 231, 302
Judah, Kingdom of—6:162, 206, 216, 265, 295, 310, 8:118, 130, 329, 16:13, 78f, 81, 85, 89f, 106, 108, 117, 126, 154, 156, 219, 221, 326, 18:5f, 200f, 208–210, 218, 236, 247, 283, 291, 319, 20:49f, 95, 110f, 117f, 121, 192, 21:356, 46:41, 104, 120, 171, 192, 195
Judah, Kings of—1:302, 6:278, 303, 38:178, 41:139, 42:161
Judah, Scepter of—see **Scepter of Judah**
Judah, Tribe of—1:194–196, 6:223, 284, 13:28, 21:327, 45:214–219, 52:159, 185f

Judaism—4:157, 9:26, 54, 81, 231, 14:29, 270, 19:102–104, 22:97, 23:28, 82, 353, 373, 390, 24:335, 25:194, 26:14, 60, 68, 101, 105, 109, 111, 120, 27:186, 189, 213f, 247, 280, 293, 30:6, 233, 47:x, 60n, 127, 132, 137n

Judaizers, Judaizing—3:77, 14:258, 28:253, 35:158, 284n, 47:126

Judas (not Iscariot), St., Apostle—24:154f

Judas Iscariot—1:293, 2:330f, 3:16f, 62, 4:32, 48, 5:154, 6:40, 47, 134, 326f, 337, 368, 370, 378, 380, 388, 393f, 398, 404, 7:11, 229, 235, 237, 257, 275, 8:40, 43, 45, 67, 216, 280, 307, 329f, 9:308, 10:170, 228, 245, 256, 332, 11:114, 325, 371, 13:382, 14:197, 235, 257, 261–263, 266, 308, 16:55, 17:47, 173, 323, 20:124f, 318f, 21:101, 249, 276f, 22:86, 180, 187, 248, 446, 483, 23:157, 188n, 190–194, 196, 351, 24:57, 103, 154f, 191, 204, 206f, 225, 237, 256, 274, 410, 412, 25:64 142, 374, 26:19, 94, 256, 339, 343, 456, 27:195, 205f, 261, 28:198, 340, 358, 29:33, 53, 144, 30:325, 33:185, 192, 195, 34:13, 192, 357, 35:190, 36:55f, 37:28, 79, 172, 188, 353f, 38:28, 142, 157f, 201, 204, 39:124, 40:66, 41:80, 84, 92, 120, 218, 239, 243, 246, 255f, 319, 332, 42:7n, 44:70, 46:101f, 47:273, 48:387, 49:102, 51:268, 304, 312, 52:77, 135, 230f, 267

Judas Maccabeus—32:96, 35:302, 352, 47:17

Judas of Meissen—5:x

Jude, St.—1:112, 343, 3:278, 300, 13:28, 24:324, 27:48, 52:206

Jude, St., Epistle of—30:ixf, 203–215, 41:364, see also **James and Jude, Epistles of**

Judea—2:187, 189, 3:61, 278, 4:373, 5:161, 174, 6:308, 10:22f, 116, 16:86f, 113, 125, 139, 142, 147, 166, 182, 186, 190, 192, 194, 197, 201, 286, 300, 17:33, 72, 89, 313, 22:84, 127, 189, 415f, 423, 492, 503, 506, 516, 520, 23:205, 207f, 217, 243–245, 256, 283f, 306, 26:52, 78, 101, 438, 441, 27:122, 161, 197, 198, 311, 314, 316, 35:338n, 47:250, 52:19

Judge, Office of—46:102, 107, 113f, 126f, 240, 266, 289, 307

Judges—2:258, 4:85, 131, 215, 295, 347, 351, 357, 5:15, 115, 122, 227, 252, 304, 311, 335, 381, 7:102f, 164, 166, 171, 184, 188 190, 255, 271, 281, 284, 300, 8:4, 146, 188, 240, 250, 267, 278, 280–283, 285f, 9:82, 161–163, 165f, 168, 170f, 182f, 195, 203, 242, 251, 296f, 16:44, 59, 17:358, 26:37f, 119, 178, 200, 229, 278, 348, 365, 368, 383, 389, 396, 405, 428, 27:10f, 22, 26, 34, 88, 120, 199, 212, 242, 287, 342, 387, 397, 29:73, 126f, 235, 30:39, 85, 178, 236f, 301, 303, 41:53f, 133f, 220, 245f, 249, 251, 253, 256, 260

Judges, Book of—4:175, 5:153, 252, 6:247, 7:165, 211, 9:49, 14:307, 16:5n, 20:17

Judges, Secular—21:32, 37, 83, 99f, 109–111, 116

Judges, Unrighteous—5:361

Judges for Luther's case—48:70f, 89, 98f, 103n, 104, 109, 127–129, 150n, 172, 196f, 201, 204–206, 208

Judging—17:67, 73, 248, 296, 21:210–212, 214f, 219f, 222, 263f, 274f, 46:27, 41, 50, 80, 94n, 107f, 113, 136, 166, 267, 286, 295, 297, 303, 314

Judging doctrine—40:31f

Judging others—11:500, 15:60, 187, 198, 200, 212, 349f, 25:14f, 173f, 301, 25:15f, 113–115, 173f, 301, 336, 489, 492f, 499–502, 25:501f

Judgment—1:173, 186, 188–190, 288f, 295–297, 302f, 308, 312, 2:7, 20, 26, 32, 47, 51–53, 61, 63, 101f, 126, 140f, 149, 167–169, 198, 208, 218, 220, 224, 237, 266, 288, 298f, 312, 314, 322, 340, 347, 352–354, 367, 398, 3:15, 25, 30, 42, 57, 62, 107, 114, 213, 220, 224f, 229f, 240, 260f, 263, 268, 275, 292, 294, 307, 310, 326, 342, 345, 4:43, 54, 95, 148, 159, 174, 205, 232, 234, 250f, 257, 311, 315, 317, 319, 355, 358, 372, 5:26, 34, 53, 59, 84, 93, 103f, 107, 119, 150, 153, 157, 164, 167, 170f, 182, 189, 284f, 368, 373, 7:29, 42, 83, 92, 98, 101f, 113, 144f, 148, 156f, 166, 207, 228, 320, 323, 343, 354f, 360, 363, 8:11, 29, 33f, 40, 44, 46, 59, 62, 71, 101, 110, 115, 125, 171, 202, 235, 238, 266, 270, 281, 283, 285, 289, 301, 316, 331, 9:144, 161f, 166–168, 171, 183, 195f, 212, 231, 245, 298, 10:24f, 30–33, 76f, 86, 172f, 206, 234, 238, 267, 278, 324, 343, 403–407, 457, 11:4, 9, 13, 111f, 247, 281–284, 288, 313, 319, 346, 381, 388, 420f, 438, 443f, 449f, 453f, 467, 483, 486f, 489, 494n, 495, 501n, 504f, 513, 516, 524–526, 533f, 544, 546–548, 12:184, 198, 207, 232, 243, 263, 410, 13:188, 14:76, 153, 182, 186, 214f, 217f, 220, 223, 256, 262, 266, 276,

302, 308f, 344f, 15:137, 16:19, 46, 52, 59, 100, 143, 192, 204, 245, 331, 17:63, 149, 198, 248, 269, 303, 375, 388, 393, 411–413, 19:109f, 155, 20:4f, 10, 74, 79, 85, 265, 277, 21:186f, 217, 219, 268f, 278, 317, 22:370, 23:57, 24:21, 38, 48, 54, 70, 122, 140, 184, 202f, 213, 229, 232f, 235f, 270, 273, 293, 324, 339–342, 349–352, 363, 390, 25:15f, 27, 26:7, 33, 44, 48, 52, 59f, 89, 94, 96, 173, 213, 216, 234, 254, 259f, 275, 311, 327, 370, 372, 375f, 380, 411, 457, 27:9, 14f, 41, 57, 74, 77, 89, 91, 98, 100, 108, 113, 117f, 120, 127, 136, 140, 155, 207, 215, 258, 263, 274, 281, 293, 300, 341f, 359, 365, 381, 393, 395, 28:67, 81f, 115f, 144, 353, 358–360, 29:53, 72, 81, 115, 138f, 145, 152, 154, 167, 172, 176, 183, 219, 32:44f, 54f, 57, 84–86, 172–176, 259f, 33:88, 173f, 35:34, 42, 136, 138, 140, 144, 185, 297, 336, 342, 407, 36:55f, 41:117, 146, 191, 198, 204, 206, 221, 241, 249–256, 365–367, 46:25, 52n, 64, 66, 70, 80, 114, 304, 51:63, 98, 275–279

Judgment, Last—see **Judgment Day**

Judgment Day—1:23, 175, 186, 243, 312, 2:26, 63, 315, 3:40, 4:136, 234, 312, 7:83, 8:12, 46, 125, 9:59, 10:25, 77, 98, 324, 343, 12:198, 232, 243, 263, 13:188, 14:184, 281, 15:187, 16:265, 292, 17:149, 269, 375, 388, 393, 411f, 18:114, 19:36, 74–76, 153, 155, 20:140, 217, 262, 301, 337–340, 347, 22:95, 130, 202, 272, 370, 380, 384f, 400, 428, 520, 23:57, 61, 143, 207, 261, 266, 336, 392, 24:14, 78, 91, 125, 220, 250, 270, 285, 25:17, 20, 176, 355, 402, 430, 502, 27:87, 358, 378, 28:108, 114, 30:179f, 211, 301f, 37:73n, 94, 101, 118, 134, 218, 222, 305, 361, 372, 38:171, 176, 199, 201, 211, 287, 41:201, 206, 321, 42:134, 43:67, 143, 175, 215f, 223, 235, 46:165, 174, 177, 205, 230, 317, 52:155

Judgment of God—see **God**—His judgment

Judgment seat—36:36, 222

Judgments—25:16, 104, 108, 233, 444, 499f

Judica Sunday—23:143n, 422

Judith—4:261f, 5:93, 6:286–288, 10:23, 19:226, 42:90

Judith, Book of—35:337–339

Jugglery—30:125f, 189

Juice—24:193f, 205, 234

Julian calendar—41:61n, 62n

Julian the Apostate, Emperor—2:213n, 13:211, 21:116, 24:198f, 26:74, 76, 103, 106, 119, 30:75n, 34:185, 40:284n, 41:41n, 45:99n

Julius II, Pope—1:323, 3:41n, 6:286, 8:6n, 13:219, 14:227, 16:349n, 25:289, 440f, 472, 29:170n, 171n, 31:21, 155, 171, 334, 34:236, 37:254, 38:191n, 44:125, 141n, 156n, 163n, 167n, 195n, 46:168n, 169, 47:38n, 48:34n, 100, 104, 172n, 49:125n, 50:32n, 121n, 54:136, 347

Julius, Duke of Braunschweig—43:260n, 261n

Julius Caesar—5:160, 236, 239, 270, 353, 6:90, 331, 335, 362, 7:117, 120, 311, 362, 8:58, 12:238, 13:68, 15:10f, 17f, 20f, 39, 90n, 103f, 117f, 143n, 16:260, 17:122, 19:217, 20:170, 22:43, 26:191, 34:238, 41:373n, 54:79, 247, 307, 314, 375, 475

Gallic War 15:102n, 16:147n

***Julius Exclusus*, ca. 1514**—4:199n

Jungen, Wife of Claus—32:285

Jungkuntz, Richard—translator of *Lectures on Galatians*, Chapters 1–6, 1519 27:153–410

Junker, Hans—28:59, 158

Junkers—16:45, 24:159, see also **Squires**

Juno—6:238, 8:297, 22:506

Jupiter—1:249, 2:192, 211, 4:87, 90, 6:113, 238, 331, 7:205, 336, 13:126, 17:24, 175, 25:158, 29:38, 77, 30:290, 31:185, 34:175

Jupiter, Priesthood of—36:199

Juridical procedures in Luther's day—1:284n

Jurisdiction, Ecclesiastical—45:276, 277n

Jurisprudence—1:94, 4:250, 5:68, 308, 9:161n, 195n, 14:35n, 26:188n

Jurists—1:240, 284, 2:5, 297, 312, 340f, 3:42, 260, 262, 326, 4:217, 219, 250, 347, 395, 5:42, 65, 189, 194, 302, 366, 6:31, 204, 213, 299, 370, 7:140, 312, 8:11, 30, 167, 171f, 224, 271, 9:164, 194, 10:19, 11:441, 12:251, 299, 13:157, 299, 398, 14:38, 283, 306, 22:125, 132, 153, 156, 227, 432, 435, 438, 440, 452, 477f, 23:39, 150n, 167, 226, 273, 297, 313, 409, 24:109, 345, 26:373, 27:245, 248, 275, 397, 28:107, 31:103f, 235, 284, 41:31, 102, 112, 115, 174f, 45:107, 118f, 128f, 276, 279, 376, 46:226f, 239f, 243f, 247, 250f, 256, 273, 275, 316, 318f, 47:7f, 181, 50:11f,

105, 248, 274n, 293f, 299, 303, see also **Lawyers**

Justice—1:67, 69, 73, 178, 2:6, 62, 126, 177, 337–339, 341, 396, 399, 3:224, 230, 242, 331, 4:87, 146, 217, 350, 375, 5:51, 65, 84, 235, 368, 376, 6:30, 198, 204, 7:89, 144, 176, 191f, 204, 365, 8:71f, 100, 160, 162f, 167, 205, 276, 9:14, 19, 49, 129, 145, 161, 163–165, 193, 196, 224, 243, 291, 10:83, 94f, 11:166, 247n, 13:152f, 163f, 204, 360, 379, 15:56f, 83f, 124, 16:19, 25, 43, 61, 63, 66, 102, 150, 231, 273, 17:260, 300, 302f, 339, 18:13, 29, 66, 260f, 19:109, 164, 23:63, 178, 305, 313, 315, 25:15, 441–443, 27:241, 388, 29:76, 100, 115, 177, 183, 30:85, 104, 212, 231, 31:93f, 35:79, 251, 41:245f, 249, 46:40, 100–103, 105, 113f, 123, 127, 131, 178, 180, 215, 237, 287f, 301, 49:9, 54, 257n, 260

Justice, Civil—37:227

Justice, Divine—see **God**—His justice

Justice and equity—45:238f

Justification—1:64, 192, 228, 257–260, 265, 2:159n, 2:269f, 3:19, 39, 67, 107, 175, 4:162f, 165, 174, 191, 243, 274, 368, 370, 400, 5:242, 257–259, 262, 6:146, 213, 7:234, 251f, 279, 294, 364, 8:45, 286, 9:ix, 49, 76, 10:32, 46, 53f, 76, 90, 130, 146f, 172, 236–238, 395, 404, 408, 12:18f, 21, 61, 75, 197, 239, 245, 250, 278–280, 294, 331f, 347, 359, 367, 375, 385, 392, 398, 407, 409, 13:90, 14:204n, 318, 331, 15:74, 111, 16:25, 101, 203, 280, 17:9, 11, 23, 50, 69f, 100, 114, 135f, 213, 222, 230f, 256, 340, 399, 18:111, 261, 412, 19:41f, 20:143f, 152, 21:72, 289, 347, 23:58, 106, 109, 112, 129, 135, 140, 171, 207, 24:8, 202, 329, 349, 25:6, 19, 26f, 29–31, 33, 35–38, 43, 76, 184f, 197–199, 201, 205f, 208–213, 217, 219, 234–236, 241f, 246, 249f, 252, 256f, 263–265, 284, 386f, 26:9, 21, 26, 28f, 31, 42, 57, 63f, 82–85, 91, 96, 108, 112f, 120f, 123f, 126f, 130, 136f, 139, 142–146, 152f, 155, 157, 160, 167–169, 172, 182, 184, 203, 209, 216, 222–224, 233, 240, 252, 261, 264, 266, 271f, 276, 279, 283, 302, 306–308, 312n, 313, 315f, 325, 334, 359, 363–366, 372, 390, 395, 403, 407, 410f, 413, 453, 461, 27:11, 15–17, 19, 28–30, 36, 46, 60, 64–66, 78, 87, 104, 106, 120, 138f, 145, 168, 203, 214, 225, 228, 238, 240, 246, 269f, 274f, 348, 28:230, 232, 234f, 269f, 29:44, 175, 192, 30:253, 287, 296, 299, 31:x, 56, 73, 79, 100, 102, 193, 257, 270, 295, 346, 348f, 358, 32:43, 53, 84f, 136, 155f, 191f, 208f, 275f, 34:66, 90, 109, 113, 126, 149–196, 311, 319, 35:64n, 178, 182, 187f, 195f, 230, 363f, 373f, 396f, 36:44, 65–67, 303, 37:xvii, 38:15, 23, 36, 261, 41:48, 110–113, 138, 42:13, 140, 44:18, 31, 281f, 285f, 296, 375, 46:60, 83, 47:ix, 54, 85f, 110n, 133, 150, 48:12f, 23f, 156f, 335f, 367, 49:238n, 263, 284n, 358f, 379, 50:20, 67, 108, 131n, 202, 204, 209n, 51:19, 29, 63, 283, 52:71, 112, 154, 54:10, 68, 176, 240, 328f, 348, 359, 456f

A gradual process 25:245f, 251f, 260f

Justification and sanctification—25:321

Justification by faith—11:10, 12f, 166, 171, 174, 442, 25:30f, 33, 35, 43f, 67f, 184, 188, 201, 206, 209–212, 233f, 237f, 256, 260f, 265f

Justin Martyr—34:301, 45:207n, 47:178n, 235n

Justinian, Code of—5:115n, 33:206

Justinian, Emperor—12:230, 15:115n, 26:227n, 27:240n, 37:367n, 46:245n

Institutes 7:21n, 8:103, 15:270n, 26:227n, 29:119n, 30:231n, 36:357n, 54:320

Jüterbog—31:19, 41:231, 48:125n, 173n, 50:115, 209n

Juvenal—4:292, 33:46n, 35:185n, 41:25n, 54:330

Satires 2:116n, 155n, 3:48n, 4:248n, 291n, 5:311n, 6:78n, 399n, 8:135n, 9:92n, 163n, 267n, 15:88n, 96n, 18:9n, 145n, 25:481, 33:20n, 34:156n, 237n, 334n, 40:43n, 347n, 46:41n

Juvenal, Bishop of Jerusalem—41:95n

Kaaden—54:381

Kabbala—see **Cabala**

Kadesh—2:367, 3:74, 318, 9:16, 10:134f

Kadesh-barnea—9:15, 20, 27f, 32, 26:438

Kairos—15:52

Kaiser, Leonhard—14:88, 28:375

Kalkoff, Paul—32:103f

Der Wormser Reichstag, 1521, Munich, 1922 32:104n

Die Depeschen des Nuntius Aleander vom Wormser Reichstage, 1521, Halle, 1886 43:74n

Kanitz, Elsa von—45:344n

Kant, Immanuel—1:47n

Kantz, Kaspar—53:xii, 53

Kappel—38:289n, 302n
Kappel, Battle of—8:134n, 46:107n
Kareah, Prince—17:166
Karg, George—54:255
Karl Victor of Braunschweig—43:255, 261n
Karlstadt, Andreas Bodenstein von—1:156n, 211n, 2:220, 3:301, 4:125, 192f, 5:109n, 7:176, 12:viii, 7, 10, 16, 24, 49, 60, 183, 218, 13:51, 64, 16:332, 17:155, 238, 23:100n, 165n, 280, 26:47n, 27:118n, 129n, 153, 28:229, 244, 267, 283, 329, 29:33, 30:28n, 307, 31:xviii, 309–325, 339, 32:259, 33:8n, 34:xiv, 333, 35:157, 165n, 362n, 36:129, 233f, 238n, 256n, 271–273, 37:xi, xiii–xv, xvii, 5, 9, 18, 24, 38–41, 45, 49, 52, 74, 80n, 87n, 101f, 129n, 135f, 145n, 155, 164f, 289f, 307n, 310, 318, 321, 323, 331, 342, 347, 371n, 38:xviii, xx, 57, 221, 284, 287, 291, 294n, 296, 302, 314, 316f, 40:xi, 63, 67, 73–223, 43:83, 44:245n, 246, 45:xiv, 13, 53, 162n, 342, 365n, 46:xi, 19n, 21n, 106n, 146, 47:104, 116, 244, 48:39n, 54, 79n, 80n, 107, 112n, 119, 136, 168n, 184, 223n, 232, 263n, 277f, 281n, 288, 311, 325, 337n, 338n, 356, 358n, 363, 386n, 400n, 49:4n, 15n, 29, 50n, 70–73, 82n, 83f, 88f, 89n, 94f, 98n, 100, 121n, 122, 141, 146n, 160n, 174n, 179, 201f, 231, 303, 50:55n, 131, 227f, 51:53, 69, 80, 53:xiii, 9, 153, 263, 54:xxii, 51, 54, 60, 64f, 81, 91, 107, 147, 232, 245, 284, 318, 379, 415
  As pastor in Wittenberg 40:75, 106, 108, 111n, 113n, 116
  At Jena with Luther 40:75, 89n, 106, 136
  His books 40:63, 76, 118n
  His gray garb 40:81n, 117, 162, 187
  Relations with Münzer 40:48, 69n, 75, 89n, 107n, 109f
  Reverses God's Order 40:147, 181f, 184, 187
  Teaching on the Lord's Supper 40:152f, 179n, 204, 206, 215f
Karlstadt, Andreas Bodenstein von, Works of—*Against the Old and the New Papistical Mass* 38:315n
  Anzeig etlicher Hauptartikel christlicher Lehre 40:149n
  Apologia 31:314
  Auhslegung dieser Wort Christi Das ist mein Leib 40:131n, 201n
  Defensio 31:314
  Dialogus oder ein Gesprächbüchlein von dem grevlichen und abgöttische Missbrauch des hochwürdigen Sakraments Jesu Christi 38:315n, 40:145n, 154n, 158n, 195n, 211n
  Edition of Augustine's "On the Spirit and the Letter" 48:25n, 54, 150n
  On Celibacy, Monastic Life, and Widowhood 44:245n, 48:283n, 290, 293f
  Theses on Celibacy and the Lord's Supper 48:277n, 279n
  Von dem alten und neuen Testament 40:102n, 166n
  Wider dem alten und neuen papistischen Messen 40:127n, 132n
Karlstadt, Anne—48:363n, 50:227n
Karlstadt, John—see **Drach, John**
Karsthans—45:56, 57n, 48:233
Kassel—50:194n
Kastenbauer, Stephen—49:238n
Kate, wife of Luther—see **Luther, Katherine von Bora**
Katherine, Duchess of Saxony—34:149
Katie von Bora Luther—see **Luther, Katherine von Bora**
Kattenbusch, Ferdinand—*Die Doppelschichtigkeit in Luthers Kirchenbegriff*, Gotha, 1928 39:xiiin
Katzenelnbogen—54:380
Kaufmann, Andrew—54:439
Kaufmann, Cyriac—49:269, 287, 419
Kaufmann, George—54:205
Kaufmann, Magdalen—50:168n, 209n
Kaufmann family—50:128
Kawerau, Gustav—10:8, 31, 45:54n, 78n, 114n, 166n, 47:102n, 107n, 48:xiiin
  Die Briefwechsel des Justus Jonas, Halle, 1884 38:145n
  Hieronymous Emser. Ein Lebensbild, Halle, 1848 39:107n, 132n
Kawerau, Gustav, and Julius Koestlin—51:295n
Kawerau, Waldemar—*Thomas Murner und die deutsche Reformation*, Halle, 1891 39:140n
Kayser, Leonhard—1:288n
Kedar—2:189, 4:331, 10:413, 11:536, 16:126, 173f, 17:72, 315, 43:109f
Kedemoth—9:35f
Keeping faith—46:150, 275
Keiser, Leonard—13:59n, 47:16
Keller, John—48:123n, 154n, 267n
Keller, Michael—50:173n
Kemberg—22:310f, 434, 23:245, 48:95n, 115n, 142n, 148, 231, 235, 278, 378
Kenan—2:28
Kenites—11:129

Kepler, Thomas S., ed.—*The Table Talk of Martin Luther*, Cleveland, 1952 54:xvn
Kerioth—18:138
Kernels—3:147, 151f
Kerygma—21:xiv
Ketch, Jack (hangman)—see **Jack Ketch**
Kettenbach, Heinrich von—47:40n
Keturah—3:112, 162, 4:43, 300–307, 320, 6:387, 389, 16:172, 25:80, 282, 384, 47:151f
Key signatures—53:xix
Keys, The—1:304, 2:286, 353, 4:70, 126, 203, 240, 323, 348f, 373, 402, 404–406, 5:21, 142, 145, 185, 196, 245, 251, 6:10, 234, 308, 8:186, 313, 12:41, 369, 14:12, 16:180, 21:153, 22:270, 285, 303, 515, 23: 340, 378, 24:179, 312, 330, 368, 31:27n, 31n, 91, 93, 103f, 106, 159, 162, 192, 196, 185, 217, 228, 239, 244f, 250, 267f, 283, 311, 388, 32:41f, 50–52, 75f, 34:53, 306, 35:xn, 11, 16f, 36:79, 83f, 93, 95n, 37:161, 368f, 38:200, 204, 211, 39:xvif, xxv, 42, 86–92, 96, 40:26, 28, 321–378, 40:337, 346, 352f, 357, 367, 41:xiv, 54, 73, 153n, 154n, 167, 195, 199, 200, 202, 207, 223, 293, 303, 306, 313–316, 317n, 318–321, 329–332, 334–337, 339, 341f, 356f, 360, 363, 367, 43:29, 44:134n, 134f, 45:111n, 46:220, 47:48f, 48:85, 144, 50:40
Kichenordnungen des sechzehnten Jahrhunderts—see **Richter, A.L.**
Kidd, B.J.—*Documents Illustrative of the Continental Reformation*, Oxford, 1911 46:xin, xiiin, 90n
Kidnappers—6:23, 44, 51, 9:146, 242
Kidneys—10:85, 108f
Kidron Valley—16:175
Kids—7:24, 31–33, 38, 40f, 46
Kierkegaard, Soren—*The Concept of Dread* 13:7n
Kiessling, Elmer Carl—*The Early Sermons of Luther*, Grand Rapids, 1935 31:295, 51:xin, 5, 17, 26
Killing—6:27, 29, 46:95f
Kimalthi, Rabbi—3:71
Kimchi, Rabbi David—10:413, 15:321n, 35:210n
Kind, Heinrich—39:303, 45:163n, 164f, 187n
Kinder Glaube—see **Creeds**—Apostles'
Kinder, Ernst—39:xiin
Gottesreich und Weltreich bei Augustin und bei Luther 41:xin
Kindness—3:12, 49–52, 59f, 68–70, 73, 83, 99, 117, 126, 137, 154, 165, 178, 183–187, 189, 197, 199, 218, 225f, 235, 247, 288, 319, 342, 4:15, 61, 63, 66f, 77, 85, 146, 148, 209, 225, 267, 273, 278–281, 290, 294, 308, 318, 408, 5:7–9, 32–34, 52, 57, 64, 81f, 86, 107, 169, 193, 196, 219, 256, 319, 371, 373, 375, 378, 8:12, 26, 35, 49, 51–53, 58, 62f, 65, 74, 77, 101, 112, 124, 127–129, 139, 158, 177, 182, 234, 265, 276, 324, 326f, 9:251, 272, 11:458f, 18:13, 19, 24:50, 247, 251, 253f, 267f, 270, 25:169, 176, 288, 27:368, 373, 376, 29:74f, 78, 227, 30:40, 50f, 91f, 157, 176, 326
King, Melchior—50:293, 54:214, 425
King's Valley—2:380f
Kingdom, Eternal—2:196, 289, 18:5f, 201, 227, 236, 240f, 250
Kingdom, Spiritual—see **Spiritual kingdom**
Kingdom of Christ—2:61, 69, 157, 179, 261, 381, 393, 3:7, 29, 77, 163, 172, 228, 317, 4:54, 5:26, 28, 38, 88, 310, 8:179, 185, 187, 207, 243–245, 248f, 254, 256, 259, 263–265, 270, 9:118, 138, 150, 184, 226, 12:16–18, 35, 42, 56–60, 66–69, 98, 103–107, 171, 204f, 215, 227, 232, 236, 239, 241f, 245, 282, 299, 13:72, 112, 132, 227f, 234, 237f, 240, 246–248, 252f, 264–266, 268–270, 274, 287f, 299, 337, 341, 344, 14:8, 13f, 27, 90f, 94, 102, 183, 185–187, 315, 321, 343, 15:259f, 262, 288f, 16:27–29, 30–32, 34, 36, 51f, 90, 100–102, 120f, 123, 132, 185, 195, 199, 298, 17:6, 62f, 78, 119f, 211f, 215, 217, 233, 325, 345, 387–389, 18:5f, 12n, 28–31, 72, 74, 76, 79, 89, 113, 121–123, 166, 188f, 194, 200–203, 207, 227, 236, 240, 248, 268, 274f, 319, 342, 344, 358, 361f, 375, 379, 381, 410–412, 417–419, 19:199, 217, 20:32, 40f, 51, 53, 69f, 87f, 94–96, 111, 136–138, 148f, 152, 158f, 181–183, 186, 193, 199, 216–220, 281, 335, 23:48, 178, 190, 291, 310, 312–318, 332, 337, 362, 375–377, 394, 406, 408, 24:21, 85, 110, 125, 135, 156, 186f, 196, 223, 229f, 263, 334–336, 398, 402, 29:5, 13, 105, 115, 123, 178, 203, 30:127, 163, 244, 251f, 259, 271, 288, 290f, 315, 35:219, 265f, 275, 277, 280, 283, 288f, 296, 303f, 316, 319f, 360, 39:76, 41:107, 330, 335, 42:135
Kingdom of God—2:62f, 177, 194, 3:49, 95, 104f, 130, 153, 170, 184, 224, 254,

299, 317, 363f, 4:42, 53, 94, 96, 124, 249, 363f, 384–387, 392, 397, 5:19, 33, 90, 138, 140, 156f, 230, 244, 247, 355, 7:163, 167, 234, 8:6, 43, 53, 181, 183–185, 189, 194, 243f, 309, 9:27, 43, 113, 169, 12:118f, 13:184, 401, 14:58, 183–185, 302, 16:203, 18:6, 61, 395, 407, 21:146, 202f, 206, 290, 23:5, 26, 100, 164, 310, 407, 24:189f, 302, 342, 356, 360f, 389, 391f, 399–402, 410, 25:4, 117, 504f, 26:220, 304, 411, 27:64, 79, 91f, 97f, 250, 329, 337, 371f, 29:115, 120, 134, 144, 156, 29:115, 120, 134, 150, 156, 30:15, 81, 197, 238, 278, 33:119, 152f, 227, 35:67, 147f, 164, 360, 382, 36:125, 135, 37:115, 164, 167, 236, 281–283, 368, 38:100, 196, 211, 230, 269, 39:66, 76, 93, 218, 42:27, 37–41, 49f, 78f, 176, 44:xiii, 46:18n, 69f, 217, 228f, 235, 254, 266, 51:71, 89, 165, 174–176, 345

Kingdom of grace—26:7, 167, 443, 457

Kingdom of heaven—2:21, 177, 391, 4:17, 65, 146, 281, 343, 345, 390, 392, 398f, 5:23, 132, 137, 140, 142, 145, 177, 244f, 247f, 250f, 285, 7:64, 229, 8:5, 7, 39, 135, 163, 166, 185, 192, 23:26, 407, 24:34, 132, 155, 158, 198, 402, 410, 27:340, 345, 29:115, 119, 130, 30:52, 69, 81, 159f, 197, 238, 36:209, 41:54, 195, 208, 225, 335, 343, 42:147, 176, 45:21, 102, 149

Kingdom of Israel—8:118, 130, 241, 300f, 47:203f

Kingdom of truth and righteousness—42:39

Kingdoms—2:35, 37, 52, 118, 170, 175, 177, 185, 187, 190, 192–194, 210, 225–227, 254, 258, 263f, 306, 362, 364f, 367, 3:14, 79, 91, 100, 107, 113–115, 126f, 150–152, 160, 229, 250f, 283, 318, 332, 336f, 339f, 346f, 357, 4:3, 29f, 35f, 38, 64, 75, 106, 127, 177, 186, 251, 264, 291, 316, 340, 344–347, 349, 367, 370–372, 376, 380, 5:20, 22, 41, 44, 51–53, 64, 81, 83–85, 94, 96, 112, 145f, 148, 185, 191, 199, 235–237, 268, 297, 344, 369, 7:53, 70, 84, 104, 109, 120, 141, 145, 149, 152, 155f, 158, 169–171, 178, 180, 182, 186f, 190, 204, 215, 223, 240, 243, 258, 266, 297, 300, 343, 346f, 355, 8:16, 20, 35, 44, 56, 62, 64–66, 95, 98–100, 104–108, 110f, 115f, 119f, 124, 128f, 144, 154, 168, 175, 186, 195, 216, 225, 235, 237f, 240, 257, 266, 276, 285, 297–299, 301, 304–306, 308, 321, 9:171, 176, 179, 203, 221, 234, 295, 298f, 305f, 12:10, 41, 13:139, 152, 193, 238, 251, 14:54, 98, 134, 16:25, 28f, 36, 47, 60, 69, 102, 107, 117, 132, 156, 183, 196, 211f, 217, 240, 285, 289, 295, 327, 18:6, 12, 28, 73, 179–186, 201, 207f, 227, 236, 249, 23:162, 257, 282, 310, 316, 319, 338, 373, 378, 382, 384–387, 389–391, 393f, 397, 404–406, 408, 24:80f, 84, 86, 89, 155, 205, 251, 303, 310, 354, 360, 26:13f, 32f, 40, 42, 54, 124, 143, 180, 200, 205, 211, 214, 250, 293, 355, 387, 391–393, 397, 409, 438, 450, 27:9, 15, 31, 62, 98, 100, 111, 139, 171, 28:124–127, 139, 141, 198, 29:5f, 13, 75, 105, 114f, 117f, 213f, 30:22, 62, 64, 66, 243, 245, 249, 252f, 275, 287f, 290, 294, 311, 41:307, 334f, 45:328f, 373, 46:18, 39, 41, 54, 69f, 171, 228, 230, 239f, 242f

Kingdoms, Two—see **Two kingdoms**

Kings—1:212, 245, 260, 280, 328, 354, 2:3–5, 7, 29, 35, 50, 58, 60, 98, 184, 192, 200, 202, 220, 250, 252, 258, 274f, 279, 281, 292, 306–308, 310, 312, 316–319, 321f, 324f, 352f, 361, 366–368, 370, 372, 374f, 378, 382f, 388–393, 395–398, 3:43, 52, 64f, 89, 113, 117, 123, 128, 147–152, 157, 159, 161, 174, 184, 188, 199, 226, 233, 245, 253, 261, 270, 303, 318f, 322, 326f, 329–333, 335–340, 344, 347–353, 356–361, 4:4, 10, 15, 35f, 73–75, 77–88, 90–92, 104–106, 113, 119, 123f, 127, 129, 151, 173–176, 186, 193–195, 204, 206f, 209f, 213, 228f, 235, 252, 275f, 284, 287, 291, 341, 351, 357, 365, 371, 381, 400, 404, 5:22, 25f, 28, 31, 41, 51f, 55, 58–60, 63–66, 80–84, 85n, 86f, 94f, 102, 112, 121f, 130, 135, 139, 143–145, 152f, 160f, 167f, 184f, 195, 200, 202, 205–207, 226f, 253, 270, 286f, 293, 311, 340–342, 352f, 378, 6:40, 195, 207, 263, 302–304, 306, 7:45, 51–53, 66, 68, 77, 89, 108, 110, 114, 116, 120, 122, 133f, 136, 140–147, 149f, 155f, 158–163, 166–168, 170–174, 179f, 182f, 186f, 189f, 197–201, 207, 214, 231, 239, 248, 253, 266, 299f, 322, 337, 346, 348f, 355f, 8:4, 31–33, 35, 41, 44, 56–60, 62–66, 77, 79, 81, 91, 93–95, 98–105, 107–110, 112, 116, 119–131, 135, 137, 143, 166, 169, 178f, 194, 200, 207, 210, 226, 233, 237f, 240f, 243f, 247, 250, 252, 264, 275, 280, 286, 291–293, 300,

305, 308, 321f, 9:4, 37, 49, 52, 111, 140, 145, 147f, 162, 167, 169–171, 194, 202, 231, 272, 304, 306–308, 10:37, 328–330, 345, 11:367, 451, 12:240f, 13:85, 147, 15:71f, 85, 135–137, 165f, 169, 16:7, 37, 59, 183, 196f, 211, 214, 243, 17:28, 32, 35, 188f, 274, 318, 322, 409, 19:129, 144f, 234f, 212, 20:200, 21:356f, 23:8, 13f, 163, 195f, 221, 226, 258, 277, 282, 320, 331f, 369f, 380, 387–390, 394f, 399, 405f, 24:35, 72, 78–84, 126, 154–156, 184, 251, 284, 302f, 306, 336, 352, 359, 366, 378, 416, 26:14, 16, 27, 43, 90, 94–96, 119, 158, 210, 231, 249, 258, 267, 281, 293, 295, 315, 346, 354, 387, 392, 408, 420, 428, 451–453, 456, 27:16, 31, 102, 122, 130 159, 210, 241f, 303, 335, 30:63f, 68, 80, 80, 94, 96f, 101, 104, 108, 137, 165, 180f, 185f, 207, 223, 249, 255, 258f, 261, 289, 311, 34:360, 38:110, 121, 131, 165, 178, 52:187, 231, see also **Rulers**

Kings, Books of—1:236, 2:217, 3:284, 345, 360, 4:10, 175, 178, 184, 310, 5:138, 6:303, 7:165, 211, 214, 10:232, 14:289, 18:26, 68n, 130, 20:250, 256

Kings and Princes—46:20, 65f, 98, 104f, 107, 113, 127f, 163, 167, 169, 180, 184, 187, 196, 199f, 202f, 221n, 223, 225, 228, 233, 243–245, 250, 266, 315, see also **Rulers**

Kingship—2:169

Kinsfolk—6:66, 79, 102, 23: 208f

Kir—16:146, 151f, 176, 18:131, 151, 187

Kirchberg, Hepp von—25:472n

Kirche—39:xiii, 57n, 305n

Kirchenordnungen—see **Church Orders**

Kirchenordnungen of the 16th century—see **Sehling, Emil**

Kiriath-arba—4:192f

Kirn, Paul—*Friedrich der Weise und die Kirche*, Leipzig, 1926 45:163n, 164n

Kirnberger, J.P.—53:226

Kisch, Guido—47:128n

Kishon River—11:129–131

Kiss of peace—30:144

Kissing—5:283, 6:46–48, 86, 164, 10:29, 38f, 12:83, 87, 89, 14:346f, 15:196, 251, 18:70

Kissing feet of pope—44:168f

Kitchens—2:134, 327, 3:204, 5:270, 342, 23:125, 168, 247, 314, 317

Kite (bird)—11:337, 339

Kittens—13:205

Kittim—2:191

Kitzingen—50:210n, 226n

Klann, H. Richard—translator of commentary on Psalm 110 13:225–348

Kleber, Leonard—53:268, 270

Kling, Melchior—see **King, Melchior**

Kluckhohn, August—"Zur Geschichte der Handelsgesellschaften und Monopole im Zeitalter der Reformation" (in *Historische Aufsätze dem Andeken Georg Waitz gewidmet*, Hannover, 1886) 45:69n, 271n, 272n

Kluckhohn, August, and A. Wrede, eds.—*Deutsche Reichstagsakten unter Karl V*, Gotha, 1893–1905 42:169n, 45:69n, 46:227n

Klug, Joseph—34:341, 41:xiiin, 43:257, 46:263, 49:418n, 53:131, 137, 172f, 176f, 179, 181, 194, 225f, 233f, 237f, 242f, 247, 252f, 258, 261, 263–265, 272, 276, 283f, 286f, 289, 292, 299, 302, 304f, 306–308, 317, 319, 325

Knappe, Hans—53:232f

Knavery—24:21, 254, 317, 385

Knebel, Victus—40:211

Kneeling—6:161, 8:144, 159, 28:271

Knighthood—14:53

Knighthood, Secularized—45:138f, 142

Knightlets—46:82n, 101f, 116

Knights—2:200, 8:105f, 13:58, 24:162, 45:141f, 46:245, 249

Knives—4:110, 112, 114, 118, 122f, 129

Knocking—6:140, 176, 259, 262

Know-it-all, Master—35:184n, 218, 221f, 281, 410

Knowledge—1:4n, 11, 19, 42, 46, 59, 68, 124, 128, 131, 136, 142, 146, 158, 161, 168, 194, 235, 241, 310, 2:5, 15f, 41, 85f, 96, 120, 133, 148f, 152, 160, 164, 177, 189f, 209, 218f, 222, 229, 233, 235, 239, 254f, 269–271, 278, 300, 305, 308, 312f, 315, 321f, 326, 338, 344, 382, 388, 3:49, 68f, 71, 73, 88, 109, 140, 149, 188, 203, 221, 265, 273, 286, 342, 347, 362f, 4:22, 29, 40, 48, 54, 79–82, 86, 116f, 120, 149, 189, 196f, 224, 226, 248f, 255, 267, 270, 285, 289, 303, 310, 313, 318, 327, 340, 356f, 361, 367, 377, 390f, 7:10, 35, 56, 64, 104, 116, 155, 157, 165, 195, 200, 230, 235, 249, 254, 259, 261, 263, 280, 294, 296, 302, 311, 336, 348, 352, 355, 8:15, 26f, 28, 45, 58, 67, 94, 108, 118, 142, 146, 164, 173, 193, 196, 233, 235, 239, 262, 266, 292, 308, 9:56, 109, 113, 169, 171, 205, 235, 10:185, 11:48, 444–446, 459f, 462, 15:9, 28, 22f, 28, 105, 122, 183, 16:77, 119, 223f, 285,

17:19f, 20:51, 136, 218f, 22:44, 88, 95, 151n, 152–154, 157n, 23:19, 44, 62, 151, 213, 239, 246, 261, 298, 329, 408, 410, 24:32f, 35, 40, 55, 57, 59, 61f, 72f, 83, 102, 109f, 118, 124, 132, 134, 137–140, 165, 175, 196, 198, 201, 209f, 228f, 234, 257, 275, 290, 306, 316, 325, 328, 338, 345, 351, 360, 367, 383f, 387, 391f, 404–406, 415, 421, 25:9, 103, 127, 135, 478f, 507, 519, 26:3, 6, 9, 11, 24, 30, 32, 35, 54, 69–73, 77, 91, 102, 114, 116f, 125f, 130f, 137, 212, 238, 245, 288, 314, 341, 346, 350, 363, 395, 401, 408, 411, 424, 431, 433, 445, 461, 27:10, 22f, 34, 53, 79, 85, 115, 124, 144, 177, 184f, 189, 238, 245, 269f, 272, 275, 292, 303, 318, 328, 350, 359, 372, 403f, 29:6–8, 10f, 35, 43, 97f, 119, 132, 165, 185, 201–203, 234, 35:361, 364

Knowledge, Ardent—40:204–206, 208, 212f

Knowledge, Evening and morning—1:4

Knowledge, Natural—25:10, 156f, 52:162f, 167, 194, 207

Knowledge of Christ—1:247, 300, 2:229, 4:141, 315, 317, 408, 5:43, 223, 8:246, 265, 269, 312, 9:98, 186, 16:123, 300, 17:229f, 24:87, 97, 131, 168, 171, 321f, 329, 340, 361, 27:17, 25, 49, 147, 52:167

Knowledge of God—2:12, 42f, 121, 123–126, 206, 250, 306, 311, 332f, 348, 363, 372, 392, 3:48, 51, 72, 75, 81, 95, 107, 114, 117, 125, 153, 162, 269, 289, 319, 335, 337f, 340, 344, 4:69, 145, 195, 213, 271, 293, 5:43, 51, 84, 95, 124, 209, 223, 259, 6:9, 93, 103, 113, 131, 151, 8:17, 35f, 79, 130f, 136, 165, 228, 9:53f, 119, 206, 12:403, 15:306f, 310, 17:12, 20, 23f, 229, 18:19, 19:45, 54, 69, 132, 22:149f, 154, 156, 23:22, 87, 355, 24:97, 150, 157, 226, 259, 282, 298, 318f, 25:9f, 103, 153, 156–158, 432, 26:39, 42, 213, 268, 274, 396, 399f, 402, 27:286, 294, 28:168f, 29:48, 111, 30:151f, 153f, 190, 238, 267, 292f, 301, 54:34f

Knowledge of God, Natural—25:157f

Knowledge of God, Negative—25:352

Knowledge of Grace—1:178, 180

Knowledge of Scripture—4:53

Knowledge of sin—6:69f, 75f, 370, 25:30, 60–62, 240, 281, 477

Koberger, J.—48:67n

Koburg—see **Coburg**

Koch—see **Hess, Eobanus**

Koeckeritz, Caspar von—13:351, 54:236, 319

Koenker, E.B.—translator of commentary on Psalm 45 12:197–302

Koepfel, Wolfgang—53:194, 302, 308

Koepphel, Wolf—35:340n, 49:200n

Koffmane, Gustav—18:ixf, 43:49n

Koheleth—15:12

Köhler, Franz—54:38

Köhler, Walter E.—*Die Quellen zu Luthers Schrift "An den christlichen Adel deutscher Nation*, Halle, 1895 45:295n

Das Marburger Religionsgespräch: Versuch einer Rekonstruction, Leipzig, 1929 38:xxi, 10n, 11n, 26n

Dokument zum Ablassstreit von 1517, Tübingen, 1934 39:273n, 275n, 287n

Dokumente zum Ablassstreit von 1517, Leipzig, 1903 31:23, 80, 183n, 260n, 262n

Luther und die Kirchengeschichte, Erlangen, 1900 21:320n

Zwingli und Luther, Leipzig, 1924 37:xiii, xivn, xvn, xxi, 52n, 38:5n, 6n, 7n, 8n, 9n, 10n, 13n, 26n, 63n

Kokhba, Bar—47:233–236, 297–299

Kokhbaites—47:243, 299, 305

Kolb, Franz—40:68n

Kolkryb—40:199n

Kollin, Conrad—*Refutation of the Lutheran Wedding Song* 28:x

Kommentar zum Neuen Testament aus Talmud und Midrash—see **Strack, Herman L., and Paul Billerbeck, eds.**

Königsberg—45:134n, 136n, 49:121n, 310n, 313n, 50:79n, 218n, 252n, 299n, 53:53, 193

University of 53:53, 103

Kooiman, Willem Jan—47:134n, 54:13, 440n

Korah—2:58, 3:15, 17, 280, 313, 6:295, 8:222, 227f, 10:194, 208f, 215, 271, 325, 11:55, 152, 451n, 13:357, 14:55, 258, 16:35, 17:156, 19:49, 182, 20:214, 21:211, 24:293, 28:244, 254, 284, 308, 30:208, 324, 38:162, 41:283, 46:41, 47:166

Korahites—47:166

Koran—2:262n, 3:63, 77, 4:29, 35, 221, 5:79n, 222n, 8:187, 225, 14:262, 15:342f, 22:17n, 330, 333n, 334, 359, 361, 24:69, 26:134, 140, 150, 397, 400, 401, 27:90, 43:235n, 46:176n, 178f, 181f, 197, 199, 47:36, 181

Koresh—17:120, 130f, 20:161

Kortzfleisch, Siegfried von—47:61n, 126n

Köstlin, Julius—36:9, 47:29n, 51:103, 295n
Martin Luther, Elberfeld, 1883 35:281n, 36:135n
Theology of Luther, Philadelphia, 1897 36:18n
Köstlin, Julius and Gustav Kawerau—*Martin Luther: His Life and Writings*, Berlin, 1903 43:116n, 169n, 235n, 45:54n, 55n, 56n, 78n, 79n, 114n, 166n, 46:106n, 51:295n
Köthen—50:78, 262n, 263
Kötteritzsch, Sebastian von—39:303, 45:163n, 165, 194
Kraft, John—54:xiii
Kram, Asa von—46:89n, 90n, 93, 137
Krapp, Katharine—54:224
Krappe, Jacob—21:xix
Krause, Dr. Johannes—26:195, 43:141, 49:181n, 54:106
Krauth, Charles Porterfield—*Vocabulary of the Philosophical Sciences*, New York, 1879 27:31n
Krautwald, Valentine—37:11, 40n, 307n, 49:141, 147, 149n
Krodel—see **Crodel**
Krodel, Gottfried G.—39:242n, 244n, 52:ix
author of Excursus (re letter to Cardinal Albrecht) 48:345–350.
author of Bibliographical Notes 48:xvii–xxi, 49:xv–xix
author of General Introduction to *Luther's Letters* 48:xiii–xxi
author of Introduction to Vols. 48, 49
author of introductory comments preceding each item included in Vols. 48, 50
editor of Vols. 48, 49, 50
presumed author of Excursus (re letter to Elector John Frederick) 50:258–261
presumed author of Excursus (re letter to Mrs. Martin Luther) 50:307f
presumed author of Excursus (re letter to Nicholas Hausmann) 49:423f
presumed author of Excursus (re letter to Philip Melanchthon) 49:391–393, 50:316–318
presumed author of introductory comments preceding each letter in Vol. 49
translator of all items included in Vols. 48, 49, 50
Kroker, Ernst—54:xvi, 117, 136, 253, 367n
Kronberg, Hartmut von—43:59f, 45:85n, 48:216, 50:98f
An Open Letter to Charles V 43:59
Letter to Mendicant Orders 43:59
Kronberg, Lorche von—50:99n
Krönlein—see **Haloes (Krönlein)**
Kropken, Andreas—45:313n, 314n
Kroyer, Theodore—53:337n
Krumbacher, Nicholas—16:210n
Küchenschreiber, Peter—22:68n
Kück, Eduard—43:59n, 60
Die Schriften Hartmut von Kronberg, Halle, 1899 43:59n
Kunheim, Christopher Albert von—50:253, 255
Kunheim, Erhard von—50:253n
Kunheim, George von—50:79n, 253n
Kunheim, Margaret von—see **Luther, Margaret**
Kunstmann, John G.—translator of Dedication to Count Mansfield and five Sermons 52:3–158
Kymaeus, John—41:126n
Kyrie eleison—53:20f, 23, 58, 72, 136, 151, 195, 240f, 258, 268

Laban—3:235, 4:264, 280–282, 294, 5:ixf, 144, 173, 179, 182, 192f, 195, 207, 209, 231, 235, 279f, 283, 285–287, 295–297, 301f, 305f, 324f, 339, 351, 363–368, 370–380, 383f, 386, 6:3, 5, 7, 11f, 14, 18, 22f, 28, 31, 35–39, 41f, 50, 62f, 82, 230, 234, 236, 268, 272, 307, 337, 7:22, 61, 65f, 68, 70, 199, 8:87, 92, 9:15, 14:273, 24:79, 42:54, 46:299
Laban, Sons of—6:3–7, 12
Labanites—5:370, 6:21, 52
Labor—1:211, 213, 300, 10:97, 255f, 15:8, 14, 46f, 52, 70, 88, 91–93, 98, 110, 150, 17:5, 99f, 111, 251, 261, 275, 348f, 392, 23:11, 15, 23:33, 222, 360, 28:20, 89f, 324, 346, 349, 30:94, 35:63, 72, 182, 42:74, 44:108, 334, 45:153f, 256f, 303, 324–328, 331–335, 370
Laborers—21:227, 266f
Labyrinths—8:88, 246
Lacedemonians—15:42
Lachish—6:33, 16:316, 18:219
Lacunae—16:58n, 223n, 225n
Lacus Asphaltites—2:366
Ladder—4:139, 178, 5:215–218, 220, 223, 242–244, 247, 250
Ladislaus III, King of Bohemia, Hungary, and Poland—32:90, 44:194n, 45:134, 46:167n, 48:190
Ladner, Gerhart B.—*The Idea of Reform. Its Impact on Christian Thought and Action in the Age of the Fathers*, Cambridge, Mass., 1959 2:144n
Lady, Our Dear—30:10f, 174

Laelius—2:297
Laemmer, Hugo—*Die vortridentinisch-katholische Theologie die Reformationszeitalters,* Berlin, 1858 22:269n
Laestrygones—2:138
Laish—8:281, 9:307
Laity—2:152, 3:128, 213, 315, 318, 322, 365, 4:21, 25, 88f, 121, 141, 182, 200, 237n, 8:267–269, 13:65, 14:116, 281, 20:x, 23:222f, 273n, 24:172, 242, 326, 360, 25:470f, 26:104, 376, 27:55, 61, 204, 29:43, 232, 30:53, 55, 105f, 170, 187, 226, 230, 31:246f, 32:7, 55–62, 81, 35:13, 80, 90, 106, 36:15–17, 49, 201–203, 314, 318, 38:114n, 120, 162, 164–166, 168f, 41:140, 224, 46:142, 182, 52:209, 212f, 233, 247, 54:120, 323
Lakes—1:54
Lamb, Paschal—11:301, 35:84f, 219, 37:36, 38, 42f, 164, 174, 197, 253, 255, 262, 264, 274, 311f, 321, 322, 362
Lamb of God—1:192, 9:157, 11:255, 26:32, 38, 143, 147, 151, 215, 278f, 285, 29:168, 194, 35:401, 407, 41:68, 111, 113, 151, 313
Lambert, Francis—49:17f
Lambert, Franz—*Commentarii in Micham, Naum, et Abacuc,* Strasbourg, 1525 19:151n
Lambert, James F.—*Luther's Hymns,* Philadelphia, 1917 53:xviii
Lambert, John—50:202n
Lambert, William A.—translator of *Avoiding the Doctrines of Men* 35:125–147
  translator of *Exhortation to the Knights of the Teutonic Order that they Lay Aside False Chastity and Assume the True Chastity of Wedlock* 45:131–158
  translator of *Freedom of a Christian* 31:327–378
  translator of *Reply to the Texts Cited in Defense of the Doctrines of Men* 35:147–153
  translator of *Sincere Admonition by Martin Luther to all Christians to Guard against Insurrection and Rebellion* 45:51–74
  translator of *Treatise on Good Works* 44:15–114
Lambs—1:63, 3:250f, 330, 4:85f, 88, 111, 5:374, 376, 383f, 6:4, 12–14, 67, 175f, 184, 7:46, 153, 281, 8:153, 166, 208, 263, 312, 9:158, 293, 16:122, 22:162, 168, 23:94, 146, 24:92, 260, 416
Lambs, Feeding—41:293, 305, 344, 346, 350f
Lame—46:224, 306
Lamech—1:303f, 316–323, 326, 342, 351, 354, 2:7f, 10, 16f, 22f, 27f, 33, 38, 44, 49, 51, 82, 141, 4:306, 41:157, 47:148
Lamentation—16:189
Lampoons—16:139
Lamps—11:485f
Lampstands—20:43, 45, 51, 222–225, 229f, 29:199–202, 204
Land—11:152–156, 163
Land as base for contracts—45:300–303, 307
Land economy—14:122n
Land of Promise—23:113f, 27:289, 314, 373, 29:147
Landlords—9:254, 46:47
Landmarks—9:198f
Landmarks, Apostolic—9:198
Landsberg, M.—48:137n, 138n
Landtsperger, John—37:10f, 41n, 87n, 38:297n
Lang, John—27:x, 177n, 33:12, 34:283n, 35:205, 36:234, 37:102n, 39:140, 44:120n, 48:14, 18, 27, 36n, 39, 41, 51, 55n, 61, 135, 148, 165n, 170n, 214, 356., 50:269n, 51:5, 12n, 49n
  Letter from Luther 33:12
Lang, Matthew, Archbishop of Salzburg and Cardinal—12:144, 34:86n, 89, 254n, 47:20n, 32, 45, 51, 48:99n, 104, 109, 131n, 138, 191n, 217, 359n, 49:48, 189n, 351n, 54:442
Langenmantel, Eitelhans—37:11
Language—30:23, 221, 35:90, 163, 189
  Knowledge of 1:293
  Rules of 37:31f, 34, 79, 165f, 171–174, 211, 239–242, 254–258, 296, 301–303, 305, 308, 339, 350, 353
Languages—2:15, 225, 32:135, 36:304, 38:167, 177, 189, 191, 44:202, 45:344, 351, 357–364, 365n, 366–369, 373f, 376, 46:215
  Biblical 14:281n
  Confusion of—see **Languages**—Division of
  Division of 2:214–216, 225, 227f, 364, 368, 371
  Study of 12:198f
  Unknown 11:106–107
Laodicea—25:254
Laodicea, Synod of—35:399n
Lap, God takes us in His—3:139
Large Catechism—see **Luther, Martin, Writings of**
Larvae Dei—see **Masks**

Lasciviousness—4:238, 303f
Lasha—2:205
Lassla—see **Ladislaus III**
Last Day—1:20, 23, 31, 65, 67, 77, 89, 100, 131, 191, 196f, 200, 204, 207n, 236, 333–336, 343, 2:11f, 49, 63, 128f, 144, 153, 177, 239, 256, 3:38, 159, 178, 182, 187, 190, 196, 296, 299, 4:16, 184, 191, 340, 356, 363, 5:22, 37f, 90, 6:102, 7:135, 8:202, 225, 260, 310, 318, 12:106f, 115, 13:188, 191, 201, 216, 258, 260, 262–265, 273, 281, 320, 324, 353, 14:145, 186, 205, 274, 306, 15:116, 187, 347, 16:102, 17:363, 18:67, 21:293, 22:27, 179, 263, 285, 317, 319, 401, 478, 486, 519, 23:42, 57, 63, 65, 74f, 77, 130, 140, 142f, 195, 238, 266, 306, 335–337, 24:82f, 85, 110, 168, 191, 214, 238, 419, 25:9, 17, 176, 355, 402, 430, 502, 26:21, 56, 239, 326, 27:68, 28:60, 69, 108, 111, 114f, 117, 119f, 122f, 129, 132, 141, 151, 160, 168, 176, 190, 193f, 197, 199f, 206, 358, 360, 29:19, 46, 30:38, 61, 111f, 114, 127f, 154, 163–166, 179, 181, 192f, 195f, 210f, 254, 35:31f, 164, 296, 300, 306, 314, 319, 325, 327, 330, 387, 392, 401f, 36:142f, 161, 41:13n, 27, 65n, 117, 45:60f, 282, 286, 288, 320, 46:51, 54n, 181, 222, 224, 235, 47:14, 115, 117, 50:220, 245, 251, 52:154, 212, 54:27, 128, 134, 402, 427f, 437, see also **End of the World; Judgment Day**
Last Judgment—see **Judgment Day**
Last rites—43:135
Last Supper—see **Lord's Supper**
Last things—10:40, 428, 450
Last times—52:248
Last will and testament—4:218, 307, 332, 15:270, 26:298f, 359, 27:265f, 314, 29:194, 213f, 54:178, 281
Last will and testament, Luther's—34:291–297
Last words of David—15:265–351
Lateran Councils—see **Councils, General Church**
Lateran Treaty, 1929—44:107n
Latimer, Hugh—50:199, 54:332
Latin—2:15, 185, 373, 3:358n, 4:36n, 107n, 259n, 298, 306, 362, 397n, 398n, 5:24n, 35, 225n, 279, 317, 370, 6:xi, 53, 87, 142, 153, 229, 274, 309, 7:53, 61, 113, 118, 251f, 258, 266, 314, 326, 353n, 8:3n, 25, 28n, 34, 54n, 64n, 66f, 76n, 84n, 107n, 152, 158, 181, 183n, 195, 212n, 216, 237, 241, 245n, 278, 295, 296n, 300, 9:49, 154f, 163, 189n, 195n, 222n, 234n, 16:55n, 61n, 146n, 150n, 239n, 251n, 259n, 276, 278n, 304n, 17:17, 24:109, 303n, 29:109, 117, 132f, 135, 145, 151, 155n, 156n, 160, 173, 30:5, 11, 132, 268, 282n, 289n, 36:13, 37:8–11, 80, 108n, 109f, 147, 153, 239–242, 327, 332, 38:10f, 32, 55n, 60, 145, 178, 185n, 189, 226, 277n, 288n, 319n, 40:300, 307, 309, 315–320, 45:342n, 343, 352, 356–360, 362n, 363, 375f, 46:231, 232n, 53:xvi–xvii, 11, 22, 36, 53f, 63, 123, 54:ix–xxii, 235, 376
Latin schools—50:190n, 199n, 209n, 230
Latin style—45:370n, 374n
Latins—1:4, 3:48, 4:153, 193, 306, 6:229, 283, 7:40, 188f, 285, 330, 16:293, 26:139, 29:59, 74, 151, 30:255, 45:377
Latomus, James (Jacobus Masson)—1:251, 32:xv–xviii, 133–259, 48:132n, 229n, 255, 54:77
Articulorum doctrinae fratis M. Lutheri per theologos Loveniensis damnatorum ratio ex sacris literis et veteribus tractoribus, 1521 32:135, 140n
Dialogue on Three Languages 32:135, 153, 186, 205
Latter times—48:104, 114n, 215
Latvia—45:313, 317n, 53:43
Lauda, Sion, Salvatorem **(hymn)**—38:293
Lauds—14:ix, 53:331n
Laughter—3:154, 212, 216, 4:10, 12, 221, 12:24f, 15:31f, 110f, 114, 149
Laurel—14:226
Lauterbach, Anthony—2:262n, 4:25n, 16:ix–xi, 312n, 17:15n, 23:x, 48:26n, 51:xin, xvi, 54:xii, xiv, xvif, 157, 203, 253, 257, 277, 287, 316, 319, 359, 368, 396
recorder of Luther's table conversation, 1536–1537, 1538–1539 54:201–364
Law—1:95f, 101, 107–110, 138, 146, 162–164, 169f, 172f, 176, 178, 181–183, 186, 190, 196, 234, 264, 269, 277, 280, 294, 304–307, 347, 351, 2:9, 34, 60, 65, 71, 99, 123f, 127, 133f, 140, 147, 150–163, 165, 175, 185, 192, 223, 227, 229, 242, 250, 253, 257, 261f, 267, 274, 277f, 309, 312f, 316, 327, 336–341, 362, 394, 399, 3:20, 22–26, 29, 32, 46–48, 59, 62, 65f, 69, 75–78, 83–85, 89–92, 94, 96, 100, 103, 106, 112f, 121, 125–128, 131–133, 135–137, 143–145, 150f, 156, 163f, 215, 221–225, 237, 241, 250f, 256, 259–262, 265, 269, 281, 309, 314, 319, 326,

330f, 333, 336, 341, 347, 352, 4:32, 49–52, 55f, 62, 79, 82, 85, 95, 99, 104, 116f, 120, 128f, 166, 175, 177, 183, 191, 201f, 205, 221, 227, 234, 240, 261, 276n, 281, 306, 345–347, 365, 368, 387f, 398, 5:19f, 22f, 34, 38f, 43, 53, 62f, 80, 88, 102, 105, 110–112, 114f, 129, 132, 162, 164, 177, 194f, 213, 230, 257, 259, 261, 264, 281, 291, 296, 307–312, 326–328, 371f, 386, 6:65f, 96, 100, 104, 239f, 285, 7:4, 18–20, 22f, 27f, 33, 39, 41–44, 47, 49, 53, 73, 107, 126, 136, 143, 152, 160, 176, 178, 181, 188, 212, 228f, 254, 256, 273, 275, 284, 331, 349, 355, 8:30, 40, 71f, 79, 125, 145, 153f, 160–164, 168, 170–172, 174–181, 184–186, 200, 205, 207–210, 216, 225f, 240f, 244, 249, 264, 268, 280f, 283f, 288, 297, 305, 311, 324–327, 329–332, 9:ix, 6n, 7f, 14–20, 26–28, 42f, 48–52, 56–58, 63n, 64, 70, 74, 76, 80–82, 84, 97, 104, 108–111, 113f, 125, 134, 136f, 140f, 144–148, 150f, 156–158, 161, 163, 166–168, 170f, 175–179, 181–184, 186–188, 193n, 195, 197, 199, 202f, 210–212, 214, 216, 219–226, 229n, 230, 232–238, 241–245, 248–250, 258–260, 267, 271–274, 278f, 283f, 290, 304f, 310f, 10:14, 30, 63, 102, 105, 109, 203, 214, 231, 11:50, 53, 96, 111, 133, 147n, 169, 190, 206, 313, 319f, 357, 385, 397, 414f, 438–441, 447, 452, 465, 469, 478, 480–484, 498, 511, 513f, 516f, 521f, 525, 527, 533, 12:39, 44–46, 139f, 162, 178, 213, 239, 257, 263, 265, 268, 275f, 280f, 291–293, 313, 320, 326, 332, 334, 337, 339, 342f, 363f, 366, 372, 374f, 386, 391, 396f, 408, 13:5, 7, 10, 12, 19, 22, 35, 55, 70, 81, 83, 110, 117, 151, 161f, 164, 250, 261, 267, 270, 288f, 292f, 296, 305, 316, 334, 359f, 381, 396, 400, 14:x, 14, 17, 19f, 22–25, 28f, 37f, 53f, 76, 83n, 91, 94, 97, 104, 114, 130, 132, 153, 170, 173, 175, 196, 202, 223f, 255, 285–290, 294–298, 300, 302f, 310, 318f, 327, 329, 331, 337, 341, 348f, 15:70, 81, 122f, 125f, 128f, 226, 245, 331, 348, 16:25, 58–61, 72f, 77, 95, 98–100, 107, 122, 137, 167, 223, 235, 321, 326f, 17:3, 5f, 8–10, 81f, 95, 97, 103, 142, 157, 179f, 189, 191, 198f, 207, 210, 233, 252, 260f, 277, 313, 331f, 387, 389, 18:12, 123, 229, 253, 357, 419, 19:41f, 96, 100, 102, 110, 112, 120, 152, 20:9, 11f, 41, 98f, 105, 109, 119f, 122f, 126f, 143f, 158, 220, 248, 291f, 315f, 21:67–69, 72, 74, 76, 82f, 118f, 352, 354, 22:39f, 139f, 142f, 146, 148, 150, 165, 285, 423, 23:22f, 28f, 34, 36, 38, 43, 57–59, 62f, 66, 71–73, 75f, 86, 98f, 106f, 114, 141, 150f, 170–172, 178, 193, 196, 215, 222, 226, 236, 238–241, 252, 267f, 271, 272, 274, 278, 280–282, 286, 296, 298, 300f, 304f, 310, 313f, 317–319, 324, 328, 351, 353, 385, 405–407, 412–414, 24:37f, 61, 64, 101, 140, 143, 145f, 153, 173, 175, 188, 228, 252, 254, 256, 264, 281f, 284f, 295f, 303–305, 308, 311f, 316, 319, 325, 329, 335f, 338, 341f, 345, 355, 357, 360f, 396, 405, 418, 25:18–20, 22–24, 30, 34, 39f, 48f, 57–69, 111, 121, 180–184, 186–190, 223, 240, 242f, 250f, 262, 266, 278–281, 302, 306f, 316, 322, 324, 326–328, 333f, 337, 344f, 347–350, 357f, 388, 474–476, 514f, 26:6, 53f, 79–81, 83, 91, 149, 181, 194, 197, 207–209, 216, 218, 272, 274, 293, 304, 306, 309f, 312, 316–318, 322f, 324, 330f, 333, 344f, 348f, 355, 361f, 366, 368–373, 376, 394, 443–448, 27:7, 18, 139, 188, 201, 217, 243, 259, 314, 319, 326, 346f, 355, 378, 28:31f, 135f, 207–209, 227–234, 236, 29:12f, 19, 23, 35, 42f, 44, 69, 67, 71, 75f, 83, 99, 102–104, 122–124, 137, 141, 143, 168, 175, 182, 189–194, 197f, 201, 206–209, 211f, 218f, 221f, 224, 30:3, 7, 10, 18–21, 51, 53, 58, 60, 70, 73, 75, 77f, 135, 138, 156, 180, 182, 183n, 188, 199, 212, 234, 238, 243, 260, 269, 285f, 288, 293, 309, 326, 31:13–15, 30, 51, 54f, 60, 69, 92, 115, 228, 231, 347f, 364, 32:10, 20–22, 79, 153–157, 177f, 189, 207–209, 223–226, 246f, 33:9f, 121, 126f, 134, 137, 147–155, 215–222, 257–266, 34:53, 112–121, 312f, 35:x, 79, 162f, 164, 168, 216, 230, 240–242, 245, 247, 268, 357, 360, 363–369, 373, 375–377, 380f, 383, 388, 393, 395, 36:75, 88, 90, 96–99, 103, 105, 114, 116, 142f, 149, 152, 221, 226, 37:26n, 67, 168, 227, 39:xvi, 37–40, 64, 80, 84, 89, 157f, 162, 169f, 177, 183–185, 187f, 200, 202, 207, 210, 214, 249n, 270, 291, 306, 40:82f, 41:18, 28–31, 34, 51, 66–68, 71–79, 113f, 120, 123, 131, 133f, 137–139, 177, 195, 202, 220, 253f, 256, 287, 295, 309, 315f, 320, 340, 343, 42:67, 162n, 43:21, 44:302f, 45:17, 29, 32,

60, 68f, 82n, 86, 89, 90n, 105, 118, 149, 229, 239f, 248, 258, 261, 270, 275–277, 292, 295, 306, 328, 341f, 392, 46:9n, 14, 18n, 25–27, 28n, 31, 34, 40, 43, 51, 64, 70, 75, 82n, 95, 100–103, 104n, 113f, 131, 159, 166, 181, 197, 209, 226, 239f, 245, 251, 261f, 265–269, 270, 272, 277, 279, 285n, 287n, 288, 289n, 290, 295, 297, 303–305, 307, 311–318, 320, 47:ixf, 8, 19–21, 30, 33, 65, 79, 87, 88n, 89n, 97, 110f, 113, 181, 272, 48:24, 50:12, 32n, 34–39, 51:78f, 104–108, 132, 227, 279, 52:22, 36, 38, 131f, 151f, 157, 173, 175, 209, 232, 241f, 54:10, 42f, 106, 111, 127, 222, 232, 241f, 246, 248, 275f, 293, 300, 313–315, 325, 349, 404, see also **Righteousness of the Law**

Exceptions to 9:70

Meaning of 9:48–50

Motivation to obey 9:55f

Outward vs. inward 25:189f

Requires grace 25:191f

Third use 3:85, 9:179

Uses of 9:113f, 179

Written in human hearts 3:84

Law, Canon—see **Canon law**

Law, Ceremonial—4:81, 12:85, 398, 401, 26:121–123, 130, 138, 147, 156f, 180f, 202f, 330, 333, 446f, 32:178, 46:146, 47:88n, see also **Ceremonies**

Law, Christian—46:8, 25f, 28–31

Law, Church—50:161n

Law, Civil—12:43, 205, 238, 13:54, 57, 150f, 164, 198, 369, 19:109, 128, 164, 169, 21:114f, 238f, 23:39, 300, 26:94n, 122, 249, 275, 297, 308, 313, 359, 364, 446–448, 38:87f, 41:40, 68, 73, 130, 133f, 248, 289, 326, 44:203n, 204, 45:68, 70, 85, 87, 89, 91–95, 105, 240f, 261, 264, 270, 275f, 389, 391, 46:261, 304, 49:74, 85f, 274f, 386, 390, 397f, 411, 430n, 432n

Law, Imperial—46:40, 265–268, 315f

Law, Mosaic—14:17–20, 23, 55, 90f, 337, 342, 23:23, 34, 36, 38f, 62, 86, 236f, 239, 268, 310, 324, 328, 366, 24:64, 46, 126, 29:8, 43f, 213, 36:65, 184, 200, 211, 214, 38:105, 39:19, 85, 40:58f, 85, 87–89, 92, 99, 41:29, 61–76, 79, 113, 138, 212, 214, 45:8, 31, 86f, 102, 119, 126, 157n, 201, 205, 228, 241, 287, 308–310, 381, 386, 391, 46:70, 145f, 197, 277f, 280, 291, 297, 300, 311, 316, 47:66, 70, 73f, 79–96, 133, 164–172, 181, 224, 269, 271f, 49:72n, 74, 86, 50:34, 37f, 52:23, 77, 178, 185, 193, 276, see also **Law, Old Testament**

Repealed 12:41, 58, 85, 272

Law, Natural—see **Natural law**

Law, New—11:312f, 319, 322, 327, 415, 442

Law, Old—11:312f, 318–320, 322, 327, 345, 379, 415, 441f, 468, 515

Law, Old Testament—35:80, 121, 164, 237f, 246f, 350, 361, 374

Law, Outside the—25:180f, 183f, 242

Law, Positive—13:160, 163f

Law, Preaching of—47:ix, 107–115

Law, Roman—46:15n, 82n, 101n, 239, 245n, 261, 274n, 50:213n

Law, Secular—see **Law, Civil**

Law, Threefold use of—47:103n

Law, Turkish—see **Turkish law**

Law and Gospel—1:234, 2:158–163, 3:23–25, 63, 125, 132f, 156, 225, 237, 240–243, 265, 4:51, 63, 4:68, 6:261, 399, 400, 7:230, 8:40f, 79–81, 161f, 164, 167, 170f, 176f, 179, 181, 264, 324f, 330, 332, 9:42, 63, 136, 178f, 194, 244, 10:36, 63, 214, 301, 399, 405, 11:160f, 286–288, 12:46, 140f, 164, 206, 317, 334, 340, 13:10, 78, 86, 93, 270, 288f, 316f, 14:294, 331, 16:32f, 17:3, 210f, 277, 18:253, 20:9, 39, 122f, 126f, 243f, 315f, 319, 21:242, 22:44, 87, 143–146, 150–152, 155, 167, 223, 23:270–272, 278, 310, 324, 25:416, 418, 26:54, 72, 91, 113, 115, 120, 150, 203, 208, 287, 301, 313, 318f, 331, 406, 442, 444f, 27:164, 183f, 318, 28:140, 32:136, 177, 223, 257, 33:105, 132–138, 158, 262, 264, 35:xn, xviiif, 119f, 157–174, 360, 36:124, 39:182–195, 40:82, 44:xiii, 45:239, 46:64, 66, 145, 47:60, 101–119, 132, 186n, 50:16, 51:20, 109, 132, 279–283, 54:42, 105f, 111

Law and Prophets—11:288

Law of Christ—see **Christ**—His law

Law of God—25:18, 30, 29:7, 118, 152, 164, 186, 219, 36:76, 79, 87, 98–100, 102, 104, 167, 197f, 201, 210, 213f, 217, 221, 38:91, 104f, 258, 46:7, 9n, 12n, 17, 24–27, 28n, 82n, 113, 268, 305, 47:33, 107, 168, 171, 174, 269

Law of love—see **Love**

Law of Moses—see **Law, Mosaic**

Law of the Lord, Delight in the—10:14f, 17, 19f, 25, 33, 25:65, 184, 223, 240, 333, 388

Law vs. Gospel—25:416, 418

Law vs. grace—25:234, 243f, 266

Law vs. spirit—25:130
Lawbooks—45:118f, 128f, 293, 376
Lawgiver—11:137
Lawless, The—28:237
Lawlessness—2:119, 30:269, 288
Lawmakers—27:358
Lawrence, St.—3:125, 11:405, 24:22, 39:232n
Laws, Human—32:7, 113, 35:136, 140, 147, 149, 240, 366, 379
Laws, Papal—see **Canon law**
Lawsuits—4:395, 9:144, 162, 165, 42:33f
Appeals to Rome 45:276, 277n, 293
Christian attitude toward 45:89, 92, 101f, 276–279, 293
Lawyers—1:47, 105, 4:116, 7:179, 182, 184, 20:9, 23:403, 25:151, 274, 439, 441, 470, 26:4, 10, 262, 359, 41:246, 248, 253f, 276, 305–307, 311–313, 317n, 360, 363, 365–367, 46:8, 39, 127, 240, 283, 54:21, 66, 69, 103, 128, 131, 144, 150f, 214, 236, 243, 246, 274, 320, 375, 449, 473f, see also **Jurists**
Lay brothers—5:342, 346, 348
Lay preaching—48:308, 311
Laying on of hands—6:132, 8:159, 26:74, 224, 28:250, 330, 354, 359, 29:17, 37:115, 38:186, 39:174
Laymen—see **Laity**
Lazare, Bernard—47:226n
Lazareth, William H.—54:192n
author of introduction to Vols. 44–46, *The Christian in Society* 44:xi–xvi
Lazarus—2:196, 3:16, 65, 4:76f, 121, 311, 330, 5:371, 6:20, 7:293f, 347, 8:315, 10:160, 334, 13:25, 14:133, 145, 221, 21:18, 22:46, 114, 120, 519, 24:76, 85, 25:228, 28:99, 148, 41:199, 42:149, 45:320, 51:44f, 48, 233, 253, 52:26, 172, 179f
Laziness—5:95, 363, 16:245n, 45:307f, 325
Lea, Henry Charles—47:51n
History of Auricular Confession and Indulgences, Philadelphia, 1894 35:68n
History of Sacerdotal Celibacy in the Christian Church, New York, 1907 45:142n, 150n
Lead—23:348
Leaders—20:34, 134f, 204, 25:155f, 171f, 238f, 242, 469, 43:236f
Leadership—45:373
Leagues of Imperial Estates—see **Alliances of Imperial Estates**
Leah—4:289, 5:270, 288–290, 293f, 296–307, 311f, 314–321, 324, 326, 329, 331f, 336–340, 343–347, 350–353, 356–358, 6:7, 12, 193, 196, 212, 215, 247, 272, 279, 287, 316, 319, 322, 337, 373, 7:8, 13, 15, 22, 45, 66, 199f, 218, 221, 8:49, 74, 87, 98, 102, 141, 154, 157, 176, 210, 272, 280, 9:258, 11:220n, 25:246, 28:14, 45:27, 381n, 388, 46:299, 51:39
Leanness, Spiritual—11:304f
Learning—23:228, 26:47n, 114, 238, 428f, 27:156, 172, 256, 375, 393, 46:163, 209n, 215, 217, 232n, 250
Leaven—9:215, 245, 25:269, 27:339–341, 364
Leaves—10:22f, 18:88, 94f, 335, 24:195, 199, 209, 341
Lebanese—16:248
Lebanon—53:40
Lebanon, Mt.—2:108, 5:372, 6:157, 8:291, 10:21, 134–136, 195f, 201, 203, 350, 11:186, 336, 14:226, 291, 299, 16:33, 37, 115, 139, 247, 281, 286, 300, 322, 17:20f, 44, 321, 396, 18:75, 288, 19:130, 223, 20:113f, 116f, 134, 306–308, 310f, 26:357, 27:315
Leclercq, Jean—*The Love of Learning and the Desire of God*, New York, 1962 15:191n
Lectors—1:235, 48:7n, 27, 31, 41, 331
Lefevre d'Etaples, Jacques—11:181, 183, 422n, 501n, 14:324n, 25:ix, xi, 13, 16f, 28, 31–33, 37, 42, 44, 47, 51, 55, 61, 70f, 73–77, 90, 107, 109, 118, 125, 127f, 131, 146, 148, 153, 168, 304, 317, 319, 385f, 388, 390, 392, 27:245, 261, 307, 314, 315n, 368, 29:159f, 163, 205, 31:157, 48:26n, 40, 55n, 185n, 222n, 49:7f
Epistolae beatissimi Pauli 29:126n, 127n, 131n, 167n, 180n, 199n
Epistolae Pauli Apostoli 25:125n, 406
Psalterium quintuplex 11:65n, 141n, 243n, 274n, 329n, 337n, 437n, 472n, 14:324n
S. Pauli Epistolae xiv ex vulgata editione, adjecta intelligentia ex Graeco cum commentariis, 1512 27:315n
Left hand—25:138
Left-wing Reformers—see **Anabaptists**; **Enthusiasts**; **Fanatics**; **Radical reformers**; **Sacramentarians**; **Schwärmer**
Legacy—38:198, 200
Legal procedures—21:77f, 107–109, 111, 113–115
Legalism—51:226, 271

Legalists—3:262, 26:10, 143, 159, 262, 274, 288, 312
Legality—6:213f
Legates—50:84, 108, 110f, 115, 155, 163
Legates, Papal—34:258, 48:73n, 84f, 87, 90n, 91n, 92, 94, 176, 216n, 272n
Legenda aurea—see **Jacobus de Voragine**
Legends—4:140, 6:222, 224, 233
Legends of the saints—54:475
Lehmann, Helmut T.—co-author of General Introduction in all volumes (except Vol. 12)
general co-editor of all volumes
general editor of Vols. 31–54
Meaning and Practice of the Lord's Supper, Philadelphia, 1961 42:171n, 43:149n
Lehmann, Martin E.—54:49n
author of introduction to Vol. 38 and presumably also of the introductory comments on each writing in that volume
editor of Vol. 38
Justus Jonas, Loyal Reformer, Minneapolis, 1963 38:142n, 266n
translator of all writings in Vol. 38
Leiffer, Georg—51:40n
Leipzig—3:66n, 249n, 5:370, 7:160, 8:120, 128, 241n, 9:14n, 23:201, 227, 323, 27:315, 31:319, 323–325, 381, 36:8, 14, 17, 38:137n, 142, 196, 217, 39:51, 53–56, 58, 67, 69, 87, 100, 103, 107f, 110, 122, 165, 176, 197n, 211n, 244, 40:53, 42:17, 45:54f, 107n, 48:72n, 75, 109, 113n, 121, 123, 137n, 138n, 164n, 192, 264n, 391, 49:7n, 104n, 115n, 291n, 358n, 50:111n, 135n, 185–187, 208n, 223n, 273n, 276, 278, 279n, 284, 296, 312, 51:xivn, 53, 55f, 303, 312n, 53:176, 193f, 284, 293, 295, 299, 305, 308f, 332, 54:197, 256, 350, 360
University of 31:310, 46:234n, 48:63n, 78, 110, 123n, 131n, 132n, 134, 136n, 138, 145n, 149, 160, 163n, 164n, 187n, 224n, 230n, 233, 236n, 267, 314n, 49:5n, 7n, 81n, 291n, 314n, 320n, 50:150n, 226n
Leipzig Colloquy, 1539—50:190n
Leipzig Debate, 1519—7:92n, 8:90n, 14:309n, 23:201n, 27:158, 392n, 28:242, 30:254n, 31:307–325, 329, 339, 32:137n, 34:272, 326, 333, 35:ix, xv, 38:xviii, 6, 39:xv, xxi, xxiii, 57, 100n, 108f, 119, 122n, 165n, 41:xiii, 5, 8n, 21n, 150n, 293n, 42:xi, 5, 18n, 85, 97, 44:xviin, 117, 222, 45:64n, 106n, 47:22n, 51:53, 48:69n, 79n, 80n, 107, 110n, 112n, 114n, 117, 123n, 125f, 131n, 134n, 136n, 137n, 145n, 183, 200n, 218, 220, 233n, 246, 249, 258n, 267n, 49:6, 7n, 34n, 120n, 50:185
Leisen—53:195, 208, 240, 252, 255, 258, 263, 265, 278
Leisentrit—53:268
Leisnig—39:xxiv, 303f, 49:28f, 45f, 53:9
Leisnig parish and town council—45:162n, 163n, 164–167, 177n, 178n, 195, 343n
Leisure—5:80f, 313, 346, 28:335f, 345, 381
Lemnius, Simon—53:324n
Lending and borrowing—9:144f, 148, 45:239, 256–261, 268f, 289–295
Length of Life—see **Dublin, Louis I., and Alfred J. Lotka**
Lenker, John Nicholas—1:vii, 29:vii, 51:xv, 52:xiii
Lent—see **Church Year**
Lenten readings—1:235
Lentils—4:394, 402, 408
Leo I, Pope—31:281n, 32:148f, 41:107n, 108n, 115n, 117n
Leo III, Emperor—41:204n, 51:82n
Leo III, Pope—41:261
Leo IV, Pope—*Decreta* 5:137n
Leo X, Pope—3:268, 14:282, 26:45n, 27:157n, 218, 31:xv–xix, 80, 87, 108, 155, 183n, 255f, 262n, 334f, 336n, 337–343, 384, 32:x, 5, 122n, 187n, 276, 34:5, 83n, 236, 259, 311n, 329n, 332, 334, 35:47, 128, 406n, 36:229n, 38:141n, 39:xxiii, 55n, 113n, 273n, 40:377, 41:xvn, 235n, 277, 308n, 371n, 372, 44:142n, 45:135, 288n, 298n, 46:xi, 162n, 164, 166, 188n, 47:34n, 37f, 48:44, 64, 69, 71n, 73, 74, 84, 86, 88, 89, 91n, 92, 98, 100, 104n, 108, 176, 315, 49:24n, 71n, 161n, 50:191
Leon—34:345, 353
Leopards—19:170
Lepanto, Battle of—50:183n
Lepers, leprosy—1:62, 64, 207, 3:50, 183, 7:118, 9:167, 242, 245, 23:221, 26:403, 46:224f, 302, 304
Lerch, David—*Isaaks Opferung christlich gedeutet*, Tübingen, 1950 4:114n
Lerna—4:280
Lernean Hydra—20:31n
Lese maiestatis—46:101n, 133
Lessons (liturgical)—53:9–14, 21, 38f, 55f, 68f, 111
Lethargy—5:142
Letter, According to the—25:20f, 23f, 130, 174, 234
Letter, Law of the—27:235, 313, 319
Letter, The—11:34, 96–98, 102, 143, 145,

167, 183n, 191, 207, 217, 223f, 239, 241, 244f, 249, 252f, 255f, 258, 286f, 291f, 313f, 318, 329, 335, 338, 357, 381, 385f, 413–415, 441, 456, 464, 470, 475, 481f, 486, 503, 505, 510, 514, 517, 530, 532, 551
Letter of recommendation—28:298
Letter to Aristeas—35:308n
Letter vs. spirit—10:4f, 30, 88f, 91f, 102, 109, 124, 212, 222, 315, 336, 439, 464, 27:312f
Letters of Luther, 1507-1522—Vol. 50
Letters of Luther, 1522-1530—Vol. 49
Letters of Luther, 1531-1546—Vol. 51
Letters of Obscure Men—48:9n, 117, 143n, 163n, 54:261
Leupold, Ulrich S.—author of Introduction to Vol. 53 53:xiii–xx
author of introductions to all items in Vol. 53 53:5, 17, 43f, 53–60, 93, 129, 149, 191–210
editor of Vol. 53
translator of *Agnus Dei* 53:151f
translator of *Gloria in excelsis* 53:184–188
translator of motet, *I shall not Die but Live* 53:335–341
translator of *Preface to Georg Rhau's Symphoniae Iucundae* 53:321–324
Levi—2:384, 393f, 3:34f, 251, 4:14, 151, 176, 230, 5:304, 319, 337, 340, 6:26, 175, 196, 201f, 210–212, 215f, 218f, 242, 246, 290, 293, 316, 318, 320, 325, 327f, 337, 342, 346, 366f, 372f, 377f, 388, 390, 392–394, 404, 7:4, 11, 57, 231, 256, 259f, 266, 268, 310, 363, 376, 8:49–51, 64, 70, 88, 89n, 91, 104, 114, 149, 151, 170, 197, 204, 215–224, 226–229, 231f, 284, 307, 323, 325, 9:258, 305, 13:154, 305, 20:144, 214, 330, 29:189f, 47:67, 203, 222
Levi, Tribe of—22:200, 238f, 36:113
Leviathan—1:51, 4:47f, 51, 56, 59, 7:321, 10:35, 273, 448, 11:70, 14:322, 327, 338, 16:211
Levirate marriage—7:18–22, 33, 9:248, 35:167, 36:102, 50:34
Levites—2:384f, 3:164, 280, 4:176f, 5:19, 261, 6:212, 233, 8:219, 222, 224, 228f, 231f, 306, 9:14, 51f, 108, 114, 125, 138–141, 144, 174f, 189, 213, 242, 245, 254, 273, 283, 10:42, 14:104, 337, 16:107, 293f, 17:213, 22:38, 43, 46, 126, 219, 229, 238f, 367, 415, 23:222, 252, 386, 409, 36:173, 45:318, 320, 321n, 373, 46:233, 47:201f
Levitical order—18:49, 63, 106, 402
Levitical priesthood—4:151, 176, 5:20, see also **Priesthood, Old Testament**
Leviticus, Book of—5:19, 7:161, 8:225, 9:138, 174, 20:144
Lewin, Reinhold—47:96n, 123n, 126n, 136n, 191n
Lex talionis—9:193n, 196n, 14:285
Lexicographers—4:71n
Liars—11:400–405, 408f, 494, 13:185, 187, 218, 16:190, 20:106, 238, 277, 25:26f, 83, 205, 209, 211–216, 284, 28:102, 310, 29:38–40, 120, 123, 148, 152, 216, 237, 35:61, 89, 137, 201, 366, see also **Lies**; **Lying**
Libanuss, Mt.—2:18n
Libations—2:166, 8:200, 18:48, 84, 100
***Liber usualis Missae et Officii*, Paris, 1929**—29:151n, 31:130n
Liberal arts—45:341, 344, 356n, 357, 376, 46:252n, 49:179, 426, 428
Liberality—23:356
Liberation—6:19f, 31, 40
Liberty—see **Freedom**
Liberty, Carnal—30:32
Liberty, Christian—see **Freedom, Christian**
Libraries—45:244, 373–377
Library of Christian Classics, Vol. 15—25:xiv
Libya, Libyans—2:194, 203, 10:412
Lice—3:52f, 8:172, 173, 23:30, 390
License—7:33, 73, 181, 286, 23:407
Licentiate—5:125
Licentiousness—3:259, 319, 4:276, 9:55, 232f, 27:48, 368, 378, 30:120, 204f
Lichtenberg, John of—17:153n, 21:272f, 48:179, 327n
Pronosticatio 6:331, 334, 43:271n
Licinius, Emperor—25:375, 41:55n, 56
Liebenwerda—31:329, 48:126, 128n, 129
Liege—48:93, 132n
Lies—6:57, 60f, 82, 11:514f, 13:179, 29:20, 39, 181, 31:175f
Lietzmann, Hans—*Die Wittenberger und Leisniger Kastenordnung, 1522–23*, Bonn, 1907 45:162n, 172n, 180n, 181n, 186n
Founding of the Church Universal, New York, 1950 35:139n
Life—1:46f, 56f, 63, 65, 68, 72f, 80–82, 86, 90, 92, 94, 96, 100, 102, 106, 110f, 121f, 131f, 135, 139, 153, 167, 196–200, 215f, 224–226, 229, 242, 246f, 270, 285, 301f, 307, 310f, 318, 331f, 341, 344f, 349f, 358, 2:155f, 164, 168, 172, 175–177, 180f, 204, 215, 217, 227, 235, 247, 249, 253f, 257, 259,

263, 267f, 271, 275f, 286, 289, 292, 294–299, 304, 308, 310, 319–322, 325, 327, 335, 338f, 341, 369, 373–375, 380, 396, 3:39f, 45, 49f, 51f, 54f, 62–65, 68, 81, 83, 86, 98, 119, 121, 125, 128f, 138–140, 160, 189, 202, 204–207, 209, 211, 214–218, 221, 228, 248, 258, 275, 280, 283f, 295, 300, 306, 311, 315, 318–321, 323–325, 329, 335, 341, 343f, 347, 351, 354, 4:6, 9, 21, 29, 38, 41, 45f, 50, 55, 73f, 85, 87, 91–94, 96–98, 103–105, 112, 114, 116–120, 122f, 132, 137, 143, 146, 149, 157f, 160f, 163, 176f, 181, 187f, 191f, 194, 197f, 202, 205, 207, 218, 223, 225, 227, 231, 233, 242f, 245, 248, 251, 253f, 262, 268, 271, 279, 287, 289, 292f, 300, 304f, 307, 309f, 312, 315–319, 322f, 329f, 332, 335, 339, 353, 356–359, 363f, 366, 368–370, 378, 380, 397, 402, 406, 5:7, 16, 26, 32f, 36, 53, 55, 58, 64, 70, 72–77, 83f, 87, 100f, 103, 112–115, 120–122, 135, 138, 142–144, 149, 155, 164f, 173, 175, 180, 184, 189f, 193, 199f, 203, 205, 218f, 233–235, 249, 254, 256, 263, 266f, 269f, 272f, 275, 277f, 282, 284f, 290f, 294, 297, 300, 312, 315, 324, 328, 331, 333, 341f, 356, 377, 382, 6:52, 189, 245, 257f, 280f, 334f, 7:17, 24, 28f, 34, 44f, 47, 49, 58, 61, 64, 68f, 73f, 88f, 91, 93, 98–101, 103, 106, 113f, 117, 125–129, 132, 135, 155, 157–159, 179–181, 184–186, 190f, 193f, 207, 209, 212, 214f, 219–222, 225f, 231–235, 238, 244, 246–248, 250, 252f, 256f, 259, 261, 264, 275f, 281, 291–293, 295f, 298, 302, 307–309, 311f, 317f, 320f, 323, 326, 337, 340–344, 347, 354f, 362, 367, 8:6, 11, 16–19, 24, 28f, 31f, 34f, 37–39, 42, 46, 50, 55, 60f, 68, 83, 95, 98, 112, 115, 125, 128, 130, 132, 147, 149, 163, 165–167, 172, 180–182, 184, 186, 191, 200, 206, 212, 221f, 229, 235, 237, 252, 254, 257, 266, 269, 274, 276f, 281, 290, 308, 314, 316, 318, 324, 331, 333, 9:26, 67, 69, 83, 93–95, 137f, 147, 156f, 163, 166, 178, 181–184, 194, 196, 212, 216, 220f, 230, 233, 235, 243, 245, 291, 297, 10:84f, 337, 11:201–204, 296–299, 309, 494, 510, 534f, 13:82f, 97, 100–103, 118–120, 121n, 122, 124, 128f, 136, 141, 413, 14:50, 71, 82, 84, 96, 103, 111, 169, 171, 179, 182, 186, 203f, 232, 254, 261f, 271, 274, 295, 297, 302, 308, 331, 335, 337, 340, 343–345, 15:10, 14f, 29f, 36f, 44, 53, 58, 71, 98, 100, 109, 148f, 16:207, 339, 341, 347, 22:30, 32, 51, 275, 290f, 336, 467, 518, 23:5, 9, 13f, 23, 30, 36, 44, 48, 62, 66, 69, 72, 75f, 83, 113f, 139, 145, 148, 150, 153, 162f, 166, 173, 175, 190, 196, 203–205, 211, 213, 219f, 235, 247, 261, 263, 269f, 275, 278, 287, 289, 299, 326, 332f, 338f, 344, 347, 352, 355–359, 365f, 376, 392–394, 399, 404, 406, 411, 417, 24:16, 21–24, 27, 36–38, 43, 45, 51, 54f, 58, 62, 64, 74–76, 86–88, 90, 94, 102, 112, 117f, 124, 139, 136–139, 144f, 147, 150, 157f, 160f, 169, 186–188, 190, 197f, 210, 214f, 218, 222, 228, 230, 232f, 249, 251, 265f, 269, 283, 291, 295, 297, 307, 324f, 329, 335, 338, 341, 343f, 348f, 351, 353f, 360, 371, 380, 383f, 400–403, 408, 418, 420f, 25:268, 26:3, 8, 12, 22, 25, 30–32, 38, 41, 49, 60, 64, 70–72, 92, 95, 99, 116, 133f, 140, 152, 155, 157, 161f, 166–168, 170f, 172, 176, 184, 187, 189, 193, 201, 212, 217f, 220, 229, 233, 235, 249–253, 256, 259f, 265f, 269–271, 273, 281–284, 287, 291f, 295f, 302, 306, 313–316, 318, 327, 329–332, 335–337, 345, 352f, 357, 361, 363f, 366, 369, 373, 376f, 379, 387f, 391, 393, 398, 405, 446, 451, 459f, 27:3, 5, 8, 13, 17, 19, 25, 33f, 37, 39, 41, 44, 46–49, 58, 60, 62–65, 73f, 81, 84–86, 88, 92, 94f, 98, 107, 109, 111f, 115, 119, 120f, 127, 135f, 141, 144, 147, 158, 161, 168, 173, 181, 186, 206, 210, 219, 222f, 226, 229, 234, 239, 258–260, 271, 273, 281, 284, 293, 295, 308, 313, 316, 329, 338, 340, 349, 351, 353f, 356, 365, 372, 386, 391, 402f, 405, 28:30, 48f, 52, 103–107, 121–123, 142f, 146, 155–157, 189, 191–196, 29:3, 10f, 57f, 60f, 63f, 97, 128, 130, 135, 137, 141, 153, 163, 168, 174, 180, 201, 214–216, 224–226, 233, 235, 30:8, 26, 28, 32f, 36, 41f, 50, 53, 73, 77f, 80, 85, 89, 91, 94, 96f, 100, 102, 110–114, 116, 124–126, 137f, 140–142, 149, 152f, 156, 164, 170–172, 177, 179, 181f, 184, 189–191, 196, 211, 219, 221, 223–225, 237–239, 241, 244f, 250, 252, 259n, 268, 276f, 281, 294–296, 300, 302, 312f, 37:84n, 123–125, 142n, 149, 180n, 199, 246–251, 38:97, 135f, 41:xv, 205, 218, 223f, 229, 279, 301, 42:73, 114, 142, 150f, 164,

46:242, 269, 52:55f, 60, 62, 259, 263, 280, see also **Christian life**
Life, Active vs. contemplative—6:260–262
Life, Ascetic—22:280, 337, 366, 461
Life, Brevity of—11:203, 298f
Life, Christian—see **Christian life**
Life, Civic—4:78f, 88, 105, 165, 188, 224, 234, 277, 284, 296, 308, 333, 400, 8:103, 163
Life, Corporate nature of—25:499
Life, Everlasting—see **Eternal life**
Life, Evil—30:15, 31, 86, 174f, 175f, 178, 206, 209, 211, 213
Life, Future—see **Life to come**
Life, Godly—52:137, 234f, 240, 243f
Life, Good—14:145, 148f, 180, 197f, 220, 262, 289f
Life, Religious—see **Religious life**
Life, Secular—5:3, 6f, 10, 15, 39, 54, 141, 163, 229, 245, 311, 21:12, 20, 23f, 35, 40:109–111, 238f, 257f, 265, 278, 41:68, 122, 195–197, 331
Life, Spiritual—1:56, 63, 65, 68, 80, 86, 89, 92, 100, 104, 111f, 115, 121, 130f, 153, 198, 226, 349
Life, Words of—20:176
Life and death—13:127
Life eternal—see **Eternal life**
Life expectancy—1:207, 340, 2:231n, 6:188–190, 8:113n, 11:203f, 13:103, 118, 120–122
16th century vs. O.T. patriarchs 3:323
Life to come—8:13, 76, 90, 115, 190, 260, 315f, 13:126, 14:38, 88, 141, 218, 252, 27:64f, 127f, 169, 224, 232f, 302, 317, 328, 28:5, 107f, 114f, 124, 127, 145, 172f, 183f, 197, 29:12, 137, 141, 145, 156, 163, 216, 30:160, 54:41, 291, 297f, 326, 400f, see also **Eternal life**
Lifting up—36:53
Lifting up of hands—11:452, 28:271f
Ligatures—53:xix
Light—1:5, 7f, 10, 16–21, 27, 34, 36, 39–42, 44, 48, 65, 78, 126, 161, 165, 170–172, 181, 218, 223, 249, 265, 267, 303, 306, 332, 11:263f, 485f, 15:92, 289f, 17:78, 311–313, 324f, 18:90, 182, 272, 290, 20:43–45, 91, 123, 128, 222f, 244, 340, 21:62, 179f, 25:112, 150, 224, 345f, 353, 424, 37:xviii, xx, 112–114, 117, 169, 259, 263, 52:56–58, 60–65, 67–70, 72f, 78, 88f, 194, 196
Lightning—16:267, 272, 284, 315, 330, 24:114, 216, 292
Lights—41:215f, 305
Likeness (Sacramental elements)—see **Similarity**
Liliencron, R. von—53:338
Lilje, Hans—*Luther and the Reformation*, Philadelphia, 1967 38:xxn
Lille—34:353
Lillies—21:199f
Limbo—4:314–316, 7:296n, 8:315f, 318, 11:175, 20:96f, 290
Limburg—34:345
Limits—6:37f, 156f, 222f, 243
Limping on both sides—11:372, 483, 524
Lindau—34:80n, 48:247n
Lindbeck, George—translator of *Against Latomus* 32:133–260
Linde, Jasper, Archbishop of Riga—45:313n, 314n
Lindemann, Caspar—50:48
Lindemann, Frederick, ed.—*Corpus grammaticorum Latinorum veterum*, Leipzig, 1831 8:181n
Linden tree—20:15, 168
Lindenau, Paul—51:312n
Lindsay, Thomas M.—*History of the Reformation*, New York, 1922 46:xiin, xiin
Linen—6:297, 323f, 7:32, 185, 187, 347, 9:221, 225
Linguists—1:295, 297, 3:81
Link, Wenceslaus—4:281n, 7:ix, 8:ix, 14:xi, 16:ix, 20:x, 21:xix, 31:330, 34:272, 35:178, 181n, 205, 229, 38:93, 42:6n, 45:58n, 135n, 376n, 48:7, 29n, 31, 162, 169f, 191n, 193, 357, 49:11, 13, 20f, 115n, 157f, 164f, 166f, 172n, 197n, 209n, 214f, 219f, 272n, 314n, 315n, 317n, 332n, 50:10, 13f, 75, 241f, 54:383
Commentary on the Pentateuch 50:242n
Linke, Johannes—18:ixf, 20:ix
Linss, Wilhelm C.—47:xi
Linz—48:217n
Lion of the tribe of Judah—18:61
Lions—1:51, 55, 62, 64, 77, 91, 103, 119, 132, 181, 189, 331, 2:69, 74f, 116, 135, 296, 3:30, 37, 271, 284, 300, 354, 4:37, 61n, 106, 128, 390f, 5:33, 131, 215, 254, 313, 327, 7:56, 143, 170, 173, 267, 8:94, 167f, 235, 238f, 240, 242, 248, 251, 274, 309, 9:188, 307, 11:3, 8, 215, 254, 338–340, 14:235, 267, 16:67, 122, 147f, 238, 254, 271, 304, 20:117, 24:196, 294, 415, 418, 420, 26:263, 308, 391, 423, 30:141, 181, 274
Lips—6:85f, 11:532, 535, 537f, 17:279f, 296
Listeners—22:5, 98, 401, 23:96
Listening—15:76f, 127, 155f, 25:3, 130, 237, 243, 447

Litany—34:53, 56, 46:172, 53:129, 153–170
Literal sense—25:209, 214
Literalism—35:xiii, 178
Literature—14:7, 46, 52, 280
Lithuania—45:134, 138, 313, 317n
Littell, Franklin H.—47:116n
Litter—6:59f
Little ones—20:150, 335
Liturgical chants adapted by Luther—53:149–188
Liturgical ornaments—43:159
Liturgical reforms—48:211n, 324f, 400–402, 49:3f, 28n, 29n, 31n, 55f, 72n, 90, 98n, 122, 134f, 204f, 263, 378n
Liturgies—14:47n, 26:83, 37:xii, xx, 28n, 260, 292n, 53:5–188
Liturgists—25:123n
Liturgy, Lutheran—38:123, 208, 313f
Liturgy for a time of crisis—43:231
Lives of the Fathers—2:11n, 3:217n, 4:123, 5:47, 310n, 6:133n, 253, 256, 7:262, 342, 7:262n, 367, 9:103n, 11:348, 13:113n, 15:9, 177n, 16:311, 333, 21:88n, 271n, 23:350, 25:353, 409, 458, 478, 26:190f, 27:14, 112, 28:291, 356, 39:45n, 44:308n, 327n, 382n
Lives of the Saints—8:191n, 28:29
Lives, Evil—4:21, 156, 311, 329
Living stones—30:52
Livonia—45:xv, 139, 313–315, 317n, 49:121, 53:41, 43, 45
Livonians—31:152, see also **Luther, Martin, Writings of**—*Christian Exhortation to the Livonians*
Livy—1:280, 5:353
Ab urbe condita 9:196n, 19:114n
History 5:317n, 8:123n, 326n
History of Rome 6:106n, 157n, 244n, 331n
***Lo, How a Rose E'er Blooming* (hymn)**—37:172n
Loans—45:290f, 236f, 304f, 357n, 315n, see also **Lending and borrowing**
Löbnitz—50:273n, 278
Local inclusion—37:65n, 93n, 290n
Location—37:6, 55n, 56–66, 69f, 73, 102, 145, 213–229, 232–235, 276–285, 293
Lochau—36:130, 41:230n, 48:138, 142, 150n, 159, 173n, 398n, 49:3, 17, 83n, 210n, 211n, 54:308
Loci communes—see **Melanchthon, Philip, Writings of**
Locusts—2:136, 357, 3:10, 11:18, 76, 83f, 358, 14:273f, 18:81f, 173f, 312f
Loffel, Martin—54:309
Logic—1:233, 3:26, 85n, 137, 205, 6:29f, 32:184f, 36:179, 38:xx, 25, 55, 241, 247, 257, 276, 41:109, 110n, 111–115, 136, 139, 48:12n, 37, 56n, see also **Dialectics**
Logical fallacies 37:34–37, 40–42, 45–48, 79, 106f, 121, 146, 170, 178–180, 194–196, 242, 256, 271, 277
Other fallacies 37:37, 39, 97f, 102, 178, 180, 191f, 194–196, 212, 232–235, 246–248, 251, 265, 271, 287, 301, 335, 339
Questions of 37:64n, 72, 75–77, 246, 271–274, 282, 295–297
Logic, Medieval—2:4n, 3:118n
Logical leap—10:160
Logos—1:13, 1:160, 15:300, 22:8n, 26, 110n, 116n, 362, 34:219n, 301, 38:255n
Logs—27:58, 81, 112
Lohmüller, John—45:314n, 315n, 317n
Lohn (geschenk)—45:322n
Lohse, Bernhard—52:xiin, 54:341n
Loi, Balthasar—54:294
Loins—10:179f
Lombard, Peter—see **Peter Lombard**
London—36:9, 50:30, 102n, 137n, 150n, 190n, 192f
Long-suffering—27:368, 373, 376f
Longing—11:446f
Lonicer, John—19:x, 39:52, 54, 62n, 101n, 44:118, 48:164n, 49:82
Against the the Romanist Friar Augustine Alveld 39:52
Loofs, Friedrich—*Leitfaden zum Studien der Dogmengeschichte*, Halle, 1906 38:115n
Lord of hosts—16:165, 240, 317
Lord's Day—26:412, 27:296, 41:64
Lord's Prayer (Pater Noster)—1:128, 3:121, 288, 362f, 4:342n, 5:52, 138, 197, 214, 271, 6:330, 7:259, 11:16, 13:334, 14:8, 60, 122, 15:310, 316, 332, 16:311, 17:360, 19:230, 20:156f, 21:101, 145–147, 22:102, 107, 258, 265, 270, 363, 392, 23:107, 191, 242, 259, 280, 386, 415, 24:121, 212, 263, 325, 368, 387, 391f, 398, 25:64, 247f, 253, 276, 309, 459, 26:109, 27:42, 28:66, 271, 319, 324, 29:31, 69, 30:103, 245, 31:46, 69, 99, 216, 32:24f, 56, 34:25n, 28, 53, 74, 35:201, 36:190, 258, 292, 357, 37:233, 296, 38:123, 171, 178, 190, 229, 40:161, 307f, 315, 318, 41:49, 107, 132, 164, 168, 185, 196, 216, 342, 358, 362, 42:15–81, 43:13f, 29–38, 190, 194–198, 200, 45:250f, 255, 46:33f, 136, 231n, 288,

47:52f, 113, 244, 50:69, 71, 84, 100, 119, 127, 186, 205, 250, 255, 283, 51:57, 99, 137, 142, 144, 169–181, 188f, 274, 277, 307, 321, 374, 380, 53:28, 64–69, 78–80, 99, 108, 125, 168, 295–299

1st Petition 21:146f

Lord's Supper—1:95, 157, 228, 248–250, 304, 309, 2:46–48, 150n, 295, 338, 353, 3:29, 37, 108f, 110f, 122, 124, 146, 155, 165f, 205, 213, 220, 272f, 281, 375, 4:16f, 32, 48, 70, 95, 126f, 142, 179, 181, 236, 240, 297, 323, 346, 349, 405, 5:21, 23, 141, 145, 185, 205, 244–246, 248, 256, 274, 6:10, 128f, 131f, 137, 234, 308, 330, 361, 364, 7:104, 132, 155, 294, 297, 304, 8:33, 144f, 182f, 186, 258, 264, 271, 10:120, 234, 337, 342, 375f, 414, 11:102, 378f, 12:16, 49, 60, 128, 255, 262, 266, 269, 278, 360, 369, 13:xii, 27, 256, 282, 312f, 324, 351–387, 16:109, 168, 241n, 264, 297, 17:113, 256, 18:39n, 258, 397, 20:68, 103, 253, 22:21n, 66, 197, 202, 227, 257f, 265, 270, 285, 297, 300, 304, 308, 314, 333n, 349, 379, 442–455, 420f, 466f, 470f, 481f, 505, 507, 512f, 515f, 523, 23:14n, 15, 46, 56, 80, 92, 99, 100n, 105, 118n, 122n, 123, 142, 165f, 169, 173, 193, 202, 206n, 207, 229, 235, 257, 275, 285–287, 344, 355, 24:7, 126n, 172, 287, 332, 386, 26:45, 222, 227, 312, 412, 424, 27:36f, 41, 62n, 82, 107f, 364n, 28:230, 244, 268f, 274f, 304f, 382, 29:33, 35, 48f, 90, 123f, 170, 172, 201–203, 213, 219, 224f, 31:210, 32:16f, 41, 51–62, 34:38–40, 56, 66, 68, 79–82, 349, 355, 35:xiii–xviii, 47–50, 50n, 51–63, 64n, 65–67, 69, 72f, 77–111, 194n, 202, 290, 405, 36:xf, 15f, 19–57, 60, 65, 81, 83, 91, 118, 124–129, 143, 149, 154, 162–198, 202, 218, 257, 271, 277–289, 293–298, 300, 300, 317, 325f, 331, 333, 335, 337, 346–352, 354, 37:xi, 8f, 11, 16, 20, 23n, 52n, 75–78, 87, 101n, 102n, 115–122, 127n, 142–145, 148n, 153, 157, 161, 163, 181–187, 199f, 204f, 252, 264f, 273–275, 312, 315, 319, 331f, 343, 351, 353f, 356–360, 367–369, 38:ix–xiii, xv–xvii, xixf, 5f, 8f, 18f, 23, 27, 34–37, 39, 42, 45, 54, 58, 62, 79–81, 88, 94f, 98–100, 101n, 102f, 105f, 109–112, 114n, 115, 117–121, 122n, 123–126, 128, 130n, 131–133, 135–137, 142, 149, 151–153, 158–160, 162f, 165, 167–169, 171, 177–183, 189, 191–194, 196–202, 204, 205n, 206–210, 212, 217, 223–225, 226n, 227f, 232, 255, 283, 290, 292, 300f, 306, 313, 315, 318n, 39:xv, xxii, 7–11, 20, 22, 75, 82, 134, 40:9, 25, 55, 63, 70, 122, 142f, 145, 178n, 266, 289–293, 309, 41:xivf, 11, 22n, 33–34, 73, 107, 122, 152, 154f, 167f, 170–173, 195, 199f, 201, 203, 207f, 211, 219, 223, 271, 335f, 352, 360, 42:xiv, xvi, 21, 57, 100, 108, 111–113, 162f, 167–177, 43:69n, 134, 141–143, 149–158, 44:55–57, 198n, 199n, 45:53f, 77f, 148n, 46:12, 117, 227n, 228, 231, 254, 47:30, 43, 52, 116n, 161, 297, 48:50, 143, 144f, 211n, 279f, 281n, 317, 324f, 380, 400f, 50:3f, 5–8, 17, 21, 24, 64–66, 76n, 108n, 111, 119n, 131, 133n, 171, 173n, 192n, 193, 198n, 201, 260, 274n, 51:69, 88–95, 99, 114, 116, 167, 182, 186f, 188–193, 226, 307f, 327f, 379, 384, 391, 53:xvii, 19–40, 64, 68, 78–84, 104f, 126, 181, 209, 249, 252, 54:12, 25, 45, 58, 89, 91f, 100, 113, 196, 199, 231, 284, 311, 342, 345f, 350, 394, 407, 417, 438, 459f, 463, 471, see also **Bread and Wine in the Sacrament**; **Body and Blood of Christ**; **Faith**—and the Sacrament of the Altar; **Promises, Divine**; **Real Presence**; **Sacramental elements**; **Words of Institution**; see Vols. 35–38 which deal primarily with the sacraments; especially 35:23–75, 36:15–57, Vol. 37, and 38

Abuse and perversion 35:65, 38:xv, 95, 98f, 110, 112–116, 119f, 126, 133f, 136, 143, 148, 151, 153, 159, 161f, 179f, 190, 192f, 197, 206f, 209f, 223, 225–227

Administration 37:xiii, 7, 65n, 86, 115–118, 120, 122, 140, 157, 166, 185, 188, 193, 274, 338, 353f, 356–359, 364, 366f

Benefits 35:65, 37:xviiif, 131–137, 139f, 38:23, 105, 108, 111f, 115f, 124–132, 136f, 154, 158

Bread (hosts) 34:365f

Christ's new testament 37:315, 320f, 323–327, 333–338, 340

Chronology according to St. Luke 37:315f, 330

Daily celebration of 9:157, 29:201, 219f, 38:154

Distribution 37:28, 43f, 108, 117f, 120,

124, 130f, 187, 192, 266, 328f, 332, 348, 363, 355f
Fraction 40:178, 181
Instituted by Christ 37:xix, 44, 86n, 88, 100, 102, 126n, 141f, 184, 187–190, 204, 264f, 291, 294, 309–313, 331f
Liturgical order 49:3n, 4n, 90, 98n, 181n, 182n, 204f, 261, 263, 328n, 351, 367, 377n, 378n, 407f, 416n, 421, 50:66, 95, 133n, 162, 192n, 193, 198n, 254
Luther's understanding—see entire Vol. 37 (the index is particularly helpful)
Modes of Christ's presence 37:xiif, xix–xxi, 6, 8, 25, 42–44, 64f, 69–73, 85–88, 93–97, 99f, 102–125, 129–136, 139f, 142, 145, 153–155, 166, 184–207, 217, 224, 230, 254f, 257f, 272f, 294n, 296, 300f, 304–317, 325–360, 367, 38:xi–xiv
Not dependent on celebrant 38:28, 42, 201, 304
Participation in the Sacrament 37:6, 43, 71, 89, 120, 124, 131f, 348–360, 38:95, 99, 101, 106, 109, 114n, 116, 128f, 135, 151, 153, 163, 40:178–180
Paul's teaching 36:xi, 16, 20, 22, 24f, 34, 37, 53, 118, 171, 173, 180, 37:310, 314, 318f, 321, 328f, 330–360
Purpose 37:xiif, xvii–xix, 18, 52, 69, 126f, 131f, 139–143, 199, 261, 264, 305f, 319, 359f, 367
Real presence of Christ 7:104f, 15:160, 16:70, 23:14n, 27:62n, 28:244, 382, 35:xiii, 47, 77, 36:xi, 271–273, 275, 276n, 294, 297n, 335, 337, 339–343, 345, 347f, 351, 37:xviiif, 6, 75, 78–88, 95–97, 101f, 127, 129f, 131–137, 139f, 236–238, 38:x–xiv, xvif, 9f, 13, 16, 18, 25, 27–30, 32, 39–42, 44f, 48, 56, 59, 61f, 74f, 78, 80f, 84, 95, 110, 115, 159, 163f, 169f, 193f, 197, 199, 205, 209, 224, 227f, 301, 304, 40:289
Remembrance in the Sacrament 36:40, 60, 147, 163, 166f, 169, 173, 317, 335, 341, 348f, 351, 37:xiif, xviii, 30, 41–45, 56, 103, 125f, 140–142, 187, 261, 319, 330, 342, 437, 38:22, 33, 51n, 61, 95, 105–119, 122, 124, 126, 151, 200, 205, 40:172f, 207f
Self-communion of celebrant 36:54, 172, 174, 38:154
Theology of the 49:3, 56, 773, 99f, 178f, 200n, 205f, 207f, 300f
Worthy and unworthy reception 37:72, 86, 132, 157, 188, 341–347, 353f, 357f, 366f
Lord's Supper, Controversy over the—38:xix, 3–90, 48:79n, 203, 205, 207f, 209n, 250, 255, 49:xviii, 50n, 88f, 89n, 94f, 122f, 141, 145f, 148f, 153, 160f, 172f, 178f, 186, 199f, 226, 228, 230n, 234f, 244, 247, 265f, 272, 300f, 414n, 420, 50:xv, see also **Marburg Colloquy**
Development of the controversy 37:xi–xx, 5–11, 18, 52, 147–150, 153–158, 161–163, 359f
Karlstadt's part 37:326, 336
Karlstad's view 37:38–41, 43, 49, 164f, 167, 310, 318, 321, 323
Letters concerning 50:xv
Luther's arguments vs. Swiss and South Germans 37:xiif, xvif, 18n, 25f, 67–69, 83f, 126, 131f, 141, 153, 155, 262, 367, see also entire Vol. 37 and major part of Vol. 38, especially the indexes
Luther's view 37:xvii, xixf, 6f, 95, 156f, 249, 288, 38:xif, xivf, xvii, xix, 17–22, 25, 27f, 30, 32, 34, 37, 45–57, 51–53, 55f, 59, 67–69, 81f, 85, 88, 95, 98, 110, 117f, 131f, 149, 151n, 152f, 154f, 158–160, 163, 166–169, 171, 192–194, 197f, 199f, 202, 205–207, 209f, 223f, 227, 300, 306, 313
Oecolampadius' views 37:ivf, xiiif, 5f, 24, 30–36, 40–46, 48f, 99n, 101n, 108, 122, 145, 154, 156–158, 165, 167f, 176, 189n, 253, 257, 273, 275, 304f, 308, 323–326, 333, 336, 339, 341–345, 348–351, 354, 38:16n, 17f, 29f, 34f, 38, 43–46, 52–54, 58, 67, 76f, 8f, 82n
Oecolampadius's "sign-concept" 37:36n, 40, 45f, 177, 259–261, 306–308, 323, 326f, 336, 339, 352
Oecolampadius vs. Pirkheimer 37:20, 22, 66f
Schwenckfeld's view 37:40, 289, 321, 323, 352f
Twentieth-century attempts at agreement 38:xi–xiv
Varied interpretations of Words of Institution 37:xi–xiii, xvi, xviiif, 6, 25f, 30–33, 41–48, 55, 65, 69, 109n, 123, 144f, 156f, 163, 166, 213, 217, 254, 257, 265, 270, 273–275, 285, 304–308, 313, 337, 339, 342, 344, 347, 351, 359f, 367
View of radical reformers 38:20, 22, 24, 28, 30, 36n, 38, 43, 47, 54, 64, 66, 68, 73, 76, 80, 82, 94, 110, 157n, 167n, 287–290, 295f, 298f, 305, 311
View of radical reformers—Twentieth century attempts at agreement 38:xi–xiv

Views of Church fathers 38:51f, 61, 123, 232
Writings opposing Luther's view 37:8–11
Zwingli's and Hoen's interpretation 37:xii–xiv, xviii, 30–41, 49, 115, 126n, 165, 167f, 170, 257, 262, 304f, 308, 326, 352, 354
Zwingli's part 37:xx, 5, 8, 21n, 24, 53n, 81, 101n, 104n, 113n, 139, 145, 153–158, 203, 226, 241n, 248n, 269, 294n, 307
Zwingli's "representation concept" 37:36n, 36–40, 48f, 122, 170, 174f, 177, 198, 204, 255f, 259, 261, 268, 306–308, 326f, 352
Zwingli's view 37:113n, 38:xi, xx, 15, 20–24, 33, 37, 39–41, 43, 47f, 51, 54–58, 61, 64f, 70–75, 79, 82f

Lord's Supper, Evangelical—36:xi, 233f, 260

Lordlings—23:292, 302, 343, 361f, 366

Lords—23:8, 13, 44, 47, 205, 226, 277, 282, 292, 297, 320, 331, 375, 392–397, 403f, 412, 417, 24:78–83, 85, 93, 123, 126, 154–156, 159, 189, 197, 249, 255, 266, 270f, 337, 366, 371, 377, 420, 38:117, 179–181, 195–197, 231, 233, 316

Lorenzo Valla—11:332, 25:ix, 27:3n, 31:157, 33:43n, 72, 35:406n, 37:225, 38:189n, 41:286n, 44:166n
Adnotationes in latinam Novi Testamentum interpretationem 25:146n, 148n, 390
In Latinem Novi Testamenti interpretationem adnotationes 11:333n
Laurentii Vallae graecae quam latinae doctissimi ... Elegantiarum libri omnes, Venice, 1543 7:252n

Lorraine—16:296, 34:345

Lortz, Joseph—*Reformation in Germany*, New York, 1968 39:xviiin

Löscher, Thomas—49:232f

Löscher, Valentin E.—51:30n

Löser, Hans von (John)—14:xii, 110, 28:x, 3, 50:73f, 54:184, 225, 400

Löser, Wedding of Hans—28:3

Loserth, Johann —*Die Reformation und Gegenreformation in den innerösterreichischen Länder im XVI Jahrhundert*, Stuttgart, 1898 45:112n

Lot—2:7f, 17, 25, 28, 217, 253, 275–277, 336–338, 342, 345, 349, 351, 357f, 362, 365, 369, 372, 374, 378, 382, 393, 3:52, 61, 131, 179, 188, 226, 230, 232, 234, 236, 240–247, 249, 252–254, 263, 265, 271f, 277, 280, 282–285, 287, 291f, 295, 309, 314, 324, 341, 344, 352, 356, 365, 4:48, 195, 215, 272, 278, 281, 292, 306, 5:207, 299f, 6:327, 389, 7:56, 172, 232, 8:84, 9:32, 34, 226, 10:282, 290, 11:122, 128, 12:34, 92, 13:353, 14:5, 19, 220, 16:45, 64, 17:35, 268, 292, 334, 381, 19:40, 168, 21:21, 22:36, 108, 23:265f, 24:80, 25:463, 27:321, 370, 29:115, 30:179, 36:187, 38:159, 162f, 42:136, 159, 45:48, 96, 156, 46:195, 248, 256

Lot, Daughters of—2:279f, 3:256–261, 264, 266–269, 278, 302–304, 306–313, 324, 346

Lot, Prayer of—3:289f, 312

Lot's wife—2:280, 3:240, 264, 267, 286, 294, 298–308, 324

Lotan—6:297

Lothar II, Emperor—28:364, 41:292n

Lotka, Alfred J., and Louis I. Dublin—see **Dublin, Louis I., and Alfred J. Lotka**

Lots, Casting—19:12, 60–62

Lotter's hymnal—53:184

Lotther, Melchior—34:333n, 35:235n, 36:130, 39:25f, 53, 110, 45:56, 48:72n, 113n, 138, 149n, 150, 155n, 164n, 171n, 172, 190n, 192n, 225n, 229n, 311n, 314n, 324, 331n, 355n, 49:13n, 14, 25, 135n, 153n, 160n

Lotther, Melchior, Jr.—54:141

Louis I, Emperor—41:281n, 333n

Louis II, King of Bohemia and Hungary—14:x, 209, 17:151n, 46:90, 157, 167n, 202n, 49:156, 240n

Louis III, Emperor—41:376n

Louis IV, Emperor—41:332n

Louis IX, King of France—41:277n

Louis V, Elector of the Palatinate—41:268n, 49:198n, 50:22, 44n, 54n, 56, 254n

Louis XI, King of France—41:266n

Louis XII, King of France—3:41n, 13:219, 16:349n, 31:285n, 44:195n, 48:104n, 50:206

Louvain—8:189, 212, 238, 261f, 264f, 267, 272, 274, 284, 288f, 310–312, 314, 332, 9:4, 31:381, 384, 48:55n, 132, 191n
Theologians of 34:346, 356f, 359
University of 31:257, 264, 32:xvi, 135–260, 34:xvi, 259, 341, 346, 36:14n, 153, 156, 163, 167, 174, 179, 199, 204, 211n, 214, 45:285n, 48:123n, 132n, 155n, 185n, 229n, 236n, 50:27n, 31f, 247n, 251n, 255f, 256n, 258f, 53:211

Love—1:60, 94, 136f, 252, 261, 272, 325, 2:42, 50, 65, 91, 122, 124–126, 159,

176, 257, 275, 297–302, 335–341, 372, 380, 387, 3:23–25, 31, 52, 58, 71, 84, 94, 99, 170, 184f, 200, 231, 233, 235, 240, 277, 308f, 330, 339f, 355–357, 359, 4:19–22, 24, 37f, 44–46, 71, 83, 85, 91, 111, 121, 132, 141, 143, 189, 195, 209, 217, 224–226, 243, 245f, 248, 255, 257, 263, 267, 285, 304f, 320, 323, 325–327, 334, 336, 343, 355, 373, 377, 381, 397, 408, 5:12, 31f, 34, 40, 49, 67, 79f, 82, 89, 95, 114, 140, 164, 189, 195, 214, 221, 232f, 262–264, 278, 281–283, 288, 290–297, 299–304, 307, 313–317, 322, 324, 327, 333–345, 347f, 351, 355, 380, 6:46f, 76f, 113, 130, 152, 171, 194f, 253, 269, 271, 320, 384, 7:11, 19–21, 24, 27, 34, 55, 73f, 76–79, 84f, 88, 92f, 96, 117, 123–125, 130–132, 134, 138, 182f, 197, 230–232, 234f, 238, 249, 252, 255f, 260–262, 266, 313, 315–317, 319, 332, 339, 344f, 353, 358, 373, 376, 8:3, 11, 13, 16f, 19, 24, 52, 70, 78, 80, 169, 202, 206, 221, 268f, 324, 327, 9:7, 17, 42n, 56, 68–71, 73f, 76, 84f, 136, 140f, 145, 150, 156, 161, 163, 166, 175f, 183–186, 193, 205, 211, 214, 219, 222, 224, 229, 243, 251, 254f, 11:3, 223f, 253f, 447, 472n, 508f, 513, 525, 527, 529f, 12:191, 194, 323–325, 347, 373, 13:5, 14, 88n, 380, 14:25, 29f, 32, 61n, 84, 130, 146, 149, 153, 172, 193, 244, 257–260, 296f, 300, 309f, 326, 15:3, 29f, 144f, 229f, 257f, 16:4, 10, 18, 20, 185, 206, 215, 246, 299, 17:88f, 286f, 346, 18:13, 83, 261, 20:19f, 79, 82, 85f, 155, 175, 277, 21:20, 103, 119–194, 127f, 310, 22:10–12, 236f, 418, 490, 496, 500, 23:15, 66f, 87, 98, 135, 213, 240, 352, 388, 24:7, 52, 61, 102, 115, 140, 146, 149f, 152, 157f, 161, 163–166, 178–181, 194, 244, 246f, 249–256, 259, 262, 264, 267, 269, 284, 361, 398f, 403, 406, 25:6f, 44, 59, 77f, 106–108, 111, 116f, 119f, 125, 226f, 262, 276, 293–205, 326, 348, 352, 364, 378–381, 444, 451f, 454f, 463, 466, 475–477, 484, 486–488, 490, 503, 509, 512–517, 519f, 26:88 90, 99f, 193, 119, 124, 126–129, 132, 136–139, 144, 147f, 155, 160, 169, 172, 177, 181, 183, 220, 223, 265, 269–273, 279, 286f, 292, 294, 327, 339f, 345, 352, 386–388, 394, 398, 414, 417, 422, 424f, 429, 27:5, 25, 28–42, 47–59, 61–68, 72, 93, 95, 99, 101, 106, 108, 113f, 159, 169, 172, 180–182, 203f, 215f, 218, 221, 233–237, 241, 260, 277–279, 290f, 295, 298, 303–307, 313, 326, 329, 333, 335–337, 346–352, 353n, 353–359, 361, 365, 368, 370–373, 375, 378, 381–387, 391–393, 395f, 400f, 408f, 28:16, 42, 47, 225f, 256f, 328, 368, 372f, 29:9, 42, 45, 48, 52–55, 65, 68f, 79, 81, 88–90, 96–100, 104, 119f, 154, 162, 177, 185, 188, 197, 207, 215, 217, 219, 225–227, 238, 30:20f, 25, 40, 42f, 47, 52, 57, 67, 72, 76, 78f, 86, 92, 96–99, 109, 117f, 122f, 136, 143, 157, 180–182, 184, 188–190, 198, 207, 212, 214, 219, 225, 238, 240–242, 249, 264–266, 268f, 272, 274, 276, 278f, 281, 292–294, 296, 298, 300–307, 310, 322, 31:13–15, 57, 124, 133, 137, 184, 202, 330, 364–377, 32:29, 31f, 35, 38, 72f, 33:10f, 88, 34:53, 184, 304–320, 35:52n, 58f, 65f, 69, 73, 86, 89, 239–241, 361, 367, 374, 379f, 390, 393, 36:23, 39f, 42, 98, 133, 175, 198, 205, 207, 210, 217, 227, 253, 256, 260, 262–264, 266, 287, 300, 350, 352f, 37:23–28, 46, 76, 92, 95, 131, 141–143, 154, 199, 262, 270, 365, 38:99, 103, 119, 125, 135, 184n, 196, 224f, 293n, 295, 41:17f, 77, 88, 123f, 126, 146f, 149, 42:99, 161f, 172, 44:9, 393, 45:27, 31, 88, 94–98, 120f, 126, 128, 136, 172f, 176, 178f, 247, 263f, 293, 296f, 328, 381f, 46:9, 12–17, 69, 96, 131, 134, 182f, 217, 250, 309–310, 312, 48:374f, 383–385, 51:8–13, 61, 71, 75, 77, 95f, 104–110, 116, 171, 266–272, 297–299, 52:28, 35f, 38, 58, 221, 223–225, 242f, 245, 250, 54:28, 70, 74, 223, 463f

Love, Brotherly—25:107, 30:42, 79, 157, 278f, 304

Love, Services of—see **Works of love**

Love, Works of—see **Works of love**

Love for Christ—22:452, 24:132–134, 147f, 151, 248

Love for God—21:300, 320, 25:293–295

Love for the neighbor—see **Neighbor, Loving and serving one's**

Love of God—see **God**—His love

Love of neighbor—25:79, 108, 122, 444, 475–477, 504–506, 512f

Love of self—18:261f, 25:475f, 512f

Love songs—15:193

Loving-kindness—29:74

Low mass—see **Mass, Low**

Löwenich, Walter von—21:xii

Luther als Ausleger der Synoptiker, Munich, 1954 51:xin
Luther und der Neuprotestantismus, Witten, 1963 39:xviiin
Lowenthal, Marvin—47:124n, 126, 135n, 266n
Lowlands—see **Netherlands (Lowlands)**
Loyalty—4:45, 24:102
Lübeck—21:xixf, 23:ix, xi, 422, 46:113f, 49:261f, 50:29–31, 199n
Lucan, Marcus Annaeus—*Civil War (Pharsalia)* 4:256, 13:140, 17:190n, 54:332
Lucas, Senior—36:272f, 275
Von der siegreichen Wahrheit 36:275n
Lucia, St.—5:304, 6:255, 8:255, 10:252, 11:220, 31:199, 32:258, 45:25n, 371n, 52:273
Lucian of Samosata—2:116, 33:24, 29, 30n, 106, 225
De morte Peregrini 15:60n, 29:58n
True History 33:102
Zeus Tragoidos 13:203n
Lucifer—1:23, 28, 2:12, 3:139, 4:255, 343, 5:168, 222, 6:219, 10:438f, 11:115, 12:47, 313, 13:196, 213, 16:140, 20:268, 22:103, 469, 25:159, 183, 26:29, 202, 28:291, 31:393, 32:30, 51, 81, 36:150n, 37:129, 38:230, 41:256, 45:112n, 122n, 50:303, 51:38, 52:86
Luck—11:339, 18:138
Lucke, Walter—53:xx, 193, 212, 225, 245, 260, 265, 271, 275, 317
Lucretia, St.—5:303, 7:90, 93, 95f, 44:327n
Lucretius—*De rerum natura* 1:13n
Lucullus, Lucius Licinis—54:163
Lucy, St.—see **Lucia, St.**
Lud—2:206
Ludim—2:203, 206
Ludovicus of Bologna—54:208
Ludwig II, King of Hungary—see **Louis II, King of Bohemia and Hungary**
Lueders—7:198
Lueker, Erwin L.—indexer of Vol. 13
Lufft, Hans—9:x, 34:108, 234, 282, 326, 363, 35:207f, 212n, 38:137n, 41:8, 184, 261, 43:9, 117, 144, 45:243, 49:146n, 187n, 318n, 344n, 418n, 434n, 50:185n, 186n, 228n, 53:194, 225f, 54:269
Luke, St., Evangelist—1:320, 2:241, 242n, 5:34, 116, 9:124, 14:168, 313, 16:251n, 276n, 22:38, 86, 107, 23:108, 268n, 25:148, 26:25, 62, 69, 77, 79, 103, 108, 203f, 209f, 363, 396, 420, 27:143, 163, 185, 193, 195, 210, 364, 29:105, 41:88, 322, 45:98n, 47:204, 298, 52:7, 19, 24, 30, 33, 37, 39, 60, 65, 90, 103, 105, 107f, 123f, 129, 131, 136f, 140, 142f, 175, 206, 267
Luke, St., Gospel according to—23:186, 25:14
Lukewarmness—25:107, 254, 402, 409, 456, 478, 495, 29:153
Luminaries—1:40, 74
Lüneberg—3:249n, 41:230n, 45:308, 49:127n
Lunn, Arnold—54:154n
Lupin, Peter—27:153, 48:168, 230, 235
Lust—2:7–10, 13f, 17, 19f, 24, 28, 30, 32, 38, 104f, 115, 119, 127, 131, 222, 241, 246, 296, 299, 305, 317, 328, 347, 366, 397, 3:22, 42f, 47f, 57, 135, 141, 210, 223, 226, 239, 259, 305, 307–311, 313f, 331, 337, 350, 4:5f, 8, 15, 82, 145f, 158, 196, 221f, 231–235, 237–239, 243, 249, 252, 273, 303, 305, 333–337, 354f, 378, 402, 5:5, 34f, 37f, 71, 112, 170, 189–191, 193, 195, 232, 282, 290f, 299, 301, 322f, 327f, 338, 341, 343, 349, 351, 355f, 358, 380, 7:19f, 27, 30, 33f, 49, 54–57, 65, 73–76, 80f, 84f, 90f, 93f, 121, 146, 198, 229, 236, 263, 381, 8:5, 9, 117f, 121, 220, 243, 251, 311, 9:74f, 137, 139, 237, 11:7, 18, 306, 309, 319, 360, 365, 472n, 513, 12:235, 327, 330, 341f, 349, 375, 378, 13:123, 392, 16:47, 216, 245n, 346, 18:140, 142, 19:187f, 20:141f, 21:86–88, 91, 180f, 24:161–163, 202, 221, 315, 341, 344, 25:13, 53, 55, 62, 64, 112, 164, 262, 264f, 484, 26:216, 230, 275f, 340, 342, 352, 27:50, 132, 141, 173, 224, 233, 235–238, 249, 257, 260, 275–278, 287, 326, 341, 361, 363f, 371f, 378, 380, 391, 399, 404, 407, 29:21, 53, 55f, 84, 214, 220, 225, 30:27, 31f, 40f, 45, 47, 68f, 70–73, 104, 118, 120, 122, 142, 155, 180, 189, 212, 232f, 238, 244, 249–251, 269, 273, 322, 42:73f, 46:77, 84, 150f, 153f
Lute—26:256
Lutenists—5:322
Luther, Elizabeth—4:16n, 5:5n, 43:116, 49:181, 184n, 203, 213, 50:73n, 54:33, 433
Luther, Haenschen—see **Luther, John**
Luther, Hans—24:ix, 43:169, 46:251n, 48:301, 329f, 49:115n, 117, 267f, 318f, 319n, 320, 54:27, 109
Luther, James—50:18, 128, 283n, 312, 54:297

Luther, Johann Ernst—10:46n

Luther, John—49:152n, 154, 169, 173f, 181, 203, 238, 271, 321f, 402, 419, 50:50, 73n, 93n, 129, 151f, 210n, 231f, 234, 239f, 246n, 273, 277, 285n, 291n, 300, 312, 54:9, 29, 157, 163, 190, 448

Luther, Katherine von Bora—13:171, 26:ix, 29:21n, 34:291, 295n, 296f, 35:177f, 46:211, 251n, 49:105n, 111n, 115n, 117, 142, 150–154, 161, 165, 169, 173, 181, 186, 203n, 218–220, 234f, 236n, 237n, 267f, 271, 310n, 311f, 312n, 319n, 321, 322n, 399f, 415f, 424f, 50:xv, 21, 47f, 72f, 74, 79f, 100, 109, 112f, 117, 124, 147, 153, 165f, 168n, 170, 174, 176, 180, 184, 207f, 209, 212f, 215n, 218f, 221f, 223f, 225n, 232n, 239, 240, 246, 250n, 273f, 278n, 280n, 284f, 287n, 290f, 293n, 297n, 299–302, 305–308, 310f, 314, 316f, 54:22, 25, 62, 89, 90, 127, 145, 153, 162, 165, 174, 191, 199, 216, 222, 226, 228, 258, 270, 315, 317, 319, 369, 374, 384, 396, 428–431, 447, 448, 470

manages Luther household 50:49, 81, 94f, 108f, 110n, 113, 126, 167n, 212–214, 216f, 220–222, 223n, 224f, 278, 286n, 312

Luther, Magdalene—4:16n, 5:5n, 49:218, 220, 238, 271, 312, 402n, 50:50, 73n, 234f, 238f, 246n, 54:9, 428–433

Luther, Margaret—48:329, 336, 49:115n, 268, 271, 50:79n, 184, 208n, 210n, 218n, 221n, 246n, 253n, 299n, 54:434

Luther, Martin, Biography of—3:ixf, 7n, 182n, 183n, 207n, 239, 241, 261n, 275n, 276n, 303, 306n, 319n, 325n, 331n, 335n, 342n, 347n 358n, 4:x–xi, 21n, 61n, 91n, 96n, 98n, 107n, 125n, 126n, 153n, 203n, 220n, 236n, 266n, 272n, 281n, 341n, 356n, 372, 375n, 404n, 5:ix–xii, 36n, 158n, 352n, 369n, 370, 380n, 382n, 384n, 6:ix, xi, 188n, 210n, 7:ixf, 3n, 9n, 97n, 228n, 234, 251, 280, 8:32f, 36, 47, 93, 231, 272, 311, 314, 13:111, 128, 204, 213f, 326, 22:ixf, 106, 135, 142, 145, 207, 242, 244f, 256, 259, 359f, 368, 377, 387–390, 399, 412n, 415f, 432n, 461, 477, 495n, 500n, 506, 510, 515, 28:51, 65, 79f, 85–87, 114, 129, 163, 165f, 229, 240–244, 246f, 290, 324, 383, 34:286f, 39:xi–xix, xxi–xxv, 47:59, 50:xiv, 73n, 84n, 110n, 128n, 224n, 269n, 281, 285f, 300n, 301n, 303, 312

A favorite story 8:101n

Abrogation of Private Mass 36:271–305

Absences from Wittenberg 50:3, 5, 9, 10, 11, 47f, 52n, 79, 90f, 135n, 154f, 157, 165f, 169, 207, 235, 260, 273, 282, 284, 285f

Abusive language defended 47:44f

Academic career 8:276

Accusations of radical reformers 37:11, 22f, 36, 138, 148f, 154, 238, 260f

Accused of being papist 40:231

Accused of heresies 39:109, 233, 247

Admits his dullness of faith 4:117f

Admits his ignorance 12:249

Admits often being imprudent 6:58

Advises death penalty for adultery 9:211

Afflicted by superstition 17:54

Agricola, Relation to 40:206, 47:101–106, 108f, 115, 49:206

Alienation of ecclesiastical properties 34:34–37

Allegory, Attitude towards 2:10, 150, 5:345, 347

Allegory, Use of 2:x, 16:xi

Alms often requested of him 7:338

Alveld, Controversy with 39:61–64, 76–85

Anabaptists, Controversy with the 29:8

And the Peasants' War 46:48f, 161n, 47:18

And the Turks 18:88n, 50:9, 46, 54f, 69f, 72, 155, 164f, 219, 224n, 225n, 227–229, 238, 243, 251, 270, 272

Antinomian rejection of the Law opposed 9:180

Appeals to imperial government 48:174n, 175f

Arranged for first doctoral examination 34:107

As academic adviser 11:175n

As bishop he would be a busy-body 17:323

As district vicar 48:14f, 18, 20f, 28, 32, 41, 60, 61n

As hermit 48:3, 234, 263n, 270, 323

As Pastor 32:xix, 42:xiv, 98, 170, 44:17, 45:xi–xiv, 51:73

As preacher 11:388n, 14:101n, 199n, 31:xxi, 36:312, 331, 333, 335, 41:350, 42:xn, xiii, xivn, 19, 85, 46:48, 213n, 47:18, 50:129n, 135n, 157, 275n, 276, 279n, 280n, 296, 303n, 317f

As priest 48:3f, 28, 142n, 281

As Professor 34:xiif, 42:ix, xiii

As Reformer 42:ix, 19, 44:xi, 45:xi–xiv

As Squire George (Junker Joerg) 48:228n, 234

As writer 46:249, 252, 54:83, 326, 342f

Asked for too little in prayer 17:364

Asks for help 48:28, 130f, 141f, 187
Asks that name "Lutheran" not be used 45:70
Assurance of salvation gained by experience 12:371
Astrology, Attitude towards 17:153n
Attack on indulgences 14:67n, 71n
Authority for his teaching 23:386, 389, 24:275, 25:472
Autobiographical remarks 37:7, 16, 18–25, 30, 33, 45, 51, 68, 70, 78, 101–104, 107, 131, 147–150, 161–163, 173, 177, 238, 248, 252, 261, 286, 288, 319, 329, 348, 350–361, 371f
Autobiography up to 1521 34:327–338
Aware of his verbosity 14:xn, 17:62, 27:147, 330
Aware of sectarians' attacks 17:96
Aware of sins and failings 22:260
Aware of those thirsting for his blood 17:298
Banned 39:7–22, 45:194, 347, 48:87f, 90, 155n, 176, 179n, 210, 233, 263, 276n, 340, 393f
Baptizes son Paul 28:3
Beginning of his theology 10:ix
Belief in imminence of the Last Day 41:13n, 244f
Believed witchcraft probable 27:245
Believed world fully evangelized 14:334n
Bernard, St., Attitude towards 17:392
Beset by four dangers 17:350
Birth 47:254, 54:458
Blamed for Mohacs defeat 46:161n
Bohemian Brethren, Relations with 36:271–305
Booklet pleases the Elector 46:163
Break with Rome 31:xx, 381
Briefs on political subjects 50:9f, 43n
Builds on Christ as his foundation 17:326
Burned in effigy 48:125, 194
Burning of papal bull 31:xix
Burns Canon Law 46:273n, 48:186f, 192
Cajetan, Hearings before 31:xvii, 255–257, 285
Cajetan, Interview with 27:156f
Call to serve whole German nation 45:348
Called a heretic 12:369, 390
Called a Hussite 48:80n, 143f, 149, 153, 249
Calls self a half-baked theologian 24:362
Calls self Eleutherius 48:55n, 59, 63, 73, 76, 96
Calls self "one little friar" 14:282
Calls self scribe, not prophet 12:205
Calls struggle with pope a family quarrel 3:57
Career 37:xi–xvi, xx, 5, 147–150, 155, 158, 161f
Career as teacher 25:ix
Cares for people 49:9, 45, 93f, 105n, 122n, 140, 141n, 151n, 158n, 210f, 310n, 320n
Changes in civil life to his credit 12:253
Character defamed 3:15f
Charged with rebellion 36:310f
Childhood memories 1:135, 2:231, 5:381n, 7:84, 335, 8:21, 288, 48:145, 330, 333, 54:235
Children 16:93n, 45:369
Christ crucified central for him 11:304, 33:82
Church, Attitude towards the 31:xix, 16, 263
Church Councils, Attitude toward 32:117, 120f, 41:119f, 50:157f
Claims Holy Spirit's presence 37:51, 149
Coat-of-arms 49:358
Coburg, His stay at 43:181f
Collected works 54:274, 311
Command to abandon Gospel would be resisted 45:84
Commends parish visitations 40:272f
Commentaries he used 25:ix
Compares self to Samson 38:233
Competence in Hebrew 9:34, 35:205
Complains of wickedness in his own day 2:62, 175
Concern for accurate maps 8:273
Concern for common man 48:102, 113n, 248f, 252, 308f, 311, 320, 336, 395
Concern for his wife and family 1:275, 7:115
Condemns mere historical faith 8:193
Conditions for peace 48:97f, 102–104, 152n, 178, 195f
Confession of faith 20:viii, x, 31:343f, 37:360–372, 38:5, 224, 284
Confidence in Bible 7:120
Confidence in doing God's work 45:347
Confidence in his teachings 39:125
Confidence in preaching given by Christ 12:296
Conflict at Diet of Speyer time 16:253
Consciousness of theological development 29:78, 80
Consequences of salvation by faith alone 41:111
Contradictions in his writings 42:140n
Contradictions in Scripture, Attitude toward seeming 2:277n
Controversies 15:43, 29:35, 60

Conversion of whole world not to be expected 12:193
Correspondence 54:206
Council, Appeals to General Church 3:355, 31:xvii, 255, 344, 48:90, 99, 171, 185
Councils, General Church, Views on 2:21, 41
Courage needed 12:387, 17:46
Created world supports his teaching 23:239
Critic of common New Testament exegesis 21:xi, xiiif
Critics 46:59–65
Critique of Church of his day 25:469
Curia vs. Roman Church 27:156–159
Danger threatens 48:69, 74, 81, 97, 148, 160, 188f, 192, 233
Death 8:x, 34:xvii, 41:5, 42:xi, 48:275n
Death, Fear of, his 17:34
Death, Last days, and funeral 50:xix, 284, 285n, 294n, 312n, 314n, 317
Death, Longs for 4:107f, 117, 50:184, 238, 242, 245f, 267, 278, 281, 284f
Death expected 1:347, 3:120, 6:401, 8:309, 9:5, 21:47f, 47:15f, 104n, 107f, 117, 49:13, 110f, 428, 54:133f, 152f
Death falsely reported 54:238
Death of daughter, Elizabeth 5:5n
Defender of Scriptural teaching 34:66
Defends his actions 3:193, 27:408, 32:8, 40:54f, 44:228, 46:31
Defiance of church and civil authority 23:47, 369f, 386, 415
Denounces pilgrimages 46:142n
Deplores lack of success 12:221
Despairs of self 48:7, 12f, 34, 53f, 156f
Development of his exegetical method 2:164
Devil fights him every day 14:7f, 36, 38:144, 149–156
Devil known well 24:71f, 51:73, 100
Devils, Crowd of, surrounds him 12:227
Devotional writings 42:xin, xiv
Difficult to free self from papal teachings 12:370
Discouraged by world's unexpected evil 17:205
Discovers evangelical meaning of penitence 48:65f
Disputations 38:xviii, xix, 144, 149–156, 237f
Distrusts jurists and law books 45:128
Doctor's degree 4:220, 13:66n, 111, 158n, 14:282f, 21:44, 23:342, 26:18n, 30:169, 34:66, 103, 40:387, 48:5, 6n, 49n, 146f, 196f, 232, 366
Does not want angels to appear to him 4:126
Does not wish to be anyone's master 45:71
Dreams, Attitude towards 6:333f, 336
Due process for blasphemers, Recommended 13:67
Duties as preacher 41:350
Earliest Sermons 51:5
Early opposed monastic vows 17:21
Early struggles for faith 10:34
Early theological development 14:67n
Ecclesiastes and Song of Solomon, Dates of lectures on 15:ix–xi
Echoes of *Ein Feste Burg* 7:132n, 8:35, 9:202, 12:172, 20:7, 44n, 162n, 163, 24:159, 28:88, 33:241, 34:52, 35:281n, 41:186, 245
Eck, John, Relations with 39:122
Economic and ecological protests 8:109, 120
Emser, Controversy with 39:107–115, 119, 121–135, 139–140, 143, 147, 198, 214f, 233
Enjoys food and drink 50:41, 81, 87, 208, 218, 221, 287, 291, 300, 304, 312
England, Contacts with 50:27–40, 104f, 126f, 179f, 192–206
Erasmus, Controversy with 9:277, 26:323n
Erasmus, Relationship with 3:67, 29:31f, 33:10, 42:64n, 46:xi
Estimates his own mental acumen 4:117f, 122, 390
Etymology of German names 7:102n
Evaluates his opposition 34:287
Excommunication 9:110, 31:311, 32:ix, xiii, 5, 115, 125, 234, 276n, 40:341n, 41:5, 42:169n, 46:xi, 48:90n, 91n, 94, 176, 179n, 210f, 224n, 226n, 393, 52:5, 54:30
Expects fall of papacy in two years 45:68
Expects Last Day in his lifetime 2:24, 239, 3:125, 218, 245, 296, 41:13n, 244f
Experience of despair 31:129, 33:190, 39:128
Experience of Law and Gospel 4:68
Experiences Anfechtungen 1:287, 3:5, 8n, 7:290f, 8:54, 251f, 10:360, 12:304, 14:49n, 84n, 17:213, 23:73n, 24:272, 26:73, 49:173, 179, 186, 312n, 329f, 50:175, 182–184, 188, 234n, 238, 291, 298
Experiences as confessor 2:314
Experiences depressions see **Luther, Martin, Biography of**—Experiences Anfechtungen

Experiences hatred and persecution 2:57
Experiences of questioning God 2:45n
Experiences with princes' Diets 17:302
Faith based on Scripture 37:360, 372
Family and relatives 37:155, 46:141n, 251n, 48:145, 227, 329, 49:106f, 183n, 269n, 291n, 319, 341, 358, 402n, 50:17f, 26f, 50, 151n, 156, 167, 210f, 222f, 231f, 246, 282n, 283n, 287, 291f, 300, 312, 54:178, 188
Fasting, His practice of 17:282
Father, Recollections of his 8:181f, 46:250, 251n, 48:303, 329f
Feared by enemies 48:84f, 108, 138n, 213
Feared calamity to strike Germany 13:352, 46:256
Fears for future of evangelical movement 26:312, 402
Fears heresy after his death 2:18
Fears his death to be followed by civil disorder 2:369
Feelings of persecution 1:280
Feels calamity threatening 18:208
Feels enemies persist 12:118
Feels old, tired, and useless 50:79, 110, 182, 188, 245, 267, 281, 284f, 290, 293f, 298, 300, 302
Feels overburdened 50:16, 124, 182, 188, 227, 242, 284f
Feels rich in inner peace 17:409
Feels unworthy 5:38
Feels world's contempt 26:423
Finds Church Fathers in error 2:55
First lectures on the Bible 10:ix
First mass celebration 4:341n, 16:216, 54:156, 234, 325, 354
Francis, St., Attitude toward 17:286n
Frederick the Wise, Recollections of 13:218, 14:282, 41:230
Freedom of the will, His views on 31:9–16, 33:288f
Friendships 49:172, 179, 183f, 186, 316f, 320, 336, 394, 399
Galatians, Commentaries on 27:ix
Genesis, Chronology of his lectures on 1:ix, 3:ix, 3n, 303n, 6:ix–xi, 148, 7:ix
Genesis, His lectures on 42:ix
Genesis, Views on authorship of 6:303n
Genesis commentary planned 13:141
Gospel, His definition of the 30:19f
Growth in knowledge of God 47:112
Guests at Luther's table 54:ix–xi
Hailed as Messiah 47:126
Hated the righteous God 34:336
Hates public attention 14:282
Health 3:342, 5:42, 23:xi, 405n, 413, 28:x, 34:291, 38:284, 43:119n, 276n, 48:16, 61, 69, 188, 198, 217, 219, 232n, 237f, 255, 257, 264, 268, 270, 276, 288, 291, 307, 316, 357, 49:147, 186, 314, 329, 400, 418, 50:47n, 48, 53f, 79, 87, 125, 128, 153f, 165f, 170, 179, 182, 208, 218, 242, 260, 267, 276, 284f, 290f, 293f, 302, 304, 306n, 307, 312, 314, 316, 318, see also **Luther, Martin, Biography of**—Illnesses
Hebrews, Authorship of, Luther's view of 8:178, 30:ix
Heidelberg disputation 32:37–39
Heresy, Attitude towards 15:120, 155, 163f
Heresy trial 48:64n, 70, 74, 76, 83, 95–97, 176
His absence brings confusion in Wittenberg 43:6
His account of indulgence controversy 34:328–337
His account of Leipzig Debate 31:xviii, 309–325
His Bible study 32:338, 40:190
His boasts 37:45, 51, 63, 140f, 161f, 282, 359f
His books burned 31:381, 42:169, 48:187n, 192, 207
His doctrine a gift from God 23:224
His doctrine of the Word 37:xv
His doubts 3:129, 31:221
His ecclesiology 39:xiv, xviii, xxiii, xxv, 115, 121–135, 143–223, 229–238, 305–314, 41:xi–xiii
His enemies 42:18, 121, 46:xii, 20n, 21, 33, 59, 61, 95, 47:113, 115–117
His exegesis of Old Testament 14:87n
His faith weak 5:327
His friends 46:xii, 60, 141
His Gospel 46:21, 30
His lectures 49:165, 176n, 181
His ordination 29:31n, 34:30
His polemics 4:130n, 240n
His prayers for Diet of Augsburg, 1530 21:233
His "scribes" 13:xi
His sense of call 23:192, 323, 332, 342f, 34:103
His sense of duty 44:216f
His sense of imperfection 2:169
His teachings 14:65, 39:124f, 133, 180, 200, 248f
His temper 3:239
His theological language 9:41n
His theology 42:ixf, 5, 49:356f
His wedding 46:61n, 49:69n, 93, 104f, 107, 111, 115f, 123, 132n

His wife 45:27n, 369n, 387n
His work 54:123, 382
History, Attitude towards 34:275–278
Holy Spirit and his writings 33:18
Hope of converting the Jews 34:225
Hospitality in his home 3:183n
Household and daily life 48:27f, 49:58, 59n, 115n, 142, 158f, 165–167, 173f, 220, 268f, 271, 312f, 321f, 356f, 416, 420n
Household and home 50:xv, 16f, 51, 93n, 96f, 110, 122, 130f, 149, 172n, 175, 211f, 214n, 216n, 223, 252, 273n, 276, 279f, 292, 302n, 314n, 54:ix
How he understood his reforms 24:368
Human sympathy 3:239
Humility 40:53, 48:xivf, 3, 5, 7, 20, 34f, 45f, 177
Hunting, Attitude toward 4:382n, 9:194, 14:xii
Hunting accident 9:194
Huss, John, Agreement with 8:90, 266
Huss, John, Opinion of 13:415, 17:44
Hussites, Attitude toward changes, 27:392
Illnesses 8:ix, 20:x, 54:23, 154f, 189, 225–228, 232, 237, 266, 293–295, 297, 314, 346, 374, 383, 448
Imperial safe-conduct 42:169
Impressed by authority 33:72f
Imprisonment threatened 48:87, 108f, 128f, 138
Income 54:181
Indulgence controversy 27:153, 386n, 31:x, xvf, 73, 79f, 255–257, 309–311
Influence of humanism 45:344
Influenced by classical antiquity 9:6n
Inner unity 34:xi
Inter-Protestant sacramental dispute 27:106
Interest in German history 34:271, 276f
Involvement in church and court business 3:3
Irony, Use of 27:153f
Isaiah, Dates of lectures on 17:ixf, 260n, 301, 312, 416
Italians, Attitude towards 8:95
James, St., Evaluation of Epistle of 2:277n, 30:13
Jena and Orlamuende, Visits to 40:69n, 100, 107n
Jews, Attitude towards 1:313, 6:293, 9:215n, 34:225, 45:xv, 47:60–62, 165n, 191f, 52:xif, 101
Jews, Relations with 45:xv, 47:60–62, 165n, 191f
Jews, Treatises on the 47:65n
John, Dates of sermons on 23:ix–xi
Karlstadt, Controversy with 23:165n, 186
Karlstadt, Relations with 40:75, 103, 107n, 129, 136, 186
Knowledge of Astronomy 10:410
Knowledge of Church History 41:7n
Knowledge of Dialectics 32:184f
Knowledge of Hebrew 2:139, 4:153n, 8:262, 47:81n
Knowledge of Near East history 45:224f
Knowledge of Physiology 1:125, 129
Knowledge of Rabbinic literature 47:68n
Language, Use of 41:183, 261
Language aimed at common people 34:281
Language study, Attitude toward 2:15
Last writings 50:317f
Leaves the planning to God 7:104
Lectures 54:207, 288
Lectures on Ecclesiastes 29:76n
Lectures on Epistle to Titus 28:228, 230f, 286
Lectures on Epistles to Titus and Philemon 29:ixf
Lectures on Galatians 26:ix, 48:28, 30
Lectures on Genesis and the Psalms 41:xi
Lectures on Habakkuk 18:xi
Lectures on Hebrews 29:xf
Lectures on I John 29:ixf, 3n
Lectures on Minor Prophets, Times and dates of 18:xi
Lectures on Romans 48:19, 23
Lectures on the Psalms 47:126
Lecturing on Isaiah 35:273n
Lecturing on the Minor Prophets 35:323n
Lecturing on Zechariah 20:ix, 48n, 68n, 157
Leipzig debate 32:318–325
Leisnig, Visits parish of 45:163
Lending, His definition of 45:290
Letters, Printing of his 45:5n
Letters to Elector John 47:6, 27n
Letters to Spalatin 42:97n, 100n
Lies told about him 39:125, 150, 45:199
Life as university student 31:27f
Life stages 34:xi
Limits of his authority 40:7
Linguistic ability 50:189, 294n, 303n
Liturgical ideas 13:xii, 351–387
Loneliness in his struggle vs. Rome 2:87
Loved Roman Church 27:159
Low regard for commerce and banking 46:244f
Luther name, Origin of 7:198

Mainz, Archbishop of, Relations with 41:231f
Makes German jingle 19:174n
Manger of Christ preferred to God's majesty 2:45, 48f
Marburg, Experiences at 17:ix
Marburg and Zwingli, Recalls 12:42
Marburg Colloquy 38:xi, 6–12, 15, 36, 52
Marriage 18:xi, 24:24n, 26:216n, 29:21, 48:290, 303, 331n
Martyrdoms, Reaction to Protestant 1:288
Medicine, Given in hour of death 11:89n
Meets with Karlstad at Jena 40:106
Melanchthon, Disagreement with 2:241f
Melanchthon's return, awaited 1539 3:303n
Method of Bible exposition 2:ix
Method of Bible interpretation 25:xi
Method of exegesis 21:xi, xiii
Method of Scripture exegesis 2:139
Methods of teaching 10:ix
Miltitz, His dealings with 31:xviiif, 310, 329f, 339f
Miniature canon of New Testament 21:xv
Misquotes Erasmus 33:38, 58n, 66, 90n, 206n
Monastic life 5:271, 6:286, 349, 404, 7:69, 8:173f, 181, 188, 267, 276, 326, 12:371–373, 17:111, 282, 22:368, 23:348, 24:24, 98, 228, 26:68, 70f, 27:13, 73, 81f, 92, 28:81, 114, 242, 290, 30:312, 31:129, 34:27, 37:371, 38:166, 228f, 41:340, 42:xiii, 44:327–331, 349, 387, 46:149, 48:xivf, 3, 5, 300f, 331f, 54:14f, 85, 87, 95, 109, 129, 182, 234, 337–340
Monastic vows 36:18
Monk in him sometimes revives 3:275f, 12:275
Motivation 23:201, 33:51, 48:7, 34f, 69, 103, 170f, 196f, 207, 306, 332
Motive for publications 27:147, 160
Motto 14:45n
Münzer, Comparison with 16:316
Münzer, Relations with 40:43, 53f
Murner, Relations with 39:141, 215–219
Mysticism, Attitude towards 31:73f
New Hymn planned 13:351
Nicholas of Lyra, Evaluation of 2:164, 383
No archivist! 45:242n
No defense vs. detractors 7:91f
No peace after Confession and Mass 5:157
No pope or counsellor helped his conscience 12:316
Observant of nature 2:146, 49:21, 158n, 216, 291n, 292n, 293f, 334, 396f
Oeclampadius, His Opinion of 37:33, 240, 252, 347
Offered military protection 48:169n, 223n, 244
Offers concessions to bishops 34:51f
Old Testament, High regard for 21:ixf, xiif, 354
Old Testament, Interpretation and use of 30:21
Old Testament Chronology, Luther's 16:5n
On use of the vernacular 44:22
Opinion of government administrators 3:53
Opponents, Attitude towards 17:188, 247, 35:47, 179, 187
Opponents in Rome 36:ix, 5, 24f
Opposition to violent reforms 36:263
Origin, preservation, and publication of Luther's Table Talk 54:x–xxvi
Original sin, Slow to learn doctrine of 12:351
Papacy, Relations with 39:55–104, 221–223, 247–299
Papal decretals, Judgment of 32:83
Paradoxes (contradictions, absurdities, etc.) in Scriptures, Views on 9:17, 37:xixf, 41, 47–54, 60, 102, 144f, 163–171, 185f, 276f
Parents 42:126n, 54:178, 188
Paul, His son 14:xii
Peasants and radicals, Rethinks ideas about 9:183n
Persecuted for Gospel's sake 12:353
Personality 14:ix
Pessimistic outlook on life 10:387f, 35:41, 45:296
Plans to translate O.T. prophets 16:ix
Pleasure at being educated 46:243
Pope, His view of obedience to 31:246, 260, 275
Pope and bishops, Attitude toward 3:57, 21:120f
Popular unrest and violence feared 48:98, 108, 126, 129, 152, 192, 213, 223, 234, 245f, 281, 351n, 396, 399
Prayer and the Reformation 3:161
Prayer learned with difficulty 6:111, 12:314f, 318, 24:385f
Prayer practice—see under Prayer in *Letters of Luther*, I, II, and III in Vols. 49–50
Prayers, An example of his 30:324

Preaching 13:163, 31:21, 36:312, 331, 333, 335, 46:48, 213n, 48:17, 27f, 113, 189, 202, 219, 221n, 226, 232f, 262, 308f, 311, 320, 51:x–xxi
Preaching style and method 51:xvif, 35, 96, 52:xif
Prefaces to his collected writings 34:xvii
Preserved 18 years by God's grace 12:175
Prierias, Interview with 27:397f
Princely plotting vs. the Gospel sensed 13:403
Princes, Attitude towards 2:36, 198f
Princes harass him 46:203
Printers 49:25, 167, 403, 417f
Private life vs. public ministry 7:181f
Process vs. him in Rome 31:xv–xviii, 255f
Progress in understanding Bible 14:140, 252n
Property and income 46:11n, 50:108n, 167n, 208n, 212f, 218, 221, 222n, 223, 227, 250, 276–278, 278n, 286, 290, 301, 305
Prophecy about him 39:135n
Prophet of the Germans 47:29
Protests tampering with author's own words 2:239
Psalm lectures, Dates and times of first 11:ix
Psalm 2:11, Hated, as youth 12:80
Psalm 90 terrified him 13:86f
Psalms, His favorite Scripture 14:98, 110, 232
Psalms, Uses Vulgate numbering of 9:23, 30:7n, 25
Public life 48:69, 75, 91, 100, 108, 110, 119, 147, 152, 177f, 363
Public reception of papal bull 44:221f
Publications 31:329
Publications pirated 28:56
Quest for salvation 42:ix, xv
Questions his call 5:119
Radical reformers, Attitude toward 12:218, 15:84, 23:230, 24:109, 26:413f, 455f, 51:337
Reaction to Erasmus 29:31f
Reactions to Augsburg Diet 47:5, 11f
Reactions to 95 theses 28:293
Reasons for breaking monastic vows 9:234
Reasons for resisting the ban 26:97
Recalls his youthful Bible reading 2:391
Recalls life as pastor and preacher 46:255
Recalls self as "one of pope's monsters" 12:392
Recalls women's self-flagellation 23:347
Recantation rumored 36:5, 12f, 18, 125
Recites Catechism or Decalog daily 14:8, 47:101–106, 108f, 115
Recognized variety among biblical writings 21:xv
Recognizes his weaknesses 17:256
Recollections of 15 years under Papacy 51:345
Recovery from illness, 1537 24:ix
Reformation beginnings 40:53, 46:xi, 157, 51:72f
Reformation foretells "restoration of all things" 9:6
Reformation progress 38:231
Reformation writings 18:viii
Regrets schism among Evangelicals 26:221
Rejects baptism of bells 14:101n
Rejects papists' charges 26:67
Rejects term "priests" for N.T. ministers 9:157
Relation to Mysticism 26:113n, 130
Renunciation of monastic vows, Second thoughts on 30:280
Repelled by Christ painted as judge 23:57n
Respects judgment of universal church 21:68
Response to attacks 32:ix, 5–260
Response to his message disappoints him 2:53
Rethinks treatment of Heresy 9:183
Reuchlin controversy 47:124
Righteousness of God misunderstood 12:313, 316
Risks life on reforms 34:49
Rome, Recalls visit to 8:260, 14:6, 16:87n, 31:233n
Rome, Visit to 4:272n, 8:260, 14:6, 16:87n, 27:157n, 384n, 31:233n, 38:166, 318n, 41:xv, 264n, 278f, 283n, 284, 322n, 54:208f, 237, 296, 427
Sacred office forced on him 28:283f
Said to flatter princes 40:90, 110, 46:40, 60, 115, 117, 163
Says Gospel has reached high-noon 14:140
Saxon Elector, Relation to 40:102
Saxon humor 39:xix, xxiv
Scholastic view of man rejected 8:91
Scholasticism, Attack on 31:5–7
Schoolman and teacher 48:3n, 4n, 5, 6n, 30n, 37n, 103, 145f, 232, 251f, 274
Scolded often by Satan 17:6
Scripture(s), Held to unity of 21:xv
Scripture(s), His views on 31:x, xviiif, 83, 295, 38:19, 28f, 37, 45
Scripture(s), Interpretation of 21:xiii–xv,

48:23, 24f, 25n, 26n, 52f, 57f, 151, 156f, 213, 396
Scripture(s), Use of 39:156, 163–165, 176, 196f, 199, 215–218
Scripture(s) his sole authority 32:x, xii, xviii, 11, 83, 93f
Seeks God for 20 years as monk 24:24
Self-evaluation 17:109, 33:16, 37:162, 45:68, 49:33, 79, 81, 390, 427, 429, 50:129f, 137f, 242, 54:26, 50, 355, 387f, 405
Sense of duty 48:3, 6n, 49n, 103f, 110, 146, 196f, 232, 248, 274, 319, 336, 343, 395
Sense of sinfulness 6:371
Sense of the Demonic 47:131
Sense of victory 39:243f
Sermons on Baptism 35:26
Sermons on John 8 concluded 23:422
Sermons on the Catholic Epistles 30:ix–xi
Sermons on the Gospel of John 24:ix
Smalcald, Return from, 1537 24:ix
Social and economic conditions in Germany 51:124f
Social classes in his day 8:99, 103
Social unrest not caused by Gospel 23:374
Sorry to be German 46:255f
Sources of temptation 16:346n
Spirit-driven 48:171
Spiritual Struggles see **Luther, Martin, Biography of**—Experiences Anfechtungen
Stages in his career 34:xif
State of Church in his day 10:359
Staupitz, Recollections of 7:192, 332n, 14:283n, 23:271, 26:66, 27:73, 113n
Struggle over the Sacrament 36:250, 40:68
Student days 12:238, 16:196n, 26:345f, 46:234n, 250n, 250f, 54:14, 39, 127
Students' notebooks 25:xiii
Studies 48:5, 12n, 25n, 30n, 36, 37n, 53n, 59n, 65n, 225, 366n
Study of biblical and patristic writings 41:19n
Subordination to the Church 48:69, 88f 98, 101, 103f, 103n, 205f, 208
Substitutes for Bugenhagen as preacher, 1530–1532 23:ix–xi, 322
Sultan's inquiry 46:205n
Summary of his teaching on the Lord's Supper 37:156, 214
Summons to Augsburg, 1518 48:71, 83
Summons to Rome, 1518 48:72, 75n, 76n
Summons to Worms, 1520–21 48:176, 193n, 196n, 198n, 204
Supporters 46:18n
Surprised at progress of the Reformation 12:175, 223
Surprised by opposition 24:288
Takes Augustine as name 6:286
Taunted by papists 2:293
Teaching his second choice as calling 46:253
Teaching methods 25:ixf
Teaching schedule 25:x
Teachings 46:5, 108, 110, 162, 213n
Techniques for conquering devil 16:333n
Temptations 3:345, 4:54, 14:37f, 17:71, 128n, 173, 343
Testimony to his life's work 1:272
Tetzel, Prays for 34:336n
The Word is his basis of confidence 12:64, 170, 220
The young Luther 1:xii
Theses proposed for debate 50:108, 131n
Thuringia, Journey to 46:6, 47, 49n, 72n
Toasts Reformation 43:116
Told to recant 48:86, 88–91, 99, 101, 103, 105f, 109, 190, 200, 202, 204–206, 208, 246, 250
Torgau, Visit to 5:46, 34:6
Tower experience 42:ixn, 54:193f, 308f, 442
Translates selected Aesop fables 16:78n
Translating New Testament 32:259
Translating the Bible 3:207f, 6:53f, 182, 8:143, 13:xvi, 135f, 138f, 259, 35:xv, 181f, 194, 205f, 222n, 227, 230, 50:72, 143n, 185f, 189n
Trip to Augsburg and Worms 46:312n
Turns to Scriptures on distress 27:79, 109
Unfamiliarity with Princely courts 13:147, 149f, 201f
University studies 46:214
Urged to recant 32:xi, xii–xvi, 108, 120, 124f, 127f
Use of Biblical Commentaries 48:26n, 54n
Use of German in lecturing 16:23n, 40n
Use of Latin 4:277n
Uses name Luder 48:17, 19, 23, 26, 36, 52
View of his calling 44:123f
View of Reformation's goal 21:68f
Views on Confession 39:27–47
Views on fanatics 38:282f, 289, 291, 296, 302, 304f, 307
Views on Usury 47:169f
Visited by Jewish rabbis 47:191n, 192
Warnings vs. sacramentarians 37:25, 27f,

70, 74, 131, 144, 150, 162f, 169, 171, 176, 206, 230f, 284, 288
Wartburg, Daily life in the 48:212, 214, 219, 221, 225, 232, 237f, 255, 263n, 267, 274, 294f, 319f, 351, 52:ix, 5
Wartburg, His stay at the 45:xiii, 13, 53, 55, 58n, 77f
Wartburg, Kidnapped to the 48:201, 209n, 210, 212, 215, 219, 223n, 227n, 233, 264n, 269, 270n, 271f, 319
Wartburg, Return from the 48:233, 263, 319, 363f, 371f, 380f, 386n, 388, 391, 393, 395f, 398n
Weariness with philosophical studies 25:361
Weary of preaching 23:xi, 264, 362, 24:247, 34:50
Wife, Role and rights of his 34:291–297
Willingness to be judged or taught 48:74n, 81, 84f, 86, 88f, 98, 103n, 105, 146, 152, 172n, 178, 195f, 205–208, 246, 249f, 390
Wittenberg, Plague in 16:107n, 35:273n
Wittenberg, Ready to leave 49:15, 158f, 194
Wittenberg, Return to 43:69f
Wittenberg disturbances, Reaction to 36:233–235
Wittenberg home 34:291
Wittenberg Law faculty, Controversy with 50:xv
Work habits 39:126
Worms, Diet of 32:101–131
Wounded in a leg 42:132n
Writes for his dear Germans 47:29, 54f, 140, 190
Writings 14:105n, 31:ix
Writings, Attitude toward his own 3:305f, 305n, 34:282–288
Writings, His evaluation of his 34:327f
Zülsdorf farm 34:295, 50:223n
Zwingli, Controversy with 41:105
Zwingli, His opinion of 37:31, 35f, 45, 97, 161, 173, 177–179, 181, 185f, 191–194, 198, 206–208, 231–236, 240, 247–249, 252, 271, 331
Zwingli, Relationship with 8:130f

Luther, Martin, Jr.—46:251n, 50:73n, 232n, 246n, 285n, 291n, 300, 312, 54:150158f, 162, 177, 334f, 451

Luther, Martin, Writings of—49:59n, 81n, 93n, 104n, 173n, 282n, 284n
A *Mighty Fortress is Our God* (Hymn) see **Luther, Martin, Writings of**—*Ein Feste Burg*
A *New Song Here shall be Begun* (Hymn) 43:74
Abomination of the Secret Mass 36:xii, 41n, 51n, 164n, 309f, 311–328 (text), 38:123n, 53:xxn
About the Wolf and the Sheep 41:235n
Abridged Response to Martin Luther 39:173n
Abrogation of the Private Mass 36:xii, 129–132, 212n, 257n, 38:141, 48:281n, 324, 327, 344, 346, 350
Ad schedulam inhibitionis sub nomine Misnensis episcopi editam responsio, 1520 45:28n
Addition to Goat Emser 39:109
Address to the Christian Nobility—see **Luther, Martin, Writings of**—*To the Christian Nobility of the German Nation*
Admonition against the Jews 50:303n
Admonition concerning the Sacrament of the Body and Blood of Our Lord 38:xv, 94f, 97–137 (text), 49:418n
Admonition to Peace, A Reply to the Twelve Articles of the Peasants in Swabia 35:403n, 36:310, 46:xii, 3–43 (text), 43n, 49n, 59n, 60f, 65n, 75n, 47:18n, 49:106
Admonition to Pray against the Turk 4:356n, 46:137n, 53:304
Admonition to the Clergy Assembled at Leipzig 21:272n
Admonition to the Clergy that they Preach against Usury 2:263n, 45:238n, 308n
Adoration of the Blessed Sacrament 36:xi, 271–274, 275–305 (text), 37:38n, 86n, 153, 296n, 40:153n, 45:342n, 365n
Advent sermons 35:115
Adversus armatum Cocleum 34:6n
Adversus execrabilis Antichristi bullam 32:5
Aesop's Fables selected and translated by Luther 16:42n, 78n, 36:17n, 46:112n, 49:288n
Against Hanswurst 22:253n, 34:326, 329n, 366n, 39:xvn, 41:xivf, 184–256 (text), 261, 43:254, 47:181n, 50:224n
Against Henry, King of England 35:128n
Against Jack Sausage see **Luther, Martin, Writings of**—*Against Hanswurst*
Against Latomus 1:251n, 15:133n, 27:252n, 32:xv–xviii, 135f, 137–260 (text), 34:139n, 305n, 37:57n, 172n, 39:168n, 44:300n, 341n, 45:371n, 48:229n, 270, 293, 319

Against Scholastic Theology 33:16n, 48:38n, 60

Against the Antinomians 3:223n, 35:157n, 41:72n, 47:101–119

Against the Assassin at Dresden 38:142

Against the Asses in Paris and Louvain 34:342

Against the Asses of Louvain and Cologne 48:155n, 162, 185n, 229n, 289n

Against the Bishop of Magdeburg, Cardinal Albrecht 41:239n, 248n, 249n

Against the Heavenly Prophets in the Matter of Images and Sacraments 9:185n, 27:105n, 28:231, 268, 345, 35:157n, 37:xi, xv, 38, 55, 74n, 80n, 86n, 101f, 125, 129n, 136, 145n, 153, 162, 193, 210n, 266, 270, 282, 288, 294, 303, 307, 318, 321, 347, 38:57n, 294n, 296, 40:73–224 (text), 44:xiv, 45:365n, 46:146n, 183n, 47:89n, 116n, 49:101n, 129n, 146n, 187n, 261n, 312n, 50:37n, 51:262, 53:53f

Against the Idol at Halle 39:241–243 (text)

Against the Mainz Brief 49:144n

Against the New Idol and the Old Devil 4:130n

Against the Perverters and Falsifiers of the Imperial Mandate 28:56

Against the Robbing and Murdering Hordes of Peasants 20:48n, 35:403n, 46:xii, 43n, 45–55 (text), 59n, 60n, 61, 72n, 47:18n, 49:107, 109n, 113n

Against the Roman Papacy, an Institution of the Devil 41:xvf, 263–376 (text), 50:162n, 250

Against the Sabbatarians 41:29n

Against the Spiritual Estate of the Pope and the Bishops, Falsely So Called 39:xxiv, 239–299 (text), 45:15, 114n, 169n, 48:349f

Against the Thirty-two Articles of the Louvain Theologists 34:341–342, 345–360 (text), 38:284, 50:255f, 317

An den christlichen Adel deutscher Nation von den christlichen Standes Besserung—see **Luther, Martin, Writings of**—*To the Christian Nobility of the German Nation*

An Italian Lie concerning Dr. Martin Luther's Death 34:363f, 365f (text)

Annotations on the Other Chapter of Matthew 41:311n

Answer to Goat Emser 36:141n, 37:367n

Answer to Several Questions on Monastic Vows 46:xiii, 139–154 (text)

Answer to the Christians at Reutlingen 37:xiv, 163n

Answer to the Dialog of Sylvester Prierias concerning the Power of the Pope 27:156n, 48:72, 75, 79, 81

Answer to the Hyperchristian, Hyperspiritual, and Hyperlearned Book by Goat Emser in Leipzig—Including some Thoughts on His Companion the Fool Murner 39:xxiiif, 137–223 (text), 227, 48:192n, 194n, 257n, 265n

Antinomian Disputations 47:102–106, 50:183

Appeal for Prayer Against the Turks 42:55n, 43:213–242 (text), 50:224n

Appeal of M. Luther from Cajetan to the Pope 48:86, 88f, 90f, 99

Appeal to a General Council of the Church 48:90, 99, 185

Army Sermon against the Turk 18:395n, 46:137n, 175n

Articles against the Whole Synagogue of Satan and All the Gates of Hell, 1530 46:227n

Assertion of all the Articles which were Condemned by the Latest Bull of Leo X 32:5, 33:8n, 15n, 16n, 160n, 212–233 (text), 45:364n, 48:190n

Asterisks 31:xvi, 309, 36:12n, 48:80n

Autobiographical fragment 41:xi

Avoiding the Doctrines of Men 28:309, 33:54n, 35:127–129, 131–147 (text), 39:308n, 45:15, 28n, 72n

Babylonian Captivity of the Church 28:24, 33, 31:xix, 285n, 329, 32:33n, 56n, 59n, 33:7, 54n, 34:315n, 35:xn, xiiin, xvi, 36:ixf, xii, 3, 5–10, 11–126 (text), 129, 135n, 271f, 37:xi, 64n, 86n, 123n, 196n, 303n, 366n, 368n, 369n, 370n, 371n, 38:141n, 313n, 314, 39:xviin, xxiii, 169n, 175n, 309n, 40:ix, 118n, 42:xiiif, 100n, 43:90n, 44:54n, 199n, 217n, 45:7n, 8n, 14n, 20n, 24n, 26n, 28n, 29n, 53n, 117n, 141n, 143n, 179n, 313n, 367n, 381n, 385n, 46:262n, 48:281n, 49:71n, 157n, 384n, 50:75, 51:75, 53:22

Bible translation see **Luther, Martin, Writings of**—German Bible

Bondage of the Will 1:269n, 2:39n, 44n, 3:306n, 5:43, 44n, 50n, 9:23n, 277n, 17:4n, 20:162n, 23:327n, 24:x, 25:372, 26:209n, 27:36n, 28:244, 29:32n, 33:xif, 5, 10f, 11n, 13, 15–295 (text), 36:20n, 37:363n, 42:48n, 46:xi, 49:140n, 145n, 50:172n

Booklet of Prayers 53:66, 82
Brief and Sound Exposition of the Lord's Prayer 48:113n
Brief Confession concerning the Holy Sacrament 35:xiv, 37:158
Brief Explanation of the Ten Commandments, the Creed, and the Lord's Prayer 35:241n, 43:14n, 53:66n
Brief Form for Understanding and Praying the Lord's Prayer 43:14n, 48:113n
Brief Instruction on How Confession should be Made 39:25f
Brief Instruction on What to Look for and Expect in the Gospels 35:115f, 117–124 (text), 45:90n
Brief on the election of Ferdinand of Austria to be German king 50:41–44, 44–50 (text)
Brief on the frequency of celebration of the Lord's Supper 49:205–210 (text)
Briefe see **Luther, Martin, Writings of**—*Letters*
Briefs in connection with the Pack affair 49:190n, 192–195 (text)
Briefs on alliances among evangelical Estates of the Empire 49:128f (text), 247–250 (text)
Briefs on armed resistance to the emperor 49:255–260 (text), 274–280 (text), 431–433 (text), 50:9–12 (text), 9f
Bull of Convocation with Luther's preface and comments 34:238n
Bull of Paul III with Luther's comments 41:140n
Bull of the Ecclesiastic in Wittenberg against the Papal Bishops, Granting God's Grace and Merit to all Who Keep and Obey It, 1523 39:245
Bulla Coena Domini (ironic) 45:85n
Burning of Brother Henry 32:xviii–xx, 263f, 265–286 (text)
Business Dealings and Usury see **Luther, Martin, Writings of**—*Trade and Usury*
Call for a Crusade against the Turks and all Opposed to the Christian Faith 46:157n
Catechisms 15:247n
Certain German Proper Names Restored to Their Original Etymology, ascribed to Luther 7:102n, 198n
Christ is Arisen (hymn) 37:144n, 260n
Christ Jesus Lay in Death's Strong Bands (hymn) 37:260n
Christ, the Letter of Indulgence 42:64n
Christian Exhortation to the Livonians concerning Public Worship—53:5, 41–50 (text)
Christian Letter of Consolation to the People of Miltenberg 43:97–112 (text)
Christian Liberty see **Luther, Martin, Writings of**—*Freedom of a Christian*
Christian Writing for W. Reissenbusch, Encouraging him to Marry 49:103n
Christmas Postil 35:115n, 52:xiif, 3–386
Chronology 27:267n
Church Postil 37:xv, 7, 10, 147, 148n, 237n, 42:5, 52:ix–xiii
Circular Letter concerning Translating and Interpreting, and Intercession of the saints 40:332n
Collected Works, 1st edition 31:ix
Collected Works, Erlangen edition 9:151n, 204n, 258n, 28:5, see also index of each Vol. for references
Collected Works, Jena edition 37:147n
Collected Works, St. Louis edition 26:169n, 28:309, see also index of each Vol. for references
Collected Works, Weimar edition 25:vii, x, xiii, 549, 26:ix, 43n, 406n, 485, see also index of each Vol. for references
Collected Works, Wittenberg edition 30:ix, 37:147n
Collection of Latin Works 48:110, 112n, 155n
Come Holy Ghost, God and Lord (hymn) 39:65n
Comfort for Women who Have Had a Miscarriage 43:243–250 (text)
Comfort When Facing Grave Temptations 42:xvi, 179–186 (text)
Comment on Giovanni Nanni's Disputation on the Rule of the Pope 41:294n
Commentaries see also **Luther, Martin, Writings of**—Expositions; **Luther, Martin, Writings of**—Lectures
Commentary on Ecclesiastes see **Luther, Martin, Writings of**—*Notes on Ecclesiastes*
Commentary on I Corinthians 7 28:3–56 (text)
Commentary on I Corinthians 15 28:59–213 (text), 45:153n
Commentary on Hosea 18:3–18 (text), 20:6
Commentary on Isaiah 16:3–349 (text), 17:3–415 (text), 45:354n
Commentary on Psalm 2 12:viif, 3–96 (text)
Commentary on Psalm 8 12:ix, 97–138 (text)

Commentary on Psalm 19 12:x, 139–146 (text)
Commentary on Psalm 23 12:x, 147–182 (text)
Commentary on Psalm 26 12:ix, 183–196 (text)
Commentary on Psalm 45 12:viii, 197–302 (text)
Commentary on Psalm 51 12:viiif, 303–410 (text)
Commentary on Psalm 68 13:ix, 1–38 (text)
Commentary on Psalm 82 13:x, 39–72 (text), 39:17n, 44:xvn
Commentary on Psalm 90 4:195n, 13:xi, 73–142 (text)
Commentary on Psalm 101 9:221n, 13:x, 143, 224 (text), 16:x, 46:239n
Commentary on Psalm 110 13:xii, 225–348 (text)
Commentary on Psalm 111 13:xii, 349–388 (text), 38:94n, 95
Commentary on Psalm 112 13:xi, 389–420 (text)
Commentary on Psalm 118 28:175
Commentaries on the Psalms 32:106
Commentary on Psalms of 1513–1516 45:316, 361n, 365n
Commentary on Romans 37:364n
Commentary on the Alleged Imperial Edict 34:65f, 67–104 (text), 47:25n, 28n
Commentary on the Lord's Prayer 32:106
Commentaries on Psalms 1, 2, 6, 32, 37, 38, 51, 62, 94, 102, 109, 117, 118, 130, 143, 147 14:x–xii, 3–349 (texts)
Commentary on the Sermon on the Mount 21:295–357 (text), 22:xi, 23:ix, 34:306n
Commentary on Zechariah 14:210n
Communion Exhortation 53:104
Computation of the Years of the World 1:207n, 2:82n, 4:300n, 5:340n, 6:ix, 179n, 188n, 255n, 282n, 340, 7:9n, 8:115n, 16:5n
Concerning Human Traditions 35:127
Concerning Leonard Keiser of Bavaria, Burned for the Sake of the Gospel 47:16n
Concerning Penitance 44:17
Concerning Rebaptism 29:81n, 37:155, 367n, 40:227–261 (text), 41:46n, 49:187n
Concerning the Answer of the Goat in Leipzig 39:xxiii, 117–135 (text)
Concerning the Ministry 39:xviin, 305n, 40:3–44 (text)
Concerning the Order of Public Worship 39:304, 45:165, 371n, 49:31n, 53:5, 7–14 (text), 95
Concerning the Papacy at Rome In Opposition to the Celebrated Romanist at Leipzig 40:26n
Condemnatio doctrinalis librorum Martini Lutheri per quosdam magistros nostros Lovaniensis et Coloniensis facta. Responsio Lutheriana ad eandem damnationem 32:141n, 306n
Condemnation by the Theologians in Paris of the Teaching of Dr. Martin Luther, a Counter-Condemnation by Doctor Luther, etc. 34:306n
Confessio et testamentum venerandi patris nostri D. Luther 34:293
Confession concerning Christ's Supper 28:265, 267, 36:8n, 81n, 37:28n, 40n, 42n, 109n, 153–159 (text), 161–372 (text), 39:xviin, 41:105n, 49:172n, 200n, 201n
Confession of the Articles of Faith 37:157, 368n
Confitendi ratio 32:44n, 44:216n
Counsel of a Committee of Several Cardinals with Luther's Preface 34:233f, 235–267 (text)
Countertheses to Eck's 48:107n
De potestate papae see **Luther, Martin, Writing of**—*On the Power of the Pope*
Decalog, Preached to the People of Wittenberg 41:169n
Dedications and Prefaces 50:176n, 242, 317
Defense against the Malignant Judgment of Johann Eck 32:67n
Defense and Explanation of All the Articles 32:x–xii, xx, 5, 7–99 (text), 33:8n, 16n, 35:407n, 36:82n, 37:369n, 39:173n, 44:198n, 46:239n, 53:24
Defense of the Translation of the Psalms 7:243n, 35:205–208, 209–223 (text)
Deuting der zwo greulichen Figuren, Bapstesels zu Rom und Mönchkalbs zu Freiberg im Meissen funden 40:271n
Deutsche Bible see **Luther, Martin, Writings of**—German Bible
Deutsche Messe see **Luther, Martin, Writings of**—*German Mass and Order of Service*
Dictations on the Psalter 30:32n
Die Propheten alle deutsch 35:229
Disavowal of Purgatory 46:257n
Discussion of Confession 36:8n, 81n, 44:216n

Discussion on How Confession should be Made 39:xxii, 23–47 (text)
Disputation against Scholastic Theology 27:292n, 31:xv, 3–16, 32:151n, 154n, 34:139n, 305n, 37:363n, 38:xvii, 41:213n, 42:48n, 44:300n
Disputation concerning Infused and Acquired Faith 44:275n, 300n
Disputation concerning Justification 4:163n, 34:147–149, 151–196 (text)
Disputation concerning Man 34:135, 137–144 (text)
Disputation concerning the Passage "The Word was made Flesh" (John 1:14) 38:xix, 238, 239–277 (text)
Disputation of Johann Eck and Martin Luther 32:64n, 65n, 82n, 95n, 97n, 138, 51:53
Donation of Constantine, Annotated translation of 41:286n, 44:166n
Dr. Luther's Retraction of the Error Forced upon Him by the Most Highly Learned Priest of God, Sir Jerome Emser, Vicar in Meissen 39:xxiv, 225–238 (text)
Dr. Martin Luther's Bull and Reformation 39:245, 278–299 (text)
Dr. Martin Luther's Opinion Concerning Erasmus of Rotterdam 49:6
Earnest Exhortation for All Christians Warning them against Insurrection and Rebellion 36:233f, 265n, 311n
Edition of Melanchthon's *Defense against the Sorbonne* 48:258n, 270, 289n, 290, 320
Editions 29:vii
Eight Wittenberg Lenten Sermons 36:234n, 235, 273, 40:51n, 45:13n
Ein Bericht an einem guten Freund von beider Gestalt des Sakraments 17:82n, 34:81
Ein Feste Burg (hymn) 5:50n, 7:132n, 17:119n, 337, 20:44n, 163n, 28:88, 41:186n, 245n, 49:175n
Eine Freiheit des Sermons päpstlichen Ablass und Gnade belangend 31:289n, 36:81n
Epistola Sancti Hieronymi de poteste papae, cum praefatione Lutheri 41:7n
Epitome of a Reply to Martin Luther 44:118n, 110, 133n, 136n
Er ging aus der Kammer sein (hymn) 10:397n
Erhalt uns, Herr (hymn) 2:181n
Erlangen edition see **Luther, Martin, Writings of**—Collected works
Exegesis of Psalm 101 41:239n
Exegetica opera 18:vii, ix, xi, 20:ix
Exhortation to All Clergy Assembled at the Diet of Augsburg 34:5–8, 9–61 (text), 38:134n, 141, 47:11n, 27n, 48n, 50n, 51n, 52n, 66f, 49:318n
Exhortation to the Communicants 53:104f, 53:54n, 104f (text)
Exhortation to the Knights of the Teutonic Order that they Lay Aside False Chastity and Assume the True Chastity of Wedlock 45:xif, 133–158 (text), 385n
Explanation of Certain Articles of Dr. Martin Luther, Regarding His Sermon on the Blessed Sacrament 36:20n, 276n, 39:82n
Explanation of Psalm 117 49:417n
Explanation of Some Articles . . . 48:149n
Explanation of the Articles Debated at Leipzig 32:80n, 83n, 176n, 48:131n
Explanation of the Book of the Prophet Zephaniah 49:160n
Explanation of the Disputation concerning Infused and Acquired Faith 44:275n
Explanation of the First 25 Psalms 49:288n, 331n
Explanations of the Ninety-five Theses 1:323n, 11:372n, 31:xvi, 37, 79f, 83–252 (text), 32:12n, 29n, 65n, 74n, 79n, 86n, 87n, 89n, 91n, 97n, 151n, 34:330, 35:8n, 36:8n, 11n, 65n, 81n, 89n, 37:369n, 370n, 38:ix, 41:71n, 175n, 235n, 42:65n, 46:157n, 158, 162n, 47:39n, 48:64, 69n, 75, 81, 88, 100n, 51:86
Exposition of Isaiah 9 37:361n
Exposition of John 20:23 48:294, 297n
Exposition of Psalm 9 32:264, 268–272 (text)
Exposition of Psalm 37 48:248, 252n, 320
Exposition of Psalm 68 48:229n, 254n, 290n, 320
Exposition of Psalm 77 44:274n
Exposition of Psalm 119 48:254n, 271n, 290
Exposition of Psalm 127 for the Christians at Riga in Livonia 45:xv, 313–337 (text)
Exposition of the Epistles and Gospels 20:287, 36:332
Exposition of the Gospel of the Ten Lepers 48:314n, 320
Exposition of the Lord's Prayer for the

Simple Layman 21:145n, 42:xv, 5, 15–81 (text)
Exposition of Zechariah 45:225n
Expositions of Scripture see **Luther, Martin, Writings of**—Commentaries; **Luther, Martin, Writings of**—Lectures on Scripture
First Lectures on the Psalms, Vols. 10 and 11, 48:12n, 18n, 19n, 26n, 28, 67n, 49:371
First Lectures on the Psalms, Dresden manuscript 10:x, 8, 231
First Lectures on the Psalms, Part I, Psalms 1–75 10:ix–xii, 3–464 (text)
First Lectures on the Psalms, Part II, Psalms 76–126 11:ixf, 3–549
First Lectures on the Psalms, Preface to the Scholia 10:8–10 (text), 27
Formula Missae see **Luther, Martin, Writings of**—*Order of Mass and Communion*
Four Psalms of Comfort 14:x, 206–277 (text), 23:7n, 49:152n
Fourteen Consolations 37:370n, 42:xv, 117–166 (text), 48:134, 328, 51:40n
Fraternal Agreement on the Common Chest of the Entire Assembly at Leisnig 39:304, 45:xii, 176–194 (text)
Freedom of a Christian 11:359n, 16:305n, 25:468, 28:42, 30:52n, 31:xix, 329–331, 333–377 (text), 32:117, 33:54n, 36:5, 117n, 126n, 39:xxiii, 148n, 308n, 40:ix, 42:165n, 45:94n, 118n, 48:12n, 180n, 402n, 51:xiii, 53:43
From Heaven Above to Earth I come (Hymn) 45:83n, 49:322
Galatians, Commentaries on see **Luther, Martin, Writings of**—*Lectures on Galatians*, 1519 and 1535
German Bible 2:242n, 5:352n, 384n, 7:188n, 18:229n, 27:345n, 28:21, 149, 164, 204, 338, 371, 32:xvi, 135f, 138n, 259, 37:101n, 40:99, 41:261n, 44:224n, 45:206n, 222n, 226n, 227n, 316, 332n, 46:232n, 49:4, 5n, 13f, 17n, 18f, 25, 69, 75, 104n, 165, 288n, 291n, 418
German Explanation of the Lord's Prayer 48:113n
German Litany 49:263n, 53:139–141, 163–170 (text)
German Litany and Latin Litany Corrected 53:154–170
German Mass and Order of Service (Deutsche Messe) 22:ix, 5n, 36:324n, 37:28n, 40:xii, 265, 43:34n, 49:135n, 163n, 50:232n, 53:xiii, xvi, xix, 5, 51–90 (text), 136f, 150f
German New Testament 35:179, 181n, 227, 37:239, 45:xiii, 77n, 81n, 84n, 86n, 87n, 112n, 278n, 332n, 343, 359n
German Theology, Preface to the Complete Edition of 7:133n, 31:73f, 75f (text), 79, 48:36n
Grund und Ursach aller Artikel D. Martin Luthers so durch römische Bulle unrechtlich verdammt sind, 1521 32:5
Handbook for Pious Prayer 43:7
Hauptstück des ewigen und neuen Testaments, von den hochwürdigen Sakrament beider Gestalt, Fleisch und Blut Christi, Zeichen und Zusage, die er uns in demselben getan hat 34:81
Heidelberg Disputation 31:xxi, 37f, 39–70 (text), 79, 32:92n, 159n, 33:16n, 34:139n, 38:xviii, 42:48n, 50:266n, 51:17, 35, 44
Heidelberg Theses 48:60
Herr, nun lässest du deinen Diener (hymn—Nunc Dimittis) 28:110
Homilies on the Lord's Prayer (Lent, 1517) 48:113n
House Postil 2:147n, 5:283n
How Christians Should Regard Moses 35:157–159, 161–174, 45:97n, 308n, 47:82n
How God Rescued an Honorable Nun 43:81–96 (text)
How One should Properly Baptize 53:95
How One should Teach the Common Folk to Shrive Themselves 53:119–121 (text)
Hymns 43:74n, 231, 53:211–309 (texts)
Hymns based on Ten Commandments 47:109n
Infiltrating and Clandestine Preachers 40:379–393 (text), 42:ix
Instruction for a Brief Confession of Sins, According to the Decalog 39:38n
Instruction to Penitents Concerning the Forbidden Books of Martin Luther 42:100n, 43:73, 44:223–229 (text)
Instructions for the Visitors of Parish Pastors in Electoral Saxony 40:263–320 (text), 43:223n, 51:136
Introduction to "Theologia Deutsch" see **Luther, Martin, Writings of**—*German Theology*
Invocavit sermons, 1537 9:187n, 37:18n, 371n, 48:400n, 402n, 49:3, 261n
Jesaia, dem Propheten (hymn) 20:60n
Judgment of Martin Luther concerning Monastic Vows 9:234n, 14:34n,

15:79n, 167n, 16:167n, 17:21n, 21:129n, 30:30n, 31:xviii, 309–325, 33:54n, 36:81n, 217, 261n, 39:285n, 40:97n, 43:83, 44:xiv, 216, 249, 251–400 (text), 45:14n, 27n, 141n, 175n, 371n, 46:141, 145n, 48:321, 328f, 331n, 336f, 344, 346, 350, 359
Kirchenpostille see **Luther, Martin, Writings of**—*Wartburg Postil*
Koran, Foreword to a German edition of the 5:79n
Large Catechism 9:69n, 13:376n, 16:35n, 321n, 17:293n, 309, 37:xx, 28n, 286n, 369n, 38:102n, 40:84n, 229n, 41:113n, 247n, 42: 61n, 43:14n, 45:247n, 254n, 308n, 46:253n, 47:92n, 109n, 51:xiii, 135f, 161n, 163n, 165n, 166n, 167n, 177n, 179n, 186n, 53:110f
Larger Treatise on Usury 32:98n
Last Words of David see **Luther, Martin, Writings of**—*Treatise on the Last Words of David*
Last writings 50:317f
Latin Advent Postil 48:152, 225, 229, 237f, 254n, 268n
Latin Litany Corrected 49:263n, 53:140f, 153–170 (text)
Lectures on Amos 18:x, 127–190 (text)
Lectures on Deuteronomy 3:237n, 9:ixf, 3–311 (text), 33:142
Lectures on Galatians 1:214n, 21:ix, 23:271n, 25:xii, xiv, 212, 27:ixf, 28:42, 36:179n, 42:5, 43n, 44:300n, 45:354n, 48:28, 30, 113, 121n, 125, 168n, Vols. 26 and 27 (text)
Lectures on Galatians, 1519 9:260n, 25:212, 39:xivn, xxi, 201n, 41:111n
Lectures on Galatians, 1519, Chapters 1–6 27:153–410 (text)
Lectures on Galatians, 1535 4:20n, 24:x, 27:67n, 240n, 30:294n, 39:xvin
Lectures on Galatians, 1535, Chapters 1–4 26:ix, x, 3–461 (text)
Lectures on Galatians, 1535, Chapters 5–6 27:3–149 (text)
Lectures on Genesis 1:ix–xii, 2:ixf, 85n, 204n, 344n, 3:ix, 3n, 47n, 249n, 303n, 4:ix–xi, 5:x, xii, 47n, 99n, 112n, 237n, 267n, 285n, 309n, 340n, 6:ix–xi, 98n, 105n, 311n, 313, 3–407 (text), 7:ixf, 9n, 61n, 276n, 308n, 312n, 3–377 (text), 8:ixf, 109n, 134n, 173n, 268n, 273n, 8:3–333 (text), 15:269n, 319n, 323n, 17:26n, 23: x, 27:384n, 38:ix, 47:60, 50:242n, (text) Vols. 1–8
Lectures on Genesis, His introduction to original Vol. 3 2:235
Lectures on Haggai 18:x, 367–389 (text), 45:225n, 228n
Lectures on Hebrews 25:xii, xiv, 29:109–241 (text), 51:17, 35
Lectures on Hosea 18:x, 3–77 (text)
Lectures on Hosea, Zwickau manuscript of 18:x, xii, 1–76 (text), 19:142, 20:17n, 37n, 59n
Lectures on Isaiah, First Book, Chapters 1–39 16:ix–xi, 3–349 (text)
Lectures on Isaiah, Second Book, Chapters 40–66 17:ixf, 3–416 (text)
Lectures on Joel 18:x, 79–125 (text)
Lectures on Malachi 18:x, 391–419 (text)
Lectures on Micah 18:x, 207–279 (text)
Lectures on Nahum 18:x, 281–317 (text)
Lectures on Obadiah 18:x, 193–205 (text)
Lectures on Philemon 29:93–105 (text)
Lectures on Romans 25:ix–xii, xiv, 3–525 (text), 28:29, 33:16n, 47:127
Lectures on Scripture see also **Luther, Martin; Writings of**—Commentaries; **Luther, Martin, Writings of**—Expositions
Lectures on the Minor Prophets 2:240n, Vols. 18, 19, and 20 (text)
Lectures on the Psalms 25:x, xiv, 15, 26, 97, 152, 163, 209, 33:16n
Lectures on the Psalms, 1513–1516 51:40, Vols. 10 and 11 (text)
Lectures on the Song of Solomon 15:xf, 191–264 (text)
Lectures on I Timothy 25:271, 28:217–384 (text)
Lectures on Titus 29:3–90 (text)
Lectures on Zechariah, German text 20:154–347 (text)
Lectures on Zechariah, Latin text 20:3–152 (text)
Lectures on Zephaniah 18:x, 319–365 (text)
Leipzig Debate 31:xviii, 309–325, 32:19n, 158n, 34:328n, 44:xviin, 18n, 117n
Leisnig Church Ordinance, 1523 edition 49:31n, 46n
Lenten Postil 38:18n, 26n, 57
Letter accompanying *An Answer to Several Questions*, May 18, 1526 46:143n
Letter concerning the Rebellious Spirit 37:70n
Letter of Consolation to All who Suffer Persecution 43:57–70 (text)
Letter of Consolation to the Christians at Halle 43:139–166 (text)
Letter of Dr. Martin Luther Concerning

His Book on the Private Mass 38:xvi, 221–233 (text)
Letter to Albrecht, Archbishop of Mainz 49:350n, 354n
Letter to Cardinal Albrecht 41:233n
Letter to Cordatus, 1530 17:366n
Letter to George Spalatin 25:15
Letter to Hans von Rechenberg 43:47–56 (text)
Letter to Herwagen 37:10, 77n, 153
Letter to Melanchthon, July 5, 1530 46:211
Letters to Nicholas Hausmann 46:158, 159n, 263n
Letter to Nicholas von Amsdorf, Oct. 27, 1529 46:184n
Letter to his father 46:141n
Letter to his wife, Aug. 15, 1530 46:211
Letter to the Archbishop of Mainz 38:141
Letter to the Christians at Strassburg in Opposition to the Fanatic Spirit 37:xin, 40:61–78 (text)
Letter to the Evangelicals in Leipzig 49:308n
Letter to the Princes of Saxony concerning the Rebellious Spirit 35:205, 40:45–60 (text), 47:14n
Letter to two Pastors concerning Rebaptism see **Luther, Martin, Writings of**—*On Rebaptism*
Letters 2:21n, 3:306n, 4:266n, 281n, 382n, 5:369n, 6:200n, 9:211n, 22:418n, 23:xi, 26:195n, 27:130n, 177n, 28:253, 30:277n, 33:6f, 11n, 12, 37:xiv, 5n, 7n, 21n, 22n, 42n, 101n, 104n, 161n, 252n, 40:230n, Vols. 48, 49, and 50
Letters on despair 49:217
Licentiate Examination of Heinrich Schmedenstede 34:301f, 303–321 (text)
Little Book on Prayer 37:260n, 368
Lives of the Fathers, Preface to 44:308n
Long Sermon on Usury 43:221n, 45:161, 175n, 176n, 235n, 240, 256n, 273n, 308n, 48:136n, 142n, 49:52n
Luther at the Diet of Worms 39:141n, 43:65n, 44:xviin
Luther's Will 34:291–293, 295–297 (text)
Lutheran Declaration concerning the Thirteenth Thesis on the Power of the Pope 40:26n
Magnificat, Exposition of 13:ixf, 21:3–294 (text), 34:306n, 43:39n, 45:121n, 124n, 48:219n, 225, 254, 288, 290, 296, 320
Marburg Articles 38:xi, 12f, 85–89 (text), 281, 288n, 291, 49:235, 236n, 238n, 239n, 303n
Meditation on Christ's Passion 25:389, 42:xiv, 3–14 (text), 48:114n
Misuse of the Mass 36:x, xii, 129–132, 133–235 (text), 37:14n, 371n, 38:313n, 42:171n, 45:26n, 68n, 82n, 179n, 47:44n, 53:22
Mitten wir im Leben sind (hymn) 10:337, 40:310n, see also indexes in Vol. 53
New Testament in German see **Luther, Martin, Writings of**—German New Testament
Ninety-five Theses 7:234n, 17:247n, 28:293n, 29:12, 31:x, xv, 19–23, 25–33 (text), 37, 278, 32:31n, 62n, 34:xi, 306n, 329, 35:205, 36:81n, 37:369n, 38:xvii, 39:xvin, 9, 42n, 241, 41:199n, 233n, 42:xiin, 143n, 44:17, 45:134n, 285n, 287n, 46:xi, 90n, 257n, 47:39n, 48:45–47, 49n, 55n, 56, 61n, 64, 68, 70, 72n, 80n, 81, 85, 97n, 101, 104, 116, 118, 49:175n, 51:31n, 53:39n, 116, 54:286, 342
Notes on Ecclesiastes 2:271n, 15:ixf, 3–187 (text), 26:386n, 30:248n
Notes on the Decalog 50:52n
Notes to Quincuplici Fabri Stapulensis Psalterio 48:26n
Now Let us Pray God the Holy Ghost (hymn) 39:69, 41:148n, 42:114n
Of Secret Masses 53:252
Of Threefold Justice 32:117
On Confession see **Luther, Martin, Writings of**—*Whether the Pope has the Authority to Make Confession Obligatory*
On Good Works 32:106
On Justification 35:198n
On Marriage Matters 21:85n, 45:385n, 46:xiv, 259–320 (text)
On Music 49:426
On Rebaptism 37:155, 367n, 49:187n
On Rogationtide Prayer and Procession 21:140n, 42:xv, 83–93 (text), 43:8
On the Abuse of the Mass 2:137n, 51:88n
On the Blessed Water and the Agnus Dei of the Pope 41:169n
On the Councils and the Church 15:339n, 38:230n, 39:xvin, 41:xiiif, 9–178 (text), 44:xviiin, 51:167n
On the Jews and Their Lies 6:212n, 9:215n, 15:280n, 349n, 22:107n, 34:225n, 42:7n, 45:214n, 213n, 216n, 229n
On the Lord's Prayer 42:17
On the Lord's Supper 42:172n, 175n

On the Councils and the Churches 32:243n

On the Papacy in Rome: Against the Most Celebrated Romanist in Leipzig 39:xxiii, 49–104 (text), 140, 159n, 172

On the Power of the Pope 44:165

On the Shem Hamphorus see **Luther, Martin, Writings of**—*On the Tetragrammaton and the Genealogy of Christ*

On the Ten Commandments 42:17

On the Tetragrammaton and the Genealogy of Christ 2:364n, 24:93n, 45:204n, 208n, 213n, 216n, 229n, 47:65n, 123, 137n, 212n, 256n

On Translating: An Open Letter 34:281n, 35:177–180, 181–202 (text), 42:113n, 49:69n

On War against the Turk 30:75n, 36:211n, 37:368n, 42:55n, 43:239n, 46:xiii, 137n, 104, 155–205 (text), 217n, 49:203n, 50:69n, 51:xiii, 53:153

Open Letter on the Harsh Book against the Peasants 35:403n, 46:xii, 57–85 (text), 47:18n, 50:125n

Open Letter to Pope Leo X 31:xix, 334–343 (text), 36:126n, 48:180n

Open Letter to the Christian Nobility see **Luther, Martin, Writings of**—*To the Christian Nobility of the German Nation*

Open Letter to the Imperial Estates 48:203, 209n, 255, 292n

Operationes in Psalmos, 1519 10:36n, 25:105

Opinion of the Parisian Theologians on Doctor Luther's Doctrine, Luther's Dissenting Opinion 44:300n, 312n, 382n

Opinion on the divorce of King Henry VIII 50:27–31, 31–40 (text), 121

Opinion on the Proposed Council 50:157f, 158–165 (text)

Order of Baptism 53:95–103 (text), 106, 117, 142–144

Order of Baptism, newly Revised 53:106–109 (text), 111, 142f

Order of Marriage for Common Pastors 53:106, 110–115 (text), 144

Order of Mass and Communion 36:324n, 37:28n, 371n, 40:xii, 265, 45:148n, 49:56n, 53:xviii, 5, 15–40 (text), 53, 104, 191f

Ordinance of a Commmon Chest, Preface 22:117n, 34:99n, 44:xiv, 45:xiif, 161–176 (text)

Ordination of Ministers of the Word 53:122–126 (text), 145

Passional (Passion History) 43:8, 42–45

Passional of Christ and Antichrist 16:139n, 23:115n

Pentecost Sermons at Wittenberg, 1525 46:60n

Personal Prayer Book 42:18n, 43:3–46 (text)

Persons Related by Consanguinity and Affinity who are Forbidden to Marry according to the Scriptures 45:xi, 5–9 (text), 46:315n

Postil see **Luther, Martin, Writings of**—*Wartburg Postil*

Postils 15:247n, 48:237–245, 52:xf, xiv, 70, 121, 371n

Praelectio in librum Judicum 44:274n

Preface, Epilog, and Marginal Notes to the Brief of Pope Adrian VI 41:265n

Preface for All Good Hymnals 53:319f (text)

Preface to book about the Council of Gangra by John Kymaeus 41:126n

Preface to "Confessio Bohemica" 26:70n

Preface to Daniel 45:144n, 224n, 226n, 227n, 329n

Preface to Galeatus Capella's History 34:271–273, 275–278 (text)

Preface to Georg Rhau's Symphoniae iucundae 53:321–324 (text)

Preface to his glosses on the Psalms 10:3–5 (text)

Preface to Justus Menius' *Oeconomia Christiana* 46:210n

Preface to *Lives of the Popes*, by Robert Barnes 41:xiiin

Preface to *Luther's German Writings*, Wittenberg edition 34:281f, 283–288 (text), 41:26n

Preface to the Bapst Hymnal 53:332–334 (text)

Preface to the Burial Hymns 53:325–331 (text)

Preface to the Catalog of all his Writings 34:281

Preface to the Complete Edition of Luther's Latin Writings 25:9, 151, 34:325f, 327–338 (text)

Preface to the Epsitle to Titus 43:42

Preface to the First Book of Maccabees 47:208n

Preface to the New Newspaper about the Anabaptists of Münster 41:242n

Preface to the Swabian Syngramma 36:332, 336n, 37:xv, 9, 42n

Preface to the Weiss Hymnal 53:317f (text)
Preface to the Wittenberg Hymnal 53:315f (text)
Preface to Wenceslaus Link's translation of Capella's history of Francesco Sforza 45:376n
Prefaces to hymnals and musical collections 53:311–334
Prefaces to the Apocrypha 35:227–232, 337–354 (text)
Prefaces to the books of the Bible 35:227–232
Prefaces to the New Testament 35:227–232, 357–411 (text)
Prefaces to the Old Testament 35:227–232, 235–333 (text)
Private Mass and the Consecration of Priests 38:xvf, 147–214 (text), 217f
Proceedings at Augsburg 31:xvii, 255–258, 259–292 (text), 32:81n, 34:330n, 48:72n, 87n, 91n, 94, 108
Proposed Commentary on Matthew 48:320
Protest and Offer 48:172n, 174n, 195n
Psalms (Psalter), German translation of the 45:320n, 321n, 322n, 335n
Questio de viribus et voluntate hominis 33:16n
Receiving Both Kinds in the Sacrament 34:81n, 36:xi, 233–235, 237–267 (text), 359n, 38:141n, 39:274n, 40:51n, 127n, 45:70n, 78n, 49:4n
Refutation of the Alcoran by Brother Richard, Translation of 5:79n, 43:235n, 46:176n
Rejection of Purgatory 16:9n, 40:332n, 47:42n, 44n
Reply of Martin Luther to the Ranting of Several Papists at the Seventeen Articles 40:332n
Reply to the Book of Our Outstanding Teacher Ambrose Catharinus 48:291, 319, 357
Reply to the Texts Cited in Defense of the Doctrines of Men 35:127–129, 147–153 (text), 36:107n
Resolution concerning the 13th Lutheran Thesis on the Power of the Pope 36:12n, 39:xiin, 92, 41:293n
Resolutiones super propositionibus suis Lipsiae disputatio 32:176n
Responsio ad Martinum Luther (per Fratrem Silvestrum de Prierio) 41:xvn
Responsio Lutheriana ad condemnationem doctrinalem per magistros nostros Lovaniensis et Coloniensis 32:135, 142n, 149n
Right and Power of a Christian Congregation or Community to Judge all Teaching and to Call, Appoint, and Dismiss Teachers 45:165, 46:37n, 49:31n, 384n
Sacrament of Penance 35:5–8, 9–22 (text)
Sayings in Which Luther Found Comfort 43:167–178 (text)
Schwabach Articles 37:157
Second Lectures on the Psalms 48:114n, 121n, 125, 131, 136, 150, 225, 49:159n
Second Sermon, March 10, 1522 44:xin, 233n
September Bible 43:7, 41n
September Testament 28:149
Sermon against the Turks 49:240n
Sermon against the offense of slander 11:388n
Sermon for 4th Sunday after Easter 20:127n, 320n
Sermon for St. John the Evangelist's Day 25:268
Sermon for the 18th Sunday after Trinity 27:57n
Sermon Notes on Some Chapters of Matthew 43:238n
Sermon on Confession and Sacrament 43:8
Sermon on Contemplating the Holy Suffering of Christ 43:6, 8
Sermon on Excommunication see **Luther, Martin, Writings of**—*Sermon on the Ban*
Sermon on Holy Baptism 37:286n
Sermon on John 2:1–11 44:11n
Sermon on Keeping Children in School 28:256, 40:314n, 41:176n, 44:xiv, 45:344, 46:xiiif, 187n, 207–258, 49:307n, 403n, 51:151n
Sermon on Preparing to Die 42:xv, 59n, 95–115 (text), 43:6, 8, 48:130
Sermon on Repentance 32:35n, 38n, 42n, 44n, 47n, 49n, 53n, 35:7n, 36:81n
Sermon on the Ban 31:255, 32:66n, 39:xiiin, xxii, 3–22, 44:182n, 48:114n, 51:xiii
Sermon on the Estate of Marriage 28:33, 55, 44:xiv, 6, 7–14 (text), 45:14n, 143n, 385n, 46:274n, 51:xiii
Sermon on the Holy and Blessed Sacrament of Baptism 35:25–27, 29–43 (text), 43:6, 8
Sermon on the Sacrament of Penance 32:50n
Sermon on the three Kinds of Good Life

for the Instruction of Consciences 44:140n, 221n, 222n, 234–242 (text)
Sermon on the Unrighteous Mammon 46:83n
Sermon on the Virtue of Excommunication 34:33n, 39:5
Sermon on the Worthy Reception of the Sacrament 32:54n, 42:xvi, 167–177 (text), 49:208n
Sermons 37:xx, 159, 237n, 360n
Sermons of Feb. 24, 1517, and March, 1518 41:232n
Sermons on Genesis 3:52n, 17:241n
Sermons on Indulgences 32:32n, 34:329, 36:81n, 44:17
Sermons on the Catechism 28:165
Sermons on the Gospel of John 5:48n, Vols. 22, 23, and 24, 50:302n
Sermons on the Ten Commandments and the Lord's Prayer 44:17
Sermons, 1520–21 48:321n
Seven Penitential Psalms 35:205n, 43:6, 44:17, 48:19n, 49:69
Short Confession on the Blessed Sacrament 2:43n
Short Form of the Ten Commandments, the Creed, and the Lord's Prayer 33:150n, 43:6f, 39n, 48:113n
Short Instruction on Confession 49:208n
Short Order of Confession 53:116–119 (text)
Short Sermon on Usury 45:xii, 235, 256n, 272n, 273n, 48:136
Simple Way to Pray 42:xvn, 18n, 43:189–212 (text)
Sincere Admonition by Martin Luther to all Christians to Guard against Insurrection and Rebellion 39:xixn, 45:xiii, 53–74 (text), 81n, 48:352, 355
Smalcald Articles 14:101n, 22:407n, 26:383n, 35:ix, 37:370n, 39:xi, 41:xiiin, 135n, 167n, 176n, 184n, 48:362n, 50:131n, 145n, 153, 51:xiii, 187n, 54:215, 356
Small Catechism 3:306n, 4:126n, 16:305n, 37:xx, 28n, 286n, 369n, 38:124, 41:247n, 42:61n, 43:7, 34n, 190, 47:109n, 48:113n, 53:106, 110f, 117, 119
Statement on right of resistance (co–author) 47:8
Summaries of the Psalms 35:205–207, 223n
Supputatio annorum mundi (Chronology of World History) 20:60n, 41:23n, 106n, 126n, 348n, 45:222n, 224n, 225n, 227n, 47:138n, 221n
Table Talk 1:45n, 78n, 129n, 166n, 239n, 326n, 2:277n, 361n, 3:114n, 144n, 4:236n, 341n, 5:346n, 6:298n, 9:211n, 14:269n, 15:12n, 16:ixf, 312n, 313n, 21:42n, 89n, 259n, 22:ix, 108n, 412n, 416n, 451n, 23:xi, 25:9, 26:46n, 28:21, 29, 35:9, 36:131, 42:x, 98n, 45:224n, 300n, 305n, 46:247n, 47:61, 96n, 104, 109, 53:265, 54:5–476
Temporal Authority: To What Extent it Should be Obeyed 45:xiii, 77–129 (text), 258, 264, 357n, 367n, 388n, 46:31, 95, 99, 115n, 136, 163, 166, 47:6, 181n, 49:18n, 276n
Ten Sermons on the Ten Commandments 48:113n
That a Christian Assembly or Congregation has the Right and the Power to Judge All Teaching and to Call, Appoint, and Dismiss Teachers, Established and Proved by Scripture 39:xxiv, 301–314 (text)
That a Christian Should Bear His Cross with Patience 43:179–186 (text)
That Jesus Christ was Born a Jew 42:7n, 45:xii, 197–229 (text), 47:73n, 124, 135, 137n, 178n, 229n
That Parents Should neither Compel nor Hinder the Marriage of their Children, and that Children Should not become Engaged without Their Parents' Consent, 1524 4:72n, 45:381–393 (text), 46:262n
That These Words of Christ, "This My Body," Still Stand Firm against the Fanatics 3:110n, 16:71n, 17:107n, 20:x, 23:14n, 80n, 101n, 122n, 27:37n, 28:367, 37:5–7, 13–150 (text), 153f, 161–163, 166, 176, 193, 206f, 209, 236–238, 249–252, 276, 280, 285, 288, 292, 38:5, 65n, 157n, 298n, 300n, 43:137n, 49:153n, 172n, 187n
The Beautiful Confitemini. The 118th of the Psalms 49:166n, 344n
The Blessed Sacrament of the Holy and True Body of Christ, and the Brotherhoods 18:396n, 32:56n, 34:26n, 35:47f, 48–73 (text), 36:ixn, xi, 8n, 13, 19n, 33n, 35n, 37n, 53n, 133n, 135n, 287n, 37:123n, 39:5f, 7n, 82n, 42:60n, 43:149n, 44:117n, 192n, 45:181n, 48:134, 143f, 149n, 51:xiii
The Estate of Marriage 36:97n, 105n, 45:xi, 5, 15, 13–49 (text), 141n, 143n, 145n, 251n, 381n, 385n, 386n, 388n, 390n

The Holy and Blessed Sacrament of Baptism 39:43n
The Keys 25:270, 34:53n, 100n, 37:368n, 39:xxv, 40:321–378 (text), 41:153n, 44:134n, 47:48n, 49:418n
The Magnificat 13:ixf, 21:297–358 (text), 21:xvif, 297–358 (text)
The Papacy at Rome: An Answer to the Celebrated Romanist at Leipzig 36:6, 48:164n, 51:167n
The Psalter 35:210n
The Sacrament of Penance 39:25
The Sacrament of the Body and Blood of Christ: Against the Fanatics 36:xii, 331–333, 335–361 (text), 37:xv, 6n, 53n, 65n, 86n, 153, 234n, 369n, 49:146n, 164n, 165
The Seven Penitential Psalms 14:ixf, 137–205 (text)
The Ten Commandments Preached to the People of Wittenberg 2:11n, 21:221n, 39:38n, 213n
The Ten Commandments, with a Brief Explanation of their Fulfillment and Violation 39:38n
The Three Symbols or Creeds of the Christian Faith 34:xii, xv, 199f, 201–229 (text), 37:212n, 41:7n, 53:171
Theses against the Council of Constance 41:6, 7n
Theses against the Whole School of Satan and All the Gates of Hell 40:332n
Theses concerning Faith and Law 34:107f, 109–132 (text)
Theses on Vows 17:21n, 43:83, 44:246n, 287n, 300n, 45:141n, 48:298f, 302n, 310, 311n
Three Letters of John Huss 41:7n
Tischreden see **Luther, Martin, Writings of**—*Table Talk*
To All Christians in Worms 43:71–80 (text)
To the Christian Nobility of the German Nation 31:xix, 329, 32:82n, 34:282, 35:408n, 36:5n, 16n, 18n, 35n, 79n, 99n, 113n, 114n, 205n, 39:xxiii, 10, 19, 95, 109, 119, 139f, 147n, 148n, 151n, 172n, 206n, 213n, 288n, 309n, 40:ix, 21n, 41:5n, 15n, 74n, 261n, 372n, 42:xiii, 90n, 43:83, 173n, 44:xiv, 6 (text), 89, 123–218 (text), 45:26n, 28n, 53n, 61n, 69n, 81n, 83n, 141n, 161, 176n, 178n, 180n, 237, 246n, 276n, 286n, 288n, 295n, 318n, 319n, 342n, 343n, 371n, 375n, 378n, 46:22n, 131n, 164n, 214n, 287n, 48:167n, 170f, 172n, 192n, 194n, 234n, 49:28n, 135n, 384n, 50:267n, 51:75
To the Christians in Riga, Reval, and Dorpat 45:315
To the Councilmen of all Cities in Germany that they Establish and Maintain Christian Schools 40:314n, 41:176n, 45:xiv, 318n, 341–378 (text), 46:210f, 217n, 218n, 232n, 49:103n, 51:151n
To the Goat in Leipzig 28:244, 39:xxiii, 56, 105–115 (text), 119, 41:150n, 48:192n
To the Saxon Princes 43:251–288 (text)
Trade and Usury 3:249n, 22:418n, 43:221n, 44:xiv, 110n, 96n, 45:xii, 233–310 (text), 308n, 358n, 388n, 46:213n, 47:169n, 51:xiii
Translations 31:vf, xxif
Translations into English see General Editors' Preface in each volume
Treatise concerning the Ban 32:66, 67n, 36:28n, 45:61n, 176n, 285n, 51:xiii
Treatise on Baptism 36:8n
Treatise on Good Works 21:305n, 33:150n, 36:47n, 39:213n, 42:xiii, 24n, 183n, 44:20, 21–114 (text), 182, 45:118n, 47:109n
Treatise on the Last Words of David 1:93n, 15:xf, 267–352 (text), 35:157, 47:65n, 72n, 137n, 192n, 290n
Treatise on the New Testament, that is, the Holy Mass 35:77f, 79–111 (text), 36:ixn, x, 8n, 36n, 46n, 135n, 37:371n, 39:140, 40:118n, 42:174n, 53:22
Two Kinds of Righteousness 31:295, 297–306 (text)
Unterricht auf etlich Artikel 32:95n
Warning to His Dear Germans 3:252n, 34:25n, 27n, 65f, 40:342n, 46:258n, 49:434n, 437
Wartburg Postil 18:247n, 28:55, 35:115, 124n, 35:xviii, 45:90n, 321n, 381n, 386n, 389n, 48:145n, 237f, 258, 271n, 276, 288, 292f, 296, 314, 320, 337, 346, 356, 359, 49:139, 50:189, 52:ix–xiii
Was fürchtest du, Feind Herodes, sehr (hymn) 36:126
What Persons are Forbidden to Marry 40:301n
Whether One May Flee from a Deadly Plague 43:113–138 (text), 49:175n
Whether Soldiers Too Can be Saved 9:232n, 21:40n, 41:34n, 44:xiv, 45:118n, 46:xiii, 87–137 (text), 158, 165f, 246n, 49:110n, 50:69n

Whether the Pope has the Authority to Make Confession Obligatory 32:159n, 35:147n, 36:258n, 43:70n, 48:225, 231n, 244, 246n, 254n, 288, 290, 292, 294, 297, 313f, 320, 50:75, 51:98n
Why Nuns May, in all Godliness, Leave the Convents: Ground and Reply 43:83n, 45:141n, 155n
Why the Books of the Pope and His Disciples were Burned by Doctor Martin Luther 31:xix, 381f, 383–395 (text), 32:137n, 34:332n, 39:126n, 158n, 45:104n, 46:273n
Wider den Eisleben (Against the Eislebener) 47:105
Wider den neuen Abgott und alten Teufel, der zu Meihsen soll erhoben werden 40:109n
Wider den rechten auffrürischen, verräterischen und morderischen Rathschlag der ganzen Mainzischen Pfafferei Unterricht und Warnung 34:46n
Wider die Bulle des Endchrists 32:5
Winter Postils 43:70n
Wittenberg Latin Bible of 1529 9:ix
Word to Penitents about the Forbidden Books 48:246f, 247n
Luther, Martin, Writings of, no longer extant --*Against the Idol at Halle* 48:316n, 320, 326n, 340f, 343–345, 350f, 353n, 365n, 372, 377
Notes on Aristotle's Physics 48:38, 112
Notes on Canon Law 48:114
Shorter Postil 48:237f, 254, 268n, 321n
Luther, Paul—25:xii, 28:3, 46:251n, 50:74n, 232n, 246n, 285n, 291n, 300, 312n
Luther als Kirchenhistoriker—see **Schäfer, Ernst**
Luther and Erasmus—Bibliography 33:xin, 5n
Luther and the Old Testament—see **Bornkamm, Heinrich**
Luther on Vocation—see **Wingren, Gustaf**
Luther seal—49:358f
Luther the Expositer—see **Pelikan, Jaroslav**
Luther und der Frühkapitalismus—see **Barge, Hermann**
Luther und Emser. Ihre Streitschriften etc.—see **Enders, Ernst Ludwig**
Luther's career as reformer—Bibliography 31:xi–xiii
***Luther's Works on the New Testament*, Introduction to (Vols. 21–30), by Jaroslav Pelikan**—21:ix–xv
Luther's World of Thought—see **Bornkamm, Heinrich**
Luthers Romfahrt—see **Böhmer, Heinrich**
Luthers Sprichwörtersammlung—see **Thiele, Ernst**
Lutheran, The name—45:70n
Lutheran Confessions—38:xix
Lutheran Protestantism—21:70
Lutheran and Presbyterian/Reformed Consultation, 1966 --Summary Statement 38:xii
Lutheran doctrine—46:20, 90n
Lutheran name decried—36:265
Lutheranism—45:135, 136n, 138, 347n, 47:59, 101, 130
Lutheranism, Scholastic—35:xn
Lutherans—3:193n, 361, 5:x, 12:213, 299, 13:190, 192, 14:98, 16:241, 256, 17:200, 234, 270, 379, 22:82, 84, 344, 408, 23: 217, 255, 303, 23:189, 26:15, 50, 75, 414, 34:30, 52, 80, 346, 38:6, 12, 91, 142f, 167, 183n, 196, 224, 230f, 281, 283, 41:231–236, 43:112, 45:77f, 161, 197, 313f, 46:xii, 20n, 228, 47:13, 24, 26, 28
Charges against 37:xx, 5, 10, 18n, 21, 22n, 23, 27, 41n, 51, 65, 71, 73, 80, 84, 86f, 96, 98f, 124f, 133, 146, 147n, 149, 165f, 198, 212n, 226, 248, 259f, 291, 308, 317, 339
Lüthi—9:308n
Luxemburg—34:345, 353
Luxury—2:12, 29, 252, 3:238, 324, 5:11, 331, 333, 7:4, 34, 45, 180, 194, 214, 8:118, 120, 133, 9:55, 92, 139, 156, 181, 11:259, 265, 294, 302f, 394, 498, 536, 16:185, 188, 18:169f, 25:174, 481
Luz—5:243, 251, 6:183, 246f, 8:151, 153f, 156, 295
Lycia—10:412
Lycurgus—15:42
Lydian stone—23: 174
Lydians—2:203, 206
Lying—1:274, 2:291, 317, 3:63, 193, 196, 258, 319f, 326f, 5:40f, 72, 110, 114, 126f, 150, 327, 6:4, 44, 57, 62, 76, 82, 177, 331, 374, 381, 7:238, 248, 10:54–57, 60, 223, 255, 317, 16:65, 229, 231, 298, 17:275, 296, 303, 26:409, 445, 28:238, 36:210, 38:103, 112, 156f, 174, 200, 202, 45:60, 66, 69, 73, 108, 199, 213, 46:179, 181f, 225, 227, 236, 301, 303, 310, 51:142, see also **Liars; Lies**
Lying spirit—25:160
Lying-in period—52:163
Lynx—1:62
Lyons—2:327f

Lyons, Council of—48:362n
Lyra—see **Nicholas of Lyra**
Lyres—7:301, 370, 11:103n, 104

Macarius—13:33
Macarius, St.—24:75, 26:191f, 194
Macaronic style—54:xixf
Maccabeans—49:380, 386
Maccabees—16:118, 19:226, 20:29, 89f, 192, 250, 314, 33:15n, 35:232, 302f, 350f, 38:195, 45:222n, 331, 47:207–209, 222f, 229
Maccabees, Books of—20:314, 36:220
Maccabees, First book of—35:350–351
Maccabees, Second book of—35:352f
Maccabees, Wars of the—11:98n
Maccabeus, John Scotus—34:301, 35:xvin, 39:xivn
Maccabeus, Judas—see **Judas Maccabeus**
MacDonald, George—53:173, 189–308
translator of Luther's hymns 53:211–309
Mace—9:149
Macedonia—2:191, 16:184
Macedonian heresy, heretics—37:361, 41:86n, 87f, 91, 95, 120–123
Macedonians—9:4, 16:182, 184, 25:126, 26:31
Macedonius, Bishop of Constantinople—38:309n, 310
Mackinnon, James—47:105n
Luther and the Reformation, 1925 31:331
Macrobius—*Commentaria in somnium Scipionis* 6:332n
Madensack—41:149n, 45:70n, 144, 151
Madness—8:118, 135, 137, 169, 173, 189, 223, 230, 243, 250, 310
Madrid—46:159n
Maecenas—14:280
Magdeburg—13:xi, 22:45, 23:227, 41:33n, 184, 229, 240, 45:342n, 344, 47:266, 48:28n, 146, 161, 183n, 218, 377, 49:82, 104, 120, 155, 187n, 219n, 314n, 50:30f, 72, 209n, 237n, 249n, 291n, 309, 312, 51:xivn, 371, 53:191, 193, 232–234, 287, 299
Augustinian Monastery 48:23
Magdeburg, Bishop of—23: 211, 48:44, 378, 49:103n
Magdeburg, League of—49:155
Magdeburg, Liborius—54:262
Magi—3:167, 13:199, 16:34, 17:314, 18:129, 198, 320, 36:294, 52:141f, 160f, 164, 167f, 171, 176, 183f, 189f, 194f, 201, 207f, 235, 239f, 243f, 249f, 270, 273f, 283f
Magic—3:264, 5:380, 384f, 22:107f, 43:17, 30, 52:162, 182, 207, 54:58, 241
Magicians—3:315, 7:140, 148, 346, 364, 9:190, 22:474, 25:124
Magistrates—2:19, 127, 173, 175, 318f, 4:23, 77, 211, 224, 285, 5:5, 15, 124, 159, 184, 186, 193, 269, 275, 326, 341, 6:20, 27, 30, 34, 168f, 194, 7:62, 67, 118, 142f, 145, 150, 158, 176, 180, 184f, 188–191, 193, 195f, 202, 205, 224, 339, 341f, 344, 356, 8:59, 62, 83, 94, 125, 181, 212, 297f, 301, 16:37, 181, 23: 5, 36, 71, 392, 26:12, 18, 95, 107, 117, 187, 208, 212, 217, 249, 275, 277, 307–309, 313, 337, 353, 355f, 439, 448, 450, 27:50, 61, 82, 90, 113, 119, 123, 148, 281, 29:27f, 71–74, 78, 54:28, 180
Magna Graecia—2:188n, 189
Magnificat **(Canticle)**—3:155, 5:316f, 6:311, 12:149, 17:341, 21:297–358, 30:26n, 50, 40:307, 47:111, 53:68f, 176–179
Use of 21:350
Magnificence, True—11:265f
Magnifying—25:3, 28, 99, 135, 426
Definition of 21:306f
Magog—3:64, 10:411
Mahanaim—6:87, 94, 117, 179
Maher-shalal-hash-baz—16:88n
Mahrenholz, Christhard—53:57n, 154n
Maids—46:114, 290, 308
Maidens—17:238, 346, 409, 26:191f
Maier, Paul L.—54:469
Maimonides—38:250n
Mainz—2:199, 14:233, 22:408, 465, 31:381, 35:133n, 38:141, 41:24, 115, 233, 369, 48:123n, 160, 194, 230n, 322n, 377
Mainz, Archbishops of—41:233n
Mainz, Archdiocese of—23: 201n, 370n, 378n, 39:60n
Mainz, Conference of—34:46
Majesty—46:133, 245, 277
Major, George—26:36n, 44:308n, 50:209n, 212, 271n, 275n, 54:386
Majorca—34:345
Majoristic controversy—12:ix, 50:209n
Majority opinion—21:242f
Malachi, Prophet—9:182, 18:391, 408, 23: 325, 35:331f, 46:221, 49:418n
Commentary on his book 18:ix, xi, 391–419 (text)
Malchus—45:274n, 46:29
Male and female—3:44, 48, 103f, 111, 128f, 133–136, 144, 147, 200–202, 255, 270, 274, 310, 353, 360, 4:243, 255, 274, 299, 333, 5:31, 329, 382, 5:6, 31, 33, 35, 39, 189, 282, 288f,

292, 298, 314, 323, 331, 357, 365, 382, 9:157, 26:354, 41:349, 45:36f, 390f, 143–146, 153, see also **Husbands and wives; Man and woman**
Male sex—4:6, 8, 162, 222, 232, 237f, 290, 362, 369
  Superiority of 42:144
Malefactor—46:172
Maler, Matthes—51:61
Males—1:69, 84, 104, 117, 123, 125, 127, 151, 182, 203, 238, 255–257, 312, 338f, 3:48, 101–104, 127, 129, 132f, 135–137, 142, 144, 148, 202, 208, 215, 228, 255, 270, 272, 274, 6:205, 367f, 377, 8:210, 9:157, 205, 249, 26:307, 354f, 359n, 39:263
Malevolence—27:395
Malice—2:161, 163, 173f, 3:51, 158, 193, 228–231, 236, 296, 307, 311, 11:303, 25:168f, 46:287, 308f
Malmsey wine—24:113, 205, 208
Mamelukes—23: 187
Mamertus, Bishop of Vienne—42:85
Mammon—3:100, 4:380f, 409, 5:58, 208, 306, 6:18f, 49, 9:70f, 14:240, 16:61, 21:11, 13, 168, 173f, 177f, 186–188, 192, 194f, 203f, 23: 17, 288, 24:19f, 22, 25, 163, 43:220, 46:130, 214–216, 243f, 251, 256, 305, 315
Mamre—2:362f, 372, 398, 3:184, 234, 244, 316, 5:236, 6:184, 280, 345, 7:4, 293
Mamre Valley—4:192
Man—Meaning of the word 14:288
Man (Mankind)—see **Human beings**
Man and wife—see **Husbands and Wives**
Man and woman—17:180, 21:84–86, 91, 28:16, 51, 171–173, 276–280, 46:152, 261, 292, 296, 304, 313, see also **Male and female**
  Created as equals 1:136f
Manasseh—6:145, 371, 7:14, 144, 200, 208–212, 229, 260, 266, 8:55f, 149, 154–156, 158–160, 169f, 174, 176, 178, 207, 233, 286, 290, 295f, 300f, 303, 306, 9:40, 60, 258, 277, 306, 10:281f, 284, 286, 290f, 296f, 434, 11:40, 96f, 20:117, 307, 25:374
Manasseh, King—1:286, 289, 2:172, 16:179, 278, 32:48, 44:83, 46:172, 230, 47:194f, 203
Manasseh, Prayer of—1:296n, 9:60n, 13:92, 43:8, 273
Manasseh, Tribe of—16:37, 50, 102, 106, 18:132
Mandates, Imperial—49:36f, 190n, 191f, 198n
  Jan. 20, 1522, against the Wittenberg disturbances 48:388, 397
  March 10, 1521, against Luther 48:198n, 201, 207
Mandrakes—5:352f, 355
Manes—22:67, 448
Manger of Christ—2:45, 48f
Manhood—3:6
Manichaeanism—13:89, 96f, 135, 25:353, 425, 31:9n, 37:81, 99, 40:154n, 41:85n, 103n, 44:283n
Manichaeans—1:213, 2:14, 39n, 3:160, 4:125, 332, 5:103, 144, 228, 348, 356, 359, 12:374, 14:125, 15:268, 17:187, 327, 20:303, 22:21–23, 112, 23:122, 27:60, 288n, 362, 28:313, 30:287, 298, 310, 33:173, 34:208, 210, 35:139n, 142, 150, 402n, 38:33, 35n, 50, 61f, 98, 39:170, 197, 43:249, 54:36
Manichaeus—52:81
Manilis, Marcus—*Astronomica* 33:41n, 54:326
Mankind—see **Human beings**
Manliness—17:406
Manna—1:248, 3:274, 8:201, 9:92f, 95, 97, 11:56–64, 66f, 73, 23: 29, 31f, 36, 42, 101, 113f, 153, 156f, 159, 54:146f
Manners—28:332f, 340
Manoah—52:219
Manschreck, Clyde L.—54:23, 260n
Mansfeld—5:370, 8:288, 35:171n, 46:48, 63, 121n, 48:4, 145, 220, 329, 49:140, 268, 271, 314n, 318n, 50:125, 281f, 282n, 284n, 288n, 289n, 291–293, 295n, 302f, 306n, 51:383
Mansfeld, Countess of—see **Dorothy of Solms, Countess of Mansfeld**
Mansfeld, Counts of—42:xi, 43:84f, 87n, 47:15n, 50:281f, 283f, 285n, 288n, 289, 293, 295f, 298f, 311, 314, 316–318
Mantovano, Baptista Spagnola—29:155n, 41:283n, 54:208
Mantua—41:6, 275n, 54:215f, 222, 230
Manure—23:38, 92, 24:194, 196, 198f, 231, 233
Many-breasted—5:197
Maps—8:273n, 278, 281
Marah, Waters of—42:141
Maranatha—9:82n
Marburg—12:42, 17:ix, 260n, 38:xi, 8f, 11, 13, 63n, 72f, 77, 83n, 85, 288f, 291–293, 301f, 41:184, 46:xii, 263, 49:239n, 389n, 414n, 50:28n, 31, 54:376
  University of 48:164n, 166n, 49:17n, 32, 100, 414n
Marburg Articles —see **Luther, Martin, Writings of**—*Marburg Articles*

Marburg Colloquy—2:18n, 35:xii, 37:xxf, 53n, 158, 241n, 38:xv, xix, 6–89, 94, 157n, 281, 298n, 300, 49:88n, 177, 200n, 229f, 234f, 239f, 243n, 244n, 264n, 266, 282n, 302
Marburg Colloquy, Reports of the—
Anonymous report 38:15–85 (text)
Brenz, Report of 38:73–80
Collin, Report of 38:52–62
Hedio, Report of 38:15–36
Osiander, Report of 38:62–73
Rhapsodie on the Marburg Colloquy 38:80–83
Summary Report 38:83–85
Marburg Revisited—see **Empie, Paul C., and James I. McCord, eds.**
Marcion—22:67, 448n, 24:204, 27:288n, 30:19n, 35:231, 399n, 402n, 37:99, 108, 110f, 113f, 227, 309
Marcolvus—see **Markolf**
Marcus Attilius Regulus—2:125
Marcus Aurelius, Emperor—21:110n
Marcus, Jacob R.—47:270n
Mardi Gras—19:211
Margaret, Duchess of Brunswick—35:5, 25, 47
Margaret, St.—8:203, 17:140n, 41:239n, 45:40n
Margaret of Austria—41:128n, 49:21, 144n
Margaret of Brandenburg—50:175n
Margaret of Navarre—54:xxii
Margaret of Savoy, Regent of the Netherlands—32:263, 272n, 275
Margaritha, Antony—*The Whole Jewish Faith* 47:130, 141n, 149n, 153n, 176n, 185n, 256n, 257, 54:436n
Mariahilf, Shrine of—6:231n
Mariners—2:69
Mariology—35:108n, 191n
Marius, Emperor—41:37n
Mark, St., Evangelist—22:107, 218, 23:268n, 24:368, 25:148, 26:101, 27:161, 196, 29:105, 30:144, 41:325, 52:30, 65, 254
Markolf—34:235f, 286, 357–359, 41:363n, 47:184, 246, 249, see also **Morolf**
Marlianus, Louis—33:6n
Marlow, A.N.—co-translator of Erasmus' *Diatribe* 33:xin, xiin
Marnholt, Ludolf—54:417
Marranos—47:184, 246, 249
Marriage—1:69, 96, 106, 116–118, 133–138, 142, 168, 198, 200f, 233, 238–240, 282, 312f, 339, 355, 357, 2:8–10, 18, 25, 30, 32, 36, 38, 55, 57, 76, 92, 131, 240f, 254, 256, 274, 301, 306, 329, 377, 3:12, 14, 16, 42f, 45, 47f, 53–55, 58, 121, 202, 204, 210f, 214, 251, 256, 259, 269, 277, 329, 331, 354, 4:6, 8, 11, 21–23, 37, 72–74, 92, 94, 127, 134, 185, 188, 218, 222–228, 232–234, 238, 242f, 246f, 250f, 253, 257, 262, 274–277, 280, 290–294, 298f, 301, 303, 306, 333, 335–338, 352, 5:4–6, 8, 31–34, 36–38, 52, 57, 85, 91, 109, 166–168, 172, 174f, 180, 182, 188–193, 195f, 198, 267, 282, 289–291, 296–298, 301–304, 306, 324, 328–330, 332, 339, 345f, 348f, 354, 356–358, 363, 6:74, 179, 188f, 198f, 246f, 369f, 7:5n, 7–9, 16–19, 22f, 25, 27f, 30, 33f, 50f, 79, 85, 143, 146, 194, 197, 199f, 223, 8:59, 61–63, 85, 114, 134, 206, 212, 9:74, 79, 84, 211, 214, 223, 230, 233, 12:260, 348f, 15:4, 35, 106, 198, 17:143, 262, 18:402–407, 21:87, 89, 93, 95–97, 263, 22:91, 94, 100, 110, 140, 217, 442, 470f, 23:67, 266, 293, 24:162, 246, 377, 25:13, 55, 57–59, 166, 320, 332f, 26:141, 216n, 243, 364, 390, 428, 434, 444, 27:69, 127f, 138, 148, 400, 28:ixf, 3, 5f, 9, 11–20, 24, 26–35, 37, 41, 50–52, 54, 79, 124, 172, 312, 315, 342f, 352, 29:21, 44, 55f, 64, 237, 30:40, 88, 92, 95, 106f, 139, 173, 193, 250, 313, 32:211f, 34:41, 48f, 55, 66, 92, 94, 350, 357, 35:41, 136f, 376, 381f, 36:48, 76, 79f, 92–106, 212f, 37:364, 370, 38:154f, 39:89f, 275f, 278f, 289–294, 40:266, 301, 41:43n, 78, 122, 156–164, 197, 204, 222, 238, 241, 272, 301, 337n, 44:xivf, 5, 7–14, 183f, 246, 313–315, 341, 391, 394, 45:xi, 7f, 13n, 14n, 15, 17, 20, 22f, 28n, 38, 144–157, 319, 323f, 367, 381–393, 46:181–183, 198, 210, 220, 227, 261f, 265–320, 274n, 47:52, 49:85, 92f, 168, 218, 50:33f, 49n, 309, 51:79–81, 84, 116, 147, 154, 357–367, 52:124f, 133, 218f, 220, 227, 230, 246, 250, 260f, 263, 268, 273, 284, 53:93, 106, 110–115, 173, 209, 242, 54:24f, 31, 64–67, 80, 138, 141f, 151, 161, 171, 176f, 181, 191, 194, 218, 222–224, 244, 271, 289, 294f, 301f, 305, 315, 416, 422, 424, 441, 444, 449, 455f, 459, see also **Clergy, Marriage of**
Among the Turks 46:181–183, 195, 294n
Church laws on 45:145, 148, 150, 152f, 158
Dissolution and remarriage 36:105n, 46:262, 277, 295, 311f, 314, 316

Impediments to 4:288, 289n, 6:293f, 36:96n, 98–104, 105n, 40:301, 45:xi, 7n, 15, 22n, 23–30, 46:262n, 281, 310, 315f
Its troubles and discomforts 4:226, 264, 292, 294, 305
Problems of 46:xiv, 261, 270f, 310
St. Paul's teaching 36:93f
Marriage, Levirate—see **Levirate marriage**
Marriage, Love in—1:104, 134
Marriage, Order of, for Common Pastors—see **Luther, Martin, Writings of**
Marriage, Parental consent in—4:72
Marriage, Secret—5:194
Marriage as allegory—25:332
Marriage feast—36:185
Marriageable age—4:335f
Marriages, Second—4:304, 307
Married life—1:117, 135, 139, 238–240, 45:xi, 14, 17–49, 101f, 141, 143n, 144n, 145–157, 385
Married persons—36:78n, 206, 213
Mars—5:349, 6:113, 17:24, 382, 29:144, 46:182n
Marsyas—25:17
Martens, Dirk—48:55n, 155n
Martha—7:174, 294, 9:25, 10:127, 204, 254, 22:128, 23:247, 251, 26:214, 28:53, 42:8n
Martha and Mary—51:46, 48
Martial—3:312, 4:291
Epigrams 4:329n, 7:90n, 13:76n, 14:235n
Martin V, Pope—41:265n, 44:91n, 45:163, 295n, 297n
Martin, Raymond—47:130f, 153n, 188n, 191, 222n
Martin of Leon—*Expositio in epistolam B. Petri* 30:73n
Martin of Tours, St.—1:179, 275, 7:272, 17:78, 24:369f, 25:460, 30:133, 296, 32:116f, 41:40n, 94n, 308, 51:306
Martyrdom—1:288, 2:270n, 4:334, 7:88n, 92, 8:7, 21, 180, 266, 9:138, 11:109, 23:301, 24:118n, 27:350, 30:239, 31:111, 199n, 215, 35:60, 343, 402, 43:73–75, 143, 174, 276n
Martyrs—1:335, 2:7f, 12, 21, 217, 230, 3:125n, 264, 4:41, 103, 126, 205, 334, 356–358, 5:54, 59, 90, 131, 156, 6:70, 124, 221, 255, 282, 363, 390, 7:80f, 99, 103, 130f, 254, 8:7, 52, 191, 226, 249, 251, 255f, 260, 9:5n, 55n, 10:286–289, 340f, 360f, 11:405f, 423–425, 467, 476f, 550, 552, 12:174, 176f, 13:24f, 281, 333, 14:16, 49, 73, 87, 292, 303, 339, 17:186f, 205, 312, 327, 20:27, 132, 21:110, 156, 22:472, 499, 23:145, 202–204, 327, 359, 24:77, 118, 122, 131, 138, 146, 171, 196f, 269, 277, 319, 400, 420, 422, 26:23n, 175, 198n, 27:8, 164, 195, 280, 296, 350, 374, 29:11, 19, 150, 30:127, 137, 31:226, 33:100f, 36:69, 37:122, 38:78, 172, 192, 203, 289, 293n, 303f, 41:44, 52n, 322, 325, 354f, 42:100n, 129, 44:112, 45:99, 276, 347n, 371n, 46:40, 48, 53f, 81, 149, 48:31n, 33n, 280, 52:271, 276f
Martyrs, Lutheran—45:347n
Martyrs, Protestant—9:5n, 13:336n
Martyrs, Reformation—32:xviii, 261–287
Martyrs of the Reformation—see **Rule, William H.**
Mary, Mother of James and Joses—27:195f, 37:298
Mary, Queen of Hungary—14:x, 209
Mary, Virgin—1:79, 109, 146, 180, 191–196, 235n, 243, 256, 297, 2:4, 28, 35, 48, 54, 72n, 114, 118, 217, 265, 312, 3:29, 109, 115, 136, 145, 152, 206, 241, 276, 4:94, 129, 151, 161, 174, 189, 269, 5:20, 161, 218, 220, 222, 234, 272, 316, 346f, 349, 363, 6:102, 226, 231, 249, 323, 336, 338, 7:202, 299, 329, 8:139, 164, 203, 242, 9:25, 71n, 11:152f, 172, 180, 185, 366f, 418, 470, 12:149, 13:326, 14:23, 101, 288, 15:225, 16:332, 17:125, 142, 160, 338, 405, 20:41, 168, 208, 219, 21:96f, 243, 272, 298f, 301–303, 307–311, 315–318, 321–323, 326f, 329–331, 335, 342, 344, 346, 350, 352–355, 357, 22:14, 18, 20, 22–25, 37, 47, 73–76, 101, 103, 107–113, 116, 118, 130, 136, 142, 146, 165, 214, 215n, 239, 248, 314, 321, 323–329, 332–334, 346f, 350–353, 356, 361–366, 368f, 377, 388, 390f, 393f, 421, 453, 467–468, 473, 476f, 485, 490, 492, 494, 496–498, 503, 526, 23:14, 16f, 55, 57, 59, 64, 67, 80f, 83, 89, 101–106, 108f, 111, 115, 120, 122f, 129, 135, 137, 139, 161f, 166f, 226, 241n, 244, 251, 283, 306n, 333, 335, 342, 366, 377, 409f, 24:24, 33f, 62, 69, 74, 76, 92, 96–98, 105–108, 139, 232, 307, 320f, 348, 369, 25:4, 129, 209, 218, 366, 438, 26:154, 214, 286, 367, 422, 460, 27:81, 195, 288, 28:247, 29:84, 114, 166, 190f, 201f, 30:10f, 26, 50, 174, 210, 221, 223, 265, 285, 288, 291, 31:173, 240, 273, 353, 368, 32:40, 79f, 128n,

157, 172, 282, 34:26f, 54, 207, 209, 35:190, 192, 275, 296, 36:299, 341, 37:37, 49, 61f, 72, 76f, 82, 84f, 89f, 92, 94, 98f, 103, 110, 172, 236f, 260n, 280, 305f, 361f, 38:20n, 22f, 25, 30, 56, 59, 61, 86, 150f, 173n, 192, 197, 200, 206, 224, 253, 255n, 256, 263, 275, 290, 307n, 310, 40:88, 96, 312, 390, 41:95–101, 104–106, 109f, 119, 144, 157, 204, 233, 264n, 326, 42:6, 8, 98, 101, 113n, 43:26f, 39f, 154n, 44:86, 182, 45:xv, 197–213, 46:141, 176f, 221, 289, 300, 311, 47:45–48, 83n, 111, 137, 139, 222, 254, 257–263, 267, 274, 279, 285, 291, 50:20, 302, 51:58, 62, 165, 212–218, 375, 390, 52:9f, 15, 31, 33, 37, 39f, 53, 81, 86, 103f, 107f, 111, 118f, 125, 128, 140f, 163, 171, 198, 53:28, 268, 54:15, 32, 84f, 247, 301, 329, 341, 420, 426

Called Holy Mother 1:235

Called Mother of God 21:308, 311, 322f, 326f, 329–332, 335, 346, 352, 355, 357

Called Queen of Heaven 21:327

Her perpetual virginity 24:320

Mary, Wife of James or Cleophas—27:195, 30:203

Mary Magdalene, St.—2:321, 3:263, 6:326, 337, 371, 10:92, 11:510, 512, 541n, 14:151, 346, 17:402, 22:104, 192, 23:247n, 251, 268, 26:43, 34:313, 35:190, 37:66, 76, 298, 42:64

Mary Magdalene's, St., Day—23:259n

Mary of Bethany, St.—11:541n

Mary of Burgundy, Princess—15:193n, 47:223

Mary of Württemberg—41:183

Mary Tudor, Queen of England—50:32f, 121, 127, 192

Masks—1:15, 2:79, 343, 4:5, 7, 33f, 53, 61–66, 159, 404, 5:135, 147, 268, 271, 7:180, 184f, 187, 190f, 238, 311, 315, 344, 371, 8:31, 33, 182, 185, 9:7, 41, 75n, 96, 109, 203, 12:193, 312f, 330, 378, 380, 13:197, 315, 14:114f, 16:9, 22, 229, 17:127, 213, 339, 21:61, 253–256, 281, 22:452, 23:75, 393, 24:67f, 264, 312, 26:95n, 96, 104, 170, 202, 256, 263, 284, 298, 321, 323f, 27:12, 17, 31, 43f, 281, 342, 351, 408, 30:212, 32:166, 37:128, 39:113, 213, 248f, 253, 270, 272, 274, 314, 40:13, 27, 126, 41:142, 291, 295, 339, 43:282, 45:331, 375, 51:251

Masons—13:268

Masquerade—22:123

Mass, The—1:250, 258, 2:65, 86, 273, 284, 290, 333n, 383, 385, 387, 3:128, 168, 215, 217, 267, 4:53, 201, 203n, 236n, 237, 398, 400, 5:137n, 157, 6:186, 228, 237, 240, 404, 7:247n, 296–299, 313, 8:182, 230, 267, 326, 9:322, 11:29, 12:400, 13:27, 313f, 324f, 327, 363, 366, 371f, 14:6, 23, 25f, 33, 76, 294f, 16:x, 76, 216, 225, 310, 312, 17:9, 25, 27, 49, 78, 173, 188, 266, 278, 283, 293f, 296, 301f, 400, 402, 18:153, 309, 396, 20:267f, 21:38, 68f, 81, 165, 183, 204f, 272, 285, 22:36, 64, 102, 135, 158, 220, 254, 267f, 278, 280, 333n, 366, 370, 387, 392, 394, 398, 405, 407, 410, 429, 515, 23:25, 85, 127, 136, 138, 154, 174, 207, 213, 264, 268, 271, 357, 366, 370, 378, 408, 411, 413, 24:38, 69, 98, 119, 121, 127, 130, 172, 229, 232, 242–244, 265, 268, 275, 279, 309, 325, 328, 363, 367, 369, 25:123, 234, 490, 26:32, 41, 70, 105, 124, 135, 140, 154, 180, 199, 221–223, 305, 27:124, 135, 28:241, 243, 312, 315, 29:6f, 9, 21, 28, 42, 45f, 58, 72, 123n, 30:61, 83, 98, 170, 174, 183f, 207, 233, 253, 280, 282, 287, 300, 31:211, 34:22f, 26, 30, 31n, 54, 82–86, 349, 355, 357, 35:13, 54, 61, 63, 65f, 72, 81f, 86f, 90, 92n, 93f, 100, 102, 105, 107n, 109f, 36:22, 35n, 36–38, 40–57, 113–115, 129–131, 134f, 143f, 147, 160f, 166, 171, 178, 180, 184, 195, 198, 203, 211, 218, 226, 257, 260, 278n, 302, 319n, 37:142–144, 322, 369–371, 38:ix, xvf, 27, 73, 88, 110, 114n, 118n, 121, 123, 142, 144, 151n, 153–155, 159, 165–169, 173, 175, 177, 181, 183, 203–205, 208–210, 213f, 224, 226–228, 230–233, 293, 310, 313n, 318, 39:22n, 38f, 41, 89, 195n, 40:119f, 121–123, 138, 141, 299, 41:33, 111, 169, 172, 199, 203, 215, 241, 271, 273, 283, 336, 340, 42:xvi, 8n, 11, 14, 57f, 146, 173–175, 44:54f, 180n, 181n, 191, 334f, 371f, 45:53–55, 72, 161n, 165, 180n, 284, 306, 351, 46:163n, 167, 172, 204, 209f, 221, 229, 303, 47:39, 43f, 53, 48:3f, 39n, 79n, 114n, 152n, 281, 317, 324f, 338n, 364n, 382n, 401, 49:11, 31n, 56, 204f, 263, 328n, 35ln, 378n, 380, 391, 408f, 416n, 421, 51:65, 69, 73, 75–77, 84, 124, 217, 226, 345, 52:27, 178, 222, 228f, 248, 254, 271f, 275, 53:13, 20, 25, 48, 321, 54:13, 20, 161, 182, 215, 234, 264–266, 295, 324f, 340, 354, 392f, 461, see also **Canon of the Mass**

Attendance at 51:64, 145, 261–263
Ceremonies see **Ceremonies of the Mass**
Daily 53:13
Frequency of celebration 36:37, 198, 278n
German 53:51–90
German language 35:90
Its abrogation 36:xii, 130, 133, 147, 309–311
Language 36:54, 254
Latin 53:91–40, 62f, 89f
Presanctified 53:24n
Propers of 53:xiv, 21, 38
Secret prayers 35:90
Votive 53:22

Mass, Canon of the—see **Canon of the Mass**
Mass, Evangelical—see **Lord's Supper, Evangelical**
Mass, High—24:21
Mass, Low—see **Mass, Private**
Mass, Private—24:281, 27:84, 89, 36:55n, 309–316, 36:x, xii, 54n, 105, 130, 257, 309–316, 38:xvf, 123, 134n, 141n, 143f, 149, 152–154, 156, 158f, 162–166, 168–170, 173, 176, 179–181, 183, 185f, 188, 193f, 203, 205, 209, 211, 213, 218, 225f, 45:161n, 51:75, 79, 53:9, see also **Hedge masses**
Mass, Requiem—see **Mass for the dead**
Mass, Sacrifice of the—35:47, 77f, 94f, 97f, 36:ix, xii, 7, 35, 37, 47–56, 114, 129–131, 142, 147f, 154, 161–198, 203, 226, 254, 260, 313–327, 38:xv, 51, 110, 117f, 121, 226f, 232, 313, 314n, 315, 40:14f, 28, 41:335f, 53:xiii, 21f, 26, 29, 122
Mass, Secret—see **Mass, Private**
Mass for the dead—23:138n, 28:315, 31:247f, 35:85, 91, 101f, 108n, 36:xif, 36n, 55n, 178, 191–193, 197, 45:180n, 47:82, 51:231, 385, 53:325–327
Mass lessons—see **Gospels and Epistles (Liturgical)**
Mass of perdition—11:468n, 25:156, 348, 386, 391, 394, 27:275n
Mass priests—36:144, 161, 171, 175, 177f, 181, 185, 189, 191
Massa perditionis—see **Mass of perdition**
Massah—9:75, 305
Masses, Endowed—36:203n, 226
Massie, Richard—*Martin Luther's Spiritual Songs*, London, 1854 53:xviii, 173, 199, 213, 233, 249, 299
Massilianism—34:209n
Masson, Jacobus—see **Latomus, James (Jacobus Masson)**
Master Eisleben—see **Agricola, John**
Master Jack (Hangman)—43:133
Master Smart Aleck—21:210n, 211–213, 219f, 332f, 343f
Master of Arts—8:276n
Master of the Sentences—see **Peter Lombard**
Masters and mistresses—29:60–66, 71, 77, 93, 100, 103, 149, 185, 232, 240, 51:140, 144, 148
Material things—15:4, 8f, 11, 13, 20, 31, 49, 88, 164, 40:70, 117, 148, 45:xii, xivf, 47f, 342
Material things, Use of—10:460, 12:80, 135, 161
Materialism—2:390n
Maternity—3:44, 7:28
Mathematical point—17:239
Mathematicians—9:109
Mathematics—1:27, 46, 2:67, 22:59n, 37:109, 278, 281, 38:45, 67, 75, 45:369n, 49:140, 220n
Mathesius, John—5:x, 8:x, 17:ix, 24:x, 38:xix, 39:129n, 42:17, 47:59, 191n, 54:x, xii, xvi, xvii, xviii, xxii, 367, 360, 393, 405, 413
D. Martin Luther's Leben in Siebzehn Predigten, Leipzig, 1887 38:xixn
recorder of Luther's table conversation, 1540 54:365–410
Matins—11:259, 455n, 525n, 51:295, 53:9, 12, 25, 38, 53, 68f, 78, 153, 171, 173, see also **Canonical Hours**
Matriarchs—4:187, 189, 272, 362, 7:46, 200f
Matricides—7:243, 256
Matrimony—see **Marriage**
Matrons—3:201, 211, 7:45f, 95, 201, 218, 310, 8:85, 110, 175, 29:54f, 60, 65
Mattathias—19:226
Matter—38:241, 246, 270f
Matter, Primary and secondary—1:6n, 8, 16
Matthew, St., Apostle and Evangelist—5:216, 294, 14:257, 262f, 20:125, 128f, 251, 318, 321f, 22:37, 107, 159f, 172, 182, 215, 217–219, 23:ix, 108f, 268n, 25:148, 26:101, 27:165, 185, 196, 310, 38:201, 41:92, 320, 324, 52:30, 144, 185, 206
Matthew, St., Gospel according to—5:216, 294
Matthias Corvinus, King of Hungary—2:319, 8:103, 13:172, 15:70f
Mattocks—24:194, 198f
Maugis, Ferdinand von—54:xiii

Maundy Thursday—4:282, 13:413, 26:45n, 30:207n
Maurer, Wilhelm—39:xvn, 47:61n, 126, 136n, 226n
Mauretania—10:412
Maurice I, Emperor—41:90n, 243f, 277n, 292
Maurice, Duke of Saxony—5:x, 43:259n, 261n, 48:33n, 54:473
Maurice, St.—41:35n, 38n, 45:99n
Maurice, St., and the Theban legion—41:35n, 38n
Mauritania—2:194
Mauritanians—2:203
Maurus, Nicholas—43:74, 79
Maxentius—31:219n
Maximilian I, Emperor—1:70, 212, 2:137, 3:41n, 6:334, 7:198, 8:105f, 205, 13:149, 214f, 219, 16:259, 349n, 29:77, 31:xviif, 255f, 285n, 287, 32:150n, 34:83n, 272, 330, 332, 36:229n, 38:27, 41:230n, 231, 276n, 372n, 376n, 44:195n, 46:108n, 116, 168, 249n, 47:223, 48:71f, 74, 93n, 96f, 99n, 104n, 163n, 175f, 194n, 49:21n, 125n, 126n, 240n, 427, 50:73, 206, 311n, 54:416, 420
The Dangers and Adventures of the Famous Hero and Knight Sir Teuerdank 15:193n
Maximilian II, Emperor—49:81n, 54:x, 213
Maximinus—31:219n
May, Gerhard, ed.—*Das Marburger Religionsgespräch 1529* (in Gerhard Ruhbach, ed., *Texte zur Kirche- und Theologiegeschichte*, 13, Gütersloh, 1970) 38:62n
Mazzolini—see **Prierias**
McCord, James I.—see **Empie, Paul C., and James I. McCord, eds.**
McDonough, Thomas M.—54:107n
McNeill, John T.—47:89n
History and Character of Calvinism, New York, 1954 37:81n
History and Character of Calvinism, New York, 1967 38:6n
McSorley, H. J.—*Luther: Right or Wrong? An Ecumenical-Theological Study of Luther's Major Work, The Bondage of the Will*, New York, 1969 33:38n, 66n, 103n, 112n
Meadows—23:225, 255
Means of grace—1:309, 2:197, 3:29f, 37, 107–111, 124, 146, 155, 165, 168, 220, 4:373, 405, 6:128, 149, 257, 308, 398, 7:132, 299, 344, 8:33, 166, 182, 184–187, 271, 12:119, 151, 156, 159, 170, 173, 255f, 259f, 262, 266, 277f, 297, 363, 13:90, 139, 272, 282, 303, 324, 342, 14:13, 55f, 91, 132, 15:276, 20:83, 172, 21:151, 22:202, 204, 304, 308, 314, 420f, 471, 507f, 513, 23:15, 226, 235, 257, 285, 24:79, 85, 109, 127, 131, 145, 151, 168, 171, 175, 178f, 183, 185, 221, 228, 230, 274, 310, 368, 394, 28:135, 141, 231, 269f, 29:83, 37:xviiif, 95, 135, 137, 140f, 188, 192, 357, 265f, 368, 370, 41:172, 52:222, see also **God**—His ordinances
Measure, Just—9:249
Measurements used in l6th century—19:208
Measuring line—20:25f, 181f
Meat—1:36, 72, 2:76, 134, 137, 141, 231, 338f, 355, 3:202, 325, 364, 4:41, 134, 245, 338, 396, 5:6, 137, 232, 7:107f, 158, 199, 344, 350f, 8:172, 174, 185, 302, 321, 9:124, 141, 24:35, 38, 106, 172, 175, 232, 26:85, 118, 405, 428, 29:41, 45, 47, 30:28, 40, 248, 35:379, 41:29, 129n, 340, 46:189, 204
Mechlin—34:345, 353
Mechtild of Magdeburg—6:132n, 17:30n, 214n, 30:255
Medea—2:219
Medes—1:323, 2:188f, 365, 7:40, 16:125, 133, 135, 137, 141, 170, 172, 316, 17:72, 18:151, 20:15, 85, 112, 193, 251, 35:295
Media (land of the Medes)—2:206n, 16:307, 20:95, 250, 47:203f
***Media vita* (hymn)**—10:337, 13:83n, 16:207n, 19:15, 53:274f
Mediator—see **Christ**—Mediator
Mediators—30:10, 12, 29, 39, 65, 152, 225, 236, 261, 285f
Medical knowledge—6:182
Medicine—1:94, 130, 2:77, 156, 170, 339f, 3:216, 223f, 232, 271, 358, 4:76, 250, 7:79, 113, 256, 308, 323, 16:342, 344, 23:13, 114, 203, 337, 24:198, 205, 26:416f, 43:131, 45:342, 376, 46:209, 252f, 319, 54:53f, 102f, 237, 266, 277
Medicine, Spiritual—42:183, 186, see also **Antidote**
Medieval man—42:xv
Meditation—10:17–20, 184, 305, 11:12, 14–16, 23, 422, 431f, 434f, 512f, 533, 46:89f
Mediterranean Sea—1:99, 2:187, 189, 194, 205, 365, 8:273, 10:412, 16:33, 17:72, 314, 317, 413f, 18:61, 103, 19:9, 52:163

Mediums—16:307
Medler, Nicholas—34:107, 50:86n, 103n, 108n, 53:184, 54:xiii, 117, 147, 396
Medo-Persian kings—18:368, 20:6n
Medusa—17:54
Meekness—10:221–223, 21:23–25, 27:106f, 109, 111, 44:100–103
Megiddo—20:141, 329
Mehetabel—6:293, 309
Mehujael—1:303, 315f
Meier, Kurt—47:127n
Meinhold, Peter—1:x–xii, 13n, 37n, 191n, 204n, 214n, 280n, 334n, 3:x, 5:ixf, 6:x, 22:x, 27:24n
Die Genesisvorlesung Luthers und ihre Herausgeber 8:134n
Meissen—4:130, 8:198, 11:105, 13:170, 206, 14:280, 16:308, 27:315, 35:47, 38:119n, 145, 45:112n, 54:351, 388
Meissen, Bishop of—39:82n, 299n, 45:5, 13, 162f, 49:389
Meissen, Nobility of—50:223n, 224, 312
Meissinger, K.A.—27:ix
Erasmus von Rotterdam, Berlin, 1948 33:5n, 8n
Meister Hans—13:66, 203
see **Jack Ketch**
Meister Kluegel—see **Master Smart Aleck**
Meistersang—53:196, 198
Melancholia—5:133f, 300
Melancholy—7:239, 54:15–18, 74f, 95f, 203, 275f
Melanchthon, Anna—54:268
Melanchthon, Catharine—48:166n, 217, 303n, 308
Melanchthon, Philip—1:xif, 25n, 27n, 28n, 2:207n, 242n, 3:x, 19n, 103n, 262n, 263n, 303n, 4:372, 4:ixf, 220n, 266n, 372, 5:ix, 73n, 9:ix, 32n, 12:ixf, 139, 12:viii–x, 13:122n, 14:xi, 281n, 15:x, 16:42n, 18:ix, 21:xixf, 22:59n, 23:ix, xi, 25:xii, 26:216n, 27:x, 377, 28:x, 3, 294, 32:xvi, 34:xiv, xvii, 5–7, 37n, 80n, 108, 127, 147, 199, 291, 301, 320, 327, 331, 341, 35:177f, 188, 206, 36:x, xii, 129, 37:5, 147n, 149, 155, 360, 364n, 38:xviiif, 7–10, 22f, 26f, 30n, 37, 41, 57, 63, 71, 74, 89n, 93f, 137n, 141n, 167n, 237, 284, 39:110n, 227, 242f, 40:76, 106n, 227, 272, 275n, 350n, 41:8, 23n, 115n, 116n, 159n, 167n, 42:64n, 43:83n, 169f, 181f, 191, 235n, 260n, 44:xi, 18, 120n, 245f, 45:8n, 77n, 127n, 128n, 137f, 161n, 188n, 224n, 241n, 343, 382n, 46:6n, 47, 210, 214n, 263, 47:5, 8, 15n, 20n, 29n, 30n, 32f, 101–103, 106, 107n, 116n, 123f, 264n, 48:xix, 55n, 63n, 77n, 78, 83n, 107, 111, 119, 122n, 123n, 134n, 136n, 143n, 148, 150, 162, 164n, 165f, 184, 210, 213, 215, 219, 221, 222n, 228, 230n, 232, 238f, 242f, 254n, 256, 264, 267n, 269, 277, 283, 290n, 292f, 296, 305n, 308f, 310f, 314, 316, 321, 322n, 323f, 337, 344f, 352f, 356n, 359, 364, 49:xviii, 13–15, 15n, 33n, 43, 52, 74f, 77n, 79n, 81n, 101, 103n, 104n, 130f, 137n, 104n, 147, 168n, 180n, 190n, 195f, 205n, 211n, 214n, 224, 225n, 226n, 228, 231n, 235, 236n, 238n, 240n, 244n, 256n, 272n, 274, 281n, 282n, 283, 284n, 285n, 287f, 287n, 291n, 295, 296n, 297f, 298n, 299n, 310n, 313n, 315n, 316f, 320f, 324f, 334n, 335–337, 339n, 340–343, 348, 350n, 351n, 352, 354n, 355, 357, 367n, 368n, 370, 372f, 373n, 374n, 377n, 378f, 391f, 394n, 395n, 397n, 399, 400n, 401n, 405n, 406n, 408n, 409n, 413n, 414n, 418n, 420n, 423, 431n, 50:xix, 47n, 68, 69n, 76n, 80n, 86n, 145n, 154, 156n, 163n, 207n, 209n, 210n, 211n, 212n, 216n, 222n, 229n, 231, 248, 250, 253n, 254n, 263n, 269n, 288n, 51:xivn, xv, 69, 77, 103, 197, 259, 303, 53:67, 275, 321, 54:ix, xi, 23f, 33f, 44, 50, 54, 64, 79, 89, 132f, 153, 155f, 158, 162, 173, 184, 187, 191, 209, 214, 217, 219f, 222, 224–225, 231, 233, 245f, 257f, 260, 268, 277, 287, 290f, 319, 331, 355f, 358, 360, 364, 371, 376–378, 380, 383, 387, 390, 393, 416, 431f, 440, 442, 449, 454
and England 50:28n, 31n, 33n, 98, 101n, 103n, 104n, 105, 106, 113f, 120f, 124n, 133n, 134n, 142n, 150n, 177f, 178n, 179n, 180n, 192, 195, 196n, 198n, 200n, 203n, 205
and France 50:, 87n, 88f, 98n, 101, 103, 106n
and Wittenberg University 50:56n, 61, 63, 67, 75, 78, 85n, 87n, 93n, 103n, 107n, 108n, 111n, 112, 118, 196n, 203f, 274f, 280n
relationship with Luther 50:11n, 43, 80, 87n, 89f, 101, 105, 107n, 108, 111n, 112, 113n, 144, 166n, 167n, 182, 208f, 210n, 212, 215, 50:219, 222, 258, 260, 263n, 269n, 274n, 280n, 281, 287n, 288, 291n, 292f, 295f, 297f, 300n, 303f, 307f, 312, 313f, 316f, 318
uses pseudonym Faventinus Didymus 39:110n
Melanchthon, Philip, Jr.—40:324

Melanchthon, Philip, Writings of—see also ***Wittenberg Articles***
Adversus Furiosum Parisiensium Theologastrorum Decretum, Phillipi Melanchthonis Pro Luther Apologia, 1521 36:276n, 277
Annotations on the Gospel of John 37:360, 38:26n
Annotations to Genesis 49:23n
Annotations to the Gospel Lessons, 1540 50:300
Answer given to papal nuncio in Smalcald, 1537 50:128n
Apology of the Augsburg Confession 2:266n, 8:110n, 9:24n, 22:444, 23:16n, 17n, 30:123n, 32:225n, 37:370n, 39:45n, 53, 110, 47:32n, 108f, 48:77n, 49:423f, 54:187, 358
Articles of Visitation 40:266, 47:101, 107n, 49:168n
Augsburg Confession 1:27n, 14:xi, 23:219n, 293n, 31:193n, 34:xiif, 6, 41n, 68n, 70n, 71, 80n, 37:61n, 81n, 120n, 157, 361n, 363n, 364n, 367n, 368n, 369n, 370n, 371n, 40:149n, 41:xiin, 18n, 116n, 167n, 362n, 43:181, 46:6n, 47:ix, 5, 22–28, 31, 42n, 108n, 109, 116n, 48:77n, 275n, 49:xvii, 51f, 87n, 282n, 296–298, 299n, 328n, 330, 343–346, 348, 349n, 350n, 351n, 353f, 354n, 359f, 362n, 368n, 374n, 375n, 391f, 397n, 403f, 404n, 423f, 435n, 50:3, 104n, 106n, 134n, 140n, 142n, 210n, 51:197, 54:34, 39, 137, 139, 186–187, 355f, 358, 362
Commonplaces (Loci communes) 33:16n, 34:327n, 48:232, 258n, 288, 297f, 320, 355, 49:331n
Das die Preester Eeweyber nemen mögen und sollen 44:246n
Defense 48:258n, 270, 289n, 315n, 320
Expostulatio 50:203n
Instructions for the Visitors of Parish Pastors in Electoral Saxony 47:101f, 49:168n, 180n, 182n, 50:63n
Letter to Erasmus 33:10
On True and Scholastic Theology 48:151n
The Passion of Christ and Antichrist 48:230n
Melanchthonian theology—1:xi
Melchizedek—2:358, 381–394, 3:35, 234, 267, 4:15, 151, 176, 383n, 7:21n, 42, 8:111, 11:368f, 393, 13:228, 304, 306, 309–315, 29:173f, 188f, 36:182, 188f, 321, 38:187, 39:81, 40:19
Meldorf—32:263–285, 48:236n
Mellerstadt, Dr. Martin Pollrich von—30:287
Melting—10:455f
Members—28:184f
Memmingen—34:80n, 46:8n, 48:247n
Augustinian Monastery 48:11
Memorial days—36:36n
Memorial sign—37:xiif, 18, 41, 73n, 141, 142n, 144
Memorials—6:79f, 128, 273, 25:450, 475
Memory—8:110, 11:11, 15–17, 388f, 17:367, 37:273, 279
Memphis—7:208, 270, 16:162
Menander—*Fragments* 4:243n
Monostichoi 5:341n
Thais 28:161n
Mendicancy—see **Begging**
Mendicant orders—2:328, 330, 9:147, 29:34, 36:220, 229n, 42:60n, 44:109f, 172f, 172n, 173n, 189f, 48:16, see also **Friars**
Meni—17:383
Menius, Justus—8:ix, 13:x, 27:130n, 34:108, 342, 40:383n, 46:210n, 263, 49:172n, 50:99n, 212n, 218n, 53:59, 54:50
Menstruation—27:220
Mentel, Johann—35:357n
Mentel Bible—35:357n
Mephibosheth—11:248, 12:237, 13:206
Merbecke, John—*Book of Common Prayer Noted,* 1550 53:149
Mercenaries—21:319, 41:36, 37n, 39f, 46:127n, 134, 49:110, 241n, 242n, 317
Merchandise, merchandizing—9:249, 21:235–237
Merchants—2:124, 194, 3:251, 4:216, 6:165, 7:6, 160, 164, 286, 8:120, 12:354, 45:240, 245f, 247n, 248, 250, 256, 260–262, 264–270, 272, 302, 46:215, 244, 312
Mercury—1:30, 17:316, 383, 20:60, 233, 25:11, 27:200, 353, 31:185, 188
Mercy—1:179, 189, 191, 200, 245, 249f, 258f, 275f, 289, 301, 306, 327, 330, 350, 352, 2:4, 16, 47, 51, 66, 71, 103, 118, 120, 149, 153, 162f, 170, 172, 175, 185f, 202, 228f, 240f, 245–248, 260, 263, 269, 276, 280, 289, 296, 306f, 310, 312, 323, 325, 333, 352, 358, 380, 398, 3:7f, 22f, 25, 33, 44, 49, 60, 65, 68f, 97, 115, 120, 128, 134, 140, 143, 145, 156–158, 166–168, 171f, 180, 221, 224f, 235, 237, 240, 242, 283, 287f, 292, 300, 305, 311, 327, 331f, 337, 345f, 348, 360, 4:43, 53, 55, 57–59, 65f, 73, 146–148, 160, 168f,

224, 228, 245, 261, 267, 294, 341, 363, 399, 404n, 5:56, 59, 74, 125, 140, 152, 154f, 157, 170, 181, 199, 219, 221, 255, 257, 277, 283, 307, 314, 316f, 319, 354, 358, 375, 6:92f, 97, 112–115, 220, 253, 354f, 7:10–12, 24, 28, 44, 47f, 57, 100, 111, 122, 131, 137, 144, 162, 175f, 196, 225f, 229f, 235, 237, 249, 251–254, 258f, 285f, 301, 316, 325, 334, 345, 360, 371, 373, 8:9, 17, 24, 26, 38–45, 51, 53, 65, 72, 74, 78, 139, 171, 176, 180, 189, 204, 227f, 231, 266, 268, 323f, 328–332, 9:16, 59f, 76, 83, 85–87, 96, 102–104, 112, 138, 146, 193–195, 198, 206, 10:39, 47, 53f, 202, 260, 302, 304–306, 367–369, 13:133, 152f, 407, 14:24f, 30, 50, 120, 122, 142f, 163, 166, 190, 192, 194, 197, 200, 203–205, 255, 264, 296, 320, 323, 345, 16:55, 80, 104, 145, 194, 198, 204, 289, 320, 17:6f, 14, 24, 26, 114, 127, 239, 252f, 279, 305, 319, 334, 356, 19:155n, 166, 20:20, 79, 86, 94, 132f, 137, 295, 304, 21:29, 125, 151f, 332–334, 341, 350, 23:12, 16, 26, 33, 76, 87, 98, 150, 183, 190, 195f, 216, 233f, 237, 240, 250, 257, 299, 310, 316, 319, 337, 339, 341, 24:8, 24, 52, 58, 61f, 71, 88f, 98, 150, 165, 180, 182, 197, 210, 218f, 222f, 228, 236, 259f, 268, 282, 284, 288, 306, 318, 337, 343, 392, 26:6, 37, 41, 48, 58f, 69, 72, 123, 175, 177f, 180, 183, 227, 229, 233, 235, 253, 265, 280f, 292, 310, 313, 322, 328f, 336, 339, 341, 352, 362, 367, 385, 396f, 460, 27:3, 15, 18, 44, 81, 100, 110, 113, 140, 142, 172, 174, 185, 220–222, 227, 266, 270, 274f, 286, 328, 345, 365f, 371, 374f, 388, 406, 409, 28:219, 225f, 243f, 248, 363, 29:50, 83, 85, 102, 104, 115, 128, 132, 142, 151, 169f, 176, 188, 194, 211, 219, 30:3, 9, 102, 104, 152, 214, 223, 233, 235, 267, 293, 312, 314, 36:39, 59, 169, 226, 46:65–75, 52:222, 229f, 252, see also **Christ**—His mercy

Mercy, Deeds of—25:106, 451, 462, 42:122

Mercy, God's Accidental—1:301n, 302–304, 306, 313–316, 325, 342, 6:281, 284, 295, 8:134n

Mercy, God's sharp—47:268, 272, 292

Mercy, Irregular—1:304

Mercy, Naked—25:137

Mercy of God—1:64, 107, 175, 180, 222, 248, 257, 265, 291, 304, 351, 359, 3:140, 7:99, 274, 9:103f, 11:159, 163–170, 174, 229, 233f, 281–284, 288, 312f, 319, 347, 349–351, 378f, 387f, 396, 410f, 438, 448, 457, 468, 497, 501, 513, 12:320f, 323–326, 331, 333, 335, 352, 358f, 371, 373, 381, 384, 387f, 390, 392, 398, 400, 408, 410, 13:5, 26f, 87, 132f, 136, 167, 373f, 406, 16:14f, 260, 325, 18:13, 61, 66, 96–100, 105, 112, 119, 128, 19:21, 28, 30, 46f, 51, 80, 91, 136, 155, 21:331, 325, 332–335, 25:28, 43, 81f, 84f, 106, 122, 137f, 179, 194, 270, 387, 391f, 27:5, 18, 44, 29:12, 15f, 79, 81f, 112, 188, 217, 31:64, 348, 360, 367, 32:44, 48, 83, 91, 172, 175, 209, 282f, 278, 285, 33:62, 289–292, 35:54, 143, 36:56, 86, 177, 187, 38:105, 223, 39:25, 36, 40f, 42:28, 42f, 63, 71, 74, 80, 87, 89f, 105, 115, 125, 129f, 132f, 150, 155f, 185n, 46:10, 66, 71, 79, 123f, 135, 47:132, 171, 239, 294, 302

Mercy seat—6:50, 127f, 11:96, 16:69, 17:61, 29:199, 201, 203–205, 37:364f

Meribah—13:80

Meribah, Waters of—9:305

Merit, Supererogatory—24:326

Merit of condignity—26:124–127, 131–135, 175f, 181, 183, 291, 293, 301, 330, 374f

Merit of congruity—26:124–127, 131–132, 134f, 172f, 175f, 181–183, 202, 210, 291, 293, 301, 330, 374f

Merits—2:122–124, 4:17, 35, 43f, 55, 59–63, 65f, 70, 109, 156–158, 162, 166, 168, 170, 361, 398, 400, 5:157, 258, 260, 316, 6:61, 67, 97, 114, 216f, 262, 7:228, 230n, 234, 359f, 362, 8:41, 161, 177f, 234, 267, 276, 332, 10:46, 11:396, 424, 532, 12:220, 314, 321, 353, 389, 394, 397, 13:325, 16:202, 329, 334, 17:3, 5f, 18, 100, 142, 157, 160, 162, 214, 252, 305, 18:277, 21:287–289, 322f, 327, 24:24, 36, 88, 258f, 282, 315, 325f, 328, 373, 397, 405, 25:35f, 75, 81, 96, 277, 360, 371, 377, 386, 26:6, 32–34, 38, 70, 124, 126, 132, 140, 149, 153f, 169, 177, 200, 265f, 280, 286, 295, 300, 302, 322, 328, 334, 371, 387f, 392, 394, 396, 460, 27:10, 19, 28, 140, 174, 179, 189, 203, 221, 240, 249, 251, 263, 266, 270, 328f, 372, 388, 29:12f, 80f, 219, 232, 30:3, 7, 18, 29, 106, 143, 174, 214, 235, 261, 265, 270, 294, 301, 31:138, 176, 212–229, 261, 264, 266–270, 282–284, 32:62–64, 97, 33:147, 149–155, 211, 266–270, 34:15n, 17,

171n, 173, 35:39, 89, 136, 143, 237, 364, 368n, 36:51, 84, 215n, 37:369, 372, 38:86, 101, 106–108, 114f, 117, 124f, 134, 175, 204, 248n, 316, 41:147, 200f, 204, 213, 215, 42:62, 88, 140n, 44:285, 287f, 46:95, 173, 254
Merits, Treasury of—26:126, 48:44, 84f
Merodach-baladan—16:346, 347n
Merom, Waters of—2:34, 19:234
Merseburg—31:381, 35:47, 50:275n, 276f, 280n, 51:357
Merseburg, Bishop of—31:319n, 48:152n, 164n, 183n, 49:23, 389
Mertz, George Karl—25:xiv, 35:158n, 230n, 47:63, 106, 136, 51:xxi
Das Schulwesen der deutschen Reformationzeit im 16. jahrhundert, Heidelberg, 1902 45:345
Meshech—2:189
Mesopotamia—1:89, 2:206, 240f, 277, 279, 4:139, 185f, 261, 298, 333, 5:99, 175, 210, 252, 280f, 339, 6:36, 39, 66, 89, 96, 98, 102, 110, 124, 179, 187, 190, 224, 234, 256, 282, 288–290, 306, 308f, 340, 7:4, 25, 270, 8:151, 17:33f, 22:200, 208, 48:67
Messengers—6:96, 100, 18:377, 30:5, 64, 177, 185
Messiah, The—2:264, 326, 397, 3:36f, 92, 4:150f, 351, 374n, 5:94, 157, 294, 6:32, 136, 162, 248, 283, 7:12–15, 17, 37, 164, 231, 8:191f, 211, 217, 239, 241, 243, 247, 251f, 284n, 285, 288, 304, 307, 316, 11:413, 12:104, 266, 14:19, 15:271f, 278–281, 283, 290, 298f, 341, 350, 16:95, 97n, 17:216, 219, 307, 330, 18:410, 22:41–43, 45, 47f, 53, 77–79, 125, 128, 156, 159f, 175, 184f, 187–189, 191, 194f, 198–200, 222, 230, 239f, 244, 251, 284f, 419, 427, 429, 432, 438f, 448–450, 463, 465–467, 477, 485–487, 505, 510f, 23:38, 195, 243–245, 261, 267, 281, 296, 396, 24:396, 26:210, 328, 27:146, 29:33, 30:270, 34:304, 35:288f, 38:xi, 41:119, 314, 45:213, 214n, 215f, 220–224, 226, 227n, 228f, 46:9, 47:6, 68–70, 73–75, 77–80, 82f, 85f, 88, 94, 132f, 139, 163, 176–254, 263, 281–283, 288, 292–305
His crucifixion 47:226, 282f, 305
His kingdom 47:73n, 79, 82f, 182, 218, 296, 302
Hoping to merit his coming 47:174, 239–241, 258, 260
Jewish beliefs 47:65, 67, 70, 80, 88, 142, 150, 157, 164, 176–254, 258, 292–295
Rejection by the Jews 47:67n, 95, 97, 138, 141f, 176–254, 281–285
Sin cannot delay 47:68–70, 73, 77f
Time of his advent 47:67, 70, 78, 94, 97, 229–253
Messianic hope—13:230, 264, 344
Messianic line—4:3
Metals, Precious—45:234
Metaphors—2:220n, 4:175n, 5:150n, 6:6, 80, 7:240, 8:168, 195f, 278, 9:250, 12:153, 169, 171, 175, 204, 13:15, 21n, 50n, 14:289, 296, 318, 324, 15:9, 16:17, 98, 104, 151, 209, 275, 327, 17:9, 64, 78, 126, 180, 182, 219, 272, 289, 312, 315, 321, 384, 18:136, 20:99–102, 105, 108, 112, 116, 118, 143, 23:116, 24:67n, 160n, 279n, 365, 26:97n, 267n, 27:127, 407, 28:176, 37:36n, 36–39, 43, 49, 52n, 170, 172, 174f, 181, 184, 204, 253n, 38:16f, 30, 37, 53, 59, see also **Figures of speech**
Metaphysics—7:279
Metasthenes Persa—45:224n, 225n
Metellus Numidicus—45:36n
Metellus of Tegernsee—*Quirinalia* 25:16f
Meters, Poetic—53:197f
Methuselah—1:334, 343–345, 2:7, 16f, 22f, 27f, 38, 44, 49, 51, 82f, 87, 228, 4:3, 13:99, 310
Metonymy—3:146, 6:274, 16:13, 219, 229, 286, 294, 27:179, 28:348n, 29:144, 30:315
Metsch, Hans—50:23f, 104n, 168n, 54:47, 159, 220, 315, 345
Metz—41:249n, 49:17n
Meyer, Johannes—*Historischer Kommentar zu Luthers kleinem Katechismus*, Gütersloh, 1929 43:13n, 14n, 15n, 16n
Meyer, Martin—41:294n
Mezentians—31:156
Micah, Prophet—2:17, 3:237, 8:300f, 16:5n, 18:207, 210, 212, 221, 225, 236, 19:215, 22:87, 511, 23:243f, 251, 283, 27:123, 335, 35:324f, 52:92, 185
Commentary on his book 18:xf, 207–277(text)
Micaiah, Prophet—11:65, 25:445
Mice—1:51f, 170, 187, 2:135, 8:135, 177, 250
Michael, St., Archangel—2:184, 3:80, 232, 4:127, 264, 7:195, 12:112, 20:17, 170, 173f, 181, 22:88, 246n, 364, 23:349, 30:206f, 41:65n, 51:80
Michael, The wealthy—47:270n
Michael's, St., Day—4:127, 18:362, 23:319n, 326n

Michal—2:292, 5:40, 6:33, 46:285
Michalec, Martin—54:45
Michelangelo—49:286n
Michmash—16:114
Mickell, Master—54:398
Midas, King—5:378, 18:183, 31:224
Middle Ages—1:118n, 235n, 2:129n, 14:69n, 22:51n, 103n, 518n, 26:28n, 122n, 45:166, 233, 235, 341
Middle class—46:251
Middle condition—1:111, 25:186, 270, 377
Middle course—4:58, 68, 275, 277, 389, 6:180, 7:248, 27:239
Midian—4:307, 8:133, 136, 306, 27:360, 364, 29:241
Midian, Land of—1:295
Midianites—4:104, 129, 235, 6:211, 309, 356, 359, 374, 382, 387–390, 396, 405, 7:51, 173, 222, 8:285f, 9:35, 10:413, 11:128–131, 14:114, 339, 16:98f, 114, 150, 17:87f, 314, 19:173, 232f, 22:263, 46:130, 47:152
Midwives—1:132
Might—see **Power**
Mighty ones—21:328, 343–345
Milan—2:365, 18:92, 22:267, 271, 417, 34:233, 38:318n, 46:204n, 48:112n, 49:156
Milan, Bishop of—41:291
Milan, Duke of—8:103
Milcah—4:184f, 280
Mildew—16:159, 195f
Mildness—9:138, 27:376f
Miles—3:293n
Milesians—25:172
Miletus—24:403
Milich, Jacob—54:268
Military law—46:95, 102
Military orders, Medieval—1:118n
Military preparedness—8:299
Military profession—46:90, 93, 97f, 100, 128n, 129, 257
Military service—2:272, 8:102, 105, 15:100, 20:8, 288, 21:102
Military strength—9:170
Milk—3:198, 4:14, 291, 323, 7:393, 8:63, 247, 253f, 256, 261, 270, 302f, 308, 317, 9:138, 293, 11:463f, 23:403f, 30:48–50, 53, 136, 54:320f
Milk faith—43:120
Miller, Walther M.—translator of commentary on Psalm 23 12:147–182
translator of German text of *Lectures on Zechariah* 20:154–347
Millstone, God's—24:196
Millstones—3:237, 9:241, 244
Miltitz, Karl von—31:xvii–xix, 310, 329f, 339f, 34:326, 332n, 334, 335n, 336, 39:25, 51, 53, 248n, 48:96n, 97n, 99–101, 101n, 103n, 108, 109n, 115n, 127–129, 138n, 146, 179f, 54:195
Mind(s)—1:234, 11:13, 15f, 417, 25:69, 71, 85, 105, 113, 130, 168, 217–219, 275, 299, 328, 332, 348, 435, 438, 442, 27:341, 29:47f, 50, 52, 123, 139, 153, 166, 196, 198, 208, 215
Minerva—11:203n, 29:144, 30:290, 38:80, 173n
Mines—5:370
Minges, Parthenus—*Ioannis Duns Scoti doctrina philosophica et theologica* 26:128n
Ministers (of the Word)—2:19–21, 37, 44f, 158, 163, 171, 175, 382, 3:48, 181f, 187, 190, 218, 220, 232, 240f, 356, 361, 4:48, 74–76, 124f, 129, 141, 200–202, 204, 210, 295, 397, 400, 407, 5:10f, 23, 49, 71, 130, 145, 192, 216, 229, 248f, 263, 265, 6:20f, 23, 224f, 257, 7:44, 68, 85, 108, 111, 146, 161f, 8:54, 63, 121, 125f, 145, 183, 185, 229–231, 269–271, 309, 331, 12:298, 25:123, 26:11, 14–16, 18, 23f, 40, 45, 49, 52, 59, 105, 107, 121, 314, 27:37, 41, 47, 62, 82, 100f, 108, 122–124, 126–129, 29:4f, 16, 20–23, 52, 30:55, 63, 164, 36:63f, 67f, 82, 120, 122, 149, 159, 171f, 183, 192, 201, 54:37, 47f, 395, 471, see also **Servants of God**
Ministers, Poverty of—41:198f
Ministers, Women—41:154
Ministers of sin—26:19, 23, 50, 56, 147f, 150f, 198, 200f
Ministry—1:135, 272, 313f, 2:19f, 36, 44, 46, 56, 82–84, 158, 160–162, 164f, 168, 171, 215, 231, 236, 249f, 272, 275, 287, 332, 358, 363, 382, 393, 5:21, 50, 62, 141, 186, 209, 245, 250, 260–264, 268, 362, 8:62, 94, 117, 119, 126, 128, 133, 166, 181f, 186f, 212, 268, 270f, 310f, 23:56, 88, 123, 157, 174, 190f, 193, 217f, 221, 223, 225, 247, 251, 257, 286, 319, 322f, 330, 332, 340, 342, 344, 375, 377, 24:66f, 131, 133, 147, 175, 180, 242, 268, 283, 301, 312, 334, 336, 340, 362, 383, 385, 399, 25:3, 5, 7, 106, 123, 126, 140, 446f, 26:15–17, 19f, 22, 24f, 55, 60–63, 74–76, 78, 93, 100, 102, 104, 108, 193, 218, 224, 313, 348, 362, 366, 402, 412, 426, 430, 440–442, 444, 27:49, 51, 98–100, 102–104, 115–120, 123, 125f, 164f, 192, 200, 209f, 226, 249, 29:5, 11, 23, 58, 101, 124, 184, 51:83, 167,

222–227, 344, 388, 54:12, 80, 90, 100f, 107, 318, 459
Ministry, Call to the—21:7, 63, 25:447, 26:17–22, 28:217f, 281, 36:116, 38:176f, 186, 190, 192–195, 197, 200f, 204, 208, 212, 214, 39:xvii, 74, 174, 233, 40:xiii, 11, 62, 111, 386n, 54:80
Ministry, Office of the—2:163, 175, 272, 3:5, 37, 165, 232, 237, 241, 272, 274, 277, 281, 342, 4:32f, 66, 72, 74, 126, 179, 181, 201f, 204, 210, 295, 385, 406, 9:22, 26f, 43, 84n, 134, 140, 151, 157n, 174, 177–180, 189, 206, 213, 235, 237, 244, 250f, 284, 304f, 310, 10:143, 180f, 223, 316, 320, 330, 13:24, 49, 80, 140, 192, 265f, 270, 331, 370, 15:4, 228f, 237, 260, 276, 327, 21:8f, 27f, 44, 54, 57f, 61, 63f, 71, 124, 136, 212f, 224f, 251f, 22:48, 56, 308, 368, 372, 420, 452, 472, 480, 482, 516, 521, 523, 526, 529, 25:446f, 32:178, 36:82f, 97, 112–117, 122, 38:27f, 41f, 58, 73, 101, 154, 176f, 180, 188, 197, 199, 204, 208, 214, 39:xiv, xvi–xviii, xxii–xxv, 28, 74, 110, 151–155, 174, 234f, 248, 250–253, 267f, 304, 40:x, xiiif, 8, 11, 19, 21, 29, 31, 35f, 39, 41, 62, 111, 384f, 386n, 41:154, 161, 221, 251, 329, 350, 46:81, 209, 233, 265n, 49:207f, 51:335f, 373, 384
Ministry and Church—see Vols. 39, 40, and 41
Ministry of the Law—9:14, 26f, 113, 170, 177, 181, 311
Ministry of the Word—1:212, 309, 3:111, 124, 155, 164, 167f, 233, 240, 288, 343, 356, 364, 6:21, 34, 227, 250, 258, 369f, 7:38, 162, 164, 171, 182, 221, 299, 318, 332, 364, 369, 11:160, 312, 323, 334, 12:186, 191, 217, 219, 242, 256, 274, 279, 295, 297f, 300, 388, 393, 14:262, 281, 331, 334, 16:33, 70, 188, 17:11, 115f, 178, 211, 213f, 243, 269, 315, 18:127, 129, 177, 228, 231f, 263, 417, 19:36, 83, 97f, 20:36, 45, 59f, 62–65, 73, 93, 110, 112, 28:281f, 323, 327f, 349, 354, 375, 377, 37:364
Minkwitz, George von—54:205
Minkwitz, Hans von—45:164, 53:54
Minkwitz, Wolfgang von—54:172f
Minnesänger—53:196
Minor Prophets, Luther's lectures on—see Vols. 18, 19, and 20
Versions and manuscripts 18:ixf
Minorites—see **Franciscans or Minorites**
Minstrels—13:26
Minucius Felix—*Octavian* 5:44n
Miracles—1:35, 37, 54, 79, 126f, 352, 2:27, 56, 75f, 97, 157, 215, 241, 255, 259, 303f, 321, 374–376, 389, 391, 3:31, 64, 68, 109, 117, 145, 206, 210, 226, 260, 262f, 270, 289, 302f, 315, 325, 4:4–6, 8f, 73, 113, 129, 140f, 168–170, 212, 229, 232, 258, 287, 330, 344, 360, 397, 5:8, 32, 45, 56f, 175, 213, 234, 252, 291, 293, 310, 353, 6:9, 124, 128, 222, 7:30, 46, 49, 56f, 70f, 84, 89, 108, 129f, 166, 220, 239, 295, 307, 310, 314f, 8:33, 44, 75, 82, 89, 129, 131, 133, 167, 183f, 200, 222, 227, 281, 302, 9:3, 22, 32, 36, 74, 96f, 117, 188f, 310, 10:61, 63, 11:12–14, 28, 14:10, 28, 80, 82f, 98f, 129, 131, 135, 210, 259f, 304, 15:333, 16:84, 325f, 336, 17:96f, 118, 120, 124, 168, 376, 19:82, 206–208, 226, 228, 20:100, 126, 158, 294, 21:270–272, 276, 279f, 22:34, 43f, 47–49, 71, 76, 78, 80, 96, 99, 108f, 112, 116, 118, 121, 126–128, 130, 172, 186, 200, 215, 219, 241f, 244, 247, 251, 276, 310, 367, 477, 479, 505, 23:5, 29–32, 34, 37, 77, 109, 114, 116, 147, 155–157, 160f, 186, 188f, 208f, 214, 220f, 227, 343, 345, 369, 375f, 24:9, 32, 67, 73–75, 78f, 135, 181, 192, 283, 285, 287, 304, 367–371, 375, 402, 411, 26:14f, 28, 93, 96, 98, 103f, 204, 219, 226, 270, 373, 27:146, 209, 251, 288, 291, 303f, 336, 354, 29:124f, 173, 30:4, 153f, 194, 206, 284, 297, 36:338–343, 37:xii, 48, 52, 58, 62, 65f, 73f, 76f, 94, 103, 133, 278, 295, 337, 41:116, 254, 46:179, 184n, 197, 203, 224f, 228f, 49:396f, 51:122, 334f, 52:192, 199, 201, 54:111, 357f, 386
Miracles, False—see **False miracles**
Mirandola—see **Pico della Mirandola, Giovanni**
Mirbt, Carl, ed.—*Quellen zur Geschichte des Papsttums und des römischen Katholizismus*, Tübingen, 1924 27:342n, 31:xixn, 330n, 381n, 32:xiiin, 61n, 79n
Mire—24:203, 368, 383f, 401
Miriam—8:222, 227, 9:242, 22:333n, 24:293, 28:277, 45:209, 219, 52:271
Mirror—24:67, 26:64, 396, 37:65, 226f
Misanthropes—3:51
Miscarriages—43:247f
Misenus, Andrew—54:403
Miserere—12:198
Misericordias Sunday—23:165n, 176n

Misers—13:399, 15:53, 67f, 86f, 90, 95f, 23:7, 12, 383
Misery—3:179, 10:368f, 13:112, 117f, 123, 125, 15:8, 13, 22, 32, 34, 44, 63, 95f, 182f, 219
Misfortunes—3:25, 33, 120, 124, 135, 180, 185, 248, 252, 264f, 288, 303, 307f, 311, 322, 324, 326, 332, 334, 346, 348f, 356, 360–362, 4:5f, 15, 36, 40f, 45–48, 56, 59, 73, 79, 161, 188, 195f, 214, 247f, 254f, 258, 270, 290, 292, 319, 323, 329, 333, 338–341, 360, 363, 375, 5:8, 10–14, 21, 30, 53, 56, 62, 77, 89, 90, 92, 96, 118, 121, 165, 168, 170f, 176f, 179f, 190, 234, 238, 270, 320, 354, 360, 368, 7:39, 47, 50, 54f, 58, 60, 72, 81, 113, 116, 124f, 127, 132, 146, 178, 184, 202f, 210, 217, 222, 237f, 256, 275, 290f, 304, 319, 327f, 367f, 8:7, 14, 17, 29, 34, 40, 53, 114, 151, 162, 231, 293, 303, 19:160, 24:11f, 14–18, 21, 26, 64, 136, 148, 185, 195f, 201, 241f, 377, 379, 404, 420, 26:50, 58, 27:67, 298, 330, 345, 30:16f, 28f, 31, 103f, 109, 173, 181f, 198, 261, 276
Mishpat—2:367
Missa privata—see **Mass, Private**
Missions—10:339, 13:342
Missions, World—2:184f, 14:9f, 334n, 50:209, 53:232
Mist—1:7f, 10, 17, 24, 83
Mitres—13:296
Mizar, Mt.—11:327n, 20:118, 22:422, 27:177
Mizpah—18:26
Moab—3:313f, 4:186, 6:64, 216, 309, 389, 7:14f, 8:11, 238, 262, 289, 9:15, 26, 43, 236, 271, 284, 297, 10:203, 282–284, 286–288, 290–292, 327, 407, 434f, 11:121f, 124f, 128, 12:258, 265, 13:185, 14:194, 317, 337, 16:126, 146–153, 198, 201, 18:9, 89, 113, 134, 137f, 342f, 27:317, 321, 29:202, 49:44, 215
Moabites—1:292, 302, 2:189, 367, 3:313, 5:207, 6:64, 228, 7:15, 8:135, 199, 228, 237f, 288f, 304, 9:14n, 32–35, 53–55, 83, 169, 230f, 235, 10:413, 16:146f, 149–151, 153, 17:72, 352, 19:144f, 233–235, 30:185f, 47:154
Moabitess—3:133, 7:22, 200, 8:228
Mob, The (Herr Omnes)—21:243f, 29:27, 45:63, 46:27, 105f, 112
Mochau, Margaret von—49:174, 181
Mockers—28:157–161, 163f, 195
Mockery—23:257n, 286, 300, 302, 371, 377, 24:314, 358
Moderation—2:16, 309, 339, 341, 3:241, 262, 331, 4:8, 146, 197, 217, 277, 296, 5:32, 116, 382f, 7:178, 182f, 204, 262, 8:59, 171, 9:204, 248, 13:153, 15:129, 25:55, 105, 26:84, 27:373, 378, 28:13–15, 51:291–299
Modernists—14:284, 318f, 33:105, 134, 45:377n
Modesty—3:201f, 246f, 249, 253, 259, 4:19, 208f, 217, 224, 235, 238, 284, 299, 5:30, 37, 193, 227, 233, 299, 301, 378, 7:28, 54, 57, 73, 80, 145, 166, 178f, 185f, 190, 240, 337, 8:58, 101, 121, 151, 158, 13:210, 28:280, 29:29, 54
Moessner, Paul H.G.—translator of *Appeal for Prayer against the Turk* 43:213–242
Moffatt, James—35:352n, 353n
Mohacs—49:156, 185n, 240n
Mohacs, Battle of—4:28n, 14:x, 16:160n, 46:90, 157, 158n, 167n, 202n
Mohammed—2:267, 5:71, 79, 347, 6:127, 8:47, 89, 106, 187, 225, 10:34, 11:227, 289, 12:115, 232, 284, 355, 13:325, 14:38, 15:340, 342f, 351, 17:331, 22:17f, 67, 70, 76, 137, 333, 351n, 365, 392n, 428–430, 464, 476, 23:129, 24:22, 69, 237, 368, 26:32, 368, 30:257, 309, 34:208, 35:267, 287, 300, 404n, 406, 410, 38:310, 41:86, 91, 43:232f, 238, 46:175–179, 181, 195f, 47:36, 161, 212, 220, 253, 268, 293, 49:289
Mohammed II, Sultan—46:200n
Mohammedanism—23:82, 24:97, 188
Mohammedans—4:21n, 29, 221, 6:105n, 8:42, 4, 6, 265, 13:258, 270f, 16:34n, 22:60, 137n, 351n, 23:56, 186n, 26:10, 33, 396, 47:80n, 128. 54:416
Möhra—46:141n, 48:227n, 329
Moibanus, Ambrose—54:470
Molech—36:219f, 224, 41:203n, 207
Molechites—36:225f
Moles—1:141, 3:316–318
Moloch—7:300, 8:131f, 186, 200, 9:131, 175, 18:260, 322, 25:218, 52:260
Möller, Wilhelm—54:107
Momus—13:203
Monarchianism—34:208n, 37:361n, 38:255n, 262n
Monarchs, monarchy—4:35, 71, 235, 284, 372n, 400, 5:94, 313, 7:145, 167, 8:93, 250
Monasteries—1:179f, 239f, 2:252, 269f, 326, 328, 339, 3:7, 62, 130, 203f, 217, 252, 275f, 284, 309, 316, 322, 357,

361f, 4:7, 21f, 37, 41n, 53, 58, 88, 165, 181, 242, 396, 399, 5:247, 271n, 292, 309, 342n, 346, 348, 6:28, 253, 286, 349, 7:63, 69, 113, 262, 296f, 307, 332, 337, 341, 8:20f, 62f, 126, 174, 182, 186, 230, 276, 9:25, 140, 14:xi, 15, 20f, 23, 25f, 51, 301, 16:96, 227, 244, 17:21, 25, 46, 69, 102, 152, 214, 222, 266, 272, 18:10, 53, 184, 214, 20:145, 238, 262, 264, 272, 330, 21:32, 72, 132f, 142, 157, 256–259, 266f, 269, 312, 22:155, 244, 271, 278, 302, 439, 23:136, 142, 346, 348, 356n, 359f, 24:24n, 26:85, 105, 200, 201, 315, 385, 27:90, 136, 204, 254, 375, 385, 28:3, 10, 28f, 49, 315, 322, 29:84, 30:55, 246, 253, 256, 288, 297, 304, 312n, 34:180, 36:142, 178, 213, 233, 260f, 38:86, 175, 190, 232, 39:296, 299, 305, 40:30, 58, 44:174n, 179, 312f, 355, 367, 45:53, 68, 161n, 170, 171n, 172, 174f, 267, 284, 304, 341, 348–360, 371, 373, 375, 46:47, 50, 82, 141, 142n, 148–151, 174, 176, 197, 209, 220, 225f, 228, 231–235, 241, 256, 298, 51:79–81, 88, 96, 116, 164, 171, 212, 239n, 266, 299, 360, 366, 52:118, 141, 212, 217f, 228f, 241, 247, 250f, 254f, 258, 262, 265f, 269, 275, 54:234f, 295, 312, 473

Monastic exegesis—1:114n

Monastic life—1:103, 230, 343f, 1:103, 343f, 2:76, 270, 3:284, 362, 4:7, 48, 56, 5:7, 9, 91, 291, 294n, 345–349, 7:34, 86, 194, 357, 371, 374, 10:15, 21, 275, 426, 11:537, 22:280, 337, 366, 401, 458, 22:366, 458, 23:68, 76, 86, 171, 204, 348n, 29:47f, 30:253, 280

Monastic orders—16:227f, 244, 326n, 21:304f, 22:50f, 57, 71f, 133, 155, 158, 165, 249, 255n, 281, 330, 335, 354, 356, 366, 369, 26:25, 27, 32, 40f, 52, 66, 140f, 154, 176, 212f, 222, 301, 307f, 332, 333n, 356, 385, 396f, 405, 458f, 28:17–21, 40, 281, 30:95f, 156, 169, 171, 189, 229, 263, 282f, 297, 32:98f, 34:257, 35:134, 142, 145, 318n, 36:213f, 38:86, 189, 213f, 46:141f, 145, 52:34, 36, 115, 172f, 222, 235f, 247, 252f, 262, 265f, 269f, 272f

Monastic properties—14:21n

Monastic vows—see **Vows**

Monastic works—29:9

Monasticism—2:269, 340, 3:203f, 325, 362, 4:333, 399, 5:4n, 6:28, 124, 262, 8:20, 60, 284, 9:74, 12:72f, 86, 187, 273f, 332, 353, 365, 389, 394, 396, 13:7, 325, 368, 15:4, 32, 83, 17:83, 88, 179, 376, 402, 21:32f, 269, 304f, 312, 22:50, 135, 155, 254, 446, 456, 481, 23:37, 24:59, 227, 231, 260, 275, 279, 281, 326, 328, 348, 363, 367f, 25:491, 494, 26:185, 199, 223, 318, 330, 460, 27:13, 61, 84, 140f, 30:295n, 34:20, 27f, 44, 257f, 35:xvii, 96, 131f, 141, 36:73n, 74f, 128, 159, 214, 37:173, 363f, 371, 38:100, 105, 231, 310f, 41:38n, 39–41, 85, 110f, 125–129, 136, 140, 147, 169, 172, 199, 213, 215, 223, 283, 336, 341, 44:173n, 251–256, 260–268, 270–272, 288–291, 319–326, 328f, 331f, 334f, 337–346, 349–354, 356–362, 365–370, 373–385, 45:85n, 144n, 170, 238, 46:141f, 145, 150, 209, 298n, 48:15f, 18, 20f, 29f, 211n, 225n, 321, 53:112, 176, 54:134, 178

Monday—23:240

Money—1:329, 2:161, 263, 317, 326, 330f, 3:283, 317, 359, 361, 4:13, 36, 41, 61, 196, 199–206, 215f, 251, 296, 315, 395–397, 400, 403, 5:13, 17, 38, 55, 58f, 61, 140, 197, 296, 332, 354n, 368f, 373, 6:68, 93, 112, 184, 231, 239f, 245, 7:32f, 145, 158, 266f, 270f, 276, 286f, 296, 298, 311, 323, 329f, 332, 334, 361f, 8:12, 23, 66, 103, 119–124, 126, 202, 267, 279f, 9:51, 141, 145, 210, 233, 242, 249, 19:183n, 202, 21:168f, 171, 189, 183f, 189, 192, 334f, 23:8f, 30, 40f, 66, 104, 152, 212f, 228, 291, 330–332, 344, 356f, 383, 392, 395, 402, 24:22, 24, 81, 118, 134, 178, 208, 251, 254, 266–268, 284, 25:172, 26:20, 71, 128, 220, 306, 364, 406, 27:58, 128, 158, 198, 216, 236f, 308, 358, 384, 28:107, 111, 133f, 137, 143, 145, 370f, 30:54, 63, 67, 174, 178, 181, 184, 186, 207f, 248, 273, 275, 278, 296, 35:211, 45:245, 246f, 251n, 301f, 304n, 46:200n, 228, 269, 281

Money economy—14:122n

Money lenders—8:128, 24:118

Moneybags—24:118

Monica, St.—3:159f, 5:103, 180f, 359, 361, 7:119, 11:350, 17:364, 21:41, 22:113, 35:102, 103n, 104n, 36:100, 45:25, 54:260, 454

Monk in us—12:274, 277, 280

Monkery—22:52, 71, 335, 360, 368, 395, 464, 24:119, 121, 169f, 173, 240

Monkeys—3:318, 4:240, 13:158, 25:235, 324

Monks—1:14, 114, 121, 135, 147f, 161,

213f, 238f, 250, 300, 339, 343, 2:21, 78, 86, 103f, 113f, 124, 150, 152, 160, 249, 251–253, 268–271, 273, 325f, 328, 331, 339, 349f, 3:51, 66n, 118, 128, 130, 139, 145, 153, 165f, 168, 170, 180, 196, 200, 203f, 218, 245, 275f, 289, 315f, 321f, 325, 329, 362f, 4:7, 21–23, 37, 39–41, 43, 46, 65, 88f, 109, 122–124, 140, 181f, 209, 216, 250, 259, 267, 276f, 284, 303, 315, 321, 327, 338, 340f, 347, 359, 368, 377, 399f, 5:3–9, 13f, 35f, 71, 80, 92, 114, 138f, 157, 193, 210, 253n, 257f, 263, 268, 271, 282, 285, 291, 301, 308, 329, 333, 342, 347, 351, 6:28, 73, 111, 114, 123, 149, 181, 230, 252–254, 260–262, 346, 348f, 407, 7:20, 34, 69, 129, 134, 193f, 199, 261f, 296, 305, 311–313, 315n, 323, 326, 337, 340–345, 350, 355–357, 361, 366f, 8:15, 21f, 60, 70, 75, 106, 132, 167, 172f, 181f, 188, 192, 231, 264, 267f, 276, 326, 9:55n, 131, 179, 10:21, 29, 12:36, 71, 313, 321, 380, 397, 13:56, 98, 146, 273f, 14:15, 23f, 39, 61, 70, 76, 94, 99, 215, 217, 257, 292, 295, 15:5, 32, 66, 79, 83, 104, 146, 176f, 16:38, 133n, 223, 227f, 293, 310, 328, 17:12, 17, 21, 52, 64, 102, 110, 112, 118f, 160, 172, 207, 297, 317, 384, 390, 18:9f, 22, 44, 55, 152, 183f, 212, 231, 260, 322f, 19:52, 21:6, 28f, 37f, 46f, 133f, 142f, 158, 182f, 204f, 256f, 262f, 267, 281–283, 292, 304f, 312, 318f, 350, 22:51f, 64, 71, 81, 132, 146f, 152, 157, 166, 169, 190n, 192, 254, 256, 258, 271, 273, 278–281, 301, 320, 331, 337, 359f, 370, 374, 386f, 389, 392, 399, 405, 421, 425, 429f, 434, 440, 456f, 459, 461, 464, 468, 477, 484, 514, 23:26f, 37f, 44f, 68, 70, 86, 127f, 134–136, 141, 174, 179, 182, 193, 196, 201, 204f, 213, 224f, 228, 234, 262, 268, 272f, 285, 290, 316, 320, 323, 331, 348, 351f, 356–359, 364, 366, 369, 386, 408–411, 413, 418, 24:13n, 22f, 35, 37f, 52, 62f, 69–71, 88, 91, 97f, 128–130, 147, 156, 170, 174, 215f, 219f, 222, 225f, 228f, 233, 237, 240, 242, 257, 259f, 266, 268, 274, 281, 288, 325f, 360, 363, 394, 406, 25:139, 476, 491, 509f, 26:25, 28, 33f, 52, 68, 104, 109, 122, 125f, 134, 140f, 153, 172, 184, 199–201, 213, 229, 231, 238, 258, 312f, 332f, 347, 356, 385f, 395–398, 400, 404, 408, 458, 460, 27:9, 13f, 25, 55, 60f, 68f, 71, 73, 75f, 81, 83–85, 88f, 91f, 101f, 135, 140f, 148, 166, 281, 329, 397, 28:40f, 53, 113f, 116, 197, 221, 227, 311, 322, 357, 365, 29:19–21, 34, 43, 45f, 54, 60–62, 66, 71–73, 88, 102, 153n, 30:6, 8, 15, 37, 77, 82f, 85, 97, 99, 168, 170, 173f, 177, 184, 188f, 191, 203, 233–235, 245, 248, 256, 266, 275, 286f, 295–297, 300, 312, 34:15, 21, 28, 35:80, 141, 144, 146, 200f, 36:36, 42, 75, 78, 115, 136, 153f, 158f, 167, 213f, 220–224, 233, 260f, 358n, 38:114, 159f, 166, 173, 176, 183n, 231, 233, 287n, 307n, 310, 311n, 42:20, 47, 55, 134, 44:255, 268f, 286–288, 378, 45:14, 19, 37, 39, 41f, 53f, 141–143, 151, 170–172, 176, 185f, 200, 318f, 348, 355, 375–377, 389n, 46:xiii, 19, 147, 149, 163, 177, 182, 189, 209, 217, 294, 298, 319, 47:15, 38, 47, 50–53, 175, 52:34f, 37, 79, 100, 203, 212, 216f, 250f, 254f, 259, 262f, 266, 272, 275, 277, 54:68, 188, 268, 281, 304, 307, 327f, see also **Friars**

Monks, Mendicant—see **Mendicant orders**

Monks and nuns—10:15, 303, 362, 378, 385, 41:34, 38–40, 71, 124, 127n, 140, 144, 164, 197, 206, 251, 337, 340f, 51:79–81, 88, 107–117, 124, 139, 171, 185, 247, 272, 296, 327, 359f, 385

Monks of Mammon—46:251

Monner, Basilius—54:245

Monogamy—2:305

Monophysitism—37:212n, 213n

Monopolies—45:xii, 234, 240, 241n, 242f, 262n, 264, 266, 270, 271n

Monopolies, Laws against—45:242f, 262n, 270

Monstrances—30:79, 129, 35:97, 38:110, 114

Monstrosities—16:343, 50:146f, 228, 262f, 54:44, 58

Mont, Christopher—50:104n, 177, 192, 193n, 195n, 196, 198n, 199n, 205n

Montanism—37:361n

Montanists—24:176, 30:306, 32:128, 211n, 34:209n, 35:402n, 36:211n

Months—20:13, 77, 166n, 259, 27:7, 52, 295f, 331

Moon—1:5, 21, 29, 39–43, 49, 54, 69, 74, 76, 90, 100, 105, 309, 327, 2:92, 147, 152, 156, 3:86, 163f, 273, 347, 4:143, 231, 276, 5:6f, 91, 97, 260, 7:111, 183, 8:67, 138, 224, 30:37, 181f, 197

Moors—14:273

Moral grammar—26:263, 294

Moral order—13:163f

Moral sense—25:141, 144, 156, 209, 212, 256, 322, 325, 330, 350, 398, 426, 431
Moralia—see **Gregory I, Pope**
Morality—1:272, 26:7, 13, 25, 294, 304, 321, 394, 44:xix
Morals—2:152, 158–160, 175, 247, 288, 305, 333, 3:201, 213, 227, 249, 252, 254, 4:81, 85, 213, 291, 396, 5:11, 20, 28f, 86, 104, 124, 187f, 285, 293, 7:30, 74, 91f, 351, 27:36, 47, 60, 109, 125, 176, 214, 256, 268, 369, 375, 399, 36:209
Moravia—2:361, 3:77, 36:272, 275, 40:5, 229n, 47:59–61, 65n, 54:239
Moravian Brethren—see **Bohemians**
Mordecai—8:93, 17:124, 45:220
More, Thomas—17:57n, 247n, 54:288, 362
Moreh, Mt.—2:382, 385f
Moresheth-gath—18:219
Moriah, Mt.—2:281, 4:98f, 100f, 110, 138, 179, 181, 231, 5:242f, 251f, 262f, 6:185, 223f, 14:152, 327, 16:28, 18:329, 20:82, 271, 26:315
Moriones, Frances, ed.—*Enchiridion Theologicum Sancti Augustini*, Madrid, 1961 4:70n
Moritz, Duke—see **Maurice, Duke of Saxony**
Moritz Castle—38:168
Mörlin, Joachim—54:383, 396
Morning watch—14:193
Morning, Threefold meaning of—11:292–294
Morolf—17:69n, 51:361, 54:389, 450, see also **Markolf**
Morone, Cardinal Giovanni—41:259f
Mortality—1:330, 2:144, 3:268, 25:65, 70
Mortar—18:329f
Mortification—4:39, 42, 44–46, 49, 101, 109, 123, 5:184, 203, 6:43, 97, 110f, 114, 121, 142, 147, 150, 152, 180, 236f, 248, 354f, 7:104, 177, 196, 209–211, 235, 8:5–7, 114, 9:185–187, 237, 250, 12:410, 17:8, 43, 50, 66f, 20:101, 140f, 143, 25:37, 51, 70, 117, 320, 407, 40:70, 81, 83, 149, 221f
Mortification of self—26:398
Mortification of the flesh—13:115, 16:59, 216, 25:37, 51, 70, 117, 320, 407, 36:90
Mosellanus, Peter—see **Schade, Peter (Mosellanus)**
Moser, Hans Joachim—*Die Melodien der Lutherlieder*, Leipzig, 1935 53:xx
Moses—1:ix, 3, 5–14, 16–23, 25f, 28–31, 35, 40, 43, 45, 48f, 53, 55f, 58f, 68–70, 72–77, 79f, 82–92, 94f, 87–101, 104f, 110, 113, 115, 119–121, 127, 129–131, 133f, 138f, 142, 144, 146–149, 152, 157, 164, 167f, 170, 173, 181f, 185, 187, 189, 191, 197, 206, 208f, 215–217, 229f, 234, 237f, 240f, 247, 249, 252, 257, 260, 263, 268f, 276–280, 282f, 287, 291f, 295, 308–310, 312, 314, 316–319, 321–324, 327f, 330, 332–335, 337–339, 342–346, 349f, 355–358, 2:3, 6, 8–10, 12, 17, 27, 29–33, 36f, 41–44, 47, 50f, 56, 58f, 61f, 67, 69f, 74, 76, 77, 82–86, 88, 90–92, 94–97, 103–106, 109f, 115–117, 119, 121–123, 128, 132, 134, 150, 152, 158, 160f, 165f, 170, 172f, 179, 182, 187, 192f, 196, 198f, 204f, 207f, 210, 212, 214, 223f, 232, 234, 240–243, 245f, 249, 258, 260, 266, 268, 271, 273, 277–279, 282, 285–287, 290, 293, 304f, 324, 331f, 337, 342, 344f, 351, 353, 359–362, 364–370, 376, 380f, 388f, 3:3, 5, 7, 10–12, 15, 18f, 23, 26–28, 32, 34–36, 41, 43, 46, 56, 58, 61–63, 74–82, 84, 86, 88, 90–94, 96–98, 100, 115, 134, 141, 143, 152, 156, 161, 163–166, 168f, 173, 177, 180f, 185f, 191, 196–198, 200f, 203, 205, 209, 218–220, 225, 229, 231, 243f, 247f, 250–253, 255, 257, 259, 261, 263, 267, 271f, 278, 280, 282, 286, 290, 292f, 295–298, 302–305, 308–312, 314–316, 320, 323, 330, 338, 344, 346, 352–354, 356f, 361, 4:4, 6–10, 13–16, 23f, 26, 30, 36, 38, 40f, 45, 48f, 66–73, 77f, 88, 90, 101, 103, 108, 111–113, 116, 118, 126, 128, 131, 136, 140, 153f, 167, 176–179, 182–189, 193–195, 198, 200, 207, 209, 214, 216–218, 221, 227, 229, 250, 259f, 263–266, 269f, 272, 274, 280, 299, 302, 306, 309f, 312f, 317, 320, 322–325, 327, 329, 331, 333, 337, 341f, 358, 360, 378, 380, 384, 386, 390, 393, 408f, 5:3, 6, 9, 19f, 44, 47, 53, 55–57, 59, 61f, 65, 69, 79, 91f, 100, 108–110, 114, 116, 123, 125, 129–131, 134, 136, 138, 145, 147, 179, 192, 199f, 210f, 223f, 227, 237f, 242, 259, 261, 266, 269, 276, 280, 283, 289, 294f, 297, 304, 307, 309, 314, 316, 325, 337–340, 348, 350, 357f, 360, 366f, 373, 378, 384, 6:25, 34, 293, 303, 330, 7:3, 7f, 11, 15, 17–19, 22–24, 26, 29, 31f, 38–41, 50f, 57f, 60, 69, 74, 78, 84, 91, 93f, 100, 102f, 108, 112, 119, 140, 158, 170, 172f, 181, 185, 189, 202, 206, 215–218, 224, 228, 239–241, 243, 250, 258f, 263f, 266f, 269–271,

278, 283, 285f, 296, 324f, 327f, 339f, 345, 348, 352, 360f, 366, 8:22f, 30, 33, 50f, 54, 64f, 68, 71–73, 75f, 82, 84, 87, 89, 97, 101, 111, 116f, 129, 131, 133, 135–137, 142f, 145, 149, 153f, 158–160, 162, 169, 178f, 203, 206, 210, 213f, 216f, 219, 221–223, 227, 229, 231–233, 240, 246, 281f, 290, 301, 304f, 307, 309, 319f, 323, 326, 332, 9:3, 6, 8, 14–16, 17n, 18–23, 26, 32, 34–36, 42f, 48, 50–52, 57, 59f, 63f, 67–71, 73, 75f, 79–86, 92, 94–97, 102, 104, 108–114, 117, 123–126, 129f, 134, 139–141, 144, 147–149, 154, 157, 161–164, 166–170, 175–184, 188f, 193, 198, 202, 205, 210f, 215, 219, 222, 229, 233, 242, 244, 258–260, 267, 271–273, 277–279, 283f, 292, 296–299, 304–306, 310f, 10:25, 293, 318f, 346, 349, 399f, 446, 11:34f, 38, 41, 129, 147n, 197, 252, 277, 288, 312f, 366, 510, 528, 537, 551, 12:170, 205, 207, 212, 267, 269, 281, 292, 360, 365, 13:34, 62, 75, 77, 79–82, 86f, 114, 119, 121, 130, 132, 134, 184, 199, 287, 200, 305, 14:29, 53, 72, 77, 79, 103, 132, 170, 244f, 258, 289, 15:299f, 312, 325–330, 332–335, 16:3, 6, 14, 16f, 24, 29, 35, 66, 74, 130, 152, 178, 206, 212, 239, 243, 17:81f, 95, 106–108, 118, 128, 179f, 189, 191, 244, 308f, 358–360, 393, 398, 18:3, 12, 101, 19:14, 49, 75f, 89, 104, 111, 127, 131, 133, 138–140, 182, 184, 187, 196f, 217, 230, 232, 20:35, 201, 214, 223, 246, 248, 256, 290, 307, 21:10, 93f, 106f, 122f, 128, 235–237, 279, 316, 329f, 352, 22:7f, 12f, 24, 28, 31, 38–41, 78, 97, 99, 116, 120, 122, 124, 129–132, 134, 138–140, 144, 147f, 151, 153–157, 161–163, 165, 184, 187, 194, 201, 223–227, 230f, 245, 249, 251, 257, 277, 284f, 289, 304, 308–311, 319, 330, 331, 334, 338–341, 344, 348f, 353, 367, 378, 385, 396, 422f, 425f, 428, 430f, 438, 440–442, 445, 448–450, 475f, 483–489, 495, 504, 510f, 23:10, 30–33, 35–37, 44, 59, 89, 98, 114, 141, 156, 174, 190, 193, 228, 247, 279–281, 311–314, 317, 319, 327, 366, 369, 373, 375f, 378, 404–406, 409f, 414, 24:24, 40, 60, 82, 101f, 115, 214, 252f, 257, 283–285, 293, 295, 345, 369, 396, 419, 25:49, 79, 143, 275, 358, 391, 476f, 26:4, 7, 10, 22, 24, 26, 28, 32, 38, 48–50, 52, 68, 72–74, 78f, 81f, 94, 111, 114, 116, 120, 139f, 142–146, 149f, 151n, 152, 155f, 175, 178, 185, 203, 207, 211f, 222, 241, 248, 252f, 257, 259–261, 268, 274, 276f, 279, 288f, 291, 293, 304, 309, 311, 313, 315, 319–325, 327, 345, 354, 357, 360, 364f, 367f, 372, 383f, 391, 400f, 433, 436, 439, 448, 27:15f, 18, 56, 59, 109, 130f, 138f, 178–180, 185, 187, 219, 222, 226, 235, 247, 255–257, 259, 261, 267, 269, 272, 274, 295f, 318, 320, 331, 334f, 341, 349, 366, 379, 392, 407, 28:9, 12, 31, 98, 282, 29:4f, 8f, 30, 34, 36, 110, 115, 140, 145f, 148, 157, 168, 186, 197–200, 204, 208, 222, 231, 240, 30:7, 19, 21, 37f, 45, 62, 100, 115, 136, 162, 177f, 187, 194, 196, 206–208, 210, 252f, 261, 306, 309, 324, 31:178, 34:xvi, 178, 35:xvii, 79, 83, 132, 141, 149, 158f, 161–174, 238n, 241f, 244–246, 257, 284, 289, 374, 377, 36:39, 40, 53, 60, 136, 149, 152, 161, 187, 198, 200, 204f, 280–282, 37:31f, 35–28, 42–44, 95, 117, 130, 184, 264, 273f, 336, 38:42, 51, 58, 80f, 84n, 105, 108, 113, 178n, 290, 314, 41:39, 68, 81, 120, 142, 155, 210, 42:137, 141, 150, 45:29f, 62f, 96, 111, 125, 212, 219, 226, 241, 322, 353, 373, 378, 390, 46:35, 51, 94, 97f, 131, 147f, 151f, 196, 253, 277, 282, 289–292, 47:67–71, 75–77, 79, 81f, 86–94, 142, 144, 147, 150, 153, 159, 165f, 168, 171, 173f, 177, 185, 206, 218, 224, 239–241, 250, 254, 262–264, 267, 269–271, 289, 304, 49:44, 331, 51:82, 87, 106, 130, 139, 153, 227, 273, 347, 52:3, 21f, 42f, 47f, 51, 54, 58, 60, 67, 87, 89f, 101, 106, 110, 126, 130, 133, 150f, 154f, 167, 170f, 177, 179f, 182, 202, 205, 212, 238f, 259, 271, 53:13

Moses, Books of—2:385, 3:237, 47:69, 165, 304

Moses, Law of—see **Law, Mosaic**

Moses, Song of—9:283, 290, 308

Moslems—see **Mohammedans**

Mossellanus, Peter—see **Schade, Peter (Mosellanus)**

Motets—53:321, 335–341

Mother, God pictured as—17:131, 183f, 410

Mother of God—see **Mary, Virgin**

Motherhood—1:199, 201–203, 3:44, 49, 4:293f, 299, 337, 353f, 358, 7:35, 39, 43

Mothers—1:104, 193, 201f, 251, 2:145, 311, 356, 4:10, 15, 17 20, 22, 24, 36–

44, 46f, 49f, 52, 58–60, 64, 66, 72, 96, 108, 110, 112f, 161, 174, 181f, 188f, 194, 197, 207, 223f, 233, 239, 265, 270, 278, 280, 287, 290–293, 296f, 299, 301, 307, 313, 320, 325, 327, 330, 337, 344, 4:349, 351–354, 357, 364, 369f, 374, 376f, 380, 383, 386f, 389f, 393, 401, 17:16, 139, 183, 410, 21:109f, 274, 308f, 26:95, 106, 265, 367, 434f, 439–446, 458, 27:58, 158, 308, 310, 317, 319, 321, 46:302

Mothers-in-law—6:290

Moths—21:168f, 172, 183

Motion—11:494, 496f, 520

Motivation—21:133–135, 180–184, 232f

Motives, Right—25:495

Motz, Philipp—34:148

Moulton, C. G.—*Life in the Middle Ages*, Cambridge, Mass., 1930 43:17n

Mount of Olives—2:110, 7:299, 20:338f, 347

Mountain dwellers—19:143

Mountains—1:8, 98, 172, 310, 10:100, 117, 171, 198f, 336, 341, 413, 11:3f, 86, 97, 268, 324, 326f, 328n, 336, 394, 16:287, 17:9f, 241, 247, 296, 363, 381f, 405, 20:46, 64, 66, 82, 184, 188, 222, 226, 248, 339, 24:24, 46, 126, 160, 259, 386, 388

Mourners, mourning—8:320, 323, 9:134, 254, 15:108f, 112, 182, 204, 17:334f, 18:48, 93, 336, 20:140f, 278, 329, 24:13, 132, 381

Mouth—37:7, 85–89, 93, 100, 134, 230

Mouth-Christians—23:399

Mozart, Wolfgang Amadeus—53:226

Mtellus—5:182

Mud—19:126, 204, 24:203, 368, 27:356, 409

Muhammad—see **Mohammed**

Mühlberg, Battle at—48:181

Mühlhapt, Erwin—*D. Martin Luthers Evangelien-Auslegung*, Gütersloh, 1938–54 51:xin, 5

Mühlhausen—40:48, 230, 46:5n, 49, 84, 49:119n, 123n, 127n

Mühlphort, Hermann—31:330, 333, 50:50

Mulberry trees—11:76f

Mulde River—5:63

Mulert, Hermann—54:xxvn

Mules—1:67, 186, 2:328, 3:149, 4:205, 208, 250, 317, 5:73, 271, 6:293, 301f

Müller, Caspar—46:60, 61n, 63, 85n, 50:124–130

Müller, Gerhard—39:xiiin

Müller, Joseph—*Die Deutschen Katechismen der Böhmischen Brüder*, Berlin, 1887 36:275n

Müller, Krafft—41:8

Müller-Blattau—53:337n

Mummery—22:123

Munich—7:192n, 42:5f, 49:315n, 318
  Augustinian Monastery 48:31f, 39n, 55, 169

Münster—5:239, 24:92, 41:242n, 44:18, 53:292

Münster, Sebastian—5:293n, 336, 349
  Christiano lectori, Hebraica Biblia 8:89n, 141n
  Dictionarium hebraicum 8:88f, 195n, 35:284n, 47:261, 54:445
  En tibi lector 5:293n, 336, 349
  Hebraica Biblia, Latina planeque 8:89n, 54:445n

Münsterberg—40:16

Münsterer, Dr. Sebald—4:ix, 91n, 96n

Münzer, Thomas—2:150, 375, 3:5, 13, 15, 30, 31n, 165, 260, 301, 4:125, 240, 5:96, 311, 325, 7:261, 315, 342, 12:7, 16, 183, 218, 223, 253, 13:51, 61n, 64, 217, 14:4, 16:316n, 17:66n, 155, 183, 20:239, 303, 21:xix, 107, 22:225, 283, 524, 23:91, 280, 348, 24:69, 26:97, 192, 28:229, 309, 329, 29:58, 82n, 83, 30:254, 285n, 310, 34:12f, 52, 35:xii, 157, 169n, 196n, 403n, 37:18n, 70, 135–137, 139, 150, 179, 290, 327n, 352, 371n, 38:167, 40:xi, 47f, 50f, 52n, 53–57, 59, 89n, 90, 103n, 41:170n, 191, 43:163, 220, 253, 271n, 45:xiv, 243n, 343, 365n, 46:xi, 5n, 19n, 21n, 49n, 59n, 64n, 72n, 84, 121n, 180, 183, 47:14, 20, 104, 110n, 116n, 118f, 235, 48:79n, 49:82n, 94, 98, 111, 119n, 120, 121n, 123, 163n, 231, 265, 51:172, 386, 53:53f, 203, 237, 260, 263, 302, 54:xxii, 41, 60, 86, 144, 233, 284, 379
  Schriften und Briefe (Deutsch-Evangelische Messe) 6:261n

Murder—2:6, 9, 55, 60, 127, 138f, 143, 161, 167, 169, 171, 197, 214, 226, 3:5, 227, 258, 294, 4:220, 285, 313, 350, 391, 5:41, 143, 162f, 172, 181, 6:30, 88, 91, 100, 193, 215, 292, 7:94, 99, 192, 195, 8:5, 217, 219f, 236, 307, 9:166, 193–197, 202, 210–212, 219, 222, 16:21f, 244, 21:74, 77, 23:58, 62, 134, 141, 238, 247, 381, 417f, 420, 24:25, 53, 79, 216, 245, 260, 270, 291, 313, 315–317, 321–323, 331, 338, 341, 350, 26:36, 40f, 49, 96, 123, 338, 340, 363f, 371, 415, 453, 455, 27:23,

31, 80, 89, 133, 297, 368, 370, 384, 36:100, 165, 207, 210, 298, 41:124, 221, 237, 240, 256, 326, 344, 42:10, 44, 73, 92, 45:26, 86f, 157, 46:8, 20, 24, 27, 48f, 53, 70, 81, 129, 178, 179n, 182, 195, 227, 252, 315, 51:152f, 374
Murderers—2:59, 139f, 172, 196f, 248, 368, 4:123, 350, 5:41, 164, 177, 181, 377, 382, 7:73, 92, 113, 181, 8:205, 215f, 220, 13:186f, 24:22, 26, 76, 195, 216, 265, 272, 275, 279f, 284, 295, 313f, 324, 329, 370, 389
Murmuring—6:73, 148f, 177, 218, 306, 352f, 406, 7:55, 61, 126f, 131, 169, 229, 263, 17:128f, 155, 189, 283, 295, 356, 358
Murner, Thomas—39:xxiv, 129n, 140, 207n, 212, 215–224, 44:xvii, 48:194n, 234
  Christian and Brotherly Admonition 39:215n
  German translation of Luther's *Babylonian Captivity of the Church* 36:9
  Guild of Fools 39:129n
Murphy, T. Austin—see **Empie, Paul C., and Austin Murphy, eds.**
Musa, Anton—34:5
Muscovites—2:189, 4:331, 47:22
Muses—49:33, 70n
Music—1:126, 318, 4:56, 6:46, 12:98, 13:5, 26f, 167, 15:36f, 273f, 16:62, 24:89, 40:316, 45:369n, 46:252n, 49:68, 426f, 54:130, 205f, 246, 420
  Use in worship 10:43, 40:141f
Music, Chant—2:164
Music in grammar school—50:231–233
Music of heavenly spheres—5:22f
Musical instruments—1:317f, 10:43f, 152f, 228, 11:101f, 103n, 104, 209, 233, 272–275, 285–288, 12:98, 16:181
Musicians—1:295, 317
Muslims—see **Mohammedans**
Muth, Conrad—54:69
Mutianus Rufus—29:125n, 34:301
Myconius, Frederick—3:x, 8:ix, 34:108, 38:11, 63, 94, 40:383n, 50:178, 190n, 195, 218, 51:312n, 54:374, 462
Myconius, Oswald—37:81n
Mylius, Kraft—50:189n, 191n
Myrrh—4:99f, 296, 8:320f, 10:217f, 15:208, 227n, 231, 235f, 238, 242, 42:140f, 143, 52:278f
Myrtle trees—20:15, 24, 167–169, 183f
Mysteries—4:133, 244, 279, 356, 5:44, 78, 217f, 294, 6:71, 126, 10:91f, 148, 156, 158, 17:306, 308, 366, 20:198f, 23:169, 193, 25:50–52, 90, 131, 429, 431, 28:296f, 303–305, 29:175, 201, 239, 36:68, 70, 93n, 37:104, 114, 123, 157
Mysteries of the Scripture(s)—2:86
Mystery, Meaning of—25:431
Mystical interpretations—see **Scripture(s)**—Interpretation, Mystical
Mystical persons—10:91f
Mystical theology—25:287
Mysticism—2:104n, 23:144n, 25:411, 26:113n, 31:73, 330, 40:77, 48:36n, 59n, 366n
Mystics—5:128n, 37:272n
Mystics, Language of—25:213f, 287
Mythology—26:230n
Myths—4:127, 28:221f, 270, 321, 345, 29:31, 42f, 59, 68f, 73

Naaman—2:178, 258, 5:287, 6:217f, 8:136, 13:155f, 165, 170, 180, 207, 16:180, 17:291, 22:99, 24:80, 25:181, 282, 38:165, 41:228, 42:123, 46:192, 248, 47:91, 157, 49:74, 340, 51:148, 52:271
Naaman the Syrian—1:302, 3:81, 89, 235, 332, 7:65, 151, 14:19, 19:84, 26:211, 27:287, 335, 28:364
Nabal—5:285, 303, 305f, 364f, 6:14, 31, 50f, 55, 63, 7:24, 8:92n, 291, 9:149, 15:141, 18:131, 41:188, 192
Nabatea—4:331
Nabib—16:276
Nabo—17:133, 137
Naboth—9:196, 11:113, 17:74, 51:161
Nadab—36:154
Naevius, C.—19:126n
Nahar River—6:309
Nahor—1:358, 2:240, 243, 3:352, 4:3, 184–186, 260, 281, 5:207–210, 280, 6:66, 79, 84f, 307f, 7:13, 45:23n, 46:316, 47:157
Nahum, Prophet—16:5n, 18:281f, 293, 295f, 35:326
  Commentary on his book 18:ix, xi, 281–315(text)
Nails—9:211, 214
Nain, Widow of—8:317, 22:46
Naked Godhead—see **God**—Naked deity
Naked mercy—25:137
Nakedness—1:165, 174, 1:165–168, 7:240, 18:215
Nakedness in marriage—5:34, 37
Name of the Lord—18:111, 141, 171, 239f, 394, 396, 399, 416, 20:86, 151f, 238, 256, 336, 36:63f
Names—6:141, 179, 248–250, 258f, 263, 286, 10:133, 230, 252f, 322, 15:102,

106f, 197, 308, 16:80, 203, 17:90, 307, 345, 362, 372, 385, 20:72, 145, 341
Namur—34:345, 353
Nannen, Peter—32:279, 282f, 285
Nanni, Giovanni—41:294n
Naomi—3:133
Naphtali—5:336–338, 340, 350, 6:275f, 319, 321, 366, 380, 8:55, 70, 102, 222, 278f, 291–293, 9:307, 11:186
Naphtali, Territory of—22:216
Naphtali, Tribe of—13:28, 18:60
Naples—3:x, 295, 34:345, 36:208, 48:73n, 49:265n
Naschhausen—40:110, 132, 136, 138, 150
Nassau—50:199n
Natalibus, Peter de—*Catalogus sanctorum* 48:17
Natalie, St.—25:462
Nathan—6:42, 377
Nathan, Prophet—2:72, 4:173, 176, 7:41, 151, 274, 8:331f, 9:52, 10:31, 163, 240, 12:368, 406, 13:207, 15:280, 286f, 288, 290, 292, 294, 20:330, 22:397, 403f, 25:16, 445, 26:108, 29:115, 30:263, 38:161, 47:240
Nathaniel—5:217, 22:128, 182, 186, 189, 194f, 197–202, 413
National Socialists (Nazis)—47:268n
Nations—19:129, 139, 20:4, 6, 15, 17–19, 22, 24, 32, 47, 50, 63, 71, 81, 87, 89, 95f, 113, 305f, 338f, 21:352f, 25:8, 39f, 122, 125, 281f, 418f, 464, see also **Gentiles**
Their boundaries 10:411
Nations along the Mediterranean—17:72, 314, 317, 413f
Nations, Great—13:342
Natural History—see **Pliny**
Natural law—6:26, 113, 13:105, 160f, 164, 369, 15:5, 25:18f, 180–183, 187, 35:159, 172, 40:97f, 104, 310, 41:155, 43:16, 44:228, 45:127n, 117, 247, 287n, 292f, 296, 309, 46:25, 27, 28n, 29, 34, 108, 110, 114, 230, 269, 305, 47:x, 21, 79n, 89n, 90–95, 110f, 168f, 228n, 49:27, 257, 50:12, 37–39, 52:208, 54:67, 103, 293
Natural limitations—25:320
Natural order—37:55n, 61, 75n, 81, 89, 97–99, 110f, 114, 119f, 121n, 130, 132–134, 145, 153, 195f, 214, 223, 253–255, 257–259, 267f, 278, 297–301, 335, 355, 361f, 366, 44:xvi
Natural phenomena—2:147
Natural relations—25:13
Nature—1:37f, 46, 62, 66, 94, 99, 109, 115, 117f, 120, 128, 130f, 139, 146, 149, 153f, 156, 162–165, 167–170, 179, 183, 191, 200f, 204, 219f, 229f, 238, 244, 256, 273, 3:8, 47f, 52f, 56, 68, 85, 127, 152, 165, 199, 206, 221, 226f, 254f, 258, 262, 298, 323, 343, 347, 360, 4:3, 27, 37, 40, 51f, 58, 66, 70, 93, 107, 144, 179, 194, 222, 250, 253, 270, 290, 292, 299, 323, 343, 346, 349f, 353, 355, 386f, 289, 400, 5:37, 49, 62, 71f, 74f, 101, 129, 190, 229, 271, 282, 291–293, 297, 325, 355, 365, 371, 375f, 378, 380, 383–385, 6:90, 94, 115, 189, 7:9f, 15, 17, 21, 30, 33, 36, 48f, 164–166, 170, 178–180, 195, 211, 226, 228f, 233f, 236, 245, 261f, 273, 280–282, 302, 305, 323, 336, 340f, 8:5, 8, 10, 12–14, 16f, 19–21, 30, 67, 89, 169f, 178f, 210, 213, 216, 218, 220, 227f, 230–233, 248, 256–258, 284, 310f, 314, 324, 332, 11:13, 12:76f, 14:236, 15:9, 17f, 24:57f, 62, 107, 117, 210f, 213n, 223f, 226, 228, 255, 258, 267, 285, 289, 316, 328, 363, 373, 25:73, 361f, 434, 26:273, 307, 368f, 373, 395, 397–400, 406, 413, 28:201f, 29:134, 149, 30:44, 96f, 156, 211, 222f, 245, 253, 259, 263, 266, 314, 38:29, 202, 45:18, 22, 127, 144, 147, 149, 155f, 205f, 303, 353, 46:305, 52:12, 108, 122, 129, 161f, 164, 168f, 196, 207, 241f, 245, 273, 54:24, 474
Nature, Corrupted and deformed—1:11, 31, 63, 71, 104, 108, 134, 141f, 161, 174f, 177, 183, 187, 254, 262, 339
Nature, Law of—16:22
Nature and grace—33:240f
Naumburg—48:63n, 104, 218, 49:123n, 50:144n, 207n, 221n, 291, 304, 53:184f, 54:190, 436
Parish Visitation in 40:267
Naumburg, Bishop of—31:339
Naumburg-Zeitz, Diocese of—45:5n
Navarre—34:345, 48:155n
Navel—15:250
Nazarenes—26:426, 452
Nazareth—1:195, 8:305, 21:301, 22:73, 128, 187, 189, 194f, 214–217, 344, 416, 485, 23:245f, 248, 289, 303, 333, 366, 24:33f, 403, 26:125, 47:222, 52:9, 144
Nazarites—5:262, 8:305, 18:143, 20:77, 102f, 106n, 38:233
Neapolis—7:5
Nebaioth—10:413
Nebo, Mt.—9:299
Nebuchadnezzar, King—1:302, 2:203, 258f, 3:10f, 89, 5:236f, 6:41, 333, 335,

7:120, 139, 141, 143, 11:524, 547, 12:34, 16:86, 141, 176, 182, 18:42n, 327, 368, 19:84, 117f, 125, 20:90, 25:421, 470, 27:335, 29:174n, 30:104, 34:192, 35:294, 297, 337, 47:85, 158, 188

Nebuzaradan—7:53

Necessity—11:332f, 333n, 524, 547, 25:371–373, 376, 33:36–44, 64–70, 151, 184f, 192–195, 36:260, 45:119n

Neco, Pharoah—20:141

Nectarius, Bishop of Constantinople—41:88, 91

Needs—4:57, 322, 340, 363, 396, 409, 7:63, 156, 159, 182, 184–186, 214, 338, 370f, 376, 8:126, 203n, 300, 302, 24:7, 11, 18, 103, 112, 119, 150, 240f, 244, 251, 264, 391f, 422, 27:125f, 237, 329, 385, 408

Needs, Physical—21:13, 143–145, 196–201, 229–231, 233–235

Neefe, John—54:369

Negation—25:383

Negative statements—25:52, 311

Negeb—2:324, 18:202f

Negligence—7:115, 239, 296

Nehemiah—16:221, 17:124, 126, 130, 133, 47:204, 249

Nehemiah, Book of—20:26, 84, 274, 342

Neighbor, The—3:25, 84, 118, 122, 125, 198, 203f, 209, 226, 240, 277f, 327, 342, 354, 4:44, 46, 74, 84, 188, 196, 222, 290, 313, 333, 353, 374, 381, 5:5, 8, 40, 65, 67, 78, 82f, 85, 97, 109, 112, 114, 181, 189, 191, 259, 263f, 286, 295, 320f, 381f, 6:197, 205, 208, 241f, 245, 248, 7:7, 24, 38–41, 57, 86f, 115, 132, 165, 182f, 185, 194, 196, 218, 222f, 310, 315, 318, 329, 338, 8:45, 64, 76, 107, 128, 152, 198f, 279, 284, 286, 288–290, 292f, 304, 14:118–120, 132, 219, 231f, 244, 300f, 16:16, 21:24f, 77f, 81, 103, 121f, 128, 135f, 149f, 152f, 179f, 186, 194, 214–216, 218f, 223, 235–237, 258, 264, 23:25, 27, 56, 65, 67, 71–73, 81, 110, 135f, 172, 240, 270, 275, 317, 320, 322, 329, 417, 24:20, 41, 50, 52, 87, 143, 157, 162, 198, 226, 250f, 254, 256, 261–263, 267f, 272, 316, 377, 385, 390, 26:161, 171, 181, 220, 247, 255, 260, 273, 285, 287, 376, 398, 449, 27:30f, 50–52, 54–58, 62–64, 66f, 71, 75, 114, 203, 295, 298, 313, 347–349, 351–357, 369, 374f, 395f, 401, 29:24, 29, 41, 55f, 78, 84, 134, 184, 197, 240, 30:20, 33, 35, 41, 46–48, 67, 76–79, 96f, 100, 117f, 120, 122–124, 152, 156–158, 182, 184, 198, 204, 214, 219, 240, 264, 269, 271, 274, 277, 292, 296f, 300, 304, 308, 325, 35:120f, 361, 36:353, 356–359, 37:24, 92, 149, 199, 281, 288, 292, 42:66–71, 45:xiii, 94–98, 101, 103, 177, 245–250, 261f, 286, 291f, 294, 296, 306f, 46:12, 16, 55, 78, 121, 129, 141, 151, 169, 182, 215, 223, 240, 246, 289, 312, 51:6, 10, 12, 37, 63, 65f, 71–74, 86, 95f, 104f, 116, 140, 152f, 158–161, 178, 180, 183, 267–270, 274, 344, 346, 351, 52:24, 26, 35f, 39, 117f, 173, 224f, 242, 246, 265

Neighbor, Loving and serving one's—24:251, 262, 25:512–517, 38:87, 95, 113, 123f, 184, 204, 41:17, 76f, 166

Neighbor, Serving the—31:302–304, 364–377

Nelson, Benjamin N.—*The Idea of Usury*, Princeton, 1949 45:237n

Neo-Arians—1:16n, 26:312

Neo-Aristotelians—47:38n

Neobulus, Jodocus—50:172n, 173n, 174n

Neophytes—9:241, 244

Neoplatonism—20:155n, 31:13n

Nephilim—7:330

Nepotism—13:184

Nero, Emperor—2:153, 7:121, 195, 13:68, 194, 14:333, 15:34, 43, 45, 72n, 25:127, 34:238, 37:254, 39:95, 203f, 306, 40:19n, 41:243, 244n, 323, 333, 348, 47:181

Nesen, Wilhelm—53:275

Nest—11:138–144, 150

Nestorianism—37:xviii, 212n, 292n, 362, 41:94n, 95n, 96–98, 99n, 100–118, 120f, 123, 136, 138f, 147, 156, 159, 163

Nestorians—22:323, 351, 24:107, 32:128, 38:307n, 310

Nestorius, Bishop of Constantinople—15:292, 339, 341, 38:307n, 310

Nests—9:220, 19:210, 213f

Net—26:222f, 28:130f

Netherlands (Lowlands)—13:336, 16:4, 31:381, 32:263, 41:128, 43:267, 45:78, 48:33n, 233n, 49:12f, 21f, 144n, 50:251, 253, 254n, 312n

Nettl, Paul—*Luther and Music*, Philadelphia, 1948 53:xxn, 55n, 59n, 319, 54:130n

translator of *A Preface to all Good Hymnals* 53:319f

Nettles—1:204f

Neudecker, C. Gotthold—*Urkunden aus der Reformationszeit*, Cassel, 1836 46:90n

Neuheler, Jodocus—54:233
Neumann, Max—*Geschichte des Wuchers in Deutschland,* Halle, 1865 45:236n, 290n, 295n
Neumark—47:135
Neustadt—1:274
Augustinian Monastery 48:20, 31
Neutralists—27:239, 256
New being—25:104
New birth—1:228, 22:92–94, 98, 100f, 277, 279, 281f, 284–286, 289f, 298f, 301, 312, 353, 364, 24:227, 230, 25:68, 104, 26:351–353, 355, 445, 30:10–12, 14, 43, 273, 326, 34:113, 37:16n, 68f, 72, 143, 364, 369, 371
New Covenant—see **Covenant**—New
New creation—13:293, 14:17, 27:138–141, 32:27, 39f, 94, 37:200–202, 51:19, 63, 243f
New creatures—11:374f, 13:378, 22:292, 29:156f
New earth—28:143f
New Israel—see **Israel, New**
New Jerusalem—11:176
New law—25:112, 486–488, 26:157, 162–164
New life—22:290
New man—6:258f, 354, 362, 11:267, 273, 296, 319f, 322f, 435, 550, 14:190–193, 22:317, 374, 23: 165, 231, 324, 333, 25:323, 25:57, 69, 104, 179, 191, 435, 25:68, 26:7f, 351, 431
New moon—11:101, 16:17, 18:28, 48, 181, 26:411
New nature—13:323
New obedience—12:381
New people and Jerusalem—47:303f
New prophets—see **Radical Reformers**
New Rome—see **Constantinople**
New Testament—see **Scripture(s), New Testament**
New things—15:20f, 164
New York City—38:xii
Newman, Louis Israel—47:60n, 126
Newness—10:154, 17:365f
Newtown—see **Eisleben**
Nicaea—26:113
Nicaea, Council of—see **Councils, General Church**
Nice—50:183n, 243n
Nicephorus I, Emperor—41:374n
Nicephorus II, Emperor—41:374n
Nicetas, Bishop of Remesiana—53:171
Nicholas I, Pope—28:364
Nicholas II, Pope—37:300, 41:331n, 334f
Nicholas III, Pope—40:353
Nicholas V, Pope—45:302n
Nicholas, St.—2:379, 14:114, 23:59, 45:285n, 53:268
Nicholas', St., Day—39:252n, 314n
Nicholas of Cusa—41:62n
Nicholas of Lyra—2:ix, 10n, 11, 13n, 14, 33n, 38, 52, 58, 67n, 69n, 71, 73, 82n, 92, 104n, 107n, 109n, 115, 129, 138, 164, 166, 179n, 182n, 189n, 190n, 194n, 201n, 203n, 211, 227n, 232n, 234, 237n, 238f, 248n, 264n, 276, 292n, 293n, 2:303n, 304n, 305n, 310n, 364, 370n, 371n, 380, 381n, 383f, 3:ix, 16n, 23, 26–28, 34, 47n, 64n, 67, 71n, 72, 188n, 205n, 230n, 232n, 246n, 250f, 257–259, 263, 266, 268, 269n, 298n, 299, 308n, 309, 313, 337n, 353n, 358, 4:xi, 9, 10n, 13n, 43n, 90, 97, 184, 187n, 205, 230n, 260, 265n, 280n, 301, 302, 327n, 331n, 341, 359n, 383, 395, 5:25n, 30n, 36n, 56n, 101n, 111n, 113, 134n, 149n, 160n, 212, 216, 241n, 243f, 251n, 253, 263, 273, 280n, 281n, 299, 301, 302n, 320, 323f, 326, 352n, 374, 379n, 381n, 385n, 6:xi, 32n, 35n, 71n, 96n 125n, 130n, 178n, 179n, 181n, 184n, 192n, 201n, 208n, 210n, 215n, 223n, 230n, 238n, 249n, 260n, 274n, 291n, 292n, 307n, 314n, 319n, 321n, 323n, 338n, 342f, 387n, 7:4, 6n, 21n, 24n, 39n, 40n, 52, 54n, 67n, 77n, 79n, 81n, 108, 113n, 119, 142, 149, 189, 205, 216n, 233n, 243, 260n, 265n, 268, 300, 347, 351n, 373n, 8:23n, 38n, 50, 56f, 65n, 85n, 86f, 90, 102n, 127, 139n, 144, 155, 156n, 175, 207, 213n, 221, 222n, 225, 246f, 280n, 281, 284n, 291n, 304n, 9:x, 36n, 69n, 135n, 222n, 10:38, 40, 42, 54, 116, 210, 247, 259, 269, 280, 300, 309, 327, 397, 410, 413, 431, 448f, 463, 11:3n, 41, 43, 65, 75, 102, 106n, 122n, 127n, 144, 166n, 180, 183, 187n, 189, 290n, 337, 365n, 367n, 368n, 378n, 384, 541, 12:200, 14:346, 15:79f, 269n, 295n, 329n, 336n, 16:69n, 97n, 100n, 117n, 252n, 255n, 272n, 330n, 18:xii, 51n, 54, 63, 132, 152, 188, 203, 219, 302, 329, 379, 20:28, 36, 96, 118, 127, 130, 186, 290n, 337n, 342n, 25:xi, 3, 9, 28, 58, 60f, 80, 97, 136, 138f, 146, 148, 152, 162, 170, 178, 191, 200, 212, 214, 246, 256, 332, 402, 435, 451, 516f, 26:243n, 27:70n, 245, 28:295, 32:161, 35:34n, 290n, 41:167n, 45:321n, 47:66, 68n, 81n, 130, 131n, 134, 138, 176n, 178n, 179n, 181n, 186n, 187n, 188n, 191, 210, 213n, 214, 216n, 222n, 225, 228,

229n, 234, 238, 283, 290n, 292n, 48:26n, 67n, 225n, 51:6n, 54:14
Postilla super epistolas Pauli Apostoli 29:163n
Postilla super Psalterium 14:346n, 29:113n, 120n, 177n, 181n, 199n, 205n, 206n, 208n, 222n
Postillae perpetuae in universa biblia 1:xi, 4n, 5n, 8n, 28n, 32n, 37n, 39, 40n, 42, 57n, 70, 88n, 91n, 93, 129n, 131, 151n, 169, 184, 187n, 188, 191, 217n, 223n, 226n, 231, 234, 251n, 269n, 270, 271n, 295, 296n, 302, 303n, 304, 312n, 317n, 327n, 337n, 338n, 339n, 350n, 352n, 353n, 356n, 10:104, 11:5n, 65n, 25:6, 155f, 29:114n, 35:350n
Nicholas of Tudesco (Panormitanus)—31:220n, 265, 32:81n, 41:313n, 319
Concerning Penance and Remission 31:147f
Lecture on the Five Books of the Decretalium 41:305n
Nicholson, John—see **Lambert, John**
Nicodemian manner—23:300
Nicodemus—9:4, 22:276–283, 285f, 280, 292–295, 298, 303f, 306, 309, 311f, 316f, 319, 331, 337, 345, 353, 355, 359, 361, 365, 381, 409, 413, 415, 23:296, 299–306, 33:86, 280, 37:20, 219, 38:28, 43, 58, 81
Nicolaitans—1:238, 30:284
Nicolaus—24:204
Nicopolis—29:88
Night—1:40, 42, 44, 170, 309, 11:19, 234, 455, 457, 510f, 20:14, 168, 25:112, 480
Night and day—Biblical meaning 25:480
Night watches—14:193
Nightingale—13:120
Nile River—1:97, 99–100, 101, 126, 2:344, 7:346, 8:38, 96, 108f, 9:117, 16:127, 161n, 182, 184, 218, 20:114, 25:156
Nimbschen, Convent at—49:115n, 50:278n
Nimrod—2:196–200, 203, 205f, 210, 212, 214, 219, 224, 230, 231f, 234, 240, 246f, 283, 364, 371, 7:267, 8:65, 13:311, 25:172, 36:12, 228
Nimrodites—2:247
Nimrods—27:158
Nineteenth Sunday after Trinity—23:352n
Ninety-five Theses—see **Luther, Martin, Writings of**
Nineveh—1:302, 314, 2:200–202, 214, 225, 232, 259, 276, 342f, 5:336, 6:227, 8:227, 13:46, 14:19, 273, 17:335, 18:3, 283f, 298, 302–307, 310, 313, 315, 345f, 19:4, 6, 22f, 31, 39f, 37, 52, 84, 89, 94, 96f, 21:156, 22:92, 26:211f, 35:326, 36:84
Nineveh, King of—1:302, 314
Ninevites—2:24, 26, 43, 178, 3:81, 89, 289, 6:284, 371, 7:152
Niobe—11:203
Nisan (Jewish month)—2:226n, 38:317n
No—18:310
Noah—1:76, 206, 208, 310, 334–336, 342, 352–358, 2:ixf, 7f, 10, 12f, 16f, 22–25, 27f, 33, 37f, 40, 44, 47, 49–59, 61–64, 66f, 70f, 73, 75–77, 80–87, 89–92f, 96–98, 101–106, 109–115, 117, 119n, 129, 131–133, 135, 143, 145, 148, 153–159, 162f, 165–167, 172–175, 177–180, 182–184, 186f, 189n, 193f, 196f, 204, 209f, 214, 216, 219–222, 225, 228, 230, 235f, 245, 249, 283, 368, 381, 383, 3:39, 141, 233, 241, 250, 268, 4:3, 15n, 98n, 100f, 303, 308, 318, 322, 5:74, 149, 207, 6:89, 233, 327, 7:36, 125, 225, 8:57, 75f, 202, 236, 315, 317, 13:34, 97, 14:126, 16:62, 17:36, 240, 292, 303, 334, 358, 413f, 19:40, 42, 221, 20:68, 253, 22:31, 33, 36, 116, 131, 449f, 453, 23:260, 265f, 27:146, 370, 29:236f, 30:113, 115f, 176, 193f, 35:xi, 31f, 79, 83, 36:39, 43, 65, 174, 38:290, 51:82, 296, 52:126f, 150, 226
Nob—13:183, 16:115
Nobility—2:5f, 19, 24, 366, 3:182, 227, 249, 260, 7:62f, 110, 118, 142, 160f, 164, 167, 180, 182, 347, 350, 8:57, 105, 321, 13:215, 353, 14:4–6, 54, 57n, 117f, 120, 122n, 231, 267, 23:5, 262f, 277, 298, 322, 356, 361f, 394, 397, 402, 417, 419, 421, 27:102, 123–126, 198, 407, 39:290, 45:61f, 177, 269n, 390, 46:7f, 11, 13f, 18n 19–21, 23, 28, 39–43, 52, 54, 59f, 67, 71, 73–75, 81, 84, 91, 98, 101n, 102, 104f, 113n, 115–117, 121f, 125f, 128–132, 135, 162f, 165f, 169, 171, 176, 180, 183–190, 193, 196, 199–204, 210, 214, 216, 223, 225, 233, 235, 239–241, 243–245, 248–251, 255, 266, 302
Nobility, The—29:22, 77
Nobility of Germany—50:98, 224f, 225n, 243n, 245, 253
Nobles—4:74, 76, 84, 90, 174, 193, 208, 211, 224, 276, 397, 5:42, 52, 368, 8:44, 56, 59, 62, 93, 100, 103, 106, 108, 128, 12:256, 24:22, 81, 123, 162, 197, 265f, 271
Nobles, Pledge of the—32:115n
Nobles, Young—13:215, 220

Nobody—6:366, 13:203
Nobody, Mr.—22:396f
Nocturnes—11:455n
Nod, Land of—1:307, 309
Noetians—34:209n
Noetus—37:361n
Nomads—5:265, 8:62
Nominalism, nominalists—31:5, 322n, 34:27n, 48:30n, 59n, 85n
Nomos—27:319, 321
Non-Christians—24:38, 71, 134, 175, 212, 217, 221, 251, 28:33–35, 38–40, 114f, 119, 46:186, 265
Nones—11:422n, 525n
Nonimputation—25:269, 271f, 278
Nonresistance—45:77, 81n
Nonwillingness—25:333, 439
Nook for the church—5:52
Noonan, John T.—*The Scholastic Analysis of Usury*, Cambridge, Mass., 1957 45:174n, 175n, 238n, 248n, 252n, 257n, 292n, 298n, 299n, 302n, 304n, 305n, 317n
Noonday devil—11:148, 199, 219, 222–224, 226, 289, 446
Noph—16:102
Nordhausen—7:299n, 41:253, 46:48, 48:173n, 275n, 49:176n, 183n, 186
Augustinian Monastery 48:16, 125n
Nördlingen—31:37, 49:100, 53:xiiin, 54, 184
North, The—20:63, 65, 67, 189f, 250, 252
North Africa—22:137n
Northeners—10:411f
Norway—54:271
Nose(s)—13:112, 169f, 27:134, 158
Notation—53:xix
Notation, Musical—53:xix, 57f, 204f
Nothing—15:14, 21f
Notker, Balbulus—53:25n, 32, 274
Nourishment—23:8, 10, 39–41, 133, 142f, 176
Novatians—25:314f, 26:197, 198n, 29:181f, 227, 37:368, 40:374n
Novationists—41:329n
Novatus—22:67, 35:403n
Novelties—11:294
Novices—28:289f, 320, 326f
Nullifying God's grace—26:179f, 184f, 198, 200
Numa Pompilius—8:134f, 38:290n, 291
Numbers, Book of—2:34
Numbers and time—1:44
Numerology—11:167, 524–527, 14:193n, 20:54, 52:134f
Numidia—2:194, 203, 10:412
***Nunc Dimittis* (Canticle)**—53:247
Nuncios, Papal—41:6, 9n
Nunneries—see **Convents**
Nuns—1:103, 135, 238f, 2:349, 3:128, 201, 204, 209, 275, 277, 321, 4:65, 207, 5:48, 253n, 329, 6:111, 132, 348, 8:175, 225n, 10:3, 14:15, 23, 39, 47, 94, 99, 257, 16:310, 312, 21:204f, 256f, 22:51, 65, 81, 108, 132, 221, 256, 258, 278f, 302, 357f, 360, 365, 374, 387, 405, 430, 456, 464, 514, 23:26f, 70, 205, 213, 234, 262, 268, 328, 356, 410f, 24:225, 360, 25:419f, 460, 26:33, 141, 199, 27:61, 28:16f, 40f, 336, 338, 341, 29:20, 54, 56, 30:6, 15, 83, 95, 97, 173, 177, 189, 36:75, 116, 159, 213, 260f, 38:173, 214, 42:47, 55, 45:14, 19, 37, 39, 41f, 53, 170, 172, 348, 387n, 46:143, 147, 189, 209, 217, 227n, 241, 52:217f, 250f, 254f, 259, 266, 54:134, 188, 312, see also **Monks and nuns**
Nuremberg—see **Nürnberg**
Nurembergers—14:ix
Nürnberg—4:91n, 5:ix, 6:ix, 320, 7:108, 16:ix, 23:x, 219n, 35:177f, 36:235, 38:6, 9, 11, 62n, 72n, 73, 93, 42:5, 46:210, 213n, 214–216, 263, 48:43n, 67n, 92, 123f, 125n, 149n, 150n, 172, 184, 227n, 388, 397, 398n, 49:xvin, 17, 24n, 30n, 32, 72n, 81n, 82n, 94, 96f, 100, 103n, 105n, 146n, 157f, 165n, 166n, 167n, 190n, 204f, 215n, 220n, 224n, 228, 236n, 244n, 245f, 250f, 256, 272, 274n, 282n, 284n, 287, 293n, 297n, 313n, 314n, 315, 317n, 318n, 332n, 350, 357, 360n, 368n, 397n, 414n, 420n, 422n, 423, 435n, 50:9f, 11n, 14n, 17n, 54n, 56f, 58n, 61f, 75f, 77n, 119, 209n, 248n, 263, 297n, 51:xiii, xivn, 83, 53:54, 191, 193, 219, 222, 232, 265, 287, 54:82, 356
Augustinian Monastery 48:41n, 51n, 60, 72, 92, 125n, 161f, 169f, 193
Churches and monasteries in 49:10, 11n, 96n, 98n, 166n, 167n, 204f, 238n, 282n
Evangelical Church in 50:13f, 61f, 65n, 75f, 241
Reformation movement in 45:135n, 136n, 162, 344
Nürnberg, Diets of, 1522-1524—12:x, 28:56, 34:12, 41:141n, 265n, 44:132n, 212n, 45:xii, xv, 33n, 69n, 135n, 138, 197n, 240–243, 246n, 247n, 310n, 46:xi, 167, 227n, 247n, 49:23n, 24n, 35f, 60, 69n, 93n, 125f
Nürnberg, League of—43:266, 50:189n, 190n

Nürnberg, Peace of—41:6
Nürnberg Mass—53:54
Nürnberg Truce—50:xiv, 54n, 82n, 155n
Nurses—43:129f
Nutrition—God's miracle 1:93
Nuts—3:147f, 150f
Nuts, Garden of—11:23, 363

***O Lord, We Praise You, Bless You and Adore You* (hymn)**—38:206
Oak, The—21:272, 22:250, 526
Oak of Mamre—3:184
Oaths—2:246, 4:75, 78, 83f, 86–88, 142–144, 146–148, 150f, 172f, 230, 231n, 244f, 252, 254, 258f, 266, 405, 6:78, 82, 7:248f, 8:139f, 143f, 196f, 322, 9:72–74, 85, 103, 14:35, 15:135, 217n, 256, 17:136, 155f, 186, 240f, 348, 20:277, 21:99–104, 24:390, 25:25, 79, 379f, 489f, 27:12, 196, 38:195, 225, 41:299f, 44:164n, 46:48, 50n, 113n, 146, 151f, 187, 193f, 282f, 303, 313n, 51:142
Oats—24:51, 385
Obadiah, Prophet—18:193f, 199, 19:157, 210f, 35:321f
Commentary on his book 18:xf, 193–204 (text)
Obduracy—17:83, 157, 159
Obedience—1:95, 104, 118n, 146, 157f, 196f, 203, 227, 313, 325, 2:36, 77f, 80, 90, 126, 173, 193, 251f, 268–273, 275, 280, 296, 349, 398, 3:80, 100, 169–175, 203f, 248, 273, 283f, 353, 4:6, 17, 21, 35, 38f, 41f, 72, 79, 81, 91, 97, 103, 105, 107, 109f, 112–115, 121–124, 132–134, 142, 150, 182, 235, 258, 267, 270, 285f, 304, 346f, 5:7, 114, 117f, 233, 263, 303, 326, 351, 6:26f, 29f, 38, 51, 168, 238f, 7:83, 105, 115, 135, 168, 180, 185, 196f, 204, 311, 319, 9:ix, 70, 110, 130, 149, 151, 177, 204, 212, 219, 10:16f, 28f, 33, 130, 189, 11:546–549, 12:85, 375, 381, 13:176, 279, 15:135f, 237, 17:157, 246, 323, 20:7, 161, 212–214, 21:269, 22:86, 93, 98f, 121, 138f, 154–156, 165, 216, 227, 229, 286, 314, 397, 452, 456–458, 509, 23:21, 24, 135, 182, 194, 214, 217, 247, 252, 292–294, 346, 356, 406, 24:35, 41, 43, 48, 50, 81, 166, 188, 192, 227, 252, 255f, 262, 306, 313, 345, 348, 361, 370, 388, 390, 395, 398, 400, 25:5, 92, 109, 132, 250, 408, 444, 488, 26:12, 70, 125, 128, 137, 148, 172, 175, 200, 249, 286, 305, 345f, 355f, 372f, 376, 386, 391, 398, 428, 448, 27:7, 14, 18, 61, 113, 120, 163, 372, 28:337f, 361, 29:46, 65, 71, 73, 77, 103f, 223, 239, 30:8, 22, 31, 40f, 73–75, 88, 170, 172, 188, 205f, 265, 288, 309, 31:369, 385, 34:307f, 320, 35:142, 145, 239, 260, 374, 379, 36:208–214, 350, 37:15, 86n, 133, 135, 284, 364f, 38:xxi, 104, 114f, 136, 150, 174, 181, 228, 239, 41:35, 39f, 146f, 225–227, 250, 287, 296, 376, 42:20, 47, 108f, 44:98, 45:31, 84, 111f, 125f, 46:95, 98f, 103, 126, 129, 180, 185, 194, 226, 277, 283f, 306, 310, 52:217f, 244, 263, 266f, 54:67
Outward vs. inward 25:347
Obedience, Willing—10:26, 325
Obedience of faith—see **Faith, Obedience of**
Obedience to God—1:65, 94–97, 109, 130, 140, 231, 308
Obedience to parents—46:277, 306, 310
Oberland—23:7
Oberman, Heiko A.—26:173n, 39:xiin
Forerunners of the Reformation, Cambridge, Mass., 1966 31:7
Harvest of Medieval Theology, Cambridge, Mass., 1963 4:58n, 31:7, 38:184n, 248n, 263n
Oblation—36:53, see also **Offering**; **Sacrifice**
Obligations—see **Duty**
Obscure terms—20:107f, 116, 192
Observantine controversy—10:75
Observants—11:232, 428, 18:55, 67, 323, 30:275
Obsopoeus, Vincentius—19:x
Obstetrical knowledge—7:14n
Obstinancy—2:17, 20:12, 23:356
Occam, William of—1:57n, 14:284n, 25:xi, 7, 325, 343, 372, 458, 26:128, 31:6, 13n, 32:153n, 34:25, 155n, 187, 34:27n, 38:263n, 272, 48:6n, 30n, 96n, 156n, 54:392
Commentarii in quattuor Sententiarum libros 25:162, 261, 34:188n
Occamism, Occamists—33:190n, 37:214n, 215n, 272n, 363n, 38:32n
Occasional services—53:91–126
Occidentals—16:33
Occupations, Secular—see **Callings**
Oceans—1:34, 207, 2:94f, 107, 245, 3:39, 343, 4:5, 201, 23:358, 385, 24:45, 49, 257, 26:107, 27:344, 392, 409
Ockham, William of—see **Occam, William of**
Octavius—see **Augustus Caesar**
October—2:92

Octonaries (Psalm 119)—11:414n, 422n
Oculi Sunday—23:422n
Oddballs—11:208f
Odors—2:116f, 236, 269, 343
Oecolampadians—34:346
Oecolampadius, John—2:243, 3:5, 12:49, 221, 16:330, 332, 17:75, 82n, 155, 238, 27:119n, 129n, 28:244, 365f, 382, 30:276, 36:332, 346, 37:xv, 21n, 22, 33, 41f, 45, 49f, 511, 66f, 70, 104–124, 147n, 148n, 165, 173, 240, 252, 274–276, 279, 285f, 289f, 347, 38:xi, 5–7, 9f, 15, 16n, 17, 18n, 19n, 20, 28, 30, 35–37, 43, 46, 51–53, 55, 58f, 61, 64, 68, 70, 74, 79–81, 89n, 157n, 247, 289, 291, 293n, 299n, 302, 48:149n, 230n, 255, 258, 49:42f, 50n, 77n, 96n, 146, 160, 188, 200n, 213, 215n, 216n, 234n, 237, 238n, 302, 303n, 50:3–5, 7, 54:12, 23, 75, 86, 95, 147, 173, 262, 376
His views attacked 37:7, 39–54, 67, 78f, 88, 93, 103–124, 127, 130, 135, 138f, 176, 252–288, 305f, 323–327, 343–352, 354
Oecolampadius, John, Works of—
Antisyngramma 37:9, 135
Apologetics 37:9, 21n, 41n, 52n, 71n, 72n, 80n, 135n, 265n
Concerning Luther's Book 37:158
Genuine Exposition 37:xiv, 9, 23n, 30n, 36n, 47n, 52n, 54n, 65n, 73n, 75n, 76n, 78n, 81n, 93n, 102n, 103n, 104n, 106n, 113n, 114n, 116n, 119n, 120n, 121n, 123n
In Jesaiam prophetam 16:4n
Luther's Incorrect Interpretation of the Eternally True Words, "This is my Body," Will Not Stand up to Criticism 49:172n, 179n, 186n
On Confession 48:230n, 253n, 254
On the Original Meaning of the Words of Institution according to the Testimony of the Fathers of the Church 49:145n
Psegmata Joannis Chrysostomi 49:45n
Reasonable Answer 36:336n, 37:9, 16n, 21n, 22n, 36n, 39n, 46n, 80n, 102n, 131n, 138n, 140n, 144n
Reply to Pirkheimer 37:9, 22n, 30n, 46n, 50n, 52n, 65n, 67n, 73n, 75n, 86n, 103n, 138n
Second Reasonable Answer 37:78n, 157, 269–288 (notes)
The Unlearned Canons 48:149
Oeden, John—45:136f
Oertel, Veit—34:301, 320n, 38:264n, 54:257
Offene Schuld—see **Confession, Public**
Offenses—6:24, 36, 163, 318, 359, 13:178, 276, 278, 16:202, 17:61, 63, 84f, 87, 95–97, 99, 106, 156, 173, 175, 216, 246, 311f, 318, 350, 20:123, 148–150, 216f, 220, 335, 21:241f, 25:113, 116f, 500f, 514, 29:57f, 60, 76, 100, 35:73, 196, 199f, 379, 54:62, 73
Offerings—2:116f, 384f, 4:99, 237, 9:174, 198, 233, 258, 298, 305, 26:263f, 27:126, 211, 335, 352, 29:168, 175, 191, 221, 223, 232, 36:173, 184f, 224, 237
Offerings, Freewill—11:487f, 18:152f
Offertory—35:57, 95, 53:21, 26
Office—2:10, 20, 102, 229, 329, 340, 353, 367, 382f, 388, 390, 3:5n, 232, 281, 364, 4:5, 30, 33, 52–54, 70, 76, 80, 173, 176, 182, 202, 204, 254, 264, 283, 407, 5:103, 119, 123, 197, 238, 265, 268, 330, 7:45, 58, 83, 89, 102f, 107f, 115, 145f, 151, 158, 167, 182n, 183–185, 189, 191, 194f, 197f, 205, 229, 246, 369, 9:3, 19, 84n, 162f, 177, 229–231, 283, 290, 13:212, 331, 370, 14:14, 263, 276, 304, 331, 334, 340, 23:193, 195, 205, 218, 222, 228, 251, 253, 286, 289, 312, 315, 317, 321–324, 340–342, 345, 352, 364, 378, 380, 409, 415, 24:66–68, 87, 106, 115, 127, 131–134, 140, 155, 161f, 166, 172f, 180, 209, 218, 220, 243, 264, 268f, 289, 291, 304, 310f, 338, 350, 353, 377, 403, 408, 25:4, 8, 138–144, 446f, 26:12, 16, 19, 60, 75, 102, 173f, 187, 353, 378, 30:30, 53–55, 63f, 76, 113, 125, 132–137, 160, 164, 172, 176, 181, 188, 192, 259, 35:260, 46:94f, 166, 226, 237, 243
Office, Dignity of—25:140f, 143
Office, Secular—6:167–169, 15:4, 7, 56f, 65, 83, 110, 223, 21:114, 168, 276–278, 26:19, 75, 173f, 249, 313, 28:256f, 330f, 52:192
Officers—23:292–296, 298f, 302
Offices, Church—4:76f, 200, 396, 41:154–160, 163f, 171
Call to 25:141–144
Officials—23:407, 46:244, 265n, 267, 272f, 283, 286, 294, 318
Offscourings—6:52, 147, 237, 18:80, 118
Offspring—4:13, 19, 26, 35, 37, 69, 109, 113, 172f, 224, 230f, 244, 290, 302–305, 307, 320f, 323–325, 337f, 340, 353f, 376, 378, 17:89, 103f, 187, 229
Og, King of Bashan—2:259, 367, 370, 9:27, 34, 40, 13:378, 14:250, 19:142, 20:117

Oholibamah—6:287–294, 309
Oil—5:133, 180, 252f, 9:174, 307, 10:217f, 11:334f, 357, 16:13, 26:260
Oil of gladness—12:246
Ointment—15:10, 107, 149, 157, 197, 209, 233
Old Adam—3:5, 6:258, 12:158, 189f, 13:27, 179, 378, 14:94, 144, 161, 167, 190f, 15:21, 16:52, 197, 18:229, 19:27, 121, 20:140, 144, 191, 231, 296, 329, 21:57, 213, 235, 22:140, 177, 180, 250, 262, 268, 312, 350, 23:107, 143, 175, 272, 24:45, 163, 226, 383, 25:59, 27:84, 380, 405, 30:8, 16f, 54, 69, 35:39, 370, 278, 36:203, 357f, 37:96, 199f, 249, 41:114, 146, 165, 42:11, 43f, 49, 61, 70, 44:76–78, 46:132, 169, 51:19, 146, 373
Old age—8:113, 158, 15:98, 117, 179f, 17:139, 19:159, 54:64f
Old Covenant—see **Covenant, Old**
Old law—25:58, 112f, 145
Old leaven—25:269
Old man—6:354, 9:26, 126, 179, 184, 250, 11:267, 273, 289, 296, 302, 319f, 322f, 325, 421, 435, 480f, 483, 485, 495, 505, 517, 525, 550f, 14:190f, 16:59, 129, 197, 25:313, 25:57–59, 69, 179, 191, 313, 407f, 26:6f, 167, 352, 29:67, 118f, 225, 30:68, 35:367, see also **Old Adam**
Old people—16:346, 28:232f, 350, 30:132
Old Testament—see **Scripture(s), Old Testament**
Olive branches—2:92f, 110, 157, 160, 162f
Olive oil—2:162
Olive tree, Hybrid—25:100f
Olive trees—2:110, 157, 162f, 185, 18:75, 20:43, 45, 51, 222, 224, 229f
Olives—9:243
Omens—17:118, 140, 181, 270
Omphale—13:205
Omri, King—18:267
On Marriage and Concupiscence—see **Augustine, St., Works of**
On the Secrets of Priests—4:236
Onagers—11:329
Onan—7:6, 9, 19–21, 23, 27, 29, 51
Onanism—7:20f
Onesimus—27:108, 29:93, 95, 97, 100–105, 35:300
Onkelos—see **Targums**
Onomatopoeia—17:266
Onyx—1:97, 101
Open questions—32:184
Opinions—16:123, 17:22, 70, 140, 251, 270, 279, 25:33, 108, 114, 116, 464, 492f, 500, 507, 28:366–368
Opinions, Legal and doctrinal—41:162
Oporin, John—50:228n
Oppenheim—32:123
Opponents—29:35, 60, 54:445
Opponents of the Reformation, Catholic—46:ii, xiif, 59, 90n, 261
Opposites—10:135, 206, 238, 421, 25:98, 200, 205, 382f, 467
Oppression, oppressors—2:12, 19, 34, 36, 119, 222, 15:62, 83, 17:286f, 289, 334, 26:72, 86, 27:158
Opus alienum—see **Alien work of God**
Opus operatum—4:236n, 346n, 5:258n, 6:234, 237, 8:192n, 11:375n, 18:396, 26:122n, 35:48, 63, 64n, 102, 36:37n, 44, 47, 55n, 38:160, 197f, 40:29, 42:8n, 47:161
Oracles—5:102, 104, 200, 248, 250, 6:80, 17:51, 53
Oracles of God—25:25, 28, 194–196, 207f, 29:4f, 18f, 22
Oral manducation—see **Eating and drinking in the Sacrament**
Oral word—see **Spoken Word, The**
Orange, Synod of—32:152n
Oranges—2:65
Orators—3:73, 26:92, 186, 227, 352, 385, 422, 432, 50:127, 160
Oratory—26:184f
Order, Divine—39:59, 64, 97, 280, see also **Ordnung**
Order for Mass and Communion for the Church at Wittenberg—see **Luther, Martin, Writings of**—*Order of Mass and Communion*
Orders, Holy—4:398, 45:8n, 28, see also **Clergy**; **Priesthood**; **Priests**
Orders, Religious—see **Monastic orders**
Orders in society—see **Stations in society**
Ordinances—11:105, 14:14, 22, 24, 91, 113, 132, 23:33, 37, 39, 137, 173f, 182, 213, 231, 273, 314, 26:296, 298, 309, 355, 378, 408, 448, 29:16, 18, 20, 77, 103, 46:98, 100
Ordinances, Extra-Biblical—24:356
Ordinances, Human—41:139
Ordinances of God—see **God**—His ordinances
Ordinaries—34:258, see also **Bishops**
Ordination—5:248, 7:146, 13:295, 22:479, 25:143f, 235, 28:250f, 354, 29:17, 180n, 30:255n, 34:45, 246, 357, 36:48, 91, 101, 106–120, 123, 213, 38:143, 186–188, 195–197, 208, 211, 213f, 40:8, 11, 23f, 36f, 40, 41:163n,

45:117n, 46:262, 48:308, 53:93, 122–126, 54:100f, 119, 359
Ordination, Impediments to—9:230n
Ordination of George of Anhalt as Bishop—50:280n
Ordination of Ministers of the Word—see **Luther, Martin, Writings of**
Ordination of women—36:152, 41:154
Ordnung—30:73, 39:57n, 59n
Oreb, Rock of—11:129f, 132, 16:114
Orestes—1:287, 3:189, 7:271, 329, 25:173, 31:284
Organ pipes—42:39
Organs—29:170, 45:54, 53:22, 62, 185
Orient—1:100, 2:382, 4:308, 5:92, 279, 7:140, 9:34, 14:273, 16:33, 22:60, 27:335, 32:69, 41:27, 299, 309, 317
Orientals—2:303, 3:251, 4:275, 6:297, 323f, 16:38
Origen—1:88, 90f, 97–99, 122, 231–233, 237, 2:14, 150–152, 158, 164, 5:88, 344f, 6:125, 153, 9:7, 25, 14:36, 15:194n, 287n, 16:xi, 327, 17:328, 373, 20:155, 282, 21:91n, 23:79, 123n, 26:121, 180, 275, 433, 27:169, 185, 202, 236, 250, 259, 312, 346, 363, 379, 30:69, 32:194, 217, 33:163n, 165, 167, 169, 172f, 213f, 275, 34:22, 35:174n, 235, 318n, 372, 403n, 36:30n, 110, 37:302n, 372n, 39:175f, 178, 181, 232, 40:190, 43:51, 48:54, 309, 51:39n, 54:22, 47, 397
Origen, ed.—*Hexapla* 15:267n
Origen, Works of—*De Principiis* 24:245n, 29:166n, 34:219n
Homilies on Genesis 1:90n, 5:58n
In Leviticum Homilia; Homilia 3 34:15, 22n
Selecta in Psalmos: Homilia 34:22n
Original sin—1:63f, 71, 102, 104f, 107f, 110, 114, 118, 124, 128, 133, 139, 141, 149, 161, 163, 165, 166n, 169, 171f, 202, 237, 326, 340, 352, 2:4–6, 9, 118f, 121n, 127, 149, 167f, 171, 308, 314f, 345, 348, 353, 3:56, 103, 133f, 136–139, 144, 206n, 350, 4:4, 6, 9, 146, 158, 161, 196, 238, 249, 252f, 289, 304, 349f, 5:22f, 30, 33, 35, 37, 42, 44, 157, 165, 190, 204, 289, 358, 380, 6:63, 115f, 258, 396, 7:13, 72, 75, 164, 166, 194f, 233–235, 240, 242, 245, 255f, 258, 262, 266, 272, 274f, 278f, 281, 283f, 360, 376, 8:5, 15, 220, 226, 228, 310f, 325f, 9:51, 10:116, 11:174, 201, 12:110, 154, 206f, 319, 348–351, 13:76, 95, 127f, 133, 196, 14:149, 169, 171, 180, 15:338f, 16:98, 17:100, 20:144, 332, 21:352, 22:100, 119, 138, 333, 376, 24:255f, 307, 328, 341f, 343, 25:45–47, 51, 53, 181, 261f, 266f, 272–274, 291, 296–302, 308, 313, 341, 386, 27:105, 28:113, 210, 29:8n, 68, 30:229, 32:21, 27, 29, 92–94, 33:272, 34:119, 151, 154f, 164f, 181, 186, 195f, 35:31, 37:8, 16, 161, 362f, 38:9, 15, 36, 79, 86, 184, 41:84, 42:43, 43:238, 44:114, 375, 45:90f, 51:42, 52, 57, 378, 378, 52:151f, 54:20, 34, 37
Orimasda—2:243, 4:237
Orion—16:134
Orla River—1:274
Orlamünde—35:165n, 40:6, 75, 100, 105, 107f, 110–112, 114f, 127, 132, 163, 182, 202, 48:79n, 49:71n, 72n, 73n, 82n
Ornaments—6:238, 287, 16:47, 38:114, 46:183, see also **Statues**; **Symbols, Religious**
Orosius—*Historiae adversus paganos* 27:227n
Orphans—2:99, 4:381, 7:194, 9:19, 112f, 138, 243, 254, 13:53, 16:19, 22, 50, 22:97, 24:130f, 29:29, 72, 30:182, 45:190, 355, 387, 50:13f, see also **Widows and orphans**
Orthodox Church—see **Greek Church**
Orthodoxy—30:289n
Oschatz—54:38, 181
Osiander, Andrew—37:154, 246n, 38:9–11, 15n, 33, 62, 66, 72n, 73, 89n, 45:136n, 47:123, 129n, 49:121, 238n, 339n, 367n, 54:107, 249, 290, 376, 382f
Osiander, John—50:13n, 16n, 67n, 75f, 77n
Osiris—24:323n
Osterlandt, James—54:279
Ostia—41:356, 368
Ostriches—9:41n, 135, 16:136, 18:215
Oswald, Hilton C.—associate editor of Vols. 6, 13, 16
author of Introduction to Vols. 10, 11, 17, 18, 19, 20, 25, 28
editor of Vols. 10, 11, 17, 18, 19, 20, 25, 28
indexer of Vols. 16, 29
Othniel—47:187
Otmar, Silvanus—31:74
Otto I, Emperor—41:292n, 333n, 374
Otto II, Emperor—41:292n, 374
Otto III, Emperor—41:292n, 374
Otto IV, Emperor—41:332n
Ottos (German Emperors)—35:296n

Our Father, The—see **Lord's Prayer**
Outcasts—16:149
Outer man—see **Outer person**
Outer person—11:460, 483, 485, 487, 493, 514, 25:109, 220, 257, 309f
Outgoings—10:314f
Outward appearance—25:28, 108, 150, 189, 230, 465, 470
Outward means—29:81–83, 85
Outward things—13:277, 292, 300, 317
Overlords—46:91, 112f, 116, 126f, 189, 194
Overseers—25:131
Overshadowing—11:214, 223
Ovid—1:5, 168n, 2:219, 3:312, 4:20, 12:28, 37:220n, 41:346, 54:150
Amores 15:10n, 116n, 16:62n, 25:184, 33:20n, 291n, 54:444n
Art of Love 2:329n, 3:47n, 248n, 6:119n, 7:178n, 314n, 8:252n, 10:86, 13:177, 380, 15:109n, 16:34n, 17:177n, 240, 19:114n, 42:151n
Fasti 7:52n, 62n, 90n, 13:118, 16:292n, 20:79n
Heroides 18:293, 19:126n, 28:321n
Metamorphoses 1:6n, 2:131n, 220n, 302n, 4:58n, 208n, 331n, 5:347n, 6:115n, 8:288, 9:25, 13:119n, 15:204n, 16:113n, 17:198n, 26:191, 28:292, 33:17n, 80n, 34:327n, 40:188, 317n, 319, 48:9n, 95, 107
Pontic Epistles 3:308n, 38:244n
Remedia amoris 4:297n, 11:294n
Tristia 7:54n, 13:153, 15:128n, 133n, 25:452
Owls—11:306–308
Oxen—1:128, 132, 188, 211, 352, 2:74, 137f, 324, 396, 3:30, 86, 128, 149, 356, 4:84f, 119, 127, 246, 276, 309, 5:73, 76, 208, 289, 291, 7:59, 69, 149f, 300, 347, 9:150f, 174, 219, 221, 225, 233, 248, 250, 15:45, 83, 133, 23:125, 133, 143, 226, 236, 241, 24:82, 260, 309, 413

Pack affair—49:189f, 195f, 199n, 210n, 211n, 215n, 222, 225–227
Pack, Otto von—47:23n, 49:189, 197f, 50:72, 54:285
Packer, J.I.—co-translator with O.R. Johnston of Luther's *Bondage of the Will* 33:xin
Padua—9:55n
University of 48:73n
Paganism—1:206
Pagans—see **Heathen**
Pagans, Conversion of—8:132–135
Pageantry—4:236
Pahl, Paul D.—translator of *Lectures on Genesis*, chapters 29–50, Vols. 5, 6, 7, and 8
translator of second half of Vol. 5 5:182n
Pain—6:197, 210
Painted godliness—16:120
Painter, F.V.N.—*Luther on Education*, St. Louis, 1889 45:344
Painters—13:168, 174f, 185
Paintings—4:34, 13:375, 434n, 14:131, 16:255, 30:250, 40:99, 43:43
Palatinate—34:345, 50:78, 147n, 254
Palatine, Count—49:23, 198n, 416
Palermo, Bishop of—41:299
Palestine—1:310, 2:187, 204, 3:176, 180, 303, 318, 4:74, 77, 5:14f, 28, 352, 8:96, 9:35, 14:263, 16:33, 114, 125, 139, 144, 20:282, 22:420, 27:340, 38:317n, 45:133, 47:80n
Palestinians—2:305, 4:73, 16:143, 18:113, 115, 118, 134, 137, 187, 220
Palladius, Peder—54:305
Palliums—4:201, 27:237, 385, 31:386, 41:168n, 233n, 234, 271n, 283, 294, 299, 337, 368f, 376, 45:288n, 289
Palm Sunday—11:176n, 14:101, 22:49, 213, 517, 23:143n
Palm trees—11:229, 232f
Palms—10:49, 134
Palus Maeotis—see **Azov, Sea of**
Pamphlets—31:xx
Pamphylia—10:412
Pan—3:201n
Paneas—16:115
Pannonia—7:145, 8:290
Panormitanus—see **Nicholas of Tudesco (Panormitanus)**
Pantheon—34:213
Papacy—1:134f, 180, 221, 238f, 249, 258, 288, 300f, 357, 2:61, 86, 113, 161, 164, 198, 271, 284, 3:37, 44, 51, 62, 107, 124, 166, 172, 179, 181, 196, 204, 210, 229, 243, 296, 325, 4:22, 54, 65, 76, 201, 204, 231, 335, 396, 398f, 5:48, 71, 91, 125, 154, 156, 242, 244, 6:127, 230, 234, 237, 308, 329, 349, 7:62, 138, 147, 155, 162, 234, 312, 329, 350, 8:20, 118, 125, 132, 144, 146, 185, 188, 192, 203, 212, 230f, 246, 256, 276, 312, 326, 9:72, 148, 167, 12:90f, 114, 117, 144, 151, 156, 168, 192, 199, 219, 253, 280, 297, 341, 344, 363, 396, 14:14, 23, 37, 39, 94, 98, 253, 261, 266, 325, 328n, 16:236, 296f, 303, 323, 17:25, 28, 36–39, 52f, 73, 76, 82f, 109f, 135, 272, 275, 18:21, 381f, 20:55, 74f,

238, 268, 313f, 328, 21:132f, 142f, 154, 157f, 165, 181f, 194, 213, 272f, 22:35, 52, 58, 67, 86, 102, 107, 109, 118, 143, 185, 222, 228, 250, 254, 257f, 268, 275, 302, 312, 320, 333, 359f, 366, 377, 386, 388, 398, 421, 424, 429, 431, 443, 450, 452, 454, 477, 500, 512, 522, 524, 527, 23:31, 37, 57, 72, 82, 134f, 137f, 140, 142, 144, 152, 154, 170f, 193, 205f, 213, 235, 257, 261–263, 269, 271–273, 280, 284, 286, 290f, 335, 348, 354f, 359f, 374, 385, 387, 390, 402, 410, 418, 24:47, 103, 117, 127–129, 180, 197, 218f, 253f, 260, 274, 294, 304f, 309, 312, 321, 348, 363, 367f, 397, 26:18, 32, 41, 70, 80, 96f, 105, 126, 135f, 200, 201, 212, 216, 221–224, 250, 302, 330, 377, 386, 402, 404, 452, 458f, 27:53, 60, 63, 84, 87, 91, 100, 110, 113, 121, 158, 29:8, 34, 42, 44, 87, 219, 30:135, 169, 181, 205, 229, 252, 254, 282, 286f, 32:68–74, 82, 34:52, 214, 249, 332, 350, 358, 35:201, 268, 405f, 36:ix, 5, 7f, 11f, 22, 24–27, 89f, 96, 123, 125f, 37:14f, 136, 143, 154, 172, 289, 300, 322, 367f, 38:27f, 42, 85, 95, 101, 110, 115–118, 120, 136, 143, 148f, 155, 159, 162, 170, 173, 175, 184, 190f, 193, 203f, 207, 211, 213, 224, 231, 233, 292, 321, 39:xv, xxiii–xxv, 7f, 55–104, 124n, 153, 192, 205, 220f, 40:x, 8–10, 12f, 15f, 18, 23–26, 28, 30, 32f, 53, 57, 67, 109, 178n, 191f, 231f, 238, 256, 327, 333, 348, 353–355, 41:xi, xiv–xvi, 5–7, 9n, 14, 20, 38, 46, 73, 86n, 90f, 105, 131, 149, 163, 191f, 199, 206–208, 211f, 223, 225f, 233n, 235, 237, 244f, 260, 266n, 271, 273, 276f, 279, 280n, 286, 291–294, 296–299, 300f, 304f, 307–309, 311, 313, 316, 323f, 325–329, 333n, 334f, 339f, 343, 345f, 351, 354, 356f, 361f, 365–369, 371f, 44:xvii, 89–91, 118, 120f, 130f, 133n, 134–137, 139–143, 142n, 161–164, 146, 148n, 152n, 158, 164–169, 184, 188n, 192–194, 210, 239, 45:61, 62n, 67n, 70n, 133, 147n, 157, 310, 320, 46:xi, xiii, 18n, 82, 163f, 166, 168f, 176, 180n, 183f, 186, 196–199, 201, 204n, 205, 227, 232, 246, 250, 255, 261, 266, 268, 272f, 286f, 298, 300, 312, 315–317, 319, 47:7, 11–55, 82, 112f, 115f, 132, 161f, 175, 177, 181, 253f, 274, 48:10, 48n, 68f, 72n, 73n, 91n, 100, 102, 109, 114, 127, 137, 141, 164n, 167n, 186n, 215, 253, 291n, 295, 49:61–68, 138n, 214n, 378f, 411, 416n, 421, 50:xiii, 9, 20, 40, 60, 82, 84, 98n, 104, 114n, 115f, 144f, 158f, 160f, 165, 176, 184, 188n, 189, 190n, 200f, 209n, 219n, 247n, 254, 256n, 257, 270, 272, 279n, 280n, 289, 312n, 51:166, 217, 294, 311, 322, 345, 379, 52:5f, 8, 25f, 35f, 74, 79f, 100, 108, 112, 118, 120, 136f, 139, 141f, 145, 151, 180f, 183, 203f, 209–219, 221f, 227, 231f, 235f, 239f, 243f, 247f, 260, 264f, 267f, 274f, 282f, 285, see also **Papists**; **Pope, The**

Proposed reform of the 50:82n, 83n, 249, 250n

Papacy and the churches—41:42, 89, 138, 210, 220, 224, 263, 283, 288, 294, 300, 321, 329, 332, 334, 346, 349, 360, 363, 368

Papal Briefs—41:289f

Pope Paul III to Emperor Charles V 41:259n, 260n, 263, 268f, 271f, 280, 282f, 286–288, 361

Papal Bulls—see **Bulls, Papal**

Papal Commandments—see **Canon Law**

Papal court—38:310

Papal decrees—10:19

Papal decrees and decretals—see **Decretals, Papal**

Papal Decretals—see ***Corpus Iuris Canonici***; **Decretals, Papal**

Papal falsehoods—41:187f, 192, 214–217, 236–238, 241, 301, 303, 307–308, 321–325, 328, 339–344, 352, 357, 363, 369f, 373, 376

Papal histories and biographies—41:xiii, 7n, 87, 107n

Papal kingdom—8:181f, 187

Papal laws—see **Canon law**

Papal lies—38:118, 121, 147f, 156, 158, 170, 174–176, 193, 198, 226, 231

Papal perversions—41:361, 362n

Papal States—31:228n, 44:166n, 167n, 49:161n, 389n

Paphnutius, St.—17:65n, 26:113, 29:19, 41:43n, 56, 60, 125n, 318n, 44:308n, 316n, 382n

Papists—1:132, 149f, 211, 216, 235, 238f, 258, 261, 355, 357, 2:22, 24, 33, 36, 51–53, 55, 64, 79, 99–103, 160f, 168, 170, 220, 222, 243, 251, 315, 383–386, 3:13, 26, 78, 84, 97f, 107, 109, 118, 153, 161, 172, 181, 193, 201–203, 210f, 213, 217, 266f, 286, 293, 295–297, 299, 304, 315, 321f, 326, 357, 361, 363–365, 4:7f, 14, 17, 25, 28, 31–33, 53f, 61, 76, 121–124, 127, 141f, 145f, 149f, 163, 165, 170f, 178, 200,

227, 233, 249, 250, 259, 269, 282, 291, 295, 303, 314f, 347f, 354, 361, 368, 392, 403, 405–407, 5:5, 7, 33, 36, 52, 90, 137, 199, 213f, 236, 245f, 249, 267f, 289–292, 299, 328, 330–333, 344, 348, 350, 353, 355f, 6:32, 50, 52, 104, 149, 165, 243, 285, 318, 347, 349f, 359, 363, 374, 7:10, 12, 34, 64, 130, 227f, 232, 234f, 253f, 265, 278, 281, 299, 311–314, 316, 324, 337f, 356, 8:6, 35, 46, 62, 70, 75, 80, 83, 90, 94, 118, 136, 191f, 218, 238, 244, 258, 263, 267, 300, 315f, 325, 9:53, 55, 167, 12:352, 13:187, 211, 272, 301, 398, 14:17, 76, 98, 102, 134, 271, 16:11, 95, 122, 162, 171, 190f, 193, 203, 205f, 217, 225–231, 236, 239, 243–246, 248, 250f, 256, 262, 270, 300–302, 314, 319, 324–327, 344, 17:17, 38, 41, 47, 63, 71, 74, 84f, 87, 92f, 104, 106, 110, 114, 127, 134, 143, 163, 172f, 178, 180, 196, 213, 224, 234, 251, 255, 275, 278, 283, 287, 295, 300, 302, 304, 323f, 329, 378, 387, 391, 400, 415, 18:9f, 21, 108, 165, 222, 225, 386, 414, 19:51, 55, 151, 167, 216, 21:70, 72, 74f, 91, 138, 157f, 219f, 243f, 274, 284, 350, 22:60, 64, 68, 107, 125, 132, 137, 142, 145, 153, 164, 168, 242–244, 262, 269–271, 278, 281, 286, 302, 334, 349, 366, 368, 370, 408, 445, 454, 523, 23:25f, 33, 38, 49, 56, 58f, 62, 66, 71, 73, 79, 86f, 101, 112f, 128, 136, 138, 157, 159, 187, 189, 194, 211, 217, 224, 237, 240, 280, 285, 304, 334–335, 348, 358, 261, 376–378, 389, 415, 24:98, 126, 172, 176, 188, 212, 217, 221, 223, 243, 274, 305, 320f, 324, 330, 349, 26:7, 9f, 23, 33, 51, 57, 67, 73, 80, 84, 90, 98, 135f, 140f, 143f, 150, 152, 155, 176, 182, 199f, 207, 213, 216, 222, 224, 247, 251, 279, 283, 286, 305, 307, 312, 330f, 340, 342, 348, 368, 372, 375, 383, 386, 396–398, 411, 413, 416, 418, 420, 429, 454–459, 27:6, 8f, 18f, 68, 87, 91, 107, 118, 126, 133, 138, 148f, 28:218, 236, 259, 364, 29:8f, 13, 36, 44, 30:7, 69, 229, 253, 300, 306, 34:187, 35:142, 151f, 166, 182f, 198, 365, 36:17–19, 21, 72, 117, 134, 137, 146, 148, 150, 163, 165, 170, 175f, 178, 180f, 188, 194, 211, 214f, 227, 229, 244f, 259–261, 288, 300, 302, 310–313, 316, 323, 347, 351, 37:xi–xvii, xx, 10, 14f, 65n, 87n, 88, 116, 142–144, 147, 154, 203, 226, 260, 361, 367–369, 38:23, 88, 110f, 117–119, 133f, 147–149, 156, 158, 161, 164, 166f, 169, 175, 180–189, 189n, 190–213, 221–223, 225–231, 233, 289, 292, 301, 313, 315, 41:13f, 23, 26, 35, 47, 77, 85, 108, 111, 132, 163, 165f, 168, 189, 191–199, 203, 205, 211, 213, 218f, 221, 225, 228, 235, 251, 256, 46:163, 167, 177, 183, 48:223f, 249, 266, 269, 272f, 281, 321, 334, 336, 396, 51:73, 75, 77, 124, 137, 165, 204, 216f, 304, 306, 333, 354, 358, 361, 52:39, 83, 88, 91, 114, 275, 281f

Papists, Their impenitence—47:11–13, 17f, 36–41, 43f, 46, 48–51, 55

Pappenheim, Ulrich von—32:105f

Parables—5:56, 158, 361, 16:92, 257, 24:54, 193, 26:406, 433

Paraclete—see **Holy Spirit, Paraclete**

Paradise—1:38, 57, 65f, 73, 78, 80, 82, 87–93, 95f, 98, 100, 103, 105, 109f, 116, 118f, 132, 138–140, 144, 146, 152, 154, 157, 169, 172, 174f, 179, 187, 209f, 218, 225, 230f, 233f, 242, 246, 249, 266, 274f, 281, 284, 300, 308–310, 324, 326f, 335, 337, 339f, 345, 349, 351–353, 2:3, 52, 57, 74, 86, 110, 136, 154, 157, 178, 194f, 219, 222, 287, 343–345, 351, 368, 380, 3:42, 61, 171, 173, 179, 184, 282, 287, 293, 303, 312, 4:7f, 17, 49, 61, 74, 87, 100n, 102, 123, 144, 175, 193, 210, 257, 281, 311, 316, 319, 401, 5:42, 49, 167, 243n, 267, 347, 355, 6:189, 255, 7:127, 194–197, 233, 277, 346, 363, 8:11, 115, 134, 225n, 259, 331, 12:160, 173, 256, 276, 308, 311, 16:337, 17:125, 22:104, 124, 193, 208, 296, 313, 329, 340f, 395, 469, 474, 23:232, 417, 24:253f, 341, 343, 359, 25:156, 26:280, 301, 27:145, 391, 29:34, 86, 30:198, 31:360, 393

Paradisus animae—43:11

Paradox—5:128f, 202, 206, 6:104, 8:20, 80, 199, 10:61, 89, 110, 421, 461, 12:173, 204f, 220, 13:252, 392, 13:6, 8, 236, 241, 254, 404, 413, 14:31f, 58, 83, 86, 100, 151, 158, 191, 203, 304, 316, 342, 18:130, 19:154, 24:420, 25:40, 232, 370, 443, 445, 26:161f, 228, 232, 252, 27:255, 319, 326, 29:127, 201, 203, 33:58f, 64f, 113

Paralytics—24:73, 26:157

Paran, Mt.—4:71, 9:15, 304, 14:244, 19:137, 230

Paranoia—15:127

Parents—1:102, 116, 127, 138, 148, 169, 222, 244–247, 249, 259, 261f, 270f,

273, 279, 283f, 301, 304f, 308f, 313, 324–329, 339, 347, 2:9f, 12, 29–32, 42, 78, 83, 120, 127f, 163, 167, 169, 173–175, 192, 251f, 270–272, 301, 321, 3:43, 45, 68, 99, 122, 131, 133, 144, 177, 198, 203, 205, 231, 233, 240, 257f, 274, 279, 284, 4:4, 14, 41, 44, 69, 72f, 92, 94, 142, 182, 195, 197, 212, 218, 223–227, 230, 247f, 251, 253, 257, 259f, 264, 270f, 273, 278, 285, 288f, 295, 298, 304, 318, 323, 331, 344, 346, 354, 362, 374, 378, 386f, 5:22, 40, 71, 86, 92, 97, 102, 106–108, 112, 114–116, 143, 162–166, 169f, 173, 175–177, 183f, 186, 193–195, 198, 200, 207, 209–212, 229, 253, 264, 273, 278, 285, 289, 299, 303, 317, 344, 371, 381, 6:16f, 25–28, 30, 193, 195, 198, 370, 8:9, 11, 16, 19–21, 50, 55, 61, 82f, 94, 116, 170f, 173, 181f, 206, 218f, 223f, 276, 303, 9:212, 219, 226, 20:19, 171, 21:76, 109f, 148, 179f, 22:93–96, 100f, 142, 157, 222, 235f, 281, 296, 313, 315, 330, 404, 418, 421, 436, 446, 478, 527, 23:25, 27, 62f, 65, 68, 71, 80, 98f, 134, 141, 204, 213, 234, 247f, 255, 321, 323, 24:345, 26:4, 36, 44, 107, 186, 191f, 208, 217, 309, 399, 417, 430, 446, 27:56, 82, 145, 149, 158, 215, 219, 320, 357, 28:55, 92, 161f, 164, 29:22, 55, 77, 30:244, 246, 37:199, 292, 364, 41:166, 248, 338, 42:147, 45:xi, 29, 36f, 46, 348f, 353–355, 367f, 381f, 385, 386n, 387–393, 46:xiv, 141, 209, 222, 226, 229, 257, 268f, 278f, 281, 285, 290, 301, 304f, 49:163, 203, 269, 319, 51:137, 137, 146–151, 159, 183f, 298, 52:216f, 218f, 220, 246, 54:355f, 424, 432, see also **Fathers**; **Mothers**

Authority of 48:331f, 54:67

Parents, First—1:108, 143, 164, 171, 181, 191, 197, 210, 243, 281f, 341, 8:11

Paris—5:9n, 8:264, 267, 272, 284, 288f, 24:156, 50:190n

University of 17:65, 28:366, 31:257, 262, 264, 34:306, 36:9, 14n, 135n, 140, 153, 156, 163, 167, 169, 174, 179, 199, 204, 205n, 206–208, 211–217, 38:238f, 242f, 248, 252, 265, 272, 44:259n, 382, 46:197, 204, 48:112n, 136n, 137, 229n, 258n, 270, 289, 314, 50:247n

Paris, Theologians of—21:4, 75, 29:88, 30:260n, 41:15n, 45:82n

Parish Visitation in Electoral Saxony—Instructions to the visitors 51:136

Parishes—4:181f, 201, 209, 396, 7:63, 299, 8:62, 125f, 229, 297, 13:48n, 64f, 38:162, 166, 176, 194, 196f, 41:xiv, 122, 135, 137, 142, 160, 46:10n, 11n, 78, 234, 214

Parishioners—22:98, 220, 24:266, 268, 272

Parisians—7:140, 36:172, 207

Parkes, James—47:128, 216n

Parminides—31:42

Paronomasia—16:239

Paroxismus—5:113n

Parricides—6:292f, 341, 356, 358, 7:243, 8:19, 24, 216, 220, 223f, 226

Parsons—7:68, 164

Partakers of divine nature—30:155

Parthians—5:210, 280, 7:14, 14:273, 16:125, 17:414

Partiality—9:110, 163f, 170, 211, 26:94–97, 104, 27:53, 61, 103

Participation, Sacramental—36:35n, 44, 47

Particularism—25:271, 337

Partisan groups—17:64

Partnership—37:349, 356–358

Party spirit—27:91

Paschal I, St., Pope—31:28, 178

Paschal II, Pope—41:299n, 300, 344n

Paschal lamb—see **Lamb, Paschal**

Passing away—25:72f

Passion—1:142, 168, 237, 28:27–30

Passion History—51:197

Passion of Christ and of Antichrist—30:193n

Passion Week—38:206, 42:12

Passional—35:253n

Passions—13:109, 29:65, 211

Passivity—27:25, 294, 33:32, 35, 67, 157, 178

Passover—3:250f, 8:116, 9:144, 154–157, 11:102, 13:xii, 349f, 355–357, 371, 14:343, 16:267, 20:47n, 22:161f, 216–218, 251, 414, 24:191, 25:72, 26:32, 155, 411, 29:127, 220, 35:x, 243, 37:36, 38, 42, 197, 264, 266, 273–275, 311–313, 316, 38:22, 24, 55f, 113, 317n, 47:86f, 48:67

Past, Recalling the—17:106f, 120, 168, 200, 202, 355

Pastor, Ludwig—47:223

Pastoral counseling—49:160n, 305f, 331f, 336f, 340f, 369f, 395f, 50:17f, 47n, 50f, 68f, 76n, 79

Pastors—1:213, 2:84, 3:174, 249, 4:25, 40, 66, 72, 76, 105, 181, 201f, 205, 212, 224, 254, 285, 295, 401, 5:21, 23, 71, 122–124, 193, 241, 249, 260, 263, 6:20, 23f, 30f, 34, 132, 148, 163, 224f, 240, 318, 7:63, 68, 97, 164, 182, 185,

221, 237, 8:54, 62f, 79, 125, 182f, 185, 227, 230f, 300, 331, 12:254f, 297, 13:52f, 14:60, 91f, 260, 266, 320, 332, 16:249, 305, 17:150, 185, 266, 289f, 337, 347, 350, 22:98f, 217, 226, 236, 239, 260, 390, 399f, 407, 419, 421, 436, 479n, 508, 510, 516, 518–521, 523, 526–528, 23:7, 57, 98, 104, 156, 192f, 195, 217f, 222, 225, 228, 247, 262, 274, 298, 321–323, 330f, 333, 342, 344, 356f, 362, 408, 421, 24:66f, 83, 221, 246, 265, 268, 288, 25:7, 138–140, 150, 155f, 238, 242, 410, 26:46, 105, 186, 413, 418, 27:109f, 112f, 115, 121f, 124f, 237, 297, 304f, 308, 385, 393, 28:62, 84, 87f, 89, 91f, 140, 142, 296, 354, 29:23, 26, 30, 41, 30:132f, 135, 34:44, 36:113, 210, 224f, 37:327, 364, 38:87, 104, 176f, 188, 193, 195f, 198f, 202f, 207–209, 262, 283, 40:40, 41:132–134, 136, 153–155, 157, 164, 176, 358f, 42:xv, 52, 59f, 79, 176, 45:177f, 186f, 315, 318, 320, 46:xiv, 10f, 22, 37f, 158, 166, 171, 174, 187, 193, 196, 218, 220, 223, 225f, 229, 231f, 234f, 254, 256, 281, 289, 293, 297, 301, 305–309, 311, 313, 318, 49:28n, 31n, 62f, 87n, 101f, 135, 138, 175n, 207f, 282n, see also **Bishops**; **Clergy**; **Elders**; **Ministers (of the Word)**; **Preachers**; **Presbyters**

Pastors, Election of—46:11, 37

Pastors, German—Their suffering during Reformation 3:232, 240, 357

Pastures—6:12, 66, 345f, 17:179f

Patches—41:63, 65, 67, 161

Patens—38:114, 168, 224

Pater Noster—see **Lord's Prayer**

Paternity—8:167

Pathros—2:203, 16:125

Patience—2:19, 57, 105, 217, 278, 322–324, 331, 335, 346, 369f, 389, 3:24, 51, 54f, 57, 68, 70, 120, 211f, 315, 354, 4:6, 18, 21, 46, 74, 115, 121f, 141, 147, 207, 217, 226, 271, 318f, 321f, 325, 334, 336, 338f, 352f, 378, 408, 5:7f, 12–15, 25, 27, 34, 58, 65, 68–70, 79, 81f, 85f, 89–91, 95, 103, 144, 192, 205, 233, 235, 270, 292, 294, 296, 298, 304, 307, 312, 326, 332–335, 345, 347f, 358, 6:70, 105, 187, 191f, 221, 402, 7:54, 58, 64, 70f, 75, 77, 98, 106, 109, 114, 116f, 123–125, 130, 132, 135, 177f, 184, 192, 202, 218, 356f, 8:7, 11f, 17, 32, 34, 229, 11:367, 529, 15:116, 16:31, 196, 259, 17:65, 74f, 187, 245, 21:98, 219–221, 22:54, 24:43, 50, 151, 198, 203, 209, 227, 250, 268, 392, 411, 25:32, 175, 177–179, 193, 290, 292, 26:43, 90f, 136, 155, 218, 220, 247, 352, 392, 394, 428f, 453, 27:20, 24f, 94, 106, 126, 157, 303, 368, 373, 376, 393, 29:53, 76, 129, 181, 185, 30:40, 101, 156f, 327, 31:224, 35:387, 396, 42:140, 143, 51:71f, 87, 171, 298, 391

Patmos—6:138

Patriarchs, Old Testament—1:4, 21, 59, 85, 243, 283, 292, 295f, 302, 314, 321, 332–335, 338, 342–345, 348, 350, 353–358, 2:x, 3, 7f, 10, 12, 18, 22f, 27f, 30f, 37, 53–55, 100, 132, 166, 175, 179, 184, 187, 206, 210, 212, 235f, 240, 242, 245, 247, 249, 251f, 254, 260f, 268f, 275, 277, 281–285, 289, 326, 332, 352, 358, 363, 368, 371, 373, 380, 382f, 389, 397, 3:14, 34, 49, 52–54, 57, 61, 81, 99, 109, 114f, 124, 131, 155, 157, 159, 164f, 167, 170, 175, 178f, 182, 185f, 190, 196f, 228, 230, 232–234, 245, 250, 302, 314f, 317, 319, 323f, 326f, 338, 344, 4:ix, 3f, 9, 24, 44, 48, 58, 74, 79, 84, 87–91, 97, 98n, 99, 101, 103, 115, 117, 125, 139, 178, 181, 184, 187, 191, 193, 196, 206f, 210, 228f, 270, 278, 281, 284, 300, 303f, 308, 318–320, 331f, 343, 350f, 355, 359f, 364, 378, 384f, 5:ix, 7, 10, 16, 22, 26, 53, 57, 59, 61, 69f, 72, 77, 89–91, 100f, 105, 110, 114, 140–142, 144, 163, 168, 177, 196f, 200f, 204f, 207, 209–214, 216f, 223f, 226f, 229, 233, 235, 242, 251, 253, 255–257, 262, 265f, 269, 271f, 274f, 279, 281, 286, 290f, 295, 298f, 301, 304, 311, 322, 324, 337, 340, 344, 356, 363, 380, 384, 386, 6:70, 72f, 87, 97, 117, 123, 149, 233, 236, 265, 278f, 284, 303, 321, 355, 366, 7:5n, 9–12, 18f, 25, 28, 32, 36f, 45, 56, 108, 116, 125, 129, 163, 203, 207, 218, 220f, 225, 288, 303, 307f, 313–315, 323, 328, 331, 354, 356f, 364, 8:17n, 21, 41f, 59f, 75, 82, 84, 91, 135, 138, 140, 150f, 157, 159, 163, 165, 174, 176, 182, 191, 198f, 211, 214, 216f, 219, 234, 245, 253f, 261, 270, 272, 285f, 291, 295, 307, 9:104, 113, 211, 11:97, 13:85, 118n, 121f, 124, 400, 21:248f, 22:22, 32f, 37, 47, 70, 92f, 116, 118, 130, 135, 156, 195, 201, 208f, 312, 354, 427, 435, 449f, 522, 23:266, 24:79, 197, 220, 305, 341, 395, 397, 26:14, 85, 121, 210, 236, 240f, 267, 275f, 287,

293, 360, 483, 29:189, 229, 30:29, 38, 212, 34:113, 121, 313, 316, 320f, 36:137, 303, 38:179, 290, 41:51, 70–72, 138, 213, 331, 353, 359, 45:203f, 206, 227f, 277, 46:39, 98n, 268f
Patricians—2:200
Patricides—4:350f, 7:55, 256, 264
Patrimony of Christ and St. Peter—31:228, 245
Patrimony of Peter—27:122n
Patripassionists—34:208n, 54:36
Patristic passages—29:xi
Patrologia, Series Graeca—see indexes in each volume for references
Patrologia, Series Latina—see indexes in each volume for references
Patronymics—8:262
Pauck, Wilhelm—*Heritage of the Reformation*, Glencoe, Ill., 1961 25:xiv, 39:xiiin, xviiin, 54:393n
Paul II and Paul III, Popes—45:305n
Paul II, Pope—40:16n, 41:7n, 278
Paul III, Pope—13:277n, 34:xv, 223, 41:xii, 5f, 9n, 11–13, 140n, 142, 232f, 235f, 240, 245, 248–255, 259, 260n, 263–265, 267–274, 275n, 277f, 280f, 282n, 283–290, 337, 345, 356, 361, 50:82n, 83n, 144, 155n, 157, 158n, 163n, 177, 184, 216, 222n, 254, 264, 266n, 289, 297, 315, 54:219, 229
  Consistory of 41:259, 263n
Paul IV, Pope—44:150n
Paul, St., Apostle—1:12, 18, 21, 41, 65, 77, 86, 89, 100, 107–110, 116, 125, 135, 137f, 155, 164, 171, 182f, 196, 198f, 203f, 211, 213, 225, 233–235, 239, 253, 261, 265f, 268f, 273, 289f, 295, 299, 308, 322, 327, 332f, 338, 340, 350, 354, 2:16f, 23, 40f, 44, 48, 50, 59, 72f, 77, 86, 88, 99, 105, 121f, 151–153, 157, 160, 168, 171, 177–179, 184f, 191, 230, 237, 247, 272f, 277, 280, 288f, 291, 295, 297, 300f, 309, 320f, 325, 329–331, 333, 335, 339, 341, 348f, 355f, 358, 365, 370, 388, 3:4–6, 14, 17–23, 26, 28f, 31, 35, 39f, 55, 59, 62, 64, 70, 76f, 80f, 83–86, 90, 93f, 96–99, 101–103, 105, 108, 117, 121, 124f, 130, 139, 147–149, 152, 155f, 158, 167, 176, 180–182, 187, 192, 197, 199–201, 213, 222, 224f, 239f, 254, 264, 269–271, 273, 275, 277, 283, 286, 288, 290–301, 320f, 325f, 334, 341, 343, 346, 348, 355, 361, 4:15, 17, 20, 25–28, 30, 32, 43, 49, 52f, 55, 59, 62, 64, 71f, 104, 114, 116, 118, 120, 123, 125, 127, 134f, 137, 141, 144f, 148, 152, 154, 156f, 159–161, 182, 188, 190f, 198, 206, 208, 231, 233, 238f, 241, 249, 269, 271–273, 282–285, 300f, 342–345, 347f, 351, 365–367, 402f, 5:5, 10f, 22f, 27, 37, 40, 52, 62, 71, 82, 85, 89, 96n, 129, 131f, 145, 155n, 156, 164, 178, 192, 204, 208, 224, 255f, 259, 264f, 275, 278, 284, 287, 293, 303, 310, 316, 320, 327, 341, 359, 361, 372, 6:103, 128, 217, 371, 7:32, 47, 59, 65, 93, 97f, 100, 109, 113, 126, 129, 131, 137f, 154f, 174f, 181, 190f, 194, 204, 212, 248f, 251f, 254–256, 273, 279, 324–326, 337, 342, 355, 357, 366, 8:5f, 10f, 13, 18, 21, 26f, 34, 39f, 46, 49, 61, 69, 73, 79f, 94, 101, 107, 116, 121, 126, 133f, 147, 159, 164, 167, 178, 191, 193, 202, 205, 217, 219, 222, 227, 230, 235, 239, 241, 244, 248, 251, 254, 256, 258, 275, 305f, 308, 312, 316, 328f, 332, 9:4f, 21f, 25f, 41, 42n, 52, 54, 63, 68, 70, 72–74, 81f, 84n, 88f, 95, 102–104, 108f, 111, 113, 125, 129f, 136, 140, 151, 157f, 171, 181, 186–188, 190, 199, 205f, 213–216, 219, 229, 235–237, 244, 248, 250f, 255, 259f, 278f, 292, 11:412, 12:132, 166, 178, 198, 208, 219, 252–254, 268, 272, 325f, 337f, 350, 353, 355, 382, 391, 398, 407, 13:111, 194, 288, 382, 400, 14:7, 9, 14, 17, 23f, 30, 36f, 39, 50, 56, 58, 79f, 86, 90f, 93f, 97, 100, 105, 115, 121, 124, 127, 130, 161, 183, 185f, 191, 196, 209, 227, 240, 243, 246, 249, 251, 259f, 265, 270f, 274, 294, 304, 314, 329f, 333, 335, 341, 343, 15:312f, 16:71, 189f, 200, 203f, 209, 212f, 215, 218, 229, 238, 305, 307, 332, 17:105, 173, 178, 185, 197, 217, 223, 260, 279f, 307f, 314, 328, 330, 366f, 19:27, 54, 123, 151f, 184, 186, 192, 195, 197f, 20:67, 77, 101, 109, 184, 199, 218, 251, 296, 21:117f, 304, 313f, 319, 330, 22:6, 20, 35, 55, 73, 87, 90, 98, 109, 118, 121, 132f, 138, 149–151, 169, 176, 178, 190, 192, 196, 203, 208, 222, 230, 235, 250, 254f, 258, 261, 264f, 272, 283, 288, 302, 307, 318, 326, 341, 344, 351, 362f, 379, 381, 385f, 404, 445, 448, 450, 468, 470, 472f, 482, 487, 489f, 498, 507, 513, 515, 524, 23:11, 22, 28, 34, 52, 57, 82, 89, 97, 102, 104, 107, 145f, 171, 181, 184, 186–188, 191f, 215f, 231, 237, 262, 273, 292, 300, 320, 328f, 343, 373f, 376f, 380, 387f, 390, 406, 408, 412f,

24:13, 16, 19, 23, 30, 32, 49, 55, 59, 64, 66f, 71, 75f, 78, 82, 85–87, 97, 106, 113, 121, 128, 133, 141, 148–151, 170, 189, 200, 228, 230, 243f, 246, 260, 263f, 276, 281, 286, 294, 303, 305f, 308, 310–312, 314, 316, 319, 325, 327f, 330, 340f, 345, 347, 358, 363, 366f 371, 376, 383f, 391, 400, 402f, 405, 407, 421, 25:8, 78, 124–126, 129, 335f, 520f, 26:15, 19f, 68–70, 74–93, 98, 100f, 110, 27:134f, 154n, 186f, 194n, 199, 407, 28:21–24, 82–91, 94, 107, 118, 152–154, 156f, 240–242, 245, 247f, 380, 29:3–5, 7, 9, 11, 13–15, 17–23, 25, 28, 32, 35f, 38–41, 43–49, 55, 63f, 66–68, 71, 74, 78–81, 85f, 88, 93–95, 97, 99–102, 104f, 109, 122, 124, 141, 173–175, 182, 200, 204, 225, 30:ix, 3f, 6–8, 11f, 14f, 18, 21, 23, 26, 32, 40, 42, 45, 51f, 55, 58, 60, 65, 68, 70, 74, 77–79, 82, 94–97, 99, 105, 107, 110–112, 115, 119f, 124, 127, 133, 136, 139, 141, 144, 149, 153, 158, 161, 163–165, 167–169, 174, 195, 197–199, 210, 222, 227, 240f, 243, 252–256, 260, 268, 275f, 279, 283, 285f, 291, 293, 297f, 302f, 307, 310, 313, 316, 321f, 325f, 31:75, 107f, 144, 178, 204, 266, 335, 368f, 34:109, 114–116, 151, 158, 178, 358, 35:30f, 33, 52, 58, 62, 87, 118, 122, 185f, 188, 196f, 359f, 366f, 369–371, 377, 384, 36:38, 70, 74, 76, 82, 91, 93f, 149f, 238, 253, 261, 263, 266, 280f, 287, 37:20, 53n, 66, 146, 172, 198–202, 257f, 265, 332, 38:28, 31, 60, 76f, 80, 99–101, 122, 126, 130, 132, 151, 160, 162, 170f, 180, 182, 184, 186f, 190, 196, 199, 202f, 211–213, 225, 239, 243, 258, 269, 290, 295, 299–301, 303, 307, 311, 319, 39:73, 81, 84, 131, 135, 143f, 174, 188, 190, 205, 210, 231, 251, 254–257, 268, 272, 277f, 291, 310f, 40:31, 41:18, 51, 61, 67f, 71, 73, 78f, 81, 88f, 105, 114–116, 121–124, 128, 130, 138f, 144, 148, 154f, 158–169, 177f, 190, 197f, 206, 209f, 213f, 216, 273, 301, 308, 311, 315f, 322–325, 339, 345, 347–355, 360–362, 364, 368–370, 42:14, 130, 137f, 161f, 164, 45:24f, 28, 34–37, 42, 44, 47, 70–72, 82n, 90, 99, 103n, 110, 169, 205, 212, 226, 243, 273, 278, 283, 352, 356, 359, 363, 365, 373, 46:25, 29, 32, 39, 50f, 64, 66, 68, 73f, 98f, 107, 118, 126f, 131f, 150, 175, 196, 198, 221, 224, 233, 235, 237f, 246, 265, 278, 286, 299, 314, 51:250f, 52:4, 18, 21f, 29, 34f, 41, 47, 51, 55, 63f, 67, 71f, 76, 78f, 86, 97, 101, 106f, 110f, 114, 122f, 126, 131f, 137f, 141, 144, 147f, 153, 156f, 166f, 172f, 175, 177, 187, 191, 197, 201, 205f, 211f, 220f, 227, 230f, 235f, 249, 253f, 256, 258, 267f, 272, 274, 277f, 285, see also **Lord's Supper**—Paul's teaching

His thorn in the flesh 26:341, 420

Love for his own people 25:379f

Paul of Burgos (Burgensis)—2:ix, 71, 234, 371, 3:358, 4:99, 138, 156f, 160, 5:374n, 6:xi, 201, 208, 212, 319, 321–323, 8:86, 10:259, 329, 409, 413, 463, 11:106n, 139n, 142, 144, 150, 179f, 187n, 196n, 201n, 207, 236, 373n, 14:346, 15:329, 331, 18:51, 25:299, 27:345, 29:113, 128, 208, 47:68n, 130, 131n, 134, 138, 153n, 176n, 178n, 179n, 181n, 191, 214, 222n, 224, 227n, 228, 234, 238, 243n, 283, 290n, 48:67

Additio I 25:435

Additio II 25:153

Additiones to *Postilla* of Nicholas of Lyra 10:104, 11:65n, 91n, 92n, 384n, 20:128n, 163n, 177n, 205n, 208n, 222n

Postilla … in Psalmos 14:346n

Scrutinium Scripturarum 29:113n

Paul of Samosata—38:255n, 266, 274

Paul of Thebes, St.—28:322

Paul the Hermit, St.—35:105n

Paula, St.—31:197, 44:306n

Paulianists—41:44n, 45n

Paulina, St.—44:306n

Paulinians—18:55

Paulinus—27:209, 308

Paulinus, St. Jerome's letter to—1:3n

Paulinus of Nola, St.—31:208, 45:289n

Paulus Orosius—45:110n

Paupers—7:71, 142, 337, 9:138, 242, 16:187

Paupers, Injustice for—18:29

Pavement—11:435f

Pavia—41:295n, 48:73n, 49:125, 161n, 221, 54:299

Pavia, Battle of—46:120n, 168, 198

Peace—4:19, 35f, 58, 78f, 85, 89, 92, 157, 162, 175, 197f, 232, 249, 254, 268, 307–309, 312–314, 316, 329f, 368, 379, 395, 402f, 5:5f, 16, 53f, 56, 58, 66f, 76, 80f, 84, 87, 89, 136, 215, 218, 238, 244, 274, 341, 7:62, 68, 97, 101, 141–143, 145, 169, 173, 176, 178, 181, 184, 232, 240, 262f, 271, 275, 284, 293f, 303, 339, 367, 8:7, 31, 33, 41, 82, 121, 191f, 238, 256, 264, 275, 278–280, 298f, 301, 313, 318, 320, 10:70–

72, 193, 351–353, 361, 370, 373, 417, 11:6f, 163, 166–170, 174, 368, 525, 527, 12:9, 12, 15, 322, 336, 13:5f, 44f, 55, 140f, 369f, 14:16f, 52–54, 57, 60, 69–72, 99f, 113, 116–121, 123f, 126, 132, 149, 161f, 212, 215, 220, 227, 239, 324, 334f, 344, 349, 15:26, 46, 195, 207, 224n, 237, 16:29, 31f, 43, 46, 79, 97, 101, 117, 123, 129, 131, 163, 173, 179, 200f, 206f, 209, 211–213, 221, 226–228, 233, 240, 248, 250, 262, 275, 279f, 289, 299, 335, 342f, 17:167f, 184, 197, 210f, 241, 245, 258, 268f, 279f, 324, 394, 408, 18:239, 250, 277, 20:9, 11, 15, 24f, 41, 45, 95f, 112, 139, 167f, 220f, 270f, 275, 278, 288f, 300, 21:305, 22:54, 384, 24:12, 15, 31, 37, 74, 78, 80, 82, 88, 141, 149, 177–180, 182, 185, 213, 228, 266, 270f, 277, 279, 289, 313, 354f, 414, 418–422, 25:6, 29, 43, 92, 108, 117, 232, 285f, 416f, 504f, 518, 27:5, 13, 18, 23, 38, 41–44, 47f, 59, 62, 66, 73, 91, 94f, 103, 108, 121, 130, 134f, 137, 141f, 144, 148, 170, 174, 184f, 204, 219, 224, 242, 289, 318, 357f, 367f, 373–376, 402, 28:38–40, 106, 220, 257, 259, 29:10, 30, 73, 77, 95, 115, 135, 141f, 167, 188f, 215, 30:8f, 40, 71, 74f, 92, 95, 100f, 139, 151f, 155, 197, 219, 226, 243, 260, 298, 303f, 31:100f, 32:193, 35:19, 109, 212, 290, 374, 379, 37:xiv, 7, 15, 17, 23–25, 27–29, 101, 135n, 161, 270, 40:312, 41:140, 225, 274f, 284, 42:12, 50, 64, 104, 45:93f, 279, 46:9, 27, 72f, 75, 90, 95–97, 100, 110, 118f, 121f, 180f, 226, 240, 243, 246f, 252, 254, 288, 51:177, 354, 52:27, 35, 208

Peace, Spiritual—25:285f

Peacemakers—21:39–41

Peacocks—1:76, 188, 11:280n

Pearls—4:275, 25:236

Pears—23:114, 139, 398

Peasants—2:6, 19, 24, 375, 3:30, 182, 227, 260, 345, 4:74, 208, 211, 227, 382, 5:121, 270, 311, 325, 334, 341, 368, 7:62, 159, 161, 164, 189, 193n, 213, 334, 8:100, 102f, 112, 128, 229f, 260, 268, 279, 9:183n, 12:240, 245, 298, 13:51, 64, 353, 14:5, 53f, 94, 113, 117f, 120, 122, 234, 19:154, 170, 209f, 214, 21:177, 202, 286, 23:6f, 9, 11, 13, 313, 322f, 356, 361f, 370f, 394, 397, 402, 417, 419, 24:79, 81, 83, 118, 133, 197, 214, 224, 236, 265f, 271, 288, 29:62, 71f, 74, 77, 30:254, 35:171, 37:149f, 335, 46:xiif, 5n, 7–9, 12n, 13n, 14, 17, 18n, 20–23, 47, 51n, 52–55, 57, 59, 61, 65, 67–79, 82n, 84, 85n, 97n, 100, 101n, 105, 110, 116, 125, 194, 201, 308, 49:50n, 268, 54:72, 132, 142, 152, 163, 180, 241, 282, 294, 435, 458

Peasants, Christian Association of—46:7n, 14, 24, 27f, 50n, 70n

Peasants' War—2:320n, 14:52n, 15:90n, 125n, 16:11n, 42n, 231n, 17:276, 19:73, 174, 176, 209n, 20:48n, 215n, 22:225n, 231n, 23:397n, 24:69n, 26:343n, 344, 26:343n, 344, 28:62, 259, 29:74n, 82n, 30:254, 34:12n, 35:169–171, 35:xix, 37:70n, 149n, 327n, 40:48, 227, 265, 286, 41:170n, 181, 235n, 43:8, 99n, 149, 163, 220n, 271n, 45:62n, 116n, 239, 46:xii, 5f, 91, 95n, 97n, 121n, 142n, 161n, 201n, 247n, 48:282n, 49:106f, 113f, 117f, 122n, 123f, 131, 132n, 135n, 145, 249n, 50:279n, 51:201, 54:180, 390

Pedagogy—4:322

Peddlers—4:398

Peffinger, Degenhard—35:67

Pelagianism—25:496, 29:32, 172, 31:9n, 11, 49, 63, 238, 317, 37:363, 41:83n, 117, 308

Pelagians—1:213, 2:39, 12:223, 14:299, 15:268, 17:66, 254, 256, 20:303, 21:259, 265, 25:496, 26:214, 412, 27:219, 314, 362, 28:253, 309, 30:69, 322n, 32:27, 33:107, 123, 129, 157, 268f, 34:27, 36:211n, 48:24n, 52:88

Pelagius—22:67, 327n, 23:231, 25:298, 327, 497, 30:253, 257, 31:9n, 33:78n, 107n, 111, 136, 35:402n, 40:80n, 364, 44:261n, 51:384

Pelagius II, Pope—31:280

Pelagius, Pope—36:20n, 148, 150, 153

Peleg—2:205, 216, 4:3

Pelicans—11:296, 305, 306n, 307–309, 18:345f

Pelikan, Jaroslav—17:x, 54:81, 356n
- author of Introduction to *Luther's Works on the New Testament* 21:ix–xv
- author of Introductions and presumed author of introductory comments preceding each item in Vols. 1–9, 12–16, 21–24, 26, 27, 29, and 30
- co-author or author of General Introduction in all 54 volumes
- editor of Vols. 1–9, 12–16, 21–24, 26, 27, 29, and 30
- general co-editor of all volumes
- general editor of Vols. 1–30
- *Luther the Expositer* (Companion

volume to Luther's Works, American edition), St. Louis, 1959 2:4n, 10n, 13n, 15n, 47n, 82n, 99n, 112n, 231n, 240n, 332n, 384n, 3:5n, 227n, 233n, 272n, 273n, 4:95n, 101n, 167n, 220n, 236n, 303n, 407n, 5:15n, 111n, 254n, 6:149n, 165n, 177n, 7:104n, 265n, 9:6n, 8n, 164n, 197n, 198n, 214n, 16:55n, 73n, 307n, 17:x, 18:290n, 24:66n, 87n, 91n, 107n, 160n, 202n, 207n, 269n, 323n, 26:15n, 18n, 65n, 139n, 281n, 383n, 435n, 27:20n, 29:97n, 184n, 30:19n, 68n, 167n, 169n, 286n, 35:232n, 37:xxi, 156n
Spirit Versus Structure: Luther and the Institutional Church, New York, 1968 39:xivn, 20
translator of commentaries on Psalms 19, 26, and 51 12:97–146, 303–410
translator of *Four Psalms of Comfort* 14:207–278
translator of *Lectures on Galatians*, 1535, Chapters 5–6 27:3–152
translator of *Lectures on Galatians*, 1535, Chapters 1–4 26:4–461
translator of *Lectures on Philemon* 29:93–108
translator of *Lectures on Titus* 29:4–92
translator of Luther's *Sermon on the Mount* 21:3–294
translator of *Notes on Ecclesiastes* 15:3–190
Pellicanus, Conrad—44:247n
De modo legendi et intelligendi Hebraeum 15:112n
Peloponnesus—3:281, 17:414
Pelt, Hans—21:xix
Pelusium—8:109
Penalties—32:33f, 37, 52, 63, 75f, 39:42
Penalty of sin—32:25, 194f, 203–217, 230, 232, 244, 246, 249–251, 255
Penance—5:154, 7:227, 232, 234f, 8:204, 267, 11:94, 14:31, 22:163, 456, 23:180, 24:128, 348, 26:182n, 211f, 29:19, 124, 31:19f, 25, 85, 87f, 90, 271, 322, 32:16, 32–34, 43, 50–53, 59–61, 136, 257, 34:19, 32, 56, 66, 92, 347f, 356, 35:x, xvii, 5–22, 38n, 36:7f, 18, 28, 58, 60, 61n, 69, 81–93, 95n, 123f, 37:370, 40:293–296, 323f, 41:33, 34n, 35n, 42:12, 20, 62, 68, 100n, 44:53n, 281n, 46:295, 48:211n, 324, 51:59, 107, 308f
Penance, Sacrament of—13:274n, 48:43f, 67f, 211n, 230f, 246f, 263n, 269, 313n, 314, 402
Penelope—28:85, 41:346n
Peniel—6:126, 130, 144f
Penitence—2:63, 5:153, 162, 7:48, 58, 225, 363f, 376, 8:7, 9, 10:31, 186, 11:8, 84, 101, 139, 141, 146, 14:197, 24:344, 29:112, 214, 34:21n, 171, 38:183, 204, 46:42
Penitential seasons—42:85
Penitential system—14:ix
Penitents—36:59f, 82f, 90
Pentateuch—2:246n, 361, 367, 9:ix, 16:5, 35:132, 161n, 228, 235n, 235f, 337n, 338–350
Pentecost—see **Church Year**—Pentecost
Penuel—6:179f
People of God—13:286, 15:23, 193, 203, 215f, 221, 223, 225, 227, 234, 246, 262f, 274, 17:3, 97f, 176, 260, 263, 361, 372f, 33:84–87, 47:76f, 96f, 132, 138–176, 200, 218f, 228f, 233f, 282, 291
Perazim, Mt.—16:234
Perception—29:145, 199, 200
Perdition—4:30, 50, 5:18, 171, 199, 8:5, 21, 185, 190, 272, 19:20n, 23:73, 24:321, 329, 372, 27:34, 98, 110, 189, 275, 288, 292, 30:190, 295
Perez—7:8f, 14, 16
Perez of Valencia, Jacobus—*Centum et quinquaginta Psalmi Davidici* 10:44n
Perfectability, Human—25:344
Perfection—1:262, 2:55, 6:372, 10:122, 161, 455, 11:479, 494, 12:381, 17:66, 224, 21:129f, 22:85, 25:8, 137, 183, 245–247, 269, 309f, 312, 32:156, 34:118, 44:294, 360, 45:88, 101, 256n, 52:268
Perfidy—2:65
Pergamum—17:123
Perils—3:6, 129, 135, 146, 179f, 188, 190, 209f, 223, 225, 243f, 258, 277, 310, 317, 327, 343, 360, 363
Peripatetics—2:346, 33:107
Perizzites—2:336, 6:201, 8:152, 197
Perjurers, perjury—2:65, 4:220, 245, 9:196f, 20:238, 46:193f, 283
Perknowsky, Ignatius—1:166n, 54:48f, 59, 92, 160, 173, 183, 823
Perlbach, Max—*Die Statuten des deutschen Ordens*, Halle, 1890 45:137n
Permission—25:83, 97, 160, 374
Persecution—1:143, 2:16, 137, 214, 334, 3:31, 179f, 184f, 198, 244, 357, 4:17, 33, 403, 5:15, 59, 186, 6:8, 38, 48, 74, 7:343n, 8:32, 180, 232, 235, 240, 314, 9:134, 184, 216, 222, 244, 11:189, 235f, 251, 308, 326, 365, 473–477, 487, 513f, 516, 519, 521, 12:183f, 190,

252, 344, 356, 13:37, 259, 275, 280f, 296, 336, 14:81, 231, 16:209, 213, 215, 285, 20:25, 28, 100f, 130–132, 134, 149, 152, 163, 210, 323–325, 336, 339, 21:29f, 45, 47, 49f, 52f, 123f, 224, 248f, 293, 338, 22:55, 80–82, 85, 205, 23:7, 74f, 158, 183, 266, 393, 24:14f, 25, 27, 29, 47, 79, 116, 123, 131, 149, 151, 163, 181, 183, 204, 209, 216, 271, 273f, 276f, 279, 282, 285f, 289, 293, 302, 322, 332, 350, 354, 366, 382, 400, 25:24, 29, 44, 77, 127, 193, 462, 518, 26:23, 58, 60f, 72, 285, 383, 418f, 428, 450–453, 455–457, 27:25, 42–44, 46, 49, 101–103, 129–131, 134f, 145, 180f, 227n, 301f, 322f, 343, 403, 28:49, 101, 129, 153, 156, 29:9, 139, 215, 30:107, 156, 176, 219, 242f, 310, 326, 35:217, 220, 386, 401, 404, 41:35n, 55, 43:59–70, 73–79, 83–96, 99–112, 120f, 141–165, 46:37, 105, 173, 52:250

Persecution of the Gospel—46:31, 41f, 104f, 115, 169

Persecutors—10:78f, 144, 319, 351, 353, 379, 16:24, 209

Perseverance—6:158, 166, 259, 262, 12:31, 13:177–179, 15:116, 213, 21:309f, 29:217, 228

Persia—2:187, 255, 365, 4:264, 5:352, 8:56, 14:114, 118, 17:3, 95, 117, 121, 138, 144, 365, 18:151, 273, 281, 343, 393, 21:344, 22:86, 246, 351n, 478, 24:80, 25:24, 35:295, 299n, 398, 41:271, 291, 45:220, 222f, 224n, 225n, 329, 46:41, 157, 52:161

Persian and Greek kingdoms—45:222, 224n, 225n

Persian Empire—20:46, 170, 179, 226, 251

Persian Gulf—1:99, 2:195

Persian kings—2:243, 259, 276, 304f, 18:368, 20:6, 83, 159, 162, 164, 167, 192, 224f, 250, 252f

Persians—1:87, 323, 2:205, 232, 243, 352, 365, 3:67, 4:29, 155, 328, 373, 6:88, 211, 8:81, 182, 301, 14:74, 118, 16:33f, 126, 133, 137f, 170–172, 176, 19:145, 147, 205, 216, 221, 20:15f, 46, 50, 62, 169, 179, 192, 38:97, 41:54n, 55, 372, 46:107

Persius—28:327

Carmina 29:24n

Satires 15:18n, 261n, 25:202, 447, 28:327, 32:196n

Person—23:343, 37:61n, 100, 206n, 211–213, 219, 230, 297, 356, 358, 361f

Persona (Latin term)—26:94n, 27:206, 210, 219f, 29:53

Personal union—24:106

Personification—1:292, 14:38n, 16:108, 17:210, 24:193, 26:162, 169, 371

Personnel—13:184, 196

Persons, Distinctions between—38:120, 186f

Perugia—University of 2:313n

Perversions, Sexual—46:198n

Pestilence—2:17, 143, 210, 289, 4:91n, 5:10, 252, 7:254, 332, 8:117, 10:13, 29f, 85, 16:63, 333, 22:416f, 419, 479, 499, 516, 23:12, 130, 152, 363, 406, 24:49, 76, 90, 315, 358, 392, 28:203f, 30:xi, 278, 42:75, 91f, 51:157, 254, 54:15, 152, 345, 434–436, see also **Plague**

Peter, St., Apostle—1:8, 21, 69, 100, 158, 221, 225, 289n, 296, 322, 341, 348, 2:3, 8, 10, 13, 28, 60, 64, 81, 84–86, 89f, 99, 151, 153, 155f, 252, 273f, 282, 286, 316, 383, 386, 3:18, 31, 40, 44, 58, 63, 112, 124, 127, 129, 169, 172, 180, 209, 231, 252, 260f, 270, 273, 291, 293–296, 299, 305, 332, 346, 353–355, 359, 4:39, 58, 71, 118, 121, 132, 141, 157, 179, 186, 189, 199f, 202, 213, 269, 271, 281, 348, 376, 386, 402, 5:11, 20, 25, 27, 31, 40, 51, 104, 116, 130, 186, 204, 250, 254f, 381, 6:101, 165, 255, 371, 7:11, 56, 73, 103f, 212, 8:21, 26f, 30, 32f, 37, 53, 94, 101, 134, 222, 249, 256, 258, 309, 316, 324, 9:52, 72, 84n, 94, 104f, 124, 135f, 145, 187, 197, 250, 273, 12:254, 325, 13:28, 194, 411, 14:12, 23, 31f, 79, 90, 92, 94, 186, 222, 231, 252, 257, 262, 283, 304, 315, 328, 336f, 16:55, 76, 80, 178, 209, 229, 332, 17:51–53, 65, 75, 86, 90, 194, 388, 18:262, 19:49, 94, 22:33, 46, 54, 86, 95, 108, 118, 121, 132, 168f, 181f, 184–187, 189, 192, 229, 255, 259, 265, 283, 359, 369, 374, 381, 442, 446, 463, 479, 501, 23:10f, 57, 72, 104f, 107, 137, 190–195, 274, 374, 385, 387f, 395, 416, 24:9, 86, 147, 178, 207, 212, 332, 366, 383, 421, 25:4, 84, 113, 143, 439, 442, 26:15, 34, 62, 66f, 74–78, 84f, 94, 96, 98f, 101–104, 106–116, 118–121, 124, 133, 135, 139, 157, 159, 163, 179, 203–207, 209–211, 239, 258, 277, 280, 297n, 344, 356, 27:3, 7, 80, 94, 156, 162, 167, 178, 185, 192–195, 197, 200, 208, 210–215, 217f, 238, 243, 247f, 297, 334, 338, 362, 386, 396, 28:76, 173, 309, 29:15, 19, 36, 79n, 182, 192, 30:ixf, 3–215, 221, 224f, 229f, 235,

237, 241, 256, 263, 272f, 285, 314, 319, 325, 31:233, 242, 265, 273, 279f, 338, 388, 32:68–74, 76, 82, 96, 34:17, 192, 350, 358, 35:11f, 22, 31, 122, 360, 372, 36:55, 61, 71, 83, 136f, 139, 141, 146, 190, 37:37, 50, 130, 133, 38:27, 57, 158, 160–162, 164, 178, 187, 204, 224, 243, 290, 293, 39:73f, 80–83, 86–90, 92, 95–100, 135, 152, 174, 191, 203–206, 222, 234–237, 248f, 256–260, 268, 272, 283f, 40:21f, 27, 54, 218, 41:38, 53f, 58, 66, 69–75, 71, 73–75, 77–79, 81, 88f, 123, 129, 137–142, 151, 155, 162, 178, 190f, 196f, 209, 213, 215, 218, 232, 245, 273, 282, 298, 300, 306, 310–319, 320n, 321f, 323n, 324f, 327, 331, 333, 342, 344–351, 353, 367–369, 42:62, 71, 154, 159, 45:25, 65f, 87, 98, 110f, 117, 153, 156, 224, 226, 274n, 288, 46:29f, 51, 73, 98, 102, 166, 172, 195f, 52:65, 78, 82, 97, 105, 137f, 175, 182f, 191, 205f, 216, 232, 241, 255, 267, 269f, 274, 282f

Peter, St., as Rock—40:218

Peter, St., Church of—see **Rome**—Basilica of St. Peter

Peter, St., Epistles of—8:268, 35:390–392, 41:321, 358

Peter, St., Second Epistle of—Authorship 30:198

Peter, St., vs. St. Paul—30:66, 68

Peter de Palude—31:146, 222

Peter Lombard—1:116, 3:133, 135, 137, 140, 193, 4:199, 25:xi, 238, 292, 458, 26:20n, 209n, 28:85, 223, 29:113, 116, 189, 192, 207, 219, 230, 34:154n, 155n, 36:63n, 37:104n, 45:376n, 54:260

Collectanea in epistolam ad Hebraeos 29:116n, 125n, 208n, 229n

Collectanea in epistolam ad Romanos 25:248

Collectanea in epistulas Pauli 25:512

Four Books of Sentences 1:xi, 56n, 68, 113n, 116n, 235n, 3:133n, 135, 137n, 139f, 193n, 4:100n, 204n, 8:16n, 91n, 186n, 14:286, 18:290n, 25:ix, 154, 162, 299, 300, 390, 26:20n, 57, 209n, 27:x, 222n, 290n, 333, 377n, 28:85, 223, 236, 29:87n, 113n, 121n, 125n, 172n, 178n, 180n, 188n, 290n, 192n, 209n, 218n, 229n, 230n, 235n, 237n, 30:204n, 31:49f, 88, 106, 202n, 273, 32:26, 259, 33:108n, 34:154n, 155n, 36:29n, 44, 62, 90, 38:251n, 39:38n, 41:48n, 49, 52, 105n, 116n, 44:204n, 281n, 48:5, 28n, 30, 37, 42, 156n, 313n, 54:26, 440

Peter of Ailly—see **D'Ailly, Pierre**

Peter of Ravenna—31:157

Peter of Spain (Pope John XXI)—37:277, 283

Summulae logicales 41:304n

Petersen, Peter—*Geschichte der aristotelischen Philosophie im protestantischen Deutschland*, Leipzig, 1921 35:186n

Petitions—29:125, 175

Petra—18:195

Petreius, Johann—35:177f

Petri, Adam—31:23

Petrus Sylvius—*Von den vier Evangelion, szo eyn lange tzeit untter der banck seynn gelegen* 20:279n

Petzensteiner, John—48:227n

Peutinger, Conrad—32:116, 120, 45:241n, 262n, 48:205

Pfefferkorn, John—25:289, 32:150n, 38:168n

Pfeffinger, Degenhard—31:319, 48:32, 50, 71f, 78, 109n, 121, 49:69n, 54:286, 334

Pfinzing, Martin—38:62n

Pflug, Caesar—31:323, 325

Pflug, Julius von—50:224n

Phaeton—5:121

Phalaris—49:198

Phantoms—24:372, 37:99, 108, 110f, 227

Phanuel—52:129f, 137

Pharisaism—26:14, 68, 72

Pharisees—2:42, 161, 4:55, 148, 159, 273, 5:26, 6:114, 249, 262, 292, 8:289, 329, 9:27, 52, 157, 272, 10:46, 74, 145, 366, 458, 11:203, 371, 470, 472, 492, 14:96, 283, 294, 16:23, 43, 94f, 228, 17:62, 69, 75, 93, 207–209, 266f, 400, 18:350, 352, 19:219, 20:53–55, 63, 80, 105, 118f, 121, 125, 233, 236–239, 242, 296, 300, 312f, 315f, 320, 332, 21:30f, 33, 67f, 70, 73f, 81, 84, 106, 130f, 138, 140f, 155–157, 22:47, 62, 128, 141, 143, 177, 194, 196, 216, 229, 277f, 289, 377, 435, 456–458, 468, 475, 483, 503, 506f, 510, 515, 23:27, 74, 207, 209, 211, 213, 217f, 221, 235, 243, 259f, 268, 285, 292f, 296–300, 303–305, 310, 313, 315, 318f, 329, 353, 409, 24:154, 156, 223, 228, 287, 395, 410f, 25:24, 28, 122, 511, 26:25, 68, 188, 204, 234, 310, 314, 363, 396, 27:112, 172, 187, 219, 340, 383, 388, 390, 394, 28:164, 29:9, 26, 34, 79, 30:26, 98, 31:246, 301, 36:75, 245, 37:173, 38:28, 42, 58, 41:69f, 75, 119f,

122, 45:71, 73, 148f, 46:63, 51:, 17, 106, 109, 114, 131, 147, 334, 342, 348, 52:115f, 202f, 226, 285

Pharmacist—23:41

Pharoah—1:314, 323, 2:17, 152–154, 259, 310–312, 314, 316–318, 322, 325, 376, 379, 4:323, 5:51, 82, 130, 236, 276, 339, 6:6, 41, 75, 101, 120, 330, 333, 335, 341, 353, 368, 405, 7:45, 52f, 69f, 113, 118, 120–122, 127, 135–139, 142, 148–150, 152f, 155–158, 162–166, 168–171, 173, 180, 186–188, 190, 197f, 201, 203–205, 223, 245, 248f, 284, 324, 349, 8:4, 17, 19, 44, 48, 56, 59f, 64, 76f, 92f, 98, 101f, 104, 110, 113, 116, 125, 128, 146, 224, 320–322, 9:87, 272, 11:31, 33, 35, 106, 134, 392, 402f, 498, 13:130, 197, 213, 359, 372, 378, 418, 14:11, 19, 64f, 77, 250, 320, 333, 16:129, 253, 17:36, 40f, 77, 95f, 184, 202, 208, 306, 363, 365, 411, 18:173, 258f, 353, 19:89, 127, 129, 136, 139, 217, 230, 20:141, 230, 240, 21:348, 22:309, 312, 23:257, 401, 403, 24:47, 49, 82, 237, 280, 25:82–84, 163, 199, 370, 374, 389, 391–394, 472, 26:22, 265, 27:16, 30:34, 261, 33:164–174, 178–183, 35:270, 38:147, 41:251, 255, 42:186, 45:212, 46:9, 35, 52:150, 238f

Phicol—4:75, 80, 86

Philanthropy—2:42

Philemon—3:181, 28:xi

Philemon, Epistle to—29:ix, 93–105, 35:390

Philip IV, King of France—28:364

Philip, Count of Mansfeld—50:282f, 302n

Philip, Daughters of—28:277

Philip, King of Macedonia—13:200, 15:39, 46:107n

Philip, Landgrave of Hesse—5:382n, 17:260n, 23:219n, 34:341, 363, 36:105n, 37:5, 158, 38:6–10, 12f, 15n, 19, 63n, 41:181n, 182, 183n, 187, 228n, 241n, 242, 260, 43:254–288, 46:161n, 162, 47:23n, 135, 255, 48:272n, 49:xviin, 88n, 127, 155, 189f, 194–198, 224–226, 228f, 234n, 235f, 244, 246n, 250f, 254, 256n, 258n, 259n, 275n, 277n, 299f, 339n, 350, 360n, 389, 414n, 429n, 430, 433f, 50:xixn, 3n, 22, 28, 30n, 31, 33n, 41f, 45n, 46n, 47n, 58n, 207n, 213, 216n, 224n, 228n, 258, 312, 54:218, 263, 284, 330, 350, 376, 379–382, 387–389, 472

Philip, St., Apostle—5:217, 8:192, 16:55, 17:405, 22:128, 186f, 192, 194f, 199, 251, 413, 494, 23:53f, 90, 346, 24:33, 56f, 59f, 63, 65, 71, 26:205, 29:172, 30:222, 286, 35:364, 37:56, 61, 41:65n, 45:98

Philip, St., the deacon—40:38

Philip Magnus of Braunschweig—43:261n

Philippi—16:115, 26:426, 41:323

Philippians—22:490, 507, 26:24, 68, 27:239

Philippians, Epistle to the—35:385

Philistia—6:389, 10:284, 286, 290–292, 376, 434, 16:144f, 19:234

Philistine woman—4:226

Philistines—2:203, 311, 3:188, 5:58, 60f, 63–65, 69, 88, 131, 155, 200, 225, 268, 6:304, 385, 7:22, 163, 165, 208, 8:78, 175, 199, 236f, 274, 281f, 287, 289, 9:89, 231, 297, 11:96, 121f, 125, 126n, 127f, 14:66, 16:126, 142–144, 18:203, 216, 341f, 20:92f, 126, 282n, 285–287, 26:263, 45:104, 46:193, 47:182, 52:122

Phillips, M. Mann—*Erasmus and the Northern Renaissance*, London, 1949 33:5n

Philo of Alexandria—2:68, 5:161, 9:25, 22:8n, 27:161, 267, 29:231, 34:219n, 35:337, 341f, 40:157n, 45:222n, 224n, 225n, 47:231

Philo, Pseudo-—*Breviarum de temporibus* 20:29n, 27:167n

Philologists—1:297f, 2:182, 237, 362, 380, 392, 3:67, 70, 83, 267, 4:10, 12, 306n, 23:160

Philology—1:298, 2:15

Philosophers—1:3–8, 11, 24–28, 30, 33, 35, 42, 44, 47, 49, 53, 84, 122–125, 127f, 131, 142f, 204, 255f, 263, 333, 2:14, 43, 123, 133, 146f, 152, 155, 160, 207, 297f, 325–330, 346–348, 3:85, 226, 268, 270, 4:116, 145, 148, 188, 5:291, 354, 6:73, 7:140, 181, 193, 281, 8:11, 14, 17, 30, 211, 261, 271, 9:109n, 13:100, 14:38, 287, 293, 303, 342, 15:3, 17f, 55, 59, 61, 132, 146, 16:342, 17:150, 22:101, 125, 152, 156, 293, 295, 301, 315, 340, 435, 442, 455, 477f, 23:96, 115n, 24:37, 72, 345, 25:72, 135, 154, 204, 206, 235, 274, 284, 307, 340, 360, 410f, 439, 26:4, 140, 188, 262, 269f, 373, 27:47, 164, 219, 240, 250, 326, 391, 28:195, 29:149, 185, 235, 34:120, 142, 282, 37:173, 45:370, 376n, 51:61f

Philosophers, Moslem—23:115n

Philosophy—1:4, 37, 123, 125, 130, 185, 2:124, 127, 148, 160, 207, 299f, 302,

308, 3:193, 4:79, 113, 146, 250, 5:201, 288, 7:180, 347, 8:11, 30, 209, 261, 276, 11:441, 14:296, 15:3, 9, 25:361f, 383, 26:30, 259f, 263, 266, 271, 285, 294, 27:24, 29, 37, 172, 285, 367f, 29:60, 155, 166, 34:111, 137f, 142, 35:403, 38:xx, 23f, 67, 238f, 240–250, 253, 255, 260–264, 266–274, 276f, 52:162, 167

Philosophy, Natural—see **Science**

Philosophy vs. Scripture—25:360f

Philosophy vs. theology—see **Theology vs. philosophy**

Philostratus—4:87

Phinehas—38:290, 45:62

Phocas, Emperor—41:90n, 244, 277n, 290n, 292, 297–299, 317

Phoebe—25:128

Phoenicia—2:18, 206

Phormio—13:155

Photinians—32:128, 41:44n

Phrygia—29:102, 31:276n

Phrygians—2:191, 4:8, 76f, 116, 188, 347, 6:195

Physical things—37:39n, 57n, 72, 81n, 82–95, 99–103, 132–136, 200–201, 215–218, 234, 274, 292, 322, 325, 334, 350–359

Physicians—1:47f, 105, 119, 127, 207, 2:117, 311, 338, 2:340, 3:10f, 206, 262, 271, 5:308, 310, 352, 380, 6:31, 7:14, 238, 285, 8:7, 51, 149, 172, 253, 23:39, 41, 119, 154, 337, 339f, 24:109, 25:202f, 26:34, 219, 233, 404, 416, 421, 27:185, 277, 30:69, 245, 253, 42:177, 43:129f, 46:96f, 221, 240, 244, 249f, 252f, 256, 273, 319, 54:24, 51, 53f, 102f, 237, 266, 277, 293f, 296

Picards—10:279, 11:492, 25:487f, 28:338, 31:125n, 126, 184, 217, 245f, 36:217, 44:198n, see also **Bohemian Brethren**; **Hussites**

Pico della Mirandola, Giovanni—31:157, 39:107

Pictures—19:139, 37:254f, 257f, 343, 345–347, 350f, see also **Paintings**

Pictures of Christ—42:6, 11, 105–108, 111, 165

Pietsch, Paul—30:ix, 43:181, 45:308n, 335n, 371n

Piety—2:6, 18, 59, 152, 170, 292, 398, 3:48, 62f, 124, 226, 4:72, 139f, 181, 194, 196, 207, 221, 276, 386, 5:55, 285, 334, 357, 7:72, 75, 156, 159, 164, 186, 208, 214, 242, 259, 343, 8:15, 20f, 38, 57, 59, 62, 103, 107f, 143, 145, 225, 231, 320, 9:67, 85, 135, 165, 190, 212, 232, 16:26, 78, 185, 230, 263, 20:38, 165f, 212, 21:138, 256f, 22:87, 98, 253, 255, 268f, 276f, 335, 349, 425, 23:20, 65, 85, 106f, 144, 209, 271f, 315, 406, 24:52, 98, 153, 228, 255, 296, 313, 322, 340, 345, 26:11, 218, 375, 399, 402, 424, 429, 459f, 27:33, 80, 154, 159f, 188, 29:44, 55, 60, 62, 64, 170f, 238, 30:7, 36f, 58f, 67, 274f, 318, 36:219, 52:55, 172f

Piety, Medieval—46:141

Pighius, Albert—7:92

Pigs—see **Hogs**; **Swine**

Pilate, Pontius—2:37, 5:220, 6:366, 388f, 391, 8:217, 10:166, 169, 192, 257, 309, 11:114, 14:97, 257, 266f, 313f, 321, 16:45, 106, 17:367, 20:219, 335, 22:239, 245, 317, 351, 459, 492f, 23:210, 24:21, 59, 96, 106, 274, 287, 25:109, 28:210, 340, 358, 377, 29:33f, 30:78, 181, 34:110, 211, 37:37, 79, 39:18, 41:104, 122, 218, 256, 42:13, 45:88, 46:51, 81, 97, 166, 195, 47:232, 271, 51:89, 52:35, 115f

Pilgrimages—1:249, 2:123, 3:202, 216, 4:130n, 181, 242, 5:233, 253, 6:129, 265, 7:299, 8:182, 326, 13:7, 325, 327, 14:23, 25, 33, 76, 16:252, 17:5, 21:272, 285, 22:51n, 168f, 220, 250, 254, 256–258, 268, 271, 278, 347, 354, 359, 366, 370, 374, 385, 392, 394, 398, 404, 410, 422, 451, 502, 504, 514, 23:15, 24, 127, 138, 171, 174, 205, 213, 263, 327, 335, 356f, 408, 411, 413, 24:35, 62, 74, 157, 172, 181, 237, 265, 281, 307, 325, 348, 356, 363, 369f, 26:26, 32, 40, 135, 180, 283, 29:55, 63n, 31:198, 226, 237, 34:25, 54, 99, 237, 351, 35:399, 38:110, 149, 159, 175, 183, 231, 40:92, 41:33, 199, 338, 42:7n, 12n, 44:27f, 40, 86, 171n, 185n, 186, 45:351, 46:142n, 47:50f, 51:107, 110, 113, 247, 264, 266, 52:264, 54:238, 340f, 422

Pillar of fire—1:252, 309, 11:50

Pillar of salt—3:298

Pillars—6:77f, 83, 274, 26:100, 102, 115

Pimps—see **Whoremongers**

Pindar—*Pythian Odes* 1:201n, 3:189n

Pious people—13:392, 406, 46:166, 180, 287f, 295, 299, 304, 309, 311, 315

Pirkheimer, Willibald—37:9, 22, 67, 70, 108n, 38:6, 45:138, 49:145f, 215n

Pisa, Council of—see **Councils, General Church**

Pisgah, Mt.—9:40, 60, 299

Pison River—1:97, 100

Pistorius, Frederick—14:45n, 49:166n, 217, 220n
Pistorius, Simon—31:323n
Pit, The—11:246f, 15:150, 160, 16:141, 191, see also **Perdition**
Pit, Waterless—20:289f
Pity—4:38, 47, 7:5, 135, 209, 231f, 259f, 266, 316, 325, 345, 9:149, 249, 251
Pius II, Pope—40:16n, 41:280n, 294n, 295, 44:152n, 50:267n
Pius III, Pope—31:334
Pius IX, Pope—32:79n
Pius V, Pope—43:10, 11n
Plague—1:ix, 2:70, 75, 77, 136, 143, 226f, 272, 274, 297, 305, 310–312, 316f, 322, 330, 3:248, 264, 271, 301, 342, 4:ix, 91n, 105f, 146, 194n, 209, 397, 5:164, 170, 363, 378, 7:177, 228, 231, 234, 255, 280, 304, 308, 8:ix, 9, 38, 113, 117, 255, 9:55n, 102, 295, 11:12, 17–19, 73–85, 87, 11:199, 217–219, 222f, 225f, 289, 446, 16:ix, 63, 66, 107, 197, 23:152, 381, 24:49, 76, 254, 261, 268, 270, 280, 289, 314f, 358, 413, 27:3, 86, 226f, 370, 409, 30:xi, 191, 205, 35:217, 281n, 360, 401, 404f, 37:5, 155, 161, 42:55, 75, 91f, 45:44, 46:78, 80, 198, 48:23, 27, 30, 274n, 316, 49:88n, 96n, 168n, 173f, 179, 181, 183f, 186, 201n, 203n, 214, 239n, 50:85–87, 93n, 100, 108, 111, 116f, 118, 120, 228, see also **Pestilence**
Plagues in Egypt—14:286n
Plaintiffs—9:165f
Plan of salvation—25:145
Planets—1:25f, 29f, 43, 48, 74, 29:199, 30:209
Planitz, Hans von der—31:325, 40:272n, 45:20n, 164n, 197n, 46:247n, 48:381n, 398n, 49:xvii, 24n, 38n, 168n
Planning—15:22f, 26, 30, 71f, 82
Plants—1:37, 53, 120, 144, 204–206, 209, 24:194, 200, 226
Platina, Bartolomeo—41:7n, 104n, 107n, 115n, 127n, 310n, 374n
Liber pontificalis 31:315n
Plato—1:4, 47, 70, 122n, 124, 255, 2:43, 142, 160, 207, 327, 358, 8:17, 12:237, 13:105, 163f, 199, 15:22n, 75, 103, 29:40, 31:5, 42, 223, 33:29, 89, 240, 37:206n, 38:245n, 249, 276, 290n, 39:144n, 47:141, 51:64, 52:52, 57, 63, 54:35, 112, 307
Cratylus 4:206n
Gorgias 4:206n, 6:398n, 54:322n
Meno 15:132n
Phaedo 15:59n
Phaedrus 3:276n, 54:401n
Republic 1:255n, 2:327, 13:123n, 33:29n, 79n
Timaeus 1:4n, 47, 2:207n
Plato, George—54:xiii
Platonic millennium—33:79
Platonists—33:107, 36:109
Plautus—54:14
Amphitruo 25:498, 27:353n
Asinaria 13:218
Aularia 4:364n
Aulularia 6:5n, 15:67n
Captivi 25:498
Miles gloriosus 5:286n
Mostellaria 29:27n
Pseudolus 5:88n, 26:406n, 31:185n
Rudens 27:125n
The Captives 4:328n
Trinummus 15:109n
Plawnitzer—see **Planitz, Hans von der**
Play—2:126, 16:81, see also **Games**
Play pleases God—20:271f, see also **God—Plays games with us**
Plays on words—5:274n, 285n, 8:280, 27:80n, 154n, 157n, 361n, 35:325
Pleasing God—15:244, 255
Pleasure—2:12, 29, 34, 51, 126, 158, 267, 353, 378, 5:6f, 14f, 37, 50, 66, 68f, 189, 199, 215, 220, 328, 331, 350, 354f, 358, 363, 381, 10:102, 160, 356, 11:17f, 13:26, 392, 394f, 402f, 15:8, 10, 29f, 36f, 46f, 53, 92f, 98, 110, 149, 29:18, 119, 173, 35:366, 376
Plebeians—2:200
Pledge, First—28:342f
Pledges—4:143, 147, 149, 226, 257, 356, 406, 35:xi, 37f, 55, 93
Pleiades—1:43, 18:160
Pleissenburg—51:303
Pleonasm—15:13, 16
Plettenberg, Walter von—45:313n
Pliny the Elder—4:xi, 329, 369, 11:89, 200, 329n, 18:160, 19:53, 28:294, 29:40, 33:291, 38:245, 48:42n, 165f
Epistles 30:72n
Letters 28:294
Natural History 1:120n, 204n, 207n, 2:192n, 299n, 3:347n, 4:331n, 339n, 5:293n, 6:301n, 7:14n, 62n, 67n, 245n, 8:253n, 9:135n, 10:217, 11:89n, 134n, 200n, 218n, 14:71n, 281n, 299n, 15:66n, 232, 16:123n, 158n, 219n, 18:346n, 19:208n, 20:167n, 25:26, 158, 401, 520, 26:453n, 33:77n, 106n, 37:30f, 30n, 44n
Pliny the Younger—*Epistolae* 29:12n, 58n
Letter to Suetonius 29:12n

Plowman—16:236
Plowshares—18:117f, 239
Plumb line—18:175
Plummet—20:49, 229
Plundering—6:3, 14, 19, 21, 23, 32, 208, 212–214
Plural of majesty—7:283n
Pluralism—54:144
Plutarch—2:296, 7:191n, 272n, 10:49n, 13:207, 28:300, 29:56n, 48:307, 374n
Conjugal Precepts 2:296n
Crassus 5:211n
De tranquillitate animi 19:187n
Lives 7:117n, 15:19n, 39n, 90n, 103n, 105n, 24:267n, 28:300, 50:228n
Morals 13:395n, 50:202n
Plutus—28:306
Poach, Andreas—12:ixf, 51:xivn, xvf, 5, 315
Podiebrad, George, King of Bohemia—40:16n, 17, 54:352
Poellet, Daniel E.—assistant editor of Vols. 2, 9, and 24
associate editor of Vol. 14
translator of commentary on Psalms 111 and 112 13:349–419
Poellet, Luther—indexer of Vols. 11 and 18
Poetic language—18:90
Poets—1:268, 287, 296, 358, 2:91, 127, 131, 149f, 189, 222, 291, 302, 329, 343, 348, 378f, 3:49, 128, 308, 4:256, 274, 291, 297, 334, 347, 383, 5:66, 172, 292, 308, 377f, 9:6, 267, 24:109, 161, 323, 26:191, 406, 29:38f, 235, 37:272, 45:370, 376, 46:41, 182, 245
Pogrom in Brandenburg—29:170n
Pogroms—47:128
Pohrt, Otto—*Reformationsgeschichte Livlands*, Leipzig, 1928 45:313n, 314n
Poison—3:210, 216, 301, 312, 5:23, 164, 289, 333, 9:184, 297, 23:337, 24:205, 208, 210, 223, 244, 246, 279, 309
Polack, C.—*Johannes Drach, ein thüringischer Reformator* 43:99n
Poland—1:254, 2:136, 17:188, 41:371, 45:133–136, 138f, 46:202f, 49:23n, 60, 77n, 265n, 50:214, 228n, 229, 54:402
Pole, Cardinal Reginald—34:233, 266
Polemic force—33:196, 203, 253
Polemics—20:viii
Polenz, George von, Bishop of Samland—9:x, 3, 49:125n
Poles—14:11
Poliander, John—42:170n, 181f, 183n, 185n, 186n
Police—1:109
Politeness—4:86
Politics—1:94, 14:x
Polner, John—38:270n, 49:402, 419, 54:428
Poltergeists—16:205, 24:76, 47:44, 54:279f
Polybius—25:24, 47:208n
Histories 34:xv
Polycarp, Bishop of Smyrna—41:62n
Polycrates, Bishop of Ephesus—2:226n, 7:65
Polygamy—1:316f, 2:305, 3:45–47, 7:19, 9:210f, 46:181, 291, 300, 50:99n, 54:109
Polyhistor—see **Solinus**
Polytheism—47:290n
Pomegranates—2:65, 4:296
Pomer, Dr. Johannes—see **Bugenhagen, John**
Pomerania—4:281n, 45:313f, 48:223n, 236n, 303n
Pomeranus—see **Bugenhagen, John**
Pomp—4:236f, 259, 397f, 6:78, 236
Pompey—12:226, 19:206n, 41:373n
Pomponazzi, Pietro (Peter)—*On the Immortality of the Soul* 13:77n, 38:238
Pomponius Atticus—26:123, 354
Pomponius Mela—25:128n
De Chorographia 10:421
Ponds—1:54, 274
Ponikau, John von—54:227f
Pontiff, Roman—26:87, 224, 233, 411, 27:3f, 110, 155f, 296, 342, 397
Pontiff, Supreme—27:155f, 385, 408
Pontiffs—2:7, 24, 234, 383, 7:16, 63, 131, 147, 8:27, 231, 266, 283, 9:183, 198, see also **Papacy**; **Pope, The**
Pontus—2:365, 30:5, 41:106, 321, 347, 351, 358
Pools—6:301f
Poor—6:114, 311
Poor, The—3:198f, 4:399, 9:19, 49, 112, 140, 144, 148–150, 182, 243, 245, 254, 10:190f, 306, 326, 328f, 13:57f, 15:83, 90, 95f, 100, 167, 172, 16:61, 20:79, 86, 94, 263f, 268, 315, 318, 21:12f, 19, 117f, 22:190f, 417, 520f, 529, 25:107f, 126, 150, 451, 463, 27:210, 28:295, 341, 31:228, 34:53, 35:68, 94, 96, 379, 36:116, 41:238, 240, 317, 44:190f, 45:172f, 177, 282, 287n, 288–291, 304, 306, 45:84, 161f, 167, 177, 182, 185f, 190n, 281f, 286f, 46:11, 38, 41–43, 83, 104, 245, 285
Poor Men of Lyons—2:327, 32:129
Pope, The—1:135, 159, 179f, 213f, 229, 238, 240, 250, 253f, 260, 271f, 276, 280, 285, 288f, 322f, 339, 2:5, 12, 20f, 33, 38, 41, 60f, 63, 84, 87–89, 99f,

102, 134, 137n, 151f, 156, 176f, 181, 196–198, 213, 220, 223f, 229, 240, 244, 256, 267, 270, 273–275, 282, 287, 290, 293, 315f, 327f, 338, 353f, 356, 390, 399, 3:13f, 17, 21, 35, 37, 40, 57, 63, 106, 109, 121–123, 128, 144, 153, 158, 166, 173f, 179, 182, 190, 202, 221f, 227, 229, 237, 268, 271, 286, 294, 319f, 322, 326, 335, 342, 349f, 355, 362, 4:7, 11, 30f, 34, 43f, 50, 52–54, 70f, 82, 89, 103, 108, 121, 125, 130, 134f, 140f, 145, 169–171, 179, 199, 201–203, 205, 210f, 218, 220, 222–225, 227, 235–237, 240, 242f, 247, 249, 252f, 257, 268, 275, 323, 339, 345–348, 351, 356–360, 363, 367f, 371–374, 389f, 392, 398–400, 402–404, 407, 5:7, 71, 73, 77, 79, 100, 102, 115, 195, 213, 245f, 251, 272, 329, 331, 354, 365, 6:9f, 27, 29f, 40, 55f, 63, 88, 127, 129, 165, 218, 223, 226, 236f, 240, 286, 347, 353, 365, 375, 404, 7:16f, 62, 73, 132, 134f, 162, 167, 188, 205, 233, 242, 255, 265, 283, 297–299, 315, 320, 369, 8:6, 21f, 27, 32, 35–37, 42, 47, 60f, 75, 89, 125, 146, 180–182, 186f, 189, 201, 212, 226, 230, 232, 238–240, 243, 246, 251f, 256, 260f, 264f, 269, 271f, 275–277, 283f, 294, 297, 310, 312, 316, 324f, 332, 9:7, 54, 167f, 188, 10:19, 303, 361, 380, 385, 11:258, 291, 328n, 481, 12:41, 85, 88, 90f, 102, 114, 227, 240, 245, 271f, 275, 298f, 351, 367, 370f, 389, 396, 406, 13:273, 281, 326, 14:12, 23, 35, 45, 55, 62–64, 76, 92–94, 215, 217, 224, 233, 237, 243, 250, 252, 263, 282f, 294, 333, 341, 16:34, 45, 137, 139, 141, 185, 188, 205, 220, 223, 236, 244f, 249, 277, 279, 283, 287, 331, 349, 17:5, 25, 52, 54, 56, 61, 74, 79, 102, 118f, 146, 196, 207, 221f, 330, 348, 18:10, 22, 27, 130, 161, 183, 198, 209, 222, 226, 281, 284, 289, 308, 322, 381, 395n, 19:41, 51, 93, 203, 20:25, 55, 141, 196, 240, 255, 257, 267, 303, 314, 324, 21:3–5, 32, 44, 58–62, 68f, 107, 119–121, 146, 158, 162, 165, 204f, 220f, 281, 22:35, 50f, 58f, 61, 64f, 67, 72, 80–85, 101f, 137, 141, 148, 153f, 163, 168, 185, 191, 193, 205, 207, 209, 211, 220, 225–227, 232, 237, 241, 244, 248f, 252, 254, 257f, 261f, 265, 267, 273–275, 277, 286, 288f, 298, 301, 306, 314, 330, 333, 335, 342f, 365–367, 369, 383f, 388f, 392–395, 404, 406–408, 411f, 426, 430–432, 434–438, 440–442, 444, 446, 450–453, 456f, 460, 463–465, 467–469, 471, 475, 478, 480, 487, 489, 491, 498f, 502, 505, 509, 512–516, 523f, 23:34, 36f, 44–47, 60, 71, 82, 85f, 100, 103, 112, 115, 117, 120, 127–129, 136, 139, 144, 147, 152, 158, 163, 170, 173, 177, 181f, 187, 191–194, 196, 211–213, 221, 224–226, 228–231, 234, 242, 250, 253, 257f, 260f, 268f, 275, 283, 285–287, 290f, 294, 297f, 305, 320, 322, 329, 332, 341, 347f, 351f, 356, 361f, 364, 369–371, 378–381, 383, 385–388, 390, 394–397, 402, 407–410, 412, 415–418, 420, 24:69, 79, 122f, 126, 128, 131, 133, 144f, 153, 155f, 161, 172, 174–176, 184, 188, 199, 205, 215, 217, 223, 229, 235, 237, 243, 265f, 268, 271, 275, 280, 285–287, 304–306, 308–311, 315, 328, 353–356, 359, 361–363, 368, 372, 394, 405, 413, 416–418, 26:4, 9, 15, 28, 44, 45n, 49, 52, 57f, 65, 67f, 70, 75, 87, 90f, 97–99, 103, 117, 125, 134–136, 140, 144, 182, 184, 212, 221, 223–226, 231, 241, 246, 250, 258f, 270, 291, 330, 335, 344, 365, 373, 377–379, 383, 385, 387f, 391, 401, 407–410, 414, 443, 448, 452, 458, 461, 27:3n, 9, 19, 31, 44f, 48–51, 89, 91, 110f, 122, 124, 129f, 133, 135, 138–140, 147, 153–155, 157, 177, 179, 206f, 215f, 236, 295n, 297, 342, 358, 385n, 397f, 407f, 28:223, 259, 308, 312, 315f, 364, 366, 29:7f, 15, 18–23, 25, 28, 31, 42, 44f, 47f, 60, 71, 89, 95, 99, 102, 30:4, 6, 8, 22, 27f, 30, 54, 62–64, 73, 77f, 80, 99, 105–107, 125, 133–135, 137f, 167f, 175, 177f, 180f, 183, 188, 191, 206, 208, 211f, 214, 252, 255, 257, 260, 285–287, 311, 31:xviii, 83, 93, 104, 154–178, 204, 226f, 229n, 243, 246, 260, 262, 265–267, 284, 314, 337, 341, 370, 384–395, 32:52, 67–79, 89, 143–148, 33:86, 90, 34:48, 69, 244f, 350, 357, 35:12f, 106, 133, 139, 141, 149, 152, 297, 405, 36:xi, 6–9, 11f, 18f, 22, 25, 27–29, 57f, 70–86, 88, 96–98, 103, 105f, 110, 114f, 117, 123, 134, 136–140, 145, 149–151, 153, 156–158, 164, 167, 174f, 182, 190, 204–218, 222, 225, 237, 251f, 360, 38:23, 29, 99–101, 114f, 120, 135f, 141, 147, 149, 151f, 161, 166f, 170n, 173, 177, 179, 182, 187, 189n, 190f, 192n, 193, 196–198, 201, 207, 213, 230–233, 251f, 261, 292, 297, 310, 317n, 318, 39:42, 72–

74, 79–84, 88–90, 92, 95–103, 123f, 126, 133–135, 139, 141, 149, 161, 172f, 194f, 198, 201f, 262, 265, 272f, 275–278, 285–287, 289, 41:xvf, 5, 10–15, 19, 23n, 25n, 30, 32–34, 36, 53f, 67, 70, 72f, 74n, 75, 85f, 91, 93f, 97, 106–108, 115, 120f, 128, 131f, 137–145, 147–159, 163, 165, 167f, 174f, 178, 189–191, 196f, 202f, 206–208, 211–213, 215, 218, 220–222, 224, 232, 233n, 234–236, 246, 248–256, 259, 260n, 261, 263–280, 284–287, 289–307, 308n, 309, 310n, 311–376, 42:169, 172f, 45:xii, 20, 22, 24, 26f, 30, 57n, 59f, 64–71, 82, 85n, 106, 109–111, 129, 144n, 146, 154, 172, 200, 297, 352, 360, 366, 47:17, 21f, 37–40, 48, 50f, 66, 112, 116, 161f, 169, 177, 181, 192, 220, 268f, 51:55, 59, 62f, 66, 73, 78, 80, 82, 87–89, 93, 98, 107f, 146, 173, 175, 183, 189, 191–193, 202f, 205, 212, 214, 223, 261f, 281, 298f, 306–308, 311, 321, 329, 347, 354, 358, 361, 363f, 366f, 378, 384–392, 54:13, 19, 41, 46, 48, 66, 130, 158, 185, 228f, 263, 265, 286, 288, 291, 323, 330, 333, 343, 346f, 421, 443, 474, see also **Papacy**; **Papists**; **Pontiff, Roman**
  As St. Peter's successor 31:21, 279–283, 321, 342
  Grants remission of penalties 31:26, 89–95, 97f, 145–151, 183–185, 191–196, 229
  His authority 31:234, 244, 262n, 311, 321f, 342
Pope's disciples—12:372
Pope's household—44:147n, 149
Popes, Deposed—41:121, 266f, 268n
Popilius, Marcus—35:312
Popularity—21:133f, 188
Porchetus, Salvagus—47:131, 179n, 187n, 256
Porcupines—16:296
Pork—26:110, 118
Porphyry—20:155n, 26:74, 76f, 103, 106, 119, 27:181, 190f, 214, 31:13n, 38:247, 250n, 48:37, 57f
  Against the Christians 33:163n
Portius Festus—23:300
Portugal—45:247n
Positions—26:94–98, 106f
Posnanski, Adolf—47:178n
Possessions—20:7, 31, 110, 162f, 193, 237f, 258, 334f, 21:12–15, 18f, 22, 114f, 126, 169f, 172f, 176, 189, 209, 237f, 335, 347, 26:96, 99, 106, 190, 218, 327, 364, 394, 439, 455, 28:133–136, 142f, 145f, 29:55, 230, 35:96, 145, 359, 45:177, 317f, 46:29, 74, 129, 237, 312, 52:215, 221, 267f, see also **Property**
Possibility—25:149, 317, 392f
Possidius—*Vita Augustini* 39:295n
Posterity—6:154
Postils—40:229n, 371n
Postils, Luther's—see **Luther, Martin, Writings of**
Pot—10:282f, 286–288
Potentates—4:268
Potentiality—1:85
Potestas—4:137n
Potiphar—3:162, 6:387, 405, 7:51–53, 59f, 62, 65, 67–71, 82, 95f, 102f, 124, 283, 346
Potiphera—7:52, 197f
Pottage—4:393–395, 403–405, 408f, 5:113, 148, 170
Potter—10:37, 12:66, 13:378, 17:371f, 20:120, 124f, 131, 319, 25:84, 309, 366, 375f, 394, 421, 27:60, 410, 29:118, 148f
Potter, God as—25:84
Potter and clay—33:191, 203–206
Potter's vessel—14:338f
Pouring out—10:200f, 211, 213, 378f, 458, 37:43f, 327–330
Poverty—2:270n, 325, 327, 330, 3:203, 5:8, 183, 258, 263, 265, 286, 332, 364, 371, 7:60, 70, 73, 338, 8:10, 20, 35, 64, 248, 9:75, 92, 95, 98, 130, 147f, 268, 11:306f, 14:149, 337, 342, 16:183, 17:160f, 384f, 398f, 21:12–15, 44f, 118, 301f, 310, 347f, 23:24, 134, 400, 24:14, 21, 27, 29, 35, 26:70, 105, 137, 172, 175, 200, 305, 403, 405–407, 27:65, 72, 122f, 262, 298, 329, 405, 29:46, 117f, 30:170, 188, 205f, 45:161, 290, 51:156–158, 177, 180, 52:263, 266f, 54:132, 137
Poverty, Vow of—see **Vows**
Power—13:42f, 72, 92, 239, 253, 16:36f, 43, 111, 137, 309, 316, 19:161f, 21:328, 332, 334, 337, 339f, 25:5, 8, 41, 78, 82f, 109f, 124, 139f, 143, 146–151, 153f, 316f, 370, 388f, 392f, 412, 468–471, 473, 28:127f, 202, 371, 46:32, 35, 305f, 308f
Prague—36:272, 40:3–44, 47:266, 48:224, 49:212n, 389, 50:112, 128n
Praise—10:22f, 46, 91f, 94, 152, 159f, 232–234, 241, 313, 344, 395, 398, 11:144, 345, 353f, 371, 13:5, 357f, 363, 366, 386, 16:71, 190, 194, 198, 344, 17:71f, 98, 117, 168, 182, 211, 234, 324, 336,

20:70, 108, 25:6, 24, 177f, 193, 267, 26:17, 43, 171, 29:143f, 176, 35:255, 260, 379

Prath River—1:97, 101

Prattlers—28:228

Prayer—1:45, 81f, 94, 180, 229, 258, 296n, 329, 340, 2:19, 42, 51, 77, 84, 123, 171, 184, 222f, 284, 293f, 304f, 318, 332–334, 349, 377, 3:6, 9, 25, 60, 75, 155, 160f, 165, 168, 174, 204, 232, 234–236, 260, 270f, 287–292, 305, 311f, 327, 329, 331f, 334–336, 339f, 351, 354, 357, 359–365, 4:21, 24, 35–37, 46, 55–57, 59, 61, 63f, 73, 81, 89, 93, 109, 126n, 139, 142, 148f, 170, 178, 209, 226, 243, 247f, 251, 260–269, 273, 279, 293, 315, 320, 334, 336, 338–343, 353f, 360–365f, 374, 5:3, 6, 109, 119, 122–124, 153, 156f, 165, 167, 171, 192, 196f, 199, 217, 252, 268, 271, 310, 318, 320f, 335, 337f, 357–361, 6:8, 69, 105, 107, 110–116, 123, 140, 166, 219, 233–235, 249, 259, 262, 264, 274, 394f, 7:44, 47f, 57, 60, 65f, 68, 112, 117, 126f, 134f, 143, 146–148, 151, 170, 181, 192, 214, 221, 228, 234, 250, 299, 305, 307, 320, 322–327, 336, 358, 360, 368–373, 375f, 8:15, 47, 60, 69, 80, 82, 84, 112, 135, 143, 267f, 275, 277, 294, 302, 9:8, 42, 105, 180, 190, 305, 10:53f, 66, 72, 121, 128, 139, 359, 391, 394, 11:295, 511f, 12:31, 91, 143, 150, 184, 188, 191, 258, 277, 305, 314, 317–319, 358, 407, 13:34, 79, 83, 87f, 141, 318, 334, 14:55, 60–62, 74, 91, 145, 178, 200, 202, 243, 247, 260, 262, 268f, 292, 313, 334, 15:198f, 204, 208, 222, 231, 236, 253f, 285, 316, 16:96, 166, 283f, 316, 318, 320f, 335, 17:70f, 127, 129, 224, 289, 302, 361, 363, 371, 393, 18:11, 14, 100f, 396f, 19:16f, 70f, 80, 227f, 20:18, 45, 80, 111, 132, 139f, 173f, 268f, 304, 21:23, 81, 123, 131, 138–140, 143–146, 154f, 228f, 232–235, 321, 325, 357f, 22:203, 381, 418, 23:15, 23–26, 58, 107, 179, 182, 235, 287, 409, 24:24, 80–83, 86–90, 98, 111, 114, 117, 197, 210, 239–242, 263f, 294, 297, 302, 368, 382–401, 405–407, 419, 25:7, 74, 107, 127, 166, 244f, 247, 251–253, 263f, 280, 365–367, 369f, 412, 458–461, 26:10, 25, 45, 65, 70, 72, 86, 114, 155, 191, 196, 210, 212, 305, 312, 318, 323, 383n, 385, 388, 27:76, 92, 97, 121, 165, 216, 286, 296, 354, 410, 28:14f, 53, 62f, 256–258, 262f, 270–273, 323, 335, 372, 29:23, 94–96, 105, 153, 172, 175, 218, 30:8, 83, 93, 101, 122, 143, 191, 230, 236, 281f, 322–324, 31:86, 91, 204, 32:13, 35, 43f, 54f, 88, 143f, 163, 34:53, 56, 35:53, 61, 69, 99, 108, 136, 178, 198f, 379, 391, 36:44, 46, 50, 52, 70, 73f, 92, 112, 116, 119, 121–124, 137, 139, 194, 198, 219, 292, 37:21n, 27, 128, 269, 284f, 369f, 38:35, 118n, 178, 211, 289, 318n, 40:29f, 273f, 278f, 283, 312, 41:52, 149, 164f, 168, 173, 252, 358, 42:xv, 15–21, 22n, 23, 24n, 25–81, 87–89, 91, 93, 113f, 137, 157, 161, 186, 43:11–13, 193f, 198f, 250, 44:xiii, 58–71, 331f, 338, 384, 45:39–42, 66, 119, 46:16, 33f, 52, 54f, 79, 149, 159, 163, 165, 167, 171, 172n, 173f, 180f, 184, 186f, 199, 203, 228, 256, 47:11–13, 17, 52, 173, 48:126, 147, 215–217, 219, 228, 235, 256f, 263, 267f, 273, 289, 308, 310, 312, 324, 342, 357, 402, 49:73, 263, 306, 355n, 365, 400, 426, 51:62, 64, 108, 110, 128, 169–181, 295f, 307f, 333, 52:139f, 230, 54:18, 38, 52f, 85, 259, 340, 439, 454, see also **Jewish Prayers; Lord's Prayer; Prayer, Intercessory**

Prayer, Daily—14:8, 54:17f, see also **Canonical Hours**

Prayer, Intercessory—1:249, 3:239, 351, 359, 361, 5:211, 8:282n, 24:127, 236, 348, 25:477f, 26:323, 28:257f, 31:46, 157–175, 175–177, 225, 35:53, 198f, 38:118n, 48:369

Prayer at reception of Sacrament, Luther's—42:174

Prayer books—42:7n, 21n, 23, 43:5–10

Prayer for the dead—see **Dead, Intercession for the**

Prayer of blessing—37:116f

Prayer of Manasseh, Book of—see **Manasseh, Prayer of**

Prayers in the Mass—36:50, 54–56, 114, 118, 120f, 180

Pre-natal influences—5:380f

Preachers—2:22, 24, 26, 40, 56, 249, 287, 383, 388f, 3:78, 129, 132, 234, 340f, 357, 5:16, 72, 216f, 238, 354, 7:145, 364, 8:106, 168, 210, 9:22, 250, 10:87, 103, 156, 189, 11:275, 331f, 336, 538, 540, 12:186, 13:12, 14–18, 25, 31, 43, 48–51, 64–66, 80, 169, 216, 272, 295f, 324, 14:8f, 54, 57, 67, 91f, 128, 187, 254f, 259–261, 266, 274, 302, 15:12, 23, 65f, 75, 92, 124, 146, 151, 170, 263, 328–331, 16:275, 281, 17:116,

141n, 172–174, 180, 213f, 249, 265, 277, 289, 315f, 323, 343, 349, 414, 18:256, 363, 377, 415, 19:157, 159, 171, 189, 20:45, 50f, 103, 105, 155f, 171, 195, 225, 230, 286, 299, 21:7–9, 26f, 44, 49, 54, 56–58, 61, 63, 71, 105, 119–121, 124f, 166f, 177f, 187f, 193f, 202f, 212f, 223f, 226, 250f, 253f, 276, 285, 312, 22:5, 99, 126, 128, 130f, 156, 210, 220, 222, 225, 227, 230, 235, 237, 304, 332, 342, 344, 370, 372f, 384, 396, 400, 410f, 416, 434, 436, 475, 479f, 482, 518, 526–528, 23:7f, 29, 40f, 52, 69, 98, 101f, 104, 113, 144, 148, 152, 155f, 157, 159, 175, 191, 193, 196, 216, 218, 224–226, 227n, 230–233, 244, 246–248, 251f, 260, 264, 267, 269, 271, 279, 281, 284, 288, 290, 292, 311, 319, 321–323, 327, 332, 336, 339, 342–344, 352–357, 362, 364, 367–370, 375, 377, 388, 417–420, 24:66–68, 70f, 78, 83, 101f, 109, 131, 134, 145, 147, 170, 197, 209, 218, 235, 268, 270, 277, 288, 295, 308, 310, 313f, 336f, 362–364, 368, 370, 25:6, 414f, 26:10, 16–18, 23, 45, 51f, 54, 78, 95, 117, 186, 220, 308, 427, 430, 27:39, 53f, 102f, 118, 121f, 125–127, 129, 164, 184, 193, 248, 308, 352, 371, 396, 399, 28:67, 153, 286f, 348f, 29:66, 96, 145, 30:10, 49, 52, 56, 60, 94, 115, 136, 143, 149, 163, 167–169, 176, 178, 188, 192, 203, 233, 272, 277f, 33:93f, 34:53, 56, 85, 96, 35:56, 99, 170f, 332, 372, 385, 388, 407, 36:94, 139, 160, 219, 224f, 252, 304, 335, 348, 38:85, 99–102, 109, 134, 137, 176f, 188, 193, 195f, 198, 201, 291, 41:28, 32, 43, 85, 151, 154f, 157, 164, 176, 251, 256, 335, 338, 349, 358f, 45:35, 136, 163, 167, 240, 363, 365, 370, 46:24, 28, 36, 38, 74, 78, 83, 97, 99, 130, 161, 168, 171, 174, 193f, 213, 215, 229, 223–226, 231f, 234, 246f, 249f, 252f, 256, 272, 301, 307, 310, 47:274, 276f, 297, 54:31, 137f, 180, 213f, 300, 384, 403f, 428

Preaching—1:82, 105, 180, 248, 327, 347, 2:16f, 20, 22, 24–27, 56, 84, 98, 202, 249, 280, 333f, 398, 3:297n, 10:87 89, 320f, 11:273, 275, 12:43, 112, 114, 141, 144, 147, 157, 170f, 183, 186, 188, 190, 258, 290, 296, 392, 394, 410, 13:5, 63f, 270–272, 289, 291, 316f, 341, 377, 16:95, 128, 203f, 218, 249, 17:4, 7f, 10, 13f, 72f, 92, 98, 145, 206, 210, 217, 260f, 277, 282, 343f, 347, 18:178, 401, 19:36f, 191, 20:18, 45, 50f, 70, 103, 155–157, 233, 292f, 21:66, 119f, 151, 226, 228, 230, 277, 22:48, 308, 480, 23:5, 8, 47, 174, 182, 192, 219, 223, 229, 234, 239, 253, 264f, 278, 289f, 296, 299, 311, 317, 320, 325, 331, 341f, 345, 360, 371f, 382–384, 387, 389f, 403, 408, 24:102, 124, 128, 134, 141f, 150, 210, 218, 242, 249, 263, 287–289, 294, 303f, 327, 336–338, 343, 364, 367, 370, 389, 25:64, 91, 106, 130, 132, 143, 150f, 154, 156, 189, 277, 372, 413–417, 520–522, 26:245, 28:66, 68f, 100f, 230, 268–270, 280, 330, 369, 29:9, 13, 95, 145, 154, 31:51, 241, 357, 364, 32:73, 35:106, 115, 119, 121, 147, 166, 179, 230, 276f, 281, 362, 387, 389, 400, 36:9, 56, 72, 91, 111–113, 115, 118, 131, 148–153, 159–161, 183, 210, 233, 299, 312, 335, 347, 37:13, 15, 88, 92, 128, 138, 140f, 150, 166, 188, 192f, 199, 225, 249, 338, 364, 38:19, 25, 28f, 36, 87, 95, 99f, 103, 107, 111, 161, 176f, 179, 186, 189, 192–196, 198, 200f, 210, 30:182 184, 186–190, 202, 298f, 310, 314, 41:186, 196, 202, 216, 221, 247, 320, 348, 359, 42:56f, 64n, 43:109, 44:55–58, 235, 239, 45:47, 79f, 46:xi, 22f, 30, 48, 142, 165, 167, 169, 174f, 179f, 186, 221, 251f, 255, 48:17, 27f, 113, 189, 202, 219, 221n, 226, 232f, 262, 308f, 311, 320, 51:35, 63f, 96, 107, 112, 115, 136–139, 143–145, 165, 178, 181f, 191, 221–227, 232, 245, 261–265, 390, 52:14, 22f, 25, 32, 40, 69, 72, 205f, 212, 243, 249f, 54:90, 100, 157f, 160, 179, 182, 192, 206, 235f, 271, 282, 292, 383f, 393, 396, 428, see also **Sermons**

Must include the Law 3:223f

Remembrance of God 3:163

Rightly dividing the Word 3:222

Preaching, Test of apostolic—35:396

Preaching Office—46:194, 196, 220, 222f, 226–229, 231, 233, 236f, 242f, 248, 253f

Prebends—1:75n, 3:362, 364, 26:68, 34:36n, 66

Precentors—12:200

Precepts—11:422, 436, 478, 485, 507

Precepts in New Testament—33:147–155

Predestination—2:50, 104, 3:171, 4:143, 320, 5:42, 44–50, 173, 178, 6:105, 149, 7:308, 321, 15:1f, 121, 16:55n, 75, 17:118, 18:75, 22:368, 23:256, 259, 24:62, 70, 25:145, 163f, 371, 373f,

25:197, 25:296, 25:4, 44, 75f, 79–81, 145, 147f, 164, 296, 371–376, 387, 389–392, 25:44, 75f, 80–82, 386–389, 26:72, 27:190, 255, 294, 29:214, 30:6, 158, 31:11, 33:41, 149, 272, 35:378, 42:102f, 105f, 108–111, 157, 43:231f, 235f, 48:187n, 291n, 52:243, 54:87, 90f, 249, 385

Prediction—3:35, 24:365

Preger, Wilhelm, ed.—54:xvi, 125n

Pregnancy—1:71, 216, 5:381f, 28:14, 36:341, 45:35, 40n

Prelates—2:152, 23:201, 375, 25:5, 7, 139, 238, 27:130, 164, 227

Prenter, Regin—54:91n
Luther on Word and Sacrament, Decorah, Iowa, 1958 35:xiif
Spiritus Creator, Philadelphia, 1953 37:xxi

Preparation for grace—25:181, 218, 241f, 246, 496

Presbyters—30:132f, 36:91, 120f, 38:196n, 307n, 40:18, 35, 41:359, see also **Elders**

Presence, Modes of—37:47, 52, 55, 57–77, 82, 83n, 84–106, 109–111, 117–119, 130–133, 156, 177–179, 194–197, 207, 213–235, 270–272, 275–286, 290n, 294n, 300, 320, 337, 344, 368

Presence of Christ—see **Lord's Supper**—Modes of Christ's presence

Presence of God—see **God**—His presence

Pressel, Theodore—*Anecdota Brentiana, Ungedruckte Briefe und Bedenken von Johannes Brenz*, Tübingen, 1868 38:74n, 76n

Prestige—2:172, 199, 238, 247, 262, 318, 329, 336f, 341, 366, 383, 395

Presumption—3:5f, 76, 176f, 226, 4:19, 50, 62, 69f, 158, 162, 180, 348f, 5:124, 175, 6:24, 104, 115, 7:44, 146, 265, 8:40, 175, 329, 331, 9:41, 42n, 87, 110, 125, 187, 232, 237, 13:148, 344, 16:121, 150, 169, 177, 204, 215–217, 219, 222, 233, 238, 256, 271, 287, 324, 332f, 335, 338, 346, 17:49, 53, 66, 78, 150, 158f, 339, 363, 23:85, 209, 253, 319, 25:82, 91, 95, 97, 100, 114, 246, 300, 377, 384, 393, 495, 27:23, 71, 115, 132, 136, 323, 372, 30:175, 230, 233f, 293, 45:254f

Pretense—2:56, 62f, 78, 268, 295, 6:44, 46, 49, 60f, 75, 77f, 82, 200, 203, 394, 16:257, 27:141, 148

Preus, Jacob A.O.—25:xiv
translator of *Lectures on Romans*, glosses and scholia for Chps. 3–16 25:25–132, 194–524

Preuss, Hans—*Die Vorstellungen vom Antichrist im späterem Mittelalter und bei Luther und in der konfessionellen Polemik*, Leipzig, 1906 13:417n
Martin Luther, Der Prophet, Gütersloh, 1933 43:223n

Prevenient mercy—25:181

Priapus—1:249, 2:18, 4:235, 6:238, 9:55, 237, 39:261, 264, 271

Prices—45:233f, 248n, 249n, 250, 262, 264, 54:209f

Pride—1:221, 245f, 255–257, 259, 266, 275, 315, 323, 2:6, 71, 127, 212, 248, 253, 285, 320, 342, 346, 355f, 3:5, 51, 63, 81, 96f, 111, 131, 176, 203, 225f, 265, 322, 4:19, 51, 58–60, 62, 65, 71, 80, 106, 154, 156, 206, 255, 257, 284f, 290, 343, 346, 349, 360, 368, 372, 379–381, 409, 5:6, 94f, 104f, 112, 279, 286, 315, 336, 6:85, 159, 180, 199, 285, 7:4, 15, 36, 45, 69, 165, 167, 179f, 183–185, 187, 190, 196, 200, 207, 228f, 232, 248, 258, 263, 265, 281, 337, 345f, 357, 359, 362, 8:16, 103, 150, 175, 187, 190, 214, 234, 9:102, 104, 110, 113, 134f, 171, 185, 206, 10:68f, 102, 118, 172, 274f, 278, 353, 387, 439, 457, 11:18, 27, 47, 49, 51, 63, 68, 71, 75f, 157, 178, 203n, 208, 220, 224, 226, 235, 259, 262n, 265, 279f, 289–292, 294, 303, 306f, 342f, 366, 371, 391, 394, 416–419, 425, 428f, 453, 462–465, 469, 471, 492f, 495–498, 500f, 510f, 522, 535f, 12:188f, 410, 402, 13:117, 208f, 213, 14:5, 21, 63, 74, 76, 133, 150, 168, 173, 293, 295, 333, 16:102f, 146, 150, 169, 182f, 192, 198, 217, 244, 245n, 286f, 333, 335, 346f, 18:394, 21:271, 308–310, 316f, 322f, 328, 339–343, 22:133, 232, 330, 23:38, 52, 241, 353, 379, 24:19f, 25, 49, 87, 108, 118, 161–164, 25:82, 88, 96–98, 135, 137, 139f, 182f, 207, 210, 214, 218, 236, 246, 269, 300, 324, 385, 425, 455, 26:15f, 21, 77, 98f, 103, 106, 118, 163, 235, 342, 345, 371, 379, 27:48, 67, 70f, 97, 113, 162, 174, 192, 217, 270, 342, 345, 359, 403, 28:21, 87, 154, 291, 340, 378, 29:26f, 70, 30:141, 160, 177, 245, 250, 256, 271f, 31:47, 86, 35:53, 266, 373, 41:18, 117, 42:37, 73, 46:123, 201, 51:14–17, 26, 43, 178f, 350, 52:58, 60, 195, 213f, 216, 226

Prierias, Cardinal Sylvester Mazzoline—

27:156, 157n, 158, 397n, 398, 31:xvi, 255, 316n, 334, 32:ix, 34:311n, 36:11n, 14, 39:55n, 173n, 41:xvn, 286n, 44:118n, 132n, 45:252n, 48:71n, 72n, 81n, 110, 167, 50:267n, 54:83, 263, 265

Dialogue against the Presumptuous Conclusions of Martin Luther, 1518 31:xvi, 255

Epitome 44:132n

Priesthood—1:299, 301, 308, 4:173, 177, 333, 345, 5:20, 93f, 102, 104, 106f, 112, 139, 141, 148, 162f, 166, 168f, 175, 183f, 238, 344, 7:47, 58, 136, 168, 194, 298, 8:118, 149, 154, 207, 210f, 213, 229, 307, 9:16, 97, 141, 168, 176, 178, 182, 214, 295, 13:294f, 304, 316f, 14:56, 98, 132, 341, 16:47, 69, 107, 163, 187, 198, 200, 217, 238, 240, 293, 295, 300, 23:223, 252, 369, 384–387, 389, 391, 405, 407–409, 24:242f, 302f, 305, 310–312, 337, 26:138, 177, 181, 293, 355, 426, 437–439, 454, 27:166, 210, 29:168f, 173, 177, 189, 191, 30:52n, 53, 55, 64, 34:357, 36:78, 101, 111–117, 131, 137–155, 183, 194, 199f, 210–222, 227, 37:20, 185, 259f, 364, 367, 370, 39:151–153, 155, 157–162, 209, 234n, 264f, 279n, 41:286f, 310, 320, 45:142n, 320, 343, 46:145, 217, 221, 233, 48:3f, 28n, 142, 265, 287, 301, 308n

Priesthood, Levitical—see **Levitical priesthood**

Priesthood, Old Testament—2:185, 197, 229, 362, 393f, 3:13, 77, 115, 126f, 356, 12:202, 272, 362, 403, 406, 13:23, 228, 294, 306f, 312, 321, 18:185, 20:39, 41, 69, 117, 205f, 214f, 22:39, 41f, 27:15, 139, 35:66, 237f, 242, 331, 36:200, 204, 219–221, 41:122, 142, 197, 45:320f, 373

Priesthood of believers—2:394, 9:124, 12:289, 403, 13:65, 294f, 329f, 348, 17:98, 337, 414f, 18:106, 109, 20:346f, 24:242f, 27:394, 30:52, 63, 31:x, 353–356, 32:50–53, 73, 35:101f, 248, 387, 36:x, 112f, 116, 131, 138–141, 145, 200, 38:186–188, 39:xvii, xxiv, 151f, 157, 159, 227–238, 304, 40:xv, 10, 19, 21f, 40:xv, 9f, 22f, 29, 35, 222, 44:120, 127–129, 135, 45:46, 179n, 342f, 46:209, 49:28n, 62, 51:335

Priesthoods, Two—12:403

Priestly ministry—16:180

Priests—1:135, 238, 280, 344, 2:19, 21f, 24, 98, 114, 116f, 160, 197f, 202, 247, 280, 282, 284, 287, 332, 336f, 381–384, 386, 388, 393f, 3:3, 60, 113, 292, 338f, 4:15, 32, 65, 76f, 111, 114, 117, 139, 151, 173, 176f, 183, 200f, 210, 236, 315, 335, 340, 343, 357, 379, 384, 397, 5:5, 58, 81, 84, 125, 136, 143, 167f, 175f, 184f, 192, 202, 205, 207, 217, 226, 253, 261f, 265, 286, 346, 6:124, 126, 212, 230, 7:34, 37, 42–44, 46, 52, 57, 61, 71, 77, 84, 110f, 120f, 136, 140, 142, 148, 151f, 156, 160, 167, 169, 176, 197–200, 266, 299f, 343, 8:6, 41, 44, 59, 63, 76, 91, 93f, 105, 119, 124–127, 129f, 133, 136, 172, 183, 185, 188, 207f, 213, 216f, 219, 221, 229–231, 240, 249f, 289, 9:14, 108, 114, 124f, 138–140, 150, 156f, 162f, 168, 174, 189, 197, 202, 242, 254, 273, 11:544, 546, 13:44, 185, 315, 329, 14:15, 39, 54, 61, 64, 70, 76, 94, 99, 105, 170, 175, 215, 217, 292, 294f, 328, 333, 341, 16:12, 16, 60f, 105, 178, 222f, 293–295, 17:72, 98, 101, 20:29, 34–39, 205–208, 331f, 21:204f, 22:38, 41, 45, 47, 65, 126, 216, 219f, 224, 229, 231, 240, 276, 302, 346, 415, 511, 23:20, 22, 25–27, 44f, 68, 136, 179, 193, 195f, 201f, 211, 218f, 222f, 241, 252, 254f, 259f, 269, 273n, 276, 292, 296, 320, 348, 353, 356f, 366, 369, 386, 408–410, 415, 418, 24:9, 21f, 24, 38, 69, 91, 103, 147, 154–156, 219f, 242, 247, 266, 287, 292f, 295, 302f, 305, 309, 311, 338, 393f, 406, 25:123, 144, 152, 234f, 238, 414, 457, 469f, 493, 509f, 26:33, 135, 199, 245, 428, 27:9, 55, 123–125, 135, 142, 166, 281, 329, 392f, 397f, 408, 28:237, 29:16, 18f, 22, 30, 33f, 44, 46, 63, 66, 88, 117, 126, 139, 142, 169–171, 175, 191–195, 200f, 204, 206, 224, 232, 30:6, 8, 15, 37, 52–55, 62–64, 68, 77, 82f, 95, 98, 105, 132, 139, 165, 168, 170f, 173f, 177, 183n, 184, 189, 191, 203f, 208f, 212, 235f, 255, 258f, 261, 275, 288, 291, 31:91, 98–107, 247, 317, 34:93, 175, 347, 349, 35:12f, 17, 66, 100f, 141, 144, 200f, 333, 388, 36:x, 15, 21–23, 26–27, 35f, 41–43, 49–54, 70, 75, 78, 82, 87, 90f, 94, 98, 103, 105n, 112–117, 120, 122, 133n, 158f, 164–167, 171f, 177–189, 184, 194, 199–230, 310, 314, 316, 318–321, 325f, 38:xv, 24, 27, 42, 56, 58, 81, 95, 108, 111, 114, 119f, 122n, 123, 141f, 150, 153, 163–165, 169f, 185n, 186, 192, 194, 198, 206, 208,

210n, 213, 314, 39:xvii, 25, 33, 154, 156, 158f, 194, 235–237, 41:87, 144, 163n, 164, 172, 201, 206f, 214, 234, 251, 42:20, 23, 47, 55, 57, 59f, 79, 101, 108, 110, 173n, 174, 45:19, 27, 46, 53, 61f, 117, 281, 319, 341n, 348, 355, 375, 46:19, 163, 167, 220f, 226, 227n, 229, 240f, 287n, 47:15, 32, 40, 42f, 45, 48, 50–53, 85, 175, 51:59f, 88, 107, 109, 151, 295, 335, 359f, 52:34f, 39, 79, 90, 100, 142f, 162f, 183, 191f, 203, 217, 229, 231, 250f, 259, 272f, 275, 277

Priests, High—4:22, 275

Priests, Marriage of—41:112, 163f, 172

Priests, Old Testament—31:106, 353, 46:147, 221

Priests, Wives of—41:60, 152, 159

Primacy—4:43, 399

Primogeniture—1:243–245, 250–252, 255, 257, 259, 264, 266f, 269, 273, 275, 281, 2:183, 190, 3:64, 4:17, 21, 379, 382, 385–390, 395, 402, 406, 5:92–97, 99, 102, 105, 108–111, 113f, 116, 150, 170, 200, 215, 238, 7:75, 168, 209, 211f, 236, 264–266, 289f, 8:155, 160f, 169f, 174f, 178, 187, 207, 210, 213, 306f, 9:211, 39:298

Prince, The Christian—41:218, 238

Princely estates—39:295

Princely succession, Principles of—8:178

Princes—1:212, 245, 260f, 288, 290, 2:5, 19, 34f, 38, 63, 84, 88, 198f, 202, 220, 262, 310, 315, 318f, 331, 334, 339, 361, 365, 380, 390, 395, 3:x, 114, 123, 126f, 131, 151, 153, 179, 182, 245, 270f, 340, 356, 4:16f, 20, 24f, 35, 67, 69, 74, 76, 80, 89, 124, 128, 155, 165, 204, 207f, 210–213, 215, 253f, 262, 264, 276, 284f, 291, 325f, 328, 341, 356, 365, 382, 402, 403n, 6:21, 29f, 40f, 88, 168, 194, 206, 211, 240, 243f, 334, 336, 7:45f, 53, 63, 66, 68, 110f, 118, 121, 123, 132, 136, 142–146, 150–152, 156, 158f, 161–168, 172, 175, 179–183, 185, 187–190, 193, 198, 200, 204, 206, 239, 244, 257, 283, 299, 322, 337, 348, 350, 371, 8:16, 22, 32, 35, 41, 44, 56–59, 62f, 68, 92–94, 98, 100, 103, 105, 109f, 117, 124–126, 128–131, 135–137, 169, 178, 200, 208, 234, 237, 240, 250, 264, 275, 291, 9:3–5, 19, 34, 36, 49, 56, 111, 139f, 145, 162, 167, 173, 272, 306f, 10:344, 358, 11:176n, 186, 367, 392, 430, 517f, 523, 12:206, 241, 244, 251, 253, 272, 290, 298, 13:x, 27f, 39f, 44, 51–53, 56–58, 60, 67f, 72, 143f, 146f, 151–153, 167f, 170, 172, 188, 193, 199–201, 212, 338, 393, 395, 16:7, 12, 22, 35, 37, 40, 42f, 48, 54, 61, 65f, 86, 90, 104, 110, 115, 139, 150f, 153, 156, 162, 176, 178, 180, 183, 186, 191f, 197, 211, 222, 232, 243, 252f, 273f, 276–278, 285, 294–296, 349, 17:14, 25, 38f, 57, 75, 78, 96f, 130, 149, 177, 188f, 318f, 322, 338, 18:60, 20:27, 46, 93, 117, 121, 133, 152, 164, 171f, 286, 314, 324, 21:227, 297f, 23:5, 7f, 13f, 44, 46f, 81, 98, 152, 158, 163f, 187, 196, 202, 205, 213, 219, 221, 226, 231, 242, 255, 257f, 260, 289, 294, 296–298, 301f, 315, 320, 322f, 331f, 341–343, 362f, 369–371, 379, 387, 389f, 393f, 397, 402, 404, 417, 420, 24:22, 71, 78, 80–82, 93, 121f, 126, 134, 154–156, 162, 166, 175, 214, 218, 220, 251, 271, 274f, 278, 286, 288, 309, 313, 315, 336, 350–352, 366, 377, 380, 25:21f, 151, 172f, 214, 404, 457, 469, 496, 26:4, 14, 18, 23, 27, 43, 54, 59f, 231, 281, 305, 308f, 408, 451, 27:44f, 69, 111, 122, 125, 130, 155, 159, 210, 303, 317, 386, 28:145, 257, 259, 300, 377, 29:29, 72–74, 77, 94, 35:407, 37:xvii, 15, 365, 38:7, 15, 36, 57, 63, 71, 73f, 79, 110, 121, 131, 141, 179f, 195f, 242f, 51:149, see also **Rulers**

Princes, German—41:xii–xiv, 5, 142, 181, 274, 332n

Princes and lords—41:xiv, 31, 36, 79, 135, 166, 171, 177, 185, 221, 225, 238f, 241, 246f, 252, 254, 269f, 292, 317, 362, 365

Princes and prince-bishops—see **Rulers**

Princes of the Empire—45:78, 84, 107, 112, 197

Princesses—3:146

Princeton, New Jersey—38:xii

Printers—54:141

Printers and printing—48:18f

Priors—23:134, 316, 348

Prisca—25:129

Priscilla—41:324

Prison—3:18, 179, 181, 4:58, 206, 8:17, 19, 29, 34, 36, 44, 53, 56f, 59, 72, 171, 191, 234, 245, 259, 261, 26:157–159, 163, 308, 335–340, 345f, 349, 359, 387

Prison wardens—7:101f, 108, 122, 250

Prisoners—46:39, 175n, 54:269

Prisons—7:43, 62, 73, 81, 98–100, 107, 109f, 114, 124–129, 133–137, 141, 172, 174–177, 179, 182f, 191, 196,

202, 210, 212, 233, 249, 276, 282f, 287–289, 326, 334, 348
Private confession—Its origin 44:229
Private judgment—9:129, 33:101
Privation—4:90
Privileges—27:3, 384f, 393
Probst, Jacob—54:338, 425
Probus—13:63
Proceedings at Augsburg—see **Luther, Martin, Writings of**
Process, Christian life as a—25:202f, 245f, 251f, 260–263, 268, 339, 341, 433f, see also **Sanctification**
Processions—18:96, 23:154, 36:110, 290, 42:90–93, 46:172n
Processus, St.—12:290
Procrastination—4:297
Procreation—1:51, 53, 56, 71f, 84, 92, 100, 104f, 112, 115–121, 125–128, 133f, 167f, 186, 191, 199, 202f, 237f, 311, 337, 2:9, 57, 115, 132, 241, 281, 3:135f, 152, 177, 205f, 208, 310, 4:235, 238, 242, 302, 304f, 307, 330, 343, 352, 355, 358, 367, 5:30, 288f, 324, 380, 7:9, 16, 21, 33, 37, 46, 86, 240, 8:42, 59, 206, 12:348, 350, 15:216, 22:91, 26:174, 237, 240, 243, 28:194f, 45:201–206, 52:151
Procurers—4:224, 226, see also **Whoremongers**
Profanity—37:46, 72, 86, 342–345
Profit—45:249–252, 261, 298–301
Profit motive—20:147
Profiteering—45:262, 263n, 264–266
Progeny—4:28, 218
Progress—10:53, 55, 21:208, 25:8, 51, 59, 62, 117, 222, 225, 433, 478
Progress, Mutual—25:117
Proles, Andrew—54:72
Promiscuity—3:47, 4:244, 275, 334, 5:34, 51, 7:57, 80, 83
Promise, Children of—25:81
Promise vs. fate—25:145
Promised land—1:78, 2:246, 361f, 3:28, 32, 317, 4:206f, 5:17, 8:55, 73, 114, 117, 150, 155, 177, 185, 188, 273, 287, 292, 9:20, 27, 32, 42n, 86, 97, 108, 117, 189, 205, 284, 304, 14:6, 337, 19:144, 29:5, 215, 239
Promises—1:81, 96, 155, 178–180, 191, 193–195, 197, 199f, 218, 220, 222, 224, 227–229, 238, 242f, 250, 259, 266, 285, 292, 301, 304–306, 308, 310, 313, 318, 321, 326, 333, 336, 346, 352, 2:26, 40, 48, 51, 54, 56f, 72, 77, 98, 100f, 103, 105, 107, 114, 129, 131, 143, 145–147, 153, 155f, 163, 170, 176–178, 183, 185f, 211, 250, 254, 256, 258, 260f, 264, 267, 269, 273, 275–277, 280, 284, 287–289, 293–295, 308–310, 312–317, 324, 333, 335–338, 341, 358–360, 362f, 377, 390, 396f, 3:4, 9, 13–29, 31–33, 35–39, 42–46, 54, 56, 58, 60, 62–64, 66f, 74–77, 82–90, 92–97, 99, 102, 104–106, 110–113, 116, 117n, 119f, 122–125, 132, 135, 138f, 144–158, 161–163, 169, 176f, 180, 185f, 192, 200, 203, 208, 214, 216, 218, 220–222, 224f, 237, 242, 265, 285, 287, 289, 291, 302, 315–319, 324, 327f, 338, 343, 345f, 356f, 359, 4:3f, 8, 15–17, 19–22, 24–27, 29–37, 42–45, 48, 52–55, 57, 59f, 62, 64f, 67f, 71–75, 88, 91–98, 103, 107, 112f, 117, 119, 124f, 127–130, 132, 143f, 146–152, 154, 156–161, 163, 167, 169, 171–176, 178, 181, 195, 199, 206f, 222, 231–238, 251–253, 258, 266f, 279, 282, 299, 302f, 309–312, 314, 318f, 321–328, 336–340, 342–345, 347–349, 354f, 360f, 363, 365–369, 371, 376–379, 387–390, 405, 5:8f, 12, 15–18, 21–23, 25, 31, 41, 43, 46, 48, 54–57, 59–63, 69, 76, 78–81, 83, 93–95, 97, 101, 103f, 106, 113, 116, 128, 131, 134, 137f, 140–145, 154, 159f, 162f, 167, 173–175, 177–179, 182–184, 186, 192, 198, 200–202, 204–209, 214–217, 224–226, 229–233, 235, 239–241, 244f, 253f, 256f, 260f, 265, 272–274, 278, 288, 291, 293, 310, 328, 332, 334, 350, 353, 358, 360, 372, 6:10, 39, 72, 85, 96f, 104, 109, 113f, 131, 135, 259, 262–264, 267, 278, 284f, 360f, 364f, 391, 397, 404, 406, 7:11, 56, 64, 79, 96, 98, 117, 128, 130–132, 136, 156, 175, 199–202, 210, 212, 219–222, 226, 230, 237, 251, 257, 291, 299, 303f, 307–314, 316, 318–320, 322–327, 329, 331, 373, 8:10, 30f, 33, 35, 40f, 45, 60f, 75f, 79–82, 92–95, 105, 107, 110, 115, 117, 130, 132, 134, 139, 143–145, 150f, 154, 156f, 160–163, 165, 167–170, 175, 177, 179–182, 184f, 187–193, 199–204, 211, 214f, 217, 220f, 232f, 235–238, 242, 251f, 254–257, 259f, 263–266, 271f, 274–276, 279, 281, 283, 286–288, 291–294, 301, 308, 310–315, 324, 329, 331, 333, 9:20, 22, 26, 28, 32, 35f, 40, 42, 57, 59, 64n, 85f, 88, 94, 97, 103f, 112, 117f, 146, 149, 194, 197, 202, 232, 243, 254, 277, 283, 12:159, 212, 266, 312f, 326, 333, 336, 342, 366f, 373,

376, 384, 14:12, 30, 34, 130, 132, 192, 211f, 228f, 295, 320, 332, 15:273, 276, 16:11, 21–23, 40, 57, 82f, 117, 157, 164, 188, 194, 200, 209, 212, 224, 236, 299, 301, 341, 17:3, 41, 52, 58, 71, 77, 89, 91f, 115, 120, 131, 137, 141–143, 157f, 163, 168f, 253, 287f, 341, 348f, 351, 358f, 361, 371, 374, 384f, 395f, 18:284, 20:21, 85, 212, 270, 272, 274–276, 282, 21:44, 48, 206f, 229f, 291, 352, 23:44, 49, 65, 70, 73f, 100, 131, 133, 275, 299, 337, 367, 372, 397, 406, 414–416, 24:18, 31, 70, 88, 90, 113, 119f, 125, 129, 131f, 137, 164, 168, 182f, 212, 239–241, 264, 294, 302f, 305, 308, 311, 336, 341, 343, 388, 390, 393f, 398, 400, 405, 415, 25:9, 18, 25f, 39f, 80f, 121, 145f, 194f, 207–209, 278–280, 26:5–7, 14, 24, 32, 53, 64, 88, 90f, 119, 121f, 125, 140, 143, 195, 206, 211, 226, 229f, 236, 238f, 241–246, 248–250, 255, 257, 270–272, 274, 289, 291, 293f, 298–304, 308, 310, 315f, 318, 327–329, 331–334, 341, 343, 357f, 360, 364f, 374, 385f, 388–392, 394, 397, 402, 404, 409, 434f, 438f, 441, 444, 450, 454, 457, 460, 27:10, 13, 16, 21, 23, 25–27, 112, 142, 146, 219, 224, 251–255, 263–268, 270–275, 278, 282f, 310, 319, 322–324, 334f, 366, 377, 28:323f, 347, 29:12f, 159, 174, 179, 185, 193, 206, 213f, 30:18, 66, 108, 116, 140, 154, 158, 193, 196, 231, 245, 274, 280, 294, 322, 34:160, 303, 35:xf, 82, 85f, 91, 122, 168f, 246, 254, 267f, 357f, 390, 45:214, 47:198

Promises, Divine—36:38–40, 42–44, 49–51, 81–85, 92, 107, 118f, 121, 123f, 169f, 174, 176, 179, 183
In the Sacrament of the Altar 36:7, 38–43, 47–49, 51f, 56f, 108, 111, 131, 171, 174–176, 178, 283
In the sacraments 36:58–64, 66f, 83

Prone, The (prayer)—44:65

Proof, Burden of—37:6f, 30–57, 67, 70, 78–82, 84–88, 105–111, 118, 120–123, 139, 144–146, 168–171, 177, 189, 227–229, 304, 342–346

Proof texts—10:189

Propagation—1:96, 125f, 2:132, 3:207, 8:210

Proper work of God—see **God**—His proper work

Property—6:23, 208f, 253, 6:3, 5f, 19, 22, 93, 95, 184, 208, 315, 7:60, 62f, 68, 82, 84, 96, 123, 132, 158, 160, 164, 191, 194, 209, 301, 9:71, 219, 233, 236, 242, 23:202f, 226, 344, 403f, 24:146, 233, 256, 267, 270, 349, 351, 360, 373, 318, 421, 29:56, 154, 156, 230, 34:42, 45:57, 60, 62, 66, 79, 105, 109, 111f, 126, 176, 238, 252–255, 302, 305, 309, 46:13, 26, 37, 39, 51, 74, 101, 108, 127, 147n, 183, 227, 235, 237, 242, 252, 295, 306, 314, 316, 319, 54:279, 299, 472f, see also **Possessions**; **Wealth**

Property, Church—21:220f, 23:6, 213

Prophecies—6:330–332, 28:250f, 330, 46:157
concerning Christ 45:214f, 219–221
concerning the Jews 45:221–228

Prophecy—2:26, 84, 151f, 157, 174–178, 184, 186, 218f, 222, 263, 3:10, 36, 141, 152, 212, 278, 330, 5:101f, 104f, 110, 112–114, 116, 118, 143, 150, 155, 160–162, 169f, 176, 223, 346n, 7:121f, 125, 137, 148–153, 156, 158, 161, 224, 366, 375, 10:xi, 7, 86, 444, 13:131, 228f, 258, 14:8, 18, 36, 16:50, 255, 17:3, 51–53, 91–93, 120f, 157f, 210, 219, 18:108, 20:4f, 30, 89, 146, 310, 333, 22:69, 78, 129, 217, 228n, 264, 487, 510, 24:303, 365–367, 371, 25:4, 91, 106, 145, 444–446, 30:22, 124, 166, 168, 309, 35:399f, 43:271

Prophetesses—5:79, 8:293

Prophetic writings—32:148f

Prophets—1:4, 15, 23, 74, 85–87, 145, 149, 181, 216, 218, 224, 244, 254, 272, 280, 291, 295, 299, 304, 320, 328, 344, 354f, 2:26, 40, 43, 45, 51f, 57, 70, 83, 85, 94, 98, 114, 136, 143, 155, 157, 162, 171, 184, 197, 200, 219–221, 243, 245, 255, 258f, 261f, 265, 282, 285f, 288f, 297, 301f, 306f, 321, 332, 336f, 353, 359f, 363, 388, 398f, 3:3, 10, 35–39, 60, 72, 76, 79, 82, 90, 94, 108f, 115f, 125, 147, 152f, 155f, 161, 163, 166–168, 191, 203, 212, 215, 218, 220f, 223f, 237, 239f, 255, 264, 274, 289, 300, 317, 338f, 345, 349f, 353, 355–357, 359f, 364, 4:7, 9, 23, 28, 48, 73, 84, 87f, 96, 102, 105, 119, 126, 131, 140, 151, 159–161, 165, 171f, 174, 176–178, 180, 186, 206f, 210, 215, 233f, 270, 278, 282, 284, 291, 312, 321, 346, 359n, 370, 373f, 5:5, 10, 12, 19, 25f, 42, 52, 73, 79, 81, 84–86, 88, 131, 153, 185, 209, 216, 229, 238, 241–243, 245, 255, 260–261, 263, 286, 340, 348, 6:81, 129, 206, 236, 264f, 332, 7:60, 111, 114, 121, 131, 149, 153, 155f, 161, 163, 168, 176, 211,

216f, 231, 240, 274, 297, 299, 312, 344, 346–352, 356, 364f, 370, 8:17n, 20, 30, 33, 60, 63, 75f, 79, 89, 111, 117f, 130, 141, 153, 155, 159, 161, 168, 179, 194, 201, 217, 221, 224, 227, 231, 242f, 245, 254f, 264, 276f, 296, 298, 300f, 304f, 308–310, 312, 314, 329, 331, 9:5f, 19, 27f, 51, 53f, 57, 82, 95, 112, 123, 131, 161f, 165, 168, 175–177, 180–184, 186f, 189, 214, 235f, 261, 273, 295, 297, 299, 307, 10:10, 19, 336, 431, 444, 11:38, 97, 288, 312f, 336, 12:361, 373, 399, 13:85, 102, 199, 14:xi, 9, 18, 20, 24, 36, 45, 47, 53, 66, 68f, 84, 90, 100, 104, 113, 116, 128, 140, 149, 168, 183, 186, 198, 211, 245, 248, 264–266, 273, 291, 298–301, 305, 308, 315f, 319, 332, 340f, 346, 348, 15:335, 16:5, 12, 23, 27, 34, 37, 40f, 59f, 63f, 73, 91, 94, 102, 104f, 117, 122, 183, 204, 225, 243, 293, 300, 17:80, 146, 260f, 18:65, 127, 129, 146, 149, 177f, 233f, 257, 260, 320, 354, 371, 374, 19:45, 83, 108, 120, 144, 152–154, 157, 190f, 199, 20:10–13, 42, 45, 51, 53, 78–80, 118, 121, 125, 127, 146, 156–159, 164, 225, 299, 21:178, 352, 354, 22:22, 34, 37f, 40–42, 46f, 57f, 64, 67, 78, 92f, 96, 98f, 109, 113f, 116, 118, 120, 128–130, 135, 138, 156, 161, 184, 187, 194f, 199f, 209f, 216, 229, 231, 239, 241, 252, 257, 259f, 277, 285, 311f, 331, 335, 346, 367, 392, 396, 401, 421, 427f, 431, 435, 437, 439–442, 447f, 450, 453f, 467, 476, 482–487, 489, 495, 509–511, 23:8, 13, 20, 29, 35, 69, 82, 89, 91, 98–100, 113, 156, 180, 184, 189, 195, 207, 216, 218, 222f, 243f, 249, 262, 266f, 269, 272, 276, 279f, 282, 284, 288–291, 286f, 300, 306, 346, 362, 365f, 369f, 373, 376, 378, 24:24, 80, 90, 114, 116, 203, 234, 239, 257, 259, 367, 369, 371, 383, 387, 395f, 411, 25:4, 131, 145f, 239, 241, 26:7, 17, 19, 108, 210f, 230, 241, 245f, 258, 267f, 270f, 275, 278–291, 293, 296, 317, 339, 359, 373, 387, 437, 442, 444, 446f, 449, 27:15, 44, 93, 123, 135, 146, 158, 179, 189, 222, 235, 245, 259, 275, 289, 295f, 317f, 323, 334, 350, 355, 366, 380, 392, 409, 29:5, 35, 100f, 114f, 124, 147, 151, 184, 197f, 229, 30:18f, 21–25, 20, 32, 37f, 41, 51f, 56–58, 60, 66, 68, 177f, 185–187, 197, 206, 208, 231, 294, 309, 32:xi, 8f, 34:113, 223, 35:118, 122, 152, 177, 194, 199, 228f, 237, 246f, 265–274, 276, 286, 317, 359, 380, 390, 36:137, 147, 149, 178, 192, 197f, 220, 38:40, 93f, 100, 107, 113, 133, 156, 161, 211, 290, 307, 41:xv, 26, 51, 59, 70–72, 116, 119, 121, 125, 138, 154f, 209, 213–218, 223, 228, 247, 303, 306, 311, 318, 325, 353, 356, 359, 42:158, 45:200f, 317, 363, 373, 389, 46:6, 19–21, 28, 33, 35, 38–40, 54, 145f, 173, 176, 196, 221, 233, 240, 258n, 47:68f, 74–78, 87, 93, 95–97, 110, 112, 114, 147, 156, 159–161, 163–166, 170f, 173, 179, 188, 194, 209–253, 291, 49:68, 288, 418, 428, 51:122, 377, 52:22, 89f, 99, 105, 116, 129, 194, 197, 205, 215, 250

Persecution of the 47:96, 156, 159–161, 163–166, 194, 211, 226

Prophets, New—see **Radical reformers**

Prophets, Our—see **Radical reformers**

Prophets, Sons of the—15:276, 18:177f, 320

Propitiation—7:281, 25:32f, 29:202, 227, 30:295f

Propitiator—27:11, 64, 68, 74–76, 86

Propriety—4:259, 28:273, 284f

Propst, James—30:xi, 32:265n, 272, 274n, 43:73f, 45:78n, 48:233n, 236, 49:12, 50:181f, 184n, 244f, 246n, 284n, 285, 51:103

Proselytes—1:302, 2:275, 3:88f, 5:83, 8:41f, 9:229, 231, 17:260–263, 22:98, 30:6

Proselytism, Jewish—47:60, 65, 80, 87, 137, 149, 191

Proselytizing—13:64f

Prospering—10:22, 34

Prosperity—5:56, 175, 201, 7:178, 196, 232, 315f, 320, 324, 339, 352, 357, 359, 8:20, 58f, 151, 294, 9:71, 74, 86, 92, 95f, 113, 170, 230, 10:22, 34, 45f, 54, 86, 174f, 352f, 361, 417, 420, 11:300, 18:281f

Prostitutes—2:198, 259, 311, 347, 3:108, 227, 249, 257, 259, 4:122, 165, 397, 5:124, 191, 293, 303, 322, 330, 335, 345, 347, 355, 357, 7:12, 30, 38–41, 43, 80f, 85, 87–89, 94, 96, 99, 101–103, 116, 199f, 254, 371, 9:147, 157, 233f, 237, 16:21, 185, 232, 24:74, 245, 399, 26:217, 283, 405, 27:14, 123, 41:158, 188, 208, 45:41, 144, 149, see also **Common woman**

Prostitution—3:243, 4:232, 9:210, 233, 235, 237, 18:3f, 23, 308, 26:40, 141,

30:26, 53, 183, 250, 269, 35:187, 317n, 318, 46:287, 293f, 301f, 50:24, 51:154
Protection—6:24, 131, 242, 311, 16:195, 213, 335
Proteron hysteron—see **Hysteron proteron**
Protest of Evangelicals at 1529 Diet of Speyer—49:223f, 227n, 228, 240n, 244n, 245n, 246, 250f, 254, 256n, 257n, 258, 260, 272, 275n, 277, 280n, 281n, 296n, 339n, 432n
Protestant Agreement on the Lord's Supper—see **Skibbe, Eugene M.**
Protestant Church—Its state in Luther's day 7:62
Protestant churches—see **Evangelical churches**
Protestant denominations—42:xi
Protestant work ethic—7:65f
Protestantism—21:70, 41:6, 181, 259f
Protestants—1:297n, 34:5, 38:6f, 46:xiiif, 59, 106n, 161n, 232n, 261, see also **Evangelicals**
Proteus—31:277, 33:17, 22, 30n, 82, 113, 162, 166, 224
Proto-Gospel—see **Seed, The promised**
Prototypes—13:9
Proverbs, Book of—3:197, 30:122, 130
Proverbs and sayings—2:302, 367, 373, 4:47, 61, 86f, 131, 236n, 272n, 275, 283, 392, 398, 6:3–5, 18, 28, 90, 115, 119, 123, 167, 194f, 197, 201, 203, 209, 213, 240, 254, 326, 333, 339, 351, 357, 370, 377, 400, 8:71, 113, 151, 253, 292, 296n, 330, 13:x, 16:x, 94n, 114, 191n, 253, 270, 277, 297, 304, 19:214n, 218n, 220, 23:253n, 272n, 362n, 405n, 28:5, 11–13, 106, 202, 46:195f, 302, 49:144, 215, 225, 250, 263n, 279n, 50:23, 25, 59, 105, 130, 164, 202, 205f, 225, 233n, 237, 250f, 256n, 287
Provosts—23:340
Prudence—4:86f, 216, 15:33, 125, 25:69, 350–354, 369–372, 375–378, 408, 428, 27:23–25, 36, 29:149, 203
Prudentius—15:274n
Pruning hook—18:117f
Prüss, J.—*Karsthans*, 1521 48:233n
Prussia—4:281n, 9:5, 45:xii, 134f, 138f, 48:134n, 49:60, 121, 122n, 140, 50:79n, 253n
Prussians—45:133f
Psalms—1:232, 295, 323, 7:56, 131, 154, 162, 359, 370, 8:228, 235, 248, 332, 9:57, 59, 105, 11:233, 272, 275, 285–289, 294, 15:273f, 17:49, 202, 355, 19:148, 151, 219, 226, 230, 226, 237, 22:229, 231, 311, 365, 387, 23:20, 188, 410, 24:385, 387, 397, 25:ix, 264–266, 26:279, 322, 337, 341, 389, 421, 433, 27:46, 75, 81, 93, 30:235, 35:177, 209–223, 239, 253–257, 277, 38:15, 36, 149, 158, 165, 173, 175, 213, 40:318, 393, 41:19, 52, 164, 251, 42:22, 156, 43:285f, 45:xvf, 361n, 362n, 365n, 46:34, 148, 191, 49:xx, 68f, 142, 253, 270, 288, 426, 428, 51:65, 125
  Exposition of individual Psalms see Vols. 10, 11, 12, 13, 14, 32, and 48
  Guidelines for interpretation 10:6f
  Hebrew text 14:324f, 346, 45:321n, 323n, 361n, 362n, 363
  Latin text 14:340
  Structure 10:51, 57
  Their titles or headings 10:42–44, 104, 147f, 156, 158, 176, 183, 194, 200, 240, 249, 259, 262, 272, 280, 321, 393, 431, 434, 447, 451f, 455
  Use in monastic life 25:ix
  Use in worship 10:43, 45, 12:5, 98, 149, 200, 304, 13:111, 228, 355f, 43:31n, 41, 53:69–71
Psalms, Book of—2:104, 3:4, 7, 160, 313, 362, 364, 9:23n, 10:ixf, 3, 6–8, 104, 228, 257, 455, 13:5, 356, 14:ix, xii, 34, 45, 47n, 51, 64, 69n, 81, 87, 112, 284–286, 290, 311, 330, 332n, 346, 20:104
Psalms, Chanting of—43:231
Psalms, Numbering of—4:x, 48:xxi
Psalter—see **Psalms**
Psalter, Roman—29:151
Psalterium quintuplex—see **Lefevre d'Etaples, Jacques**
Psaltery—7:370, 10:37, 152–154, 228f, 265, 18:170
Pseudapostles—27:331
Pseudosaints—22:81, 125, 141, 24:25, 231, 256, 258, 370
Pseudo-Dionysius—see **Dionysius the Areopagite**
Pseudo-Primasius—see **Cassiodorus (Pseudo-Primasius)**
Pseudo-Tertullian—see **Tertullian, (Pseudo-)**
Pseudorighteousness—32:173, 175
Ptolemais—8:96, 273f, 248
Ptolemy I, King of Egypt—8:320
Ptolemy II, King of Egypt—35:308, 348n
Ptolemy III, King of Egypt—35:348n
Ptolemy VI—35:348n
Ptolemy VII, King of Egypt—35:348n
Ptolemy Publius—2:108n, 188n, 8:320, 26:436
Public affairs—12:395

Public health measures—43:117–138
Public works—45:350, 355
Publicans—24:89, 31:246, 33:80, 46:172
Publilius Syrus—*Sententiae* 4:61n, 272n, 5:378n, 6:4n, 7:123n, 15:88n, 168n, 19:202n
Publishers—3:x
Puerstinger, Berthold—*Onus ecclesiae* 25:171n
Pugilists—3:146
Pulpit—5:246, 311, 7:182, 13:49, 22:238, 24:91, 179, 218, 266, 304, 326, 349, 364, 28:62f, 101, 103, 105, 46:78, 234
Pulpit, Adam's—1:95
Punishment—2:3, 9, 11, 18, 20, 22f, 25f, 35, 43, 58, 60–62, 65f, 70f, 81, 84–86, 117, 124, 131, 136, 139f, 145, 148f, 158, 175f, 182, 212, 215f, 219–221, 223f, 226, 261, 280, 287, 290, 310–312, 314–316, 318f, 321, 342, 354, 360, 369f, 2:373, 377, 380, 3:10, 37, 40, 48, 59f, 68, 123, 132f, 135, 160, 166, 190, 218, 221f, 225f, 230, 234, 239, 243, 250, 252, 255–257, 264f, 267, 277, 279–281, 294f, 298, 300–302, 311, 328, 335, 341, 360, 4:5, 77, 80, 125, 141, 146, 214, 244, 250, 255, 290f, 299, 313, 315, 318, 335f, 355, 5:12, 51, 65, 71, 124, 152–155, 164f, 169–171, 190f, 195, 372, 6:43, 78, 83f, 91, 206, 209, 211, 220, 276, 367f, 373, 377, 7:20f, 31, 42, 62, 79, 83, 88, 96, 98f, 108, 113, 172, 178, 191, 194–196, 204, 214, 225, 227f, 230, 232, 237f, 249, 254f, 260, 281, 283f, 289, 296–298, 301, 303, 329–331, 8:11, 18, 37, 39, 51f, 73, 81, 104, 108, 121, 124, 126, 128, 133, 137, 150, 170f, 185, 202, 204–206, 214–218, 221, 224, 226, 231, 234f, 237, 240, 272, 323, 330, 10:24, 81, 86, 115, 206, 354, 376f, 379, 416f, 12:92, 364, 13:101, 115, 152–154, 172, 342, 14:143, 172f, 186, 244, 261, 266, 295, 323, 344f, 15:11, 23–25, 48, 80, 125, 136–138, 140f, 16:25, 45f, 50, 61–63, 104, 106, 112f, 141, 154–156, 163, 175, 177, 191, 193, 217, 226 228, 240, 244, 246, 257, 259, 267, 19:111, 161f, 170, 20:12, 19f, 119, 129, 134, 158, 161, 164f, 175, 215, 239f, 242, 265, 283, 343, 21:77, 123f, 191, 22:144, 146, 233, 23:12, 58, 63, 157, 253, 260, 266, 310–312, 315, 381, 383, 399, 406, 24:194, 237, 252, 262, 280, 284, 314, 349f, 389f, 25:9, 13, 17, 97, 110, 160–162, 164f, 183, 205, 27:8, 12, 33, 44, 50, 86, 107, 110, 124, 170, 188, 219, 245, 278, 284, 286, 291, 311, 332, 345, 409, 28:159f, 255, 29:122f, 164f, 176, 208f, 30:35, 76, 109, 130, 175, 177, 179, 191, 233, 239, 303, 31:90–95, 103, 112, 121–123, 125, 128, 132, 143, 151f, 178, 185, 189, 197, 201, 317, 32:33f, 61, 65, 201, 34:15n, 35:9, 281, 367, 380, 39:18, 148, 42:150f, 162, 45:26, 58f, 62, 86f, 91, 95, 99f, 104f, 123f, 126, 136, 150n, 157, 178, 203, 228, 254f, 277f, 46:25, 27, 32, 41, 48, 52f, 59n, 68f, 73f, 77f, 80, 82, 85, 94f, 98f, 101–103, 109f, 114–116, 118, 126, 165, 198, 211, 248, 255, 278, 282, 284, 292, 296f, 49:85f, 96f, see also **Eternal punishment; Penalties**
Pupils—5:6, 24, 71, 84, 261, 262, 264, 27:119, 247, 306
Puppies—1:62, 77, 171, 186, 25:16
Purgatory—1:250, 2:86, 161, 386, 4:203, 312, 314f, 5:354n, 7:250, 293f, 296–298, 8:111, 189, 230, 316, 318, 10:364, 13:314, 325, 14:6, 26, 76, 142, 15:147, 16:205, 17:196, 21:165, 272, 22:96n, 158, 168, 211, 254, 392, 394, 407, 23:138, 154, 327, 370, 24:172, 265, 275, 279, 356, 363, 369, 25:381f, 26:135, 221f, 408n, 27:401, 30:174, 31:21, 27f, 90, 111f, 125f, 135, 137, 139, 143, 175f, 317f, 322, 32:31f, 75, 95–98, 97, 136, 143, 34:15n, 16, 54, 85, 351, 358, 35:98n, 102, 406, 36:131, 171, 192, 299, 37:161, 369, 38:15, 36, 149, 158, 173, 175, 42:11n, 75, 43:36, 46:54, 257n, 47:39, 42, 48:43f, 46, 48n, 362f, 49:345, 347, 52:180f, 54:259
Purgatory, True—12:387
Purification—4:39, 22:424–426, 430–440, 447f, 29:112, 211
Purity—4:238, 305, 5:214, 345, 12:367, 21:35, 37, 219f, 29:208f
Purity of heart—28:225–227
Purple—6:297, 323f, 7:32, 180, 185, 187, 193, 195, 347
Purpose—25:75, 371–374
Puteoli—3:x, 295
Pyrrhus—7:164
Pythagoras—1:126, 2:189, 5:22, 23n, 30:268, 31:42, 146
Pythagoreans—48:37, 52:40
Pythian spirit—6:331

Quacks, Religious—13:64
Quadragesima—11:210, 214
Quadratus—12:298
Quadrupeds—1:51, 2:324
Quail—4:136

Quanbeck, Warren A.—54:406

Quarrels—2:127, 302, 3:53–55, 57, 80, 83, 354, 5:15, 55, 65, 67f, 96, 104, 106, 116, 181, 200, 329, 350, 353, 355, 7:20, 40, 85, 265, 8:69f, 100, 149, 169, 194, 208, 24:245, 321, 27:368f, 377, 407

Quasimodogeniti—23:155n

Quatember fasts—20:74n, 279n

Queen of heaven—2:290, 16:225, 18:9, 323

Queens—5:95, 102, 166, 331, 339, 343, 380, 7:19, 46, 51f, 299, 355

Quentel, Peter—41:7n

Quentell Press—48:9n

Questioning God—25:390f

Questionings—28:223

Quinquepartition—7:158, 160f, 213

Quintillian—5:381n, 32:202, 234, 33:36, 97, 37:75n, 253n

Institutiones oratoriae 1:274n, 3:73n, 5:118n, 6:229n, 381n, 7:291n, 8:195n, 26:389n, 29:39n, 116n, 152n, 32:241, 34:69n

Institutiones rhetoricae 26:169n

Quirinus—1:249

Raamah—2:195

Raamses—8:96, 109, 116, 137

Rabbah—18:136

Rabbis—1:3, 32, 37n, 57n, 131, 169, 227, 263, 265f, 269–271, 295–298, 302f, 307, 327, 338, 349, 352f, 2:14f, 33f, 58, 67, 104, 107, 138, 234, 238, 3:16, 21, 68, 70–73, 147, 209, 299, 312, 4:12, 70, 113, 147, 154, 184n, 351, 359, 383n, 393, 406, 409, 5:88, 113n, 149n, 349f, 384, 6:52–54, 63, 68, 73, 182f, 266, 291f, 301, 7:4n, 21n, 39n, 40, 77n, 81, 216, 252, 260, 268n, 285, 8:65, 71, 85, 88f, 102, 141f, 157, 195f, 209–214, 241, 243f, 246, 278, 303f, 315, 11:384, 16:227n, 296, 35:211n, 213f, 220, 284, 45:275n, 47:65, 68, 176f, 190–192, 207, 226–228, 243–246, 265, 269, 282, 290, 293, 296

Rabbits—5:33, 107, 9:137, 14:274

Rabble, The—26:305, 376, 46:75, 293, see also **Mob, The (Herr Omnes)**

Rabies—22:341n

Rabshakeh—16:308, 312, 315f, 18:283f, 286, 290

Raca—21:78

Rachel—1:132, 3:134, 4:189, 354, 5:270, 281–283, 288f, 294–302, 304f, 307, 312–316, 318–321, 324, 327–340, 343–347, 350, 352f, 357f, 360–362, 364, 368, 6:6f, 12, 23, 25, 27, 29–32, 57, 59, 68, 116, 215, 230, 237, 247, 266, 268–278, 280, 282, 320, 322, 338, 340–342, 367, 380, 7:6, 8, 13, 15, 17, 22, 35, 45, 48, 66, 74, 125, 199f, 220, 236, 256, 277, 288–290, 338, 8:13, 49, 56, 74, 86f, 92, 114, 138, 153, 156f, 170, 176, 206, 295, 9:258, 11:96, 22:208, 28:173, 45:27, 46:299

Radical reformers—9:7n, 79, 82, 129, 161f, 185, 188, 306, 18:107f, 109, 112, 378, 38:xviii

Rahab—2:259, 5:40, 6:227, 246, 7:14, 22, 39, 200f, 207, 346, 8:135f, 9:79, 11:46, 177f, 185, 16:255, 18:115, 19:138, 25:234

Rain—1:83, 140, 293, 2:69, 89, 92f, 95, 105f, 129, 136, 142, 343, 4:34, 136, 9:6, 117, 119, 290, 16:159, 18:32, 104, 160, 224, 20:60, 105f, 299f, 345, 21:125, 144, 26:11, 251, 329, 42:56, 58, 46:28, 169, 195

Rainbow—1:43, 76f, 348, 359, 2:66, 71, 145–149, 163, 8:269, 26:37

Rainbow, Noah's—36:39, 43, 65, 174

Ram—4:135–137, 183, 18:271

Rama—2:195, 16:192

Ramah—16:115, 18:28, 22:215

Ramminger, Melchior—53:240

Ramoth—8:290

Rams—10:133f, 136, 320–322, 413, 23:125, 284, 378

Ramsau—Augustinian Monastery 48:124

Rank—27:162, 193, 208–210, 250, 281, 393, 398

Ranke, Leopold von—*History of the Reformation in Germany*, London, 1845 36:246n, 43:265n, 266n, 268n

Ransom—10:226, 228

Rantzau, Paul—54:418

Rape—3:279, 6:190, 193, 196f, 201, 207

Raphael, Archangel—3:80, 232, 35:346

Rapine—3:62, 182, 203, 364

Rapture—25:288, 432

Rashi (Rabbi Solomon ben Isaac)—1:32, 131, 303, 2:14, 234, 238, 3:71, 4:184n, 393, 5:149n, 8:71, 10:42, 116, 11:384, 15:269n, 35:210n, 45:23n, 214n, 47:66n, 134, 238n, 243n, 265n

Rashness—6:24, 48, 109, 217, 253

Ratisbon—see **Regensburg (Ratisbon)**

Ratisbon, Colloquy of—see **Regensburg, Colloquy of, 1541**

Ratisbon, Council of—see **Regensburg, Council of, 1524**

Ratzeberger, Matthew—43:169, 50:274n, 275n, 276f, 306n, 314n, 53:337f

Rau, George—46:211
Raugsdorf, Andreas—39:283
Raun, James—translator of *Comfort for Women who have had a Miscarriage* 43:243–250
Rauscher, Andrew—53:171, 194, 283, 286, 317
Ravenna—54:347
Ravens—2:108f, 135, 147, 158–163
Razor—3:193
Readiness—10:32f
Reading—28:328f, 44:204f, 45:369, 373
Reading of Scripture, Public—18:39
Real presence in the Sacrament—see **Lord's Supper**
Realism—31:5f
Reality (Scholastic term)—29:111, 230
Realms—see **Two kingdoms**
Reason—1:3f, 17, 32, 42, 45, 47, 49, 62f, 65, 70, 84, 96, 98, 108, 121–125, 128, 131, 136, 142f, 153, 157, 159f, 165f, 184f, 300, 305, 328, 2:13, 41–43, 46, 64f, 67, 78, 88, 119, 121, 123, 125–128, 135, 152, 160, 166, 173, 176, 180, 184, 207f, 236, 242f, 246, 250, 254, 263, 267f, 288, 290, 293, 298, 308, 313f, 346–348, 354, 369, 3:85f, 100, 107f, 131, 145, 170–174, 203, 221, 257, 265, 268, 282, 295, 320, 322, 323, 4:37, 50, 95–97, 109, 113, 116f, 121, 144, 159, 164, 180, 182, 219f, 229, 232, 251, 274, 290, 319–321, 330, 345–347, 350, 353, 360, 371, 374f, 391, 5:44f, 72–74, 129f, 132, 174, 186, 190, 194, 202, 213, 219, 235, 303, 371, 6:24f, 73, 89f, 93, 104, 117f, 135, 141, 261f, 362, 7:95, 105, 137, 175, 226, 308, 316, 8:8, 10, 22, 79, 83, 95f, 166, 250, 270, 317, 9:18, 27, 51, 248, 10:430, 452, 11:8, 17, 127, 12:21, 23, 49, 54, 57f, 64, 86, 88, 110, 115, 133, 153, 173, 203, 255, 282–285, 303, 321, 323, 325, 329, 341–343, 346, 349, 356–359, 364, 378, 389, 404, 13:5n, 46, 98, 105, 107, 141, 148, 150, 163, 198, 200, 204, 237, 247, 263, 304, 392, 14:15, 30, 82f, 99, 119, 153, 201, 250, 252f, 261, 287, 309, 344, 15:5, 240, 279, 292, 295, 300, 310f, 318, 342, 16:72f, 100, 214, 307, 309, 311, 315f, 17:7, 9, 12, 28, 110, 219, 243, 356, 18:64n, 183, 363, 409f, 19:11f, 53–55, 112, 116, 190, 20:3–5, 9f, 52, 57, 151, 168, 172, 244, 21:9, 54, 115, 186f, 206, 249, 255, 260–268, 303, 307, 353, 22:8, 12–15, 60, 65, 74–76, 111, 125, 145, 153, 155f, 165, 190, 248, 268, 292, 294f, 297, 300f, 303, 316, 318–324, 330, 349, 424, 439, 441, 443, 455–458, 462f, 466f, 472, 475, 477f, 481, 503f, 23:21, 23, 51, 55, 70f, 78–81, 83–87, 90–92, 94–97, 99–101, 103, 108f, 113, 115f, 119, 124, 126, 131, 133, 139–141, 145, 150, 159, 163–165, 167–170, 173, 175–178, 184, 219, 223, 229, 240, 249, 263, 283, 291, 299, 301, 319, 320, 333f, 346, 364, 367, 377, 382, 400, 402, 24:22, 35, 37f, 45, 48f, 54, 56f, 64, 68, 71f, 80f, 91f, 95, 99, 103, 107, 109, 175f, 213, 215, 226, 256, 268, 296f, 319, 323, 345, 347, 356, 358–360, 362, 372, 25:5, 157, 344, 26:5, 26, 34, 54, 64f, 73, 88f, 113, 117, 119f, 127, 139f, 155–157, 159, 161, 173–175, 184, 210, 213–216, 227–231, 233f, 238, 240f, 247f, 256, 261–263, 265–268, 274, 285, 287, 280, 294, 303, 305, 307, 316, 322f, 326, 328, 339f, 350, 368f, 375f, 391, 396, 400, 419, 421, 443, 27:6, 26, 47, 53f, 56f, 85f, 88f, 138, 181, 189, 219, 285, 293, 28:59, 63, 68–70, 76–80, 100, 107, 118, 169, 172, 174, 184f, 201, 234, 269, 29:33, 90, 145, 165, 179, 199f, 235, 30:14–16, 32, 36, 65, 69, 104, 107, 119f, 159, 165f, 196, 226f, 229, 236, 247, 290f, 310, 323, 31:84, 94, 238, 318, 376, 33:120–127, 144–146, 154–158, 171–175, 189f, 206–211, 290f, 34:111, 135, 137, 144, 160, 166, 35:239, 242, 378f, 403, 410, 36:279, 343f, 37:xviii, xx, 32, 39, 47–53, 59–63, 75, 81, 128f, 131, 137f, 208, 210, 212, 216, 221–224, 228, 231f, 278, 292, 294n, 295–297, 318, 359, 363, 38:16, 44f, 67, 128n, 240–244, 257, 259n, 260, 262, 264, 268–270, 272, 274, 276f, 306n, 316, 39:63, 79, 166, 219, 40:77, 80, 101, 153, 202, 41:25, 53, 57f, 60, 92, 106, 122, 174f, 220, 263, 359–361, 43:52–55, 44:xii, 73f, 336f, 45:39, 129, 141, 143n, 144, 201, 256, 261, 279n, 307, 310, 323, 328, 335, 355, 360, 372, 46:177, 237, 239, 242, 266, 268–270, 47:25, 28, 139, 163, 176, 213, 228, 49:411, 51:7, 249f, 323, 375–379, 52:6, 18f, 48–51, 57–60, 62f, 67f, 71, 75, 78f, 83f, 88–91, 107, 122, 149f, 162, 164f, 177, 182f, 194f, 207, 223, 283, 54:60, 71, 105, 183f, 323, 326, 377f, see also **Frau Hulda**
Reason illumined by faith—26:285, 287

Rebaptism—27:84n, 149, 35:26, 37:155, 366f, 41:44n, 45f, 68, 241f
Rebecca—1:308, 2:231, 305, 311, 4:10, 139, 184, 223, 225, 255f, 262, 265, 269–272, 274f, 277f, 293–295, 297, 299, 301, 303, 320, 323, 333, 335–343, 349, 352–354, 357–359, 361–365, 367f, 376, 378, 386–390, 393, 5:x, 14, 24f, 28–30, 34, 40f, 51, 59, 76f, 79, 91–93, 95, 97f, 101–108, 110–118, 120f, 125, 127, 132, 134, 141, 147, 163, 166–170, 172–182, 194, 199f, 207, 209, 256, 273, 280f, 6:188, 197, 255f, 283, 287f, 302, 304, 367, 7:13, 17, 25, 45, 66, 199, 338, 8:169, 175, 10:37, 268, 23:397, 25:81, 385f, 38:252, 45:209, 382, 392, 46:269, 47:140, 145f, 264, 52:219
Rebel—17:159, 377
Rebellion—2:168, 271, 336, 3:13, 16, 301, 5:161, 13:274, 368, 15:200, 203, 238, 16:22, 42–44, 181, 19:161, 24:337f, 26:250, 45:xiii, 57, 58n, 59, 61, 62n, 63–69, 74, 94, 46:xii, 19, 20n, 21f, 25, 31, 33, 41f, 48, 50, 55, 72, 75f, 81f, 91, 101, 108, 116, 161, 201, 47:13–15, 19f, 55, 48:399, see also **Peasants' War**
Rebellion, Fear of—52:209f
Rebellion charged vs. Luther—36:310f
Rebels—46:35, 41, 47, 50, 59, 61, 65f, 68, 71, 80–83, 101f, 225f
Rebenstock, Henry Peter, ed.—*Colloquia, meditationes, consilia, judicia, sententiae, narrationes, responsa, facetiae D. Martrini Lutheri, piae et sanctae memoriae, in mensa, prandii et coenae, et in perigrinationibus observata et fidelitur transcripta*, Frankfurt-am-Main, 1571 54:xivn
Rebirth—22:91, 94, 282, 284, 286, 295, 298, 303, 316, 320, 355, 358, 26:352
Rebuke(s)—6:27, 62f, 65, 70f, 320, 394, 15:113, 119f, 169, 241, 245, 28:332f, 336, 352, 367
Recantation of Luther rumored—36:5, 12f, 18, 125
Recapitulation—5:338, 357, 7:268f
Recess of Diet of Augsburg—see **Augsburg, Recess of Diet of, 1530**
***Recess* of 1544 Imperial Diet**—41:259n
Rechabites—25:488, 26:297
Rechenberg, Hans von—17:150n, 43:49–55
Reckoning—25:35f, 46
Recompense—21:293
Reconciliation—3:12, 4:86, 92, 6:158, 164–166, 170, 200, 8:54, 12:85, 319, 367, 13:277, 14:83n, 19:161, 21:43, 81–83, 96, 219–221, 22:56, 25:45, 26:30, 151, 28:31–33, 38, 29:101, 201, 30:236, 261, 274, 293, 37:142n
Recreation—4:273, 277
Red—17:352n, 353
Red earth—4:xi, 5, 369
Red Sea—1:35, 99, 248, 342, 2:77, 107, 153–155, 259, 3:221, 4:5, 307, 331f, 5:131f, 6:101, 109, 135, 353, 7:324, 346, 348, 8:33, 96, 9:15, 20, 23, 26, 32f, 202, 10:318, 327, 412f, 447, 11:32f, 37, 13:114, 14:11, 65, 16:114, 158, 184, 315, 17:88, 120, 182, 192, 200, 202, 314, 317, 358, 18:73, 287, 19:43f, 138, 231f, 20:307f, 22:310, 312, 430, 448, 24:46, 49, 53, 280, 26:383, 29:137, 150, 35:66f, 38:113, 41:255, 42:90, 52:198
Redeemer—4:53, 116
Redemption—1:106, 192, 196, 229, 243, 310, 328, 2:17, 3:38f, 43, 214, 338, 344, 4:157, 164, 174, 5:18, 196, 7:13, 133, 138, 278, 281, 296, 298, 328, 8:46, 171, 252, 10:226–228, 11:10, 12, 12:155, 13:79, 136, 260, 372, 382, 14:83n, 100, 194, 16:130, 203, 305, 19:135, 21:350, 22:321, 324, 351, 365, 466, 468, 481, 484, 489, 527, 23:58, 110, 137, 148, 171f, 278, 330, 338, 354, 357, 365, 24:91, 102, 220, 269, 281, 287, 307, 344, 347, 387, 408, 25:31, 47, 26:8, 182, 154, 269, 282, 286, 295, 360, 365, 374, 27:34, 82, 144, 147, 241, 260, 328, 28:264, 267–270, 308f, 319, 376, 29:80, 98, 144, 234, 30:35, 301, 31:177, 295, 351, 36:217, 352, 38:xi, 113, 125, 41:113f, 140, 166, 42:58, 80, 164, 46:166, 51:63, 162, 164f, 279
Reed, Elizabeth S.—indexer of Vol. 32
Reed, Luther D.—*The Lutheran Liturgy*, Philadelphia, 1960 53:28n
Reeds—6:107f, 135, 218, 16:213, 309
Refining—11:506
Reform—15:27, 56f, 64f, 119, 143
Reformatio ecclesiarum Hassiae—49:17n
Reformation, The—2:63, 340, 361n, 3:6, 213n, 275n, 4:125n, 204n, 209n, 5:x, 109n, 115n, 6:x, 228, 230–232, 237, 7:108n, 9:215, 14:x, 26:47n, 455n, 31:37, 250, 394, 34:8, 15n, 38:xi, xiv, 7, 114n, 142f, 157n, 218, 232, 42:xi, xiiin, 121n, 44:xi, xvii–xix, 90f, 123f, 156–216, 45:313n, 314, 342, 344, 46:xif, 5n, 18n, 39n, 89, 90n, 106n, 141, 142n, 209f, 239n, 247n, 294n,

298n, 47:7, 52f, 60f, 125f, 133, 51:303, 333, 54:231, 273, 356
Bibliography 31:xi–xiii
Causes and effects 3:153
Reformation, Need for—41:11, 13–16, 19, 223, 259
Reformation, Progress of the—12:4, 41:xii, xiv, 110n, 181
Reformation, Radical—1:6n, 2:361n, 22:225n, 367n
Reformation controversies—30:123n
Reformation in Germany—Sufferings of pastors 3:232, 240, 357
Reformation writings (Luther's)—34:xii
Reformationsgeschichte, Vereins für—Halle, 1880– 32:274n
Reformed Church—48:230n, 322n
Reformed tradition—49:17n, 88n, 215n
Reformer without a Church: Thomas Münzer **etc.**—see **Gritsch, Eric W.**
Reformers—23:105n, 24:347, 38:xixf, 12, 93, 142f, 282, 41:xiiif
Reformers, Radical—14:4n, 19f
Reforms, Imperial—48:49, 216n, 244
Refuge, Cities of—9:193–197
Refuge, The believer's—10:396f, 16:195, 208
Regency, Imperial Council of—36:246n, 45:77, 78n, 84n, 197, 242, 48:70n, 85n, 129n, 144n, 381n, 398n
Regeneration—3:167, 4:27f, 343–345, 347, 401, 12:386, 22:35, 96, 100, 277f, 283, 298, 24:256, 26:228, 352f, 29:81, 83f, 30:264, 292, 38:43, 87
Regensburg (Ratisbon)—6:ix, 231n, 16:323, 34:25, 28, 44:185n, 47:266, 48:139f, 248, 49:313n
Regensburg, Colloquy of, 1541—28:257n, 34:301, 50:190n, 230n
Regensburg, Colloquy of, 1546—50:250n, 265n, 288n, 321n
Regensburg, Council of, 1524—28:257
Regensburg, Diet of, 1471—41:270n
Regensburg, Diet of, 1524—12:x
Regensburg, Diet of, 1532—50:54n, 55, 68, 82n
Regensburg, Diet of, 1546—50:312n
Regensburg, Diets of, 1541, 1543—43:253–255
Regensburg, League of—49:119n, 126f, 131n, 190n
Regia via—see **Royal road**
Regicides—18:42, 47
Regiment (German term)—13:147n, 193, 23:313n, 24:82n, 26:116n, 30:20
Regina coeli laetare (hymn) 21:327
Regulus, Marcus Atilius—33:225
Rehoboam, King—6:223, 15:43, 72, 47:187, 194f, 207
Rehoboth—2:202, 5:69, 76, 80, 6:309
Reichert, O.—35:207n
Reichskammergericht—see **Supreme Court, Imperial (Reichskammergericht)**
Reichstag—45:161
Reifenstein, William—38:79
Reinicke, Hans—49:314, 318, 319n, 320n
Reisch, Gregorius—*Margarita philosophica nova* 29:149n, 166n, 231n
Reissenbusch, Wolfgang—54:83n
Rejoicing—see **Joy**
Relatives—2:139, 251f, 254, 268, 336, 357, 6:4, 66, 83, 272, 390f
Release, Year of—9:144, 148, 150
Relics—4:231, 7:299, 8:144, 9:130n, 25:476, 26:222, 31:225f, 41:149n, 151–156, 164–169, 173, 205, 42:142n, 143n, 146, 48:33f, 50, 161, 387, 51:40, 53:39, 54:131, 247, 273, 288
Religion—1:106, 275, 292, 344, 2:6, 52, 60f, 65, 87, 165, 170, 186, 192, 197f, 202, 208, 210, 213–216, 219, 227, 229, 247, 250f, 264, 269f, 274, 276, 279f, 280, 282f, 285f, 289–291, 293, 314, 328, 335, 339, 349, 355, 388, 393, 3:108, 118, 162, 188, 219, 316, 340, 4:3, 25, 29, 35, 78, 88f, 135, 178, 180, 236, 239, 271, 273, 284, 288, 315, 344, 346, 348, 350, 352, 356, 365f, 384, 386, 392, 401, 5:3, 7, 43, 80, 96f, 108, 115, 176, 208, 263, 329, 6:33, 49f, 52, 60, 66, 79, 7:14, 85, 140, 145, 163, 199f, 202, 207, 212, 298, 253, 311, 343–347, 349, 351f, 355, 357, 364, 8:32, 36, 41, 59, 129, 131, 133, 172, 305, 9:3, 56–58, 83, 164, 186, 226, 291, 12:85, 198, 222, 265, 352, 355, 358, 16:10, 16, 21, 36, 38, 78, 82f, 153, 156, 293, 17:78, 95, 107, 111f, 145, 158, 225, 271, 274, 375, 382, 412, 20:57, 74, 86, 142, 198f, 241, 264, 23:85f, 232, 351, 24:337, 348, 26:3, 7, 13, 30, 32, 41, 47, 58, 96f, 104, 106, 140, 185, 192, 199, 210, 224f, 227, 229, 231, 270, 307, 332f, 354, 373, 375, 396f, 399, 420f, 426f, 437, 446, 454, 458f, 27:87–89, 91, 135f, 141, 146, 148, 161, 239, 281, 337, 374f, 396, 28:303f, 308, 29:9f, 48, 41:34n, 38n, 39f
Religion, Near Eastern—5:352n
Religion, Old Testament view of—48:24f
Religionists—17:149f

Religions, True (pure)—2:201, 206, 212, 234f, 242, 245, 262, 269, 321, 332, 363
Religious, The—see **Monks and nuns**
Religious life—52:254f, 257f, 265f, 270
Religious orders—see **Monastic orders**
Rem, Alexander—45:271n
Remembrance—6:110, 112f, 10:179, 393f, 13:371n, 16:184, 207, 17:347, 367, 20:113, 145, 306, 21:350
Remembrance in the Sacrament—see **Lord's Supper**—Remembrance in the Sacrament
Remembrance of sacrifice—see **Sacrifice of Remembrance**
Reminder—28:64, 67, 72, 175f
Reminiscere Sunday—23:131n
Remission of sins—see **Forgiveness of sins**
Remnant—10:19, 11:5, 9, 22, 71, 95, 99f, 193, 293, 367, 472f, 476, 492f, 551, 16:26, 51, 75, 77, 80, 81, 85, 90, 112f, 144, 153, 155, 159, 221, 235, 326, 328, 17:212, 306–398, 344, 381, 413, 18:51, 101, 148f, 154, 158, 177, 187, 194, 207, 228, 241, 251f, 276, 281f, 319, 338f, 342f, 358, 406, 419, 20:3, 27f, 37, 66, 82, 85, 92f, 108f, 116, 123, 148, 150, 210f, 323, 336, 25:85f, 96, 394f, 421, 423
Remorse—6:84, 369–371, 10:64–67, 74, 141f, 293, 11:19–22, 24–26, 36f, 84
Renewal of man—16:208
Rengstorf, Karl Heinrich—47:61n, 126n
Rents (Rente, Rentenkauf)—8:127, 9:254, 45:236f, 238n, 295n, 46:14, 39, see also **Zins and Zinskauf**
Renunciation—53:99, 108f
Repair work—15:167
Reparation—9:197
Repentance—1:82, 148, 181, 231, 283, 297, 301, 307, 2:23, 26f, 40, 51f, 176, 223, 297, 358, 3:40, 170, 268, 340, 4:49, 51, 367, 409, 5:82, 151–155, 157, 162f, 6:40–43, 51, 62, 69, 75, 195, 200, 368, 7:11, 227, 229, 234, 236, 237n, 256f, 287, 8:27, 41, 45, 118, 216, 332, 9:21, 27, 59f, 210, 277, 10:64f, 75, 106, 147, 207, 11:25, 368, 12:143f, 303–305, 316, 330f, 347, 14:ix, 158, 166, 16:60, 104, 235, 18:3, 53, 79, 82, 85, 95, 100, 103, 105, 127f, 131, 146f, 157, 173, 208, 213, 220, 238, 281, 285, 338, 356, 409, 19:58f, 22:63, 65, 172, 176f, 180, 23:407, 24:236, 287, 402, 25:17, 176, 229, 434, 478f, 26:126, 131, 197, 27:184, 189, 29:182, 219, 227, 30:248, 31:25f, 83–88, 96, 186–188, 364, 32:13, 21, 24, 27f, 33, 35, 37–43, 49, 34:19n, 53, 35:xi, 7, 40, 298, 394, 37:192, 38:97, 118, 305, 40:274–276, 364, 41:232, 241, 342f, 42:148, 46:42, 159, 171f, 174, 184, 255, 47:16, 39f, 43f, 85, 101–104, 110–112, 140, 239–242, 51:21, 318, see also **Contrition**
Repentance, Daily—12:330
Repentance, Esauitic—5:170
Repetitions—20:47
Rephaim—2:366f, 370, 374, 388, 9:34, 52:202
Rephaim, Valley of—16:155
Rephan—8:131, 200, 18:167n, 322
Reports—25:92, 418
Reproaches—6:3, 45 52, 55f, 77, 215, 318, 11:443f
Reprobates—24:345
Reproduction—see **Procreation**
Reproduction as duty—see **Creation**—God's ordinance at
Reptiles—1:54, 2:74, 8:133, 24:317, 378
Repurchase (Widderkauf)—45:174n, 175n
Reputation—10:84f, 303, 11:353, 21:236f, 271, 292, 25:177, 465, 503f, 46:302
Reredos—42:119
Resemblence (Sacramental elements)—see **Similarity**
Resen—2:201
Reservation of benefices—34:251, 44:152f, 161f
Reservation of the Sacrament—36:xf, 257, 50:66f
Reservations, Luther's—34:67
Reserved cases—35:13, 36:86n, 88
Resignation—25:381, 25:381f, 384
Resignation to hell—25:381f
Resistance—21:337
Resistance to authority—31:234f, 47:ix, 6–9, 13–20, 34–55
Resistance, Armed, to the Emperor—49:xvin, 193, 244f, 251, 254, 257f, 264, 272f, 376, 397f, 429f, 433f, 50:9f, 66
Respect—6:98, 160f, 163, 167–169, 329
Respect of persons—9:145, 163, 211, 298, 20:79, 326, 333, 33:56
Respectability—4:259, 276, 7:42f, 59, 78, 85, 242, 8:59
Responsibility—21:318–321
Responsories—53:12, 14, 38, 321, 328, 331
Respublica—2:272n
Rest—6:120, 281, 29:147, 159–161, 173
Restitution—6:77, 13:103f
Restoration of all things—9:5
Restraint—3:201f, 281, 24:81
Resumption—12:274, 355, 389, 406
Resurrection—1:52, 68, 80, 111, 196, 198,

214, 285, 330, 333, 338, 345, 350, 354, 2:151f, 155, 232, 3:10, 38f, 141f, 148, 4:45, 96, 105, 113, 119, 121, 124, 156–158, 190, 192, 205, 309–311, 314, 316f, 329, 330f, 366, 5:17, 19, 39, 42, 73–75, 353, 6:273f, 281, 354, 7:116f, 212, 298, 8:19, 26, 82, 140, 144, 162, 168, 189f, 194, 236, 315f, 320f, 9:158, 279, 10:24, 31f, 71, 138, 327, 12:118f, 128, 231, 13:85, 126f, 240, 291, 14:12, 87, 307, 331, 16:73, 102, 124, 177, 17:227, 365, 18:240f, 22:297, 479, 24:125, 205, 321, 25:5, 45, 50–51, 70, 89f, 115f, 121, 146f, 284, 406, 26:21f, 24, 392, 27:87, 296, 372, 28:59f, 69, 71f, 75f, 93–96, 98–100, 102, 110f, 114–117, 119, 121–123, 132f, 147f, 150, 163, 167–172, 193, 196–198, 202f, 253, 29:14, 125, 137f, 230, 30:118, 35:381, 387, 36:67–70, 147, 299, 37:100, 114–116, 118, 134, 155, 366, 372, 38:57, 41:65, 127, 241, 46:177, 224, 51:19, 166–168, 52:279f, see also **Christ**—His resurrection

Resurrection of the flesh—28:150, 168, 196–198

Retaliation—9:193, 197, 199

Return to God—20:9, 161f, 164, 33:132–135

Return to homeland—6:3, 7f, 11, 109f

Reu, J. Michael—47:5n, 25n, 54:39, 440, 445

Augsburg Confession, The, Chicago, 1930 4:166n, 16:201n, 22:444n, 23:16n, 33n, 173n, 26:137n, 35:222n, 340n

Luther's German Bible, Columbus, Ohio, 1934 35:191n, 227n, 229n, 253n, 279n, 339n, 340n, 345n, 349n, 350n, 352n, 357n, 394n

Reuben—3:16, 5:90, 304, 317f, 337, 339f, 351, 6:77, 161, 175, 204, 246, 270, 275–277, 279–281, 292, 305, 315f, 318f, 328, 340, 362, 366f, 372, 376–380, 392–395, 404, 7:11, 42, 57, 125, 201, 218, 259f, 264–266, 270, 289, 310, 362, 376, 8:51f, 91, 104, 114, 154f, 170, 204–207, 210–216, 218, 222–224, 233, 285, 295, 307, 9:35f, 40, 258, 305, 13:154, 16:154

Reubenites—3:280, 9:81

Reuchlin, John—4:xi, 7:217, 10:37, 43f, 65, 146, 237, 256, 320, 449, 11:43, 125n, 184, 459, 15:112n, 322n, 25:xi, 289, 388, 435, 454, 498, 31:157, 259, 44:118n, 47:124, 127, 129–130, 48:9f, 31, 38n, 57, 69, 77n, 99n, 123n, 132n, 143n, 172n, 230n, 318, 54:261, 445n

De arte cabbalistica, 1517 26:290n

De verbo mirifico 11:422n

First Principles of Hebrew, Pforzheim, 1506 2:34n, 4:393n, 10:37, 43f, 329, 449, 11:29n, 128n, 312n, 369n, 459n, 463n, 14:335n, 339n, 18:300f, 29:117n, 35:263n

Lexicon hebraicum 29:128n

Septem psalmi poenitentiales 10:44, 146, 237, 258, 11:262n, 309n, 25:211n, 264n

Vocabularius breviloquus 25:72n, 123n, 496n

Reuchlin controversy—32:150, 176, 186n

Reuel—6:290

Reutlingen—23:219n, 36:310, 37:xiiif, 38:11, 73n, 49:88n, 350, 53:53

Reval—45:314

Reval, Bishop of—45:313f

Revelation of St. John, The—2:150, 20:155f, 24:366, 36:140, 310

Authorship—30:ix

Preface to the 35:398f

Revelations, Special—1:350, 2:83, 86, 162–164, 174, 249, 283, 320, 3:5f, 10–12, 71n, 92, 120, 167, 170, 219, 275f, 280, 285, 302, 330, 350, 4:97, 101, 125–127, 178, 240, 5:73, 216, 238, 245, 261, 346, 348, 6:226, 251, 264, 329f, 334, 9:26, 89, 123, 12:339, 341, 365, 14:8, 13n, 14, 30, 36, 90, 100, 341, 22:156, 161, 24:68f, 115, 175, 257f, 290, 296, 303, 366–368, 371, 402, 405, 25:9, 154, 214, 223, 26:16, 62f, 67, 72–75, 77f, 81–83, 98, 108, 302, 440, 27:9, 24f, 90, 101, 142, 171, 182f, 190–193, 196, 199, 277, 28:75, 35:295, 372

Revelry—2:127

Revenge—see **Vengeance**

Revenue—23:394

Reverence—3:14, 99, 185f, 189, 218, 228, 234, 247, 281, 25:11, 143, 167

Reviling—17:269f

Revolution—49:40, 53f, 99, 191f, 196, 234, 259, 298f, 309, 369

Rewards—3:132, 257, 263, 361, 11:491, 13:382, 419, 16:25, 17:15, 53, 340, 348f, 351, 410, 21:20, 290f, 315, 26:261, 264–266, 272, 294, 334, 397, 29:122f, 33:9f, 149–154, 197, 199, 210, 37:142f, 372

Rhadinus, Thomas—39:110, 112, 126, 157, 162, 166

Rhaeticus, Joachim—22:59n

Rhapsodies on the Marburg Colloquy—38:11f, 80–83 (text)
Rhau, George—14:xi, 49:403, 418, 53:123, 284, 295n, 319, 321
Rhegius, Urbanus—37:5, 8, 49:160n, 213, 54:391
Rhegius, Urbanus, Works of—*Serfdom and Slavery: A Discussion of the Christian Relationship between Lords and Serfs on the Basis of Divine Law. A Sermon preached at Augsburg* 46:39n
Rhenanus, Beatus—31:38n, 42:17, 45:54n
Rhetoric—1:46, 233, 3:9, 191, 196, 288, 341, 343, 347, 4:153, 192, 5:24, 147, 182, 306, 6:36, 43, 69, 83, 120, 171, 208, 384, 7:89f, 287–289, 291, 359, 14:89, 24:104, 109, 26:92, 169n, 218, 412, 430, 27:23f, 31, 390, 37:123, 156f, 171–189, 239–246, 253, 267, 301f, 307, 331, 38:22–24, 55, 49:100, 212, 326n, 331
Rhetoric, Medieval—2:4n
Rhetorical arts—46:252n
Rhetorical inversion—26:100
Rhetoricians—1:177, 279, 2:393, 3:73, 195, 213f, 5:24, 337
Rhine River—6:309, 14:73, 22:387, 422, 38:93, 46:83n
Rhineland—22:59n, 41:xii, 48:33f, 134n, 216n
Rhinelanders—54:387
Rhodes—2:380n, 19:43, 27:154n, 46:157, 166n
Rhymes—53:198f
Ribbick, Otto, ed.—*Scenicae Romanorum Poesis Fragmenta* 15:78n
Rich, The—46:255, 257, 285
Richenthal, Ulrich von—*Das Conciliam, so zu Constanz gehalten ist worden,* Augsburg, 1536 54:215
Riches—see **Wealth**
Richter, Aemilius Ludovicus, and Aemilius Friedberg, eds.—see ***Corpus Iuris Canonici***
Richter, Aemilius Ludwig—*Die evangelischen Kirchenordnungen des sechzehnten Jahrhunderts,* Weimar, 1846 45:162n
Ricius, Paul—54:377
Ridicule—2:71, 17:270f, 343
Rieder, Henry—54:316, 398
Riederer, Johann Bartholomaeus—*Nachrichten zur Kirchen-, Gelehrten- und Büchergeschichte aus gedruckten und ungedruckten Schriften gesammelt,* Altdorf, 1764–1768 38:62n
Rieger—see **Rhegius, Urbanus**
Rietesel, John—50:50
Rietschel, Georg—53:93, 123
Lehrbuch der Liturgik, Berlin, 1900 36:278n
Riga—23:xi, 45:313n, 314n, 315n, 317n, 318n, 49:121
Right, To be in the—21:333f, 336, 347
Right and left hand—25:138n
Right hand—11:221, 226, 369
Right hand of God—see **God**—His right hand
Righteous, The—2:3, 12, 84, 100, 197, 307, 349, 3:36, 227, 234f, 243, 295, 6:26, 44, 48, 73, 75–77, 79, 89, 165, 10:25, 39, 47, 174f, 399, 423, 11:372–375, 386, 504–506, 13:4, 370f, 398, 410–412, 414, 416–419, 15:121f, 126, 134, 16:250, 17:268f, 35:xi, 217f, 251f, 258, 268, 297f, 342, 359, 42:140, 156f, 46:70, 73, 95, 174, 286
Righteous works—25:138, 152
Righteousness—1:64f, 141, 154, 160, 162, 179, 181, 197f, 234, 245, 260, 264, 275, 341, 2:3, 8, 12f, 18, 24, 28, 41, 43, 56, 60–63, 119n, 135, 159–161, 171, 246, 249f, 267, 269f, 303, 349f, 378, 382–384, 3:5, 9, 20–26, 28f, 78–80, 82, 84f, 87f, 90, 93f, 96, 101–107, 112f, 122, 148, 156, 167, 177, 179, 242, 252, 305, 331n, 4:7, 44, 49f, 52, 55, 59, 68, 109, 123, 134, 146, 148, 156–159, 162–171, 177, 203, 232, 235, 238–243, 246, 264, 318, 323, 344, 348, 368, 370, 375, 401, 5:3, 18, 51, 154, 158, 196, 213f, 232, 263, 267, 271, 7:11, 43, 73, 96, 248, 256, 274, 281, 313, 356, 359f, 362, 366, 375, 8:21, 39, 49, 79, 121, 171, 175–177, 187, 263, 277, 9:26–28, 76, 105, 178, 185, 198, 213, 216, 236f, 251, 255, 273, 284, 291, 11:6, 26, 37, 116, 163, 165–174, 266, 268, 313, 319, 346, 368, 375, 377, 485, 494, 496, 505, 507, 522, 546–548, 12:19–21, 61f, 74, 92, 148, 197, 203, 207, 215, 218, 220–222, 226, 239f, 243–247, 255, 267, 272f, 279, 282–285, 311, 313f, 320f, 326, 329f, 333, 335, 337–340, 343, 346f, 354–356, 359, 362–364, 367, 370, 373, 376, 378, 385, 12:389, 392, 397, 400, 402, 409, 13:11, 53, 72, 136, 341, 402, 406f, 14:36f, 39, 82, 90f, 93, 97–99, 101, 141f, 150f, 158, 163, 169–171, 173–175, 182, 186, 194, 198, 200, 202–205, 232, 252f, 262, 275, 291f, 294, 297f, 307, 318, 326f, 331, 337–340, 345,

16:3, 11, 14, 19f, 21f, 24, 25n, 31f, 37f, 56f, 61, 69, 72f, 74f, 77, 98, 102, 107, 112, 121–124, 128, 137, 155, 166, 204, 206, 216, 219, 225, 228, 230, 232, 235f, 239, 248f, 262f, 280, 332, 17:11, 38, 64, 68, 103, 113, 126f, 136, 162, 229f, 245, 251, 260f, 276, 305, 323f, 344, 369, 18:13, 207, 259, 276, 336, 20:273, 21:xi, 26f, 46f, 60, 73, 122–124, 150, 205f, 223, 332, 22:23, 34, 39, 43, 55, 63, 77, 89, 117, 122, 124, 134, 136, 144f, 278, 287, 320, 330, 341, 407, 459, 461, 474, 488, 491, 23:23f, 30, 34, 37, 39, 53, 56, 58, 62, 65f, 71–73, 76, 79, 85f, 106–108, 117, 136, 141, 143f, 146, 148, 154, 178, 247, 250, 263, 278, 339, 355, 359, 366, 375f, 388, 24:50, 74, 141, 144, 148, 226, 228, 255, 281, 292, 334, 337, 339, 345–347, 349f, 421, 25:19, 23, 30n, 31, 46, 48, 54, 65, 70, 80, 86, 136f, 168, 184f, 193, 220, 241f, 246, 252, 254, 256f, 263f, 267f, 274, 285f, 299, 316, 328, 406, 410f, 440, 504, 26:4–11, 14, 21, 44, 72, 113, 115f, 118, 121, 127–130, 132, 166, 169, 176f, 183, 186, 198, 209, 222, 225f, 229, 231–233, 249, 251, 261, 280f, 302f, 310, 312, 314, 331, 335, 354, 356, 363, 367, 396, 27:13f, 22, 111, 141, 172, 203, 240n, 260, 325, 344, 349, 28:83, 372, 29:6f, 9–11, 41f, 44f, 48f, 50, 53, 63, 67f, 78, 80, 84f, 98, 112, 115, 119f, 123, 134, 141f, 144, 154, 172, 182, 188f, 192, 206, 209, 211f, 216, 236f, 30:6, 24, 26, 59f, 69, 151, 155, 164, 176, 178, 197, 224, 226, 229–231, 234–236, 240, 247, 252f, 255f, 263f, 268, 271, 283, 285f, 294, 296, 299, 313, 324f, 31:x, 45f, 55, 59–70, 96, 191, 224, 297–306, 345, 394, 32:28, 172–176, 33:249f, 263f, 270–276, 290, 34:152, 161, 167f, 196, 337, 35:xi, 80, 111, 145, 197, 230, 251, 359f, 362, 366, 371, 373f, 380f, 385, 390, 402, 36:75f, 94, 221, 37:132, 134f, 168, 248f, 362–364, 366, 38:86, 102, 107, 113, 117, 125, 128, 259n, 42:42f, 51, 58f, 140, 150f, 158, 164f, 391, 44:206, 200, 301, 45:221, 223, 226, 46:64, 95, 99f, 153, 224, 299n, 51:29, 63, 98, 112, 164, 318f, 52:96, 112, 254f, 54:121, 193, 308f, 324, 329, 348, 373f, 403, 442

Righteousness, Alien—16:120, 22:157

Righteousness, Civil—12:363, 400, 17:63, 25:86, 410

Righteousness, Imputed—25:20, 36, 79, 85f, 151f, 188, 201, 233, 256, 260f, 265, 271f

Righteousness, Original—1:113f, 117, 144, 164f, 167, 169, 171, 326

Righteousness, True—14:86, 92f, 148, 197, 200, 329, 25:136f, 278

Righteousness of Christ—see **Christ**—His righteousness

Righteousness of Faith—9:28, 141, 151, 214, 235, 278f, 19:48, 197, 25:9, 38, 89, 97, 151, 168, 205f, 209, 211, 237f, 242, 278–280, 406f, 410f, 26:4f, 12f, 21, 74, 98f, 104, 113, 122f, 136, 145, 231, 234, 249, 253, 272, 274, 278, 295, 307, 313, 344, 396, 436, 445, 449, 27:7, 42, 229, 240, 242, 264, 348, 382

Righteousness of God—7:251f, 279, 284, 10:33f, 47f, 53, 59, 129f, 143–145, 171–173, 221–223, 234, 241, 273, 395, 398f, 401–404, 408, 416, 11:3f, 26, 524–526, 12:313f, 320f, 351, 17:27, 42, 47, 80f, 83, 100, 103, 115, 145, 176, 251, 253, 255, 261, 277, 25:xif, 3, 9, 14, 27, 30–32, 89, 135f, 151–153, 200f, 205–207, 212, 218, 229, 243, 249, 259, 394, 440, 442, 29:119f, 154, 188f, 31:x, 63, 33:249, 290, 46:66, 146, 191

Righteousness of the flesh—26:44, 249, 280, 302, 363

Righteousness of the Law—4:52, 159, 162f, 26:4, 7–10, 44, 52, 54f, 68f, 73, 83, 99f, 115, 119f, 122f, 158, 172, 175, 177, 179f, 182–185, 189, 197, 199, 202, 204–207, 216–219, 222, 234, 240, 242, 247, 254, 256, 261, 272, 274, 280, 283, 289, 302, 309, 325, 334, 349, 353, 364, 401, 445, 449, 458, 27:7, 16f, 189, 198, 218, 225, 239, 246, 249, 264–267, 276, 283, 286, 291, 311, 317f, 328, 48:24f

Righteousness of works—see **Works righteousness**

Rights, Individual—21:24f, 235–237

Rights of a Christian—49:29, 46n

Rights of men—6:17, 19, 25, 28, 30, 35, 44, 57, 27:375–377, 46:67, 125f, 132, 134, 165, 190

Rihel, Wendelin—50:172n

Rimmon—20:341

Rings—26:132, 134

Riots—45:xiii, 54–56, 64n, 74n

Rischmann, John—50:49n

Risk—45:252n, 256, 260, 299, 301, 303, 304n, 307, 309

Rissdorf—50:291n, 302

Rites—2:116, 255, 285, 6:40, 229, 237,

16:201n, 256, 300, 29:200, 206, 36:64, 73, 108, 110f, 113, 117
Rites and ritual—see also **Ceremonies; Ceremonies of the Mass**
Ritter, Gerhard—41:xii
Ritual—1:292, 14:292, 20:10, 143f, 26:312, 396, 398, 400, 448, 32:7
River gates—18:302
Rivers—1:8, 33f, 90, 97–101, 206, 310, 19:142f
Road to Reformation—see **Böhmer, Heinrich**
Robbers—7:49, 59, 83, 91, 93, 128, 181, 186, 190, 214, 243, 254, 267, 338, 38:148f, 159–161, 175, 205, 207, 46:26, 37f, 42, 52, 68, 74, 182, 276, 306, 313, see also **Highwaymen; Thieves**
Robbert, George S.—indexer of Vol. 31
Robbery—2:6, 60, 127, 141, 214, 319, 6:27, 29, 31, 35, 47, 55, 68f, 7:94, 115, 191f, 195, 234, 255, 266, 276, 287, 330, 361, 365, 367, 9:167, 211, 232f, 14:149, 21:235–237, 23:58, 62, 69, 134, 141, 213, 247, 298, 312, 317, 399, 402, 24:14, 317, 339, 341, 26:36, 41, 125, 340, 28:13, 237f, 30:245, 46:19, 27, 38f, 48f, 70, 72, 95f, 164, 170, 178, 179n, 181, 252, 276, 317, 51:155–158, 299
Robert of Melun—34:xvi
Robigalia—42:85n
Rock (figure)—10:30 104, 188, 449
Rock (metaphor)—9:13, 197, 290, 293f, 296, 298, 17:86, 92f, 106n, 197, 21:282, 25:86f, 104, 236, 390, 401
Rock, Christ as—see **Christ—Rock**
Rock, Meaning of the, Matt. 16:18—32:68–74
Rock, St. Peter as—41:293, 303, 313f, 327f
Rock of Israel—15:276, 313, 330, 345
Rod—8:73, 10:35f, 283, 452, 16:111, 113, 159, 208, 240, 20:158, 161f, 175, 226, 46:65n
Rod vs. reed—11:283, 362–366
Rödinger—53:299
Rogate Sunday—42:85, 91n
Rogationtide—42:85, 87n, 90, 91n
Rogge, Joachim—47:102n
Roland—37:176, 226, 248
Romagna—41:308n
Roman Breviary—36:181n
Roman captivity—18:16
Roman Catholicism—3:67n
Roman Church—see **Church, Roman**
Roman cities—9:145
Roman consuls—25:165
Roman court—34:249, 332
Roman Curia—see **Curia, Roman**
Roman emperor—Emperor, Roman
Roman Empire—2:177, 194n, 195, 255, 259, 6:244, 283, 331f, 8:178, 250, 261, 13:217, 256, 259, 281, 283, 342, 15:26, 42, 156, 16:275, 17:74, 95f, 318, 351, 18:187, 20:27, 62, 179, 187, 251, 328, 343, 22:86, 188, 23:219, 390, 24:86, 26:185, 451f, 29:105, 30:101, 31:390, 34:169f, 35:295–314, 387, 406, 41:25, 37, 40, 90, 332f, 356, 372–374, 42:123, 44:167n, 45:151f, 329, 356n, 359, 367, 46:41, 104f, 107, 119, 127, 199, 261, 274n, 47:233f, 297, 48:105, 52:7f
  Transferred to Germans 36:18n
Roman Empire, Holy—26:97n, 37:15, 41:225, 230, 240, 248, 265, 274–276, 279, 289f, 294, 308, 333f, 367, 371–376, 41:246, 289, 290n, 371, 44:207–211, 45:84, 46:184, 188, 198, 241f, 47:9, 97, 223n, 48:44, 49, 128, 140, 145, 163n, 176, 209, 244, 49:88n, 265n, 286, 289, 349, 350n, 363, 368f, 397, 425, 50:46, 65n, 68, 73, 115, 183n, 190n, 219n, 228n, 245, 254, 263n, 270
  Electors 22:188n
  Its circuits 50:68
  Its supreme court 50:68n
  Law of the 50:9f, 12, 66
  Laws see **Law, Imperial**
Roman gods—45:152
Roman Law—see **Law, Roman**
Roman rule—16:211f
Roman See—41:24, 87, 259, 267, 270, 272, 275, 277f, 280, 282, 285f, 289, 296, 320f, 323, 326, 333, 337, 345, 349, 351, 355–357, 361–363, see also **Church, Roman; Papacy; Pope; Rome**
Romanists—see **Church, Roman; Papacy**
Romans—1:7, 249, 255, 261, 276, 305, 310, 323, 2:17, 179, 205, 208, 221, 229, 305, 343, 346, 352, 360, 3:6, 18, 23, 67, 84, 94, 4:29, 221, 237, 275, 328, 347, 372f, 5:12, 24, 161, 209, 297, 6:88n, 106, 244, 297, 8:250, 254, 300f, 9:26, 28, 34, 42n, 103, 145, 163, 196, 204, 295, 297, 10:23, 84f, 106, 169, 249, 308f, 357, 441, 11:98, 134, 191, 12:109, 224, 253f, 266, 13:346, 14:10, 22, 64, 70, 74f, 118, 247, 250, 253, 263, 266, 322f, 16:28, 35, 47, 60, 63, 66f, 75, 118, 187, 296, 211, 240f, 258, 292f, 302, 17:7, 35, 74, 113, 122, 190, 241, 396, 404, 411f, 18:183, 198, 200, 245, 253, 281, 343, 354f, 19:195, 211,

217, 20:67, 120, 132f, 139, 164, 168, 171, 179, 184, 192f, 285, 311, 314, 343, 22:81, 84f, 150, 188, 426, 23:204, 300, 377, 381, 387, 390, 394, 24:80, 269, 25:6, 8, 28, 126, 128, 155f, 171, 470, 26:76, 428, 456f, 27:219, 385, 28:130, 183, 299, 30:225, 290, 34:179, 38:166, 317n, 318f, 41:204, 349, 46:104, 107f, 110, 119n, 123f, 127, 198, 236, 308n, 47:173, 190, 200, 221f, 225, 230–239, 250–252, 299, 48:82, 92, 109, 167, 202f, 213, 52:159, 171

Romans, Epistle to the—3:23, 4:342–344, 365, 7:46, 93, 118, 140, 166, 280, 350, 8:165, 308, 10:145, 14:91, 294, 349, 19:50, 151, 20:126, 212, 23:28, 24:340, 25:xi, 3, 8, 28, 61, 127f, 131, 135, 138, 156, 26:264, 27:167, 177, 269, 285, 306, 325, 357, 381, 29: 4, 193, 30:1–4, 313, 35:365–380

Latin text 25:4, 14, 20, 76

Romanticism—53:xiv

Rome—1:7n, 88, 206, 239f, 250, 2:192, 200, 217, 220, 225, 243, 286, 319, 339n, 3:108f, 168, 252, 254, 342, 344, 362, 4:20, 201, 279, 396, 398, 5:x, 11, 156, 244, 317, 323, 339, 369n, 6:157, 244, 353, 7:90n, 91, 8:5, 250, 260n, 283f, 9:92n, 167f, 196, 221, 11:122, 134, 177f, 13:24, 208, 339, 343, 14:6, 22, 97, 111, 114, 118, 325, 333, 16:20, 42, 87n, 137, 159, 189, 194, 241, 286, 302, 323, 17:51, 89, 123, 149, 151f, 217, 18:6, 92, 19:89, 203, 20:117, 285, 324, 21:204, 344, 22:42, 69, 85, 102, 136, 249f, 258, 266, 287, 365, 374, 417, 440, 478, 499, 513f, 523, 23:43, 201, 211, 353, 356, 374, 387–390, 395, 412, 24:146, 156, 159, 169, 171, 174, 196, 237, 262, 277, 307, 339, 25:8, 128f, 138, 156, 481f, 493, 523, 26:23f, 76, 420, 27:108, 124, 147, 154f, 177, 218, 337, 28:156, 29:102, 30:40, 64, 144, 180, 190, 193, 31:156, 198, 226, 311, 388, 393, 34:xv, 233, 358, 38:105, 110, 166, 172, 262n, 290, 310, 317n, 319, 39:25, 43, 51, 53, 67, 87f, 93, 96, 102, 107, 112, 171, 204, 241, 271, 41:5f, 24, 33, 42, 51, 74, 87–90, 94, 121, 134, 154, 204, 243, 260, 279, 295n, 304f, 322–325, 327, 333, 341f, 346, 353, 356, 372, 42:40, 64, 45:110n, 235, 276, 352, 46:106n, 120n, 164n, 169, 188, 198, 236n, 239, 47:190, 192, 234n, 275, 282, 48:18n, 44, 46, 73n, 76n, 82, 87n, 92n, 109, 125, 127–129, 172n, 49:78n, 169, 176, 220n, 221, 265n, 286n, 315n, 350n, 374n, 414n, 423, 51:107, 109, 207, 327, 52:5, 183, 223, 264, 54:208f, 237f, 272, 286, 299, 332, 427

Basilica of St. Peter 5:369, 27:386n, 29:89, 31:xv, 30, 33, 206, 248, 34:264, 329n, 42:62n, 65, 45:264, 265n, 51:61

Church of St. John Lateran 17:339, 41:354n

Church of St. Sixtus 31:264, 289

Churches in or near 41:41f, 232, 283n, 299, 322n, 354n

Rome, Bishops of—41:xv, 22n, 23–26, 41f, 49, 62, 87–91, 93n, 94, 121, 263, 281, 290n, 291f, 297–299, 307f, 321, 325f, 333f, 347f, 351, 354n, 366, 368, 374f

Rome, Sack of—16:331n, 35:408n, 41:295n, 50:150n

Romulus—9:196

Ronciglione—41:278

Room—10:48f, 51

Root of Jesse—see **Jesse, Root of**

Roots—10:14, 19f, 23, 25, 436, 24:194, 199, 233, 235, 238, 342, 25:121, 516f

Rörer, George—9:x, 12:ixf, 13:xi, 14:xi, 15:x, 17:x, 301n, 312n, 18:x, 22:xi, 23:x, 24:ix, 25:61, 26:ix, 29:x, 30:ix–xi, 226n, 230n, 242n, 248n, 285n, 307n, 34:108, 282, 35:206, 294n, 35:212n, 213n, 36:309, 355n, 37:147n, 38:9, 11, 94, 143, 43:115, 49:173n, 183n, 50:38n, 40n, 311n, 317, 51:xii, xin, xvf, 121f, 136, 197, 211, 221, 231, 239n, 247n, 291, 315, 333, 337f, 371, 53:122, 302, 54:xii, 117, 120, 150, 163, 392, 408, 431

recorder of Luther's table conversation, 1531–1535 54:115–122

Rörer, Hanna—49:173n, 174n

Rosary—2:114, 21:38, 60, 164, 229, 274, 23:85, 124, 263f, 409, 24:325, 26:283, 42:7n, 22n, 23, 72n, 51:55, 65, 108, 116

Roscher, Wilhelm—45:239n

Rose (figure)—12:202

Rose-colored glasses—17:108n, 140

***Rosegarden of Spiritual Exercises*, 1404**—10:320f

Rosenblatt, Wilibrandis—49:188n

Rosenburg, Albrecht von—50:263n

Roses—2:168f, 10:208f, 11:153, 24:205, 420

Rosheim, Josel—54:239n

Rossig, Gregory—54:250n

Rostock—53:172

University of 48:223n

Roth, Stephen—28:xi, 36:309, 38:94, 43:182, 271n, 51:xv, 70, 121f, 52:xi
Roth, Ursula—22:417
Rothenburg—46:47n, 49:100n, 122n, 50:214n
Rotten—see **Sects**
Rottengeister—13:147, see also **Sectarian spirits**
Rouen—35:133n
Rouge and lipstick—16:47
Royal priesthood—14:32
Royal road—2:77f, 282, 286, 299, 370, 4:277n, 7:44f, 357, 8:329, 15:42, 74, 77, 111, 122, 16:334, 17:17, 43, 223, 25:186, 267, 270, 377, 26:343, 28:320
Rubies—1:101
Ruccius, Walter M.—54:257
Rückert, Hanns—49:xv
Rudolph I, Emperor—41:376n
Rufinus—24:245, 26:191n
  Commentary on the Apostles' Creed 13:346n
  Eleven Books of Ecclesiastical History 41:7n, 33n, 34n, 56n, 57n, 59n, 60n, 61n, 93n, 106n, 115n, 125n
  Lives of the Fathers 24:75n
Rufus Festus Avienus—*Arati phenomena* 4:5n
Rühel, John—46:48, 59n, 60n, 49:106–108, 113n, 115n, 117n, 151f
Rule, William H.—*Martyrs of the Reformation* 43:73n
Rulers—4:74f, 81, 87f, 128, 185, 276, 327, 365, 382f, 389, 7:184, 195f, 8:106, 169, 212, 13:42–53, 55, 61–64, 67–71, 161, 165f, 169, 172, 175, 181f, 188f, 192, 200, 206, 209f, 224, 274, 340, 342, 413, 15:276f, 345f, 16:181, 188, 274, 17:56, 216, 291, 323, 368, 19:176f, 201, 203, 206, 20:79, 176, 277, 345f, 21:12, 31, 79f, 109f, 120, 132–135, 148, 182, 186, 188, 227, 269, 278, 297f, 336f, 356, 22:84, 95, 128, 189, 193, 435, 477, 511, 23:201, 218, 222, 302, 304, 345, 395, 25:11, 21n, 110, 171f, 443, 450f, 469, 471, 496, 28: 127f, 29:72f, 75, 174, 241, 35:39, 298, 360, 389, 41:9f, 15, 24f, 35f, 41, 54, 62, 84, 121, 128, 138, 140–142, 153, 195, 197, 206, 214, 227, 239f, 246f, 254, 295–297, 312, 328f, 332, 334f, 337, 344f, 349, 352, 354, 357, 365f, 45:67, 78f, 82–84, 105–107, 109–129, 161, 215f, 246f, 270f, 297, 310, 330, 368, 389, 46:xiii, 12, 17, 19, 22f, 25–27, 31f, 34, 36, 38, 40, 47f, 50, 52n, 53, 59, 61, 64f, 68f, 76, 82f, 90f, 95, 98n, 99f, 101n, 103f, 106f, 110, 112–114, 117, 125f, 130f, 135, 161, 163, 166, 169, 175, 180, 183n, 184, 187, 193, 200, 215, 238, 250, 265–267, 51:149–151, 349, 352, 387, see also **Emperors**; **Kings**; **Princes**
  Authority of 25:443
Rulers vs. laws—36:98
Rules—27:184, 29:7, 33, 52:174
Rültz, Peter—40:156n, 158, 161, 167, 177, 182, 185, 195, 201, 211
Rumor—9:165f
Running—10:276
Rupp, E. Gordon—54:xvn
  author of the Introduction to Vol. 41
  co-translator with Philip Watson of Erasmus' *Diatribe* 33:xin, xiin
  Luther and Erasmus: Free Will and Salvation, Philadelphia, 1969 20:161n
  Luther's Progress to the Diet of Worms, Chicago, 1951 37:371n
Rupsch, Conrad—53:55
Russian Orthodox Church—39:58n
Russians, White—22:60n
Rust—11:75f, 83, 21:168f, 183
Ruth—1:302, 2:276, 3:133, 313, 6:228, 246, 7:14, 20, 22, 35, 200f, 207, 8:135f, 9:230, 25:265
Ruysbroeck, John of (Ruunsbroeck, Jan van)—*Dat boec van den gheesteleken Tabernacule* 20:347n
Rye—1:37f
Ryss, Konrad (John Landtsperger)—37:10, 41n

Saale River—40:105, 109, 112, 115, 50:286f, 289n, 302, 307
Saalfeld—2:381, 49:69n, 128, 291n
Saba—18:310n, 27:317
Sabbatarians—2:362, 3:77, 7:152, 41:29n, 47:x, 59f, 65, 93n, 95, 126, 158, 188, 206, 54:239
Sabbath—1:5, 70, 73, 75, 79–82, 94, 105, 140, 144, 2:129, 214, 361f, 3:77, 141f, 5:20, 348, 6:35, 177, 231, 264, 406, 7:262, 8:66f, 9:67, 82, 10:437, 12:398, 401, 13:25, 17:261, 292f, 415, 22:41, 141, 223f, 229, 432, 23:222, 235–237, 239–242, 366, 24:410, 26:7, 64, 203, 295, 330, 411f, 27:55, 249, 257, 295f, 332, 29:6f, 163, 35:165, 36:99, 240, 249, 259, 40:93, 98, 41:64, 66f, 43:15n, 44:54n, 171f, 47:59f, 91–93, 168, 254, 51:334–336, 52:23, 246, 54:51f
Sabbatical Year—26:411
Sabeans—10:412f, 18:116

Sabellianism—37:361, 40:197n
Sabellians—12:282
Sabellius—15:186n, 303, 24:204, 34:209n, 38:262n, 52:48f, 53, 116
Sabinianus, Pope—41:292n
Sabinus, George—54:268
Sachs, Curt—53:205
Sachs, Hans—53:196, 54:450n
Sachs, John—54:429, 451
Sachsenhausen—31:73
Sachsenspiegel—13:402n, 21:90n, 34:291, 35:159, 167, 40:98n
Sack (body)—17:387f, 28:112
Sackcloth—18:182, 19:24, 53, 86, 88, 97, 20:146, 333
Sacks—7:189, 237, 266–268, 270f, 286f, 323, 329, 333f, 361f, 37:65n, 228, 230, 285
Sacrament, Desire for the—32:49f
Sacrament, Validity of the—49:101f
Sacrament of the Altar—see **Lord's Supper**
Sacramental elements—36:129, 147, 235, 295f, 319f, 323–326, 336–338, 341f, 347–350, 38:xiiif, xvii, 18f, 22f, 27, 30, 40f, 44, 47f, 54, 60, 68, 71f, 74f, 79, 85, 88, 95, 110, 114n, 131f, 137, 143, 149, 151n, 153, 155, 158, 166f, 169, 171, 176, 178, 182n, 191, 193, 197, 199f, 202, 205f, 208, 225, 291–293, 295f, 305, 42:53f, 56–58, 162f, 53:24, 26, 28, 34f, see also **Bread and wine in the Sacrament**
  Blood of Christ 38:114n, 205–208, 224f, 228, 306
  Body of Christ 38:19, 21, 23, 25–27, 29, 31–33, 40–59, 61, 70f, 74–76, 78, 80–85, 95, 109, 136, 205f, 208, 217, 223–225, 228, 287n, 294n, 295–298, 306
  Consecration 37:22n, 185, 260, 294n, 300n, 38:xv, 120f, 143f, 147, 149–152, 155f, 158, 161, 164, 166, 173, 176f, 180, 185–189, 192f, 195, 197, 200, 203f, 213f
Sacramental grace (res sacramenti)—36:23n, 54, 68, 99, 125
Sacramental Signs—19:193, 36:8, 13, 43f, 52f, 56, 64n, 65–67, 68–70, 92–94, 95n, 118f, 124, 303, 38:23, 26, 34f, 41, 62, 68, 81, 87, 131, 42:111, 144
Sacramental union—35:50, 37:xix, 103, 299f, 303, 325f, 330, 334f, 338f
Sacramentarians—1:145, 149, 153, 228, 2:15, 18, 87, 243, 3:5, 13, 191, 272, 301, 4:71, 95, 125, 240, 295, 380, 392, 5:240, 6:81, 7:73, 104, 131, 200, 8:133, 144, 12:23, 223, 253, 280, 397, 17:57, 92, 100, 108, 113f, 193f, 244, 256, 289, 327, 20:303, 22:22, 316, 383, 467, 525, 23:71, 80, 99, 119, 147, 157, 163, 165, 187, 194, 230, 263, 285, 356, 26:52, 176, 192, 194, 221, 395, 413, 424, 455, 27:37, 39, 60, 106, 111f, 29:8, 33, 35, 47, 30:262, 286, 306, 34:xv, 356, 35:xii, 157, 37:150, 157, 206f, 360, 367, 38:157n, 282, 299, 302n, 304n, 47:5, 110n, 54:43, 89, 91, 100, 138, 162f, 274, 284, 318, 390, 463, 471, see also **Enthusiasts**; **Fanatics**; **Iconoclasts**; **Radical reformers**; **Schwärmer**; **Zwinglians**
Sacraments—1:213, 228, 248, 330, 355, 2:72, 84, 197, 286, 301n, 338, 341, 3:37, 85, 87, 92, 107, 110, 122, 155, 213, 272, 275, 288, 4:32, 34, 72, 79, 121, 179, 191f, 240, 358, 360, 398, 401–403, 406, 5:21, 23, 42f, 45–47, 49, 124, 141, 184, 197, 208, 223, 247f, 250, 258, 277, 348, 7:62, 73, 205, 226, 297, 299, 311, 328, 344, 8:42, 146, 186–188, 192, 235, 258, 264f, 271, 310, 313, 315, 10:156, 221, 234, 339, 345, 11:177, 401, 12:300, 363f, 369f, 375, 14:13, 39, 55f, 91f, 132, 261, 16:73, 168, 17:163, 193, 341, 18:375, 20:172, 21:154, 276, 22:48, 81, 102, 120, 202, 220, 227, 229, 257, 269, 303, 308, 368, 372, 421, 470–472, 480, 482, 505, 508, 512, 514–516, 23:46, 81f, 92, 118, 123, 169, 207, 226, 229, 247, 253, 257, 285f, 349, 386, 392, 24:12, 45, 66f, 70, 79, 85, 99, 102, 109, 127, 130f, 143, 145, 151, 155, 168–171, 179f, 182f, 185, 202, 222, 225, 228, 230, 236, 242, 250, 252, 257, 274, 280, 284, 296, 304, 307, 309f, 312, 321, 368, 394, 25:45, 52, 284, 309f, 26:11, 19, 24–26, 45, 70f, 122n, 136, 222–224, 245, 350, 388, 439, 27:10, 37, 41, 82f, 86f, 91, 102, 105f, 117f, 238, 28:60, 62, 67, 70, 78, 81, 124f, 167, 305, 384, 29:17, 23, 48, 83, 172, 192f, 207, 224f, 30:63, 72, 170, 174, 286, 299, 314, 31:102, 193, 257, 271–275, 32:13–19, 24, 41f, 49–53, 34:347, 354, 35:x, xiif, xviif, 5, 54, 67, 93n, 94f, 36:ix, 5–9, 23, 44, 59–62, 64–66, 72–74, 81, 83, 90–92, 93n, 94f, 107f, 109n, 114f, 122, 124f, 168, 181, 201, 272, 302f, 37:7, 48, 86, 102n, 104–106, 119, 123, 185f, 188, 193, 273f, 300n, 338, 343, 367, 38:ix, 154, 189, 212, 41:116n, 131, 154, 156–164, 166, 173, 195, 199, 201, 42:100f, 108–111, 113f, 45:8n, 24f, 53,

177, 371, 381, 46:219f, 261f, 271, 47:35, 116n, 162, 51:168f, 172, 181, 187, 242, 52:151, 222, 271, 53:110, 115n, 122, 54:47, 119f, 358, 394, 470

Depend on the Word 37:7, 11, 86–88, 111, 116f, 119, 127f, 132–134, 141f, 149n, 193, 238, 274, 338

Faith needed 29:172, 193, 207, 38:x, 29, 35, 43, 47, 55, 58, 80, 88, 101, 103, 125, 152, 159, 181, 206f, 209

Sacraments, Captivity of the—36:48, 67, 250

Sacred, The—Meaning of 25:436

Sacred letters—33:25n

Sacred vs. profane—33:45

Sacredness of the secular—13:41f, 146

Sacrifice, Human—7:300f, 8:132

Sacrifice, New Testament—17:315, 414

Sacrifice, True—25:435

Sacrifice of Christ, Repetition of—37:142f, 328f

Sacrifice of praise—17:72, 98, 168, 182, 212, 324, 336, 18:74, 397, 36:162

Sacrifice of Remembrance—38:33, 118f, 122

Sacrifice of thanksgiving—3:70, 227, 6:86, 112, 114, 233, 237, 9:238, 12:410, 16:70, 128, 166, 18:397, 19:21, 81, 38:xv, 111, 117, 121f, 187, 314, 46:148, 153

Sacrifice of the Mass—see **Mass, Sacrifice of the**

Sacrifices—1:247–253, 258f, 262, 264–267, 291, 310, 328, 2:73, 80, 88, 114, 116–118, 132, 138f, 142, 166, 173, 197, 242, 272, 284, 362, 384, 386, 3:15, 22, 32f, 41, 80, 91, 106, 111f, 122, 128, 143, 145, 164, 218, 237, 242, 250, 328, 359, 4:67, 69, 100, 106, 110f, 115, 122f, 128, 135, 137–139, 168, 178f, 181–183, 200, 237, 252, 258, 279, 315, 320, 322, 328, 361f, 5:5f, 8, 20, 52, 77f, 103, 109f, 242, 252, 258f, 261–266, 283, 357, 6:50, 110f, 114, 123, 141, 232–234, 236f, 247, 7:34, 42, 53, 58f, 75, 82, 87f, 99f, 103, 107, 258, 278, 280, 282, 285f, 297f, 301, 315, 344, 354, 8:11, 22, 75–78, 80, 83, 132, 136f, 153, 188, 200, 210, 228, 275, 293f, 9:53, 81, 123–125, 130, 138, 164, 174, 189, 233, 254, 258, 298, 305, 10:67, 153, 173, 232, 320f, 12:18, 360f, 396f, 399f, 402f, 406, 408–410, 13:318f, 321, 333, 371, 14:33, 35, 51, 60, 78, 92, 94f, 105, 111, 132, 145, 174, 198, 15:75f, 281, 284f, 16:14, 16, 105, 128, 166f, 195, 238, 331, 17:99, 222, 271f, 275, 377f, 380, 401, 412, 18:46, 48, 74, 152, 336f, 357, 397, 19:21, 81f, 20:41, 101f, 166, 219, 237, 266, 296, 300, 21:81, 22:135, 219, 234, 238f, 285, 320, 397, 428, 430–432, 458, 464, 23:26, 213, 241, 366, 369, 412, 24:242–244, 252, 259f, 309, 314, 327, 25:6, 104, 123, 247, 338, 377f, 407, 433, 435–437, 26:7, 17, 32, 70, 177, 180–182, 205, 211, 217, 226–229, 233, 245, 263f, 275, 322, 333, 338, 342, 363, 454, 27:7, 25, 55, 89, 132, 145, 314, 335, 29:6, 42, 148, 175f, 179, 183, 191, 206f, 219f, 223, 227, 232f, 30:30, 52–55, 111, 143, 186, 207, 35:57, 78, 94f, 219n, 220, 248f, 305, 333, 36:51, 53, 56f, 65f, 95n, 139, 145–147, 151, 153, 159–162, 169, 171, 173–175, 179, 181–185, 189, 214, 218, 227, 313–315, 318, 37:44, 123, 128, 142–144, 264, 356f, 38:51n, 105f, 118, 120f, 152, 158, 160, 162, 169, 175, 181f, 194, 218, 313, 40:28f, 122, 138, 41:28, 287, 314, 42:133, 46:67, 221, 227, 229, 233, 52:277, 54:139

Sacrifices, Jewish—47:66, 68, 75, 239, 303f

Sacrilege—6:49, 55, 57, 7:44, 297, 9:4, 211, 17:340, 380, 25:192, 26:135, 200, 371, 390, 399, 38:173, 176–183, 187, 190, 192–194, 197, 204, 207–209, 211, 213

Sacristans—38:213, 45:187, 46:220, 231, 234, 244

Sadducees—3:118, 6:249, 7:336, 13:62, 16:94f, 18:350, 20:53f, 119–121, 233, 296, 314–316, 332, 22:62, 151, 456, 23:268, 28:59, 100, 29:12, 33f, 34:211, 47:227–229, 52:115f, 202

Sadness—3:7, 4:15, 67, 223, 285, 7:74, 127, 231, 262, 291, 316, 332, 359, 363, 374, 8:7, 25f, 52f, 56, 11:253, 521, 24:12f, 16, 112, 114, 117, 149, 178, 183f, 198, 210, 273, 276, 333, 335, 354, 377f, 382, 384, 399–401, 26:8, 64, 152, 167, 178, 341, 350, 393, 420, 27:22, 26, 51, 70, 74, 111

Sadoleto, Jacobo Cardinal—3:67n, 12:335, 339, 398, 31:289, 33:13n, 34:165, 233, 266, 50:191n, 54:329

Three Books of Commentaries on the Epistle of Paul to the Romans 34:165n

Safe-conduct, Imperial—32:xiv, 115, 120–122, 47:135, 270, 274, 285, 48:392, 49:18, 282, 332n

Sages—22:101, 125, 153, 189, 295, 24:72, 79, 99, 131, 138, 167

Sailors—2:106, 181

Saintlets—16:11, 72f

Saintliness—2:12f, 59f, 135, 188, 372, 4:7, 22, 103, 181f, 236, 238, 242, 276, 282, 322f, 332f, 356, 5:153, 213f, 266f, 334, 26:335, 27:14f, 136, 206f, see also **Holiness**

Saints—2:8, 21, 31, 35, 44, 61, 81, 104, 112f, 120, 128, 136, 145, 154, 167, 169–172, 178f, 181, 199, 216f, 240, 243, 245, 247, 249, 267f, 273, 275, 281, 287, 289f, 294, 306f, 312, 320, 330, 346, 354, 357, 369–371, 375, 378, 391, 398f, 3:4f, 8f, 12–14, 16f, 19, 25, 30f, 42, 51f, 76, 81n, 96, 109, 134, 139f, 167f, 171, 174, 181, 188, 202, 215, 222, 225, 229, 233, 254, 259, 261, 264f, 267, 269, 271, 283, 292, 300, 305, 311, 317, 320f, 325, 328f, 333–337, 345, 351, 354f, 357, 4:14f, 18f, 37, 53, 61, 63, 73, 78, 80, 83f, 89, 103, 112, 115, 120, 122, 131, 147f, 151, 157, 168–170, 172, 174, 177, 189f, 192, 196, 202, 231, 246, 257, 261, 269, 271, 278, 282, 291, 309–311, 316, 319, 326, 329, 331, 333, 336, 354, 356f, 371, 376f, 396, 398, 5:4, 8, 12, 14f, 22, 25, 28, 32, 53, 57, 65, 69, 75, 79, 87, 89f, 94, 117, 119–121, 125, 128, 131, 147, 150, 186f, 212, 232–234, 236, 248, 254f, 257, 266, 276–280, 284f, 298, 304, 312, 327, 329, 341, 346, 353, 359f, 371, 6:9, 18, 56f, 59, 73, 97, 123, 131, 149, 171f, 177, 181, 213, 217f, 221f, 225, 359, 404, 7:11, 28, 44, 47, 64, 68, 78, 88, 96, 98f, 101, 103f, 106, 112, 119, 124, 126f, 129, 131, 163, 176, 224f, 230–232, 252, 261, 262f, 272f, 275, 284, 293, 295f, 298f, 303, 305, 310–312, 314–316, 319, 326, 329, 337, 341f, 344, 349, 352, 366, 370, 8:5, 7, 10, 12–14, 21, 30, 69, 74f, 77, 82f, 89f, 96, 117, 132–134, 144, 158, 163, 184f, 188, 203n, 218f, 222, 232, 237, 258, 266, 300, 314–318, 326, 333, 9:56, 68, 71n, 82, 126, 129f, 164, 181, 188f, 237f, 304, 10:52, 89, 105, 116, 121f, 151, 156, 170, 188, 196, 251, 331f, 343, 346, 379, 11:144, 360, 550, 12:360, 375, 388, 394, 13:11, 36, 85, 112, 115, 138, 179, 184, 188, 326, 381, 384, 410, 14:6, 10, 13, 19n, 20, 24, 36f, 45, 50f, 61, 63, 73, 79–81, 83, 85, 87f, 96f, 103, 141, 143f, 151, 161–163, 167, 174, 176f, 186, 194, 196–198, 205, 221f, 290, 303f, 339, 16:6, 51, 60, 204, 210, 227, 238, 17:12, 23, 181, 224, 266, 268f, 300, 326f, 360, 376, 18:159, 263, 323, 19:4–6, 27f, 45, 47, 206f, 21:272, 329, 22:55, 57, 64–66, 72, 107, 118, 120f, 124, 131, 135, 137, 146, 164f, 169, 190, 203, 217, 237, 254–256, 259–264, 267, 270, 272–274, 304, 310, 336, 347, 356, 377, 380, 385, 388, 392, 398, 430, 438, 440, 464, 475, 490, 525, 23:15, 50, 58–60, 72f, 75, 87, 89, 105, 107, 113, 128, 137, 139, 182, 191, 235, 239, 273, 304, 314f, 318, 325, 330, 333, 336, 350f, 409–411, 24:11, 22, 24, 30, 37, 40, 42, 52, 65, 69, 74–76, 88, 90, 108, 118n, 119, 121, 126n, 134, 138, 141, 153f, 158, 169–172, 182, 198, 226, 228f, 233, 244, 259, 265f, 295, 304, 307–309, 325, 328, 347f, 356, 369, 413f, 422, 25:6, 60f, 75, 107, 126, 128, 257f, 264, 267, 277f, 286–289, 336, 409, 434, 461f, 26:19, 34f, 65, 70, 91, 108f, 125, 133, 135, 148f, 154, 168, 200, 222, 230, 263f, 268, 276, 286, 311, 314, 337, 342, 352, 356, 369, 383, 389, 393, 459, 27:35, 42, 50, 54, 61, 64, 66, 70f, 73, 75–77, 79–87, 96, 109, 115, 122, 136, 161, 169, 172, 192, 210, 214, 247, 262, 344, 254, 361f, 372, 379, 28:121–123, 133, 248, 317, 322f, 358, 29:28, 80, 94–96, 98, 105, 139f, 150, 164, 178, 184, 187, 195, 218f, 229, 240, 30:7, 10f, 32, 43, 47, 51, 60, 63, 68–71, 75, 94, 99, 104, 110, 130, 133, 152, 156, 174f, 183, 189, 207, 211, 223, 226, 232, 236, 244, 261, 275, 288, 298, 301, 303, 314, 31:46, 91, 104, 175, 212–228, 239, 266–270, 32:xif, 9, 31, 62, 71, 83, 96, 258, 33:71f, 76f, 87f, 34:24f, 54, 351, 359, 35:40, 51–53, 68f, 119, 146, 151, 182, 198f, 253–256, 300, 321, 375, 380f, 36:87, 131, 136f, 171, 186–190, 193–196, 199, 220, 299, 317, 322, 37:70, 75, 95, 112, 147, 149, 161, 185, 210, 222, 251, 260, 265, 353f, 363f, 369f, 38:77, 106, 109, 121f, 128f, 150f, 160, 176, 178, 180, 189, 192, 194, 197, 289, 295, 39:86, 96, 101, 193, 40:91, 96, 300, 41:44, 50, 71f, 81, 107, 110, 124–126, 128, 140, 147, 165, 191, 204, 213, 215, 316, 324, 336, 348, 355, 359, 42:14n, 20f, 31f, 47, 55, 62, 72f, 75, 98, 100n, 104–106, 111f, 113n, 114, 121, 126, 129, 135n, 137–140, 149, 157–160, 172, 44:55, 186n, 290, 354, 363f, 372f, 383, 46:23, 34, 43, 135, 141f, 172, 174, 177, 240, 225, 255, 47:35, 43, 45–47, 50f, 54, 111, 157, 169, 171, 198, 253, 51:48f,

62, 90, 107, 167, 246–248, 276, 345, 380, 52:91, 124f, 127, 129, 131, 138f, 143, 173f, 177, 181, 190f, 211, 226, 268f, 276, 281, 54:70, 92, 259f, 324, 340, 353, 475
Auxiliary 8:203n
Communion of 11:292, 329, 541
Counterfeit 21:28–39, 22:457
Invocation of 2:273, 354, 35:198f, 46:172, 50:20, 53:153f, 268
Legends of the 24:266
Mad 13:44, 23:409, 24:22
Super- 11:492
Their deaths 11:405, 449
Veneration of 38:159, 175, 183
Worship of 2:273, 8:203, 9:54–56
Saints' days—35:69, 134, 198f
Salbach, Franz—45:165
Salbach, Hans—39:303
Sale, Margaret von der—54:379, 388, 390
Salem—2:247, 281, 382f, 4:99, 6:181–183, 11:6, 368
Salem, King of—2:381, 386, 394
Salim—22:415, 421n, 423
Sallust—3:283, 15:88, 34:277n
Bellum Catilinarium 3:284n, 4:297n
Bellum Iugurthinum 2:227n, 9:221n, 28:152n
Catiline 15:102n
Salmon—6:246
Salome—27:195f
Salt—3:200, 298, 300, 21:54f, 59f, 53:97, 102, 106
Salt, Blessing—36:108n, 122
Salt, Holy—34:55, 100, 41:168n, 200n
Salt Sea—2:366, 3:298
Salt wells—2:94
Salting the world—22:63
Salting, Ministry of—21:56
Saltpeter—20:66n
Salutation—29:4, 11, 13f, 16, 95, 53:29, 106
Salvation—2:24, 39–41, 43, 72, 112, 153, 155, 178, 249, 261, 267, 323, 345, 369, 391, 3:76f, 79, 89f, 96f, 104, 106, 110–112, 114, 120, 124, 128f, 133f, 143, 145, 154, 156, 161–163, 167, 220, 225, 262, 272f, 283, 286, 299, 359, 4:6f, 9, 34, 50, 55, 58, 64, 125, 131, 143, 152, 154, 157f, 160, 163f, 166, 197, 210f, 232, 242f, 315, 323, 347, 350, 359, 368, 392, 400, 405, 5:11f, 21, 42f, 45, 50, 144, 154–156, 203, 216, 230, 253n, 258f, 287, 6:50, 89, 95, 128, 146, 152, 258, 284, 7:10, 12, 64, 67, 80, 92, 98, 105, 127, 154, 167, 177, 184, 186, 229, 248, 251f, 257, 265, 273, 275, 326, 328, 339, 356, 8:5f, 9, 28f, 31, 35, 37–39, 42f, 126, 133n, 136, 145, 189–191, 211, 244, 256, 264, 271f, 284f, 287, 289, 312, 329, 331f, 9:67, 105, 139f, 156, 178, 180, 182–184, 189, 214, 245, 268, 293, 11:13f, 174, 496f, 510, 516, 529, 533f, 12:358, 361, 365, 13:21, 36, 85, 131, 14:16f, 21f, 28, 30, 34–36, 71, 77–82, 91, 95, 98, 100, 163, 172, 204, 222, 228f, 233f, 236f, 259, 270, 286, 329, 331, 335, 348, 16:29, 131, 200, 224, 17:176, 199, 210, 261, 279, 317, 324, 332, 344, 18:70, 98, 111f, 117, 259, 20:96, 98f, 101f, 123, 276f, 290–292, 21:4, 228, 258, 282, 288, 290, 22:25, 35, 43f, 50f, 54, 59–61, 63f, 67–72, 74, 76, 84, 100f, 118, 122, 132, 134, 136, 156, 165, 187, 220, 234, 248, 268, 272, 287, 302, 313, 320f, 324, 336, 340f, 343, 346, 351f, 357, 359, 361, 364, 366, 368, 381, 386, 388, 391f, 395, 405, 413, 424, 426, 435, 438, 456, 462, 464, 466, 471, 478, 481, 484, 487–489, 491, 513, 523, 528, 23:12, 17f, 23f, 35f, 38f, 41, 47, 58, 60f, 69f, 73, 76f, 80, 82, 84f, 91, 106, 108, 117, 134–137, 142, 155, 159, 170f, 175, 177, 189, 194, 225, 230, 233f, 246, 250, 262, 278, 284, 291, 319f, 325, 337f, 340, 348f, 352, 354–357, 360, 366, 399, 24:36, 47f, 55, 58, 72, 82f, 97, 99, 120, 141, 156, 172, 174, 183, 200, 209, 229, 236, 252, 257, 261, 263, 275, 281, 285, 288, 293, 296, 302, 319, 322, 326, 334f, 343f, 349, 353, 355, 357, 368, 372, 385, 411, 25:7, 41, 80, 88, 98, 111, 145, 202f, 268, 371f, 413f, 419, 426f, 480, 516, 26:3, 8, 11, 14, 28–30, 35f, 42, 44, 48f, 52, 71, 77, 86–89, 92, 105, 120, 126, 132, 135, 138, 151–153, 162f, 167f, 171, 183, 199f, 204–207, 211, 215, 220, 225, 237, 239, 242, 246f, 291, 295, 302, 304, 312f, 315f, 331–333, 338, 342, 352–356, 385, 388, 404, 406, 408f, 421f, 424, 426, 428f, 451, 458f, 27:9, 11, 19, 35, 38, 46f, 56f, 73f, 98f, 102–104, 117, 119–121, 130, 139, 143, 154, 161, 171f, 178, 184f, 189f, 198, 202, 204, 222, 248, 259, 269, 288, 290, 334, 357f, 384, 392, 402, 405, 28:261–264, 325f, 29:17, 24, 37f, 63f, 66, 87, 97f, 118, 131, 142, 178, 188, 214, 217f, 223, 30:14–16, 38, 45, 47, 58, 67, 77, 80, 106, 134, 143, 165f, 168, 184, 189, 205, 207, 210, 225, 229, 246, 254, 256f, 261, 286, 294f, 299, 307, 315,

325–327, 31:351f, 32:217, 33:64, 103–106, 250, 286, 288f, 35:xiii, 91, 146, 200, 359, 362, 373, 378f, 390, 36:30, 40, 59–61, 69, 75, 77f, 82, 88, 95n, 103, 116, 139, 164, 166, 175f, 186, 202, 277f, 303, 312, 37:16n, 26, 46, 92–94, 134, 136, 231, 364f, 368, 38:xiv, 39, 55, 86, 101, 105, 113, 132, 160, 165, 177, 184, 196, 207, 311n, 41:31, 35, 49–51, 67, 70–71, 75, 77, 106, 115, 123, 137, 140–142, 149, 161, 169, 190, 214, 234, 285, 296, 315–317, 336, 338, 42:ix, xv, 36, 59, 88, 109n, 114, 129, 183, 44:xii, 45:21, 35, 46, 72, 78, 103, 106, 118, 205, 280, 293, 349, 357, 367f, 46:36, 83, 108, 136, 141, 148, 170, 175, 210, 254, 306, 51:54, 59, 61f, 105, 109, 112, 114f, 164, 192, 318f, 52:15, 53, 56, 62, 70, 76, 130, 175, 204, 240, 244, 250, 257f, 277, 283, 286

Salvation by faith—25:8, 47

Salzburg—8:105, 34:86n, 46:248n, 48:108n, 191n, 49:10, 48f

Salzungen—46:47

Sam, Konrad—37:11, 65n, 126n

Samaria—3:263, 5:241, 10:29, 13:270, 16:33, 111, 165, 218f, 17:405, 18:43, 54f, 147, 149, 160, 168, 184, 203, 213, 217, 291, 19:38, 22:210, 216, 517, 36:44, 115, 174, 223, 41:220, 46:107n

Samaritan, Good—10:191f, 30:68, 118, 41:218n

Samaritan woman—2:285, 9:258, 22:521, 524, 36:220, 290, 42:20

Samaritans—11:69, 335, 20:264, 307, 22:521–525, 38:150, 42:46, 47:254, 52:33, 70

Samland—9:x, 3, 49:121

Samland, Bishop of—see **Polenz, George von, Bishop of Samland**

Samosatenes—12:282, 284, 34:80n, 47:116n

Samson—2:258, 375, 3:30, 4:104, 128, 226, 5:131, 257, 311, 325–327, 6:275, 7:7, 24, 8:281, 284f, 13:155, 161, 17:147, 22:274, 316f, 319, 26:109, 27:149n, 38:233, 45:44, 104, 382, 46:83, 193, 269, 52:126, 210

Samuel—2:19, 50, 91, 102, 270, 3:285, 4:117, 6:42, 183, 323f, 7:356, 367, 8:203, 208, 219, 221f, 227, 229, 231, 262, 265, 11:277, 13:172, 16:115, 17:248, 19:234, 22:99, 116, 215, 347, 397, 26:293, 27:204, 28:173, 284, 36:196f, 221, 38:290, 40:87, 41:250, 42:156, 45:96, 373, 46:83, 97, 148n, 153, 52:180, 187

Samuel, Books of—9:162

Sanctification—3:344, 4:157, 164, 341, 352, 5:18, 274, 7:281, 8:5, 56, 59, 65, 259, 261, 266–269, 329, 9:184–186, 10:121f, 11:261, 264, 441, 12:247, 327–331, 343, 377f, 381f, 384, 13:89f, 136, 138, 290f, 366f, 378–380, 14:94, 16:29, 21:245f, 22:55, 459, 23:58, 24:347, 25:5f, 8, 55, 70f, 123, 144, 147f, 248, 308f, 313f, 319–321, 356, 436, 26:350f, 360, 26:8, 27:21, 34, 82, 227, 241, 29:143, 195, 30:17, 69f, 118, 268, 30:7, 27, 119, 252, 264, 31:295, 32:23, 136, 229, 232, 235, 239, 254, 37:365, 38:208, 41:113n, 114, 145, 165f, 218, 42:140, 164, 46:153f, 51:162, 164, 166–169, see also **Holiness**

a life-long process 35:32f, 378

Sanctification and justification—25:321

Sanctity—see **Holiness**

Sanctuary—4:59, 64, 90, 136, 332, 7:39, 10:8, 418f, 428, 435, 443, 452, 11:393, 18:175f, 23:369, 29:142, 168, 224

Sanctuary, Places of—see **Refuge, Cities of**

Sanctus bell—42:174

Sanctus **(hymn)**—3:155, 16:76, 35:87, 38:123, 42:146n, 53:21, 28, 36, 55, 57, 60, 81f, 149, 209, 282

Sand—3:18

Sanhedrin—2:248n, 8:241, 24:303, 29:81, 47:181, 222n

Santes Pagninus—1:236n, 297f, 2:14n, 3:358, 5:336, 6:292, 35:284n

Santiago de Compostella—see **James of Compostella, St.**

Sap—24:201, 205, 210, 221, 226, 230, 236

Saphra—47:179–183, 189, 197, 206, 221, 223

Sapphires—1:101

Saracens—3:63, 65, 76, 161, 4:21, 35, 70n, 71, 108, 328, 7:323, 11:92, 32:129, 35:404n, 406, 41:372, 47:180, 212

Sarah—2:238, 240f, 251–254, 277, 279f, 294–296, 303–306, 309–312, 314, 321, 325, 374f, 3:9, 13f, 42–46, 49, 51–55, 57–59, 61–65, 68, 70, 74f, 99, 135, 144–148, 150–154, 156–158, 161, 176, 188, 192, 200–212, 215–217, 228, 317, 319, 322–324, 327, 331–333, 336f, 349, 352, 354, 356–359, 361, 4:4, 6, 9–13, 17–24, 35f, 38, 40, 45, 49, 51, 79, 98, 102, 104, 109, 113, 183–185, 187–194, 196–199, 205–207, 210, 215,

217, 223, 250, 265, 271, 287, 301–303, 306, 323f, 327, 330, 335, 337, 339, 348, 351, 353f, 367, 376, 389f, 5:17, 29, 36, 93, 95, 325, 334f, 6:146, 184, 263, 272, 283, 303, 7:66, 114, 199, 220, 241, 263, 8:84, 150, 169f, 297, 303, 13:355, 17:197f, 18:405, 23:401, 24:220f, 25:40f, 81, 384f, 26:226–228, 433–436, 438f, 441–446, 457, 461, 27:310f, 317, 322, 28:49, 173, 29:62, 239, 30:90, 323, 37:37, 91, 251, 292, 38:252, 45:23n, 47:140, 142, 145–147, 264, 48:32n

Sarai—see **Sarah**

Sarcasm—1:222, 4:356, 16:169, 23:245

Sarcerius, Erasmus—50:198f
Loci communes 50:198n
Postil 50:198n

Sardanapalus—2:206, 13:76

Sardinia—41:41n

Sargon II (King of Assyria)—35:326n

Sasse, Hermann—54:91n
This is My Body, Minneapolis, 1959 35:xvn, 37:xxi, 52n, 53n, 101n, 143n, 147n, 204n, 214n, 241n, 294n, 300n, 370n, 38:xxi, 5n, 6n, 8n, 10n, 12n, 14n, 18n, 26n, 32n, 63n, 87n, 115n

Satan—1:15, 49, 61, 67, 70, 74, 82, 96, 106f, 109–111, 113, 133, 135, 138, 142, 144–151, 153, 155f, 158–163, 165, 170f, 180, 183–196, 198–200, 203, 206, 215, 218, 220, 223, 225, 242, 271, 273, 275f, 281, 301, 310–312, 322f, 328, 340, 344, 346, 349, 2:8, 11, 17f, 21, 48, 102, 115, 128, 150, 154, 157, 168f, 172, 174, 184, 197, 213, 216–219, 222, 228, 230, 235f, 258f, 266, 268, 273, 275, 292, 302, 319f, 334, 354, 356, 369, 387f, 3:5f, 8, 11, 17, 19, 21, 34, 44f, 51, 57f, 63, 76, 108f, 120, 124, 138–140, 146, 158, 161, 166–168, 172–174, 179f, 184f, 214, 227, 234, 255f, 264–266, 270f, 276f, 282, 291, 296, 301, 319, 327, 330, 341f, 345, 347, 350, 357, 363f, 4:3, 5, 31, 47f, 56, 71f, 74, 92–95, 110, 116, 126, 129f, 132, 144, 170, 175, 191, 204, 236, 256, 264, 294, 319, 324, 358, 371, 375, 5:10f, 18, 46, 48f, 67, 131, 145, 151, 189f, 194, 205, 215, 219, 221, 222n, 224, 234, 239, 246, 251f, 255, 271, 290, 310, 321, 348, 6:20, 37f, 59, 63, 88, 90, 94f, 132, 228f, 271, 331, 380, 7:16, 20, 55, 57, 75, 85f, 89, 110, 121, 128, 131f, 140, 179, 191, 195, 261f, 298f, 309, 311, 332, 364, 369, 8:8, 10, 22, 33, 37, 44, 73, 83, 93, 126, 131, 135, 162, 164, 173, 224, 226, 239f, 251, 271, 275, 277, 284, 294, 314, 9:4f, 18, 41n, 54, 59, 72, 74, 82, 93, 111, 130, 140, 147, 183, 185–189, 198, 237, 10:28, 130, 270, 418, 438, 12:9, 17, 22, 24, 26f, 36, 38, 41, 46, 59, 65, 93, 125, 189, 214, 216, 218, 226–228, 233, 237, 245, 264, 266, 281, 283, 287, 318f, 330, 335f, 346f, 354, 358, 365, 374f, 379, 382–384, 387, 393f, 404f, 408, 13:109, 112f, 117, 137, 184, 188, 262, 14:186, 258, 261, 264f, 15:65, 244, 274, 317f, 339, 16:6, 17, 24, 28, 41, 54–56, 72, 75, 90, 113, 119n, 124, 129–131, 143, 152, 160, 170, 189, 201f, 213f, 225, 263, 275, 298, 300–302, 306–312, 314, 317, 319, 321, 331, 343f, 17:6, 27, 30, 34, 41–43, 47, 106f, 116, 177, 199, 214, 224, 340, 350, 394, 18:72, 79, 127, 166, 229, 261, 360f, 364, 371f, 383f, 399, 401, 20:8, 13, 31f, 35–37, 46, 48, 74, 93, 139f, 173, 183, 204–207, 226, 228, 234, 321, 22:55, 63, 67, 82, 416, 442, 513, 23:145, 327, 24:350, 352, 384, 25:244, 254, 275, 337, 472, 484, 26:5, 14, 18f, 21, 24, 31, 33, 35–37, 39f, 45f, 49, 52f, 56, 59, 65, 70, 125, 137, 168, 190–193, 196, 285, 296, 334, 387, 408, 418, 420, 424, 450, 27:3, 12, 19, 34f, 40, 43, 48f, 53, 58, 84, 99, 101; 109f, 118f, 123f, 137, 143–147, 345, 388, 392, 28:219f, 250, 254, 291, 303, 350f, 373f, 381, 29:11, 20, 33f, 41, 50, 54, 56, 66, 68f, 76, 78, 81, 87, 90, 95–97, 182, 30:224–226, 230, 236, 244, 246f, 258, 260–263, 275f, 280–283, 286f, 291f, 295f, 305f, 312, 317, 325f, 33:25, 65, 98f, 115, 130, 175–178, 227, 238, 256, 287f, 34:117, 120, 139, 36:17f, 41–44, 57, 106, 115, 138, 221, 237f, 256, 344, 37:13–18, 122f, 133–135, 194, 261f, 345, 349, 356–358, 372, 38:99, 142, 182, 269, 40:34, 42, 41:84, 124, 171, 199, 278f, 290, 334, 42:67, 128, 43:52, 64–66, 103, 106f, 112, 127–129, 133, 137f, 143, 145–148, 161, 163f, 181, 184f, 194f, 197, 205f, 228f, 232–234, 237f, 271, 277, 279n, 284, 44:xvi, 62, 66, 73, 79, 132, 138, 265, 369, 371f, 45:13, 169, 176, 46:24, 150, 215, 217, 300, 47:107, 48:16, 152, 166, 168, 214, 230, 235, 265–267, 269, 273, 278, 295, 301, 306n, 307f, 319, 321, 328, 333, 336, 354f, 366, 368, 371, 387, 390, 395, 401, 49:230f, 289,

301, 309, 361, 52:227, 53:33, see also **Devil**; **Lucifer**
Satan, Church of—2:27, 52f, 101, 176, 213, 224, 240, 247
Satan and Christ—33:282, 287–291
Satiety—28:64, 66, 165, 167
Satisfaction—5:155, 162, 6:201, 368, 371, 7:135, 227–229, 232, 234f, 237, 246, 254, 258, 275, 281, 8:6, 41, 181, 189, 267, 332, 12:364, 373, 389, 17:5, 99, 300, 370, 23:23, 154, 178, 180, 334, 24:348, 25:31f, 249, 284, 411, 26:182n, 411, 30:3, 110, 171, 237, 252f, 263, 287, 295, 31:85–87, 95, 103, 113, 134, 151, 32:32–34, 62–64, 34:111, 180, 347, 35:6–24, 37, 40, 42, 103n, 38:183, 204, 40:297, 41:199, 215, 236f, 48:43f, 68, 51:30, 60, 317, 319
Satre, Lowell J.—translator of *Two Kinds of Righteousness* 31:293–306
Satyrs—4:394, 16:297
Sauer, Alfred von Rohr—translator of commentary on Psalm 101 13:143–224
Saul (called Paul)—see **Paul, St., Apostle**
Saul, King—1:271, 316, 2:50, 78–80, 91, 355, 3:30, 62, 172, 283, 285, 327, 339, 360, 4:44, 5:94, 145, 152, 184f, 6:42f, 75, 134, 211, 213, 324, 366, 368, 370, 385, 7:229, 235, 257, 273f, 356f, 8:40, 43, 208, 235, 242, 285, 306, 329f, 9:40, 155, 163, 168, 202, 272, 10:16, 28, 31, 86, 130, 147, 240, 278, 334, 11:73, 132, 200, 359, 13:172, 183, 197, 205, 214, 304, 14:130, 203, 221, 226, 231–237, 239–241, 319f, 16:115, 143, 17:122, 279, 18:216, 262, 19:62, 144, 227, 234, 20:137, 140, 213, 22:81, 188, 397, 399, 405, 23:149, 24:276n, 25:142, 374, 408, 459, 26:63, 73, 94, 339f, 343, 27:134, 204, 29:152, 30:231, 325, 34:77, 357, 36:196f, 221, 37:135, 259, 38:312, 41:80, 250, 42:156, 46:66, 112, 131, 193, 285, 47:186f, 51:159, 52:93
Saulites—14:241
Sausages—23:119
Savior—see **Christ**—Savior
Saviors—18:204, 46:221n, 223, 240
Savonarola, Girolamo—32:88, 48:291n
Saxenburg—4:99
Saxo, Johannes—38:265
Saxon Circuit, Lower—50:68f
Saxon dynasty—49:15n, 58n, 120n, 170n, 183, 383n, 380n, 414n, 50:80n, 129n, 213n, 214n, 280n
Saxons—2:188, 366, 8:108, 14:ix, 38:8, 41:xiv, 374, 54:310, 331, 336, 351
Saxony—3:66n, 340, 341n, 350, 4:99, 210, 281, 382, 5:x, 63, 263, 341, 369, 6:21n, 240, 7:121n, 158, 193, 198, 8:124, 178n, 11:105, 14:110, 233, 280, 21:356, 23:201n, 208, 226, 258, 295, 298, 321, 342, 344, 26:190, 27:315, 28:3, 6, 34:333n, 36:8, 129, 227, 309, 38:93, 142, 40:102f, 115f, 41:xiv, 221n, 222, 230, 371, 45:107n, 308, 46:59, 239, 47:89n, 51:136, 160, 333, 53:39, 54:402
Albertine 23:201n
Ernestine family 48:49, 110n, 181
Saxony, Church visitation in—see **Visitation of parishes**
Saxony, Ducal—46:90, 47:6, 48:xviii, 110n, 49:7n, 50:134n, 135n, 185, 214n, 772
Saxony, Electoral—46:89f, 142, 234n, 47:101, 106, 134, 48:46n, 49, 70n, 79n, 94n, 128, 131n, 275, 393, 50:22n, 41n, 80n, 87n, 112n, 123n, 131n, 145n, 168n, 170n, 198n, 213n, 214f, 214n, 219n, 222, 231, 236, 254n, 259
Court and residence 49:3n, 4, 15n, 17, 69n, 70, 72, 83, 91f, 103, 229, 234n, 50:10, 42n, 47n, 48, 57, 86f, 88f, 94n, 104n, 107n, 112n, 128n, 129n, 138n, 148n, 160n, 163n, 180n, 190n, 207, 213n, 214, 258, 265n, 274, 276
Government 48:8, 28, 33n, 70, 79, 83, 85n, 90n, 108, 130n, 138n, 154, 162, 163n, 167f, 173n, 179n, 180, 186, 188, 198, 228, 253, 263, 264n, 268f, 271f, 275n, 313n, 314n, 326n, 344, 354f, 366n, 380n, 383f, 393n, 398n, 49:29, 51f, 69n, 122n, 132, 133f, 137, 152n, 189f, 197n, 236n, 240n, 246n, 281f, 295, 349n, 373n, 413, 429f, 434
Rulers 49:54, 103n, 118n, 291n, 50:, 74n, 209n, see also **Frederick the Wise, Elector of Saxony**; **John, Elector of Saxony**; **John Frederick, Elector of Saxony**
Territory 49:30, 50n, 96, 122n, 129n, 140, 160n, 168n, 190f, 307f
Saxony, Electors of—see **Electors of Saxony**
Sayings, Popular—see **Proverbs and sayings**
Scabs—3:52
Scales—9:137, 24:279, 26:97
Scandals—3:234, 6:94, 229, 306, 317f, 358f, 374, 394, 11:50, 189, 27:19, 117
Scandinavia—41:xii, 46:106n
Scepter of Judah—45:213, 214n, 215–217,

219f, 47:178–190, 197, 200–207, 222, 300
Scepters—4:87, 5:110, 161, 184f, 6:54, 7:67, 109, 184, 187, 190, 196f, 205, 223, 8:142f, 146, 238–240, 244, 10:35, 436, 47:178–208, 221–223f, 231f, 235, 250, 281, 298, 300
Sceptre, God's—Scriptures as 14:131
Schade, Oskar—*Satiren und Pasquille aus der Reformationszeit*, Hannover, 1863 36:228n
Schade, Peter (Mosellanus)—39:54, 40:316n, 49:7f, 78n
Schade, Sebastian—50:213n
Schadewald, Bartholomew—50:108, 54:434
Schäfer, Ernest—*Luther als Kirchenhistoriker*, Gütersloh, 1897 13:62n, 281, 47:234n, 51:306n
Schalbe family—48:3n, 4n
Schamhaperes—15:323, 342f, see also **Shem Hamphorus**
Schantz, Hans—43:142
Schart, Mark—42:97f
Schatzgeyer, Caspar—*Scrutinium divinae Scripturae pro conciliatione dissedentium dogmatum* 23:74n
Schaumberg, Sylvester—48:169, 223n
Scheel, Otto—54:193n
Dokumente zu Luthers Entwicklung, Tübingen, 1929 37:371n
Martin Luther. Vom Katholizismus zur Reformation, Tübingen, 1921 1:26n, 22:296n
Schem Hamphoras—see **Shem Hamphorus**
Schenck, W.—48:12n
Schenk, Jacob—3:243n, 6:76n, 34:148, 54:289, 313f, 378, 391, 396
Scherl, Henry—50:278, 54:402
Scheurl, Christopher—31:6, 43:189, 48:42n, 43n
Schick, George V.—translator of *Lectures on Genesis*, Chapters 1–28 Vols. 1–4
translator of first half of Vol. 5 5:xii, 182n
Schiefer, Wolfgang—50:211n, 216, 219, 54:x, 371–374, 376f, 381f
Schilling, John—54:417n
Schimmelpfennig—21:320n
Schindel, Jeremiah J.—35:45, 75, 78, 103n
translator of *Temporal Authority: to What Extent it should be Obeyed* 45:75–130
translator of *The Blessed Sacrament of the Holy and True Body of Christ, and the Brotherhoods* 35:45–74
translator of *Treatise on the New Testament* 35:75–112
Schindler, Carl J.—translator of *A Simple Way to Pray* 43:187–212
translator of *Sayings in which Luther found Comfort* 43:167–178
translator of *Whether One may Flee from the Deadly Plague* 43:113–138
Schirlentz, Nickel—34:342, 35:127, 39:303, 45:80, 46:211, 48:283n, 349, 49:18n, 403
Schism, Papal—41:266n
Schismatic preachers—21:66
Schismatic spirits—7:261, 305, 309, 315, 21:63, 127, 178, 219f, 225, 253–255, 261–268, 270, 22:17, 21, 25, 36, 48, 54f, 58, 66, 167f, 173, 180, 226, 237, 252, 283, 308, 324, 349, 361, 364, 366, 369f, 377, 384, 390, 433, 509, 513, 524f, 23:19, 51, 59, 65f, 68, 79, 86, 88, 97, 104, 119, 122, 124, 126, 137, 147, 152, 157, 163, 168, 170, 173, 180, 188f, 225, 229f, 249f, 267–270, 279, 281, 322, 333, 342, 347, 349, 354, 358, 360, 367, 371, 408, 24:8, 13, 46, 52, 58, 62, 118, 145, 201, 206, 212, 229, 232f, 236, 246, 294, 320, 404, see also **Schwärmer**
Schismatics—11:526, 12:185, 187, 192f, 13:146f, 204, 14:257, 261, 266, 271, 16:241, 249, 251, 301, 319, 333, 17:6, 8, 25:142, 176, see also **Reformers, Radical**
Schism(s)—14:7, 55, 16:202, 205, 24:47, 101f, 246, 249, 251, 320n, 25:120, 27:60, 169, 357, 382, 29:226, 35:381f, 36:20, 24, 37:27, 167, 360, 38:74, 317, see also **Dissension**
Schlaginhaufen, John—50:78f, 51:xvi, 54:xii, xvi, xxiii, 5, 125, 129, 132, 149, 154–156, 164, 169
recorder of Luther's table conversation, 1531–1532 54:123–166
Schleiff, A.—35:207n
Schleiz—49:236n, 240n, 243n, 244n
Schleswig-Holstein—50:49n, 147n
Schleynitz, John von, Bishop of Meissen—39:109
Schlick zu Falkenau, Count Wolfgang—40:5, 47:59, 65, 95n, 133, 137n
Schlieben—50:93n, 107n, 110n
Schlisske, Otto—*Handbuch der Lutherlieder*, Göttingen, 1948 53:xxn
Schmalzing, George—16:x, 184n
Schmedenstede, Heinrich—34:301–303, 38:266
Schmid, Johann Heigerlin—see **Faber, John, Archbishop of Vienna**
Schmid, Kunz—52:6

Schmid, Ulrich—46:6n
Schmoller, Gustav—*Zur Geschichte der national-öconomische Ansichten in Deutschland während der Reformations-Periode*, Tübingen, 1860 45:246n, 252n, 262n, 268n
Schnabel, Tilemann—45:167n
Schneider, John—see **Agricola, John**
Schneidewein, Henry—54:75, 265
Schnell, George—50:214, 220n
Schnepf, Erhard—49:414n
Schnewil, John—37:11
Schoeps, Hans Joachim—*The Jewish-Christian Argument*, New York, 1963 47:132n
Schöffer, Peter—43:75
Scholars—16:63, 20:73, 155, 233, 21:344f, 24:79, 131, 134, 138, 153, 156, 297, 38:11, 80, 277n, 46:111, 172, 218, 239f, 243, 257, 52:37, 117, 162f, 172
Scholarship—2:x, 33n
Scholastic teachers—3:137
Scholastic theologians—2:110n, 119n, 121n, 122n, 124f, 12:341, 345, 377, 381
Scholastic theology—4:199, 220, 6:182, 8:209, 261n, 16:276n, 32:xviii, 257–259, 41:217n
Scholasticism—30:300n, 31:5–7, 41f, 83, 105n, 194, 225, 238, 242, 276, 321, 38:xviii, 84n, 45:341, 376n, 48:28n, 37f, 42, 56f, 82, 96, 156f, 165n, 318, 49:7n, 15, 44, 71, 90n, 382n
Scholasticism, Thomistic—1:57n
Scholastics—1:164, 167, 2:13n, 39, 43, 46–48, 121n, 314f, 3:274, 358, 5:194, 7:12n, 298, 8:16, 42, 263, 9:51, 71f, 14:17n, 16:34, 276n, 22:141n, 23:102n, 103, 110, 112, 147, 151, 154, 183, 24:347, 26:4, 88, 109, 122, 126, 129, 181, 446, 29:188, 34:109n, 154, 171f, 185, 282, 35:xi, 48, 64n, 36:28, 124, 37:180, 214, 295–303, 38:32n, 84, 119n, 189, 246, 263, 271, 41:116, 46:226n, 273n, 52:41, 50, 54:9, 63, 249, 260, 264, 275, 290, 344, 352, 391f, see also **Sophists**
Scholia—10:ix–xi, 31, 173, 298, 11:ix, 16:x, 119n, 139n, 245n, 275n, 294n, 311n, 326n, 329n, 25:xf, xiiif, 133, 26:436, 29:xif
Schönberg, Anthony von—54:406
Schönberg, Cardinal Nicholas von—51:291, 406
Schönberg, Dietrich von—45:134n, 135n
Schönburg, Grafschaft of—50:142n
Schönfeld, Ave and Margaret—49:105n
Schönfeld, Ernst, Ave, and Margarete von—50:278n
Schönitz, Anthony von—54:310
Schönitz, Hans—41:248n
Schoolboys—26:346n, 37:33f, 36f, 79, 98, 102f, 107, 150, 165, 171, 174f, 178f, 196, 238, 271, 285, 302, 335, 339f, 343
Schoolmasters—1:109, 3:117, 9:25, 48, 11:145, 23:35f, 98, 100, 168, 220, 26:345f, 27:114, 154, 45:188n, 318, 350, 354f, 356n, 368, 46:218, 220, 225, 231, 234, 244, 246, 249, 252f, 256, 54:403f, 459
Schoolmistresses—27:156, 45:189, 368
Schools, Cathedral—45:341f
Schools, Latin—49:81n, 103n, 104, 106, 152n
Schools—3:42, 50, 118, 164, 248, 259, 274, 326, 331, 356, 4:34, 59, 384, 397, 5:109, 136, 250, 260f, 263–265, 6:20f, 31, 186, 240, 407, 7:140, 142, 163, 190, 254, 8:59, 62, 76, 125, 230, 261, 283, 14:21f, 91, 301, 15:65, 250, 22:229, 277, 518, 521, 26:20, 105, 313, 342, 346, 409, 427, 448, 27:123, 206, 30:30, 68, 99, 169–171, 34:53, 40:314–319, 41:xiv, 27, 112n, 122, 132–135, 137, 142, 176, 202, 221, 238, 240, 355, 45:xivf, 175n, 187f, 188n, 318f, 341–374, 46:47, 164, 187, 197, 209f, 213–258, 54:403f, 452, 473
Schools for girls—see **Girls, Schools for**
Schott, Hans—45:382n, 385
Schradin, Hans—38:11, 73n, 79
Schradin, John—5:x
Schreiber, Clara S.—54:7n
Schreiber, Edmund—45:235n
Schröter, Laurentius—38:135n
Schubert, Hans von—27:ix, 47:5n
Schultz, Hieronymus—see **Scultetus (Schultz), Jerome, Bishop of Brandenburg**
Schulz, Robert C.—47:106n
  author of Introduction and presumed author of introductions to all items included in Vol. 46
  editor of Vol. 46
  translator of *Answer to Several Questions on Monastic Vows* 46:139–154
Schumann, Valentin—53:184, 194, 269f, 287, 289, 295f, 299
Schürer—48:318
Schurf, Augustine—34:108
Schurf, Augustine and Anne—49:174n, 181
Schurf, Jerome (Hieronymus)—32:103, 106, 119f, 123, 40:272n, 48:74n, 200n,

219n, 227, 394, 398n, 49:13, 36, 168n, 184, 51:69, 54:150, 180, 236, 246, 262, 264, 275, 338
Schwabach—49:236n, 244, 246
Schwabach Articles—37:157, 38:8, 12, 49:236n, 246, 250, 256n, 268n, 272, 296
Schwäbisch-Hall—38:963n, 47:46n, 49:177f, 394n, 50:213n
Schwärmer—1:21n, 22:367n, 37:18n, 39:xix, 47:132, 48:79n, 211f, 49:xviii, 17n, 50n, 53n, 56n, 72n, 82, 94–97, 100, 141, 146, 148f, 164, 186f, 200n, 202, 226, 231, 264, 266, 300f, 370, 423, 54:48, 50, see also **Enthusiasts**; **Fanatics**
Schwartz, Reinhard—10:xif
Fides, Spes, und Caritas beim jungen Luther, Berlin, 1962 31:7
Schwartz, W.—54:445n
Schwarzburg, John Henry, Count of—49:17n, 19
Schwarzenberg, Christopher von—43:9f
Schwarzenberg, John von—41:141n, 43:10, 45:78n, 46:247, 49:13n, 17, 18n
Schwarzerdt, George—54:416
Schwebel, Johann—53:53
Schweinfurt—50:42n, 54n, 58n
Schwenkfeld, Caspar von—3:273, 276, 22:21n, 29:83n, 35:xiv, 37:xv, 11, 40n, 157f, 288–294, 307n, 321–323, 327n, 339, 352, 38:xx, 5, 282, 284, 287n, 288n, 291, 293n, 295, 298, 302, 304, 307n, 47:59f, 48:143n, 49:121, 141n, 147–149, 54:186f, 469
Schwertfeger, John—48:230, 236
Schwiebert, Ernest G.—*Luther and His Times*, St. Louis, 1950 3:183n, 31:38, 258, 312, 32:115n, 35:xiv, 123n, 37:xxi, 39:xxin, 25n, 83n, 108n, 113n, 123n, 141n, 248n, 303n, 42:169n, 43:59n, 70n, 99n, 45:13n, 53n, 54n, 106n, 271n, 284n, 285n, 288n, 347n, 387n, 46:5n, 6n, 11n, 13n, 47n, 60n, 131n, 157n, 183n, 186n
Schwolle, Jerome—54:459
Science—12:310, 15:18, 16:342, 25:361f, 38:75, 241
Science, Natural—1:94, 52:162–164, 168f
Scientific questions—22:296, 315
Scipio Africanus—2:374, 5:270, 354, 7:142, 144, 170, 178, 185, 311, 8:48, 134, 211, 237, 31:245, 34:169f, 179
Scipios, The—38:290n, 291
Scoffers—2:62, 13:191, 16:228, 23:369, 371
Scorpions—9:97, 24:84
Scotists—14:264, 25:324, 33:134, 37:363n, 48:96
***Scotus Academicus*, Rome, 1901**—7:12n
Scotus, John Duns—see **Duns Scotus, John**
Scotus, John Machabeus—see **Maccabeus, John Scotus**
Scoundrels—24:205, 279, 305f, 313f, 316, 326, 378, 387
Scribes—4:117, 138, 6:373, 378, 16:107, 228, 249, 290, 20:53, 117f, 121, 125, 242, 296, 311f, 316, 21:284, 22:47, 114, 229, 277, 456, 23:20, 177, 211, 223, 350, 353, 24:223, 309, 38:42, 58, 41:170, 52:90, 183
Scripture verses—a defense when challenged 30:108, 296
Scripture(s)—1:7, 14f, 19, 20, 22, 29–33, 40, 43f, 47, 49, 51, 55, 58f, 65, 78, 81, 85, 95, 100, 105, 107, 109, 122f, 125, 130–132, 135, 145, 173, 183, 189, 192, 194, 198, 206, 217, 225, 231–235, 239, 243, 245, 247, 264, 269f, 296, 297n, 298, 304, 306f, 309, 311, 319f, 322f, 326, 333, 337, 339, 341, 346, 349, 353, 357, 2:ixf, 5, 15–17, 22, 24, 29, 34f, 37, 40, 43f, 46, 49, 59, 74, 77, 91, 93–95, 104, 117, 119, 122f, 126, 128, 132, 150, 153, 155–158, 162, 164, 187, 189, 198, 202, 209, 223, 227, 233, 237, 239n, 240f, 245, 247, 253, 257, 263, 265, 276f, 294, 296–300, 302, 308, 310f, 315, 326, 328, 333, 336, 348f, 351, 355f, 359, 363, 365f, 372f, 382f, 387f, 392, 3:ix, 6, 8, 10–12, 15f, 18f, 24f, 27, 29, 35, 37f, 45, 51, 59, 68–70, 73, 84, 87, 98, 114, 141, 149, 164, 166, 168, 177f, 191f, 194f, 207n, 210, 217, 219f, 225, 229, 232, 237n, 239, 242, 247, 249f, 261, 267, 270, 272, 275, 289, 297, 300, 304, 306–310, 312, 316f, 319, 321–323, 325f, 338, 347, 353, 357f, 364, 4:15, 20, 49f, 53, 61, 76, 78f, 91f, 95, 98n, 100, 105, 111, 113, 119, 126, 128, 132–134, 136, 138, 140, 142, 145–147, 150n, 153–155, 159, 171f, 174, 177, 184f, 189, 195f, 207, 214, 219f, 222, 224f, 227–232, 238, 240, 249f, 252, 259–263, 269f, 274, 277, 280, 284, 290, 294, 296, 299, 307–310, 312, 318f, 331–336, 344f, 348f, 351f, 365, 374n, 375, 379, 386, 392–394, 406, 408f, 5:4, 18, 20f, 24, 26f, 42f, 61, 68, 73, 79f, 88, 92, 104, 106, 109, 111, 122, 125, 128, 140, 146f, 149, 152, 158f, 182, 185, 192, 194f, 199, 206f, 227, 236, 241, 244,

258, 261, 275, 278f, 294f, 299, 310, 312, 333, 338, 344f, 357, 372, 6:7f, 36, 52, 99, 170, 278, 292, 314, 329, 335, 343, 7:x, 5–7, 10, 12, 17, 29, 31, 34f, 51f, 71, 99, 112, 118, 120, 132f, 143, 150, 156, 173, 194, 198, 207, 216, 222f, 232, 243, 251f, 260, 264, 268, 271, 276, 278, 280f, 285, 290, 292f, 295, 298, 302–304, 335, 343–345, 348, 350, 353, 375, 8:5–7, 10, 27, 32, 35, 41, 49, 52, 54, 71, 75, 84, 86f, 90f, 130, 141f, 146f, 149f, 153, 155, 198–202, 209–211, 224f, 228, 235, 238, 243, 246, 253, 257, 262f, 269, 270n, 272f, 277, 281, 285, 287f, 292, 297, 299f, 304, 308–310, 312, 314, 316, 325, 9:14, 17, 21, 25, 27, 33, 49f, 53, 57n, 108f, 110n, 135, 149, 164, 171, 185, 187f, 199, 205f, 214f, 226, 233, 235, 244, 250, 10:19–21, 40f, 49, 109f, 219, 332f, 397, 452, 460f, 464, 11:50, 54, 87, 131, 150, 177, 320, 368, 517, 12:48, 53, 142, 152, 173, 185, 199, 203, 216–218, 226, 232, 237, 242, 257, 283, 285, 306, 311, 335, 338f, 351, 353, 356, 374, 394, 398, 13:16, 352, 360, 380f, 393, 14:x, xii, 4, 6, 8, 10, 14, 18, 34–38, 45f, 51f, 55, 66, 75, 80f, 87–88, 92f, 99, 118f, 130f, 156, 168, 171, 181, 191, 193, 196, 199, 204, 209f, 222–226, 229, 236, 244, 250f, 254, 257, 260f, 265f, 281, 283–286, 290, 295f, 299f, 305, 311, 313, 320, 324, 336, 338, 15:9, 184–186, 194, 206, 214, 245, 268, 275, 280, 292, 339, 16:5, 16, 28, 34, 44f, 57, 70, 75, 83, 86, 93, 95–97, 99, 102, 107f, 127, 134, 136f, 141, 155, 158, 163, 166, 222–224, 227n, 232, 243f, 246, 248, 260, 265, 270, 276, 283, 287f, 292, 317, 325, 327, 332, 336, 17:18, 38, 115, 183, 250, 307, 367, 375f, 18:89, 97, 100, 108, 354, 20:x, 126, 249, 279, 22:6, 8, 14, 19–22, 218, 229f, 274, 283, 312, 316, 339, 362, 394, 414f, 23:13, 16f, 27, 31, 35, 42, 82f, 101, 103, 108, 128, 138, 156, 163, 174, 184, 187f, 193, 195f, 208, 220–223, 226, 229f, 235, 240, 243, 245, 252, 259, 273, 277, 279–281, 283f, 297, 300f, 306, 355, 360, 369, 378, 386, 418, 24:x, 7, 19, 26, 32, 37, 46, 50, 54, 69, 80, 91–96, 98, 104f, 107, 109f, 112, 121, 131, 170, 173, 187, 203–205, 207f, 214, 218, 228, 259f, 280f, 293, 304, 319, 324f, 334f, 339, 351, 355, 359, 362, 364f, 367f, 395–397, 419, 25:3f, 97f, 120, 145f, 192, 218, 424f, 515f, 26:x, 15, 24, 28f, 33, 38, 46f, 57f, 62, 64, 73, 75, 84, 96, 102, 114, 123, 128f, 146–149, 155, 169, 176, 187, 189, 192, 194–196, 198, 205f, 213, 223, 226, 230f, 237, 240–244, 249, 251, 254f, 259, 261–268, 275f, 280, 282, 289f, 292, 294f, 299, 332f, 341, 346, 357, 359, 386, 393, 397, 406, 414, 418, 433, 436, 457, 27:x, 11, 15, 20, 22, 25, 27, 29, 34f, 38f, 42, 46, 51, 60, 75, 77, 79, 115, 126, 128, 136, 150, 154, 156f, 176, 181, 183, 191, 200f, 206, 212, 214, 220, 228–230, 233, 235, 240, 242, 244f, 251–254, 258, 261, 264, 268, 273f, 280, 308, 312, 317, 321, 323f, 329, 333, 336f, 340, 342, 344f, 360, 370, 386, 398, 28:56, 72, 75–78, 80f, 96f, 168, 230, 268, 290, 329, 365, 29:30f, 37, 43, 69, 87, 127, 159, 179, 186, 188, 194, 200, 234, 236, 30:7, 10f, 14, 17–19, 22f, 25f, 30–32, 34, 37, 41, 44, 49, 56f, 59–63, 65f, 68–71, 83, 90, 93, 96, 99, 105–108, 111, 115, 117f, 126, 128, 133, 138, 151f, 158, 160, 165–169, 175, 177, 187, 194, 199, 206, 210, 212, 222, 235, 241, 244, 259, 262, 266, 270, 280, 287, 290, 296, 307, 310, 321, 31:x, xviii, 75, 83, 93f, 126f, 176, 238, 255, 274, 338, 394, 32:11f, 81, 96, 159, 194, 215–217, 230, 237, 257, 33:25n, 70f, 89–99, 277, 282, 34:xvi, 95, 119, 125, 160, 227, 282, 286, 360, 35:ixf, xiii, 115, 122f, 132, 137, 150, 153, 199, 227, 230f, 236, 267, 284, 289, 330, 380, 403, 409, 36:9f, 15f, 18–21, 23f, 26, 29, 38, 44, 84, 93f, 96–99, 110, 117, 119, 123–125, 134–137, 148, 150, 155, 162f, 171, 181, 191f, 196f, 200, 219n, 222, 228n, 289, 302, 304, 337, 347, 352, 37:14n, 33f, 101n, 148, 156f, 38:18, 21, 33, 44f, 52, 82, 120, 129f, 170, 191, 210n, 252, 259, 265, 290, 303, 306, 314, 39:xif, xvf, xxv, 36, 52, 55f, 63f, 69, 75, 77–83, 85, 94, 97, 101, 103f, 108, 111–114, 131, 133, 139, 147, 153, 158–161, 164f, 169, 173–201, 205, 207, 211, 214, 217, 228, 230–232, 235, 254, 258, 263, 266f, 270, 306, 309, 313, 41:xiii, 5f, 11, 19–21, 25–27, 30, 43, 45, 49–52, 54, 58f, 67, 81, 83f, 86, 88, 96, 105, 115f, 118–120, 122–125, 130f, 133, 135f, 140, 151, 155, 157, 160–162, 166, 170, 174f, 190, 193, 201, 207, 213, 219–221, 231, 235–237, 247, 255, 269–272, 286, 288, 295,

303–306, 308f, 313f, 327, 332, 339, 342–346, 349, 351f, 358, 360, 362, 370, 42:xiv, 23, 25, 29, 33, 51, 56, 60f, 63n, 66, 78n, 113, 122, 124, 129, 150, 156, 160f, 185n, 43:43, 70, 44:xiii, 204, 45:xiv, 5, 8, 14, 23, 43f, 53, 58f, 62, 86, 88, 93, 136, 145–148, 164, 177, 198, 200–202, 205f, 208, 212f, 219, 221, 223f, 226, 228f, 253, 261, 263, 275, 321, 323f, 329, 344, 357–359, 361, 364–366, 368, 373–376, 381, 390, 46:6f, 10f, 13, 15f, 33f, 38, 40f, 70, 73, 77, 84, 98, 120, 141, 148, 150, 153, 167f, 171, 173, 178, 197, 217, 220, 231f, 252f, 262, 284, 289, 304, 312, 315, 47:16, 20–22, 26f, 31, 65f, 124, 132, 156, 178, 51:89, 108, 148, 204, 224, 324f, 347, 377, 388, 52:14, 21f, 39, 49, 55, 60, 93, 95, 98, 105, 125, 136, 170f, 175f, 180, 183, 187, 205f, 210f, 216, 224, 235, 271, 286, 54:11, 13, 42f, 50f, 121, 127, 165, 185, 198, 260, 344, 352f, 361, 378, 392, 406, 408, 440f, 446, 476
Absurdities and paradoxes see **Scripture(s)**—Contradictory passages
Allegorical interpretation see **Scripture(s)**—Interpretation
And faith 52:127, 146, 154, 163, 187
And the Word 52:205
As treated by the Church Fathers 39:163–168, 176, 192f, 217, 222
Authority 3:27, 57, 297, 26:15, 240, 33:19, 22, 71, 83n, 89, 37:13–19, 23, 25–28, 33, 40, 47–51, 53, 55, 59, 63, 69, 109, 304f, 352, 363, 369f, 372, 38:34, 38, 69, 76, 129, 172, 51:7–10
Authorized version 4:x, 7:285n, 26:147n
Bring comfort and hope 25:515
Called letters of God 3:114f
Canon 15:185, 30:ix, 32:118, 38:33, see also **Scripture(s), Old Testament**
Christ the key 25:xi, 4, 405f
Christ's swaddling cloths 35:122, 236
Clarity of 33:24–27, 89–99
Codex Sinaiticus 35:405n
Contradictory passages 4:92, 96, 131, 6:26, 314, 9:17n, 15:313, 37:xviii–xx, 5, 46–57, 60, 82, 155, 164, 171, 185, 191–207, 276f, 296n, see also **Paradox; Scripture(s)**—Inconsistencies
Douay version 1:87n, 97n, 152n, 160n, 263n, 297n, 2:109n, 365n, 5:272n, 8:119n, 289n, 18:viii, 22:300, 25:85n, 26:319n, 35:210n, 37:113n, 172n
Evaluation of writings 35:231f
Final authority 3:325f
German Bible see **Luther, Martin, Writings of**
German translation, Luther's 3:66, 6:54n, 301, 323, 8:290, 15:270, 20:52n, 70n, 28:21, 204, 338, 371, 35:206, 227, 229, 249, 357n, 38:314, 48:201, 303n, 320n, 352n, 355n, 359, 363, 372
German translations before Luther's 35:357n, 46:232n, 48:352n, 356, 363n, 381
Glosses 45:364n
God's book 3:297
Holy Spirit the best interpreter 10:211, 25:324
Inconsistencies 22:218f, 283, 312, 316, 339
Inerrancy 2:223
Inspiration 5:275, 352f, 6:225, 7:35, 10:10, 22, 11:160f, 364, 15:275, 280, 292, 19:16, 23, 35:152f
Inspiration, Verbal 41:49, 83f
Instruction in 37:364, 371
Interpretation 1:10, 237, 269f, 2:16, 45, 47, 121, 150n, 188n, 342, 3:15, 27, 67, 72f, 232n, 275n, 299n, 319, 353, 4:10, 14, 6:66, 68, 249, 276, 8:147, 153, 209, 224, 288, 9:6f, 89, 97, 157n, 204n, 215n, 268, 271, 310n, 10:xif, 3–5, 7, 25, 52, 54, 56, 92, 95, 109, 155, 244, 265, 312, 455, 462, 11:12, 64, 327, 366, 13:309, 14:36n, 66, 68, 74n, 87, 16:100, 325n, 18:xii, 20:21n, 99, 102, 108, 155–157, 243, 307, 337, 21:68–71, 22:230, 283, 299, 364, 484, 24:104, 173, 367, 25:xi, 26f, 141, 144, 155f, 192, 212, 238, 310, 405, 429f, 499, 26:439n, 440, 27:29, 51, 57f, 311–313, 373, 387, 28:79, 167, 189, 198, 208, 382, 30:166f, 31:280f, 32:168, 183, 223, 236–238, 243–245, 33:90f, 162, 166, 179, 34:53, 112, 228, 317, 36:xf, 30, 95, 279, 281, 37:xii, xvii–xx, 5–7, 26f, 30f, 37, 41–57, 64, 73–77, 81–85, 135f, 146, 155, 163–172, 182, 185, 190–207, 211, 246f, 249f, 252–255, 268, 270–273, 283f, 290f, 296n, 304, 327n, 332f, 350f, 38:253, 39:36, 87, 111–114, 164f, 174–201, 231f, 40:154f, 190, 374, 41:xiii, 133, 159n, 45:361–365, 47:134, 155n, 49:154f, 52:44, 86, 95, 107, 122f, 136, 191
Interpretation, Allegorical 9:7, 25, 238, 10:xi, 3f, 7, 23, 50, 54, 88f, 96, 143, 150, 153, 165, 171f, 195–198, 204, 225, 247, 318, 359, 404, 408, 450

Interpretation, Anagogical 10:xi, 3f, 86, 114, 122, 165, 173, 210, 343, 406, 451
Interpretation, Historical 10:x, 4, 7, 265
Interpretation, Literal 10:xi, 7, 54, 56, 95, 155
Interpretation, Mystical 10:24, 142, 149, 153, 158, 194, 229, 324, 326, 336
Interpretation, Tropological 10:xi, 3f, 7, 52, 74, 85, 94f, 114, 117, 122, 130, 139, 144, 150, 165, 194, 197, 204, 223, 297, 318, 372, 376, 379, 382–384, 402, 404, 440, 450, 461
Jerusalem Bible version 19:143n
Knowledge of 51:71, 74, 80, 86, 96
Language and style 37:31, 258, 276f, 296, 350
Latin version, Older 28:267, 275
Latin versions 1:191, 2:122
Not contradictory 15:313
Perversions of 1:166, 9:268, 10:15, 18, 58, 116, 187, 375
Polyglot editions 48:223n
Prefaces by Luther 35:227–411
Proofs and warrants 36:30f, 76f, 86, 91f, 107, 139, 141–144, 146f, 149, 153f, 157, 160, 174, 179, 186, 188, 195, 276, 280, 283–285, 299
Proper use 25:324f
Relation to Christ 52:127, 171f, 173, 194, 207
Revised Standard version 1:270n, 4:154n, 9:x, 15:36n, 16:88n, 20:vii, 191n, 198n, 205n, 218n, 329n, 26:147n, 28:vii, 164, 30:315n, 32:162n
Sceptre, God's 14:131
Source of encouragement 6:52, 99
Source of hope 25:120
Study of 10:461–463, 14:385, 44:204f
Teachings 37:xii, xviiif, 8, 49, 55, 57f, 60f, 63–66, 69, 79, 95, 97, 135, 156, 171, 178, 185f, 191–206, 211, 216f, 234–236, 275f, 291f, 297–299, 359, 369, 38:248
Translations 34:vi, 283
Understanding them 3:358, 4:53, 126, 277, 35:119, 170, 181, 213, 395
Unity and diversity 21:xiiif
Use as proof texts 37:29–40, 44–57, 60, 70, 78f, 81, 97, 102, 144f, 168–171, 176, 186, 189f, 207f, 254, 276, 280, 285, 304f, 341
Use by Church fathers 37:328, 330
Use in argument 37:34, 212, 228, 231, 295f, 318
Versions 6:vii, 15:vii, 36n, 267, 29:vii, 45:xvi
Vulgate version 2:158n, 185n, 190n, 286n, 324n, 373n, 386n, 4:x, 99n, 186n, 5:97, 241n, 272, 349, 352, 356n, 6:64n, 7:148, 267, 8:65, 71, 158n, 245, 289, 9:ix, 41n, 49f, 155, 10:ix, 38f, 48f, 91, 126, 155, 168, 193, 208, 237, 255, 259, 264, 284, 309, 321, 339, 363, 373, 389, 398, 412, 13:x, 14:xii, 116n, 143n, 232n, 309n, 15:181n, 267n, 298n, 320n, 322n, 330, 331n, 334n, 16:9n, 33n, 57n, 124n, 17:14n, 33, 46, 105, 19:108n, 130n, 136n, 137n, 138n, 140n, 141n, 198n, 20:6n, 12n, 21n, 43n, 46n, 52n, 57n, 58n, 59n, 65n, 69n, 70n, 80n, 86n, 87n, 93n, 95n, 104n, 124n, 131n, 212n, 218n, 221n, 224n, 240n, 263n, 264n, 267n, 329n, 22:232n, 300n, 396n, 25:ix, 12, 16, 36, 41, 43, 52, 65, 85, 125, 148, 168, 179, 211f, 245, 271, 273, 319, 385f, 428, 479, 492, 501, 27:x, 239n, 374, 407, 28:66, 164, 218, 220, 239, 267, 273, 288, 292, 298, 303, 335, 358, 370f, 29:140, 156n, 159n, 30:24n, 31:47, 272n, 32:20n, 146n, 162n, 182n, 197n, 34:22n, 41n, 35:32n, 210n, 221n, 231, 240, 340n, 36:10, 18n, 22n, 37n, 39n, 78n, 85n, 93n, 100n, 150n, 187n, 312n, 318n, 37:26n, 73n, 172n, 197n, 274n, 322n, 327n, 38:254n, 274n, 45:xvi, 58n, 87n, 144n, 173n, 210n, 227n, 320n, 361n, 362n, 365n, 46:148n, 48:363, 49:xx, 19f, 51:21, 40n, 78n
Womb which bears Christ 10:397
Zainer Bible 48:363n
Zürich Bible 49:89n
Scripture(s), New Testament—1:18, 21, 23, 59, 88, 157, 194, 223, 228, 233, 248, 250, 257, 269, 299, 303, 309, 350f, 354, 2:12, 16, 46, 105, 162f, 215, 228–230, 353, 387, 3:46, 69, 73, 92, 101, 103, 109f, 146f, 166, 169, 174, 194, 222, 297, 353, 4:33, 89, 103, 119f, 124, 151, 160, 177, 257, 309–311, 314, 316, 372, 5:8, 140f, 244, 357, 362f, 6:54, 108, 111, 155, 181, 185, 232, 237, 239, 249f, 330, 352, 7:11, 116, 129, 280n, 288n, 8:65, 132, 141f, 159, 165, 179–181, 186, 188, 223, 235, 308, 312, 317, 9:ix, 27, 43n, 63, 107, 178f, 11:274, 294, 312, 13:17, 323, 14:34, 79f, 90f, 94, 99, 246, 326n, 331, 341, 15:268, 287, 314, 333, 343, 16:37, 126, 225, 265, 18:11, 74, 119, 19:152f, 193, 23:52, 24:ix, 91, 366, 395, 26:146, 198n, 224n, 233, 245, 261, 297, 438, 32:17–19, 28f, 33:147–155, 35:ix, xiii,

179, 181n, 198, 227, 231, 236, 304, 357–411, 36:40, 107, 131, 138f, 144f, 162, 179, 182f, 217, 304, 37:31, 43f, 95, 109, 143, 168, 254f, 264, 290–292, 38:60, 95, 188, 205, 45:87, 97f, 359f, 53:13, 38, 68f, 333

German translation, Luther's 28:149, 164, 371, 35:179, 181n, 227

Greek edition of Erasmus 28:22, 30:316n, 35:231

Greek text 26:147n, see also **Erasmus, Desiderius, Works of; Gerbel, Nicholas**

Interpretation 17:10, 41, 69, 95, 209, 308f, 333, 21:xi, xiiif, 27:236, 341, 373, 389, 29:12, 22, 80f, 182, 197f, 207f, 220, 223, 30:ix, 4, 18f, 21, 54, 94n, 113, 155, 180, 256, 309, 316n, 31:349, 46:10, 26, 98, 146, 149, 172, 233, 265, 47:53, 132, 134, 173n, 279, 281, 304f, 52:41, 44f, 205f

Its nature 35:236, 357f

Scripture(s), Old Testament—1:18n, 218, 223, 232, 263n, 295n, 297n, 303, 309, 2:x, 58, 228, 237, 330, 364n, 3:31, 39n, 46, 73, 88, 103f, 147, 297n, 353, 4:117, 119, 124, 126, 128, 133, 310, 5:244, 357, 6:54, 72, 125, 184, 250, 7:10, 16, 116f, 296n, 8:186, 205, 210, 223, 241n, 270n, 310, 317, 9:ix, 6, 26, 63, 123n, 131n, 167, 11:274, 294, 13:17, 38, 48, 292, 323, 14:xi, 19n, 33, 45n, 87n, 90f, 95, 104, 113n, 170, 246, 331, 341, 15:267f, 287, 295, 299, 318, 333, 16:xi, 50, 128, 18:74, 20:41, 212, 220f, 280, 317, 23:120, 24:160, 366, 369, 395, 397, 26:85, 210, 239, 258, 261, 460, 29:20, 23, 31, 33, 38, 55, 60, 69, 80, 82f, 87, 110, 113f, 116, 122, 124, 131, 134, 149, 154f, 165, 174, 179, 181, 183f, 190, 195, 198f, 202f, 210, 223, 227, 230f, 234, 32:18f, 196f, 33:110, 35:ix, 123, 169, 235f, 252, 358, 380, 36:40, 182, 204, 279, 304, 37:26, 31, 42f, 104, 109, 144, 155, 168, 254f, 264, 273, 290–292, 323–326, 335–337, 39:xv, 52, 77f, 84f, 133, 158, 182f, 193, 254, 281n, 291, 41:51, 144, 42:89, 45:24, 96f, 200, 281, 289, 331, 359f, 373, 381, 47:132, 134, 200, 53:12f, 38, 68f, 315

Aramaic version 6:321, 32:193n, 47:179, 183, 185–190

Canon 8:130, 33:110, 45:375

Canon, Hebrew 33:110

Chaldean version 6:321

Errors in transmission or transcription of text 8:88

Frequent repetitions 9:48

Fulfillment 37:114, 234, 254, 264, 292, 323

Hebrew text 25:29, 40, 108, 211, 234, 264, 271, 273, 281, 387f, 392f, 400f, 416f, 430, 45:321n, 323n, 361n, 362n, 363, 47:132, 179, 183, 186, 261

Hebrew text, Pointing of 8:141f

Interpretation 15:191–195, 220n, 268, 269, 270, 287, 299, 318, 19:96, 110, 120, 151n, 152, 21:ixf, xiiif, 354, 27:55, 202, 236, 272, 357, 389, 399, 29:9, 151, 182, 208, 215, 30:18–21, 31, 49, 52, 54, 80n, 139, 155, 165, 31:353, 46:10, 26, 97, 107, 146, 148, 172, 197, 233, 47:126, 132, 134, 173n, 186n, 200, 52:21f, 41f, 91, 93, 126, 133, 143, 205

Interpretation, Christological 15:xif, 267f, 343–350

Interpretation, Jewish 1:296f, 302f, 313, 331, 337f, 349f, 352f, 356, 2:10–13, 34f, 107f, 311, 313, 3:299n, 304–312, 337, 353, 357f, 4:25, 351f, 392, 406, 409, 5:101–104, 6:136, 144, 170, 181f, 185, 215, 248f, 266, 291–293, 7:4f, 7f, 21, 40, 52f, 67f, 70, 187f, 198, 216, 250, 285, 8:139, 225, 239, 243, 246, 287f, 291, 303f, 10:7, 456, 15:xi, 194n, 267f, 278, 292, 319, 329, 343, 16:97n, 117n, 17:97, 373, 25:192, 34:227, 35:284n, 45:207–221, 47:127, 137, 140, 155–158, 163, 171, 177f, 192, 200, 203, 210, 213, 215, 238f, 244, 253

Liturgical divisions of the text 2:54n

Luther's translation 1:193n

Masoretic text 5:356n, 7:109n, 35:213n

Septuagint version 1:263, 4:100, 136n, 5:356n, 374, 6:136n, 266n, 323, 7:267n, 8:48n, 88, 142f, 149, 10:307, 330, 413f, 12:90, 13:x, 15:36n, 181n, 16:13, 57n, 97, 19:110n, 123, 136, 198n, 20:6, 104n, 106, 121, 131, 25:29, 121, 212, 401, 517, 27:261, 29:127, 221–223, 35:232, 350n, 37:206n, 45:361n, 362n, 51:40n

Scrolls—20:54, 233f, 35:405, 407, 409

Scultetus (Schultz), Jerome, Bishop of Brandenburg—12:387, 25:441, 510, 31:23, 79, 32:116, 34:325, 329, 41:234n, 48:64, 82n, 125n, 54:341

Scylla and Charybdis—33:17, 33f, 268

Scythia—2:108n, 20:159, 26:441, 54:474

Scythians—2:188f, 4:328, 14:333, 16:125

Sea—1:34f, 49, 55f, 66, 71, 73–76, 79, 85,

99, 321, 341, 3:18, 31, 33, 39, 89, 261, 6:38, 101, 151, 156, 223, 243, 11:31f, 53, 85f, 236, 258f, 341f, 394, 24:46–48, 51, 53, 383, 27:18, 143, 140

Sea, Depths of the—18:277

Sea, Sons of the—18:61f

Sea monsters—1:51

Seafarers—2:207

Seal—23:13, 15–19, 22, 39, 246, 370

Seal, Luther's—49:358f

Seals and letters—38:118, 121, 147, 158, 170

Search—6:57–59, 65

Seasons—2:129, 136, 208, 10:21, 23, 25, 26:410–412, 27:7, 15, 53–55, 132, 286, 295f, 331, 357

Seba—2:195, 17:87, 131, 314

Sebastian, St.—3:125, 17:78, 24:90, 35:68n, 40:279n, 44:74n

Seberger, Wolfgang—34:295, 49:158n, 167, 50:212n, 302, 54:22

Seckendorf, Veit von—25:xii

Second Coming—see **Advent, Second**

Second Gate—18:329

Second Quarter—18:329

Secret betrothals—see **Betrothals, secret**

Secrets—6:297, 301, 28:197, 199, 201

Sectarian spirits—41:80n, 81, 235n

Sectarianism—22:71, 26:44, 428f, 450, 35:xix

Sectarians—8:310, 15:43, 84, 140, 144, 155, 186, 17:96, 98, 26:9f, 17–20, 28–30, 33, 50f, 67, 87, 222, 228, 340, 342, 344, 353, 357, 396, 402, 414, 429, 456, 27:9, 20, 33f, 36, 52f, 91, 107, 29:32, 82, 30:242, 257, 299f, 43:137, 160, 162, 203, 220, 51:142, 165, 173, 189, 213f, 222–224, 232, 237, 310, 318, 322, 324, 378, 388

Sects—1:95, 150, 2:18, 269, 388, 3:17, 55f, 76, 78, 147, 229, 4:135, 295, 328, 363, 5:96f, 103, 123, 359, 6:32, 129, 230, 249, 293, 7:86n, 119, 140, 343, 8:137, 9:58, 72, 126, 186, 198, 235, 237, 244, 13:7, 50, 368n, 14:10f, 15, 23, 37, 39, 55f, 62, 68, 98, 245f, 284, 290, 293, 16:10, 30, 54, 106, 188, 202, 205, 227, 250, 297, 304, 317, 17:11, 17, 19, 25, 40, 46, 64, 96, 99–101, 108–110, 159, 175, 214, 238, 241, 327, 20:54, 156, 240, 313–316, 341, 343, 21:211f, 224f, 304f, 22:25, 53, 66f, 71, 337, 377, 384, 390, 393, 442, 465, 524, 23:56, 79, 120, 122n, 135, 157, 187, 194, 225, 249, 262, 272, 276, 279f, 290f, 378, 408, 24:142, 144, 153, 161, 168, 215f, 221–223, 231, 235–237, 246, 271, 292–294, 358, 368, 400, 26:14, 31, 47, 71, 97, 176, 195, 198, 347, 425f, 429, 443, 450, 452f, 455, 27:19, 43, 47, 60, 62, 91, 99, 101, 107, 109, 114, 117, 148, 265, 280, 370, 29:8f, 34, 83, 87, 96, 30:31, 169, 171–173, 175, 225, 228, 244, 257n, 259, 283, 287f, 295, 301, 319, 34:xv, 13, 35:80, 143, 145, 36:73n, 159, 264, 337, 353, 37:13, 16f, 41f, 149f, 163, 170, 194, 230, 323, 333, 363, 38:178, 229, 41:66n, 218n, 45:79, 88n, 50:183

Secular duties—3:202–204, 211

Secular life—28:17, 31, 92, 123–125, 41:68, 122, 195–197, 331, see also **Callings**; **Government**; **Stations in society**

Secular order and the church—25:109

Secular sanctity—6:166, 297

Secularism—44:xiv

Secularity, Sacred—13:41f, 146, 44:xvi

Security—4:36, 104, 9:169, 194, 298, 10:351–353, 361, 370, 373f, 387, 389, 392, 16:66, 246, 20:176, 312, 21:193f, 25:20, 142, 263, 267f, 28:61f, 105, 165, 200, 325, 35:63, 92, 200, 256, 268, 281, 290, 47:40, 105, 111, 119, 51:15, 20, 24f, 31, 128

Sedition—4:79, 6:27, 52, 56, 13:44f, 50, 26:48, 97, 443, 450, 28:308f, 362, 32:147f, 37:137, 150, 47:19, 51

Seduction—28:67, 75

Sedulius—15:274n

Seeberg, Reinhold—*History of Doctrines*, Grand Rapids, 1952 35:59n

Lehrbuch der Dogmengeschichte, III, 5th ed., Basel, 1953 12:345n

Seeburg—49:106n

Seed(s)—1:36f, 53f, 72f, 91, 93, 126, 166, 184, 205, 219, 291, 293, 325, 2:23, 27, 53, 56f, 66, 97, 100, 103f, 120, 178, 265, 283f, 287, 304, 317, 359, 378, 382, 390, 3:12–15, 18–21, 24, 28, 33, 35–37, 42f, 45f, 57, 60, 66, 81f, 89f, 95, 100, 123, 134, 143f, 151, 163, 177, 200, 206, 208, 215, 220, 227, 281, 327, 338f, 346, 353, 359, 6:72f, 116, 155, 235, 258, 283f, 289, 295, 338–340, 343, 9:221, 225, 248, 11:385, 513, 16:182, 196, 25:19, 38f, 81, 279–281, 28:173–178, 186, 188, 195, 37:16, 59, 65, 68f, 335

Seed, Abraham's—2:236f, 254, 257–262, 264f, 271, 280, 283, 288, 294, 300–302, 359, 361, 21:352–354, 23:378, 385, 395f, 404f, 412, 415, 417–419, 25:38, 80, 41:51, 119, 45:197f, 203f,

213, 219, 47:74, 86f, 96f, 140–152, 167, 231, 258, 260, 264, 300–302
Seed, Holy—16:76
Seed, Satan's—2:213
Seed, The blessed—see **Seed, The promised**
Seed, The promised—1:180, 221, 225, 237, 241–243, 245, 248, 252, 265f, 268–271, 273, 285, 290–292, 294, 300, 305, 311, 314, 328, 330, 332–335, 341f, 347f, 2:10, 12, 31, 52f, 55, 63f, 71, 144, 162, 164, 144, 178–180, 235f, 247, 278, 281, 303, 391, 396, 398, 3:11, 42, 94, 111–113, 152, 175, 225, 340, 4:27, 73, 92, 109, 152, 166f, 237f, 241, 265, 326, 368, 376, 5:23, 226, 328, 334, 338, 350, 7:36, 221, 365, 8:143, 12:39, 361f, 13:90, 261, 15:24, 317f, 323f, 22:17, 31, 33, 70, 93, 154, 340, 420, 427, 430, 432, 449, 455, 460, 495, 23:414, 28:98, 34:303, 35:359f, 45:201, 203, 206, 47:219–221, 52:128
Seed of the woman—1:188, 190, 193–197, 199, 217, 220, 229, 234, 256, 259, 265, 285, 310, 328, 330f, 340, 346f, 349, 351f, 3:19, 39, 92, 25:314, 47:219–221
Seedtime—2:136
Seehofer, Arsacius—49:313n
Seeing—11:271f
Seeing God—21:37
Seeking—10:247, 11:417, 439f, 17:375–377, 382, 412, 25:29, 86, 223–225, 246, 251–254, 260, 263, 267, 275, 352
Seeking God—25:224f, 252
Seers—9:175, 19:157, 193
Sees, Episcopal—11:291, 544–548
Sehling, Emil—51:136
Die evangelischen Kirchenordnungen des XVI. Jahrhunderts, Leipzig, 1902 45:164n, 166n, 53:173
Seidemann, Johann Karl—54:xvi, 253
Dresden Psalter 11:40n, 42n
Seidler, Jacob—44:245n
Seir, Mt.—4:394, 6:118, 177f, 285, 289–291, 294–297, 302, 305f, 6:303, 9:15f, 27, 34f, 304, 14:244, 16:173
Sela—18:195
Selah—7:154, 9:34 11:144, 13:37, 19:142n
Seleucia—2:200, 202
Seleucus (King of Syria)—35:309
Seleucus Philopator—7:204
Self-accusation—10:27, 31f, 237f, 240, 368, 25:15, 423
Self-castigation—24:222
Self-communion—see **Lord's Supper**
Self-confidence—26:150, 27:132
Self-control—27:373, 378, 28:26f, 30:40, 156f
Self-defense—21:106–108, 110f, 45:275, 278, 46:91, 120f, 47:8, 19f, 54, 49:257f
Self-denial—4:39, 25:411, 27:14
Self-discipline—45:319
Self-estimation—25:218
Self-examination—21:218, 235–237, 36:264, 37:347
Self-glorification—16:204, 25:202
Self-justification—27:348
Self-love—14:149, 25:381f, 29:24, 69, 119, see also **Incurvatus in se**
Self-made spirituality—13:271
Self-praise—23:320, 322f, 328
Self-punishment—32:33f, 65
Self-reliance—16:216, 279
Self-righteous persons—4:159, 5:210, 6:44, 123, 9:108, 214, 12:285, 338, 343, 397, 16:14, 32, 57, 64, 152, 171, 231, 244, 17:5, 16–18, 18n, 22, 25f, 31, 50, 64, 67, 108, 110–112, 225, 251f, 262, 275, 27:14, 25, 53, 87, 321
Self-righteousness—7:356, 360, 14:81, 21:132f, 220, 263f, 268, 270f, 23:70, 24:52, 25:3, 28, 61, 82, 86, 135, 168, 174, 193, 244, 293, 352, 383, 405, 510f, 26:459, 27:17f, 146, 185, 41:199, 44:304f
Self-satisfaction—25:136, 159, 222, 226, 428, 509f
Self-will—46:12, 18, 69, 84
Selfishness—18:270, 23:5
Selflessness—44:106n
Semen—1:83f, 126f, 4:70, 173, 330, 8:210
Semi-Pelagianism—3:67n, 34:209n
Semiramis, Queen—19:215
Semitic—22:421n
Senate—3:233
Senators—3:253
Seneca—3:287, 4:180, 242, 10:421, 41:247n, 50:145, 51:10
Ad Lucilium epistulae morales 7:34n
De Ira 19:126
Epistles 2:319n, 3:254, 4:242n, 13:222, 25:361, 48:351n
Hercules 2:348n
Medea 19:125n
Quaestiones naturales 1:43n
Troades 34:242n
Senfl, Louis—49:426f, 53:337
Senility—2:169, 3:268
Sennacherib—2:202, 4:29, 6:41, 13:130, 213, 16:24, 97n, 108f, 111, 142, 272, 292, 308, 319, 321, 330f, 17:306, 18:64, 102, 289, 293–295, 298, 300,

22:92, 210, 23:257, 35:276, 326, 36:227, 47:203
Sense experience—37:xii, xviii, 29, 47–51, 53n, 55, 68–71, 76f, 80, 82–102, 109–111, 130, 133–137, 139–141, 202, 208, 215f, 221, 238f, 278–283, 298–300
Sense organs—3:10
Senses—11:8, 15, 127, 28:98f, 107, 111, 174, 189, 191, 196
Senses, Five—12:169
Sensuality—27:249, 321
Sent—20:195, 248f
Sent, To be—25:91f, 413f
Sentences—see **Peter Lombard**
Sententiarum libri quatuor—see **Peter Lombard**
Separation—25:116, 144, 380, 436, 498f
Separation of Church and State—41:226f, 248
Sephar, Mt.—2:207
Septuagint version—see **Scripture(s), Old Testament**
Sepulchers—7:291–294, 300, 303, 8:35, 140, 157, 314, 318, 16:179
Sepulchre, Holy—36:32
Sequences—53:21, 24, 25, 240, 252, 263, 265, 274
Sequestration—49:30n, 46f, 47n, 134n, 135
Serah—8:84, 86
Seraphim—1:235f, 3:123, 16:69–72, 76f, 20:59f, 22:338
Serapis—1:249
Serfdom—8:123, 23:404
Serfs—46:12n, 39, 51n
Sergius Paulus—12:259, 26:205, 35:364
Sermon on the Mount—5:9n, 21:xviif, 3–294, 24:ixf, 45:238, 240
Sermones in cantica—see **Bernard of Clairvaux, St.**
Sermons—6:86, 116, 127, 170, 228, 233, 279, 363, 13:5, 12, 14:8, 23, 81, 101n, 131, 266, 296, 299n, 307, 20:21, 127, 157, 320, 35:x, 93, 105, 161f, 36:56, 331, 333, 37:67, 166, 370, 38:xix, 103, 177, 189, 199, 40:12, 142, 41:173, 45:376, 46:172, 210n, 236, 49:163f, 411, 52:22, 53:xiv, xvi, 11, 13, 24, 26, 38f, 53, 66f, 78, 80, 82, 111, 153, 304, see also **Preaching**
Sermons, Luther's—see entire Vols. 51 and 52
Note: His commentaries on Genesis and on the Gospel according to St. John were originally sermons or sermonic lectures
See Table of Contents of Vols. 31–47 for occasional sermons included with other writings
Serpent, Brass—42:104, 142, 150
Serpent, Brazen—40:87
Serpent, Flying—16:254
Serpent's head—41:119, 178, 314
Serpents—1:63, 66, 76f, 115, 141, 144–146, 149–152, 155, 171, 177–179, 181–184, 186–188, 192f, 196–198, 200, 207, 215, 217–221, 229, 237, 242, 269, 275, 281, 285, 300, 305, 326–328, 334f, 344, 350f, 2:27, 71, 135, 151, 157, 163, 204, 229, 265, 3:347, 4:95, 97, 102, 109, 129, 137, 175, 242, 311, 344, 374, 5:58, 153, 366, 6:209, 228, 7:14, 8:76, 168, 236, 243, 251, 281f, 326, 9:137, 206, 295, 297, 10:268, 11:551, 13:186, 15:317f, 339, 16:211, 303, 17:106, 215, 394, 23:291, 24:84, 267, 343, 411, 26:37, 188f, 192, 246, 287, 307, 332f, 357, 453n, 27:5, 11, 262, 30:95, 100, 115, 263, 311, 35:83, 369, 45:201–203, see also **Asps**; **Vipers**
Serpents, Fiery—2:136, 22:337, 42:104
Serug—3:233, 319
Servants—2:176, 198, 252, 279f, 336f, 340, 373, 383, 389, 396, 399, 6:6, 66–68, 70, 98, 121, 169, 13:180f, 196, 213, 26:12, 14, 28:236, 361–363, 29:4f, 10, 25f, 60–63, 72, 101, 232, 35:71, 391, 37:364f, 42:78, 155, 46:39, 80, 114, 240, 265, 316, 51:148f, 151, 157, 160f, 348, 54:270, 337
Servants and masters—30:82f
Servants of God—19:69, 25:3f, 6, 110, 138–141, 481
Servants of God, Duties of—25:138f
Servetus, Michael—2:18, 47:116, 54:32
Service—3:118, 186f, 190, 197f, 203, 218, 245, 253, 270f, 273f, 279, 284, 25:106, 141f, 457, 29:25, 60f, 63f, 72, 93, 121, 184, 35:17, 215
Service, Christian—45:126
Serving God—see **God**—Serving Him
Serving others—25:509, 38:108, 109f, 180, 224, 230, 304, see also **Neighbor, Loving and serving one's**
Servitude—2:174, 176, 186, 204, 341, 5:143, 150, 292, 294, 305, 312f, 324, 333, 337, 339, 341, 358, 364f, 370, 385, 6:3, 6, 8, 16, 26, 35, 38, 55, 29:61, 100f, 103
Servus servorum Dei—2:198n, 3:188n
Seth—1:241, 282, 291, 299, 324, 326–328, 332, 334, 337–341, 342, 345, 347, 351, 2:28f, 114, 178, 180, 209, 228, 235, 3:96, 6:281

Setzer, John—49:33n
Seven, Number—3:141, 4:87n, 11:524–527, 29:200
Seven wonders of the world—19:208
Seventeenth Sunday after Trinity—23:337n
Severin, St.—31:28, 178, 39:39n
Severus, Sulpitius—*De vita beati Martini* 7:272n
Sex—1:104, 115f, 118, 134, 137, 151, 199f, 202, 240, 2:29–31, 356, 377, 9:74, 219, 224, 248, 14:288, 15:130, 132, 25:13, 26:367, 385, 27:67, 69, 281, 288f, 52:259f, 268, 273, 54:161, 324, 422
Sex, Extra-marital—21:85, 46:282, 284f, 290f, 293, 296f, 320
Sex, Old Testament view of—48:285, 334
Sex in marriage—25:320
Sex roles—9:219f
Sexes—see **Male and female**
Sexual abstinence dangerous—45:45
Sexual desire—4:6, 333, 5:323f, 7:80, 83f, 13:109, 114, 21:86, 89, 99, 26:216, 418, 420, 27:13, 48, 67–71, 73f, 78, 80f, 87, 89, 92, 96, 39:33f, 297, 44:8, 394, 45:20, 45f, 52:260f, 268, 273
Sexual intercourse—see **Coitus**
Sexual offenses—9:223, 229
Sexual perversions—46:198
Sexual sins—25:13, 165f
Sexual union—see **Coitus**
Sexuality—2:18n, 39:297
Sforza, Francesco II, Duke of Milan—8:103, 34:272
Shade—10:338, 342
Shadows—10:111, 338, 11:98, 311, 313, 357f
Shallum, King—8:233, 18:47
Shalmaneser—16:96, 108, 35:326
Shame—4:146, 149, 232, 235, 10:31, 79, 241, 363, 386f, 392, 18:50, 19:127, 130, 221, 25:162–166, 400, 402f, 509f, 521–523
Shame, Being put to—11:439
Shamelessness—9:232f, 249
Sharezer—16:331, 20:77
Sharon, Plain of—16:286, 300, 17:382f
Shaul—6:309, 8:85f, 88
Sheba—6:308, 10:412f, 14:53, 18:116, 52:160, 163
Sheba, Queen of—3:112
Shebaniah—16:175
Shebat—20:13
Shebet—see **Scepters**
Shebna—16:178–180
Shechem—2:244, 282, 353, 5:84, 6:181–184, 187f, 223f, 247, 257, 264, 340, 345f, 7:4f, 7f, 24, 8:85, 114, 197f, 220, 303, 10:280, 282, 285, 294f, 342, 421, 11:394, 13:154, 14:227, 22:421n, 30:260, 40:87, 47:187
Shechem (personal name)—6:190, 193–197, 200, 207f, 220, 276, 305
Shechemites—2:285f, 4:15, 5:297, 6:201f, 210f, 213–215, 219, 221f, 227, 238, 246f, 282, 316, 340, 345f, 362, 392, 7:7, 125, 8:114, 151, 221, 225, 227, 295
Sheep—1:81, 132, 186f, 255, 312, 2:66, 74, 88, 116, 137f, 144, 324, 336, 390, 3:30, 78, 80, 197, 240, 347, 356, 4:46, 84–86, 114, 138, 246, 276, 332, 356, 382, 5:30, 47, 107, 115, 152, 269, 289, 368, 371, 374, 376f, 379f, 383f, 6:4, 14, 24, 68, 119, 175f, 7:6, 46, 300, 339, 347, 8:53, 63, 75, 94, 105, 162, 271, 302, 306, 9:150f, 174, 11:85, 534, 19:184, 20:106f, 118, 120, 299, 301, 23:92, 125, 132, 24:17, 46, 82, 26:177, 430, 27:164, 236, 304, 308, 29:15, 17, 147, 169, 30:86, 134–137, 209, 286, 314
Sheep, Feeding Christ's—41:xiii, 46f, 85f, 302, 344–347, 349–358
Sheep, Tending the—32:71–73, 87
Sheep and goats—12:153, 171
Sheep's clothing—21:251, 253f, 257, 318f
Sheep-gate pool—11:286
Shelah—3:319, 323, 338, 4:3, 303, 343, 359, 384f, 7:6, 9, 22, 27–29, 39, 43, 45, 47
Shells—3:149–151
Shem—1:355–358, 2:25, 58, 71, 170, 175f, 178–181, 183–187, 193–198, 201f, 204, 206, 208f, 212, 217, 219, 225, 228–232, 234–236, 240, 242, 249–251, 277, 281, 283, 358, 368, 371, 381, 383, 393, 3:3, 97, 233f, 319, 321, 323f, 338, 4:3, 15, 24, 98n, 99–101, 139, 230, 281, 303f, 343, 359f, 362–365, 384f, 388, 5:15, 20, 101, 242, 252, 262, 281, 283, 368, 6:89, 255, 288, 308, 7:15, 21, 125, 8:76, 13:310, 16:171, 17:413, 22:33, 36, 47:144, 147f, 52:174
Shem Hamphorus—3:296n, 47:256, see also **Luther, Martin, Writings of; Schamhaperes**
Shema—4:55n
Sheol—3:348, 4:50, 95, 6:120, 142, 218, 292, 363, 405, 407n, 7:232, 246, 249, 291–293, 374, 8:5, 10, 315, 10:81, 11:175n, 16:63, 140, 197, 214, 228, 337, 343, 345, 18:71, 100, 30:51, 172, 208

Shepherds—1:318, 2:34, 215, 306, 3:78, 270, 285, 318, 4:47, 245, 253, 280, 5:55, 65, 81, 87, 200, 281, 283, 368, 6:67–70, 74, 79, 102, 121, 205, 7:24f, 37f, 40f, 45, 47, 158, 166f, 179, 185, 192, 207, 209, 346f, 8:15, 19f, 35, 41, 48, 55, 57, 59–62, 64, 99, 102–105, 107, 109f, 116, 162, 164, 228, 233, 272, 282, 299f, 306, 16:202, 262, 305, 347, 20:107, 117f, 120, 127, 148–150, 168, 301, 311, 313, 320f, 21:320, 24:17, 108, 26:191, 424, 430, 27:164, 236, 304, 337f, 380, 383, 398, 30:86, 134f, 137, 209, 286, 314, 35:148, 150, 37:82, 90, 94, 52:32f, 171
Sherman, Franklin—52:xiin
author of Introduction to Vol. 47 and presumed author of introductions to individual writings included in Vol. 47
editor of Vol. 47
Shields—18:25
Shiloah—27:163, 330
Shiloah, Waters of—14:337, 16:89, 91
Shiloh—5:162, 6:72, 162, 183f, 265, 8:240, 242, 245–247, 249, 252, 254–256, 258, 261, 264f, 272, 274, 277, 286–288, 292, 304, 307f, 310, 313, 9:50, 20:30, 192, 27:163, 45:213, 214n, 216n, 217–220, 46:308, 47:73n, 178–192, 197, 220, 232, 250, 298, 300
Shimei—19:227, 20:330, 27:262, 33:178
Shinar—2:199f, 205, 217, 16:126, 20:59, 61, 245
Ship of Fools—see **Brant, Sebastian**
Ships—2:66, 68, 147, 16:158, 27:18, 29
Shipwreck—3:290, 7:235, 334, 27:18, 62, 28:253f, 366
Shittim—18:122, 259
Shoes—3:130, 10:284, 297, 463, 23:403f
Shoots—24:201, 225, 342
Shoulders—10:280, 285f, 295, 421
Showbread—18:394, 395n
Shrines—46:142f
Shrove Tuesday—30:53, 32:31
Shrovetide—22:123, 281, 23:254
Shrubs—1:83
Shua—7:3, 6
Shulammite—15:248
Shultan—see **Scepters**
Shunammite—4:213, 7:370
Shur—3:61, 318
Si papa—see **Canon Law**
Sibyl, Cumaean—4:403n
Sicilian tyrants—14:317
Sicily—4:202n, 31:199n, 34:345, 41:41n, 200
Sick, Communion of the—54:407
Sick, Visitation of the—34:53
Sick man—25:202f, 260, 263, 307, 336, 340f, 350, 433
Sickingen, Francis von—42:xi, 43:70, 45:58n, 48:163n, 169n, 174n, 205n, 216n, 230n, 244f, 247n, 254, 49:23, 43n, 231, 54:217
Sickness—1:113, 207, 352, 2:118, 136n, 314, 320, 379, 3:5, 156, 224, 4:5, 59, 76, 241, 290, 336, 23:12f, 131, 405, 51:171, 173, 180, 192, 374, see also **Diseases**
Sicut universitatis Conditor—see **Bulls, Papal**; **Innocent III, Pope**
Sidon—2:194, 204f, 8:273f, 277, 291, 16:182–184, 27:288, 34:170, 192, 47:208
Sidonians—26:436, 27:315
Siggins, Ian—translator of *Lectures on the Song of Solomon* 15:191–264
Sight, Physical—37:20, 29, 47, 49, 55f, 59, 61, 65, 76f, 90, 92, 94, 123f, 134f, 207f, 214, 217, 222, 224, 234, 277f, 292, 298–300, 337
Sight, Spiritual—37:56, 61, 90, 92, 94, 111, 137
Sigismund I, King of Poland—41:183, 49:77n
Sigismund, Emperor—13:173, 34:236n, 41:267n, 268, 44:194n, 47:18n, 48:189, 54:220
Sign of Christ (Isaiah)—45:206–208, 211
Sign of Jonah—19:102
Signification—37:xiif, 16n, 34n, 35–39, 115, 135n, 170–175, 253–259, 264f, 274f, 326, 335, 349, 351–354, 38:38, 240n
Signs—2:144–149, 255, 259, 376, 3:17, 29–32, 38, 70, 86f, 90, 93, 97, 99, 101, 105–108, 110–114, 116f, 123–126, 129, 131, 134–136, 143, 145f, 150, 156, 166, 300, 337, 4:105, 125–127, 137, 145f, 178, 239f, 261–263, 326, 360, 374–377, 406, 6:33, 128, 130, 233f, 10:15f, 30, 259, 285, 438–440, 16:83f, 88f, 168f, 255, 260, 302, 325f, 336, 344, 18:107, 375, 19:102, 121, 192f, 20:67f, 83, 100, 127, 208, 222f, 230, 240, 253, 320, 22:420, 464, 479, 23:10, 29f, 32, 113f, 259, 343, 398, 24:75f, 122, 146, 252, 255, 263, 273, 275, 294, 368f, 371, 25:37, 124, 396, 398, 477, 517, 26:14, 204, 296, 374f, 379, 27:235, 29:11, 112, 124f, 130, 30:22, 169, 195, 205, 292, 297, 310, 32:15, 78, 35:x, xiii, 14, 49, 51, 60f, 86, 91, 194, 36:43f, 174, 192f, 198,

37:xix, 49n, 77, 104–106, 109, 112, 126n, 135n, 141, 164, 174, 188, 253–255, 274n, 294n, 309, 323–326, 333–339, 345, 38:22, 34, 55, 62, 103, 117, 121, 134f, 185n, 195, 41:170, 173, 46:18n, 19, 26, 35, 43, 48:155, 49:216, 51:179, 328, 52:154f, 168
Signs, External—12:352, 35:49
Signs, Visible—13:272
Sihon—2:259
Sihon, King—9:27, 35f, 13:378, 16:154, 19:142, 233
Siirala, Aarne—47:xi, 133, 52:xiin
"Luther on the Jews" in *Lutheran World*, XI, 3 (July 1964) 47:133n
Silas—26:452, 27:163
Silence—3:200n, 10:128, 183f, 249, 313, 18:180, 20:202f, 25:234, 46:122n, 48:37, see also **God**—His silence before the Lord 25:234
Silesia—2:136, 202, 16:308, 38:288, 294n, 48:143n, 230, 49:141, 147, 148f, 284n, 50:99
Silesians—see **Schwenkfeld, Caspar von, and Krautwald, Valentine**
Siloam—18:219, 27:163f, 28:159, 260
Siloam, Tower of—9:102, 24:14, 42:133
Silvanus—7:366, 15:177, 44:382n
Silver—2:279, 324f, 329–331, 334, 395, 3:190, 199, 359, 4:92, 103, 201f, 211, 229, 260, 275f, 287, 397, 6:49, 238f, 7:97, 184, 231, 268, 286, 297, 8:123, 230, 238, 245, 256, 280, 10:102f, 332, 335, 16:22, 24, 34, 61, 24:83f, 90, 177, 26:32, 177, 27:49, 51, 55, 122, 171
Simeon—4:14, 5:304, 318, 337, 340, 6:196, 201f, 210–212, 215f, 218f, 242, 246, 316, 318, 320, 325–329, 337, 342, 346, 366f, 372f, 377f, 388, 390, 392–394, 404, 7:4, 11, 57, 231, 256, 259f, 264–266, 282, 284, 287–289, 291, 310, 313, 317, 322, 325f, 334, 361–363, 367, 376, 8:49–52, 55, 64, 70, 85, 91, 104, 114, 151, 154f, 170, 197, 204, 207, 215–224, 226–228, 231, 233, 281, 284, 307, 323, 325, 9:258, 308, 13:154
Simeon, St.—2:217, 3:70, 120, 7:202, 11:163, 474, 16:332, 17:63, 338, 20:291, 22:17, 76, 28:305, 37:82, 90, 94, 131, 39:133, 46:64, 52:102–112, 114f, 125, 128f, 140f, 170, 172
Simeon Stylites, St.—25:409, 28:29
Simeonites—8:219, 224, 232
Similarity—37:44, 109, 252–269, 327, 333f, 343, 355
Similes—13:102f, 105, 119f, 14:339, 16:179, 195, 29:235
Simon, St., Apostle—see **Peter, St., Apostle**
Simon Maccabeus—47:221n
Simon Magus—4:199f, 397, 9:273, 21:226, 22:108, 24:204, 27:46, 27:47, 30:247, 34:318
Simon Peter, St., Apostle—see **Peter, St., Apostle**
Simon the leper—14:151, 27:390, 42:64
Simon the Zealot, St., Apostle—27:195
Simonists—4:201–203, 205, 395, 400f
Simony—4:199–203, 205, 395–402, 407, 26:458, 27:46, 237, 31:201, 237, 34:34, 37, 242, 262, 41:120n, 237, 268, 272, 285, 337, 44:152n
Simpleton, Mr.—13:367, 372
Simpletons—9:236
Simplicity—9:221, 25:106, 449f, 30:275
Simul justus et peccator—2:166, 168f, 171f, 204, 240, 3:70, 259–261, 355, 6:18, 57–59, 102, 172, 177, 181, 404, 7:28, 234f, 281, 8:10, 259, 267f, 9:185, 10:123, 12:143, 186, 234–236, 262f, 319f, 325, 327f, 330, 344, 350, 357f, 376, 384, 13:138, 271, 321, 393, 14:141, 16:179, 333, 17:181, 326f, 18:263, 19:4–6, 27f, 45, 47, 178, 22:127, 140, 178f, 258f, 262, 270, 272, 304, 394, 23:49, 107, 146, 235, 24:340, 344, 359, 25:239, 247, 258f, 262f, 268, 332f, 335f, 338, 453, 26:108f, 133, 188, 230–232, 235, 260, 285, 376, 27:21f, 40f, 54f, 68, 71, 73f, 78f, 82, 84, 86f, 96f, 109, 227, 230–233, 237, 361, 365f, 372, 30:17, 27, 40, 47, 68–71, 118f, 229f, 236, 269, 326, 31:214, 32:19–29, 37f, 43f, 53, 84, 93, 151, 159f, 176, 180f, 188f, 210f, 216, 254, 34:152, 167, 181, 35:xi, 31, 377, 36:355, 37:233, 365, 44:37, 268, 47:ix, 102, 54:374
Sin—1:11, 15, 57, 61f, 64, 68, 72–74, 77–80, 82, 86, 88–90, 93, 96–101, 103, 105, 109–111, 115, 117f, 120f, 132–136, 138, 142–144, 146–148, 150–153, 159f, 162–164, 166–170, 173–177, 179, 181, 183, 185–189, 191–193, 196–198, 200f, 203–206, 208f, 212f, 216f, 219, 222f, 225–227, 230f, 233f, 238, 240–242, 245, 255f, 264–267, 269f, 272–278, 281, 283, 285f, 288, 290, 292, 294–296, 299f, 308, 310, 313f, 321f, 325, 332, 335, 341, 347, 349, 351, 353f, 358f, 2:ix, 6, 8, 10, 13f, 16, 21f, 26, 30–33, 39f, 42f, 48f, 52f, 55, 58–60, 65, 70, 74, 85, 95, 100, 113, 123, 127f, 131, 133–137, 139–143, 154, 157f, 160f, 167, 170, 172f,

182, 194, 205, 209–212, 214, 216, 219f, 222f, 263f, 269, 271, 274, 278, 280, 287, 289, 292f, 297, 300, 311, 316, 319, 334, 344, 354, 358, 360, 369, 377, 380, 382, 397, 3:5f, 9, 21f, 28, 30, 48, 54, 57, 60f, 63, 65, 73, 75, 84, 87, 95, 99, 103–105, 110, 112, 115, 131, 135, 141, 143, 154, 159f, 167, 173f, 181, 202, 208, 211, 214, 216, 221–224, 226, 233, 238–240, 242, 249, 251f, 254–261, 269, 278–282, 294–296, 301–304, 307, 309, 311–314, 323f, 326, 332–337, 339, 342f, 346f, 349, 352, 356, 360, 362f, 4:7, 32, 50, 55, 57, 60, 63, 68, 80f, 83, 90n, 109, 113, 116f, 119f, 123f, 129, 137, 145–147, 149f, 156, 159f, 170, 173, 175, 177, 180, 191, 197, 204, 211, 214, 222, 225, 232, 234, 239f, 242, 244, 251, 255f, 260, 278f, 288, 290, 292, 299, 305, 315, 341, 343, 350, 355, 374, 380–383, 388, 391, 397, 399, 401, 404, 5:4f, 11, 18, 21, 24, 27f, 34, 36, 39, 41, 45, 49, 51f, 62, 67, 73, 82, 85f, 93, 113f, 125, 132, 140, 146, 149f, 152, 154, 157, 164, 170f, 178f, 185, 193f, 205, 208, 210, 215, 219f, 222, 228, 230, 235, 248, 254, 256f, 263, 267, 274, 278, 282, 302n, 303f, 326–328, 330f, 6:7, 43, 61, 63f, 75, 192, 194, 199f, 206, 208f, 211, 275, 326f, 368–370f, 377, 381, 395, 7:10, 13, 16, 18f, 21, 24, 26, 31, 34, 36, 43–45, 47f, 58, 73, 79, 82–84, 91, 94, 108, 110, 113, 116, 123, 132, 154–156, 179–181, 183, 188, 193, 196, 199f, 219, 225, 227, 229f, 232, 236–238, 241, 247–250, 254, 256f, 259, 260, 263–266, 271–273, 276–282, 286, 290, 294, 305, 312f, 320f, 330f, 344, 358, 360f, 363f, 375, 377, 8:6–9, 11f, 16, 21, 23, 27, 30, 34, 39f, 42–45, 48, 51–54, 67, 72–74, 78f, 80n, 83, 103f, 121, 124, 153, 162–165, 171, 181f, 184f, 189, 193, 195, 202, 204, 206–210, 218, 220, 227, 231, 234f, 237, 244, 256, 263, 266f, 271, 275–277, 283f, 300, 314, 323–329, 331f, 9:23f, 26, 37, 43, 48, 64, 79f, 97f, 105, 109, 111, 114, 134, 136f, 139, 147f, 157f, 164–166, 170f, 178f, 181, 184–186, 197, 213, 215f, 226, 232–234, 236–238, 243–245, 250, 254, 259–261, 267, 284, 290f, 299, 10:11–13, 34, 109, 140, 142, 145, 147, 151, 162f, 235, 267, 277f, 368–370, 435f, 11:9, 13, 17, 85, 105, 250, 262n, 303n, 345, 496, 498, 513, 12:251, 303–306, 308, 310, 314f, 318f, 323, 326–329, 332f, 335f, 337–339, 341, 343, 346–348, 355, 373, 394, 13:7, 21f, 77, 106f, 112f, 116–118, 183, 242, 373, 383, 14:9, 13, 17, 25–29, 31, 54, 60, 66, 76, 82, 84–87, 93, 98, 100f, 104, 143, 145, 148–150, 157f, 160–162, 167, 171n, 172–175, 190, 196f, 201, 205n, 262, 265–268, 276, 294, 316, 324, 331, 16:3, 6, 10, 20, 27f, 30, 35–37, 43f, 56, 60f, 73, 95f, 98, 104f, 108, 121, 124, 130, 170, 177f, 215, 245, 258, 287, 305, 321, 333f, 338, 343, 346, 17:5–7, 26f, 99f, 116, 146, 148, 181, 222f, 282–284, 297, 300, 302f, 354, 359, 383, 389, 18:3, 19, 73, 200, 273, 414, 19:6, 24, 46f, 53, 57–59, 66, 98, 101, 175, 212, 222, 20:41, 50, 92, 98f, 137, 164, 205, 207, 219f, 291, 21:31, 76–81, 88f, 92–94, 99–101, 110, 149f, 152f, 189, 193f, 218, 267f, 288, 293, 327f, 352, 22:22, 111, 163, 165–167, 170, 178f, 312, 333, 354, 382, 394, 507, 23:11, 16, 18, 23, 33f, 43, 48, 57, 59f, 70, 73, 83, 87, 106f, 109f, 113, 122, 127, 131, 134–136, 139, 141, 144f, 153f, 170–172, 178, 180, 183–185, 194–197, 206, 213, 236, 238, 242, 246f, 260, 272–275, 282, 293, 297, 304, 310, 312–316, 318, 324f, 328, 334, 336, 351, 355f, 358f, 361–365, 368, 374–377, 390, 396, 399, 402, 404, 406–421, 24:21, 34f, 41, 50, 52, 61f, 64, 68, 73f, 79, 84, 90, 98, 100, 102, 105, 108–110, 112–114, 116, 119, 121f, 124, 132, 139–146, 151, 153, 168, 175, 185, 201, 219, 221, 229, 233, 237, 246, 250, 258, 262f, 266, 268f, 271, 279, 281–284, 289, 291–293, 295, 307, 315, 318, 325f, 329, 334–336, 339f, 342–345, 348–350, 360f, 387–389, 391, 394–397, 399f, 405, 407, 422, 25:3, 11, 28, 22f, 30, 32, 46f, 49, 53, 55, 60, 62, 64f, 102f, 112, 118, 135, 160f, 168, 175, 184, 213–216, 221, 240, 245, 247–249, 259, 261f, 264f, 268, 270, 273, 275f, 281, 284, 298, 302f, 307, 309–311, 313f, 317, 319, 435, 477, 506–508, 26:9f, 28, 33, 40, 124f, 129, 133, 158, 197, 269, 281, 341, 348, 352, 363, 381, 403, 453, 27:26, 28, 55, 76n, 184, 214, 226, 238, 318, 325, 328, 349, 28:46f, 69–71, 99, 102f, 115–118, 120, 135f, 206f, 210, 351f, 355, 358, 29:7, 10–12, 24, 26, 34, 43, 47, 51, 62, 67f, 77, 80f, 83, 86, 95, 97, 100, 102f, 112, 122, 130, 134, 137–142, 144, 154, 168–172, 181–183,

190, 206–209, 211f, 215, 219f, 223–225, 227f, 236, 240, 30:3f, 7, 11, 13, 29, 32, 49f, 52, 57, 63–65, 68, 70f, 80, 85f, 95, 106f, 110f, 117–119, 122f, 126, 130, 154, 156f, 164f, 170–173, 176–179, 189f, 197, 204, 212, 219, 224f, 228–237, 245, 247, 249, 253, 263, 266–269, 271–274, 276, 283, 285f, 288, 295f, 301, 309, 314, 319, 324f, 31:20, 26, 28n, 40, 45–50, 59, 64f, 98–107, 136, 179, 192, 196, 216, 225, 241, 317, 32:19–31, 34–38, 42–44, 84f, 136, 160–217, 219–221, 223–229, 231, 234f, 238–242, 246–256, 33:215–222, 248–257, 34:53, 114, 123, 155, 179, 182, 349, 35:xi, 11–19, 20n, 21, 31, 33–35, 37n, 53, 60f, 64n, 105, 134, 197, 201, 230, 237f, 242f, 359, 362, 366, 369–372, 376–378, 387, 407, 36:22, 28, 43, 55, 57–61, 65, 68f, 71, 75, 84n, 85–88, 90, 94, 102, 135, 143, 165f, 177, 181, 186f, 189, 194, 198, 200–204, 207, 209f, 215, 217, 219, 222, 225, 312f, 316, 320, 344, 350, 354, 357f, 360, 37:16n, 20, 26, 67, 96, 101, 123, 130, 133–135, 143–144, 191, 233, 329, 342f, 346, 362–364, 371, 38:xf, 79, 86f, 98, 110, 112f, 116, 125–130, 155, 158, 160, 171, 178, 184, 191–194, 204, 226–228, 245f, 316f, 39:11, 19–21, 30–35, 39, 41, 42n, 43, 45, 183–185, 202, 212, 241, 251, 267, 290, 41:66f, 74, 78, 84, 111, 127, 140, 143f, 146f, 153, 157, 163, 168f, 174, 193, 195, 199f, 202, 216f, 222f, 232, 241, 255, 273, 282, 288, 314, 316f, 320, 329n, 336–343, 359, 364, 366, 370, 45:18f, 26, 37, 45, 49, 66, 90, 97, 108n, 125, 149, 202–204, 226, 247, 251f, 353, 354n, 364, 46:20, 22f, 42, 49f, 53, 77, 109, 115, 130, 135, 153, 158, 162, 165f, 171, 193f, 198, 220, 224, 226, 229f, 255, 258, 283, 304–306, 310, 312, 315, 48:12f, 48n, 65f, 282, 303f, 367, 51:11, 62, 92f, 114, 128, 164f, 178, 200, 317, 319, 378, 54:60f, 321, see also **Fall, The**; **Original sin**; **Weakness as sin**

Conquered in Baptism—25:51, 61

Definition 25:222, 259, 264f

Sin, Law of—25:63–66, 320, 323, 336

Sin, Original—see **Original sin**

Sin, Penalty of—see **Penalty of sin**

Sin, Secret—36:86–88

Sin, Unforgivable—3:296, 33:35

Sin, Venial—25:268, 276, 507

Sin against the Holy Spirit—see **Holy Spirit, Sin against the**

Sin and grace—15:347

Sin boldly—48:282

Sin vs. natural law—25:180

Sinai, Mt.—1:172, 180, 3:223, 4:66, 129, 9:14, 16f, 57, 104, 108, 156, 176, 292, 304, 10:134, 324, 338, 343, 11:105, 282f, 343, 13:8f, 17, 19, 85f, 93, 14:244, 15:348, 16:31, 19:59, 20:246, 22:308f, 504f, 511, 527, 26:64, 130, 241, 309–311, 313, 315, 319, 321–323, 436–438, 27:314–316, 318f, 382, 35:159, 162f, 215n, 38:93, 41:39, 177, 47:89, 165, 168, 171, 176, 49:288

Sincerity—3:246f, 10:73, 92, 13:365, 21:206, 324

Sindringen, Bleikard von—50:112, 213

Sinews—6:91, 145f, 154f

Sinfulness—Outward vs. inward 25:219f

Singing—10:3–5, 42f, 344, 16:76, 19:148, 36:219, 41:137, 196, 42:60, 43:231, 45:369n, see also **Hymns**; **Songs**

Singularity (vice)—28:221

Sinners—2:41, 43, 49, 53, 66, 87, 96, 100, 154, 167, 172, 182, 221, 248, 297, 300, 345, 384, 3:26, 65, 107, 130, 134, 144, 159f, 214f, 224, 239, 243, 265, 269, 277, 295, 4:54, 57, 80, 144, 148, 159, 161, 168, 231, 241f, 255f, 315, 5:38, 86, 154, 157f, 214, 216, 6:48, 62, 75, 91, 377, 7:11f, 28, 31, 37, 44, 83, 138, 154, 197, 215, 226, 228–230, 274, 276n, 277, 280, 294, 320f, 361, 8:40f, 176, 209, 227f, 263, 271, 326, 328–330, 332, 9:3, 43, 83, 105, 111f, 157, 214, 244f, 10:11f, 23f, 29, 162f, 233, 235–238, 11:294, 494, 13:92f, 110, 124f, 131f, 373f, 14:61f, 83, 92–96, 120, 130, 141, 150, 163, 168f, 171, 180, 184, 197, 203, 288–293, 307f, 310, 326, 348, 16:11, 73, 22:280, 354, 364, 23:58, 60, 127, 146, 178, 251, 271, 274, 312, 314, 316–318, 339, 347, 350, 24:61f, 89, 106, 112, 124, 130, 141, 153f, 170f, 213, 258, 269f, 289, 292, 295, 336f, 340f, 343f, 347f, 359, 378, 403, 25:17, 206, 211, 213–218, 240f, 246f, 253f, 258, 516, 26:5, 7, 9, 29, 34–37, 39, 59, 109, 120f, 126, 131, 134, 137, 141–143, 145, 147, 150f, 159, 163, 168, 176f, 179, 205, 232f, 235, 257, 259, 277f, 280f, 284, 288, 291f, 300, 304, 314, 318, 325, 330, 339, 349, 352, 365, 367, 369f, 376, 379f, 386, 405, 412, 27:12, 14, 26, 34f, 68f, 72, 77, 170, 176, 181, 185, 190,

205, 218–222, 225–227, 230–233, 236, 272, 274, 279, 288, 303, 319f, 324–326, 329, 351, 364f, 372, 389–391, 393, 400, 29:24, 127, 184, 196, 30:8, 51, 58, 60, 68, 70, 130, 211, 228, 230, 236f, 269, 278, 280, 285, 287, 293, 296, 299, 307, 314, 324f, 36:86, 134, 199, 208, 354f, 38:111, 158, 171, 179, 181, 293n, 295, 41:xi, 316f, 42:8f, 30, 42, 70, 134, 136, 157f, 165, 169, 46:132, 172, 237

Sinners, All are—25:28, 30f, 219f, 223–225, 274–276, 302, 35:370, 373

Sins—42:6, 9n, 10–13, 34f, 38f, 43, 63–66, 68–71, 74, 76, 78, 80, 92, 100–103, 105–111, 114f, 122, 129f, 134–137, 140, 150f, 157–160, 162n, 164f, 171–175, 44:xii, xiv–xvi, 50f, 189–191, 214–216, 47:68–73, 101–104, 110–113, 148f, 168, 171, 185, 198, 230, 240f, 297, 303f, 52:12, 35, 55, 57, 88, 108, 120, 130, 152f, 157, 203, 224f, 237f, 242, 257, 260, 279f, 285

Sins, Forgiveness of—see **Forgiveness of sins**

Sirach—8:248

Sirach, Book of Jesus—see **Wisdom, Book of** in this index and Ecclesiasticus in Scripture Index

Sirion—10:134, 136, 196, 198, 203

Sisera—8:293, 9:307, 10:334, 11:129–131, 16:66, 18:120

Sisinnius, St.—10:287

Sisters—9:230, 260, 23:208f, 244

Sisyphus—26:406

Sittler, Edward V.—translator of commentaries on Psalms 117 and 147 14:1–40, 107–136
translator of *Commentary on I Corinthians 7* 28:3–56
translator of *Letter of Consolation to the Christians in Halle* 43:139–166

Situation ethics—44:26

Six, Number—11:167

Six Articles—50:30, 193–195, 197n, 198n, 199n, 200n, 54:384

Sixtus II, Pope—4:140n, 141, 41:44n, 354n

Sixtus IV, Pope—31:21, 109, 172n, 173, 262, 32:79n, 36:63n

Skeptics—33:19f, 22f, 89

Skibbe, Eugene M.—*Protestant Agreement on the Lord's Supper*, Minneapolis, 1968 38:xii–xiv

Skin—11:319f

Skydsgaard, Kristen E.—54:356n

Slander—2:168, 297, 11:388n, 494f, 502, 13:201f, 204, 414, 15:115, 163, 17:245, 297, 303, 21:41f, 49, 81, 25:231f, 26:40, 60, 63, 84, 169, 200, 218, 27:102f, 120, 29:54, 237, 30:48, 128, 35:62, 181, 217, 41:191f, 196f, 242, 45:65f, 46:300f, 52:224, 226

Slanderers—9:166, 10:77, 28:291–295, 298

Slaughter—6:106, 193, 201, 205f, 210f, 222, 16:329

Slave woman—See Hagar

Slavery—3:32f, 63, 5:313, 6:54, 74, 406, 7:20f, 54, 57, 60, 70, 74, 92, 105, 180, 191, 202, 266, 363, 365, 368, 374, 8:18, 20, 26, 31, 33, 44, 59, 115n, 119, 124, 126, 128f, 17:147, 26:9, 149, 208, 225, 346, 352, 361f, 389–392, 395, 409, 411, 419, 436, 438–440, 442, 444, 460f, 27:4–7, 9f, 19, 49, 51, 104, 201, 203f, 217, 232f, 267f, 284, 291, 314–317, 319, 324–326, 346, 348, 28:46, 236f, 363

Slavery, Spirit of—25:356

Slaves—2:21, 102, 176f, 247, 296, 361, 374, 379, 381, 391, 3:52, 55, 64f, 127, 132, 142f, 147, 162, 175, 252, 281, 334, 360, 7:55, 57–60, 62, 65, 69, 71, 78, 82, 94f, 113, 164, 178, 182, 187, 218, 330, 346, 361, 365, 367f, 9:72, 148f, 151, 232f, 237, 243f, 15:36, 17:99, 148f, 23:403f, 406f, 412–415, 417, 420f, 25:53–55, 70f, 226, 356–358, 473f, 496, 28:42–45, 55, 191, 361–363, 29:60f, 64–66, 93f, 100–103, 109

Slavs—45:133

Sleep—1:129, 214, 267, 4:119n, 277, 309, 313, 329, 5:74f, 103, 127, 215, 229, 240, 252, 308, 324, 7:65, 113, 137, 154, 172, 294f, 320, 331, 8:71f, 191, 317–319, 324, 10:70–72, 99f, 333–336, 360f, 16:171, 19:10, 57, 20:43, 223, 25:111, 478f, 517, 28:110, 200, 43:286

Sleeping—Biblical meaning 25:479f

Sleeplessness—4:17, 391, 54:306

Sloth—11:259, 303n

Sluggishness—6:165, 362, 10:53, 314, 352, 360

Smalcald—3:335, 24:ix, 47:107, 49:198n, 199n, 246, 250, 253f, 264n, 266n, 272, 291n, 54:225, 228, 231f, 238, 266, 283, 321, 374, 383

Smalcald, League of—34:148, 41:xiin, 6, 36n, 181, 183, 260, 43:254–257, 259, 47:9, 48:269n, 49:52, 50:22, 41n, 82f, 104, 108, 110n, 111n, 128n, 145n, 153n, 155n, 157f, 162n, 163n, 177, 189n, 206n, 224n, 269n, 282n, 312n, 54:271, 362

And England 50:xii, xviii, xx, 29f, 98n, 100f, 103f, 104n, 108n, 111n, 114f, 117f, 119n, 120f, 124, 126f, 131–133, 134n, 136–141, 177–179, 189f, 192–194, 195n, 196n, 198n, 199n, 200n, 201n, 203n, 204–206

And France 50:55n, 87n, 88f, 103, 160n

Meetings 50:9f, 117f, 120, 127f, 138n, 142n, 154, 155n, 157, 163n, 165f, 166n, 168n, 171n, 177f, 189n, 191n, 193n, 198n, 199n, 203n, 213n

Smalcald Articles—see **Luther, Martin, Writings of**

Smalcaldic War—41:xiin, 47:9, 48:33n, 181, 218, 219n, 275n, 49:127, 140, 177, 238n, 274, 414n, 50:xiii, 80n, 213n, 312n

Smallpox—1:110

Smart alecks—22:53, 408, 24:32, 40, 338, 350

Smend, Julius—*Kelchversagung und Kelchspendung in der abendländischen Kirche*, Göttingen, 1898 43:150n

Smith, Preserved—47:6n, 23n, 48:xiv, xix, 54:x, xxvi, 13n

Life and Letters of Martin Luther, Boston, 1911 46:209n, 51:53

The Age of the Reformation, New York, 1920 45:44n, 161n, 197n, 270n, 272n

Smith, Preserved, and Charles Michael Jacobs, trans. and eds.—*Luther's Correspondence and Other Contemporary Letters*, 2 vols., Philadelphia, 1913–1918 31:xxi, 38n, 286n, 312, 32:5n, 34:6n, 35:157n, 188n, 228n, 229n, 294n, 36:6, 7n, 8n, 39:xivn, 52, 108n, 109n, 139n, 140n, 243n, 43:74n, 46:18n, 20n, 51:40n, 49n, 55n

Smoke—3:304, 354, 7:134f, 174, 327, 10:118, 121, 11:296f, 300f, 303, 313, 315, 473, 475

Smoking flax—6:107–109, 135f, 166, 172, 218–220, 271

Smugness—2:23f, 26, 28, 38, 50f, 53, 58, 64, 73, 119, 175, 181, 212, 223, 225, 240, 256, 3:14, 174, 222f, 226, 229, 238, 267, 311, 314, 336, 4:28, 52, 56, 129, 154, 158, 241, 264, 317, 391, 6:8, 10, 24, 85, 98, 115, 159, 207, 356, 367, 7:176, 227f, 233, 236, 238, 329, 362, 8:7, 9, 324, 331, 9:273, 294, 12:328f, 358, 16:47, 49, 220, 229, 293, 324, 17:42, 148f, 151, 156, 177f, 326, 350, 412, 23:8, 266, 24:117, 25:268–270, 478, 495, 26:23, 60, 310, 347, 387, 27:7, 50, 59, 125, 30:193, 234, 273

Snakes—see **Serpents**

Snares—10:376–378, 23:350f, 25:86, 98, 353, 424f, 495

Sneaks, Religious—13:64

Snicken, Master John—32:278, 281

Snow—1:140, 144

Sobriety—25:112, 481, 30:27

Social classes—see **Stations in society**

Social climbing—21:185

Social existence—15:68f, 106, 146, 177

Social gatherings—4:251

Social justice—13:53f

Social orders or estates—see **Stations in society**

Social responsibility—52:223

Society—4:250, 380, 21:24f, 32, 85f, 99f, 258, 269, 26:7, 30, 116n, 316f, 363, 392, 27:97, 114, 30:248, 250, 45:77, 239, 46:xiv, 261

Society, Civil—9:144, 241, 12:237, 253

Society, Orders of—see **Stations of society**

Society, The Christian in—see Vols. 45–48 introduction by William H. Lazareth 44:xi–xvi

Society, Urban—45:341

Socrates Scholasticus (Church historian)—2:43, 125, 5:190, 269f, 6:398, 7:281, 25:136, 33:29, 225, 37:128, 39:144n, 41:7n, 47:117n, 54:218

Ecclesiastical History 2:18n, 26:113n

Socrates of Athens—15:132

Sodalities—34:26n, 35:48, 67n, see also **Brotherhoods**

Sodom—1:78, 135, 206, 231, 240, 341, 2:7, 17, 28, 48, 50, 61, 205, 269, 279, 315, 342, 344f, 380–383, 388, 394–397, 399, 3:x, 61, 131, 176, 181, 187f, 190, 218, 222–228, 231–234, 237–240, 242–244, 247–250, 252f, 255–257, 262–266, 268, 285, 287, 292–294, 296, 303, 305f, 309, 311, 316, 319, 324, 330f, 333, 338, 341f, 344–346, 351f, 365, 4:3, 274, 5:34, 283, 300, 6:126, 353, 9:5, 79, 226, 273, 297, 10:353, 374, 11:83, 12:34, 92, 315, 13:310, 325, 14:5, 57, 112, 18:50, 95, 154, 343, 21:21, 22:36, 108, 186, 390, 419, 423, 425, 23:265, 24:80, 270, 25:12, 86, 481, 26:24, 43, 143, 28:246, 271, 30:175, 177–180, 31:336, 34:225

Sodom and Gomorrah—6:218, 404, 7:232, 13:192, 311, 16:14, 44f, 135, 267f, 330, 17:268, 292, 19:40, 77, 89, 36:305, 38:159, 162, 170, 41:221, 243, 283f, 337, 341, 42:134, 45:44, 138, 156, 158,

355, 46:24, 171, 173, 195, 198, 254, 256, 47:15, 37, 262f, 50:279, 52:273

Sodomites—2:9, 136, 217, 224, 346, 378–380, 3:98, 140, 240f, 249, 264, 294, 296, 321, 324, 4:37f, 196, 214f, 217, 6:326, 404, 7:18, 125, 239, 16:14, 44, 36:219, 41:227n, 287n, 288, 361, 42:159

Sodomy—26:141, 458, 41:285, see also **Homosexuality, homosexuals**

Softness—25:139

Soil—24:47, 194

Sojourner—9:243

Solafideists—4:163, 167, 26:138n

Solarii—4:163n

Soldiers—3:228, 251, 4:298, 9:83, 204, 232, 13:191, 20:8, 93, 21:102, 23:254, 301, 389, 24:22, 117, 26:157, 191, 28:251f, 41:34n, 35–37, 39f, 45:87, 98, 46:89, 91, 93–98, 119, 124, 127n, 128f, 131, 134, 135n, 136, 168f, 181, 50:70f, see also **Military profession**

Solemnity—10:437

Solinus, Gaius Julius—*Collectanea rerum memorobilium*, later called *Polyhistor* 11:89n

Solinus, Gregory—22:xi

Solitary life—6:112, 123, 15:4, 68f, 89, 106f, 176f

Solitude—11:306, 54:140, 203, 268, 277

Solitude, Dangers of—3:17f

Solomon, King—1:20, 265, 272, 299, 2:29, 39, 93, 117, 143, 148, 154, 157, 218, 264, 296, 321, 3:27, 112, 152, 165, 197, 227, 246, 249, 256, 285, 334, 4:99, 213, 216, 5:81, 122, 203, 241, 252, 261, 277, 6:16f, 62, 158, 223, 265, 7:17, 19, 66, 109, 151, 162, 169, 185, 193, 217, 243, 321, 327, 355, 359, 371, 8:9, 25, 33, 52, 69, 103, 110, 113, 144, 148, 224f, 245, 254, 260, 285, 291, 300, 9:19, 75, 96, 149, 163, 169, 267, 11:89, 540, 13:104, 154, 161, 172, 189, 199, 203, 212, 305, 14:9, 65, 119, 221, 237f, 273, 327, 15:7, 11f, 22f, 28, 33, 36f, 94, 144, 193, 195f, 201, 224n, 245, 16:21, 28, 59, 62, 65, 71, 80, 176, 180, 232, 275, 18:135, 19:42, 85, 99, 20:54, 235, 280, 289, 311, 21:16, 199f, 313, 358, 22:42, 97, 188, 200, 235, 241, 247, 333, 347, 23:92, 25:275, 26:108, 386f, 27:165, 167, 28:84, 29:18, 77f, 114, 128, 206, 30:94, 96, 122f, 187, 292, 323, 34:67, 35:40, 181, 258, 262, 341, 37:56, 173, 45:26, 34, 37–41, 44, 46, 71n, 93n, 119, 124, 126, 206, 220, 223, 252, 255, 283, 306n, 320n, 321n, 323, 325, 327, 330, 332, 372, 46:65, 72, 100, 107, 128, 131, 152, 192, 238, 245, 276, 288, 47:86, 170, 173, 186, 197f, 213, 222–225, 228f, 266, 52:3f, 27f, 44, 86f, 118, 126, 161, 170, 172, 271

Solomon ben Isaac, Rabbi—see **Rashi (Rabbi Solomon ben Isaac)**

Solon—13:210

Solstices—2:92

Soltau, Battle of—41:230n

Sommerlath, Ernst—Articles in *Die Religion in Geschichte und Gegenwart* and in *Evangelisches Kirchenlexikon* 35:xivn

Son of God—1:9f, 12, 15, 18–20, 50, 57–59, 68, 77, 79, 95, 112, 134, 146, 156f, 161f, 164, 180, 189–192, 195, 197f, 200, 223, 229, 244, 253, 275, 278, 336, 351, 353, 2:28, 48f, 154, 181, 184, 195, 248, 253, 260, 265, 269, 289, 321, 344, 356f, 383f, 3:7, 22, 25, 39, 87, 92, 95, 109, 115f, 118, 124, 154, 163, 168, 178, 189, 196, 199, 204, 214f, 219f, 222, 225, 265, 268, 276, 287, 293, 296f, 338, 343, 353, 355, 359, 363, 4:6, 29, 32, 34, 53f, 60, 66f, 96, 105, 125, 146, 149, 161f, 166, 173f, 191, 196, 201, 214, 241, 244, 256–258, 281, 316, 318, 351, 358, 367, 399, 401f, 408, 5:18f, 27, 42f, 45–50, 56, 72, 142, 146, 220–223, 231, 278, 303, 310, 348, 6:52, 72f, 126, 129f, 147, 149, 185, 206, 232, 263, 311, 7:12, 17f, 98, 109, 124f, 127–129, 132, 154, 177, 225, 234f, 242, 256, 278, 280f, 285, 294, 298, 304, 328, 344, 8:9f, 12, 40, 75f, 136, 139, 162f, 165, 183, 195, 233, 256, 258, 266, 268f, 272, 308f, 320, 324–326, 332, 14:72, 328–331, 347, 15:276–278, 280f, 283, 285–287, 289–294, 303, 305f, 311, 330, 338f, 16:118, 229, 23:72, 77, 81–83, 89, 93, 101–104, 108, 111, 115, 120, 132, 150, 155, 160–162, 195, 230, 250, 260, 264, 346, 354, 357, 372, 410, 413, 24:15, 74, 84, 93, 96, 99, 105–107, 138f, 143, 179, 185, 188, 190, 241, 251, 254, 258, 269, 281f, 290, 292, 319, 325, 342, 364f, 372f, 375, 378, 380, 388, 393, 402, 25:xi, 4f, 7, 112, 131, 146–148, 326, 26:9, 11, 21, 31–37, 39, 42, 72–74, 88, 126, 133, 141, 147, 160, 162, 171–173, 175, 177, 182, 183, 199f, 202, 231f, 238, 262, 277–280, 290, 292, 341, 357, 367, 369f, 372–374, 377f, 380, 386, 388, 460, 27:5, 15, 18, 107, 136, 145f,

178, 185f, 189–191, 239f, 302, 29:24, 110, 114, 227, 30:12, 30, 36, 86, 170, 222–224, 227, 246, 251, 253, 257–259, 266f, 282, 287, 290, 294–297, 299, 304, 318–321, 327, 35:249, 368, 37:xix, 31, 62, 72, 77, 88f, 115, 137, 210f, 229, 297, 330, 337, 361f, 365f, 39:86, 41:80, 98, 103, 105, 109, 119, 129, 241, 271, 296, 308f, 312–315, 327f, 355f, 359, 370, 42:8–10, 13, 51, 107, 114, 141, 157, 46:51, 135, 176f, 219, 254f, 47:43, 110, 113, 268, 280, 285f, 52:94, 103

His death 26:90, 176, 228, 371, 387, 453, 26:90, 176, 228, 387

Son of Man—see **Christ**—Son of Man

Song of Moses—9:283, 290, 308

Song of Solomon—4:225n, 14:144, 347, 24:404, see also **Luther, Martin, Writings of**—*Lectures on the Song of Solomon*

Song of Songs—11:330, 510, see also **Song of Solomon**

Song of the Three Young Men—35:353

Songs—10:154, 208, 455, 16:76, 130, 203, 337f, 17:71–73, 117, 137f, 168, 211, 341, 355, 375, 34:59, see also **Hymns**

Songs of Ascent—42:21n

Sonnenwalde—53:54

Sons, Educating—46:222, 224f, 228f, 233–236, 241f, 249, 251

Sons for the ministry—46:229

Sons of God—2:5, 9, 11f, 20f, 27, 29–33, 37, 54, 180, 195, 224, 25:43, 71, 74, 356, 359

Sonship—22:91f, 98f, 101, 363

Soothsayers—7:110, 141f, 346, 351, 364, 9:175, 190, 16:94, see also **Sorcerers and soothsayers**

Sophia of Poland—41:183

Sophistry—26:228, 238f, 377

Sophists—1:107, 113f, 143, 146f, 187, 227f, 2:42, 72, 121–123, 266, 3:24, 29, 118, 336, 339, 4:13, 23, 58, 113, 117, 134, 7:168, 229f, 234, 8:189, 211f, 239, 264f, 267f, 272, 288, 310, 312, 316, 319, 325f, 330, 9:4, 56, 71n, 198, 277, 13:81, 14:17, 25–27, 30, 34, 16:56n, 226, 17:8, 142, 229, 18:39n, 19:85–87, 20:9, 64, 161f, 21:288, 292, 22:125, 141, 23:16, 112, 24:67, 71, 354, 26:127f, 130–133, 136, 139, 157, 159f, 168f, 172–174, 177, 189, 182, 210, 228, 230, 232f, 246, 249, 256, 262f, 265–268, 270f, 273, 276–279, 282, 285–288, 294, 307, 309, 321, 330, 334, 356, 368, 377, 439, 448, 27:22, 28, 51, 63–65, 67, 70f, 75–77, 81–83, 86, 113, 339, 370, 28:241, 29:19, 33, 30:107, 277, 31:70, 107, 32:ix, xviii, 94, 135–260, 33:16n, 27f, 34, 37, 39f, 44, 67, 103, 108–110, 115, 129, 194, 225, 234, 271, 279f, 34:184, 356, 35:367, 38:30, 32, 49, 84, 114, 134, 174, 40:207, 41:73, 99, 350, 45:82n, 87, 95, 101, 107, 200n, 213, 363, 366, 367, 370, 375, 377, 46:226n, 228f, 50:201f, 229, 251, 299, see also **Scholastic theology**; **Scholastics**

Sophocles—13:123

Oedipus Coloneus 15:63n

Sophronius—25:127

Sorbonne—see **Paris, University of**

Sorbonnists—5:9

Sorbs—4:37n

Sorcerers, sorceresses—2:11, 4:324, 9:175, 190, 17:149f, 22:107, 241, 245, 474

Sorcerers and soothsayers—41:168–170

Sorcery—21:272, 22:107, 397, 26:190, 27:85, 87, 90, 368f, 36:196f, 51:139, 142, 155, 174, 180, 321, 52:160f, 163, 180, 182, see also **Magic**; **Witchcraft**

Sorcery and witchcraft—47:131, 242

Sorrow—3:7f, 12, 14, 68, 154, 238, 305, 309, 312, 314, 324, 356, 4:7, 11, 37, 49, 63, 109, 112, 197f, 278, 285, 327, 338, 352f, 7:5, 28, 55, 110, 117, 131, 138, 194, 222, 246, 264, 280, 291, 304f, 316, 368, 371, 376, 8:7, 12–14, 15n, 24–27, 43, 47, 80, 97, 113, 157, 206, 221, 10:86, 114–116, 191, 15:22f, 28, 30, 91f, 105, 110f, 178, 16:340, 21:18, 20, 22, 24:12, 17, 29, 35, 132, 158, 166, 183, 185, 201, 280, 289, 332, 335, 377, 379–383, 399–401, 26:195, 317, 379, 416f, 420f, 426, 27:32, 65, 67, 72, 81, 93, 110f, 118, 134f, 350, 397

Sosia—27:353

Soteriology—51:44–49

Soul—1:13, 85f, 106, 113f, 157, 163, 177, 180, 185, 250, 333f, 336, 2:14, 37, 58, 73, 85f, 98, 100f, 131, 138, 144, 161, 207f, 217, 222, 262, 273, 275, 279, 296, 301, 340, 354, 356, 391, 395, 3:103, 132, 149, 168, 235f, 243, 271, 277, 285f, 300, 308, 327, 337, 346f, 4:115, 131, 141f, 153, 158, 175, 203, 206, 208, 211, 273, 277, 290, 310, 312–316, 324, 329f, 5:xii, 18, 40, 43, 62, 74–76, 88, 106, 135f, 140, 143f, 155, 190, 203, 228f, 277, 346, 7:48, 99f, 121, 128, 135, 137, 163, 174, 202,

217, 227, 237, 241, 248, 276, 279, 292–295, 298, 300, 303, 332, 364, 375, 8:7, 14f, 22, 88, 90f, 112, 219, 223f, 268, 272, 274, 276, 284, 289, 317f, 331, 9:57n, 68f, 93, 175, 189, 198f, 225, 236, 241, 245, 267, 10:142f, 11:12, 14f, 185, 435–437, 465f, 533f, 14:142–145, 151, 154, 157, 162, 179, 181f, 190, 192, 198, 200–202, 222, 233f, 290, 293, 296, 302, 323, 343, 348, 15:59–61, 109, 150, 247, 16:203, 19:127, 21:302–304, 23:23, 32, 43f, 56, 76, 107f, 116, 133, 136, 138, 143f, 175, 189, 219, 225f, 230, 232, 265, 267–269, 295, 340, 348, 352, 355, 417, 24:106f, 109, 114, 158, 171f, 174, 181, 209, 253, 255, 268, 271, 293, 313, 349, 369, 371, 413, 25:11, 180, 424, 468f, 473, 28:34, 69, 110, 133, 135, 150, 189, 191f, 29:9f, 38, 79, 110, 126, 128, 139, 153, 164, 166, 181, 192, 216f, 219, 230f, 233f, 30:26, 40, 42, 48, 68f, 86, 90, 101, 113–115, 119, 125, 130f, 134, 137, 160–162, 164, 167, 170n, 174, 186f, 189, 212, 268n, 297, 312, 34:85, 138, 186n, 211n, 352, 35:56, 61, 103, 36:31, 74, 338, 37:6, 18n, 21, 27f, 51, 83n, 87f, 92f, 114f, 125, 131f, 134–136, 138n, 143f, 211, 219, 368f, 38:21, 23, 26, 35, 55–57, 83, 101, 107, 110, 134–136, 148, 150, 158, 163, 173n, 175, 177, 179, 185f, 192, 208, 276, 296, 42:50, 78–81, 92, 99, 148, 176f, 184f, 45:105–111, 115, 147, 149, 154, 354, 386, 46:8, 23, 54, 67, 81n, 91, 93, 108, 146n, 165, 179, 195, 224, 230, 236, 303, 319, 54:297, 446–448

Perfume bottle of the Holy Spirit 10:219

Soul and body—see **Body and soul**

Soul-sleep—4:312f, 5:73, 8:318, 15:147f, 150

South—11:551f

South German reformers—36:xii

South Germany, Evangelicals in—46:xii

Southern Europe—14:48n

Southerners—10:411f

Sowing—2:129, 28:185–188

Sows—23:8, 32, 43, 116, 119, 164, 208, 210, 275, 291, 402f, 416

Sozomen—41:7n, 47:117n

Ecclesiastical History 2:272n, 27:216n

Space—6:120, 122, 266f, 15:195f, 37:xviii, 6, 215–229

Spain—1:254, 2:189, 191, 346, 353f, 3:16, 41n, 108, 168, 6:x, 128, 7:160n, 355, 8:120, 255n, 10:412, 14:209, 17:414, 18:204, 19:43, 22:386, 25:125, 127, 34:247, 37:154, 248, 38:110, 41:267, 350, 374, 46:202, 47:31, 128, 222f, 266, 272, 48:24n, 97n, 132, 150, 176, 203, 270n, 49:156, 265f, 363, 50:193n, 54:402

Spalatin, Anne and Catherine—50:170n

Spalatin, George—10:x, 11:ix, 13:352n, 16:ix, 18:xf, 20:x, 21:xviif, 22:x, 25:15, 28:294, 31:xviii, 295, 311, 318f, 321n, 32:xii, xivf, 103, 121n, 33:12, 34:5, 7, 199, 301, 325, 330n, 35:5, 93n, 127, 228, 36:x, 6–8, 130f, 229n, 234f, 239n, 37:21n, 38:12, 84, 145, 39:25f, 27n, 51, 109f, 139, 227, 241–244, 40:102, 41:190n, 230n, 42:5, 17n, 97, 100n, 119f, 123, 43:9, 44:xi, xvii, 17, 119n, 222, 246f, 45:53, 55f, 64n, 74n, 78, 79n, 138, 157n, 163n, 166n, 197n, 198n, 241n, 242, 347n, 382, 387n, 46:61, 263n, 47:8, 124n, 48:8f, 17f, 23, 32, 42, 50, 52, 56, 60, 70, 73, 76, 80, 83n, 90, 93, 95, 98, 106, 108n, 111, 122n, 126, 130, 132f, 134n, 141, 143, 148n, 151, 154, 156, 159, 161, 163, 165n, 167, 171, 173, 179, 181, 186, 188, 193n, 197, 203, 216f, 219, 222, 230n, 231, 237f, 242f, 253, 263, 268, 270n, 272, 274, 288f, 291, 305n, 311f, 315, 319, 322n, 323, 325, 337, 344f, 350, 353, 366n, 380, 382, 398n, 49:xviii, 3f, 5f, 8f, 13f, 17f, 45n, 47n, 57n, 68f, 70f, 72f, 82n, 91f, 95f, 95n, 102f, 115f, 115n, 118n, 122n, 131n, 132n, 134n, 135n, 138n, 143f, 164n, 178–180, 203n, 212n, 265n, 287, 291–293, 330n, 333f, 347, 367n, 372n, 373n, 375n, 401n, 405n, 412f, 431n, 50:xx, 65n, 97f, 141f, 169f, 53:191, 221, 295, 54:19, 195, 286, 334

Letters from Luther 33:6, 11n, 12

Span, Laurentius—20:x

Spangenberg, Johann—53:287n

Spaniards—2:189f, 5:381, 6:247, 8:95, 266, 24:271, 47:275, 51:292f, 54:229, 269, 309, 332, 338, 347

Spaniards at Worms—32:114

Spanish—54:338

Sparrows—2:96, 11:138f, 142, 150, 306n, 307–309, 336f

Spatial categories—37:58f, 62, 65n, 228, 234

Spear, Dr.—13:160n, 163

Spears—2:147, 3:191, 18:17, 118, 24:117, 137, 276, 417f

Speculation—3:275f, 5:44f, 47, 133, 216, 345, 347f, 354, 6:128, 261f, 17:8, 331 375f, 396, 25:389f, 28:60, 223f, 252,

254, 269, 290, 304, 381f, 29:80f, 217, 231, 37:23n, 29, 47, 52f, 60f, 64, 103, 127–129, 131, 138–140, 194, 214, 220f, 223–225, 261, 312, 54:35, 44, 112
Speech—12:141, 13:119
God's gift 35:163
Spengler, Lazarus—13:x, 34:20n, 45:135n, 316, 337n, 46:211, 213n, 227n, 48:149n, 184, 49:24n, 77n, 96f, 165, 204f, 224n, 244n, 245n, 246n, 272n, 356f, 50:9f, 17n, 55n
Spenlein, George—48:11f, 51:38n
Speratus, Paul—36:272f, 276, 40:5, 28n, 45:365n, 53:17, 20, 192, 232
Speyer—6:ixf, 38:7, 15n, 49:251n, 253, 50:312n, 54:473
Council of, Proposed 34:12
Diet of, 1526 13:403, 22:412n, 38:6, 41:254n, 43:265, 46:xiii, 167n, 204n, 49:138n, 153f, 189, 222f
Diet of, 1529 16:253n, 22:412n, 34:86n, 38:7, 15n, 46:167n, 204n, 49:220, 222f, 230n, 231n, 244, 248n, 260, 264n, 414n, 50:9, 25n
Diet of, 1542 50:228n, 229
Diet of, 1544 41:259, 282–285, 43:255, 50:245n, 248n, 250n, 253n, 263n, 265n
Ghosts of 49:413n
Speyer Alliance of Evangelical Estates—49:251n, 253, 413
Spheres—1:47, 126, 235
Sphinx—11:508
Spice trade—45:246n, 247n, 270f
Spices—2:65, 195, 231, 325, 6:382f, 23:119
Spider web—28:130
Spiders—1:77, 2:168, 11:202, 203n, 24:36, 205, 277, 368
Spiegel, Erasmus—54:313
Spies—7:231, 240, 243, 245f, 249, 282, 284, 288, 329
Spinka, Matthew—54:142, 372
Advocates of Reform, Philadelphia, 1953 9:130n
Spires—see **Speyer**
Spiridon, St.—27:216, 29:43f, 31:154, 35:402n, 36:158n, 54:271
Spirit, Free—11:367
Spirit, Holy—see **Holy Spirit**
Spirit, Human—see **Human spirit**
Spirit, Inner—45:xiv
Spirit, Law of the—27:235, 312, 319, 355
Spirit, Walking by the—27:97f, 141f, 360f, 365f, 371f, 381f
Spirit and body, Unity of—25:340–343
Spirit as wind—20:64, 248, 305
Spirit of God—see **Holy Spirit**
Spirit or soul—30:68, 111, 121
Spirit Versus Structure: Luther and the Institutional Church—see **Pelikan, Jaroslav**
Spirit vs. flesh—see **Flesh vs. spirit**
Spirit vs. letter—11:7, 34, 161, 195, 201–203, 215, 239, 244, 249f, 255, 286, 293, 299, 311f, 319f, 332, 378, 395, 415f, 422, 424, 428, 433–435, 440, 442, 471, 473, 477, 491n, 497f, 506, 528, 27:312f
Spiritism—28:67
Spirits—2:11n, 83, 321, 29:116, 134, 166, 182, 203, 225, 37:136
Spirits, Deceitful—28:309, 314
Spirits, Erring—see **Factious spirits**
Spirits, Frivolous—20:155–157, 223, 234, 239, 320, 346f
Spirits (dispositions), Human—38:7, 11, 21, 24, 38, 40, 55, 70f, 97, 100, 102, 120, 207, 213, 294n, 296–298, 315f
Spirits of the dead—36:131, 190–192, 194–198
Spiritual aspects of life—37:xviii, 11, 13, 15, 27, 52, 60, 83–95, 120f, 135, 220, 245–247, 284, 292f, 322
Spiritual birth—29:191
Spiritual blindness—35:62, 242, 244
Spiritual body—24:207, 28:189f, 193–194, 196, 198f
Spiritual death—27:239
Spiritual estate—45:157, 279f, 349, 367, see also **Clergy**
Spiritual fathers—6:28, 50, 72, 89, 221f, 262
Spiritual food and drink—36:44, 280
Spiritual grasp—37:68f, 87–94, 202, 221, 272, 337f, 366
Spiritual kingdom—18:12, 73, 200f, 207, 227, 241, 249, 251, 275, 380
Spiritual life—22:94, 290, 25:52, 314f, 435, 468, 28:190, 192f, 196
Spiritual man—29:162, 200, 216, 240
Spiritual manner—37:38f, 83–86, 89–96, 99, 135, 145, 201f, 275, 283f, 292, 325, 349–359
Spiritual meaning—see **Allegory**
Spiritual persons—25:327–330, 332, 335f, 339, 37:95, 101, 180n, 196, 248f, 322
Spiritual pride—21:332f, 339f
Spiritual relationship—45:8, 15, 21, 24, see also **Godparents**
Spiritual rulers—45:101
Spiritual sleep—13:15, 25:111, 478f
Spiritual struggles—12:380
Spiritual things—11:369, 378, 540f, 41:286, 310, 335, 370

Understanding of 37:7, 20, 73, 97, 126–129, 135n, 137f, 142, 223, 368
Spiritual thirst—23:267, 278
Spirituality—28:15, 19, 94, 35:59, 62, 137, 141f, 372, 378, 382, 402f
Spirituality, Self-made—13:271
Spitta, Friedrich—53:193n, 271n
Spitz, Lewis W.—39:xin
author of Introduction and presumed author of introductory comments to writings included in Vol. 34
editor of Vol. 34
translator of *An Italian Lie concerning Dr. Martin Luther's Death* 34:361–366
translator of commentary on Psalm 2 12:3–96
translator of *Disputation concerning Justification* 34:145–196
translator of *Disputation concerning Man* 34:133–144
translator of *Exhortation to All Clergy Assembled at Augsburg* 34:3–62
translator of *Luther's Will* 34:289–298
translator of *Preface to Galeatius Capella's History* 34:269–278
translator of *The Licentiate Examination of Heinrich Schmedensted* 34:299–322
translator of *Theses concerning Faith and Law* 34:105–132
translator of *Why the Books of the Pope and His Disciples were Burned* 31:379–395
Spitz, Lewis W., Sr.—indexer of Vol. 34
translator of *Against the Thirty-two Articles of the Louvain Theologists* 34:339–360
translator of *Preface to the Complete Edition of Luther's Latin Writings* of 1545 34:323–338
Spoken word, The—2:112, 3:273, 10:399, 12:369, 13:266, 14:131, 16:121, 19:8, 82, 22:48, 421, 473, 527f, 26:375, 29:200, 30:313, 317, 321, 35:123, 36:339–341, 38:24, 81, 87, 106, 157, 40:55, 52:45f, 205, 206
Spoliations—6:19–24, 31
Sponsors—see **Godparents**
Spouses—see **Husbands and wives**
Spouses, Separation of—28:31–33, 361
Spouses, Unbelieving—28:33f, 36, 38f
Spreng, Jacob—53:211
Spring—1:144, 23:398, 24:70f
Spring rain—20:106, 299f
Springtime—2:93, 15:219f, 347f
Sprinklings—12:359f, 362f, 366, 368, 373, 30:7f
Sprout—20:29f, 40, 215, 217, 258
Spyridon, Bishop of Cyprus—see **Spiridon, St.**
Squires—21:117, 135, 224, 237f
St. Louis edition of Luther's works—see index in each volume
Stabreim—53:198
Stadion, Christopher von, Bishop of Augsburg—13:352n, 32:116, 47:16n, 49:350n, 416, 50:264n
Staff of God (Psalm 23)—11:283
Staffs—20:119f, 122f, 126f, 315
Staggering—20:132, 134, 324
Stähelin, Ernst—37:xxi, 78n
Stalk—24:203, 224–226
Stange, Carl—31:38
Die Anfänge der Theologie Luthers, Berlin, 1957 31:7
Quellenschriften zur Geschichte des Protestantismus, Leipzig, 1904 31:7
Studien der Theologie Luthers, Gütersloh, 1928 32:78n
Stapel, Wilhelm *Luthers Lieder und Gedichte*, Stuttgart, 1950 53:xxn
Stapulensis, Faber—see **Lefevre d'Etaples, Jacques**
Stars—1:5, 7f, 10, 23, 30, 32, 38, 40–43, 47–49, 53f, 66, 69, 74f, 105, 127, 2:192, 256f, 305, 359, 3:10, 17f, 34, 164, 209, 261n, 5:6, 186, 222, 225, 245, 7:11, 111, 211, 332, 8:138, 221, 224, 17:26f, 153, 21:287, 24:257, 371, 25:11, 35, 41, 145, 255, 50:86, 120, 52:168f, 193, 205, 273f
State, The—1:168, 173, 184, 202f, 212–214, 233n, 240, 253, 255, 305, 4:5, 7, 22f, 76f, 82, 88, 126f, 164, 180f, 188, 200, 202, 212, 221, 245, 249, 252, 276f, 284, 287, 292, 302, 306, 354, 380n, 383, 5:6, 15, 31, 38, 106, 108, 112, 121–124, 139, 143, 155, 159, 161, 188f, 267, 269, 272, 274f, 290, 309, 333, 341f, 345, 368, 7:231, 347–349, 355, 366, 15:5, 24, 162, 191f, 200, 225f, 257
States—2:32f, 36–38, 64f, 79, 83, 119, 131, 137, 165, 167, 169–172, 193, 197–199, 253, 263, 398
Stationaries (mendicant monks)—34:261, 45:69n, 186, 318n, see also **Mendicant orders**
Stations in society—2:83, 3:62, 12:407, 13:42f, 60, 71, 131, 146f, 220f, 358, 368–370, 14:56f, 76, 17:13, 21:20, 23f, 32f, 35, 43, 99f, 106f, 110f, 123f, 185f, 214, 257f, 265–269, 274, 286f, 346, 356f, 22:93–95, 100, 140, 405, 436, 25:509f, 27:102f, 281, 29:19, 52, 64,

73, 30:6, 55, 74, 76, 82, 88, 169f, 172f, 177f, 184, 188f, 204, 206, 211, 213, 250, 35:259, 386, 388, 37:364f, 371, 41:176f, 224n, 301, 44:xvf, 46:128, 176, 182, 188, 215, 220, 226, 248f, 352f, 48:70n, 203, 205, 207f, 209n, 250, 255, 50:68n, 189n, 190n, 51:48, 150, 299, 347–354, see also **Clerical estate**
Statius—*Silvae* 2:150n
Statues—1:328, 337, 3:109, 4:35, 6:33, 49, 61, 230f, 237f, 9:82, 10:432, see also **Images**
Status quo ante—49:123, 285, 362n, 372n, 374n, 404n, 416n, 420n
Statutes—11:105, 419, 422, 430f, 436, 471, 476, 491, 507, 510, 516, 20:12
Stauffenberg Castle—41:183
Staupitz, Günther von—48:115n, 268
Staupitz, John von—5:47, 333, 341, 346, 7:159, 192, 332n, 10:ix, 13:213, 222, 14:283, 15:57n, 83, 204, 16:55n, 23:271, 25:ix, 476, 26:66, 114, 27:x, 73, 113n, 31:xvi, 37, 80, 256f, 277, 325, 330, 34:272, 335n, 35:7, 181n, 41:129n, 236, 42:97, 44:xvii, 48:5, 6n, 7, 12, 19n, 29n, 31–34, 36n, 39, 41, 51, 55, 61, 64n, 72, 86, 108, 115n, 125, 138, 153, 162, 170, 171n, 191, 268n, 359, 49:10f, 21, 25n, 48f, 51:xi, 54:11, 19, 30, 72, 94, 97, 133, 230, 320, 383, 406, 449
Steadfast love, God's—see **God**—His steadfast love
Steadfastness—25:120
Stealing—6:25–27, 31, 35f, 44–46, 48f, 58, 63, 29:100, 104, 36:205, 210, 44:106–110, 391
Steam—1:83
Steck, Karl Gerhard—*Luther und die Schwärmer*, Zürich, 1955 13:368n
Steimle, Augustus S.—39:54, 110, 51:70
Stein, Wolfgang—35:158, 40:107n, 45:79, 240n, 49:15n, 83f, 51:103
Steinhäuser, Albert T.W.—36:xii, 10, 42:120n, 126n
translator of Luther's *The Magnificat* 21:295–358
translator of *Ordinance of a Common Chest* 45:159–175
translator of *The Burning of Brother Henry* 32:261–285
translator of *To the Councilmen of All Cities in Germany that they Establish and Maintain Christian Schools* 45:339–378
Stem—24:199, 221, 224, 235, 342
Stench—8:320f
Stenckefeld (Luther's name for Caspar Schwenkfeld)—see **Schwenkfeld, Caspar von**
Stepchildren—22:97
Stephen II, Pope—44:167n
Stephen, St.—1:74, 236, 295, 2:241f, 277f, 283, 305, 3:119, 125, 4:184, 6:34, 184, 7:269, 348, 8:88, 131, 197, 200, 306, 9:125, 196, 10:68, 129, 160, 167, 11:256, 412, 13:185, 245, 14:265, 16:43, 17:395, 397, 18:322, 19:187, 20:200, 250, 22:202f, 396, 25:181, 190, 26:205, 319, 27:195, 197, 268, 271, 28:242, 258, 295, 29:81, 240, 33:96, 35:364, 36:74, 266, 342, 37:66, 279f, 39:149, 218, 310, 41:322, 348
Stepmothers—8:26, 213, 215, 9:229, 260
Sterility—7:9, 28, 33, 45, 18:51
Stern, Selma—47:61n, 129n, 135n, 264n
Sternberg, Hans von—14:xi, 4
Sternberg, Monastery of—44:185n
Stettin—49:25–28
Stewards—7:53, 107, 297, 333, 354f, 358, 22:373, 25:131n, 36:70, 82, 94, 113, 155, 192f
Stewardship—2:329, 5:260, 7:323, 17:317, 21:318–321, 22:519–520, 29:22, 32, 30:249, 31:356, 370, 45:319
Stiefel, Michael—20:x, 37:102n, 39:224n, 49:139f, 153f, 210f, 50:26f, 38n, 40n
Stiff-necked—25:198, 464
Stigmata—27:142–144, 407
Stillness before Spirit's work—25:368
Stimulus—10:43–45
Stiphelius, Laurentius—53:186
Stock—24:199, 216, 221, 224, 234, 239
Stöckel, Wolfgang—49:358n
Stoics—2:292, 326, 330, 346f, 4:273, 276, 6:254, 7:261f, 315, 345, 354f, 358, 15:127, 27:81, 396, 33:76
Stolberg, Count Henry the Elder of—1:78n
Stolberg, Count Henry the Younger of—1:78n
Stolt, Birgit—54:xxn
Stoltz, Johannes—51:xvi, 291, 197, 297n, 54:xii
Stolze, Wilhelm—*Der deutsche Bauernkrieg*, Halle, 1907 and Darmstadt, 1956 46:72n
Stomach—2:231, 279, 9:55, 174, 189f
Stone of offense—25:87, 116, 408
Stones—6:80, 137, 210, 266, 19:128, 213, 20:40, 47, 50f, 133, 148, 150, 218f, 226, 229, 324f, 24:93, 280, 310, 323, 386

Storch, Nicholas—36:233, 37:18n, 40:47, 51n, 46:19n, 51:69
Storge—6:16n
Storks—11:337, 339
Storms—1:206, 6:38, 92, 156, 162, 223, 226, 11:108f, 42:ixn
Stotternheim—48:155n, 332n
Stotternheim, Storm near—42:ixn
Strabo (Greek Geographer)—25:128n
Strabo, Walafrid—see ***Glossa ordinaria***
Strack, Hermann L., and Paul Billerbeck, eds.—*Kommentar zum Neuen Testament aus Talmud und Midrash* 9:177n, 13:230n
Strange work of God—see **God**—His alien work
Strangers—9:112f, 118, 137f, 145, 150, 157, 219f, 230, 234, 238, 243, 254, 272, 29:78, 95f, 99, 238
Strasbourg—3:306n, 9:x, 23:262, 25:472, 31:37, 32:95, 34:80n, 35:340n, 37:xif, xivf, xxf, 5, 9, 23n, 24n, 42n, 203, 38:6f, 9, 11, 13, 15, 36n, 70, 78, 95, 281, 40:63, 76, 41:8, 266n, 42:5, 45:162, 198, 47:129, 135, 48:167n, 194n, 222n, 247n, 305n, 318, 322n, 373, 49:6, 17n, 30n, 44n, 82, 90n, 94f, 96n, 100, 200, 201, 224, 225n, 226n, 236n, 238n, 251, 264, 303n, 50:3, 46n, 95n, 172n, 189n, 190n, 195n, 219, 242n, 53:53f, 193, 222f, 229, 255, 260, 271, 278, 302f, 308f
Strassburg Gymnasium—50:190n
Strassburg Kirchenamt—53:54
Strauss, Jacob—35:157f, 37:9, 11, 45:240n, 241n, 242n, 49:50f, 50n
Straw—3:149, 295, 344
Streams—11:551–553, 15:16f, 97
Strength—2:9, 174, 181, 304, 6:53f, 107f, 134, 136f, 150, 172, 189, 10:49, 250–252, 11:313, 444–446, 25:82, 110, 112f, 116, 149–151, 153, 392f
Strengthening—28:239f
Strieder, J.—45:234n, 241n, 242n
Striving, Human—15:8, 10, 14, 17f, 20, 22, 101f
Strodach, Paul Zeller—translator and editor of Luther's liturgical writings in Philadelphia edition of Luther's Works 53:59n
translator of *Christian Exhortation to the Livonians concerning Public Worship and Concord* 53:41–50
translator of *Concerning the Order of Public Worship* 53:7–14
translator of *Exhortation to Communicants* 53:104f
translator of *German Litany and the Latin Litany Corrected* 53:153–170
translator of *German Mass and Order of Service* 53:51–90
translator of *Order of Baptism* 53:95–103
translator of *Order of Baptism Newly Revised* 53:106–109
translator of *Order of Marriage for Common Pastors* 53:110–115
translator of *Order of Mass and Communion for the Church in Wittenberg* 53:15–40
translator of *Ordination of Ministers of the Word* 53:122–126
translator of prefaces to the Wittenberg, Weiss, Bapst and burial hymnbooks 53:313–318, 321–334
translator of *Short Order of Confession* 53:116–118
translator of the Collects 53:129–146
Stronghold—20:97f, 291
Struggling—6:116, 135–137, 143–145, 180, 349
Stubble—17:153, 200, 296f
Stubbornness—16:64, 248, 20:60f, 80, 116, 27:106, 108, 29:35, 49
Stübner, Mark Thomas—36:233, 40:47, 51n, 51:69, 54:455
Student notebooks—25:x, xiii, 45, 97, 257
Students—3:x, 48:168f, 214, 223, 270n, 51:49n, 292, 54:179, 221, 287, 311, 320, 353, 362, 433
Students, University—12:189
Studium generale—48:5, 6n, 7n, 25n, 28n, 30n
Study—15:64f
Stumbling blocks—7:91, 252, 357, 11:525–528, 543, 36:51, 94, 336
Stump, Joseph—translator of *How One should Teach Common Folk to Shrive themselves* 53:119–121
Stupidity—23:9, 296f
Sturm, Caspar—32:106, 123, 48:197n, 208n
Sturm, Jacob (John)—34:234, 38:8f, 70, 50:190n, 191n
Sturtz, Dr. George—50:167n, 54:294
Stuttgart—47:46, 49:414n
Subdeacons—1:235, 23:273n
Subjects of rulers—13:45–47, 22:95, 45:83, 120f, 126f, 142f, 46:39, 91, 99, 103, 106f, 110f, 114–116, 125f, 186–190
Substance—10:355f, 384, 29:111, 155–158, 229–231, 37:43, 57n, 119–120, 157, 254, 295 297, 300n, 301, 302n, 334f,

353, 38:29, 32, 48, 59, 82, 251n, 253, 277
Substance of the act—25:266, 326, 344
Substance vs. accidents—36:31, 32n, 33f, 40, 52
Substantive verb—37:65n, 255n, 256, 331n
Success—21:11, 208, 242
Succoth—6:178f, 181, 187, 14:104
Succubi—2:11
Suckers—24:201, 203f
Sucklings—10:87, 89
Suetonius—19:126n, 27:385n, 29:12, 31:208n, 41:244n
Augustus or *Octavius* 13:57n, 158n, 28:300
Caligula 13:210n
Life of Caesar 26:191
Lives of the Caesars 1:245n, 261n, 5:309n, 7:120n, 121n, 8:321n, 15:72n, 116n, 25:481, 26:191n, 34:265n
Tiberius 54:400
Suffering—3:33, 102, 4:305, 336, 352, 360, 6:268, 271, 363, 398f, 405, 7:74, 92, 111, 129–131, 133, 137, 210, 254, 315, 362, 8:8, 29f, 52, 147, 260, 319, 10:39f, 81, 106f, 179, 289, 351, 11:404–406, 13:10f, 110, 279, 333, 378, 20:151, 196, 323, 21:46f, 52f, 107f, 205, 291, 22:86, 166, 204, 206, 208, 24:13, 17, 36, 87f, 110, 122, 132, 138, 146f, 149, 151f, 163, 181f, 190, 193f, 196, 198, 201, 210, 212, 217, 234, 247, 273f, 302, 314, 334, 355–358, 366, 377f, 380–383, 415, 422, 25:44, 72, 77, 137, 177, 232, 288–291, 293, 378f, 462, 26:133, 144, 148, 175, 218f, 419, 27:101, 128f, 133, 143f, 268, 401, 405, 28:11, 29f, 50f, 103–106, 108, 123, 152f, 325, 374, 29:130, 132f, 147, 176, 210, 30:16–18, 23, 84, 109, 126f, 129–131, 312, 31:225f, 35:39, 41, 54f, 105, 251, 299, 377f, 387, 391, 38:95, 302f, 41:197, 42:61, 139f, 142, 148, 154, 163, 43:181–186, 44:79f, 46:29, 40, 52:246, 260, see also **Christ**—His suffering and death; **Cross, Christian's**; **Trials and tribulations**
Sugar—23:94, 119f, 122–124, 143, 24:113, 205, 377
Sugar water—23:119f, 122f, 125, 148f
Suicide—2:138, 7:90n, 13:257, 23:203, 361, 26:150, 195, 43:131, 50:215, 54:29
Suicide of John Krauss—49:181f
Suidas—1:87
Suits—9:144
Suleiman the Magnificent, Sultan of Turkey—34:34n, 43:215, 46:157, 161n, 49:156, 221n, 240n, 50:54n, 70, 228f, 243n
Sulla—6:331
Sulpicius Severus—*Dialogues* 30:133n
Life of St. Martin of Tours 30:296n
Sultan, Turkish—23:9, 331, 390
Sultans—14:233, 15:136, 46:118, 183n, 202n, 205n, 251, 47:80n, 180–184, 189, 221
Sulzbach—49:238n
Sulzer, Simon—54:283
Summa de casibus conscientiae (Summa angelica)—see **Angelo Carletti de Chivasso**
Summa Theologica—see **Thomas Aquinas, St.**
Summary Report concerning the Marburg Colloquy—38:12, 83–85 (text)
Summenhart, Conrad—45:252n, 307n
Summer—2:129, 14:125f, 128, 23:256, 364
Sun—1:5, 19–22, 24f, 30, 39–44, 49, 51, 53f, 58, 64, 69, 74, 76, 78, 90, 100, 105, 124, 126f, 140, 161, 236, 249, 265, 309, 327, 2:92, 107, 148, 152, 156, 192, 236, 315, 343, 354, 356, 3:50, 86, 91, 129, 184, 193, 273, 289, 292f, 316, 342, 347, 4:141, 143, 190, 192, 231, 234, 236, 238, 276, 296, 328, 5:6–8, 91, 97, 121n, 176, 186, 260, 277f, 304, 383, 7:11, 71, 99, 111, 124, 140, 143, 148, 183, 210f, 293, 309, 332, 366, 8:67, 138, 221, 224, 300, 302, 11:101, 110, 225, 339, 15:9, 14–17, 23, 58, 96, 177, 203, 347f, 18:403, 417, 21:125f, 144, 22:296, 405f, 23:6, 138, 174, 180–182, 217, 241, 279–282, 314f, 324f, 358, 393, 24:67, 92, 149, 180, 321, 359, 371, 378, 416, 25:72, 112, 267, 363f, 27:39, 57, 64, 69, 149, 28:184f, 190, 195, 263, 379, 30:37, 112, 127, 162, 181f, 197, 37:68, 112f, 277, 52:168
Darkened by sin 25:363
Revolves around the earth 1:44
Sun and moon—10:409–411, 19:143, 243
Sunday—5:137n, 23:236, 240, 27:296, 37:38, 38:317n, 41:64, 51:143f, 155, 261–265, 334–346, 53:13, 23, 38, 68, 321, see also **Sabbath**
Sunshine—2:142
Supererogation, Works of—22:51, 360, 456f, 23:359, 38:117, 41:72n
Superintendence—41:294n, 298
Superintendent, Office of—40:xii, 313f, 48:218, 220, 275n, 303n
Superintendents—49:15n, 178, 284n,

291n, 50:78, 97, 99n, 178, 218n, 233n, 252n

Superstition—1:45, 247, 249, 2:192, 213, 215, 244, 247, 250, 272, 355, 3:11, 4:239, 277, 328, 5:96, 7:110f, 154, 245, 249, 355, 364, 367, 8:21, 25, 36, 51, 172, 181, 276, 11:401, 12:360, 13:178, 16:21, 33f, 302, 17:54, 56f, 102, 140n, 141, 146, 151, 233, 271, 273, 412, 19:56, 21:272, 23:135, 24:139, 327n, 25:158, 254, 271, 485, 489, 493, 26:105, 376, 443, 27:31, 52, 54, 57f, 60, 83, 89, 161, 201, 244f, 285, 292, 296, 338, 350, 31:376, 36:88, 100, 115, 123, 221, 37:16n, 41:169, 338, 42:7, 91, 137, 174, 43:17, 30, 44:48, 46:135, 47:131, 226n, 242, 51:143, 180, 52:168, 208, 54:241, 332, 435f

Supplication—20:139f, 164, 328, 24:87, 239, 405f, 419, 29:175

Support of churches and pastors—5:260f, 6:20f, 23f, 7:62f, 164, 8:62f, 117, 229f, 11:332, 21:31, 161, 167f, 177, 192, 202, 224, 277, 22:220, 518–522, 23:152, 356, 26:104f, 27:121, 126, 398, 28:257, 335

Suppositions—38:240n

Supreme Court, Imperial (Reichskammergericht)—41:249, 253f, 256, 259

Surety—45:252n, 253n, 254n

Surgeons—1:129

Sursum corda—42:141n

Susanna—35:353f, 37:322

Suspension of grace—2:104

Suspicion—2:297, 300–302, 4:78–80, 83, 85, 303, 6:59, 77f, 83, 106, 7:241–243, 253, 276, 287f, 290, 334

Swabia—34:345, 37:xiv, 9, 244, 46:6, 17, 248n, 53:43

Swabia, League of—46:7n, 59, 49:107n, 118n, 119n

Swabian Peasants' *Twelve Articles*—see ***Twelve Articles of the Swabian Peasants***

Swabian Syngramma—36:332, 335-354, 37:xivf, 9, 38n, 78n, 135n, 139n

Swabians—6:183, 10:412, 54:310, 387

Swaddling cloths—Scriptures as Christ's 35:122, 236

Swallows—1:52

Swawe, Peter—48:227n, 236n, 267

Swearing—6:85, 9:72f, 298, 11:486, 16:165, 21:99–104

Sweat—24:206, 266, 378

Sweating sickness—2:136n

Swine—1:217, 2:36, 109, 116, 169, 270, 3:199, 210, 249, 308, 354, 4:29, 42, 208, 271, 275, 303, 348, 5:30, 33, 37, 292, 323, 363, 7:10, 8:266, 310, 312, 9:118, 136f, 16:10, 110, 23:402, 26:263, 306, 405

Swineherd—8:61, 102

Swiss—2:202, 8:133, 38:7f, 10, 64, 79, 281, 49:88, 110n, 264, 50:55, 173n, 242, 54:361, 387

Swiss dialect—37:246

Swiss Reformers—36:xii, 271, 273, 331, 333, see also **Zwinglians**

Switzerland—36:229, 38:7, 26, 57, 94, 157n, 283, 294n, 41:xii, 46:xii, 106n, 107n, 108, 48:163n, 247n

Sword, The—3:59, 132, 190–192, 232, 271, 281, 328, 348, 357, 4:34, 110, 285, 332, 6:29, 45, 164, 210, 9:74, 204, 10:85f, 94, 165, 15:85, 16:211, 17:171, 193, 18:117f, 239, 20:128, 148–150, 172, 321, 335, 21:102, 106, 110, 22:225–228, 24:9, 43, 49, 70, 80, 86, 117, 216, 266, 271, 276, 336, 417–420, 33:49, 35:405, 36:207, 41:205, 338, 45:17, 62f, 77f, 80–104, 117f, 127, 141, 258, 278, 46:xiii, 19, 25, 29f, 34, 41, 52f, 61, 66, 68, 70f, 73f, 76, 80, 84, 90, 95–99, 112, 118, 121f, 126, 130, 136, 161, 165–168, 171, 176f, 178f, 184, 186, 197f, 247f, 265

Sword, Two kinds of—30:180n, 31:244

Sword, Two-edged—29:164f

Sybaris—3:281

Sybille of Saxony—50:246n

Sychar—8:198

Sycophants—4:375, 395, 8:57, 14:231f, 234, 282, 27:130, 133, 369

Syllogisms—4:25f, 5:73, 128, 6:9f, 7:336, 17:193, 38:204, 259, 270f, 38:240f, 244, 246, 264, 266f, 269, 272, 274, see also **Dialectics**; **Logic**

Sylvester I, Pope—41:23n, 57n, 286n, 333, 354n

Symachus—10:210

Symbolism of numbers and letters—10:428

Symbols—4:87, 12:121, 141, 37:xiii, xviii, 18, 48, 75n, 83n, 141, 164, 273, 345, 352, 38:34, 62, see also **Creeds**

Symbols, Biblical—32:18f

Symbols, Religious—48:401f

Symmachus—29:233n

Symplegades rocks—36:75n

Synagog(s)—1:206, 2:265, 278, 3:70, 115, 164, 192, 4:52, 8:284, 317, 9:27f, 213f, 225f, 235, 244, 250, 304, 10:4, 12, 25, 194, 196, 225, 245, 318f, 339, 432,

436, 11:7, 11, 17, 62, 68, 73, 76, 79, 81, 92, 95f, 98–102, 106, 116f, 124, 132, 136, 152, 172, 176f, 179f, 183f, 186, 190–192, 194, 200, 203, 205, 221, 224, 238, 243f, 255, 288, 293, 330, 338f, 358, 364, 366, 370, 374, 381, 385, 394, 402, 413, 415f, 428, 437, 475f, 488, 497, 503, 509f, 521, 535, 537, 539, 547, 552, 12:353, 14:91, 93, 270, 341, 15:254, 16:186, 191, 198f, 207, 212, 249, 280, 299f, 17:62, 75f, 79, 85, 103, 191, 209, 233, 270, 337, 352, 381, 384, 18:6, 8, 20, 33, 106, 114, 246, 252, 391, 408, 417, 20:141f, 184, 330, 21:138, 22:46, 229, 277, 23:156, 408, 24:276n, 302, 350, 25:100, 129, 153, 174, 191, 336, 396, 26:52, 101, 409, 442, 27:132, 146, 190, 193, 200, 311, 317–321, 29:102, 144, 183, 200, 203, 36:58, 115, 131, 145, 219, 221, 225, 47:140, 149, 153, 156, 169, 171f, 216n, 228, 264, 267, 273

Synagogues, Burning of—47:135, 268f, 285, 287, 292

Synaxis—see **Communion**

Syncope—6:54

Syndics—49:97n, 284n

Synecdoche—1:195, 218f, 2:395, 3:360, 5:374f, 379, 6:13, 34, 50, 342, 7:213, 215, 348f, 8:84, 93, 102, 122, 196, 198, 220, 282, 286, 9:125, 214, 268, 271, 12:390, 408, 13:217, 14:113, 326, 16:300, 18:27, 51, 71, 116, 122, 166, 320, 19:16, 143, 26:24, 101f, 27:31, 139, 29:39, 147f, 30:114, 32:161, 165–172, 179, 189f, 195, 249, 34:166, 37:157, 209n, 211, 214, 302, 330, 335, 338, 346, 357, 38:30, 47, 59, 82, 40:197f, 49:201, see also **Figures of speech**

Syngramma Suevicum—49:145, 146n, 178, 179n, 414n

Synods—38:317n

Synoptic Gospels—2:337n

Synteresis—10:49, 99, 197, 11:8, 17, 108, 389

Syphilis—see **Venereal disease**

Syracuse—4:202n, 46:110n

Syria—1:89, 2:108, 204, 206, 257f, 3:16, 235, 332, 4:105, 183, 185f, 195, 258, 333, 5:91, 143, 287, 6:39, 217f, 256, 269, 7:65, 125, 8:275, 291f, 9:70, 10:412, 14:19, 16:79, 81, 96, 103, 106, 154f, 181, 211, 218, 18:68, 187, 291, 19:39f, 84, 235, 20:90f, 112, 120, 163, 250f, 282–285, 22:252, 24:80, 26:78, 27:197, 29:129, 30:185, 35:301, 306f, 36:44, 88, 174, 38:195, 41:42, 281, 291, 42:123, 45:220, 46:66, 157, 192, 202, 232, 248, 47:223, 50:126n, 229, 52:271

Syria, Kings of (Antiochus line)—35:301f, 306–313, 351f

Syria Felix—16:125

Syriac—6:80, 308, 7:188

Syrian Wars—35:308f

Syrians—3:260, 263f, 4:155, 175, 185, 284, 5:155, 279, 7:22, 163, 8:237f, 274, 287–289, 291, 293, 298, 304, 22:210f, 29:233, 46:120, 47:182

Syrup—23:119

Syrus, Publius—*Sententiae* 54:449

Tabeel—16:81

Tabernacle—1:43, 2:46, 67, 179, 255, 285, 3:163, 4:178f, 182, 5:19, 78–81, 83f, 6:33, 50, 183f, 265, 9:16, 51, 123, 157, 167, 174f, 304, 10:296, 298, 304, 338, 12:360, 20:45, 51, 156, 21:304, 29:179, 195, 204–207, 44:233, 235, 47:76, 224

Tabernacles—38:93

Tabernacles, Feast of—9:14, 154, 156f, 22:216, 23:206f, 214, 35:219f

Table—29:200–202, 204

Table, The Lord's—see **Lord's Supper**

Table Talk—see **Luther, Martin, Writings of**

Tabor, Mt.—1:236, 4:178, 6:265, 8:278f, 291, 9:307, 18:26, 20:248, 22:119, 201, 319, 340, 23:229, 35:162, 245, 48:361

Taborites—40:47

Tacitus, Cornelius—*Annals* 8:326n
Germania 13:218, 41:239n, 54:277f

Tailors—54:298

Talmud—11:75, 14:262, 15:342, 20:236, 35:284n, 45:214n, 321n, 47:129, 191, 226, 269, 286, 293n

Talmud, Babylonian—41:28n

Talmud, Becharoth—14:118n

Talmudic tales—1:70

Talmudists—47:228, 234, 236, 243

Tamar—5:91, 6:227, 267, 282, 313f, 323f, 7:6, 8–11, 13–23, 26–35, 38–45, 47–49, 51, 200f, 207, 310, 318, 8:234, 9:224, 45:23

Tambach—50:166n

Tanis—11:52, 73

Tann, Eberhard—40:383n

Tannenburg, Battle of—45:134

Tantalus—13:107, 15:67

Tapestry—3:199

Tapinosis—2:156n, 16:310n, 315n, 18:43, 26:362n, 27:187n, 286, 294, 29:42f

Tappert, Theodore G.—39:54, 47:92n, 49:xv
author of Introduction to Vol. 54 and of introductory comments to all items included in Vol. 54
editor and translator of *Book of Concord*, Philadelphia, 1959 35:xin, 38:102n, 124n, 39:xin, 45n
editor of Vol. 54
Luther: Letters of Spiritual Counsel, Philadelphia, 1955 42:xin, 43:116n, 117f, 191, 216, 51:38, 237n, 54:27n
The Lord's Supper: Past and Present Practices, Philadelphia, 1961 43:150n
translator of letter 116 48:386–388
translator of letter 117 48:388–393
translator of Vol. 54
Targums—2:380, 20:245n, 32:196, 35:210n, 45:23n, 214n
Tarquin—5:303
Tarshish—2:191, 10:412f, 16:37, 182, 17:317, 413, 19:9, 43f
Tarsus—2:191, 19:43f, 23:343, 26:16, 27:197
Tartars—2:188–191, 3:183, 4:29, 331, 5:347, 13:283, 343, 14:62, 17:235, 18:200, 22:17, 68, 75, 145, 153, 157, 197, 383, 391, 468, 23:41, 56, 24:304, 417, 26:147, 31:92, 152, 34:11, 35:271, 409n, 37:32, 367, 38:97, 113, 46:107, 217n, 218, 244, 254, 47:22, 35, 52:160, 182
Tartary—26:441
Tartu—53:43
Tassels—9:221, 225
Tatian—1:238, 27:399, 32:211, 39:210n, 292n
Tatian, Works of—*Diatessaron* 44:101n
Oratio ad Graecos 44:101n
Tatianists, Tatians—see **Encratites (Tatianists)**
Taubenheim, John von—48:163n, 316, 323, 50:215, 54:205
Tauber, Caspar—32:266, 49:91
Tauber River Valley—49:118n
Tauler, John—7:133, 25:213, 366, 368, 31:73, 128f, 178, 32:95, 48:36
Taunts, Prophet's—17:22, 33, 35, 50f, 53, 55, 59, 134, 151f
Taunts vs. prophets and preachers—19:131, 186, 216, 223f
Taurus—2:108
Tautology—2:91, 3:177, 205, 7:156, 8:224, 248, 257, 305, 14:320, 322, 334, 336, 343
Taverns—37:67, 141, 335
Tax collectors—2:42, 303, 26:35, 405, 27:13f, 383, 388, 390, 394, 49:9n, 57n, 170n, 290n
Taxes—1:212, 2:263, 4:200, 7:160f, 8:58n, 119f, 122f, 127f, 9:138f, 150, 23:394, 399, 404, 25:110, 172f, 469, 25:12, 45:109f, 321n, 46:11n, 15n, 22f, 39, 48:51f, 82, 84n, 142, 224, 393n
***Te Deum laudamus* (hymn)**—3:7, 6:218n, 10:263, 455, 22:255, 24:314, 26:66n, 34:199f, 205–207, 40:307, 41:7, 53:xx, 39, 68, 136, 138, 149, 171–175, 184, 288
Teachers—2:18f, 22, 32, 39, 78, 83f, 122, 128, 138, 158f, 161, 167, 189, 243, 259, 272, 282, 312f, 338, 360, 364, 391, 3:8, 50, 68f, 87, 121, 128, 131f, 138, 143, 147, 160f, 164, 185, 192–194, 198, 210, 217, 222, 233–236, 260, 269, 272, 280f, 284, 301, 319, 324, 326, 338–341, 344, 357, 363, 4:3, 29, 51, 127, 130, 168, 170, 186, 208, 210–212, 215, 221, 250, 254, 264, 285, 295, 331, 342, 5:6, 21, 49, 71, 73, 79f, 83, 96, 123, 136, 158f, 245, 261f, 274, 6:21, 89, 93, 165, 240, 7:37, 43, 45, 54, 72f, 91, 125, 135, 140, 142, 145, 150, 152, 162f, 167–169, 181–186, 231f, 254f, 265, 335, 355f, 8:9, 18, 20, 44f, 54, 62, 113, 119, 129, 131, 171, 186, 199, 201, 212, 219, 224, 231, 269, 271, 283, 289, 315, 9:28, 50, 53, 114, 118, 135f, 176–179, 190, 207, 215, 225f, 229, 236, 245, 273, 307, 11:3, 149, 336, 480f, 13:15, 178, 184, 16:41f, 60, 64, 104, 186, 188, 249, 261, 275, 277f, 281, 293, 17:7, 13, 40, 79, 82, 91, 110f, 126, 208, 265, 337, 22:53, 57, 60, 63f, 67, 70, 73, 78, 98f, 130, 137, 156, 209, 223, 227, 230, 233, 259, 335, 337, 351, 370, 372, 377, 385, 512, 518, 23:5, 10, 15, 20, 27, 29, 37, 56, 69, 79, 95, 98, 100, 106, 112, 165, 168, 170, 172, 193, 209, 223, 225f, 230–232, 234, 252, 269, 272f, 280, 288, 293, 319, 325, 327f, 330f, 341, 349, 373, 378, 398, 412, 420, 24:40, 46, 50, 58, 60, 101, 107, 123, 155, 174, 226, 257, 278, 293f, 304, 321, 332, 363, 410f, 25:113, 228f, 449, 26:4, 10, 46, 53, 57f, 60, 74, 76, 95, 97, 117, 142, 145, 148–151, 180, 202f, 212, 220, 224, 294, 305, 309, 337, 346, 354, 356, 372, 394, 402, 408f, 414, 416, 424, 430, 27:32f, 36, 40, 47, 52, 59, 61, 99, 116, 119, 124f, 129–132, 148, 153, 167, 174, 182f, 188, 194, 197f, 207, 244, 292, 299, 305f, 355, 339f, 345, 351f, 354,

386, 398–402, 404, 28:60, 84f, 228f, 285f, 280f, 320, 327f, 29:54, 59, 72, 79, 124f, 157, 179, 186, 192, 194, 237, 30:62, 70, 163, 167, 187–189, 205, 237, 240–242, 244, 246, 248, 252, 254, 261, 284, 287, 291, 297, 300, 313, 35:148, 401, 36:144, 216f, 222, 37:17, 67, 126, 164, 168f, 246, 38:30, 34f, 50, 59, 81, 84n, 110, 188, 41:132–135, 154, 176, 294, 307, 325, 349, 42:25, 45:363, 365, 370, 375, 46:19, 75, 97f, 112, 218n, 220, 223, 240, 247, 252f, 52:40, 212, see also **Schoolmasters**; **Schoolmistresses**; **Schools**

Teaching—6:30f, 74, 124, 186, 248, 264, 10:13, 27, 29, 38, 15:183, 229, 17:61, 92, 99, 138, 163, 180, 243f, 340, 350, 20:57, 60, 103, 121, 126, 155f, 171, 230, 236–238, 276f, 297, 300f, 333, 25:7, 106, 120, 138, 447, 472, 29:5, 14, 23, 30–32, 37, 54, 59f, 68, 70, 73, 34:77, 38:98–101, 112, 116, 117, 180

Teaching, Ministry of—2:272, 332, 25:7, 106, 447

Teaching, Office of—12:4, 220, 395, 25:447

Teachings—2:18, 23, 86f, 112, 122, 159, 161, 166, 192, 199, 210, 229, 235, 313, 327, 334, 338, 340, 3:27f, 118, 137, 164, 178, 192, 221, 230, 292, 297, 299f, 349, 363, 7:54f, 61, 72, 91, 104, 111, 132, 140, 146, 154, 193, 200, 205, 207, 212, 214, 349, 355, 16:21, 94f, 209, 224f, 251, 300, 303, 23:5, 11, 47, 51, 59, 112, 137, 201, 219, 223f, 226f, 229, 231f, 253, 269, 271f, 297, 331, 381, 30:3f, 16, 22, 26, 49, 75n, 76f, 81, 84, 94, 96, 107, 124, 164, 168, 192, 198f, 203, 209, 230, 242, 251f, 277, 287, 289, 313, 37:164, 248f, 261f, 287, 38:112, 115–117, 119, 123, 134, 141, 164, 170, 175, 184, 231, 301, 307n, 314, 41:287, 296, 301f, 307, 341, 44:235–242

Teachings, Evil—16:107

Teachings, False—21:181f, 248f, 251, 261–263, 280, 293

Teachings, Fanatics'—37:19, 110, 125f, 128, 130f, 137, 146, 164, 167, 231

Teachings, Human—52:130, 136f, 171, 191f

Tears—6:19, 23, 102, 124, 196, 256, 10:80, 200, 11:503f, 551

Tedium—25:244f, 456, 494

Teeth—10:264, 268f

Tekoa—13:181

Tekoah, Woman of—1:308

Tema—16:174

Teman, Temanites—3:96, 6:291, 307f, 18:135f, 198, 19:137n

Temerity—15:7, 39, 41

Temperance—6:188, 190, 8:120, 25:112, 27:174, 378, 30:312

Templar, Knights—45:133, 137n

Temple—4:70, 99, 136, 236, 281, 322, 373, 375, 390, 9:73f, 237, 304, 14:92, 15:75, 220, 228, 232, 281, 283f, 16:69, 71, 217, 319, 345, 17:145, 156, 263, 271, 274, 309, 315f, 321, 373, 395f, 18:142, 237, 242, 273f, 329, 344, 367–369, 371f, 374–377, 380, 383f, 409, 19:19, 20:3, 6, 46–50, 53, 72, 76, 87, 90, 107, 116f, 159f, 177, 227, 257, 259f, 279f, 310f, 21:187, 23:20, 22, 25f, 120f, 154, 171, 218, 220, 243, 245, 292, 310, 314, 319, 353, 360, 366, 369f, 378, 390, 409, 412, 24:9, 24, 160, 301, 303–305, 308, 310–312, 337, 29:195, 206, 208, 35:293, 302, 305, 313f, 329f, 331, 405n, 36:184, 222, 38:174, 176, 183, 190, 192, 211, 41:64, 80, 167, 209, 214, 286f, 339

Temple, Haggai's—47:210–229, 234, 237, 298

Temple, Jerusalem—1:95, 11:190, 193, 13:30, 37, 45:93, 227f, 321n

Temple, Jewish—47:66, 73f, 79f, 83f, 97, 138, 173f, 176, 187, 210–213, 221–229, 233, 239, 303f

Temple, Second—see **Temple, Haggai's**

Temple, Solomon's—1:248, 47:198, 213, 223, 225, 228f

Temples—2:67, 71, 98–100, 112, 179, 192, 202n, 255, 278, 285f, 3:81, 89, 101, 108, 121f, 126, 150, 188, 263, 364, 6:223, 226, 232, 236, 250, 265, 274, 7:39, 53, 142, 297f, 300, 309, 375

Temporal goods—13:15, 408, 42:99, 158

Temptation—1:95, 144–147, 149, 152f, 156, 158, 160f, 163, 168, 220, 229, 267, 281, 350, 2:7, 48, 104, 106, 165, 216, 278, 282, 290, 335, 3:6, 42, 172, 278, 288, 307, 4:57, 94, 108, 126, 295, 323, 389, 5:207, 215, 6:11, 37–40, 90, 95, 99, 101, 104, 110, 115, 125, 131, 133, 135, 162f, 179f, 234, 241, 256, 271, 280, 362, 364, 7:76, 86, 126, 8:34, 167, 268, 9:23, 138, 236f, 11:248f, 424f, 12:365, 370, 372, 407, 13:95, 109f, 113, 14:7, 27, 127, 130, 143, 211f, 254, 340, 15:205, 239, 304, 16:213, 312, 17:47, 127, 249, 369f, 18:99, 20:5, 142, 21:86, 88f, 177–179, 193, 231, 271, 22:106, 115, 142n, 143f,

146, 283, 307f, 394, 404, 456, 472, 491, 501f, 23:68, 76, 107, 171, 179, 183, 268, 400, 24:8, 12, 47, 58, 63, 89, 114, 116, 149, 247, 289, 347, 362, 391, 400, 404, 415, 25:254, 318f, 26:3, 5, 10, 27, 35, 37, 46, 113–115, 127, 134, 166, 178, 193, 195f, 292, 294, 301, 318, 338, 382–385, 407, 418, 27:6, 11f, 23, 33f, 80f, 94, 106, 113, 167, 290, 302f, 359f, 390, 28:10, 12f, 61, 70f, 77, 135, 371, 373f, 30:17, 236, 241, 288, 312f, 35:89, 200, 260, 36:190, 37:155, 233, 372, 38:128, 131, 41:17, 46:149, 286, 51:24, 49, 129, 131, 179f, 191, 52:120, 196, 200, 54:75, 133, 158, see also **Anfechtungen; Trials**

Tempting God—6:24, 104–106, 117f, 159f, 168, 217, 404, 11:55, 57, 61, 64, 16:83, 41:69–72, 137f, 46:172, 191, 202f, 49:268, 410

Ten Articles—50:150n, 177n

Ten Commandments—1:6, 147, 238, 240, 278, 2:47f, 5:20, 92, 214, 233, 348, 6:26, 177, 262, 330, 374, 7:311, 344, 8:186, 284, 294, 9:14, 63f, 67, 176, 254, 12:44, 88, 306, 313f, 320, 323, 402, 408, 14:8, 111, 15:269, 313, 332, 17:108, 20:156f, 21:4, 33, 74f, 81–83, 99f, 236f, 22:38, 102, 141, 143, 150f, 165, 174, 267, 273, 277, 284, 306, 367, 423, 425, 430, 433, 446, 456f, 460, 463, 487f, 504, 23:24, 34f, 56, 58, 62f, 68–70, 72–74, 77, 134, 141, 157, 170, 176f, 191, 213, 271, 280, 286, 324, 415, 24:50, 188, 242f, 261, 284, 287, 294–296, 329, 346, 348, 391, 394, 25:180, 325, 26:4, 121n, 122f, 138f, 163, 181, 200, 203, 293, 330, 333, 364, 426, 443, 447, 27:51, 188, 219, 223, 230, 265, 268, 286, 288, 313, 327, 335, 357, 378, 28:66, 29:212, 33:258f, 34:53, 74, 112, 118, 167, 35:159, 165, 173, 243f, 36:131, 204–218, 38:178, 180, 190, 39:16, 37n, 137, 274, 286, 40:82f, 93, 247, 276–278, 308, 318, 329, 333, 41:17f, 67n, 71f, 75, 78, 132, 144–148, 164, 166f, 204n, 247f, 342, 362, 366, 43:13f, 16n, 21–24, 200–209, 44:10, 23, 63, 68, 113, 46:231n, 47:x, 52f, 88–95, 101f, 107 109, 160, 169f, 226f, 49:233, 51:xii, 14, 137, 146, 149f, 158, 161f, 169, 188, 335, 372, 53:64–68, 120, 195, 277–281, 54:9f, 25, 282

1st commandment 1:149, 329, 2:6n, 3:80, 116, 237, 4:68, 119, 121, 324, 328, 5:115, 125, 262, 264, 6:228, 231, 9:59, 67f, 70f, 75f, 79–81, 84–86, 92–94, 96, 102, 109–114, 117, 123, 144, 12:19f, 87, 166, 266, 286f, 306, 315, 340, 350, 13:151, 235, 14:34f, 66, 68, 74, 87, 15:282f, 295, 313f, 332, 16:215, 269f, 17:22, 52, 143, 271, 273, 277, 303, 341, 397, 401f, 21:141, 190, 22:141, 144, 494, 26:184, 253, 257f, 275, 293, 28:242, 30:57, 35:199, 266f, 345, 36:217f, 38:107, 39:262, 276, 40:86, 277, 41:342, 43:17, 22, 200f, 44:30–39, 46:222, 47:90f, 93f, 167, 51:82, 138–141, 150, 161, 52:250, 252

2nd commandment 1:149, 329, 4:30–34, 78, 245, 361, 6:85, 8:209, 12:306, 13:218, 14:74, 15:314, 21:141, 190, 22:84, 141, 144, 174, 26:253, 27:119, 292, 36:217f, 39:262, 40:85, 88, 277, 42:28, 34, 43:18, 22, 201, 44:39–54, 46:22, 33, 276, 47:226, 286, 51:141–143, 169, 173

3rd commandment 1:149, 329, 6:177, 12:306, 398, 401, 26:253, 35:165, 36:217f, 39:262, 40:279f, 43:18, 22, 202f, 44:54–80, 47:91–93, 51:143–145, 261, 335, 342

4th commandment 4:72, 94, 293, 5:107, 145, 165, 6:16f, 25f, 61, 339, 7:341, 8:16, 18, 21f, 61, 9:219, 12:39, 276, 306, 36:208f, 211, 218, 39:16, 262, 40:280–286, 43:18, 22, 203f, 44:80–100, 45:154n, 353, 390, 46:310, 47:94f, 51:146–152, 183, 365

5th commandment 2:139, 4:102, 6:20, 376, 9:70, 219, 12:306, 21:76f, 99f, 22:403, 29:228, 34:43, 36:207f, 210, 218, 43:19, 22, 205f, 44:100–103, 47:264, 51:152f

6th commandment 3:331, 350, 6:374, 8:18, 9:219, 222, 229, 12:306, 21:84f, 92f, 94f, 99f, 22:407, 29:228, 34:42, 36:206f, 210, 218, 39:262, 43:19, 23, 206f, 44:103–106, 51:153–155, 378

7th commandment 3:350, 6:25–27, 8:18, 9:219, 222, 229, 244, 21:236, 22:402, 34:42, 36:205, 210, 218, 39:262, 43:20, 23, 208f, 44:106–110, 51:155–158

8th commandment 5:40, 6:27f, 36:204f, 210, 218, 39:262, 43:20, 23, 208, 44:110–114, 47:258, 51:158–160

9th and 10th commandments 36:204, 210, 218, 43:21, 23, 208, 44:114, 47:95, 51:160f

First Table 1:68, 183, 327–330, 2:6, 8f, 12, 30, 55, 58f, 61, 65, 86f, 89, 159, 212, 250, 3:4–6, 98, 101, 159, 240, 296, 4:36, 44, 88, 102, 109, 127, 381, 391f, 5:80, 94, 114 125, 263, 6:28–30,

36, 49f, 79, 228f, 239, 267, 294, 374, 7:341, 343, 8:76, 12:276f, 386, 398, 13:81, 235, 17:108, 21:66f, 22:141, 147, 267, 273, 286, 304, 371, 404, 406, 23:25, 317, 24:188n, 242, 26:35f, 27:132, 36:214, 217

Second Table 1:6f, 163, 183, 327–330, 2:6, 8f, 12, 30, 42, 55, 58f, 61, 65, 86f, 89, 141, 159, 212, 248, 3:5f, 98, 100, 159, 227, 240, 4:36, 44f, 88, 109, 5:80, 94, 114f, 120, 125, 6:26–29, 50, 79, 231, 294, 367, 374, 9:67, 193, 12:44, 276, 279, 14:132, 17:397, 21:66f, 166, 190, 236, 240, 22:141f, 267, 286, 371, 23:25, 58, 62, 317, 24:188, 242, 26:36, 364, 27:132, 36:208, 214

Luther's explanations 2:6n

Ten thousand—11:220, 226–228

Tent of Moses—29:199, 200

Tent pegs—20:108f

Tents—6:58f, 287, 11:318–321, 16:291, 339, 19:140f

Teppen, Henning—49:16

Terah—2:238–240, 242f, 249, 276f, 3:319, 352, 4:3, 184f, 250, 281, 5:210, 6:66, 84f, 7:269, 8:57, 150, 22:316

Teraphim—6:25f, 28, 31–35, 59, 237, 20:106f, 300

Terebinth—3:199, 18:23n

Terence—2:15, 339, 3:303, 13:147, 14:118, 17:389, 40:317n, 45:45n, 46:100n, 47:228, 54:80, 348

Adelphoi 4:221n, 5:38n, 120n, 305n, 10:14, 15:106n, 54:390n, 457n

Andria 2:127n, 3:47n, 4:144n, 6:47n, 7:65n, 10:325, 11:488n, 16:21n, 17:147n, 20:175n, 24:161n, 25:223

Eunuchus 2:149n, 4:375n, 13:182, 15:87n, 154n, 17:45n, 18:115n, 301n, 23:217n, 27:59n, 98n, 31:338n, 33:23n, 50:96n, 97n, 112n, 54:246

Heautontimorumenos 2:97n, 348n, 4:400n, 5:119n, 184n, 369n, 6:254n, 8:14n, 20:8n, 25:223, 33:246n

Hecyra 5:95n

Phormio 4:67n, 5:118n, 120n, 121n, 136n, 7:33n, 144n, 290n, 13:123, 15:99n, 160n, 25:448, 29:61n, 50:249n

Terrestial bodies—28:184, 190, 195f

Terror—3:3, 63, 135, 237, 330f, 345, 6:72, 83, 100, 137, 143, 151, 162, 173, 241f, 245, 271, 24:10f, 16–18, 20, 44, 46, 61, 71n, 98, 102, 111–114, 117, 119, 137, 143, 145, 149f, 157, 166, 183–185, 210, 279, 291f, 298, 352, 361, 405

Tertius—25:128, 131

Tertullian—5:129n, 12:174, 24:320, 32:128n, 34:209n, 219n, 275n, 35:280, 37:108–114, 258, 361n, 43:156, 45:82n, 102n, 207n

Ad scapulam 21:110n

Adversus Judaeos 8:50n

Adversus Marcionem 1:310n, 27:201n, 50:36n

Apologeticus 13:25n, 17:407n

De resurrectione 5:222n

On Baptism 2:270n

On Monogamy 30:306n

On the Veiling of Virgins 30:306n

Tertullian, (Pseudo-)—*Against All Heresies* 30:257n

Tertullus—29:74

Testament (Covenant)—36:37f, 40–57, 180, 195

Testament, Last will and—see **Last will and testament**

Testator—27:264f, 314

Testicles—27:345f

Testimony—6:62f, 80f, 84, 10:280f, 11:421, 429–435, 438, 443, 451, 479, 490, 499f, 505f, 508, 516, 529–531, 12:386, 16:95, 28:267–269, 29:145f, 171f, 233, 46:298, 301, 307

Testimony of Israel—11:542f

Testing the spirits—23:174f, 40:52

Testing, God's—25:177

Testings—25:13, 319, 452f, 28:290, 297f

Tetleben, Caspar von—49:181n, 322n

Tetragrammaton—3:296n, 6:185, 248, 9:67n, 11:271n, 15:324, 22:107, 27:221, 35:248n, 271, 47:242, 256

Tetrapolis—2:200–202, 4:192

Tetrapolitana—see ***Confessio Tetrapolitana***

Tetzel, John—5:354, 31:xvf, 19, 21f, 87n, 34:6n, 335, 336n, 41:231–235, 48:45, 68n, 70, 71n, 109, 181n, 340, 342, 49:107, 51:35, 49n, 54:341f

Teutleben, Caspar von—54:156

Teutonic Knights—1:118n, 9:5n, 31:73, 45:xii, 133n, 134n, 135f, 137n, 138f, 141–144, 152n, 157, 48:134, 49:125n

Teutonic Order—see **Teutonic Knights**

Teutonicus, John—see **Zemecke, John**

Textbooks used in schools—45:374n

Textual criticism—27:373

Thales of Miletus—15:122n

Thalhofer, Valentin—*Handbuch der katholishe Liturgik*, II, 2nd ed., Freiburg i. Br., 1912 12:71n

Thamar—13:223

Thanklessness—see **Ingratitude**

Thankofferings—9:258, 38:106, 112f, 116

Thanks—3:50, 120, 122, 145f, 227, 243, 276, 288, 336, 342, 344, 364

Thanksgiving—2:76f, 178, 333, 348, 357, 392f, 3:70, 99, 118, 128, 4:98n, 269, 277, 279, 397, 5:109, 258–261, 264, 335, 357, 6:185f, 226f, 7:57f, 124, 127, 150, 8:47, 115, 158, 249, 294, 9:157, 254f, 10:45, 234, 368f, 11:410f, 15:10, 199, 215f, 227, 231, 252, 16:70, 344, 17:72, 117, 182, 324, 336, 24:273, 26:17, 43, 155, 171, 27:93, 28:316f, 29:95f, 35:95n, 98, 104, 136, 255, 36:53, 77, 162f, 170f, 37:xii, 116–118, 126, 142n, 144, 161, 313, 319, 38:95, 106–108, 111, 119, 121–125, 133, 136, 208, 51:164, 52:277, see also **Sacrifice of Thanksgiving**
Thanksgiving, Sacrifice of—see **Sacrifice of Thanksgiving**
Thartan—16:168
The King's Primer—43:10
Theaters—2:139
Thebaid—8:48
Thebes—8:96n, 11:508, 18:310
Thedotians—34:208n
Theft—see **Robbery**
Themistocles—2:125, 15:154n
Theocracy—3:31n, 9:169
Theocritus—2:385
Theodore of Mopsuestia—15:194n
Theodoret—35:318n, 41:7n, 60n, 106n, 47:117n, 50:126n
  In Exodum 10:258fn
Theodoric I, King of the Ostrogoths—34:277n, 42:57n, 51:64n, see also **Dietrich of Bern**
Theodosia—6:309
Theodosius I, Emperor—3:329, 22:267, 31:119, 41:23n, 24f, 38n, 86n, 87n, 93n, 281, 374n, 44:211n, 54:260
Theodosius II, Emperor—41:24n, 93n, 94, 106, 281
Theodotion—15:267, 29:233n
Theologians—1:4, 28, 31, 53, 90, 105, 113n, 166, 202n, 232, 234f, 235n, 296n, 301, 316, 339, 2:5, 86, 119, 124f, 148, 150f, 159, 288, 291, 313, 328, 330, 337, 340f, 349, 383, 391, 3:27, 29, 42, 153, 267, 306, 358n, 4:108n, 118, 233, 264, 327, 351, 396, 5:9n, 25, 42, 345, 7:140, 179, 278, 320, 365, 370, 8:25, 28, 51, 108, 167, 192, 209, 268, 311f, 325, 9:164, 215n, 12:4f, 77, 199, 288, 313, 351, 14:xii, 23, 149, 215, 283f, 295, 306, 15:4, 16:335, 22:304, 23:45, 102, 115n, 271, 273, 284, 410, 24:98, 291, 362, 398, 25:289, 429, 454, 26:20, 115, 125, 130, 140, 144, 156, 263, 313, 342, 398, 407, 410, 414, 429, 443, 27:22, 91, 100, 116, 155, 158, 177, 181, 236, 248f, 267, 271, 289, 335f, 352, 370, 404, 28:219, 228, 233, 290, 292, 294, 306, 308f, 367, 369, 382, 29:35, 98, 180, 30:235, 260n, 33:70, 36:125, 38:xiiif, xvi, 9, 114n, 169, 243f, 246, 248, 252, 263, 265, 269, 271–273, 41:xi, 162, 170, 175, 221, 269, 306f, 319, 360, 362f, 365, 45:376, 46:226n, 239f, 251, 270, 273, 54:22, 31, 39, 69, 111, 144, 150, 214, 439f
Theological knowledge—12:311, 334, 339f
Theological questions—12:366
Theological study—18:185
  Its aim 28:223–225
Theological terms—12:378
Theology—1:xi, 27, 94, 131, 143, 185, 255, 269, 2:42, 148, 164, 220, 3:26, 94, 132, 136, 160, 262, 4:13, 108n, 145, 199, 220, 222, 331, 5:63, 136, 194, 201, 302f, 309, 345f, 6:31, 141f, 182, 230, 7:58, 180, 181n, 216, 227, 268, 280f, 8:30, 135, 170, 181, 191, 209, 261, 267, 312, 9:24, 71n, 185n, 10:313, 12:68, 204, 310f, 316, 322, 335, 351, 373, 405, 13:110f, 14:x, 7f, 35n, 153n, 281, 284, 295, 23:192, 233, 26:7, 10, 28, 73, 94, 114, 124, 127, 140, 161, 196, 228, 234, 256, 260–264, 266–268, 271, 285f, 294, 298, 307, 326f, 331, 366, 378, 387, 414, 435, 27:23, 25, 37, 59, 62n, 153, 156, 159f, 219, 222, 225, 230, 240, 328, 389, 29:163, 179, 200, 30:259n, 300n, 31:x, 12, 40–42, 52f, 76, 225, 227, 256, 276, 34:128, 131f, 46:209, 273n, 51:213, 54:22, 50f, 71, 112, 157, 448
  Affirmative 13:111
  Doctors of 2:220
  Melanchthonian 1:xi
  Modern 32:153f
  Mystical see **Mystical theology**
  Negative 13:110f
  Rhetoric vs. true arguments 3:194, 213
  Scholastic see **Scholastic theology**
  Skeptical 33:35
Theology vs. philosophy—31:41f, 38:xx, 75, 239f, 242, 247–250, 253, 255, 258–277
Theophania, Empress—41:374n
Theophilus—*To Autolycus* 23:169n
Theotokos (Mother of God)—37:292n
Theses—34:xiv
Theseus—3:189
Thessalonians—25:402, 30:18

Thessalonians, Epistles to the—35:386–389
Thessalonica—41:273, 323
Thief on the cross—17:81, 84, 29:176
Thiele, Ernst—12:x, 47:28n, 30n, 37n, 51:246n, 376n
Luthers Sprichwörtersammlung, Weimar, 1900 35:103n, 37:57n, 125n, 38:101n, 127n, 164n, 165n, 173n, 223n, 39:15n, 87n, 121n, 123n, 127n, 146n, 147n, 153n, 159n, 160n, 162n, 167n, 197n, 207n, 213n, 216n, 267n, 43:208n, 46:35n, 39, 51n, 64n, 67n, 78n, 80n, 103n, 109n, 112n, 117n, 118n, 164n, 177n, 186n, 196n, 199n, 235n, 266n, 287n, 288n, 290n, 302n, 305n, 308n
Thievery—see **Robbery**
Thieves—2:59, 313, 4:51, 202, 381, 7:59, 73, 128, 181, 190, 214, 243f, 254, 338, 365, 13:60, 20:55, 238, 25:21, 38:159–161, 202, 46:71, 74, 98, 240, 276, 306, 313
Thieves, Crucified—42:140
Thighs—4:230f, 233–235, 238f, 241f, 244, 259, 6:137f, 146, 153f, 182
Thinking—25:69, 105, 167, 218, 236, 350, 415, 428, 438f
Thirst—3:179f, 184, 4:40–42, 44, 46f, 49, 23:267–274, 276–278
Thirteen Articles—50:178n, 192
Thirty pieces of silver—20:124f, 127, 318f
Thirty Years' War—29:xi, 47:9
Thistledown—11:134n
Thistles—see **Thorns and thistles**
Thomas, Brother—see **Badia, Thomas**
Thomas, Doubting—2:21
Thomas, St., Apostle—20:250, 22:422, 24:31–33, 35f, 42, 57, 94, 332
Thomas Aquinas, St.—1:29n, 227, 5:36n, 8:261n, 316, 12:377, 14:171n, 284n, 17:112, 22:255f, 23:115n, 25:227, 372, 497, 26:446f, 28:85, 29:63, 30:36n, 99n, 107n, 188n, 277n, 31:83, 146, 194n, 218, 221f, 262, 321n, 32:xviii, 79n, 257f, 33:46n, 112n, 266n, 34:27f, 35:6, 64n, 318n, 368n, 36:29n, 37:214n, 215n, 256n, 38:189, 293n, 39:168n, 40:75, 179n, 200n, 44:199n, 273n, 274–277, 391n, 45:8n, 82n, 83, 119n, 233n, 299n, 377n, 48:30n, 73n, 85, 96n, 49:410n, 51:22n, 54:12, 38, 39, 264
Adoro Te devote (hymn) 22:459n, 30:36n
Commentaries on Aristotle's Works 48:95, 107, 112
De malo 2:315n
Summa Theologica 1:3n, 113n, 159n, 228n, 2:44n, 313n, 314n, 4:117n, 137n, 289n, 5:72n, 205n, 303n, 6:42n, 7:219n, 8:261n, 11:396n, 14:171n, 16:227n, 17:70n, 250n, 21:88n, 289n, 22:175n, 26:4n, 73n, 88n, 121n, 127n, 128n, 200n, 230n, 256n, 267n, 406n, 410n, 427n, 447n, 27:52n, 113n, 234n, 29:153n, 198n, 30:99n, 107n, 188n, 189n, 277n, 31:5, 33:38n, 34:154n, 155n, 305n, 36:287n, 44:273n, 391n, 48:156n, 157n, 362n, 52:46, 50, 115, 229n
"Super epistolam S. Pauli ad Hebraeos expositio" (in his *In omnes S. Pauli apostili epopstolas commentaria,* Turin, 1929) 29:126n
Verbum supernum prodiens (hymn) 32:57n
Thomists—14:284, 25:324, 27:390, 36:29n, 48:58n, 81, 96n, 168n, 291n
Thompson, Harrison S.—39:108n
Thorn, Lambert—53:211
Thorn, Peace of—45:134
Thorn in the flesh—8:73, 26:341, 420
Thorns and thistles—1:38, 64, 76–78, 89, 102, 203–206, 208f, 293, 353, 3:6, 319, 4:9, 380, 8:248, 302, 323, 10:21, 270, 275, 16:213, 332f, 24:200, 225, 227, 232f, 26:296, 27:79, 373, 391
Thoughts—11:4f, 9, 493f, 13:114, 17:30, 129, 255–257, 25:20, 185, 187–189, 324
Evil 16:56
Impure 15:191–195, 231, 249
Thousand years—11:195f, 203f
Thrace—18:203
Thracians—2:189
Thraso—4:375n, 13:182, 15:87n, 156, 159, 17:45n, 18:301, 23:217, 50:96, 112n
Thrasons—41:244n
Threats—4:34, 147, 154, 6:38, 42, 56f, 243, 245, 16:11, 21–23, 57, 82f, 87–89, 95, 117, 259f, 266, 269, 271, 17:71, 254, 275, 278, 375f, 379f, 384, 20:11, 107, 162, 243, 23:133, 361, 363, 371f
Three Kings—see **Magi**
Threshing—17:45f
Throats—25:227f
Thunder—9:155, 308, 16:207, 267, 271, 284, 315, 330, 20:106, 294, 24:114, 184
Thüngen, Conrad von, Bishop of Würzburg—48:30n, 49:383, 385, 389
Thuringia—1:78n, 274, 2:344, 7:299, 8:109, 124, 11:105, 14:280, 17:382, 35:171n, 46:6, 47, 59, 72n, 47:15n,

48:228n, 49:106, 114, 118n, 168n, 214n, 389, 50:222n, 54:351
Thuringian Forest—20:310, 48:219n, 227n, 50:222
Thuringians—8:124, 54:387
Thyesteans—38:72n, 292f, 305
Tiara, Triple—23:269
Tiber River—2:188n
Tiberius, Emperor—31:208n, 39:203, 41:356n, 47:298
Tibullus—*Corpus Tibullianum* 16:162n
Ticinus River—6:244
Ticonius—39:196n
Tidal, King—2:365
Tigers—1:119, 2:69, 75, 135
Tiglath-pileser—16:96, 108, 18:223
Tigris River—1:97f, 101, 2:279, 4:186, 5:210, 8:38, 16:184, 17:96
Tillmans, Walter G.—25:xiii
The World and Men around Luther, Minneapolis, 1959 43:73n
translator of *Lectures on Romans, Glosses and Scholia for Chps. 1–2* 25:4–24, 135–193
Timann, John—32:272n
Timbrel—11:102–104
Time—10:17f, 21, 159, 258, 13:99f, 118, 15:49f, 52f, 57, 73, 150, 152f, 17:238f, 368–370, 21:208, 30:114, 122, 196, 35:392n
Depends on sun's revolutions 1:44
Time signatures—53:xix
Timnah—7:7, 24, 26, 32, 38
Timon of Athens—3:51, 6:291, 297, 14:51, 15:105n, 24:267
Timothy, Epistles to—35:388f
Timothy, First Epistle to—28:ix, xi, 215–383
Timothy, St.—13:79, 111, 14:50, 20:109, 22:98, 24:327, 25:474, 488, 26:17, 55, 61, 80, 82, 85, 156, 27:16, 211, 303, 334f, 343, 29:10, 14, 88, 94, 105, 182, 30:144, 31:368, 36:155, 266, 38:99, 186, 41:78, 42:161, 45:73, 373
Tinder (Fomes)—7:234f, 278, 13:81n, 114n, 25:57, 62f, 65, 259, 265, 268, 270f, 273f, 276f, 300, 320, 339, 26:189n, 27:228
Tinder of concupiscence—51:25
Tinder of sin—25:339, 32:29–31, 214, 233
Tischreden—see **Luther, Martin, Writings of**—*Table Talk*
Tithes—1:211, 2:22, 384, 388, 393f, 3:35, 5:24, 260–262, 264f, 267, 7:160, 8:127, 9:124f, 138f, 141, 144, 174, 221, 254f, 12:410, 18:84, 414, 45:161, 308f, 46:10n, 11n, 22, 38, 233
Tithing—28:349, 30:54
Titus, Emperor—8:321, 16:187, 45:222f, 227, 228n, 47:138
Titus, Epistle to—27:243, 29: ix, 3–90, 35:386, 43:41
Titus, St.—13:111, 20:109, 22:98, 24:71, 26:55, 81, 85, 87, 89, 91, 27:200, 201, 215, 28:xi, 281, 286, 29:14, 16, 69, 87, 105, 182, 30:144, 31:368, 373, 39:281, 41:19, 324, 45:71, 73
Titus Pomponious Atticus—5:104n, 269f
Tjernagel, Neelak—54:362
Toads—1:54, 77, 23:255, 285
Tobern, Anden—50:252n
Tobias (Tobiah, Tobijah)—5:203, 206, 7:132, 20:68, 72, 162, 228, 253f, 28:14, 35:346n
Tobit—5:77
Tobit, Book of—35:326, 345–347
Today—20:98, 292
Toil—see **Labor**
Toil and trouble—19:140, 159f
Toledo—5:369
Tolerance—9:183, 12:241, 245, 13:66f, 15:126, 21:213–215, 219–221, 24:317, 26:67, 27:46, 376, 386, 34:213, 37:xiv, 11, 22, 27, 40:32, 57, 230, 257, 44:199, 46:22, 47:279n, 48:401, 49:99
Tolerance is indifference—33:35
Tollet—49:140, 141n, 210n
Tolls—2:263
Tombs—see **Sepulchers**
Tomfoolery—24:174, 181, 225
Tomvernus—see **Tobern, Anden**
Tomyris, Queen—17:122n, 20:159
Tondalo, Legend of—21:245
Tongue, The—3:130, 136, 4:68, 254, 352, 9:249, 10:97, 211f, 214, 220, 255, 257, 264, 309, 322, 340f, 400, 442, 11:532f, 535, 537f, 13:204, 23:382, 44:110, 46:240, 300
Tongue, Misuse of the—3:194, 362, 11:353
Tongues of fire—16:168
Tongues, Confusion of—see **Languages**—Division of
Tongues, Speaking in—36:115, 40:142, 389, 53:11n, 38
Tonsures—17:5, 50, 57, 99, 112, 158, 316, 23:24f, 68, 135, 171, 182, 196, 204, 261, 351, 409, 24:38, 98, 147, 174f, 225, 260, 326, 356, 360f, 26:29, 91f, 175, 185, 199, 238, 295, 27:31, 87, 141, 286, 375, 30:6, 206, 212, 34:20, 55, 36:112, 115, 177, 179, 201f, 38:119, 185, 195, 197, 203, 40:38f, 129, 41:168, 211, 213, 270, 340, 48:308, 334

Topheth—7:299f, 303, 8:186, 16:267
Torah—11:439n, 27:309
Torgau—2:85n, 5:46, 22:45, 34:6, 38:135, 196, 42:119n, 45:13, 382, 46:89n, 90, 48:28, 39n, 51, 95, 138, 180, 264n, 269, 378n, 49:115n, 132n, 142, 152n, 155, 174n, 180, 182, 240n, 277, 280f, 28ln, 282f, 298, 315n, 335, 422, 429n, 430n, 431, 433, 435n, 50:151n, 154n, 156n, 169n, 231, 232n, 233n, 234, 239f, 240n, 271, 275n, 280n, 287, 51:295n, 326n, 333, 54:37, 219, 277, 448
Torgau Articles—34:7, 49:282n, 295f
Torment—8:6
Torquati—6:297, 324, 15:166n
Torquemada, Juan de—11:180n
Torture—1:106, 2:123, 3:8, 125, 264, 342
Torun, Peace of—49:60
Total depravity—32:83, 93
Touto, tauta—40:159–177, 192f
Karlstad's exegesis 37:326, 336
Tower of David—15:230
Trachtenberg, Joshua—47:131n, 212n, 214n, 217n, 226n
Tracts (Liturgical anthems)—53:24n
Trade and commerce—8:274, 45:171f, 233–273, 295–305, 46:134, 209, 213n, 236
Trade, Foreign—44:212–214
Trading companies—45:133, 234, 240–245, 246n, 270–272
Tradition—2:116n, 161, 3:121f, 145, 155, 203f, 206n, 250, 321, 326, 4:50, 90, 141, 163, 165, 167, 211, 236, 5:79, 96f, 246, 249, 251, 253, 294n, 6:30, 85, 89, 7:x, 3n, 17, 19, 32n, 87, 92n, 109n, 173n, 323, 341, 350, 8:83, 130, 133, 186, 283, 332, 9:3, 52–55, 58, 64n, 72, 125, 157, 179, 188, 224, 226, 235, 268, 13:79, 118n, 14:16, 16:21, 203, 223f, 228, 245f, 248f, 262, 334, 18:30, 20:10, 74f, 86, 105, 234, 236, 264, 22:61, 452, 26:3, 30, 33, 47, 49, 52, 68, 79f, 86, 91, 112, 120, 122n, 135, 140f, 152f, 182, 184f, 197, 199, 208, 212, 221, 224, 248f, 306, 330, 351, 363, 365, 390, 394, 399f, 405, 408, 411, 428, 443, 461, 27:9f, 13f, 18f, 25, 44, 55, 110, 122, 138, 140, 157, 165, 177, 187f, 219, 227, 276, 285, 298, 312, 329, 341, 350, 354, 375, 408, 28:221, 223, 225, 230, 29:7, 9, 10f, 16, 18, 20, 42–45, 47f, 30:26n, 253, 280, 301, 33:71–84, 34:351, 356, 40:7, 38f, 52:257
Tradition, Exegetical—4:xi, 97n, 187n, 388n
Traditionalists—48:10, 37f, 40, 53n, 110, 117f, 122, 132, 150n, 156f, 178, 250f, 362
Traditions of men—20:234, 236, 264
Traducianism—11:466n, 22:327n
Tragedies, Greek—2:8
Training—28:279f, 321f, 335–337
Traitors—52:230f
Trajan, Emperor—2:77, 13:200, 28:294, 29:58, 30:72, 47:234, 236
Tranquility—6:179f, 186, 190, 15:11, 29, 48, 142, 219, 223f
Transference (figure of speech)—27:312
Transfiguration—30:162f, 35:162
Transformation—28:182, 200f
Transforming minds—Work of the Spirit 25:438
Transforming power of Christ—37:100f, 132
Transgressions—29:122, 212, 219
Transgressions, Three—10:12f
Transgressions, Four—10:12f, 380, 397
Transgressors—12:387
Translating—8:3n, 25:52, 37:xv, 7, 9f, 101, 113, 147f, 155, 162n, 239–241, 321, 331, 356, 54:42f, 135, 210, 375f, 408, 445f
Errors in 12:351
Problems in 7:7, 24f, 37, 40, 251, 292, 16:49, 19:110, 122f, 20:70, 80, 131f, 230f, 283, 21:340, 29:160, 36:276
Translating the Bible—35:xvii, 177–194, 223, 249, 265–279
Translators—see **Ahrens, Frederick C.; Atkinson, James; Bachmann, E. Theodore; Bergendoff, Conrad J.; Bertram, Martin H.; Beto, George; Beyer, Earl; Bouman, Herbert J.A.; Brandt, Walther L.; Bretscher, Paul M.; Caemmerer, Richard R.; Dinda, Richard J.; Doberstein, John W.; Erling, Bernhard; Fischer, Robert Harley; Flesner, Dorris A.; Folkemer, Carl W.; Froelich, Charles D.; Grimm, Harold J.; Gritsch, Eric W.; Gritsch, Ruth C.; Guebert, Arnold; Hansen, Walter A.; Hebart, S.P.; Heitner, Robert R.; Hornsby, Roger A.; Jacobs, Charles Michael; Jungkuntz, Richard; Klann, H. Richard; Koenker, E.B.; Krodel, Gottfried G.; Kunstmann, John G.; Lambert, William A.; Lehmann, Martin E.; Leupold, Ulrich S.; Lindbeck, George; MacDonald,**

George; Miller, Walther M.; Moessner, Paul H.G.; Nettl, Paul; Pahl, Paul D.; Pelikan, Jaroslav; Poellet, Daniel E.; Preus, Jacob A.O.; Raun, James; Satre, Lowell J.; Sauer, Alfred von Rohr; Schick, George V.; Schindel, Jeremiah J.; Schindler, Carl J.; Schultz, Robert C.; Siggins, Ian; Sittler, Edward V.; Spitz, Lewis W.; Spitz, Lewis W., Sr.; Steinhäuser, Albert T.W.; Strodach, Paul Zeller; Stump, Joseph; Tappert, Theodore G.; Tillmans, Walter G.; Watson, Philip S.
Transubstantiation—34:355, 35:47, 59n, 77, 36:ix, 7, 31n, 32–35, 44–45, 52, 129, 181n, 271f, 37:xvi, xix, 64, 116, 294n, 295–298, 300n, 317, 38:143, 151n, 164f, 167, 210n, 40:25, 42:174, 44:199n, 50:202
Transvestism—9:219f
Transylvania—49:185n, 240n
Traps for married penitents—39:45
Travail—18:92, 243, 249
Treachery—2:127, 199, 6:69f, 203f, 7:60, 82f, 11:502, 535f
Treason—7:225, 240, 46:80, 114, 240
Treasure—22:87, 89, 109, 340, 359, 363, 369, 462, 466, 473, 488f, 491, 525–528
Treasure, Christian's—28:115, 125, 137, 191, 297
Treasures of the church—32:62f
Treasury, Common—28:285, 295, 337, 347, 380, see also **Common chest**
Treasury of merits—31:20f, 30f, 167–169, 211, 224, 261, 266–269
Treaties—6:77–80, 82, 199, 16:89, 106, 36:210, 212
Tree, Forbidden—1:144, 151, 164, 173f, 176, 218
Tree of death—1:225–227, 234
Tree of knowledge—4:193
Tree of knowledge of good and evil—1:81, 92–96, 103, 105, 109f, 122, 140, 144, 146, 149, 226, 229, 231, 310, 7:302
Tree of life—1:92–96, 105, 144, 222, 225–227, 229, 234, 249, 29:116
Trees—7:68, 109, 211, 272, 299, 302, 10:25, 83, 442, 11:335, 17:49, 259, 271, 321, 336, 391, 22:198, 24:193f, 224, 230, 253f, 262, 265, 342f, 368, 26:255, 257, 261, 264, 277, 279, 288, 290, 30:43, 58, 86, 97, 108, 196, 209, 242, 263f
Trent—54:215
Trent, Bishop of—49:119
Trent, Council of—see **Councils, General Church**
Treptow—45:313n
Trespasses—21:152, 154
Trials and tribulations—3:3, 5–10, 12–15, 17, 36, 42f, 46, 55f, 58, 71, 76, 128f, 135, 159, 174, 185, 190, 229, 239, 265, 282, 301–303, 312, 325, 333f, 348, 356, 4:9, 21, 44–47, 54, 63, 65, 67f, 73, 80, 91–97, 104, 106, 112, 128, 132, 149, 183, 188, 254, 259, 274, 277, 309, 314, 319–321, 325, 329, 336f, 353–355, 359f, 376, 378, 5:5–8, 12–16, 21, 24, 46–49, 53–64, 69f, 76f, 79f, 87, 89f, 92, 144–146, 166, 171, 175f, 183, 195, 199f, 202, 205, 210, 212, 215, 223, 231, 234, 254f, 266, 278, 320f, 326f, 333, 347, 358, 362, 6:89, 92, 95, 99, 104, 123, 142, 180, 187, 190f, 219, 267, 354, 364, 7:55–57, 75f, 84, 87, 94, 106, 109, 126–129, 131, 137, 163, 172, 174–178, 183f, 210, 221, 225f, 229, 233, 235, 237f, 249, 257, 259, 278, 282, 303, 307, 315, 321, 324, 326, 332, 365, 368f, 371, 8:5–8, 12f, 20, 27, 33f, 53, 57, 67, 69, 74, 78, 83, 113f, 193, 204, 228, 240, 267, 279, 294, 309, 324f, 9:138, 222, 251, 10:40, 48–50, 55f, 59, 149, 287, 319, 340, 356, 12:148, 167f, 189, 296, 318, 326, 330, 406, 13:22f, 108f, 16:31, 111, 157, 167, 208, 213f, 287, 326, 335, 343, 17:3, 30, 49, 86, 103, 127f, 132, 135, 160, 183f, 196, 203f, 212, 238f, 241, 290, 325, 372, 411, 19:136f, 146, 20:24, 32, 163f, 23:76, 145, 400, 24:8, 10, 55, 70, 98, 145, 149–151, 153, 166, 183, 195, 209f, 213, 244, 247, 263, 293, 301, 311, 359f, 362, 388, 393, 415, 25:18, 44, 72, 77, 107, 176, 179, 232, 248, 286, 289–293, 379, 26:27, 178, 27:22, 25, 27, 32, 34, 49, 54, 71–73, 78f, 113, 170, 253, 316, 318, 361, 374, 28:219, 248, 29:25, 69, 118, 129f, 146, 176, 181, 189, 234–237, 30:70f, 109, 126, 156, 303f, 309, 311, 321, 34:121, 35:52, 402, 410, 40:287, 42:71–76, 79f, 127, 183n, 184, 44:28, 47f, 291
Tribulations—see **Trials and tribulations**
Tribute—17:274, 23:394, 404
Tricks—5:107, 117, 127, 151, 295, 365f, 370, 6:58, 203f, 208, 365
Trier—21:272, 31:198, 256, 34:25, 28, 44:141, 185n, 48:128f, 138, 51:207, 390
Trier, Archbishop of—23:192, 31:329, 339, 32:116, 120–122
Trier, Holy Coat of—47:50

Trier-Cologne, Diet of, 1512—45:241n, 262n, 271n

Trinity, Doctrine of the—1:11f, 1:12, 14, 16n, 20f, 58, 60, 223, 2:18n, 227f, 3:61, 190–195, 219, 232, 245, 299, 353, 4:171, 198, 244, 279, 5:39, 72, 74f, 78, 212n, 280, 6:72f, 113, 126, 185, 230, 232, 250f, 333, 7:109, 167, 283, 294, 8:12, 145, 164f, 168, 264, 325, 11:226, 406, 497, 12:43, 99, 101, 283, 286, 288, 15:275–280, 282, 286, 289, 291, 293, 295, 297f, 300–307, 309–311, 315f, 325, 327, 338–340, 343, 345, 17:165, 18:394, 20:163f, 194, 208, 22:5f, 14–17, 19, 74–76, 115, 156, 173f, 181, 283, 297, 314, 316, 319, 321, 328, 361, 364, 23:54, 65n, 89, 102, 105, 115f, 24:8, 23, 290, 364, 372–374, 408, 25:295, 27:206n, 290, 340, 30:223, 320, 34:201n, 208, 217–219, 223, 227, 36:63, 298, 37:157, 297, 361, 368, 38:15, 34, 36, 78, 251f, 255–257, 261–263, 265–267, 273, 275, 277, 307, 310f, 38:36, 298n, 309n, 41:80, 93, 178, 271f, 315, 355, 47:290n, 54:31, 371, 376, 418
- God the Father see **God the Father**
- Second Person 1:9

Trinity Sunday—22:275n

Tripartite Ecclesiastical History—see **Cassiodorus, Flavius**

Trishagion **(hymn)**—16:70, 53:274

Triumph—25:65

Triumphis Veritatis **(poem)**—36:228n

Troglodytes—16:158f

Trojan War—28:321

Trojans—6:204, 207

Trondheim—50:252n

Tropes—33:160–170, 37:174, 252–258, 326, 336, 349–352, 355, 37:52n, 53n, 171–176, 209–214, 231, 252–269, 273, 313, 323–327, 336f, 344, 349–352, 354f, 359f, 38:21, 25, 28, 30, 43–45, 47, 55f, 59, 81f, 53:21n, see also **Figures of speech**

Tropological sense—25:xi, 141, 212, 398, 26:440, see also **Scripture(s), Interpretation**

Tropology—14:339, 343, 27:312

Trott, Eva von—41:183, 239n

Troubadors—see **Minnesänger**

Trouble makers—15:65f

Troubles—4:5, 20, 22, 58, 74, 76f, 127, 148, 190, 227, 249f, 277, 292, 294, 312, 318, 336, 340, 361, 371, 395, 402, 7:55, 58, 64–66, 71, 75, 125f, 128f, 131, 146, 149, 177–179, 190, 194–196, 203, 208–210, 225f, 228, 230, 235, 237, 246, 248, 256, 278, 287, 290, 308, 311, 313, 315, 320, 324, 327, 330, 338, 340, 347, 356, 359, 365, 367, 369, 373f, 8:13f, 27, 33, 36, 44, 46f, 74, 83, 96–98, 100, 106, 111, 113f, 126, 138, 143, 157, 163, 188, 197, 199, 228, 231, 275, 278, 290, 294, 312, 318, 11:19, 507f, 15:5, 10, 24f, 46, 56f, 71, 106, 110, 161, 204, 223, 16:209, 212, 19:136f, 146, 21:95, 209, 309f, 24:7, 11, 84, 87, 134, 141, 206, 239, 241, 262, 318, 328, 341, 357, 383, 385, 391, 422, 30:39, 96f, 130f, 135, 176, 326

Troy—1:99, 2:189, 6:201, 9:221, 13:208, 16:42, 17:148, 367, 379, 20:343, 45:329

Trumpet sounds—28:200f

Trumpets—11:101f, 272–275, 286–288, 18:89f, 146, 26:191, 310f

Trumpets, Feast of—9:154, 11:101f, 16:267

Trust—10:68, 12:362, 406, 408, 16:90, 195, 329n, 349, 37:xvi–xx, 7, 84n, 88–94, 111, 121, 124, 127–132, 138n, 192, 337f, 363, 365f, 45:120f, 123, 126, 280f, see also **Faith**

Trustees—26:361, 369

Trusting God—21:196–198, 200f, 309, 325, 346

Truth—2:125f, 147, 158, 184, 241, 243, 269, 290, 297, 299, 317f, 349, 386, 3:16, 22, 36, 62, 174, 213f, 265, 268, 281, 286, 295–297, 313, 316, 332f, 345, 5:4, 11, 38, 41, 48f, 71, 73f, 80, 144f, 177, 208, 213, 236, 291, 366, 6:55f, 73, 113, 8:17n, 44, 118, 132, 139, 230, 238f, 241, 275, 10:221–223, 325, 375, 11:6, 31, 34, 116f, 164–171, 174, 177, 215, 223f, 229, 233f, 239, 313, 381f, 396, 470f, 477, 488, 505f, 514, 517, 13:379, 16:21, 29, 82, 150, 227, 246, 18:19, 19:198n, 21:102f, 112, 247, 22:88, 471–474, 479, 491, 23:13, 70, 84, 95, 100, 113, 117, 158, 211–213, 223, 229, 235, 237, 240f, 249f, 253, 275f, 287, 300, 304, 319, 321, 326, 330f, 341, 358, 364, 368, 378–381, 392–397, 399–402, 409, 416f, 419–422, 24:16, 23, 36, 38, 40, 43–45, 47–55, 58, 76, 94–96, 117, 119–124, 129, 153, 166, 169, 177, 187f, 194, 203, 206, 209, 216, 222f, 235, 271, 283, 290–294, 313, 321, 323f, 327, 357–363, 368, 370, 399, 25:9, 16, 26, 157, 198f, 217, 230, 236, 26:3, 18, 29, 50, 53f, 67, 71, 77f, 80f, 87–89, 91–93, 96, 98, 107f, 110–115, 118, 135, 142,

176, 182, 186, 189, 195–198, 201f, 213, 218, 221f, 228, 250, 302, 328f, 354, 368, 375, 378, 387, 400, 407f, 413f, 416, 423f, 432, 29:6–11, 13, 42, 44f, 60, 156, 172, 182, 219, 31:223, 239, 277, 318, 333, 395, 32:149, 36:49f, 84f, 94, 108, 209f, 220, 223, 37:22, 29f, 50, 60, 70, 77, 81, 96, 104–112, 116, 123, 125, 129, 141, 168–170, 293, 38:84, 118, 120, 147, 157, 160, 170, 173, 175, 190, 196n, 201, 210, 222, 230f, 238f, 247, 265, 273, 277, 294n, 296, 41:215f, 234, 339, 42:77, 89, 133, 147, 149, 174, 45:57, 59, 64, 70, 177, 366, 46:180f, 236, 52:49, 60, 88, 90, 144, 172f, 194, 212, 238, 254, 273f

Truth, Hidden—12:354, 357

Truth, The Christian faith as—37:13, 20, 39, 56, 74, 101, 103, 118, 143f, 149f, 206, 330, 345

Truthfulness—22:399, 404, 474, 27:377, see also **Honesty**

Trutvetter, Jodocus—25:235, 343, 372, 25:343, 372, 48:37f, 41, 57f, 62
- *Summa in totam physicen* 1:26n, 25:235
- *Summulae totius logicae* 48:12n

Tschakert, Paul—*Urkundenbuch zur Reformationsgeschichte des Herzogthums Preussen*, Leipzig, 1890 45:136n, 137n

Tubal Cain—1:303, 317

Tübingen—7:192n, 50:83n
- Augustinian Monastery 48:64n
- University of 31:6, 48:64n, 77n, 99n, 123n, 132n, 137n, 154n, 219n, 230n, 317, 49:43n, 414n, 50:253n

Tucher, Stephen—50:277n, 51:371

Tucker, Anthony—*Henry VIII and the Lutherans*, St. Louis, 1965 54:457

Tuesday—23:240

Tulich, Hermann—36:11n, 13, 15

Tullia—7:303n

Tumults—33:50–57

Tunics—6:379f

Tunisia—50:95n

Turkey—4:275, 5:244, 347, 7:26, 8:84, 16:126, 17:188, 407, 22:60, 335, 359, 386, 499, 20:441, 38:207, 46:175, 198, 205n, 47:36, 293f

Turkish Book, 1522—46:157n

Turkish law—46:178, 181

Turks—1:59, 2:12, 52f, 60, 137n, 181, 188, 191f, 195–197, 210, 223f, 226, 256, 262f, 266, 346, 353f, 358, 378, 380, 3:14, 35, 37, 40, 59, 63f, 69, 98, 121f, 158, 161f, 173f, 183, 229, 271, 290, 4:28f, 31–33, 35, 44, 52–54, 99, 105f, 108, 124, 145f, 165, 170, 180, 221, 223, 242, 268, 275, 295, 323, 328f, 345–348, 351, 356–360, 363, 367f, 371–374, 376–382, 391f, 400, 407, 5:12, 22f, 27, 43, 70–73, 77, 130, 170, 199, 262, 343, 347, 6:ixf, 9f, 14, 24, 31, 40, 105n, 106, 117, 127, 138, 149, 157, 159, 206, 210, 218, 223, 228, 229n, 236, 243–245, 250, 253, 274, 307, 334, 353f, 363, 365, 375, 390, 7:26, 32, 61, 64, 72f, 118, 123, 132, 145, 166, 171, 172, 233, 346f, 349, 369, 8:6, 32, 36f, 42, 84n, 89, 136, 182, 187, 193, 230, 243f, 254, 256, 259, 261, 265, 298, 312, 10:14, 431, 436, 438, 449, 453f, 11:92, 98, 100, 339, 12:15, 23, 25f, 70, 84f, 89, 313, 341, 343, 351–354, 357, 13:61, 218f, 234, 236, 258, 271, 273, 281f, 343, 14:x, 11, 26f, 30, 35, 37f, 45, 55, 62, 74, 84, 94, 102, 118, 121n, 125, 209, 250, 262, 266, 333f, 15:340, 16:34, 60, 63, 82, 87, 126, 160, 172, 240, 282, 348, 17:5, 28, 31, 95, 118, 138, 148, 150, 153, 223, 235, 268, 280, 293f, 301, 304f, 309, 314, 317, 331, 365, 369, 375, 392, 401, 403, 18:55, 71, 88n, 91, 153, 197f, 200, 216, 308, 19:43, 51, 168, 20:187, 21:11f, 243, 22:17f, 68, 75, 81–85, 137, 142, 145, 148, 153, 157, 163, 168, 191, 197, 205, 209, 211, 237, 248, 250, 275, 277, 281, 286, 289, 298, 301, 314, 330, 333–335, 337, 342, 351, 365f, 370, 383, 385, 389–393, 399, 404f, 426, 428f, 432, 438, 440, 463f, 466, 468–470, 475f, 486f, 494, 497–499, 501, 505, 514, 23:6, 27, 36, 41, 56, 66, 79, 82, 86f, 99–101, 103, 115, 117f, 120, 122, 124, 128f, 139, 142, 163, 167, 169f, 181, 196, 230, 246, 269, 286, 304, 346–348, 352, 354, 358, 361f, 370, 377, 403, 24:21f, 67, 69, 71, 79, 88, 97, 168, 175, 184, 213f, 219f, 228f, 233, 243, 271, 280, 304, 315, 323, 328, 349, 372, 405f, 408, 417, 26:9f, 26, 28, 125, 130, 134, 138, 140, 147, 150, 231, 270, 283, 368, 395–398, 400f, 27:9, 89, 159, 179, 237, 335, 409, 28:97, 117, 130, 154, 257f, 29:89, 30:5, 12, 29, 55, 75, 152, 189, 309, 311, 31:92, 152, 187, 226, 235, 237f, 337, 32:10, 60, 72, 88–91, 129, 149, 34:5, 11n, 16, 19f, 34n, 48, 35:177, 266f, 271, 296, 300n, 409, 36:28, 71, 211n, 37:32, 77, 232, 272, 359, 367, 38:62n, 97, 102f, 113, 150, 159, 183, 287, 307, 39:11, 13, 15, 19,

69, 76, 82, 93f, 101, 161, 280, 41:xii, 11, 37n, 91, 140n, 141, 145, 165, 202, 207, 241, 251, 259, 274, 284, 331, 339, 344, 352, 366, 371n, 42:38n, 55n, 43:215f, 221, 237f, 240, 44:70, 45:44n, 116n, 137, 199, 201, 350, 352n, 359, 364, 378, 388, 393, 46:xiii, 11n, 18n, 27, 81, 90n, 127, 135, 136n, 137n, 157n, 158n, 161n, 162–178, 179n, 180–182, 183n, 184–201, 202n, 203–205, 217n, 242, 244, 254, 257n, 285, 308, 317, 47:22, 34–36, 49, 51, 80n, 129, 164, 175, 177, 266n, 274, 277, 301, 303, 305, 48:82n, 189n, 49:24n, 37n, 99, 109, 156, 185, 217, 221f, 240f, 251, 253, 255n, 258n, 265, 281, 286, 289, 330n, 352n, 368, 410, 425, 427, 50:55n, 144n, 155n, 219n, 228n, 243n, 248n, 51:150, 157, 203, 205, 212–214, 217, 292, 296f, 346f, 354, 391, 52:83, 108, 114, 231, 53:63, 304, 54:27, 40, 46, 55, 58, 131, 143, 148f, 269, 299, 336, 416, 419–422, 454f

their carnal living 46:175f

Turning the other cheek—45:87, 96, 274, 388

Turtledoves—11:138f, 142, 150

Twelve, Number—11:167

Twelve, The—29:37, see also **Apostles**

***Twelve Articles of the Swabian Peasants*, 1525**—46:6n, 8–16 (text), 17, 18n, 22f, 34, 37–43, 49n, 51, 104n, 49:106

Twenty-first Sunday after Trinity—23:372n

Twenty-third Sunday after Trinity—23:281n

Twenty-fourth Sunday after Trinity—23:390n

Twins—1:217, 243, 312, 2:233, 4:353, 369f, 387, 395, 5:101, 176, 199, 7:8f, 12, 35, 47–49

Two kingdoms—7:254, 8:264, 12:42, 57, 67, 103, 242, 13:42f, 139, 150, 193f, 217, 14:23, 17:325, 387, 21:5, 9, 105n, 210f, 22:225f, 372, 437, 23:178, 295, 311–313, 316, 24:155, 25:109, 26:116n, 28:125–128, 30:20, 75, 180, 212, 33:118f, 287f, 35:164, 238, 289f, 40:355f, 41:226f, 248, 301, 42:38f, 44:xii–xiv, 45:31f, 62, 88, 91–93, 105, 117, 46:69f, 99, 178, 251, 54:199

Tychicus—29:88

Tyndale, William—50:28n

Typhoeus—28:292

Typographical errors—7:x, 7n

Typology—52:127f, 130

Tyranny—2:7f, 20, 30, 32–34, 37, 48, 61f, 84, 197f, 210, 212, 214, 219f, 261, 275, 292, 306, 310, 317f, 364, 368, 3:172, 240, 326, 329, 339, 342, 349, 356, 5:130, 150, 161, 209, 227f, 301, 303, 6:23, 30, 208, 211, 7:4, 135, 200, 331, 8:40, 117, 184, 220, 222, 226, 244, 246, 250, 292, 9:4, 58, 139, 161, 179, 196, 245, 10:7, 431, 12:184, 216f, 238, 347, 394, 15:139, 16:28, 46, 61, 105, 123, 170, 207, 249, 18:140, 147, 161, 180, 230, 20:105, 130f, 133, 135, 257, 26:40f, 96, 162, 221, 306, 344, 461, 27:23, 26, 48, 50, 110, 113, 147, 154, 236f, 276, 286, 297, 358, 382, 408, 29:25, 27, 234, 30:178, 180, 35:202, 287, 352

Tyrants—2:5, 23, 30, 32, 36, 38, 53, 59, 85, 132, 177, 198f, 224, 260, 275, 296, 310, 367, 369, 383, 391, 3:34, 190, 235, 242, 256, 319, 327, 329, 356f, 4:81f, 94, 132, 140f, 182, 202n, 224, 335, 403, 5:18, 130, 171, 186, 262, 265, 7:61, 68, 70, 84, 103, 151, 183, 192, 204, 225, 330, 346, 349, 363, 8:4, 8, 15, 32f, 106, 216, 220, 226, 251f, 265, 267, 288, 9:112f, 226, 245, 13:67, 209, 211, 213, 419, 16:61, 100, 122, 139, 142, 161, 179, 183, 195f, 205–207, 210, 216f, 221, 224, 230, 241, 248–250, 265, 269, 301, 324, 329, 331, 17:5, 25, 57, 67, 71, 74, 86, 88, 120, 132, 154, 171, 175, 177, 183, 185f, 188f, 200, 208, 238, 241, 246, 318, 320, 338, 365, 392f, 407, 19:128, 201f, 208, 213, 215, 218, 24:20, 30f, 81, 112, 114, 116, 118f, 136, 138, 141f, 153, 198f, 224, 265, 280, 286f, 293, 400, 419–421, 25:139, 26:14, 22–24, 33, 44, 128f, 149f, 160, 164, 177, 278, 281, 283, 322, 346, 362, 368–370, 383, 389, 415, 418, 27:5, 43, 45, 72, 110, 123f, 198, 237, 29:62, 72, 90, 235, 35:151, 297, 303, 343, 36:253f, 266, 45:57f, 60, 73, 109, 115, 46:20, 31, 41–43, 84, 104–116, 125, 127, 169, 173, 205, 238, 254, 279, 288, 306, 49:157, 387f, 398

Tyre—2:191, 194, 205, 6:389, 8:273f, 277, 9:169, 11:121f, 125, 127, 185, 16:182–186, 18:52, 134f, 34:170, 192, 47:86

Tyre and Sidon—20:89, 91, 113, 126, 282, 284f, 42:134

Tyrian purple—16:20

Tyrol—49:119

Tyrrhenian Sea—41:356n

Ubiquity of Christ—see **Christ**—His omnipresence

Ulm—49:149, 224, 225n, 236n, 266n, 54:272
Ulrich, Duke of Württemberg—43:261n, 49:414n
Ulrich, St., Bishop of Augsburg—1:239, 3:361f, 39:211
Ultimogeniture—8:208n
Ulysses—4:208, 14:280, 15:5
Unam sanctam—see **Bulls, Papal**
Unbelief—1:64, 147–149, 155, 159, 161, 164, 171, 177, 183, 275, 2:119, 176, 254, 264, 310, 3:30, 37, 136, 148, 158, 170, 187, 190, 199, 214, 229, 4:146, 158, 254, 265, 315, 5:6, 14, 45f, 131, 157, 205, 255, 269, 278, 327, 332, 6:10, 116, 131f, 134, 175, 177, 246, 7:126f, 132, 171, 221, 229, 327, 348, 8:8, 72, 311f, 314, 325, 9:20–23, 27, 97, 112, 135, 149f, 245, 299, 11:13, 46, 71f, 462, 13:22, 117, 16:89, 103, 255, 293, 18:38, 20:164, 21:62, 141, 196–198, 347, 23:175, 238, 288, 295, 350, 360, 24:16, 47, 65, 97, 130, 170, 219, 229, 237, 244, 339, 341, 343f, 346, 379, 394, 396, 400, 25:25, 32f, 53, 93, 97, 108, 208, 228, 284, 310f, 26:189, 227, 230f, 383, 27:8, 67, 70f, 81, 109, 140, 214, 232, 29:65, 109, 124, 150, 153–155, 159, 182, 236, 30:26, 31, 34f, 70, 100, 190, 211, 233, 266, 303, 325f, 35:14, 243, 322, 369, 371, 384, 36:60f, 67, 178, 201, 203, 303, 38:103, 112, 155, 191, 313, 41:250, 287, 45:25, 102, 327f, 354n, 46:186, 219, 265, 286, 290
Unbelievers—2:24, 261, 304, 3:269, 286, 4:147, 330, 5:138, 332, 372, 8:9, 59, 136, 185, 9:97, 19:197, 23:31, 336, 358, 418, 24:80, 164, 168, 214, 316, 345, 25:9, 85f, 151, 168, 198, 26:25, 240, 242, 374, 413, 27:34, 76, 245, 281, 310, 28:33f, 36, 38f, 94f, 102, 201, 29:103, 163–165, 237, 30:15, 20, 23, 60f, 74–76, 87f, 100, 115, 121, 155, 172, 210, 278, 35:13, 370, 36:93, 134, 145, 193, 38:39, 42f, 71, 104, 153
Unbelieving spouses—28:33f, 36, 38f
Unborn, Nurture of the—27:308
Uncertainty—28:223, 240
Unchastity—30:25, 31, 119, 141, 189, 233, 35:53, 372, 382, 36:201, 203, 206, 208, 210, 227, 42:14, 38f, 44, 72–74, 92, 44:104f, 45:30f, 43, 142, 145, 148, 150, 155, 324, 391, 48:342
Uncircumcision—25:193, 26:92, 95, 101f, 104, 27:30, 137–139, 141, 209, 280, 330, 333–335, 405, 29:158, 219
Uncleanness—4:9, 5:4, 34, 37f, 7:230, 20:144f, 331f, 25:11f, 116, 164–166, 498–500, 27:86, 260, 276, 29:152f, 191f, 211
Unction—see **Anointing**
Unction, Extreme—11:401, 28:62, 29:180n, 34:55, 87, 349, 357, 36:48, 117–123
Unction in Baptism—36:118n
Understanding—4:20, 104, 106, 117, 123, 125, 133, 146, 148, 161, 178, 188, 216, 220, 222, 230, 244, 264, 268, 295, 310f, 319, 351, 361, 363, 369, 376, 7:10, 12, 120, 134, 137, 173, 175, 178, 254, 280, 289, 298, 10:107, 109, 119, 147f, 190, 310f, 452, 459, 11:440, 445f, 461, 465f, 497f, 508, 512, 531f, 14:152, 280, 285, 310, 316, 342f, 16:109, 119f, 224, 246, 251, 21:260f, 25:xi, 4, 28f, 61f, 213, 223f, 263, 329, 412f, 28:228f, 290, 29:126, 145, 186, 237, 30:155f, 327, 38:18, 22–24, 28, 38, 43, 53, 55, 110
Understatement—see **Tapinosis**
Underworld—11:175
Unfaithfulness—16:18, 47, 25:26, 208
Unforgiveable sin—16:84
Ungodliness—1:312, 318, 2:23, 25, 27f, 30, 44, 55, 59, 61f, 71, 84, 117, 180, 204, 209, 211, 214, 220, 224f, 229, 244f, 248, 262, 290, 310, 327, 373, 3:136, 324, 335, 352, 4:43, 88, 315, 391, 5:115, 157, 6:4, 63, 85, 229, 8:59, 11:510, 16:8, 11, 17f, 24, 27, 47, 63f, 80, 105f, 160, 185, 190, 194, 204, 226, 234, 243, 246, 255f, 270, 303, 17:70, 280, 285f, 304f, 378, 385f, 25:271, 273, 277, 26:225, 456, 27:173, 337, 42:135
Ungodly persons—2:4, 7f, 20, 26, 30, 35, 38, 42, 44, 51, 53, 55–57, 62, 70, 76, 82, 84, 89, 93, 127, 133, 153f, 170, 172, 176f, 180, 182, 192, 194–196, 198, 204, 212, 214, 218–227, 230, 235, 241, 246, 248, 251, 283, 289f, 310, 320, 2:347, 349, 351, 378f, 382, 3:13–15, 22, 40, 60, 70, 140, 173, 235, 241, 244, 264f, 268–270, 284, 292–296, 302, 304, 311, 318, 320, 333, 336, 340f, 347, 4:78, 117f, 121, 134, 154, 156, 172, 196, 229, 246, 248, 261–263, 309f, 316, 322, 338, 343, 373, 375, 404, 5:10, 121, 143, 171, 6:51, 90f, 124, 217f, 310f, 7:62, 81, 113, 119, 215, 232f, 252, 287, 292–296, 298, 303, 320, 347, 350, 8:52, 96, 202, 219, 276, 300, 315, 9:4, 83, 135, 161, 179, 183, 268, 10:7, 12, 17, 23f, 29, 32, 59, 71, 200, 423f, 11:494, 529, 14:287–

293, 297, 301f, 305–309, 316–319, 323f, 15:61, 246f, 16:10f, 15, 23, 36, 40f, 45f, 57, 62, 64f, 67, 70, 72, 79f, 83, 85, 91, 95, 102, 108, 110, 120f, 129, 137, 139, 141, 143, 150, 152, 156, 162f, 167, 173, 185f, 191, 194, 196, 204–208, 217, 220–222, 225–229, 231, 16:232–236, 239f, 242–246, 248–250, 254–257, 260, 269, 272, 281, 283, 287–290, 324, 326, 338, 340, 17:14, 17, 18n, 21f, 38, 43, 54, 70, 92, 110f, 196, 242, 278, 280–283, 287, 297, 300, 302f, 334f, 360, 377f, 416, 19:183, 23:6, 10, 18, 31, 50, 61, 86, 113, 306, 327, 24:359, 369, 25:44f, 77, 179f, 205, 225f, 265, 273, 277, 435, 496, 26:24, 251, 27:172, 185, 291, 329, 346, 28:237, 261, 29:11f, 30:177, 179f, 233, 32:144, 37:22, 24, 26, 31, 53, 70, 88, 100, 121, 145, 147, 261f, 354f, 365, 372, 38:28, 42, 58, see also **Godless, The**

Unhappiness—9:185

Unicorns—10:113, 11:88, 89n

Union with Christ—23:147f, 35:50

United States of America—38:xif

Unity of Christians—3:147, 9:72, 221, 250f, 12:295, 13:7, 13, 18, 20:147, 327, 334, 23:388, 25:104–106, 464, 483, 27:38f, 41f, 60f, 91, 107, 215, 265, 280f, 392, 30:94f, 32:74, 82, 35:67, 80, 201, 383, 37:xiiif, xvi, 13–15, 17, 23–38, 41, 143, 154, 158, 167f, 275, 289, 367, 38:195, 319, 39:62, 65–67, 139, 181, 41:48, 107, 143, 311, 316, 348, 358, 45:360f, 46:9, 50:6f, 62f, 171, 173f, 188, 227, 52:34f, 54:283f

Universal salvation—8:134, 10:457, 25:376, 37:372

Universals—27:390

Universe—1:18, 46, 235n, 25:158, 38:32, 60, 75

Universities—4:x, 226, 14:23, 16:243, 17:14, 152, 18:184, 23:27, 96, 112, 329, 351, 26:23, 134, 184, 309, 28:366, 30:266, 309, 311, 32:141, 34:165, 259, 36:123, 134, 135n, 136n, 139n, 156, 163f, 166f, 173, 199, 207, 209f, 216, 220, 224f, 44:200–207, 45:82n, 343f, 348, 351f, 358, 360, 375, 46:164, 197, 214n, 226, 232, 234, 52:82, 84, 108, 118, 141, 145, 162, 166f, 178, 183, 194, 196, 241, 258, 265, 275, 282, see also individual universities listed under names of cities where located; **Schools**

Unjust commands—29:73

Unjust persons—3:234f, 11:491f

Unleavened bread—9:154, 158

Unmarried persons—28:47–50, 52f

Unrighteous persons—10:76, 267f, 273f

Unrighteousness—2:28, 383, 7:275, 279, 283, 8:230, 24:346, 25:9f, 13, 27, 53, 83, 168, 205, 270–273, 278, 284, 319, 26:35, 182, 217, 230, 308, 376

Unrighteousness vs. iniquity—25:168

Unworthiness—3:25, 158, 160f, 291, 11:512, 24:386–388, 398, 394, 26:214, 311

Upright persons—10:154f, 11:385f, 13:357, 381, 399, 402, 405

Uprightness—7:58, 15:133, 16:24, 120, 204, 25:405, 513, 26:141

Uprisings—see **Insurrection; Rebellion**

Ur of the Chaldees—2:242, 248f, 268f, 276–278, 281, 290, 3:29, 34f, 43, 112, 180, 244, 4:185, 237, 250, 308, 348, 352, 5:209f, 6:84, 7:199, 22:108

Urban II, Pope—44:144n, 46:186n, 227n

Urban IV, Pope—23:82n, 45:133

Urban V, Pope—31:238n

Urban VI, Pope—34:24n, 31

Urbino—41:308n, 367n

Uriah—7:35, 274, 8:236, 14:173, 22:397, 29:113f, 30:229, 45:26, 389

Uriel, Archangel—3:80

Urim and Thummim—9:168n, 305n

Ursula, St., Monastery of—42:17

Ursula von Portzig—28:3n

Usages—14:14, 290

Use of Salvation, Making—28:34f, 230–232, 267f, 304f

Using and enjoying God's gifts—25:292, 295, 313, 350, 363, 28:316, 54:54

Usurers—8:27, 120, 126, 128, 45:301, 305n

Usury—2:263, 326, 3:222, 231, 249, 279, 324, 4:206, 214, 227, 381, 5:368f, 6:24, 32, 206, 211, 356, 7:160f, 8:109, 117, 9:144–148, 234, 238, 242, 14:113, 123, 264, 20:55, 267, 22:418, 518f, 23:235, 291, 297, 399, 24:250, 27:386, 28:315, 358, 35:127f, 41:18, 43:20, 221, 279, 44:96, 213, 45:xii, 115, 174n, 175f, 229, 233–236, 239n, 240f, 243, 245n, 247, 257n, 268, 273, 290n, 291–300, 302, 304n, 306f, 47:125, 167, 169n, 217f, 227f, 242, 255, 270–276, 284, 285n, 288, 49:50–55, 51:93, 97, 124, 294, 374, 52:215, 228, 54:369, 398, see also **Luther, Martin, Writings of—*Trade and Usury***

Usury, Scholastics on—45:233f, 237, 290n, 292n, 307n

Utinger, Heinrich—38:12, 83n
Utraquists—40:4f, 48:144n, 153n, 49:56n
Utrecht—54:472
Utrecht, Territory of—34:345, 353
Utterance—10:210–212, 219
Uz—2:206, 4:185, 5:207
Uzziah, King—4:261, 16:6, 69, 78, 143, 18:130, 19:38, 20:339

V.D.M.I.E.—17:109n, 118f, 309n, 395
Vacuums—2:207
Vadianus (Joachim von Watt)—45:57n, 343n
Vagabonds—4:319
Vagrants—3:179f, 182, 7:49, 244, 337f, 8:89, 209, 212
Vain endeavors—15:7f, 9, 14, 94, 102f
Vainglory—2:119, 3:4–6, 9, 27:80, 99, 102–105, 106n, 115, 120f, 142, 371, 394f, 403
Vajta, Vilmos—48:xviin, 54:69n
Luther on Worship, Philadelphia, 1958 53:59n
Vale of tears—28:122
Valens, Emperor—41:38n, 127n
Valentin, Emperor—23:301n
Valentin, Veit—*The German People: Their History and Civilization from the Holy Roman Empire to the Third Reich*, New York, 1952 46:6n
Valentine's, St., Day—23:117n
Valentinian, Emperor—41:38n, 127n
Valentinians—see **Gnosticism, Valentinian**
Valentinus—30:287
Valerian, Emperor—3:125n, 15:71n
Valerius Gratus, Procurator—34:52n
Valerius Maximus—*Factorum et dictorum memorabilium libri* 25:175n
Valla—see **Lorenzo Valla**
Valley of the shadow 12:166f
Valleys—11:145f, 326f, 328n, 329
Van den Esschen, John—see **Esschen, John van den**
Van Gelder, H.A. Enno—*The Two Reformations of the 16th Century*, The Hague, 1961 26:65n
Vandals—2:189, 12:33, 13:282, 23:388, 28:130, 41:372
Vanity—3:63, 9:201, 10:54 57, 59, 74, 122, 139, 186, 300f, 11:66, 68, 300, 442, 12:192, 14:5, 15:4, 11, 13–16, 34, 48, 82, 129, 16:143, 25:13, 159, 361–363, 28:327, 29:123, 235, 30:31
Vapor—2:147
Varna, Battle of 32:90, 44:194n, 46:167n
Varro, Marcus Terentius—2:328n
Antiquitates Rerum Humanorum et Divinarum 34:275n
Vashti—11:281
Vatican City—44:167n
Vatican Council, Second—42:xiii
Vatican library—25:xiif, 29:xi
Vaughn, E.T.—early translator of Luther's *Bondage of the Will* 33:xin
Vegetables—1:206, 210
Vegetius—3:132n
Vehe Hymnal—53:268
Vehus, Dr., Chancellor of Baden—32:116–118, 120
Veil—3:98, 4:296, 299, 26:322, 324
Veil of the temple—29:224
Veil over Scriptures—47:155n, 171
Veit, Brother—5:369, 18:395n
Veneration of saints—see **Saints**—Veneration of
Venereal disease—13:76n, 22:132, 500
Venetian printer—42:17
Venetians—16:126, 259, 19:43, 25:464, 472, 46:120, 199n
Vengeance—1:261, 271, 289f, 339, 5:8, 65, 67, 327, 365, 373, 6:30, 201, 368, 7:116, 227, 232, 237, 263, 265, 271, 275, 8:24, 70, 162, 219, 9:112, 145, 183, 195, 211, 248–250, 297–299, 10:58f, 11:9, 242f, 411–413, 13:416f, 14:244, 258, 316, 16:139, 17:75f, 83, 147, 305f, 308, 334, 353f, 411, 21:24, 40f, 106f, 114, 124, 25:108, 444, 26:428, 27:376f, 29:121, 169, 30:75, 101, 31:305, 43:104f, 46:25, 27–29, 73, 107f, 110, 113f, 165, 185, 54:301
Veni, Creator Spiritus **(hymn)**—30:256n
Veni, Sancte Spiritus **(hymn)**—15:316, 30:256n, 39:65n
Venial sin—42:162n
Venice—2:137, 3:41n, 5:74, 8:274, 16:286, 17:144, 22:417, 25:124, 34:48n, 36:208, 41:181, 260, 340, 374n, 45:134, 46:204n, 48:57n, 49:156, 185, 220f, 286n, 50:54n, 83n, 183, 184n, 190n, 219n, 229n, 242n, 248, 269n, 270, 272, 54:347
Venom—2:163, 9:297, 23:144, 361, 26:17, 23
Ventriloquists—16:239
Venus—1:203, 249, 2:18n, 3:201, 7:75, 120, 17:24, 22:25, 27:371, 29:56, 46:182n
Verbal inspiration—see **Scripture(s)**—Inspiration, Verbal
Verbosity—54:136
Vercellae, Woman of—25:465n
Verden—32:274n

Vergerio, Peter Paul—34:238n, 41:6, 9n, 50:83n, 108, 110, 115, 127, 128n, 160
Vermin—1:54, 204, 3:52, 24:216, 221, 277, 323, 368
Vernacular language—40:288, 300, 307, 310, 53:24, 36, 39, 101
Veronica, St., Veil of—41:322f
Verres—4:202, 205
Versicles—53:129–145, 154, 168–170
Vertumnus—33:82, 163
Vespasian, Emperor—1:245, 12:254, 13:155, 15:141, 47:138, 237
Vespers—11:525n, 16:331, 21:298, 53:9, 13, 25, 30, 38, 53, 68f, 153, 308, 321, see also **Canonical Hours**
Vessels—1:79, 84, 16:158, 181
Vestiges of divinity—4:195
Vestments—5:110, 125, 6:324, 10:436, 13:289f, 294f, 14:333, 20:156, 205f, 255, 24:176, 25:487, 491, 27:31, 53, 29:22, 23, 120, 191f, 195, 32:7, 18, 35:82, 36:201f, 38:109f, 114, 39:253f, 40:41, 129f, 148, 45:78, 166, 179n, 53:22, 31, 69, 260, 327
Vexations—4:5f, 9, 8:7, 54, 113f, 279, 293
Via regia—see **Royal road**
Vicars of God—11:111
Vicenza—34:235, 238n, 41:6, 9n, 11n, 275n
Vices—3:132, 254, 4:78, 88, 193, 242, 380, 396, 5:4, 83, 181, 207f, 293, 364, 7:30, 34, 83, 124, 229, 258, 281, 13:67f, 222, 15:202, 246f, 25:65, 139, 160, 164, 167, 452, 481, 26:141, 188f, 217, 307, 459, 29:18f, 25, 27, 39, 53f, 62, 65, 74, 77, 119, 139, 154f, 42:40, 72, 177
***Victimae paschali laudes* (hymn)**—29:136n
Victor I, Pope—2:226n, 26:411, 38:317n, 41:61n, 62
Victor of Carben—47:130, 176n
Victory—3:3f, 6f, 9, 13, 31, 76, 160, 225f, 4:191f, 5:18f, 39, 72, 90, 92, 131f, 143, 185, 227f, 230f, 234, 239, 6:157f, 167–169, 180, 225, 242, 244, 7:81, 87, 132, 170–172, 221, 313, 369, 9:202, 205, 268, 272, 305, 10:42–45, 209, 451, 17:123, 206, 277, 324, 19:148, 20:132–135, 302f, 305, 309, 327, 24:138, 192, 383, 389, 403, 415, 421f, 25:53, 65, 317, 26:22, 27, 31, 86, 125, 138, 146, 167, 185, 218, 223, 228, 280, 282, 284f, 295, 303, 317, 342, 357, 369, 371, 421, 27:71, 87, 158
Victory, Spiritual—25:318, 28:111f, 202f, 206, 210–212
Victory of faith—30:311f
Victory over sin—38:xf, 129
Victory through Christ—12:59, 172–175, 217, 219, 231
Vienna—4:391, 7:91n, 14:121, 16:160n, 22:83, 23:6n, 32:266, 40:229n, 46:161n, 184n, 48:155, 199, 49:81n, 91, 187n, 240n, 241, 330, 368f, 50:186n, 243n
University of 48:99n, 199, 49:88n, 284n, 50:211n
Vienna, Concordat of—44:147n
Vigilance—28:165–169
Vigilius of Thapsus—41:83n
Vigils—2:161, 339, 3:316, 4:57, 61, 140, 165, 5:3f, 6, 271, 7:113, 234, 323, 8:267, 276, 326, 14:23, 16:227, 23:85, 138, 268, 356, 24:24, 222, 26:26, 68, 70, 212, 222, 386, 27:55, 68, 124, 174, 350, 352, 29:7, 9, 28, 72, 30:170, 174, 34:26, 54, 36:89, 198n, 299, 37:369f, 38:118, 173, 213, 41:241, 283, 42:75, 44:181, 45:284, 286, 351n, 53:327
Villages—20:186f
Villains—46:288, 302, 311, 313f
Villainy—52:232
Vincent of Lerins—27:310, 34:209n
Commonitorium 3:125n
Letters from St. Augustine 32:167n, 216n
Vincentius, St.—6:230, 8:255f, 259, 31:142, 51:392
Vindictiveness—2:104, 25:112
Vinedresser—24:193f, 198–202, 204, 209f, 224
Vinegar—5:67, 88, 24:379, 401
Vines—2:134, 7:97, 112, 124, 302, 8:247–249, 251f, 254f, 257, 259, 261, 266, 268f, 272, 308, 310, 11:76f, 83, 24:193–196, 198–203, 205, 208f, 212, 216–219, 222, 224–227, 231f, 234–239, 248f
Vineyards—2:166, 188, 373, 3:129, 4:62, 136, 5:136, 138, 8:248, 251f, 259, 266, 295, 9:204, 206f, 214, 221, 225, 238, 241, 243, 245, 15:203, 221, 262f, 16:57f, 60, 87, 186, 189, 212, 214, 18:268, 24:195, 198–200, 216, 235
Violence—4:85, 332, 9:80, 13:58, 14:309, 17:324, 19:16, 108, 125f, 128, 130, 158, 160, 222f, 29:27f, 58, 62, 170, 45:61f, 87, 46:48, 61, 157, 252, 270, 281, 308, 47:14, see also **Force**
Violence opposed—36:263
Vipers—3:193, 4:222, 24:272, 410f, 26:19, 21, 188, 422, see also **Asps**; **Serpents**
Vipo—53:255
Virgil—1:247, 2:106, 5:353, 8:210, 12:7, 33, 76, 220, 13:119, 199f, 14:250,

280n, 296n, 17:379, 19:174, 27:179, 33:33, 41, 37:56, 39:151n, 178, 40:43n, 298, 319n, 320, 41:145n, 346n, 43:240, 45:285n, 329n, 54:14, 375, 476

Aeneid 1:42n, 99n, 214n, 303n, 3:359n, 4:289n, 347n, 383n, 403n, 5:132n, 172n, 247n, 377n, 6:83n, 111n, 203n, 7:40n, 41n, 46n, 48n, 62n, 74n, 79n, 178n, 203n, 295n, 8:58n, 97n, 214n, 297n, 9:203n, 10:159, 14:250n, 15:38n, 43n, 102n, 108n, 156n, 159n, 16:48n, 72n, 128n, 171n, 280n, 17:42n, 51n, 123n, 148n, 240n, 367n, 18:20, 49, 180, 246n, 298n, 19:114n, 20:60n, 25:300, 317, 451, 26:134n, 187n, 27:24n, 61n, 28:292, 29:39n, 144n, 31:156n, 164n, 32:167n, 168n, 33:41n, 51n, 56n, 72n, 85n, 50:172n, 216n, 54:80, 356

Bucolics 2:385n, 14:296n, 54:476

Eclogues 2:15, 3:308n, 4:90n, 398n, 5:53n, 292n, 6:15n, 267n, 305n, 7:76n, 15:258n, 347n, 16:171n, 18:363f, 25:364, 27:244n, 29:67n, 33:19n, 226n, 36:125n, 54:375

Georgics 1:212n, 2:304n, 352n, 7:193, 8:147n, 10:412, 11:203n, 13:103n, 15:114n, 18:82f, 20:16n, 169n, 31:277n, 337, 33:33n, 34:336n, 54:476

Virgin birth—8:242, 307f, 12:123, 15:325, 16:84, 20:195, 21:353, 23:83, 244, 250, 27:288, 29:190f, 36:32, 152, 275, 280, 283, 298f, 337f, 341, 344f, 45:xv, 207–209, 213n, 52:153

Virgin vs. maiden—see **Almah (Hebrew word for virgin or maiden)**

Virginity—3:204, 208, 4:233, 5:307, 348, 362, 9:162, 222f, 226, 10:91, 156, 223, 397f, 17:236f, 262, 24:320, 26:113, 367, 27:95, 288, 28:15f, 48f, 29:190, 30:96, 170, 225n, 260, 35:382, 37:37, 371, 44:307, 346, 45:46f, 205, 210, 275, 391, 46:282, 291, 48:284, 334, 52:108, 144, 218, 239, 273

Virgins—1:220, 233, 2:7, 18, 72, 97, 3:147, 202, 211, 257, 259, 4:160f, 212, 224f, 233f, 255, 262, 270f, 275, 299, 5:35f, 40, 294, 296f, 357, 6:18, 114, 193, 201, 211, 323, 7:12f, 25, 31, 36, 77, 272, 21:6, 310, 24:34, 75, 90, 92f, 97, 105, 107f, 118, 138, 171, 215, 319, 324, 26:28–30, 37, 39, 228, 277, 349, 367, 372, 444, 459, 28:11, 48f, 54, 29:19, 202, 30:26, 95, 225n, 41:156–164, 208, 45:207n, 208–210, 353n, 46:281f, 292, 289, 298

Virgins, Foolish—5:158, 42:36

Virgins, Wise and foolish—11:372

Virtue—3:22, 24–26, 44, 49, 58, 132, 185, 198, 200f, 203, 208–210, 306, 351, 354, 357, 7:55, 58, 62, 67, 70f, 74, 77f, 83, 88, 90–92, 96, 98, 100f, 103, 125, 130, 133, 142, 164–166, 177f, 182f, 185, 194, 204f, 234, 318, 359f, 371, 8:17, 19, 21, 49f, 56–58, 62, 100f, 103, 107f, 110, 171, 174, 179, 194, 228, 267, 13:54, 214, 25:135, 27:58f, 84, 93–95, 115, 129f, 145, 154, 156, 169, 172, 174, 196, 220, 240–242, 259, 289, 291, 303, 404, 42:36, 41, 101n, 46:102, 284

Virtues—4:18, 21f, 78, 83, 103, 157, 170, 187, 193–197, 213, 216f, 223, 242, 255f, 270–272, 278, 282, 295, 309, 318, 327, 338f, 352, 384, 390, 397, 5:5–9, 12, 25, 41, 65, 81, 83, 89, 91, 233f, 254, 269, 275f, 278, 287, 293, 307, 332f, 351, 369, 378, 382, 6:36, 45, 50, 70, 114, 180, 10:74, 100, 11:4, 9, 12, 313, 325, 336, 15:202, 234, 246f, 21:41f, 183f, 314, 321, 25:108, 135–137, 152, 160, 178, 222, 354, 385, 410, 476, 479, 26:107, 124, 247, 270, 308, 352, 354, 363, 379, 398, 421, 28:372, 29:25, 30, 36, 61f, 76f, 119, 144, 155, 30:98, 100, 156, 229, 313, 31:350, 32:136, 225f

Virtues, Chorus of—25:160

Virtues, Theological—41:146

Visibility—37:xii, 47, 76f, 89, 94, 99, 104, 109

Visible things—29:181, 185, 216, 240

Visions—3:10–12, 17f, 164, 167, 177n, 275, 330, 350f, 4:313, 5:71, 211, 236–238, 244, 254, 264, 288, 318, 346f, 6:144, 264, 329–331, 7:119f, 143, 149–151, 153, 212, 295, 367, 8:79, 201, 16:5, 28, 69, 71–73, 18:108, 20:14, 17f, 21, 36–38, 42f, 45, 51, 56, 69, 105, 146, 157f, 167f, 178f, 222f, 252f, 25:92, 106, 26:28, 29:191, 30:296n, 297, 35:285, 330, 398, 54:259, see also **Dreams**

Visitation, Divine—16:240

Visitation of parishes—13:x, 15:247, 37:155, 40:263–320, 45:166, 180n, 48:163n, 182, 211n, 275n, 400, 49:30n, 47n, 55n, 135, 137f, 159f, 163, 168, 214, 291n, 209, 50:61, 63n, 93n, 97n, 54:308

Visitation of the sick—37:370

Vistula River—45:133

Vitae patrum—see ***Lives of the Fathers***

Vocations—see **Callings**

Voes, Heinrich—53:211, 217
Vogelsang, Erich—51:5
Vogt (or Voigt), James—48:33n, 43, 51, 313n
Vogt, Wilhelm—*Die Vorgeschichte des Bauernkrieges,* Halle, 1887 45:62n
Vogtland—50:97n
Voice—13:35, 17:8, 211, 308, 25:31, 92, 192f, 239f, 407, 417f
Volta, Gabriel della—31:37, 255
Voluntary nature of faith—40:230f, 45:106–108, 114
Voluntas—33:xii
Voluptuousness—2:60
Volz, Hans—49:xv, 50:xvi
Volz, Paul—30:259n
Vomit—2:157, 19:130, 219, 222
Voragine, Jacobus de—see **Jacobus de Voragine**
Vorst, Peter van der, Papal legate—50:145n, 155n, 163n, 54:228, 232
Vorstius, Peter—see **Vorst, Peter van der, Papal legate**
Vos, Henry—13:336n, 32:263, 266, 43:74
Vows—1:106, 118n, 161, 238, 249, 2:79, 270n, 379, 3:128, 158, 203, 4:40, 121, 139, 156, 288, 400, 5:253, 257–265, 342n, 8:182, 186, 305, 9:64n, 89, 234f, 238, 10:15, 14:33, 34n, 35, 36n, 15:79f, 16:167, 18:10, 142, 296, 19:81f, 20:260, 262, 277, 22:456, 23:24, 25:489–491, 26:26, 28, 32, 41, 70n, 175, 185, 221–223, 238, 283, 287, 295, 312, 332, 27:10, 18f, 25, 71, 73, 89, 135, 211, 28:9f, 17, 43, 344, 29:6, 9, 19f, 46, 30:89, 246, 280n, 295, 34:66, 94, 306, 352, 358, 35:84, 138, 142, 36:7f, 18, 58f, 73–75, 76n, 77, 78n, 79–81, 101f, 134, 158–160, 212f, 217, 260, 37:363, 371, 38:86, 118n, 39:43f, 286–289, 42:20, 43:83–96, 44:212, 215, 243–400, 45:14, 19, 22, 27, 53, 141f, 145–155, 155n, 158, 46:141f, 145, 146n, 147–151, 152n, 153f, 48:277f, 281n, 285, 297f, 310f, 321, 331f, 337f, 354, 357f, 50:133n, 192n, 51:81, 116, 361–363, 52:251–270, 273, 54:13
Vows, Old Testament view of—48:285
Vulgar speech—23:298
Vulgate version—see **Scripture(s)**—Vulgate version
Vultures—9:242

Wace and Buchheim, trans.—*Babylonian Captivity of the Church* by Luther, London, 1896 36:9f, 105n
Wages—5:287, 364–368, 370, 373–377, 385f, 6:17f, 20, 68, 70, 80, 96, 8:280, 9:243, 245, 248, 307, 46:14, 127–132, 233
Wagons—5:121, 215, 24:37, 203, 383f
Wahl, Adalbert—54:xxiiin
Waiting—10:78, 100
Waldberg, Otto Truchsess von—50:264n, 265n
Waldensians—2:327n, 17:67, 28:339, 349, 32:129n, 36:271, 275, 37:14n, 38n, 40:153n, 154n, 255, 50:172n, 54:115, 176f
Waldo, Peter—32:129n
Waldshut—40:229n
Walk—11:322
Walking with God—18:261–263
Wallachia—49:240n
Walls, City—20:186
Walpurgis Night—18:362n
Walter, Johann—see **Walther, Johann**
Walter, Johannes von—47:5n
Walther, Jerome—39:211n
Walther, Johann—50:232, 53:55f, 58–60, 177, 193f, 204, 212, 214, 218, 222, 225, 227, 229f, 232f, 235, 237f, 240, 252f, 255f, 258, 260, 263–265, 268, 271–273, 275, 278, 280f, 284, 299f, 315, 319
Walther, Wilhelm—*Für Luther wider Rom,* Halle, 1906 45:33n
Walz, Otto—21:xvii
Wanckel, Matthis—51:357
Wander, Karl F.W., ed.—*Deutsche Sprichtwörter Lexikon,* Leipzig, 1867–1880 31:158n, 35:52n, 142n, 166n, 184n, 188n, 195n, 200n, 249n, 36:230n, 255n, 260n, 346n, 347n, 355n, 37:57n, 133n, 45:17n, 21n, 33n, 35n, 37n, 38n, 44n, 45n, 46n, 47f, 63n, 108n, 113n, 114n, 119n, 120n, 123n, 124n, 125n, 250n, 253n, 256n, 272n, 275n, 279n, 324n, 325n, 353n, 375n, 46:21n, 25n, 26n, 28n, 29n, 32n, 64n, 65n, 68n, 69n, 76n, 78n, 83n, 84n, 104n, 108n, 121n, 122n, 123n, 125n, 169n, 172n, 272n, 290n, 319n
Wantonness—2:62, 126, 141, 3:179, 231, 24:14, 25:12, 367, 481f, 488, 27:92, 96, 368f, 46:72, 150, 153, 286f, 309, 311
Wants—24:24, 87, 90, 113, 354
War—2:60, 70, 142, 198, 215f, 225f, 272, 289, 336, 338, 358, 363, 365f, 368f, 373f, 377, 380, 382, 396, 3:30, 66, 114, 171, 191, 225, 290, 293, 4:3, 58, 105, 202n, 263, 292, 335, 344f, 368, 377, 380, 405, 5:10, 61, 68, 124, 131, 150,

179, 227, 230, 238, 251, 268, 297, 349f, 6:41, 229, 242, 334, 7:40, 121, 126, 141, 169–173, 176, 178, 181, 183, 186, 228, 240, 266, 304, 313, 8:103, 169, 253, 256, 264f, 279f, 282, 290, 299, 306, 9:202–206, 210, 231f, 241, 306, 11:5–7, 12, 13:13f, 55–57, 140, 395, 15:21, 26, 39, 41, 138, 151, 156, 16:32, 67, 134, 176, 221, 284, 17:4f, 21:30f, 81, 110, 113, 169, 175, 335–338, 23:12, 21, 274, 291, 301, 349, 363, 380, 24:12, 14, 26, 80, 90, 315, 336, 392, 25:55, 63–65, 112, 506, 26:307, 27:47, 70–72, 170, 239, 361–363, 374, 29:9, 73, 30:71, 75, 235, 247, 259, 269, 303f, 311, 36:207, 210, 41:34f, 36n, 37, 121, 45:123–125, 134f, 276, 279, 46:8, 11n, 78, 89–91, 95–98, 103, 109, 115, 118–121, 122n, 125, 127, 130, 132–136, 159, 164f, 168, 180–183, 185, 192, 201, 226, 238, 245, 257, 50:69f, 51:157, 177, 52:222, 231, 54:279, 283, 335f

War, Doctrine of just—47:7

War against Evangelical states feared—47:6, 13–19, 29, 32–54

Warfare, Christians'—12:174f, 218

Warfare, Spiritual—44:69–71, 105f

Warnings—4:57, 140, 176, 219, 264, 343, 7:110, 213, 338, 23:80, 265, 362

Warriors—4:7, 327, 30:255, 311

Wartburg—6:138n, 13:ix, 21:xviif, 32:xvi, 135, 138, 34:xv, 283n, 35:115f, 127, 206, 228, 36:x, 129f, 233, 38:93, 39:xxi, 227, 242f, 40:xi, 42:xi, xiii, 46:19n, 48:4n, 39n, 79n, 210, 213, 214n, 215, 220, 222n, 227n, 228, 243f, 246, 248, 253, 255f, 264, 268f, 272, 274, 277, 283, 289, 291, 296, 305, 310, 312, 315, 317, 319, 321, 322n, 323, 325, 337, 339, 346, 348, 353, 356f, 360, 364, 372, 380, 382, 386, 388, 393, 49:xiii, 4n, 13, 40, 71n, 94, 287n, 51:xivf, 69

***Wartburg Postil*, Luther's**—see **Luther, Martin, Writings of**

Warts—2:108

Waste—8:120

Watches of the night—14:193

Watchfulness—25:112, 45:328–331, 336

Watchmen—17:265, 18:271, 28:283

Watchtower—6:81f, 274

Water—1:6–9, 16, 24, 26, 28f, 32–37, 40, 43, 49, 52, 54f, 64, 96, 126, 160f, 208, 227f, 309f, 351, 2:64, 66f, 70f, 74, 76, 85, 89, 93–98, 102f, 105, 107, 110–112, 129, 149, 154f, 157f, 162, 231, 266f, 269, 293, 344, 349f, 357, 360, 385, 3:34, 59, 86f, 95, 105, 108, 149, 181, 184–186, 190, 202, 204, 225, 245, 249, 274, 355, 4:5, 7, 9, 36, 40, 45, 47f, 51f, 67, 74, 77, 136, 172, 262, 270f, 317, 354, 370, 379f, 409, 5:8, 49, 58–60, 64f, 68, 82, 137, 150, 248f, 255, 281f, 284, 287, 7:68, 70, 103, 127, 141, 262, 302, 309, 338, 8:38, 108, 120, 145, 153, 179, 192, 211f, 230, 254, 267f, 296, 9:230, 235, 272, 290, 10:20f, 23, 88, 133, 149f, 155f, 171, 195, 201–203, 351f, 354, 11:17f, 30–33, 320, 357, 15:17, 97, 17:47f, 86, 97, 103, 113, 192f, 217, 290, 317, 413, 19:146, 233, 20:143, 331, 340, 23:85, 92, 114, 119, 122–124, 143, 205, 258, 263, 265, 269, 300, 315, 334, 358, 377, 412f, 24:39, 41, 43, 46–48, 53, 70, 75, 82, 109, 129, 215, 291, 361, 369, 383, 26:107, 315, 329, 362, 384, 406, 27:26, 58, 69, 81f, 149, 163f, 220, 222, 227, 276, 284, 330, 356, 364, 410, 36:92, 108, 122, 202, 37:11, 16n, 38, 76, 95, 317, 53:26f, see also **Baptism**

Water, Consecrated—12:360

Water, Holy—2:161, 15:324, 34:55, 100, 35:292n, 41:168f, 172, 200, 339

Water, Living—23:273–277

Watson, Philip S.—26:x, 54:328n
author of Introduction and of introductory comments in Vol. 33
co-editor of *Luther and Erasmus: Free Will and Salvation* 33:xin
editor of Vol. 33
Let God be God, Philadelphia, 1949 51:17, 40n
translator of *Bondage of the Will* 33:5–295

Watt, Joachim von—see **Vadianus (Joachim von Watt)**

Watzdorf, Kaspar von—43:84n, 94

Watzdorf, Katharina von—43:88, 89n

Waves—11:235, 19:18

Waving—20:198

Wax—3:28, 191, 7:72, 237

Way, The—10:29, 39, 17:8–10, 181, 256f, 279

Way of salvation—12:90f

Way of the Lord—18:408f

Ways of the Lord—12:386

We Condemn—see **Gensichen, Hans-Werner**

Weakness—6:11, 18f, 26, 102, 107f, 110, 116, 139, 150, 171f, 177, 218f, 241, 8:11, 14, 58f, 73, 138, 143, 149, 237, 256, 312, 314, 10:79–81, 89, 93, 177f,

325f, 351, 390f, 395, 12:63, 112, 117, 13:253, 16:89, 17:15, 32, 64–66, 75, 87, 172, 276, 192, 201, 224, 318, 335, 340, 398, 20:7, 14, 22, 26, 31, 36, 52, 151, 222, 304n, 323, 327, 25:30, 63, 67, 113, 116, 119, 153f, 340, 347, 349f, 369, 392, 485, 489, 492, 499–502, 506–508, 516, 28:14, 32, 187f, 29:18, 83, 144, 187, 224
Weakness as sin—32:158, 203–220, 230–232, 246, 255
Wealth—2:6, 9, 34, 37, 59–61, 64f, 87, 102, 124, 172, 181f, 186, 247, 252, 255, 257, 262f, 279, 307, 318, 324–328, 331, 341, 352, 354, 358, 366, 373, 383, 395, 397f, 3:33, 96, 100, 125, 153, 168, 227, 239, 243, 248, 326, 328, 362, 364f, 4:29f, 38, 41, 53, 74, 76, 103, 105, 127, 132, 146, 156, 158, 160, 163, 179, 194, 202, 204, 206f, 210f, 225, 227–229, 245, 255, 260, 270, 275, 287f, 291, 305, 344–346, 350, 368, 379–381, 400f, 404, 5:11, 16, 56f, 66, 72, 77, 80, 86, 112, 199, 260, 369f, 6:3–7, 112f, 7:4, 34f, 62, 68f, 84, 149, 179f, 297, 320, 347, 8:10, 42, 100, 105f, 120, 203, 229f, 248, 258f, 294, 305, 309, 321, 13:393, 400, 15:8f, 37, 68, 86f, 89f, 93f, 119, 157, 259, 17:315, 317, 322, 337f, 18:168, 170, 20:90f, 117, 311, 344, 21:14, 18f, 75, 169f, 172, 174f, 195, 332, 346, 349, 24:19, 79, 84, 162, 181, 354, 25:90, 104, 150, 226, 353, 410–412, 432, 469f, 26:28, 40, 251, 392f, 403, 406, 408, 418, 420f, 439f, 458, 27:65, 121, 130, 134, 219, 250, 286, 393f, 405, 28:371, 378f, 46:94, 129f, 132, 185, 236, 243f, 251, 54:452, see also **Possessions**; **Property**
Wealth, Ecclesiastical—45:161, 297
Wealth, Eternal—23:13
Weaning—4:13, 15, 17
Weapons—1:320f, 9:205, 219, 10:165f, 13:55, 20:95f, 99, 104, 109f, 249, 288, 294, 29:4, 170, 179, 32:89, 46:xiii, 89, 245
Weapons of Christian warfare—12:174f, 218
Weasels—1:77
Weather—2:136, 146, 211, 13:405, 23:203
Weber, James—54:xii
Weber, Max—44:xii, 45:239n
Wedding at Cana—23:114
Wedding rings—53:113
Wedding song—28:3
Weddings—4:243, 252, 254, 257–260, 275–277, 288, 300, 5:100, 295, 24:118, 196, 28:3, 274–276, 341, 45:390, 46:281, 291, 293–295, 298, 300, 54:269, 435, see also **Loeser, Hans**
Wednesday—27:296
Weeds—1:204f, 209
Weekday Services—53:12f, 37f, 68f, 89, 277
Weeks, Feast of—9:155, 26:411
Weeks of years—45:221, 224n, 225, 226n, 227n, 228
Weeping—8:3, 72, 11:503f, 551, 18:96, 25:107
Weight, Just—9:249, 251
Weimar—35:158, 40:48, 45:79, 46:72n, 48:188n, 198n, 313n, 49:15n, 69n, 83, 131n, 152, 190n, 195, 211n, 50:169n, 170n, 207n, 209n, 212f, 214n, 219n, 221n, 231, 51:103f, 111
Weimar edition of Luther's works—see indexes in each volume for references
Weisensee—50:214n
Weisse, Michael—36:275, 53:295, 331, 334
Weissenberg—16:254
Weissestadt, Magister—39:107
Weisz, Hans—14:xi, 34:199, 35:159, 49:203n, 417
  Hymnal 53:194, 283, 317
Welcome—25:120f, 485–487, 492, 501
Welfare, Social—21:118, 172
Well-being, Physical—23:7
Weller, Jerome—34:107, 128, 49:321n, 322n, 340n, 402n, 50:86n, 93n, 103n, 108n, 135n, 149, 54:xiii, 275
  recorder of Luther's table conversation, 1536–1537 54:201–250
Weller, Nicholas—34:107
Weller, Peter—49:321n, 322n, 400n, 401f, 419, 54:75, 150, 152, 203, 367
Welser, Hans—34:363
Wendish boor—4:37
Wends—4:37n, 13:258, 14:74, 118, 50:208n, 54:387
Wentz, Abdul Ross—author of Introduction and presumed author of introductory comments to all items in Vol. 36
  editor of Vol. 36
  translator of *Receiving Both Kinds in the Sacrament* 36:233–267
Werdenberg, Felix von—54:139
Werdermann, Hermann—51:xin, 44n, 52:xn
Werner, Guenther—32:270, 286
Werra River—48:227n
Wertheim—49:50n, 90n, 53:53
Werthern, Dietrich von—45:14, 33n
Wesel, John of—41:115n, 48:185n

Wesley, John—35:365n
West, The—5:71
West Prussia—45:134
Western Church—1:202n
Western Sea—18:61, 103
Westphalia—48:43n, 50:312
Wetzel, George—41:150n, 151n, 189
Weyer, Martin—54:353
Weygand, Frederick—43:99f
Whales—1:51, 2:77, 90, 8:225, 19:67f, 82
Wheat—1:36–38, 2:24, 157, 8:68, 218, 9:243, 293, 23:9, 161
Wheat and chaff—11:293, 374, 381f
Wheel of fortune—16:162, 282
Whips—26:345f
Whisperers—25:13, 170
Whistle—20:112, 305
White—6:323f
White robes—9:149
Whitmonday—22:370
Whitsun week—22:275
Whitsunday—see **Church Year—Pentecost**
Whole man—28:189, 190, 193
Whoredom—see **Prostitution**
Whoremongers—5:330, 332, 345, 8:303, 311, 28:6, 23, 315
Whores—see **Prostitutes**
Whoring—see **Prostitution**
Why?—10:15f, 51, 57, 17:125, 127f
Wicked persons—1:17, 22, 181, 209, 265, 273, 295, 6:42, 78, 90f, 10:174f, 416f, 11:198, 13:112, 179, 186, 419, 16:305, 18:271, 19:110, 117, 129, 144, 160f, 164, 172, 180, 20:42, 52f, 134, 24:73, 235, 368, 46:66, 70f, 73
Wicked teachings—20:53f, 56f, 60, 63, 118f, 127f, 145, 234, 242
Wickedness—1:78, 108, 134, 175, 247, 249, 278, 311, 335, 358, 2:6, 8, 14, 17, 22, 24f, 28, 32, 39, 41, 44f, 47, 52, 61–63, 65, 84, 113, 120, 127f, 134, 170, 173, 201, 210, 217, 219–221, 229, 248, 281, 285, 290, 292, 304, 344, 382, 4:77, 88, 159, 168, 219, 224, 229, 283, 304, 330, 336, 5:5, 11f, 23, 40, 58, 65, 68f, 82, 145, 153, 165, 174, 200, 208, 210, 291, 320, 364f, 375, 380, 7:11, 83, 86, 138, 230, 235, 255, 281, 289, 297, 337, 350, 8:55, 58f, 95, 108f, 114, 215f, 220, 230, 330, 9:233, 13:182f, 275f, 14:11, 47, 72, 106, 167, 211, 213, 216, 226, 244, 256, 267, 275, 292, 309, 315, 336, 18:161, 257, 20:57, 263, 22:117, 123, 125, 234, 236, 253, 378, 23:145, 260, 340, 419, 24:15, 31, 131, 195, 199, 207, 264, 268, 286–288, 290, 317, 341, 378, 25:13, 65, 169f, 200f, 212–214, 453f, 26:39, 71, 86, 105f, 136, 174, 182, 185, 201, 221, 309, 329, 336, 344, 368f, 376, 385, 395, 409, 458f, 27:10, 31, 44, 82, 131f, 136, 175, 260, 350, 375, 387f, 395, 408, 29:84, 119, 153, 196, 30:36, 47, 144, 156, 176, 190, 325–327, 46:68, 81, 248
Widderkauf—see **Repurchase (Widderkauf)**
Widow, Marrying a—22:451
Widowers—8:68, 74, 28:21f, 31, 339
Widowhood—7:23, 28, 35, 28:15, 21, 31, 48:279, 284f, 52:123f, 131, 133
Widows—3:47, 182, 183n, 202 204, 4:233f, 271, 6:246f, 345, 7:8f, 25, 27, 39, 194, 267, 337, 9:19, 111–113, 137f, 243, 248, 254, 13:53, 16:22, 50, 24:171, 25:488, 26:444, 28:334–337, 341f, 345f, 29:29, 38, 72, 30:182, 35:388, 37:365, 371, 41:157, 159, 162–164, 221, 286, 44:396–400, 54:242
Widows and orphans—46:15, 42, 50, 78, 101, 111, 150, 153, 290, 309
Wieck, Johann von der—44:121n
Wied, Hermann von, Archbishop of Cologne—48:34, 247n, 50:253f, 315
Wiederkehrer, Heinz Probst—54:350
Wiencke, Gustav K.—author of Introduction and presumed author of introductions to individual writings in Vol. 43
editor of Vol. 43
Wife and children—46:71, 117, 254, 315
Wild grapes—16:61f, 64, 67
Wild oats—1:204
Wild oxen—9:306
Wildenauer, John Sylvius (called Egranus)—31:333, 34:162, 190, 335n, 54:401
Wilderness—3:31, 60, 64, 66, 69, 71, 74, 107, 4:5, 40, 71, 324, 11:85, 520, 24:45, 48, 62, 75, 35:177, 202n, 47:75–77, 153, 185, 292
Wilhelm III, Count of Honstein—44:149n
Wilhelm V, Duke of Bavaria—45:112n
Wilhelm VI, Count of Henneberg—46:141, 142n
Will—2:118, 123, 125f, 270, 326, 10:11, 25f, 30, 32f, 25:19, 21–24, 77, 183f, 189, 217, 220f, 241, 245, 266–268, 328, 348f, 372, 375, 433, 453, 27:22–25, 69, 77, 89, 91, 165, 173f, 224, 235, 356, 375, 406, 409, 30:32, 119, 224, 246, 52:62, 94f
Will, Bound—25:375f, 32:92
Will, Free—see **Free Will**
Will, Human—12:357, 25:21f, 77, 184,

217, 220f, 241, 245, 328, 372, 375, 433, 453, 29:99, 125, 154, 164, 213, 31:9–16, 48, 58, 323, 33:64–69, 278f, 34:111, 184, 196, 37:81, 121, 363, 42:44–51, 46:18n, 76f, 274, 304
Will, Neutral—33:68f, 114f, 237, 264
Will and testament, Last—see **Last will and testament**
Will of God—1:95, 114, 141, 143, 146–148, 151f, 154, 158, 210, 2:44, 46–49, 112, 124f, 142f, 145, 173, 251, 255, 286, 305, 313, 333, 346, 3:14, 4:6, 8, 36, 40, 72, 89, 95, 103, 112, 116, 123, 125, 141, 144f, 219, 221f, 227f, 248, 262, 268, 304, 325, 353f, 360f, 364, 367, 395, 6:130, 133, 152, 173, 274, 352, 362, 7:73, 113, 115, 122, 128, 151, 154, 175, 177, 182, 184–186, 190, 192, 195f, 214, 219, 232, 238, 308, 314, 322, 357, 8:8, 17f, 30, 33, 37, 60, 92, 114, 165, 200, 259, 14:153, 192f, 201, 212, 281, 15:24f, 28, 40, 65, 148, 16:187, 20:3f, 48f, 131, 21:146, 269, 281, 309, 23:63, 25:83, 198, 375, 381, 386f, 437–439, 442f, 29:4, 61, 71f, 82, 185–187, 30:6, 14, 16, 82f, 110, 117, 124, 140, 249, 251, 303, 322f, 33:37f, 138–147, 181, 184, 190, 35:50, 264, 37:44, 75, 94, 127, 140, 38:23, 54, 56, 102, 187, 39:128, 41:164, 173, 242, 249, 289, 298, 334, 359, 376, 42:27, 42–52, 59, 61, 75f, 79, 89, 102f, 108, 130, 151, 154, 183, 45:37f, 85, 87, 122, 126, 145, 148, 150n, 202, 204, 271, 307, 334, 46:18n, 2l, 33f, 52, 66, 75, 132, 134f, 153f, 250, 317f
William IV, Duke of Bavaria—13:352n, 15:90n, 41:190n, 49:187, 188n, 189n, 318, 332, 427, 50:158n, 54:441
William of Occam—see **Occam, William of**
William, Duke of Braunschweig-Wolfenbüttel—41:182, 240n
William, Prince of Anhalt—48:183n
Williams, George H.—47:116n, 235n
The Radical Reformation, Philadelphia, 1918 37:289n, 38:298n, 46:6n, 7n, 15n
Willingness—10:32f, 12:384
Willingness and Necessity—33:39, 64f, 192f
Wilsnack—44:185n
Wimfeling, Jacob—44:161n
Wimpheling, Jacob—see **Wimfeling, Jacob**
Wimpina, Conrad—31:87n, 51:35
Confutation 34:6n
Winckel Messen—13:366n
Wind—1:9, 170, 2:106n, 10:23f, 11:322f, 14:130, 15:16, 91, 173, 306, 18:23, 25, 44, 49, 64, 227, 20:13, 64, 248, 305, 22:213f, 279, 301, 318, 26:170, 172, 27:27, 100, 149, 367, 385, 410, 30:187, 209, 244, 284
Windstorms—50:189
Wine—1:210, 2:46, 166f, 173, 230f, 243, 350, 357, 383–388, 3:190, 197, 204, 220, 248, 267, 309, 311f, 364, 4:15, 21, 36, 95, 277, 396, 406, 5:6, 16, 21, 49, 59, 133, 135–138, 197, 248f, 260, 277, 294, 300, 7:97, 104f, 107, 158, 281, 351, 367, 8:54, 69, 120, 133, 144, 247–249, 251, 253f, 256–260, 266–268, 270, 272, 277, 290, 302, 305, 308, 9:174, 203, 272, 293, 297f, 308, 10:156f, 460f, 463f, 11:286, 334f, 16:22, 62, 188f, 212, 222, 19:124f, 199f, 23:14, 40, 45, 68, 80, 114, 123, 128, 165, 226, 267, 275, 347, 24:188, 194f, 199, 205, 208, 224, 237, 26:96, 110, 260, 27:83, 184, 290, 321, 364, 28:286, 296, 299, 313, 316, 355–357, 29:27, 54, 30:26, 28, 40f, 45, 49, 177, 258, 291, 306, 35:86, 100, 106, 378, 36:108n, 182, 250f, 37:43–45, 60, 65, 76, 84, 97, 101, 110, 146, 150, 267, 302, 315, 327, 42:41, 50:304, 51:158, 171, 182, 323, 53:24, 26, 28f, 54:71, 163, 172, 178, 424f, 438
Wine, Malmsey—see **Malmsey wine**
Wine, Rhine—50:287
Wine, Sacramental—see **Sacramental elements**
Winepresses—11:102, 142f, 146, 286, 17:353f
Wineskins—11:472–475, 36:250–253, 262
Wingren, Gustaf—*Luther on Vocation*, Philadelphia, 1957 39:xviin
Wings—10:111, 119, 254, 331–333, 11:214f, 225f, 319, 322f, 20:59f, 233, 244
Winkler, George—34:20n, 43:141–165, 46:227n, 49:182n
Winkworth, Catherine—*Lyra Germanica* (1855–1858) and *Chorale Book for England* (1863) 53:199n, 247
Winsheim, Veit—38:264, 272
Winter—1:144, 2:92, 129, 14:125f, 15:347, 23:254, 256, 364, 24:235, 378
Winter, E.F.—*Erasmus and Luther: Discourse on Free Will*, New York, 1961 33:xiin
Wisdom—2:3–6, 9, 12, 15, 18, 46, 63, 65, 78, 110, 160, 171, 208, 258, 305, 313, 329, 340, 342, 354, 376, 3:5, 9, 96, 108f, 114, 125–128, 137, 162, 172f, 209, 226, 241–243, 261f, 274, 300,

306, 338, 342, 353, 4:53f, 65, 76, 86, 118, 120, 125, 130, 147, 154, 156–160, 162–164, 166, 180, 193, 201, 229, 242, 251, 255, 257, 287, 295, 319, 333, 344–347, 350, 352, 357, 368, 370, 372, 382, 5:3f, 24f, 28, 45, 58, 72, 120–122, 124, 128, 186, 194, 208, 215, 219, 224, 226f, 230, 235, 329, 338, 341, 346, 382, 6:8, 24, 73, 88–90, 99f, 102f, 194, 321, 360f, 375, 7:11, 62, 93, 96, 101, 104f, 108f, 111f, 119, 122, 125, 132, 136, 142f, 146, 148–151, 156f, 159, 164–166, 171, 174f, 177, 187–189, 204–206, 212, 215, 217, 223, 225, 233, 240, 246–248, 258, 271, 281, 285, 295, 308–310, 317, 347, 351, 354, 359, 371, 8:6, 10f, 17f, 29f, 56f, 62, 88, 95f, 111, 128–130, 136, 169, 175, 191, 226, 233, 244, 251, 263, 266, 9:6, 14, 18f, 27, 40f, 57, 97, 113, 171, 196, 205, 213, 11:265, 313, 320f, 383, 445f, 460f, 12:353, 356, 360, 404, 13:72, 82, 129f, 136, 214, 253, 362, 385, 14:15, 24f, 53–56, 59, 62, 78, 81, 83, 90, 94f, 98, 105, 112, 42, 45, 158, 163, 169, 170, 174, 197–199, 202–205, 223f, 288, 314, 327f, 342, 344f, 15:22f, 28, 38f, 99, 119, 132, 134, 148, 153f, 156, 16:9, 32, 36f, 70, 100, 109, 111, 118–120, 124, 128, 137, 149, 153, 162, 223f, 246, 251, 276, 285, 318, 17:17, 21, 25, 57, 76, 80, 130, 150f, 194, 243, 366, 18:198, 20:91, 234, 21:210f, 299, 332, 341f, 344, 22:463, 23:23, 33, 38, 47, 51–53, 68, 79, 85f, 90, 94, 100, 115, 120, 144, 146, 148, 151, 160, 164f, 167f, 177, 193, 213, 229, 233, 254, 283, 297, 302, 306, 334, 347, 366, 375–377, 387, 400, 413, 24:32, 53, 99, 101, 103, 109, 156, 228, 297, 322, 328, 337, 347, 352, 358, 365, 392, 25:5, 69, 106, 139, 145, 223, 278, 370, 26:6, 8, 13, 26, 29f, 35, 37, 40–42, 54, 58, 66, 73, 95, 114, 140, 156f, 184, 196, 216, 227, 229, 238, 262, 294, 314, 326, 338, 354, 356, 393, 396, 420, 433, 449, 27:10, 24f, 34, 39, 42, 76, 82, 89, 98, 115, 117, 134, 136, 138–140, 145, 148, 153, 156, 166f, 169, 181, 196, 207, 209, 220, 241f, 244, 275, 310, 341, 343, 345, 384, 393, 396, 404f, 28:84, 117f, 190, 197, 249f, 294, 317, 367, 29:31, 97, 115, 119, 134, 142, 144f, 149, 154, 165, 202, 235, 30:14, 16, 65, 155, 164, 166, 252, 257, 266f, 289, 310, 322, 31:53f, 35:215, 217, 259–261, 344, 380f, 38:170, 173n, 255n, 264, 276, 42:58f, 61, 149, 153, 46:102n, 228, 238f, 245, 51:26f, 104, 123, 125, 164, 383–392

Wisdom, Book of—9:51, 28:250, 29:231, 35:347–349

Wisdom of God—2:79f, 120, 130, 170, 266, 120, 130, 170, 266, 8:28, 79, 160, 317, 11:3, 16, 39, 231, 250, 338, 341f, 499, 14:329, 343, 15:25, 23:275, 25:8, 103, 150f, 153f, 223, 249, 338, 432, 29:145, 190, 35:261, 344, 37:71, 127, 132, 138, 207f, 42:9, 32, 85, 89, 131, 163

Wisdom of Sirach—see **Wisdom, Book of**

Wisdom of the flesh—11:301, 320, 324, 408, 464, 25:xi, 3, 9, 29, 40, 68–70, 77, 106, 135f, 211, 224, 293, 317, 345f, 348f, 351, 375, 396, 399, 407f, 428, 433, 513, 26:54, 216, 449

Wisdom of the world—34:128

Wiseacres—2:172, 16:73, 203, 24:32, 96, 103, 209, 297

Wisemen—see **Magi**

Wishes vs. actions—see **Actions vs. wishes**

Wisloff, Carl F.—54:91n
The Gift of Communion, Minneapolis, 1964 38:315n

Wissenburger, Wolfgang—53:53

Witchcraft—22:106, 24:74f, 245, 26:190, 192, 197, 27:90, 243–245, 30:91, 43:17, 54:188, 298, 346

Witches—4:324n, 16:297, 41:172, 52:160f, 182

Witnessing—4:87, 216, 244, 248, 395, 6:77, 80, 9:161f, 165f, 171, 195–197, 199, 222, 10:41, 45–48, 87, 91f, 153, 443, 455, 11:16, 12:383–387, 394f, 409, 17:93, 109, 253f, 20:213, 307, 28:102, 350–352, 354, 359, 29:145f, 213f, 33:20, 37:xii, 126n, 290, 41:249, 253, 46:261n, 268, 271, 284, 290, 307, 52:277, see also **Testimony**

Wittenberg—1:30, 47n, 166n, 207n, 2:137n, 147, 3:x, 303n, 4:ix, 91n, 194n, 318n, 5:x, 35n, 63n, 194n, 380n, 381, 6:34n, 76, 93, 320, 7:107n, 8:ix, 120n, 124, 9:ixf, 8, 14n, 10:ix, 12:189, 255f, 14:xi, 116, 210, 281, 284, 286, 16:ixf, 107n, 264, 286, 288, 17:ix, 83, 117, 128n, 186, 268, 319, 322, 338, 407, 20:310, 21:ix, 22:xf, 45, 54, 59n, 68n, 70, 207, 310f, 338n, 390, 417n, 418n, 434, 465, 512, 23:ix, xi, 27, 137, 201, 245, 289, 303, 311, 324, 356, 422, 24:ix, 171, 25:ix, 441, 450, 456, 461, 510, 26:14, 24, 45, 27:113n, 123, 153, 315, 28:xf, 84, 30:xf, 254n, 31:325, 329, 333, 381–395, 32:5, 105, 263–

265, 272, 276n, 35:115, 325, 36:xii, 6, 129f, 133, 227, 233–235, 256n, 272f, 275n, 309–321, 333, 37:x, xii–xvi, 10f, 40n, 138n, 148f, 154f, 161, 283, 38:xix, 6–9, 13, 63, 94, 142, 197, 270n, 183n, 39:xii, xxif, 6, 25, 52f, 67, 69, 110, 120, 139, 141, 227f, 242f, 245, 303, 40:xi, 5, 47, 52, 41:xiin, 8, 23n, 33n, 49n, 170, 253, 262, 325f, 350, 358, 42:5, 17, 120, 169, 170n, 44:119, 247, 45:xiif, 13–15, 53–56, 58n, 59n, 74n, 78–80, 83, 107n, 135–138, 161n, 165, 197f, 243, 313n, 316, 344n, 345, 383, 46:xi, 19n, 21n, 48, 89, 106n, 143, 211, 234n, 263, 47:106, 108, 115, 116n, 165n, 191, 212n, 245, 48:19n, 29f, 42n, 69n, 77n, 78, 88n, 90n, 94n, 113n, 114n, 120, 121n, 123, 125, 130n, 131n, 134n, 136n, 138, 148n, 149n, 150n, 155n, 161f, 164n, 165, 166n, 168f, 171n, 180n, 186, 190n, 192n, 197n, 202, 212, 215, 219n, 221, 223, 225n, 229n, 230n, 232n, 238, 246n, 247n, 248, 250, 252n, 256, 258n, 274, 281n, 283n, 284, 288, 290, 291n, 302, 308, 311n, 314n, 316n, 320, 322n, 324, 327, 331n, 344, 348f, 353n, 355n, 356n, 359, 372, 380, 391, 393f, 401, 50:23–25, 29, 31, 55n, 85, 98n, 101n, 103n, 108n, 110n, 113n, 118, 130, 135n, 137n, 142, 150n, 153, 168n, 170n, 175n, 178, 182, 185f, 189n, 198n, 209n, 210n, 211n, 214n, 215n, 220n, 221, 225n, 228n, 237n, 239, 246n, 248n, 269n, 273n, 274n, 275n, 278n, 279, 282n, 283n, 285n, 318, 51:xi–xiv, xvn, 35, 69, 91, 167, 175, 224, 303, 315, 357, 371, 383, 53:xiii, 5, 7, 15, 17, 23, 39, 43, 50, 53f, 58, 60, 62, 68, 82, 96, 106, 117, 122f, 131, 137, 151, 153f, 172, 176f, 181, 184, 192–194, 212, 214, 218, 222, 225f, 232f, 235, 237, 240, 242, 245, 249f, 252, 255, 271, 277f, 280, 283f, 286, 292, 295, 299, 302, 304f, 315, 317f, 319, 321, 325, 54:15, 134, 169, 282, 391, 419

A holy city 26:24f

All Saints' Church—see **Wittenberg, Castle Church of All Saints**

Augustinian Monastery 34:149, 42:x, 97n, 48:5, 6n, 8n, 11, 17f, 20, 23, 27, 29n, 30n, 31n, 32, 36, 39, 41–43, 49, 52, 56, 60, 64n, 70, 73, 76, 80, 90, 93, 95, 103, 106, 108, 111, 115n, 116, 120, 122, 124f, 125n, 126f, 130, 132f, 135, 141, 143, 145f, 148, 149n, 151, 154, 156, 159, 161, 163, 165, 167, 169, 171, 173, 175, 181, 186, 188, 191, 194, 233n, 268n, 324, 337f, 352n, 356, 358n, 359, 399, 49:11n, 22, 24f, 57f, 115, 50:216n, 278n, see also **Wittenberg**—Black Cloister

Black Cloister 27:122n, 32:278, 46:132, 54:ix, 181, 193, 267

Castle Church of All Saints' 12:ix, 27:153, 36:227n, 42:x, 142n, 48:33n, 45, 46n, 50, 55n, 79n, 142n, 161, 202n, 235n, 275n, 310, 338, 360, 387n, 49:71n, 73n, 84n, 104n, 134n, 151n, 219, 50:110n, 111, 209n, 210n, 226n, 236n, 318, 51:xii, xivn, 80n, 231

City Church 42:x, 48:28, 221n, 303n, 309n, 311n, 49:115n, 135n, 151n, 386, 51:xii, 15, 69, 121, 221, 291

Disturbances of 1521–22 36:233f, 48:33n, 77n, 79n, 199, 211f, 281n, 311n, 364n, 381n, 386n, 388–390, 395, 401f, 49:3, 6, 11n, 46n, 71n, 94, 130, 163n

Government 49:14, 15n, 22, 24, 29, 40, 59, 68n, 77n, 82, 83n, 94, 105n, 106, 107n, 111n, 115n, 120, 121n, 135n, 136, 140, 146n, 149n, 152n, 153n, 160n, 169f, 173f, 177, 183f, 186, 187n, 201n, 203n, 210n, 214n, 218n, 266n, 271n, 292n, 294n, 310n, 312, 318n, 320, 327n, 332n, 344n, 351n, 355n, 400n, 401, 403n, 416, 417n, 418n, 420n, 422n, 425

Luther's home 34:xiii, 65, 108

Reforms 36:233, 249

University 1:ix, 5:263, 6:93, 10:xi, 27:377n, 30:287n, 32:106n, 34:xiii, xvii, 107, 125, 272, 38:xviiif, 237, 264n, 42:ixf, xiii, 97n, 45:315, 343, 46:19n, 210, 234n, 47:101f, 105, 48:5, 8, 14, 19, 29n, 30n, 31n, 39n, 41n, 43n, 54n, 59n, 61n, 63n, 64n, 71, 74n, 79n, 83n, 90, 92n, 94n, 95n, 96n, 115n, 123, 125n, 130n, 135n, 136, 138, 143n, 145f, 154n, 161, 162n, 164n, 166n, 168f, 169, 173n, 179n, 185n, 202n, 218, 219n, 220, 223n, 227n, 230n, 232, 233n, 235n, 236n, 266n, 269, 274n, 275n, 284, 303n, 311, 378n, 393n, 49:xix, 12n, 15, 17n, 22n, 36, 51, 58n, 71n, 73, 74f, 84, 85f, 103, 104f, 107, 121, 128–131, 152n, 158n, 159, 167n, 168n, 174n, 175n, 181n, 184n, 201, 247, 272, 281, 284n, 291n, 313n, 314n, 321n, 402n, 431, 50:xx, 25, 27n, 28, 30, 31n, 51, 80n, 108n, 209n, 210n, 211n, 212n, 217, 218n,

226n, 231, 252n, 253n, 273n, 274n, 275, 277n, 279n, 294n, 318
University, Chair of Greek and Hebrew 48:42n, 63n, 77n, 123n, 132, 154n, 160f
University, Disputations 50:86n, 93, 94n, 103n, 108n, 131n, 183n
University, Faculty of Law 50:112n, 213n, 274n, 293n
University, Faculty of Theology 34:xiv, 14, 50:xix, 61, 77n, 82n, 94n, 106n, 127, 133n, 144n, 194, 196n, 209n, 210n, 242n, 274n
University, Humanistic influences 48:37n, 38, 41f, 57f, 78n, 82f, 95f, 106f, 112, 165f
Visited by Plague 48:23, 30, 274n, 316
Wittenberg Articles—50:4f, 117f, 132f, 138n, 139f, 142n, 198n
Wittenberg Concord—35:xii, 37:xxi, 38:281, 48:247n, 49:414n, 50:171n, 173n, 242n, 54:205
Wittenberg edition of Luther's works—see index to each volume
Wittenberg Hymnal (Bapst)—37:260n
Wittenberg Latin Bible—see **Luther, Martin, Writings of**
Wittenbergers—41:231
Witz, John—48:222n
Witzel, George—3:193n, 275, 4:209, 23:212n, 38:142f, 167n, 183n, 47:102, 54:108, 304
Postil 50:185, 186n
Wives—1:69f, 96, 116–118, 132, 134–139, 159f, 169, 178, 182, 199–204, 215, 217, 220, 238–241, 245, 267, 270, 301f, 305, 309f, 312–314, 317, 324, 338f, 344, 356, 358, 3:13f, 42, 45–47, 49, 51, 53, 55, 57f, 133, 147, 179, 201, 204, 209f, 213, 227, 231, 253, 258, 261, 283, 288, 315, 317f, 320f, 323, 325–327, 329f, 333, 335, 340, 342, 349–354, 360f, 4:6, 12, 18, 22–24, 36–42, 56, 58, 69, 72, 78f, 103, 141, 164f, 181f, 184, 189, 193–198, 216, 221–228, 243f, 246–248, 251f, 254, 258, 262, 265 267, 270, 283, 287, 291f, 294, 299–307, 320, 324, 326, 332–338, 340–342, 348, 351f, 365, 379, 383, 385, 5:3, 5–7, 9, 13f, 16f, 24f, 27–41, 51–53, 55, 60, 66, 70, 72, 77f, 82f, 89f, 92–97, 99f, 102–104, 107f, 112, 114, 124, 138, 160, 166, 169, 172, 174–176, 178f, 185, 190n, 191–193, 195, 199f, 202f, 206f, 210, 229, 261, 269, 272, 277, 281 297, 302, 304n, 306f, 313–315, 319, 322–326, 329–335, 337, 339, 341, 343–345, 350f, 353, 359, 362–365, 370f, 378, 381f, 6:15–20, 22f, 44f, 56, 66, 76, 82, 102, 196, 112, 123, 247, 269, 7:5–9, 17–20, 22f, 27–29, 32, 34f, 40, 42f, 45, 52, 56, 68, 76f, 80, 82f, 85, 95f, 115, 117, 124, 132, 146, 192f, 197, 199, 202, 218, 220, 222, 241, 249, 261, 270, 272, 274, 288, 290, 307, 310, 326, 341, 343, 372, 8:20f, 31f, 35f, 60, 63–65, 68, 84–88, 97, 110, 114, 137, 150, 153f, 156f, 160, 163, 169, 174, 194, 204–206, 213, 223, 273, 284, 295, 304, 306, 9:146, 149, 205, 207, 210f, 213f, 222–224, 226, 229, 235, 241, 244, 250, 13:13, 18:402–405, 21:37, 87, 94–97, 109, 256f, 263, 334f, 23:8, 35, 66f, 71, 92f, 196, 201–205, 224, 295, 322f, 332, 356, 401, 403, 24:161, 163, 165, 186, 216, 231, 245, 280, 360, 380, 26:143, 168, 216–218, 250, 305, 327, 376, 397, 425, 434, 27:56, 67f, 127, 195, 204, 232, 252, 281, 320, 408, 28:5, 11–13, 21f, 50–52, 59, 276f, 298f, 338, 29:18–20, 22, 43, 53–57, 60, 64–66, 71, 30:20, 50, 71, 86–89, 91–93, 98, 104, 115, 118, 176, 178, 183, 203, 206, 249, 271, 273, 296, 304, 35:388, 391, 41:217, 45:7f, 23f, 27, 33, 38, 144, 46:154, 181, 237, 287n, 291f, 298–300, 302, 313–316
Wives, Foreign—11:30
Wives and husbands—see **Husbands and wives**
Wives of apostles and bishops—41:60, 152, 156–163
Wizards—9:175, 190, 22:474, 27:369, 36:196f
Woes—35:404f
Wolf and sheep—37:23f, 98, 101, 164f, 280
Wolfenbüttel—10:x, 22:xi, 50:178n, 226n, 236n
Ducal library 42:98
Wolfenbüttel manuscript—28:237
Wolfenbüttel Psalter—10:x, 3
Wolff, Thomas—18:x
Wolff von Lindau—13:354
Wolfgang, Count of the Palatinate—48:61
Wolfgang, Prince of Anhalt—23:218n, 49:350
Wolgast, Eike—49:xv
Wollensecker, Andreas—54:369
Wolmar—53:43
Wolmar Landtag—45:314
Wolsey, Thomas—34:83n
Wolves—1:55, 77, 2:74f, 116, 135, 138, 3:17, 67, 78, 271, 347, 4:37, 71, 74, 382, 5:107, 6:17, 20, 68f, 7:158, 205,

267, 9:3, 52, 135, 157, 187, 229, 11:85, 16:122, 144, 19:113, 20:313, 21:260, 319, 23:119, 132, 193, 211, 26:407, 413, 424, 429, 30:134–136, 169, 181, 188, 209, 311
Wolves, Evening—18:350
Woman's seed—see **Seed, The promised**
Womanly honor—46:280, 291f, 302, 308, 316
Womb—3:45, 55, 64, 134, 148, 152, 205f, 208, 360, 4:271, 291, 294, 330, 337, 344, 351, 353f, 361, 363f, 368f, 377f, 388, 5:75f, 101, 105, 176, 316, 335, 342, 356, 381, 7:14, 17, 28, 31, 41, 46–48, 179, 295, 325, 10:143, 268, 342, 397f, 11:181, 366–368, 17:139, 183, 24:92f, 27:345, 42:99, 153
Women—1:33, 68–70, 116–120, 123f, 126, 128–132, 134, 136f, 146, 154f, 160, 177f, 181–183, 185f, 188, 190, 192f, 198, 200, 202f, 205, 216, 219, 238, 241f, 255, 257, 270, 300, 325, 3:44f, 47f, 111, 128f, 132–136, 200–202, 209, 215, 255, 270, 272, 274, 310, 360, 4:10–13, 18–20, 23, 40, 47, 50, 65f, 92, 137, 148, 161, 164, 175, 189, 191, 199, 222, 228, 233, 238, 242–244, 246f, 255, 258f, 261, 263, 270, 275, 280, 290–293, 302, 305–307, 311, 333f, 336–339, 342, 344f, 347, 352–354, 360, 369f, 386f, 5:289, 314, 217, 382, 6:60, 132, 193, 210, 254f, 270, 349, 7:9, 17, 20, 33, 46, 57, 80, 85, 88, 148, 325, 8:25, 86, 89, 110, 131, 176, 203, 241f, 250f, 254, 259, 294, 308–310, 316, 331, 9:204, 210f, 213f, 219f, 222–224, 230, 235, 248f, 251, 272f, 15:8, 100, 130–132, 231, 249, 317f, 16:45, 47f, 50, 52, 146, 163, 278, 17:183f, 213, 18:311–313, 397, 403, 20:57, 60, 141f, 242, 244, 283, 298, 21:84–87, 91, 286, 329, 25:13, 57f, 465, 509f, 26:307, 311, 332, 356, 367, 404, 27:289, 204, 28:5–7, 10–12, 16, 44, 49, 51, 79, 171, 178, 194, 271–280, 298f, 321, 341, 345, 29:53–57, 30:88f, 91, 35:381, 388, 405, 37:364f, 39:63, 68, 234, 296f, 40:23, 25, 369, 388, 389–391, 41:42n, 52, 154f, 362, 42:100, 144, 44:388, 45:36f, 144, 153, 201–206, 324, 333, 368, 46:42, 71, 133, 182, 232, 271, 276, 280, 291f, 295f, 51:292, 352, 52:230f, 237f, 54:8, 15, 59, 135, 160f, 171, 175, 183, 205, 221, 223, 317, 320f, 428, 438, see also **Husbands and wives; Male and female; Man and woman; Mothers; Virgins; Widows; Wives**
Jewish view 47:141f
Women, Ordination of—36:152
Women, Unmarried—28:54
Women followers of Christ—42:7–9
Women ministers—40:23, 41:154
Women preachers—30:54f, 135, 39:234
Wonders—1:24, 126, 3:117, 166, 4:120, 125, 199, 10:61, 67, 105, 24:76, 368f
Wondrous things—11:427, 436f
Wood—3:86, 153, 191, 206, 214, 303, 4:92, 98, 107f, 110f, 114, 185, 330, 6:238f, 24:93, 234, 250, 323, 27:52, 55, 62, 134, 37:113f
Wood carving—14:191
Woodcuts—42:6, 46:220n
Woodcuts by Lucas Cranach—35:179
Wool—4:370, 6:67–69, 112, 324, 7:45, 219, 9:174, 221, 225
Woolf, Bertram Lee, ed.—*Reformation Writings of Martin Luther*, New York, 1953 31:23, 330, 36:10, 81n, 105n, 110n, 126n, 51:61
Word (of God), The—1:13, 16, 75, 79, 81, 84, 95f, 105, 123, 125, 130, 143, 146–149, 157–160, 197, 222, 227f, 247–250, 262, 300, 2:23, 30, 32f, 35, 40f, 47, 82, 104, 112, 132f, 146, 171, 173, 209, 218, 222, 236, 248, 250, 271, 274f, 285, 292, 295, 309, 334, 351f, 355–358, 361, 369, 387, 3:14, 16, 19, 30, 37, 55, 64, 69f, 77f, 86, 98, 108, 111, 116–118, 120f, 138, 140, 145f, 148, 155, 160, 163f, 167, 174, 180, 182, 214, 216, 219f, 227f, 232, 237, 239, 241, 273, 284, 286, 291, 297, 299, 302, 307, 326, 338, 343f, 348, 353, 357, 4:4f, 7f, 16f, 24, 27, 35, 39, 49, 58, 60, 67f, 89f, 97, 100f, 103–107, 122, 127f, 130, 135, 140–142, 150, 179–182, 186, 205, 219, 229, 251, 266, 294f, 311, 314, 319, 334, 341, 345, 355, 357, 361f, 373, 376f, 384–386, 389–391, 398, 5:3–6, 10f, 14, 16, 22f, 49, 51, 54, 70, 72, 78, 83f, 86, 88, 128f, 131, 133, 144f, 156, 164, 178f, 183, 185f, 192, 232f, 238, 240, 244–246, 248f, 253, 258, 261, 265f, 325, 330, 348, 353–355, 357, 362, 6:x, 8, 22, 24, 30f, 40f, 70, 73f, 95, 99, 116f, 124, 147, 224f, 227f, 233f, 248, 261, 305, 336, 344, 361, 363, 7:22, 43, 57, 71, 77, 105f, 117, 128, 138f, 147f, 151f, 161f, 166, 179, 226, 261, 309, 315, 318, 320, 336, 339, 8:27, 32, 73, 82–84, 92f, 118, 132, 144f, 220, 244f, 265,

269, 271f, 293, 298, 301, 312, 9:3, 7f, 15, 20–23, 33, 35, 37, 40, 48n, 50–53, 64, 69, 75, 83f, 88f, 92f, 95, 118, 123, 125, 129, 131, 136f, 140, 155f, 168–170, 176, 187, 202f, 213, 226, 258, 272, 10:10, 154f, 219, 230f, 286, 293, 407, 11:142, 149, 183, 202, 297, 334, 362–365, 394, 401, 477f, 481, 501n, 508, 517–521, 532f, 12:4, 8, 10, 13f, 22–27, 34f, 39, 42–44, 46f, 49, 51, 53, 63, 65–67, 71, 78, 90, 108, 111–117, 136, 139–142, 144, 147f, 156f, 159–179, 183–191, 193f, 203, 210f, 214–225, 227–229, 235, 237–239, 242f, 245, 247, 251f, 254f, 262f, 268–271, 277–279, 281, 283f, 287, 291f, 296f, 300, 304f, 310, 316, 319, 322, 329f, 336, 339, 341–345, 352, 358, 360f, 363–371, 373, 386, 389, 392, 405, 13:3n, 4, 7, 12, 16f, 27, 29f, 36, 70f, 86, 92, 99, 140, 155, 168, 178, 183–185, 189, 234, 237, 247, 266, 275, 341f, 360, 381–383, 385, 410, 14:131, 133–135, 180, 192, 247, 251, 257f, 261f, 272, 281, 284, 290, 292, 297, 302–305, 310, 323, 326f, 333–336, 338f, 343f, 15:10, 24f, 74–78, 172f, 191f, 197f, 203, 207, 217f, 222, 229, 232f, 238, 242, 253f, 257, 264, 272f, 299f, 312f, 317, 341, 16:10, 13, 16, 21, 27–31, 33f, 37, 54, 59f, 64f, 68, 72f, 77, 79, 81f, 84, 91–96, 101, 103, 106f, 119, 121–123, 130, 152, 155, 157, 160, 163f, 166, 168, 179 183, 190, 204, 221, 223–226, 228f, 233f, 239, 241, 244–246, 249–251, 256, 262, 292, 295, 298, 300–304, 308, 320f, 327, 329, 331f, 334, 338f, 341f, 17:3, 8, 12f, 15, 27, 29, 40, 42f, 45, 47, 51, 59, 62, 77, 89, 93f, 109, 118f, 133–136, 138f, 159f, 170–172, 178, 180f, 187, 193–195, 199f, 202f, 221, 249, 252, 258, 264, 270, 275, 308–310, 316, 328, 333, 350, 374–376, 405, 413, 18:3–5, 119, 166, 245, 250, 253, 367, 376, 401, 19:7–9, 25, 30, 35–37, 40, 45f, 51, 67, 80, 83, 89, 97f, 124, 167, 173f, 192, 203, 20:3–5, 7, 10–12, 18, 22, 45, 49, 64, 67f, 73, 83, 85, 100–103, 105, 108, 110, 113, 127, 135, 143, 172, 177, 190, 208, 216, 222f, 253, 267, 294, 320, 346, 21:10, 47, 34f, 99f, 120, 145f, 150f, 177–180, 187, 205, 221, 232f, 241f, 246, 250, 258–260, 265, 269, 275f, 290, 338, 347, 22:6, 8–14, 17, 25, 48, 56, 76, 155, 177, 204, 208f, 211, 223, 229, 271, 283, 290f, 295, 304f, 307, 309f, 312f, 316, 338f, 400, 421, 470, 472f, 477, 484f, 505, 508, 515f, 526–528, 23:12, 30, 35, 78f, 82, 95–97, 99f, 115, 150, 152, 159, 167, 173–175, 177, 191, 193, 204, 208, 211, 215, 223, 225–235, 248, 255f, 263, 266, 274–277, 287, 290f, 296–299, 303f, 321, 331, 333, 344, 349, 367, 371, 374, 378f, 386–388, 390f, 399, 401f, 413, 416f, 420f, 24:12, 14, 16–18, 23f, 34, 37, 39, 46, 53f, 66, 68f, 75, 79, 81f, 91f, 112, 115, 121, 123, 129, 131, 147, 166, 171, 173, 176, 179, 182, 197, 200–202, 204, 208–212, 214, 219, 222, 227, 230, 236, 250, 263f, 268, 274f, 286f, 293, 297, 301–303, 305, 308–312, 317, 321, 328–330, 343, 350–353, 362, 368, 374, 383, 385, 388–391, 394–396, 399, 25:8f, 54, 80, 85f, 89f, 93, 143, 150, 211, 226, 317f, 377, 396–400, 408f, 415f, 425, 439, 459f, 26:20f, 36, 47, 49, 50, 52, 56, 58–60, 66f, 72, 76f, 93f, 97f, 104, 107, 126, 141, 192–194, 197, 211, 213, 228f, 276, 287, 302, 312, 318, 364, 383, 399, 407, 425, 434f, 448, 452, 455, 27:6, 23, 26–28, 53, 56f, 70, 78, 82, 85, 87f, 101, 105, 138, 140, 159, 164, 200, 205, 209, 249, 296, 303, 305, 340, 346, 380, 387, 396, 398, 28:6, 19, 53, 61f, 67, 69f, 72–74, 76f, 79, 97, 100, 144–146, 163f, 166f, 169, 217, 239, 246, 269, 365, 375–377, 384, 29:3–5, 8–10, 13–17, 21, 25, 28, 30–35, 37, 46, 48, 50, 57, 59, 62–64, 69, 71f, 80–83, 86, 95–97, 100, 109f, 118, 124, 133, 145, 149f, 152–155, 160, 162f, 165, 171, 182, 198, 200, 202, 210, 224, 228, 230, 237f, 30:7, 28, 31, 41f, 44, 48f, 54–56, 62, 65, 68f, 72, 76, 99, 105–107, 115, 125f, 132, 134, 142, 151, 163–168, 176–178, 187f, 190, 192–194, 199, 210, 213, 239, 247, 250, 260f, 272f, 282, 291, 307, 311f, 326, 31:ix, 76, 209f, 238, 311, 335, 341, 345, 349, 356, 32:xii, xvf, xviiif, 111, 259, 33:50–52, 56f, 105, 139, 155, 178, 286, 34:31, 52, 82, 122f, 160, 316, 354, 35:xif, xvi, 7, 12, 19, 52, 64, 82, 92, 105, 107, 131f, 151f, 158, 170f, 200, 218, 262, 267, 333, 343f, 382, 390, 399, 402, 409, 36:15, 18, 22, 30f, 35f, 39, 42, 44, 46, 49, 57, 65, 67, 71, 73, 91f, 106f, 111, 113, 116, 122–124, 134–136, 142, 144f, 151–153, 158f, 163, 167, 179, 182f, 185, 191f, 194f, 198, 219f, 225, 229, 234f, 244f, 247f, 257f, 263, 267, 278, 287–289, 296–

298, 302f, 311f, 321, 325, 327, 337, 341–343, 345f, 355, 37:xv, 20f, 25f, 29, 42, 45, 47, 50f, 55, 68–70, 72, 77, 88, 96, 109, 127–129, 132–137, 139–142, 145, 156, 169, 175, 177, 184–186, 188, 193f, 202, 214, 216, 230, 253, 293, 296, 304–308, 322, 352, 359, 361, 364f, 367, 38:ixf, xvii, xxf, 5, 9, 16, 18, 21–29, 36–44, 54–56, 58, 65, 67, 69, 76, 79, 81, 87f, 93, 100, 105f, 128, 131, 134, 148f, 155–159, 161, 163, 164n, 170–174, 189–191, 195f, 198f, 204, 208, 211f, 222f, 225, 227, 229, 241, 243f, 247, 250f, 263, 268, 274, 303, 306, 308, 312f, 317, 39:xi, xiv–xvi, xviii, xxi, xxiii, xxv, 19, 22, 28, 56, 61, 64, 90f, 94, 130f, 139f, 146, 151, 159f, 162, 165–168, 174, 178f, 193, 200, 213f, 237, 250–253, 270f, 277, 279, 284, 292, 298, 306f, 309, 40:xf, 10, 21, 34, 49, 55, 59, 68, 80, 91, 132, 135, 146f, 149, 157, 176, 190, 212–214, 249, 251, 298, 349, 352, 41:xi, xiv–xvi, 5, 13, 42, 51, 69f, 109, 132–135, 148–152, 154–156, 164f, 168, 170, 172, 176, 189f, 196, 203, 211f, 214–219, 221, 223, 227–229, 235, 238, 242, 249, 269, 272, 281, 286f, 293, 295, 303, 306f, 309f, 318f, 323, 331, 335, 339, 344–347, 355, 359f, 364, 370, 42:20, 37, 42, 52–61, 69, 77, 79f, 91n, 101, 106, 108–112, 124, 147, 158, 44:xi–xiii, xvii, 38, 72, 112, 139, 227, 379, 400, 45:9, 19, 22, 37f, 40–43, 47, 58, 66f, 69f, 74, 84, 100–102, 105, 107, 109, 114–118, 121, 144–155, 177f, 187, 202, 204, 261, 277, 317–319, 343, 347–350, 352, 357, 359n, 363f, 371, 46:6f, 9, 12, 14f, 18, 20, 24f, 53, 61, 65f, 76, 98f, 115, 119, 136, 141, 148, 161, 165, 173–175, 183f, 186f, 197f, 209, 213, 220, 222, 224, 226, 228, 231, 235f, 243, 248, 251, 255f, 276f, 281, 283f, 299, 305, 315f, 47:35–51, 73, 75f, 92f, 96, 115, 117, 137, 145, 147, 154f, 159–164, 168, 190, 192f, 196, 200, 202, 209, 212f, 225, 227, 245, 247, 250, 270, 274, 284, 287, 48:30, 103f, 146, 152f, 206f, 226, 232, 251f, 306, 309, 327, 374f, 402f, 51:59, 73, 76–78, 83, 86, 88, 90, 95f, 104, 111, 122, 124, 135, 139, 142, 144–146, 149, 155, 168, 172–174, 180, 182–186, 188f, 200, 202–205, 207, 212, 223, 231, 247, 251, 262, 264f, 272, 276, 296, 299, 320–323, 338, 342f, 346, 358, 388, 390, 52:14, 31f, 32f, 37, 39, 42f, 45–50, 54, 54–58, 83, 86, 104f, 137, 147, 172, 174, 174, 181f, 194, 197, 199, 201f, 205f, 209, 248, 250, 275, 286, 54:13, 18, 55, 57, 63, 192f, 197f, 244, 313, 318, 322f, 334, 394f, see also **Spoken word, The**; **Written word**

Contempt for 50:182f, 189, 215, 279

Requires faith 8:8, 10, 12, 135

Suffering and death for its sake possible 48:201, 214, 221, 228, 232, 249, 307, 319

Word, External—12:369

Word, The spoken—see **Spoken Word, The**

Word, The weak—26:72, 452

Word, Written—see **Written Word**

Word and Sacrament—see Vols. 35–38

Word and sacrament—1:247f, 4:201, 349f, 358, 360, 6:128f, 147–149, 173, 225f, 356, 398, 7:299, 344, 13:90, 272, 342, 22:515f, 526–528, 40:10, 176, 212–214, 46:220

Word made flesh, The—41:105n, 346

Word of Christ, The—36:45, 57, 133f, 165, 168, 210, 266, 41:11, 91, 111, 123, 300, 319, 329–331, 341, 343, 351, 353, 364

Wordiness—2:88, 96, 16:94

Words—6:53, 58, 71, 73, 76, 84, 112, 115, 120f, 163, 182, 37:42, 65, 81, 103, 109, 111–113, 116, 135n, 146, 262, 270–275, 305–309, 341, 359

Words and the Word—17:93

Words of God—see **God**—His words

Words of Institution (Communion Liturgy)—35:xiiif, 55, 82n, 88, 90, 92, 36:xf, 20f, 22n, 23, 27, 33–36, 37n, 38, 40f, 43f, 51, 53, 83, 111, 162f, 164, 166–184, 254f, 272, 277–288, 298, 319n, 331f, 335–338, 341, 345–352, 37:xii–xiv, xviiif, 6, 9, 11, 18f, 21, 25, 28–46, 64f, 69, 72, 74, 78, 82, 85–87, 93, 197, 102, 106–110, 112, 125–127, 129f, 132, 134, 137, 139f, 144f, 150, 153f, 156f, 161–163, 165–171, 177–182, 184–195, 197, 203, 207, 213, 217, 230, 254, 257–261, 263, 266, 268, 270–273, 278, 285, 289–291, 294n, 295f, 298–300, 303–360, 367, 38:10, 20, 48, 80f, 168, 199, 204, 209f, 212, 309n, 313n, 314, 42:173–175, 53:xviii, 26f, 31f, 55f, 59, 80f

Fanatics lack clear text 37:40f, 97, 107, 112, 125f, 163–171, 176, 259f, 268, 271, 304, 308–310, 335–337, 343f

Text clear 37:18f, 28, 33–35, 45, 72, 74, 97, 106f, 112, 150, 163, 167, 203, 213,

270–273, 278, 304–306, 308f, 313f, 337, 341, 348, 353, 359f
Textual criticism 37:126f, 310f, 313, 315, 327n
Words of the Days—3:361
Work—see **Labor**
Work ethic, Protestant—7:65f
Work of Christ—35:360, 362, 372, 377
Workman—20:179f
Works—1:258f, 265, 300, 2:103, 113, 122, 124, 149, 158f, 184, 222, 241, 246, 249, 269, 271, 273, 281, 315, 349–352, 355–357, 387, 392, 3:20–23, 25f, 29f, 34, 50, 80, 84, 87, 100–102, 106, 118, 120, 122, 128, 136, 146, 156, 162, 172, 176f, 202, 210–212, 216, 218, 271, 290, 292, 315, 318, 320–322, 336, 348, 359, 362, 4:5f, 8f, 17, 21, 32, 37, 50, 54f, 57, 60–66, 68, 73, 88, 94, 96, 100, 102, 104, 109, 113f, 122f, 131, 133f, 140–142, 157–160, 162–165, 167, 169f, 171, 173f, 177, 181f, 204, 216, 235, 238f, 242f, 253, 265, 269f, 272, 276, 284, 289f, 297, 304, 307, 315, 320f, 326, 328–330, 340, 344, 346f, 349f, 355, 358, 360, 368, 371, 376, 398–401, 5:3–7, 13f, 42, 47, 49, 70f, 84, 94, 103, 115, 118, 122, 132, 141f, 149, 157, 173, 175, 214f, 223, 233, 247, 250, 257, 259f, 264, 267–271, 276–280, 282–286, 330f, 334, 342, 349, 6:35, 73f, 115, 124, 128, 177, 181, 262f, 347f, 364f, 7:28, 65, 70f, 129, 136, 152, 166, 196, 221f, 229, 236, 245, 253, 311f, 315, 319, 323, 326, 332, 341, 344, 357f, 366f, 8:22, 29f, 45, 50, 69, 75, 96, 132, 137, 165, 179, 230, 267, 276, 284, 288, 316, 325, 331, 9:7, 26f, 59, 63, 72f, 76, 79, 82, 84, 86, 89, 97, 103f, 108–111, 117, 123, 125f, 135–137, 141, 151, 158, 166, 170f, 179, 183, 185–187, 190, 199, 205f, 224–226, 235, 238, 244f, 250f, 255, 259, 261, 284, 291, 294, 10:21–23, 128–131, 213f, 219f, 267, 11:9, 80, 524, 12:80, 269f, 274, 279, 385f, 388f, 397, 400–402, 406f, 409, 13:35, 51f, 56, 139f, 292, 300, 319, 385, 14:24, 27, 30, 33, 35, 37–39, 81, 84, 86, 91, 94–98, 102, 112, 141, 145, 168f, 171, 173, 193, 196f, 199, 203, 244, 255, 262, 287, 293f, 297, 301, 304, 327, 335, 337, 344f, 348, 16:15, 18, 27, 31, 35, 71, 73, 79f, 109, 120f, 155, 202, 206, 223, 226, 228, 230, 235, 305, 319, 327, 331, 334, 344, 17:5, 26, 73, 85, 114, 213, 222, 225, 273, 286, 296, 378, 380, 18:37, 375, 20:62, 75f, 78, 85f, 259, 261, 264f, 21:4, 15f, 65–67, 130–132, 145, 150, 161, 164f, 205, 258, 285, 288–290, 305, 318f, 324f, 331f, 352, 22:146, 149, 360, 381, 456f, 459–462, 23:21f, 25, 28, 39, 49, 52, 70, 98, 120, 122, 124, 130, 138, 141, 152, 182, 211, 214, 233, 236, 239, 241, 250, 256f, 264, 270, 277, 298, 315f, 356–360, 392, 396, 403, 419, 24:24, 39–41, 47, 52, 62, 66, 71–75, 77–79, 83, 85–87, 90, 94, 98–100, 106, 111, 115f, 122, 126, 128–130, 132, 135, 139, 147, 153, 156f, 169, 173, 182, 184, 193, 209, 214, 216f, 220–222, 225–234, 238, 240–244, 249, 253, 256, 259, 262, 264, 271, 282f, 286, 288, 292, 295, 297f, 313f, 319, 325f, 328, 330, 335, 346f, 349, 372, 385, 389, 397, 405, 25:3, 64, 68, 96, 104, 135–138, 152, 174, 234–236, 241f, 251f, 259, 407f, 420, 474, 26:4–6, 9–11, 20f, 25–30, 34f, 41, 48, 52–55, 58f, 64, 72, 79f, 88, 90, 112, 115f, 118–123, 125, 132, 135, 138f, 141f, 144, 150, 152, 154f, 159f, 166–168, 170, 173, 176f, 179–181, 183–185, 190, 197, 199, 201, 205f, 215, 208, 210, 212f, 216, 221, 223, 225f, 228f, 232, 235f, 238, 244f, 247–250, 252–267, 272–276, 279, 283, 287, 291, 293, 295f, 299–305, 307, 312f, 322, 331–333, 336, 338, 344, 347f, 351–355, 371, 375f, 387–390, 392, 394–398, 402f, 405f, 430f, 433, 438f, 441f, 444–446, 450, 457, 459f, 27:6, 10, 18, 25, 31, 52f, 57, 83, 85, 90, 114, 140f, 189, 327, 329, 363, 400, 28:81f, 113, 115, 119, 173, 234, 309, 337, 29:9f, 46, 50, 55–57, 61, 63–65, 67, 71–74, 79, 85, 88, 123f, 135f, 144, 161, 165, 186, 190, 208f, 218, 232, 236, 239, 30:8, 10, 13, 16–18, 26f, 299, 32, 36, 43–45, 47, 50, 52f, 56, 58, 60, 65–72, 75, 77, 82f, 86, 88, 91f, 94–96, 98–100, 103, 106, 116, 119, 125, 128, 132, 136, 142, 154, 157, 166, 170–173, 177f, 180, 184, 186, 189, 195, 199, 204f, 207–209, 211, 214, 226, 228, 230, 232f, 237, 245, 253, 255f, 263–265, 272f, 279f, 285, 293, 295f, 298f, 301, 307, 309, 318, 322, 31:39–41, 43–45, 52, 55, 68, 86f, 99, 117, 175, 200, 221, 267, 317, 346, 349, 353, 358–377, 33:257–266, 270f, 34:20f, 32, 159, 161, 315, 317, 35:6, 12, 57, 60, 69, 92, 111, 143, 149, 196–198, 270, 361, 363, 368, 371f, 375, 383f, 393, 37:13, 26, 42, 81, 96,

148, 168, 202, 364, 38:86, 101, 106, 108, 114–116, 118, 150, 152, 158f, 160, 163, 175, 177f, 181, 183f, 190, 194, 198f, 202f, 207, 41:17, 18n, 19, 70–72, 113, 139, 147, 149, 172, 199, 213, 310, 315f, 328, 336, 338, 343, 46:83, 95, 224, 226, 52:16f, 23, 37f, 40, 59, 70, 75f, 79f, 82f, 88f, 91, 99, 109, 112f, 120–124, 131f, 136, 138, 154f, 172–174, 177, 181, 191f, 203, 208, 210, 228f, 240f, 250, 253f, 258f, 282f, see also **Good works**

Works, Evil—41:124, 136

Works, Good—see **Good works**

Works, Human—15:23, 36, 51f, 70, 74, 111, 135, 148, 244, 255

Works, Self-chosen—11:502, 12:367

Works of God—1:24, 113f, 127, 13, 136, 147, 324, 329, 2:111f, 147–149, 306, 4:232, 270, 7:46, 103f, 109, 133, 137, 148, 155, 162, 169, 203, 210, 216, 246, 252, 353, 8:5n, 10, 42, 44, 46, 66, 103, 158, 160, 165, 200, 248, 252, 255, 303, 309, 328, 10:310–312, 11:3, 5, 10–20, 22f, 26–30, 34–37, 39, 340f, 350f, 374, 379f, 553, 13:6–8, 16, 22, 96f, 106, 135, 401, 412n, 15:14f, 21, 55f, 119, 143, 173f, 16:31, 43, 78, 84, 109, 183, 206, 236, 21:332f, 23:182, 24:68, 73, 226, 26:32, 40, 48, 73, 204, 373, 29:19, 49, 123f, 135, 140, 149f, 190, 31:39–41, 43–45, 52, 55, 99, 175, 36:56n, 63, 163, 344, 37:7, 42, 58, 72f, 75f, 92, 138, 141, 207f, 296, 299, 337, 354, 38:106, 225, 39:93, 188, 41:19, 155, 315, 42:89, 113–115, 132, 45:37–41, 144f, 157, 207, 319, 328f, 331, 333, 347, 376, 46:96, 183, 186, 228, 231, 240, 246, 248, 51:18–21

Works of love—3:125, 170, 180, 189, 196, 225, 272, 16:185, 24:41, 147f, 227f, 252, 263, 25:490, 27:52, 140, 29:45, 50, 53, 30:117, 274, 31:29, 240, 364f, 35:69, 368, 379, 384, 36:194, 205–208, 40:83

Works of Satan—3:264

Works of the Holy Spirit—2:267, 11:13, 287

Works of the Law—25:30, 59, 187f, 219, 233, 241f, 252, 256, 27:7, 12f, 75, 78, 173, 175, 202f, 214, 218, 222f, 224f, 228, 231f, 234, 238f, 242f, 245, 247, 249, 250–252, 255–258, 260, 264–266, 272, 274, 283f, 286, 291, 321f, 327, 329, 331, 334–336, 340, 381, 404

Works righteous persons—9:244, 273, 279, 11:266, 16:203, 22:132, 501, 23:30, 60, 85, 135, 264

Works righteousness—9:26f, 97, 102–104, 141, 158, 170f, 186, 213f, 226, 235, 244f, 273, 284, 12:74, 13:8, 185, 325, 328, 17:23, 43, 99, 108, 163, 214, 222f, 237, 296, 19:80, 90, 99f, 21:38, 254f, 263, 285, 289, 304f, 318f, 23:23, 58, 60, 24:59, 63, 171, 229, 343, 25:xi, 3, 9, 28f, 89, 104, 135f, 177, 263, 279f, 406, 26:4, 74, 172, 202, 225, 242, 253, 268, 273, 280, 286, 295, 436, 443, 458f, 27:167, 35:375, 42:xiii, xvi, 51:20, 30, 53:11

Works vs. faith—25:130, 234, 251

World—1:18, 22, 34f, 37, 39, 43, 78, 87, 107, 123f, 126, 128, 131, 139, 172, 194f, 208, 210, 216, 220–222, 224, 230, 240f, 243, 248, 255f, 268, 272, 289, 298, 301, 310, 315, 318, 321–323, 328, 330, 332, 336, 341, 348, 351–355, 357–359, 2:3, 7f, 13, 16f, 20, 22f, 25, 27f, 30, 36–38, 43, 49, 55–62, 64–66, 68, 71, 81f, 84–89, 92, 97, 99, 102, 140, 142–144, 148f, 153f, 163, 167–170, 172f, 175–177, 180f, 184, 186f, 191, 193–196, 198, 200, 204, 208, 211f, 216–219, 223f, 226, 228–230, 235, 237, 239, 243–245, 247, 253f, 257f, 260f, 265, 268, 273f, 290, 295, 302, 304, 312, 326f, 331, 333f, 338, 345f, 352, 354–356, 368, 370, 375, 377–380, 382–384, 388, 390f, 395, 398, 3:10, 13f, 19, 33, 38, 43, 48f, 51f, 57, 59, 63, 66, 81f, 84, 91, 96, 105f, 108, 112, 114, 118, 120, 123f, 126, 129, 134, 141f, 145f, 150–154, 159, 161, 179f, 189, 199f, 208, 212, 218, 221, 229, 231, 234, 237f, 240, 246–248, 262, 267f, 270, 276, 279, 292–295, 300f, 315–317, 319, 327, 329, 331, 338–340, 342–346, 362f, 365, 4:3, 6f, 8f, 11, 18, 23f, 28–30, 33, 38, 41–43, 54, 60, 62, 67, 73, 76–78, 90, 92, 100f, 106, 108, 111, 118–123, 125, 127, 135, 137, 141–143, 146–148, 160f, 163, 174–177, 179, 181, 190, 193, 195, 198, 202, 204–206, 210, 214, 216, 219–221, 224, 227, 229, 231, 234, 236f, 239, 249, 251, 258, 275, 291–295, 303, 307–309, 315, 318f, 322, 327–330, 332, 335, 338, 340, 343–347, 350, 352, 355f, 364, 366, 370–374, 376, 379, 386, 392, 398–402, 404–406, 408, 5:6f, 11f, 17–19, 26, 28, 32, 34, 42f, 49, 55, 57, 62, 67, 70, 72, 74, 84f, 88, 100, 109f, 112, 119, 130, 142f, 146,

150, 155, 186–188, 192, 197, 199, 201, 206, 208, 219f, 222, 224–228, 231, 234, 240, 247, 251, 262, 264f, 268, 272, 274–276, 297, 306, 309, 313–316, 320, 329, 341–343, 350f, 353f, 368–370, 372, 6:3, 9, 23, 31, 74, 92, 217, 243, 344, 354, 399, 7:12, 21, 33f, 38, 46, 56, 62–64, 67, 69–71, 89, 96, 98f, 115, 128, 131f, 134, 146, 149, 154, 162f, 167, 170, 178, 181–183, 189f, 192, 214, 225, 231, 248, 255f, 265, 274f, 280, 295, 297f, 320, 332f, 338, 341f, 345, 348f, 351, 362, 364, 370, 376, 8:6f, 10, 17–20, 28–30, 32f, 36, 41, 45, 60, 67, 69, 71–73, 75, 81, 83, 89f, 97, 114f, 117–119, 138, 152f, 163f, 168, 176, 182, 186, 194f, 202, 204, 208, 217, 220, 223f, 226, 230f, 233, 236–239, 244f, 247f, 251–253, 260f, 263–266, 270–272, 274, 276, 283, 287, 292, 300, 303–306, 308f, 312, 321, 324, 326, 9:4f, 19, 22f, 28, 33, 56, 68, 80, 111, 139f, 144f, 148, 154, 157f, 166, 184, 203, 213, 216, 225, 235, 238, 243, 273, 299, 305f, 308, 11:12f, 17f, 307, 424, 435, 447, 519, 12:167f, 215, 220, 246, 344, 354, 375, 377f, 380, 384, 394, 13:13, 15, 164, 198, 248, 262, 14:4, 9–11, 15–17, 24–26, 30–33, 46f, 52, 55–59, 63f, 66–68, 73, 78, 81–83, 87–89, 91, 99–104, 111, 121, 124, 126, 130–135, 144, 181, 186f, 198f, 210, 213–215, 220f, 223, 225, 231, 235–237, 239f, 248f, 252, 260f, 264, 267, 273–276, 290, 285, 298–300, 304, 306f, 322, 329, 334, 337, 343f, 15:4, 9, 31, 48, 53, 67, 117f, 140, 142, 145, 159, 161f, 176, 211, 214, 16:30, 124, 17:43f, 47, 169, 194, 243, 18:119, 229, 20:25, 28, 41, 43, 50, 115, 152, 210, 21:17, 20, 61, 115, 126, 132f, 163, 172–175, 180, 184, 193, 203, 214f, 230, 244f, 275, 307f, 311–313, 331f, 352, 22:25, 32, 35f, 56, 75, 106, 165, 167f, 198, 275, 306, 321, 356, 370, 373, 376, 382, 386, 390, 411, 459, 23:6, 8f, 11, 13, 20, 25f, 30, 33, 39–41, 47, 50, 52, 58, 60–62, 68, 70, 75, 78, 83–85, 87, 89, 93, 104, 119–121, 123–126, 132, 135, 140f, 146, 150, 156–158, 160, 162–164, 166, 174, 176–180, 183, 186, 192, 195, 208–212, 214, 218f, 221, 230, 233, 238–242, 244, 249f, 255, 257, 260, 262, 264f, 274, 277, 281f, 288, 290–292, 302, 306, 310, 314–317, 321f, 326, 333–336, 346f, 354f, 358–364, 366, 368, 370, 372, 375f, 382f, 387, 389f, 393–397, 399, 404, 407f, 412, 420, 24:7, 10–12, 16–21, 25–31, 35, 37, 40, 43f, 48–50, 55, 64, 67–69, 71, 73, 77f, 80–85, 87, 90f, 96f, 99, 101, 103, 109f, 112–114, 116–121, 123–138, 141f, 145, 149, 152–156, 158–166, 168, 172, 177, 179–183, 185, 189, 192f, 195–202, 204, 209–211, 214–216, 221, 225, 228–231, 233, 238, 241, 247–249, 251, 259–263, 265–271, 273f, 276–278, 280, 285–292, 294, 297, 301f, 306, 310f, 313–316, 319f, 322f, 325, 332, 335–342, 345–347, 350–354, 358–361, 366, 368–370, 372, 377–379, 382, 384, 389f, 395–397, 399, 401f, 408, 413–422, 25:30, 46, 295, 297, 26:4, 8, 13f, 17f, 20–22, 24, 26–31, 33f, 37, 39–43, 47f, 54, 58–60, 63, 65, 71, 90, 93, 95f, 99, 105, 107, 112, 130–134, 140f, 151, 162, 166, 171, 175f, 180, 182–185, 187, 190, 193, 212f, 225, 228, 231, 234, 238, 240–247, 251, 255, 258f, 262, 277–282, 284–287, 289, 301, 304f, 307–309, 311, 315, 319–322, 326, 334f, 337, 348–351, 354–356, 361–366, 368–370, 373, 375f, 379f, 384–387, 390, 393f, 402, 408f, 414, 418–421, 423, 426, 439, 441, 443f, 446, 450–453, 456, 458, 27:5, 11, 15, 18f, 24f, 27, 31, 35, 39f, 43–45, 47, 54, 56, 59, 61, 68f, 86, 91, 97, 100, 102–105, 107, 110, 117f, 122, 125, 130, 132–138, 140–144, 146, 148, 156, 158, 163, 165, 170, 173, 174, 178, 210, 242, 269, 274, 277, 283, 285–287, 301, 336, 340, 345, 354f, 358, 374, 390f, 397, 404f, 28:5, 11f, 38, 50–52, 71, 97, 106, 111, 114, 117, 135–137, 145, 306, 29:10, 69, 137, 199, 30:3, 8, 15–17, 19, 29–31, 36f, 42–54, 58, 61, 66f, 70, 72, 74, 76, 78, 80, 88, 90, 95, 101, 103, 109, 114, 119, 121, 128, 144, 151, 153f, 156, 163, 165f, 169–171, 173–176, 178f, 184, 188, 190f, 193, 195–197, 199, 209–211, 219, 223, 226f, 235, 237, 241f, 248–251, 254, 256, 259, 261f, 266f, 272, 274, 276, 279, 281, 283–287, 289–292, 294f, 298–302, 304, 309, 311–313, 317f, 326, 33:98, 177, 277–287, 35:52, 55, 151, 281, 285f, 299, 331, 380, 389, 36:237, 37:21n, 30, 40, 81n, 82, 94, 115, 131n, 195f, 204, 233, 293, 308, 361, 367, 38:5, 68, 85, 105f, 108, 111f, 115f, 128, 130, 159f, 175, 184, 187, 189f, 204, 230, 41:xi, 82, 103, 127, 169, 334,

42:50, 78, 80, 99, 104, 129, 143, 159, 45:88, 90, 92, 95f, 102, 105, 111, 113–116, 118, 142, 149f, 156, 158, 176, 264, 279f, 323, 328, 331f, 333, 350, 368f, 46:27, 35, 77, 141, 154, 166, 171, 176, 179, 182, 196, 211, 225, 236, 246f, 254, 265, 305, 317, 48:206, 259, 52:115, 117
Degenerating 8:131
Growing old 8:67
World, First (Primal or original)—1:77, 88, 90, 206f, 237, 333–336, 342, 344, 346, 349–351, 354–356, 358f, 2:3–6, 10, 19, 24, 26, 32, 40, 52f, 63f, 66, 70, 81, 83f, 89, 114, 165, 209, 232, 234, 236
World, Kingdom of the—45:88, 90, 96, 102, 105n, 111, 118
World, Ruling powers of the—37:21n, 131n
World missions—see **Missions, World**
Worldliness—23:167
Worldlings—2:37
Worldly-wise persons—14:146, 196, 22:119, 125, 23:13, 41, 54, 283
Wörlitz—51:257
Worms (City)—43:77–79, 51:60f
House of the Knights of Rhodes 32:105f
Printing of Bibles in 46:239n
Worms (creatures)—1:54, 131, 207, 5:130, 206, 7:210f, 237, 334, 8:93, 173, 190, 236, 252, 9:137, 17:45f, 19:29, 94, 23:131, 24:205, 207, 221, 223, 314f, 359, 417, 419, 26:267, 421
Worms, Bag of—12:105, 21:13, 230, 24:44, see also **Madensack**; **Sacks**
Worms, Colloquy of, 1540—48:248, 50:190n
Worms, Colloquy of, 1541—34:310n
Worms, Diet of, 1122—44:164n
Worms, Diet of, 1520—35:228f
Worms, Diet of, 1521—6:ix, 138n, 7:ix, 370n, 21:xvi, xviii, 22:412n, 26:97n, 32:xii–xv, 101–131, 34:xi, 5, 12, 14, 33n, 65, 338, 36:129, 38:93, 39:141, 227, 248n, 41:xii, xvi, 230n, 264, 42:xi, xvi, 169, 181f, 43:59, 65–67, 69, 99, 265, 269n, 44:xvii, 132n, 142n, 144n, 150n, 152n, 153n, 157n, 212n, 45:69n, 77, 135n, 241n, 272n, 46:142, 213n, 227n, 247n, 48:74n, 129n, 143n, 174n, 176, 188n, 189n, 192, 196f, 199f, 203f, 208n, 210f, 216n, 218f, 222n, 224n, 225f, 231n, 234, 236n, 244, 246, 255, 256n, 272n, 275n, 292n, 307, 321, 322n, 324, 390, 49:xvii, 35, 51, 285n, 352n, 364, 51:66n, 53:211f, 54:30, 160, see also **Kalkoff, Paul**
Account of Aleander 32:123–130
Account of Luther's supporters 32:105–123
Luther's appearance 32:xii–xv, 103–131
Luther's speech 32:109–113 (text)
Worms, Diet of, 1545—41:260, 43:255, 50:248, 250n, 253n, 254n, 265, 267n, 269n, 312n
Worms, Edict of, 1521—28:257, 32:123–130, 276, 34:12n, 83n, 39:xxi, 247n, 41:xii, 245n, 284, 288n, 43:63, 73, 142, 254n, 265n, 45:xiii, 77f, 83n, 169n, 314, 347n, 46:xi, xiii, 204n, 247n, 48:210f, 216n, 220n, 223, 253n, 255, 340n, 392n, 393, 50:219n, 285f
Worms Translation of the Prophets—49:165
Worms, Wood—3:310, 17:239
Worry—21:190–192, 207, 24:117, 157, 162, 222, 318, 384f, 395, 28:103–105, 372
Worship—1:79–81, 94f, 97, 101, 106, 109, 115, 140, 146, 154, 159, 161, 180, 192, 227, 231, 246f, 249f, 272, 292, 301, 314, 316, 321, 327–330, 358, 2:6, 18, 29, 32, 40, 42, 52f, 55, 60, 71, 112f, 128, 160, 165, 170, 173, 176, 192, 197–199, 201, 205, 213f, 219, 230, 235, 242–244, 246, 256–258, 263, 269, 282f, 285f, 305f, 326, 333–335, 349, 355f, 361, 363, 371, 383, 388f, 393f, 3:36, 74, 84, 94, 98, 108f, 116–118, 120–122, 144, 146, 150, 164, 172, 174, 181, 200–204, 210, 242, 250, 275, 294, 319, 325, 329, 339, 344f, 357, 362, 364, 4:6, 8f, 22, 34, 53, 56f, 70, 89, 98n, 99–102, 134f, 39, 150, 178f, 182, 230, 235–237, 246, 279, 308, 320–323, 327f, 333, 347, 359, 366, 384f, 391, 401, 5:7, 9, 20, 49, 71, 80, 82–84, 94–97, 155, 188, 241f, 252, 259, 264, 358, 6:30, 33, 71–73, 85, 113, 126f, 185, 225, 230–232, 236f, 248, 250, 264, 324, 347, 349, 7:15, 37, 72, 91, 136, 155f, 163, 199f, 218, 299f, 311, 341, 343f, 355, 8:6, 21, 65, 69, 82, 126, 129f, 132, 143, 146, 177, 194, 201, 229f, 275f, 294, 301, 304, 9:53, 63, 67, 71–73, 81f, 85, 109, 123, 131, 134, 138, 140, 144, 156, 161, 164, 166, 175f, 193, 229, 237, 291f, 294, 10:38, 233f, 351, 353f, 359, 12:4, 79f, 87, 89, 92f, 144, 192, 200, 222, 289, 300, 306, 315, 361, 397, 402, 404, 406, 13:34, 167, 182, 191, 291–293, 397, 14:17, 22, 33f, 132, 237, 347f, 16:10, 26, 35,

69f, 78f, 107, 128, 147, 149, 152, 155, 163, 165, 167, 198, 216f, 244f, 263, 293, 318f, 338f, 17:12f, 70–73, 97, 111–114, 134, 136, 141, 271, 373, 378, 18:5, 12, 166, 260, 324f, 19:11, 13, 161, 187, 20:10, 39, 84, 87, 177, 300, 21:81, 139f, 145, 279, 322, 325f, 350, 23:20, 22, 27, 85, 120f, 298, 327, 348, 353, 355, 360, 366, 373, 377f, 388, 405, 24:154, 213, 242f, 304, 308, 313, 337, 341, 357, 367, 396f, 25:10, 145, 157f, 422f, 437, 26:32, 43, 64, 70, 82, 92, 104f, 121f, 125, 138, 140, 153, 173, 181, 185, 205f, 208, 222, 226, 228f, 231, 257–259, 293, 300, 331, 333, 347, 355, 373, 377, 396f, 408, 426, 428f, 437–439, 454, 499, 27:9f, 25, 30, 44, 56, 83f, 88–91, 122, 135f, 139, 141, 176, 204, 293, 298, 28:271, 369–372, 29:9, 177, 200, 30:36f, 239, 35:62, 81, 132, 145, 199, 239, 269f, 272f, 329, 351, 378, 401, 36:42, 290–297, 37:10, 22n, 52f, 73n, 76, 180, 265, 283f, 369–371, 38:95, 99, 105f, 108, 110, 112, 149, 152, 159, 165, 178, 190, 207, 210, 232, 40:xii, 44, 86f, 306–310, 301–303, 42:60, 77, 44:xiv, 32, 54f, 323–326, 329–331, 46:148, 229, 236n, 51:333, 52:17, 90, 245f, 249f, 272, 54:84, 195, see especially Volume 53, *Liturgy and Hymns*

Established places of—3:163f

Worship, False—see **False worship**

Worship, Forms of—6:128, 226, 229f, 237, 372

Worship, Heathen—26:330, 354, 395

Worship, Jewish—Only in Jerusalem 6:126–129, 166, 265

Worship, New forms of—41:xii, 136f, 139, 164, 206, 285

Worship, Old Testament—26:317

Worship, Orders of—45:165, 169

Worship, True—2:12, 19, 31, 54, 56f, 59, 63, 240, 247, 250, 284, 334, 382, 6:85, 247f, 233–235, 237, 248

Worship, Uniformity in—38:317

Worth—11:396

Worthiness—6:114, 166, 21:314, 323f, 26:5, 328, 379, 402, 437, 27:205, 35:12, 55f, 89f, 368n, 36:45f

Wrath—1:189, 195, 200, 260–262, 266, 270–273, 275, 281, 291, 332, 2:4f, 21–23, 30, 47, 49–54, 57, 60, 64–66, 70, 72, 81f, 85f, 89, 91, 96, 99, 103, 111, 117f, 120–123, 131, 134, 143, 145, 148–150, 154, 155, 157f, 163, 176, 186, 210f, 216, 223f, 229, 248, 252, 265f, 280, 287, 317, 321f, 344, 352, 356, 358, 377f, 382f, 389, 3:6, 21f, 59, 135f, 138, 180, 220–222, 225, 227, 235, 242, 256, 296, 305, 320, 4:44, 70, 261, 309, 5:38, 77, 88, 171f, 198, 222, 327, 6:37, 43, 107, 370, 7:102, 179, 181, 191f, 196, 228f, 237, 254–257, 262f, 274, 281, 8:9, 16, 31, 65, 124, 227, 240, 330, 9:4, 16, 21, 23f, 33, 57n, 58f, 81, 83, 97, 104, 112f, 145f, 158, 170, 178, 181, 184f, 204, 212, 215, 244f, 251, 290, 293–296, 10:23, 36, 39–41, 117, 145, 177, 378f, 433f, 14:30, 58f, 64, 69, 73, 91, 140, 142, 153, 156f, 178, 258, 270, 323, 331, 16:108, 200, 212, 17:83, 126, 203, 238, 240, 277–279, 318f, 354, 20:6, 11, 19, 107, 132f, 161, 175, 294f, 22:87, 131, 456, 23:62, 106, 180, 206, 221, 251, 256, 267f, 302f, 341, 24:88, 98, 113, 136, 146, 153, 157, 179f, 194, 196, 220, 222, 268, 273, 275, 279, 288, 307, 343, 361, 420, 25:9, 39f, 57, 59, 161, 175, 262, 279–281, 26:42, 48f, 59, 64, 126, 147f, 151, 166, 230, 235f, 251, 254, 275, 290, 292, 301, 310f, 314, 325f, 331, 334, 342, 352, 364, 372, 395, 397f, 402, 404, 438, 27:18, 34, 109, 164, 184, 235, 257, 260, 266, 269, 303, 313, 324, 370, 407, 29:169, 198, 209, 30:12, 97, 101, 141, 179, 276, 35:200, 210, 374, 41:140, 206

Wrath, Kingdom of—5:38

Wrath, Twofold—25:288

Wrath of God—2:14, 17, 26, 3:8, 44, 60, 72, 134, 203, 214, 224, 233f, 236–239, 242f, 264, 269, 278, 281, 292, 294f, 302, 304, 308, 310, 313, 348, 351, 364, 4:11, 159f, 166, 210, 222, 232, 241f, 245, 337, 360, 5:10, 59, 71, 140, 152–158, 161, 163, 167–170, 194, 199, 219, 259, 6:43, 139, 141, 143, 210, 7:80, 83, 180, 183, 227, 233, 271, 275, 277, 332, 8:38, 40, 43, 52, 166, 171, 204f, 224, 227, 256, 10:81, 118, 11:4, 80–82, 84, 93, 204f, 319, 536, 12:63, 112, 117, 310, 315, 321, 334f, 356, 358, 365, 406f, 410, 13:77, 85, 91f, 96, 100f, 106f, 124f, 130, 242, 275, 14:20, 29, 31, 84f, 89, 141, 144f, 150, 160, 306, 322, 329, 336, 349, 16:7, 34, 54, 60, 74, 102, 128, 191, 213, 231, 266, 292, 18:97, 212, 217, 230, 283, 19:10, 18, 66f, 76, 85, 100, 141f, 144, 20:128, 313, 22:366, 368, 375f, 378, 382, 391, 419, 430, 490, 500, 23:34, 59, 64, 89, 127, 196, 265, 278, 313, 317, 361, 371,

404, 24:53, 70, 73, 110, 113, 140, 162, 158, 164, 219, 296, 315, 319, 328, 340, 342, 370, 405, 25:17, 176, 179, 392, 26:10, 33, 36, 49, 65, 72, 120, 126, 136, 140, 146, 148, 150, 152, 179, 217, 222, 225, 229, 231, 252, 256, 258, 282–284, 287f, 291, 293, 305–318, 321f, 324, 327, 330, 337, 339, 341, 348, 355, 361, 363, 365, 370, 381, 386, 388, 390, 403, 405, 439, 443, 448, 458–460, 27:4f, 7f, 19, 21, 26f, 50, 78, 154, 170, 376, 409, 28:70, 103–105, 107, 136, 140, 209, 245f, 264, 29:41f, 81, 130, 151, 159f, 30:10, 184, 191, 225, 278, 302, 325, 31:47, 100, 131, 203, 244, 346, 32:154, 172–176, 224–226, 228, 33:212f, 247f, 34:126, 35:106, 109, 252, 256, 281, 328, 366, 372f, 407, 36:46f, 50, 84f, 142–144, 154, 161, 175, 177, 182, 217, 224f, 37:19, 33, 72, 362, 38:113, 131, 160f, 39:188, 275, 290, 41:xv, 13, 111, 130, 146, 148, 201, 210, 229, 236, 241, 245, 255, 292f, 295, 335, 339, 342, 42:55, 74, 88, 92f, 101–104, 115, 135, 151, 156, 44:28f, 69, 44:79, 45:59, 61f, 87, 113, 327, 46:18f, 21f, 24, 29, 40–43, 52f, 61, 66, 68–70, 72, 79, 99, 115, 153, 168, 170f, 174, 179, 184, 186, 188, 255, 47:13, 15, 29, 44, 51, 67n, 69, 71–75, 110–115, 132, 138f, 143, 148, 154–156, 164, 172, 192, 213, 241, 253, 261, 268, 272f, 293, 296, 52:168, 54:15, 34, 190, 270, 308, 420

Wrede, Adolf—see **Kluckhohn, August**

Wrede, Adolf, and August Kluckhohn, eds.—*Deutsche Reichstagsakten unter Karl V*, Gotha, 1893–1905 46:227n

Wrestlers—3:146, 6:137f, 143, 154

Wrestling with God—6:125f, 130, 136, 143f, 180, 14:193

Wretchedness—24:29, 61, 73, 152, 413

Writers—2:ix, 116n, 237, 46:187, 245–252, 256, 46:246–252, 256, 48:35

Writings, Human—32:148, 216f, 236–238, 243–245, 257

Written code—25:60f, 67, 180f, 324–326

Written word—10:211–213, 220, 399, 25:4, 120, 145f, 414f, 515

Württemberg—23:7n, 31:37, 46:85n, 49:118, 177f, 414n, 54:380, 382, 390

Würzburg—31:37, 44:141, 46:47n, 49:118n, 313n, 54:308, 472

Augustinian Monastery 48:60

Würzburg, Bishop of—48:30n

Wurzen—5:xi, 369

Wuttke, Adolf—*Der Deutsche Volksaberglaube der Gegenwart*, Leipzig, 1925 22:107n

Wuttke, Gottfrid—*Melchisedech der Priesterkönig von Salem*, Giessen, 1927 13:310n

Wycliffe, John—28:242, 267, 30:295, 32:83, 129, 33:72, 116, 160, 231, 37:157, 294n, 295f, 299, 301f, 39:20n, 45:60n, 48:147n, 149n, 249, 54:110

De potestate papae 30:295n

On the Pastoral Office 9:130n

Wycliffites—34:50, 36:28n, 30

Xenophon—1:204, 2:43, 160, 26:123, 354

Cyropaedia 1:204n

Xerxes—18:368, 371, 20:187, 35:299, 306n

Yahweh—see **Tetragrammaton**

Yardarm, Golden—16:134n

Years—2:92f, 208, 239, 304, 13:99, 118n, 27:7, 285, 295, 331, 357

Yeast—3:5, 7:233, 235, 27:36f, 39, 45f, 339f

Yehudith—35:338n

Yield—9:221

Yoke—9:213, 225, 236, 26:133, 207, 304, 370, 404, 27:7f, 10, 13, 50, 135, 155, 326, 28:361, 363

Yoke of Israel—18:194

Yokefellow—28:22, 218

Young people—3:6, 186, 279, 323, 327, 4:141, 182, 213, 250, 333, 5:164, 192, 260, 282, 289, 304, 347, 7:55, 58, 74–79, 84f, 88, 93–96, 101, 125, 130, 140f, 165, 198, 281, 312, 325, 8:113, 175, 187, 221, 223, 291, 298, 311, 9:212, 10:91, 345, 12:77f, 13:114, 402, 13:215, 220, 14:76, 15:176f, 231, 17:31, 224, 20:104, 297f, 28:3, 10f, 160, 327, 333, 357, 29:21, 58, 30:138f, 246f, 35:258f, 262, 339, 345, 36:77, 208f, 224, 42:74, 133, 45:335f, 349–353, 367f, 370f, 54:64f

Young woman (Almah)—16:84, 17:236

Zaanan—18:217f

Zabarella, Cardinal Francis—39:134n

Zacchaeus—9:180, 22:407, 38:100

Zacharias—see **Zechariah, Father of John the Baptist**

Zack, John—39:108

Zadok—3:13, 13:207

Zahn, Johannes—*Die Melodien der deutschen evangelischen Kirchenlieder*, Gütersloh, 1892 53:25n, 173, 192n, 290n, 302n

Zahna—54:436

Zahrnt, Hans—*Luther deutet Geschichte*, Munich, 1952 46:159n
Zainer Bible—see **Scripture(s)**
Zalmon, Mt.—10:331, 338, 342, 11:98, 13:17
Zapolya, John, Prince of Transylvania and King of Hungary—43:217, 49:185n, 221n, 240n, 242n, 50:55n
Zarephath—18:203
Zarephath, Widow of—2:178, 259, 3:81, 89, 4:137, 9:93, 14:19, 19:38, 21:346f, 27:288, 335
Zeal—2:125, 150, 171, 185, 292, 331, 399, 3:13, 15, 137, 146, 197f, 218, 232, 246, 276, 290, 4:100, 151, 178, 238, 254, 272, 342, 384, 390f, 5:107, 119, 169, 207, 242, 287, 328f, 344, 348, 350, 370, 7:5, 11, 34, 63, 65, 75f, 83, 97, 114, 125, 164, 193, 204, 215, 219, 223, 240, 255, 298, 317, 319, 321, 335, 342–344, 355, 8:24, 33, 44, 54, 59, 62, 98, 107, 119, 137, 150, 197, 203f, 219, 223, 264, 275f, 279f, 283, 293, 309, 315, 320, 9:53, 59, 171, 175, 10:78, 365, 370, 15:76, 245, 314, 17:3, 5, 37–39, 74, 146, 263, 275, 376, 378, 22:230–237, 263f, 267–269, 301, 307, 330, 367, 484f, 506, 23:174f, 186, 204f, 264, 328, 348, 354, 356, 360, 24:54, 58, 154, 229, 363, 25:88, 93, 96f, 107, 127, 226, 231, 244, 269, 379, 402, 404f, 422, 440, 455f, 513, 26:13, 18, 21, 43f, 55, 68f, 103, 125, 155, 162, 186f, 202–204, 276, 395, 403f, 415, 424f, 428f, 27:9, 39, 49, 53, 133, 178, 187, 189, 214, 217, 240, 243, 300f, 305–307, 327, 342, 369–371, 375, 391, 409, 29:232, 30:242, 244, 310, 41:117n
Zeal, False—see **False Zeal**
Zealots—21:333, 26:68, 429, 31:306
Zebedee—27:195f
Zebedee, Sons of—25:369
Zebulon—5:340, 6:321, 366, 378, 8:55, 70, 102, 222, 272–274, 277–279, 281, 286, 9:258n, 306f
Zebulon, Territory of—22:216
Zebulon, Tribe of—13:28
Zebulonites—16:96
Zechariah, Father of John the Baptist—1:321, 2:178, 3:208, 284, 4:151, 6:358, 22:32, 38f, 44, 76, 172, 27:185, 29:6, 205, 218, 37:337
Zechariah, King—18:4, 176
Zechariah, Prophet—2:191, 8:227, 11:474, 13:184, 17:69, 18:xi, 371, 379, 20:3f, 6, 13, 53f, 83, 102, 157, 159, 161, 167, 22:70, 23:149, 24:87, 90, 239, 275, 25:41, 29:113f, 30:41, 35:330f, 45:215, 274, 47:298, 49:160, 52:74, 92f
  Interpretations of his book 20:62, 73, 130, 155–157, 181
  Luther's commentary on his book 14:210n
Zedekiah, King—13:172, 18:209, 319, 19:166, 25:445, 46:194, 47:250, 258
Zeeb—11:129f, 132f
Zell, Matthew and Catherine—49:95n
Zemah—16:53, 117, 20:215, 217, 255, 258
Zemecke, John—41:313n, 319
Zenan—see **Zaanan**
Zenas—29:87f
Zeno—33:76n
Zephaniah, Prophet—14:10, 18:319, 35:328f
  Commentary on his book 18:ix, xi, 319–364 (text)
Zephthah—18:351
Zerah—5:91, 7:8
Zerbst—9:211n, 31:19, 41:230f, 48:148n, 150n, 49:25, 85f, 54:310
Zerubbabel—8:26, 16:221, 18:378, 386f, 20:34, 42, 44–48, 50f, 60, 68, 204, 222f, 226–230, 35:303, 45:214n, 47:225
Zeus—5:121n
Ziba—11:248, 13:180, 206
Zibeon—6:291f, 294
Zieger, Balthasar—54:155
Ziegler, Bernard—8:241, 15:286n, 34:301, 319, 35:206, 54:375f, 446
Zieglers—48:329n
Zilla—1:316–318
Zilpah—5:338, 340, 344, 350, 7:218, 221, 8:52, 87, 98, 9:258
Zimri, King—46:41
Zin—9:16
Zink, Albert—50:52n
Zink, John—50:50f
Zink, Thomas—50:50f
Zinna—50:115
Zins and Zinskauf—44:96n, 213, 45:174n, 175n, 176, 179, 235, 236n, 237f, 240n, 247, 252n, 258–261, 268, 289, 291, 295n, 301, 304f, 307n, 308f, 46:220n, 49:52n, 52:215, see also **Rents (Rente, Rentenkauf)**
Zion—5:342, 8:89, 183, 224, 244f, 297, 10:95, 230f, 314, 441, 12:37f, 29:140, 173, 30:301
Zion, Daughter of—18:219, 242, 244, 246, 358, 20:94, 125, 191
Zion, Mother—11:178–181
Zion, Mt.—2:101, 4:99, 6:173, 274, 9:60, 182, 11:147, 178–185, 313, 362, 365f,

389, 550, 12:37f, 13:234, 264f, 270f, 284, 14:111f, 135, 174, 183–185, 226, 324–328, 332f, 335f, 16:27f, 53f, 131, 141, 145, 149, 227, 229, 261, 272, 284, 295, 305, 321, 17:13f, 58, 203, 307, 343, 345, 405, 18:7, 112, 121, 200–202, 238f, 241, 329, 22:43, 46, 195, 27:93, 177, 221, 318, 393, 410, 35:291, 321, 38:93, 49:288, 52:286

Zittau—2:202n

Zoan—11:52n, 16:254

Zoar—2:265, 378, 3:290, 292f, 298, 302, 306f, 16:147, 46:248

Zoch, Lorenz—54:138, 268

Zoilus—11:123, 15:186n

Zophar—6:307, 16:113

Zor—11:127

Zoroastrianism—13:96n

Zülsdorf (Zölsdorf)—34:295, 50:233n

Zürich—35:227, 36:235, 37:xii, xiv, xvii, 8, 81n, 149n, 203, 226n, 38:6–8, 11, 14f, 83n, 86n, 288, 302n, 303n, 40:76, 229n, 42:5, 46:90n, 106n, 47:123, 49:88n, 89n, 94f, 96n, 100, 215n, 251, 264n, 303n, 427, 50:3, 46, 55n, 242

Zütphen, Gerhard Zerbolt von—*De spiritualibus ascensionibus* 11:145n

Zütphen, Henry of—see **Henry of Zuetphen**

Zuzim—2:367, 374

Zwickau—22:417n, 31:330, 34:107, 38:94, 40:47, 119, 227, 45:5, 8n, 13f, 46:19n, 21n, 60n, 158n, 48:xiv, 180n, 399, 49:55, 87, 159, 161f, 168, 240n, 264, 283, 284n, 348, 420, 50:50, 222n, 277n, 51:xvn, 5, 69, 53:17, 19, 104, 106, 193, 245, 250n, 272, 304, 337, 54:145f

Zwickau prophets—34:12n, 36:233, 256n, 43:64, 45:55, 365n, 47:116n, 48:39n, 364–366, 380f, 386n, 401, 49:121n, 163n

Zwilling, Gabriel Didymus—36:129, 233f, 256n, 37:18n, 45:13n, 53, 382, 46:89n, 48:39n, 79n, 281n, 325, 337n, 356, 358n, 380n, 386n, 400, 49:4n, 71n, 142, 355n, 50:233n, 51:69, 80, 54:244

Zwingli, Ulrich—2:43n, 243, 3:5, 8:41n, 133n, 134f, 136n, 12:viii, 7, 10, 16, 42, 49, 60, 218, 223, 287, 16:168n, 241n, 303, 329, 332, 346, 17:75, 93, 155, 238, 260n, 393, 22:316n, 23:100n, 101, 102n, 285n, 26:192, 242n, 27:20n, 62n, 119n, 28:228f, 244, 252, 258, 264, 290, 345, 365f, 368, 382, 30:229, 276, 34:301, 35:x, xii, xiv, 36:272, 331f, 346, 38:xi, 5–13, 20, 21n, 22–27, 30n, 31, 32n, 33–35, 39, 41f, 47, 49f, 54–56, 58–60, 64, 66–68, 70, 72, 74f, 79, 80f, 83n, 84f, 89, 157n, 167n, 221, 284, 287n, 288f, 291, 293n, 294n, 299n, 300–304, 40:xi, 63, 76, 259n, 41:37n, 105n, 42:17n, 43:70n, 138n, 220, 46:5n, 263, 47:104, 48:123n, 163n, 212, 230n, 247n, 318, 322n, 49:xviiin, 50n, 88n, 89n, 94f, 122, 124n, 141, 146n, 160n, 164, 165n, 179, 200n, 215n, 226n, 228, 230n, 234n, 237, 238n, 266n, 300f, 303n, 370n, 414n, 50:3–5, 7, 28, 55n, 131, 242n, 53:xv, 54:11, 22f, 41, 51, 60, 65, 73, 75, 86, 88, 92f, 147, 152, 173, 232, 262, 284, 376, 379, 391, 417

Attacks on his views 37:6f, 24, 34–41, 97, 100, 130, 156f, 163–188, 189n, 190–252, 305f, 326, 330, 352, 354, 363n

Teachings 37:xiif, xviif, xx, 16n, 53n, 94n, 126n, 139, 145, 153, 155, 206n, 213n, 227, 250, 252n

Zwingli, Ulrich, Works of—*Answer to Eck* 37:8, 81n, 97n, 102n

Answer to Strauss 37:9, 180n

Christian Answer 37:18n, 36n, 161n, 163n, 170n, 171n, 177n, 180n, 187n, 189n, 191n, 193n, 194n, 197n, 198n, 203n, 206n, 212n, 213n, 220n, 231n, 232n, 234n, 236n, 237n, 242n, 247n, 249n, 250n, 280n

Clear Instruction 37:xxi, 8, 22n, 52n, 61n, 64n, 68n, 73n, 77n, 83n, 84n, 85n, 99n, 102n, 104n, 123n, 139n, 144n, 145n, 178n, 187n, 206n, 300n

Commentary on True and False Religion 37:xiv, xxi, 8, 16n, 29n, 30n, 39n, 45n, 46n, 52n, 53n, 61n, 68n, 73n, 78n, 80n, 83n, 84n, 85n, 86n, 102n, 104n, 113n, 126n, 128n, 141n, 142n, 294n, 296n, 300n, 49:88n, 122n

Concerning Luther's Book 37:158, 206n

Exposition of the Christian Faith 8:134n, 37:16n, 38:289

Friendly Exposition 37:xv, xviiin, 153, 157, 206n, 234n, 249n, 49:164n

Friendly Rejoinder and Rebuttal 37:83n, 102n, 178n, 211n, 234n, 295n

Huldrici Zuinglii Opera, Zurich, 1832 38:73n

Letter to Alber 37:xiii, 8, 22n, 30n, 46n, 48n, 52n, 76n, 78n, 81n, 102n, 126n

Letters 37:21n, 149n, 154, 246n, 248n

Of the clarity of the Word 38:37n

On Baptism 37:211n

On Original Sin 37:8, 16n

Rearguard or Supplement 37:xiv, 8, 36n, 52
Reply to a Certain Friend 37:8, 75n
Reply to Billican and Rhegius 37:8, 22n, 36n, 41n, 65n, 73n, 77n, 130n, 139n, 145n, 211n
Reply to Bugenhagen 37:8, 36n, 52n, 53n
These Words of Christ, "This is my Body which is given for you" will Retain their Only and Original Meaning 49:172n, 179n, 186n
Zwinglian Reformation—46:xii
Zwinglians—8:135f, 17:66, 247, 26:143, 34:356, 36:273, 37:xiv, xvii, xxf, 5–7, 10, 16n, 24n, 39n, 68n, 80n, 81, 87n, 104, 129n, 145n, 155, 300n, 38:6, 12f, 94f, 167, 205n, 217f, 283, 287, 307n, 47:59

SCRIPTURE INDEX

OLD TESTAMENT

Genesis
Complete commentary in Volumes 1–8
Chp. 1—1:3–73, 12:32, 118, 13:46–48, 15:313, 18:363, 22:477, 28:55, 317, 29:147, 37:58, 61, 117, 41:304, 46:11, 13, 51, 47:184, 48:342n, 52:28, 130, 154, 199
1:1—5:72, 15:320, 34:223, 37:31, 88, 272, 361, 40:190, 43:44, 52:43, 54:159
1:1–3—22:7
1:1–31—54:89
1:2—16:296, 25:367, 433, 31:142, 33:98, 157, 52:44, 60
1:2–5—34:219
1:3—4:155, 13:92, 14:123, 15:276, 300, 22:10, 116, 37:61n, 117, 180, 40:203, 52:47, 51
1:4—7:82
1:5—10:315, 11:115, 288, 12:127, 18:371, 52:24
1:6—1:28n, 13:98, 15:300, 37:61n, 52:51
1:6f—11:318
1:7—14:304, 52:51
1:8—1:32n
1:9—4:5, 11:323, 15:300, 30:194, 37:61n, 54:200
1:10—19:43
1:11—1:37n, 14:300, 15:300, 38:202
1:11f—46:12
1:12—28:313
1:14—1:39n, 40n, 42n, 3:163, 13:98, 15:300, 18:48, 362, 22:59, 37:180–181, 183
1:14–18—52:167
1:16—12:122
1:18—7:194
1:20—2:74
1:22—54:200
1:24—1:85, 2:74
1:25—6:293
1:26—1:57n, 3:353, 12:134, 13:98, 15:49, 22:439, 33:118, 34:223, 45:111
1:27—1:70n, 238, 330, 2:121, 3:202, 4:8, 34:177, 37:49, 40:157, 43:44, 45:17
1:27f—5:362, 22:91, 45:150, 51:358, 53:115
1:28—1:237, 238, 240, 2:64, 236, 330, 3:205, 4:4, 8, 52, 89, 303, 337, 5:325, 335, 7:17, 194, 8:95, 12:133, 311, 13:97, 98, 131, 141, 238, 15:5, 324, 21:93, 22:441, 470, 23:404, 24:214, 28:25f, 33:230, 34:89, 137, 37:49, 38:202, 40:236, 43:88, 44:339, 45:18, 38, 45, 49:411, 51:154, 52:199, 54:59, 175
1:28f—23:6
1:29—1:92, 13:46
1:29f—4:276, 13:45, 45:327
1:31—1:150, 227, 2:51, 64, 4:290, 15:56, 101, 20:123, 22:496, 25:362, 383, 27:396, 31:55, 33:173, 35:63, 264, 42:146, 43:44, 45:17, 53:115, 54:198
Chp. 2—1:74–140, 15:49n, 22:477, 28:55, 46:51, 48:342n, 49:411
2:2—29:147, 33:157, 43:44
2:3—44:71
2:5—4:299
2:7—14:183, 15:182, 18:376, 28:191, 194, 45:204, 207, 54:377, 400f
2:8—1:88n, 91n, 16:33, 18:91, 49:411n
2:8f—13:198
2:10—6:189
2:10–14—54:438
2:11—2:195
2:13—18:271
2:14—46:181
2:15—23:8, 31:360, 46:242, 49:411n
2:16—54:308
2:16f—38:80, 43:44
2:17—1:155, 330, 8:190, 331, 12:310, 13:94, 97, 185, 15:318, 25:69, 37:129, 43:183
2:18—4:6, 8, 5:32, 12:257, 15:8, 34:223, 37:49, 40:301, 45:37, 143, 145, 153, 53:114
2:18f—25:332
2:18–24—44:7–9
2:18–25—45:150
2:21—1:129n, 131n, 4:263, 34:224
2:21f—45:204, 207, 49:112
2:21–23—48:221n
2:21–24—53:114
2:22—6:71, 49:147, 154, 202
2:22f—1:238, 43:44, 45:390
2:23—1:113, 11:182, 29:129, 48:217n, 50:100n, 246n
2:23f—4:362, 6:257
2:24—1:133, 313, 7:14, 11:537, 13:183, 18:404, 406, 22:111, 29:160, 31:190, 297, 36:95, 39:181, 50:34, 35n, 51:154
Chp. 3—1:141–236, 25:46, 298, 28:55
3:1—1:151n, 10:16, 13:113, 21:252, 22:340, 23:81, 24:343, 25:513, 37:129
3:1–7—54:175
3:1–20—54:399
3:2—3:282
3:2f—12:287
3:3—1:66n
3:4f—13:185, 43:44
3:5—1:223, 5:42, 7:195, 13:196, 17:19, 22:314, 27:145, 49:337, 51:38, 54:418

3:7—3:50, 4:257, 8:66, 10:22, 21:316, 25:69, 346, 28:291, 37:29, 39:169, 41:90, 48:309n
3:8—1:169, 34:10, 172, 174
3:8–10—13:90
3:9—1:284, 4:61, 6:235, 45:203
3:9–12—7:272
3:12—5:153, 7:272, 22:397, 46:276
3:14—1:ix, 76, 151, 17:394, 27:262, 37:129n
3:15—1:184n, 217n, 242, 252, 311, 330, 332, 403, 2:64, 178, 229, 265, 4:95, 97, 175, 242, 311, 5:58, 226, 6:72, 235, 7:77, 8:76, 242, 243, 331, 10:262, 11:294, 385, 473, 12:109, 327, 13:90, 134, 231, 251, 280, 14:39, 15:317, 324, 16:169, 337, 17:395, 20:209, 22:17, 31, 63, 70, 76, 79, 127, 154, 178, 340, 427, 448, 449, 460, 24:319, 343, 25:65, 314, 26:189, 246, 307, 332, 27:5, 148, 28:98, 203, 30:263, 272, 294, 32:20, 34:187, 188, 209, 303, 35:83, 169, 359, 369, 36:39, 41:110, 178, 314, 43:44, 45:201, 202, 203, 51:375n, 52:127, 54:41, 342, 438
3:16—2:49, 6:197, 235, 270, 8:24, 12:131, 15:131, 16:138, 28:26, 51, 279, 30:88, 109, 33:126, 36:152, 41:155, 52:11f, 53:114
3:17—1:290, 27:262, 28:50, 54:105
3:17f—1:78, 12:121, 38:202
3:17–19—15:150, 44:214, 53:115
3:18—1:38, 76, 7:219, 8:302, 21:86, 54:198
3:18f—6:190, 7:194, 41:177
3:19—4:97, 7:219, 222, 281, 13:97, 98, 14:15, 123, 15:14, 182, 18:336, 21:209, 256, 23:8, 10, 24:161, 27:298, 28:194, 28:20, 30:109, 39:259, 42:62, 151, 44:108, 395, 45:47, 154, 326, 328, 333, 47:145, 272, 54:267
3:19—28:50
3:20—54:223
3:21—22:420
3:22—1:223n, 226n, 6:250, 7:195, 34:224
3:22–24—1:255
3:24—1:231n, 3:61n, 5:50
Chp. 4—1:237–331, 19:25
4:1—1:193n, 353, 2:185, 4:374, 6:269, 8:242f, 15:24, 319, 20:147, 41:314, 54:437
4:1–16—34:171
4:2—1:103
4:3—1:251n, 312, 12:86
4:3f—26:263
4:3–5—6:119
4:3–8—52:90
4:4—7:322, 8:63, 21:321, 25:3, 256, 29:232f, 30:207, 31:186, 32:84, 34:303, 36:321, 48:25, 54:56
4:4f—2:116, 26:454, 32:109
4:5—6:345, 20:212, 21:321, 36:56
4:6—3:272, 30:275, 54:121
4:7—1:164, 269n, 304, 6:368, 377, 7:126, 227, 8:325, 32:213, 33:125, 34:141, 54:121
4:8—1:270n, 271n, 13:186, 30:207, 43:148n
4:8–16—51:246, 54:41
4:9—6:385, 13:413, 26:338, 34:29, 43:176, 52:110
4:10—1:283, 333, 2:61, 7:100, 13:25, 14:88, 17:285, 20:133, 26:338, 43:143n, 145n, 51:246f, 54:406
4:10–14—39:135
4:11—1:298, 27:262
4:13—1:296n, 6:134, 26:338, 38:157
4:14—1:11, 282, 307, 18:188
4:14f—45:86
4:15—1:282, 302n, 303n, 304n, 307n, 2:140, 26:139
4:17—1:282, 312n, 2:196, 200
4:17–24—21:259
4:19—1:316n, 4:306, 41:157, 54:244
4:22—1:317n
4:23—54:41
4:25—54:437
4:26—1:327n, 343, 5:79, 15:329
4:30—8:169
Chp. 5—1:332–359, 5:200, 47:248
5:1—1:337n
5:1–5—54:437
5:2—1:338n
5:3—1:282, 339n, 35:288n
5:6f—47:248
5:22—15:322
5:24—1:350n, 4:310, 29:234, 30:210
5:29—1:352n
5:32—1:356n
Chp. 6—2:3–80, 19:40, 43:277
6:1f—2:10
6:1–4—21:259
6:1–13—45:44
6:2—30:176, 178, 50:310
6:2f—2:224
6:3—8:283, 17:329, 23:166, 27:250, 363, 29:134, 30:118, 176, 32:93, 182, 33:212f, 37:95
6:4—1:299, 321, 7:330, 9:34, 30:176, 178, 31:393, 32:146, 43:240n, 50:243n, 52:202
6:4f—13:213
6:5—2:120, 122, 127, 31:64, 32:93, 225, 33:215f, 39:63, 52:58
6:5f—43:44
6:6—2:117, 6:197, 52:95
6:6f—49:23
6:7—11:368, 13:97, 17:358, 30:176
6:8—2:26
6:9—2:245, 15:322
6:10—4:214
6:11—1:321
6:11–13—34:212
6:12—2:55, 42:159, 43:223
6:14f—52:150
6:15—3:229
6:17—25:424
6:18—13:97, 52:127
Chp. 7—2:81–102, 46:171, 49:397n
7:2—2:134
7:11—1:98, 2:89, 10:379
7:11–24—41:29n

7:17—43:44
7:17–24—46:24
7:18—20:111
7:20—54:256
7:21—2:74, 4:317
7:21f—20:210
7:23—43:44
Chp. 8—2:103–130, 17:358n, 29:134, 49:397n
8:4—2:116
8:5—11:325
8:7—10:254, 50:94n
8:18—43:162n
8:20—51:82
8:21—2:39, 145, 14:295, 25:219, 275, 299, 348, 31:59, 64, 32:93, 182, 225, 33:215, 42:78, 44:72
8:22—16:75
Chp. 9—2:131–186
9:1—2:115, 22:91
9:6—1:283, 40:305, 45:86f
9:8f—37:135
9:8–17—36:43
9:9–11—35:83
9:11–13—36:174
9:12f—20:253
9:12–17—35:86, 36:39
9:13—1:76, 54:56
9:18—47:147n
9:21—19:221, 51:296
9:21f—27:370, 52:226, 174
9:21–23—19:130
9:25—21:101, 40:280
9:27—17:413
Chp. 10—1:357n, 2:187–209, 19:22, 47:144n, 147
10:2f—47:147n
10:4—17:413
10:7—10:412
10:8—27:158
10:8f—25:172, 36:12, 97, 228, 48:342
10:9—7:267, 8:65, 10:290, 19:184, 27:158, 32:64, 40:284, 46:178
10:10—2:202, 217, 13:311
10:10f—2:364
10:11—2:214
10:12f—7:238
10:21—1:358, 2:234, 4:385, 5:265
10:22—2:201, 232
10:25f—2:371
Chp. 11—1:210–244, 4:3, 184, 20:59, 47:144n, 248
11:1f—13:148
11:1–9—32:89, 45:328
11:2—20:245
11:5—1:284, 52:95
11:6f—20:245
11:7—3:230, 6:250, 10:255, 39:216, 44:351, 50:299
11:8—9:292, 17:305
11:9—30:144
11:10f—13:310
11:17—47:248
11:20—1:357
11:26—8:90, 47:157n
11:28—2:248
11:29—4:185, 46:316, 50:34n
11:31—2:277, 4:250, 17:137, 34:303
11:32—7:269
Chp. 12—2:245–323, 4:152, 5:40, 143, 25:255, 30:106
12:1—2:242, 351, 4:350, 10:204, 12:275, 25:136, 48:233, 51:29
12:1f—3:316n, 14:152, 21:243, 43:277, 48:371n
12:1–3—26:328, 34:303, 35:83
12:2—7:103, 22:92, 25:424, 26:246
12:2f—2:316, 4:172, 27:264
12:3—2:363, 389, 3:28, 4:152, 154, 6:72, 7:201, 10:38, 13:27, 308, 318, 21:352, 22:31, 63, 449, 464, 26:243f, 246, 27:253, 267, 30:106, 31:298, 35:173, 42:106, 52:128
12:4—2:271, 7:269, 48:94
12:5—8:84
12:6—2:381, 48:67n
12:7—2:351, 37:91, 51:82
12:8—5:243, 15:329
12:10—7:309, 18:307, 313, 29:230, 46:235
12:10f—52:200
12:11f—5:28
12:13—43:123n
12:15—29:239
12:18—2:376
12:20—3:356
Chp. 13—2:324–363, 25:255
13:1—29:239
13:1f—6:6
13:2—18:307, 21:169
13:4—15:329, 51:82
13:6—41:284
13:10—30:177
13:10–13—46:195n
13:15—4:246
13:15f—54:41
13:16—4:172, 18:313, 30:323
13:18—3:316n, 51:82
13:20—1:78
Chp. 14—2:364–399, 4:214, 13:309, 17:35, 45:125, 46:10
14:2—22:423
14:5—17:35n
14:5f—9:34
14:6—6:294
14:7—2:364
14:8–16—45:96
14:10—18:312
14:13—5:52, 6:280, 7:4
14:13–16—22:316
14:14—2:279, 4:109, 24:80
14:14f—7:172, 13:21
14:15—9:70
14:17—46:193
14:18—2:247, 3:267, 6:183, 13:313, 36:182, 321
14:18f—29:173
14:19—4:151, 8:112, 13:318
14:19f—13:318
14:22—28:271
Chp. 15—3:3–41, 4:113, 134, 26:239, 47:142, 145
15:1—3:116, 6:357, 375, 397, 26:244, 33:153f
15:1–6—48:285n
15:2—4:108, 35:248n, 249n
15:4—3:16n, 27:253
15:4f—37:135
15:5—2:359, 4:152, 18:313, 25:41, 255, 26:244, 30:323
15:5f—25:35
15:6—3:23n, 4:168, 8:139, 19:197, 25:255, 26:226, 229, 238, 242f, 31:271, 32:15, 35:152, 374, 396, 37:134, 52:153
15:7—3:27n
15:13—3:34n, 27:268
15:13f—8:110, 47:74
15:13–16—3:36
15:15—4:308, 310, 7:293
15:16—1:206, 4:246, 5:91, 6:214, 8:111, 35:83, 49:73
15:17—6:123
Chp. 16—3:42–74, 4:109
16:1f—20:434
16:1–4—35:333, 54:109
16:2—1:132, 4:20, 353f, 5:325, 328, 334, 26:446, 29:239
16:3—4:306, 337
16:4—3:47n, 5:92, 335, 26:435

16:5—8:169
16:10—4:155, 388
16:11—3:64n, 27:310
16:12—3:71n, 4:71, 328, 332
16:13—4:324, 7:103, 8:30
16:14—5:59
16:16—3:72n
Chp. 17—3:75–175, 47:142, 151, 160
17:1—5:197, 10:418, 11:173, 50:158n
17:1f—27:264
17:3–11—36:44
17:4—3:102, 4:303, 29:239
17:5—14:18, 25:39, 40f, 26:244, 47:301
17:6—9:169
17:7—40:244, 257, 288, 47:162
17:7–9—3:91
17:8—47:159
17:9—47:81n
17:9–13—47:85n
17:10—20:253, 22:420, 26:242, 36:174, 37:275, 51:106, 54:68
17:10f—26:120, 37:26, 274n, 48:371n, 50:35
17:11—25:37, 27:235, 35:86, 47:159
17:12—23:236
17:12f—47:150, 152
17:14—27:131, 32:183, 47:142
17:15—25:39
17:17—2:238, 5:29
17:19—26:435, 441
17:20—4:20, 35, 155, 326, 6:303
17:23—46:39, 52:153, 54:56
Chp. 18—3:176–238, 5:20, 6:125, 25:463, 47:145
18:1—4:192, 278, 5:236
18:1–4—34:225
18:2—1:21, 2:249, 3:188n, 37:298n
18:2f—6:250, 20:208
18:7—5:294
18:8—4:37
18:10—3:205n, 10:296, 25:81, 30:90, 323, 37:91
18:10–14—35:83
18:12—4:210, 5:36, 12:99, 30:90
18:18—4:154
18:19—14:220, 36:136n, 51:98n
18:20—43:44
18:20f—2:61
18:21—3:230n, 29:115
18:22—3:232n
18:22f—46:174n
18:23—16:45, 17:381
18:23–32—2:50
18:23–33—4:37, 51:338
18:24–33—46:193
18:27—22:120, 47:145
18:32—44:67, 54:439
Chp. 19—3:239–314, 4:272, 19:40, 25:463
19:1—4:278, 29:115, 34:225, 37:298n
19:1f—3:61n, 188
19:1–13—35:281
19:1–24—45:44
19:1–25—45:355
19:2—3:246n
19:2f—4:281
19:3—3:250n
19:4—13:311
19:4–8—45:148
19:9—3:257n, 4:215, 12:92, 16:44, 41:361
19:11—3:263n, 7:239, 41:227, 51:296
19:12—3:266n, 40:276
19:14—3:269n, 19:168, 37:293n, 52:150
19:15—41:296
19:15–19—44:328
19:15–23—44:352n
19:16—13:193
19:17—45:156
19:19—13:133
19:21—46:248
19:22—2:378, 24:80
19:24—4:274, 15:280, 336, 16:330, 18:171, 34:226, 44:148, 46:198, 254, 50:222n
19:24f—30:177, 43:44
19:24–28—46:24, 171
19:24–29—43:162
19:26—3:298n, 299n, 13:125, 45:156
19:27—4:196
19:29—46:256
19:30f—27:370
19:33—3:308n, 313n, 28:286
19:33–35—36:187
Chp. 20—3:315–365, 5:81, 6:21
20:1—3:303
20:2—5:28, 7:114, 241, 263, 10:158, 23:401, 29:239
20:2–7—45:126
20:3f—19:227
20:6—3:337n, 31:62
20:11—2:293, 3:128, 303, 7:114, 241
20:12—2:29, 45:23n
20:13—3:353n
20:15—7:4
20:16—4:265
20:18—2:311
Chp. 21—4:3–90, 5:88, 6:21, 26:454, 27:264
21:3—6:112
21:5—27:267
21:7—4:13
21:9—4:403, 5:36
21:9f—5:94
21:9–14—35:333
21:10—8:169, 26:441, 27:322, 38:252
21:10–12—9:241
21:11f—4:325, 26:457
21:12—3:94, 4:92, 129, 350, 19:52, 25:80, 26:237, 44:136
21:14—21:185, 27:284
21:15—4:299
21:15f—4:43
21:16—7:153
21:17—11:123
21:20—4:387, 11:217
21:22f—5:81
21:25—12:164
21:25f—4:74, 5:63
21:27—4:90
21:29f—8:197
21:34—20:189
Chp. 22—4:91–186, 359, 5:19, 143, 242, 23:169, 25:255, 38:80
22:1f—4:97
22:1–13—54:68
22:1–20—48:300n, 51:105
22:2—4:99, 5:161, 202, 6:185, 35:170, 36:182, 321, 37:129, 40:58, 46:310
22:2f—4:274, 19:52
22:3—4:108
22:5—26:116, 34:223, 48:57
22:12—1:241, 2:222, 5:202, 34:124
22:13—11:102, 20:54, 233
22:14—4:138, 14:152, 327
22:16—4:232, 7:82, 11:368, 13:308, 34:124
22:16f—45:391
22:17—2:256f
22:18—4:154, 156, 311, 387, 5:17, 84, 217, 6:155, 8:60, 183, 10:38, 13:230, 308, 15:323, 338, 16:29, 17:395, 20:54, 21:352, 22:31, 79, 92, 127, 23:339, 395, 414, 26:289, 304, 328, 332, 357, 374, 27:253, 275,

30:21, 29, 106, 31:298n, 35:83, 169, 359, 36:39, 41:119, 45:203, 204, 47:301, 52:30, 128
22:21—47:157n
Chp. 23—4:187–217, 395, 5:78
23:1—4:187
23:3–16—21:115
23:4—4:205
23:7—5:146
23:8—5:211
23:9—43:136n
23:13—32:146
23:15—7:25
23:16—3:317, 5:17, 7:286
23:17—6:184
Chp. 24—4:218–299, 6:256
24:1f—22:209
24:1–4—45:390
24:1–10—46:269n
24:1–35:29—54:91
24:2—8:139
24:2f—4:230
24:3—2:10
24:10—4:260, 5:273
24:12—35:248n
24:14—4:265
24:15–50—46:269n
24:16—45:209n
24:18—4:297
24:18–20—10:37
24:28—4:297
24:32—7:338
24:43—45:208n, 209n
24:57—52:219
24:57f—45:392
24:58—46:304
24:65—7:25
Chp. 25—4:300–409, 5:160
25:1f—4:301f, 47:151
25:5—21:325
25:5f—27:284
25:6—21:325
25:7—47:248
25:8—4:329, 7:293, 14:186, 53:328
25:9—4:327, 7:293
25:11—5:200
25:12–16—4:327
25:13—16:173
25:14—16:172
25:17—8:315, 13:76
25:18—4:331
25:21—4:341
25:21f—18:135, 33:197
25:21–28—54:458
25:22—2:231, 4:139, 10:268, 397, 48:170, 54:88
25:23—1:295, 4:24, 350, 5:15, 94, 101, 129, 150f, 160, 169, 176, 8:175, 23:397, 26:237, 33:196, 198, 47:146
25:23f—25:81
25:24—33:200
25:25—4:394, 10:225, 11:123, 517
25:26—10:193, 27:267
25:27—4:383, 10:290, 296, 11:217
25:28—8:169
25:30—10:290, 11:121, 123
25:31–34—4:395
25:33—22:34
25:34—4:393
Chp. 26—5:3–98, 6:21, 11:312
26:1—10:158, 46:235
26:1f—52:200
26:3—5:57
26:4—5:225, 228, 11:312, 22:31, 92
26:6f—5:25
26:7—43:123n
26:8—4:10, 5:30, 21:34
26:9—2:45
26:11—2:305
26:12–14—5:56
26:19–22—12:164
26:34—6:286, 35:338n
26:34f—45:392n
26:35—5:166, 6:287
26:47—7:218
Chp. 27—5:99–187, 256, 273
27:1—5:101, 9:310n
27:4—8:65
27:6—38:252
27:7—10:287
27:16–29—22:528
27:22—22:453
27:23—5:134
27:25—8:65
27:27f—33:198
27:28—8:302
27:29—6:121, 304, 328, 25:82, 231
27:32—5:149
27:33—5:134
27:34f—5:149
27:39f—5:160, 6:164
27:40—4:365, 6:283, 295, 10:85
27:41—21:259
27:43–45—43:123n
27:45—1:308, 6:256
27:46–28:9—45:293n
Chp. 28—5:188–265, 7:114, 45:48n
28:1f—5:256, 45:300
28:1–5—46:269n
28:9—6:287
28:10f—22:200, 207
28:11—5:212
28:12—10:120, 153, 11:321, 24:48, 26:30, 29:111, 36:109
28:12f—6:126
28:12–14—5:216
28:13—5:225, 6:256, 8:151, 17:61
28:14—22:31, 92
28:14f—7:307
28:15—45:212
28:16—5:241
28:17—2:284, 4:139, 5:239, 6:226, 10:346, 18:110
28:18—4:178, 26:446
28:19—2:286, 5:243, 251, 6:183, 247, 36:221
28:20–22—5:253
28:21—9:67, 14:34
Chp. 29—5:266–321, 7:68, 45:48n
29:1–3—5:273, 280
29:8–10—10:121
29:16—3:266n
29:17—5:293, 15:100
29:20—13:118
29:21—5:299
29:21–28—45:388
29:21–30—46:299
29:21–30:13—54:244
29:21–30:24—51:39
29:23—8:87, 50:34n
29:23–25—45:27
29:25—5:302
29:28—50:34n
29:31–35—5:320
29:35—10:46, 25:246
Chp. 30—5:298, 322–385
30:1—3:134, 5:326, 345, 7:17
30:1–24—48:285n
30:3—1:132, 4:354, 6:71
30:7f—8:291
30:13—52:130
30:14—5:352, 15:253
30:20—8:273
30:23—5:335
30:24—5:323, 11:95
30:27—5:374
30:30—5:291, 6:4, 6, 7:61, 24:79
30:32f—5:374, 378
30:33—42:54
30:37—8:143
30:37–39—52:161
30:37–42—5:381
30:39—20:64n
Chp. 31—3:146, 6:ix, 3–86, 7:22, 45:48n
31:3—6:397
31:7—5:365, 6:12
31:8—6:14
31:14f—5:332
31:15—7:66
31:16—6:26, 71
31:19—6:32n, 35n
31:20—14:273
31:22–24—6:ix
31:25—15:228
31:33—6:207n
31:34—18:17
31:40—5:324
31:41—5:377
31:42—4:134, 5:371,

385, 6:6, 22, 71n, 10:346, 29:178
31:46—6:66
31:47—10:280
31:47f—13:28
31:53—5:331, 15:217
Chp. 32—6:ix, 87–155, 7:114, 18:64, 45:48n, 48:320
32:3–5—6:96n
32:8—14:193
32:10—8:143, 9:104, 42:109, 45:48n
32:11—6:100
32:24—6:125n, 130n, 8:163, 28:374
32:24–29—21:351, 35:199
32:25—8:139
32:26—5:161, 18:65
32:26f—4:322
32:28—5:160, 6:260, 7:303, 21:351, 32:193, 36:134
32:30—6:131, 264, 8:163, 52:129
Chp. 33—6:ix, 156–186, 45:48n
33:1–3—5:160
33:5—4:228, 30:249, 54:59
33:10—6:170
33:13f—8:64, 48:402
33:14—17:16
33:17—1:78n, 6:178n
33:18—6:181n, 182n, 22:421
33:19—6:184n, 21:115
33:20—6:249, 51:82
Chp. 34—4:252, 5:297, 6:ix, 181, 187–221
34:1—6:192n, ix, xi, 30:260
34:2—8:198
34:3—17:4, 33:217
34:13—8:197
34:13–17—6:201n
34:20–22—6:208n
34:25—4:14, 6:210n
34:26—13:154
34:26f—8:197, 152
34:30—6:201, 215n, 8:152, 197
Chp. 35—5:200, 6:ix, 221–281, 18:65
35:1—5:265, 6:223n, 8:151
35:2—6:x, 8:76
35:4—6:238n, 40:89
35:5—6:x, 20:22
35:6—6:183
35:9f—6:260n
35:10—8:162
35:11—6:397, 8:152–154
35:11f—8:31
35:16–19—4:189
35:17—7:48
35:18—8:206
35:20f—6:274n
35:21—6:287, 18:242
35:22—10:398
35:27f—6:282
35:28—5:201, 6:314
35:28f—7:3, 270
35:29—6:313, 7:130
Chp. 36—4:365, 6:ix, 282–311, 30:260
36:1—6:179n
36:4—5:273
36:11—18:198
36:14—6:291n
36:15—18:198
36:20—11:122
36:20–30—6:x, 7:x
36:24—6:293
36:42—18:198
Chp. 37—6:ix, 282, 312–407, 8:49, 21:43
37:2—3:280, 6:319n, 8:222, 52:225
37:3—5:288, 6:321n, 323n, 7:323, 372
37:5—7:119
37:6f—7:339
37:9—8:138, 13:414
37:9–11—6:338n
37:10—7:102
37:12—6:247
37:12–17—6:x
37:14—7:339, 14:227
37:18—7:253
37:20—8:223
37:23—7:259
37:26f—6:387
37:28—20:318, 25:430
37:29f—7:259
37:32f—7:245
37:33—6:380
37:34f—4:195
37:35—4:350, 6:292, 363, 7:3, 293, 10:373, 19:75
37:36—7:52
Chp. 38—6:282, 345, 7:3–50
38:1—7:4, 269
38:1–5—7:6
38:6—7:5
38:9—48:293n
38:11—7:21, 39
38:18—7:25
38:23—7:40
38:29—5:225
38:44—7:ixf
Chp. 39—6:282, 7:51–106, 8:57
39:1—7:198
39:2—7:109, 15:323
39:2–23—41:227
39:3—7:111
39:5—46:192
39:6—7:67, 103
39:7—6:277
39:7f—52:271
39:8—7:79, 81, 12:99
39:9—7:111
39:13–15—7:ix
39:16—7:283
39:17—7:346
39:21—7:99
Chp. 40—6:282, 7:107–129, 43:124
40:1—7:54, 108
40:8—7:150
40:12—7:113
40:15—7:348
40:16—35:210n
40:22—7:99
Chp. 41—7:53, 130–215, 20:230, 43:124
41:1–7—3:177n
41:12—7:348
41:14—7:142
41:16—7:190
41:17–21—3:177n
41:25—7:149, 19:74, 37:175
41:26—20:240, 37:xii, 175
41:32—11:392, 14:320
41:34—45:309
41:36—7:200, 45:263f
41:40—45:220
41:42f—8:64, 146
41:43—8:4
41:45—7:52, 189, 8:64
41:46f—7:205, 24:80
41:48—45:263
41:48–57—45:262
41:51—7:236, 8:21, 55, 10:281, 12:273
41:52—8:154
41:53–56—46:248
41:56—46:235
41:57—7:216
Chp. 42—7:216–305, 20:133, 43:124
42:1—37:333
42:7—7:233
42:13—7:317
42:18—7:351
42:21f—6:386, 8:228
42:22—6:378, 394, 8:223
42:23—7:260
42:24—6:378, 7:265, 305
42:27—7:266, 268
42:33—7:285
42:34—27:155
42:35—7:270
42:38—6:293, 7:246, 292, 293, 15:150
Chp. 43—7:306–353, 43:124
43:8f—45:254
43:11—6:383, 52:160
43:21—7:268
43:30—7:183
43:32—7:347, 8:16
43:33—7:350, 351
43:34—16:165n
Chp. 44—7:ixf, 354–377, 20:133, 31:119, 43:124
44:4—15:322

44:4f—7:351
44:5—9:175
44:6—7:356
44:14–34—45:254
44:16—10:170
44:18f—8:91
44:20—6:321, 7:373
44:29—7:292, 15:150
Chp. 45—8:3–74, 43:124
45:2—8:23
45:4—7:319, 247
45:5—8:23
45:6—7:214, 8:38
45:7—6:344, 7:215, 8:52
45:8—8:64, 12:99
45:9—8:57, 12:131
45:14—8:54
45:16—8:56
45:18—8:63
45:20—8:65
45:26–28—42:164
45:27—3:154, 8:208
Chp. 46—8:75–99, 43:124
46:1—8:76
46:10—8:85
46:15—8:86
46:23—8:84
46:25–27—28:191
46:26—4:230
46:27—8:62, 90
46:32—2:324
46:33f—7:346
46:34—7:166, 8:16, 48, 57, 61
Chp. 47—8:100–148, 43:124
47:2—8:102
47:3—7:45
47:6—8:102
47:9—8:147, 13:344
47:12—15:97
47:13–26—13:197, 21:169, 45:262
47:14—21:171
47:16f—8:108
47:22—7:197
47:23–25—8:127
47:24—7:160, 45:309
47:26—45:309
47:29—6:342
47:31—8:144, 147, 14:336, 29:118, 222
Chp. 48—6:267, 8:149–198
48:1–7—46:269n
48:3f—8:295
48:5—8:207
48:6—8:155
48:7—6:266, 8:157
48:9—4:155
48:10—9:310n
48:14—10:421
48:15f—8:164
48:16—16:50, 47:46
48:17f—25:75
48:19—18:51
48:22—6:202, 8:198
Chp. 49—7:266, 8:199–319, 19:140n, 20:193, 29:118, 222, 47:134, 181n, 210, 218, 220, 222n, 234, 237f, 298, 300
49:3—8:207, 10:398, 12:108, 13:154, 18:50, 66
49:3–7—21:101
49:4—6:277, 8:295, 9:305, 10:168, 13:154, 18:351, 40:280
49:4f—6:201
49:5—6:212, 7:266, 8:65, 10:165
49:5f—8:50
49:5–7—6:372, 13:154
49:6—8:222, 11:533
49:6f—8:307
49:7—32:197
49:8—6:328, 8:272, 47:182
49:8–12—8:91
49:9—10:71, 11:3, 8, 47:182
49:10—5:161f, 6:53, 72, 162, 7:318, 9:50, 11:474, 12:266, 15:272, 338, 16:118, 19:116, 20:30, 71, 192, 22:39, 79, 448, 511, 25:122, 27:163, 29:223, 30:25f, 45:213n, 215, 217, 47:73n, 176n, 178–192, 196, 207, 214, 301, 52:159, 170
49:10f—5:160, 8:200
49:10–12—45:213, 215, 220, 221n, 229n
49:11—10:218, 18:110, 37:43, 45:218
49:11f—8:247
49:12—5:293, 18:123, 28:367, 45:218
49:13f—17:51n
49:14—8:106
49:15—8:280, 40:120
49:16—8:272, 282
49:17—8:281
49:19—5:350, 8:272
49:22—8:225, 18:51, 20:191
49:23—8:63, 16:8n
49:24—13:31, 19:233, 48:213
49:26—8:304, 19:140
49:33—4:317
Chp. 50—8:320–333
50:11—11:159
50:15–17—8:51
50:18—7:241
50:19f—8:34
50:20—3:334, 6:344, 8:39, 24:197
50:26—27:267

Exodus
Chp. 1—6:368
1:5—6:154
1:8—3:34, 182, 8:33, 111
1:8–14—42:186n
1:10—15:224
1:10–16—42:38
1:11—8:95, 109, 9:163
1:11–14—54:270
1:20f—2:259, 45:322
1:21—6:71, 45:323n, 47:197
2:3—3:34
2:8—45:208n, 209
2:14—7:173
2:15—29:241, 43:124n
2:22—6:308
Chp. 3—22:309, 28:282, 46:9, 54:12
3:1—12:154
3:2—26:319
3:2–5—29:115
3:5—10:25, 17:244n, 29:189, 231, 37:219n
3:6—5:91, 10:346, 13:36, 33:96, 53:329
3:6–8—35:83
3:7f—46:9
3:8—27:314
3:11—16:74n
3:13f—33:125
3:14—25:387, 49:337
3:15—11:544
3:17—50:35n
3:19f—33:182
3:22—1:96, 27:126, 29:40
Chp. 4—25:358, 28:282, 54:12
4:3f—10:448, 11:551
4:6f—10:446
4:10—12:205, 372, 23:228, 29:198
4:11—35:163
4:12—10:160, 14:331, 30:45
4:13—17:128
4:14—28:282
4:15f—52:90
4:16—9:176, 10:87
4:21—33:164, 40:186, 48:341
4:22—8:84
Chp. 5—52:150
5:1—50:35n
5:2—13:130, 41:255
5:2f—12:216
5:5f—25:370
5:6–21—35:281
5:7–19—54:270
5:21—10:178, 48:367
Chp. 6—52:150
6:1—41:251
6:3—11:544, 13:9, 30:38
6:5–7—46:35

6:13—50:35n
6:14-27—13:312
6:16—6:290
6:16f—3:34
6:20—6:293, 32:200
Chp. 7—35:270, 45:270
7:1—24:82, 30:261, 52:170
7:3—32:276, 48:341
7:10-12—1:187
7:11—7:140, 10:448
7:13—48:341, 54:385
7:14—6:6, 11:218
7:14f—34:212
7:17f—11:17
Chp. 8—11:75, 30:261, 35:270, 45:270
8:2f—11:18
8:7—33:75
8:14—7:84
8:15—6:120
8:16f—11:18
8:18—11:18, 33:75
8:19—52:239
8:21—11:75
8:21f—11:18
8:26—7:347
Chp. 9—35:270, 45:270
9:3—18:72
9:3f—11:18
9:5—11:498
9:9f—11:18
9:12—33:161
9:16—19:129, 217, 230, 21:348, 25:82, 374, 33:182
9:18f—11:18, 33:169n
9:24—33:169n
9:29—15:322
9:35—33:183
Chp. 10—35:270, 45:270
10:4f—11:18
10:5—20:241
10:6—33:169n
10:12-19—14:273
10:13—19:113
10:14—33:169n
10:15—20:57
10:17—32:253
10:21f—11:18, 27:31, 29:18, 40:137
10:21-23—1:209
10:26—5:130, 276, 8:90, 16:125
Chp. 11—35:270, 45:270
11:2—5:150
11:2f—6:19
11:4—11:397
11:6—33:169n
Chp. 12—17:214, 35:270, 45:270, 51:30n
12:1f—35:243
12:2—1:37f, 2:92, 9:154, 18:386
12:3—37:274, 43:44
12:3f—37:274n
12:3-5—22:162
12:4—15:98
12:5f—36:182, 43:44
12:6—13:371
12:8—48:231
12:8-11—35:56
12:10—9:158
12:11—9:155, 10:463, 11:146, 20:47n, 37:36, 38, 45n, 52n, 78n, 197n, 275, 48:67
12:11f—27:289
12:13—42:141
12:15—32:183
12:15-20—36:299
12:17—37:319
12:21f—37:264
12:22—11:46, 18:186, 20:132
12:27—38:22, 24, 55
12:27f—19:231
12:29—27:16
12:29f—11:19
12:33f—30:37
12:36—3:259
12:37—8:116
12:38—2:324
12:40—2:277, 3:34, 27:268
12:42—13:355
12:43f—47:86
12:46—37:130
12:50—29:158
Chp. 13—17:214
13:2—25:499
13:3—50:85n
13:9—11:173, 44:46
13:13—11:81, 36:79
13:18—14:337, 19:232, 32:30, 43:282
13:21—26:232, 44:74
13:21f—13:5, 8
Chp. 14—10:319, 17:411, 19:139, 182, 22:310, 46:9
14:10—31:161
14:11—6:101, 30:323
14:11f—26:384
14:12—47:74
14:14—48:213
14:15—4:322, 5:131f, 6:101, 108, 7:324, 13:114, 22:310, 26:383, 43:248, 54:129
14:15f—22:348
14:15-22—43:226
14:16—6:101, 17:192, 20:308
14:16f—17:192
14:19f—16:114, 19:139, 20:188
14:20—12:228
14:21—2:107, 19:113, 20:315, 29:137
14:21f—35:66
14:21-29—42:90
14:22—31:161
14:24f—19:139
14:25—9:202, 297, 19:140, 41:255, 47:18
14:26-28—43:248n, 277
14:27—13:130
14:27-29—43:44
14:28—2:259, 13:378, 43:67n
14:31—11:134
Chp. 15—10:319, 15:191, 18:299, 43:261n
15:1—14:245, 16:130, 18:299, 20:117
15:1f—14:79, 16:51
15:2—14:77, 16:129, 38:108, 53:316
15:3—43:281
15:9—19:127
15:13—7:172
15:14f—19:232
15:15—19:233
15:20—36:152
15:23f—11:109
15:23-25—42:141, 46:253
15:27—10:344, 39:83
Chp. 16—23:30
16:1-3—38:84n
16:3—11:55, 12:274, 15:264, 16:288, 43:78
16:4—44:74
16:14—54:147
16:14f—43:44
16:15—36:182
16:21—54:147
16:33—29:205
16:34—29:206
Chp. 17—29:191
17:2—9:75, 15:313
17:3—11:55
17:6—11:54, 20:315, 23:114, 36:280f
17:7—9:75, 11:55
17:8-16—35:169
17:11—46:256
17:12—14:337
17:13—19:233
17:14—26:55
17:15—6:185, 249, 20:103
17:16—10:129
18:13f—10:102, 33:295n
18:13-26—35:164
18:14—9:17
18:17—9:21
18:17-24—45:378
18:19-22—13:167
18:20—40:89
18:21—9:163, 52:185
Chp. 19—11:173, 22:308, 26:149, 321, 403, 29:5, 186, 35:161
19:5—18:187, 22:78, 26:437, 29:67, 40:197
19:5f—11:393, 23:405, 29:117, 30:62
19:6—14:11, 15:284

19:8—15:82, 25:350, 26:311
19:9—9:57
19:10—25:436
19:12—34:223
19:16—13:85, 26:64, 30:10
19:16–18—13:93
19:16–19—13:8
19:17f—44:351
19:17–20:17—54:114
19:18—11:343, 13:137
Chp. 20—9:180, 22:308, 25:357, 26:149, 321, 403, 29:5, 35:161
20:1—35:163, 165, 40:280
20:1f—43:44
20:1–17—39:182
20:2—3:117, 237, 5:115, 125, 14:87, 15:47, 22:142, 33:232, 40:86, 54:9, 75
20:2f—13:185, 15:313, 26:293, 41:173
20:2–12—26:326, 45:154n
20:3—15:47, 277, 282, 16:270, 21:190, 22:494, 504, 33:125, 37:180, 40:86, 95, 49:365
20:3f—4:135
20:3–12—22:141
20:3–17—35:168
20:4—12:87, 15:317, 17:22, 25:422, 36:148, 40:86, 51:82
20:4f—48:401n
20:5—3:80, 6:368, 10:365, 12:286, 313, 315, 16:142, 270, 17:92, 21:190, 25:483, 36:259, 40:340, 47:72n, 51:82, 54:339
20:5f—12:166, 21:331, 35:266
20:6—1:304, 3:237, 7:96, 15:332, 33:136, 51:155
20:7—4:245, 336, 361, 6:84, 8:209, 10:462, 13:218, 22:504, 27:119, 29:58, 34:85, 36:300f, 360, 38:309, 40:292, 43:195n, 47:286, 54:12
20:8—43:15n, 50:35, 51:335
20:9—6:177
20:11—1:6, 7:94
20:12—1:238, 240, 4:72, 293, 21:36, 22:510, 26:208, 36:208, 45:154, 278, 390n, 51:364, 54:67, 109, 161, 267, 354
20:13—2:139, 6:27, 21:76, 23:270, 27:235, 36:207, 50:36, 54:66, 128
20:13f—33:125
20:13–15—51:20
20:14—36:206
20:15—1:96, 6:25, 21:236, 36:205, 50:36
20:16—5:40, 36:204, 43:176
20:17—25:63, 243, 262, 274, 299, 27:235, 31:348, 36:204
20:18—29:143
20:19—9:180f, 181, 10:293, 11:255, 12:50, 13:19, 22:504, 511, 25:350, 26:149, 319f, 327f, 29:186, 30:10, 47:171
20:20—26:335
20:22—8:61
20:23—40:86, 41:204n
20:24—3:146, 6:128, 265, 9:258, 10:38, 14:103, 16:319, 19:80
20:25—10:29, 11:140
21:1—7:113
21:2—7:301, 23:404, 49:93n
21:2f—9:148
21:5f—10:189, 47:81
21:6—2:361, 20:11, 29:126, 47:206
21:9—7:113, 9:49, 18:66, 45:390, 46:269
21:13—45:126n
21:14—9:195, 45:86, 46:70
21:15—54:68
21:17—5:164, 54:68, 180
21:22—7:222
21:23–25—14:285f, 45:87n
21:24—21:105, 50:12n
21:26—9:233
21:28—1:152
22:1—40:285
22:1–15—45:157n
22:6—14:72, 35:221
22:8—13:43
22:9—9:162
22:15—2:182
22:16—9:224
22:16f—4:227, 45:29, 391, 46:277
22:18—9:175, 54:173
22:20—34:223n
22:25—47:169n
22:27—25:412
22:28—13:202, 46:107
22:29—9:221
Chp. 23—29:154
23:2—21:241, 45:294
23:4f—21:128
23:8—4:85
23:9—29:78
23:12—6:177
23:15—10:46, 18:395, 36:43
23:15f—9:154–156
23:20–23—27:222
23:21—10:133
23:22—16:23, 18:284, 30:128
23:23—40:59
23:26—5:325, 12:257
23:32–34—13:345
24:3—7:113
24:5f—37:264n
24:6—20:296
24:6–8—30:7
24:8—27:314
24:12—39:182
Chp. 25—20:43
25:9—20:246
25:11—29:201
25:17f—37:364n
25:18—20:243, 36:259
25:19—27:22
25:20—20:233
25:23f—50:35f
25:25—28:48
25:30—12:172, 18:394
25:31f—20:223
25:37f—20:52n
25:38—20:230
25:40—4:176, 8:153
26:33—21:304
Chp. 27—29:204
Chp. 28—13:294
28:1—13:312, 36:219
28:2—13:294, 368, 20:70, 205
28:2f—5:125, 12:215, 20:255
28:2–43—39:91
28:17–21—39:83
28:18—20:80n
28:21—12:202
28:30—2:242, 4:143, 9:305
28:38—29:142, 168
29:7—10:218
29:18—2:116
29:21—12:359, 401
29:27—9:174
29:36—45:226n
Chp. 30—29:204
30:6f—29:204
30:22f—47:250
30:23—6:382, 10:217
30:23f—10:218
30:24—6:382
30:25–32—21:329
30:29—21:330
30:31f—12:249
Chp. 31—46:10n
31:18—39:182
Chp. 32—25:218

32:1—17:161, 40:387
32:1-4—45:152
32:1-33—44:103
32:2f—4:275
32:4—11:41, 36:222
32:6—4:10, 15, 5:36
32:11-14—44:69n
32:12—18:101
32:19—35:245
32:22—12:99
32:24—25:301
32:25—32:198
32:27f—45:62
32:28—3:280
32:31—11:271
32:32—2:50, 25:79, 31:178, 42:137
32:34—15:81, 17:380
32:38—9:166
Chp. 33—5:44, 15:333
33:5—18:355, 19:59
33:7-10—14:342
33:8—32:176, 44:269
33:12—6:258
33:14—10:6
33:15—1:252, 5:123, 10:6, 25:296
33:17-23—22:157
33:18—15:326
33:18-20—22:157
33:18-23—6:151
33:19—12:323, 15:328, 329n, 336, 19:28, 25:163, 374, 387f, 391
33:19f—15:326
33:20—2:46, 4:66, 5:47, 7:103, 8:74, 15:329, 16:71, 23:123, 26:28, 34:216, 41:171, 43:239, 47:160, 48:367
33:21-23—15:329
33:22—25:390
33:23—4:371, 5:44, 7:103, 8:30-32, 8:74, 11:88, 43:239
Chp. 34—47:171
34:5—15:331n
34:5-7—15:330
34:6—12:323
34:7—25:247, 275, 39:145
34:9f—15:333f
34:10—37:42n
34:11—18:159
34:14—10:365
34:18—9:154
34:20—10:46, 36:43, 79
34:29—15:334n, 19:138, 231
34:29-35—35:245, 377
34:33f—47:171
34:33-35—39:185
34:34f—35:245
35:5—40:136
35:22—29:154, 40:136
35:26—11:19
36:4—17:104
36:5f—9:140
36:10—11:286
37:7—51:82
37:7f—13:14
37:9—11:286
37:23—20:52n
38:8—15:100, 28:338, 33:218
40:1-11—21:304
40:9—1:79f
40:20—14:337, 20:235
40:23—12:172
40:30f—20:331
40:34—16:77
Chp. 44—29:222
49:24—48:213

Leviticus
Chp. 1—13:9
1:6—10:288, 18:93
1:9—36:173
1:12—18:93
1:13—2:116
Chp. 2—13:9
2:1-3—36:173
2:12f—9:156
2:14—9:154
Chp. 3—13:9
4:5f—20:296
6:2—7:161
6:3—27:109
6:4—7:161
6:12—2:242
6:21—10:67
Chp. 7—9:174f
7:12f—18:152
7:28-36—4:183
7:30—20:198
Chp. 8—9:174f
8:9—20:38
8:15—45:226n
8:27—36:53
8:27-29—38:314n
8:35—20:213n
Chp. 9—9:174f
9:24—1:249
10:1f—3:300
10:2—3:285
10:3—36:154
10:9—18:141
10:14—38:314, 314n
Chp. 11—2:74, 25:487, 48:286n
11:1f—35:243
11:2f—52:177
11:3—11:23, 33:89
11:3f—25:140
11:3-8—36:188
11:4—44:29n
11:13-19—49:19n
11:14—20:59n
11:18—11:306
11:19—20:244, 35:131n
11:22—18:312
11:44—1:135
12:2-5—22:176
12:2-8—4:98
12:3f—20:332
12:4—40:310
12:5—40:244
Chp. 13—43:133
13:45—18:232
Chp. 14—43:133
14:4f—10:251
14:21—10:244
14:52—45:226n
15:16-33—48:293
Chp. 16—11:101, 37:264n
16:5f—10:251
16:12f—29:204
16:29—21:160
16:29f—20:260
16:31—17:285
17:7—4:394
17:8f—36:184
17:11—38:35
17:11-14—38:35
Chp. 18—7:286, 45:3, 6f, 8n
18:3—4:14
18:4f—40:135
18:5—13:269, 22:143, 25:89, 26:398, 437, 27:258, 54:454
18:6f—7:240, 9:229
18:6-13—45:23
18:6-18—36:97, 99
18:7—6:251
18:14-18—45:23
18:16—50:32n, 34, 35n, 36, 38f
18:18—5:307, 45:8n, 50:34
18:21—9:176, 44:83n, 48:283, 293, 300n
18:22f—43:20
18:30—18:139
19:2—30:31
19:8—18:384
19:15—26:94
19:18—1:277, 3:25, 21:103, 122, 25:475, 27:51, 114, 348f, 30:20, 45:292f
19:28—35:243
19:29—44:96n
19:32—2:175, 5:86, 28:332, 351
20:2—13:28, 22:224, 48:283, 293, 300n
20:6—43:17
20:8—19:178
20:9—5:164
20:10—21:96, 23:310, 49:86
20:10-16—43:20
20:17—7:286
20:20—48:285n
20:21—50:32n
20:24—25:499
20:25—36:224
20:27—13:28
21:5—39:84
21:9—7:21
21:14—39:83
21:16—37:104n
21:16-23—18:397
21:17—13:32
21:18—13:32
22:4-6—22:176
Chp. 23—26:411
23:8—7:300
23:10—34:23
23:17—21:156

23:18—34:23
23:24—9:154, 11:101, 34:23
23:27–32—11:101
23:32—17:285
23:33–36—23:206
23:39–43—35:220
23:42—14:104
24:5f—50:35f
24:6—7:267
24:8—18:394
24:14—13:28
24:16—5:367, 13:28, 62
24:17—21:77
24:23—13:28
25:2–7—40:98
25:8—40:98n, 45:224n
25:8–55—35:167n
25:10f—45:310
25:18f—1:304
25:28—10:244, 37:42n
25:35f—45:261, 47:169n
26:1—9:81, 25:422, 40:87
26:4—40:312
26:6—18:239
26:8—9:296
26:11f—10:315
26:18—18:132
26:18f—1:216
26:21—18:132
26:24—18:132
26:30—18:295
26:34—16:87, 19:237
26:36—1:170, 174, 3:8f, 264, 6:78, 7:271, 276, 326, 329, 9:267, 10:140, 16:12, 230, 272, 18:88, 19:75, 23:147, 24:112, 182, 184, 25:401, 26:148, 31:128, 40:144, 43:261, 45:58, 46:22, 47:18
26:40f—47:240
26:41—47:153
Chp. 27—46:147n
27:9—4:200
27:9f—28:17
27:14f—28:17
27:14–25—15:79
27:16–24—46:147n
27:17f—28:17
27:28—18:269, 26:55
27:28f—15:79
27:29—9:83

Numbers

1:3—9:271
1:53—20:213n
2:18–24—11:96
3:13—22:216
4:7—50:35f
4:31—10:36, 14:337
5:11–31—35:240, 50:16
5:15—31:203
Chp. 6—20:102
6:1–21—8:305, 20:77n, 46:177
6:2—54:40
6:2f—8:305
6:3—18:143
6:3f—20:260
6:22f—20:297
6:24–27—53:30, 232
7:2f—19:142
7:89—20:59n
8:16—13:305
Chp. 10—18:89
10:1–10—10:229, 11:101
10:2—11:102
10:2f—11:274
10:7—10:229
10:12—4:71
10:35—50:289n
11:1–3—11:62
11:4–6—21:312
11:5—32:223, 43:78
11:11–15—54:64
11:12—29:112, 54:30, 450
11:16—9:162
11:16f—22:487
11:17—29:109
11:20—43:77
11:29—24:367
11:33f—11:67
Chp. 12—8:222, 28:277
12:1—10:349
12:2—24:293
12:3—3:58, 5:316
12:6—50:271
12:6–8—3:10, 5:237, 6:330
12:14—9:242
12:16—19:137
Chp. 13—2:367
13:2f—9:21
13:3—4:71, 9:21
13:26—4:71
13:30—20:203
13:32—6:319
13:32f—16:286, 50:243n
13:33—4:71, 9:22, 40
13:34—2:33, 50:243n
14:1f—19:83
14:9—25:355
14:12—9:103f
14:13–19—44:69n
14:21—19:129, 217
14:22—15:313
14:30—29:147
14:34—47:75
14:40–45—46:120
15:38f—51:109
Chp. 16—3:15, 8:222, 228, 10:194, 13:357, 16:35, 19:182, 20:214
16:1—28:254
16:1f—10:271, 14:55, 30:208, 37:173n
16:1–40—54:300, 389
16:3—21:211, 24:293
16:5—13:32
16:14—11:55
16:15—9:198, 14:258, 19:49, 28:284, 30:136, 324, 51:273
16:15f—21:101
16:24f—3:280, 10:325
16:28f—30:208
16:30—15:21, 41:251
16:31—40:282
16:31–33—13:360
16:31–34—44:320
16:31–35—46:41
16:32—2:58, 41:283
16:32f—40:111n
16:35—13:360
17:2—10:329, 20:141, 28:308, 47:76n, 166
17:6—20:141
17:8—52:31
17:10—29:206
18:1—29:142, 168
18:8—40:136
18:11—40:136
18:12–24—12:381, 410, 13:90
18:20—5:261, 25:449
18:23—2:361
18:28—9:138n
18:30—35:95
18:30–32—36:53
18:31—17:15
18:32—35:95
19:2f—20:207
19:2–10—51:326
19:4—8:153
19:6—8:153
19:9—12:360, 366, 29:207
19:11f—29:207
19:17–19—29:207
19:18f—14:170
19:19—45:226n
20:1—9:16
20:2f—19:233
20:4—11:55
20:11—1:96, 11:23, 37:184
20:11f—9:299
20:12—2:293, 9:23, 22:120
20:12f—29:5
20:13—13:80, 29:191
20:21—9:32, 33:200n
20:23–29—13:312
Chp. 21—14:250, 22:337, 25:68
21:1f—19:233
21:4—10:276
21:4–9—54:97
21:5—4:214
21:5f—35:257
21:6—1:236, 2:136, 13:360
21:6–9—39:78, 42:104
21:7—44:69n

21:8—1:227, 22:338, 348, 40:87, 43:44
21:8f—36:259, 42:142, 150
21:9—1:96, 30:253, 31:161, 43:157, 51:82
21:13—10:203
21:14—54:373
21:18—45:214n
21:21–30—46:120
21:21–35—19:142
21:22—25:270
21:23f—19:233
21:28—9:35
21:33—13:24, 378, 28:235
21:33f—54:389
21:34—13:378
21:35—3:197
Chp. 22—9:297, 18:259, 30:185, 54:303
22:1—34:316n
22:1f—32:150
22:21—36:182, 40:391
22:21f—25:445
22:21–30—51:389
22:21–35—41:361, 43:68, 44:136, 205
22:28—13:146, 23:97, 32:10, 40:212, 351, 45:121
22:28f—37:28
22:38—35:163n
Chp. 23—4:185, 9:236, 18:259, 30:185, 41:191, 54:303
23:3—54:88
23:4—54:303
23:5f—33:233, 37:52n
23:7—4:186
23:11–30—43:157n
23:19—4:127, 5:135, 25:41, 32:26, 36:176, 52:180
23:21–23—18:166
23:23—6:34, 7:348, 9:175, 18:322
Chp. 24—30:185, 41:191, 47:234n
24:1—5:366, 54:88
24:1f—22:187
24:2—21:276
24:5—6:34, 11:86, 121, 177
24:5f—47:241
24:6–9—9:125
24:13—39:260
24:16—41:120
24:17—10:436, 25:121, 29:202, 40:251, 44:207, 52:169
24:17f—52:191
24:17–19—47:235
24:19—44:207
24:20—6:291
24:21—25:393
24:24—2:191, 44:207
24:25—34:316n
Chp. 25—18:50
25:1—10:135, 18:259, 37:173n, 42:159
25:1f—39:263
25:1–5—47:68n
25:2—44:380n
25:2–9—39:260
25:3—13:185, 32:140, 40:16n, 48:315
25:3–5—36:219
25:6–15—39:263
25:7–8—45:62
25:15—52:120
26:9f—37:173n
26:11—12:201, 44:320
26:65—41:210
27:20—5:109, 20:70n
27:23—5:109
28:1–10—26:411
28:9f—51:345
29:1—11:101
Chp. 30—46:151
30:1f—46:151
30:2—5:257, 46:146n, 152
30:2f—48:285n
30:2–8—39:286
30:3–8—46:151
30:8—30:89
30:9—46:151
30:10–15—46:152
30:13—28:17
30:16—46:152
Chp. 31—19:233
31:8—34:316n
31:16—34:316n, 39:260
31:17f—6:210
Chp. 32—35:292n
33:6—10:449
33:17—9:35
33:52—1:337
Chp. 34—35:292n
34:16—9:162
35:1–8—46:233n
35:6—54:301
35:10–25—45:126n
35:19f—17:308
35:27—9:197
35:33—18:244
36:9—18:202

Deuteronomy
Complete commentary in Vol. 9
Chp. 1—9:11–28, 37
1:1—9:14
1:3—9:15
1:5—16:146
1:6—9:27
1:6f—9:16
1:9—9:17
1:12—9:17
1:13—9:18
1:15—18:247
1:17—9:19, 18:66, 29:30
1:19–46—46:190
1:20—9:20
1:27—9:22
1:29—9:22
1:31—9:97, 51:72
1:34—9:23
1:40–42—9:23
1:41f—19:83
Chp. 2—9:29–37
2:1—9:32, 10:276
2:2–4—18:195
2:3—9:32
2:4f—6:294
2:7—9:32
2:10f—2:367, 50:243n, 52:202
2:20—17:35n
2:20f—50:243n
2:23—9:34
2:24—9:35
2:24–3:11—19:142
2:25—9:297, 54:336
2:26—9:35
2:26–37—46:120
2:30—9:36
2:33—2:259
2:34—21:118
2:36—9:36
Chp. 3—9:38–43, 60, 33:128
3:2—21:118
3:3—2:259
3:8f—10:136
3:8–10—10:203
3:9—10:196, 198, 27:315
3:11—9:40, 10:200, 13:24
3:18—9:40
3:21—9:42
3:23–26—8:73
3:28—20:70n
Chp. 4—8:73, 9:44–60
4:1—9:48, 13:269
4:2—9:50, 22:257, 35:132, 149, 239, 37:304n, 39:193, 262, 40:275, 41:214, 47:153, 269, 52:136
4:3—9:52
4:5—9:55
4:6f—2:258, 353, 9:56, 12:210, 272, 15:240
4:7—2:255, 2:258, 3:169, 4:66, 8:301, 9:57, 22:53
4:10—9:57
4:11—12:224, 19:18
4:12—9:58, 35:163
4:13—43:44
4:14f—12:252
4:15—40:87
4:16—9:58
4:19—32:196, 51:85
4:20—9:58, 17:107, 44:251n, 52:119
4:24—2:7, 4:66, 9:58, 12:313, 317, 22:249, 26:175, 40:295, 48:367
4:26—9:59
4:29f—47:240
4:30—9:59
4:30f—25:429, 52:101
4:36—9:60n

4:41—9:60
4:44—9:60
4:45—9:49
4:46—8:198
Chp. 5—9:61–64
5:1—9:63
5:3—9:63
5:5f—9:63
5:7—22:7, 41:214
5:8—15:317, 25:422
5:9—47:72n
5:10—26:270
5:11—46:24, 33
5:21—8:304, 25:299
5:22—9:64
5:25—9:180n, 29:148
5:29—45:294n
5:32—9:64, 35:273n, 41:214
Chp. 6—9:65–76, 46:12
6:2—9:67
6:4—4:279, 9:67, 15:282, 22:7, 28:238, 29:148, 34:225, 47:289, 52:43
6:5—5:106, 9:68, 21:69, 25:262, 26:294, 296, 364, 27:65, 31:61
6:6—9:69
6:6f—25:476, 28:166
6:7—5:145, 26:26, 32:197
6:8f—10:393, 51:139f, 142
6:10—9:70
6:12f—9:71f
6:13—8:139, 12:84, 18:324, 21:99, 29:211
6:13–14—15:298
6:15—13:273
6:16—9:74
6:20—9:75
6:21f—17:214
6:25—9:76
Chp. 7—9:77–89
7:1f—9:79
7:1–5—21:118
7:2—9:82
7:2f—48:286n
7:4—9:84
7:6—22:78, 30:62
7:6f—9:84
7:8f—9:85
7:12—9:86
7:16—40:104
7:17—9:86
7:21—9:87
7:22—9:88
7:25—6:239
Chp. 8—9:90–98
8:1–3—9:92
8:2—40:66
8:3—5:206, 6:261, 7:128, 8:204, 9:272, 18:127, 28:143, 36:45, 43:44
8:3f—8:201
8:4—6:364, 9:94
8:15–17—9:95
8:17—9:96
8:19—9:97
8:20—8:177
Chp. 9—9:99–105, 47:70
9:4f—47:241
9:4–6—9:118n
9:5—9:102f, 12:333, 47:185
9:6—9:103, 29:34, 43:278
9:10—25:67
9:24—9:105, 47:71
9:26–29—47:71
9:27f—9:105
Chp. 10—9:106–115, 46:10
10:9—8:228
10:12–14—9:109
10:16—3:76, 82, 36:66, 47:153
10:16–18—9:110f
10:18—9:118
10:20—15:298
10:21—9:113
10:22—8:88
Chp. 11—9:115–119
11:10—20:345
11:10f—29:183
11:25—9:117
11:29—22:522
11:44—40:312
Chp. 12—9:x, 120–126, 150, 46:10
12:1—9:123
12:2–13—34:201n
12:4–6—6:127
12:4–28—35:270
12:5—4:128, 16:59
12:8—9:125, 27:305, 35:239, 36:223, 37:290, 39:63, 44:46, 73, 52:182
12:13f—4:178, 17:378, 23:121
12:13–21—9:141
12:18—16:164
12:19—25:449
12:31—18:260, 48:300n
12:32—9:125, 129, 35:149, 239, 39:205, 41:214, 44:46, 47:153, 269, 52:136
Chp. 13—3:166, 9:127–131, 188
13:1—9:129
13:1f—4:131, 24:75, 369, 48:364
13:1–3—21:279
13:3—5:237, 7:119, 9:188, 16:166, 21:280, 40:66
13:6–10—28:34
13:9f—4:140
13:12f—47:269
13:13—13:178
Chp. 14—9:132–141, 25:487
14:1—9:134
14:1f—35:243
14:2—9:137
14:4f—49:19n, 20n, 52:177
14:6f—25:140
14:6–8—36:188
14:8—9:137
14:12–19—49:19n
14:13—20:59n
14:18—11:306, 35:131n
14:21—9:137, 30:49
14:21f—9:138
14:23—9:140
14:24–26—9:124
14:28—9:141
14:29—9:144, 174
Chp. 15—9:142–151
15:1—9:144
15:1f—17:332, 49:93n
15:1–11—45:241, 49:51f
15:4—9:147, 45:161, 281
15:5f—9:146
15:6—9:145
15:7—9:148
15:7f—45:289, 51:153
15:7–11—45:241
15:11—9:150, 21:117, 27:389, 45:161, 281, 287
15:12—9:148
15:16—9:149
15:17—18:329
15:18—9:148f
15:19f—9:150
Chp. 16—9:152–158, 174, 254
16:1—9:154
16:3—9:154
16:5f—2:285
16:8—9:155
16:10—40:119n, 120f
16:11—4:16
16:16—36:43
16:17—44:384n
16:18—9:161
16:19—4:85, 9:163, 19:28, 26:94
16:20—45:63n
16:21—9:164
Chp. 17—9:159–171, 46:10
17:3—18:323
17:4—9:165
17:6—9:196, 30:317, 35:329n, 39:89
17:8—9:167
17:8f—33:91
17:10f—47:269
17:11—9:168
17:14—9:169
17:16—21:169
17:16f—9:169
17:17—21:169
17:18—45:373
17:18f—9:14
Chp. 18—9:172–190, 46:10, 15
18:1—9:174
18:1–4—22:219
18:6—9:174
18:9–11—52:180
18:10—48:300n
18:10f—18:254, 22:245
18:11—18:22, 36:197f, 52:180

18:14—36:195
18:15—3:90f, 8:153, 9:176, 177n, 16:3, 22:78, 129, 308, 510, 23:35, 26:293, 27:334, 29:186, 47:74, 52:106
18:15f—35:169
18:15–19—22:485, 35:246
18:16—9:180
18:17f—22:511
18:18—1:304, 9:177n, 182, 311, 22:284, 448, 487, 511, 36:39
18:18f—8:310, 34:74, 37:42n
18:19—9:165, 182, 22:78
18:20—9:129, 187
18:20–22—21:270
18:21—9:188
18:22—9:129, 183n, 24:368, 28:309, 33:75, 40:113
Chp. 19—9:191–199
19:1—9:193
19:3—54:301
19:4—9:193
19:6—9:194
19:8–10—9:194
19:11–13—9:195
19:14—9:198, 18:29
19:14f—9:196
19:15—9:165, 11:211, 29:203, 40:236, 239, 41:249
19:15–21—9:166n
19:19—9:196
Chp. 20—9:200–207, 231
20:1—9:202
20:5—1:314, 9:203f, 241
20:8—4:91, 16:134
20:10f—9:36, 203
20:10–12—45:125
20:16—9:36
20:17—2:10
20:19—9:204
20:34—9:202
Chp. 21—9:208–216
21:1—9:210
21:1–9—41:251
21:10f—9:210
21:12f—9:211
21:15–17—8:160
21:15–20—9:211
21:17—8:206f, 35:122, 40:285
21:18–21—9:162, 45:353
21:21f—9:212
21:22f—26:277
21:23—10:364, 11:242, 22:230, 27:261, 51:62
Chp. 22—9:217–226, 29:112
22:1—6:372, 9:219
22:5—9:219, 26:307
22:6–8—9:220
22:9—9:221
22:9–11—6:324
22:12—9:221
22:13—9:222
22:20f—9:162, 46:300
22:22—46:278, 49:86
22:22f—9:223
22:22–24—45:32, 46:311
22:23—7:93
22:23f—46:289
22:23–25—46:297n
22:28f—9:223f, 46:280,282
22:29—3:46
22:30—9:227, 229
Chp. 23—9:227–238
23:1—9:229, 12:186, 16:169, 27:345
23:2f—9:230
23:3—1:302, 12:186, 15:139, 17:206
23:6—9:230, 21:118
23:7—9:231, 47:264
23:9—9:231
23:12f—35:131
23:15—9:232
23:17—7:40, 44:96n
23:17f—9:233
23:18—44:96n
23:19—9:234, 45:233n
23:19f—47:169n
23:20—47:270
23:21—5:261, 9:234
23:21f—5:257, 48:285n
23:21–23—5:257, 46:152
23:22f—5:263
23:24—9:235
Chp. 24—9:239–245
24:1—9:241, 18:406, 21:93, 30:20, 31:338, 35:240, 40:98
24:1f—28:31, 339
24:1–4—10:102, 31:203, 46:277
24:3f—28:37
24:4—21:93
24:5—28:12, 30:49
24:5f—9:241
24:6—3:237, 12:334, 14:245, 54:276
24:7f—9:242
24:10—9:242
24:12—18:141
24:14—9:243
24:15—43:20
24:16—16:141, 25:298
24:16–19—9:243
Chp. 25—9:246–251, 46:11
25:4—1:211, 8:225, 13:11
25:4f—9:248
25:5—3:47, 7:18f, 16:50, 36:102, 50:34, 36–39, 54:301
25:5f—30:21, 35:167
25:5–9—45:24
25:5–10—54:109
25:10—7:20
25:11—9:249
25:11f—27:345
25:13—9:249
25:15—43:20
25:17—9:249
25:17–19—35:169
Chp. 26—9:252–255, 18:84
26:1—9:254
26:2–4—34:23
26:10—40:121
26:11—18:404
26:11–14—18:48
26:13—9:254, 40:121
26:14—18:336
26:16—9:254
Chp. 27—9:256–261, 26:288
27:1—9:258
27:12f—9:259
27:15—44:380n
27:15f—14:173
27:16—5:164, 27:255
27:26—12:165, 26:251, 332, 27:18, 33:259f
Chp. 28—9:146, 261–268, 20:275
28:1—9:129, 267
28:4—5:325
28:6—16:263, 18:168
28:9—26:437
28:10—13:361
28:12—40:312
28:13—21:24, 23:397, 405
28:14—31:372, 35:273n, 44:46
28:15f—10:30, 16:188, 297
28:18—47:262
28:20—46:94
28:21—18:72
28:23—9:110, 45:59
28:25—22:83, 85, 46:94, 47:18
28:26—1:55n
28:31—3:80
28:32—6:53
28:33f—16:206
28:36—16:152
28:49—11:106
28:57—45:216n
28:64f—34:131n
28:64–66—44:294
28:65—9:267, 25:401, 29:235, 31:127, 32:31, 38:231
28:65–67—7:276, 29:141, 31:143, 42:137, 45:58f
28:66—16:340, 18:186
28:67—25:401
Chp. 29—9:269–274
29:3—29:124
29:4—9:271
29:5—9:272, 44:74
29:6—3:197
29:7–10—9:272

29:13—2:246
29:18—8:131, 13:86, 18:160
29:18f—9:273
29:19—2:243, 4:154, 7:348, 18:231, 22:385, 28:66
29:23—16:295
29:29—9:274
Chp. 30—9:275–279, 33:128
30:1—9:277
30:1f—47:240
30:8—9:277
30:11—9:277
30:11–14—30:45, 33:141
30:12f—9:279, 25:89, 405, 52:67
30:14—25:90, 27:352, 52:67
30:15—9:277n
30:15–19—33:126, 128
30:19—9:277n
Chp. 31—9:280–284
31:6—9:283, 43:176
31:10f—9:14, 283
31:14f—9:283
31:16—22:453
31:17f—18:230
31:25f—45:373
31:26—29:206
31:26f—9:283
31:27—17:159, 47:166
31:29—2:59
Chp. 32—9:x, 283, 285–299, 22:385, 47:189
32:1—16:6
32:1–4—9:290
32:3—9:6
32:4—1:37n, 19:199
32:4–6—9:291
32:6—4:214, 18:258
32:7—10:205, 11:64, 480, 45:353
32:7–12—9:292
32:8—17:185
32:9—18:341
32:10—20:339, 42:131, 146
32:11—11:322, 15:9, 16:100, 17:357, 25:404, 20:112, 226
32:13—11:23, 331, 338, 44:39
32:13–16—9:293
32:14—8:257, 18:110, 37:43
32:15—1:355, 2:345, 3:249, 5:138, 9:92, 10:202, 11:238, 319, 12:229, 19:187, 44:47
32:17—1:148, 8:131
32:17–21—9:294
32:18—10:202
32:20—10:419
32:21—2:170, 3:152, 4:406, 8:168, 10:121, 11:257, 521, 16:75, 97, 17:402, 18:355, 25:93, 35:365, 39:126, 41:142, 46:64, 47:161, 174, 218, 233
32:22—16:206
32:22–26—9:295
32:24—1:37n, 2:135, 10:30, 11:219
32:25—45:63n
32:27—8:217
32:27–31—9:296
32:29—6:268n, 10:377, 420, 11:205
32:30—38:231, 43:278
32:32—11:83, 18:268
32:32–35—9:297
32:33—10:375, 14:293, 22:337
32:35—6:29, 204, 9:195, 11:205, 242, 21:124, 25:108, 29:121, 40:285, 46:25
32:36—10:433, 31:44
32:36–41—9:298
32:37—16:152, 19:131n
32:37f—17:276
32:39—10:206, 11:256, 13:135, 31:99, 39:188, 42:79, 49:173, 51:19, 25
32:41–43—9:19
32:42—16:294, 19:145n
32:42f—9:299
32:48—9:299
32:50f—13:80
32:51f—54:145
Chp. 33—8:50, 9:283, 300–308
33:1–4—9:304
33:2—14:244
33:5—7:174
33:6—8:154, 213, 214, 233
33:6–11—9:305
33:9—5:114, 6:26, 7:341, 8:22
33:9f—8:232
33:12–18—9:306
33:13f—4:296
33:15—19:149n
33:17—8:225
33:19–25—9:307
33:20f—8:200
33:26–29—9:308
33:29—34:201n
Chp. 34—9:283, 309–311
34:1—9:299, 310, 49:44
34:1f—14:337
34:5—29:5, 49:44
34:5f—16:146, 48:361n
34:6—9:310, 26:151, 27:15, 30:206, 41:67
34:7—13:121
34:9—5:109, 8:159
34:10—6:303, 30:207
34:10f—9:310

Joshua
1:5—45:256
1:7—35:270n
1:17—9:272
Chp. 2—6:227
2:5—5:40
2:9–11—19:138
2:11—7:39
2:18—2:395, 11:46
3:1—18:259
3:5—25:436
3:8—19:232
3:14–17—35:66
3:16—19:233, 25:137
5:1—19:143
5:5f—50:35
5:8f—4:14, 36:220
5:9—18:159, 48:102, 54:303
5:14—29:115, 40:57
Chp. 6—25:399, 54:187
6:17—9:79n, 26:55, 27:177
6:25—2:259, 9:81n
6:26—11:523
Chp. 7—19:14
7:1–5—46:125
7:1–26—32:90
7:2—18:28, 27:220
7:3—43:283
7:9—9:105
7:18—19:62
7:19—10:317, 39:29
7:21—4:370
7:24—18:11
7:26—29:51
8:1—5:243
8:3–29—31:278
8:9—5:243
8:30f—9:258
8:33—22:523
8:33f—9:259
Chp. 9—48:278
9:18—9:36
9:21—31:205
9:27—11:359, 31:205
10:10—47:236
10:11—19:234
10:12—54:359
10:12f—19:143, 43:226
10:13—19:234, 54:373
10:22f—52:156
10:28f—19:234
11:7—2:34, 19:234
11:19—9:79n
11:19f—48:245
11:23—20:17
12:4—2:367
12:21—20:329
Chp. 13—35:292n
13:11—6:81
13:16—16:154
13:18—9:35
13:20—9:40

13:24—9:36
Chp. 14—35:292n
14:15—4:193
Chp. 15—35:292n
15:8—7:301, 20:286
15:19—11:320
15:37—18:218
15:44—18:210, 220
15:45f—20:191
15:63—10:381, 25:247, 32:249
Chp. 16—35:292n
16:10—20:347
Chp. 17—35:292n
17:14-18—54:175
17:15—18:341
Chp. 18—35:292n
18:23—9:35
18:28—35:292
Chp. 19—35:292n
19:1—9:308
19:9—18:341
19:10f—8:278
19:13—19:38, 35:323
19:29—19:114
Chp. 20—35:292n
20:7—2:282, 4:193
Chp. 21-22—35:292n
22:10f—3:280
22:10-34—9:81
22:21—40:87
23:6—44:46
23:13—32:249
24:2—2:239, 243, 246, 249, 4:3, 6:84, 7:199, 22:120, 26:328
24:2f—47:144
24:9-11—43:277
24:12—2:246
24:19—18:63, 34:226, 54:302
24:20—54:302
24:26—40:87, 91
24:32—22:421

Judges
Chp. 1—32:203
1:13f—50:37
1:15—11:132
1:21—10:381, 32:249
1:21f—38:131
1:28—20:347
1:33—27:211
2:10—8:131
3:1-6—31:245
3:1-11—44:47
3:3—10:291
3:9—18:204, 47:187
3:15—10:109
3:15-30—46:192
Chp. 4—18:26
4:1—40:390
4:4f—9:307
4:4-7—36:152
4:4-5:31—46:193
4:6—8:293
4:13-15—11:129
4:14—28:276
4:17—28:276
4:17-21—11:129
4:18f—10:334
Chp. 5—8:285, 293, 15:191, 19:134
5:1f—14:79
5:9—14:283
5:14—45:214n
5:16—8:214
5:16f—8:285
5:20—7:332, 18:120
5:31—16:265
6:4—11:130
6:6—18:9
6:11-8:28—46:193
6:12—37:298n
6:17—3:30n
6:27—39:271, 40:89
6:36—36:40
6:36f—4:261
6:36-40—22:348, 35:86, 36:65
6:37f—52:31
6:38—11:319
Chp. 7—9:123n, 16:98, 114
7:1—2:282
7:1-23—54:47
7:4—11:109, 126
7:12—11:109, 126, 19:173
7:13f—10:304
7:14—29:129
7:15-23—22:316
7:16—16:99, 27:330
7:16-21—10:37, 14:339
7:16-22—42:106
7:19f—11:129
7:20—46:130
7:22—10:86, 250, 16:130, 27:364, 33:122
7:24—44:273
7:25—11:129, 132
8:1—8:285, 306, 11:40
8:6f—20:190
8:16f—6:179
8:22—12:131
8:22-27—35:271
8:23—15:345, 35:271n, 47:187, 52:187
8:24-27—22:263
8:27—35:271n
8:30—22:263
9:5—22:263
9:8f—11:335
9:13—8:248
9:22-57—46:41
9:48—13:17
9:48f—10:342, 432
9:53—15:153, 40:282
10:15—5:153
Chp. 11—6:309, 15:79
11:3—18:351
11:29-40—2:113
11:30-39—54:59
11:37f—45:205n
11:38—54:59
12:1—8:285, 11:40
12:1-6—46:120
12:3—11:489
Chp. 13—9:123n
13:2-16:31—46:193
13:11—37:298n
13:16-23—36:65
Chp. 14—54:79
14:1—7:24
14:1f—7:24, 44:12
14:1-3—7:7, 46:269n
14:1-4—4:226
14:3—52:219
14:4—45:104
14:6—4:128, 32:146
Chp. 15—54:79
15:4—27:149, 47:175
15:11—10:376, 445, 31:395, 45:104
15:15—4:128
Chp. 16—54:79
16:1—54:31
16:1-21—45:44
16:21—17:147
16:23f—38:233
16:30—39:135
17:1—18:56
17:2f—35:271n
17:3—6:33
17:5—20:300
18:27—9:307
18:27f—8:281
Chp. 19—3:279, 18:50, 45:355
19:10—20:286
19:22—45:149n
Chp. 20—3:279, 6:279, 45:355
20:12-48—32:90
20:12f—13:151
20:13—13:178
20:18-25—43:283, 46:191
20:21f—9:231, 44:125n
20:22—46:191n
20:38—18:362
Chp. 21—6:279, 47:186
21:1—44:392
21:1-24—54:301
21:7—46:308
21:19-23—44:392
21:23—46:308
21:25—46:75n

Ruth
1:4—1:302
1:16—2:276, 3:133
2:1—8:100
3:1-4:17—54:301
3:7—25:265
3:9—25:265, 31:190
3:10f—22:214
4:1—7:20
4:5—50:38
4:10—50:38
4:11—8:176
4:13—7:200

I Samuel
1:1-11—54:13
1:2-18—54:59
1:4—27:322
1:5—26:446, 27:322
1:9—28:338
1:10—3:134
1:11—4:339
1:15—10:200
1:17f—44:26

1:18—31:273
1:22–28—46:148, 153
Chp. 2—15:191, 25:377, 28:335, 338
2:1f—10:50, 14:79
2:3—14:247, 16:108
2:4—10:49
2:4f—26:442
2:5—21:347, 27:322
2:6—3:348, 4:50, 95, 6:142, 151, 10:349, 372, 13:97, 16:214, 20:50, 25:176, 443, 25:365, 31:44, 99, 141, 33:62, 34:172, 174, 42:125
2:6f—8:5, 10, 14:335, 17:319, 19:154, 228
2:6–8—39:188
2:7—7:249, 25:365
2:9—21:328, 27:322, 42:79
2:12—40:387
2:12–17—41:284, 286
2:17—31:249
2:19—6:323
2:22—15:100, 28:338, 33:218, 41:284, 286
2:24—29:22
2:25—54:303
2:27–36—41:282
2:28—8:208
2:30—5:84, 148, 9:56, 11:262, 13:396f, 14:5, 26:141, 27:119, 31:351, 38:111, 40:281, 43:177, 46:133, 49:365n, 376n
Chp. 3—9:123n
3:1—31:195
3:2—9:310n
3:4f—48:366
3:10—10:293
3:18—48:233
3:19—18:188
4:3—47:186
4:4—13:34
4:18—43:175
Chp. 5—11:96
5:1–5—18:328
5:2—40:30n
5:6—9:231, 11:127, 14:6, 52:122
5:7—9:297
5:12—53:26
6:5—11:88, 127
6:16–18—10:291
6:18—11:128
7:9—50:311n
7:12—40:87, 91
7:16f—22:215
7:17—40:269
8:4f—20:200
8:7—6:263, 9:169, 52:187
8:19f—18:324
9:1—13:304
9:2—18:262
9:3f—22:188
9:9—16:5, 19:193
9:15f—2:79
9:25—36:221
Chp. 10—47:187
10:1—36:221, 44:211n
10:5—18:186, 49:428n
10:6—12:401, 25:323, 27:204
10:6f—15:151, 44:26
10:7—7:356, 367, 12:401, 27:204
10:8—40:269
10:10—18:186
10:24—15:217
10:27—11:73, 13:178
Chp. 11—3:30
11:2—3:228
11:14—40:269
12:2f—51:273
12:3—8:229, 17:195, 28:284, 30:136
12:15—46:168n
12:23—2:19
12:23f—43:229
13:8—40:269
13:14—5:255
Chp. 14—17:192n
14:2—16:114
14:5—16:114
14:6—9:202, 43:278, 46:193, 54:149
14:20—10:86
14:42f—19:62
14:44—29:152
14:45—8:285, 16:129
Chp. 15—2:355, 3:283, 30:231
15:1–31—22:397
15:1–35—51:159n
15:2f—37:135
15:3—5:152, 6:211
15:4–24—46:66
15:9—2:78, 10:147, 10:16
15:12—10:147, 40:269
15:13f—34:29
15:15—5:152, 38:312, 44:347n
15:15f—10:130
15:17—5:94
15:20—10:240, 278
15:22—2:270, 2:272, 3:172, 10:16, 11:417, 18:165, 20:10n, 28:337, 30:30, 44:332n, 347n, 54:84
15:22f—30:30
15:23—2:270, 5:153, 17:19, 34:77, 47:269
15:24—6:42
15:29—1:304, 38:295
15:30—6:43, 7:273, 8:208
15:33—45:96
15:34—46:148
15:35—2:91, 41:250, 48:368
16:1—2:50, 5:184, 13:304, 42:156
16:6–13—32:10
16:7—2:102, 5:107, 9:260, 27:206, 29:232
16:12f—29:5
16:13—5:202, 44:211n
16:13f—5:184
16:14—14:203, 37:259
16:15—10:12
16:23—10:154, 14:310n, 15:274, 53:320, 323
17:4—37:63n
17:7—35:245
17:24—35:245
17:32—35:245
17:34—22:188
17:37—26:263
17:38f—13:156
17:43—17:400
17:45—39:156, 50:70f
17:45–47—26:263
17:50—20:295, 327
17:50f—37:63n
17:51—39:94, 42:151
17:55—18:324
18:10—10:154, 205
18:15—9:272
18:16—35:358
18:17—6:385, 10:129, 21:74
18:30—9:272, 12:202
Chp. 19—10:28
19:5—11:489
19:10–17—43:123n
19:11f—5:40
19:11–17—3:327
19:13—6:33
19:17—2:292
20:1—13:223
Chp. 21—10:158
21:1—40:269
21:1–6—51:106
21:4f—25:436, 44:389
21:6—27:55, 35:240, 50:36
21:9—42:152
21:10f—10:158
22:9—41:84
22:11f—16:115
22:18—9:163, 13:172, 183, 46:193
22:19—13:183
22:22—27:135
23:26—9:155
24:1–7—46:112n
24:4—6:324
24:6—17:122
24:7—13:197
24:16f—41:80
24:20—1:271
Chp. 25—9:149, 41:192, 237
25:3—5:285, 18:131
25:8–11—7:24
25:13—15:141

25:22—29:152
25:28—10:129, 23:21
25:29–31—6:369
25:36—8:291
25:44—46:285
26:5f—10:334
26:6–12—46:112n
26:15—14:288
28:6—9:168, 9:168n
28:7—11:132
28:8–14—36:196
28:12f—52:180
28:15—9:168n
29:8—54:303
29:9—21:297
30:11f—25:396
31:3f—44:327n
31:4—36:197, 40:297
31:4f—10:86
31:4–9—43:175

II Samuel
1:1–10—14:232n
1:1–16—54:21
1:2–16—36:196
1:10—41:343
1:15—9:163
1:16—40:372
1:20—16:143, 18:216
2:14—4:10, 5:35
2:22—8:209
3:8—9:233
3:9—29:152
3:27—13:154, 25:452, 35:240, 45:123
3:28f—18:68
5:6f—42:39
5:20—5:225
6:2—13:34
6:2f—13:166
6:16—3:44n, 6:193
Chp. 7—47:198
7:2f—13:167
7:3—26:108
7:3f—25:445
7:4–13—45:93
7:5—47:196
7:6f—8:242
7:6–11—51:42
7:7—8:282
7:8—47:197
7:11f—1:132, 29:114, 47:196
7:11–16—15:279
7:12—23:283, 48:360, 50:245n
7:12f—47:176n, 194
7:12–14—35:359, 45:206
7:12–16—36:39, 47:197
7:13—35:170
7:14—3:27, 29:114, 47:198
7:16—13:304
7:18–29—51:42
7:19—15:291, 298
7:21—22:31, 449
7:22–29—42:46n
7:23—34:226
Chp. 8—13:172
8:9—9:169
10:2—9:231
10:3f—11:355
10:4—16:86
10:11f—43:236
10:12—4:107, 43:237
Chp. 11—27:80, 45:26, 45:44
11:1–27—36:100
11:2f—13:80
11:2–12:25—54:145
11:4—2:293, 10:147
11:13—10:147
11:15—10:147, 12:237, 30:229
11:21—40:282
Chp. 12—12:305, 45:44
12:1f—10:163
12:1–15—22:403, 31:102, 35:22
12:5–13—7:41
12:7—7:274, 8:331, 12:406
12:9—29:227
12:13—6:42, 377, 7:274, 8:331, 10:31, 240, 12:368, 373, 389, 406, 20:138, 22:397, 30:263, 31:102, 34:172, 174, 39:29, 40:295, 47:240
12:14—12:306
12:16f—24:390, 48:368
12:25—10:208, 45:321n
Chp. 13—9:224
13:5—6:267
13:13—35:240, 45:23
13:18f—6:323
13:21—15:110
13:22—25:453, 456
13:30—15:110
13:31—7:303
14:4—12:286
14:5–7—1:308
14:6—22:85
14:11—35:240
14:14—10:133
14:17—16:274, 27:102
14:20—15:251
14:21–24—35:240
14:26—10:342, 13:23
Chp. 15—43:274
15:1–11—44:289
15:2f—12:242
15:2–4—13:148
15:4—7:144
15:14—14:273, 43:123n
15:25—3:13, 21:311
15:25f—5:145, 206, 43:274
15:26—3:13, 21:311
15:31—13:179
15:32–37—46:102
15:34—2:292, 50:189n
Chp. 16—13:180
16:1f—11:248, 12:237
16:1–4—10:189
16:2—15:271
16:3f—36:187
16:4—13:206
16:7f—19:227
16:10—14:323, 27:262
16:10f—25:160
16:11—33:178
16:16–19—46:102
16:22–17:23—46:193
16:23—13:171, 179, 45:122
Chp. 17—10:28
17:1–14—23:301
17:1–23—45:122
17:20—2:292, 10:367
17:23—13:170, 43:274
17:24—6:117
17:27—6:117
18:1–33—54:398
18:5—6:176, 22:236
18:7—47:18n
18:9—40:280, 282
18:9–15—15:143
18:14—43:274
18:14f—46:41
18:33—2:91, 7:303, 22:236
19:6—42:157
19:15—43:275
19:17–20—45:158
19:21—17:122
19:24f—11:248
19:24–30—10:189
19:29—13:206
20:8—39:156
20:10—35:240, 45:123
20:13—40:390
20:14–21—28:276
20:22—40:282, 46:41
21:1f—11:359
21:16f—32:137
Chp. 22—20:58n
22:31—18:25
22:46—11:127
22:51—13:230
Chp. 23—1:93, 47:134
23:1f—10:214
23:1–4—10:9
23:1–7—15:xi, 265–351, 47:72n
23:2—15:295
23:2f—47:192
23:3—9:171, 16:121, 29:178
23:3f—10:89
23:4—18:31, 47:194
23:5—8:285, 47:72, 78, 176n, 192–209, 300
23:6—18:271
23:6f—10:270, 47:72
23:8—8:54, 12:316, 37:172n
Chp. 24—15:271
24:1–15—21:356

24:10—46:172n, 173n
24:13f—17:278, 44:94n
24:15—6:206
24:17—31:197
24:18f—5:252
24:21f—5:252

I Kings

Chp. 1—15:271, 47:198
1:1–4—54:75
1:16—29:115
1:21—7:321
1:23—29:115
1:30f—52:3
1:38—36:182
1:39—44:211n
1:47f—8:143
2:2—4:310
2:5f—35:240, 45:124
2:6—13:154
2:10—48:360
2:12—12:380
2:13—9:196
2:31–33—1:299
2:33—13:230
2:46—7:243, 16:28
Chp. 3—15:36, 47:181
3:4—36:221
3:5—5:122
3:5–11—30:323
3:5–14—21:358
3:5–15—45:321n
3:6–10—46:173n
3:7—5:122
3:7f—5:122
3:9—45:119, 126, 50:190n
3:10–13—5:122
3:11f—15:22
3:16f—30:96
3:16–27—52:161
3:16–28—15:262n
3:26—6:17, 7:343, 371, 29:101, 30:97
Chp. 4—35:341
4:5—5:85
4:7—15:46
4:22—15:46
4:24f—20:221
4:25—22:198
4:26—9:169, 15:46
4:30—2:217
Chp. 5—18:135, 19:193n, 47:91n
5:1–12—47:86
5:12—9:169
6:3—20:235
6:5—35:405n
6:7—45:93
6:16—35:405n
6:24—11:319
6:29—1:236
Chp. 7—15:36
7:46—20:311
8:9—29:205f
8:10—16:71, 77
8:12—44:269, 49:331
8:25—17:397, 18:326
8:27—15:281, 33:48
8:39—50:85n
8:46—25:247, 275f, 32:181, 183
8:48—8:144
Chp. 9—47:186
9:3—47:173
9:6f—47:173
9:7—17:397
9:16—14:333
9:26–28—19:44
Chp. 10—35:341
10:1—18:116
10:7f—10:413
10:19f—39:83
10:23—9:169
Chp. 11—47:203
11:1—12:258
11:1–8—2:29
11:1–13—45:44
11:3—15:245, 54:109
11:4—40:387
11:5—18:137, 36:219
11:5–7—36:220
11:31f—8:300
11:41—18:130
Chp. 12—6:183, 47:187, 203
12:10f—40:284
12:12–14—48:216n
12:19—13:305
12:26–28—35:272
12:26–32—36:87
12:28—2:286, 6:49, 19:56, 26:258, 35:269n, 36:219
12:28f—5:241, 11:40, 37:22n
12:28–33—24:327n
12:29—2:286, 6:264, 36:222
12:31—36:113, 219
12:32—40:19
13:1f—9:188
13:24—3:284, 300
13:33—38:150
14:8—12:237
14:15f—8:179
14:16—41:288
14:23—12:352, 51:374
14:29—10:314
15:5—32:188
15:13—7:343, 39:271
15:25–29—46:104n
16:3f—20:163
16:8—40:282
16:8–10—46:104n
16:18—46:41
16:29f—26:80
16:31—43:93n
16:31f—36:219
16:31–33—2:29
16:32—52:107
16:34—2:113, 11:523
Chp. 17—6:177, 19:3, 38, 40:269
17:1—8:290
17:6—21:347, 50:94n
17:8–24—2:259, 35:323
17:9—18:203, 35:322
17:14—4:137
17:15—21:347
17:24—19:38, 35:323
Chp. 18—6:177, 9:123n, 40:269
18:1f—22:57
18:2—46:235
18:3f—18:193
18:4—45:389
18:13—8:300
18:17—2:20, 25:96, 422, 33:52
18:17f—43:110n, 48:307
18:17–40—41:207n
18:17–46—54:300
18:18—5:12
18:19—8:230, 13:59, 183, 24:24
18:20–40—54:313
18:21—5:246, 7:155, 11:69, 372, 483, 18:324, 356, 29:123, 31:346, 41:139
18:22—33:85
18:24—9:130
18:25–29—31:316
18:26—44:315n
18:26–28—25:422
18:27—33:75, 34:359n, 36:146, 37:259, 39:162, 208, 40:155, 43:281
18:28—3:144, 4:135, 7:355, 27:154, 36:223
18:38—1:249, 2:242
18:40—3:320, 45:62, 96, 54:287
18:44—18:160
Chp. 19—6:177, 40:269
19:1–3—5:25
19:1–4—3:320
19:2f—45:389
19:3—43:123
19:4—26:109, 34:284n, 49:428, 50:245n
19:6—36:182
19:8—5:30
19:9–18—41:210
19:10—13:89, 25:95, 31:342, 35:200
19:11—14:340
19:11f—27:367, 29:143
19:11–13—26:311
19:14—26:425, 35:200
19:18—2:101, 3:345, 8:180, 300f, 13:89, 211, 14:347, 18:70, 27:176, 33:86, 35:201, 36:220, 38:159, 44:383
Chp. 20—31:316, 40:269, 47:276
20:3f—48:217n

20:10—16:33, 43:263
20:28–34—43:263
20:30—30:290
20:31—29:170
20:32—43:263
20:34f—9:70
20:42—43:263f, 46:66
Chp. 21—40:269
21:1—18:4
21:1–16—51:161
21:7—8:297
21:9—49:381n
21:10—11:113, 13:178
21:17f—48:307n
21:19—17:74
21:20—36:223
21:27–29—46:172n
21:29—12:333
Chp. 22—17:301n
22:1f—22:57
22:2–40—46:120
22:14f—25:445
22:22—25:160, 41:84
22:23—11:65
22:24—25:445, 36:178, 39:81
22:32—43:264
22:34—43:263f
22:34f—8:298

II Kings
1:2—32:140, 39:263
1:2f—10:385
1:9–12—43:226
1:10—50:222n
1:17—47:199n
Chp. 2—40:269
2:4—15:217
2:8—4:370
2:9—48:232
2:11—29:234, 48:361
2:11–12—1:346
2:12—6:61, 16:64
2:23—23:265
2:24—2:136, 14:258, 27:262, 344
Chp. 3—40:269
3:5—6:64
3:9f—6:216
3:13—6:216
3:14—46:192
3:14f—25:459
3:15—10:43, 15:274, 16:62, 130, 53:320, 323
Chp. 4—40:269
4:1—18:320
4:1–7—13:401, 46:173n
4:27—4:213, 7:370
4:30—15:217
4:38—46:236
4:38–41—13:401
4:40—1:272, 13:80, 25:151, 39:31
4:42—4:137
4:42–44—13:400
Chp. 5—40:269, 47:157n, 49:74
5:1—7:65, 13:155, 16:180, 19:84, 24:80, 28:364, 34:67, 41:228, 42:123, 46:248
5:1f—52:271
5:1–27—46:192
5:3—22:99
5:10—10:283
5:13—16:180, 22:99, 25:282, 51:148
5:15—26:211
5:17—2:258
5:17f—26:211, 38:165
5:18—49:340n
5:18f—40:95
5:19—26:211, 6:266
5:22—13:103
5:22–23—29:120
Chp. 6—40:269
6:8–9—22:252
6:13f—22:209
6:16—6:241, 12:227, 20:27, 21:46, 30:290
6:16f—20:188, 42:112, 173
6:17—6:246, 15:212
6:18—3:263
6:23—8:288, 18:34, 105, 291
6:31f—13:403
Chp. 7—40:269
7:1f—13:403
7:19—44:57
Chp. 8—40:269
8:6—7:52
8:7–15—43:261n
8:11—19:39
8:19—47:194, 207
8:20—5:160
Chp. 9—40:269, 47:194n, 54:339
9:6—44:211n
9:11—21:53, 35:278
9:13—16:130
9:27f—46:104n
9:30–37—43:93n
Chp. 10—40:269, 47:194n, 54:339
10:24f—41:220
10:26—40:90
10:27—9:81n
10:32–33—35:324
Chp. 11—40:269
11:1f—47:208n
11:1–3—52:3
11:12—15:217
11:31—40:284
Chp. 12—40:269
12:2—13:184
12:17—40:284
Chp. 13—40:269
13:3—35:324
13:7—35:324
14:8–14—46:120
14:23–27—35:317
14:25—18:128, 19:3, 38, 35:323f
15:8–10—18:176
15:8–11—18:4
15:10f—18:42
16:1f—16:78
16:1–3—54:310
16:3—2:113, 3:216, 4:100, 102, 124, 180, 7:314, 341
16:10–14—53:21
16:14—36:154n
16:20—47:199n
Chp. 17—20:264n
17:1–7—35:326n
17:3—16:108
17:4—7:110
17:6—46:107n
17:18—19:77
17:28f—11:69
17:33—20:264n
Chp. 18—16:142, 17:306n
18:1f—45:207n
18:1–3—54:310
18:4—9:81n, 11:524, 22:347f, 40:87, 90, 43:157, 51:83, 53:90
18:9–12—35:326n
18:13—43:261n
18:13–19:36—35:326n
18:17—16:177n, 308
18:19—16:283
18:21—14:338
18:22—36:227
18:28–35—43:159n
18:33–35—19:176
18:35—13:130
Chp. 19—17:306n, 18:294
19:10f—16:283
19:12—16:316
19:14–19—46:173n
19:15—13:34
19:20f—12:30
19:28—32:161
19:32—16:109
19:32–34—43:282
19:35—3:270, 13:130, 16:266, 22:210
19:35f—19:165
19:35–37—54:148
19:37—16:330n, 22:92, 49:340n
20:3—12:240, 32:191
20:3f—48:220n
20:8—3:156, 4:261
20:13—15:107
20:20—16:80
21:6—44:83n, 48:300
21:16—35:278n
22:8—29:206, 34:283n
22:14—18:329, 28:276, 40:390
22:14–20—36:152
Chp. 23—8:186, 16:45
23:3f—35:278n
23:4—9:81n
23:5—7:343, 18:322, 21:6, 40:90
23:7—9:237
23:10—36:219, 224, 39:296, 41:203n, 44:83n, 48:300
23:10–12—43:278
23:15—34:31
23:20—41:220
23:29—46:120
23:34f—52:93

Chp. 24—35:294, 326n
24:1—29:174
24:2—8:288
24:6–15—45:214n
24:12—49:279n
24:14—18:320, 45:367
24:15—18:208
24:20—19:77
24:20–25:1—25:440
Chp. 25—35:326n, 48:396n
25:8f—7:53, 20:260
25:11f—19:162
25:17–41—52:70
25:25f—20:260
25:27—49:279
25:27–30—18:208

I Chronicles
1:32—4:306
3:16–19—45:214n
5:1—6:277, 7:201, 8:154, 207, 213
Chp. 6—8:207
6:33—53:221
6:39—53:221
7:20f—8:107, 150
7:21f—8:175
8:13—7:165
9:16—12:201
9:19—12:201
10:13—11:132
11:15—35:291n
13:3—13:166
13:6—13:34
Chp. 14—16:234
Chp. 15—13:188
15:19—12:201
15:21—10:43
16:33—10:76
16:34—53:139
16:41—53:221
Chp. 17—15:294, 298, 349
17:4f—9:52, 15:281
17:7f—17:253
17:10–14—15:279
17:11—15:282
17:11–14—47:197
17:12—15:308, 338
17:13f—15:286, 290, 296
17:14—15:283, 288, 292, 337
17:14–17—15:298
17:15f—15:285
17:16—15:294, 326
17:16f—15:286, 296
17:17—15:291, 298
Chp. 18–19—13:172
20:3—18:131
21:16—37:298n
Chp. 22—15:271
22:9—25:285
22:12—17:216
22:14—27:165
23:1—14:186
23:4—12:199
Chp. 25—14:231
27:33—5:85
Chp. 28—47:198
28:6f—9:52
Chp. 29—47:198
29:14—15:284

II Chronicles
3:1—4:99, 18:329, 35:291n
5:2—35:291n
5:13—47:224
6:1—47:224
6:36—25:275
7:1—47:224
7:14—54:244
7:16—5:242
9:4—15:28
9:21—19:9
10:4—15:144
11:4—6:223
14:9–12—54:148
14:11f—46:173n
15:2–4—52:101
15:7—15:147n, 33:153
19:4–7—45:121
19:4–8—9:162n
19:6—9:163, 13:44
20:3—49:381
20:5–12—46:173n
20:7—3:31, 23:414
20:17—40:43
20:36—19:9
21:7—47:194
22:11—47:222
24:2—46:173n
24:20–22—52:93
24:21—52:92
24:22—13:184, 45:274n
28:1f—16:78
28:3—8:244, 275
28:22–25—36:154n
28:23—18:9
28:23f—11:496
28:27—47:199n
28:27–29:1—45:207n
Chp. 30–31—47:203
32:7—16:113
32:8f—16:349
32:13–15—4:29
33:1–6—1:289
33:10–13—46:172n
33:10–16—6:371
33:13—43:275
34:28—7:298
34:33—46:173n
Chp. 35—20:141
35:13—11:301
35:21f—12:240
35:22f—9:203
35:24—43:162
35:24f—20:329
Chp. 36—35:294, 43:69, 47:246f
36:4f—52:93
36:9f—45:214n
36:22—47:246
36:22f—35:286n, 45:225, 47:86, 48:359

Ezra
Chp. 1—35:304, 47:247, 48:359
1:1–3—45:225
1:1–4—35:329
1:1–8—35:286n
1:2—2:128, 258, 47:86
1:2f—19:218
1:5—18:237, 241
1:8–11—45:214n
Chp. 2—35:304, 48:359
2:1f—47:203n
2:1–65—35:288
2:2f—20:190
2:60—20:254
2:70—47:203
Chp. 3—35:304, 48:359
3:7—20:116
3:8—10:129, 12:199, 23:21
3:12f—20:227
3:13—18:237
Chp. 4—35:304
4:4f—20:160
4:4–6:15—35:329
4:6—45:225n
4:7f—20:160
4:12—20:186
4:24—45:225n
Chp. 5—35:304
5:11—25:470
Chp. 6—20:160, 35:304
6:2—34:276
6:6–15—35:303
6:16—47:249
6:19–22—13:372
9:8f—20:109
9:9—17:291
10:2—35:332n
10:18—20:254
37:12—53:329

Nehemiah
2:1—45:225
2:1–8—35:304n
2:1–11—45:225
2:6—45:226
2:10—20:162, 35:305
2:16—7:118
2:19—20:228
Chp. 3—18:329
4:6—35:305
4:17—29:30
5:13—9:223
6:15—20:186
11:30—7:301
12:36—40:30
13:10—8:229, 45:318
13:24—32:245
13:38—20:186

Esther
Chp. 1—29:222
1:1–7—1:100
1:2–2:17—45:34
1:3f—11:265, 34:130
1:4—52:87
1:5—35:61
1:8—7:350
1:10—7:52
1:12f—11:281
2:2f—2:304
2:7f—25:511
2:12—30:89
2:17—30:89
3:8—11:508
3:13—49:193
5:2—8:142, 10:35,

14:336, 29:118, 222
6:1—44:95
8:10—2:264
8:15—7:118
10:3—45:220
14:16—30:89, 44:84n
14:16(Vulgate)—21:316

Job

Chp. 1—15:221, 25:275
1:1—2:206, 4:185, 5:207, 11:376, 34:125, 47:157n
1:6—6:380, 8:131, 21:212, 22:206, 26:24, 29:87, 34:216, 41:228, 43:64, 53:45
1:8—26:193, 27:231
1:9–12—12:125
1:10—6:95
1:12—10:418, 13:135, 15:136, 23:77
1:13f—16:240
1:20—6:324
1:21—7:133, 14:50, 345, 15:91, 28:370, 30:104, 32:122, 42:32, 54:225
2:3—2:319, 12:373
2:4—12:125, 23:330
2:6—11:369, 54:129
2:9—3:44n, 4:326, 5:14, 30, 203, 7:132, 12:126, 42:146
2:10—5:206, 7:133, 11:283, 12:126, 14:50, 30:104, 42:146, 46:78, 79n, 54:183, 225
Chp. 3—17:129, 25:69
3:1—10:162
3:1f—10:381, 25:346
3:1–3—13:108
3:1–10—47:113n
3:3—1:178, 11:53, 12:126, 17:47, 127
3:3f—26:109
3:11—1:178
3:14—1:103n
3:15—51:6
3:21—7:334
3:23—29:187
Chp. 4—29:187
4:17–19—4:61
4:18—4:61
4:18f—10:37
4:20—28:103, 45:255n
Chp. 5—11:138, 29:36
5:5—20:102, 35:252
5:7—7:208, 13:123, 44:108
5:9—25:103
5:12—49:253n
5:13—32:112, 40:166
5:17–19—51:42
5:18—10:63
6:3—42:134
6:5—18:146
6:16—10:319, 31:132
6:19—18:136
7:1—11:19, 42, 535, 20:8, 30:142, 33:217, 42:73, 127
7:3—10:426
7:15—10:170, 202
7:17—25:391
7:18—11:246, 456
7:19—25:391
7:20f—25:275
7:21—27:231
8:14—11:203
Chp. 9—32:173
9:2f—7:360, 25:275
9:3—32:85, 42:70
9:5—1:241n, 10:336, 462, 32:112
9:10—25:103
9:15—25:275, 31:214, 32:86
9:20—10:380, 27:231
9:21—19:133, 25:222, 32:91
9:22—32:172
9:28—10:368, 13:116, 14:344, 25:222, 278, 497, 31:67, 160, 205, 32:91, 182, 259, 39:33
10:8f—7:232
10:10—1:126, 29:191
10:12—11:109
10:18—25:391
10:21—10:126
11:2—10:183
11:11–17—14:141
11:12—10:307
11:16f—16:113
12:5—34:214n, 35:221
12:6—33:291
12:7—11:138
12:18—17:123, 18:273
12:21—46:19n
13:14—15:66
13:15—4:132, 6:131, 354, 7:132, 137, 8:9, 204
13:25—11:192, 13:117, 19:76, 25:391
13:26—30:244
14:1—13:101, 34:129
14:1f—6:335, 14:272
14:4—33:174
14:5—15:51
14:11—16:161
14:13—18:340, 31:127
15:15—10:239
15:16—10:354, 11:74, 29:120
15:32—15:141
15:32f—45:255n
16:2—11:467
17:12—11:199
17:13—11:175, 19:75
17:14—6:401
18:8—35:252
18:14—45:255n
19:2–22—10:380
19:19—1:241n
19:20—11:319, 14:180
19:21—29:140, 31:122
19:22—31:110, 122
19:25—8:162, 53:134
19:25f—53:328, 331
19:26—10:32
20:11—45:255n
20:13—13:112
20:15—19:222
20:22—45:255n
20:29—13:134
Chp. 21—13:112
21:5—10:73
21:9—13:112
21:13—2:351, 7:232
21:14—2:315, 8:239
21:17—2:351
21:18—14:306, 18:329
22:9—19:219n
22:23–27—51:42
22:29—11:21, 290, 21:315
23:15—3:348
24:3—19:219n
24:5—18:45
24:9—13:16
24:21—19:219n
24:24—45:255n
25:5—10:239
26:7f—2:94
26:11—10:346
26:14—10:286
27:6—25:275
28:8—35:252
28:13—5:215, 6:8
28:26—20:106
29:6—8:247
29:9—10:73
29:15—10:143, 27:244, 29:200
30:21—12:374
30:29—1:51n
31:17—4:380
31:24—4:380, 28:378, 44:107
31:27—11:292, 18:70, 27:175, 31:346
31:27f—10:29, 14:348
31:28—27:175, 31:346
31:33—22:403
Chp. 32—29:36, 32:218
32:2–22—39:159
32:18f—20:234
32:19—10:211
Chp. 33—32:218
34:5—18:359
34:11—17:340
34:30—7:143,

11:356, 33:233, 46:109
37:18—1:24
38:4—22:363
38:7—22:363, 29:117, 41:81n
38:8—11:325
38:10—1:34, 11:325
38:10f—6:38
38:11—2:93, 6:156, 243, 11:325, 42:129
38:25—20:106
38:31f—27:245
39:5–8—11:329
39:6—18:45
39:13—9:41n, 25:256
39:13–18—18:215
39:14–16—45:353, 355
39:21—20:168
39:23—8:253
39:25—10:43
40:15—10:321, 13:31, 14:289, 21:333, 39:124n, 43:269n
40:15f—48:306n
40:16—15:250, 29:114
40:17—10:130
40:19—10:85, 29:140
40:21f—26:428
40:23—10:199
40:24—4:47, 29:135
Chp. 41—7:321, 29:240
41:1—1:51n, 21:333, 26:267, 29:140, 32:146
41:1–7—29:135
41:3—11:70
41:6—10:165, 270, 448
41:11—25:103, 376, 42:32
41:14—32:146
41:15–17—45:85n
41:16f—21:334
41:17–19—14:322
41:18—21:333
41:19—7:85
41:20—10:165
41:21—42:74, 44:387
41:24—21:334, 45:154n
41:25—11:391
41:25–34—45:115n
41:26f—10:189
41:26–28—21:334
41:31—26:452
42:1—32:146
42:8—31:64, 225
42:10—45:280
42:12—45:280

Psalms

Numbers in parentheses indicate verse numbering in Hebrew text and as used by Luther.

Ps. 1—3:138, 10:11–34, 173, 14:287 312, 17:104, 391, 18:66, 25:15, 139, 334
1:1 5:159, 7:260, 10:7, 274, 366, 11:217, 249, 356, 494, 12:193, 13:178, 17:101, 18:56, 20:242, 25:218, 27:235, 244, 329, 341, 43:194
1:1f—5:111
1:1–3—11:146, 336
1:2—2:21, 7:143, 9:69, 278, 10:25, 359, 11:51, 145, 452, 15:50, 17:347, 22:275, 25:65, 184, 223, 240, 333, 388, 43:194, 44:46, 52:137
1:2f—1:329
1:3—2:163, 5:82, 8:206, 10:420, 14:315, 16:83, 17:369, 391, 32:165, 35:219, 44:26, 45:365
1:4—5:22, 11:233, 14:63, 17:25, 18:70, 339, 19:26, 135, 20:21, 347, 24:320, 25:232, 285, 400, 27:19, 100, 31:126, 51:46
1:5—9:49, 10:407, 20:146, 243, 24:235, 25:218, 27:100, 41:219
1:6—9:33, 11:342, 14:348, 18:289f, 352, 25:74, 388, 27:280, 51:46, 52:95, 158
Ps. 2—10:35–41, 11:17, 363, 12:3–96, 13:168, 182, 14:313–349, 18:139, 26:451, 34:128n, 41:253, 49:350n
2:1—2:35, 8:69, 10:7, 13:167, 249, 335, 26:27, 30:257, 40:49, 377
2:1f—12:290, 14:249, 277, 16:321, 26:231, 48:189, 49:336n
2:1–3—14:16
2:2—2:35, 5:251, 6:389, 9:4, 147, 11:370, 393, 12:292, 13:167, 249, 335, 13:168, 188, 190, 14:70, 15:278, 16:286, 19:37, 20:25, 21:344, 23:387, 40:49, 41:122, 43:177, 46:185, 47:220, 50:215n, 52:35
2:2f—41:122, 49:253n
2:3—6:375, 8:240, 14:30, 18:270, 294, 30:258, 41:178, 50:215n
2:4—2:224, 6:304, 375, 397, 10:41, 102, 15:279, 16:225, 286, 19:203, 21:176, 23:302, 27:125, 40:49, 45:347, 48:189, 220f, 49:337, 50:216n, 266n, 300n
2:4f—9:4
2:5—2:224, 6:398, 8:240, 10:36, 40f, 14:156, 15:279, 21:176, 31:126, 32:31
2:6—15:278, 337, 45:88
2:6f—18:273, 338
2:7—5:20, 8:240, 9:48, 10:323, 15:278, 311, 336, 22:46, 23:281, 24:94, 34:217, 226, 38:257, 51:390
2:8—8:304, 10:107, 11:115, 13:33, 378, 14:183, 15:338, 20:311, 25:5, 31:228, 37:281, 367, 39:88, 45:215, 220
2:9—2:3, 8:300, 10:278, 13:338, 340, 14:22, 17:63, 20:124, 23:380, 29:118, 48:321, 50:216n
2:10—10:65, 12:203, 243, 13:167, 16:273, 21:120, 25:243, 32:145, 34:360, 54:128
2:10f—26:119, 48:189
2:11—2:307, 6:159, 8:202, 10:346, 13:261, 15:278, 16:38, 45, 18:70, 21:120, 25:497, 26:72, 32:165, 39:41, 54:21
2:11(12)—19:212
2:11f—25:278, 43:151, 47:281
2:12—13:338, 14:22, 22:85, 23:22, 380, 27:176, 29:129, 130, 30:266, 44:25, 52:115
2:24—40:49
Ps. 3—42:21n
3:1—10:7
3:2f—11:398
3:3—25:248, 202, 32:181
3:5—10:334, 53:328

3:6—12:176, 18:372, 45:331, 46:24
3:7—10:41, 269, 324, 27:360
3:8—20:91, 25:152, 237
Ps. 4—5:69, 10:42–75, 11:237, 45:321n
4:1—2:185, 6:103, 10:52, 252, 373, 11:127, 143, 237, 514, 14:163, 259, 25:288
4:2—10:59, 460, 11:41, 218, 239, 290, 314, 505, 515, 13:182, 25:142, 179, 27:54, 37:108n
4:2f—11:418
4:3—2:288, 3:4, 8, 334, 336, 4:120, 6:150, 354, 359, 7:129, 224, 226, 230, 285, 316, 352, 8:163, 10:258, 463, 11:236, 351, 374, 378, 499, 514, 25:367, 498, 29:135, 36:187, 44:268
4:4—4:168, 8:69, 11:24, 84, 93, 219, 237, 277, 343, 407, 16:209, 313, 18:196, 19:137, 183, 27:70, 48:213n
4:4f—11:5
4:5—25:424, 36:146
4:6—2:121, 8:16, 10:30, 60, 93, 144, 324, 387, 11:207, 249, 252, 299, 515, 13:43, 17:350, 21:321, 25:203, 33:111, 51:27
4:6f—6:172, 44:37, 52:129, 274
4:7—11:332, 18:40
4:8—16:342, 17:258, 42:149, 49:428, 53:328, 337
4:15—10:21
Ps. 5—10:76f
5:3—1:82, 11:272
5:4—10:76, 12:356, 16:35, 29:196, 34:123, 44:309
5:4f—47:156
5:4–6—10:48
5:5—9:53, 198, 10:76, 14:307, 51:46, 52:257
5:6—10:76, 11:292, 32:165, 226
5:7—47:156
5:8—10:162, 276, 11:260, 48:21, 51:27
5:9—2:158, 7:153, 243, 11:132, 213, 18:231, 20:237, 25:495, 26:379, 28:366, 31:208, 32:197, 33:231
5:10—5:52, 9:236, 10:58, 308
5:11—10:257
Ps. 6—10:44, 76, 78–82, 139, 14:139–146, 42:126, 49:69, 53:221
6:1—2:321, 3:358, 4:265, 5:255, 10:81, 140, 142, 26:317, 31:129, 42:63, 44:29, 54:275
6:2—10:141, 326, 14:157, 17:411, 25:179, 392
6:2f—31:128, 32:31
6:2–5—18:100
6:3—10:142, 11:158, 34:311
6:4—18:112, 132
6:5—10:197, 16:343, 26:337, 29:176, 31:145, 42:49
6:6—10:92, 14:159
6:7—8:113, 10:142, 11:108, 14:180, 20:57, 241
6:8—10:77
6:10—14:161, 32:139
Ps. 7—10:83–86, 349, 15:81, 19:133, 47:18
7:1—19:227
7:2—10:84, 21:383
7:3—19:133
7:6—2:61, 4:106, 356, 11:110, 17:173, 32:x
7:8—14:245, 32:192, 45:107, 52:187
7:9—11:290, 21:346, 27:206, 31:43, 33:24, 36:189, 45:107
7:10—25:346, 29:232
7:11—21:346
7:12—16:46
7:12f—46:171
7:13—10:165f, 18:40
7:14—6:64, 17:356, 392, 27:350, 35:298, 43:269
7:15—29:232, 46:286
7:15f—43:268
7:16—6:66, 10:86, 11:219, 27:350, 35:298, 43:196, 46:43n, 49:248
7:17—2:388
Ps. 8—4:223, 8:97–138, 10:87–90, 11:139, 272, 22:491
8:1—10:133, 19:138, 20:64
8:2—8:208, 10:87f, 256, 11:507, 14:71, 29:144, 31:75, 43:106, 49:7, 51:125
8:3—11:272, 374, 22:318, 34:132, 50:135
8:4—1:327, 10:224, 16:124, 345
8:4–6—15:276
8:5—3:4, 5:218, 10:232, 11:387, 13:382, 20:255
8:5f—20:149
8:5–8—21:167
8:6—8:180, 12:285, 290, 15:345, 20:248, 255, 22:491, 496, 498, 24:82, 25:148, 27:171, 28:139, 29:120, 37:64, 52:51, 278, 54:280
8:6–8—25:5, 34:140
8:7—10:89, 27:171
8:7f—4:276
8:8—10:89, 20:290
8:9—25:83
Ps. 9—10:91–97, 156, 183, 13:ix, 16:344n, 32:268–272, 42:21n
9:1—11:37, 427
9:2—2:388
9:3—10:94, 105, 26:384
9:4—10:369, 11:37
9:5—10:108, 18:322, 20:209, 25:83, 31:232
9:6—10:94, 409, 11:22, 389, 14:182, 20:145, 25:517, 40:208
9:8—10:94
9:9—1:329, 2:283, 11:514, 12:29, 14:218, 16:118, 283, 18:288
9:9f—6:221
9:10—19:57, 24:392, 43:171
9:12—5:276, 11:193, 51:245f
9:13—2:61, 10:94f
9:13f—11:176
9:15—10:94
9:17—10:94, 372, 27:46, 43:264
9:19—10:94
9:20—2:282, 4:62, 10:97, 12:122
Ps. 10—10:99f, 13:ix, 35:206n, 43:41
10:1—4:356
10:1f—16:207
10:2—7:330
10:3—13:43
10:5—10:407, 14:344, 21:333, 32:213
10:5f—14:190
10:6—21:333, 42:63–64
10:7—10:255, 257, 264, 11:213, 524, 19:108, 159,

26:379, 27:350, 407
10:8—10:166
10:9—2:34, 10:252, 265
10:11—1:322, 2:61, 221, 4:379, 10:112, 277, 16:247, 18:162
10:12—2:222, 20:198
10:12-15—45:66
10:13—10:277
10:14—1:253, 12:29, 42:156n
10:15—16:249, 39:253, 45:60
10:17—12:316, 53:141
Ps. 11—10:99-101, 13:ix, 18:162, 167, 270
11:1f—10:100
11:2—10:166, 29:232
11:3—10:101, 17:248, 25:250, 27:230
11:4—19:58
11:4-7—45:269
11:5—25:291, 313
11:6—10:106, 459, 19:129
11:7—10:112, 42:80
Ps. 12—10:102f, 11:243, 244, 13:ix, 35:206n, 43:41, 53:225
12:1—3:345, 11:243, 245, 11:506, 14:291, 16:344, 29:232
12:2—10:66, 301, 11:244, 246, 292, 506
12:3—7:92, 25:233
12:4—2:33, 11:245, 13:43, 17:33
12:5—1:322, 3:345, 10:51, 324, 427, 11:243, 14:307, 19:122
12:6—11:243f, 506, 13:14, 17.161, 18:411, 19:195, 20:72, 25:02
12:6-8—40:80
12:7—11:506
12:8—13:183
Ps. 13—13:ix, 29:177
13:1—2:222
13:2—2:61
13:3—10:264, 11:132, 213, 14:320, 15:92
13:3f—43:32n
13:49—16:167
Ps. 14—13:ix, 18:255, 20:221, 53:229
14:1—1:156, 2:83, 3:229, 4:261, 10:178, 180, 191, 11:524, 13:365, 16:247, 18:354, 25:225, 409, 29:51, 33:28, 235, 34:308, 37:59, 44:241, 51:124, 52:196
14:2—1:161, 2:40, 83, 167, 171, 301, 25:252, 29:51
14:2f—29:177, 33:253
14:3—2:40, 59, 83, 301, 3:108, 10:238, 11:132, 197, 213, 14:196, 16:57, 18:255, 25:247, 299, 363, 27:174, 224, 274, 29:189, 32:169, 41:216, 44:294, 45:279n, 51:46
14:4—7:217, 11:132, 18:325, 20:102, 237, 25:228
14:4f—53:334
14:5—4:134, 6:70, 7:329, 11:528, 14:345n, 18:255, 31:127, 35:90, 136, 45:58n
14:6—25:521, 31:75, 32:10
14:7—33:135
Ps. 15—10:265, 13:ix, 35:206n
15:1—27:280
15:2—10:48, 65, 73f, 160, 14:288, 27:280, 32:173
15:3—10:66, 264, 11:292
15:4—11:486, 530, 13:411, 20:277, 52:35
15:5—10:117, 25:218, 45:233n
Ps. 16—10:104-110, 259, 13:ix, 29:51, 31:226, 35:206n
16:1f—11:351
16:2—11:374
16:3—6:354, 25:311, 367, 44:268
16:4—8:22, 10:26, 11:291, 339, 12:273, 14:266, 20:145, 32:163, 40:208, 47:304
16:5—10:106, 333, 458
16:6—10:458, 11:86
16:7—10:109, 459, 16:119
16:8—10:162, 11:369, 383, 29:177
16:8f—10:71
16:10—7:292, 10:115, 14:324, 19:20, 75, 37:124, 130, 52:280
16:10f—8:35
16:11—10:115, 12:246, 375, 32:168
16:12—52:251
16:13—11:351
Ps. 17—10:111f, 176, 11:127, 13:ix
17:2—9:49, 10:112
17:3—25:291, 30:126
17:3f—38:227, 51:18
17:4—5:225, 10:255
17:5—53:328
17:6—10:176
17:7—4:168, 6:354, 7:230, 10:146
17:8—7:96, 48:379n
17:9—33:219
17:10—11:304, 464
17:14—6:306
17:15—10:112
17:36—10:373
Ps. 18—5:338, 10:113-124, 11:344, 13:ix, 14:75, 35:206n
18:1—11:364
18:2—10:113
18:3—14:144, 29:130, 40:157, 42:183, 44:49, 49:253n
18:5—6:209, 10:114, 35:285n
18:7—10:120, 19:134
18:7f—11:343
18:8—8:159, 11:343, 36:85
18:9—10:120, 14:201
18:10—10:119, 11:95, 322, 25:434, 29:203
18:11—25:287
18:12—11:322, 49:331
18:13—2:388, 11:76
18:14—10:120, 19:234
18:15—11:176, 324, 31:99
18:16—22:283
18:17f—10:114
18:19—11:127, 20:58
18:20—28:273, 29:232, 54:62
18:23—20:55
18:24—28:273, 29:232, 54:62
18:25—3:334, 336, 12:193
18:25f—19:11
18:26—3:334f, 5:336, 6:214, 9:67, 12:193, 14:319, 17:402, 18:266, 25:219, 405, 29:195, 35:70, 36:76, 166, 37:238, 322, 38:110, 42:31, 44:183, 46:64, 186, 47:291, 52:6, 29
18:26f—28:35, 44:317
18:27—43:249n, 44:294
18:28—30:164

18:29—9:87
18:33—10:276, 19:147, 237
18:35—10:49, 74
18:36—25:250, 27:229
18:37—32:219
18:40—14:53
18:41—11:438, 20:269, 25:91, 413
18:42—20:303, 40:278
18:43—11:106, 18:253
18:44—10:189, 11:218, 25:92
18:45—14:301, 20:58n
18:49—25:121
18:50—6:284, 13:230
Ps. 19—11:201, 12:139–146, 13:ix, 26:58, 36:95
19:1—13:136, 14:13, 184, 200, 17:172, 26:58, 29:215, 32:195f, 51:17–23
19:2—10:8, 131, 201, 294, 329, 427, 11:234, 455, 25:480
19:3—12:56
19:3f—47:220
19:4—8:304, 10:103, 314, 11:329, 364, 13:269, 18:238, 296, 357, 25:31, 92, 417, 26:245, 29:117, 33:172, 34:111, 35:284, 37:367, 39:88
19:5—10:276, 397, 14:10, 18:32, 20:109, 43:45, 49:375
19:6—10:11, 11:457, 25:312, 27:337, 52:73
19:7—10:30, 109, 281, 11:422, 12:108, 29:152
19:8—29:164, 31:372
19:9—10:407, 12:83, 19:13, 33:92, 39:64
19:10—10:240
19:10f—25:191
19:11—12:161
19:12—3:348, 350, 4:80, 6:192, 7:360, 10:109, 237, 11:201, 13:383, 14:28, 25:61, 215, 291, 31:160, 209, 32:23, 43f, 53, 55, 91, 34:75, 35:20, 36:187, 39:35f, 43:197, 44:240, 46:288, 51:276
19:12f—10:369, 25:240
19:13—10:109, 11:502, 14:202, 18:43, 30:245, 32:252, 40:296, 51:11
19:14—52:131
19:19—10:346
Ps. 20—13:ix, 35:206n, 43:41, 231
20:7—20:325, 50:70n
Ps. 21—13:ix, 34:338n, 42:171n
21:1—3:4, 5:145, 8:237
21:2—10:33, 17:393
21:3—29:118
21:5—10:232, 33:139n
21:6—21:301
21:9—29:165, 31:127
21:11—14:249, 18:291
21:12—10:285, 464, 11:107, 194, 25:322, 51:40n
21:13—16:144
Ps. 22—10:259, 13:ix
22:1—6:54
22:5—4:267
22:6—6:52, 10:326, 11:67, 140, 150, 367, 377, 430, 12:110, 123, 298, 15:342, 16:94, 19:103, 22:340, 26:420f, 29:126, 30:24, 48:281
22:7—14:275, 49:177
22:9—29:191
22:10f—45:213n
22:11—26:421
22:12—11:304, 19:110
22:14f—14:159
22:21—21:333, 24:413, 31:130
22:22—12:393, 24:407, 27:221, 29:133, 30:265, 38:187
22:23—36:240, 40:20
22:26—52:251
22:28—12:131, 15:345
22:29—15:44
22:30—25:281
22:30f—11:385
22:31—13:270, 29:221
Ps. 23—10:458, 12:147–182, 13:ix
23:1—6:176
23:2—36:45
23:3—20:317n, 33:135n
23:4—3:190, 5:355, 11:283, 292, 530, 20:315, 29:11, 136, 42:149
23:5—7:353, 10:110, 367, 458, 19:219n, 20:45, 29:201, 35:61, 109, 36:45
Ps. 24—13:ix, 382, 42:21n
24:1—10:33, 13:47, 18:171
24:2—8:296, 13:47
24:3—14:307
24:4—29:195
24:5—9:76, 16:19, 18:104
24:6—8:299
24:7—10:442, 11:176, 19:140
24:7f—4:126
24:8—25:393, 29:146, 30:71, 32:252, 45:329
24:9—11:176
24:10—30:71, 32:252, 36:338
Ps. 25—10:173, 13:ix, 35:206n, 43:41
25:1—18:21, 28:271
25:3—14:67, 16:171, 17:159, 363n, 18:351
25:5—29:188
25:6—5:170, 10:146
25:7—21:218, 25:62, 215, 30:244
25:9—25:405
25:10—7:252, 10:403, 11:167, 13:25, 29:219, 42:89
25:11—9:105, 13:383, 27:221, 30:245, 32:47, 39:28
25:14—10:232, 11:164, 29:214
25:15—25:352
25:16—14:253
Ps. 26—12:183–196, 13:ix
26:2—30:126
26:3—11:167, 44:37
26:4—15:187
26:8—17:316
26:9—3:235, 18:20, 321
26:12—10:132, 11:314, 372
26:59f—10:309
Ps. 27—10:125–127, 11:110, 13:ix, 29:148
27:1—15:92, 34:131
27:1–3—45:331
27:3—51:202
27:4—12:179
27:5—11:34, 109, 29:167
27:9—4:132, 17:370, 21:321
27:10—7:336, 8:9, 9:113, 10:159, 24:414
27:12—11:218
27:13—11:241
27:14—2:308, 3:223, 4:105, 147, 321, 5:56, 131, 6:354, 7:56, 99, 126, 131,

174, 176, 233, 8:13, 20, 29, 201, 234, 287, 10:100, 11:529, 13:179, 25:365, 29:236, 43:172, 51:392
Ps. 28—10:128–132, 13:ix
28:1—3:230, 10:84, 31:128, 42:183
28:3—1:272, 10:66, 73, 168, 17:174, 25:286, 347, 27:351, 37:24
28:4—10:311
28:5—10:131, 310, 11:340, 14:200, 303, 18:5, 21:347, 32:169, 42:132, 43:85, 44:268, 51:19
28:7—10:14, 39:41
28:8—10:146
Ps. 29—10:133–137, 155, 13:ix, 21:120, 43:245, 247n
29:6—10:134, 198
29:9—18:45, 45:365n, 366n
29:10—10:151, 35:32
Ps. 30—10:138f, 13:ix, 22:375
30:5—2:143, 223, 3:140, 10:39, 12:77f, 369, 16:113, 153, 156, 29:135, 31:364, 33:136, 42:151, 53:169
30:6—5:23, 6:97, 101, 15:210
30:6f—5:26
30:6–9—3:4
30:7—5:23, 27, 6:101, 14:142
30:7–9—6:218
Ps. 31—10:139–144, 13:ix
31:1—7:251, 27:241, 29:188, 31:299, 51:309, 374
31:2—25:271, 286
31:3—6:176
31:5—4:119, 19:199
31:6—36:137
31:6f—7:315
31:8—11:127, 148
31:9—10:140
31:9–20—10:139
31:11—14:159, 24:413
31:12—26:389
31:13f—10:265
31:15—6:13, 243, 14:218
31:16—3:72, 21:321, 23:258
31:18—14:247
31:19—8:12, 10:50, 11:484, 25:370
31:20—10:91, 29:216, 240
31:22—3:72, 4:132, 7:225, 232, 8:8, 19:19, 77, 26:389, 30:303, 31:129, 42:183, 48:367
31:23—19:198
31:23f—4:147
31:24—5:56, 13:179, 51:392
Ps. 32—10:145–151, 12:305, 13:ix, 14:147–154, 49:69, 53:221
32:1—1:265, 297, 6:9, 8:209, 10:112, 25:258f, 34:128, 42:134
32:1f—25:264, 32:169, 35:36, 374, 47:171
32:2—8:275, 10:135, 233, 25:266, 271f, 27:362, 31:60, 214
32:3—7:274, 11:238, 406, 510, 19:59, 87, 100
32:5—4:54, 7:236, 275, 10:31, 350, 11:262, 371, 12:324, 340, 17:228, 22:397, 399, 25:62, 215, 258, 265, 272, 27:76, 31:46, 36:258, 39:29, 47:240
32:5f—25:246, 259, 263, 36:355, 51:98
32:6—10:258, 18:289, 25:214, 221, 239, 258, 272, 275, 292, 313, 336, 26:109, 27:76, 31:63, 214, 42:62, 47:171, 54:328
32:7—44:62
32:8—11:440, 14:201, 21:313, 42:112
32:9—1:67, 3:149, 4:250, 317, 5:73, 271, 10:190, 428, 11:15, 440, 461, 515, 14:342, 29:149
32:10—10:150, 11:206, 284, 25:273
32:11—7:315, 10:149, 11:334, 27:93, 43:173, 176
32:16f—25:150
Ps. 33—10:152–157, 265, 13:ix, 49:70n, 53:221
33:2—10:266
33:4—37:51n, 139
33:5—10:34, 407, 42:146
33:6—1:20, 10:252, 11:340, 15:301, 314, 22:12, 25:76, 29:118, 133, 34:240, 51:77, 52:44
33:7—10:171, 196, 11:31
33:9—1:76, 93, 5:234, 10:202, 11:39, 13:29, 92, 14:123, 323, 18:294, 19:82f, 20:209, 22:11, 25:216, 33:178, 37:117, 181
33:10—15:25, 18:198, 23:221, 292, 25:305, 29:186, 31:66, 34:70n, 45:329, 49:248, 253n, 286, 52:190
33:10f—14:249
33:11—19:211
33:12—2:352
33:15—23:292
33:16—34:92
33:16f—9:202, 43:278
33:17—6:242, 19:115, 45:329
33:18—43:229, 44:67
33:19—21:207
Ps. 34—9:50, 10:158–164, 13:ix, 37:106, 49:70n, 53:57, 70f, 181, 221
34:1—4:133, 6:218, 7:124, 127, 315f, 10:162, 11:525, 40:319, 44:41
34:1f—5:18
34:2—5:228, 10:9, 163, 48:35
34:3—7:364, 11:265, 316, 25:24
34:4—2:307
34:5—4:267, 10:6
34:6—2:307
34:7—4:253, 5:61f, 6:41, 94, 245, 8:60, 12:125, 20:93n, 22:207, 30:224, 42:112
34:8—6:131, 152, 357, 21:302, 25:358, 48:36
34:9—25:252
34:9f—5:144
34:10—9:94, 14:196, 20:7, 117, 21:347
34:11—10:38, 323
34:12—49:196, 369
34:13f—30:100, 43:164
34:14—10:160, 18:31, 49:196, 369
34:15—10:99, 14:152
34:16—18:322
34:16–21—51:42
34:17—47:167
34:18—11:453, 468, 14:145, 27:26, 33:130, 44:78
34:19—2:307, 13:392, 14:161, 40:280
34:20—8:90
34:21—5:52, 25:311, 27:181, 42:140

34:22—29:138, 31:131, 44:25
Ps. 35—10:165–169, 13:ix
35:3—2:373
35:4—10:241
35:5f—10:59
35:8—25:425
35:10—11:300
35:15—10:40
35:16—3:197
35:17—17:186
35:18—10:103, 198
35:19—26:433
35:20—10:73
35:21—14:102, 226, 49:46
35:23—16:103n
35:28—52:36
Ps. 36—10:170–173, 13:ix, 17:392
36:1—10:277, 16:57, 83, 121, 25:269, 29:177
36:1f—16:207, 17:333, 34:71n
36:2—25:276, 40:8, 144, 45:58n
36:3—11:292
36:4—18:222, 25:329
36:5—6:391
36:6—10:4, 196, 11:4, 28:325, 348, 29:187
36:8—6:391, 8:249
36:11f—10:131
36:21—14:344
36:22—25:231
Ps. 37—8:49, 10:174–176, 13:ix, 14:211–230, 21:25, 29:239, 35:206n
37:2—5:144, 10:174, 17:391
37:3—10:174
37:5—7:246, 8:47, 21:164, 25:365, 49:271, 54:381
37:6—18:364, 21:164, 27:120
37:7—7:104, 133, 25:234, 25:365, 27:170
37:7f—10:311
37:9—10:175
37:10—10:174, 18:267
37:11—10:175
37:12f—10:174, 14:321
37:12–14—6:397
37:13f—48:220f, 50:266n
37:15—41:192, 205, 225, 343n, 351
37:16—5:66, 369, 14:134, 17:384, 45:245, 332
37:18—6:391, 10:175
37:19—2:289, 8:117, 177, 9:94, 13:399, 401, 15:171, 215, 21:207
37:20—40:66
37:21—36:357
37:21f—10:174f
37:22—21:22
37:23f—5:278
37:24—10:174, 428, 31:131
37:25—2:289, 5:12, 372, 9:94, 13:399, 21:207, 347, 28:323, 44:108, 45:48, 280
37:26—15:171
37:27—10:175, 16:18, 25:464, 26:265, 51:7f, 12
37:28—10:31, 175, 407, 18:267, 25:95
37:29—10:175
37:30—10:244, 14:199, 296
37:31—9:278, 11:145
37:32f—52:190
37:34—10:175, 21:22
37:35—14:291, 16:249, 259, 20:134, 21:341
37:35f—5:372, 18:267
37:36—17:44, 21:341
37:38—10:174
Ps. 38—10:177–182, 13:ix, 14:155–164, 15:173n, 25:258
38:3—10:179, 16:280, 31:99
38:4—27:342
38:5—10:177
38:6—6:160, 18:267
38:7—10:179, 30:25
38:9—8:71, 25:74
38:10—10:140, 11:108, 18:182
38:11—8:9, 10:453, 24:413, 25:289
38:17—31:225
38:18—25:258
Ps. 39—4:199, 10:183–187, 11:313, 13:ix, 103, 30:245, 48:67, 49:69n
39:2—11:19, 240, 407
39:3—10:205, 11:407
39:4—10:185, 11:205
39:4–12—10:183
39:5—10:185, 11:300, 25:362, 29:123, 33:75
39:6—5:368, 9:51n, 10:334, 13:103, 16:151, 27:220, 31:175, 42:125, 52:88
39:7—10:183
39:10–11—29:139
39:12—2:252, 281, 4:198, 206, 8:115, 10:183, 21:13, 30:249
39:13—7:25, 18:160
Ps. 40—10:188f, 11:36, 13:ix
40:1—11:472, 14:192
40:2—11:36, 148
40:5—11:26, 39
40:6—16:14, 18:166, 29:221
40:6f—47:304
40:6–8—29:221, 54:84
40:7—10:6, 52, 11:517, 30:286
40:7f—34:119
40:8—10:11, 14, 33, 22:138
40:8–11—51:42
40:9—11:36
40:10—11:400
40:10f—30:270
40:12—7:280, 8:263, 15:342, 25:102, 26:279, 30:280
40:14—10:241
40:17—42:153
Ps. 41—10:190–193, 13:ix, 21:101, 43:130
41:1—2:289, 5:261, 11:392, 31:57
41:1–3—43:128f
41:4—15:342, 24:105, 26:279, 28:211
41:5—11:121, 48:216
41:6–9—54:107
41:9—3:50f, 10:170, 14:235, 26:456
Ps. 42—10:194–204, 209, 13:ix
42:1—11:390, 15:9, 27:275, 38:128, 42:176, 52:162
42:1f—51:58
42:2—18:87
42:3—10:200, 27:275
42:4—10:197f, 200, 12:151, 14:90, 51:337
42:5—11:398, 18:100, 26:341, 38:109
42:6—5:203, 10:34, 197, 201, 203, 11:327, 16:127, 19:131, 223, 20:118, 22:422, 25:380, 27:177
42:7—10:20, 156, 201, 379, 13:346, 19:76
42:8—3:18n, 10:427, 29:176, 48:233
42:9—11:398
42:10—4:356, 11:398, 14:182n
42:11—10:195, 24:114
Ps. 43—1:295n, 13:ix, 29:176

43:1—10:408, 18:257
43:4—10:154, 265, 11:141
43:5—10:195, 11:475, 19:20, 147
Ps. 44—10:205–207, 11:193, 13:ix, 17:207, 29:150
44:1—10:205, 19:135, 228
44:1–3—11:26, 14:199
44:1–8—23:21
44:3—43:282
44:4–6—8:237
44:4–7—43:283
44:5—10:113, 249
44:6—8:299, 9:75, 170, 202, 10:249, 43:237, 45:331, 50:70n, 54:183
44:6f—46:191
44:7f—21:301
44:8—43:283
44:9—10:206, 11:193
44:10—10:205, 11:451
44:10f—11:194
44:13—11:194
44:15—10:386
44:17f—32:173
44:18—18:405
44:19—1:51n
44:22—1:323, 10:430, 11:190, 194, 19:184, 20:101, 25:77, 26:207, 27:134, 30:24, 31:225, 36:70, 50:18, 155, 54:276
44:23—2:222, 4:61, 133, 358, 7:176, 225, 14:197, 18:355, 34:240n
44:24—9:59, 11:22
44:42—49:248
Ps. 45—10:43, 208–223, 231, 12:130, 197–302, 13:ix, 233, 18:123, 45:321n
45:1—10:20, 210, 219, 255, 294, 399, 16:290, 25:267, 52:36
45:2—10:21, 209f, 215, 11:149, 365, 437, 18:123, 25:267, 326, 459, 27:184, 29:197
45:3—2:182, 11:387, 20:109, 32:168, 54:186
45:4—10:22, 34, 111, 221, 346, 420, 11:30, 551, 14:315, 20:104, 25:267, 437
45:5—11:217, 14:13, 19:18, 20:100, 200
45:6—8:240, 10:210, 11:292, 13:29, 267, 14:336, 20:315, 21:64, 25:405
45:6f—33:56
45:7—6:385, 10:210, 11:173, 12:148, 177, 13:29, 15:336, 20:208, 21:64, 22:117, 123, 25:65, 247, 32:190, 39:309, 48:72, 51:46, 52:4
45:8—25:265, 27:165, 366, 30:255, 40:20
45:9—10:76, 11:357, 18:302, 25:265, 36:200
45:10—2:250, 4:44, 46, 7:208, 8:22, 232, 10:204, 281, 12:368, 25:136, 243, 29:238, 44:327, 51:6, 54:323
45:10f—10:239, 22:42
45:11—2:250, 15:336
45:13—10:209, 42:147
45:14—10:91
45:15—29:192
45:16—11:95, 18:253, 25:281
45:17—11:22, 18:171
Ps. 46—13:ix, 53:283
46:1—11:364, 493, 514, 19:57, 43:171
46:2—12:14
46:3—11:119
46:4—10:20, 196, 201, 11:328
46:5—18:352, 46:10
46:7—11:369
46:8—11:37, 12:393
46:8f—11:5, 7
46:9—7:172, 18:12
46:10—6:35
Ps. 47—10:231, 13:ix
47:2—10:346
47:3—11:380
47:4—10:231
Ps. 48—8:296, 10:412, 13:ix
48:2—8:296, 10:436, 11:221, 327, 14:327, 35:291n
48:5—10:117
48:7—19:44
48:8—10:412
48:10—10:241, 11:411
48:19—29:176
Ps. 49—10:308, 13:ix
49:1—12:122
49:2—10:210, 12:122, 16:35
49:5—10:225
49:6—10:226, 25:150, 30:280
49:7—10:308, 18:286
49:9—10:255
49:10—15:44
49:11—22:193
49:11–13—18:383
49:12—16:71
49:14—6:120
49:15—53:328
49:18—10:159f, 11:371, 404, 21:307, 310, 27:374
49:18f—11:70
49:20—18:196
Ps. 50—10:230–234, 13:ix, 15:284, 29:176
50:1—10:230, 15:336
50:2—10:329
50:3—11:119
50:7—54:75
50:7–14—52:276
50:8—4:265, 12:361, 399, 17:285, 396
50:8f—22:428
50:8–14—14:33
50:8–15—51:42
50:9—7:322
50:9–12—12:397
50:10—17:398
50:12—20:78
50:13—5:258, 260, 16:14, 19:81, 20:78
50:14—6:237, 8:294, 9:238, 14:95, 15:82, 19:21, 82, 29:176, 36:146, 43:77, 44:46, 46:148, 153
50:15—2:307, 3:328, 4:58, 336, 361, 5:79, 7:246, 320, 369, 8:275, 11:236f, 12:393, 16:215, 341, 17:359, 18:288, 20:268, 304, 40:277, 287, 43:226, 250, 44:46, 46:34, 47:167, 51:142, 171, 52:199, 53:139, 169f
50:16—9:3, 10:463, 38:313
50:16–20—13:64
50:22—18:199
50:23—10:239, 241, 11:263, 14:35, 51, 16:70, 19:21, 29:176, 36:146, 38:106, 40:277, 46:149
Ps. 51—3:45, 117n, 6:43, 10:235–243, 12:303–410, 13:ix, 14:33, 165–176, 22:399, 25:26, 212, 28:306, 43:41, 47:172, 49:70, 53:221
51:1—6:108, 7:272,

280, 360, 8:332, 9:291n, 11:388, 16:16, 26:385, 34:316, 320, 43:232
51:1-5—25:273
51:2—25:264, 274
51:3—1:241, 10:240, 14:161, 18:262, 25:62, 206, 214, 247, 257, 259, 274, 34:176, 42:102
51:4—1:181, 277, 5:157, 170, 7:228, 275, 279f, 10:144, 163, 233, 235, 317, 350, 11:262, 522, 529, 17:283, 22:402, 468f, 23:249, 25:26f, 29, 102, 200f, 204, 210f, 214, 217, 257, 259, 26:131, 29:152, 30:230, 31:194, 34:117, 35:373, 36:355, 37:296, 38:293n, 306, 43:228, 232, 54:457
51:5—4:70, 239, 7:31, 10:146, 163, 235, 12:154, 13:95, 15:325, 17:271, 296, 22:138, 23:79, 25:273, 32:211, 33:174, 35:31, 36:354, 37:363, 41:84, 43:26, 40, 44:376, 45:49, 47:148, 52:15, 152, 53:66f
51:6—10:236, 25:62, 214, 278
51:7—5:380, 8:153, 10:331, 29:208, 30:7, 41:216, 45:226n
51:8—10:294, 11:300, 389, 14:201
51:9—10:112, 12:321, 25:273
51:10—7:153, 155, 243, 8:212, 13:139, 21:303, 23:180, 25:346, 26:380, 27:405, 29:152, 31:97, 32:23, 39:35, 44:240, 53:124, 135
51:11—8:237, 34:117
51:12—4:63, 10:325, 11:367, 527, 13:136
51:13—11:30, 36, 17:328, 25:273, 27:185, 39:310
51:14—11:36, 121, 16:20, 25:215, 27:185, 44:40
51:15—10:244, 11:36, 25:215, 338
51:16—25:338
51:17—3:236, 6:110, 7:217, 11:5, 281, 12:316, 14:94, 145, 198, 16:59, 25:247, 338, 378, 27:26, 30:235, 31:85, 89, 36:146, 40:209
51:18—6:173, 8:224, 10:325, 27:174, 52:276
51:18f—51:42
51:19—3:242, 10:136, 11:141, 17:398, 49:340, 52:276
51:21—18:74
Ps. 52—10:244–246, 13:ix
52:2—3:193, 16:86, 34:32
52:4—27:360
52:9—10:252
Ps. 53—10:247f, 13:ix, 27:181, 29:116
53:2—11:171, 12:325
53:3—12:325
53:4f—53:334
53:5—9:268n, 11:384, 16:83, 25:178, 28:311, 36:166, 40:361
Ps. 54—10:249–253, 13:ix
54:1—10:252, 11:209
54:3—29:177
54:4—7:274
54:4f—10:252
54:6—10:14, 33, 44:47
54:7—2:9, 14:226, 18:245, 273, 44:47
Ps. 55—10:254–258, 13:ix, 21:101
55:2—34:311
55:4f—29:139
55:10—10:97, 255f
55:13—10:170
55:13f—23:188
55:15—27:46
55:17—10:305
55:19—10:75
55:20f—11:56
55:22—8:47, 94, 14:127, 222, 17:299, 18:392, 42:154, 43:172, 174, 45:333, 49:259, 50:306
55:23—10:269, 11:315, 12:91, 15:141, 16:67, 140, 221, 18:291, 333, 29:163, 30:172, 31:132, 45:255, 49:398n
Ps. 56—10:153, 259–263, 265, 13:ix
56:7—10:260
56:8—1:288, 5:276, 278, 6:23, 124, 7:138, 8:90
56:11—10:262
Ps. 57—10:264–266, 273, 13:ix
57:1—10:259, 11:98, 25:314
57:4—10:94, 165, 13:204, 14:216, 27:360, 51:16
57:6—25:231
57:10—35:210
Ps. 58—10:267–271, 273, 13:ix, 35:209
58:1—25:314
58:2f—10:267
58:4—10:301, 21:333, 31:373, 32:215, 44:251
58:4f—37:270
58:5—9:175, 21:333
58:6—25:231
58:8—28:83, 43:247
58:9—15:114, 35:206n, 209f
58:10—10:419, 35:297, 42:156
58:11—13:182, 54:28
Ps. 59—10:272–279, 13:ix
59:1—6:13, 25:314
59:6-17—10:279
59:8—50:266n
59:10f—11:360
59:11—10:273, 427
59:13—12:131, 15:345
Ps. 60—10:280–297, 11:121, 124, 13:ix, 189
60:1—10:259, 273, 288, 357, 434, 11:42, 25:179, 314
60:3—10:288, 19:221, 20:132
60:4f—10:285
60:6—2:353, 5:84, 10:284, 421, 13:167, 189, 29:4, 41:225, 54:21
60:7—8:150, 296
60:8—4:365, 10:463, 11:450, 33:200n
60:10-12—46:191
60:11—10:289
60:11f—25:149
60:12—9:170
Ps. 61—13:ix
61:2—34:311
61:4—10:298
61:5—49:355n
Ps. 62—10:298–301, 13:ix, 14:231–242, 44:269f, 49:355
62:1f—10:313, 36:137
62:3—36:137
62:3f—52:271
62:5-7—36:137
62:8—10:200, 39:31, 43:176
62:9—10:300, 11:149, 17:84, 33:75
62:10—2:328, 398,

3:248, 4:380f, 9:71, 95, 21:192, 28:378, 44:108
62:11—18:161
Ps. 63—10:302–306, 13:ix
63:1—10:306, 14:182, 200, 300
63:1f—11:449
63:2—10:306, 11:272
63:3—11:315, 449, 44:304
63:4—36:53
63:5—10:111, 304, 35:206n, 212
63:6—11:457
63:7—11:109, 25:265, 29:167
63:9—10:439
63:10—11:356
63:11—4:245, 5:185, 7:248, 10:143, 16:165, 45:103
Ps. 64—10:307–312, 11:505, 13:ix, 36:78n, 41:252f, 343n, 43:256, 285
64:1—18:360
64:3—29:174
64:5—33:111n
64:6–8—10:309f
64:8–10—10:308
64:9—10:128, 131, 132, 310, 318
Ps. 65—10:313–316, 13:ix
65:1—25:234
65:2—10:316
65:3—14:157, 16:26
65:4—10:316, 42:103n
65:4f—10:61, 11:236
65:5—10:316
65:6—5:27
65:7—6:243, 18:334, 20:114
65:8—10:338, 11:288, 35:206n, 212f
65:9—7:353
65:11—10:258
65:12—19:143
65:13—10:316, 11:328
Ps. 66—10:317–323, 13:ix
66:3—40:129
66:5—9:21
66:6—25:12
66:8—8:112
66:11f—10:320
66:12—17:86, 30:126, 32:95
66:13f—46:153
66:14—10:205
66:15—11:336
66:16—11:36
66:16–20—6:235
66:20—4:267
Ps. 67—13:ix, 35:206n, 43:41, 53:232
67:1—6:172, 10:324, 31:377, 42:21n
67:1–4—44:251
67:2—31:377
67:4—25:516
67:6f—53:30, 232
67:7—10:346
67:14—27:392
Ps. 68—10:324–350, 11:272, 13:ix, 1–37, 19:230, 25:97, 35:206n, 213f
68:1—13:3, 16:47
68:2—10:456, 13:3
68:3—10:162, 11:260, 334, 13:4
68:4—13:4
68:5—9:112, 12:184, 13:6, 195, 24:131, 31:305, 42:156n, 44:269, 45:355
68:6—11:68, 541, 13:7, 21:305, 52:34
68:7—13:8, 42:21n
68:7–10—19:134
68:8—10:324, 13:9
68:9—10:79, 179, 251, 331, 13:9, 20:198n, 25:392
68:10—11:329, 13:11, 29:183
68:11—13:12, 16:76, 53:126, 145
68:12—10:210, 11:285, 393, 13:13, 20, 18:52, 30:12, 35:214, 40:57, 46:221n
68:13—2:157, 8:278, 10:103, 11:327, 13:14, 25:479, 29:185, 35:206n, 214
68:14—10:37, 11:98, 13:15
68:15—10:171, 13:17
68:16—13:18, 20:21
68:17—13:ix, 19
68:18—10:345, 13:ix, 20, 241, 25:311, 26:155, 371, 27:171, 32:206, 35:216f, 41:154n
68:19—13:21
68:20—1:197, 2:156, 13:22, 19:57, 25:311
68:21—13:23, 18:185
68:22—10:198, 13:24
68:23—10:188, 12:29, 13:24
68:24—11:30, 103, 13:25
68:25—10:359, 13:26, 18:303, 45:208n
68:26—11:372, 13:27
68:27—13:27, 20:293
68:28—13:29, 15:236, 254
68:29—13:30
68:30—7:150, 13:30, 16:147, 35:206n, 211, 40:312, 46:118, 120
68:31—10:345, 13:33
68:32—13:33
68:33—8:244, 13:34
68:34—13:35
68:35—5:186, 10:102, 239, 346, 463, 11:236, 13:36, 19:92n, 25:246, 258, 277, 379, 29:135, 240, 31:135, 33:295n, 36:187, 44:268, 291
Ps. 69—10:351–384, 13:ix
69:1—10:351
69:1f—19:146
69:1–3—10:382, 22:283
69:3—27:397
69:4—7:301, 24:286, 27:182, 32:200
69:4f—10:383
69:5—10:363, 15:342, 25:521, 26:279, 32:200
69:6—10:363
69:7—10:390, 25:521
69:8—10:363
69:9—9:216, 10:365, 370, 390, 11:74, 15:342, 22:229, 25:119, 26:187, 28:211, 31:302, 32:200
69:10—27:389
69:11—18:182
69:12—10:367
69:13—10:258, 367
69:14—10:363, 383
69:15—10:363
69:16—10:382, 27:279
69:20—10:357
69:21—12:115
69:22—3:37, 16:113, 20:45
69:22f—25:97
69:23—10:376, 386
69:24—10:376, 378
69:25—10:376
69:26—29:140, 31:122
69:27f—34:101
69:28—9:251, 11:22
69:29—10:381
69:30f—14:157
Ps. 70—10:385–394, 13:ix
70:1—43:199n, 51:171n
70:2—8:299, 10:241, 387, 389
70:3—10:387
70:5—10:393
Ps. 71—10:395–402, 13:ix, 25:511, 27:312
71:1—10:395, 29:188

71:2—10:395, 11:148
71:3—10:396
71:8—11:525
71:15—10:399
71:17—10:399, 29:113
71:19—10:403
71:20—31:128
71:20f—18:223
71:24—10:241
Ps. 72—10:403–414, 13:ix, 29:148
72:1—9:49, 27:241
72:2—10:190, 403
72:3—11:312, 331
72:4—10:403, 408, 14:307
72:5—11:172
72:7—10:417, 11:368, 25:285, 27:241
72:8—8:304, 10:4, 11:259, 20:24, 96, 289, 29:125
72:8-11—45:215
72:9—10:349, 11:126
72:10—14:14, 19:9, 43
72:10f—10:37
72:11—13:235
72:12f—9:238
72:14—1:253, 25:275, 313, 32:266, 51:245
72:15—10:412
72:16—10:134, 11:287, 497, 12:163, 14:179, 18:252
72:17—14:184, 29:113
Ps. 73—2:351, 10:415–430, 13:ix, 103, 29:239
73:1—10:417, 42:158
73:2—2:307, 10:117, 311, 415, 417, 15:75
73:2f—19:180, 29:239, 32:226, 42:158
73:3—2:307, 10:417, 25:286, 27:170
73:3-5—21:241
73:3-6—2:346
73:4—10:422, 426
73:4f—2:33
73:5—8:5, 10:56, 390, 426, 21:17
73:5f—28:20
73:6—10:390, 422, 426
73:7—10:112, 174, 390, 422, 11:304
73:8—10:422
73:9—10:390, 423
73:10—10:419, 422
73:11—2:222, 10:422f
73:12—33:291, 34:358n, 42:158
73:13—6:306
73:14—2:196, 346, 10:427, 21:242, 30:272
73:15—42:161
73:16f—10:8, 311, 14:250
73:16-20—21:341
73:18—6:304–306, 375, 7:359, 10:51, 415, 18:333, 19:181
73:19f—13:103
73:20—10:334, 428
73:22—2:347, 29:148
73:22f—33:65, 66n
73:23—10:430, 12:69
73:25—51:216
73:25f—7:336
73:26—25:449
73:27—10:430
73:28—29:231, 42:158
Ps. 74—10:431–454, 13:ix, 47:183
74:1—10:292, 433
74:2—11:22
74:3—10:435f, 452
74:4—3:164
74:4f—10:453, 462
74:5—4:136, 16:115, 43:160n
74:6—10:453
74:7f—10:434
74:8—3:164, 10:443, 44:319
74:11—25:152
74:13—10:447, 21:333
74:13f—10:448
74:14—1:51n, 323, 10:448
74:16—10:447
74:17—10:25
74:19—10:449, 11:22
74:20—10:438, 449
74:22—32:x
74:23—10:301, 439
Ps. 75—10:273, 455–464, 13:ix
75:2—11:505
75:5—10:144, 456, 14:247
75:6—10:457
75:8—10:106, 109, 273, 458, 461, 13:345, 18:310
75:9—19:219n
75:10—10:113
Ps. 76—11:3–9, 339, 13:ix, 43:256, 284–288
76:1—8:292, 11:6
76:2—13:20, 84
76:4—11:258, 14:133, 18:304, 19:172, 204, 20:184, 43:288n, 46:178
76:4f—11:31
76:5—6:242, 7:172, 10:334, 11:324, 13:103, 21:174, 346, 25:479, 43:286n
76:6—6:242, 10:334
76:8—43:261
76:10—11:9, 22, 57, 14:307
76:11—5:261, 44:298, 303, 309, 311n, 337, 342, 46:153, 48:297, 52:260
76:12—6:41, 7:172, 371, 11:9, 31, 13:404, 19:213, 43:287n, 45:329
Ps. 77—11:10–37, 73, 313, 13:ix, 18:96, 167, 22:396, 29:137, 140, 163, 236, 48:293, 49:69n
77:2—11:17, 238
77:3—11:22, 44:274n
77:3-6—11:18f
77:7f—43:51
77:10—10:41, 11:17, 26:377
77:11—11:14, 23, 39, 15:206, 17:355, 18:287, 42:131
77:11f—11:11, 14, 340, 19:226, 29:150
77:12—11:12, 14
77:13—11:26, 32
77:14—11:13
77:15—8:149, 11:95
77:16—11:324
77:16-20—18:287
77:19—7:103, 10:316, 11:27, 13:136, 22:311, 31:101, 38:22, 44:268f
77:20—11:34, 29:168
Ps. 78—10:38–89, 11:10, 23, 118, 13:ix, 18:167
78:1—10:210, 11:44
78:2—10:92, 11:44
78:3—11:45, 50
78:4—11:45, 47, 50
78:5—11:39, 45, 11:47, 16:344, 27:187
78:5f—44:83, 45:353
78:5-8—51:137
78:6—11:45
78:7—11:11
78:8—8:200, 11:46, 47, 22:396, 42:80
78:9—14:344, 19:142, 233, 42:79, 53:170
78:10—11:50
78:10f—42:79
78:11f—11:51
78:12—29:124
78:18—11:59, 18:167, 32:171
78:18f—7:308, 8:32
78:19f—8:185

78:20—10:202, 11:552
78:21—11:56
78:23—29:183
78:27—11:57
78:31—25:395, 27:375, 33:86, 48:153, 52:113
78:33—1:243, 2:310, 8:185, 11:300, 14:179
78:34—11:297, 18:96, 354
78:36—27:374
78:36f—9:92, 10:92
78:37—11:69, 21:303
78:39—11:192, 52:81
78:43—29:124
78:45—14:123n
78:47—11:473
78:51—18:104
78:57—11:42, 217, 289, 386, 17:171
78:63f—10:326
78:64—11:87, 37:320
78:66—14:66, 53:26
78:67f—8:300, 42:103n
78:68f—2:101
78:69—10:113
78:70—13:243
78:70f—14:51
78:72—12:307
Ps. 79—11:90–94, 13:ix, 35:206n, 43:41, 231
79:1—18:213
79:4—18:41
79:6—19:93
79:7—10:248, 11:148, 19:183, 20:102
79:8—11:94, 43:231n
79:9—18:112, 43:231n
79:10—1:288, 11:94, 43:233
79:11—12:203, 208
79:11f—11:94
79:13—10:457
Ps. 80—11:95–100, 277, 12:202, 13:ix, 25:271, 31:226
80:1—13:34, 29:199
80:2—11:296, 11:95
80:3—9:294, 11:107, 296, 299, 18:230, 52:129
80:5—42:138
80:7—11:296
80:8—18:300
80:9—43:287
80:10—2:342, 5:336, 11:335
80:11—18:300
80:12—11:99f
80:12f—32:x
80:13—11:98, 339, 25:271
80:14—7:302, 11:99
80:15—7:302, 8:295
80:16—11:99
80:17—7:302, 8:295, 20:52
80:19—11:296
Ps. 81—11:101–109, 139, 13:ix
81:2—11:102
81:6—25:322, 341, 31:144
81:6f—7:72
81:7—11:237, 25:370
81:8—20:213, 29:145, 51:111, 115
81:8f—30:246
81:10—10:87, 14:331, 25:412, 30:45, 51:111, 115
81:11f—41:130, 47:161
81:12—2:26, 38, 10:33, 275, 11:14, 200, 12:382, 20:313, 31:66, 34:216
Ps. 82—11:110–117, 13:xf, 39–72, 146, 19:355n
82:1—13:44, 34:223
82:1–8—13:41
82:2—6:122, 13:51
82:2–4—44:51, 45:278
82:3—13:57
82:4—11:114, 13:58
82:5—11:114, 13:67, 29:72, 44:51
82:6—1:12, 2:390, 4:81, 5:124, 9:162n, 13:69, 21:297, 23:184, 27:181, 333, 34:223, 41:81n, 43:62, 52:157
82:6f—54:36
82:7—10:438, 13:71, 32:182
82:8—8:208, 10:408, 13:72
Ps. 83—11:118–135, 13:ix
83:1—17:380
83:1–8—21:259
83:4—16:24, 18:322, 40:208
83:5–8—6:389
83:6–8—52:115
83:7—11:109
83:9f—16:66
83:10—20:303
83:16—10:79, 11:133
Ps. 84—10:136–151, 11:139, 13:ix
84:1—16:345, 29:128, 177
84:3—11:94, 336
84:4—44:40
84:6—2:282, 25:300, 30:187
84:7—25:246
84:8—25:153
84:10—11:142, 146, 315, 34:129n
Ps. 85—11:152–174, 13:ix
85:1f—11:164
85:3—10:379
85:3–8—11:164
85:5—17:238
85:8—10:419, 11:183, 389, 19:137, 24:156, 419, 52:286
85:9—11:153, 29:171
85:9–13—11:164
85:10—8:121, 10:417, 11:368, 15:238, 256, 25:285, 27:170, 29:189, 42:89
85:11—25:209
85:12—11:153
85:13—11:209
Ps. 86—11:175f, 13:ix
86:2—30:32, 31:62, 54:70
86:4—18:21, 28:271
86:5—25:412, 30:235
86:15—11:378, 35:16n
86:16—7:292
86:17—3:30n, 7:292
Ps. 87—11:176–186, 13:ix, 17:104
87:1—11:115, 185, 326
87:1f—17:321
87:2—10:96, 11:185
87:3—11:185
87:4—7:345, 10:349, 11:22, 185, 389, 16:255, 20:113, 126
87:6—11:159
87:6f—11:186f
Ps. 88—11:187f, 13:ix, 49:69n
88:1—17:173
88:2—19:198n, 32:x
88:3—19:198n, 29:139, 31:128, 48:367
88:4—11:114
88:5—25:228
88:6—10:84, 19:198n
88:7—26:290, 317
88:8—11:114
88:9—19:198n
88:10–12—11:187f
88:13—11:253
88:15—19:198n
88:16—26:290, 317
88:25—19:198n
88:34—19:198n
88:50—19:198n
Ps. 89—11:189–194, 13:ix, 47:199
89:1—20:115
89:1–4—47:199
89:2—15:346
89:4—22:31, 45:215
89:4f—52:30
89:4–52—47:78
89:6—11:118, 14:330
89:7—11:372, 25:75
89:10—20:135

89:14—10:295, 406, 11:172, 12:55
89:15—11:299
89:17—10:328, 27:104, 29:146, 32:181
89:18—14:324, 19:178
89:19—11:212, 47:199
89:22—42:160
89:26—3:27, 10:322, 14:259
89:27—3:27, 14:324
89:29—17:415, 45:215
89:30—2:223
89:30-33—2:257, 31:91
89:32—2:223, 32:33, 64
89:33—11:190
89:35—4:150, 11:368, 29:152
89:35-37—47:206
89:36f—45:215
89:38-46—11:189
89:42f—11:194
89:47f—3:302, 48:215, 52:142
89:48—10:227, 11:193, 32:186
89:49—11:193
89:50—11:192
Ps. 90—4:195, 6:189, 7:181, 11:195-207, 313, 13:ix, xi, 73-141
90:1—13:83, 85, 87, 25:286
90:1-5a—11:197
90:2—11:195, 314, 13:91, 18:248
90:3—11:196f, 13:94, 105, 22:28, 30
90:3f—11:192
90:4—11:195, 299, 13:99, 17:239, 30:114, 196, 35:392n
90:5—6:335, 7:320, 11:196, 13:102, 133, 16:232n
90:6—11:198, 297, 303, 13:102
90:7—13:106, 130
90:8—7:228, 12:350, 13:116, 46:22
90:9—11:200, 217, 13:118, 133
90:10—2:304, 6:189, 12:185, 13:120, 18:159, 221, 19:108, 140, 159, 20:183, 28:240, 44:27n
90:11—13:78, 124
90:12—13:78, 126
90:13—13:130, 134f, 18:133
90:14—13:132, 136
90:15—13:133
90:16—13:134
90:17—13:137
Ps. 91—11:208-228, 13:ix, 367, 49:270
91:1—8:152, 10:338, 25:286
91:1-7—52:97
91:3—11:362, 18:270, 25:352, 424
91:4—25:286, 29:167, 52:98
91:5—11:255
91:5f—11:199, 446, 32:117, 35:206n, 216
91:5-8—11:224
91:6—10:28, 274, 11:148, 289f, 502, 18:72, 31:206
91:7—3:223, 4:107, 11:224, 230, 255, 12:30, 17:84, 42:73, 44:47
91:8—12:30, 13:416f, 14:226, 252, 18:273
91:8f—12:43
91:9—35:206n, 218
91:10—10:149
91:11—4:107, 253, 5:62, 6:41, 246, 11:211, 17:357, 20:16
91:11f—1:107, 22:207
91:11-13—43:129
91:11-16—42:112
91:13—8:94, 167, 251, 10:340, 16:129, 25:417, 30:261, 34:104n, 41:178, 359, 49:113n
91:14—30:246, 44:47
91:14-16—14:228, 43:173
91:15—5:77, 10:258, 11:237, 44:78, 46:34, 50:311n, 51:172
91:16—4:58
Ps. 92—11:229-234, 13:ix
92:2—10:203, 427, 11:217, 229, 29:194
92:3—11:233
92:3f—10:311
92:4—10:122, 11:229, 13:367, 42:146
92:4f—10:128
92:5—11:230
92:5f—11:227, 236
92:6—10:369, 11:229
92:7—2:196, 11:198, 229f, 233
92:11—2:9
92:12—10:134, 11:229, 232f, 302, 14:299
92:13—10:22, 17:241n
92:14—35:206n, 218f
92:14f—29:186
Ps. 93—10:75, 202, 11:235-241, 13:ix
93:1—10:138, 11:387, 394, 33:139n
93:4—10:155, 201f, 11:235, 19:18, 48:153
93:19—6:99
Ps. 94—11:242-251, 13:ix, 14:243-256
94:2—11:243
94:3—2:180
94:4—11:250
94:5—11:243
94:5f—11:251
94:7—11:242
94:9—11:245, 249, 345
94:11—7:138, 18:254, 25:365, 31:66, 33:99, 45:329, 48:332
94:12—27:368, 42:184n
94:12f—11:236
94:13—27:368
94:14—11:256, 25:95
94:16—11:251
94:17—16:72, 31:128
94:19—11:236, 16:116
94:21—8:289
Ps. 95—11:252-259, 399, 13:ix
95:1—10:43
95:2—11:260
95:3—10:33
95:4f—11:257
95:5—14:304
95:6f—12:100
95:7—13:79, 26:437
95:7-9—11:60, 72
95:7-11—29:147
95:8—25:192
95:10—4:78, 9:125, 18:167, 25:257, 29:151, 47:166
95:10f—25:192
95:11—1:80, 4:150, 9:23, 19:141
Ps. 96—11:260-266, 13:ix
96:1—17:305, 53:332f
96:6—10:239, 350, 13:136, 29:143, 51:18
96:10—9:83n, 27:206
96:12—10:442, 20:184
96:13—10:83, 407, 14:307, 27:242, 44:396
Ps. 97—10:267-269, 13:ix
97:1—17:305, 25:516, 29:115
97:2—10:31, 295, 407, 11:263, 267, 548, 29:115
97:3—29:115

97:6—29:115, 51:19n
97:7—11:268, 399, 15:337
97:8—11:282, 25:355
97:9—11:268, 17:305
97:10—11:283, 29:116
97:11—11:263, 18:272
Ps. 98—11:270–276, 13:ix
98:1f—17:212
98:3—11:268
98:5—10:329, 11:285
98:5f—11:287, 294
98:9—2:62, 10:76, 95, 407f, 11:292
Ps. 99—11:277f, 13:ix
99:4—10:21, 237, 407
99:5—11:361, 37:123n
Ps. 100—13:ix
100:2—11:260, 264, 14:343
100:3—3:35, 4:62, 13:214, 33:235, 34:114
Ps. 101—2:226, 9:19n, 11:276, 279–294, 13:x, 143–224, 15:345, 34:271
101:1—13:147
101:2—22:289
101:2-4—13:166
101:3—13:177
101:4—13:184, 25:346
101:5—10:277, 13:193, 201, 208, 35:262n
101:6—13:213, 14:288
101:7—11:173, 208, 13:217
101:8—13:220
Ps. 102—4:299, 10:200, 11:295–315, 13:ix, 14:177–188, 15:338
102:2—11:295
102:3—11:299, 313, 11:535
102:3–5—11:302
102:4—11:299, 29:153
102:5—11:319
102:6—14:198
102:7—11:139, 296
102:8—25:289
102:9—11:309
102:10f—11:299
102:11—13:103
102:12–14—11:313
102:13—10:258
102:16—11:313
102:21—27:221
102:21f—35:105, 53:11
102:23f—11:315
102:24—11:314
102:25f—6:189, 8:66, 15:337
102:26—13:103, 16:37, 23:22, 25:73, 50:245
102:27—11:68
Ps. 103—1:236n, 18:359, 35:206n, 43:41, 49:70, 53:221
103:1—8:112
103:5—3:323, 11:343, 15:9, 18:220
103:6—9:49, 41:256n, 43:240
103:7—9:51, 29:185, 47:165, 52:131
103:8—3:283, 11:378, 18:97
103:9—12:77, 43:54
103:10—43:231n, 53:168
103:11—25:365
103:11f—10:403
103:14—10:392, 11:192, 12:342, 20:124
103:14f—25:366
103:15—3:159, 12:122
103:17—10:329
103:19—11:192
Ps. 104—11:316–344, 19:82, 43:31n
104:1—10:239, 11:326, 20:70n, 255, 33:139n
104:2—1:26, 11:326, 357, 475
104:3—11:318, 29:116, 33:139n
104:4—1:236, 4:129, 5:216, 16:70, 20:248, 37:298f, 301
104:5—10:188
104:6—11:326
104:7—9:155
104:8—5:57, 6:94
104:10—10:331
104:12—11:334, 53:322
104:13—11:340
104:15—4:15, 277, 10:414, 13:216, 15:197, 214, 22:6, 27:318, 35:53, 110, 36:91, 42:52
104:16f—2:342
104:17—11:336, 20:59n
104:18—11:339
104:19—18:362
104:22f—12:122, 15:14
104:23—15:88
104:24—11:316, 326, 341, 42:146
104:25—19:184, 42:74n
104:26—1:51n, 8:225, 10:448, 14:327n
104:27f—28:19, 45:326n
104:27–30—13:16
104:29—25:424
104:31—25:311, 46:246
104:32—10:121, 19:11
Ps. 105—5:26, 43:31n
105:3—4:162, 27:104, 48:35
105:4—14:196, 25:225, 252
105:6f—7:348
105:12–15—2:306
105:13—17:33
105:14—3:330, 18:359, 370
105:15—20:30, 36:150
105:17—6:343, 397, 8:34
105:17f—8:57
105:18—7:202, 52:119
105:18–20—7:133
105:20–22—8:129f
105:21—6:401
105:21f—7:136
105:22—7:152, 163, 200, 347, 349, 8:135f, 47:85, 158
105:31—14:123
105:37—16:125, 20:327, 32:30
105:40—18:167, 32:171
105:45—25:252
Ps. 106—11:345f, 43:31n
106:3—11:237, 31:96, 42:42, 51:98
106:4—10:258
106:4f—42:103n
106:6—53:169
106:7—11:23
106:8—19:82n
106:13—6:353, 8:32, 200f, 25:366, 29:149, 236, 42:51
106:20—14:237, 18:21
106:21—7:348
106:23—29:140, 44:69n
106:24—25:366, 29:137, 163, 42:146
106:24f—6:353
106:26—9:103, 20:198
106:27—48:293
106:28—48:315
106:34—11:329
106:37—36:224, 40:242, 244
106:37f—7:300f, 16:331, 51:105
106:38—18:244
106:39—6:129n
Ps. 107—11:347–353, 28:261f
107:1—43:176
107:2—11:37

107:4—15:165
107:6—11:351
107:6f—3:328
107:9—52:85
107:10—37:259n, 52:119
107:11—2:310, 8:30, 25:438
107:18—29:153
107:20—14:123, 27:164, 31:346, 33:140, 36:39n
107:26—10:372
107:27—3:8, 6:102f, 136, 225, 7:246, 16:163, 17:203, 18:198, 29:235, 42:61
107:32—11:372
107:33f—8:108, 10:23
107:34—1:78, 99, 18:343
107:39—11:487
107:40—18:309, 45:116n, 46:19, 22
107:42—10:143
107:43—13:385, 15:202
Ps. 108—13:189, 17:380n, 29:140
108:1—3:283
108:7—13:167
108:10–12—9:170
Ps. 109—11:353–358, 14:257–278, 46:10
109:1—17:340
109:1f—10:380
109:2—11:354
109:2f—7:92, 25:4
109:3—11:355
109:3f—26:388
109:4—2:50, 11:355, 26:223, 27:182, 30:275, 50:267
109:6—11:355, 369, 20:207, 321, 34:101
109:7—4:55, 11:356, 20:269, 24:394, 396, 32:163, 42:66, 43:41, 281, 52:272
109:8—9:49, 17:323
109:8f—11:356
109:10—1:294
109:11—2:262
109:13—14:228, 18:322
109:14—17:380
109:16—9:251, 11:238, 49:172
109:17—10:260, 14:30, 16:92, 20:236, 43:67, 46:72, 48:252, 52:99
109:17f—15:326
109:18—11:353, 47:216
109:19—11:357
109:20—11:353, 13:134, 17:340, 50:267n
109:21—26:329, 33:136
109:22—11:357
109:24—17:141n
109:28—11:353, 27:262, 39:20, 40:16, 361
Ps. 110—4:150, 172, 11:359–370, 13:xii, 225–348, 18:241, 35:206n, 43:31n
110:1—4:174, 6:338, 11:110, 12:132, 134, 285, 13:230, 246, 14:321, 325, 15:294f, 16:75, 18:241, 22:493, 498, 25:5, 102, 28:128, 132, 136f, 29:120, 34:226, 35:249n, 37:50n, 73n, 145n, 43:241n, 45:212, 46:236, 49:369, 371f, 50:216, 52:278, 281, 54:389
110:2—5:240, 8:244, 10:210, 252, 436, 11:180, 341, 508, 12:38, 108, 293, 13:264, 273, 14:13, 336, 16:31, 17:322, 18:274, 20:200, 315, 25:91, 26:24, 27:43, 318, 391, 29:118, 39:150, 180, 48:13, 49:375
110:2f—25:413
110:3—1:10, 7:325, 10:13, 397f, 11:498, 13:10, 284, 297, 17:72, 18:226, 29:190, 39:180, 45:93, 213n, 361n
110:4—2:384, 387, 393, 4:150, 8:196, 9:182, 11:393, 13:304, 307, 309, 15:58, 120, 24:243, 25:435, 31:388, 35:99f, 38:187, 39:81, 40:19, 47:83, 206, 52:279, 281
110:5—13:335, 25:176
110:6—2:16, 11:370, 13:341, 14:307, 16:32, 18:307, 355, 25:215
110:7—2:156, 10:106, 11:36, 370, 13:344, 52:281
Ps. 111—11:371–384, 13:xii, 349–387, 38:94f, 43:31n, 53:137, 181–183
111:1—13:356, 363, 27:281
111:1(2)—13:365
111:2—10:22, 11:316, 553, 13:357, 21:348, 25:311, 367, 42:114
111:2(3)—13:366
111:2(4)—13:366
111:3—10:23, 239, 241, 11:4, 13:358, 27:270, 29:143, 31:108, 37:73, 39:28, 42:36, 46:246n, 47:194, 49:262, 51:18, 52:96
111:3(5)—13:368
111:3(6)—13:369
111:4—13:359, 29:201
111:4(7)—13:371
111:4(8)—13:373
111:4–5—35:105, 110
111:5—10:377, 11:389, 13:359
111:5(9)—13:376
111:5(10)—13:377
111:6—11:28, 13:359
111:6(11)—13:377
111:6(12)—13:378
111:7—7:157, 10:83, 310, 13:360, 21:348, 32:26
111:7(13)—13:378
111:7(14)—13:380
111:8—13:360
111:8(15)—13:380
111:8(16)—13:381
111:9—10:63, 13:361
111:9(17)—13:382
111:9(18)—13:382
111:9(19)—13:384
111:10—13:362, 396, 14:307, 31:99, 40:276
111:10(20)—13:385
111:10(21)—13:386
111:10(22)—13:286
111:12—36:45f
Ps. 112—13:xi, 389–420, 43:31n
112:1—10:14, 33, 11:145, 384–389, 25:334, 377, 31:205, 34:127, 40:208, 319, 54:136
112:1f—14:225
112:2—11:316, 332, 13:398f
112:3—13:400, 402, 27:270, 32:236, 52:96
112:4—11:378, 13:402, 404f, 15:179, 18:272
112:5—11:525, 13:406, 410, 16:44
112:6—10:332, 13:412, 16:80, 29:233
112:6–8—14:226
112:7—2:289, 7:335, 13:414, 416,

25:92, 29:208, 31:127, 32:32
112:7–8—7:333, 39:188
112:8—7:336, 10:117, 13:416
112:9—10:113, 13:418, 52:96
112:10—10:23, 124, 13:419, 14:63, 25:97, 48:308, 51:18
Ps. 113—11:30, 390–392, 43:31n
113:1—10:241
113:2—11:390
113:4—14:321, 25:122
113:5—21:299
113:5f—51:14f, 54:xviii
113:5–8—7:166, 8:103, 46:250
113:6—5:354, 21:299, 317
113:7—11:391, 12:316
113:7f—7:142, 8:57, 11:391
113:8f—11:392
Ps. 114—11:30, 393–395, 25:227, 43:31n
114:1—17:355
114:1f—10:203, 29:117
114:1–3—25:137
114:2—4:332, 10:23, 113, 204, 18:176
114:3—10:199, 318
114:4—10:133, 17:258, 18:92, 19:143
114:5—17:120
114:8—10:19
114:14—11:408
Ps. 115—11:30, 396–400, 43:31n
115:1—11:30, 32:252, 39:28
115:2—5:203, 11:397
115:3—25:83, 374, 33:68
115:3–6—19:131
115:4—5:377, 7:162
115:5—17:107
115:6—7:162, 37:265, 40:279
115:8—5:377
115:11—35:366n
115:16—9:110, 11:393, 41:225, 45:111
115:17f—14:143
Ps. 116—11:400–409, 43:31n
116:3—10:115, 11:411, 24:149, 25:180, 29:139, 31:128
116:3f—11:237
116:4—11:271
116:5—53:328
116:7—33:135n
116:10—7:111, 10:233, 242, 359, 11:449, 12:383, 393, 14:81, 15:199, 17:176, 21:313, 26:375, 27:25, 43, 28:306, 30:224, 283, 39:309, 43:62, 52:143
116:11—2:40, 297, 300, 4:54, 5:49, 6:74, 9:51n, 155, 10:233, 11:299, 12:322, 383, 13:152, 206, 22:125, 27:165, 174, 181, 220, 275, 29:120, 123, 148, 30:257, 31:175, 36:187, 37:246n, 39:167, 40:191, 42:125, 44:52, 50:46, 52:88, 248
116:12—30:265
116:12f—36:326, 52:277
116:12–14—14:84
116:13—10:459, 11:449, 19:219n, 36:326, 44:49
116:14—9:238, 19:82, 52:251
116:15—1:253, 285, 323, 2:154, 3:292, 4:309, 5:276, 284, 6:9, 123, 7:357, 8:318, 11:378, 449, 31:111, 131, 32:266, 42:149, 44:28, 78, 51:245, 248
116:16—11:271
116:16f—36:146, 52:277
Ps. 117—1:253n, 14:1–40, 90n, 43:31n, 49:288n, 53:176
117:1—25:121
117:2—11:167, 18:418
117:13f—22:193
Ps. 118—3:120n, 10:33, 11:410–413, 13:358, 14:41–106, 28:175, 43:31n, 49:344n, 364
118:5—10:50, 11:127, 19:72, 50:311n
118:6—21:246
118:8—27:39, 34:98
118:8f—23:297
118:9—16:106
118:10–12—3:132
118:12—10:270, 15:114, 16:86, 288, 21:246, 35:220, 50:300n
118:13—6:135, 152, 10:299, 21:246
118:13f—5:144
118:14—7:127
118:15—11:372, 454, 18:360, 38:109, 50:295n
118:15f—37:58
118:16—10:111, 31:243
118:17—3:120, 4:120, 6:110, 135, 355, 11:37, 16:113, 24:116, 148, 30:301, 43:169, 49:426, 53:337
118:17f—4:118
118:18—6:152, 8:9, 14:90n, 18:359, 19:6, 46
118:21—6:142, 152
118:22—5:201, 12:62, 124, 18:117, 20:40, 30:60, 34:208n
118:22f—11:240, 499, 20:150, 29:128, 30:51, 49:344f
118:23—10:67, 11:351, 12:124, 30:52
118:24—12:122, 22:66
118:25—10:22, 11:271, 29:221
118:25f—14:315
118:26—35:219
118:27—10:64, 11:98, 18:100, 270, 35:206n, 219f
Ps. 119—3:138, 11:209, 413–534, 549, 13:178, 25:253, 29:124, 186, 31:345, 33:92, 35:206n
119:1—4:383, 11:483, 18:161, 29:33
119:2—11:417, 436, 437, 441, 18:158
119:5—25:253
119:6—14:298
119:7—11:432, 450
119:8—11:432
119:10—18:158, 25:253
119:11—11:145, 27:340
119:12—43:77
119:13—43:77, 48:21
119:15—11:437, 32:198
119:18—11:437, 43:202
119:20—11:434
119:21—11:417, 27:262
119:22—25:522
119:23—11:437
119:25(?)—4:67
119:26—11:456
119:26 *et al.*—34:286n
119:27—11:437
119:28—29:153, 32:198, 42:52
119:29—54:59

119:30—11:450, 33:92
119:31—11:435
119:32—9:49, 11:552, 20:58, 25:388
119:33f—11:442
119:35—10:14, 11:443, 445, 44:73
119:36—10:17, 11:443f
119:37—11:443f, 44:73
119:38—11:444
119:39—11:268, 430, 444, 450, 525, 25:522
119:42—11:421
119:43—11:452, 30:282
119:44—11:440
119:46—25:522, 32:145, 49:354
119:49—31:194
119:50—4:103f, 106, 11:454, 23:275
119:51—11:417
119:52—11:443, 19:69, 226, 42:131f
119:53—10:366
119:54—11:450, 14:298, 29:176
119:55—11:457
119:56—11:454
119:58—11:422
119:59—11:395, 482
119:60—4:297
119:66—9:50, 11:438, 15:28
119:67—36:187
119:70—32:226
119:71—6:152
119:72—10:240, 12:161, 25:334, 34:287, 42:56
119:74—11:467
119:75—11:168, 411
119:81—11:474, 31:194
119:84—11:513
119:85—11:474, 36:100
119:86—11:513, 32:26
119:87—11:479
119:88—25:225
119:89—10:286, 25:54, 49:155
119:89f—31:108
119:92—12:163
119:97—25:240
119:98-100—34:287
119:100—51:140
119:102—10:407
119:103—25:191, 334
119:104—10:49
119:105—4:378, 6:335, 8:83, 16:95, 17:77, 33:92, 36:191, 39:164, 40:135, 41:215, 42:56, 109
119:106—11:450
119:107—11:402
119:108—18:153
119:111—10:110, 11:455
119:113—25:191, 26:378
119:116—11:439
119:121—32:173
119:126—25:250
119:129—11:427
119:130—11:462
119:132—7:113
119:133—51:27
119:137—11:411, 513, 27:393, 29:176, 31:245, 54:457
119:140—11:323, 21:326
119:141—37:329n
119:143—11:478
119:145—25:253
119:150—11:503
119:151f—11:516
119:158—10:366, 18:351
119:160—11:450
119:162—11:539
119:164—11:450, 43:77
119:165—24:418, 25:232, 30:243
119:171—21:326, 43:77, 52:36
Ps. 120—11:535–538, 35:206n, 42:21n, 43:101, 103, 108–110, 45:320n
120:1—10:60
120:2—11:475, 535, 14:202
120:4—11:77, 25:466, 48:66
120:5—2:189, 4:331, 11:475, 537, 29:163
120:5-7—11:537
120:6—16:123
120:7—23:291, 27:182
Ps. 121—29:190, 191, 42:21n, 45:320n
121:1—46:33n
121:2—25:257
121:4—6:360, 10:99, 11:110, 12:408, 18:288
121:5f—11:219
121:6—12:163, 15:203
121:8—11:539
Ps. 122—11:539–549, 42:21n, 45:320n
122:1—10:160, 201, 11:490
122:4—10:281, 328f, 20:213, 25:225, 29:145
122:5—11:291, 14:262, 307, 25:215
122:6—7:339, 29:167
122:7—45:216
122:8—5:215
Ps. 123—42:21n, 45:320n
123:2—14:192, 30:82
123:3—11:430
123:4—11:140, 430, 25:522
Ps. 124—42:21n, 45:320n, 47:118, 53:245
124:1-3—48:249
124:3—6:40
124:7—14:204
124:8—8:299
Ps. 125—42:21n, 45:320n
125:1—40:319
125:1f—20:187, 42:112
125:2—6:244, 8:60, 20:27, 42:163
125:3—5:215, 13:382
125:4f—25:405
125:5—16:104
Ps. 126—8:298, 11:550–554, 42:21n, 45:320n
126:1—11:158
126:2—11:551
126:3—18:103
126:5f—11:551
Ps. 127—13:146, 42:21n, 45:311, 315–317, 320n
127:1—4:264, 9:96, 11:374, 13:47, 14:113, 19:209, 20:171, 40:312, 319, 41:177, 45:327
127:1a—45:323n, 325
127:1b—45:328n
127:1f—45:321n
127:2—2:49, 7:65, 8:25, 10:334, 11:414, 552, 15:88, 16:342, 18:69, 25:479, 45:332–334
127:2f—25:281
127:3—2:132, 3:134, 8:298, 11:542, 14:116, 17:15, 29:190, 30:249, 45:333f, 335n
127:4—10:165, 194, 198, 464, 17:171, 246, 42:78, 45:334, 335n
127:5—19:122, 45:336
Ps. 128—13:146, 17:380n, 42:21n, 45:320n, 53:242
128:1—40:319
128:1-4—44:85
128:3—18:52, 29:126, 37:252, 49:213
128:3f—4:355
Ps. 129—42:21n, 45:320n

129:6—16:220
Ps. 130—12:305, 14:189–194, 29:185, 42:21n, 45:320n, 49:70, 53:221f
130:1—10:372
130:3—7:360, 22:66, 133, 27:74, 77, 31:97, 47:185
130:3f—17:9, 31:97
130:4—12:323, 27:77, 53:334
130:5—4:324, 10:283, 31:194, 42:52
130:6—16:92
130:7—13:134
130:7f—31:97
130:8—25:275
Ps. 131—8:68, 42:21n, 45:320n
131:1—21:315, 27:280
131:2—16:224
Ps. 132—11:540, 42:21n, 45:320n
132:1—1:298
132:2—8:299, 13:31
132:5—8:299, 13:31
132:7—10:315, 11:361
132:9—18:412, 20:206, 255, 29:191, 39:79
132:11—4:150, 173, 11:368, 16:118, 18:241, 22:31, 92, 25:4, 29:114, 190, 47:206, 52:30
132:12—12:266
132:14—2:98, 100
132:15—7:267, 8:66, 68
132:18—8:305
Ps. 133—42:21n, 45:320n
133:1—21:305, 27:280, 40:319, 52:34
133:2—10:218, 12:249, 16:86
133:3—10:34, 195, 25:380, 27:177
Ps. 134—42:21n, 43:31n, 45:320n
134:2—36:53
Ps. 135—43:31n
135:7—10:171, 11:65, 22:293
135:11—19:142
135:14—50:299n
135:15f—7:162, 31:164
135:17—41:193n
136:1—53:20
136:4—2:389
136:8–9—11:101
136:19–20—19:142
136:25—9:96, 118
Ps. 137—36:265
137:1—17:148
137:1f—36:83
137:2—10:197, 36:106n
137:3—13:211
137:4—13:34, 20:306
137:5—11:22
137:7—1:280, 8:298, 18:116, 193, 245, 342, 393, 19:116, 20:20, 35:322
137:8—10:376, 13:93, 16:170
137:9—11:293, 44:105
138:2—11:167
138:6—5:316, 21:299, 32:9, 51:14
138:7—19:136
Ps. 139—15:173, 29:164
139:1—3:36
139:1–3—42:152
139:7—11:360, 457, 13:93, 19:44, 26:339, 37:62
139:7–10—37:58
139:8—5:355, 19:44, 33:47, 38:77
139:8f—34:207n
139:11—10:427, 11:455
139:12—10:427, 42:142
139:13—10:108
139:15—15:173
139:15f—42:153
139:16—3:36, 10:427
139:17—10:49, 11:95
139:19—49:398n
139:22—2:174, 12:193, 30:242
139:23f—25:291
140:2—14:345
140:3—11:213, 14:293, 37:270
140:4f—52:137
140:5—10:166
140:9—10:97, 255, 27:350
140:11—10:183, 31:131, 42:149, 48:361
140:12—42:156n
141:4—31:48
141:5—11:354
141:6—27:229
141:7—31:128
Ps. 142—42:184f, 49:364
142:1–2—44:62
142:2—10:200
142:4—11:114, 18:143, 24:149
142:5—10:333, 11:427, 18:159
Ps. 143—14:195–206, 49:69, 53:221
143:1—27:241
143:2—4:43, 54, 7:360, 10:242, 12:321, 335, 14:190, 17:369, 22:65, 379, 25:185, 206, 275f, 26:260, 27:73, 77, 225, 275, 365, 28:233, 30:230, 233, 31:43, 46, 61, 209, 242, 266, 32:43, 53, 84, 172, 190, 193, 259, 36:85, 39:35f, 131, 42:70, 43:36, 44:37, 47:171, 185, 51:277, 316, 53:169
143:4–6—29:150
143:5—10:132, 369, 42:131f
143:6—11:475
143:7—10:84, 14:143
143:8—18:21, 28:271, 29:186
143:9—6:13
143:10—33:92
144:1—9:202
144:2—54:451
144:4—13:103
144:5—32:146
144:6—19:144, 25:377
144:8—11:255
144:10—6:242, 9:202, 43:278, 50:70n, 54:451
144:11–15—12:123
144:12f—22:193
144:12–15—2:390
144:13—8:68
144:13–15—21:11
144:14—11:408
144:15—2:352, 7:347, 22:193
Ps. 145—43:31n
145:5—20:70, 29:143
145:6—29:124
145:7—43:240
145:10–12—8:179
145:11—8:187
145:13—10:237
145:14—27:111
145:15f—28:19, 45:326
145:16—4:133
145:17—10:155, 30:103
145:18—9:57n, 25:91, 44:67
145:18f—43:173, 54:192
145:19—3:289, 4:69, 6:259, 8:275, 14:225, 47:167
Ps. 146—14:79, 43:31n
146:2—48:70
146:3—2:297, 5:49, 6:74, 8:92, 14:67, 239, 24:19n, 32:120, 46:284n, 49:364n
146:3f—14:65, 232, 48:206
146:4—16:270, 23:225, 49:253n
Ps. 147—14:107–136, 28:3, 43:31n
147:3—20:329
147:5—48:333, 49:279n, 54:9

147:8—18:160
147:9—45:326, 50:94n
147:10—9:170, 202, 11:13, 15:179, 19:115, 45:329, 46:170
147:11—4:64, 5:276, 278, 283, 6:131, 7:44, 8:202, 12:75, 316, 322, 334, 375, 390, 406, 14:320, 16:121, 169, 26:339, 30:293, 40:294, 43:224, 284, 44:38, 46:191, 51:133
147:12f—27:317
147:15—10:20, 414, 12:32, 13:14, 25:417, 27:200, 39:132
147:16—11:311
147:17—11:84
147:19—8:133, 15:196, 17:58, 26:437, 41:51
147:19f—14:24, 22:53, 25:25, 26:357, 40:99, 45:201, 359, 47:165, 52:131
147:20—1:291, 6:284, 8:292, 10:457, 461, 20:319, 25:22, 207
Ps. 148—1:105, 43:31n
148:3—7:124, 10:159
148:5—4:155, 7:105, 13:29
148:8—10:459, 14:123
148:10—10:159
148:18—8:275
Ps. 149—1:105, 43:31n
149:1—11:314, 372
149:4—11:374
149:6—40:21
149:6–9—10:407
149:8f—4:174
149:9—40:21
Ps. 150—43:31n
150:1—39:169n

Proverbs
1:5—10:462
1:7—11:9, 163f, 40:276
1:8—11:181
1:9—20:47
1:10—2:182
1:12—27:360
1:16—13:186, 27:337
1:20—44:99
1:24–26—45:320n, 372
1:24–28—5:170
1:25f—38:135
1:25–27—39:253
1:26—16:63, 17:276, 32:147
1:27—14:349
1:28—11:70, 238, 16:63, 25:91, 413, 45:320n, 372
1:29f—25:269
1:30—32:148
1:31—45:320n, 372
1:32—9:92, 10:56, 14:304, 18:128
1:33—13:401, 16:79, 20:176, 31:126
2:7—18:25
2:14—3:249, 38:288n, 41:229
3:5—10:462, 16:65, 31:39, 66, 32:141, 52:182
3:7—16:65
3:9—5:264, 10:356, 29:156, 46:38
3:11—10:49, 29:55
3:11f—6:150
3:12—16:167, 17:410
3:16—17:384
3:25—18:334
3:27—3:80
3:28—7:310
3:32—27:244
3:32–34—10:366
3:34—1:256, 51:43
Chp. 4—5:170
4:23—27:349
4:27—25:226, 35:273n
Chp. 5—29:156
5:15—7:68
5:18—45:41
5:18–19—5:34, 15:230
5:19—8:291
6:1–5—45:252
6:6—10:200, 15:9
6:6–11—45:325n
6:10f—15:66
6:11—16:287
6:17—33:69
6:23—16:95
6:27—31:375
6:30–32—44:391
6:30–35—45:157n
7:10—15:134
7:10f—3:108
7:11—3:201
7:13—15:134
7:20—10:410
8:8—5:338
8:14—7:146, 217, 310, 13:148, 18:263, 24:383
8:14f—46:238
8:15—7:143, 145, 7:150, 21:277
8:16—7:150
8:22—20:147
8:22–27—1:20
8:22–31—7:109, 52:44
8:23—25:145
8:25—29:113
8:27—1:13, 2:93, 18:273
8:29—6:243
8:30—1:248
8:30f—11:341, 32:199
8:31—11:338
9:1f—11:265
9:5—8:249, 10:459
9:8—27:169
9:10—13:130, 51:22
9:12—10:366
10:1—16:180, 22:235
10:4—7:66, 9:74, 21:209, 45:325n
10:12—30:122, 51:298
10:13—3:59
10:16—36:357
10:19—10:183
10:20—20:72, 31:75
10:22—9:75, 96, 15:88, 45:325, 54:450
10:24—2:218, 14:322, 45:319
10:25—18:289
11:1—51:158
11:2—14:158, 39:64
11:6—25:495
11:8—18:392
11:15—25:323, 45:253n
11:22—4:275, 28:273, 47:170
11:25—7:353
11:26—7:217, 35:181
11:31—30:130
12:4—48:334n
12:18—5:180
12:21—25:400, 31:128
12:24—45:325n
12:27—45:325n
13:1—16:180
13:4—45:325n
13:9—18:290
13:10—52:27
13:12—5:203, 7:131, 8:319, 14:320, 16:95
13:24—15:238, 44:13
13:25—20:119
14:6—10:46, 27:350
14:10—8:25, 11:457, 484
14:12—11:348, 482, 41:227
14:13—10:181, 12:164
14:15—5:120
14:16—25:497
14:23—6:84, 39:217
14:28—11:377
14:30—11:300, 15:178, 29:78
14:31—9:149, 51:353
14:34—7:286
15:1—3:256
15:8—1:265, 31:48, 36:56
15:11—29:164
15:13—9:267
15:15—8:25, 42f, 52
15:17—45:332
15:20—16:180
16:1—10:203, 13:173, 33:231

16:2—13:173, 21:346
16:3f—33:232
16:4—12:374, 14:106, 33:174, 232
16:7—5:81, 6:158, 20:224
16:9—42:131
16:10—21:277, 40:286, 47:32
16:11—18:265
16:14—40:282
16:14f—15:170
16:18—3:227, 7:359
16:24—11:300
16:25—11:482
16:28—43:19
16:32—7:185
16:33—19:61
17:5—51:353
17:7—13:219
17:12—15:156
17:18—45:253n
17:22—8:113, 21:21
17:25—22:235
Chp. 18—45:31n
18:2—12:269, 15:155, 16:75, 39:289
18:3—1:272, 2:39, 16:65
18:9—25:456
18:10—4:34, 16:59, 17:196, 30:310, 43:201, 44:49
18:17—10:31f, 25:15, 39:29
18:19—10:24
18:22—2:143, 17:288, 40:301, 45:38–40, 46, 53:115
19:13—18:84
19:14—4:225, 44:8
19:17—9:149, 15:171
20:2—40:282
20:4—45:325n
20:6—9:19, 25:451
20:9—25:247, 31:61
20:12—7:162, 12:388, 16:181, 20:215
20:16—45:253
20:21—25:402
20:22—45:104
20:25—46:148, 152
21:1—21:297, 33:233, 48:69, 49:256, 50:85n, 190n
21:19—2:297
21:27—18:165
21:29—15:134
21:30—34:69, 40:145
21:31—7:169, 20:168
22:4—16:111
22:14—11:247
22:15—2:321, 7:233, 8:9, 40:281, 42:125, 44:13
22:26—45:253
Chp. 23—8:260
23:6f—3:246
23:13—29:55, 35:259n
23:14—44:13
23:20–30—8:253
23:26—14:202, 25:435, 29:232, 31:134
23:27—11:92, 247
23:29—8:269
23:31f—11:309
23:32—44:228n
23:35—1:208, 3:285
24:12—8:331
24:16—3:261, 334, 10:31f, 11:248, 14:221, 289, 25:316, 31:45, 60, 36:186f, 44:37, 51:63, 52:86
24:21—18:324, 45:107n
24:21f—40:281, 46:65f
24:29—45:104
24:30f—29:179
24:30–34—45:325n
24:32—10:200
24:34—16:287
25:1–7—46:277n
25:6f—21:313
25:11—10:21, 11:366
25:14—30:187
25:21—21:122, 25:108
25:21f—5:82, 25:108, 45:283
25:22—12:194
25:27—3:138, 140, 23:92
26:1—17:312
26:2—40:16, 41:189
26:4f—6:62, 25:467
26:5—28:29
26:7—10:21, 11:366
26:9—10:21, 11:366
26:11—30:190
26:12—10:438, 25:17, 176
26:16—10:438, 13:163, 54:360
26:23—50:47n
26:27—45:66n, 46:103n
26:28—32:31
27:1—45:255
27:2—23:320
27:4—16:134
27:6—26:188, 51:298
27:9—2:117
27:10—14:119
27:13—45:253
27:14—21:325
27:21—25:346, 31:137, 44:44
27:22—12:269, 16:232, 18:330, 51:376n
27:23—54:76
Chp. 28—18:90, 290
28:1—1:181, 6:71, 78, 7:170, 330, 335, 16:79, 25:400, 31:127, 32:67, 45:58
28:2—7:143, 19:163, 27:398
28:3—13:176
28:9—38:303
28:14—14:339, 345, 25:497, 31:206
28:15—7:143
28:16—45:118n
28:23—32:142
28:26—29:153, 48:206
29:9—22:241, 30:243, 292
29:12—13:182
29:15—6:194
29:18—7:151
29:21—25:484
Chp. 30—16:62n
30:5—1:21, 36:142
30:5f—35:146
30:13—11:21, 290, 21:300
30:14—10:248, 27:360
30:15—10:354, 36:90
30:15f—19:125
30:16—7:17, 25:228
30:17—8:244
30:18—11:33, 13:116
30:18f—11:414
30:19—10:316, 13:116, 17:346, 45:208n
30:20—10:12, 238, 25:191, 41:295, 44:257
30:21f—46:72
30:24–28—10:186, 29:167
30:27—14:273, 18:312
30:33—27:158, 46:288, 50:45, 58
31:6—4:15, 12:116, 14:159, 16:62
31:6f—8:248
31:10—8:110, 48:334n
31:10–31—29:56
31:11—10:356
31:18—10:18, 18:90, 290
31:19—15:66
31:23—10:95, 14:91
31:24—7:6, 18:66
31:26—25:31, 27:274
31:30—20:47, 48:334n

Ecclesiastes

Complete commentary—15:3–190
Chp. 1—15:12–28
1:1f—54:98
1:2—10:122, 14:238, 33:75, 36:61, 42:127, 154, 54:98
1:2f—25:363, 45:255n
1:4—15:97, 17:227
1:5—13:104, 15:97

1:7—15:97
1:8—10:300, 354, 11:290, 15:3, 86, 99, 129, 31:54
1:9—1:148, 11:494, 13:212, 15:34, 55
1:13—29:128
1:14—11:125, 197, 36:61, 42:127, 154, 45:255n
1:15—15:143, 25:17, 313, 405
1:16—15:21
1:17—11:197
1:18—15:105
Chp. 2—15:29–48
2:2—31:220
2:3f—10:56
2:8—21:169
2:11—45:255n
2:16—1:153f
2:21—45:255n
2:24f—45:255n
2:26—54:98
Chp. 3—15:49–61
3:1—11:42, 15:350, 31:313
3:1f—23:254
3:2—26:117
3:2–8—10:159
3:3—7:316
3:8—11:42
3:9—13:269
3:11–14—45:255n
3:19—15:3
3:22—45:255n
Chp. 4—15:62–73
4:6—8:279, 17:385
4:10—26:318, 54:16, 276
4:14—8:103
4:17—11:289, 15:74n
Chp. 5—15:74–93
5:1—19:99, 38:313
5:3—37:56
5:4—5:261, 46:148
5:4f—46:152
5:7—6:330
5:8f—46:128
5:9—1:103f
5:17—37:259n
5:18—15:8, 110, 42:154n
5:18–20—45:255n
Chp. 6—15:94–104
6:2—21:16, 44:57, 54:299
Chp. 7—15:105–133
7:6—35:210
7:8—5:83, 42:76
7:13—13:168
7:15—14:65, 46:247n
7:16—46:100, 288
7:18—15:145
7:20—25:221, 242, 275, 27:259, 31:45, 59f, 32:83, 40:295
7:26—45:34
7:29—32:212
Chp. 8—15:134–143
8:8—25:430
8:9—7:223
8:10—14:291
8:14—8:300, 10:57
Chp. 9—15:144–154
9:1—15:3, 25:71, 78, 26:386, 29:217, 31:220, 34:310n
9:1f—29:217f
9:2—31:220
9:7—7:367, 20:206, 42:154n
9:7–9—5:277, 8:69, 15:10, 44:24
9:8—6:324, 8:254, 20:206
9:8f—7:355
9:9—35:264, 42:154n, 45:41
9:10—7:292, 11:520, 29:165
9:11—13:165, 269, 15:8, 25:388, 45:329
9:12—11:115
9:14–18—34:67n
9:15f—46:245
9:16—46:238
9:18—46:192, 238
Chp. 10—15:155–168
10:1—46:100
10:4—10:100
10:7—44:312n
10:9—51:30
10:10—32:198
10:14—10:46, 46:65n
10:15—10:256, 25:503, 27:350, 35:40, 51:30
10:16—10:222, 45:119
10:20—46:107n
Chp. 11—15:169–175
11:2—18:251
11:3—31:138, 140
11:6—33:232
11:9—8:113
11:11–13—45:325n
11:28—15:116n
Chp. 12—15:176–190
12:3—8:148
12:4—7:302
12:7—25:424
12:11—10:18, 22, 11:130, 208, 15:12, 27:380
12:11f—35:263
12:12—13:220, 16:107, 27:349, 28:84
12:13—45:255n, 294n
21:30—52:190
30:23—8:13
38:2—40:315

Song of Solomon
Commentary—15:191–264
Chp. 1—15:196–210
1:1—11:158
1:2—12:83, 14:346n, 27:184
1:3—10:91, 378, 27:184, 31:57, 45:208n
1:4—10:412, 11:475, 25:267, 27:366, 31:57
1:5—10:350, 380, 448, 11:319
1:6—11:33
1:9—11:138
1:12—11:141
1:13—30:49
1:14—2:157
1:16—10:191
Chp. 2—15:211–222
2:1—11:328
2:2—11:33, 27:391, 29:237, 39:150, 43:78
2:3—10:111
2:5—25:294, 378
2:6—11:360, 523
2:8—18:328
2:9—3:8, 4:358, 6:259, 24:404, 44:28
2:10—2:157
2:12—11:138, 25:252
2:13—10:414
2:14—10:383, 11:140, 25:390, 27:184, 29:167, 32:240, 44:298
2:15—32:x
2:16—8:263, 10:208, 329, 31:190, 300, 352
Chp. 3—15:223–226, 30:49
3:1—10:191, 25:252
3:6—6:111, 221, 7:134, 327, 10:121
3:8—10:307f
3:9—10:342
3:11—51:42
Chp. 4—15:227–235
4:2—16:20, 25:229
4:3—2:396, 11:46
4:4—40:39
4:5—30:49
4:6—42:140
4:8—10:134, 196, 198, 203, 25:136, 27:315
4:9—25:295
4:11—10:257, 25:459
4:14—10:217
4:15—10:201, 14:299
4:16—11:552
Chp. 5—15:236–242
5:1—10:460
5:2—10:334, 25:479, 29:216
5:2–6—3:283, 4:297
5:5—6:383, 10:217, 11:46
5:6—4:405, 10:128, 25:252
5:11—10:259
5:12—10:359
5:13—10:217, 11:46, 42:141
Chp. 6—15:243–248

6:4—1:191
6:4–6—10:215
6:5—16:20
6:8—10:91, 11:95, 548, 45:208n
6:9—18:349
6:10—10:257, 397, 11:293, 368, 37:172n
6:11—11:23, 363
6:13—10:208
Chp. 7—15:249–253
7:1—10:180, 284, 463
7:1f—10:215
7:2—10:143, 11:368
7:4—10:359, 31:282, 53:40
7:5—11:46, 42:141
Chp. 8—15:254–264
8:3—11:360
8:5—29:226
8:6—11:46, 14:144, 22:333, 25:349, 378, 483, 29:138, 31:127, 137, 42:141
8:6f—11:451
8:12—15:350
8:14—10:136
10:12—30:126

Isaiah
Commentary in Volumes 16 and 17.
Chp. 1—16:5–26, 18:165
1:1—12:399, 19:157, 25:92, 35:273f, 317n
1:2—6:64, 10:210, 16:23
1:3—6:372, 13:48, 41:304
1:4—10:129, 14:11, 19:178
1:5—32:170, 179
1:6—11:191, 13:48, 32:170
1:8—2:229, 11:192
1:9—2:229, 6:218, 11:193, 16:26, 18:343, 19:179, 20:150n, 25:83
1:10f—25:407
1:10–17—51:42
1:11—18:33, 19:41, 22:428, 27:335, 29:176, 34:152n, 52:277
1:11f—7:354, 11:411, 18:259
1:11–17—14:33
1:12—18:396
1:13—12:361
1:13f—25:487
1:14—16:24
1:14f—34:152n
1:15—11:74, 16:21, 28:272, 29:232
1:16—11:4
1:17—9:19n, 11:112
1:18—3:358, 51:297
1:19—1:304, 25:407
1:19f—33:131
1:21—16:22, 18:349
1:22—10:460f, 13:14, 16:24, 35:42, 53:26
1:23—45:271
1:23–26—45:278
1:24—13:31, 16:26
1:29f—10:129, 11:268, 24:259f
1:30—10:23, 14:302, 17:290n
Chp. 2—11:376, 16:27–39, 18:236, 47:296
2:2—14:326, 20:66, 184
2:2f—35:291n, 47:215, 296
2:2–4—35:324
2:3—4:99, 8:244, 9:182, 10:230, 314, 11:86, 12:38, 16:164, 18:112, 201, 383, 22:41, 27:318, 29:118
2:4—8:265, 11:6f, 18:12, 118, 20:95, 288, 32:88, 45:93, 47:296, 52:28
2:7—18:147
2:8—13:292, 14:348, 19:186, 27:176, 32:181, 36:76, 41:303
2:9–22—25:345
2:10—29:165, 31:127, 32:240
2:12f—48:341
2:13—10:339, 20:117
2:20—13:14
2:21—29:165
2:22—14:64, 48:365n
Chp. 3—16:40–50
3:1—50:245n, 299
3:2—39:18
3:4—25:496, 39:18, 291, 45:113
3:5—2:175, 5:86
3:5f—10:308
3:6—18:93
3:8—18:93
3:9—3:249, 255, 52:121
3:12—10:105, 11:472, 31:342
3:14—11:472
3:16—18:150
3:17—10:341, 18:293
3:17f—10:443
3:20—10:189
3:24—10:194, 341, 13:23, 15:228n
Chp. 4—16:50–56
4:1—7:22, 15:148, 45:205n
4:2—16:53, 20:40, 217
4:3—7:315, 25:395
4:4—8:270
4:6—2:48, 10:338
Chp. 5—15:221, 16:57–68, 17:290, 18:148, 268
5:1—7:302, 8:295, 10:459, 16:81, 20:52, 230, 49:428n
5:1–7—9:214, 43:287
5:2—18:268
5:4—42:79
5:5—11:99, 190, 19:236
5:5f—52:99
5:6—14:270, 16:295, 17:290n, 18:8, 20:60, 345, 29:183, 30:188
5:7—3:230, 29:183
5:8—10:300, 18:169, 197, 20:119
5:11—8:248
5:12—11:26
5:13f—36:117
5:14—19:125, 32:139, 41:206
5:14f—48:213n
5:20—4:166, 10:57, 406, 417, 11:130, 404, 18:269, 20:79, 30:165, 33:279, 281
5:20f—11:231
5:21—16:95
5:24—6:136
5:28—10:36, 321
Chp. 6—16:69–77, 20:59, 25:97, 28:251
6:1—1:15, 265
6:1f—5:238
6:1–4—53:60
6:2—20:59n
6:3—3:123, 7:39, 9:237, 42:146
6:5—16:146, 18:356, 20:35, 29:195
6:6—1:236, 20:52n
6:9—15:287, 25:97, 29:204, 37:20, 47:175
6:9f—22:245, 33:98, 37:20
6:10—3:155, 193, 4:257, 6:251, 8:158, 9:272, 10:425, 13:150, 16:242, 21:163, 25:97, 32:199
Chp. 7—4:105, 13:346, 16:78–87, 29:177, 35:275
7:2—4:105, 20:283
7:3—11:286
7:3f—16:54
7:4—4:105, 18:331, 20:37, 48:381n
7:4–7—49:227n
7:8—16:83n
7:9—1:157, 11:245, 14:343, 19:196, 22:315, 39:63, 49:227n, 249n
7:10f—36:174
7:10–14—3:30n, 36:65
7:10–17—36:44
7:12—4:105
7:13—11:183

7:14—1:193f, 8:242, 18:381, 21:327, 24:93n, 32:140, 35:275n, 37:361n, 43:44, 45:206n, 208n, 209f, 52:24, 54:xviii
7:18—20:112, 305, 27:366
7:20—10:194, 342, 15:228, 16:169, 18:293
7:22—11:464
7:23f—10:275
7:24f—10:270
Chp. 8—16:84, 88–96, 29:114, 133, 47:164
8:1f—19:121
8:2f—29:113
8:6—27:163
8:6f—7:70, 14:337, 27:330
8:7—13:346, 27:164
8:10—13:150, 404, 23:258, 41:344
8:11—16:253
8:11-15—52:112
8:12—18:57
8:12f—6:85, 30:103, 49:227n
8:12-14—29:178
8:13—6:85, 31:136
8:13f—25:86, 30:60
8:13-15—27:344
8:14—3:70, 20:40, 25:236, 34:208, 47:237, 48:189
8:14f—32:118
8:15—47:237, 52:116
8:16—16:95
8:16f—29:134
8:17f—29:133
8:18—11:390, 20:39, 216
8:19—16:125
8:19f—36:197f, 52:181
8:20—33:92, 36:197
8:21—15:313, 25:359, 41:229
8:23—16:97n
Chp. 9—6:x, 7:x, 8:293, 11:68, 16:xi, 97–106, 17:x, 135, 413
9:1—8:278, 16:97n, 22:216
9:2—37:259n, 43:77
9:3—11:3, 12:170, 16:248
9:4—10:250, 285, 295, 304, 11:363, 14:83, 20:109, 25:58, 27:224, 29:194, 42:106, 49:21n, 173n
9:5—10:249, 11:3, 7, 108, 214, 363, 16:97n
9:6—5:186, 6:54, 141, 250, 392, 10:250, 11:3, 363, 13:239, 20:288, 25:285, 27:203, 224, 31:14, 224, 298, 35:120, 37:74, 164n, 361n, 42:164, 52:16, 53:131, 54:xviii
9:6f—15:288, 47:182, 202
9:7—10:159, 406, 13:233, 14:262, 20:51, 22:31, 47:78n, 83, 206
9:12—11:68, 31:316
9:13—5:170, 12:374, 404, 13:113, 17:278, 18:385, 19:72, 20:215, 44:31
9:14—16:163, 31:182
9:14f—17:374, 38:22
9:15—10:341
9:17—11:68
9:18—10:270, 50:300n
9:19—10:308
9:20-22—36:88
9:21—11:68, 31:245
Chp. 10—11:68, 16:107–117, 17:413, 46:14
10:4—11:68
10:5—8:240, 19:116, 178, 29:140, 31:92, 46:170
10:5f—14:322, 16:86
10:6—10:30, 11:191
10:8f—32:164
10:10f—26:260
10:13f—25:389
10:14—16:149
10:15—6:157, 25:389, 27:29
10:17—50:300n
10:17f—25:396
10:20—2:229, 20:317
10:20f—16:113, 25:85
10:21—8:217, 20:108
10:22—10:295, 11:98, 16:155, 18:6, 177, 188, 209, 20:210, 25:400, 31:347, 33:86, 35:111, 41:210n
10:22f—10:95
10:23—16:235
10:24—29:140
Chp. 11—16:117-127, 17:393, 46:15
11:1—1:194, 2:72, 10:436, 16:104, 18:189, 20:29, 40, 21:301, 25:516, 29:202
11:2—4:100, 8:266, 11:441, 20:67, 21:301, 25:31, 324, 377, 29:161, 48:287
11:2f—11:444
11:3—29:177, 40:123
11:3f—51:37
11:4—9:88, 10:406, 22:222, 40:58, 45:59, 60n, 115n
11:5—11:357, 25:321, 30:26, 41, 32:206, 39:268
11:6—8:265, 309, 17:393, 32:88
11:8—8:309
11:9—8:265, 11:357, 14:184, 16:99, 18:19, 19:129, 217, 30:151, 36:139, 45:93, 47:296, 52:28
11:10—3:107, 8:35, 10:259, 25:121, 517, 29:132, 178, 52:61
11:11—2:203
11:12—29:132, 178
11:14—8:289
Chp. 12—16:128–132
12:2—14:77
12:3—9:137
12:26—27:294
Chp. 13—16:132–137
13:1—20:283n
13:4—7:169, 16:159
13:15—32:170
13:19—18:50
13:19-22—1:99
13:21—6:296, 27:245, 281, 40:9
13:22—27:245, 281, 40:9
Chp. 14—16:138–145
14:5f—46:70
14:9—50:243n
14:10—19:220
14:10f—16:24
14:12—1:112n, 2:12, 12:313, 13:196, 213, 21:308, 25:159, 26:29, 36:150n, 37:129n, 45:112, 121n
14:12-14—15:339
14:13—5:222, 32:164
14:13f—6:169
14:17—10:239
14:24—4:150
Chp. 15—10:292, 16:146–148
15:1—20:283n
15:2—15:228n
15:4—10:200
Chp. 16—10:292, 16:149–153
16:6—10:407, 435, 11:42, 14:317, 21:333, 32:216, 49:215n
16:9—10:200
Chp. 17—16:154–157
17:1—20:283n
17:7f—1:251, 32:199
17:10—16:156
Chp. 18—16:158f
18:2—3:69n

18:6—1:55n
Chp. 19—16:160–167
19:1—11:321, 20:283n
19:11—15:166
19:24f—25:424
19:25—11:375, 13:48, 14:304
Chp. 20—5:349, 16:168f, 20:67
20:2—18:116, 19:24, 193, 20:127, 146, 333
20:2f—19:121, 20:253
20:2–4—7:351, 22:420
20:3—16:88, 18:215
Chp. 21—16:170–174
21:12—18:158, 25:252, 33:131
Chp. 22—16:175–181
22:8–11—16:177n
22:13—28:157
22:23f—20:109, 29:178
Chp. 23—16:ixf, 182–185
23:1—2:191, 19:44
23:11—13:84
Chp. 24—16:186–193
24:2—40:112
Chp. 25—16:194–200
25:2—2:35
25:6—10:464, 11:378, 42:56
25:7f—53:328
25:8—22:34
25:19—10:207
Chp. 26—16:201–210
26:4—29:174
26:9—11:238
26:10—3:318, 7:311, 15:202, 21:163
26:12—10:41, 123, 213, 11:375, 37:42n
26:16f—8:294
26:16–18—11:24
26:19—5:76, 53:329
26:20—4:309, 5:75, 32:235, 53:329
27:1—1:51n, 10:35, 14:337, 16:211–218, 31:363n
27:2—10:459
27:2–4—29:169
27:4—50:300n
27:13—13:34
Chp. 28—16:67, 219–237, 47:192
28:1—9:274n, 40:28
28:8—10:46, 41:203
28:10—8:212
28:11—4:352
28:13—4:321, 19:195, 52:116
28:14—10:258, 366, 36:115
28:14f—10:150
28:14–16—30:51
28:15—16:64, 17:295, 18:57, 289
28:16—11:529, 18:117, 19:72, 20:40, 218, 21:282, 25:86f, 90, 30:56, 105, 301, 31:126, 41:310, 50:19n, 51:281, 52:43, 106, 113
28:17–19—10:150
28:19—2:321, 4:20, 8:7, 293, 18:27, 337, 20:12, 43:224
28:20—5:246, 11:130, 25:400, 26:366, 31:139, 45:272
28:21—2:134, 4:94, 8:5, 11:236, 451, 13:79, 135, 14:335, 25:365, 26:38, 29:135, 31:44, 225, 36:56n, 44:77, 51:19, 21
28:26—16:111
28:29—3:54
Chp. 29—16:238–251
29:7f—6:335
29:8—10:334, 14:180, 40:213
29:10—10:202, 25:97
29:11—3:37, 7:149
29:11f—35:284, 288
29:11–21—54:408
29:12—3:37, 69, 15:269
29:13—4:100, 6:85, 11:252, 372, 13:70, 19:64, 22:81, 24:327, 25:357, 458, 35:132, 36:240, 40:30, 42:23f, 79, 53:334
29:14—4:351f, 51:39
29:15—10:162, 277, 11:31, 18:27, 162
29:18—16:92
Chp. 30—16:89, 252–268
30:1—10:29, 48:35
30:2—10:385
30:7—7:345
30:9f—17:343
30:9–13—44:272
30:10—3:269n, 11:56, 18:20, 25:230
30:10f—11:241
30:12—11:7
30:12f—10:299
30:14—10:37, 12:64, 14:340, 47:84
30:15—10:73, 183, 313, 16:89, 17:188n, 18:75, 40:43, 44:272, 49:227n, 279
30:15f—10:249, 319, 25:401
30:20—2:282, 8:230, 11:451
30:20f—7:103
30:21—11:107, 21:311, 36:237
30:24—11:102
30:26—1:20, 8:67, 10:411, 25:363, 30:197
30:27—11:57
30:32f—7:301
Chp. 31—16:89, 269–272
31:1—10:385
31:3—7:369, 10:385, 11:4, 50:46n
31:5—18:234
31:7–9—8:245
31:9—2:98, 255, 3:169, 8:183, 13:68, 16:272n, 22:195, 25:466, 27:393, 51:304
Chp. 32—16:273–281
32:2—13:68
32:7—21:178
32:8—7:150, 9:5
32:20—25:417
Chp. 33—16:282–291
33:1—11:3, 8, 48:342
33:4—14:273
33:11—14:63, 17:35, 54, 296, 39:151
33:12—50:300n
33:13—10:171
33:24—1:297, 47:304
Chp. 34—16:292–298, 47:227n
34:6—17:352
34:11—1:7
34:13—27:245
34:15—20:59n
34:24—6:296n
Chp. 35—16:299–306
35:1—25:516
35:2—10:134, 200
35:4—25:377, 31:231
35:5—22:79
35:5f—30:22
35:6—10:63
35:8—10:285
Chp. 36—16:307–313, 17:306n, 18:290
36:4f—32:164
36:6—10:35, 14:338, 17:274, 48:110n, 50:46
36:7—34:201n
36:8f—18:283
36:10—18:284, 286
36:11—36:227
36:14—18:284
Chp. 37—16:314–331, 17:306n, 18:102, 293, 21:232
37:4—10:202, 36:53, 43:248n
37:10—10:232

37:16—13:34, 29:199
37:21f—2:202
37:22—35:339
37:23—27:135
37:24—6:157
37:27—17:391
37:29—6:157, 32:161
37:29–35—18:291
37:35—18:235
37:36—18:292
37:36f—54:130
37:38—16:330n
Chp. 38—16:332–345
38:4—10:44
38:4–8—31:102
38:6—31:100
38:8—36:154n
38:10—10:371, 14:143, 186, 30:172, 31:128
38:10–20—31:141
38:11—18:159
38:12—11:315
38:13—31:128, 48:367
38:14—10:359
38:16—10:242
38:17—10:352, 371, 27:43
38:18—11:520
38:19—10:329, 362
38:22—29:128
Chp. 39—16:346–350
39:1—16:347n
39:4f—16:86
39:7—7:52
Chp. 40—11:161, 16:xi, 17:3–32, 25:32, 35:17
40:1—17:60, 68, 31:231
40:1f—35:121
40:2—8:209, 18:11, 20:98, 292, 33:216
40:3—25:137, 218, 27:397
40:3f—47:281
40:4—17:181, 20:341
40:5—11:272, 18:33, 30:118
40:6—4:69f, 346f, 7:285, 11:134, 297, 333, 408, 13:103, 16:324, 17:187
40:6f—10:56, 414, 33:220, 37:95n
40:6–8—22:101, 321, 30:44
40:6–9—11:197, 40:247, 260
40:7—11:521, 24:340, 44:279
40:7f—45:348
40:8—11:297, 13:381, 14:77, 15:272, 17:187, 195, 25:54, 37:19, 40:198, 333, 41:134, 189, 212, 49:155
40:9—27:144, 31:231
40:10—13:134, 16:45, 17:53
40:11—12:154f
40:12—4:314, 23:258
40:13—25:103, 33:25, 27, 27n
40:16—16:33
40:17—10:233, 14:63
40:18—9:54
40:18f—17:71, 25:11
40:19—31:238
40:25—10:425
40:26—22:12
40:30f—10:256
40:31—3:323
Chp. 41—16:xi, 17:33–59
41:1—10:72, 313, 19:131, 25:234
41:2—2:246, 303
41:3—31:99, 101, 32:40
41:8—3:164, 5:26, 7:312, 11:390
41:10—11:468
41:11—10:93, 387
41:14—3:310, 4:374
41:22f—17:71
41:23—25:262, 389
41:24—10:317, 25:389
Chp. 42—13:269, 16:xi, 17:60–83
42:1—11:390, 15:275, 342, 20:217, 22:119, 29:143
42:1f—17:215
42:2—12:207, 211
42:3—3:242, 5:26, 327, 360f, 6:107f, 135f, 166, 172, 218, 271, 7:135, 137, 174, 233, 320, 322, 324, 12:211, 226, 316, 409, 13:111, 16:213, 24:411, 26:315, 381, 27:12, 27, 29:143, 30:159, 33:137
42:4—45:212
42:6—22:32
42:8—12:55, 61, 84, 100, 15:277, 292f, 22:494, 52:188
42:14—16:134n
42:20—10:360, 42:80
42:23—22:184
Chp. 43—11:375, 13:269, 16:xi, 17:84–102, 226, 29:216
43:2—31:144
43:3—51:63
43:6—12:293
43:10—29:145
43:11f—17:132
43:19—38:192
43:21—25:6, 29:144
43:24—31:224f, 298, 42:122
43:25—12:333, 31:97, 224f, 318
43:26—31:48
43:26f—25:302
Chp. 44—13:269, 16:xi, 17:103–121, 29:209
44:6f—13:235
44:8—10:280
44:9—10:425, 18:22
44:9f—10:57
44:9–17—14:99
44:20—25:496f
44:23—25:516
44:25—5:341
44:28—2:34
Chp. 45—13:269, 16:xi, 17:122–136, 47:77, 86
45:1—35:277, 45:222n
45:3—12:132
45:4—8:93
45:7—11:389, 12:374
45:8—11:162, 331, 29:183, 216, 34:31n
45:9—25:83, 33:203
45:12—22:12
45:15—3:121, 4:7, 356, 6:398, 10:445, 31:53
45:16—10:425
45:18—2:142
45:20—33:132
45:22—33:132
45:22f—25:115
Chp. 46—13:269, 16:xi, 17:137–145
46:1—17:133, 19:186, 224
46:3—10:397, 25:395, 52:79
46:3f—7:325, 18:362, 29:112
46:4—43:171
46:5—12:48
46:8—10:419, 42:148, 49:265n
46:10—25:83, 31:118, 33:40
46:13—11:153f
Chp. 47—13:269, 16:xi, 17:144n, 146–154
47:1—10:207, 19:88
47:6—19:220
47:8—19:208, 21:348
47:8f—51:24
47:9—21:348
47:10f—10:124
47:11—51:24
47:14—48:35
Chp. 48—13:269, 16:xi, 17:155–168
48:1—10:354, 462, 20:238, 52:84
48:1f—44:42
48:4—2:220, 47:166, 173, 52:164
48:5—25:139, 145, 29:35

48:8—18:59
48:9—14:144, 29:130, 176, 187, 32:48, 42:115n
48:10—30:126
48:11—1:244, 32:48
48:13—22:12
48:17—39:270
48:18—18:166
48:19—11:181
48:22—1:181, 7:271, 11:169, 12:149, 18:69, 20:221, 25:286, 27:170, 29:141, 51:30
Chp. 49—13:269, 16:xi, 17:169–190
49:2—17:193
49:3—25:6
49:4—2:24, 3:59, 30:237
49:6—22:32, 69, 25:395, 48:100
49:8—3:283, 10:258, 14:151, 16:33, 18:14, 22:39, 45:157
49:10—30:187
49:14f—5:342, 11:388
49:14–16—8:89
49:15—6:360, 18:362, 54:432
49:15f—49:396
49:17—18:292
49:18—10:316
49:20—17:235
49:21—12:290, 27:320
49:22—4:204, 27:320
49:23—1:181, 12:290, 13:30, 54:309
49:26—13:31, 18:107
49:32—7:131
Chp. 50—13:269, 16:xi, 17:191–196
50:1—15:336n
50:2—18:225
50:3—19:24, 88
50:4—11:365, 520, 12:212, 42:52
50:6—15:337
50:7—12:217, 25:393
50:8—9:57n
Chp. 51—13:269, 16:xi, 17:197–205
51:4f—15:289
51:6—15:289f
51:8—17:195n
51:10—10:318
51:12—49:227
51:12f—21:47
51:15—15:290, 18:155
51:17—18:310, 19:221
51:17–22—13:345
51:19—2:360
51:22—19:221
Chp. 52—13:269, 16:xi, 17:206–218, 20:219
52:1—10:285, 21:104, 34:152
52:1f—33:132
52:2f—11:189
52:3—5:103, 7:301
52:5—25:22, 30:270, 42:78
52:6—10:6, 11:182
52:7—9:182, 11:161, 13:24, 16:345, 17:316, 18:295, 25:91, 27:200, 31:231, 35:326, 51:20
52:11—4:234, 51:361
52:12—10:249, 51:93
52:13—1:161, 15:297, 342, 20:217
52:14—12:123
52:14f—47:282
52:15—12:68f, 25:124, 521, 35:324n
Chp. 53—1:161n, 7:x, 12:129, 13:269, 16:xi, 17:x, 215n, 219–232, 20:148, 29:144, 35:118, 275, 46:12, 47:214
53:1—8:245, 10:70, 205, 13:284, 21:339, 25:92, 27:248, 29:145, 34:111, 52:116
53:1–3—22:79
53:2—14:300, 20:40, 217, 25:121, 230, 516, 29:203, 31:44
53:2f—4:6, 12:123, 208, 21:339, 47:282, 54:262
53:3—5:185, 7:210, 11:67, 14:298, 26:132
53:4—10:176, 379, 20:41, 25:515, 27:342, 389, 29:169, 32:63
53:4f—25:32
53:4–6—34:111
53:5—30:85, 53:133
53:5f—22:34
53:6—12:154, 15:343, 20:107, 301, 22:163, 168, 26:37, 278, 286, 292, 27:342, 29:77, 112, 30:86, 42:12, 47:171
53:7—30:37
53:8—3:116, 6:392, 7:99, 9:216, 10:144, 11:35, 12:128, 22:168, 26:37, 34:128, 42:9, 47:110
53:9—4:382, 12:239, 22:109, 113, 120f, 140, 265, 495, 29:195, 30:85, 34:75, 119, 51:277
53:10—7:258, 9:216, 11:385, 22:111
53:11—12:127, 326, 386, 16:123, 166, 18:19, 20:51, 140, 26:402, 30:119, 40:206, 208, 47:297
53:12—13:320, 22:230, 248, 341, 26:277, 27:44, 261, 31:190, 32:267
Chp. 54—13:269, 16:xi, 17:233–249
54:1—27:319
54:2—10:50
54:6—10:304
54:7—2:310, 29:187, 42:131, 43:185
54:7f—10:39, 29:128
54:8—2:310, 3:71, 17:319, 27:5
54:11—13:260
54:13—14:341, 18:67, 107, 20:346, 23:97, 100, 25:374, 29:16, 36:139, 40:21, 54:19
54:18—29:183, 198
Chp. 55—13:269, 16:xi, 17:249–259, 260n
55:1—40:146
55:3—10:151, 15:346, 29:114, 47:78n
55:6—2:18, 23:262
55:7—10:12, 34:119
55:8—2:5, 25:365, 49:397n, 50:242n
55:8f—8:29, 25:365
55:9—9:51, 54, 10:403, 27:348, 29:149, 35:153, 39:214, 45:42
55:10f—4:34, 6:124, 39:305, 42:58
55:11—7:138, 8:93, 10:216, 12:150, 219, 13:378, 15:320, 16:29, 204, 17:405, 18:376, 31:271, 35:214, 37:132, 38:100, 134, 40:38, 243, 41:150, 43:62, 280, 46:136, 174, 52:104
Chp. 56—13:269, 16:xi, 17:260–267
56:3—7:52, 44:374
56:3–5—44:374
56:7—15:283, 44:65n
56:10—4:105, 11:407, 32:146, 36:58
56:11—11:411, 29:38, 36:58
Chp. 57—13:269, 16:xi, 17:268, 269n, 271–281
57:1—2:24, 8:266,

18:98, 32:166, 43:163, 54:310
57:1f—4:309, 312, 49:319, 53:329
57:2—4:341, 5:75, 6:281, 7:293, 297
57:4—2:262, 4:210, 8:131, 21:53, 23:265, 35:278n
57:5—6:127
57:7—11:362
57:7–10—15:223
57:15—3:350n, 4:56, 26:315
57:19—25:285
57:20—1:181, 9:268, 16:89, 25:400, 37:29
57:20f—31:128, 42:136
57:21—9:267, 18:69, 20:58, 25:286, 400, 51:30
Chp. 58—13:269, 16:xi, 17:282–294, 21:131, 35:278
58:1—11:105, 274, 18:42, 43:227, 46:49
58:2—6:85, 33:147, 51:14
58:2f—7:354, 20:262
58:3—6:262, 20:261, 21:161
58:3–7—21:81
58:4—21:161, 51:341
58:6—20:263n
58:7—4:381, 7:216, 34:301, 312, 37:43n, 40:178
58:8—11:172, 27:317
58:9—35:278n
58:11—30:187
Chp. 59—11:331, 13:269, 16:xi, 17:295–310
59:1—8:158, 17:302
59:2—32:85
59:3f—11:239
59:5—10:29, 11:202, 14:88
59:5f—10:95, 185
59:6—41:245
59:7—7:217, 8:265, 11:132, 197, 13:186, 27:337
59:7f—11:524, 527
59:8—45:279n
59:9—17:x
59:13—11:224
59:16—11:270
59:17—11:5
59:20—12:38, 25:430
59:20f—25:101
Chp. 60—13:269, 16:xi, 17:311, 312n, 313–328
60:1—52:207
60:1–7—13:269
60:3—14:130n, 22:32
60:3f—2:245
60:4—10:457, 20:24, 113
60:5—22:313
60:5–7—10:413
60:6—4:307, 11:97, 52:281
60:7—11:155
60:8—2:157, 163, 10:255
60:11—12:130
60:16—13:30, 32
60:19—51:240, 52:68
60:19f—15:289
60:22—6:107
Chp. 61—13:269, 16:xi, 17:63, 329–342, 29:115, 33:130
61:1—3:222, 281, 14:184, 15:275, 328, 16:118, 20:40, 318, 26:315, 40:288
61:1f—3:241, 9:182
61:1–7—22:195
61:2—10:258, 406, 22:39
61:8—9:233, 11:417, 13:410, 21:183, 34:33, 36:79, 39:274, 45:306, 46:38
61:10—11:376, 12:130, 294
Chp. 62—13:269, 16:xi, 17:343–351
62:1—45:347
62:3—11:377
62:4—13:260
62:8—4:150
62:11—29:83
Chp. 63—13:269, 16:xi, 17:352–362
63:1—6:307
63:3—18:119, 32:x
63:5f—11:270
63:10—10:276
63:14–19—27:410
63:16—4:316
63:17—32:177, 33:167, 167n
63:19—32:177
Chp. 64—11:239, 13:269, 16:xi, 17:355n, 363–374, 22:313, 30:197
64:1–12—27:410
64:4—11:39, 29:231, 33:105, 40:277
64:5—4:264, 18:171, 32:173f
64:5–12—32:162
64:6—10:406, 11:522, 22:133, 25:275, 423, 26:41, 31:59, 32:83, 161, 169
64:7—18:155, 19:147, 32:166, 43:235, 44:69, 48:215
64:8—1:84f, 10:37, 12:342, 25:366, 32:164, 44:347
64:9—29:209, 32:164
64:10—17:126
Chp. 65—5:349, 12:121, 13:269, 16:xi, 17:375–394
65:1—3:107, 5:258, 10:19, 25:252, 253, 33:276
65:1f—47:295
65:2—3:107, 30:314, 45:372
65:3—44:33
65:5—10:118, 434, 25:511
65:8—18:148, 20:211, 25:424
65:8f—25:395
65:11—5:349
65:12f—5:170
65:13—17:411
65:13–15—42:155
65:14f—47:295
65:15—11:293
65:16—4:172
65:17—12:121, 15:20, 17:411, 25:73, 30:197
65:18—12:121, 54:326
65:20—6:321
65:24—4:267, 321, 7:369, 10:258, 18:14, 30:322, 36:139, 53:141
Chp. 66—13:269, 16:xi, 17:394–415, 25:487, 47:196
66:1—10:33, 13:405, 15:281, 284, 17:18, 19:44, 20:200, 22:325, 29:117, 33:96, 37:58f, 39:218
66:1f—10:129, 51:42, 94
66:2—3:236, 4:277, 6:85, 11:340, 14:305, 15:281, 18:383, 20:176, 25:377, 27:27, 29:176, 31:100, 37:58, 39:149, 219, 40:276n, 47:164, 54:xviii
66:2f—25:407
66:3—3:108, 15:281, 17:411, 24:259f
66:3f—11:438
66:4—31:227, 51:39n
66:7f—20:298
66:10—25:516
66:12—1:251, 5:334, 32:198
66:12f—29:171
66:13—16:343
66:14—11:300
66:17—44:33
66:19—10:171, 285, 339
66:19f—10:345, 14:332
66:20—29:192
66:22—10:22
66:23—9:82, 10:437, 27:296, 35:166n,

40:93, 44:72, 47:93
66:24—22:89

Jeremiah
1:4—11:382
1:5—22:159, 25:144
1:6—16:74n, 17:14, 128
1:10—10:273, 25:136, 314, 415, 39:251, 42:37, 48:375
1:11—11:382, 35:279
1:13—16:144, 25:142, 35:279
1:14—20:252, 29:201
1:16—4:165
1:18—12:217, 383, 18:372, 37:78n
1:18f—39:251
2:2—40:145
2:10—18:413
2:11—18:47
2:13—6:64, 10:12, 17:292, 23:276, 25:220, 27:220, 30:256, 31:50
2:20—11:413, 14:318, 51:374
2:21—43:287
2:23—10:12, 27:220
2:23f—8:118
2:24—18:23
2:24f—13:24
2:27—10:432
2:28—17:276, 18:21, 53, 35:80, 36:200
2:28–30—9:54n
2:32—36:45, 58
2:33—18:58
2:34—11:74
2:35—8:11, 18:58
3:1f—18:244
3:3—10:386, 41:224, 52:121
3:8f—30:26
3:9—18:244
3:12—33:136
3:12f—7:232
3:15—31:251
3:16—11:379
3:17—13:34
4:1—33:135
4:4—25:23, 36:66, 47:154, 263
4:19—17:344, 54:460
4:28—19:88
4:30—44:257
4:31—42:10n
5:2—10:354, 462, 20:238, 52:84
5:3—21:333, 22:396, 29:223, 36:78, 44:308
5:4f—14:318, 32:10
5:5f—42:80
5:12—10:150
5:16—15:229
5:21—42:80
5:31—11:224
6:2—13:13
6:8—10:207
6:10—47:154
6:13—11:441
6:14—10:150, 417, 16:46, 18:231, 233, 271, 20:11n, 31:33, 251, 32:12, 40:294
6:15—40:294
Chp. 7—18:46
7:2—40:284
7:4—1:258, 17:396, 18:326
7:5—18:260
7:16—43:234, 47:11
7:18—18:323
7:21—17:285, 20:78, 37:141
7:21f—20:261, 25:407
7:21–23—14:33, 17:402, 29:148, 44:46
7:22—16:14
7:22f—20:10n, 4:100
7:23—54:84
7:25—3:60
7:30–32—7:298
7:31—4:23, 7:298, 314, 36:224f, 41:203n, 51:322
7:31f—7:300, 53:39
7:32—7:301
7:34—31:301
8:2—9:58n
8:6f—16:46
8:8—11:41, 250, 399
8:10—10:357, 11:441
8:11—10:417, 20:11n, 27:289, 32:12, 48:375
8:15—10:417
8:17—20:59n
8:22—6:80, 383
9:1—32:139, 48:215n
9:21—51:25
9:23—21:317, 331, 32:181, 226
9:23f—4:154
9:24—3:96, 4:156, 17:230, 18:275, 358, 21:317, 331, 29:27
9:25f—47:154
9:26—3:76, 82, 9:110, 25:23, 27:330, 33:200n
10:2—54:173
10:7—25:122
10:8—11:399
10:9—10:432
10:10—18:63
10:14—11:399
10:19—10:178
10:23—25:388, 33:230, 48:22
10:24—2:322, 12:236, 16:108, 48:367
11:10–13—9:53n
11:13—25:388
11:19—14:77, 37:113f, 7:68
11:20—33:24
Chp. 12—1:295n, 2:62, 14:162
12:1—2:35, 29:239, 42:158
12:1f—19:180
12:2—6:327, 7:176, 19:203
12:3—2:35, 351, 19:181, 185
12:7—10:260
12:16—10:354
Chp. 13—20:68
13:11—29:178
14:7—31:250
14:8—11:391
14:12—10:30
14:17—35:339
14:19—10:417, 19:153
15:1—43:234, 46:43n, 47:11
15:3—10:30
15:10—2:17, 17:383, 23:291, 25:359
15:11—17:120
15:15—11:433
15:16—9:105, 35:286n
15:18—35:325
15:19—16:121, 25:238, 29:200, 33:132, 132n, 134
15:20—32:139, 37:78n
16:2—28:17, 45:21
16:19—12:130, 30:37
16:21—10:64
17:1—17:380
17:2—5:77
17:5—16:270, 17:274, 27:262, 30:231, 31:180, 32:120, 48:206, 50:269
17:5f—46:284n
17:9—15:19, 22:253, 25:291, 51:85
17:9f—29:152, 45:107
17:10—22:253
17:16—10:427, 32:191f, 41:216
17:17—48:367
17:18—11:242, 16:227, 21:247
17:25—47:78n
18:1–8—17:371
18:2f—11:256
18:4f—25:309
18:4–6—35:32, 41
18:6—20:124, 29:149, 33:203
18:7—14:322
18:7f—46:171
18:8—18:97, 39:29
18:9–11—46:171
18:11—11:249, 33:134
18:13—35:339
18:17—10:126, 16:215n
18:18—11:480, 14:341, 18:129,

20:316, 24:303, 32:9, 36:220, 43:78
18:20—51:273
18:21—14:116n
19:5—34:201n, 39:195
19:6—53:39
19:9—27:158
19:13—1:74
Chp. 20—2:62
20:2—2:20
20:7—2:182, 33:167n
20:7–12—54:64
20:8—16:204, 17:343, 24:301, 25:521
20:8f—10:184
20:9—10:211, 23:291, 24:301
20:14—2:20, 17:47, 128, 383, 25:346, 26:109, 54:30
20:14f—17:127
20:14–18—47:113n, 51:222
20:15—2:20
20:17—13:108
20:18—25:391
Chp. 21—18:33
21:1f—47:258
21:7—46:194
21:8f—35:282n
Chp. 22—18:33
22:6—10:281, 296, 18:33
22:9—8:203
Chp. 23—16:19
23:3—35:286n
23:5—14:262, 20:40, 32:173, 41:119n, 47:93
23:5f—6:185, 15:336, 35:248, 280
23:5–8—6:248
23:6—6:185, 248f, 30:270, 47:191
23:7f—47:94
23:8—35:286n
23:9f—18:34
23:11—9:175n
23:14—18:60, 147, 343, 48:375
23:14f—16:270
23:16—35:249
23:16–32—35:147n
23:20—11:38, 229, 25:367
23:21—8:211, 19:83, 25:142, 414, 27:166, 200, 28:218, 281, 39:186, 40:222, 387, 51:73, 54:471
23:21f—39:194
23:23—52:63
23:23f—29:164, 37:58, 62, 216
23:24—13:405, 33:47, 52:63
23:26f—27:18
23:28—10:462
23:29—3:348, 8:27, 13:4, 25:415, 26:310, 33:257, 52:13
23:32—8:212, 15:351, 18:351, 39:194
23:33—19:158
23:33f—10:404, 20:283
23:36—10:443
23:38–40—14:319
Chp. 24—35:282
24:1—45:214n
24:2—10:375
25:5—33:134
25:9—19:84, 34:169, 48:260
25:11f—20:173, 35:280
25:11–14—18:244
25:15—2:157, 13:345, 18:16, 344, 20:68
25:15f—19:219
25:16—13:345
25:17—35:318
25:27—9:274n, 18:310
25:29—10:206, 19:227, 30:129, 31:91
25:32—13:404
Chp. 26—46:14
26:3—43:225n
26:4—24:302
26:9—3:237n
26:15—54:65
26:18—3:237n, 18:210
26:21—43:123n
26:21–23—45:389
26:23—52:93
26:24—49:279n
27:2—7:351, 16:88, 169, 255, 17:289, 18:16, 20:68, 22:420, 35:318
27:2f—20:253
27:6f—44:92n
27:11–17—35:282n
28:1f—10:102, 25:445
28:4—18:327
28:10—16:88
28:10f—19:193
28:12–17—22:57
28:13—17:289
29:2—20:127
29:6—45:390, 52:220
29:7—39:19, 44:65, 47:229, 265, 48:259
29:10—2:100, 16:184, 20:18, 173, 35:280, 47:246
29:10f—7:202, 20:159
29:11—11:38
29:13—31:11
29:22—11:301
29:26f—54:261
29:31—41:303
Chp. 30—47:77
30:6—11:76
30:8f—15:298
30:11—25:275, 32:173
30:14—18:197
Chp. 31—18:67, 47:77
31:4—35:339
31:15—8:157
31:16—21:291
31:18—17:372
31:22—3:253, 10:154, 45:213n
31:23—10:171
31:31—25:4
31:31f—9:182, 35:287, 47:87, 88n, 96
31:31–33—25:243
31:31–34—35:280, 47:69
31:32—25:250
31:33—1:304, 9:157, 10:30, 293, 18:108, 27:234, 34:127, 36:200
31:33f—18:106, 29:198
31:34—25:374, 29:16, 36:139, 47:304
32:2—7:110
32:4f—18:209
32:6–15—19:124
32:7—17:364, 18:236
32:8—19:193
32:15—25:445
32:19—25:445
32:24f—18:237, 19:190
32:35—28:29, 34:201n
32:37—35:286n
32:40—11:379
33:15—20:217, 37:281
33:15f—6:185
33:16—6:248
33:17—3:36, 47:78n
33:17f—47:201
33:25—47:205
34:8f—3:41n
35:5f—25:488
35:14—25:250, 27:229
35:15—3:60, 33:134
35:16—25:39, 250, 26:297, 27:229
36:21–24—52:90
36:27—17:374
37:3—10:232
37:17—19:166
Chp. 38—49:279n
38:2—35:282
38:6—20:97n
38:7–13—2:259
38:14f—19:166
Chp. 39—20:76n
39:11—49:279n
39:16–18—51:49
Chp. 40—20:76n
40:5f—48:359
40:8f—17:166
Chp. 41—20:76n
41:1–3—20:76n
41:8—7:334
Chp. 42–44—20:76n

44:16f—46:236
44:16-18—8:200
44:17—2:290, 8:201, 18:9
44:17f—16:11
44:17-19—18:323
44:18—16:225, 17:295
46:20f—5:77
46:21—48:223n
46:25—18:309
46:28—10:242, 16:108
48:1—16:146
48:1f—10:292
48:10—27:262, 31:335, 33:246, 48:307, 375, 52:238
48:14f—11:42
48:24—6:307, 17:352
48:26—9:274n
48:29—14:317, 16:150, 21:333
48:30—21:333, 25:64
48:36—25:64
49:3—16:114
49:7—6:291
49:12—5:171, 8:11, 10:106, 110, 206, 2:320, 30:130, 31:91, 32:173, 42:139
49:13—6:307
49:14—27:248
49:18—18:60
49:22—6:307
50:12—15:197n
51:7—10:458, 16:222n
51:8—6:383
51:9—2:17, 31:337
51:11—13:174, 48:260
51:25—10.198
51:27—2:190
51:28—7:40
51:34—21:298
52:6f—20:259

Lamentations

Chp. 1 31:356
1:1—31:243
1:1f—36:73
1:3—29:208
1:4—18:234, 32:237, 44:323
1:8—10:12
1:12—12:123
1:15—10:260
2:2—32:169
2:11f—44:206
2:14—25:229, 27:189
2:15—18:342
2:18—8:72
2:20—17:173
3:12—12:229
3:13—12:293, 8:295
3:22—6:95, 236, 20:210f, 25:86, 42:128, 46:78n
3:28—11:300
3:32—7:232
3:32f—44:28
3:33—27:215
3:49—8:72
3:51—11:8, 25:69, 51:25
4:1—10:443, 13:14, 33:44
4:3—16:297
4:4—7:216, 40:178
4:5—18:183
4:21—13:345
5:2—41:340
5:4—37:320
5:6—10:349
5:12f—37:320
5:41—41:340

Ezekiel

Chp. 1—35:357n
1:3—11:533
1:4-28—35:284, 290, 293
1:5—2:74, 35:117
1:6f—27:200
1:7—11:362
1:10—35:117
1:23—11:319
1:26—35:284n
2:4—22:396
2:5—11:212
2:6 31:336, 43:78
2:7—46:49
Chp. 3—28:251
3:9—11:212
3:10—34:125
3:17—18:49
3:17f—22:372
3:17-19—39:250
3:18—3:280, 40:294
3:18-20—51:246
3:19—3:240, 46:204
3:26—11:212
4:4f—45:224n
4:12—32:223
5:1f—38:22, 24, 40, 55
5:5—13:201, 38:40
6:2f—10:117
6:3-6—34:201n
6:12—2:70
6:13—10:64
7:26—25:92
Chp. 8—29:135, 35:286
8:3—11:495
8:12—18:162
8:18—10:445
Chp. 9—11:193, 21:21, 35:286
9:1f—10:353
9:4-6—3:60
9:6—10:206, 18:145, 30:130
9:9—18:162
10—35:285
11:8f—2:218
11:13—11:193
11:19—25:186
12:1f—47:258
12:2—11:212
12:12f—18:209
Chp. 13—10:438
13:4f—43:235
13:5—2:51, 3:292, 18:155, 29:140, 46:174, 48:215, 397
13:10—32:12
13:16—32:12
13:18f—20:119, 33:49
13:19—2:161, 3:242, 29:38, 40:119
13:22—3:243
Chp. 14—10:438
14:4—7:84, 20:47, 31:223
14:7—10:27, 329
14:8—10:149
14:9—31:223, 39:193, 44:307
14:12-23—54:439
14:13-19—21:298
14:13-21—44:94
14:14—34:125, 43:234, 46:43n
14:20—10:297, 34:125
14:21—21:298, 43:124n
15:2—24:234
15:9—19:212
16:3—6:290, 11:82, 18:331
16:7f—11:509
16:8—25:265
16:10—10:284, 463
16:17—11:280, 17:17, 25:192
16:20f—41:203n
16:32—35:270
16:33f—11:488
16:38—35:270
16:42—10:273, 365, 373, 445
16:48—18:147
16:49—3:181, 3:247, 10:353, 15:90, 43:126
16:49f—30:177, 44:370
16:50—3:247
18:2—10:284, 404
18:2-4—9:245
18:3—10:416
18:4—10:416, 15:284
18:4-20—54:339
18:19f—10:285
18:20—9:245, 10:416, 25:297
18:21—31:96, 33:135, 135n
18:23—3:140, 7:229f, 8:329, 18:173, 33:136
18:24—33:135n
18:25—10:404, 415
18:30-32—34:141
18:31—10:65, 33:162f
18:32—29:135, 33:135n, 136
19:12—16:215n
20:25—16:14, 32:177f
20:26—11:415
20:30—11:415
20:40—35:288
20:43—31:63
20:43f—10:64

20:44—39:28
21:31—50:222n
22:20—45:272
22:25—14:116n
22:30—3:292, 18:155, 29:140, 36:182, 48:215, 397
22:30f—43:235, 44:69, 46:174
Chp. 23—41:208, 217n
23:4—6:287
23:19—30:49
23:19f—39:260
23:21—10:219
23:22—18:197
23:25—10:189
23:29—7:240
23:45—35:270
Chp. 24—29:140
24:3—10:287
24:3–14—43:225
24:6—7:231
24:12—7:231
24:14—33:200n
Chp. 25—35:283
25:15—19:212
26:7—48:260
26:17—2:194
27:7—2:191
27:14—2:191
27:26—16:215n
28:3—10:347, 20:284
29:3—10:447, 16:211, 17:200, 32:164
29:6—9:24
29:6f—48:110n
29:18—19:114, 20:90
29:18–20—34:169
29:19f—30:104
30:14f—18:309
31:9—2:201
32:2—10:447
32:7—10:338, 29:115
32:27—50:243n
33:7f—22:372
33:8—51:65
33:9—46:204
33:11—2:22, 3:277, 5:57, 12:322, 333, 336, 369, 378, 18:277, 19:30, 26:339, 29:135, 33:135n, 43:91, 54:14, 16
33:21—20:260
Chp. 34—35:283
34:2f—20:119, 127n, 320, 320n, 25:450
34:2–5—29:169
34:3f—3:223
34:4—10:222, 25:139, 27:111
34:10—51:65
34:11—20:107
34:16—12:155
34:23f—15:297
Chp. 35—35:283
35:6—11:74
Chp. 36–48—35:283
Chp. 38—35:117, 49:217n, 289n
38:2—2:188, 2:189, 46:202n
38:3—2:189
38:6—2:188
39—35:117, 49:217n, 289n
40:2—35:290, 291n
40:2–48:35—35:284
40:5—35:293n
40:6—1:230
43:7—10:315
43:13—35:293n
43:13–17—35:292
44:2—21:327
45:1–6—35:292n
47:1–12—35:292
47:13–20—35:292n
48:8–22—35:292n
48:35—35:290, 291n, 292n

Daniel
Chp. 1—31:84
1:2—36:250
1:6—25:511, 52:192
1:6f—44:210n
1:6–21—36:77
1:7—25:441
Chp. 2—35:314
2:1f—19:218
2:2—17:151
2:16—36:223
2:18f—7:143
2:20—49:209n
2:21—2:190, 254, 5:94, 19:163, 44:208
2:28—30:22
2:29—5:237
2:31–34—35:299
2:32—1:216
2:34—12:36, 13:342, 25:136, 29:191
2:35—12:36
2:35f—16:241
2:36f—9:204n
2:36–45—4:372
2:40—10:36, 13:217, 14:336, 338
2:41–45—35:295
2:44—9:83, 44:207
2:45—12:36, 35:296
2:46—30:80
2:48—44:210n, 47:195n
2:48f—42:161
Chp. 3—16:70, 25:217, 31:84, 48:189
3:1—19:224
3:1f—19:218
3:6—44:251n
3:8–21—36:302
3:8–30—4:137
3:13f—12:240
3:15—50:200
3:19f—11:15, 52:271
3:20f—52:192
3:21—44:351
3:22—44:268
3:23–27—44:287
3:25—3:274
3:26—39:281
3:27f—30:103
3:28—12:293
3:55(Vulgate)—21:299
3:60—1:31
4:9f—7:68
4:10–27—11:524
4:17—14:54
4:21f—35:298
4:24—16:19, 26:294, 50:108n
4:25—43:278
4:27—23:16–18, 26:265, 34:112n, 318n
4:28–37—54:386
4:30—14:114, 19:215
4:31f—2:258
4:34—44:208
4:34–36—47:85
4:34–37—35:308n
4:35—44:208f
Chp. 5—19:206
5:2—36:250
5:21—14:54
5:23—2:391
5:29—44:210n, 45:220
5:30—16:141, 19:205, 22:92
5:31—45:225n
6:1–3—45:220
6:10—8:144, 13:34
6:16—11:33, 28:156, 31:336, 49:207
6:22—37:298n
6:24—2:58
6:25–27—15:227
6:26—2:258
6:28—45:225n
Chp. 7—13:342, 28:119, 35:314
7:1–8—6:332
7:4—15:227
7:6–26—47:82
7:8f—41:198
7:9—7:118
7:10—5:216, 11:220, 20:64, 29:121
7:12—18:120
7:13f—15:291
7:14—47:206
7:21—10:114
7:27—14:93
8:2–14—35:311
8:3—37:138n
8:3f—20:179
8:5—29:27
8:9—35:301
8:10—2:359, 5:245, 37:138n
8:12—17:304, 40:79
8:14—35:302
8:15f—20:170
8:16—1:109
8:16f—48:367
8:17—4:129
8:19—52:142
8:23—15:134, 43:231
8:23–25—39:191, 192
8:24—25:124, 54:347
8:24f—11:128, 39:202
8:25—10:34, 353,

13:258, 35:302, 36:263, 39:279, 40:58, 45:59, 67, 49:12
8:27—23:21, 46:245
Chp. 9—19:121n, 29:121, 35:314, 47:134, 225, 237, 246f, 251, 303
9:1—45:225n
9:2—35:279
9:5—22:79, 30:103
9:7—8:11, 10:163, 27:275, 30:103, 230
9:10—47:231n
9:14—30:103
9:18—8:176
9:20f—4:268
9:21f—20:170
9:23—5:125, 361, 7:369f, 375, 19:121, 35:192n
9:24—3:90, 7:375, 9:178, 11:474, 15:289, 19:121, 193, 27:270, 29:212, 35:303n, 45:224n, 225, 226n, 47:176n, 229–253
9:24–27—22:511, 45:221, 229n
9:25—20:160, 22:39, 35:303, 305n, 45:224, 226
9:25f—47:242
9:25–27—30:22
9:26—1:310, 15:352, 20:311, 45:227, 47:282, 304
9:27—8:22, 31:392, 32:16, 163, 35:305, 39:202, 212, 45:228, 47:231, 251
10:3—11:298, 310
10:11—35:192n
10:13—2:181, 4:264f, 22:246
10:19—35:192n
10:20—6:88, 8:56, 22:246, 35:305
Chp. 11—47:225
11:2—35:306
11:2–35—35:303n
11:5f—35:308
11:13–19—35:310
11:20—7:204, 35:311
11:21–24—35:311
11:27–29—35:312
11:28–35—35:350
11:30–35—35:313
11:31—32:16
11:31–35—13:284
11:31–12:11—40:121
11:32–34—35:351
11:34—47:222
11:36—34:237, 38:161, 190, 40:32, 41:212, 245, 54:110, 343
11:36–39—35:313
11:36–45—45:144n
11:36–12:13—35:303n, 54:46
11:37—16:119, 28:5, 24, 30:206, 34:40, 93, 41:163, 203, 45:114n, 153n
11:37f—38:232, 39:195
11:38—8:208, 320, 13:314, 54:110
11:39—44:141
11:43—44:141
11:45—54:46, 388
Chp. 12—35:294n, 47:225
12:1—19:121n, 20:17, 173, 41:210, 50:70
12:2—35:313, 53:329
12:3—12:254, 16:293, 22:63, 26:296, 46:224, 51:240
12:7—8:42
12:8—11:551
12:9—18:120
12:10—35:316, 20:53
12:11—31:392, 32:16, 163, 54:346
13:54f—10:255

Hosea
Complete commentary—18:3–78
Chp. 1—18:3–7
1:1—10:44, 35:317
1:2—41:207
1:2f—10:130, 35:318
1:4—17:345n
1:5—35:317
1:6—11:389, 18:158, 20:61, 25:85
1:7—10:325, 15:336
1:9—18:355, 32:164, 47:139, 174, 218, 233
1:10—24:305, 25:85
1:11—20:288
Chp. 2—18:8–15, 47:170
2:1—25:84
2:1–5—30:26
2:2f—35:270
2:4f—51:341n
2:5—18:214, 44:87
2:6f—44:104
2:8—9:55, 37:42
2:12—18:47, 153
2:14—2:183
2:15—17:382, 35:319n
2:16—10:354, 19:56, 25:422
2:16f—35:272
2:17—3:330
2:19—16:25n
2:19f—31:352
2:20—10:91, 25:243, 29:155
2:23—3:152, 4:406, 13:286, 24:305, 25:84f, 30:66, 35:365, 47:218, 233
Chp. 3—18:16–18
3:1—10:464, 25:85, 52:123
3:4—6:33, 20:300
3:4f—25:429, 52:101
3:5—12:70, 15:297
Chp. 4—18:19–25
4:1—18:269
4:2—49:91
4:5—18:196
4:5f—11:509
4:6—3:153, 10:435, 16:8, 36:113, 41:142
4:6–13—13:284
4:12—6:129n
4:14—2:13
4:15—5:242, 6:264, 27:220, 350, 36:88, 221, 48:338n
4:15f—39:194
Chp. 5—18:26–30
5:2—13:182
5:3—11:40
5:5—11:40, 18:38, 18:63
5:9—11:40
5:10—18:63
5:11–14—11:40
5:12—25:429, 32:178
5:14—16:144n, 25:439, 32:178
5:15—25:429
Chp. 6—18:31–34
6:1—13:97
6:4—18:70, 42:56
6:5—7:231, 20:80
6:6—3:153, 6:113, 7:285, 315, 12:323, 18:23, 404, 19:161, 21:131
6:8—11:250, 18:114, 25:192
6:10—10:13
Chp. 7—18:35–41
7:12—2:221
Chp. 8—18:42–46
8:4—18:47, 25:192
8:5f—10:29
8:6—10:432
8:7—18:227, 25:285
8:9—11:329
8:11—35:80
Chp. 9—18:47–52
9:4—18:336
9:7—18:53
9:9—18:56
9:10—48:315
9:14—8:303
9:16—17:109
9:17—18:188
Chp. 10—2:285, 18:53–58
10:2—10:24
10:3—25:260
10:5—2:243, 21:6, 36:88, 221, 48:338n
10:7—11:22, 15:184n
10:8—25:293, 31:127, 34:201n

10:11—16:64
Chp. 11—18:59–62
11:1f—47:241
11:8f—8:179
11:9—11:180
Chp. 12—18:63–68
12:1—2:106
12:3–5—6:125f, 129
12:4—5:241
12:11—27:385
12:12—18:213, 233, 33:219, 37:320
Chp. 13—18:69–73
13:2—13:292
13:7f—34:49n
13:8—39:249, 49:101
13:9—11:25, 249, 25:257, 31:49, 65, 348, 44:297
13:11—45:114
13:14—8:147, 162, 12:231, 13:262, 16:144n, 197, 22:357, 25:310, 26:246, 281, 28:98, 203, 29:135, 137, 35:360, 53:329
13:15—2:107
13:16—18:74
Chp. 14—18:74–78
14:1f—52:276
14:2—10:321, 12:409, 18:261, 296, 29:176, 36:146
14:4—10:325
14:14—26:155

Joel
Complete commentary—18:79–126
Chp. 1—18:81–87
1:4—14:273n, 36:73
1:7—11:471, 43:287
1:9–13—27:123
1:19—18:103
Chp. 2—18:67, 88–112
2:1—11:274, 50:270n
2:5—7:169
2:6—10:126, 18:304
2:13—10:65, 75, 18:158, 23:98, 25:412
2:23—9:118n, 10:20, 11:149, 46:221n
2:25—14:273n
2:28—6:330, 7:119, 121, 20:182, 24:405, 35:401, 36:152, 40:391
2:28f—18:114
2:28–32—35:319n
2:28–3:21—35:319
2:32—2:287, 18:190, 201, 20:151n, 25:91, 27:275
Chp. 3—18:113–126
3:10—20:327, 21:340
3:19—33:200n

Amos
Complete commentary—18:127–192
Chp. 1—10:12, 18:129–137
1:1—20:339, 32:9, 35:317n, 320
1:2—10:341, 18:61
1:3—35:320
1:5—14:113n
1:13—10:380, 397
Chp. 2—10:12, 18:138–143
2:6—10:12
Chp. 3—18:144–149
3:6—12:374
3:7—25:4, 145, 31:117, 36:192, 47:96
3:8—41:xvi
3:12—9:3, 18:158, 20:37, 25:395
Chp. 4—18:150–156
4:1—29:38
4:9—11:68, 18:158
4:11—15:124, 48:47
Chp. 5—18:157–167
5:5—36:220
5:6—18:265
5:10—10:149
5:13—13:60, 31:155
5:21—34:152n
5:23—14:310, 40:30
5:25f—6:34, 9:125
5:25–27—35:321
5:26—13:185
Chp. 6—18:168–172
6:1—10:341, 12:186, 15:139, 36:115
6:1f—10:300
6:4—10:357
6:4–6—36:74
6:5—14:310, 16:62, 29:27, 40:30
6:6—10:357, 17:265, 27:165, 29:27
6:10—10:433
6:13—10:114
Chp. 7—18:173–178
7:1—10:25
7:5—11:193
7:7—41:217n
7:10—39:43
7:10–17—35:320
7:12—19:157
7:12f—6:265
7:14—10:9, 18:129, 35:320
Chp. 8—18:179–184
8:4f—18:233
8:4–6—21:178
8:11—10:30, 17:161, 31:346
8:13—19:30
Chp. 9—18:185–192
9:6—18:186
9:7—10:349, 449
9:8—2:190, 9:83
9:11f—35:321
9:13—8:255

Obadiah
Complete commentary—18:193–206
1—19:157, 25:92, 27:248
2—10:23
5—43:287
7—10:23, 11:309
11—10:98
19—20:114
20—47:265
21—12:38, 13:48

Jonah
Complete commentary—19:3–106
Chp. 1—13:46, 19:8–14, 38–69
1:1—19:38, 35:323
1:2—2:43, 19:8
1:3—15:136, 16:74n
1:5—17:140
1:9—19:9, 38, 44
Chp. 2—19:15–21, 70–82
2:2—19:6, 79
2:2f—24:387
2:3—10:372, 19:78
2:8—10:372
2:9—19:101
Chp. 3—19:22–25, 83–90
3:3—2:201, 342, 5:336, 13:46
3:4—2:24, 19:84, 43:225
3:5—2:24, 21:156, 36:84
3:5–10—35:326n, 47:85
3:6—17:335, 21:156
3:6–10—31:91
3:7—49:380
3:8—19:24
3:9—6:371, 34:301, 310
3:10—2:43, 8:227, 12:333, 19:86
Chp. 4—19:26–34, 91–106
4:1f—19:39
4:2—19:51
4:3—17:383
4:5—19:50, 26:211
4:6—15:268
4:8—26:109
4:11—19:22, 51

Micah
Complete commentary—18:207–281
Chp. 1—18:210–220
1:1—35:317n
1:2—10:232
1:6—18:234
1:7—4:397, 13:292, 27:123, 34:99
1:10–16—35:325
1:11—2:243
1:12—12:374
1:13—6:34
1:14—7:6
1:16—10:194
Chp. 2—18:221–229
2:1—6:53, 21:178

2:2—10:307, 21:178
2:3-6—35:324
2:6—2:20, 16:46, 18:57
2:6f—18:162
2:7—2:53, 18:163, 19:163
2:9—32:91
2:11—10:378, 29:183, 31:195
2:12—25:395, 35:288
Chp. 3—18:230–235
3:3—10:287, 18:93
3:5—10:264
3:10—19:215
3:11—20:11
Chp. 4—18:236–246
4:1—14:326
4:1f—35:291n, 47:215
4:1–3—35:324
4:2—10:230, 314, 20:28, 22:41, 20:118
4:3—11:6
4:4—22:198
4:6—18:364
4:8—6:274, 16:265n
4:10—11:177
4:11—14:226
4:13—10:36, 321, 11:133, 20:66, 128, 25:417
Chp. 5—18:247–256
5:1—6:295, 40:57, 52:186
5:2—22:511, 23:243, 251, 283, 29:174, 35:324, 361, 52:185, 187f
5:3f—52:189
5:7—10:410, 11:367, 13:298, 18:75, 25:395
5:8—25:78
5:15—9:183
6:1f—39:250
6:6—27:235, 31:97
6:7—4:124, 8:276, 31:97
6:8—8:276, 25:478, 31:96, 117, 40:277
7:1—43:223n
7:2—10:307, 14:291, 29:119
7:3—11:112, 19:164, 29:119
7:4—29:119, 33:55
7:5—2:297, 301f
7:6—2:297, 6:391
7:8f—11:450
7:9—49:172
7:10—25:232
7:19—22:87
7:20—6:113, 11:396, 14:332n, 40:278

Nahum
Chp. 1—18:283–297
1:3—31:99, 32:40
1:15—20:32n, 35:326
Chp. 2—18:298–305
2:10—10:126, 18:93
Chp. 3—18:306–318
3:15–17—14:273n

Habakkuk
Complete commentary—19:107–236
Chp. 1—14:162, 18:108–118, 157–188
1:4—8:71f, 25:250
1:5—11:179, 14:98, 16:242, 19:117, 29:136
1:8—18:350
1:12—19:129
1:13—10:112, 52:257
1:14—19:200, 48:179
1:16—21:344
1:17—13:395
Chp. 2—18:119–132, 189–226
2:3—2:176, 5:57, 7:99, 131, 8:20, 201, 14:320, 16:88, 29:236, 50:173n, 175n
2:4—1:181, 5:158, 6:165, 11:442, 19:151, 25:9, 243, 26:238, 268, 27:258, 30:151, 32:14, 52:114, 54:403
2:5—19:199n, 20:132
2:6—27:409, 43:223, 48:10
2:9—21:178
2:16—13:345, 20:132, 134
2:18f—13:292
2:20—26:355, 33:60
Chp. 3—18:133–150, 227–237
3:1—15:81
3:2—10:39, 273, 357, 11:111, 25:92, 179, 27:248, 31:44
3:2–19—19:151n
3:3—10:134, 11:98, 19:142n, 42:146
3:4—11:380, 21:339
3:7—10:296, 420, 428, 449
3:8—7:103, 19:146, 24:383
3:9—10:165, 19:142n
3:10—10:155, 11:324
3:13—18:185, 19:142n
3:14—27:262
3:15—4:7, 9, 24:383
3:17—18:47
3:19—10:276, 12:199

Zephaniah
Chp. 1—18:320–337
1:1—35:328
1:3—1:99
1:4—21:6
1:5—1:74
1:12—18:271
1:14-16—25:176
Chp. 2—18:338–347
2:11—14:10
Chp. 3—18:348–366, 376
3:3—19:170, 21:298
3:4—8:211
3:6—16:265n
3:9—8:196, 15:336

Haggai
Chp. 1—18:371–378, 20:84
1:1—18:380, 35:329n, 45:214n, 225n
1:1–15—35:303
1:2—20:227, 374
1:5f—20:162
1:6—5:367, 370, 18:395, 20:274, 35:330
1:9—17:396
1:13—46:221
Chp. 2—18:379–390, 47:134, 188, 237
2:6—18:121, 52:7
2:6f—35:330, 47:219
2:6–9—47:176n, 201n, 209–229, 234n
2:7—11:533, 15:268, 20:71, 81
2:7f—47:223
2:8—1:355, 20:50
2:9—11:154, 16:28, 17:395, 20:47, 50, 280, 32:163, 47:213n, 214n
2:9b—47:229
2:10–23—35:329n
2:21—52:7
2:23—45:214n
2:91—45: 228

Zechariah
Complete commentary—20:3–347
Chp. 1—20:6–25, 64, 74, 82n, 158–181
1:1—35:329n, 45:225n
1:1–17—35:303
1:3—9:86, 11:158, 31:11, 33:132n
1:7–17—35:304
1:8—6:15
1:11—20:15
1:13—10:211
1:14f—29:140
1:15—10:379, 19:220
1:16—20:194
1:21—20:22
Chp. 2—20:24–33, 74, 181–203
2:4—20:185
2:5—12:228, 20:187
2:8—10:81, 13:37, 202, 14:316,

16:79, 91, 324, 17:357, 20:101, 23:149, 24:275, 27:134, 28:138, 35:52, 36:267, 42:161
2:9—20:198n
2:10—20:87n, 191
Chp. 3—20:4, 34–41, 50f, 69, 74, 148, 204–221, 255
3:1—4:264
3:2—14:258, 19:192, 20:46, 34:226, 48:47
3:4—29:120
3:8—16:93, 20:69n
3:10—20:202, 22:198
Chp. 4—20:42–52, 74, 222–232
4:6f—8:26
4:7—10:417, 20:66
4:9—20:257
4:10—20:190, 29:200
4:11f—20:231n
Chp. 5—20:53–61, 86, 233–246, 47:227n
5:2—47:226
5:4—10:462, 38:307
5:6—47:226
5:6f—10:443
5:8—20:122
Chp. 6—20:62–74, 247–258
6:1—11:326
6:2f—6:15
6:3—20:65n
Chp. 7—18:236, 20:74–81, 259–269
7:5—17:104n
7:10—9:19n
7:14—18:236
Chp. 8—18:236, 20:74, 76, 82–88, 270–281
8:4f—18:236
8:5—16:326
8:6—20:190n, 228
8:10—20:160
8:16—10:66, 31:391
8:19—17:140n, 20:75n
8:21—20:87n
8:23—10:196, 29:178, 45:228
Chp. 9—20:89–104, 108f, 282–298
9:1—10:6, 20:89n, 90n
9:1–6—35:331
9:6—20:92n
9:7—20:89
9:9—1:298, 3:58, 8:297, 10:190, 12:38, 15:346, 20:125, 191, 22:43, 79, 195, 27:93, 35:331
9:9f—47:282
9:10—20:99f
9:11—6:379, 387, 20:96n
9:13—10:165
9:15—20:103
9:17—11:460, 30:41, 44:370
Chp. 10—20:105–115, 299–309
10:2–7—20:106n
10:3—20:183
Chp. 11—20:116–129, 310–322
11:1—10:134, 17:396
11:3—10:199, 11:394
11:7—10:452
11:9—20:323
11:11—20:323
11:12—6:391, 47:226, 52:90
11:12f—35:331
11:13—20:120
11:16f—29:169
11:17—10:222, 11:399, 14:308, 25:139, 38:180
Chp. 12—20:130–142, 310, 323–330
12:4—21:313
12:8—24:90
12:10—2:19, 333, 12:358, 21:138, 229, 24:87, 239, 405, 419, 47:226, 7:57, 371
12:10f—20:145
Chp. 13—20:143–157, 331–336
13:3—25:414
13:9—30:17
Chp. 14—20:337–348, 47:251
14:2—15:352, 20:337n
14:5—18:130
14:16f—10:437
14:17—20:186n, 342n

Malachi
Complete commentary—18:391–420
Chp. 1—18:391–398
1:2f—4:366, 25:82, 26:237, 33:161, 198
1:4—10:39, 245, 33:257
1:6—33:200, 42:78
1:7f—9:151, 25:295
1:8—10:352
1:8–14—35:332
1:10—25:295, 29:102, 35:80, 53:332f
1:10f—14:33, 53:333
1:11—36:316
1:13—10:256
1:14—6:365
Chp. 2—18:399–407
2:2—4:159, 20:209, 27:262
2:3—35:219
2:6–10—35:333
2:7—13:315, 18:377, 25:238, 29:200, 31:265, 33:92n, 34:129, 36:113, 148, 39:193, 46:221
2:10—34:114
2:11—35:332n
2:13—12:81
2:13–16—35:333
2:14–16—47:95
2:15—4:303, 305
2:17—18:413
Chp. 3—18:408–416
3:1—9:182, 18:377, 19:225, 35:332
3:2—7:231, 30:17
3:3—7:231
3:4—7:320
3:6—5:43, 135, 41:116
3:8—2:22, 10:18
3:8f—8:229
3:8–10—35:332
3:9—27:262
3:14—20:78
3:16—10:66
3:17—35:42
Chp. 4—18:417–420
4:2—2:315, 11:164, 12:122, 134, 239, 14:99, 15:347, 23:282, 325, 25:286, 26:296, 29:167, 189, 32:236, 37:164n, 172n, 52:97
4:5—17:166, 35:332
4:6—18:249

NEW TESTAMENT

Matthew

1:1—4:151, 29:5, 31:140, 35:183n, 37:240
1:1f—32:281
1:2—5:73, 37:240
1:5—7:200, 8:136
1:12—45:214n
1:16—14:288
1:18—45:210, 212
1:18–25—54:341
1:19—21:96, 45:31, 46:300, 311
1:20—35:248n, 37:98, 236, 46:289
1:21—11:271, 459, 510, 14:101n, 22:44, 74, 44:287, 52:157f
1:21f—16:84
1:23—35:275n, 37:240, 45:208n
1:24—37:240
1:25—16:75, 32:119, 45:211f, 54:341
Chp. 2—46:290
2:1—10:457, 13:199, 16:34
2:1–3—43:44
2:1–12—28:55
2:2—52:164
2:3—11:31, 52:170
2:4—40:251
2:4–6—23:222, 52:171
2:6—18:247, 40:57, 52:186, 54:301
2:7f—52:189
2:9—46:36
2:9f—52:190
2:11—6:383, 8:321, 17:274, 315, 36:294, 40:96, 43:44, 52:160, 194, 275f
2:12—52:198, 283
2:16—25:182, 40:242, 45:112n
2:16–18—42:160, 43:44
2:21–23—22:214
2:23—8:305
3:1—54:276
3:1–12—39:188
3:2—9:27, 18:356, 22:45, 62, 176, 25:241, 31:87, 96, 364, 32:232, 35:6, 48:66n, 68n
3:3—16:70, 22:62, 25:218, 29:194, 37:240, 51:21
3:4—11:84, 14:273
3:5—22:45
3:6—36:86
3:7—3:96, 10:448, 12:394, 16:23, 17:297f, 22:62, 177, 27:4, 47:141
3:7f—51:21
3:8—32:232
3:9—3:96, 4:26f, 12:112, 17:197, 22:93, 26:435, 47:141
3:9f—8:218
3:10—6:228, 21:208, 22:62, 93, 46:199n
3:11—22:45, 46:75, 52:74
3:12—2:24, 3:150, 8:118, 218, 16:198, 22:62, 85, 51:315
3:13—43:44
3:13f—37:286n
3:13–17—22:173, 51:315–329
3:14f—14:340
3:15—22:160, 25:441, 51:318
3:16—2:45, 7:130, 10:255, 400, 26:374, 34:218, 37:299n, 51:184, 52:65
3:16f—22:117, 160, 201, 35:26, 43:44
3:17—2:48, 13:320, 16:71, 18:375, 22:39, 77, 119, 172, 23:124, 27:88, 35:162
3:31—53:25
Chp. 4—20:105, 46:12
4:1—43:44
4:1f—4:389, 11:223, 24:294, 37:315, 49:110
4:1–11—54:79, 276
4:3—7:127, 22:71, 23:114
4:3–7—1:149
4:4—5:54, 61, 137, 144, 202, 7:128, 9:93, 14:192, 15:173, 25:238, 26:95, 28:143, 29:162, 216, 31:210, 345, 33:155, 35:344, 36:45, 39:200, 43:44, 48:206
4:5—10:84, 11:208
4:5f—11:210
4:5–8—1:107
4:6—1:146n, 11:211, 28:219, 30:312
4:7—7:309, 30:312, 31:87, 35:200, 43:44, 52:200
4:8—29:45
4:8–10—38:201, 41:334, 51:377
4:9—6:134, 22:204, 34:40
4:10—3:118, 5:49, 9:72, 12:72, 286, 28:219, 30:310, 43:44, 54:469
4:12—22:49
4:12–16—22:216
4:13—13:28, 22:214
4:14f—16:97
4:15—8:278
4:16—16:97
4:17—18:356, 24:14, 31:25, 83, 317, 364, 32:232, 34:192, 37:283, 45:88, 51:21
4:18—13:28, 22:181
4:18–22—22:413
4:19—10:38, 31:232
4:21—35:397n
Chp. 5—6:91, 21:7–129, 29:197, 31:86, 34:306, 41:123, 300, 44:256, 46:11f, 47:227, 51:21
5:1f—44:258
5:2—36:208
5:3—2:330, 8:255, 9:147, 10:190, 306, 11:47, 143, 441, 465, 12:226, 406, 16:46, 121, 21:285, 293, 27:298, 35:121, 43:22f, 44:356, 46:83, 52:25, 266
5:3–5—26:38
5:4—6:311, 356, 10:56, 152, 11:139, 237, 551, 14:198, 17:334, 25:457, 31:84
5:5—11:8, 146, 17:327, 35:121, 49:196
5:6—2:41, 330, 10:53, 354, 11:290, 533, 12:319, 332, 14:37, 25:252, 38:101f
5:7—9:181, 21:285
5:8—7:332, 336, 11:385, 12:378, 28:225
5:9—13:56, 17:323, 27:375, 43:19, 49:369
5:10—9:216, 11:468, 25:177, 43:164, 44:227, 47:16
5:11—14:12, 16:103, 21:285, 293, 27:44, 134, 262, 405, 37:21n, 41:165, 191, 43:33, 53:67
5:11f—6:52, 356, 24:277, 30:102, 41:165, 189, 46:83, 47:305
5:12—10:288, 11:468, 21:285, 292f, 25:177, 27:44f, 134, 33:150f, 54:96

5:13—22:63, 35:361, 39:232, 48:266
5:13f—39:180
5:14—1:343, 10:171, 20:225, 21:8, 22:63, 25:136
5:15—21:8, 25:136, 32:11
5:16—10:335, 13:295, 15:230, 25:108, 515, 29:57, 31:87, 44:45, 45:306
5:17—21:3, 29:35, 193, 32:33, 34:127, 44:258, 46:145
5:17f—39:52
5:17–22—45:88n
5:17–48—10:72
5:18—19:45, 26:403, 27:37, 41, 46, 114, 31:61f, 32:32, 34:77, 118, 39:77, 88, 40:333, 43:200, 44:348, 45:58, 214n, 52:265
5:18f—14:271, 34:74
5:19—21:4, 36:209, 41:18, 43:151, 44:258, 348, 49:67, 52:264
5:20—11:111, 20:315, 21:123, 22:456, 23:213, 25:184, 44:258
5:20f—30:173
5:20–44—46:197
5:21f—11:201, 25:290
5:21–26—31:143, 51:152
5:22—6:376, 7:286, 30:276, 36:225n, 43:19, 44:102, 47:40, 51:132
5:22–24—36:358
5:23—13:411
5:23f—43:274, 54:316
5:23–25—36:356
5:24—19:161, 28:272, 31:98
5:25—9:163, 10:18, 35, 11:57, 64, 25:54, 439, 31:235, 39:21, 42:44, 44:257, 45:81, 388
5:25f—44:259
5:26—51:49
5:27—11:57
5:27f—54:218
5:28—25:22
5:29—12:285, 21:341, 27:304, 51:39
5:29f—46:74
5:31f—46:277
5:32—36:105
5:34—4:78, 9:72, 19:66, 41:300
5:34f—4:142, 16:35
5:34–36—7:248
5:34–37—4:77, 15:216, 45:103
5:35f—9:73
5:38f—45:102
5:38–41—45:xii, 77, 87, 92n, 95n
5:38–42—9:144n
5:38–45—20:95n
5:39—30:75, 31:235, 36:71, 266n, 40:286, 43:33, 45:77, 81, 90, 95, 101, 274, 46:165, 49:340, 387
5:39f—36:207, 45:96, 49:54n
5:39–41—45:387, 388n, 46:28, 164
5:39–42—39:201, 46:99
5:39–44—36:208, 44:257
5:40—27:375, 30:80, 31:305, 390, 42:45, 45:81, 256n, 273, 276n, 279f, 305n, 48:140
5:42—3:178, 13:408, 45:256, 263, 280, 282, 289
5:43–47—29:227
5:44—7:124, 12:194, 281, 14:244, 28:257f, 373, 31:306, 36:266n, 43:19, 110, 44:101, 45:87, 102, 291n, 46:29
5:44f—43:163
5:45—2:299, 343, 3:50, 7:124, 140, 143, 8:300, 305, 11:381, 14:51, 15:115, 146, 22:192, 405, 25:72, 26:251, 28:379, 31:65, 367, 33:168, 43:36, 44:109, 45:171, 46:169, 49:159, 51:267
5:46—21:285, 25:128, 27:401, 36:208, 44:259
5:48—7:97, 124, 10:83, 25:169, 29:227, 45:102
Chp. 6—21:150–209, 28:271, 324, 30:102, 31:86, 44:256f
6:1—10:73f, 14:50
6:2—10:74, 25:378, 450, 26:60, 35:80, 44:44
6:3–5—18:263
6:4—21:285
6:5—9:144, 10:66, 10:73f, 25:450, 44:259, 51:12, 170
6:6—3:18n, 10:66, 73, 12:318, 21:232, 285, 34:285
6:7—6:111, 7:154, 177, 10:66, 12:358, 16:17, 283, 21:325, 28:335, 40:31, 42:24, 43:12, 44:61
6:7–13—42:19
6:8—6:115, 17:204
6:9—1:128, 5:214, 6:258, 8:268, 19:230n, 25:253, 370, 27:408, 29:80, 30:245, 46:33, 48:391, 54:9
6:9f—4:364, 26:86
6:9–13—34:118
6:10—4:261, 6:258, 15:25, 19:46, 25:248, 309, 35:98, 46:34
6:11—29:156, 45:255f
6:12—3:349, 5:22, 8:268, 10:394, 13:89, 21:108, 23:314, 25:247, 253, 276, 26:66, 109, 235, 27:85, 184, 30:245, 31:46, 85, 99, 266, 36:137, 258, 356, 37:233, 43:164, 45:250, 51:99, 54:422, 457
6:12–15—27:66, 36:357
6:13—8:167, 268, 26:196, 36:190, 46:34, 54:416
6:14—36:258, 51:99
6:14f—36:356, 42:65
6:15—31:46
6:16—10:67, 73, 367, 10:74, 12:246, 15:30, 134, 17:67, 25:450, 29:7, 31:84, 41:127, 51:12
6:17—12:175, 12:246, 17:335, 20:206
6:18—21:285
6:19—31:390, 35:289, 46:245
6:20—13:408
6:21—9:69, 11:418, 21:190
6:22f—46:73, 74n
6:23—4:243, 21:222, 33:152n, 38:31, 311
6:24—4:381, 10:195, 11:69, 371, 482, 16:61, 31:390, 41:216, 45:307, 46:130n, 215, 52:25, 54:360
6:24–34—53:86–89
6:25—7:65, 28:357, 40:25, 43:123, 45:48, 334
6:26—45:326, 48:235
6:26–30—42:158
6:28f—52:87

6:29—14:237, 15:157, 17:312
6:29f—16:324
6:30—11:198, 33:92
6:31—5:137, 28:371, 43:174, 45:47
6:31f—44:108
6:31–33—46:235
6:33—4:384, 5:137, 7:163, 8:183, 187, 11:253, 13:169, 189, 401, 16:20, 203, 17:375, 18:395, 23:5, 24:399, 28:323, 370, 40:315, 42:39, 45:48, 88, 51:175
6:34—5:195, 11:458, 15:10, 25, 46, 71, 19:26, 31:110, 35:264, 42:62, 45:332n
Chp. 7—17:380n, 21:210–284, 44:256
7:1—2:297, 13:50, 25:115, 174, 42:30, 46:49, 107, 113
7:1f—10:457, 23:335
7:2—43:130, 51:13
7:2f—10:123
7:3—2:297, 9:231, 12:237, 245, 14:76, 15:122, 126, 21:155, 217, 219, 22:55, 23:238, 27:112, 31:186, 34:35, 35:367, 38:54, 39:61, 40:24, 46:26
7:3f—37:138n
7:3–5—6:292, 12:349, 13:50, 14:167, 15:169, 41:16, 192, 42:66, 45:65n, 46:109
7:4—16:300
7:5—16:143, 34:98, 40:120, 131, 48:343
7:6—15:154, 27:48, 33:88, 36:263, 37:68n, 131, 38:134, 40:148, 255, 42:80, 43:64, 134, 44:251, 45:71, 53:105
7:7—4:339, 5:156, 158, 6:159, 7:376, 10:20, 14:61, 21:144, 31:11, 40:278, 43:226, 234, 49:270, 51:171
7:7f—5:361, 11:396, 23:355, 29:125
7:8—11:512, 533, 25:460, 40:40
7:11—3:138, 14:249, 19:30, 26:235, 297, 33:275
7:12—1:277, 25:180, 183, 475, 27:53, 56, 355f, 29:197, 30:21, 238, 31:203, 304, 34:21, 35:171n, 40:97, 42:68, 43:16, 122, 127, 44:42, 393, 45:127n, 287n, 292f, 46:111, 114, 51:5–13
7:13—11:342, 16:30
7:14—14:58, 23:401, 31:179, 306, 42:99, 48:47
7:15—5:107, 9:52, 129, 135, 11:215, 338, 12:165, 13:19, 16:122, 262, 17:350, 18:269, 19:113, 22:484, 26:407, 413, 424f, 429, 28:363, 29:89, 31:363, 33:49, 34:40, 36:116, 158, 209f, 39:192, 307, 40:32, 172, 41:85, 194, 286, 295, 42:30, 44:21, 31
7:16—4:407, 10:83, 16:59, 18:271, 27:79, 33:156, 34:89, 37:137, 40:250, 41:85, 42:30, 46:180
7:16f—27:373, 33:268n
7:16–20—40:84, 41:238, 45:297
7:17—11:233, 21:150, 22:280, 26:155, 27:79, 32:84, 33:216, 35:215, 40:34, 43:281
7:17f—10:25, 11:373, 14:299, 31:9, 45:89n
7:18—10:83, 17:286, 19:23, 20:38, 25:169, 30:242, 31:65, 270, 361, 33:275, 34:111
7:19—31:270
7:20—2:21, 14:298, 23:18, 27:158, 31:362, 32:193, 35:391, 42:30, 44:288
7:21—2:21, 10:26, 38, 348, 13:70, 386, 23:411, 34:118, 45:74
7:22—10:274, 348, 14:145, 22:64, 25:18, 26:14
7:22f—39:128, 41:358
7:23—10:77, 274, 14:302, 22:64, 24:250, 25:168, 34:307
7:24—25:104, 401
7:24f—11:163, 14:344, 36:134
7:24–27—36:134, 44:36
7:25—12:187, 15:258, 16:54, 41:30
7:26—25:104, 27:52, 62, 29:13, 32:83, 35:15, 36:208, 49:309, 51:29
7:26f—10:279, 44:29
7:27—12:372, 16:232, 25:288
7:28—12:225
7:28f—23:223
7:29—12:225, 14:283, 21:77
Chp. 8—13:355, 30:242, 46:15
8:3—22:114, 37:133
8:4—52:23
8:5–13—32:116
8:8—31:272, 32:48, 42:173
8:10—19:85, 22:196, 41:40
8:11—12:152, 13:33, 269, 16:300
8:11f—16:64
8:12—12:293, 16:300, 26:461, 50:249n
8:13—6:141, 8:18, 9:87n, 12:322, 29:217, 32:49, 35:11, 36:123, 53:121
8:15—33:18n
8:20—11:258, 12:110, 259, 13:194, 345, 22:102, 505, 23:40, 27:122, 38:190, 41:365
8:21—3:299
8:22—12:385, 46:265, 266n, 49:265
8:23–27—51:23–31
8:24—13:274
8:25—5:174
8:26—31:273, 42:80
8:28f—37:215n
Chp. 9—23:268, 30:292
9:1—23:156
9:1–8—24:74n
9:2—3:155, 4:50, 6:172, 7:281, 8:54, 12:368, 14:170, 201, 16:153, 321, 22:120, 23:75, 311, 26:132, 324, 27:6, 12, 32:13, 32, 46, 35:18, 22, 39:275
9:6—5:140, 233, 22:114, 40:366
9:6–8—35:22
9:8—8:182, 40:366
9:12—10:328, 339, 25:204, 26:34, 27:185, 33:282, 42:177
9:13—6:113, 7:285, 10:142, 11:522,

13:321, 17:80, 18:144, 261, 385, 404, 19:28, 20:79, 21:131, 27:12, 29:6, 58, 31:57, 46:67, 51:46
9:14—21:156
9:15—9:244, 29:7, 46:235
9:16f—10:273, 41:63
9:17—10:157, 218, 11:323, 36:250f, 262, 43:53
9:18f—11:534
9:18-26—51:44
9:20—10:350
9:20f—17:299, 37:239
9:20-22—1:13
9:21—4:261, 37:91
9:22—35:18, 54:460
9:24—7:296, 8:319, 10:334, 42:150n, 53:326
9:25—51:45, 254
9:26—11:534
9:28—31:196, 272
9:29—25:71, 31:272, 35:11
9:36—17:279, 337, 20:118, 48:234
9:36f—20:299, 301
9:37—17:337, 48:262
9:37f—41:355, 53:126, 145
9:38—13:15, 21:227, 25:447, 26:18, 28:62, 32:272, 36:135, 42:60, 43:78, 203, 49:214
Chp. 10—46:11, 14
10:2—37:37
10:3—51:217n
10:4—41:120
10:5—4:9
10:7—20:182, 35:147n, 45:88
10:8—4:204, 22:219, 31:386, 34:245, 258, 36:36, 39:59, 41:237, 353
10:9—21:167
10:10—3:361, 4:204, 5:386, 21:167, 25:449, 34:28n, 40:315, 41:353, 46:129, 130n, 233n, 49:138
10:13—2:363, 34:11, 47:12, 12n
10:14—13:63, 14:55, 24:270, 29:70, 47:276, 49:340
10:15—3:294, 24:270
10:16—2:163, 10:254, 12:110, 227, 15:220, 17:215, 19:97, 21:223, 22:517, 24:160, 31:336, 54:379
10:18—11:451, 29:146
10:19—10:87, 11:451
10:19f—30:108
10:20—10:285, 11:161, 183f, 364, 13:12, 14:303, 27:166, 192, 404, 54:318
10:21—2:271
10:22—12:159, 377, 14:100, 15:116, 20:336, 25:225, 27:400, 44:50, 54:402
10:23—23:261, 46:37, 105, 49:340
10:24—40:66
10:24f—14:96, 39:124, 43:79
10:25—23:158, 241, 38:305, 40:66, 51:198
10:26—1:267, 41:256n
10:27—8:45, 9:221, 12:384
10:28—5:27, 10:39, 225, 251, 283, 11:70, 519, 12:111, 228, 25:78, 309, 29:140, 31:244, 32:108, 43:121, 174, 238, 45:106n, 48:58n
10:30—5:276, 283, 6:74, 123, 7:137, 8:89, 251, 16:325, 20:101, 23:299, 54:24
10:31—46:318n
10:32—4:147, 11:263, 402, 18:364, 31:244, 33:20, 41:149, 43:177, 46:175n, 49:355, 365, 376, 51:240
10:32f—52:141
10:33—11:263, 32:107, 43:121
10:34—2:297, 10:250, 10:36, 13:12, 23:292, 294, 25:285, 29:10, 31:84, 33:52, 37:27, 47:219, 48:153n
10:34f—18:251
10:34-36—13:278, 39:132
10:35—10:250, 28:334
10:35-37—45:278
10:36—10:453, 22:81
10:37—2:341, 4:41, 44, 6:26, 23:202, 25:318, 26:106, 28:33, 37:27, 44:327, 46:306, 48:335, 379, 52:218, 54:463
10:37f—23:205
10:38—4:147, 8:5, 11:139, 141, 25:289, 318, 442, 31:84, 137, 225, 51:30, 198
10:39—4:46, 31:84
10:40—4:281f, 30:128, 35:147, 36:266n, 47:278
10:41f—22:517
10:42—3:203, 21:31, 49:308
11:3—22:49
11:5—10:88, 190, 424, 450, 11:28, 12:45, 14:183, 15:331, 16:224, 17:212, 330, 20:315, 318, 22:79, 102, 24:283, 26:105, 29:79, 160, 30:22, 40:277, 42:34n, 46:224, 52:25
11:5f—11:221
11:6—11:221, 15:75, 18:410, 22:49, 23:282, 26:419, 427, 35:44, 52:197
11:7—8:212, 12:187, 13:31, 14:338, 16:180, 21:252, 28:346, 29:11, 33:17n, 37:29, 30n, 40:219, 41:212
11:7f—11:363
11:8—11:140
11:9—22:43, 64, 42:139
11:9f—22:440
11:9-11—45:87n
11:10—18:377, 408, 35:332, 37:290n, 46:221
11:11—12:394, 22:49, 57, 64, 130, 438, 42:139, 52:3
11:12—6:110, 10:278, 392, 11:23, 365, 12:114, 16:29, 17:254, 409, 22:191, 25:460, 26:257, 317, 36:252, 38:101, 42:176, 52:65
11:13—10:431, 20:317, 22:38, 423, 26:317, 35:286, 46:145, 52:105
11:14—35:332, 37:xii, 170, 173, 176, 253, 38:37
11:15—27:249, 43:229
11:16f—48:146, 51:122
11:16-19—22:241
11:17—5:13, 17:297, 20:316, 23:50, 30:292, 38:100, 39:162
11:18—11:112, 39:125, 47:141, 254, 51:21
11:19—4:295,

11:354, 17:283, 21:342, 24:156, 28:84
11:20–24—45:148, 51:126
11:21—12:212, 20:90
11:21–23—22:186
11:21–24—22:390, 42:134
11:23—2:315, 30:180, 46:254, 51:71
11:24—2:315, 30:180
11:25—4:356, 10:70, 156, 11:156, 499, 12:108, 356, 17:79, 30:266, 33:88, 35:236, 51:387, 389
11:25f—51:125
11:25–30—51:26–31, 121–132, 383–392
11:26—11:500, 51:127n
11:27—4:176, 15:293, 26:402, 37:291n, 51:27, 126–128, 389
11:28—3:223, 4:51, 5:319, 10:72, 142, 178, 191, 256, 11:17, 13:321, 14:184, 16:31, 195, 17:129, 22:52, 379, 23:248, 271, 311, 350, 414, 24:60, 26:30, 316, 329, 370, 27:12, 27, 407, 29:172, 30:266, 30:309, 33:136, 35:18, 42:35, 52, 105, 176, 51:29, 129, 187, 391
11:28f—10:255
11:28–30—21:246, 51:129
11:29—3:346, 10:87, 11:466, 12:55, 76, 258, 27:34, 42:28, 51:30
11:29f—34:132n
11:30—3:346, 6:236, 10:36, 13:22, 14:62, 337, 18:59, 26:133, 27:135, 30:309, 35:40, 111, 41:22, 177, 51:60
Chp. 12—1:79n
12:1—27:55, 40:98
12:1f—24:410n
12:1–8—22:223, 31:373, 51:106
12:1–12—35:165
12:2–10—23:235
12:3—51:106
12:3f—29:7, 50:36
12:5—44:390, 50:35, 51:345
12:6—29:7
12:7—14:50, 28:363
12:8—22:223, 36:240, 242, 41:66, 51:335
12:10—51:335
12:11—35:241
12:18—15:275, 17:63, 20:217
12:20—4:51, 57, 5:26, 17:66
12:24—10:60, 11:335, 22:433, 43:85
12:25—9:221, 21:127
12:25f—37:169
12:26—21:127
12:28—12:118, 37:313
12:30—33:54, 38:250, 41:122
12:31—19:48
12:31f—48:303
12:32—3:295, 29:110, 30:325, 32:95f
12:33—12:385, 21:265, 23:152, 25:69, 354, 31:362, 32:116, 43:280
12:34—10:211, 11:407, 526, 21:343, 22:12, 26:21, 28:202, 29:39, 97, 33:275, 34:69, 35:179, 189, 45:66, 287n, 46:65, 47:277, 52:46
12:35—3:252, 13:185
12:36—10:175, 14:205
12:37—1:297, 13:224, 25:188, 33:100, 34:69, 40:372, 41:254, 343, 48:376
12:38—43:86
12:38–41—22:241
12:39—9:291, 10:15, 16:84, 19:36, 102, 49:113
12:39f—10:373, 19:31, 102, 22:242
12:40—12:224, 32:171
12:41—19:37, 89
12:42—18:116
12:43—40:48
12:43–45—1:225, 13:213, 16:325n, 27:50
12:44—1:132
12:45—2:348, 12:389, 26:71, 37:231, 40:274, 41:120, 44:400, 49:365, 50:222n
12:48—17:115
12:49—3:165
12:50—2:48, 38:187
13:3—37:175
13:3f—3:225
13:4—11:530, 40:260
13:4–8—41:150
13:5–7—24:47
13:6—15:203
13:7—28:371
13:8—5:56, 54:19
13:9—11:530
13:11—12:298
13:13—25:324, 27:20, 256, 310
13:13f—11:123
13:14—9:272n, 33:98
13:14f—16:74n
13:15—10:435
13:16f—35:257n
13:20—27:32, 30:261
13:20f—10:14
13:21—22:252, 24:150
13:22—9:137, 28:370, 45:318
13:24–30—1:234, 53:48f
13:25—1:219, 6:32, 11:293, 13:222, 15:351, 21:212, 25:142, 26:46, 31:116, 49:141
13:28—31:245
13:29—9:243, 20:199, 21:338, 31:245
13:30—11:293, 45:357n
13:31f—54:88
13:33—27:340, 364, 28:206, 30:69, 32:24, 227, 232, 35:338
13:34—37:175
13:34f—11:38
13:35—10:92
13:36—37:262n
13:38—37:175
13:39—9:187
13:41—11:293, 25:383, 35:351, 36:135, 40:325, 49:12
13:43—30:197, 32:30, 46:224
13:44—10:17, 156, 11:150, 414, 519, 31:230
13:45—35:338
13:45f—16:124, 22:526, 26:89, 28:149, 34:130
13:46—11:103, 12:161
13:47–49—35:338
13:47–50—7:364
13:52—10:315, 11:322, 14:331, 27:345, 31:364
13:54–56—52:146
13:55—35:397n, 41:101
13:57—52:146
13:58—32:13
14:1–11—7:99
14:1–12—42:139n
14:3f—50:310
14:3–12—52:00

14:4—12:394
14:5—8:132
14:6-11—43:44
14:8—12:395
14:8f—20:196
14:13—42:139
14:19—1:33
14:20—12:151, 45:360
14:25—6:151, 11:32
14:25-32—54:197
14:26—31:125
14:27—40:188
14:28—5:255
14:29—36:190
14:30—11:248, 31:125, 43:120n
14:30f—11:248
14:31—6:101, 37:133, 44:60n
Chp. 15—28:311
15:1—40:299
15:1f—24:410n
15:2—36:242, 44:355
15:2f—16:294
15:3—14:294, 20:234, 236, 264, 40:304
15:3-9—39:158
15:4—45:278
15:4f—28:334, 29:42, 47:227
15:5—4:182, 20:237, 300, 51:147
15:7-9—14:294, 36:240
15:8—6:85, 10:66, 11:372, 19:64, 22:82, 25:357, 458, 27:85, 28:311, 38:307, 40:30, 256, 42:24
15:8f—39:190
15:9—3:273, 4:100, 134, 11:442, 12:403, 27:85, 28:311, 29:7, 30:280, 35:136, 36:241f, 38:164, 39:270, 40:299, 304, 361, 41:190, 301, 45:42, 49:408, 53:334, 54:97
15:11—35:132, 35:135
15:12-14—46:63
15:13—11:335, 17:25, 18:393, 19:83, 20:239, 21:268, 29:53, 35:219, 51:73
15:14—7:162, 16:191n, 19:111, 22:58, 26:61, 124, 283, 427f, 27:20, 28:164, 29:58, 31:362, 35:18, 37:128n, 38:168, 222, 39:124, 40:348, 41:30, 217, 43:86n, 44:37, 45:108
15:15f—37:262n
15:18—35:132
15:18-20—35:135
15:19—15:180, 21:86, 91, 25:301, 51:132
15:22—6:262
15:22-28—43:250n
15:24—15:328, 54:451
15:26—6:139, 42:80
15:26f—17:400
15:27—1:292, 4:55, 6:285, 18:99, 23:403, 41:51
15:28—6:140f, 153, 172, 6:262, 12:253, 31:272, 42:76, 109n
Chp. 16—28:229, 41:293f, 304-329, 341, 343, 345, 347, 363
16:1—11:59, 19:61, 43:86
16:2f—1:43
16:4—11:59, 16:84
16:5—40:154n
16:6—9:52, 157, 16:94, 20:105, 27:340, 40:32
16:9—36:71
16:11—16:94
16:13—11:115
16:13f—41:311
16:13-19—31:324, 51:53-60
16:14—19:11
16:15—11:115, 41:312
16:15f—14:328, 37:287, 39:85
16:16—38:29, 58, 41:312, 51:49
16:16f—11:156
16:17—11:245, 14:346, 20:256, 25:224, 27:192, 250, 28:198, 44:297, 356, 51:49, 52:175, 194
16:17-20—41:313
16:18—1:58, 190, 2:64, 260, 283, 4:141, 348, 5:25, 130, 143, 231, 234, 6:40, 165, 241, 245, 365, 399, 7:369, 8:240, 277, 9:24, 87, 10:22, 95, 188, 11:49, 12:168, 214, 227, 372, 13:140, 307, 14:125, 329, 15:213, 260, 16:28f, 56, 200, 20:133, 22:11, 186, 332, 359, 442, 446, 512, 23:60, 24:160, 297, 26:20, 224, 27:155, 338, 28:270, 29:229, 30:167, 291, 31:321, 388, 32:68f, 33:96, 237, 245, 35:11f, 36:190, 281f, 39:52, 82, 86, 88, 141, 221, 40:158, 218, 304, 348, 41:10, 12, 30, 90, 214, 296, 301f, 319n, 346, 352, 367, 371, 43:107, 171, 45:68, 105, 46:228, 47:117, 269, 48:327, 340, 49:8n, 12, 61, 129, 341, 50:9, 52:113
16:18f—14:12, 31:280, 37:38n, 39:86, 89, 41:293f, 43:29
16:19—2:274, 5:251, 8:79, 193, 26:408, 27:330, 31:93, 98, 100-103, 149, 162, 164, 191, 193, 212, 229f, 235, 271, 281, 389, 32:39, 42, 45, 35:11, 16, 22, 38, 152, 36:82f, 39:42n, 171, 40:27, 325, 357, 365, 377, 41:53, 195, 315, 317, 329, 44:134n, 45:111, 50:40n, 51:60
16:22—33:83
16:23—5:348, 6:131, 11:257, 16:34, 26:228, 27:319, 363, 367, 42:147n, 51:49
16:24—3:317, 20:142, 21:90, 31:85, 52:234
16:24f—11:528
16:25—37:135
16:26—1:220, 33:52
16:27—43:45
17:1—11:327, 25:288
17:1f—22:201
17:1-9—30:162
17:2—1:236, 6:323
17:3—7:296, 11:288, 20:248, 22:340, 29:197, 48:361, 52:21
17:4—29:197, 49:288n
17:5—2:274, 3:82, 4:126f, 5:45, 348, 6:173, 8:271f, 12:83f, 271, 365, 13:78, 15:77, 16:55, 21:280, 22:77, 119, 257, 259f, 445, 23:16, 121, 229, 281, 343, 345, 24:58, 63, 65, 71, 27:35, 88, 29:223, 30:164, 34:74, 35:135, 162, 37:66, 279, 299n, 38:161, 240, 259, 41:130, 173,

46:51, 49:66, 51:375–377, 379f, 388, 54:89, 323
17:15—36:135n
17:20—10:336, 18:12, 22:313, 31:273, 38:24, 56
17:24f—30:78
17:24–27—30:181, 31:369, 36:241, 49:26, 52:7
17:25—45:235
17:27—27:358, 40:96, 45:94, 52:215
Chp. 18—28:254, 272, 351, 36:64n, 41:318, 320f, 341
18:3—12:114, 16:312, 24:410, 54:105, 120, 159
18:4—44:133
18:5—45:372
18:6—39:186, 45:354, 372
18:7—2:230, 9:187, 27:344, 34:215, 42:159, 45:354
18:8—21:92
18:8f—36:320
18:9—21:85, 92, 23:164, 27:244
18:10—1:113n, 5:221, 6:93, 17:357, 20:16, 37:232, 233, 39:17, 40:243, 45:372
18:11—20:26
18:12–14—35:338
18:13—29:142
18:14—8:27
18:15—21:43, 215, 28:353, 29:28, 34:21, 40:262, 374, 42:68, 48:383, 51:97, 52:225, 54:300
18:15f—49:103
18:15–17—14:76, 21:103, 215, 29:28, 36:86f, 39:8, 40:327, 369, 42:69, 44:130, 45:33, 46:286, 51:159, 53:64, 54:316
18:15–18—28:286, 36:79, 41:364
18:15–20—41:153
18:16—9:196, 11:211, 35:329n, 39:89, 40:239, 41:249, 46:268
18:16–20—54:66
18:17—9:137, 171, 205, 14:55, 21:226, 23:340, 31:121, 34:33, 35:382, 38:304, 40:26, 54, 311, 41:153, 194, 317, 370f, 48:340, 49:388
18:18—3:124, 8:27, 21:153, 22:433, 23:340, 29:193, 31:281, 388, 34:53n, 35:22, 36:82f, 87, 258, 39:86, 88f, 40:54, 334, 346, 357, 364, 377, 41:317, 43:29, 44:134n, 51:326
18:19—31:280, 35:103, 36:87, 258, 38:212, 40:27f, 325, 48:368, 51:99, 338
18:19f—35:98, 36:106, 41:318, 44:199
18:20—2:335, 5:247, 250, 15:233, 26:318, 36:87, 38:212, 40:27f, 51:310, 338
18:21—25:314
18:21f—54:107
18:21–35—36:357
18:22—2:298, 300, 25:316, 30:324, 34:174
18:23f—7:258
18:23–25—12:381
18:23–28—31:134
18:23–30—39:11
18:23–35—27:115
18:25—2:58, 46:315
18:28—11:264, 15:136, 45:253n, 48:13
18:30—10:418
18:31—21:112
18:32–35—51:54
18:35—7:258, 8:26, 43:27
Chp. 19—21:94
19:3–9—21:93, 45:30, 46:277
19:3–10—18:406
19:4—3:272
19:4f—4:362
19:4–6—41:197
19:5—1:136–138, 3:272, 6:257, 33:215, 36:98, 46:314, 49:221n, 50:100n, 54:67
19:6—1:134, 3:204, 5:33, 7:27, 21:94, 23:203, 36:98, 40:301, 46:275, 48:280, 50:34, 35n, 51:154, 53:113, 54:66
19:7—21:94
19:8—1:138, 9:210, 241, 18:406, 21:94, 31:203, 46:278, 50:34
19:8f—28:31
19:9—21:96, 40:301, 46:311
19:10f—48:334
19:10–12—44:9n
19:11—28:313, 44:261
19:11f—44:175, 48:294
19:12—5:355, 7:52, 21:90f, 28:340, 35:382, 44:261, 45:18, 21, 46:149, 153
19:14—8:192, 30:247, 36:301, 40:242f, 257
19:16–22—44:23
19:17—3:132, 17:23, 22:425, 451, 24:188, 25:61, 26:143, 145, 156, 252, 265, 33:147, 34:112, 118, 196, 301, 312n, 44:23, 298, 51:285
19:19—25:475, 51:269
19:21—2:330, 23:202, 33:148, 45:233n, 54:357
19:23f—10:292
19:24—32:156
19:25—22:350, 32:156
19:26—32:156
19:27f—11:222, 24:334
19:29—13:192, 16:20, 17:288, 21:14, 292, 24:26, 28:78f, 361, 32:141, 168, 44:327, 46:130, 197
19:30—2:194, 10:421, 11:78
19:31—45:149n
Chp. 20—30:169
20:1f—37:164
20:2—40:387
20:6—27:155
20:10–12—10:95
20:11—21:319
20:11f—25:98
20:11–15—33:207
20:12—3:129, 131, 10:280, 19:51, 93, 21:319, 22:461, 26:206, 231, 304, 446, 27:321
20:13f—40:117
20:14—51:15
20:15—19:94, 25:218
20:16—10:154, 421, 11:341, 22:55, 27:393, 31:31, 232, 44:294
20:20–28—3:56
20:22—3:159, 7:175, 25:74, 369
20:24—40:291
20:25—40:51, 52:214
20:26—2:337, 12:42, 31:387, 52:214
20:26–28—41:326
20:27—2:337, 31:387
20:28—22:166, 24:105, 30:294, 54:112
Chp. 21—48:67n
21:1–9—22:216
21:1–11—13:11

21:2—11:64
21:5—18:339, 20:94, 125, 43:44, 51:164n
21:6–9—35:219
21:8f—43:44
21:9—11:153, 22:49, 29:221, 35:87
21:12—20:237
21:13—8:172, 188, 11:8, 15:283, 26:201, 31:336, 41:202, 44:65n, 47:227
21:14—20:237
21:15—10:87
21:19—6:77, 10:22, 19:103, 27:262, 344, 48:214
21:21—10:336, 11:29, 37:183f, 188, 42:109n
21:22—42:76f, 87, 186, 44:384, 48:368
21:23–27—22:240
21:27—10:268
21:31—12:343, 16:232, 32:37, 51:127
21:31f—45:354n
21:33f—43:287
21:38—11:133
21:42—5:201, 11:499, 12:62f, 20:218, 30:51, 61
21:43—3:152, 10:458, 11:110, 13:355, 18:8, 185, 355, 19:98, 35:324
21:44—11:499, 12:62, 30:61, 37:146
Chp. 22—20:7, 7n
22:1–7—39:299
22:1–10—42:56
22:2—2:163, 18:13
22:2–4—35:61, 36:137
22:7—2:378, 17:379, 24:284
22:10—45:149n
22:11—12:294
22:11f—53:33
22:13—14:80, 16:235, 30:175, 40:335, 46:84
22:14—25:6, 75, 33:59, 54:86
22:15f—10:72, 24:410n
22:16—10:168, 277
22:16f—35:149
22:17—45:235
22:17–21—30:181, 52:7
22:19—40:96, 49:129
22:21—10:268, 13:48, 370, 21:108, 25:111, 31:99, 112, 39:149, 41:225, 45:111, 46:134, 316, 47:19, 49:26, 276, 375, 50:11
22:23f—33:95, 50:38
22:24—45:8
22:25—7:19
22:29–32—13:127
22:30—1:111, 12:120, 28:172, 41:223
22:32—1:285, 3:110, 118, 4:96, 312f, 5:73, 224, 7:116, 8:81, 12:369, 13:81f, 14:87, 28:120, 47:301, 53:329, 54:447
22:34–46—51:104n
22:35—39:56
22:36–39—34:184
22:37—12:164, 23:240, 26:122, 128, 270, 28:78, 30:278, 34:112, 46:197
22:37f—23:270
22:37–39—27:63, 51:104–117
22:39—7:24, 12:164, 23:240, 27:55, 43:130, 45:293, 51:10
22:40—26:270, 33:134, 44:393, 51:106
22:41–46—13:231
22:42—13:231f
22:43—13:232
22:43f—15:294
22:43–45—12:132, 41:119
22:44—13:228, 35:249n, 39:81
22:45—8:140, 15:295
22:46—15:295n
Chp. 23—20:55, 21:101, 119, 38:28, 46:15, 47:227
23:1–3—39:128
23:2—12:21, 14:289, 16:239, 20:57, 242, 22:277, 483, 25:189, 40:32, 54:323
23:2f—10:29, 35:129, 148, 38:42, 58, 81, 39:194, 41:120, 52:191
23:3—10:25, 25:64, 40:231
23:3f—20:315, 35:149
23:4—10:423, 11:78, 14:255, 20:235, 31:388, 36:261, 41:16, 44:345
23:4f—20:320
23:5—10:67, 74, 25:190, 193
23:6—10:423
23:6f—51:348
23:7—10:74
23:7f—10:160
23:8—3:147, 20:249, 39:xix, 270, 40:33, 49:62
23:9f—29:14
23:10—2:220, 15:77, 16:95, 27:167, 404, 32:77, 34:xiv, 35:147, 36:248, 40:33, 54:54
23:11—2:274, 27:208, 31:387
23:12—25:420, 27:208, 30:139, 31:51
23:13—6:385, 31:335, 33:57, 61, 40:358, 44:182
23:13f—23:213
23:13–15—51:348
23:13–29—15:187
23:14—7:194, 14:262, 18:222, 19:219, 42:35
23:15—3:89, 36:75
23:16—32:142
23:16f—11:112, 20:237
23:16–22—9:73
23:17—31:335, 36:245
23:18—45:71
23:19—36:245
23:20—16:35
23:23—5:267, 13:175, 15:124, 25:488, 28:322, 44:344
23:23f—11:112, 44:237
23:24—3:321, 6:292, 11:203, 25:489, 34:38, 38:114, 39:61, 40:275, 44:344, 48:47
23:25—21:33
23:25–27—27:172
23:25–28—35:372
23:26—15:76, 25:321
23:27—10:17, 11:111, 12:192, 21:33, 25:24, 27:188, 259, 28:246, 31:43
23:32—20:318
23:33—16:105, 254, 303, 26:188, 30:51, 31:335, 32:141, 37:269n, 42:67, 45:71
23:34—27:169, 43:78n, 46:37
23:35—1:252, 255, 282, 13:184, 188, 48:266, 52:92
23:37—10:78, 106, 11:181, 22:237, 25:29, 28:244, 29:167, 33:140, 144f, 184n, 43:78n, 48:375, 52:92
23:37–39—2:50, 16:50
23:38—52:99
23:38f—25:429
23:39—41:77

Chp. 24—13:262, 46:18n
24:1—20:257
24:2—1:323, 9:295, 10:24, 12:213, 16:199, 23:303, 369, 374, 24:280, 310, 25:232, 26:105
24:4f—39:308
24:5—15:183, 16:34, 20:233, 21:270, 22:439, 444, 23:280, 26:258f, 30:172, 32:64, 36:63, 38:117, 39:261, 40:15, 44:286, 320
24:6—33:52
24:9—24:167, 43:62, 44:112, 227
24:10—44:112
24:11—11:482, 25:486
24:12—44:252n
24:13—2:105, 176, 7:77, 131, 203, 11:361, 13:177
24:15—7:297, 8:22, 187, 11:522, 26:200, 259, 31:392, 32:16, 77, 92, 36:97, 138, 218, 38:174, 211, 39:191, 202, 40:15, 41:201, 303, 308, 339, 44:273, 379, 47:51, 49:65, 52:234, 53:19, 54:343, 346
24:15f—10:16, 362, 45:223n
24:16—10:362
24:19—10:362
24:21—54:76
24:22—2:229, 283, 10:39, 453, 16:112, 26:316, 342, 29:187, 38:159, 39:280, 52:81, 54:76
24:23—3:108, 9:167, 13:33, 21:270, 22:451, 24:63, 215, 37:xii, 102, 145, 275, 281f, 39:195, 40:219, 41:295, 44:33, 99, 52:235, 52:255
24:23f—30:169, 42:40f, 52:255, 270
24:23–26—23:280, 35:145, 39:191, 44:381
24:24—9:188, 10:279, 438, 13:33, 14:291, 21:270f, 275, 22:57, 257, 259, 24:215, 225, 294, 305, 369, 28:302, 31:291, 32:77, 36:143, 189, 192, 194, 210, 220, 227, 289, 37:367, 38:159, 171, 39:193, 195, 43:147, 44:99, 138, 354, 382f, 52:102, 249, 257
24:24f—36:198
24:24–26—22:442, 39:66
24:25—21:273, 22:57
24:26—25:486, 44:99, 52:235
24:27—51:294
24:29—13:191
24:30—11:159, 20:140, 48:366n
24:31—20:24, 179, 191, 248, 35:31
24:32—9:154
24:35—7:370, 10:22, 11:389, 17:199, 25:72, 29:120, 45:58, 214n
24:36–44—44:214n
24:37—1:336, 2:25, 37
24:37f—54:77
24:37–39—30:193
24:38—2:58, 92
24:41—17:147
24:42—33:18
24:44—30:193
24:45—25:139
24:45–51—39:154
24:48–50—14:349
24:48–51—39:90
24:50—45:255
24:50f—10:40
Chp. 25—28:341
25:1f—16:164, 31:65
25:1–13—35:338, 42:36n, 54:343
25:2—10:52, 16:165n
25:3—10:360
25:3f—28:50
25:6—34:211, 49:221
25:8f—11:372
25:9—22:370, 31:213, 266
25:11—5:158, 10:420, 43:193n
25:12—9:33, 10:25, 126, 18:352, 52:158
25:13—31:188
25:14—25:447, 27:167, 40:386
25:14f—23:228, 35:148
25:14–30—51:8
25:15—16:164
25:15f—10:174
25:18—48:13
25:21—28:282, 29:64, 34:124, 54:74
25:24—25:358
25:24–30—15:123
25:25f—35:181
25:26–30—27:159, 167
25:31—12:130
25:31–45—46:12n
25:31–46—3:187, 45:172
25:32—12:130, 20:107
25:32f—16:122
25:33—20:301
25:33f—10:111
25:34—11:389, 22:380, 25:154, 29:12, 33:152f
25:34–36—46:83
25:34–40—44:329
25:35—3:178, 187, 244, 26:106, 34:124
25:35f—21:30, 37:365n, 44:85n, 51:152
25:35–40—22:417
25:35–46—44:85n, 109
25:40—3:178, 184, 187, 271, 5:261, 282, 10:179, 13:262, 22:520, 23:149, 35:52, 42:122, 163, 43:130, 44:71, 49:171, 51:9, 53:66
25:41—11:389, 21:31, 22:96, 380, 23:350, 24:14, 27:262f, 33:153, 51:16
25:41–45—42:122
25:41–46—43:122
25:42—14:274, 16:18, 21:31, 22:519, 51:8, 153
25:42f—45:286, 46:230n
25:42–45—51:153
25:43—9:147, 31:122, 43:126, 51:9, 153
25:45—44:71
25:46—6:173
Chp. 26—13:415, 36:20
26:2—51:94
26:4—41:122n
26:6f—27:390
26:8—6:337, 35:179, 190
26:8f—6:326
26:11—5:261, 28:382, 37:196, 275, 38:30, 45, 58f, 82
26:14–16—35:108
26:20—37:205
26:21—51:94
26:23–25—36:56
26:24—6:351, 15:62f, 17:47, 41:332, 47:294
26:25—37:138n
26:26—3:124, 4:95, 8:194, 310, 32:16, 56, 36:31, 40, 295, 37:28, 312, 313n, 328, 38:292, 40:142, 154, 175, 289, 51:89, 188, 370, 51:417

26:26f—34:85n, 38:63f, 54:196
26:26–28—34:81n, 35:82n, 246n, 36:37n, 162, 286, 335, 37:307–310, 38:205n, 42:173, 43:151, 44:55n
26:27—3:124, 32:56, 34:68n, 36:20f, 23, 319, 37:310f
26:28—8:194, 310, 25:376, 29:209, 36:22n, 38, 320, 37:44, 313, 319–321, 328–330, 336, 40:148, 175
26:28f—29:213
26:29—35:67, 36:125, 37:315
26:29f—33:182
26:31—20:335, 33:86, 49:113n
26:34—27:344
26:36f—6:251, 43:44
26:36–46—54:107
26:37f—2:335
26:38—8:14, 12:126, 24:7, 54:430
26:39—13:345, 30:303, 54:65
26:40f—42:80
26:41—3:8, 5:320, 10:92, 11:443, 13:138, 14:58, 25:339, 26:46, 36:112, 48:308, 54:430
26:47–50—54:37, 106f
26:47–56—43:44, 66n
26:49—6:47, 14:347, 30:144, 41:80, 46:102
26:52—9:74, 83, 21:148, 22:221, 38:303, 40:282, 45:87, 46:25, 30, 41, 166, 198, 54:152
26:52f—45:93n
26:53—3:270, 6:41, 23:302
26:56—33:86, 43:66n
26:57—48:387
26:57f—37:20n
26:57–68—36:288
26:60—9:196
26:61—22:238, 39:123
26:63—25:12
26:64—11:116, 43:45
26:65—11:113
26:66—11:113, 33:84
26:68—44:352
26:69–75—43:66n
26:70f—20:238
27:3–7—20:125
27:3–10—34:171, 173
27:4—6:134, 11:114, 54:276
27:5—40:297, 41:343
27:7—20:318
27:7f—11:73
27:9—20:125, 321
27:9f—20:125n, 318
27:10—20:124
27:15–23—42:51
27:18—11:114, 13:415
27:22—47:271
27:24—49:150
27:25—11:42f, 14:267
27:26—36:204, 207
27:27–31—43:45
27:28–38—27:122
27:29—10:168, 36:291f, 39:161
27:31—43:45
27:34—10:375, 12:243, 22:517, 27:111, 38:190, 49:308, 51:90
27:34f—43:45
27:37—48:145
27:40—19:176, 51:41
27:40–42—42:107
27:42—17:192, 226, 19:176, 28:108, 47:282
27:42f—24:378
27:43—10:141, 364, 16:310, 19:177, 42:107
27:44—32:171
27:45—32:170, 38:192
27:46—6:54, 7:211, 10:144, 12:126, 128, 17:128, 26:372, 30:303, 42:105, 108n, 54:430
27:49—14:89
27:50—25:312, 424
27:50f—38:192
27:51—29:203
27:52—13:85
27:52f—8:313, 333
27:56—27:195
27:64—10:13, 36:228
27:66—33:26, 37:50n
27:69–75—27:156
28:1—1:5, 27:196
28:1f—37:315
28:1–4—43:45
28:2—33:26, 36:32n, 37:66n, 216–218
28:3—6:323, 29:117
28:5—37:298n
28:5–7—43:45
28:6—22:104
28:10—22:512, 513, 30:265
28:18—12:56, 132, 13:235, 15:293f, 20:203, 24:85, 26:228, 38:176
28:18f—35:26
28:19—3:91, 104, 12:288, 369, 13:272, 20:338, 23:79, 25:8, 26:101, 28:263, 35:91, 148, 36:112, 37:183, 38:24, 27, 87, 161, 198, 40:245, 252, 50:203, 51:308, 320, 376, 54:113
28:19f—6:128, 13:49, 34:74, 38:212, 41:196, 54:55
28:20—2:99, 6:311, 8:81, 183, 187f, 11:453, 13:18f, 49, 15:350, 17:309, 374, 27:156, 30:308, 33:85, 36:351, 37:331, 38:161f, 196, 41:48, 58, 107, 132, 148, 155, 202, 330, 46:222, 47:117
28:30—49:331n
29:5—12:92

Mark

1:1–15—45:224
1:2—18:408
1:3—25:218, 37:240f, 53:131
1:5—22:449
1:7—2:395, 22:475, 52:74
1:14—45:88n
1:23–26—41:150
1:25—7:242, 10:463
1:30—54:271
1:34—31:142n
1:44—54:111
Chp. 2—23:268
2:3f—48:369n
2:3–12—36:72
2:4—2:67
2:20—54:357
2:25f—35:241
2:25–28—44:389
2:27—1:79n, 29:6, 36:99
2:27f—51:335f, 342
2:28—36:99, 240n
3:1–5—36:240n
3:2—40:98
3:2f—23:235
3:4–12—54:53
3:5—7:262, 52:147
3:18—51:217n
3:29—19:48, 32:95, 37:20n
3:34f—52:107
3:35—11:185
4:8—5:56, 37:313
4:9—14:241
4:10f—37:262n
4:11—43:43
4:12—9:272n
4:15—46:9n
4:21—10:125
4:26–29—51:77
4:28—12:112
4:33f—37:262n
4:40—44:60n
5:1–10—41:185

5:9f—37:215n
5:23—31:190
5:25—27:220
5:25f—26:404, 33:18
5:25-34—31:103
5:26—27:220
5:30—19:74
5:34—27:304, 53:121
5:41—22:114
6:2f—22:47
6:3—27:195, 30:203
6:11—35:147
6:13—36:121, 37:370
6:17—2:32
6:18—50:36n
6:20—13:184, 50:200
6:27-35—36:208n
6:33—36:208
6:49—20:168
6:50—11:149
7:6—25:458
7:8f—51:107
7:9—44:330
7:9-13—51:147n
7:11—29:38
7:25—6:140
7:31—11:483
7:34—7:277, 29:223, 53:99
7:36—12:385
8:15—33:203
8:18—16:74n
8:19—37:43n
8:22-25—54:53
8:24—11:335
8:34f—27:356
8:35—25:512
8:38—26:451, 49:365, 52:142, 278
9:5-7—46:214n
9:7—43:151
9:17-29—41:150
9:19—10:55, 78, 54:30
9:23—6:154, 156, 9:87, 11:29, 149, 21:307, 31:196, 32:49, 36:73, 122, 40:260, 42:100, 43:249, 280, 46:136, 48:369, 52:157
9:23f—42:81
9:24—10:360, 22:90, 35:19, 43:173
9:26—13:409
9:32—8:37
9:34—51:304
9:35—31:301
9:39—21:279
9:40—38:264, 273, 40:241
9:48—17:415, 24:238
10:4—10:102
10:5—36:144
10:13-16—53:98, 108
10:14—22:174, 31:51, 35:111, 54:55
10:16—31:51, 36:91
10:17—41:264
10:17-19—34:187
10:20—22:141
10:23f—10:366
10:27—36:144
10:29—4:182, 28:79
10:29f—14:225
10:30—20:7
10:39—2:153
10:42f—40:356
10:48—12:317
10:52—27:304
11:16—22:224
11:23f—29:217
11:24—11:149, 25:71, 31:272, 374, 32:13, 36:121, 40:278, 42:76, 87, 113, 186, 44:58, 226, 53:79
11:25—28:272
12:7—14:314
12:14—27:206
12:15—40:96
12:25—2:130
12:30—22:179, 34:112
12:30f—34:309
12:32—51:109
12:34—10:14
12:36—13:228, 18:241
12:40—21:178
Chp. 13—46:18n
13:1—20:72, 117
13:8—25:464
13:14—40:121
13:21—37:145
13:22—36:220
13:32—2:26, 33:25
Chp. 14—36:20
14:1f—41:122n
14:3—10:13
14:4—35:190n
14:4f—6:337
14:13—10:37
14:21—15:63
14:22—4:95, 36:31, 37:28, 312f, 328, 40:175, 289, 51:187
14:22f—32:56, 53:30
14:22-24—35:82n, 36:37n, 162, 286, 37:310-314, 38:205n
14:23—36:20, 37:310f, 313
14:23f—37:315
14:24—25:376, 29:213f, 35:246n, 36:34, 38, 37:319f, 328-330, 336, 40:148, 175
14:25—36:125, 37:315
14:29—24:9
14:46—43:44
14:52—18:215
14:53—43:44
14:55—43:44
14:58—22:238
14:61—25:12
14:72—46:172n
15:15—14:314, 36:204, 207
15:19—11:363
15:23—12:115, 51:89
15:28—19:177, 48:147, 49:344
15:37—25:312
15:40—27:195
Chp. 16—28:306
16:4—36:32n
16:5—3:61n, 106, 8:254
16:7—8:26
16:14-19—43:45
16:15—2:260, 8:45, 244, 12:111, 112, 13:64, 272, 325, 14:13, 17:279, 20:338, 25:8, 26:101, 29:65, 30:121, 32:145, 33:27, 56, 35:148, 171, 36:112, 301, 40:55, 41:345, 44:256, 49:66, 52:73
16:15f—22:420, 43:45, 51:182
16:16—1:228, 266, 2:260, 3:273, 5:45, 6:128, 140, 148, 8:184, 190, 193, 255, 9:97, 10:63, 76, 237, 11:243, 12:90, 369, 13:19, 268, 15:332, 348, 16:231, 17:352, 18:15, 356, 19:196, 21:205, 22:175, 226, 283, 301, 318-320, 425, 426, 449, 512, 523, 23:92, 130, 24:215, 222, 25:9, 151, 168, 198, 26:241, 28:199, 29:223, 30:58, 31:193, 347, 32:16, 50, 34:125, 35:26, 171, 36:49, 58, 67, 82, 178, 37:192, 38:87, 40:239, 345, 41:315, 43:53, 44:242, 47:304, 48:367, 371, 371n, 49:66, 51:183f, 278, 306f, 376, 52:130, 253, 54:114
16:17—10:438, 11:28f, 16:302, 37:188
16:17f—29:125
16:18—16:302, 32:245, 36:92, 121, 43:120, 52:249
16:19—15:294, 28:230, 37:46, 195, 38:25, 56, 68
16:20—8:264, 17:243, 24:368, 36:172, 43:45

Luke
Chp. 1—29:121
1:1–4—52:206, 53:318
1:3—37:315
1:5—29:205
1:6—29:218
1:11—37:337
1:15—12:350, 22:44, 27:370
1:17—15:254, 17:166, 18:249, 22:510, 37:262, 51:20f, 52:74
1:18–22—3:208
1:19—23:366
1:20—3:284, 22:44
1:25—3:134, 5:362, 17:236, 26:446
1:26—1:109, 51:375n, 54:85
1:26f—4:255, 21:243, 37:361n
1:26–37—32:40
1:27—37:49, 45:208n
1:28—11:153, 21:322, 35:179, 191, 192, 37:260n, 43:39, 51:215
1:29—4:129, 20:168, 21:315, 327, 30:265, 48:367
1:30—2:54
1:30f—43:44
1:31—6:336, 24:92, 36:341, 37:49, 89
1:32—10:159, 12:38, 13:233, 24:94, 41:105
1:33—12:38
1:34—36:341, 38:56
1:34f—37:37n, 98
1:35—1:194, 4:161, 6:336, 7:13, 31, 8:242, 10:338, 15:275, 305, 341, 22:23, 25:149, 366, 30:222, 37:236, 362, 38:23, 25
1:36—3:29, 5:363
1:37—3:212, 6:102, 37:47
1:38—31:273, 35:152, 42:101, 45:213n, 54:329
1:39—5:272, 18:296, 40:269, 54:329
1:39–41—43:69n
1:39–56—43:44
1:41—40:242, 257
1:42—14:101, 22:23, 76, 109, 29:190, 37:172n, 260n, 45:213n
1:43—41:105
1:44—22:76
1:45—31:273
1:46—11:47, 265, 316, 341, 36:55, 152, 40:390
1:46–55—21:299–355, 43:39
1:47f—10:163
1:48—1:298, 5:270, 316, 320, 10:239, 17:160, 18:339, 20:94, 22:109, 25:463, 26:422, 41:326, 47:222, 54:329
1:49—10:163, 11:316, 29:222
1:50—3:115
1:50–53—47:111
1:51—2:4, 3:17, 10:308, 11:157, 418, 21:357, 25:198, 214, 218, 404, 29:166, 30:27
1:51f—10:347, 17:341, 33:221
1:51–53—2:35
1:52—1:256, 2:118, 3:241, 5:94, 6:311, 7:11, 11:149, 13:46, 213, 14:240f, 277, 19:162, 20:208, 31:342, 43:275, 46:23
1:53—1:245, 10:328, 11:351, 387, 533, 14:163, 30:50, 35:55, 36:226, 51:58, 52:85
1:54—11:493, 51:215
1:54f—11:259
1:55—4:151
1:56—54:329
1:58—14:101
1:64f—22:44
1:65—18:296
1:67f—10:69
1:68—2:178, 22:76, 27:185
1:69—10:113, 22:189
1:70—4:373, 35:161
1:71—6:358
1:73—4:150f
1:74—17:69
1:76f—22:159
1:77—27:185, 29:6
1:78—18:135, 20:69, 69n, 27:185
1:79—22:32, 126
1:80—22:45
Chp. 2—1:241n, 11:271, 13:233, 28:338
2:1—32:170, 44:94n
2:1–10—51:211n
2:1–14—51:211–218
2:1–20—51:211
2:4—17:253, 52:186
2:6f—43:44
2:7—27:122, 35:122, 52:10
2:8f—37:82, 90
2:8–14—54:249
2:9—1:236, 20:168
2:10—16:45, 52:15, 20
2:10f—5:220, 22:203, 51:213f
2:11—13:233–235, 22:74, 362, 24:108, 27:108, 41:105, 51:214, 52:15, 20, 53:132
2:12—13:224, 35:236, 51:375, 52:21, 171
2:13—3:270, 6:87, 29:121, 51:254
2:13f—41:365n
2:14—2:388, 392, 5:218, 6:174, 22:203, 25:126, 27:144, 174, 35:36, 44:29, 51:254, 52:27, 53:21, 54:327
2:15—38:274
2:17—22:76
2:19—2:312
2:21—43:44
2:22—31:368
2:22f—37:82, 90
2:22–24—4:98
2:25—11:163, 474, 20:291
2:29—3:120
2:29f—22:77, 53:132
2:29–32—28:110, 45:113n, 53:247, 330
2:29–33—52:103
2:30—28:305
2:31—18:107
2:32—17:63, 20:167n
2:33—52:102
2:34—3:70, 241, 10:93, 11:109, 191, 220, 394, 12:68, 13:274, 15:75, 22:17, 77, 25:87, 198, 27:343, 28:364, 29:130, 31:333, 32:141, 34:208, 36:94, 37:131, 39:133, 48:16, 189, 52:108
2:34f—10:16, 46:64, 52:110
2:35—2:217, 7:174, 202, 16:332, 27:81
2:36—40:390
2:36f—52:122
2:37—15:100, 41:286
2:38—11:474, 22:77, 28:306, 52:140
2:39—52:144
2:40—22:73, 52:145
2:41–51—22:519
2:43—6:359, 43:44
2:44—6:387
2:46—43:44
2:46f—22:73
2:47—12:113
2:48—27:81
2:49—37:306, 43:44
2:51—6:338, 22:73, 52:146
2:51f—22:73
Chp. 3—46:14
3:1—39:203
3:1–20—22:39
3:2—22:159, 172, 26:19
3:2f—22:415
3:3—22:127, 43:44

3:4—17:7, 18:210, 25:218, 37:240
3:6—11:272
3:7—10:268, 21:343, 22:45, 32:141, 39:180
3:8—2:295, 25:282, 31:96
3:9—18:52, 21:268
3:11—31:96, 45:259
3:12f—31:96
3:14—17:262, 31:96, 41:40, 45:77f, 98, 46:97, 129, 48:259
3:15—22:44
3:16—13:3f, 22:127, 52:74
3:17—13:3, 14:306, 47:263
3:20—22:49
3:21–23—45:224
3:22—15:304, 307, 19:97, 22:78, 172, 37:66, 41:271n, 302n
3:23—35:304, 45:224
3:31—15:296
Chp. 4—46:12
4:4—29:162
4:10—11:211
4:18—4:127, 15:275, 16:195, 17:329, 26:329, 27:35, 33:130
4:20—12:210
4:22—22:34
4:23—13:170, 23:209, 26:421, 28:282, 33:82, 41:16, 31
4:25f—25:93, 35:323
4:26—19:38, 27:288, 35:322f
4:30—22:207
4:41—7:242, 13:65
4:47—10:176
Chp. 5—23:268
5:1f—6:301
5:8—4:213, 12:318, 404, 31:125, 33:83, 40:125
5:10—10:38, 12:405, 31:233n
5:11—11:212
5:10—37:83n
5:19—9:220
5:31—34:153
5:32—10:230, 31:271
5:36—41:73
Chp. 6—46:11, 15
6:7—10:78
6:12—26:318
6:14—51:217n
6:20—42:34n
6:20–38—44:259
6:21—14:181, 21:346
6:22f—43:79
6:23—21:206
6:24—10:55, 152, 21:44
6:24f—6:271, 311
6:24–26—21:11
6:25—10:55, 152, 11:146, 14:181, 16:133, 21:18, 29, 21:44
6:26—25:137
6:27—16:276n, 36:205, 207
6:27f—45:275
6:27–29—36:266n
6:27–35—45:291n
6:29f—45:256n
6:30—5:264, 9:242n, 39:13, 45:256, 282
6:30f—45:263
6:31—45:128n, 287n, 292f
6:32–35—45:288
6:32–36—44:109
6:33—11:403, 54:91, 454
6:34—45:290
6:34f—45:241
6:35—2:263, 9:144, 17:410, 25:169, 45:257, 283, 290n, 291f, 294f, 51:267
6:35–38—15:171n
6:36—6:254, 31:84, 42:28, 122, 46:67
6:37—11:232, 12:356
6:37f—23:17
6:38—4:61f, 5:305, 9:149, 13:410, 14:267, 15:171, 16:20, 25, 17:380, 20:49, 21:188, 22:451
6:39—10:435, 14:224, 341, 16:104, 22:471, 44:192, 45:107, 47:172
6:40—24:278
6:41f—45:65n, 154
6:42—40:120, 41:228, 54:314
6:43—21:265
6:44—21:265, 37:149
6:45—35:189
6:46—27:257, 52:142
7:4—5:125
7:11–17—43:250n, 51:44
7:12—43:136
7:12–14—11:254
7:14—22:114, 51:45, 254
7:16—10:63, 51:90
7:22—25:150
7:27—18:408
7:29—22:46, 28:306
7:30—22:47, 62
7:32—18:385
7:34—17:402
7:35—51:335, 384
7:36f—4:148
7:36–48—29:26
7:36–50—31:303
7:37—40:125n
7:38—10:80, 14:346
7:44–47—14:151
7:45—14:347
7:47—27:277, 31:101, 34:160, 189, 313, 40:278, 42:64
7:48—16:129, 31:101, 37:183, 40:125
7:49—23:268
7:50—6:141, 31:101, 274, 32:46, 34:313, 42:64, 53:121
Chp. 8—28:302
8:2—2:321
8:5f—25:19
8:5–7—11:56
8:5–15—3:281
8:6—3:317, 23:393
8:7—20:345
8:8—37:314
8:10—9:272n, 16:92, 24:402
8:11—6:292, 18:7, 37:175, 253, 38:37
8:13—10:18, 22:472
8:14—9:169, 50:300n, 51:294
8:15—7:54, 12:387, 29:181, 41:167
8:21—52:107
8:22f—6:301
8:39—11:17
8:43—29:156, 230
8:43f—25:307
8:46—19:17
8:48—53:12
8:50—6:73, 11:149
8:53—10:366
9:2—49:66
9:3—8:146
9:6—37:83n
9:23—14:58, 20:329f
9:23f—33:148
9:26—25:521
9:32—35:245
9:35—41:271n
9:45—37:305n
9:49—21:278
9:50—21:278
9:51f—27:388
9:54—36:320, 40:291, 50:222n
9:54f—42:46
9:54–56—32:88
9:55—25:464, 31:304
9:56—12:218, 25:465, 31:304, 39:12
9:58—5:7, 18:118
9:60—46:266n, 49:265
9:62—3:299, 25:478
10:1f—23:186
10:3—35:147n
10:4—21:170
10:5–7—1:211
10:6—47:12
10:7—1:213, 2:76, 5:137, 7:63, 8:126, 229, 9:248, 27:120, 396, 28:347, 349, 40:315, 44:191, 45:249, 252, 40:129n, 40:138

10:7f—8:180, 46:233n
10:8—5:137, 22:220
10:9—20:182, 35:147n
10:10—31:97, 234
10:11—40:384
10:16—2:175, 250, 274, 358, 3:271, 9:141, 12:43, 13:80, 15:275, 17:357, 22:401, 420, 25:3, 238, 28:96, 29:6, 30:128, 297, 35:129, 147, 36:71, 148, 150, 266n, 39:170, 43:151n, 223, 44:52, 45:348, 47:278, 49:66, 52:141, 54:395
10:18—1:150, 16:140n, 28:291, 36:150n, 45:112n, 121n
10:19—24:84
10:20—27:93
10:21—10:70, 12:246
10:22—37:64
10:23—2:353, 10:368
10:23f—11:136, 14:90, 35:257n
10:24—1:354, 2:353, 12:364, 14:183, 15:260, 26:293, 52:126
10:27—12:45, 25:262, 34:112, 51:340
10:27f—22:425
10:28—2:159, 13:269, 23:74, 26:143, 145, 265, 272, 34:112, 313, 46:151, 51:109, 285
10:29—25:185
10:29–37—32:24, 41:218n
10:30—18:34, 27:227, 31:246
10:30f—25:340, 27:364, 32:232
10:30–35—8:54, 26:260
10:30–37—27:58, 29:134, 51:340, 373
10:31–37—51:344
10:33f—25:507, 30:118
10:34—7:281, 10:63, 11:335, 35:383
10:34f—10:192, 30:68
10:35—49:158
10:36—24:256
10:37—24:256, 42:140
10:38—16:327, 25:352
10:38–42—16:327n
10:41—10:204, 254
10:41f—10:127, 26:214
10:42—11:541, 15:76, 23:247, 24:97, 26:460, 28:314, 40:10, 53:14
11:4—29:18
11:5–13—36:124
11:8—38:133
11:9—17:375, 40:278
11:9–13—42:87, 186, 43:192n, 44:58
11:10—3:359
11:13—3:138, 5:23, 10:317, 243, 11:458
11:15—10:60, 47:256
11:16—9:74
11:17—2:225, 16:161, 44:336
11:17–20—45:213
11:18—1:113, 14:158, 33:65, 39:277
11:18–20—39:150
11:20—20:182, 33:237, 37:313
11:21—3:179, 12:9, 20, 114, 13:14, 409, 26:452, 27:43, 29:34, 33:65, 177, 287, 40:18, 43
11:21f—12:215, 23:290, 25:293, 26:193, 428, 34:89, 213
11:22—1:190, 11:8, 12:9, 20, 114, 13:14, 278, 409, 14:339, 18:246, 40:32, 47:219
11:23—16:124, 23:189, 31:65, 33:115, 34:207, 36:160
11:24—12:382
11:24–26—26:283, 415
11:25—11:24
11:26—12:166, 21:218, 40:18, 66
11:27—21:242, 32:108, 46:221
11:28—36:124, 44:356
11:34—15:227, 27:37, 244, 29:200
11:35f—38:311, 41:216
11:36—27:37
11:36–50—32:33
11:41—28:380, 31:86, 134, 198, 45:259n
11:42—11:112, 25:488
11:44—45:306n
11:49—52:94
11:52—31:238, 40:357
Chp. 12—16:124n
12:1—27:340, 40:32
12:4f—45:106n
12:8—11:527
12:11f—32:108
12:14—13:177, 17:115, 44:168
12:15—9:94
12:16–20—16:341
12:16–21—21:14, 174, 42:148, 45:255
12:20—15:123, 16:61, 28:370
12:21—19:214
12:24—50:94n
12:29—16:37, 28:371
12:32—3:160, 241, 5:226, 22:90, 208, 350, 25:377, 26:214, 28:375, 29:12, 66, 30:290, 35:90, 36:46, 51:115, 127
12:33—11:148
12:34—51:294
12:35—10:161, 11:261, 30:25
12:36—18:58, 25:355
12:42—31:251, 34:243
12:45—44:214n
12:46—18:333
12:48—4:381, 16:49, 19:166, 27:103, 28:330, 380, 36:356, 54:418
12:49—14:310, 16:144, 26:452, 33:52
12:50—2:153, 10:78, 42:142
Chp. 13—18:58
13:1–5—42:133
13:2–5—10:77
13:3—26:39
13:4—9:102, 24:14
13:5—9:102, 24:14, 28:159
13:6–9—48:214n
13:11—25:313, 26:70, 310, 314, 363
13:11f—48:286
13:11–17—51:339
13:14—27:55, 51:345
13:15—44:390
13:15f—51:339
13:24—44:294
13:27—10:77, 27:34
13:28—7:303, 27:34
13:33—22:80
13:34—47:133n
14:1—51:348
14:1–11—51:333–354, 54:314
14:5—35:241
14:7—13:32, 51:348
14:7–10—53:47
14:7–9—36:185
14:8—21:320
14:8–10—30:139
14:10—10:233, 348,

25:455, 44:307, 45:117
14:11—11:263, 19:111, 23:350, 30:139, 43:275
14:12f—25:449
14:12-14—13:418, 45:282
14:16—2:163
14:18—11:253
14:18f—20:163
14:18-20—18:325
14:19f—20:7n
14:20—17:116
14:23—12:243, 25:493
14:24—19:123
14:26—5:114, 6:29, 36, 252, 9:70, 45:278
14:27—25:442, 34:121
14:28—33:34n
14:28f—27:242
14:31—46:202f
14:33—21:90, 25:516, 27:242
15:2—10:145
15:4—12:154f, 25:204
15:4f—3:240
15:6—42:185
15:7—46:172n
15:8—29:142
15:10—10:287, 11:394
15:11f—19:99
15:11-32—31:224, 38:230n
15:16—12:161
15:19—4:55, 43:275
15:20—11:108
15:21—4:56, 43:275
15:25f—25:98
15:25-30—22:104
Chp. 16—21:18, 32
16:1f—30:250
16:7—18:17
16:8—1:318, 6:164, 10:21, 289, 11:523, 12:219, 13:198, 18:354, 20:128, 244, 22:31, 88, 33:87, 51:125
16:9—4:399, 7:347, 11:136, 22:521, 23:17, 28:380, 36:227
16:10—21:320, 41:187, 45:281n
16:11—4:380
16:12—11:263
16:14—10:366, 11:442
16:15—10:92, 105, 16:37, 27:181, 54:xviii
16:16—18:381
16:19—6:297, 7:118, 8:254, 10:366, 28:147
16:19f—10:160, 14:145
16:19-21—3:65, 45:320
16:19-31—41:199, 51:8, 52:26
16:20f—22:519
16:21—2:196, 13:25, 14:221
16:22—1:89, 4:311, 7:293f, 206, 8:315, 12:125, 21:352, 29:239, 35:83, 36:39, 196, 52:128
16:23f—48:361
16:24—4:28, 12:375
16:24f—54:162
16:25—21:18, 42:149
16:29—2:83, 4:126, 5:348, 36:197f, 40:146, 52:179, 54:48, 259
16:29-31—52:172
17:5—10:360, 22:90, 26:114, 35:19, 43:173, 44:60
17:6—10:336
17:10—2:160, 4:166, 8:176, 17:369, 21:289, 28:233, 30:229, 31:213
17:11f—48:313
17:11-19—3:183
17:12-19—31:94
17:14—22:114, 223, 35:174
17:18—3:50
17:19—33:232, 34:122
17:20—5:20, 14:94, 18:61, 26:411, 31:281, 37:283, 40:220, 51:89
17:20f—35:146, 36:89n, 37:282, 39:66, 218, 40:329, 42:40, 52:38
17:21—10:419, 25:383, 27:337, 39:218, 42:147
17:21f—25:486
17:24—30:193
17:26—50:244
17:26f—10:374, 29:237
17:27f—18:332, 35:327
17:31f—45:156
17:32—3:294, 299f
17:34—39:86
Chp. 18—12:29, 46:9
18:1—7:327, 21:138, 28:15, 40:278f, 42:24, 44:61
18:1-3—26:383
18:1-8—21:234
18:2f—5:361, 49:301n
18:5—4:340
18:7—4:363, 12:91, 21:234, 39:281
18:7f—6:352, 43:241
18:8—1:336, 2:84, 10:384, 13:191, 36:143, 39:280, 40:192, 44:252n, 52:248, 54:402
18:9f—10:145
18:9-13—45:354n
18:9-14—3:9, 51:14-17
18:10—12:72, 25:511
18:10-14—46:172n
18:11—2:42, 4:159, 11:371, 12:356, 359, 13:407, 17:298, 21:28, 24:89, 27:112, 390, 31:246, 301, 34:117, 42:31
18:11f—6:262, 26:25, 396, 27:383, 30:26, 45:73
18:12—6:114, 10:46, 74, 12:321, 13:407, 17:283, 21:260, 22:141, 519, 27:390
18:13—12:406, 14:158, 26:35, 405, 27:220
18:14—10:31, 16:37, 27:220, 30:139
18:19—40:203
18:26—10:366
18:27—20:222
18:34—8:37, 11:239
18:35—43:44
18:38—43:44
Chp. 19—18:110
19:1-10—39:xiiin
19:2f—9:180
19:2-10—54:398
19:2-11—32:116
19:8—22:407
19:9—10:355
19:10—10:339, 23:248, 27:12, 46:67
19:11—46:195
19:12-27—32:281, 54:80
19:14—2:315, 6:373, 8:239, 12:21, 232, 14:30, 318, 16:38, 22:84, 44:379, 49:343, 345
19:20—28:321
19:21—1:277
19:22—1:274, 277, 3:290, 4:397, 13:224, 41:13, 371, 54:78
19:40—4:77, 10:260, 27:147, 31:156, 33:17n, 224, 49:362
19:41—22:236
19:41f—10:150
19:42—10:367
19:43—11:127, 16:239
19:43f—15:352, 42:107
19:44—13:339, 16:192, 20:310, 337, 22:41, 23:380, 24:11, 39:283
19:46—15:283, 47:227

20:18—12:36
20:24—40:96
20:25—46:50f
20:38—25:411, 52:52
20:39—51:109
20:42f—13:228
Chp. 21—46:18n
21:6—22:85
21:8—30:295
21:11—39:34
21:15—11:452, 13:12, 27:166, 29:31, 33:94f, 49:375
21:18—25:310
21:19—5:146, 7:77, 11:142f, 365
21:20—47:139
21:22f—36:143, 47:139
21:23f—25:429
21:24—20:245
21:25—18:334, 39:132, 52:168
21:25f—8:115, 32:280
21:25–27—35:162
21:26—6:177
21:27f—50:245n
21:28—12:24, 17:334, 25:355, 29:138, 30:301, 35:316
21:33—36:143, 40:333
21:34—8:187, 27:370, 31:141, 44:214n, 51:293f
21:34f—30:193
21:35—28:200, 51:291
Chp. 22—36:20
22:2—41:122n
22:10—10:37
22:11—52:10
22:14f—37:316, 48:317
22:15—35:87, 43:44
22:17—37:311
22:17f—32:56, 37:314
22:17–19—36:286, 44:55n
22:18—36:125, 37:312, 316f
22:19—3:163, 4:95, 7:217, 12:369, 13:27, 16:130, 18:171, 20:113, 145, 23:92, 29:214, 220, 31:298, 36:31, 41, 44, 111, 37:28n, 45, 142, 187–189, 273, 313n, 317–319, 331, 38:24, 56, 40:22, 24, 175, 289
22:19f—35:82n, 36:37n, 38, 163, 335, 37:44, 314–330, 38:205n, 43:44
22:20—23:92, 29:209, 213, 35:84, 246n, 36:22, 34, 37, 40, 319, 37:43, 318–320, 336f, 40:148, 165, 175, 217, 53:30, 81
22:25—2:274, 6:168, 13:194, 14:68, 31:387, 45:118
22:25f—30:137, 36:157, 39:284, 295n
22:26—2:274, 31:387, 41:131, 49:383, 52:39
22:27—31:298
22:28—26:420
22:29—29:214
22:29f—33:182
22:31—1:145, 16:314, 22:259, 42:128, 51:310
22:32—2:99, 8:27, 11:177, 31:321, 44:135, 48:289
22:33—8:53, 24:332
22:35—21:169
22:36—18:118
22:37—27:261
22:38—28:364, 32:168
22:40—40:303
22:41—12:126
22:41f—26:372
22:42—32:285, 42:45, 75, 183
22:42–44—42:129
22:43—54:430
22:43f—22:111, 43:44
22:44—7:302, 13:263, 280, 345, 22:236, 26:370, 42:89, 54:65, 430
22:45—5:211
22:48—37:28
22:51—6:223
22:53—20:335, 22:207, 23:256, 48:233
22:55—46:102
22:56—24:10n
22:61—5:342, 34:171, 173
22:66—43:44
23:1—43:44
23:2—10:126, 166, 264, 22:89, 33:84, 39:123, 43:78n
23:3—43:44
23:5—43:78n
23:6–12—48:146
23:7—45:112n
23:12—16:106, 34:88, 52:115
23:13—43:45, 52:35
23:16—43:45
23:18—24:200
23:18–21—14:315
23:24—13:341, 33:156
23:27f—42:8
23:28—27:300, 32:285, 41:13, 42:9
23:30—18:56, 25:293, 402
23:31—11:468, 40:297, 42:9n, 10, 128
23:33—42:67
23:34—7:44, 14:257, 21:75, 153, 29:175, 220, 31:306, 32:285, 42:108, 43:45, 164, 44:71, 45:275, 46:30, 50:269
23:36—40:287, 51:90
23:39–43—42:140, 54:17, 198
23:40–42—46:172n
23:41—10:241, 41:252
23:42—17:81, 30:291
23:43—1:88, 4:314, 316, 28:305, 41:365, 54:446
23:46—25:312, 43:45
23:47—11:114
23:5—18:177
23:50–53—43:45
24:2—36:32n
24:5—8:46
24:16—3:263
24:17–24—51:234
24:19—14:302, 52:60
24:21—18:243, 249, 28:72, 37:202, 54:149
24:25—21:78, 28:367
24:26—10:40, 11:239, 13:347, 20:219, 290, 35:331, 37:209, 51:206
24:27—20:248, 22:339
24:28—3:327, 4:96
24:30f—7:216
24:34—21:319
24:35—7:251, 21:319
24:36—11:80, 37:66
24:37—31:125
24:39—2:45, 35:162, 37:136, 236, 279, 38:305
24:44—24:408, 37:195, 197, 276, 283, 38:30, 44, 46
24:44f—15:268
24:44–47—35:359
24:45—33:27, 35:123
24:46—24:402
24:46f—14:168, 27:184, 35:106, 37:192
24:47—1:148, 10:230, 13:271, 18:238, 356, 382, 24:402, 28:230, 32:231, 40:82, 274, 373

24:48—13:271
24:49—10:252, 25:149, 54:149
24:50f—53:30
26:46f—18:112

John
Sermonic commentaries in Vols. 22–24
Chp. 1—15:300, 22:5–216, 37:61
1:1—1:16, 157, 5:130, 12:285, 18:248, 24:364, 28:229, 37:133, 52:47f, 53
1:1–14—7:109, 46:135n, 51:211, 54:435
1:1–18—44:284n
1:1–67—54:435, 445
1:2—37:242n, 52:50
1:3—12:285, 15:276, 312, 19:82f, 22:19, 74, 87, 30:293, 33:235, 37:61n, 41:82, 109, 52:50f, 74
1:4—10:219, 15:318, 22:68, 80, 87, 30:223, 34:219, 52:52f, 56, 60
1:4f—15:290
1:5—11:3, 500, 18:80, 22:62, 69, 26:48, 33:98, 146, 277, 52:62
1:6—25:414, 37:241, 52:56, 65
1:6f—43:44
1:7—28:261, 52:68
1:8—32:248, 52:56, 69
1:9—4:177, 16:77, 52:70
1:10—22:74, 37:61n, 40:167, 52:73
1:10f—33:277
1:11—11:171, 189, 13:284, 17:191, 33:146, 52:56, 73
1:12—12:350, 22:100, 26:351, 27:184, 221, 270, 29:155, 214, 30:45, 31:349, 33:157, 36:240, 43:62, 51:71, 52:75, 153
1:12f—1:269, 4:367, 18:358, 33:278, 34:113, 35:370, 41:82
1:13—1:268, 3:93, 4:28, 65, 235, 241, 344f, 6:154f, 7:13, 18, 36, 167, 8:232, 11:121, 12:277, 359, 13:302, 22:330, 25:281, 26:42, 29:191, 52:76, 153, 54:348
1:14—10:434, 11:163, 12:206, 15:341, 20:70, 21:353, 22:6, 346, 25:223, 317, 29:190, 32:228, 33:215, 37:31, 133, 206, 211, 250, 38:xix, 237, 239, 275, 41:109, 346, 52:56, 80, 53:131, 54:197, 395
1:14f—37:290n
1:16—3:90, 9:6, 10:11, 52, 12:247, 15:263, 16:118, 22:48, 120, 426, 434, 438, 495, 31:231, 32:228, 33:279f
1:17—10:403, 12:61, 15:328, 22:161, 426, 23:237, 25:244, 26:354, 27:15, 226, 407, 32:228, 44:257
1:18—1:18, 59, 5:50, 12:140, 15:218, 317, 20:149, 335, 22:9, 26:396, 400, 30:297, 34:216, 38:267
1:19—22:126, 434
1:19–28—53:76–78
1:20—22:44, 62, 126, 439
1:21—22:509
1:23—17:277, 22:172, 439
1:24—41:105n
1:26—22:43, 433, 37:274
1:26f—22:48, 65
1:26–30—18:409
1:27—12:394, 22:48, 62, 447, 476, 52:74
1:28—22:422
1:29—1:192, 8:153, 208, 263, 312, 12:127, 365, 389, 16:129, 338, 17:99, 222, 22:44, 51, 62, 72, 80, 87, 344, 421, 425, 24:92, 25:416, 26:32, 132, 138, 143, 147, 151, 278, 379, 28:305, 29:138, 168, 194, 30:309, 31:97, 190, 224, 231, 33:228, 37:104f, 174, 253, 255, 39:188, 40:193, 299, 41:111, 48:282, 51:376, 53:67
1:30—12:394
1:32—19:97, 22:78, 37:337
1:32f—37:301
1:32–34—52:65
1:33—11:459, 22:78, 160, 171, 37:299, 38:31, 59
1:38—22:184
1:42—20:256, 22:182, 185, 41:314
1:43–51—22:413
1:45—22:128
1:46—22:128
1:47—5:217, 22:183, 187
1:50—5:217
1:51—5:217f, 22:187, 31:371
Chp. 2—22:217–274
2:1f—12:259, 52:146
2:1–11—4:257, 53:242
2:2f—43:44
2:4—52:53
2:6—10:37
2:7—23:114
2:7f—37:183n
2:9—11:286
2:10—43:44
2:14–17—31:306
2:15–17—52:147
2:16—22:221
2:17—26:187
2:18—10:15
2:19—10:15
2:20—20:160, 35:305, 45:225n
2:23–25—7:242
2:24—15:27
2:24f—22:266
2:29—30:273
Chp. 3—11:466, 22:275–502, 28:236, 37:237
3:1—40:154n
3:1f—33:280, 37:20n, 38:58
3:1–15—22:275
3:3—3:95, 13:299f, 33:227, 34:113, 36:354, 37:219n, 237n, 38:81
3:3f—25:104, 28:198
3:3–5—35:30
3:3–6—52:15
3:5—1:228, 3:105, 11:152, 13:302, 19:11, 22:118, 280, 429, 25:226, 281, 29:119, 156, 34:320, 37:237n, 40:56, 43:53
3:5f—33:214, 281
3:6—3:95, 4:345, 8:140, 11:322, 13:299, 22:97, 110, 365, 23:166, 26:139, 27:366, 28:192, 31:300, 33:214, 223, 225, 227, 260, 274, 35:371, 37:81, 95, 97–99, 236f, 39:218, 40:19, 47:144
3:7—25:281, 31:55
3:8—1:170, 9:184, 11:33, 65, 13:302, 16:76, 20:13, 25:243, 26:159, 170, 172, 33:18,

155n, 34:171, 173, 41:326n
3:9—33:281, 37:219
3:10—32:146
3:11—12:268, 16:5, 23:93, 28:80, 29:145
3:12—37:220, 44:336, 46:63
3:13—10:119, 12:365, 16:76, 22:365, 454, 24:39, 29:225, 37:66, 231n, 232, 280f, 42:23, 44:319n
3:14—2:151, 12:88, 16:144n, 23:374, 26:166, 357, 30:115, 39:78f
3:14f—22:331, 26:159, 287, 33:281, 43:44
3:16—1:242, 4:257, 8:309, 12:171, 369, 22:63, 23:63, 87, 24:60, 179, 282, 25:297, 26:37, 146, 386, 30:321, 37:210, 42:13, 43:67n, 51:278
3:16–18—53:66
3:16–21—22:275
3:17—8:326, 12:226, 16:19, 23:60, 338, 31:304, 46:166
3:18—9:183, 11:112, 12:89, 18:356, 22:74, 361, 381, 24:164, 26:443, 27:19, 34, 31:270, 33:283, 34:319n, 43:53, 51:279, 54:152
3:19—2:354, 9:184, 16:33, 91, 243, 22:35, 69, 26:48, 59, 30:226, 33:214, 52:64, 117
3:20—1:181, 39:101, 45:122
3:20f—47:25
3:21—39:101, 45:122
3:25—22:416
3:26—22:424
3:27—22:484, 27:292, 29:125, 33:240, 284
3:28—22:64
3:29—22:425, 441, 29:18, 38:187, 41:160, 227, 42:139, 46:289
3:30—22:64, 439, 515, 34:284, 48:288n
3:31—8:29, 22:455, 465, 484, 33:285, 36:142, 52:46
3:33—22:468
3:34—22:488
3:35—12:83, 22:475, 488, 51:128
3:36—5:50, 11:201, 12:89, 14:329, 22:53, 480, 495, 503, 26:147, 27:13, 33:284
Chp. 4—11:131, 22:503–530
4:2—40:36, 51:319
4:5—6:202, 8:198
4:7—6:183
4:9—22:517
4:10—16:130
4:13—10:354, 11:290, 31:54
4:13f—11:146
4:14—9:97, 11:131, 326, 357, 13:27, 20:143, 331, 340, 22:134f, 27:222, 31:343, 35:92, 36:45, 37:164n
4:16—14:288
4:20—2:285, 9:258, 36:220, 37:284
4:20f—37:283
4:20–24—13:270, 36:290, 292n
4:21—9:167, 12:360, 14:325, 20:114, 32:163, 36:290
4:21–23—18:357, 22:250, 44:33
4:22—2:178, 3:97, 4:367, 6:284, 8:136, 9:180, 214, 12:293, 297, 18:386, 20:99, 22:92, 25:100, 195, 41:51, 47:140, 302
4:23—9:167, 27:155, 32:163, 40:31
4:23f—9:157
4:24—4:213, 12:360, 21:325, 40:31, 42:20, 44:30
4:25—22:284
4:27—54:154
4:34—11:59, 291, 14:183, 20:217, 29:216, 37:44
4:35—16:98, 18:119
4:37—15:34, 41:375
4:38—54:85
4:42—52:33
4:44—32:13
4:46–53—43:250
4:50—29:35, 31:272
Chp. 5—30:115, 271
5:2—11:286
5:10—33:283
5:14—1:225
5:16—22:223, 23:235, 35:165
5:17—1:74, 76, 2:148, 8:163, 12:55, 84, 15:334, 21:328, 22:20f, 26f, 29:161, 34:276
5:17f—15:312
5:18—10:267
5:19—3:297, 12:285, 15:334, 22:469
5:19–27—12:84
5:21—8:165, 12:285, 15:293, 334, 54:65
5:22—10:77, 11:111
5:23—10:135, 15:293, 311, 316, 334, 22:392, 26:141, 30:258, 47:278
5:24—54:65
5:26—15:293, 24:373
5:27—10:403, 41:118
5:28f—22:344, 51:254
5:29—4:316
5:30—22:120
5:31f—48:366
5:32–37—22:449
5:33–35—22:239
5:35—22:62, 33:93, 52:56, 61
5:36—10:63, 20:217
5:39—10:7, 33:93, 188, 35:122, 235, 52:106, 172
5:43—10:432, 14:261, 20:127, 31:205, 37:143, 39:82, 40:230, 52:74, 54:198
5:44—10:455, 13:384, 25:31, 43, 26:60, 29:154, 54:360
5:46—15:268, 299, 326, 23:35, 35:122, 132, 37:290, 52:22, 106
Chp. 6—23:5–197, 36:15f, 19f, 37:xiif, xviii, 11, 84n, 93n, 98, 100, 114, 123, 153, 234, 248f, 360, 38:16f, 17n, 20, 24f, 26n, 57, 46:10f, 49:149f
6:9—54:377
6:10—22:414
6:11—36:170, 37:117
6:12—7:251
6:13—43:282
6:14—22:114
6:15—31:390, 40:305, 46:166
6:17—19:43, 40:96
6:24—37:93n
6:25—40:154n
6:26—21:310, 23:398
6:26–28—37:360n
6:27—22:135, 31:347, 35:194n, 37:99, 118, 145
6:27f—37:83n
6:28—10:129, 11:29, 29:123, 31:347
6:28f—11:375
6:29—29:123, 30:233, 263, 31:347, 36:15, 39:169, 44:23, 296
6:32—9:97, 11:165, 38:51, 42:58
6:33—37:100, 145
6:34—23:44

6:35—23:50, 29:201, 36:15, 37:113, 46:175n
6:35f—23:118
6:36—23:49
6:37—16:31, 23:246, 39:12, 54:330
6:38—31:298
6:38–40—51:176
6:39—17:94, 39:12, 53:329
6:40—2:48, 23:63, 24:61, 30:271
6:41—17:244, 23:155, 36:15, 37:114
6:43—23:90
6:44—5:47, 11:156, 17:244, 23:23, 183, 246, 25:224, 374, 27:179, 292, 366, 29:111, 223, 33:285, 42:57, 43:87, 44:296, 52:194
6:45—10:293, 11:156, 161, 364, 440, 17:243, 18:107, 25:374, 27:320, 28:375, 29:198, 31:376, 36:139, 151, 39:309, 40:21, 32, 42:57, 44:134, 205, 296, 48:54
6:49—23:31
6:51—23:126, 29:136, 32:63, 36:15, 37:100, 164, 42:54, 56, 43:34
6:51f—37:234
6:51–54—23:138
6:52—8:185, 38:21n, 40f, 72n
6:52f—37:286, 288
6:53—6:155, 22:317, 23:170, 36:15, 20, 37:79
6:54–57—9:136
6:55—10:460, 23:119, 33:215, 36:15, 37:79, 84, 118, 242f, 247, 251, 40:203, 52:54
6:55f—20:210, 37:121
6:55–58—37:237n
6:56—25:67, 26:137, 30:223, 37:79, 132
6:58—23:41, 37:118, 42:54
6:60—11:395, 31:232, 38:25, 57
6:61—33:180
6:61f—22:326
6:62—22:317, 321, 24:105f, 37:246
6:63—3:272, 4:95, 10:22, 460, 11:81, 439, 442, 16:55, 55n, 23:101, 162, 27:271, 28:221, 230, 265, 30:286, 315, 31:84, 33:215, 35:362, 36:19, 37:6, 11, 46, 48, 78–80, 92, 95–98, 100–102, 112f, 127n, 129, 134, 138, 145, 155f, 206, 286–288, 308, 38:20, 24, 26, 26n, 54f, 57, 64, 74, 299, 39:96, 40:202f, 41:309, 45:153, 49:200n, 52:54, 54:318
6:64—37:247
6:65—5:44, 18:378, 23:23, 42:57, 44:297
6:66—23:157
6:66f—17:208n, 33:180
6:68—15:229, 20:318, 23:10, 36:201, 37:247
6:69—29:78
6:70—21:277, 23:190
6:71—8:50, 10:256, 54:108
Chp. 7—23:198–306
7:3—38:54
7:5—52:77
7:7—3:221, 26:59, 33:277
7:15—52:146
7:16—3:297, 12:84, 14:329, 22:469, 25:388, 38:258, 267, 276, 43:151, 45:70
7:16f—16:118
7:17—23:224
7:18—27:101
7:19—15:328, 32:221, 41:70
7:20—10:126, 32:141
7:22—34:114n, 47:85, 50:35
7:22f—35:165
7:24—11:112, 27:214
7:30—15:49
7:31—31:393, 47:281
7:32–34—23:259
7:33—11:131, 23:354
7:37—16:212, 18:8, 23:50, 26:329
7:37f—22:136
7:37–39—51:129
7:38—16:130, 20:143, 35:92, 36:45n
7:38f—20:331
7:39—13:4, 15:294
7:40f—22:128
7:41—22:128, 47:281
7:41–43—52:184
7:45f—22:129
7:45–49—22:47
7:46—14:283
7:48—3:341, 24:156
7:49—3:341
Chp. 8—23:307–422
8:1–11—31:335
8:2–11—54:154
8:3–11—31:101, 54:218
8:7—46:312
8:10—31:101
8:11—23:337, 31:101, 32:32, 36:90
8:12—8:287, 12:122, 22:32, 33:93, 34:131, 35:221, 36:191
8:13f—48:366
8:14f—19:192
8:15—26:368
8:17—37:314
8:20—47:254
8:21—10:260
8:23—33:277, 285
8:24—14:329, 15:328, 23:350, 52:54, 54:148
8:25—1:10, 10:6
8:27—22:114, 23:365
8:28—12:50, 26:59
8:29—44:25
8:32–36—51:57
8:33—25:80, 109, 26:121, 236
8:33–36—32:92
8:34—25:53, 356f, 31:49, 65
8:35—14:187, 25:356, 26:443, 27:284, 317
8:36—2:123, 14:348, 17:119, 25:317, 26:447, 27:6, 31:49, 343, 40:303, 52:54
8:37—10:51, 25:85, 26:435
8:39—4:368, 7:165f, 9:26, 11:239, 16:46, 22:196, 47:141
8:39f—4:28, 26:449
8:41—22:196, 24:318, 26:121
8:42—24:308
8:42–44—26:449
8:43—24:308, 32:255
8:44—1:22, 112, 150f, 165, 189, 191, 218f, 275, 322, 2:172, 197, 3:179, 6:293, 9:53, 11:356, 12:374, 13:185, 20:314, 21:39, 22:196, 24:26, 216, 313, 329, 363, 26:14, 41, 188, 194, 429, 455, 27:11, 136, 145, 166, 29:34, 30:285, 31:335, 32:141, 34:39n, 97, 142, 36:153, 40:287, 356, 385, 41:217, 296, 340, 43:125, 146,

46:49, 81n, 179, 227, 47:141, 49:329n, 50:249, 54:41, 128
8:46—11:112, 29:229, 40:54
8:46-59—23:422
8:47—16:6, 92, 30:291, 36:142
8:48—10:126, 11:112, 12:245, 33:84, 39:125
8:49—6:56, 7:115
8:50—26:59, 31:343
8:51—4:314, 6:262, 7:298, 12:84, 13:268, 14:87, 17:13, 18:360, 41:310, 42:142, 47:295
8:52—52:55
8:54f—15:314, 17:23, 22:150
8:55—30:239, 32:141
8:56—2:260f, 353, 377, 3:153, 194, 219, 5:18, 15:326, 23:326, 26:239, 244, 27:268, 34:225, 47:301, 52:125
8:58—1:13, 14:330, 18:248, 22:321
8:59—22:207, 37:178
9:1—2:321
9:1-38—51:35-43
9:3—35:251
9:4—27:128, 401, 31:138, 44:80
9:5—33:93, 52:56
9:7—18:219, 27:163f, 28:260
9:14-16—35:165
9:16—10:62, 25:203, 51:342
9:24—10:60, 10:62, 25:203
9:26-37—28:266
9:28f—13:19, 29:110
9:31—12:313, 29:196, 31:355, 36:56
9:32—51:43
9:34—10:387, 14:341
9:38—22:128, 36:294, 37:284
9:39—11:111, 16:248
9:40f—10:145, 25:203, 51:37
9:41—10:243, 317, 11:234, 351, 17:76, 78, 23:350
Chp. 10—25:4
10:1—9:229, 11:336, 20:312, 25:142, 28:281, 31:207, 34:40, 36:141, 39:171, 40:8, 222, 41:191
10:1f—34:143
10:1-16—13:11
10:3—13:16, 17:85, 124, 35:123, 39:xi, 48:35
10:3-5—51:310
10:4—4:280, 12:153, 158, 17:209, 39:306
10:4f—20:145
10:5—5:115, 8:272, 12:155, 29:15, 36:71, 39:306, 40:32, 41:302, 45:105
10:7—29:111, 37:xii, 38, 44:253, 51:46
10:8—9:245, 13:64, 27:164, 166, 33:49, 36:141, 39:100, 39:171, 39:306, 41:302, 44:254
10:9—10:6, 31:53, 35:123
10:10—11:532, 26:19, 57, 29:135, 40:10
10:11—12:317, 30:270, 37:xii, 38, 40:194, 43:121, 46:146, 48:396
10:11f—49:428n
10:12—12:155, 13:16, 25:295, 32:146, 33:152n, 39:100
10:12-16—20:127n, 320n
10:14—12:158, 45:105
10:15—2:138, 12:158, 40:194
10:16—2:215, 14:10, 16:167
10:17—11:177
10:18—22:116, 247
10:20—22:128
10:22—31:281
10:25—10:72
10:26f—17:179
10:27—5:47, 115, 8:271, 36:71, 40:32, 41:302, 45:105
10:27f—25:78
10:28—5:47, 12:157-159, 17:94, 18:202, 23:60, 40:194, 43:171
10:28f—33:85, 289
10:28-30—51:128
10:29—25:78, 374
10:30—12:51, 84, 285, 15:311
10:31—15:312
10:32—7:288
10:34—2:390, 41:81n, 43:62
10:35—9:17, 26:457, 40:333, 43:62, 44:390
10:38—10:72, 52:199
10:39—3:263
10:41—22:128
Chp. 11—16:124n, 22:335
11:1-45—51:44-49
11:3—51:46
11:4—12:405
11:5f—50:269
11:8—51:48
11:9—3:345, 5:174, 15:96, 34:131
11:9f—22:59
11:11—10:334, 25:479, 53:326
11:12—5:75, 51:48
11:16—22:422
11:21—51:48
11:25—4:157, 8:144, 163, 14:86, 16:31, 22:335, 344, 419, 23:44, 25:78, 26:22, 29:136, 31:297, 31:345, 37:xii, 38, 41:310, 47:295, 301, 52:53, 55, 54:294, 447
11:25f—4:105, 7:298, 43:44, 53:330
11:26—4:115, 10:298, 25:314, 29:136, 31:297, 35:359, 41:315
11:27—22:128
11:33—51:233
11:36—51:46
11:39—7:264
11:40—7:174
11:41—51:45, 47, 254
11:42—10:72
11:43—10:169, 22:114, 120, 37:133, 51:45, 47, 254
11:43f—43:44
11:44—19:70
11:45—4:121
11:47—47:282
11:47-53—41:122n, 54:441
11:48—2:221, 361, 9:28, 11:224, 355, 12:253, 14:322, 26:428
11:49—14:314, 40:251
11:49f—14:72, 39:132, 51:386
11:49-51—2:218
11:49-52—36:138
11:50—11:224, 13:186, 14:322, 21:276, 52:191
11:51—21:276, 34:95, 43:157n, 52:192
11:52—28:129
11:55—22:414
Chp. 12—29:215
12:1-8—42:8n
12:3—12:175
12:3f—12:249
12:6—21:169, 52:267, 54:108
12:8—9:148, 29:226, 38:23
12:15—20:94
12:21—22:251

12:24—5:146, 6:95, 355, 7:136, 203, 210, 8:37, 11:194, 12:112, 23:161, 25:51, 28:181, 39:135
12:24f—11:385
12:25—8:5, 10:31, 14:162, 21:90, 25:51, 318, 382, 27:181, 38:260
12:25f—4:147
12:26—13:245
12:27–29—54:127
12:31—6:88, 90, 11:4, 267, 33:236n, 287, 37:17n, 40:303, 41:169, 48:267, 49:110n, 140, 173n, 50:19
12:32—16:124, 22:331, 23:161, 374, 24:21, 86, 414, 27:366, 51:28
12:35—13:152, 15:96, 17:177, 212, 254, 22:32, 40:129
12:35f—5:157
12:36—3:283, 4:214, 16:33
12:38—34:111
12:39—54:63
12:40—9:272n, 16:74n, 17:91, 37:20
12:44—54:470
12:47—12:218, 26:368
12:48—25:9
12:49—12:84, 14:329
12:49f—14:329
Chp. 13—29:215, 46:12
13:1f—3:245, 37:83, 210
13:1–14—35:372
13:4f—43:44
13:4–17—3:245n
13:5—7:337
13:6—3:172, 7:288
13:7—7:103, 8:8, 30, 32, 37, 25:74
13:10—30:69, 32:158, 232
13:13—37:164n
13:14—32:158
13:15—26:246, 36:166, 40:132
13:15f—2:337
13:16—11:365, 16:52, 26:456, 37:252n, 48:221
13:17—44:356
13:18—3:50, 10:193, 25:374, 28:261, 33:25, 59, 34:13n, 49:73
13:19—33:182n
13:20—3:186, 43:151n
13:21–30—54:107
13:23—37:267
13:25f—54:404
13:27—25:64, 38:142, 41:239
13:29—54:108
13:34—11:482, 27:113, 52:17
13:34f—35:361
13:35—24:249, 27:113
Chp. 14—24:5–192, 29:215
14:1—5:18, 12:84, 212, 54:112
14:1f—29:12
14:2—1:39, 348, 10:456, 12:212, 17:133, 42:100, 44:374
14:2f—24:183
14:3—1:351, 12:232, 22:118, 37:234f
14:4—24:332
14:5—24:57
14:6—5:44, 48, 12:372, 13:136, 15:269, 17:331, 377, 386, 22:61, 132, 331, 335, 494, 23:110, 24:23, 139n, 25:224, 26:29, 29:111, 30:45, 223, 31:53, 297, 33:281, 36:109, 37:291n, 39:156, 41:48, 215, 43:55, 153, 44:253, 51:46, 52:53
14:8—17:386, 23:53, 346, 30:286, 31:53, 54:291
14:8f—12:84
14:9—2:49, 3:297, 5:45–47, 16:53, 55, 17:386, 22:488, 494, 24:23, 30:222, 286, 31:53
14:9f—15:311, 23:90, 37:56, 61
14:9–11—12:51
14:10—3:297, 5:223, 14:329, 22:420, 24:61
14:11—22:364
14:12—3:364, 4:104, 120, 162, 167, 170, 357, 5:132, 142, 7:136, 332, 22:462, 24:148, 26:373, 43:227, 230, 288, 46:224, 54:88
14:13—9:42n, 24:89, 29:16
14:14—43:230, 46:33
14:15—24:127, 33:148
14:16—11:156, 25:368
14:16f—44:285
14:17—4:121, 6:74, 8:271, 11:454, 12:380, 24:357, 33:277, 41:327
14:18—2:99, 11:453, 17:410, 24:125
14:19—5:18, 6:401, 8:189, 12:231, 13:245, 14:63, 22:118, 465, 50:21
14:20—5:223
14:21—11:544, 44:102, 51:304
14:22—51:304
14:23—4:31, 5:245, 6:259, 8:195, 10:348, 11:453, 12:279, 377, 18:360, 23:154, 29:215, 37:196, 38:190, 41:318, 327
14:23f—39:97
14:23–31—24:8n, 51:304–312
14:24—12:55, 23:64, 38:258, 267
14:26—24:291, 297, 356, 365, 29:186, 198, 34:73, 39:170, 40:33, 41:202, 51:128
14:27—25:6, 26:27, 29:189, 49:359, 54:96
14:28—1:152, 8:183, 12:55, 32:119
14:29—25:367, 33:182n
14:30—13:251, 16:211, 19:74, 20:8, 27:45, 29:131, 33:236n, 36:204, 40:303, 41:169, 43:146, 45:349, 350, 49:110n
14:31—20:148, 51:47
Chp. 15—24:115, 193–298, 29:215
15:1—11:165, 332, 20:202, 31:317, 37:xii, 38, 170, 174, 253, 38:37, 53, 51:10
15:1f—8:267, 32:23
15:1–6—21:265
15:2—15:243, 24:213, 28:321, 31:317, 32:232, 36:194
15:3—5:213, 11:357, 15:232, 24:203, 211, 217, 29:152, 32:23, 41:218
15:4—24:216, 219, 33:235, 37:262
15:5—2:40, 4:169, 11:375, 13:381, 18:76, 22:132, 331, 24:225, 227, 30:240, 33:234, 34:112, 267, 37:252f, 38:17n, 43:35, 280, 46:156f
15:6—5:284, 20:49, 24:230, 240,

31:65, 33:238, 48:158
15:7—5:284, 6:235, 17:392, 33:148, 43:280
15:8—5:274, 284, 24:209
15:9—6:271
15:10—44:102
15:12—11:482, 29:215, 35:173
15:15—24:252, 356, 30:308
15:16—5:85, 6:355, 7:136, 13:320, 25:59, 30:133, 33:277, 49:262
15:18—6:245, 25:297
15:18f—22:433, 33:277
15:19—7:63, 12:24, 224, 246, 14:70, 24:160, 25:297, 26:234, 456, 27:135, 36:237, 40:43, 43:79, 282, 49:173
15:20—13:260, 21:46, 27:159, 39:124, 146
15:22—24:318, 29:236
15:23—47:284
15:24—24:173
15:25—26:433
15:26—24:115n, 364f, 29:214, 34:217, 39:5
15:26f—40:195
15:26–16:4—24:8n
15:27—30:307, 35:396
Chp. 16—13:381, 24:299–422, 29:215
16:1—5:235
16:2—1:253, 280, 288, 322, 4:375, 6:48, 10:195, 12:167, 257, 13:186, 250, 370, 14:95, 247, 255, 292, 18:286, 19:176, 183, 21:49, 333, 22:80, 82, 342, 23:237, 25:29, 380, 26:13, 70, 421, 450f, 454, 27:44, 165, 35:272, 37:128n, 43:104n, 44:227, 51:347, 52:91, 54:441
16:3—24:306, 51:28
16:4—5:235, 12:221, 17:124, 33:182n, 39:5
16:5–7—3:205
16:5–15—24:8n
16:7—10:425, 13:20, 20:205, 23:162, 24:186, 37:xii, 38:44, 40:202, 44:241n
16:7–9—51:113
16:8—2:19, 40, 9:158, 11:276, 429, 16:32, 76, 17:11f, 171f, 18:407, 20:101, 21:56, 119, 23:317, 28:238, 29:28, 30:249, 32:206, 33:21, 35:319, 40:82, 149, 41:364, 48:375
16:8f—22:301, 33:286
16:11—1:188, 5:227, 240, 11:4, 12:25, 20:173, 183, 21:193, 22:24, 26:190, 27:24, 32:206, 40:303, 41:169, 42:38, 43:146, 45:158, 49:140
16:12—30:306
16:12f—4:125
16:13—24:364, 30:307, 41:122
16:13f—14:204, 34:73, 54:70
16:14—2:356, 11:252, 23:161, 24:173, 356, 364, 402, 25:147, 33:74, 47:54
16:15—12:285, 15:293, 316, 54:112
16:16—17:185, 201, 48:202
16:16–22—51:200
16:16–23—24:8n
16:18—11:276
16:20—3:238, 19:185, 43:184
16:20–22—43:185
16:21—4:10, 7:49, 8:24, 15:49, 16:134n, 208, 18:243, 25:73, 42:100
16:21f—18:244, 52:189
16:22—17:41, 201, 50:21
16:23—3:359, 6:140, 245, 6:235, 9:73, 12:56, 43:226, 54:192
16:23–30—24:8n
16:24—3:339, 6:235, 18:14, 25:369, 49:179n, 53:139
16:26—25:370, 44:241n
16:27—6:245, 17:346, 26:234f
16:28—4:169, 12:231, 13:345, 18:248, 37:195, 222, 38:44
16:29—19:122
16:31—49:110n
16:32—2:88, 24:409
16:33—5:18, 12:25, 212, 224, 231, 262, 15:350, 18:229, 20:8, 24, 22:132, 25:53, 78, 285, 317, 26:27, 456, 27:12, 170, 28:220, 40:43, 42:50, 104, 43:63, 79, 172, 176, 184, 50:19, 51:131, 203, 205, 52:28
Chp. 17—13:320, 25:178, 29:215
17:1—14:259, 51:28
17:1–5—25:178
17:2—52:81
17:3—1:161, 12:161, 15:306, 310, 29:163, 30:271, 327, 51:126
17:5—10:231, 12:129
17:9—29:214, 44:135
17:11—11:101, 22:356, 37:195
17:12—23:75, 50:237n
17:14—36:237
17:17—5:213, 6:73, 17:95, 34:131, 36:245, 44:312
17:19—11:261, 40:194
17:20—29:214, 30:321, 44:135
17:21—1:64, 5:223
17:22—13:331
Chp. 18—13:20, 29:215
18:2–5—54:107
18:5—28:109
18:10—36:224, 45:274n, 46:29
18:12f—48:387
18:15–18—54:108
18:19f—19:192
18:19–23—32:111
18:20—11:111, 21:8, 28:376
18:22—21:106, 45:274n
18:22f—35:107
18:23—3:57, 7:115, 21:106, 112, 40:55, 45:274
18:25–27—54:108
18:28—6:385, 21:74, 25:24
18:30—6:388, 32:159
18:31—6:366
18:36—2:37, 12:103, 31:353, 373, 34:211, 37:293, 39:65, 40:51, 355, 44:140, 45:93n, 46:81, 97, 166
18:36f—45:88
18:37—28:376, 34:82n
18:38—24:287
19:1—43:45
19:4f—43:45
19:7—8:162, 22:80
19:9—48:146
19:11—10:244,

14:257, 20:335, 25:109, 28:377, 30:78, 45:274, 46:195, 48:262, 395
19:15—10:264, 269, 11:41, 43, 49, 46:20, 47:271
19:16—43:277
19:17–19—43:45
19:19—6:27, 10:92
19:21—11:42
19:23f—42:143n
19:25—27:195
19:25–27—42:8n
19:26—38:61, 52:53
19:28—12:115
19:29—43:62
19:30—10:78, 27:228, 29:220
19:33f—37:266
19:34—8:258, 51:324, 53:27
19:35—51:325
19:36—11:432, 37:130
19:37—20:140
19:38—37:20n
19:39—10:217, 22:353
19:40–42—43:45
Chp. 20—41:320f
20:1—11:512, 36:32n
20:1–9—37:329n
20:11–17—43:45
20:14—37:66
20:15—3:263, 10:92, 37:76
20:17—26:43, 41:352n, 43:65, 53:135, 54:208
20:19—14:227, 36:32, 37:66n, 216–218, 51:61, 54:149
20:19f—51:60–66
20:19–31—51:60, 315, 54:149
20:21—51:61
20:21–23—41:319
20:22—54:470
20:22f—37:183, 39:86, 88f
20:23—8:185, 31:104, 281, 36:82, 39:42n, 41:195, 343, 44:134n, 48:288, 294, 51:326
20:24–29—28:283
20:25—50:85n
20:26—36:32, 37:66n, 216–218
20:26f—43:45, 51:62
20:27—12:365, 32:11, 51:61
20:28—24:94
20:29—9:87n
20:30f—22:252
20:31—30:321, 39:169
21:15—41:293, 305, 344, 352, 371, 54:31
21:15f—25:120, 27:397
21:15–17—8:53, 24:147, 31:268, 36:190, 39:95, 44:149n, 51:64, 54:86
21:15–19—32:71, 46:172n
21:16—8:94, 30:134, 41:46, 126n
21:17—14:284, 27:338, 31:321, 41:313
21:17f—41:353
21:18—3:127, 25:439
21:19f—19:49
21:19–22—45:153
21:20—3:299
21:21—3:129, 15:133, 21:318
21:21f—4:39
21:22—3:129, 21:318, 31:321, 36:345, 45:156
21:25—22:251, 32:78, 39:168, 169n

Acts

Chp. 1—41:321
1:1—10:285, 11:47, 14:302, 52:60
1:4—8:254
1:6—5:44
1:7—1:243, 5:44, 47, 33:25, 45:255
1:8—8:254, 10:230, 232, 20:213, 25:149, 29:9, 214, 35:399
1:9—11:321, 38:28
1:10—3:61n
1:12—37:234n
1:13—51:217n
1:15–26—32:74
1:16—6:378, 11:325
1:19—11:73
1:20—14:257
1:22—45:224, 52:65, 146
1:23–26—26:19, 39:87
1:24—43:274, 45:107n
1:24–26—27:165
1:25—11:325
1:26—19:61, 41:92, 320
Chp. 2—2:215, 10:201, 11:268, 18:252, 23:105, 31:281
2:1f—12:177
2:1–4—30:255, 43:45
2:1–11—45:359
2:1–13—34:218
2:1–16—35:319
2:2—11:65
2:2f—37:299n
2:2–4—35:161
2:3—1:230, 10:400, 16:168, 18:110, 26:374
2:4—8:248, 36:163, 45:361n
2:5—16:159, 18:344, 20:87, 281, 41:347
2:5f—47:204
2:9–11—16:125
2:11—8:248
2:13—8:249, 270
2:15—36:163
2:15–18—11:446
2:17—29:109, 30:22, 35:401
2:17f—18:105
2:17–21—35:319n
2:21—49:270
2:22f—24:403
2:22–24—54:371
2:24—10:115, 12:231, 17:227, 19:31, 75, 22:356, 28:130, 37:130
2:27—19:75
2:31—10:71
2:33—12:131, 13:21, 25:306
2:34—13:228
2:35—13:228
2:36—25:5, 147, 26:427
2:36f—42:9, 10
2:37—9:88, 158, 10:117, 196, 11:4, 277, 348, 14:336, 16:77
2:38—3:101n, 28:149, 36:63, 43:45
2:38f—45:226
2:41—22:86, 23:274, 26:204, 41:348, 43:45
2:41f—40:125
2:44—44:357
2:44f—35:363, 45:169
2:44–46—35:94
2:46—35:61, 36:31, 184
Chp. 3—47:298
3:6—3:270, 27:122
3:15—1:348, 23:105, 29:214
3:17—17:86n, 30:325
3:21—1:59, 100, 117, 243, 4:257, 9:6
3:22—35:246, 52:106
3:22f—9:176
3:23—27:334
3:24—10:6, 431, 19:152, 52:105
Chp. 4—10:167, 47:298
4:2—10:167
4:3–24—35:123
4:10—25:24
4:11—17:86n, 30:51
4:12—4:130, 8:312, 10:63, 16:130, 24:92, 325n, 26:427, 31:180, 37:364, 41:213
4:13—19:195, 52:90
4:19—31:395

4:20—12:394
4:24–28—14:313
4:25—12:5
4:26—41:122
4:27—11:390, 14:324, 20:217
4:31—13:12, 14:313
4:32—27:210, 32:117, 48:20, 52:267
4:32–35—45:169
4:32–37—35:363, 46:51
4:33—10:196, 281, 12:386, 25:149
4:34—9:147
4:34f—35:94, 384
4:35—36:35, 53
Chp. 5—46:12
5:5—39:12, 54:405
5:9—48:377
5:12—5:357
5:15—4:121, 11:98, 22:46, 26:103
5:28—16:44, 21:74, 25:190
5:29—5:115, 6:168, 12:276, 13:250, 21:121, 26:97, 297, 426, 29:74, 31:115, 275, 32:118, 146, 279, 36:102, 39:291, 298, 40:42, 299, 42:171, 44:100, 139, 360, 45:111, 125, 46:77, 130, 47:54, 49:279, 364, 385n, 52:267
5:29f—48:395
5:31—37:58
5:34f—48:366, 49:350n
5:38f—14:67, 32:121, 48:208n
5:41—8:250, 10:288, 11:283, 12:177, 21:48, 25:522, 27:133, 405, 30:127
5:42—39:275
Chp. 6—18:375
6:1–6—28:295, 36:116, 39:312
6:2—10:358
6:2–4—44:159
6:3—11:332f
6:4—28:324, 39:314
6:5—24:204
6:5f—40:38
6:6—36:91
6:7—8:219, 11:268
6:8—40:38
6:10–12—33:96
6:13—9:196, 24:338, 39:149
6:13f—11:256
6:15—1:236, 12:207, 29:81
Chp. 7—10:167, 18:322, 375
7:1f—27:197
7:2—2:241, 277
7:2–53—54:344
7:3—2:241
7:4—4:184, 34:303
7:5—2:283, 359, 373, 3:119, 5:224, 6:184, 8:197, 29:239
7:6—27:268
7:8—20:200
7:14—8:88
7:22—2:305
7:22f—29:240
7:27—29:241
7:37—9:176, 35:246, 52:106
7:38—22:140
7:41—10:137, 19:186
7:42—7:348, 9:125, 18:166
7:42f—6:34, 18:322, 35:321
7:43—7:349, 8:131, 200, 13:185, 18:167
7:45—9:43n
7:48—17:397, 39:149, 218
7:48–50—10:129
7:49—17:395, 39:218
7:51—14:265, 16:43, 18:59, 22:396, 33:96
7:51–53—21:120
7:52—10:167, 25:24, 190, 32:89
7:53—25:181, 26:319, 27:271, 36:182
7:54—10:268, 25:191
7:55—22:202, 37:279, 40:216
7:55f—37:66, 112
7:56—13:245, 36:342, 40:221
7:56–60—28:258
7:57—10:160, 268, 36:266
7:58–8:1—36:74
7:59f—41:322, 54:453
7:60—20:97n
Chp. 8—13:245, 19:50, 93, 29:239
8:4—19:93n
8:5—39:310, 40:38
8:9–24—24:204, 31:201n, 34:34n
8:13—30:247
8:14—20:201, 31:387, 32:73, 40:41, 269
8:16—3:101n
8:17—36:91
8:17f—4:199
8:18f—22:108
8:18–24—41:120n
8:19—4:397
8:20—22:108, 27:46, 31:188
8:21—21:226
8:22—34:318
8:23—9:273, 18:160
8:26—20:285
8:27—15:131, 20:280, 28:276
8:27f—10:349, 16:159
8:27–39—45:98
8:33—11:35
8:35–37—35:151
8:36—40:38
8:36f—8:192, 32:14
8:37—40:253
8:38—37:274n
8:40—40:38
Chp. 9—26:62, 27:193
9:1—6:42, 100, 7:99, 8:217, 16:38, 266, 48:193
9:1f—37:20n
9:1–3—24:276n
9:1–19—35:364
9:1–22—43:64n
9:3–5—24:16n
9:3–6—41:324
9:4—3:348, 10:179, 379, 13:262, 17:85, 147, 357, 20:149, 23:149, 24:276, 26:73, 27:134, 40:125, 216
9:4f—27:165
9:4–6—27:183
9:5—8:27, 13:262, 39:111n, 49:304n
9:6—3:63, 4:55, 9:88, 158, 11:348, 26:62, 32:40
9:7—11:124, 24:309
9:10—25:92
9:10f—33:295n
9:11—19:43
9:12—4:72
9:15—5:254, 17:357, 25:78, 26:45, 236, 366, 27:70, 145, 29:78, 105, 34:266, 35:136
9:16—24:358
9:17—26:63
9:18f—35:53
9:19—20:250, 27:190, 36:91
9:20—27:190
9:22—30:22
9:25—43:121
9:26f—26:75, 27:195
9:28—18:168
9:29f—27:196
9:31—13:382
9:32—40:41, 269
9:40—21:287
Chp. 10—14:23, 19:93, 25:99, 27:156, 30:298, 34:126, 41:40
10:1f—17:194, 26:101, 45:98
10:1–8—35:364
10:1–48—54:63
10:1–11:18—41:69n
10:4—33:220
10:5—26:211
10:9f—19:50, 48:286n
10:9–13—46:12
10:10—5:116, 10:367
10:10f—20:201

10:10–20—34:168
10:11f—19:94
10:12—50:94n
10:13—9:124, 29:192
10:14—50:94n
10:15—21:32, 25:116, 499, 28:318, 34:192, 50:94n
10:22—33:220
10:26—3:355, 5:27, 130, 41:368
10:28—7:212, 26:209
10:30f—20:346
10:30–33—35:364
10:34—3:129f, 4:33, 60, 7:201, 9:145, 10:76, 22:186, 27:281, 32:145, 41:325n, 46:285n
10:34f—4:64, 5:51, 12:293, 18:187, 52:175
10:34–43—45:98
10:34–47—35:363
10:35—43:225
10:37f—22:217
10:38—54:53
10:41—30:225
10:42—29:13
10:43—8:312, 24:92, 51:278
10:44—18:110, 22:54, 26:203f, 27:248, 30:256, 315, 36:201
10:44f—27:247, 49:63
10:44–47—54:113
10:44–48—45:98
10:45—18:110, 20:201, 26:206
10:47—18:110
10:48—3:101n
Chp. 11—14:23, 19:93
11:2—20:201
11:3—7:212, 26:206, 41:368
11:9—25:116, 499
11:17—26:207
11:18—26:206
11:19—41:348
11:26—20:250, 284, 39:68, 41:88, 314, 348
11:28—2:288, 27:210, 46:236
12:2—35:397n, 38:110n, 39:43n, 41:172n
12:3—14:231, 44:337
12:7—37:222
12:7f—3:18
12:9—4:58
Chp. 13—17:45, 26:103, 28:330
13:1—41:325
13:1f—48:262
13:1–4—28:251
13:2—20:297, 25:4, 143, 26:101, 27:165, 190, 28:90, 39:87
13:2f—19:50, 41:325
13:3—38:186
13:6–12—26:205
13:7—20:346, 35:364
13:7–12—45:99
13:10—21:119, 31:335, 32:142, 49:388
13:10f—45:71
13:14—40:389, 392
13:17—47:302
13:18—5:34, 9:125, 18:59
13:22—5:255, 268, 12:237, 34:125
13:26—37:132n
13:34—29:114
13:36—7:181, 195, 9:72
13:38—26:82
13:38f—32:155, 50:67
13:39—19:151n, 26:82
13:40f—19:167
13:41—10:242, 19:110
13:45f—19:94
13:46—10:339, 12:293, 13:286, 16:60, 17:174, 376, 414, 20:317, 25:99, 195, 28:164, 54:451
13:47—22:69
Chp. 14—17:45, 46:10
14:3—37:132n
14:12—36:149
14:15—3:320, 322, 355, 19:27, 44:168
14:15–18—9:118n
14:16—27:146, 33:88
14:17—3:225, 4:15f, 5:138, 236, 7:325, 9:118, 15:53
14:22—5:145, 6:99, 12:216, 14:58, 25:289, 31:33, 251, 43:165, 171, 49:330
14:23—5:89, 39:311
Chp. 15—3:83, 14:23, 17:45, 25:113, 26:79, 29:114, 41:5, 44:136
15:1—7:212, 19:50, 25:488, 26:50, 52, 145, 28:232
15:1f—20:201, 49:90
15:1–19—31:265
15:1–29—41:27
15:1–35—45:227n
15:2—24:244, 40:269
15:2f—52:175
15:3–21—44:376
15:4–12—44:319
15:4–29—34:38
15:5—3:83, 9:168, 25:489, 28:232, 29:36, 32:156, 41:69
15:7–11—26:112, 27:161, 35:363, 41:69
15:8—9:180, 22:252f, 40:256, 45:107
15:8–10—26:207
15:9—13:16, 16:72, 20:307, 22:374, 24:212, 27:188, 219, 29:45, 152, 164, 172, 237, 31:43, 32:54, 34:167, 191, 41:145
15:9–11—4:65
15:10—9:84n, 10:36, 12:170, 14:90, 337, 17:46, 23:72, 26:84, 404, 27:7, 28:235, 32:155, 33:218, 35:321, 37:75n, 40:285, 41:137, 178, 54:355
15:10f—26:239, 40:92, 41:138n, 46:197, 48:285
15:11—26:210, 30:263, 31:180, 32:18, 156, 41:123, 138
15:12—21:319
15:13—10:117, 35:397n, 40:389, 392
15:13–21—41:72n, 54:355
15:14f—30:22
15:16f—35:321
15:16–18—18:188
15:19—25:505
15:20—29:40
15:22—27:163, 48:262
15:28—27:211
15:28f—41:28, 75
15:29—28:341, 40:304
15:39—26:108, 119
Chp. 16—16:67, 26:103
16:3—25:474, 488, 26:61, 27:211, 36:253, 40:139, 152, 41:78, 45:73, 48:298n, 49:381n, 51:87
16:4—41:27
16:7—44:337
16:13—51:337
16:15—40:257
16:16—9:175
16:20—26:452
16:20f—26:426
16:31—19:151n
16:37—16:67
17:2f—30:18
17:5—29:6, 32:12
17:6—33:52, 41:273
17:6f—26:452
17:11—30:18, 33:93, 35:122, 236, 52:105

17:16-32—51:77, 83
17:18—32:12, 33:106
17:18-32—35:392n
17:22-31—9:118n
17:25—1:125
17:26—9:292, 14:14
17:27—22:208
17:27f—37:58
17:28—11:390, 17:36, 26:357, 27:290, 37:56, 40:251n, 52:55, 63, 54:472
17:29—25:11
17:34—17:187n, 36:109n, 39:175n
Chp. 18—30:298
18:2—25:128, 39:204, 41:324
18:6—37:131n
18:12—32:12
18:14f—14:76
18:18—26:61, 27:211
18:24—40:37
18:24-28—25:149
18:25—39:310
18:26—19:195
18:27—7:337
18:28—30:22
Chp. 19—30:298
19:1—7:337
19:4—22:176
19:5—36:63
19:6—36:91
19:11f—26:103
19:12—7:32
19:13—22:107
19:15—24:264
19:19—31:383, 32:150
19:20—20:294
19:23-41—32:12
19:26—14:15
19:27—7:325
19:30—43:121
19:34—3:83n
19:39—41:143
19:41—41:143
Chp. 20—25:127, 26:103
20:8-12—51:337
20:11—4:271
20:17—39:281
20:17f—39:155
20:19—21:314
20:20—30:307
20:27—24:403, 30:307
20:28—14:333, 21:44, 29:17, 34:47, 39:155, 281, 40:12, 41:105, 46:221, 48:235n
20:28-31—53:125
20:29—3:17, 4:71, 9:135, 187, 21:63, 27:247, 39:289, 44:299
20:29f—22:52, 513, 29:33, 30:168
20:30—3:17, 17:208, 21:248
20:32—37:132n
20:33—30:136
20:35—6:174, 13:410, 25:449, 31:57, 45:278n
Chp. 21—25:127
21:8f—36:152
21:9—28:277, 40:391
21:22f—48:298n
21:23f—27:211
21:23-26—20:77, 44:253
21:24—26:61
21:26—20:78, 25:474, 488, 41:79, 49:381n
21:27f—25:34
21:28—24:338
21:28f—24:311
Chp. 22—16:67, 25:127
22:3—8:241
22:17f—37:66
22:17-21—26:62
22:22—10:160, 24:200
Chp. 23—25:127
23:2—39:279
23:3—14:258, 39:269, 48:170
23:4f—39:269
Chp. 24—25:127
24:4—29:74
24:5—12:252, 23:292, 26:426, 452, 33:52
Chp. 25—25:127
25:10—28:358
25:16—23:300, 47:21
25:24—29:6
Chp. 26—25:127
26:7—33:252, 35:272
26:8—4:120
26:14—15:102, 158
26:20—28:83, 30:248
26:24—27:256, 33:106
26:26—19:122n
26:29—43:62
Chp. 27—19:43, 25:127
27:21—15:163
27:23f—54:146
27:24—6:217
27:33—54:277
27:37—6:217
27:43—3:290
Chp. 28—19:43, 25:127, 26:103
28:5—5:310
28:11—36:263n, 51:83
28:14—41:322, 348
28:14f—54:146
28:15—2:335, 3:264, 13:111, 26:420, 54:277
28:22—26:443
28:23—27:179
28:26f—16:242
28:26-28—16:74n
28:31—19:195
29:28—36:155

Romans
Complete commentary—25:3-524
Chp. 1—11:463, 14:196, 25:3-14, 28, 135-170, 153, 156, 28:234, 31:346, 46:9
1:1—13:80, 20:297, 23:343, 25:499, 523, 35:359, 44:256
1:1f—14:335, 27:165, 35:122
1:1-3—25:131
1:1-4—12:44, 35:118
1:1-6—52:65
1:2—11:159, 183, 18:6, 21:69, 25:414, 30:18, 33:92, 35:118, 44:256, 45:359, 52:41, 106
1:3—15:317, 27:185, 302, 35:235n, 38:50n, 41:348
1:3-6—31:231
1:4—12:56, 101, 13:4, 236, 15:294, 22:115, 334, 24:402, 27:167, 185, 302, 28:303, 29:110, 30:224
1:5—8:254, 20:197, 25:123, 29:223, 30:30, 36:63
1:7—10:151, 416, 25:6, 462, 29:189
1:8—18:359, 25:128, 130
1:8-15—41:324
1:9—29:4, 32:280
1:11—25:125, 127f
1:13—25:125, 44:337
1:14—25:522, 31:252, 33:18, 249
1:15—10:33
1:16—4:106, 152, 5:130, 7:177, 8:244, 9:22, 187, 234, 10:250, 252, 281, 12:63, 170, 176, 13:19, 13:266, 291, 14:10, 290, 16:33n, 18:62, 238, 250, 254, 20:99, 22:345, 25:138, 522, 26:426, 27:56, 290, 29:118, 30:45, 33:248, 259, 34:115, 36:280, 37:132, 176, 40:146, 198, 41:149, 44:256, 49:101, 51:11, 54:12, 318, 395
1:16f—27:241, 54:309
1:17—5:158, 6:165, 9:76, 10:145, 273,

404, 408, 452,
11:147, 442,
13:19, 14:80, 337,
16:321, 17:80,
18:19, 350,
19:123, 151, 197,
21:xi, 25:168, 209,
211, 26:210,
29:188, 230,
30:105, 151,
31:55, 102, 270,
298, 340, 32:14,
33:275, 34:326,
336, 41:346,
42:43n, 44:31,
45:226, 49:359,
52:114, 54:193,
287, 309, 403, 442
1:17f—25:151
1:18—9:158, 10:145,
11:4, 12:356,
14:336, 16:128,
18:120, 157, 356,
20:294, 22:149,
33:247, 252,
38:264, 47:114,
54:308
1:18f—24:340,
27:218
1:19—5:258, 6:113,
17:12, 19:53f,
22:155, 38:249,
41:116
1:19f—11:10,
22:149, 26:399,
28:304, 40:97
1:20—10:190, 11:39,
25:14, 156,
29:185, 231, 235,
31:40, 52, 227,
34:144, 36:144,
38:249, 258,
40:97, 49:375
1:20f—22:149
1:21—3:117, 5:259,
10:45, 17:172,
25:9, 492, 26:400,
28:272, 34:140,
38:248, 50:131n
1:21f—7:336, 9:54,
33:41, 251
1:22—13:253,
22:157, 25:136,
28:249, 31:52,
50:131, 51:35n
1:23—25:219,
27:292, 51:124
1:24—9:36, 11:62,
67, 12:382,
25:162, 31:198,
33:175, 51:126
1:24f—25:164,
26:141
1:24–28—45:37
1:25—10:52, 11:45,
398, 25:164,
38:264
1:26f—41:289, 43:20
1:27—11:62
1:28—2:399, 6:293,
7:292, 8:246, 272,
16:191, 226, 243,
25:159, 164,
36:97, 184, 39:39,
41:280, 45:109,
46:198
1:28f—25:164
1:29—25:155
1:20f—25:170
1:31—2:300, 6:253,
18:269
1:32—6:209, 22:155,
376, 36:312n,
37:149, 41:191,
288, 44:162
Chp. 2—11:463,
14:173, 196,
18:285, 25:15–24,
165, 171–193,
336, 347, 28:234,
31:52, 44:303
2:1—3:240, 10:24,
35:366
2:1f—9:111n,
17:208, 34:48
2:2—11:44, 25:11
2:3—9:102, 10:24,
10:457, 11:43, 51,
22:151, 25:172
2:4—3:40, 10:33,
18:285, 27:376,
30:97, 31:161,
33:159, 166,
42:148, 47:112
2:5—2:43, 9:21,
10:173, 403, 406,
25:175, 43:64
2:6—8:331, 32:172,
33:152, 42:133
2:6f—33:153
2:7—25:193, 33:153,
48:383n
2:8—19:196, 25:178,
217, 52:144
2:8f—9:158
2:9—16:33n,
25:182, 29:208
2:9f—33:253
2:10—25:182,
27:290
2:11—3:64, 4:33,
20:79n, 25:16,
137, 233, 27:61,
103, 33:56n,
39:218
2:12—25:22, 31:54
2:13—22:141,
25:234, 416,
26:252f, 256,
27:257, 34:313,
35:366
2:13f—47:170n
2:14—19:41, 25:181,
219, 27:53, 34:113
2:14f—35:168,
47:111, 52:208
2:15—2:160, 6:116,
9:81, 108, 22:150,
25:76, 180, 186,
27:53, 33:191,
40:97, 44:298,
45:127n, 54:442
2:16—25:125, 149,
27:120
2:17—2:99, 4:406,
18:234, 25:248,
26:121, 33:222n
2:17f—27:218
2:20f—22:151
2:21—18:234, 25:21,
27:188, 274, 31:44
2:21f—25:189,
33:252
2:22—17:339, 380,
25:16, 26:399,
27:285, 29:24,
35:366, 40:95,
44:319, 52:187
2:23—14:24, 25:22,
29:219, 31:55,
44:41
2:23f—25:119, 175,
515
2:24—18:394, 26:25,
275, 277, 344,
28:294, 30:270,
34:242, 43:219,
234, 44:319
2:25—3:90, 25:24,
191, 193, 27:327,
330, 20:218f
2:26—25:182
2:26f—9:110
2:27—25:23, 182,
191, 27:284
2:27f—33:251
2:28—25:22, 23,
191, 193
2:28f—11:543,
20:126n, 33:251,
252n
2:29—9:110, 27:284,
33:251, 36:137
Chp. 3—10:233,
11:410, 463,
14:196, 15:325,
348, 16:33, 19:23,
25:19, 25–34, 181,
194–254, 317,
26:132, 27:8,
44:303, 47:159
3:1—25:207,
33:222n
3:1f—9:125, 10:237,
25:79, 45:359,
47:159
3:2—4:64, 8:133,
9:215, 304,
10:172, 14:24,
15:196, 18:238,
19:102, 25:194,
207, 41:51,
45:201, 52:131
3:3—22:174, 25:25,
80, 95, 97, 195f,
199, 208, 40:367
3:4—3:214, 10:235,
243, 317, 11:403,
12:322, 338,
22:404, 468,
25:29, 33, 197,
209, 210, 213,
249, 284, 28:238,
33:42, 75, 36:344,
41:48, 44:396,
48:207, 50:46n
3:5—10:162, 235,
25:11, 28, 200,
206, 212, 32:182
3:5f—12:339
3:6—25:201, 297
3:7—25:28
3:7f—8:40, 328
3:8—3:258, 8:40,
330, 10:34, 317,
25:50, 201, 488,
26:169, 305,
35:196, 40:113,

45:389, 46:26,
49:387, 51:29
3:9—25:26, 155,
186, 27:274,
30:233, 31:52,
32:177, 33:252
3:9f—27:224
3:9–12—12:342
3:9–20—34:114
3:10—2:40, 11:403,
25:247, 271,
27:174, 44:241
3:10f—10:238,
29:127, 33:253
3:10–12—2:83,
12:389, 26:131,
27:274, 31:43,
347, 51:57
3:10–18—11:213
3:11—25:220,
26:396, 400
3:11f—32:169
3:12—11:403,
25:247
3:13—28:369
3:15—8:265, 34:354
3:16—11:197
3:17—29:189,
45:279n
3:18—29:177
3:19—10:5, 422,
11:284, 14:265,
290, 18:358,
25:28, 394,
27:274, 31:62,
33:253
3:19f—32:91, 33:256
3:20—1:164, 3:22,
9:141, 10:105,
12:165, 15:346,
16:77, 19:41,
22:44, 132, 25:60,
185, 275, 281,
26:6, 333, 27:184,
274, 318, 29:43,
168, 31:51, 56,
32:195, 223,
33:121, 127, 137,
154, 257, 260,
261, 263, 34:117,
35:195, 242, 367,
397n, 40:82, 135,
276, 44:280, 289,
298, 302, 45:90n,
51:22, 109, 316
3:21—9:27, 235,
11:286, 288, 433,
20:248, 25:249f,
27:266, 28:232,
30:18, 31:42,
32:227, 33:92,
260, 40:99,
46:146, 52:21,
106, 172
3:21f—10:403,
33:263f
3:22—24:340,
33:265, 35:168
3:23—11:376, 14:94,
15:332, 20:188,
22:133, 288,
24:340, 26:131,
355, 27:104, 29:9,
31:347, 32:171,
36:354, 41:216,
51:20, 57
3:24—30:230, 252,
32:47
3:24f—26:132
3:24–26—32:28
3:25—10:258,
13:383, 15:330,
22:249, 25:175,
26:362, 27:64, 86,
29:202, 210,
32:239, 35:368,
37:364, 39:80,
50:20, 51:278,
52:280
3:25f—11:269
3:27—18:357,
28:232, 36:200,
47:144
3:27f—25:316
3:28—1:266, 7:251,
9:141, 12:398,
19:41, 25:252,
26:79, 27:234,
30:26, 199, 285,
31:56, 274, 298,
32:227, 33:260,
263, 34:109, 114,
123, 135, 139,
147, 151, 154,
158f, 35:179, 182,
187f, 195, 44:32n
3:29—7:15, 19:4,
40, 50, 28:262,
40:244, 47:94
3:30—25:112
3:31—21:70, 25:67,
250, 27:229,
29:122, 34:126,
312, 315, 35:369,
40:97, 44:298
3:35—40:296
3:38—14:349
Chp. 4—11:463,
15:325, 19:23,
25:19, 35–42,
255–284, 322,
336, 26:132f, 242,
27:8, 263, 29:122,
30:270, 36:38
4:1—25:38, 48:371n
4:1f—3:176, 9:103,
27:248, 33:270
4:1–5—31:274
4:2—4:68, 25:31,
248, 26:226,
30:256, 35:195
4:2–22—35:396
4:3—8:139, 10:146,
25:410, 438,
26:138, 28:240,
31:271, 351,
34:167
4:4—3:22, 33:269
4:4f—19:52, 33:271
4:5—3:22, 156,
13:300, 25:211,
34:167, 51:63
4:6f—33:271
4:7—25:259, 32:169,
44:10n
4:8—25:256
4:9—25:37, 27:251
4:11—3:85, 101f,
105, 26:83, 121,
27:251, 36:66,
52:153
4:12—3:105, 4:367,
25:280
4:13—26:240, 358
4:13f—37:92
4:14—26:303,
27:264, 267
4:14f—9:104
4:15—1:107f, 2:158,
3:59, 5:113,
7:254, 9:48, 114,
184, 10:292,
11:419, 12:165,
13:7, 85, 316,
14:91, 16:72, 128,
20:316, 22:139,
25:19, 38, 40, 46,
57, 59, 262, 280f,
26:8, 398, 27:184,
226, 266f, 28:135f,
29:198, 212,
31:41, 54, 231,
32:154, 224,
33:272, 34:116,
310, 35:238n,
397n, 47:114
4:16—22:139,
25:121, 29:239
4:17—1:18, 21,
3:35, 4:27, 120,
323, 376, 6:103,
7:247, 8:39,
12:112, 14:124,
20:5, 49, 210,
22:247, 23:216,
24:198, 26:240,
37:117, 38:66,
54:146
4:17f—29:239
4:18—2:288, 8:235,
12:409, 26:365,
27:27, 29:131,
38:25
4:19—4:300, 17:197,
25:283
4:19f—3:147
4:19–24—26:226
4:20—16:82, 22:139,
473, 25:11, 26:229
4:20f—25:283,
34:124
4:21—25:393, 37:47,
38:306
4:22—37:134
4:23—3:19, 39, 148,
34:167, 52:107
4:24—3:39, 148,
34:167
4:25—1:192, 4:191,
5:196, 10:327,
11:378, 12:329,
25:90, 26:21,
27:168, 238, 29:7,
34:110, 35:197,
368, 36:298,
37:191n, 42:13,
43:174, 51:19,
53:67
Chp. 5—6:236,
11:463, 17:100,
19:23, 25:43–49,
240, 285–307,
27:269, 40:83,
48:24
5:1—14:100, 16:200,
250, 18:12, 358,
20:221, 289,

25:504, 30:286, 303, 31:102, 274, 32:54, 227, 235, 51:131
5:1f—16:129, 280, 52:279
5:1–3—9:184
5:1–5—41:165
5:2—25:44, 30:12, 32:228, 236, 36:139
5:2f—42:165
5:3—2:157, 289, 12:177, 264, 13:11, 14:344, 16:99, 17:161, 18:118, 20:25, 27:133, 28:374, 29:84, 146, 51:244, 52:29
5:3f—25:458
5:3–5—10:52, 288, 27:25
5:4—10:283, 11:450, 453, 13:11, 24:151, 25:518, 51:71
5:4f—29:181
5:5—12:246, 14:30, 328, 20:139, 24:151, 25:67, 187, 27:221, 234, 326, 31:367, 35:368
5:6—25:45, 294
5:7—11:389, 458, 32:267
5:8—11:361, 25:44, 30:308, 44:38
5:8–11—44:38
5:10—11:361, 18:111, 25:51, 296, 27:171
5:11—20:188, 25:248
5:12—1:332, 2:121, 22:121, 137f, 25:46, 49, 50, 208, 304, 27:240, 32:224, 41:84, 43:238, 53:66, 54:36
5:12f—3:133, 12:350, 25:317
5:12–14—43:159
5:12–19—34:119
5:12–21—51:62
5:13—7:257, 25:298, 32:37, 224, 35:397n, 47:110
5:14—1:234, 3:103, 10:224, 25:48, 298, 304, 513, 28:113, 37:109n
5:14f—39:79
5:15—12:376, 25:299, 32:227, 239, 33:279, 35:369, 49:263n, 267n
5:15–17—34:320
5:15–21—53:66
5:16–19—25:298f
5:17—42:165
5:18—25:299, 52:71
5:18f—34:119
5:19—22:138, 25:75, 297, 302, 27:222, 31:282
5:20—2:158, 8:40, 329, 10:105, 12:358, 14:166, 22:44, 25:50, 26:308, 321, 27:269, 277, 325, 28:245, 29:122, 212, 30:199, 31:42, 32:154, 33:219, 262, 35:238n, 244, 367, 397n
5:20f—34:116, 156
5:22—27:325
Chp. 6—10:377, 11:463, 20:140, 23:48, 25:50–56, 70f, 154, 308–321, 27:234, 238, 31:84, 32:194, 248, 40:83, 41:114n
6:1—17:99
6:2—5:274
6:3—2:153, 3:101n, 8:5, 12:59, 363, 14:185, 19:121, 25:314
6:3f—25:45, 29:138, 37:274n
6:3–5—44:319n
6:3–11—22:298
6:4—13:15, 25:57, 26:398, 28:132, 29:225, 35:31, 36:68, 43:27
6:4f—10:405
6:5—30:127, 49:269n
6:6—8:6, 10:67, 25:52, 58, 70, 112, 308f, 313, 317, 435, 26:235, 27:229, 379, 29:130, 31:89, 225, 32:208, 214, 233, 37:200, 42:43, 43:37
6:6f—36:68
6:6–11—13:27
6:7—6:402, 10:406, 11:486, 525, 547, 14:197, 25:51
6:8—10:93, 25:315, 37:200n
6:9—10:138, 269, 13:245, 25:310, 315, 26:201, 286, 29:136, 37:50n, 42:163, 51:244, 53:134
6:9f—26:342, 36:320
6:10—15:323, 25:314f, 27:238, 43:174
6:12—10:377, 382, 11:33, 360, 12:233, 25:64, 308, 27:361, 30:270, 32:20, 208, 210, 212, 214, 231, 233, 42:39, 44:106
6:12f—35:37, 46:153
6:13—10:67, 165, 18:323, 25:320
6:14—7:131, 12:262, 25:58, 301, 317, 26:7, 27:347, 32:208, 211, 233
6:15—25:249, 27:347, 44:32n
6:15–22—35:397n
6:16—26:131
6:17—25:322, 32:256
6:17f—11:550
6:18—25:70, 32:256
6:19—10:67, 14:339, 25:436, 31:300, 46:153
6:19f—42:40
6:20—10:217, 11:329
6:21—9:104n, 25:56
6:22—23:33, 136, 406
6:23—2:322, 8:121, 10:304, 12:340, 13:116, 20:293, 21:324, 29:10, 34, 32:224, 229, 34:89, 37:363
Chp. 7—9:185, 10:105, 377, 11:121, 463, 19:5, 23:48, 25:40, 57–66, 240, 259, 300, 322–343, 26:309, 27:8, 269, 29:84, 31:62, 32:158, 218, 248, 40:83, 41:114n
7:1—10:405, 27:233, 31:107
7:1f—35:370
7:1–6—26:446
7:2—25:67, 31:107, 46:278, 52:131
7:2f—27:232, 28:55
7:2–4—9:235
7:4—25:318, 333
7:4f—17:81
7:5—1:269, 25:59f, 259, 27:320, 366, 31:231
7:5f—22:178, 35:369
7:5–13—35:397n
7:6—25:60, 28:209
7:7—9:114, 171, 12:340, 13:7, 16:98, 25:46, 240, 259, 27:313, 30:228, 32:19, 26, 194f, 223, 33:262, 34:114, 35:242, 36:204, 39:177, 185, 40:82, 44:114, 51:22
7:7–9—35:238n
7:7–10—35:244
7:8—7:47, 13:7, 14:161, 16:98, 25:62, 28:136, 30:232, 34:78n, 40:328, 51:22
7:9—1:164, 7:47,

257, 25:58, 31:42, 51:22
7:9f—27:226
7:10—27:70, 269, 31:54, 51:115
7:10–12—22:140
7:11—26:149, 27:226, 269
7:12—9:170, 19:100, 26:321, 31:55, 32:178, 39:188
7:13—1:171, 8:329, 25:59, 26:5, 314, 335, 31:14, 231, 32:233
7:14—5:131, 12:178, 18:308, 352, 25:32, 327, 329, 331, 26:33, 174, 189, 27:70, 227, 235, 364, 32:237, 242, 246, 34:75n, 35:367, 39:177, 39:35, 40:82
7:14f—9:89, 260, 30:233, 33:288
7:15—21:220, 25:329, 26:260, 32:246
7:15–25—32:242f
7:16—25:68, 190, 329, 28:235, 32:248, 250, 44:341
7:17—21:89, 32:248
7:17–20—35:33
7:17–24—51:275
7:18—2:41, 4:239, 12:307, 13:383, 16:35, 20:191, 21:89, 24:384, 25:64, 190, 268, 328, 331–333, 342, 27:174, 250, 361, 28:302, 31:64, 32:19, 158, 249, 34:75n, 38:129, 39:35, 44:104, 291, 50:137n
7:18f—11:487, 23:413, 43:63
7:18–20—11:305
7:18–23—22:260, 44:375
7:19—4:241, 5:22, 208, 327, 7:255, 22:254, 24:384, 25:70, 275, 309, 328, 330f, 27:365, 31:60, 32:246, 34:75, 39:35, 42:49, 130, 44:340f
7:19f—32:250
7:20—25:259, 331, 32:25
7:21—25:328, 334, 32:251
7:21–23—11:435
7:22—2:127, 11:402, 12:76, 25:328, 333f, 32:20, 22, 237, 251
7:22f—5:22, 27:231, 362, 30:70, 31:60, 359, 39:70
7:23—1:197, 2:309, 3:6, 333, 5:24, 62, 132, 230, 248, 326f, 6:100, 7:126, 304, 8:311, 9:184, 12:76, 343, 357, 14:162, 295, 22:154, 23:171, 25:311, 327, 335, 26:64, 148, 164, 189, 235, 276, 340, 349, 393, 27:21, 70, 72, 227, 236, 28:136, 29:65, 130, 32:233, 34:181f, 310, 42:71, 47:119, 51:25, 275
7:23f—11:402, 22:264
7:24—3:334, 4:241, 5:23f, 7:255, 8:167, 12:178, 16:52, 25:67, 245, 335, 26:393, 27:70, 30:70, 32:253f, 42:130, 51:22, 275
7:24f—11:298, 28:118
7:25—4:241, 5:328, 12:78, 25:247, 328, 335, 26:349, 27:77, 81, 379, 29:198, 30:326, 32:21, 25, 233, 237, 246, 254, 34:118, 41:316, 42:130, 51:22
Chp. 8—10:377, 11:463, 486, 525, 23:48, 25:67–78, 121, 259, 344–379, 27:234, 238, 31:84, 32:194, 248, 37:95, 46:9
8:1—4:239f, 11:32, 14:288, 19:27, 23:48, 24:345, 26:235, 447, 27:227, 32:27, 239, 255, 35:34, 370
8:2—1:104, 24:325, 25:474, 27:227, 234, 29:198, 31:42, 32:79, 207, 233, 35:397n, 36:200, 44:26, 51:115
8:2f—35:286
8:2–4—39:183
8:2–27—35:285
8:3—9:260, 17:81, 22:109, 24:325, 25:121, 250, 262, 305, 311, 26:155, 371, 27:65, 229, 28:238, 265, 29:122, 30:222, 32:200, 206, 33:275, 38:59, 65, 41:177
8:3f—25:243, 32:155, 52:241
8:4—14:288, 24:345, 26:252, 27:65, 227, 40:56, 51:81
8:5—25:329, 428, 33:274, 37:94, 99
8:6—10:61, 148, 25:369, 27:341, 30:120, 33:274, 37:201, 40:203
8:6f—25:428
8:7—2:14, 4:95, 13:289, 17:12, 20:128, 24:341, 25:71, 150, 348, 26:230, 321, 28:135, 33:215, 274, 288, 40:302
8:8—3:224, 254, 27:239, 33:274
8:9—10:15, 18:397, 26:378, 27:239, 290, 33:274, 51:112
8:10—16:37, 25:68, 70, 29:225, 32:21
8:10f—10:405
8:11—38:44, 46:224
8:12f—46:150, 153
8:13—1:269, 12:329, 27:70, 360, 30:269, 32:21, 207, 36:146, 37:94, 201, 40:56, 222, 44:315n, 46:150
8:14—10:15, 18:253, 20:32, 25:437, 27:366, 33:85, 160, 242, 34:320
8:15—7:324, 369, 9:184, 10:325, 22:209, 24:405, 27:290, 29:141, 33:231, 36:165, 40:31, 44:278n
8:15f—48:391
8:16—15:148, 22:88, 24:405, 407, 25:167, 26:381, 27:172, 30:283, 31:104
8:17—4:27, 10:289, 13:236, 347, 16:52, 22:41, 87f, 24:407, 25:77, 26:304, 352, 27:291, 29:98, 30:266, 36:240, 43:184, 49:269n, 51:206, 373
8:17–25—27:25
8:18—3:344, 7:137, 11:397, 468, 17:241, 21:194, 28:154, 31:212, 266
8:19—5:196
8:20—1:77, 100, 204, 290, 292, 4:355, 5:38, 7:97, 10:56, 301, 12:119, 15:14, 26:251, 30:248, 31:88, 34:139, 46:248
8:20–23—43:208

8:21—12:119, 30:197, 41:361
8:22—1:106, 354, 18:45, 92
8:22f—43:63
8:23—1:333, 12:320, 359, 381f, 13:90, 25:341, 26:290, 350, 394, 461, 27:65, 67, 31:358, 33:229, 40:55
8:24—8:186, 11:453, 20:98, 25:515, 27:20f, 29:10f, 86, 52:158
8:24f—38:244, 43:103
8:25—27:20
8:26—3:363, 4:59, 70, 268, 5:132, 320, 359, 6:107, 135, 180, 7:174, 320, 325, 369f, 9:42, 181, 12:319, 394, 13:110, 14:286, 16:208, 335, 17:4, 47, 182, 204, 364, 18:14, 243, 19:87, 20:328, 21:143f, 25:95, 365, 369, 412, 26:380f, 384, 393, 395, 29:187, 31:131, 142, 32:164, 37:128, 44:59, 49:397
8:26f—6:159, 24:391, 43:248
8:27—5:108, 132, 7:324, 9:181, 26:382, 39:44
8:28—2:378, 3:334, 336, 5:117, 276, 304, 6:59, 73, 181, 236, 7:222, 273, 8:37, 328, 10:56, 108, 159, 200, 11:247, 350, 379, 17:185, 19:16, 21, 27, 25:73, 319, 360, 468, 27:327, 28:34, 279, 374, 29:219, 31:137, 354f, 32:66, 34:11, 36:72, 42:158, 43:22, 26, 44:34, 48:159
8:29—1:253, 10:11, 52, 11:118, 13:379, 16:229, 20:41, 22:118, 25:112, 164, 31:153, 225, 33:293n, 38:31, 47, 76, 82, 43:184, 51:19, 206
8:30—5:256, 10:417, 18:240
8:31—5:16, 14:195, 17:195, 246, 18:250, 358, 360, 370, 20:270, 24:141, 25:189, 34:132, 36:60, 40:349, 43:26, 224, 44:278n, 49:332, 51:216
8:32—8:6, 16:203, 26:42, 182, 202, 341, 27:100, 221, 28:211, 247, 29:85, 30:222, 31:190, 224, 208, 35:120, 37:210, 40:20, 42:164, 43:172
8:32–35—12:178
8:33—12:231, 25:189, 360
8:33f—25:164
8:33–35—25:371
8:34—13:320, 326, 25:189, 29:46, 32:28, 35:99, 38:184, 40:300, 50:20
8:35—10:353, 12:383, 19:21, 39:7, 52:278
8:35f—4:104
8:35–39—14:82
8:36—4:356, 10:227, 11:190, 194, 13:97, 14:185, 17:322, 19:184, 36:70, 49:4, 50:18
8:37—4:175, 27:24
8:38—12:380, 29:11, 39:7
8:38f—17:408, 18:378, 22:497, 25:360, 43:27
8:39—18:361, 52:278
8:84—52:279
Chp. 9—4:25, 6:259, 11:463, 12:266, 271, 16:235, 25:25, 79–87, 197, 199, 207f, 219, 379–403, 26:237, 28:290
9:1—9:73, 16:113
9:1–3—11:504
9:2—16:190, 18:72, 47:291
9:3—2:50, 19:104, 26:426, 28:16, 31:178, 42:137, 43:62, 54:393
9:3f—9:215
9:4—11:190, 12:90, 268, 17:156, 24:304, 341, 25:9, 207, 26:53, 206, 27:142, 33:222n, 40:99, 216
9:4f—9:214, 11:239, 22:196, 41:51
9:5—5:19, 12:268, 16:300, 24:94, 341, 27:142, 37:166, 45:201, 47:140
9:6—2:179, 6:259, 17:355, 20:130, 25:26, 95, 195, 33:42
9:6f—11:121, 27:255, 33:252
9:6–8—3:94n
9:7—6:72, 153, 24:305, 25:199, 26:435, 27:251
9:8—3:19, 4:367, 6:153, 7:18, 36, 8:165, 167, 232, 17:104, 18:8, 27:251, 282, 33:279
9:8f—25:374
9:10—30:42
9:10f—4:366
9:10–13—4:342
9:11—3:103, 33:197
9:11f—4:344f, 347
9:11–13—33:197
9:11–21—33:161, 165n
9:12—33:196
9:12f—4:366
9:13—33:198
9:14—18:146
9:15—19:28, 25:163, 374, 386, 422, 54:87, 90
9:15–18—33:184
9:16—2:248, 9:194, 15:55, 25:138, 421, 26:42, 27:174, 294, 33:187, 34:113, 36:42, 54:87
9:17—25:163, 374, 392
9:17f—25:394
9:18—4:61, 9:36, 25:374, 33:59, 167, 54:385
9:19f—33:147
9:20—25:163, 375, 390, 33:60, 140, 155, 186
9:20f—33:203, 54:322
9:21—25:83, 375, 393, 422, 33:295n, 54:260
9:22—25:392, 33:59, 45:115n
9:22f—8:65
9:23—27:174
9:24—4:406, 18:138
9:25—17:104, 30:66
9:26—18:6
9:27—16:113, 20:317
9:28—10:77, 95, 18:120, 20:123
9:29—16:14, 19:179, 32:170
9:30—25:93, 33:276
9:30f—33:191
9:30–32—44:301
9:31—2:160, 26:204, 33:252, 44:280
9:31f—48:24
9:32—25:06
9:32f—25:236, 32:118, 36:94
9:33—16:91, 20:246, 25:90, 27:72, 30:51, 51:281
Chp. 10—11:463, 16:235, 17:375, 25:88:94, 374, 404–420, 27:255,

35:106, 41:210, 46:13
10:1—16:190
10:2—10:74, 12:352, 16:78, 96, 17:5, 376, 23:328, 25:96, 231, 244, 27:305, 33:252, 276, 35:272, 47:175
10:3—10:58, 399, 20:246, 26:204, 254, 27:241, 30:60, 39:287, 48:24, 52:112
10:4—23:28, 25:405, 26:143, 338, 344, 348, 364, 398, 27:34, 96, 29:193, 31:344, 46:145, 51:287
10:5—25:416, 27:258, 54:134
10:5f—26:274
10:6—25:406
10:6f—33:142
10:6–8—9:278, 52:67
10:9—14:35, 22:248, 25:45, 31:344, 35:368, 46:175, 52:277
10:10—3:273, 7:37, 9:184, 186, 10:206, 11:407, 420, 14:78, 27:241, 29:9, 31:55, 347f, 32:15, 33:20, 34:163, 165, 311n, 39:xiv, 40:208, 47:54, 48:370, 49:358, 52:277, 54:402
10:11—16:229f
10:12—12:293
10:13—25:418, 26:427, 27:275, 30:313, 35:319
10:13f—18:111, 20:151
10:13–15—1:327
10:14—2:287, 14:9, 17:8, 18:111, 356, 25:418, 27:248, 29:46, 54:318
10:14f—10:52, 38:87
10:15—10:284, 11:161, 362, 13:16, 370, 17:209, 316, 18:295, 27:164, 184, 51:20, 52:68
10:16—8:254, 10:295, 11:460, 15:124, 16:224, 25:192, 49:101
10:17—9:184, 10:188, 11:159, 16:335, 22:54, 25:418, 27:220, 29:35, 148, 31:364, 40:21, 146, 45:117
10:18—16:32, 190, 17:203, 18:357, 33:27, 34:111
10:19—11:82, 17:254, 25:97, 54:62
10:20—9:5, 25:253, 419, 498, 30:314, 33:276
10:21—9:6
Chp. 11—3:94n, 10:77, 149, 11:463, 16:235, 20:59, 25:95–103, 195, 199, 374, 421–432, 46:9, 47:253, 267
11:1—16:113, 18:177, 209, 25:26, 199, 27:155
11:1f—14:270, 25:26
11:2—25:196, 421
11:4—52:137
11:5—11:71, 16:218, 17:69
11:6—14:25, 21:285, 33:269, 41:113, 138
11:7—17:401
11:7f—27:285
11:8—11:18, 81, 14:203, 16:98, 27:344
11:9—16:113
11:11—2:178, 10:173, 11:191, 13:24, 19:104, 25:98, 163
11:11f—8:81, 9:294
11:13—26:16, 19, 51:83
11:14—1:12
11:16—34:111
11:17—2:185, 3:152, 339, 17:191
11:17f—12:297
11:20—10:277, 16:293, 33:192, 202n, 42:128, 52:114
11:20f—10:245
11:21—7:18, 41:51
11:21f—9:102
11:22—10:48, 277
11:22–24—20:61
11:23—10:379, 33:192
11:24—25:100, 51:372
11:25—10:173, 376, 13:24, 17:306, 25:103, 428, 33:202n
11:25f—18:16, 52:101
11:26—9:59, 17:306, 308, 25:430
11:27—25:430
11:29—5:43, 135, 10:146, 29:218, 41:273
11:31—25:103
11:32—2:40, 11:410, 12:322, 335, 22:288, 25:82, 103, 192, 27:274, 30:233, 267, 31:349, 32:91, 34:113, 139, 154n, 317
11:33—3:276, 348, 4:355, 358, 11:229, 29:26, 33:25, 27, 180, 290n, 41:117, 43:239, 54:91
11:33f—8:79, 33:26n
11:34—25:214, 33:27n
11:35—4:42, 61, 13:91, 15:40, 25:376
11:36—10:305, 37:58, 43:22
Chp. 12—11:463, 12:294, 16:59, 17:414n, 25:104–108, 433–469, 27:381, 47:29
12:1—5:266, 6:237, 9:124, 10:67, 153, 232, 320, 11:103, 261, 13:333, 18:357, 20:296, 346, 24:243, 29:16, 175, 31:86, 35:248, 36:145, 173, 201, 227, 318, 38:187, 39:235, 40:28, 51:374
12:2—2:48, 4:123, 6:130, 152, 352, 362, 7:115, 175, 177, 238, 8:18, 30, 9:126, 24:243, 29:30, 30:119, 31:84, 51:372
12:3—2:168, 10:296, 11:402, 21:271, 25:428, 438, 27:359, 29:29, 41:358, 44:259n, 51:371–380
12:3f—20:182
12:3–6—30:124
12:3–21—31:86
12:4—21:98, 31:302, 46:166
12:4f—27:359, 44:130, 375
12:5—21:98, 31:302, 35:70, 36:283, 42:123
12:6—1:354, 2:151, 3:130, 6:131, 7:118, 9:25, 220, 12:250, 20:225, 22:105, 34:96, 36:195, 37:262, 40:189, 51:378
12:6f—20:172
12:6–8—44:99
12:7—13:176, 22:255, 257, 264, 272, 30:124
12:7f—9:119f, 30:160
12:8—5:6, 7:191, 8:107, 11:335, 15:226, 20:231, 21:134, 193, 298, 25:462, 29:102, 45:330n, 51:271

12:9—27:374, 29:53, 30:278
12:9f—20:147n
12:10—3:197, 199, 4:208, 10:190, 12:188, 17:13, 18:324, 21:330, 22:98, 25:7, 27:93, 98, 102, 30:79, 139, 31:387, 36:294, 45:117n
12:11—3:290, 4:272, 14:7, 21:326
12:12—21:234, 25:504
12:13—6:254
12:14—25:429, 44:101
12:15—4:195, 6:253, 7:342, 15:30, 21:18, 27:300
12:16—10:102, 11:290, 417, 431, 523, 21:300, 25:217, 38:319, 51:14, 52:34f, 269
12:17—14:244, 25:504, 44:44, 140
12:18—4:403, 17:324, 27:375, 50:45
12:19—3:286, 6:29, 204, 9:83, 21:124, 148, 31:235, 39:19, 41:255, 43:33, 45:63n, 77, 81, 85, 87, 46:25n, 28f, 107, 113, 49:248, 54:301
12:20—5:82, 21:122, 43:19, 45:283, 49:243
12:21—5:85, 12:281, 16:258, 21:123, 27:59, 43:33, 45:283
Chp. 13—11:463, 25:109–112, 468–484, 27:381, 28:236, 318, 30:267, 46:12, 47:34, 49:109n, 245, 254, 277n, 53:66
13:1—2:272, 3:328, 12:36, 13:44, 48, 61, 21:102, 262, 31:282, 40:83, 237, 284, 286, 304, 43:149, 44:131, 45:77, 93, 99, 110, 46:25, 50f, 55, 96, 125, 134, 47:91n, 49:381n
13:1f—20:172, 37:137, 45:86n, 48:178, 258n, 260, 49:193, 275n, 49:26f, 381n, 387n
13:1–4—5:6, 45:63, 46:95, 98
13:1–5—46:99
13:1–6—43:15
13:1–7—31:112, 239, 369, 41:35, 37n, 197, 44:91, 46:103
13:2—3:328, 13:61, 15:136, 137, 18:359, 31:234, 46:25, 50, 55, 66, 127
13:3—2:318, 9:170, 11:443, 29:72, 30:74, 40:286, 45:91, 110, 51:372
13:3f—7:191, 44:35, 45:278, 46:70, 74
13:4—1:104, 7:181, 8:205, 9:74, 12:41, 13:44, 154, 16:274, 20:346, 21:23, 37, 22:372, 31:305, 33:49, 39:252, 40:51, 305, 43:121, 272, 44:92, 131, 45:99, 258, 46:25, 52f, 66, 68, 73, 99, 118, 121, 238, 48:260, 49:108
13:5—18:324, 26:448
13:6—13:213, 40:281
13:6f—45:94n
13:7—7:184, 190, 204, 45:110, 49:398n
13:8—18:261, 25:474, 27:204, 384, 28:46, 30:78, 238, 31:344, 36:241
13:8f—48:402n
13:8–10—21:262, 269, 27:348, 43:21
13:9—20:235, 27:357, 29:197, 40:97
13:9f—36:227
13:10—27:63, 65, 235, 28:233, 235, 29:197, 31:353, 35:73, 36:39, 207, 210, 41:18, 54:233
13:11—8:312, 10:302, 334, 452
13:12—10:165, 25:480, 40:17, 45:245, 50:270n
13:12–14—44:104
13:13—25:112, 480, 40:17
13:13f—4:15
13:14—15:10, 24:407, 25:50, 308, 26:352, 27:69, 280, 361, 30:110, 31:190
13:27—40:281
Chp. 14—11:463, 25:113–118, 131, 485–508, 27:382, 40:291, 48:402n
14:1—5:230, 6:241, 9:138, 13:25, 16:9, 17:64f, 20:187, 27:381, 29:139, 31:369, 373, 36:189, 38:171, 44:36, 45:72n, 278n, 48:375, 50:197, 51:3, 72, 372
14:1f—38:319, 40:57
14:1–3—36:229
14:1–4—44:226
14:1–12—13:35
14:1–15:1—45:70
14:2f—44:304n
14:2–6—40:127
14:3—25:501, 31:372
14:4—2:171, 3:261, 14:289, 25:501, 510, 27:82, 395, 31:121, 374
14:5—7:154, 10:62, 25:493, 36:74, 38:319, 53:31
14:6—2:348, 27:180
14:7—25:501, 511, 31:364, 43:136, 53:38
14:7f—5:88
14:7–9—53:329
14:8—2:348, 7:113, 13:245, 31:364, 42:149, 47:302, 54:431, 447
14:9—13:245, 25:502, 43:63
14:10—4:316, 22:388, 25:502, 27:120, 43:27
14:11—17:136
14:12—27:395
14:13—25:113, 36:239
14:14—25:122, 28:319, 31:374
14:15—25:502f, 27:383, 40:291, 45:73n
14:16—18:18, 25:503, 27:102, 104
14:17—10:69, 12:176, 21:204, 25:504, 38:319, 45:293n, 49:65, 51:89, 53:31
14:18–20—25:505
14:19—25:514, 37:202, 38:319
14:21—25:514
14:21f—31:374
14:22—23:48, 27:395, 51:66
14:23—1:265, 2:113, 3:30, 7:155, 8:273, 18:385, 19:24f, 20:110, 26:126, 378, 27:76, 132, 250, 29:236, 30:267, 31:66, 32:14, 35, 55, 92, 33:275, 34:115, 315, 36:57, 37:130, 347, 40:291, 345, 44:25, 273n, 45:354n, 52:254, 256

14:26f—53:38
Chp. 15—11:463, 25:119–127, 509–524, 29:139, 40:291, 48:402n
15:1—9:186, 10:368, 20:26, 187, 21:213f, 216, 271, 25:485, 27:381, 389, 31:302, 32:280, 38:171, 40:57, 43:120, 45:72n
15:1f—23:48
15:1–6—52:285
15:2—27:182, 52:29, 53:48
15:2f—51:348
15:3—10:370, 372, 383, 390, 27:389, 31:301f
15:4—1:225, 2:225, 325, 3:19, 222, 4:274, 5:12, 27, 67, 192, 275, 278, 6:51f, 99, 187, 241, 402, 7:202, 221, 9:23, 104, 10:283, 373, 384, 11:365, 12:149, 14:209, 251, 320, 15:206, 17:183, 22:498, 27:25, 28:241, 29:69, 30:310, 321, 33:27, 35:374, 42:124, 43:103, 157, 49:16, 52:107, 110
15:5—14:244, 24:113, 50:21
15:5f—53:61
15:6—10:89, 30:94
15:7—48:13
15:8—1:313, 15:328, 17:69, 25:208, 54:451
15:8f—6:113, 284, 14:332, 25:194, 196
15:9—52:114, 54:451
15:12—16:124, 25:517
15:13—25:521
15:16—9:151, 13:195, 17:414, 18:74, 396, 20:101, 25:124, 520
15:17—25:520, 522
15:18—25:519, 36:195
15:19—2:184, 28:90
15:20—21:8
15:21—25:520
15:22—17:217
15:23—25:128
15:25—29:184
15:26—27:210, 30:257
15:26f—25:126
15:31—32:139
15:33—28:38
Chp. 16—11:463, 25:128–132, 41:324
16:4–7—25:129
16:6f—41:348
16:8f—35:369
16:9—25:129, 30:30
16:16—14:347, 25:129, 30:144
16:17—7:357, 10:58, 12:175, 20:237
16:17f—39:308, 44:378
16:18—3:197, 269, 9:52, 54, 15:67, 18:270, 20:237, 21:349, 26:424, 27:49, 376, 28:369, 29:37, 59, 35:380n, 40:259
16:20—20:209, 36:305, 48:372, 49:113n, 231n, 50:149n, 180
16:22—25:128, 131, 27:402
16:25—12:298, 25:149, 431, 33:281
16:25f—30:21
16:26—28:267
Chp. 17—41:26

I Corinthians

Chp. 1—10:148
1:1—54:119
1:2—33:251, 37:95n, 43:152
1:4—15:205n
1:4f—9:98, 26:24
1:5—11:215, 28:217
1:5–7—30:153
1:7—37:95n
1:9—37:358
1:10—3:147, 9:251n, 37:167, 38:319, 41:216, 43:119, 53:61
1:10f—41:79n
1:12—26:431, 45:70n
1:13—25:236, 238, 36:136
1:14f—38:28
1:17—22:515, 25:144, 289, 27:42, 392, 29:9, 31:75, 90, 210, 36:71, 118, 38:42, 40:36, 252
1:18—16:124, 26:228, 27:118, 29:12, 33:251, 36:237, 37:53, 40:145, 45:70, 49:101n, 51:114
1:18f—17:15, 80, 49:13n, 318n, 371, 50:266n
1:18–2:13—54:472
1:19—2:3, 5:341, 19:211, 27:404, 51:39, 125
1:19f—52:197f
1:19–25—35:187
1:19–31—51:125
1:20—10:61, 37:71
1:20f—18:129
1:21—11:231, 14:343, 17:80, 22:342, 25:154, 26:29, 228, 28:249, 31:52, 363, 33:251, 34:307, 36:336, 40:197
1:22—11:59
1:22–25—46:196n
1:23—7:249, 9:225, 10:105, 11:162, 220, 13:344, 14:342, 16:91, 18:255, 20:216, 335, 22:344, 25:8, 26:419, 27:179, 343, 31:333, 33:70, 99, 158, 173, 250, 36:94, 173, 237, 336, 37:71, 44:140
1:23f—10:346, 11:28, 145, 388, 499, 14:329, 25:8, 51:113, 125
1:23–26—54:119
1:24—10:111, 180, 11:395, 25:145, 26:29, 27:179, 343, 36:94, 38:257, 49:209n
1:25—10:250, 406, 13:253, 19:43, 25:150, 153, 463, 28:250, 31:52, 37:71, 49:7
1:26—3:341, 10:325f
1:26f—11:521, 13:198, 20:150
1:27—8:69, 10:87, 89, 112, 325, 351, 11:13, 151, 14:98, 18:130, 257, 21:313, 22:190, 25:150, 463, 31:227, 51:39, 125
1:27f—10:61, 92, 224, 11:263, 29:240
1:28—10:429, 430, 11:140, 21:313, 345, 34:156
1:29—25:248
1:29–31—21:271
1:30—4:164, 5:18, 10:111, 12:89, 311, 13:136, 15:289, 325, 17:389, 22:55, 459, 24:347, 25:267, 26:8, 27:34, 82, 241, 328, 29:6, 44, 67, 202, 30:252, 31:56, 231, 297, 34:119, 37:95, 155, 38:258, 42:58, 164, 49:414n, 51:28, 63
1:30f—4:157, 15:346
1:31—4:59, 162, 14:154, 25:394, 420, 27:207, 31:66, 32:181, 51:127

Chp. 2—10:148, 15:205
2:2—3:139, 276f, 10:6, 11:101, 237, 304, 17:60, 24:32, 25:361, 26:184, 27:155, 29:42, 130, 31:227, 33:70, 36:109, 41:122, 44:140, 52:4, 274, 280, 53:316
2:3—5:254, 12:178, 22:90, 29:13, 40:53
2:4f—19:192
2:5—2:102, 38:170
2:6—25:390
2:6f—33:70
2:6-9—51:125
2:7—10:156, 11:216, 12:25, 356, 16:118, 17:366, 25:278, 26:262, 30:266, 31:377, 33:281
2:7f—10:148, 14:90, 36:94
2:7-15—39:xiii
2:8—5:303, 11:250, 446, 499, 14:24, 16:124, 22:113, 351, 362, 477, 23:105, 24:106, 316, 27:146, 30:222, 325, 33:88, 99, 37:210, 38:254, 41:105
2:9—11:205, 12:284, 14:342, 17:63, 365n, 22:301, 26:24, 28:297, 29:231, 30:267, 320, 40:277, 54:51
2:9f—33:105
2:10—10:155, 13:136, 20:219, 25:167, 29:186, 231
2:11—9:58, 10:196, 22:9, 253, 25:103, 424, 29:186, 48:301
2:12—12:256, 13:136, 364, 15:205n, 28:138, 328, 33:27, 36:125, 37:95n
2:14—4:371, 8:270, 10:171, 11:33, 330, 14:343, 25:150, 329, 26:376, 396, 450, 453, 461, 27:138, 43:61, 47:175, 51:124, 52:167
2:15—2:61, 9:167, 11:117, 481, 484, 17:248, 20:219, 22:253, 503, 23:231, 25:336, 27:89, 136, 28:365, 29:240, 33:90, 37:95n, 41:286, 370, 44:135, 49:28n, 52:79, 122
2:16—8:80, 10:7, 11:417, 16:300, 29:186, 33:27n, 36:108, 38:155, 39:72, 41:370
2:18—52:64
Chp. 3—13:70, 386, 52:29
3:1f—25:390, 39:73
3:2—11:464, 18:122, 22:251, 43:120, 51:40n, 72
3:3—27:250, 33:213, 215
3:3f—41:349
3:4—27:181, 32:182, 45:70n
3:4f—9:250
3:5—39:74, 41:160
3:5-9—14:56
3:6—11:331f, 460, 17:243, 18:252, 25:448, 40:258, 43:282, 49:102n
3:6f—7:350, 45:325
3:7—10:212, 13:149, 14:115, 20:110, 21:345, 33:18, 239, 38:202
3:8—18:58, 21:318, 30:316, 31:213, 44:374
3:9—3:270, 8:95, 11:332, 374, 18:252, 20:171, 25:505, 33:155, 242, 51:10
3:10—16:229, 25:448, 28:224
3:11—11:146, 14:39n, 97, 20:40, 21:282, 22:272, 24:371, 25:104, 27:51, 29:229, 49:61
3:11f—9:25
3:11-15—46:182n
3:12—1:234, 5:238, 347, 6:146, 12:255, 20:102, 25:104, 27:51f, 55, 62, 29:38, 35:362n, 395, 39:198, 41:49, 61n
3:12f—15:270, 48:35
3:12-14—41:148
3:12-15—2:164
3:13—30:195, 35:381
3:13-15—30:17, 32:95
3:14—18:58
3:15—13:383
3:16—17:316, 22:208, 30:52, 79
3:16f—1:132n
3:17—10:16, 25:505, 40:232, 41:214, 51:311
3:18—10:243, 12:115, 25:214, 383, 506, 44:122, 51:27, 35n
3:19—40:166, 41:343, 352
3:20—11:246, 14:249, 19:211, 33:99
3:21—19:151, 20:327, 29:8
3:21f—31:190
3:21-23—12:135, 31:354, 36:240, 44:10n
3:22—25:468, 40:8, 45:70n
3:22f—27:158, 48:335, 51:350
3:23—29:8, 40:8
Chp. 4—26:419, 29:182
4:1—12:171, 27:62, 31:356, 34:243, 36:70, 82, 93f, 113, 39:xvii, 154, 40:35, 46:221, 49:62, 385, 51:305n
4:1-5—53:73
4:1-8—53:84-86
4:2—23:191, 27:119
4:3—25:141, 28:244, 32:182, 191
4:3-5—25:137
4:4—4:159, 14:148, 19:227, 25:215, 26:124, 453, 28:233, 284, 31:246, 32:53, 55, 191, 235, 39:131, 41:316
4:5—25:221, 28:358, 31:394
4:5f—45:70
4:7—6:114, 10:47, 25:221, 27:102, 33:156, 37:347, 47:302, 51:15
4:8—24:367, 29:69, 46:64
4:9—4:120, 17:322, 20:39, 216, 27:143, 301, 28:153, 282, 38:243, 43:78n, 48:294, 49:172
4:9f—4:373, 25:521
4:9-13—24:358
4:10—51:35n, 225
4:10f—12:111
4:11—1:295, 14:274, 18:118, 254, 29:88, 41:198, 46:37
4:11-13—27:143
4:12f—25:429
4:13—2:177, 3:180, 5:52, 6:52, 10:195, 11:67, 140, 367, 13:419, 16:300, 17:176, 18:80, 118, 364, 22:344, 24:314, 25:312, 26:334, 419, 28:306, 29:8, 37:23n, 52:110
4:14f—30:144
4:15—10:136, 12:203, 14:304,

17:139, 243, 20:298, 26:430, 29:14, 35:288, 36:100, 45:24, 52:78, 107
4:16—35:288n, 51:374
4:19f—30:15
4:20—8:6, 13:70, 386, 21:205, 26:220, 30:278, 43:68, 44:268, 48:306, 51:71, 89, 52:36
4:21—31:306
5:1—6:279, 9:229, 29:28, 40:372
5:1f—8:26
5:1–5—24:16n
5:3—11:373, 28:286
5:5—3:300, 27:345, 29:182, 38:303, 39:11, 12n, 40:311, 41:193, 238
5:6—9:21, 113, 215, 245, 11:483, 27:36, 339, 33:203, 48:384, 49:212
5:6f—27:339
5:7—9:157n, 13:355, 22:178, 25:269, 27:339, 35:85, 36:299, 37:197, 253, 274n, 48:67
5:7f—32:248, 33:213, 49:160n
5:8—9:157, 15:220, 27:339, 32:233
5:9–11—10:161
5:10—5:208, 27:173
5:11—34:161, 39:8
5:12—34:33
5:13—9:215, 48:342
Chp. 6—48:299
6:1f—10:385, 46:29
6:1–8—46:31
6:2f—39:22, 41:359
6:3—8:252, 22:380, 39:249
6:4—45:278n
6:5—45:278
6:5f—44:203
6:7—31:305, 36:207, 45:258, 278
6:9—3:224, 254, 25:165, 48:293n, 54:160
6:9f—6:173, 51:293
6:10—3:224
6:11—8:257, 37:192
6:12—10:385, 25:473, 503, 31:305, 33:50, 55, 51:72f, 53:47
6:13—10:207, 291, 385, 28:135
6:17—10:127, 29:155
6:18—7:93, 10:100
6:19—11:261, 13:84, 17:316, 25:499, 26:376, 27:367
6:19f—42:39
6:20—10:342, 25:499, 27:367, 48:282
Chp. 7—28:ix, 3–56, 339, 29:155, 48:299
7:1—28:49
7:1f—5:33, 37, 28:9–12
7:1–24—28:9–47, 46:265
7:2—1:116, 3:47, 5:326, 25:320, 41:43, 45:36, 44, 48:279, 51:154
7:3—32:211
7:4—44:314
7:4f—45:34
7:5—25:320, 32:211, 233, 248, 35:138n
7:6—25:320
7:7—25:106, 320, 29:19, 44:175, 216n, 262, 308, 45:145
7:8—41:162n, 54:271
7:8f—36:260
7:8–10—44:9n
7:9—1:239, 17:271, 27:69, 28:339, 342, 36:104f, 45:36, 48:279, 304, 52:268
7:10f—45:34
7:11—46:206, 209, 314
7:12f—45:25
7:13—40:250
7:13–15—21:97
7:14—25:462, 45:47, 48:372
7:15—36:106, 46:285f, 296, 54:302
7:17—51:8
7:18—14:17, 26:83, 27:334
7:18f—44:304n
7:18–24—51:78
7:19—14:17, 25:486, 26:92, 95, 27:334, 29:6, 40:69, 94, 139, 45:97
7:21—7:113, 25:473, 29:60
7:21–24—46:39n
7:22—28:47
7:23—25:473, 36:71, 44:198n
7:24—13:386
7:25—44:261
7:25f—48:294
7:25–28—45:275
7:25–40—28:47–56
7:26—44:374
7:28—32:188, 210, 45:42, 153n, 48:291
7:30f—9:95
7:31—2:253, 10:334, 11:126, 306, 13:15, 14:240, 25:516
7:32—44:264
7:32–34—45:47
7:32–35—46:299
7:34—25:436, 28:331, 34:76, 44:264
7:36–38—36:260
7:38—44:307, 374
7:39—9:72, 29:99
7:40—51:41
Chp. 8—2:329, 25:113, 48:298n, 402n, 48:299
8:1—11:86, 460, 25:293, 27:359, 396, 28:294, 317, 53:47
8:1f—16:119, 25:486
8:1–13—14:36
8:2—10:53, 20:155, 25:479, 29:68
8:4—6:239, 9:81, 18:255, 25:500, 28:310, 29:40, 211, 36:91, 40:69, 94
8:5—9:109, 16:36, 41:81n
8:5f—2:388
8:7—25:500
8:7–10—40:95
8:7–13—51:72, 78
8:8—20:78, 25:117, 26:87, 33:259, 53:31
8:8–10—40:127
8:9—25:116, 28:317
8:11—25:503
8:12—25:503, 29:27, 51:78
8:13—25:117, 27:384, 31:374
8:21–23—31:354
Chp. 9—11:332, 25:113, 27:123, 28:22, 46:11, 48:299
9:1—14:304, 25:505
9:2—22:472, 48:119
9:5—29:19, 20, 39:84n, 41:162
9:5f—28:21
9:7—45:252, 46:131
9:7f—9:140
9:9—3:149, 13:11, 31, 132, 27:396, 28:348, 36:228n
9:9f—9:248
9:11—25:126, 27:124
9:12—29:37
9:13—5:265, 27:126, 28:349
9:13f—8:125
9:14—1:211, 7:63, 8:180, 229, 27:126, 28:350, 41:353, 44:191, 46:130n, 233
9:15—25:520, 522
9:16—2:272
9:17—28:238
9:19—31:301, 344, 45:98n
9:19f—25:473, 33:18n
9:19–22—26:76, 45:201n

9:19–23—25:8
9:20—7:212, 26:82, 27:202, 211, 36:253, 41:78, 44:36, 49:381n, 52:132
9:20f—25:113
9:20–22—26:110
9:21—27:202, 28:83
9:22—1:12, 7:212, 16:119, 25:473, 501, 26:81, 27:300, 36:287, 45:287n, 52:29
9:24—27:337, 33:151, 217, 37:148n
9:24f—48:287
9:24–26—2:115
9:24–10:4—38:26n
9:24–10:5—37:10, 148n, 237n
9:26—7:154, 13:140, 15:91, 152, 18:64, 24:230, 25:447, 28:239, 29:218, 32:193, 33:288n, 49:407
9:27—4:238, 9:137, 151, 10:382, 13:169, 25:7, 328, 29:30, 31:359, 32:21, 43:22, 52:138
9:28f—26:77
Chp. 10—3:222, 25:113, 27:123, 48:299
10:1—40:197
10:1–4—21:354, 29:157, 36:95n, 52:126
10:1–12—1:308
10:2—2:152, 11:53, 22:448, 29:158
10:3—37:148n, 54:107
10:3f—20:97, 32:18, 39:78, 45:96
10:4—2:151, 4:120, 7:109, 9:60n, 13:4, 14:304, 15:313, 18:111, 118, 26:239, 31:388, 32:70, 200, 36:280f, 282, 37:xii, 36–38, 78n, 164n, 170, 173f, 176, 253, 275, 38:35, 57, 39:79, 41:330
10:6—3:239, 11:59, 64, 39:52, 80
10:9—5:178, 15:313
10:11—11:44
10:12—2:72, 171, 10:53, 14:38, 16:179, 25:509, 26:45, 112, 27:112, 390, 28:61, 29:158, 218, 38:129, 42:68, 129
10:13—2:325, 6:37, 99, 133, 180, 280, 7:126, 8:34, 9:138, 11:249, 14:127, 16:116, 18:288, 19:137, 20:142, 24:149, 25:318f, 42:138, 48:72, 49:330, 51:200, 203
10:14—39:308
10:14f—37:122n
10:16—36:31, 34, 283–286, 37:xiif, 43n, 266, 328f, 348–350, 352–356, 360, 40:177, 180, 289
10:16f—25:486, 36:xi, 37:157, 348–357, 42:162n
10:17—11:369, 27:340, 31:190, 32:57, 35:51, 36:283, 285, 287, 353, 37:350n, 353, 355, 40:20, 293, 41:195
10:18—27:406, 36:285, 37:355f
10:18f—37:349f
10:19—19:186
10:20—36:284, 37:356
10:20f—37:356f
10:22—25:484
10:23—25:117, 33:50, 44:179, 184n
10:24—25:125
10:25—25:113
10:30—46:12
10:31—24:407, 32:189, 44:34, 41
10:32f—25:465, 514
10:33—25:514, 27:182
Chp. 11—36:20
11:1—22:261, 29:15, 52:4
11:3—12:13, 13:296, 28:277
11:5—36:152, 44:336
11:6—49:390n
11:7—16:50, 20:242, 34:177, 44:321
11:7f—10:341
11:12—9:72n
11:14—11:424, 40:310
11:14f—44:336
11:16—16:201n, 27:406, 28:261
11:17—40:132
11:17f—37:188n
11:19—2:230, 9:130, 251, 11:492, 536, 17:247, 22:375, 31:245, 34:215, 40:50, 66, 53:45, 49
11:20—13:313, 366
11:20f—37:343, 38:299
11:21—35:94, 36:53
11:21f—36:24
11:22—26:187, 40:165
11:22f—38:199
11:23—29:90, 35:57, 36:16, 24, 31, 118, 37:187, 38:213, 40:24, 54:113, 196
11:23f—36:34, 284, 37:266, 38:51n, 151, 44:55n
11:23–25—36:37n, 163, 286, 37:330–338, 38:205n
11:23–26—32:57, 36:37
11:23–30—43:152
11:24—4:95, 236, 13:366, 371, 377, 18:171, 29:214, 220, 36:38, 41, 37:28n, 43, 45, 129n, 142, 187–189, 265, 273, 317–319, 327–329, 331f, 342, 348, 38:105, 151, 300, 40:22, 24, 122, 133, 154, 175, 180, 208, 215, 289, 43:151, 54:91, 92, 462
11:24f—2:385, 387, 16:184, 34:73, 35:82n, 105, 36:44, 83, 111, 166f, 317, 37:331, 340f, 49:408
11:25—13:356, 377, 16:13n, 29:201, 35:84f, 246, 36:27, 34, 37, 40, 350, 37:319–321, 328, 333–335, 40:122, 150, 175, 292, 42:57, 53:30, 81, 54:463
11:25f—37:329f, 53:34
11:26—9:157n, 13:366, 29:214, 31:210, 32:58, 34:85, 35:87, 106, 36:173, 183, 349, 37:126, 188–190, 195, 338–340, 358, 38:58, 40:22, 208, 216, 53:137
11:26f—48:317
11:26–28—36:31
11:26–29—37:157, 338–348
11:27—29:172, 30:36, 32:58, 37:86, 341–343, 358, 38:132, 40:182, 289, 292, 296
11:27f—37:122n, 38:301
11:27–29—51:94n
11:28—32:55, 58, 36:264, 37:339, 341, 346f, 358, 43:152, 54:58
11:28f—40:185, 42:171n
11:29—2:47, 31:194, 35:62, 36:43,

37:124, 347f, 360, 40:180f, 53:105
11:30—35:65n
11:31—3:225, 6:370, 7:238, 10:240, 407, 11:263, 18:359, 25:384, 31:44, 90, 32:33, 64
11:31f—22:379
11:32—3:300, 10:24, 13:115, 16:167, 38:303, 40:287
11:33—35:94, 36:53, 37:343
Chp. 12—12:294, 16:83n, 20:26, 45, 22:487, 25:105, 29:218, 30:268, 35:399
12:3—12:232, 13:364f, 21:66, 23:270, 29:34, 30:299, 33:242
12:3–13—35:285
12:4—11:423, 12:118, 213, 250, 281, 16:130, 17:242, 20:225, 22:489, 33:19, 35:215
12:4f—10:330, 16:299, 20:182, 25:106, 27:168, 208
12:4–6—44:375
12:4–11—10:70, 41:358, 44:308
12:4–30—45:363
12:4–31—52:34
12:5—20:172, 40:44
12:6—9:8, 12:281, 21:214, 22:529, 25:388, 33:35, 175, 189, 210, 40:44, 42:152
12:7—11:86, 392, 13:295, 18:107
12:7f—25:296
12:7–11—13:14
12:8—12:250, 37:132n
12:8f—12:294
12:10—40:250, 45:361n
12:11—13:18, 20:157, 25:296
12:12—30:124, 44:130
12:12f—27:359
12:12–26—21:98
12:12–27—31:302, 34:73
12:13—45:98n
12:14f—12:295
12:14–26—44:130, 46:166
12:21–26—43:123
12:22—13:112
12:22f—25:509, 43:120
12:22–24—51:159
12:22–26—42:162
12:23—27:59, 393
12:24—21:42
12:25—31:303
12:25f—35:52
12:26—23:149, 42:161
12:27—31:190, 36:283
12:28—11:336, 340, 25:447, 449, 31:32, 243, 34:357, 40:36, 46:221
12:28f—22:489, 26:19
12:28–30—45:363
12:29f—29:124
12:31—25:296, 484
Chp. 13—44:326, 334, 50:108
13:1—26:352, 39:231, 51:71, 96
13:1f—26:136
13:1–3—44:260, 52:18
13:2—10:348, 25:326, 503, 27:115, 336, 33:239, 34:183, 195, 307–309, 315f, 318, 34:301, 36:353, 40:299, 44:298n, 50:108n
13:2f—51:96
13:3—12:89, 21:80, 44:25n
13:4—2:300, 27:93, 291, 51:297
13:4–6—30:277, 34:309
13:4–7—46:131
13:5—1:261, 9:219, 10:254, 15:67, 21:194, 25:107, 117, 125, 352, 378, 477, 512, 27:308, 355, 29:84, 30:243, 249, 269, 31:65, 304, 371, 33:153, 37:201n, 43:23, 45:293n, 296, 51:123, 297, 52:224
13:6—28:244, 38:295, 43:19
13:7—2:300, 3:31, 5:172, 9:166, 13:14, 25:119, 294, 378, 509, 26:99, 119, 27:41, 59, 95, 106, 114, 353, 357, 29:228, 30:123, 37:76, 48:375, 51:297
13:8—11:3, 143, 481, 27:64, 29:115, 228, 30:243
13:9—24:400
13:10—10:411, 11:542
13:10f—44:369
13:11—4:188, 14:288
13:12—10:106, 11:96, 212, 318, 548, 12:106, 13:237, 20:138, 24:67, 25:318, 26:113, 391, 27:171, 30:268, 33:208n, 51:71, 52:72
13:13—24:246, 27:25, 72, 34:183, 301, 309n, 36:303, 40:56, 41:146n, 43:22, 50:108n
Chp. 14—28:277, 35:399, 40:391
14:1f—16:236, 28:329
14:1–9—44:323
14:2—25:459, 39:180
14:2–19—39:181, 45:361n
14:2–29—40:142
14:4—40:391
14:6—11:461, 14:36
14:7—44:324
14:8—10:229
14:9—15:91, 16:223n, 44:324
14:12—40:391
14:13—2:333
14:15—10:3, 53, 25:459f, 29:166, 53:316
14:16—12:200, 17:53, 40:300, 392
14:16f—28:87
14:19—29:47
14:22—26:374, 27:180, 310
14:23—36:115, 44:324
14:24—40:41
14:24f—36:145
14:25—40:41
14:26—40:22, 300
14:26–31—53:11
14:26–32—45:363
14:27—45:365, 53:12
14:27f—40:141
14:27–31—36:149
14:28—40:36
14:29—32:217, 33:23, 40:392, 45:365
14:29f—52:40
14:30—10:102, 14:341, 31:266, 391, 34:102, 39:310, 40:32, 37, 388, 44:134, 48:262
14:31—20:334, 30:165, 39:311, 40:23, 32
14:32—40:32
14:33—28:38, 34:125, 37:167, 49:141n
14:34—12:54, 30:55, 38:240, 252, 259, 40:388–390, 41:154, 362
14:38—53:34
14:39f—39:311
14:40—6:231, 12:200, 26:448, 27:139, 36:149,

40:34, 298, 390, 41:131, 173, 46:166, 49:205, 53:47
Chp. 15—3:239n, 28:ixf, 57–214, 47:244
15:1f—17:253
15:1–8—42:164
15:3—37:191
15:3f—35:235n
15:4—18:31
15:8—38:77, 43:247n
15:9—27:155, 192, 40:125, 49:301n
15:10—8:227, 20:67, 21:287, 34:178f, 44:374
15:11—28:82
15:12—26:426, 29:14
15:15—18:399
15:17—30:13
15:19—5:317, 17:182, 28:61, 53:329
15:20—1:348, 10:11, 11:188, 30:112
15:22—12:230, 22:30, 25:305, 53:329
15:23f—30:163
15:24—10:106, 11:212, 12:232, 27:64, 46:127, 52:72
15:24–28—27:171
15:25—4:357, 12:285, 13:259
15:25f—13:261
15:26—22:385, 27:319, 43:27
15:27—12:133, 285, 28:113, 29:120, 52:51
15:27f—38:254
15:28—10:106, 11:458, 548, 27:64, 29:162, 30:163
15:29—37:329
15:31—1:196, 7:248, 9:73, 10:227, 13:280, 18:324, 24:49, 51:238, 241, 54:37
15:32—5:43, 16:177, 28:105
15:34—25:478, 30:270
15:38—37:43
15:39—21:287, 51:252
15:40—37:43
15:41—1:41, 21:287, 290, 35:215, 44:374, 51:252
15:42—27:4
15:42f—4:234
15:42–44—7:210, 53:326
15:42–50—51:236
15:43—4:190, 27:4, 50:318, 51:168, 236, 255
15:44—1:198, 30:111, 302, 37:101, 196
15:45—1:65, 86, 30:112
15:46—6:304, 52:143
15:47—22:459
15:47–49—29:215
15:48—38:31, 47
15:49—10:88, 224, 25:112, 26:8, 30:112, 41:110, 42:11n
15:50—27:250, 28:168, 193, 29:134, 37:115, 38:260, 269, 40:203
15:53—8:162, 258, 11:326, 21:291, 41:110
15:54—13:22, 25:308, 309, 35:216
15:54f—18:72, 50:20
15:54–57—53:329
15:55—4:118, 120, 191, 8:147, 193, 13:262
15:55f—1:349
15:55–57—31:358, 42:164, 52:157, 279
15:56—9:170, 236, 13:261, 316, 14:91, 16:98, 17:331, 371, 18:73, 19:58, 65, 101, 20:99, 316, 25:19, 316, 26:26, 27:226, 238f, 269, 28:135, 29:138, 212, 31:231, 352, 32:37, 33:219, 272, 35:242–244, 245n, 397, 37:363, 53:274
15:56f—25:184
15:57—16:99, 25:65, 317, 26:22, 280, 371, 29:137f, 31:352, 42:105, 51:22
15:58—6:325, 15:147, 16:45, 17:349, 33:154
Chp. 16—25:496
16:9—15:261, 16:305n
16:10—48:374
16:13—33:154
16:19—48:236
16:21—27:129, 402
16:22—9:82, 27:345, 34:319n
18:23—52:150

II Corinthians

1:3—8:12, 12:373f, 14:210, 15:316, 31:297, 36:40, 43:77, 48:390, 49:219n, 262, 301, 310, 319, 50:238n
1:3f—10:50, 43:103
1:4—10:152, 23:273, 25:179
1:5—11:454, 14:80, 27:134
1:6f—10:289
1:7—10:362
1:8—6:99, 103, 24:150
1:8f—6:219
1:9—3:4, 4:115, 6:103, 241, 11:248, 24:150
1:12—13:382, 17:174, 288, 25:522, 27:117, 395, 29:171, 39:144
1:19—37:107
1:19f—37:126n
1:20—3:88
1:23—7:249
1:24—3:326, 9:151, 20:313, 29:69, 49:385n, 53:48
2:5f—8:26
2:6–8—27:110
2:7—9:245, 27:108, 28:246
2:8—27:108
2:11—19:35, 30:141, 36:237, 48:376n, 49:8n, 54:41
2:14—9:205, 12:229, 26:193, 27:302, 30:311
2:15—15:107, 18:75
2:15f—16:91, 27:366, 48:16, 35
2:16—10:9, 94, 178, 12:248, 250, 252, 16:226, 38:39, 40:205, 46:162, 49:4
2:17—17:270, 31:335, 52:18
Chp. 3—32:178, 33:252n
3:1f—10:158, 51:222
3:2—22:472
3:3—9:108, 25:186, 26:430, 27:234, 29:198, 36:200, 41:145, 43:104
3:3f—11:89
3:3–6—39:182, 48:25n
3:4—51:222
3:4–3—51:221–227
3:5—21:328, 27:371, 51:223f
3:6—2:158, 164, 10:92, 11:312, 13:12, 15:327, 25:62, 67, 326, 27:236, 271, 284, 313, 31:42, 32:79, 178, 35:286, 36:62, 149, 38:18n, 39:111, 157, 175, 181–183, 231, 41:177, 44:378, 46:145, 51:225
3:6–9—33:230
3:7—1:234, 10:401, 12:356, 13:280,

15:334, 16:93, 243, 26:148, 28:209, 35:238n, 242, 39:184, 46:145
3:7f—9:26, 26:147
3:7–11—29:5, 34:113, 39:82
3:7–14—35:244
3:7–18—26:322
3:9—12:205, 14:91, 15:327, 17:68
3:10—32:177
3:12–16—35:377
3:13—11:252, 16:93, 32:177, 39:185
3:13f—47:171
3:13–15—35:213
3:14—27:77, 30:7, 35:246
3:14–16—4:176, 35:284, 52:22
3:14–18—10:108
3:15—13:288, 363, 26:244, 33:27
3:17—22:487, 26:349, 27:226, 39:189, 44:135
3:18—7:138f, 11:252, 433, 12:120, 14:285, 18:350, 25:105, 153, 246, 29:132, 203, 215, 31:300, 33:208n
Chp. 4—13:363, 26:419, 29:198, 203, 46:237
4:2—10:162, 25:108, 44:44, 52:18
4:3—10:297, 400, 16:243, 44:256, 45:147
4:3f—15:287, 33:27, 52:207
4:4—5:227, 240, 313, 6:90, 358, 390, 13:251, 20:173, 22:24, 24:80, 316, 26:41, 190, 376, 452, 27:143, 30:311, 33:287, 37:17n, 172n, 40:303, 41:169, 285, 52:205
4:5—27:143, 29:25, 69, 49:61, 64
4:6—1:17, 5:205, 8:39, 34:219, 35:245
4:7—2:73, 10:37, 12:150, 14:338, 16:131, 27:19, 94, 29:97, 43:161, 51:206
4:8—14:86, 17:97
4:8f—6:108, 354, 7:326
4:8–10—12:296
4:9—6:95, 180, 305, 26:193, 29:132
4:11—5:341, 6:355, 13:280
4:13—11:408, 17:212, 26:428, 32:18, 140, 176, 36:95n, 200, 39:309, 43:62, 44:135
4:16—25:435, 26:350, 31:124, 344
4:16–18—6:355
4:17—1:199, 3:343, 346, 6:356, 382, 10:39, 12:164, 13:117, 43:185, 51:200
4:18—3:343, 11:408, 35:65
5:1—16:339
5:1f—9:157, 30:161
5:4—8:258, 28:193, 30:161
5:6—4:206
5:7—29:156
5:9—28:325
5:10—4:314, 31:138, 213
5:11—11:70, 25:497
5:12—25:138
5:14—2:16, 37:200
5:15—11:270, 37:200
5:16—22:99, 24:55, 28:383, 37:202, 38:30n, 46, 75
5:16f—37:200
5:17—16:53, 34:113, 37:201f, 43:77
5:19—22:56, 37:166
5:20—13:272, 25:5, 29:5, 39:74, 46:221, 50:226n, 236n
5:21—9:216, 10:171, 408, 16:144n, 22:109, 111, 168, 25:68, 26:160, 278, 288, 371, 27:260, 32:206, 34:126, 38:258, 42:12
Chp. 6—25:481, 26:419
6:1—3:288, 17:177, 20:171, 25:433, 45:157
6:1f—5:156, 23:262, 25:480, 45:351
6:1–3—34:9
6:2—3:283, 4:405, 10:258, 14:217n, 16:33, 118, 17:254, 18:14, 22:39, 45:157n, 50:270n
6:3—25:504, 27:104, 29:58, 45:65
6:3–7—25:481
6:4—31:84, 86, 48:387, 54:58
6:4f—11:142, 25:433
6:4–10—18:254
6:5—31:84, 86, 33:52, 48:387, 52:138f
6:6—27:376, 30:97
6:7—27:117, 29:4
6:7f—7:91
6:8—5:57, 7:98, 10:318, 13:415, 17:182, 409, 27:102, 118, 43:18, 44:395
6:8–10—21:19
6:9—4:116, 16:209, 307, 20:306, 49:181
6:9f—31:44
6:10—2:330, 13:240, 400, 15:44, 112, 17:385, 18:118, 21:13, 24:78, 27:27, 31:302, 42:34n, 51:350
6:11f—6:103
6:13—30:144
6:14—11:90
6:14f—16:262, 37:263
6:15—5:246, 32:63, 34:212, 37:27, 212, 39:222, 49:367n, 413n
6:16—10:340
6:17—3:286, 17:212
6:19—24:82
7:1—1:183, 12:330f, 366
7:4—9:113
7:5—5:27, 254, 8:46, 12:248, 387, 13:115, 16:313, 22:90, 26:420, 27:81, 135, 30:303
7:6—13:111
7:10—8:13, 54:75
Chp. 8—16:29n, 27:123, 29:102
8:1f—9:4
8:2—50:182n
8:12—44:384n
8:13—21:117
8:18—25:149, 37:316
8:21—10:162
Chp. 9—27:123, 53:64
9:2—20:198, 45:169
9:6—5:368, 13:418, 15:171, 18:58, 27:399
9:7—9:254, 10:15, 11:335, 13:418, 15:171, 16:29, 21:134, 25:450, 29:102, 38:101, 44:240
9:8—13:418, 25:412
9:8f—25:367
9:9—13:418
9:13—43:22
9:15—5:230, 8:184, 12:161, 26:134, 379, 392, 32:240
10:1—29:74f, 41:129n
10:2f—41:79n
10:3—6:97, 10:125, 27:239, 31:373, 32:256, 37:201, 282
10:4—5:227, 8:244, 9:205, 10:165, 11:6f, 13:12,

16:122, 20:294, 46:32
10:4f—20:185, 45:114
10:5—1:157, 9:206, 10:121, 202, 11:63, 12:216, 269, 23:91, 31:245, 36:34, 37:296, 38:239
10:7–12—51:251
10:8—44:138, 53:48
10:10—31:75
10:12—30:275
10:14—14:334, 41:89
10:16—20:136
10:17—6:284, 13:37, 20:136, 21:318, 29:146
10:18—11:353, 30:276, 32:53
Chp. 11—26:419, 27:187, 28:156
11:2—1:233, 25:483, 26:120, 27:306
11:2–4—9:68n
11:3—13:30, 27:306, 30:95, 36:159, 37:129
11:5—27:192
11:6—33:16
11:12–15—18:377
11:13—16:94, 24:330, 27:166, 31:335, 48:170
11:13–15—39:284
11:14—2:213, 3:108, 167, 4:389, 7:279, 10:28, 348, 11:416, 424, 12:165, 13:110, 178, 14:32, 261, 288, 22:71, 24:13, 26:41, 65, 178, 27:35, 392, 30:241f, 296, 38:201, 311, 41:85
11:16f—40:54
11:17—10:356
11:18f—27:302
11:20—28:294, 46:29
11:21f—35:186
11:22f—20:136, 24:330
11:23f—17:238, 28:153, 39:154
11:23–27—13:382, 26:419, 27:143, 299
11:25f—28:155
11:26—23:188, 27:186
11:27—46:235
11:28—27:81, 36:115
11:28f—25:501
11:29—10:390, 48:304
11:30—21:271
11:31—10:52, 31:377, 45:103n, 49:178n
Chp. 12—26:419
12:1f—27:302
12:1–4—54:36
12:1–6—45:366n
12:2—2:86, 13:28, 31:129, 38:77, 48:360, 366
12:2–4—22:307
12:3—2:86, 22:318
12:4—1:88, 13:28
12:5—22:319
12:6—11:279, 281
12:7—1:350, 2:105, 320, 3:5f, 5:131, 145, 255, 271, 8:73, 80, 9:89, 12:297, 16:332, 18:377, 21:271, 22:416, 26:341, 420, 27:101, 28:374, 36:17, 39:34, 49:172, 329n, 50:184n, 51:207, 54:95, 378
12:7–9—8:10, 12:117, 126
12:8f—8:73
12:9—2:174, 3:130, 5:28, 196, 227, 256, 6:107, 172, 7:101, 8:59, 10:49, 74, 79, 325, 11:364, 522, 12:79, 13:253, 14:134, 16:213, 17:398, 19:19, 20:323, 21:336, 23:215, 24:87, 358, 25:178, 392, 26:341, 382, 384, 27:133, 137, 302, 404, 31:137, 355, 46:32, 47:112, 54:95
12:9f—6:107, 10:251, 26:419
12:10—6:150, 12:220, 16:307, 18:391, 20:327, 25:178, 26:193, 27:137, 302
12:11—27:193, 28:83
12:12—16:83
12:14—10:110, 31:188, 230, 232
12:15—25:380
12:16—26:359
12:18—28:219, 29:14
12:20—10:58, 30:268
12:21—25:166
12:21f—29:182
13:1—35:320n
13:3—10:251, 12:186, 16:23, 25:519
13:3f—11:364
13:8—44:326
13:10—34:60, 39:11, 21, 53:39
13:11—9:251n, 36:160, 43:119
13:13—24:170

Galatians

Complete commentary in Vols. 26 and 27
Chp. 1—9:213, 26:13–78, 27:163–198
1:1—25:143, 28:83, 35:394
1:2—40:197
1:2–16—35:195
1:3—29:189
1:4—33:287n, 39:287
1:6—3:301, 27:339, 46:40n
1:7—13:387, 26:88
1:8—4:130, 9:129, 188, 14:89, 21:120, 274, 22:71, 256, 445, 23:191, 329, 24:128, 369, 26:67, 82, 93, 27:45, 108, 129, 214, 30:310, 31:267, 32:56, 81, 119, 141, 35:151, 36:21, 29, 52, 136, 143, 247, 277, 289, 39:135, 192, 276, 40:32, 134, 41:178, 190, 219, 226, 370, 42:113n, 45:208, 48:206f, 51:58, 80, 391, 52:267
1:8f—35:144
1:9—21:101, 22:266, 26:44, 46:147n, 49:63, 67
1:10—2:184, 15:322, 27:170, 343, 402, 39:xvi
1:11—27:179, 28:75
1:11f—48:390, 52:175
1:12—27:179, 28:75, 36:136
1:13—32:252, 54:17
1:13–24—34:179
1:14—26:120, 28:83
1:15f—25:144, 37:287
1:16—29:134
1:17—27:191, 28:75
1:18—39:204, 206, 41:323
1:19—35:397n
1:20—5:40, 27:212, 29:181, 45:103n
Chp. 2—9:213, 26:79–185, 27:199–242, 46:10
2:1–10—39:204
2:2—13:24, 27:159, 28:239, 29:130
2:3—25:489, 26:91, 28:341, 31:368, 372, 40:152, 291, 45:73, 51:87
2:3–5—36:253
2:4—25:473
2:6—14:290, 25:428, 41:348
2:7—25:123, 27:165, 28:238

2:7f—46:196n
2:8—26:220
2:9—22:255, 26:100, 27:165
2:9f—25:126
2:10—30:257
2:11—22:264, 26:67, 30:235, 41:323, 49:78, 51:87, 54:300
2:11f—25:316, 38:161f, 44:136
2:11–14—27:156, 30:229, 45:97n, 47:112
2:11–21—28:309, 31:387
2:12—36:187
2:14—9:250, 25:489, 27:214, 403, 31:265f, 40:32f, 51:88
2:14f—25:113
2:15—26:205, 41:75
2:16—3:21, 14:349, 19:197, 20:309, 26:333, 27:63, 243
2:17—14:91, 28:232, 35:242, 54:321
2:19—26:410, 35:216, 46:145
2:20—4:154, 10:93, 123, 12:178, 13:381, 15:323, 16:92, 23:145, 25:388, 499, 26:234, 356, 27:65, 168, 246, 308, 379, 405, 28:266, 31:269, 299, 366, 373, 34:111, 37:201, 42:39, 43:27, 44:73, 319, 51:29, 112
2:21—10:6, 17:162, 252, 25:348, 27:246, 29:6, 30:253, 35:64, 40:330, 41:113, 52:253
Chp. 3—4:25, 9:213, 15:325, 348, 26:186–358, 27:90, 127, 36:38
3:1—2:184, 21:78, 24:16n, 27:32, 243–282, 28:367, 32:26, 35:261n
3:1f—9:68n
3:1–9—26:436
3:2—14:9, 22:54, 27:133, 291, 336, 33:260, 36:201, 44:26
3:2f—9:103
3:3—49:45
3:4—3:213n, 26:216, 27:129, 29:50
3:7—1:269, 2:179, 3:29, 20:130
3:8—26:450, 31:298n, 35:359
3:9—2:280, 3:29, 26:401, 27:142
3:10—3:29, 4:159, 8:164, 9:259, 12:165, 20:54, 25:416, 26:148, 332, 27:12, 63, 274, 31:43, 54, 32:224, 33:258n, 259
3:10–22—26:320
3:11—10:273, 17:307, 19:151, 26:238, 34:117, 42:43n
3:11f—25:416
3:12—25:89, 26:265, 48:298
3:13—9:215f, 10:258, 364, 11:242, 16:144n, 17:307, 22:39, 109, 111, 230, 25:68, 26:234, 366, 374, 447f, 27:36, 31:54, 51:62, 317
3:15—30:317, 36:142, 39:205, 40:289
3:15f—17:142
3:15–22—26:320
3:16—4:152, 160, 231, 21:352, 35:359
3:17—2:277, 3:34, 21:352, 26:241
3:18—5:105, 22:139, 29:12
3:19—9:57, 13:10, 15:81, 327, 23:98, 25:306, 26:335, 343, 346, 27:146, 29:212, 33:262, 35:163, 45:90n
3:19f—48:299
3:21—12:400, 26:318, 27:270, 32:37
3:22—4:159, 10:234, 11:410, 12:335, 25:103, 26:131, 346, 27:285, 30:233, 267, 32:177, 224, 34:154n, 39:185
3:23—11:269, 377, 415, 26:346
3:23f—17:82
3:23–4:7—26:436
3:23–5:1—35:397n
3:24—1:109, 7:254, 9:48, 17:5, 19:41, 152, 20:158, 23:35, 26:7, 27:16, 29:194, 38:268, 40:302, 43:159, 45:90n, 356n
3:24f—45:113n
3:25—26:390, 27:16
3:27—3:101n, 30:32
3:28—13:331, 20:326, 23:25, 26:98, 390, 27:204, 28:44, 30:55, 34:214, 36:139, 253n, 39:68, 40:20, 41:349, 44:308, 373, 45:88n, 46:39n
Chp. 4—4:20, 9:213, 11:410, 13:10, 26:359–461, 27:283–324, 29:194, 36:38
4:1—12:367
4:1f—9:151n, 27:202
4:1–7—52:102
4:2—12:367
4:3—26:390, 402, 34:140
4:4—9:43, 12:48, 15:317, 22:6, 109, 323, 23:28, 24:319, 26:274, 317, 27:65, 77, 31:344, 41:105, 45:205
4:4f—26:360, 43:159, 52:156
4:5—12:48, 22:39, 27:65, 77, 284, 52:157
4:6—5:361, 27:189
4:6f—25:359
4:7—36:240
4:9—25:318, 26:366, 34:157
4:9f—25:486
4:10—13:35, 18:48, 27:331, 41:67
4:10f—40:93
4:12—26:424
4:13—29:13
4:14—3:187, 30:177
4:14f—26:220
4:15—9:140
4:16—27:301
4:17—27:104
4:19—1:340, 10:143, 14:304, 17:139, 243, 20:298, 29:90, 30:318, 37:20n, 41:206, 52:202
4:19–22—27:400
4:20—10:390, 18:401, 26:415, 27:301
4:21–31—4:28, 20:143
4:22—6:146, 30:115, 39:175
4:22f—4:52, 16:327, 33:252
4:22–28—13:355
4:23—3:64
4:24—1:234, 13:19, 39:176, 180
4:24f—10:134, 28:383
4:24–31—27:180, 54:340
4:25—13:19, 27:382
4:27—17:186, 233f
4:28—17:104
4:29—3:55, 4:17, 11:121, 18:175
4:30—3:55, 70, 4:49f, 26:441, 446
4:31—53:31
Chp. 5—9:213,

13:19, 27:3–105, 325–387
5:1—28:45, 31:388, 40:134, 152, 44:179, 198n, 51:78, 52:258
5:1f—48:299
5:2—26:411
5:2-4—3:77
5:3—9:84n, 27:256, 403, 34:304, 318, 35:166, 38:311f, 40:94, 41:68, 73, 78, 46:145, 50:34
5:4—7:288, 17:252, 27:343, 32:198, 40:249, 44:280
5:5—20:292
5:6—10:335, 23:25, 25:234, 27:25, 280, 291, 405, 31:365, 38:184, 39:68, 40:250, 44:298, 45:88n, 54:74
5:7—26:216, 40:249
5:9—27:46, 29:40, 33:203
5:10—26:44, 27:108, 395, 44:309
5:11—25:289, 32:198
5:12—25:505, 26:44, 27:108, 41:79n
5:13—9:126, 255, 25:249, 473f, 493, 27:65, 31:302, 389, 33:55, 36:241, 40:301, 44:35, 309, 400, 46:39n, 53:67
5:14—29:197, 41:123
5:15—49:81
5:16—25:64, 342, 27:96, 44:375
5:16f—32:248, 33:288, 34:76
5:17—1:269, 5:129, 7:126, 11:402, 448, 12:178, 20:191, 21:213, 22:178f, 260, 272, 24:384, 25:61, 65, 309, 314, 328, 26:64, 189, 341, 29:166, 31:61, 344, 32:20, 93, 231, 33:229, 35:369, 397, 37:95, 38:129, 40:56, 44:340, 51:275
5:17f—9:89, 198
5:19—4:252, 10:129, 24:263, 29:58, 30:273, 32:22, 39:298, 48:293n, 304
5:19f—10:55, 11:524, 25:68, 26:139, 37:99
5:19-21—13:220, 18:221, 30:119, 35:372, 51:293
5:19-23—36:201
5:20—10:58, 26:190, 27:67, 29:231
5:20f—11:445
5:21—4:249, 27:97
5:22—9:184f, 219, 10:128, 179, 11:103, 133, 186, 389, 444, 458, 529, 13:5, 16:305, 25:169, 29:135, 30:97, 31:300, 32:193, 34:123, 36:101n, 40:56, 48:383n, 52:38, 147
5:22f—10:155, 11:485, 30:40, 37:95, 41:123
5:23—29:62, 156
5:24—6:97, 7:65, 11:406, 13:27, 20:140, 24:345, 27:237, 30:270, 31:84, 299, 359, 32:20, 40:56, 42:14, 44:73
5:25—27:406
5:26—26:224, 28:301
Chp. 6—9:213, 27:106–144, 387–410
6:1—6:404, 9:245, 11:252, 18:362, 20:334, 25:509, 26:44, 27:80, 29:28, 41:115, 43:93, 52:225
6:2—9:138, 186, 10:370, 426, 17:66, 25:248, 509, 511, 27:66, 94, 31:168, 246, 365, 33:19, 35:54, 36:201, 42:105, 161, 43:28, 48:216, 385, 49:80, 51:298, 52:36, 53:33
6:3—25:428, 509f
6:4—15:68n, 22:264, 31:213
6:5—31:213, 250, 36:49
6:6—4:204, 5:264, 9:140, 248, 25:449
6:7—18:58, 22:198, 25:449, 31:138, 33:34, 37:28n, 46:82, 117, 48:383, 51:90, 53:105
6:8—16:111, 156, 28:312
6:9—11:293
6:10—3:185, 15:174, 25:454, 31:138, 42:122
6:12—7:288, 11:222, 14:94, 25:290, 27:42, 180
6:12-16—34:118
6:13—13:57, 387, 17:70, 172, 274, 25:130, 26:431, 27:12, 256, 307, 403, 28:368f, 32:198, 40:94, 48:331
6:14—9:216, 10:195, 383, 11:427, 14:340, 22:89, 25:291
6:15—11:229, 13:293, 14:17, 25:486, 29:156, 32:39, 36:253n, 45:97
6:16—8:219, 13:36, 16:202, 17:257, 27:382
6:17—4:135, 14:105, 347, 29:130, 49:209

Ephesians

Chp. 1—9:104, 21:328
1:3—4:156, 11:385, 26:440, 31:298n, 36:57, 37:233, 51:47
1:4—1:18, 22:120, 24:148, 52:47
1:4f—18:248
1:4-6—51:127
1:5—22:363
1:6—22:136, 490, 32:139
1:7—8:258, 36:57
1:9—49:63n
1:10—12:68
1:11—21:328, 33:175n
1:13f—22:473
1:17—40:288
1:17-19—30:14
1:18—51:123
1:19—33:175n
1:20—36:241, 37:308, 38:254
1:20-22—43:27
1:20-23—12:133
1:21—29:110
1:22—20:255, 23:22, 34:207n, 36:342, 38:254
1:23—9:168, 21:328, 22:498, 40:216, 220
Chp. 2—9:104
2:2—3:271, 8:239, 316, 32:11, 33:236n, 40:330, 46:52, 48:147n, 49:8n, 54:93
2:3—1:273, 2:121, 3:136, 4:70, 6:258, 7:179, 8:220, 12:154, 166, 22:87, 131, 26:59, 292, 352, 370, 404, 27:324, 30:12, 33:174, 289n, 35:30, 41:84, 45:202, 51:70
2:5—12:263
2:5f—37:233
2:6—5:278, 11:359, 12:263, 15:60,

17:387, 24:85,
41:359, 51:245
2:7—22:489, 51:93
2:8—8:332, 15:277,
33:123, 34:308n,
36:62, 44:297
2:8f—4:62, 400,
22:288, 23:52, 181
2:10—7:366, 11:229,
25:323, 29:156
2:11f—4:43
2:11-18—16:228n
2:12—10:171,
13:191, 20:58n,
319, 24:259,
25:45, 100, 30:158
2:13—24:259
2:14—2:215, 12:293,
16:58, 123, 230,
20:66, 71, 289,
25:285
2:14f—26:371
2:16—8:258, 12:293
2:17—17:280, 20:29,
25:285
2:18—51:46
2:19—3:152, 4:198,
8:185, 11:124,
139, 427, 14:102,
17:263, 22:203,
24:30, 25:100,
27:317
2:19-22—30:58,
41:311, 315
2:20—3:152, 11:97,
14:39n, 16:162,
28:224, 29:229,
37:164n
2:21—25:341,
41:217
2:22—12:382
Chp. 3—9:104,
16:58
3:1—20:98n
3:3—49:63n
3:5—14:23, 28:267,
34:320
3:8—2:247, 26:21
3:8f—11:38
3:9—22:20
3:14-17—31:299
3:15—43:26
3:16f—42:61
3:17—8:193, 20:32,
200, 25:78,
37:196, 38:305,
51:114
3:18—29:187
3:18f—25:438
3:20—3:158, 4:268,
361, 364, 5:359,
6:159, 7:134, 138,
174f, 9:181,
16:335, 17:364,
20:35, 21:233,
328, 336, 25:367,
412, 28:72, 36:46,
42:87, 90, 43:177,
235, 248, 44:59,
49:114n, 337, 397
Chp. 4—9:104,
15:260, 17:186n,
20:45, 25:5
4:1—30:248
4:1-10—51:333
4:2—21:314, 25:464,
48:383n, 51:351
4:2f—34:125
4:3—21:154, 25:464,
37:167, 52:34
4:3f—37:27
4:4—24:397, 35:285,
40:20
4:4f—35:70, 51:351
4:4-6—13:331,
26:356, 35:358n,
45:24
4:4-16—32:74
4:5—10:151, 21:354,
30:3, 32:51f,
36:353, 39:65,
41:195, 44:373
4:5f—36:64n, 38:203
4:6—24:397, 43:22,
46:163
4:7—11:86, 20:26,
225, 30:124,
49:78, 50:180n
4:7f—20:182
4:8—4:318, 11:3,
13:20, 241,
25:306, 311,
26:155, 371,
41:154n, 53:135
4:8-10—22:326
4:9—5:218, 13:20
4:10—11:457,
13:233, 22:498,
36:342, 37:234,
38:77
4:11—11:423,
12:294, 13:295,
332, 20:172,
22:489, 26:19,
45:363, 54:288
4:12—10:330,
13:295, 332,
27:103
4:13—16:327,
18:350, 363,
26:442
4:13-15—6:258,
29:6
4:14—5:71, 6:129,
8:212, 9:190,
10:35, 12:380,
13:177, 14:306,
313, 16:94, 17:92,
18:23, 351,
20:235, 21:252,
30:241, 32:26,
36:37, 188, 44:380
4:15—16:212
4:15f—11:341,
39:72, 76, 41:309
4:16—34:73, 35:215
4:18f—37:29
4:19—13:86, 93,
19:181, 25:293,
32:23, 48:304
4:22—26:167, 352,
32:233, 248
4:22f—29:225
4:22-24—36:66
4:23—1:338, 25:435,
38:126
4:23f—26:431
4:24—13:123,
27:140f, 280, 405,
30:6
4:25—10:66, 30:48
4:26—4:15, 11:57,
27:69
4:28—31:365,
51:156
4:29—20:156n
4:30—2:17, 44,
22:473, 50:245n,
270n
4:31f—27:359
4:32—2:341
Chp. 5—9:104
5:1—31:57, 35:36
5:2—32:266
5:3—16:61, 25:165,
40:17
5:4—10:168
5:5—21:177, 190,
200, 22:425,
27:64, 369,
28:378, 40:294,
41:360
5:8—17:312
5:11—2:356
5:12—52:272
5:14—10:302, 334,
17:307, 311,
25:478, 43:161
5:15—4:391, 6:318,
49:388n
5:16—14:251,
20:228, 43:197
5:17—14:251,
27:168
5:18—12:176,
13:215, 40:17,
41:237n
5:18-20—8:248
5:19—10:43
5:19f—41:353
5:21-24—34:177
5:21-27—46:304n
5:21-6:9—45:94
5:22—9:72, 22:444,
40:301
5:22f—44:99n
5:22-24—53:114
5:23—37:164n
5:25—2:30, 301,
4:247, 22:445
5:25-27—30:270,
316
5:25-29—53:114
5:25-30—22:450
5:26—14:93, 22:138,
176, 27:26, 32:30,
51:320
5:26f—25:6, 31:352
5:27—8:268, 13:383,
22:176, 26:233,
27:85, 32:30
5:28—2:295
5:28f—48:217n,
221n
5:29—11:537,
43:123
5:29-32—31:297,
36:95
5:30—24:407,
26:168, 357, 40:20
5:31—1:138
5:31f—31:190, 351,
36:93f, 41:158,
163
5:32—1:233, 22:445,
28:296f, 35:58n,
36:94, 37:109n,

39:181, 41:158n, 44:10, 49:63n, 53:115
5:33—15:82
Chp. 6—9:104, 46:14
6:1—48:335
6:1f—45:390n
6:4—7:255, 13:45, 22:95, 40:281, 51:140, 54:457
6:5—9:72, 36:194, 51:270
6:5–7—30:82
6:5–8—29:61, 43:15
6:5–9—43:122n, 46:39n
6:6—7:59
6:7—15:135
6:9—3:64, 4:33, 12:85, 33:56n
6:10—49:337
6:10f—16:122
6:10–17—28:217
6:11—10:165, 51:90
6:11–17—27:97, 39:143
6:12—5:230, 11:6f, 42, 65, 77, 19:74, 20:8, 26:51, 28:373, 29:134, 30:225, 258, 33:99, 236n, 36:247, 37:15, 23, 34, 270, 40:44, 149, 303, 42:92, 43:111, 45:115, 46:52, 168, 48:267, 319, 49:110n, 51:23, 73
6:13—27:26
6:13f—26:283, 33:218
6:15—9:250, 10:284, 463, 11:161, 12:217, 17:147, 27:200
6:16—2:88, 217, 4:305, 338, 5:16, 48, 203, 210, 215, 6:64, 135, 271, 7:56, 127f, 290, 8:79, 330, 12:65, 127, 175, 216, 226, 228, 233, 374, 13:114, 117, 279, 16:310, 17:48, 21:49, 88, 231, 22:90, 369, 502, 24:70, 379, 26:65, 285, 381, 418, 455, 27:21f, 26, 35, 78, 84, 137, 144, 29:69, 81, 37:17n, 39:145, 49:289, 301f, 310
6:17—9:79, 88, 212, 10:35, 165, 11:365, 478, 12:216, 18:251, 20:287, 22:222, 27:26, 78, 31:244, 35:105, 39:8, 64, 42:56, 45:360, 46:197, 49:302
6:18—17:305
6:19—49:63n

Philippians
1:1—36:155
1:1f—39:282
1:6—9:8, 10:306, 12:175, 32:8, 35:251, 44:375, 49:262, 267, 269, 337, 365, 50:21, 173, 175
1:8—18:135
1:10—43: 27, 77
1:13—20:98n
1:15—10:348, 39:129, 49:101
1:15f—33:55
1:15–18—32:49
1:18—35:185, 43:63
1:21—36:121, 42:149, 53:329
1:23—10:204, 12:178, 14:186, 25:335, 26:393, 29:163
1:24—27:239
1:27—30:94
1:28–30—41:100
2:1—18:135
2:1f—25:433
2:1–4—27:359, 31:365, 53:46
2:2—11:417, 15:229, 25:464, 30:94, 40:272, 43:119, 53:61
2:3—3:100, 4:208, 11:328, 524, 21:314, 22:98, 25:455, 463, 26:224, 27:97, 44:259n
2:4—9:219, 25:107, 117, 477, 512, 27:356, 31:304, 37:202, 48:385, 52:36
2:4–7—42:135
2:5—25:515, 31:301
2:5f—27:389, 31:295, 297
2:5–7—15:297, 25:509, 44:140, 48:13
2:5–8—31:366, 51:37
2:5–11—39:xiv
2:6—12:127, 17:162, 340, 22:112, 27:393, 41:226
2:6f—9:171, 11:104, 25:140, 29:142, 31:301, 344, 41:106
2:6–8—22:507, 52:147
2:7—10:88, 11:316, 12:123, 127, 13:344, 15:286, 307, 22:73, 112, 24:189, 25:147, 305, 317, 26:284, 28:264, 29:23f, 130, 31:55, 365, 32:145, 35:58, 37:231n, 38:31, 49, 59, 45:120
2:7f—38:47, 59f, 65, 52:86
2:8—12:123, 22:121, 138, 26:171, 175, 370, 29:72, 34:119, 43:149
2:8f—11:36
2:9—10:133, 12:131, 13:233, 236, 37:293
2:9f—43:27
2:9–11—12:101
2:10—6:163, 342, 13:233, 236, 13:257, 24:376
2:10f—25:116, 36:294
2:12—25:497, 34:348, 36:116, 43:171
2:12f—15:55, 48:46
2:13—11:207, 24:384, 25:388, 40:40
2:14—3:291
2:15—17:312, 26:24, 29:30, 57, 60, 36:305, 49:178
2:15f—6:31, 18:397
2:16—17:210, 312, 33:93, 37:132n
2:20—28:218
2:21—10:58, 27:116, 28:282f, 369, 32:165, 171, 33:153n, 39:129, 45:318, 51:30
2:25—13:111
2:25–27—27:81
2:27—26:421, 49:173, 327n, 51:233
Chp. 3—27:187
3:2—28:369, 31:335, 32:142, 39:180, 48:170
3:4—45:366n
3:4f—4:157
3:4–7—27:187
3:5—8:306, 12:355, 17:84
3:5f—26:68
3:5–7—44:300
3:6—28:83, 29:211, 33:252
3:7—30:283
3:7f—9:214, 22:89
3:8—2:7, 4:52, 59, 11:87, 310, 12:162, 16:263, 17:9, 18:336, 22:133, 25:236, 26:41, 44:303
3:8f—26:154
3:8–10—13:346
3:9—4:157, 10:34, 26:460, 27:187, 29:13, 79
3:10f—29:225
3:12—5:230, 10:161, 11:400, 12:359, 407, 14:37, 21:205, 25:153

3:12–14—25:253, 45:201n
3:13—2:73, 3:300, 10:53, 281, 392, 11:293, 298, 542, 12:273, 25:246, 275, 352, 30:227, 34:157
3:16—9:251n, 34:11
3:18—2:50, 3:14, 11:310, 517, 16:305n, 25:289, 27:131, 31:53
3:19—3:14, 4:408, 9:54, 10:279, 291, 16:34, 59, 17:280, 20:56, 237, 21:349, 26:458, 27:100, 120, 131, 369, 28:369, 29:37, 35:380n, 43:105, 49:113
3:20—7:68, 9:157, 10:334, 11:531, 12:81, 105, 22:203, 291, 26:439, 27:337, 29:117, 215, 225, 35:411, 37:283, 39:219
3:20f—8:202
3:21—4:158, 12:105
4:1—49:177, 180n
4:3—13:354, 28:22, 218, 41:161n
4:4—10:152, 16:305, 21:18, 27:93, 54:16
4:4f—29:75, 78
4:4–6—8:47
4:4–7—22:159
4:5—2:341, 28:287
4:5f—20:139, 328, 43:177
4:6—14:260, 15:7, 20:152, 29:175, 30:322
4:7—20:25, 25:413, 26:293, 27:170, 375, 29:11, 189, 30:95, 36:135
4:11—21:18, 43:17
4:11–13—2:370
4:12—2:349, 9:41, 95, 13:400, 21:18, 310
4:13—5:293, 31:355f, 34:132, 36:117, 51:110
4:18—49:341

Colossians

1:2—26:101
1:5—27:20
1:6—16:29, 77
1:7—29:105
1:9—51:123
1:10—12:375, 17:230, 30:298, 34:157, 48:401
1:12f—4:156
1:13—24:30, 26:14, 42, 51:307, 373
1:13f—33:287n
1:15—1:224, 12:48, 15:339, 22:13, 29:111, 41:82
1:15f—22:20
1:15–17—15:312
1:16—1:18, 22:14, 363
1:16f—8:275
1:17—1:224
1:18—7:294, 23:22, 30:112
1:19—24:23n, 30:223
1:19f—32:236
1:23—30:121, 52:73
1:24—11:187, 20:151, 27:134, 30:23, 51:198
1:25—46:237
1:25–27—11:38
1:26—13:131, 25:431
2:2—12:352, 381, 384, 33:20n, 37:107n, 49:63n
2:3—3:276, 5:224, 9:171, 11:96, 17:62, 22:488f, 491, 24:328, 26:30, 27:10, 34, 29:202, 30:310, 33:146, 34:207, 41:122, 43:55, 54:378
2:4—32:142
2:5—11:373
2:7f—39:192
2:8—25:362, 27:285, 32:77, 142, 259, 39:191, 308, 51:65, 52:166, 274
2:9—3:90, 5:224, 10:426, 11:268, 12:87, 281, 289, 15:305, 16:55, 118, 22:23, 247, 250, 488, 495, 24:23, 59, 66, 97, 26:30, 29:202, 30:223, 310, 33:47, 34:207, 36:35, 37:56, 61, 234, 38:307, 40:197
2:10—22:55, 124, 23:28
2:11—3:103n, 13:35, 37:274n
2:12f—3:103n, 37:274n
2:13f—16:189
2:14—12:26, 326, 376, 26:38, 349, 28:135
2:14f—26:161, 325
2:15—4:116, 191, 5:151, 9:41, 11:243, 12:110, 25:78, 26:9, 282, 371f, 30:272
2:16—9:82, 26:411, 27:298, 29:7, 35:165, 40:298, 41:67, 130, 202, 44:72, 184n
2:16f—25:486, 40:93
2:16–19—46:12
2:16–23—35:140
2:17—12:399
2:18—2:355, 3:103, 275, 4:135, 5:71, 329, 17:111, 298, 20:74n, 142, 21:314, 24:260, 27:89, 239, 28:80, 365, 30:297
2:19—34:73
2:20—27:285, 37:131n, 199, 40:299, 44:175n
2:20f—41:339
2:20–23—39:152n, 44:310
2:22—36:66
2:23—2:59, 339, 356, 3:108, 4:273, 7:113, 9:237n, 12:363, 16:227, 20:75n, 76n, 234, 21:314, 24:260, 30:110, 40:235, 41:130, 44:312
Chp. 3—27:238, 30:110
3:1—16:34, 25:310, 29:202, 35:411, 37:101, 112
3:1f—14:342, 29:196, 37:198
3:1–3—12:330
3:1–4—37:283n
3:2—21:14, 37:131n
3:2f—29:215
3:3—6:147, 12:107, 13:84, 14:210, 25:278, 383, 29:224f, 37:200, 233, 39:69
3:4—12:107, 37:222
3:5—9:70n, 10:67, 16:61, 21:177, 190, 200, 25:70, 314, 28:288, 29:175, 30:26, 31:225, 32:21, 207, 233, 248, 37:109, 44:315n
3:5f—46:150, 153
3:8—32:233
3:9—26:352
3:9f—8:258, 13:90, 36:66
3:10—25:435, 26:431, 27:139, 51:374
3:11—40:286
3:12—21:314, 30:97, 48:383n
3:14—13:63, 24:246, 34:125
3:15—44:108
3:16—16:30, 203, 18:127, 34:157, 53:36, 316
3:17—4:269, 5:284, 7:355, 8:69, 12:72, 289, 32:189, 38:299, 44:41, 51:54n
3:18—44:99n
3:20—48:335
3:21—7:255
3:22—4:283, 36:194

3:22–24—29:61
3:22–25—46:39n
3:23—4:284, 5:287, 29:61
3:24—4:285, 30:82, 36:157
3:25—3:64, 4:33, 20:79n, 33:56n
4:1—40:284, 44:98
4:3—31:144, 32:139
4:5—6:318
4:6—3:200, 20:156n
4:8—16:275
4:10—29:105
4:12—29:105
4:17—29:95
4:18—27:129, 402

I Thessalonians
1:5—7:154, 12:381, 26:179, 33:20n, 37:107n
2:4—54:318
2:13—2:358, 54:318
2:14f—27:180
2:16—41:148, 45:59, 50:184
2:18—28:291
2:19f—17:314
3:5—28:220
3:6f—13:111
3:8—28:220
4:3f—6:152, 11:261
4:3–5—46:153, 51:358
4:4—5:38
4:4f—8:65, 9:237n
4:5—28:280, 45:36
4:6—6:173, 19:164, 36:101
4:13—4:116, 190, 311, 9:134, 42:150n, 50:52
4:13f—28:x, 29:137, 51:231–243
4:13–18—51:231n, 243–255, 53:325
4:14—6:274, 20:97n, 53:330f
4:15—41:216, 51:250
4:15–17—28:200
4:16—12:120, 28:201
4:16f—43:27
4:16–18—51:253
4:17—12:120, 18:114, 20:338, 51:252
4:18—51:232
5:2—1:336, 13:192, 31:141, 35:387, 51:291
5:2f—14:349
5:3—2:93, 10:361, 374, 13:93, 16:65, 162, 240, 18:91, 182, 332, 35:268, 282, 43:163, 45:61
5:5—20:225
5:6—14:180
5:6f—25:479
5:7—10:334
5:8—16:122, 33:218
5:12–14—25:505
5:14—13:111, 17:410, 31:231, 41:353, 45:278n
5:16—14:345
5:17—5:357, 22:381, 26:51, 41:353n, 43:12, 194n, 50:175n
5:18—11:11
5:19f—20:156
5:21—25:13, 452f, 27:155, 206, 307, 31:83, 146, 223, 32:11, 119, 217, 36:194, 39:165, 307, 40:363, 41:47, 48:105, 266, 52:177, 53:22
5:22—25:108, 44:214, 45:296
5:23—18:58, 21:303, 27:363, 29:166, 52:134
5:28—36:305

II Thessalonians
Chp. 1—30:195
1:7—12:115
1:7f—20:340, 30:195
1:7–10—31:392
1:8—8:202, 26:428
1:8f—29:165, 31:127
1:9—54:33
1:10—12:130
Chp. 2—48:114n
2:3—2:383, 3:326, 7:188, 344, 8:185, 13:190, 20:192, 26:335, 27:110, 28:237, 32:63, 92, 36:72, 39:191, 201, 212, 40:10, 16, 353, 41:288, 327, 358, 366, 43:86, 50:237n
2:3f—8:21, 34:89, 36:151, 37:367, 39:194, 307, 41:205, 209, 245, 330, 53:19, 35
2:3–10—44:133n, 45:60n, 46:180n
2:3–12—2:101, 31:392, 36:138, 192
2:4—2:383, 3:121, 8:283, 9:67, 13:190f, 16:109, 17:19, 20:123, 207, 264, 21:63, 22:470, 26:24f, 180, 258f, 408, 28:373, 377, 29:23, 102, 30:99, 253, 288, 31:392, 32:46, 66, 139, 33:88, 139, 34:67n, 36:72, 222, 38:174, 180, 190, 211, 40:32, 130, 232, 257, 349, 41:203, 212, 339, 364, 46:180, 49:68, 54:46, 77, 101, 343
2:7—30:149, 252, 288, 37:16
2:8—8:226, 11:100, 13:178, 258, 17:404, 28:237, 31:394, 35:407, 409, 36:219, 263, 40:32, 41:245, 273, 361, 45:59f, 67, 69
2:8–12—41:210
2:9—9:188, 10:438, 21:271, 24:75, 32:71, 36:251, 39:191, 43:86, 44:138
2:9–12—21:275, 36:103
2:10—10:462, 21:271, 22:385f, 24:370, 28:310, 32:94, 45:66
2:10f—4:127, 141, 5:71, 22:35, 30:191, 37:19, 143
2:10–12—8:230, 38:160
2:11—2:354, 7:297, 8:21, 9:22, 130, 11:65, 14:246, 261, 22:137, 24:76, 370, 368, 31:175, 206, 39:134n, 41:339, 44:189, 45:66
2:11f—22:58, 385, 51:123
2:26—36:193n
Chp. 3—36:193, 52:177
3:2—12:386, 19:225, 22:55, 23:52, 29:9, 32:139, 51:93
3:5—25:495
3:6—25:505
3:6–13—21:117
3:10—1:213, 7:69, 8:116, 10:362, 28:324, 349, 44:191
3:12—15:148, 16:50
3:14—39:8
3:15—39:9, 12n
3:17—27:129, 402
5:3—30:197

I Timothy
Complete commentary—28:215–384
Chp. 1—28:217–255, 383
1:1—28:238
1:1–5—25:512
1:2—22:98, 29:15, 30:144
1:3f—25:485
1:4—2:237, 6:179
1:5—9:70, 16:112, 25:486, 26:147, 269, 27:235, 335, 355, 28:223, 297, 48:355
1:5–7—51:259–287
1:6—26:131

1:6f—28:381, 37:137n
1:7—15:78, 20:235, 24:363, 25:113, 28:169, 29:31, 30:297, 31:314, 36:120, 39:265, 52:147
1:8—26:180, 306, 409, 28:235, 40:82
1:9—1:107, 5:164, 6:358, 9:70, 170, 179, 238, 11:385, 22:235, 26:344, 27:96, 235, 320, 378, 29:193, 30:77f, 31:349, 371, 35:361, 39:189, 40:92, 302, 44:35, 45:89f
1:11—28:238
1:12—28:381
1:13—12:391, 28:243, 30:325
1:15—10:34, 123, 163, 233, 239, 12:171, 15:183, 25:275, 27:35, 28:243, 30:270, 285, 293, 299
1:16—12:305, 392, 28:241
1:19—27:62, 149, 28:366
1:19f—54:386
Chp. 2—25:482, 28:256–280
2:1—3:291n, 12:237, 40:283
2:1f—4:35, 36:50, 46:107, 48:259
2:1–3—44:65
2:2—4:36, 13:140, 22:95, 48:260
2:4—3:138, 4:177, 10:95, 19:96, 25:375, 28:261, 325, 33:140, 43:51, 54
2:5—13:323, 22:137, 26:236, 50:20
2:7—23:320, 24:294, 25:123, 29:14
2:8—16:17, 25:482, 36:53
2:9—21:162, 28:341
2:12—20:242, 28:276, 38:252, 40:391
2:13—1:137
2:13f—1:182
2:15—4:242, 5:5, 312, 21:162, 25:420
Chp. 3—25:281–307, 482, 46:10
3:1—7:194, 29:173, 34:132, 41:355, 54:95
3:1–7—39:254, 53:124
3:2—3:98, 4:351, 17:211, 25:462, 28:273, 338, 29:169, 34:47, 39:291f, 40:40, 314, 41:154n, 159, 161, 45:28
3:2f—32:143, 52:270
3:3—13:15, 25:483
3:4—15:110, 29:22, 39:291
3:5—13:169, 29:182, 34:51
3:6—9:206, 244, 13:331, 28:320
3:6f—52:227
3:7—6:318, 26:307
3:8—13:15
3:9—18:411
3:10—39:312
3:11—23:196
3:12—45:28
3:13—9:140n
3:15—4:407, 33:85, 41:213f
3:16—4:125, 12:129, 20:198f, 37:274, 288, 42:108n, 43:157, 49:63n
Chp. 4—28:262, 308–331, 364
4:1—1:134, 240, 5:330, 6:28, 12:346, 14:16, 24, 29, 21:251, 263, 22:58, 61, 80f, 85, 136, 342, 406, 23:204, 319, 24:279, 26:80, 140, 152, 199, 364, 27:44, 123, 29:20, 30:106, 32:36, 77, 34:94, 40:299, 44:89, 288, 332, 45:296
4:1f—29:20, 30:169, 37:364, 48:277f
4:1–3—36:97, 261, 39:84, 149, 207, 292, 40:304, 41:204, 44:282, 51:80
4:1–5—14:91n
4:1–7—28:309, 35:136
4:2—4:134, 10:32, 58, 36:210, 39:36, 44:283, 285n
4:2f—36:77
4:3—2:77, 29:20, 30:106, 36:260f, 44:246, 280, 45:99
4:3–5—46:12
4:4—2:77, 22:258, 25:362, 28:270, 29:7, 30:248, 31:55, 35:264, 38:122, 45:99, 54:353
4:4f—15:8, 35:95, 41:168, 42:91, 53:31, 124
4:5—2:77, 285, 4:34, 10:348, 12:360, 36:53f, 41:149, 164, 43:202, 54:244
4:6—28:321, 29:10, 40:314
4:7—29:3, 33:95n
4:8—5:192, 7:117, 8:61, 180, 12:395, 13:402, 404, 15:214, 17:288, 21:17, 28:347, 370, 372, 29:9, 43:128
4:10—28:261f, 46:34, 50:20
4:11—28:331
4:11f—48:377
4:12—29:6
4:13—28:53, 29:30, 30:321, 38:99, 39:311, 45:373
4:14—28:250
4:15—29:30
4:16—28:252, 44:325, 378n
Chp. 5—28:279, 332–360, 44:396–400, 46:11
5:1—39:252, 49:163
5:1f—22:98
5:2—29:55, 48:284
5:3–6—52:123
5:3–16—48:279, 284f, 293, 299, 302
5:4—44:326, 52:124
5:6—9:137, 44:370
5:8—2:330, 5:13, 372, 21:97, 28:342, 30:278, 31:204, 40:250, 43:122, 44:326
5:9—28:337, 44:388
5:10—4:271, 282, 7:337, 24:170
5:11f—25:488, 46:150, 153
5:12—28:343, 345
5:13—28:343f, 29:56
5:14—25:465, 28:342f
5:15—1:155, 46:150
5:16—3:182, 28:337, 370
5:17—3:361, 4:204, 5:264, 7:63, 9:140, 11:333, 22:65, 28:334, 40:281, 44:374
5:18—13:11, 18:58, 25:449, 27:396
5:20—39:251
5:21—28:350
5:22—8:159, 9:137, 28:359, 36:91, 38:186
5:23—31:90
5:24—1:268
Chp. 6—28:361–384
6:1—25:108, 44:97
6:1f—46:39n
6:2—7:100, 12:323, 14:50, 49:263n
6:4—2:297, 3:213, 18:72, 28:381, 40:119
6:5—3:301, 24:327, 27:99
6:6—28:372
6:7—15:91
6:8—15:149, 16:37, 28:288, 30:251
6:9—11:213, 21:202,

25:341, 28:372, 45:245
6:9f—28:370
6:10—6:7, 9:70n, 10:55, 11:339, 444, 45:245, 46:154
6:11—13:79, 48:383n
6:12—33:217, 49:354n
6:15—30:297, 37:222, 49:370
6:16—2:46, 3:122, 138, 10:119, 12:52, 104, 23:93, 27:84, 33:145, 34:216, 41:116
6:17—3:83, 14:121, 15:53, 28:380, 42:161
6:20—3:301, 13:62, 32:223, 33:190
6:20f—52:166

II Timothy
1:2—30:144
1:5—16:112
1:8—36:266
1:10—15:319, 26:282, 35:216, 43:27
1:12—1:214, 15:272, 25:498, 43:177
1:13—18:161
1:15—12:166, 17:173, 26:426, 27:117, 36:238, 48:302
1:15f—28:381
2:2—36:152, 38:212, 40:36
2:3—33:217
2:4—13:176, 41:130, 44:167n
2:5—25:318, 33:217
2:8—25:149, 35:235n
2:9—20:295, 31:341, 32:145, 33:56, 48:206, 49:362, 50:161n
2:10—25:376, 26:306
2:11—6:150, 30:127
2:11f—10:289, 51:206
2:12—3:334, 11:187, 20:329
2:13—5:48, 6:154, 10:240, 36:60, 41:212, 331, 43:53
2:14—10:441, 33:95n, 40:119
2:15—3:222, 239n, 241, 9:136, 10:462, 13:86, 93, 15:229, 26:302, 27:63, 36:158, 54:313
2:17—10:426, 441, 11:363, 14:259n, 290, 20:57, 234, 25:29, 228
2:19—25:374, 33:25, 42, 205, 48:270
2:20—18:44, 25:84, 53:49
2:20f—33:204
2:21—53:50
2:24—10:222, 39:154
2:24-26—32:02
2:25—22:524, 29:182, 31:59
2:25f—26:6
2:26—1:273, 3:271, 8:294, 31:59, 33:65, 34:89, 43:78, 46:77
3:1—38:160, 178, 44:89, 45:273, 54:101
3:1f—10:382, 36:209, 50:244n
3:1-4—52:141
3:1-5—39:256
3:1-6—44:373
3:1-7—44:299
3:1-9—36:25, 161, 45:296, 52:211
3:2—4:372, 16:333, 346, 48:335, 51:377n
3:2f—10:373, 20:256, 25:469
3:3—2:300, 4:368, 18:269
3:5—10:389, 11:416, 462, 15:187, 16:245, 20:57, 241, 24:308, 25:478, 31:362, 376, 36:210, 39:192, 44:365, 51:16
3:6—52:236
3:7—7:155, 357, 15:185, 28:67, 222, 270, 31:362, 376, 34:118, 36:123, 223, 39:187, 192
3:8—10:448, 14:246, 25:438, 30:210, 36:30, 162n, 40:255, 52:238f
3:9—20:146, 239, 27:120, 30:174, 36:327, 45:151, 49:365
3:10f—28:218
3:12—6:99, 9:57, 10:51, 289, 11:307, 365, 12:216, 14:58, 20:41, 21:46, 43:171, 184
3:13—10:13, 14:246, 259, 15:85, 18:176, 31:362, 36:55
3:14—44:353
3:15—30:321
3:16—2:325, 3:70, 239, 15:230, 30:310, 321, 33:27, 94
3:16f—8:49, 14:338, 15:194
3:17—3:239, 4:279, 15:197, 17:245
4:1—10:403
4:1-4—41:223
4:2—2:23, 6:105, 400, 8:121, 15:113, 16:204, 17:12, 116, 26:186, 27:303, 28:321, 29:86, 30:291, 32:197, 33:18, 21, 214, 38:99
4:2f—43:227
4:3—9:225, 11:241, 15:303, 22:385, 25:229, 27:116, 29:59, 34:214, 38:100, 41:128n, 43:78
4:3f—4:127, 11:56, 28:309
4:4—20:157, 22:36
4:7—15:152, 33:218, 50:245
4:7f—32:192
4:8—6:401, 25:355
4:10—23:186, 29:105, 36:238, 44:397, 48:302
4:13—29:87, 32:189, 45:373

Titus
Complete commentary—29:3–91
1—13:62, 25:130, 482, 28:267, 29:4–51, 46:10
1:1—36:180, 54:73, 146
1:2—4:137, 145, 148, 6:360, 8:191, 9:63, 14:30, 25:145, 28:267, 33:42, 37:51n
1:3—28:238
1:4—22:98, 29:175, 30:144
1:5—13:64, 14:287, 18:264, 26:81, 39:155, 160, 311, 41:324
1:5f—26:17
1:5-7—36:155, 39:277–279
1:5-9—39:255
1:6—39:291f, 40:40, 41:154n, 45:28, 54:107
1:7—13:15, 25:483, 27:97, 28:287, 29:32, 69, 169, 38:196, 39:155n, 312, 39:160
1:7f—20:256, 29:182
1:8—16:3, 25:462, 27:96
1:9—9:171, 206, 235, 13:28, 15:230, 16:119, 20:185, 25:485, 28:286, 31:217, 390, 32:149, 194, 34:47, 39:165, 254
1:9f—33:94, 45:114n

1:10—16:305n, 20:244, 25:113, 485, 28:228, 381, 30:234, 32:142, 34:118, 48:170
1:10f—33:102
1:10-13—45:71
1:11—20:234, 27:178, 28:271, 40:393, 45:66n
1:12—13:199, 26:188, 27:243, 40:251n, 46:84
1:13—25:485
1:13f—41:301
1:14—9:52, 18:21, 20:236f, 264, 28:223, 29:68, 34:354, 35:144, 36:37, 39:39, 44:310
1:15—9:135, 216, 21:35, 25:113, 362f, 424, 26:265, 27:188, 204, 216, 256, 28:34, 225, 270, 279, 317, 29:6, 153, 193, 209, 37:130, 238, 44:317, 389, 48:158, 372, 51:17
1:16—10:185, 389, 13:386, 18:354, 20:321, 265, 21:35, 24:121, 281, 327, 25:244, 26:258, 29:49, 52:173
Chp. 2—14:227, 25:482, 29:52–70
2:1—14:36, 25:485
2:1-10—44:88
2:2—25:485, 29:75
2:3-5—28:299
2:5—1:203, 3:201, 25:108, 27:96, 29:63, 65
2:7—29:169
2:7f—48:294
2:8—9:151, 25:485, 28:294, 33:70
2:9f—44:97, 46:39n
2:10—29:57
2:11—11:6, 30
2:11-14—48:237f, 255n
2:12—5:54, 16:3, 27:173, 31:299
2:12f—11:397, 25:355
2:13—24:19, 29:62, 32:192
2:14—2:292, 15:135, 20:47, 21:350, 29:65, 30:270, 52:172
2:15—11:30
Chp. 3—13:386, 29:71–91
3:1—44:91, 46:99
3:1f—25:465
3:3—25:53
3:3f—29:211
3:4—3:155, 11:6
3:4f—3:167, 8:176
3:5—1:94, 22:176, 283, 515, 26:228, 352f, 31:363, 33:110, 34:113, 35:30, 36:60, 40:19, 146, 41:151, 43:159, 51:323
3:6—8:308, 10:378
3:8—28:239, 260
3:8f—15:186
3:9—6:179, 33:95n
3:9-11—29:81
3:10—3:286, 13:62, 407, 15:84, 120, 155, 19:192, 28:368, 29:182, 30:243, 260, 324, 37:20, 162, 288n, 38:295, 54:417
3:10f—14:271, 38:288, 41:50, 48:252, 304, 50:197, 201, 242n
3:11—3:286, 9:198, 30:260, 38:304, 41:12n, 193n
3:15—29:93

Philemon
Complete commentary—29:93–107
1—20:98n
2—28:271
4—29:98
7—3:181n, 29:94
10—27:108, 44:333n
12—29:103
13—20:98n
14—25:496
20—9:72

Hebrews
Complete commentary—29:109–241
Chp. 1—29:109–121
1:1f—10:230, 11:38
1:2—1:18, 5:142, 11:116, 22:20, 25:5, 148, 26:319
1:3—1:21, 15:339, 25:76, 34:219, 219n, 36:39, 42:56, 52:63
1:5—12:48, 61, 13:235, 14:330
1:6—5:220, 12:134, 13:234, 15:337, 29:121
1:7—10:210, 11:323, 12:202, 16:27, 18:81, 29:167, 194
1:8—10:210, 12:230, 20:209n, 29:118
1:10—14:186, 15:337
1:14—5:216, 6:89, 11:220, 20:16, 22:204, 42:113, 54:9
Chp. 2—16:92f, 29:122–142
2:1—29:110
2:2—16:229, 26:318, 27:271
2:3—31:181, 35:394
2:4—36:192
2:5—10:22, 11:272, 20:16
2:5-8—12:133
2:7—29:127, 129, 48:55n
2:8—12:133, 52:51
2:9—11:36, 12:129, 54:430
2:9f—20:219
2:10—40:57
2:13—16:92f
2:14—12:123, 13:135, 261, 51:250
2:16—4:161, 9:171, 11:232, 12:123, 22:103
2:16f—38:31, 47, 76
2:17—12:123, 38:31, 59, 76
2:18—29:226
Chp. 3—11:60, 29:143–158
3:1—25:120, 27:163
3:2—16:26, 35:327
3:2f—17:210
3:3—13:305
3:4—29:147
3:5—29:5
3:6—25:505, 29:147
3:7—10:349, 20:98n, 292
3:8-12—18:167
3:11—1:80, 4:150
3:16—29:157
3:16f—9:28
3:18—1:75
Chp. 4—29:159-167
4:2—29:159
4:3—1:75, 29:157
4:3f—9:23
4:3-9—8:67
4:7—13:79, 20:292
4:8—9:43n
4:11—11:253, 31:188
4:12—3:348, 10:30, 136, 296, 11:89, 160, 438, 12:216, 225, 29:163, 41:352n, 42:56
4:13—1:173, 11:260, 29:194
4:14—30:236, 38:184
4:15—5:205, 312, 29:226, 32:200, 38:31, 65, 51:131
4:16—13:322, 40:40, 50:20
Chp. 5—29:168–179, 30:236
5:1—13:318, 323, 36:138
5:2—29:18
5:3—43:174
5:4f—14:325, 35:247
5:6—31:388, 39:81
5:7—11:240, 13:319f, 341, 29:177
5:8—10:108

5:9—29:131
5:12—22:251, 27:285, 51:40n, 72
Chp. 6—29:180–187, 31:354
6:1—29:182
6:1–6—44:398n
6:4—35:395n
6:4f—33:66n
6:4–6—26:197, 34:174, 35:394, 52:282
6:4–7—13:306
6:6—10:19, 22:362, 26:199, 27:246, 29:181, 30:253, 36:147, 37:210, 44:294n
6:7—33:172
6:10—25:178
6:11—29:181, 33:20n
6:13—4:142, 13:308, 17:136, 348
6:16—4:78, 231, 7:249, 16:165, 21:102
6:16–18—4:144
6:17—4:150
6:18—38:306
6:19—13:308
6:20—31:388, 37:293
Chp. 7—20:41, 29:188–196, 31:354, 32:156
7:1f—11:368
7:1–17—15:58
7:2—2:393, 29:189
7:3—2:381, 11:369, 13:312, 29:189
7:7—8:111, 13:311
7:9—3:35, 13:312
7:10—3:35, 13:312, 37:65
7:11—12:362
7:12—9:178, 31:279, 36:137, 142, 199
7:12–19—29:191
7:17—13:311, 25:435
7:19—9:43, 16:72, 18:123
7:20–22—29:191
7:21–28—31:388
7:22—29:193
7:23f—32:281
7:23–25—29:191
7:24—13:315
7:25—26:11, 50:20
7:26—13:319, 32:28
7:26–28—29:191
7:27—13:319, 29:219, 36:147
Chp. 8—29:197f, 37:325
8:6—27:272
8:10—27:234
8:13—9:310, 35:85, 246n
Chp. 9—20:220, 29:199–220, 35:247, 36:38, 37:325
9:1f—37:264n
9:2—29:199
9:4—29:201f, 205
9:5—26:273, 29:201f, 37:364n
9:6—29:194
9:6–12—39:81
9:10—27:250, 335, 20:212, 39:178
9:10f—20:143
9:11f—35:246n, 36:145
9:12—2:384, 20:96, 25:52, 26:132, 360, 35:85, 216, 247, 36:313, 37:142n, 40:14
9:13f—30:8
9:14—31:124
9:15—20:97, 27:268, 29:214
9:16—36:38
9:16f—35:84, 36:179
9:17—27:268
9:19—30:7
9:22—13:319
9:24—35:99
9:25f—36:147, 320
9:26—36:313
9:27—31:138, 38:130
9:28—25:52, 40:14, 43:174
Chp. 10—29:221–228, 35:247, 37:325
10:1—10:56
10:3—29:220
10:4—13:318, 29:206
10:10—34:119, 36:162
10:12—40:14
10:14—2:384, 386, 36:138, 40:14
10:16—27:234
10:19—31:355
10:20—9:141, 26:232, 29:226
10:22—29:193, 31:124, 355, 33:20n
10:23—36:42, 60
10:24—11:253
10:25—11:373
10:26—13:306, 29:182, 35:395n
10:26f—35:394
10:27—13:306, 22:232
10:28—29:122, 46:70
10:29—10:62, 21:288, 29:227, 44:294n
10:30—6:201, 204, 9:83n
10:33f—25:462
10:34—10:356, 29:156, 230f
10:35—21:292
10:36—25:178, 458
10:37—6:158, 34:240n
10:38—11:442, 19:123, 151n, 32:14, 52:114
10:39—29:231
Chp. 11—6:8, 11:454, 18:74, 19:197, 22:310, 25:255, 26:263, 267, 29:229–241, 52:126
11:1—5:183, 7:106, 8:166, 236, 9:203, 10:69, 356, 440, 11:406f, 421, 513, 12:285, 13:241, 15:272, 17:240, 365, 25:41, 163, 215, 369, 399, 446, 27:377, 28:18, 297, 29:156f, 33:62, 35:410, 37:47, 272n, 38:50, 39:xiii, 102, 220, 43:52, 48:232, 49:62, 331, 52:197
11:2—2:113f, 34:112n
11:3—3:33, 22:28, 49:331
11:4—1:246, 251, 257, 264, 266, 14:88, 17:401, 26:263f, 294, 27:145, 34:303, 36:66, 95n
11:4f—7:28, 16:307, 22:273
11:5—26:264
11:5f—3:79
11:6—3:20, 105, 13:127, 26:264, 29:148, 31:102, 107, 271, 362, 33:42, 35:101, 43:53, 44:373
11:8—2:246, 17:401, 26:264, 34:303, 48:94, 233
11:8–10—3:318, 8:114
11:9—2:246
11:9f—2:362
11:10—1:315, 3:157
11:11—3:206, 36:60
11:13—12:113, 36:95n
11:14—5:198
11:14f—16:331
11:19—2:294, 4:96, 13:180, 34:124
11:21—6:342, 8:146, 178, 11:107, 29:118
11:25—11:151
11:31—18:115
11:32—22:263
11:32f—22:274
11:33—5:235
11:34—11:42
11:35—10:226
11:36f—27:210
11:38—17:264, 21:161
11:39f—12:120
11:40—13:259, 36:95n
Chp. 12—11:454, 13:259, 42:53
12:1—5:248, 8:309,

12:233, 16:153, 25:339, 30:228, 32:23, 233, 248, 35:38
12:2—32:265
12:3—39:146, 42:14, 143
12:4-11—42:138
12:5-7—7:226
12:5-11—14:347
12:6—6:356, 7:235, 10:206, 11:467, 12:296, 16:167, 18:145, 25:292, 31:91, 42:125, 184n, 50:18n, 53:67
12:6f—16:215
12:7—7:131
12:8—10:289, 31:91, 43:184
12:11—6:150, 19:92, 26:416, 50:18n
12:12—7:155
12:14—30:268
12:15—9:273, 18:160, 31:375
12:16—4:406, 22:34
12:16f—1:297, 5:151
12:17—4:405, 409, 5:154, 156, 13:306, 35:394, 395n
12:20—9:57n
12:21—26:320, 29:5
12:22—29:169
12:24—29:169, 31:225
12:29—3:122, 6:400, 9:58, 16:144n, 26:311
13:2—3:178, 220, 244n, 25:462, 463
13:3—54:113
13:4—3:224, 254, 4:233, 5:193, 26:351, 29:19, 55, 51:357-367
13:5—28:323, 370, 29:16, 46:29, 233
13:7—8:132, 22:65, 273, 388, 29:26, 36:188, 40:58, 300, 44:269
13:8—12:362, 19:198, 21:354, 22:427, 448, 24:397, 26:361, 34:126, 301, 304, 47:118, 52:126, 281
13:9—10:56, 25:486, 40:329
13:10—16:165, 35:247, 42:54
13:11—11:28
13:13—10:195, 11:66, 41:190n
13:14—1:351, 16:3, 30:35, 42:39
13:15—9:157, 18:74, 25:6, 29:176, 35:99f, 36:146, 162, 52:276
13:17—4:286, 21:44, 212, 44:368

James
1:1—54:424
1:2—10:288, 320, 29:130, 31:226, 51:24
1:4—6:402, 12:281, 25:178, 29:181
1:5—30:322
1:5f—32:13
1:5-8—31:273
1:6—16:320, 17:289n, 30:322, 36:51, 121, 40:279, 345
1:6f—29:217
1:6-8—42:76, 88, 44:58
1:7—30:322
1:8—13:140
1:12—6:355, 7:226, 42:75, 159
1:13—4:92, 132
1:14f—11:309
1:15—13:85
1:17—10:26, 69, 13:104, 27:371, 38:255
1:18—11:229, 25:73, 245, 323, 341, 27:406, 29:120, 156, 32:24, 33:243, 34:113, 152n, 36:39, 52:15, 78
1:19—25:402
1:22—2:159, 26:203, 51:71
1:23f—17:231, 26:65
1:25—10:26, 35:397
1:26—42:68
2:1—20:79n, 54:424
2:1-9—28:302
2:5—42:34n
2:10—11:435, 25:236, 411, 27:38, 331, 33:44, 37:26n, 39:59, 67, 96
2:10f—38:312
2:13—19:47, 21:31
2:17—29:235, 34:175
2:19—1:296, 7:229, 26:168, 27:172, 291, 29:235, 30:12, 31:127, 34:109, 173, 36:301, 38:150
2:20—44:298n, 54:176
2:21—4:96, 133, 35:396
2:22—34:301, 317
2:23—35:396
2:23-25—25:234
2:24—34:125, 35:396, 36:303
2:25—18:115
2:26—10:25, 25:234, 34:175, 54:425
3:1—3:147, 15:77, 186, 29:14, 32:77
3:2—3:348f, 10:22, 295, 382, 25:221, 276, 30:233, 31:59, 46:288, 53:33
3:11—33:122
3:12—10:83
3:15—11:216, 15:99
3:17—11:332, 12:87
4:1—25:309
4:3—28:272, 44:59
4:4—27:170, 30:249
4:6—30:293, 51:43
4:7—29:20, 30:260
4:8—31:11
4:13-16—45:254
4:15—45:257
5:1—10:288, 16:18, 51:24
5:7—42:56
5:8—19:6, 14, 27
5:13—7:326
5:14—36:120, 37:370
5:14f—29:228, 36:118
5:14-16—31:91
5:15—36:119-121
5:16—3:292, 4:340, 342, 21:234f, 36:50, 120, 356, 44:67, 46:174, 54:52, 454
5:16f—46:33
5:16-18—17:158
5:17—3:354, 21:235, 46:173
5:17f—44:67
5:20—35:397

I Peter
Complete commentary—30:3-147
Chp. 1—30:5-47, 221, 46:12
1:1—18:357, 41:321, 347
1:2—8:257f, 268, 12:363, 17:217, 30:314, 51:326
1:3—15:316
1:5—49:209n
1:6—10:39, 13:382, 18:14, 25:289, 30:109, 43:185, 51:200
1:6f—25:44
1:7—24:47n, 30:126
1:8—25:43
1:9—17:388
1:10—16:4, 30:58
1:10-12—35:122
1:11—1:145, 6:268, 8:46, 11:237, 12:246, 35:314
1:11f—35:266
1:12—4:120, 319, 5:218, 6:126, 11:296, 12:118, 15:310, 18:108, 42:108n, 48:206, 51:111, 52:107
1:13—17:117, 22:307
1:16—25:462
1:17—43:27
1:18f—46:219, 48:282

1:19—41:314
1:23—30:273
1:24—40:247, 260
1:24f—11:198
1:25—4:60, 8:190, 11:198, 14:11, 303, 22:14, 26:54, 66, 444, 456, 27:144, 35:219, 40:198
Chp. 2—8:83, 30:47–86, 46:12
2:1–5—36:139, 39:235
2:2—10:87, 11:368, 497, 12:109, 375, 16:93, 22:251, 36:141, 43:52, 51:72, 116, 52:78
2:3—25:358, 39:220
2:3–5—41:310
2:4–7—41:315
2:5—10:232, 25:6, 341, 29:16, 32:70, 36:141, 146, 40:29, 51:295n, 335, 52:138
2:5–10—48:265
2:6—16:229, 20:218, 21:282, 30:105f, 50:19n
2:6–10—39:236, 41:310
2:7f—11:394, 14:96, 16:230, 25:86
2:8—10:445, 451, 11:221, 16:91, 25:236, 32:118
2:9—10:24, 11:37, 86, 393, 13:295, 14:32, 16:9, 21:350, 22:479, 24:243, 26:394, 29:16, 67, 117, 30:52, 31:354, 35:101, 36:113, 140f, 149, 38:187, 39:xvii, 152, 179, 227f, 234, 279, 309, 40:21, 37f, 44:130, 49:209n, 51:295n, 335
2:10—10:171, 25:84, 26:101, 35:36
2:11—25:309, 27:363, 32:20, 214, 231, 44:106
2:12—15:187, 18:85, 90, 25:465, 30:109, 45:73
2:13—6:168, 12:36, 80, 13:48, 214, 15:170, 25:469, 31:385, 34:334, 39:97, 40:285, 304, 40:83, 43:22, 44:131, 45:94, 111, 46:51
2:13f—25:109, 26:448, 44:91, 45:63, 86, 110, 46:95, 98, 238, 48:260, 49:27
2:13–17—31:112
2:14—9:145, 13:154, 21:23, 22:95, 132, 40:306, 43:272, 45:91, 46:25, 70n, 73
2:15—25:110, 44:131, 45:66n
2:16—25:54, 109, 249, 493, 26:344, 27:49, 347, 36:261, 44:35, 400, 45:192, 46:32n, 36n
2:17—8:321, 25:497, 40:83, 49:257, 276
2:18—28:361, 40:285, 46:28
2:18f—44:97
2:19f—44:92n
2:21—13:379, 26:165, 352, 27:238, 29:123, 159, 31:300, 35:119, 36:146, 40:149
2:22—12:134, 262, 22:109, 113, 121, 244, 265, 495, 26:189, 370, 27:64, 29:195, 38:161, 51:277
2:23—5:108, 13:341, 14:257, 315, 15:27, 16:209, 17:226, 18:256, 43:164, 45:274, 46:30
2:24—13:321, 17:224, 22:51, 25:52, 26:126, 27:238, 389, 29:68, 34:111, 42:12, 51:297
2:25—4:310, 7:99f, 8:268, 12:155, 22:51, 61, 30:134, 40:40, 41:330, 48:286, 49:428n, 50:20
Chp. 3—13:48, 154, 30:87–116, 40:83
3:1—9:72n, 28:346, 29:71, 45:25
3:1f—28:39
3:1–7—44:99n
3:2—23:416
3:5—40:300
3:6—2:252, 3:44, 209, 4:189, 271, 386
3:7—1:69, 201, 3:58, 353, 5:31, 18:403, 28:51, 272, 29:57, 30:161, 41:155, 51:292
3:8—35:392n
3:9—8:325, 25:464, 37:138n, 45:87
3:10—43:164
3:12—10:99
3:13—36:72, 39:8, 42:160
3:13f—6:398
3:13–15—43:238
3:14—43:105
3:15—30:107, 31:159, 217, 32:276, 33:21, 80, 38:243, 39:249, 40:53, 54, 45:72, 48:105
3:16—45:66n
3:17—5:381, 30:16
3:18—27:302, 30:117, 36:138, 37:250
3:18–20—2:85, 43:27
3:19—42:105, 137, 48:301
3:20—29:237
3:20–24—35:31
3:21—2:151, 155, 12:134, 20:82, 31:67
3:22—2:151, 13:236
Chp. 4—28:290, 29:123, 30:117–131
4:1—27:237, 35:119, 42:14, 143
4:2—15:323, 27:239
4:3f—25:481
4:4—10:125, 366, 25:481, 30:144
4:6—30:111
4:7–11—51:291–299
4:8—27:352, 31:133, 198, 35:397
4:8–11—31:181
4:9—4:281
4:10—3:130, 13:295, 27:359, 35:397, 44:375, 51:8, 299
4:10–12—44:379
4:11—5:248, 250, 13:139, 16:334, 19:83, 22:255, 29:5, 32, 30:132, 36:142, 194, 37:50, 38:164, 40:40, 41:301, 44:353, 386, 45:106, 49:67, 51:305f, 311
4:12—16:310, 44:380n
4:15—7:73, 17:323, 21:46, 27:133, 31:239, 40:392, 49:385n
4:15f—39:144
4:17—5:171, 10:206, 14:186, 16:143, 17:148, 18:145, 344, 31:91, 43:163
4:17f—11:205, 468
4:18—25:142, 318, 35:43, 41:298n, 43:151, 48:46, 52:97, 137
4:19—42:154
Chp. 5—30:132–147
5:1—10:19, 13:331
5:1f—39:154, 41:358
5:1–4—30:157, 39:283
5:2—13:15, 41:85
5:2f—44:163
5:2–4—53:126
5:3—2:274, 13:64, 20:313, 20:25, 60,

41:131, 353n,
49:385n
5:4—4:358, 9:8,
17:206, 26:24,
29:23
5:5—1:244, 2:4,
4:63, 5:104,
7:167, 11:149,
264, 12:317,
13:151, 213,
16:109, 21:300,
23:303, 350,
30:293, 31:51,
340, 387, 33:61,
34:10, 288,
39:154, 41:117,
43:275, 44:312,
45:117, 49:259,
51:43
5:6—2:316, 3:14,
6:285, 30:161,
35:397
5:7—2:316, 4:340,
5:56, 7:115, 9:94,
14:222, 42:131,
154, 43:174,
44:84, 45:333,
49:227
5:8—1:189, 4:391,
5:215, 10:84,
11:369, 12:150,
13:178, 18:275,
19:35, 20:8, 93,
207, 26:3, 46, 193,
380, 428, 27:3,
28:74, 217, 376,
29:90, 30:161,
224, 244, 274,
296, 32:188,
33:236, 37:17n,
40:43, 80, 287,
42:71, 47:118,
51:295, 53:45
5:9—1:158, 3:180,
13:178, 14:79,
27:3, 32:70,
41:197, 42:137,
183, 54:275
5:10—13:139,
29:129, 31:347,
46:30n
5:13—11:177

II Peter
Complete
commentary—
30:149–201
Chp. 1—30:151–167
1:3—30:177
1:3f—17:163, 29:214
1:3–7—49:209n
1:4—26:100, 27:173,
30:163, 225,
31:192, 297
1:5—28:328, 44:298
1:7—25:107, 30:42
1:9—1:221, 225,
9:41n, 105,
12:326, 26:71,
36:61
1:10—3:169, 4:132,
7:155, 15:272,
17:288, 21:149,
26:260, 44:40
1:12—1:221
1:13—29:89
1:13f—8:258
1:14—22:412
1:15—29:89
1:16—30:221
1:17—15:304
1:19—2:81, 4:378,
5:186, 255, 8:33,
83, 309, 14:31,
16:95, 17:77, 89,
203, 29:200,
33:93, 95, 36:191,
41:215, 42:109,
51:311, 52:182,
205, 274
1:20—13:65
1:21—9:52, 10:444,
13:65, 15:275,
20:80, 22:23,
24:366, 25:131,
35:285, 391
Chp. 2—28:328,
30:168–191,
41:280
2:1—9:187, 14:94,
252, 21:288,
22:57, 26:135,
201, 258, 30:204,
213, 285, 299,
30:319, 32:77, 93,
35:143, 36:135,
41:245, 44:131,
378, 50:189,
51:366, 52:82,
241, 255, 282
2:1f—36:216,
44:321, 52:270
2:1–3—35:145,
39:256, 289,
44:131, 151,
54:343
2:2—16:10, 20:54,
39:257, 52:216
2:3—16:105, 277,
20:312, 39:220,
44:332, 51:366,
52:269
2:3–10—39:257
2:4—4:314, 8:316,
19:74, 54:447
2:4f—1:341
2:5—2:3, 10, 13, 24,
56, 83f, 89, 383,
13:311, 22:33,
27:146, 29:236,
35:31
2:6—3:293f, 296,
40:233
2:7—2:217, 21:21,
38:159
2:7f—7:56, 42:159,
46:195
2:8—2:8, 17, 28,
3:252, 346, 21:21,
42:136
2:9—3:295, 13:353,
38:162
2:10—12:240,
22:283, 30:319,
40:16, 41:197,
48:261
2:11—1:296, 11:284
2:11–14—39:258
2:12—11:126,
33:152n, 41:279,
43:105, 44:387
2:13—9:136, 14:92,
25:481f, 36:156,
44:335
2:14—3:231, 40:360,
41:273, 45:22
2:14–17—39:259
2:14–19—39:265
2:14–22—41:129
2:15—4:186, 30:208
2:15f—34:316n
2:18—34:32,
39:266f, 288,
41:151, 44:291,
52:232
2:18f—38:160,
39:260, 41:209
2:18–20—34:44
2:19—32:256
2:19–22—41:209
2:20—39:288
2:21—3:112
2:22—1:225, 2:379,
9:135, 137,
12:273, 26:283,
44:288, 47:162
Chp. 3—30:192–201
3:3—3:305, 13:43,
44:359
3:4—18:163, 29:14
3:5f—1:8, 2:64
3:7—3:40, 36:154
3:8—12:52, 13:101,
17:412, 30:38,
114, 122, 38:77
3:9—30:198
3:10—28:135,
31:141
3:11f—25:355,
31:188
3:12—15:290
3:13—12:121, 25:73,
263, 309, 28:143,
32:29, 48:282
3:14f—25:27
3:16—26:169
3:18—4:376, 12:248,
16:300, 17:230,
25:127, 507,
26:351, 29:97,
30:230, 34:157,
36:188, 41:166,
47:112, 54:143

I John
Complete
commentary—
30:219–327
Chp. 1—17:312n,
30:221–234
1:1—3:229, 22:112,
124, 23:14,
38:275, 54:198
1:1–3—28:80
1:5—2:247, 30:239
1:6—17:x, 301n
1:7—30:285, 38:184
1:8—3:333, 11:458,
496, 14:168,
23:350, 25:215,
221, 259, 276,
27:230, 372,
31:62, 215, 32:23,
34:118, 41:216
1:8f—25:247
1:9—16:73, 25:215,
39:29
1:9f—36:86

1:10—10:144, 14:168, 25:215, 32:25, 33:283, 41:216
1:24—3:300n
Chp. 2—30:235–264
2:1—16:73, 40:300
2:1f—35:34, 38:184, 44:37
2:2—20:332, 26:238, 431, 29:68, 40:297
2:4—29:216
2:9—29:68
2:12—40:257
2:14—40:245
2:15—10:292
2:15–17—46:154
2:16—10:35, 275, 287, 429, 11:306, 13:392, 14:337, 24:161, 33:277
2:18—8:282, 22:67, 30:38, 122, 38:180, 44:133n, 45:60n, 46:8, 180, 48:114n
2:18f—50:243n
2:19—14:308, 24:206, 41:219
2:22—44:133n, 45:60n, 46:180
2:23—15:316, 30:308, 38:309
2:24—28:345, 30:262
2:27—24:124, 357, 29:198, 40:33, 44:106
2:28—30:262
2:29—30:264
Chp. 3—30:265–283
3:2—11:386, 421, 548, 12:107, 382, 25:73, 26:274, 29:115, 225, 30:11, 35:59
3:3—28:198
3:3f—34:127
3:6—14:92, 28:198
3:8—3:170, 5:47, 49, 12:215, 270, 13:135, 278, 14:92, 15:173, 24:15, 74, 27:136, 29:93, 135, 30:285
3:9—4:241, 11:497, 18:358, 20:8, 27:230, 372, 29:228, 31:62, 32:211, 44:25
3:14—16:197, 34:319
3:15—6:376, 16:18, 43:126
3:16—43:127
3:17—16:18, 29:156, 230, 30:30, 250, 31:203, 43:126
3:18—13:33, 25:106, 27:52, 30:281
3:20—14:194, 15:237, 23:60, 25:188
3:23—30:251
Chp. 4—30:284–305
4:1—22:67, 23:174, 26:331, 31:219, 223, 37:150, 40:52, 44:307, 46:24, 48:304, 366
4:2f—37:150
4:2–6—24:124
4:3—20:207, 22:67, 44:133n, 45:60n, 46:180, 48:114n
4:4—6:280, 9:5, 87, 12:224, 16:23, 131, 18:293, 20:8, 32, 25:78, 26:193, 30:274, 36:167, 239, 40:43, 303, 43:172
4:10—22:368, 25:78, 27:65
4:11—48:301
4:12—38:267
4:18—10:14, 25:357, 31:124, 136, 32:31
4:19—24:148
Chp. 5—30:11, 306–327
5:1—30:45, 34:113
5:2—45:294n
5:3—20:235
5:4—5:206, 231, 6:225, 9:42n, 10:114, 11:29, 16:122, 23:183, 25:317, 26:31, 282, 369, 27:5, 30:281, 313
5:4f—26:162
5:5—25:317
5:6—10:401, 51:325, 327
5:8—10:407
5:10—25:284
5:14—24:391, 30:313, 46:33, 54:58
5:15f—10:436
5:16—2:19, 9:198, 16:35, 19:48, 26:197, 38:296, 41:255, 47:12, 48:304
5:17—11:292
5:18—10:298, 16:73, 25:276, 27:230, 372, 29:219
5:19—3:189, 15:145, 22:125, 25:297, 26:40, 348, 33:277
5:39—30:18
5:46—30:19

II John

1—10:19
7—12:363, 34:208, 46:180, 48:114n
10—38:295, 39:9
11—38:295, 39:9, 41:370

III John

1—10:19
7—12:363, 34:208, 46:180, 48:114n
10—38:295, 39:9
11—38:295, 39:9, 41:370

Jude

3—3:301, 4:181, 28:221, 29:32
4—15:100, 27:48, 41:364
6—1:112, 34:171
7—48:361
8—15:78, 20:106, 24:324, 40:16, 48:261
11—34:316n
13—47:37
14f—1:242
16—13:57
22f—3:278

Revelation

1:6—4:357, 35:101
1:7—25:116
1:8—22:429, 47:118
1:16—22:222, 45:59n
1:18—8:37
1:20—29:200, 30:177
Chp. 2—29:184
2:9—3:227, 14:93, 22:513, 26:52, 27:110, 34:39n, 36:115, 221, 41:199, 201, 217, 237, 311, 49:62n
2:14—34:316n
2:17—29:202
2:23—11:290
2:27—50:216n
Chp. 3—29:184, 202
3:7—10:6, 16:180
3:9—36:221
3:11—12:91
3:14f—25:254
3:15f—10:374, 14:7, 25:107
3:16—31:143
3:16f—10:352
3:17—10:382, 11:237, 379, 428, 21:217, 25:269, 27:115
3:19—6:150, 10:206, 283, 16:167, 18:145, 19:178, 31:91, 42:184n, 50:18n
3:20—10:99, 11:291, 32:40, 45:352n
4:4—12:258, 38:208
4:7f—35:117
5:1–5—52:41
5:3—12:296
5:3f—52:205
5:5—11:254, 25:78
5:9f—39:236, 48:265
5:10—11:356, 25:468, 35:101, 36:140, 40:21
5:12—37:262
6:4—27:376
6:8—21:298, 22:375
6:9f—11:141
6:10—13:260, 35:402, 51:246
6:11—13:260, 41:175n
6:12—18:110, 19:88

7:15—36:222
7:17—7:211
8:3—12:258, 32:139
8:3f—10:121
8:4—12:258
8:8—35:403
9:3—29:232
9:3-5—36:225
9:10—30:276
9:11—29:135
9:12—49:289n
9:13—48:114n
9:15—17:353
10:1—35:405, 407
10:1-3—40:354
10:3—26:391
10:8-10—35:407
10:9f—35:405
11:1f—35:405n
11:2—14:316, 35:405n, 44:242
11:7—48:114n
11:15-19—35:405n
Chp. 12—48:114n, 53:292
12:1—25:468
12:3—49:146n
12:3f—10:449, 37:138n
12:7f—16:140n
12:9—10:154, 25:404, 26:192, 27:11
12:10—4:48, 10:408, 12:346, 20:205, 27:11, 33:109n
12:14—10:333, 11:215, 319
Chp. 13—36:201, 44:50n, 45:60n
13:1—4:31, 48:114n, 49:146n
13:1f—20:179
13:1-18—32:82
13:5—41:90
13:7—10:114
13:8—34:313, 40:215
13:11—37:138n, 39:195
13:16f—45:9
14:2—12:258
14:8—34:104n, 35:407, 39:43
14:10—19:219
14:11—10:118, 121
14:12—33:109n
14:13—4:312, 5:272, 7:297, 10:332, 31:138, 42:104, 43:149, 47:42n
15:1—43:238
16:1f—27:227
16:19—5:171, 10:458
Chp. 17—41:206, 48:62n
17:2—16:222n
17:3-5—52:89
17:4—10:458, 39:102
17:5—13:327
17:8—32:66, 48:114n
17:10—49:146n
17:14—12:104, 28:277
17:15—10:133
17:16—13:190
Chp. 18—50:289n, 54:76
18:2—34:104n
18:4—2:274, 3:280, 285, 4:396
18:4f—41:206
18:5—2:274
18:6f—19:219
18:11-13—28:191
19:2—51:246
19:3—10:121
19:15—45:59n
19:16—12:66, 41:356, 49:370
19:20—40:17, 43:239
19:20f—22:222
19:21—45:59n
20:2—1:23, 25:404
20:6—36:140, 39:236, 48:265
20:7—1:23
20:11-14—43:27
20:14—10:298
Chp. 21—35:283, 49:4
21:1—26:235
21:2—5:250, 31:237n
21:4—1:236, 54:134
21:5—10:22, 154, 11:229, 375, 15:20f
21:9—31:237n
21:12—11:176
21:14—25:124
21:27—7:229, 12:239, 25:381, 29:130, 31:46, 62, 153
22:2—10:22
22:9—35:199
22:11—1:217, 3:170, 8:267, 10:53, 11:428, 458, 25:153, 246, 276, 26:428, 31:338, 38:221
22:13—44:295n
22:16—25:516, 37:164n

APOCRYPHA

I Esdras
4:38–41—5:144
4:43—45:225
5:63—18:237
6:27–34—20:6

II Esdras
5:26—11:95

Tobit
1:1–3:6—35:346
2:14—5:203, 206
2:22—5:77
3:8—3:58n, 50:143n
3:17—50:143n
4:6—34:11
4:7—45:306n
4:20—48:21
5:12—35:348n
5:17—3:44n
8:4—28:14
14:13—35:326n

Judith
1:1—14:114n
1:2–4—19:207
6:15—31:340
7:23—4:261
8:9–14—42:90
8:10f—11:351
8:12—4:261
8:13—4:261
8:21f—19:226
9:11—5:315
10:3f—30:89
13:9—20:160
16:14—25:75

Wisdom of Solomon
1:2—10:247
1:4—8:193
1:6–11—35:342
1:13f—29:135
2:1—19:70
2:5—10:362
2:8—10:362
2:10—11:114
2:10–20—35:342
2:11—2:33
2:15—10:261, 11:487
2:16—51:18
2:21—10:62, 11:114
2:24—2:143, 25:297, 29:134, 42:29
3:1—4:316, 8:317, 36:196
3:2f—42:142
3:6—29:238
3:7—3:8
3:13—48:334
4:7—31:132, 42:149
4:10–14—42:150
4:10–15—43:162
4:16—32:71
4:17f—43:162
5:4—11:67
5:6—44:28
5:7—10:255
5:18f—10:86
Chp. 6—16:318n, 46:12
6:1f—35:343
6:3—35:343
6:4–6—35:343
6:6—29:165, 31:127
6:7—13:342
6:8—39:16
6:9—35:343
6:22—35:343
6:26—14:290
7:1–6—7:179
7:12—11:172
7:14—31:282
7:16—42:152
7:26—29:111
7:27—34:129, 35:344
8:1—42:146
8:12—10:73
8:15—10:100, 11:365
8:21—25:243
9:4—5:123
9:7—35:341
9:13—29:186
9:13f—9:51
9:14—44:278
9:15—10:178, 25:328
10:1–11:1—35:344n
10:7—7:128
10:8—7:129
10:10—9:113
10:12—1:145, 16:318, 28:74, 40:43
10:13—7:122
10:13f—7:109, 125
10:14—7:187
10:15–19—35:342
10:21—49:34
11:16—2:311
11:18—29:231
15:2—44:37
16:12—35:344
16:20—42:54
17:11—28:227
18:5–19—35:342
19:1–16—35:342
19:7—32:74

Ecclesiasticus or Wisdom of Sirach
1:13—54:22
2:1—10:48, 11:456, 13:179
2:2—13:179
2:5—44:79
2:10—43:171, 51:49
2:10f—14:67
2:14—2:310, 7:132
2:16—4:322, 12:31
2:18—14:67
3:3f—22:235
3:18—7:183
3:20—18:263
3:22—3:138, 171, 5:47
3:26—35:200, 43:132
3:34—22:384
Chp. 4—8:279
4:30—2:296
5:2–6—8:40
5:4—8:330
5:5—31:209
5:5f—8:330
5:7—29:151, 39:32
5:8—31:47n, 188
5:8f—7:193
6:7—2:297
7:9—38:312
7:24—27:215
7:31—18:400
7:36—42:129
Chp. 8—8:300
8:3—28:308
9:14—43:205
9:17—35:253n
10:2—13:189
10:5—13:170
10:7—5:377, 44:312n
10:9—7:181
10:13—2:6
10:14f—31:362
10:20—7:190
11:25—42:119n, 124
11:27—17:355
12:10—41:80
12:15–19—13:208
14:6—6:3
15:3—11:357
15:9—10:395
15:14—12:356, 15:50
15:14–17—2:350, 33:110, 117, 162f
17:14—51:10
17:17—41:225
17:26—6:199
17:28—7:273
18:6—40:79
18:7—10:53, 11:428, 494, 542, 25:478, 26:3, 27:169
18:23—16:320, 24:394, 43:198
18:30—25:342, 44:73, 46:153
19:2—51:85
19:10—42:68
20:30—11:459
21:1—39:32
21:26—16:275, 39:212
22:7—13:277
22:10f—4:197
23:5—11:430
24:8—11:154
24:12—38:261
24:18—10:374
24:19—11:498
24:20—4:319, 27:366
24:21—4:319
24:29—14:8
25:1—2:301, 6:269, 7:85
25:2—14:119
26:15—44:346, 48:333
26:25–27—13:181

26:29—45:245, 250
27:5—11:140
27:25—46:67n
28:3—28:272
28:12—41:89
28:15—25:170
29:6—24:267
29:14–20—45:253n
30:1—29:55
30:21—25:513
30:23—8:13
30:25—21:21
31:8—25:291
31:12f—28:189
31:14—3:186
31:30—51:85
31:34—13:216
32:4—44:251
32:6—7:162, 45:71n, 49:92
32:7f—29:222
32:32—36:78
33:13—51:76
33:24—46:76n
33:31—4:229, 29:62
34:1f—7:119, 122
34:4—5:237, 14:293
34:6—3:11
34:7—3:11, 6:330
34:9—7:176
34:10—10:49
34:11–13—32:94
34:12f—48:335
34:13—28:367
34:23—39:251
35:4—10:46
35:15—54:181
35:17—7:375
35:21—13:110
36:25—5:181
Chp. 37—50:202
37:20f—50:202n
37:22f—26:64
38:1–8—46:253
38:24f—8:269, 50:202n
38:36—14:15
39:5—25:246, 258
39:6—25:246
39:29f—10:30
40:10—13:213
40:20—13:216
41:1—16:337, 28:381
41:26—4:381
42:14—7:86, 10:406, 11:309, 522, 25:66, 311, 513
44:16f—25:291
45:4—44:103
47:10—10:332
50:26—2:285, 6:183

Baruch
1:11—39:19, 40:283
1:11f—44:65
1:15—10:233
2:35—10:298
3:17—9:70
3:18—28:378
3:35f—51:28
3:36—11:27
3:38—31:365
6:16—17:134

Story of Susanna
Chp. 5—44:223n
Chp. 21—11:113
Chp. 56—11:82, 18:331

Prayer of Manasseh
1–15—39:46f
4—13:92
5—2:172
7—39:29n
8—7:229
9—26:36, 46:230
14—32:48

I Maccabees
Chp. 1—47:225
1:1–7—35:300n
1:10—35:311
1:10f—47:207
1:11—18:9
1:20–24—35:302
1:20–28—35:312
1:41–53—35:301
1:43f—50:201n
2:18—5:85
2:34–38—45:331
2:61—43:171
3:18f—43:278
3:19—46:191
4:9—19:226, 29:150
4:36–61—35:351
4:59—49:380, 386n
5:55–60—46:120
5:55f—34:103
5:62—34:103
6:1–3—35:310
6:1–16—35:302n, 353
Chp. 7—35:352
10:19—7:283
11:31—7:283

II Maccabees
2:18—10:357
4:9—44:200n
4:12—36:220
4:15—36:220
8:24—35:302n
8:30—35:302n
10:17—35:302n
10:23—35:302n
10:31—35:302n
11:11—35:302n
12:19—35:302n
12:23—35:302n
12:26—35:302n
12:28—35:302n
12:43—32:96
13:15—35:302n
13:23f—38:195
14:23—38:195
14:26—38:195
14:41–46—35:353
15:27—35:302n

Prayer of Azariah or Song of the Three Children (or Three Young Men)
Chp. 3–10—16:70
Chp. 6—25:217, 441
Chp. 8—25:217, 441